INTERNATIONAL ENCYCLOPEDIA OF
HOUSING AND HOME

INTERNATIONAL ENCYCLOPEDIA OF HOUSING AND HOME

Editor-in-Chief
SUSAN J. SMITH
*Girton College and Cambridge University,
Cambridge, UK*

Associate Editors-in-Chief
MARJA ELSINGA
*Delft University of Technology,
Delft, The Netherlands*

ONG SEOW ENG
*National University of Singapore,
Singapore*

LORNA FOX O'MAHONY
*University of Durham,
Durham, UK*

SUSAN WACHTER
*University of Pennsylvania,
Philadelphia, PA, USA*

ELSEVIER

AMSTERDAM BOSTON HEIDELBERG LONDON NEW YORK OXFORD
PARIS SAN DIEGO SAN FRANCISCO SINGAPORE SYDNEY TOKYO

Elsevier
Radarweg 29, PO Box 211, 1000 AE Amsterdam, Netherlands
The Boulevard, Langford Lane, Kidlington, Oxford OX5 1GB, UK
225 Wyman Street, Waltham, MA 02451, USA

Copyright © 2012 Elsevier Ltd. All rights reserved

The following articles are US Government works in the public domain and not subject to copyright.
Housing Subsidies and Work Incentives
Mortgage Choice: Behavioural Finance
Mortgage Default: Determinants

No part of this publication may be reproduced, stored in a retrieval system or transmitted in any form or by any means electronic, mechanical, photocopying, recording or otherwise without the prior written permission of the publisher

Permissions may be sought directly from Elsevier's Science & Technology Rights Department in Oxford, UK: phone (+44) (0) 1865 843830; fax (+44) (0) 1865 853333; email: permissions@elsevier.com. Alternatively you can submit your request online by visiting the Elsevier web site at http://elsevier.com/locate/permissions, and selecting *Obtaining permission to use Elsevier material*

Notice
No responsibility is assumed by the publisher for any injury and/or damage to persons or property as a matter of products liability, negligence or otherwise, or from any use or operation of any methods, products, instructions or ideas contained in the material herein, Because of rapid advances in the medical sciences, in particular, independent verification of diagnoses and drug dosages should be made

British Library Cataloguing in Publication Data
A catalogue record for this book is available from the British Library

Library of Congress Catalog Number: 2012935706

ISBN (print): 978-0-08-047163-1

For information on all Elsevier publications
visit our website at books.elsevier.com

Printed and bound in Spain

12 11 10 9 8 7 6 5 4 3 2 1

Working together to grow
libraries in developing countries

www.elsevier.com | www.bookaid.org | www.sabre.org

ELSEVIER   BOOK AID International   Sabre Foundation

Editorial: Richard Berryman, Scott Bentley
Production: Mike Nicholls

EDITORS

EDITOR-IN-CHIEF
Susan J. Smith
Cambridge University
Cambridge
UK

ASSOCIATE EDITORS-IN-CHIEF
Marja Elsinga
Delft University of Technology
Delft
The Netherlands

Ong Seow Eng
National University of Singapore
Singapore

Lorna Fox O'Mahony
Durham Law School
Durham
UK

Susan Wachter
University of Pennsylvania
Philadelphia, PA
USA

SECTION EDITORS
David Clapham (Approaches)
Cardiff University
Cardiff
UK

Kavita Datta (Policy)
Queen Mary University of London
London
UK

Robyn Dowling (Home/Homelessness)
Macquarie University
Sydney, NSW
Australia

Suzanne Fitzpatrick (Home/Homelessness)
Heriot-Watt University
Edinburgh
UK

Kenneth Gibb (Approaches)
University of Glasgow
Glasgow
UK

Richard K. Green (Economics/Finance)
University of Southern California
Los Angeles, CA
USA

Chris Hamnett (Welfare/Well-Being)
Kings College London
London
UK

Kyung-Hwan Kim (Economics/Finance)
Sogang University
Republic of Korea
and
Singapore Management University
Singapore

Heather Lovell (Environment)
University of Edinburgh
Edinburgh
UK

Montserrat Pareja Eastaway (Environment)
University of Barcelona
Barcelona
Spain

Richard Ronald (Institutions)
Delft University of Technology
Delft
The Netherlands

Anthony B. Sanders (Economics/Finance)
George Mason University
Fairfax, AZ
USA

Sasha Tsenkova (Institutions)
University of Calgary
Calgary, AB
Canada

Peter M. Ward (Welfare/Well-Being)
University of Texas at Austin
Austin, TX
USA

Gavin Wood (Policy)
RMIT University
Melbourne, VIC
Australia

EDITORIAL ADVISORY BOARD

Antonio Azuela
National Autonomous University of Mexico
Mexico

Robert Buckley
The New School
New York, NY
USA

Karl E Case
Wellesley College
Wellesley, MA
USA

Rebecca L H Chiu
University of Hong Kong
Hong Kong

Alan Gilbert
University College London
London
UK

Deniz O Igan
International Monetary Fund
Washington
USA

Hugo Priemus
Delft University of Technology
Delft
The Netherlands

Freek Spinnewijn
FEANTSA
Brussels
Belgium

Judith Yates
University of Sydney
Sydney, NSW
Australia

GUIDE TO USING THE ENCYCLOPEDIA

STRUCTURE OF THE ENCYCLOPEDIA

The encyclopedia contains 521 entries, arranged in alphabetical order, and split across 7 volumes. There are five features to help you either browse the contents or to access specific topics which interest you.

1. ALPHABETICAL CONTENTS LIST

The full alphabetical contents list follows the editorial introductions. Titles, authors, volume and page numbers are provided.

2. SECTION IDENTIFIERS

The encyclopedia was developed around 7 thematic Sections, each with its own commissioning and editorial team. A list of entries organised by Section appears next. This is useful in providing a conceptual map of the contents, as well as for making quick connections between entries.

Most entries are around 4000 words. However, in every Section there are up to seven rather longer scene setting or 'overview' articles. These are identified in the main contents list.

On an entry by entry basis, a Section identifier is listed at the foot of the opening page, where there is also an indicator to identify Overview articles.

3. CROSS REFERENCES

Most entries in the encyclopedia are cross-referenced. The cross references, which appear at the end of an entry as a 'See also' list, serve four different functions:

i. To draw the reader's attention to related material in other entries
ii. To indicate material that broadens and extends the scope of the article
iii. To indicate material that covers a topic in more depth
iv. To direct readers to other articles by the same author(s)

4. CONTRIBUTORS

In addition to the comprehensive contents and author list, each of the seven alphabetical volumes includes a list of the specific authors whose entries appear in its pages.

5. INDEX

There is a comprehensive index for the whole work provided at the back of Volume 7. This index includes page numbers for quick reference to the information you are looking for. The index differentiates between references to a whole entry, a part of an entry, and a table or figure.

LIST OF ARTICLES BY SECTION

APPROACHES

Actor–Network Theory
Appraisal and Cost-Benefit Analysis
Austrian Economics
Behavioural Economics
Case Studies
Comparative Housing Research
Complexity
Construction of Housing Knowledge
Critical Realism
Cultural Analysis of Housing and Space
Democracy and Accountability
Demographic Perspectives in Economic Housing Research
Difference
Discourse Analysis
Econometric Modeling
Economic Approaches to Housing Research
Ethnography
Evolutionary Economics
Filtering
Forecasting in Housing Research
Foucauldian Analysis
Game Theory
Gentrification
Globalisation
House Biographies
House Price Indexes: Methodologies
House Prices and Quality of Life: An Economic Analysis
Housing Careers
Housing Classes and Consumption Cleavages
Housing Indicators
Housing Market Search
Housing Preferences
Housing Statistics
Inequalities in European Cities
Institutional Economics: New
Institutional Economics: Traditional
Life Course
Neighbourhood Effects: Approaches
Neoclassical Models of the Housing Market
Neural Networks and Analytic Hierarchy Processes
New Urban Economics and Residential Location
Path Dependency
People and the Built Form
Political Ideologies
Post-Bubble Housing in Japan
Power
Property Rights Approaches
Qualitative Interviewing
Qualitative Methods in Housing Research
Regulation Theory
Residential Segregation: Measurement
Rurality and Housing
Simulation Models for Housing Analysis
Small-Area Spatial Statistics
Social Class and Housing
Social Construction
Social History
Social Policy Approaches
Social Theory and Housing
Socio-Legal Perspectives
Spatial Economics
Stakeholder Analysis for Housing
Structure and Agency
Sustainability
Systems Theory
Textual and Linguistic Analysis
Visual Research Methods
Welfare States and Housing

ECONOMICS/FINANCE

Covered Bonds
Credit Derivatives
Credit Derivatives and the Housing Market
Discrimination in Mortgage Markets
Economics of Housing Choice
Economics of Housing Externalities
Economics of Housing Market Segmentation
Economics of Social Housing
Financial Deregulation
Financial Regulation
Hedging Housing Risk
Home Ownership: Economic Benefits
Home Ownership: Non-Shelter Benefits
House Price Expectations
House Price Indexes
Housing and Wealth Portfolios
Housing Demand
Housing Equity Withdrawal in the United Kingdom
Housing Finance: Mexico
Housing Finance: Global South
Housing Markets and Macroeconomic Policy

Housing Subsidies in the Developing World
Housing Wealth and Consumption
Housing Wealth and Inheritance in the United Kingdom
Housing Wealth as Precautionary Savings
Housing Wealth Over the Life Course
Housing Wealth Distribution in the United Kingdom
Industrial Organisation of the US Residential Mortgage Market
Islamic Housing Finance
Microfinance for Housing
Mortgage Choice: Behavioural Finance
Mortgage Choice: Classical Economics
Mortgage Contracts: Flexible
Mortgage Contracts: Traditional
Mortgage Default: Consequences
Mortgage Default: Determinants
Mortgage Equity Withdrawal
Mortgage Innovation
Mortgage Insurance
Mortgage Market Functioning
Mortgage Market Regulation: Europe
Mortgage Market Regulation: North America
Mortgage Market, Character and Trends: Africa
Mortgage Market, Character and Trends: Brazil
Mortgage Market, Character and Trends: China
Mortgage Market, Character and Trends: France
Mortgage Market, Character and Trends: Germany
Mortgage Market, Character and Trends: India
Mortgage Market, Character and Trends: Italy
Mortgage Market, Character and Trends: Japan
Mortgage Market, Character and Trends: Korea
Mortgage Market, Character and Trends: Mexico
Mortgage Market, Character and Trends: United Kingdom
Mortgage Market, Character and Trends: United States
Mortgage Markets and Macro-Instability
Mortgage Payment Protection Insurance
Neighbourhood Effects
Price Determination in Housing Markets
Price Dynamics in Housing Markets
Residential Property Derivatives
Residential Real Estate Investment Trusts
Risk in Housing Markets
Simulation Models for Urban Economies
Social Housing: Finance
Spatial Mismatch
Submarkets
Subprime Mortgages
Supply Elasticity of Housing
Taxation and Subsidies: The US Case
Time and the Economic Analysis of Housing Systems
Transaction Costs in Housing Markets
User Cost, Home Ownership and Housing Prices: United States

ENVIRONMENT

Abandonment
Adaptable Housing
Building Regulations for Energy Conservation
Climate Change
Climate Change: Adaptations
Community Energy Systems
Construction and Demolition Waste
Construction Methods
Crime Prevention Through Environmental Design
Defensible Space
Demolition
Eco-Communities
Ecological Footprint
Eco-Renovation
Energy Saving
Environmental Consciousness
Environmental Risks: Earthquakes
Environmental Risks: Flooding
Ethnic Minorities and Housing
Eviction
Fuel Poverty
Gated Communities
Gender and Space
Gentrification and Neighbourhood Change
Ghetto
Gypsy/Roma Settlements
Health and Housing
Health Risks: Damp and Cold
Health Risks: Overcrowding
High Rise
Household Waste Recycling
Housing and Sustainable Transport
Housing Developers and Sustainability
Housing Dynamics: Environmental Aspects
Housing Estates
Housing Pathology
Maintenance and Repair
Modern Methods of Construction
Multiple Homes
Neighbourhood Design: Green Space and Parks
Neighbourhood Design: Public Spaces
Neighbourhood Design: Urban Outdoor Experience
Neighbourhood Disadvantage
Neighbourhood Governance
Neighbourhood Incivilities
Neighbourhood Planning
Neighbourhood Reputation

Neighbourhood Watch
NIMBYism
Peripheral Neighbourhoods
Place Attachment
Residential Segregation
Residential Urban Form and Transport
Restorative Housing Environments
Rural Communities
Rural Housing
Second Homes
Self-Build: Global North
Self-Build: Global South
Shanty Towns
Slums
Social Spaces and Urban Policies
Social Sustainability
Sustainable Communities
Sustainable Housing Cultures
Sustainable Lifestyles
Sustainable Regeneration
Sustainable Urban Development
Temporary Housing
Vacancy Chains
Vernacular Housing
Water Supply and Sanitation

HOME/HOMELESSNESS

Anthropological Perspectives on Home
Children and Parenting
Cost Analyses of Homelessness: Limits and Opportunities
Criminological Perspectives on Homelessness
Do-it-Yourself
Domestic Technologies and the Modern Home
Domestic Violence
Domesticity
Domestic Pets
Domicide
Economic Perspectives on Homelessness
Emotions at Home
Ethnographies of Home and Homelessness
Experiencing Home
Experiencing Home: Sexuality
Feminist Perspectives on Home
Feminist Perspectives on Homelessness
Gender Divisions in the Home
Hidden Homelessness
High-Rise Homes
Home and Homelessness
Home as a Space of Care
Home as Inheritance
Home as Investment
Home as Leisure Space

Home as Workplace
Home Environments: Aesthetics, Fashion, Status
Home in Temporary Dwellings
Home Objects
Home: Paid Domestic Labour
Home: Unpaid Domestic Labour
Homeless Families: United Kingdom
Homeless Families: United States
Homelessness: Causation
Homelessness: Definitions
Homelessness: Measurement Questions
Homelessness: Prevention in the United States
Homeless People in China/East Asia
Homeless People: African Americans in the United States
Homeless People: Care Leavers
Homeless People: Care Leavers in the United Kingdom
Homeless People: Disasters and Displacement
Homeless People: Economic Migrants in Southern Europe
Homeless People: Ex-Prisoners in England and Wales
Homeless People: Ex-Service Personnel/Veterans in the United Kingdom
Homeless People: Indigenous/Aboriginal
Homeless People: Older People
Homeless People: Polish Migrants in the United Kingdom
Homeless People: Refugees and Asylum Seekers
Homeless People: Single Men in Japan
Homeless People: Street Children in Africa
Homeless People: Street Children in Asia
Homeless People: Street Children in Mexico
Homeless People: Street Children in the United Kingdom
Homeless People: Youth in Australia
Homeless People: Youth in the United Kingdom
Homes as a Space of Worship
Homestead and Other Legal Protections
Ideal Homes
Illicit Drug Use and Homelessness
Impairment and Experience of Home
Kitchens
Living Rooms
Material Cultures of Domestic Interiors: Africa
Material Cultures of Domestic Interiors: India
Material Cultures of Domestic Interiors: Japan
Material Cultures of Domestic Interiors: Transnationalism
Material Cultures of Home
Meanings of Home
Meanings of Home for Moveable Habitats
Meanings of Home for Older People
Meanings of Home: Gender Dimensions

Meanings of Home in Popular Culture
Memory and Nostalgia at Home
Mental Health and Homelessness
Migration: Ethnicity, Race and Mobility
Nature in the Home
Ontological Security
Philosophical Perspectives on Home
Policies to Address Homelessness
Policies to Address Homelessness: Criminalisation and Control of Public Space
Policies to Address Homelessness: Housing First Approaches
Policies to Address Homelessness: Partnership-Based Approaches in Ireland
Policies to Address Homelessness: Prevention in the United Kingdom
Policies to Address Homelessness: Rights-Based Approaches
Policies to Address Homelessness: 'Staircase' Models
Privacy, Sanctuary and Privatism
Representations of Home: Literature and Language
Representations of Home: Painting
Representations of Home: Photos and Film
Representations of Homelessness
Rural Homelessness in India
Rural Homelessness: An International Perspective
Shelter and Development
Social Psychological Perspectives on Homelessness
Squatting: Developing World
Squatting: United Kingdom
Suburban Homes
Technology and Surveillance in the Home

INSTITUTIONS

Affordable Housing Strategies
Architects
Central Government Institutions
Civil Sector Institutions and Informal Settlements
Community- and Neighbourhood-Based Organisations in the United States
Cooperative Housing/Ownership
Demand Subsidies for Low-Income Households
Ethnicity and Housing Organisations
Government Mortgage Guarantee Institutions
Government/Public Lending Institutions: Asia-Pacific
Government Sponsored Enterprises in the United States
Homeowners' Associations in Post-Socialist Countries

House Building Industries: Africa
House Building Industries: Asia Pacific
House Building Industries: Latin America
House Building Industries: Post-Socialist
House Building Industries: Western Europe and North America
Households and Families
Housing Agents and Housing Submarkets
Housing Auctions
Housing Developers: Developed World
Housing Developers: Developing World
Housing Finance Institutions: Africa
Housing Finance Institutions: Asia
Housing Finance Institutions: Latin America
Housing Finance Institutions: Transition Societies
Housing Institutions in Developing Countries
Housing Market Institutions
Housing Paradigms
Housing Policy: Agents and Regulators
Human Rights and Housing
Informal Housing: Asia
Informal Housing: Latin America
Institutions and Governance Networks in Housing and Urban Regeneration
Institutions for Housing Supply
Institutions for Neighbourhood Renewal
Institutions that Represent Housing Professionals
Land Owners
Land Registration Institutions: Developed World
Master Plan Developers
Mortgage Lenders and Loans
Neighbourhood Improvement: The Role of Housing and Housing Institutions
New Urbanism and Smart Growth Movements
Notaries and Legal Professionals
Older People: Housing Institutions
Planning Institutions: Canada/United States
Planning Institutions: China
Planning Institutions: Post-Socialist
Post-Conflict Housing Restitutions
Private Protection and Housing Property Insurers in the United States
Private Rental Landlords: Developing Countries
Private Rental Landlords: Europe
Private Rental Landlords: North America
Private Sector Housing Management: Asia Pacific
Private Sector Housing Management: Europe
Private Sector Housing Management: North America
Private Sector Housing Management: Post-Socialist
Public-Private Partnerships
Real Estate Agents
Research Networks and Professional Institutions in Housing
Resident and Neighbourhood Movements

Rights to Housing Tenure
Rights to Housing: Developing Societies
Rights to Housing: International Instruments
Rights to Housing: Marginalised Housing Groups
Rights to Land Tenure
Security of Tenure in Muslim Communities
Self-Help Housing Organisations
Self-Provided Housing in Developed Societies
Social Housing Institutions in Europe
Social Housing Landlords: Asia Pacific
Social Housing Landlords: China
Social Housing Landlords: Europe
Social Housing Landlords: Latin America
Social Housing Landlords: North America
Social Housing Landlords: Post-Socialist
Subprime and Predatory Lending: Legal Regulation
Supply-Side Subsidies for Affordable Rental Housing
Taxation
Tenant Cooperatives, Shareholders' Housing Companies
Tenure as an Institution
Welfare Agencies and Assistance: United States
Women and Housing Organisations

POLICY

Access and Affordability: Homeowner Taxation
Access and Affordability: House Purchase Certificates
Access and Affordability: Housing Allowances
Access and Affordability: Housing Vouchers
Access and Affordability: Mortgage Guarantees
Access and Affordability: Rent Regulation
Brownfield Development and Housing Supply
Choice and Government Intervention in Housing Markets
Contract Saving Schemes
Deposit Assistance Schemes for Private Rental in the United Kingdom
Development Land Tax
Discrimination in Housing Markets
Education Programmes for Home Buyers and Tenants
Energy Consumption, Housing, and Urban Development Policy
Exclusionary Zoning
First Home Owner Grants
Foreclosure Prevention Measures
HOPE VI
Housing and Labour Markets
Housing and Neighbourhood Quality: Home Improvement Grants
Housing and Neighbourhood Quality: Urban Regeneration
Housing Construction Industry, Competition and Regulation
Housing Finance Deposit Guarantees
Housing Governance
Housing Markets and Macroeconomic Policy
Housing Policies in Developing Countries
Housing Policies in Developing Countries: Microfinance
Housing Policies in Developing Countries: Sites-and-Services and Aided Self-Help
Housing Policy and Regeneration
Housing Policy Trends
Housing Standards: Regulation
Housing Subsidies and Work Incentives
Housing Supply
Housing Supply: Green Belts
Housing Supply: Urban Growth Boundaries
Housing Trust Funds
Immigration and Housing Policy
Impact Fees
Inclusionary Zoning to Support Affordable Housing
Intermediate Housing Tenures
Key Worker Housing Policies
Local Government Property Taxes
Low-Income Housing Tax Credits
Mobility Programmes for Disadvantaged Populations: The Moving to Opportunity Programme
Monetary Policy, Wealth Effects and Housing
Mortgage Interest Rate Regulation
Mortgage Markets: Regulation and intervention
Policies to Address Redlining
Policies to Address Social Mix in Communities
Policies to Address Spatial Mismatch
Policies to Promote Housing Choice in Transition Countries
Policies to Promote the Environmental Efficiency of Housing
Policies to Support Access and Affordability of Housing
Policy Instruments that Support Housing Supply: Social Housing
Policy Instruments that Support Housing Supply: Supply-Side Subsidies
Privatisation of Social Housing
Rent Policies For Social Housing
Securing Land Rights and Housing Delivery
Security of Tenure Legislation in Private Rental Housing
Self-Help: Policy Assistance
Shared Equity
Social Housing and Employment
Social Housing: Measures to Attract Private Finance
Taxation Policy and Housing
Upgrading Informal Settlements

WELFARE/WELLBEING

Access and Affordability: Developed Countries
Asset-Based Welfare
Asset-Based Well-Being: Use Versus Exchange Value
Collective Ownership
Disability and Enablement
Foreclosure Vulnerability
Gated Communities: Developed Countries
Gated Communities: Global South
Gender and Urban Housing in the Global South
Gentrification and Well-Being
Health and Well-Being
Health and Well-Being: Vulnerable Populations
Household Organisation and Survival in Developing Countries
Housing and the State in Australasia
Housing and the State in China
Housing and the State in Latin America
Housing and the State in South Africa
Housing and the State in South Asia
Housing and the State in the Middle East
Housing and the State in the Soviet Union and Eastern Europe
Housing and the State in Western Europe
Housing Need in the United Kingdom
Housing Subsidies and Welfare
Immigration and Housing: North-Western Europe
Immigration and Housing: United States
Informal Housing: Colonias in the United States
Migration and Housing: Global South
Migration and Population Mobility
Migration and Urban Living in Less Developed Countries
Mobility and Community
Mortage Default and Well-Being in the United States
Older People: Well-Being
Older People: Well-Being, Housing and Neighbourhoods
Politics of Housing
Post-Disaster Housing and Reconstruction
Privatisation of Housing: Implications for Well-Being
Remittances and Well-Being
Rental Market and Rental Policies in Less Developed Countries
Residential Segregation and Education
Residential Segregation and Ethnic Diversity in US Housing
Residential Segregation: Apartheid
Residential Segregation: Experiences of African Americans
Residential Segregation: Race and Ethnicity
Rights, Citizenship, and Shelter
Rights to the City
Self-Build: Latin America
Self-Help: Land Development
Self-Help and Informal Sector Housing in the United States and Canada
Shelter and Settlement for Forcibly Displaced People
Slum Clearance
Social Exclusion and Housing
Social Housing and Social Problems
Social Housing in the United States: Overview
Social Housing: Allocation
Social Justice
Social Mix in Western Countries
Social Movements and Housing
Squatter Settlement Clearance
Supported Housing
Urbanisation and Housing the Poor: Overview
Urban Regeneration in Latin America
Well-Being and Housing in the Caribbean

CONTRIBUTORS TO VOLUME 3: H–I

Marianne Abramsson
University of Linköping, Linköping, Sweden

Claudio Acioly Jr.
United Nations Human Settlement Programme (UN-HABITAT), Nairobi, Kenya

David Adams
University of Glasgow, Glasgow, UK

Wolfgang Amann
Institute for Real Estate, Construction and Housing, Vienna, Austria

Jocelyn Apicello
Columbia University, New York, NY, USA

Blair Badcock
Housing New Zealand Corporation, New Zealand

Claire Baker
National Care Advisory Service, London, UK

Benjamin Barros
Widener University School of Law, Harrisburg, PA, USA

James Barth
Auburn University, Auburn, AL, USA

Ellen Bassuk
The National Center on Family Homelessness, Newton Center, MA, USA

Susan Baxter
National Care Advisory Service, London, UK

Andrew Beer
University of Adelaide, Adelaide, SA, Australia

Peter Boelhouwer
Delft University of Technology, Delft, The Netherlands

Steven Bourassa
University of Louisville, Louisville, KY, USA

João Branco
National Laboratory for Civil Engineering, Lisbon, Portugal; Delft University of Technology, Delft, The Netherlands

Susan Breau
Flinders Law School, Adelaide, SA, Australia

Joanne Bretherton
University of York, York, UK

Dirk Brounen
Rotterdam School of Management, Rotterdam, The Netherlands

Michael Buxton
RMIT University, Melbourne, VIC, Australia

Chris Chamberlain
RMIT University, Melbourne, VIC, Australia

C Chambers
University of Queensland, Brisbane, QLD, Australia

Sylvia Chant
London School of Economics and Political Science, London, UK

Tony Chapman
Durham University, Durham, UK

Fucai Cheng
Shanghai Academy of Social Sciences, Shanghai, China

Anna Clarke
Cambridge University, Cambridge, UK

William Clark
University of California, Los Angeles, CA, USA

Alina Congreve
University of Hertfordshire, Hatfield, UK

Henny Coolen
Delft University of Technology, Delft, The Netherlands

Edward Coulson
Penn State University, University Park, PA, USA

Maureen Crane
Sheffield Institute for Studies on Ageing, Sheffield, UK

Kavita Datta
Queen Mary University of London, London, UK

Thomas Davidoff
University of British Columbia, Vancouver, BC, Canada

Alejandro de Castro
Columbia University, New York, USA

John Doling
University of Birmingham, Birmingham, UK

Christian Donner
Formerly Lecturer at Technical University Vienna, Vienna, Austria

Suzanne Fitzpatrick
University of York, York, UK

Paul Flatau
University of Western Australia, Perth, WA, Australia

Marjorie Flavin
University of California, San Diego, CA, USA

Joe Flood
AHURI-RMIT, Melbourne, VIC, Australia

Matthew French
United Nations Human Settlement Programme (UN-HABITAT), Nairobi, Kenya

Vincent Fusaro
The National Center on Family Homelessness, Newton Center, MA, USA

Alan Gilbert
University College London, London, UK

Megan Grandin
The National Center on Family Homelessness, Newton Center, MA, USA

Lucy Groenhart
University of Sydney, Sydney, NSW, Australia

Latease Guilderson
The National Center on Family Homelessness, Newton Center, MA, USA

William Gwinner
International Finance Corporation, Washington, DC, USA

Chris Hamnett
Kings College London, London, UK

Kim Hawtrey
Hope College, Holland, MI, USA

Maureen Hayes
The National Center on Family Homelessness, Newton Center, MA, USA

David Hayward
RMIT University, Melbourne, VIC, Australia

Jozsef Hegedüs
Metropolitan Research Institute, Budapest, Hungary

Joris Hoekstra
Delft University of Technology, Delft, The Netherlands

Erling Holden
Sogn and Fjordane University College, Sogndal, Norway

Harris Hollans
Auburn University, Auburn, AL, USA

Alan Holmans
University of Cambridge, Cambridge, UK

Matteo Iacoviello
Federal Reserve Board, Washington, DC, USA

Tim Iglesias
University of San Francisco, San Francisco, CA, USA

Sylvia Jansen
Delft University of Technology, Delft, The Netherlands

Helen Jarvis
Newcastle University, Newcastle upon Tyne, UK

Hong-Gyu Jeon
Osaka City University, Osaka, Japan

Sarah Johnsen
Heriot-Watt University, Edinburgh, UK

Guy Johnson
RMIT University, Melbourne, VIC, Australia

Roberta Johnson
University of San Francisco, San Francisco, CA, USA

Anwen Jones
University of York, York, UK

Gareth Jones
The London School of Economics and Political Science, London, UK

Padraic Kenna
National University of Ireland, Galway, Ireland

Patricia Kennett
University of Bristol, Bristol, UK

Kyung-Hwan Kim
Sogang University, Seoul, Korea; Singapore Management University, Singapore

Peter King
De Montfort University, Leicester, UK

Reinout Kleinhans
Delft University of Technology, Delft, The Netherlands

Sunil Kumar
London School of Economics and Political Science, London, UK

Debbie Lam
The University of Hong Kong, Hong Kong, China

Kristin Larsen
University of Florida, Gainesville, FL, USA

Michael Lea
San Diego State University, San Diego, CA, USA

Philip Leather
University of Manchester, Manchester, UK

Charlotte Lemanski
University College London, London, UK

Diane Levy
Urban Institute, Washington, DC, USA

Kristin Linnerud
Cicero Centre for International Climate and Environmental Research, Oslo, Norway

Stuart Lowe
University of York, York, UK

David MacKenzie
Swinburne University, Melbourne, VIC, Australia

Steven Malpezzi
University of Wisconsin-Madison, Madison, WI, USA

Robert Martin
Federal Reserve Board of Governors, Washington, DC, USA

William McAllister
Columbia University, New York, NY, USA

John McDonald
Roosevelt University, Chicago, IL, USA

Carol McNaughton Nicholls
National Centre for Social Research, London, UK

Frits Meijer
Delft University of Technology, Delft, The Netherlands

Paul Memmott
University of Queensland, Brisbane, QLD, Australia

Philip Mendes
Monash University, Clayton, VIC, Australia

Diane Mitlin
University of Manchester, Manchester, UK; The International Institute for Environment and Development, London, UK

Toshio Mizuuchi
Osaka City University, Osaka, Japan

Craig Moore
University of Glasgow, Glasgow, UK

John Muellbauer
University of Oxford, Oxford, UK

Alexis Mundt
Institute for Real Estate, Construction and Housing, Vienna, Austria

Joanne Neale
Oxford Brookes University, Oxford, UK

Brendan O'Flaherty
Columbia University, New York, NY, USA

Yoshihiro Okamoto
Chukyo University, Nagoya, Japan

Don Okpala
Idoplin Ltd, Nairobi, Kenya

Ronan Paddison
University of Glasgow, Glasgow, UK

Anirban Pal
Erasmus University, Rotterdam, The Netherlands

Gareth Powells
Durham University, Durham, UK

Gwilym Pryce
University of Glasgow, Glasgow, UK

Deborah Quilgars
University of York, York, UK

Friedman Roy
World Bank, Washington, DC, USA

Mark Shroder
HUD-PD&R, Washington, DC, USA

Roona Simpson
University of Edinburgh, Edinburgh, UK

Emilie Smeaton
York, UK

Peer Smets
VU University, Amsterdam, The Netherlands

Ahmed Soliman
University of Alexandria, Alexandria, Egypt

Elisabeth Springler
Vienna University of Economics and Business Administration, Vienna, Austria

Marion Steele
University of Guelph, Guelph, ON, Canada

James Sweeney
Durham University, County Durham, UK

Sarah Thomas de Benítez
The London School of Economics and Political Science, London, UK

Andre Thomsen
Delft University of Technology, Delft, The Netherlands

Antonio Tosi
Polytechnic of Milan, Milan, Italy

Ivan Tosics
Metropolitan Research Institute, Budapest, Hungary

Sasha Tsenkova
University of Calgary, Calgary, AB, Canada

Lorraine Van Blerk
University of Dundee, Dundee, UK

Willem Van Vliet
University of Colorado, Boulder, CO, USA

Kerry Vandell
University of California Irvine, Irvine, CA, USA

Henk Visscher
Delft University of Technology, Delft, The Netherlands

Susan Wachter
University of Pennsylvania, Philadelphia, PA, USA

Peter Ward
University of Texas at Austin, Austin, TX, USA

Anthony Warnes
Sheffield Institute for Studies on Ageing, Sheffield, UK

Frank Wassenberg
Delft University of Technology, Delft, The Netherlands; Nicis Institute, The Hague, The Netherlands

Matt Watson
University of Sheffield, Sheffield, UK

Stephen Whelan
University of Sydney, Sydney, NSW, Australia

Fulong Wu
Cardiff University, Cardiff, UK

Simon Yung Yau
City University of Hong Kong, Kowloon, Hong Kong

Cecilia Zanetta
University of Tennessee, Knoxville, TN, USA

Haibin Zhu
Bank for International Settlements, Hong Kong, China

PREFACE AND ACKNOWLEDGEMENTS

The urge to collect and catalogue is as old as humanity itself. Perhaps there is something about being human that insists on scholars pausing from time to time to gather up everything they know and set it down en masse. Certainly, encyclopedias have existed, pretty much in the form we know them now, for at least two millennia. Furthermore, most dictionary definitions of the term 'encyclopedia' contain phrases like 'complete education', 'comprehensive', and 'covering all knowledge'. Roget's Thesaurus likewise directs those looking for synonyms and antonyms of 'encylopedical' to the headings 'generality' and 'knowledge'. In short, anyone with an encyclopedic knowledge of a subject simply knows it all.

It cannot be denied that there is something satisfying about the thought of coordinating a project designed to pull the housing world together in this way. Housing studies, after all, is a quintessentially interdisciplinary and international enterprise whose research and teaching spans a wide range of social science, health, and environmental disciplines. Its relevance ranges from sociology and geography to law, from politics to public health, from economics to accountancy, and from architecture to planning, engineering, and environmental science. The meaning and materiality of home has likewise moved to centre stage in a broad sweep of cultural studies, English, and humanities research. Housing and home together are hot media topics, the staple diet of dinner parties, the heart of practical politics, and very big business in the sale of financial services, do-it-yourself (DIY), home interiors, and garden design. The thought of gathering 'everything you ever wanted to know' about housing and home together into a single massive reference work is enticing.

The *International Encyclopedia of Housing and Home* is not, however, an oracle of this kind. To pretend that it is would be tantamount to claiming that a map of Spain were as complete as Spain itself. But if the map were that comprehensive, it would *be* Spain! Subjects as diverse, dynamic, lively, changeable, topical, and important as housing and home could never be crammed into, or pinned onto, the pages of a book, no matter how many volumes or innovative media platforms were brought to bear. So, in a sense, we have broken the encyclopedic mould. The aim was always to produce a work that is wide-ranging enough to embrace the cutting edges of research, to probe the inner core and outer limits of the worlds of housing and home, to capture the sheer colour and vibrancy wrapped into these subjects, and to recognise the critical importance they hold for economic management, social policy, and public well-being. At the same time, however, the enterprise is designed to set hares running: to identify, as much as to fill, key gaps in the literature; to point to new themes and research agendas which might, in time, make the current work redundant.

Cataloguing the spheres of housing and home is, then, a dynamic and open-ended project. It is a venture that began in earlier works, for example, in Willem van Vliet's (1998) single-volumed *Encyclopedia of Housing*, and its companion work, David Levinson's (1998) *Encyclopedia of Homelessness* (both published by Sage). It is a process extended into more specialised compilations, such Jack Guttentag's (2004) *Mortgage Encyclopedia* (McGraw-Hill) and Andrew Arden's (1997) *Encyclopedia of Housing Law and Practice* (Sweet and Maxwell). Then there are Jack Rostron and Michael Nutt's *Dictionary of Housing* and Jack Rostron, Robert Hardy-Pickering, Laura Tatham and Linda Wright's *Dictionary of Property and Construction Law* (published by Arena in 1997, and Routledge in 2001, respectively). And there are numerous single-volume collections, most notably and recently, the *Handbook of Housing Studies* (Sage, 2011), edited by David Clapham, William Clark and Kenneth Gibb. Who knows where it might end? Not here, and not yet; I am sure. But one other thing is certain: there is nothing published, in press, or yet planned, which offers the sheer scale, complexity, and range of content now packed into the *International Encyclopedia of Housing and Home*. This is a massive work, equivalent in size to around 25 standard edited collections. We offer it, therefore, notwithstanding its partial, uneven, and evolving character, as the major single reference work for housing professionals – for academics and practitioners – for all teaching, learning, and research needs.

It is probably clear, but the words should be said, that the encyclopedia is very much a collective enterprise and a labour of love. Academic authors get little credit for an undertaking like this in the counting and ranking exercises that so many governments now engage in. To be sure, small payments have been made, and the publisher no doubt seeks a profit. But you can be certain that those who brought this project to life did so, above all, as a service to colleagues, reflecting absolute passion for the subject. That sense of imagination and excitement is, I think, reflected in the quality of the articles and the coherence of the work.

The project has been ongoing since 2007; fully 20 senior scholars have spent, on and off, at least 5 years planning, commissioning, debating, and editing the 2 million words that are published herein. They have worked with over

350 authors, and been supported by an enthusiastic international advisory board drawn from all walks of life around housing and home. There is input from most world regions and from every key centre for housing research as well as from the non-university sector. The result is in every sense a collaborative work: it reflects the expertise of the authors, the insight and efficiency of the section editors, the vigilance of the associate editors-in-chief, and the good humoured energy of the entire scholarly team. That, I feel is the main strength of the work, and key to its endurance.

I am sure there are many acknowledgements to funding agencies, institutions, projects, colleagues, and friends that everyone involved with this work would wish to make. My personal debt is to the UK's Economic and Social Research Council, whose Professorial Fellowships scheme made time for the plot to be hatched (RES 051-27-0126); to the members of the first Think Tank on Housing Wealth who debated its feasibility; and to Elsevier's Mary Malin who turned a modest proposal into a Major Reference Work.

If I had enough space, and readers had the patience, I would wish at this point to mention every editor, and many authors, by name, and list the distinctive qualities that each has brought to this amazing collective work. It has been a privilege to be part of that team. The work of the authors is, I feel sure, clear from the content of the articles. The achievements of the section editors can been seen from the coherence of the thematic volumes and the energy in their introductory statements. The role of the associate editors-in-chief is perhaps less obvious, because they have worked between sections to explore synergies, look for overlap, encourage themes that cross section boundaries, and of course they have worked as a resource for the sections themselves. Marja Elsinga steered 'Environment' and 'Policy'; Lorna Fox O'Mahony anchored 'Home and Homelessness' and 'Institutions'; Susan Wachter and Ong Seow Eng kept an eye on 'Economics and Finance' across the board. The editors in turn owe special thanks to Jim Follain and Jim Shilling for their work as reviewers in 'Economics and Finance'. We are all grateful to Mike Nicholls for his meticulous coordination of the proofs. If, however, there is one person without whom the project would have foundered, it is Richard Berryman, development editor for Elsevier's Major Reference Works. He has far exceeded his brief, keeping track of all the articles, managing the process of electronic manuscript submission (circumventing it where necessary), and bringing unfailing energy, good humour, and consummate professionalism to an otherwise impossible task.

Susan J Smith
Cambridge, October 2011

INTRODUCTION

Housing has never been more squarely in the spotlight; homes have rarely been closer to people's hearts. For the first time ever, we appreciate the full extent to which housing market dynamics can challenge macroeconomic stability, and expose the fragility of households' primary asset base. Residential mortgage markets have proved sufficiently volatile to trigger a global credit crisis, and to bankrupt entire residential neighbourhoods; yet, they have also added unprecedented financial flexibility to home-occupiers' domestic accounts. Meanwhile, the social aspects of housing (including issues around exclusion, inequality, and identity) are under intense scrutiny by politicians and social researchers alike. Many governments have rekindled their in-house, and commissioned, housing research programmes and revitalised housing policy. The search is on for housing solutions to a wide range of enduring social problems and for ways to manage a new suite of financial and environmental risks. As a result, the inherently multidisciplinary field of housing studies is undergoing a major renaissance. The time seems right to publish a comprehensive *International Encyclopedia of Housing and Home* designed to meet a suite of teaching, research, practical, professional, and policy needs among a wide-ranging readership.

Encyclopedias come in many shapes and sizes: some are little more than elaborate dictionaries, full of long words and short definitions; others seem more like edited books, with extended manuscripts covering a few core themes. This encyclopedia occupies neither extreme. It is, well, 'encyclopedic' in every sense. It is based on over 500 substantial contributions, enough to touch practically every core theme relating to housing and home. Most articles run to at least 4000 words, sufficient for subject experts to address their topics in depth, without sacrificing accessibility. This melée is structured around a series of longer keynote or overview articles, which set the scene for the seven thematic volumes or sections comprising the larger work. The result is a comprehensive, authoritative source of facts, ideas, and concepts anchored on housing and home. The contents are international in scope, engaging with trends in every world region; the authors are drawn from a wide range of countries, and the work as a whole collates a mix of expertise from academics, policy-makers, professionals and practitioners.

There is an infinite number of ways to collect and organise the contents of a publication like this. In the end, the encyclopedic tradition is to list articles alphabetically, and we feel this works for housing and home. 'Housing studies' is, after all, a tradition founded on 'mix and match' across sectors and disciplines; the uneasy jostling of incongruous ideas has already proved to be an exciting route to new knowledge. With that in mind, why not experiment with the alphabet?

For those who seek more structure, there are other ways of navigating the text. For example, readers may wish to search by 'discipline' (there are contributions from housing economics, housing law, the sociology of housing, psychology and housing, housing and health, cultures of housing, and politics of housing), by 'world region' (coverage extends to Europe, Australasia, North and South America, Africa, and Asia), 'thematically' (through topics such as housing finance, housing policy, and housing management), 'sectorally' (owner-occupation, social renting, private renting, buy-to-let, co-operative housing, self-build, etc.), 'conceptually' (housing markets, price mechanisms, housing need, housing allocation, housing consumption, and meanings of home), 'theoretically' (housing and the macroeconomy, the microstructures of housing markets, social theory and housing), 'methodologically' (life-course approach, behavioural economics, hedonic analysis, microsociology, ethnography, and synoptic reading), and 'practically' (housing interventions, planning, buying and selling, professional training, needs assessment, price index construction, taxation, etc.).

Notwithstanding these multiple organisational possibilities, the main conceptual map of the encyclopedia is constructed from seven broad themes, each of which was commissioned, written, and edited as a separate volume or section. Other than an alphabetical list, section headings are the main way in which the work is structured. Introductions to each section, written by the editors who devised them, appear next. In brief, the sections are as follows. 'Approaches' contains articles on the main concepts and theories used in housing research, and on the methodologies commonly used to explore key themes around housing, home, and homelessness. 'Economics and Finance' engages with all aspects of housing and economy, including housing economics, housing market dynamics, housing wealth, and housing finance. 'Environment' includes articles on the physical and social environments, including environmental sustainability, energy efficiency, neighbourhood trajectories, and residential segregation. 'Home and Homelessness' addresses the full range of ideas about homemaking, home cultures, home values, domestic interiors, design, and meanings of home; it also considers the absence of home – the predicament of homelessness – in its many and varied forms. 'Institutions' documents all the main institutions of the housing system: legal frameworks, housing tenures, lenders, insurers, valuation, marketing, intermediation, and so on. 'Policy' is concerned with all aspects of housing governance and regulation: access and affordability of housing, housing production, tax policies, and links between housing, labour markets, and mortgage markets. 'Welfare and Well-Being' is concerned with the social aspects of housing. It examines the links between housing, welfare, and well-being; it considers housing needs, risks, and affordability; and it touches on health, safety, and security.

There are, of course, aspects of housing and home that this work does not cover. Some areas are simply not in the brief: they would have made the project too large, and in some important respects unbalanced. These include: commercial real estate; aspects of welfare, urban studies and planning that do not pertain to housing; technical building regulations; and aspects of home not relating to dwelling or residential property. Some topics cried out for attention, but simply refused to be attached to an author: maybe that will change next time round, as key themes blossom; perhaps it is already a pointer to topics that will in future fail to thrive. Some authors, bluntly put, did not submit their articles, despite extended deadlines. But that is the messy reality of creating a major reference work. Encyclopedias can no longer be produced by a single person; the shape they take is in every sense a reflection of the busy worlds they inhabit. One thing is clear, however: the encyclopedia is not only the print in your hands or the text on an electronic platform. It has created the community that made it and that network will hopefully widen as time goes on: connecting scholars across spaces, disciplines, and languages; sparking new alliances, friendships, and debates; indeed, giving shape to areas of scholarship that were overlooked or taken for granted before. In that sense, the encyclopedia can never be finished. It has a life of its own which has already burst free of its covers.

M Elsinga, L Fox O'Mahony, SE Ong, SJ Smith, and S Wachter

APPROACHES

Housing is a complex entity that has many different dimensions and impacts on many areas of private and public life. Housing is at the same time shelter, the scene of people's most emotional moments, the place we call home, an indicator of status, and a point of access to employment as well as to a range of public and private facilities. Housing is also the most expensive purchase the majority of households will make and a repository for the majority of personal wealth. The complexity of housing is fascinating, but this presents problems as well as opportunities for housing analysts.

The peculiarities of housing (as a locationally fixed commodity, a strangely indivisible investment, an object of consumption, and a crucible of housing services) demand special methodological and conceptual attention. That is one reason why we have devoted an entire section of the encyclopedia to it. Some aspects of housing can readily be explored using tried and tested tools borrowed from cognate areas of social and economic research. Others demand a more bespoke range of approaches. More than anything else, while acknowledging that certain elements of housing – one or two attributes at once, perhaps – can readily and productively be subject to discipline-specific analyses, the articles in this section of the encyclopedia point to the opportunity, and incentive, which housing studies provides to undertake comprehensive and transdisciplinary research.

There are 67 articles in this section. They provide both theoretical depth and methodological detail; they span qualitative and quantitative, as well as social and economic, approaches to housing research. They can therefore be used in conjunction with substantive articles in many other sections. For example, the article on the methodology of house price indexes in this section has a counterpart in the section 'Economics and Finance' on the uses and application of such indexes. Similarly, an article on neighbourhood effects in this section has a bearing on several substantive articles in the section 'Environment'. By way of a more systematic introduction to the diverse approaches collected here, we briefly consider theories, methods, and social and economic approaches as applied to housing studies.

Theory has become increasingly important in housing studies in recent years. Only two decades ago, Jim Kemeny (1992) made a haunting plea for more theoretically-aware housing research. He was critical of the then-dominant empirical paradigm for its excessively policy-driven approach, around an agenda shaped by government agencies. He argued that this style of housing studies lacked an explicit research epistemology or ontology and was isolated from the societal context within which specific problems were situated. Instead, most research addressed questions set and problems defined by powerful agents – most notably by governments. This made housing studies useful in an instrumental sense (and this is still the case), but limited its explanatory power and capacity to imagine change.

To an extent, Kemeny solved the problem himself, taking a lead role in establishing the journal *Housing and Social Theory*. However, the success of that journal is just one indicator of a steady increase in the amount of theoretically aware housing research now under way. Many articles in this section testify to this continuing trend, profiling the wide array of theoretical perspectives that are now used to illuminate housing and home. Some of those ideas are 'borrowed' – drawn from the wider social sciences, as epitomised in the application of the concept of ontological security, drawn from the work of the sociologist Anthony Giddens (1984), to research on owner-occupation. But others are, or have been made, very specific to housing research. The scene is set in Jago Dodson's overview article: Social Theory and Housing.

The 'theoretical' picture is fairly comprehensive. Articles range from actor–network theory through constructionism, critical realism, Foucauldian approaches, housing classes, and welfare regimes. There are, inevitably, gaps in this coverage, and it is important to be aware that new theoretical ideas are coming to light all the time. The articles in this section pick up on that dynamism. For example, there is no consensus on the nature of the microfoundations of housing market dynamics. Traditional neoclassical economic approaches have their place in this section, but they have been increasingly criticised by adherents of institutional economics, behavioural economics, and other approaches such as material sociology. Some of this jostling is apparent in the selection of articles herein.

Hence, one question that arises is whether there can, or should, be any comprehensive or all-embracing 'grand theory' to guide housing research. On the one hand, the lack of a 'general' theory of housing may be something to worry about. Some regard the absence of a coherent and comprehensive theoretical framework as a substantial weakness, making it impossible to transcend individual partial analyses. How do you put different insights together and understand how they relate or make up a larger whole? How do you devise a policy when all you have to go on are partial findings from varying approaches? On the other hand, the theoretical eclecticism that now exists is a fair reflection of the complexity of housing and of the many different analytical or policy questions that it poses. Even single issues, such as consumer market behaviour (e.g., the notion of housing choice), can be viewed in many different ways, and each can offer its own particular inspiration. The theoretical angle adopted in a specific piece of housing research may therefore rightly be adjusted to or dictated by the precise research question being addressed.

If the lack of a comprehensive theoretical framework in housing studies is problematic, it reflects a wider challenge for the social sciences more broadly. What is exciting, and to an extent reflected in the ideas in this section, is that housing is already the focus of transdisciplinary work in a variety of areas – for example, in behavioural and institutional economics – because of its unique features. Perhaps this is why King (2009) has argued that housing provides a good base from which to devise theory from a vantage point at the forefront of transdisciplinary research. Clearly, there is much work to be done before progress can be made in this direction, but the scope of this encyclopedia, if nothing else, provides a good testing ground for such endeavours.

Methods are as important to 'Approaches' as theories, and the articles in this section also illustrate the application of many different elements of the methodological toolkit to a range of housing topics. Reflecting a broad array of disciplines and approaches, these 'how-to' articles range widely, and they are not just about practicalities; they include some fundamental methodological concerns. For example, Flood's analysis of housing indicators reflects on their intrinsic meaningfulness as well as commenting on good and bad practice at a more prosaic level. Other articles relevant at this juncture include those on housing statistics, small area spatial statistics, forecasting, and econometric modelling. There are also reflections on comparative methods, qualitative methods, cultural analysis, visual methods, and so on. There is probably something here for everyone who is in search of a methodological starting point for research on housing and home.

There is insufficient space to profile all the 'how-to' articles, but it is perhaps worth taking one example from an overview article by Mike Oxley that provides a critique of comparative housing research. This article shows that an important development in housing research in the past 20 years has been an increase in international research, comparing housing systems for deeper insights about policy, process, and practice. While it is relatively easy to provide a superficial analysis of different national housing systems, going 'deep' into contexts, institutions, and markets requires ongoing commitment, as well as exceptional conceptual and methodological clarity. Such articles encourage commentators on housing research to recognise the scope for policy transfer and to be more willing to address the complexities of housing systems in other countries.

A sea change in the social sciences across the last decade has been the reconciliation between economics and other styles of social research. Some of this rapprochement is evident in articles of this section. However, 'housing economics' (like economics generally) addresses some very specific problems using some very distinctive tools, and this particularity is well-reflected among contributors to the encyclopedia. Approximately 17 articles are apposite here, spanning the neoclassical mainstream as well as the emerging heterodox panoply. Interestingly, while the section 'Economics and Finance' properly contains articles with a mainstream flavour, a large part of the discussion in 'Approaches' represents the heterodox challenge. At the very least, it grapples with the heterogeneity of housing research and aptly illustrates the wealth of alternative economics approaches now in play. There is, for example, discussion of institutions, property rights, Austrian economics, evolutionary perspectives, new institutional economics, behavioural economics, and neural networks. The sheer range of these ideas is pulled together in a compelling overview article by Alex Marsh on economic approaches.

More than any other applied area of economics, the housing and land market seems disposed to nonmainstream approaches, even if only a few such approaches are commonly published in key disciplinary journals (with the exception of behavioural economics which has taken the discipline by storm). Perhaps there are specific features of housing and human interactions with real estate that lend themselves to broader analyses of economics – analyses which take appropriate account of local context, bounded rationality, power over resources, the importance of the elapsing of real time, durability and spatial fixity, the joint nature of housing (with neighbourhoods, local government, and finance markets, to name three important links), and the way households, firms, and the state cope with decision-making in the face of this complexity. Other commodities have some of these attributes but, as has often been said, housing is unique in possessing them all. This, however, is not to deny the continuing importance of the insights of neoclassical economics and the evidence base built up around it, including in the sphere of housing economics. Regardless of philosophical and methodological disputes, the study of housing would be much poorer if we were to ignore the mainstream, just as housing research would be sorely limited if we only had 'orthodox' economics to rely on.

Social research in housing has a heterodox history and there is no parallel here to the challenge now facing orthodox housing economics. However, there is no shortage of articles illustrating the diversity of social approaches, and capturing the tensions, as well as opportunities, these engender. We have attempted to make it clear that the distinction between economic and social approaches is one of practicality rather than ontology. It is equally important to avoid characterising one as demanding quantitative methods and the other as more fitted to qualitative understandings. However, notwithstanding recent interests among economists in focus groups and related approaches, some of the major contributions to the development of qualitative methods have come from the sociological and anthropological disciplines. It is these cutting-edge approaches that are profiled herein. That is why there is an overview article on qualitative methods in housing research by Henry Coolen, providing context for other articles on ethnography, discourse, house biographies, life-course perspectives, and so on. There is also an emphasis in the social research articles on approaches relating to welfare, well-being, and the monitoring of inequality. While 'approaches' are not usually thought of in terms of normative theory, by sensitising readers to historical methods, matters of sustainability, and questions of power, political ideology, and policy futures, this section builds a platform for articles elsewhere in the encyclopedia to take on this broader mantle.

To return, in conclusion, to the start. Even given the extensive section that 'Approaches' has become, there is more to say, gaps to fill, and potential to realise. There is no objective sense of resolution to many key debates, and no conclusion to the various conversations the articles open up. And nor should there be. Housing studies has blossomed through diversity, and a diverse array of 'approaches' is key to this continuing. To be sure, such breadth may pose a challenge to readers and their disciplinary priors. However, the section editors, themselves coming from different disciplines, have shaped this volume with engagement and rapprochement firmly in mind.

D Clapham and K Gibb

References

Giddens A (1984) *The Constitution of Society*. Polity Press: Cambridge.
Kemeny J (1992) *Housing and Social Theory*. Routledge: London.
King P (2009) Using theory or making theory: Can there be theories of housing? *Housing, Theory and Society* 26.1: 41–52.

ECONOMICS AND FINANCE

Overview

Economics as a discipline has a long history of engagement with housing research. However, it is fair to say that, until the last decade, housing rarely took the centre stage. Now, however, it is clear how crucial housing, mortgage, and related capital markets are for the financial fortunes of whole economies and for individual households. This section consists of 72 articles, selected to illustrate this. The essays cover a wide range of topics concerning the real (physical) side of housing, as well as housing finance. They address microeconomic issues as well as macroeconomic concerns, and are complementary to articles in the sections 'Policy' (in areas such as housing supply, zoning and land-use regulation, and taxation), 'Institutions' (where there are common themes around taxes and subsidies), and 'Approaches' which, for example, contains methodological details on the calculation of housing price indexes, as well as an overview of institutional, behavioural, and neoclassical analyses of the housing economy). Although most of the articles in this section are based on the US and UK literature, reflecting the bulk of academic research, some articles cover both developed and developing countries, especially on the subject of mortgage markets and their regulations as well as housing subsidies.

This brief introduction is organised around the major themes addressed in the collection. These may be grouped into seven categories: housing demand, supply, and markets; house prices; government intervention in housing markets in the form of regulations and the direct provision of social housing; government intervention in the form of taxes and subsidies; housing wealth; housing and the macroeconomy; and housing finance (which has traditionally been jurisdiction-specific) together with an emerging international perspective on mortgage markets. Each is introduced below.

Thematic Review

Housing Demand, Supply, and Markets

Housing is not a simple commodity, like grains or metals. It is rather a complex, composite commodity, which is hard to price and whose supply is determined by policy and politics as much as markets. Moreover, housing is an investment asset as well as a consumption good. And when people discuss house 'prices', they often refer to an asset price, rather than a commodity price: the true 'price' of the commodity known as housing is rent.

Many of the articles in this section engage with this dilemma, recognising that when households demand housing, they are in fact demanding a bundle of services. Part of the bundle is physical: houses embody different quantities of interior space, exterior space, materials, plumbing, heating, and so on. Some part of the bundle is not physical. The location of a house, for example, determines the government services that it and its occupants receive. To give but one instance, it has been known that the demand for houses in 'good' school districts exceeds the demand for housing in less good school districts. Housing demand changes with price and income, just as with any other good, and in this, a remarkable similarity of housing demand is found across countries. But house price is also sensitive to household type, household tastes, and a host of other variables.

Housing demand also involves the choice of tenure, that is, whether to own or to rent, which is often made simultaneously with choices about the quantity of housing. The tenure decision is affected by the relative price of owning and renting, access to housing finance, and terms of mortgage loans. Homeownership is attractive to individual households because it generates private economic benefits. Social benefits emanating from homeownership form a basis for government support to it. Renting is more difficult in that landlords essentially serve as a financial intermediary between users of property and property itself. Rental housing therefore produces principal–agent issues that are solved via home-owning. Homeownership also allows the hedging of rent increases as the owner-occupant household is effectively renting to itself. All these themes are covered by the articles in this section.

Housing supply is more complicated. It includes new construction and alteration of the existing stock, and these two sources of supply are determined by two distinct sets of players, with different motivations: developers, on the one hand, and owner-occupiers, on the other hand. New homes are generally manufactured at the place where they are occupied, and the materials used for construction can vary from one part of the world to another. Even when manufactured homes and materials for home buildings are shipped around, the land component of supply is fixed locally. Natural barriers can also create impediments to housing supply. Bangladesh, for example, a country that is especially susceptible to flooding, faces supply challenges that are considerably greater than most other countries, and topography constrains housing supply in some coastal cities in the United States.

Political attitudes have, arguably, the greatest impact on housing supply. That is why there are synergies between the section economics and finance, on the one hand, and that on policy, on the other hand. The American city of Houston has virtually no limitations on housing construction, and as such, the supply curve for housing there is highly elastic. Mumbai, on the other hand, is among the densest large cities in the world, and yet has for many years imposed regulations and requirements that substantially limit its ability to supply housing. The elasticity of housing supply is affected by both natural constraints and regulatory barriers; the balance is weighed up by the relevant articles.

Finally, the articles in this section recognise that there is no single national housing market but a large number of local housing markets; such markets are also segmented. Identifying the submarkets is an important issue for both market analysis and policy formulation; a number of articles on housing supply, demand, and markets investigate the implications of such heterogeneity.

House Prices

The recent global financial crisis has shown that understanding house price fundamentals and dynamics has many important implications for wealth profiles, for lending and borrowing, and for policy. But understanding house price trends and volatilities is not a trivial matter. This is clear from the cluster of articles concerned with the measurement and determinants of house prices through time and spatially.

One can view house prices from several perspectives. Even terminology is not straightforward: from an economic perspective, the 'price' of a house is the rent one pays (or implicit rent in the case of owner-occupied housing) to receive the flow of housing services. To be precise, the term housing price or rent in its common use is in fact expenditure on housing and equals the unit price of housing multiplied by the quantity of housing consumed in a particular housing unit. Differentiating housing expenditure into price and quantity of housing is itself a challenge for housing researchers. The transaction price of a house is its asset value, which can be looked at as the present discounted value of its service flow.

Measuring discounted value is difficult, particularly for owner-occupied housing. In the first place, one would need to measure and forecast the rent that a particular owner-occupied house might fetch in the market; second, one would need to choose a correct discount rate. A further complication is the tendency for the market price of housing assets in any given point in time to deviate from what is explained by fundamental values. The discrepancy is called a bubble, which is often driven by expectations about future price appreciation. The difficulties in establishing fundamental values may explain why, at the time housing bubbles appeared to be developing around the world in the middle of the first decade of the twenty-first century, there was no consensus among economists as to whether this was, or was not, a departure from fundamentals.

Another method for determining fundamental house price is simply to sum the construction costs of improvements with land value. But getting construction costs right is difficult enough; getting land value right as well requires one to determine the fundamental value of land. This in turn depends on calculating land rent and a discount rate, which puts us in the same predicament mentioned in the previous paragraph. Residential property prices are, as a result, still one of the most researched, yet least understood, topics in housing economics.

Government Interventions: Regulations and Direct Provision of Social Housing

Government intervenes in the housing market in a variety of ways: land-use regulation and the provision of social housing are two of the most critical factors where economics and finance are concerned. Planning regulations, for example, directly affect how housing developers meet housing demand. It is almost certain that the demand for large blocks of flats in cities in India exceeds supply. Important reasons for the shortage are that regulations have made it difficult for developers to assemble parcels of vacant land and have produced binding limits on floor area ratios. Washington, DC, is a city whose housing supply is shaped in part by height limits, which in turn leaves demand unmet. Government regulation, in short, does much to shape both the price of housing and development densities in cities around the world.

The social housing sector is important because it effectively (to an extent) suspends the price mechanism in housing markets. The size and significance of this sector varies across countries, and is covered in most detail in other sections (see 'Institutions', 'Policy', and 'Home and Homelessness'). However, there are articles in this section on the economics and the financing of social housing which provide important points of contrast with a literature more generally focused on owner-occupation.

Government Interventions: Taxation and Subsidies

Taxation exerts a powerful effect on the shape of the world's housing systems. Most interest, in practice, centres on the implications of taxation for the role and relevance of owner-occupation. This in turn varies across countries. Many countries provide homeowners with a subsidy in the form of mortgage interest deduction; almost all countries give a tax break to owner-occupied housing by not taxing imputed rents, or capital gains, on primary residences. The mortgage interest deduction can affect the user cost of housing (i.e., the economic cost of owning a house) and make homeownership more attractive than it would otherwise be. However, it almost certainly will get capitalised into house prices to a varying extent depending on the supply elasticity. So it is not really clear how mortgage interest deductibility affects homeownership rates or home prices. Some argue that its impact is more on the size of properties than on whether they are purchased or not.

Many, if not most, countries provide some form of subsidy (other than tax breaks) to some households, and while the nature of the subsidy varies, generally the subsidy favours homeownership. This is done because homeownership is believed to generate social benefits. Some countries, such as Singapore, have a long history of directly subsidising owner-occupied housing, and this has helped drive ownership rates to high levels. Other countries also subsidise renters, through provision of social housing (supply-side subsidy), through vouchers (demand-side subsidy), or through tax incentives to landlords. Several such themes are aired in this section.

Housing Wealth

A number of articles address the various dimensions of housing wealth, the ways households can tap into it, and the impact of housing wealth on consumption. We now know with a great deal of confidence that housing wealth is important – it is the world's largest single asset class, it makes up an enormous share of global wealth, accounts for the bulk of personal wealth in most national economies, and for the majority of owner-occupiers, is by far their largest, sometimes their only, asset. We do not, on the other hand, have as much confidence in knowing the total value of individual, national, or global housing assets, not least because of uncertainty about the fundamental value of houses.

This section also reflects the fact that there is not yet any consensus concerning the implications of housing wealth for the broader economy. There is, to be sure, extensive debate on the link between home prices and consumption, and on what the causal mechanisms might be. There have also been a number of estimates of the marginal propensity to consume out of housing wealth (rather than other parts of the wealth portfolio), but these estimates have a wide range. Part of the difficulty is that the fungibility of housing wealth – the ability to mobilise or 'cash in' home equity – varies between jurisdictions, according to the 'completeness' of mortgage markets, and the transactions costs in housing markets. The means of extracting equity also varies across the life course. For example, for households attached to a job, it is difficult to cash in on house value by moving from an expensive city to an inexpensive city; retirees, conversely, do have that option. On the other hand, home-buyers in work have more opportunities to borrow-up against owned homes (to engage in mortgage equity withdrawal) than do older outright owners without an income stream. There is some agreement that the collateral channel has increased in importance; that increased leverage together with equity borrowing accounts for a significant proportion of housing's wealth effects. However, on the subject of tapping into home equity via loans, there is a mix of evidence, some of which suggests that the ability to use that mechanism can be fleeting.

That is, mortgage equity withdrawal may not improve the household balance sheet in the long run, because the asset extracted (cash) is offset by a new liability (a future stream of mortgage payments). Nevertheless, as the articles in this section show, mortgage equity withdrawal is one means by which some homeowners smooth both incomes and consumption across the life course.

Housing and the Macroeconomy

The interplay between the housing sector and the macroeconomy has attracted growing attention in recent years. Research indicates that the housing sector interacts with the macroeconomy through three major channels: the investment, consumption, and banking channels. Regarding the first channel, it is sometimes argued that housing 'is the business cycle'. Indeed, variations in housing construction explain a disproportionate amount of variation in the broader economy. The question is why. The second channel, the housing wealth effect, has been discussed above. As for the third channel, the performance of mortgage loans, conditioned by the fluctuation in housing price, influences the balance sheet of lending institutions. This affects their ability to expand new credit to households and businesses, and hence the level of consumption and investment activities. The housing–macroeconomy linkages operate in the other direction as well. For example, changes in the interest rate and the supply of credit have an impact on housing demand and the supply of new housing.

Mortgage Markets: Character and Trends

Because housing is a long-lived and 'lumpy' (indivisible) consumer durable, and because households generally wish to smooth consumption over the lifetime, it is only natural that mortgage markets have expanded hand in hand with housing markets. When housing finance is not available, households must save for many years before they have the opportunity to purchase a house. The behaviour of borrowers regarding the choice of mortgage products and repayment of mortgage debt (or default there on) and the factors that affect their behaviour are covered by several articles in this section.

The size of the housing finance sector varies considerably across countries. Some developed countries, particularly the United States, the United Kingdom, Denmark, and the Netherlands, have very large mortgage markets relative to their economies. Most emerging countries have relatively small mortgage markets, but some high-income countries, including Italy and France, have relatively small markets too. Mortgage products are highly heterogeneous across countries and jurisdictions vary in the 'completeness' of the mortgage markets they support. The United States features a large variety of mortgage products, even now, and is, like Denmark, unusual in that fixed-rate, long-term, freely-prepayable mortgages are common. In Canada mortgages generally have terms of medium length (5 years is usual). The UK and Australian mortgage markets, in contrast, where long-term fixes are less common, support a wide range of loan products in the amortising adjustable rate and equity borrowing ranges.

In short, and until recently, mortgage markets have been stubbornly national in character, notwithstanding an otherwise-globalising economy. To illustrate that diversity, there are several articles on mortgage markets, character, and trends in specific illustrative jurisdictions, from Germany (with notably low rates of homeownership) to the United Kingdom and the United States (with reasonably high rates of highly mortgaged owner-occupation) in the developed world, and spanning all other world regions, from Africa to China.

Mortgages, because they are secured debt, allow households with a relatively small asset base to borrow at narrow spreads over risk-free assets. This is because properly underwritten loans consider both the ability of the borrower to repay the loan and the quality of the collateral underpinning it. In recent years, many lenders departed from good underwriting practices, for reasons that are currently subject to debate. Nevertheless, during those years when mortgages were carefully underwritten, they were very safe investments for lenders.

This might explain why, to meet a growing demand for credit in some parts of the more developed world, mortgage-linked instruments emerged during the 2000s as an important financial market. Mortgage-linked securities helped lending institutions tap the capital market as well as contributing to the development of capital markets. Countries vary in how mortgage finance is sourced, the major division being between those that rely on capital markets for housing finance and those that rely on depositories. Germany, Denmark, and the United States tend to rely on capital markets, while Australia, the United Kingdom, and Canada rely more on depositories. These themes are taken up in the remaining articles for this section.

Research Agenda Going Forward

The articles collected here cover a wide range of subjects in the economics and finance of housing. Already, however, they point out new directions and identify areas in which further research is needed. For example, a clear and encouraging trend in housing research in recent years is increased interest in housing supply. Additional research on supply elasticity, the role of regulations on supply, and the impact of the supply elasticity on the volatility in housing price and quantity would be helpful. Second, the effects of ageing, and cohorts, on the place of housing and mortgage debt in the household portfolio, have important policy implications and merit greater attention. Third, the relationship between the structure of mortgage markets (funding mechanisms and mortgage products) and the stability of housing markets requires far more careful study. A related topic worth exploring is the role of macroprudential measures in promoting housing market stability. Finally, explaining the driving forces of the co-movement of housing prices in many developed countries during the latest housing boom, and the different pathways to unwinding the boom, is a pressing topic for research, which may be feasible once internationally comparable housing price data become more widely available.

RK Green, K-H Kim, AB Sanders, and S Wachter

ENVIRONMENT

Aims and Objectives

The broad aims of this section echo that of the overall encyclopedia, namely to provide an international perspective on housing and to engage with academic and practitioner audiences. The objective is to provide an insight into the main issues associated with housing and the environment. This section brings together the key environmental issues for housing globally, including those relating to the physical and the social spheres, and the interaction between them. The dynamic relationship established between space and society over time is explored, with many of the articles covering issues at the intersection of the social and the physical, and recognising that this relationship is multidirectional. How do individuals and communities affect the housing and wider environment? How do physical circumstances, including housing environments, influence behaviours and social relationships?

The section comprises 68 core articles written by recognised experts in the field and providing comprehensive overviews of a wide range of environmental topics from climate change to ghettos, and from health risks to household waste recycling. To provide orientation, we commissioned a small number of longer overview articles on Sustainable Communities by Alina Congreve, Climate Change by Tina Fawcett, Housing Dynamics: Environmental Aspects by Gareth Powells, and Social Spaces and Urban Policies by Wim Ostendorf. The breadth and depth of the articles in this section provide evidence of a growing interest in environmental issues for housing research and practice.

Structure and Organisation

The articles in this section are broadly divided into two categories: social and physical. The reciprocal influences created around the physical and social domains in housing are barely extricable; however, a distinction was made to facilitate the design of the section, the identification of authors, and the categorising of key concepts and issues covered by the term 'environment'. The articles were commissioned as being primarily about either the social environment or the physical environment, though in practice, of course, the two themes often overlap.

The more physical-oriented articles (encompassing both the dwelling and the built environment) cover topics about housing and environmental change, the impact of housing on the biosphere, and housing environmental sustainability issues as well as articles about the material infrastructure of housing: the bricks and mortar and its physical layout. The articles concentrate on either the dwelling or the neighbourhood/city scale, or undertake a more generic 'theory and approaches' review. Thus, for instance, we have an article by Erling Holden that is primarily about the dwelling (Ecological Footprint), Gordon Walker deals with the scale of the neighbourhood (Community Energy Systems), and Rajat Gupta deals with more general matters of theory and approaches (Climate Change: Adaptations). For essays concentrating on built environment issues, topics relating to the dwelling are explained and developed in articles on rural housing by Mark Shucksmith and on second homes by Fernando Diaz Orueta. Built environment concepts associated with the neighbourhood and the city are also discussed, for example in articles on Green Space and Parks by Nicola Dempsey and on Housing and Sustainable Transport by Erling Holden.

Essays addressing the social perspective are concerned with the interactions between housing and householders, and more broadly with environment and society. The social dimension comprises both the individual and the community, and includes topics and ideas that go from individual perceptions to collective actions related to the physical environment, embodying several scales like the dwelling, the neighbourhood, or the city. For instance, the scale of the dwelling and the role of householders are evidenced in a few articles (Place Attachment by Barbara Brown, Irwin Altman, and Carol Werner and Household Waste Recycling by Matt Watson), while others concentrate on a larger environmental scale (Neighbourhood Design: Urban Outdoor Experience by Nicola Dempsey, Neighbourhood Watch by Richard Yarwood, and Eco-Communities by Heather Lovell). This perspective also includes articles that are more conceptually focused on 'theories and approaches' (Sustainable Housing Cultures by Eli Støa).

Certain entries reflect more than others the difficulties associated with disentangling the predominance of one approach or another. Examples of this include essays on the undesired effects on the environment of negative behaviours like crime (see Neighbourhood Incivilities by Ralph Taylor), the individual health risks associated with poor environmental conditions (see Health Risks: Damp and Cold by Jeroen Douwes), and the particularities and specificities of the relationship established between groups or collectives and the environment (see Vernacular Housing by Laida Memba Ikuga or Gypsy/Roma Settlements by Teresa San Román).

Over time, housing research has changed its focus to embrace problems and issues in the real world. Until the mid- to late 1990s, the majority of the wider housing studies literature tended to concentrate on either social issues (such as low-income housing and welfare) or economic issues (notably housing finance and the operation of housing markets), and the physical environment was rather overlooked. But in the last few decades, this has begun to change with a growing body of work researching environmental issues, including householder studies (on energy and water consumption and waste management), the design and production of sustainable housing, and attitudes in the house building industry towards the environment. Exemplifying this, the articles broadly grouped as pertaining to the physical environment section consider both traditional research issues related to housing and urban studies (Maintenance and Repair by Ad Straub, Housing Estates by Frank Wassenberg, and Ethnic Minorities and Housing by Gideon Bolt) as well as newer more contemporary housing research topics (Defensible Space by Paul Cozen and David Hillier, Eco-Renovation by Gavin Killip, and Eco-Communities by Heather Lovell).

The physical environment articles address a wide range of international perspectives covering the environmental issues at stake not only in the rich and developed part of the world but also in poorer, developing countries. To this end, leading researchers from around the world discuss international debates and case studies which include examples of community planning in Vancouver, Canada, in Seattle, USA and in Brisbane, Australia (see Neighbourhood Planning by Simon Pinnegar). There is also a comparison of self-build techniques between the Gaza Strip (Autonomous Palestinian Territories), Khartoum (Sudan), Kigali (Rwanda), Rio de Janeiro (Brazil), and Buenos Aires (Argentina) (see the article on Self-Build: Global South by Fernando Murillo).

Several transversal concepts of paramount importance for the whole section feature as a *leitmotiv* across many of the articles. They are mainly related to the impact of recent changes and shifts in societal cultures and lifestyles and its relation to the environment. The three pillars of sustainability, for instance, have been acknowledged in many of the articles as has the growing attention researchers pay to safety-related issues and environmental impacts on health. Another topic that demands attention is the way deprivation and persistent inequalities at the social level are reflected in territorial outcomes.

This section deals explicitly with processes and dynamics over the territory inspired (or not) by certain attitudes and behaviours of the population and its evolution over time. In that sense, the section puts a particular emphasis on the preconditions, requirements, and determinants over time for processes to develop. A few articles (Temporary Housing by Claire Lévy-Vroelant, Gated Communities by Rowland Atkinson and Sarah Blandy, and Gentrification and Neighbourhood Change by Marco van der Land, Alexander Curley and G van Eijk) are key examples here relating to social issues, whilst others (Adaptable Housing by Eli Støa or Construction and Demolition Waste by Vivian Tam) show a certain degree of progression and development on the physical side.

More than just theoretical analysis, many of the articles in this section discuss and debate the impact of policies, programmes, and actions: that is, both analytic and normative approaches are incorporated within the section. This is perhaps most evident in a series of case studies: for instance, Amsterdam's pattern of social segregation (Social Spaces and Urban Policies by Wim Ostendorf and Sako Musterd), Danish practices related to energy consumption (Sustainable Lifestyles by Kirsten Gram-Hanssen), the design of teahouses in Shanghai or the *favelas* in Brazil (Vernacular Housing by Laida Memba Ikuga), and the evolution of second homes at the Spanish Mediterranean coast (Second Homes by Fernando Diaz Orueta).

Finally, a few umbrella concepts considered in this section are also reflected in other sections of the encyclopedia. This is the case, for instance, with neighbourhood governance (Ali Madanipour), social sustainability (Monterrat Pareja-Eastaway), and sustainabe housing cultures (Eli Støa). There are also essays on sustainable lifestyles (Kirsten Gram-Hanssen) and on gender and space (Irene Molina).

In summary, housing and the home cannot be seen, experienced, or studied apart from in their environmental contexts and effects. The physical and the social environment contribute to what housing and home represents for individuals; that wider environment is itself shaped by the practices associated with housing and home. This section aims to provide the reader with an overview of the many different international dimensions of this interplay. The hope is that it provides a way into these issues for the nonexpert, that it opens new dimensions for those already well-read in the field, and that it inspires the research community towards fresh ways of thinking.

H Lovell, M Pareja Eastaway, and M Elsinga

HOME AND HOMELESSNESS

'Home' is a concept found across the natural and social sciences, referring in its broadest sense to the habitats of animals and plants. In the context of housing, home denotes the feelings, values, cultures, and practices associated with the physical structures of human dwelling. This concept of home refers to the ways in which dwelling structures become sites of emotional, cultural, and personal significance; the ways in which a sense of belonging in the world is constructed in and through the residential environment. The articles in this section reflect and expand upon this conceptualisation of home, and on the impacts (largely in the material sense) of absence of home ('homelessness'). There are 98 articles in this section, spread more or less evenly across topics relating to home and to homelessness.

Home: A Multidisciplinary Affair

Reflecting on the multiple meanings and experiences of the term 'home', a hallmark of the scholarship in this section – perhaps more so than in any other part of the encyclopedia – is its multidisciplinary character. To illustrate this, particular editorial effort has been made to ensure that all principal disciplinary perspectives on home are elaborated to some extent, each taking different theoretical points and hence conceptualising home in subtly different ways. Philosophical perspectives, for example, are primarily concerned with the ways in which homes – material or imaginative – are connected with our sense of 'being-in-the-world', with personhood most generally. Anthropology is more focused on the collective, rather than the self, in its emphasis on the built forms of housing and different meanings of home associated with different cultures and, more recently, with its recognition of the importance of objects and material culture more generally in making home. In literature, film studies, and popular culture, the creation and maintenance of normative definitions of home is paramount, highlighting, for example, the omnipresence of representations of home across diverse forms like Flemish painting, American postwar television, and women's magazines. Feminist perspectives are critical in understanding the 'house-as-home', initially in refuting the overly romanticised and gender-blind perspectives that dominated early housing studies, and more recently in elaborating the complex links between home and both masculinity and femininity. Feminist frameworks in fact underpin a number of articles in this section, including those on sexuality, emotions, home and work, and meanings of home.

Although the individual lenses through which home is comprehended varies across these disciplines, collectively three key themes emerge.

The first, reflecting the importance of feminism in scholarship on home, is the centrality of gender when both experiencing and conceptualising home. Men and women experience home in different ways. Whether home is a place of relaxation or a place of unpaid (or paid) work, whether a safe haven or site of violence and antagonism, for example, are experiences strongly correlated with gender. While gender differences remain critical to understanding home, recent feminist scholarship has also turned attention to new types of relations between gender and home, such as through migration, temporary dwelling, and technology. Furthermore, gender is central to key concepts used to understand home. The chain of association linking home with the domestic sphere, and infusing the domestic sphere with connotations of privacy, for instance, can be traced back to the eighteenth-century notion of separate spheres in which it was presumed that the realms of daily life for men and women were, and should be, completely different. Feminist critiques of this public–private dichotomy, and the reformulation of this dualism to stress the necessary interconnections of public and private, drive contemporary feminist theorisations of house-as-home.

A second key theme concerns the ways in which experiences of home reflect and reproduce patterns of historical, geographical, and social differentiation. How home is understood, practiced, and represented varies considerably depending on age (compare the way home is imagined by a child and by an elderly person), race, religion, and sexuality, as many of the articles demonstrate. These socially differentiated experiences of home are critical in shaping both people's life chances and their senses of themselves. Historical variations are also implicit in this section, exemplified in the changing representations of home in literature and film, and the altering technological foundations of the modern house-as-home. Perhaps not surprisingly, given the volume's emphasis on houses, the importance of geographical context in shaping home underpins many of the articles. Geographical context is approached at a number of scales: national–regional differences as exemplified in the different material cultures of home and home objects; the common and varying elements of home found in high-rise and suburban housing; and the experiences of domestic workers across the global North and South. This section also advances scholarship on home through its emphasis on the importance of transnational movements of people and ideas in transforming home.

A final key theme concerns the strong linkages between home and the myriad economic, political, and legal institutions of housing. While home is a more cultural concept than house, and scholarship on home draws less on political science, law, and economics than other dimensions of housing studies, what home means remains strongly connected to socioeconomic, political, and legal differentiation. Homeownership is a critical investment and wealth-building activity across the Western world that underpins many national economies and has been linked to a sense of 'ontological security'. The legal protection of homeownership underpins the experience of homeownership, and may even be the basis for claiming new legal rights, for example, through 'defensive homeownership'. Finally, institutions such as planning and welfare systems silently support homeownership and middle-class definitions of home through their continuing preference for homeownership and nuclear family/individualised patterns of social life.

Future scholarship on home will probably be influenced by broader intellectual trends across the social sciences, in concert with the changing social, political, cultural, and economic context. Within this frame, a number of likely directions can be identified. Empirically, many of the recent trends identified in this section will endure impacts of transnational movements on housing and home, imprint of social constructions of home across diverse policy and institutional fields, and increasingly complex identity formation in and through home. The implications of climate change for experiences of home are likely to become a key issue, as scholars explore the links between carbon-intensive practices and meanings of home, on the one hand, and the meanings of home (shared living spaces, more high rises?) that could underpin a carbon-reduced future, on the other hand.

Theoretically, the trend towards more integrative approaches is also likely to continue. While much scholarship on home already draws upon diverse social science and humanities disciplines, the current moment sees increasing dialogue across natural and social sciences through perspectives such as 'science and technology' studies in which the processes of the natural and social worlds are considered simultaneously. In relation to home, it may be that existing scholarship on material cultures and pets, which draw from an understanding of the 'more-than-human' world and dispute the separation of nature and culture, will take housing studies in new directions, such as recent work on the ways in which social networks and technologies are assembled to constitute home in an increasingly technologically embedded world. These new frameworks will enable housing studies to address changing contours of home into the future.

Homelessness: A Multifaceted Condition

'Homelessness' can, conceptually, be understood as the absence of 'home', but practical definitions tend to prioritise the material aspects of inadequate housing conditions. Such definitions vary in breadth across the developed world, from the categorisation of 'literal homelessness' traditionally found in the United States and elsewhere, which is confined to those sleeping rough or in homeless shelters, to the much wider definition employed in the United Kingdom, for example, which covers all those without a legal right to occupy 'reasonable' accommodation, and the 'cultural' definition used in Australia. The European Federation of National Organisations Working with the Homeless (FEANTSA) 'ETHOS' typology, which offers a homelessness definition encompassing aspects of 'rooflessness', 'houselessness', 'insecure housing', and 'inadequate housing', has been increasingly influential in Europe and beyond. But such broad-ranging definitions are inappropriate in the developing world, where the imposition of such 'Western' notions of housing security and adequacy would label most of the population as homeless. In India, for example, reference is more often made to those who are 'houseless' or 'shelterless', emphasising the absence of any form of shelter.

Homelessness is recognised as a major social policy concern in many developed countries, and as a feature of extreme poverty throughout the developing world. Homelessness can also happen dramatically as the result of human conflicts or natural disasters, with the needs of refugees and internally displaced people representing a major humanitarian challenge in many parts of the world. The material circumstances giving rise to homelessness differ across the globe, and its manifestations differ too: street children, informal settlements, and large refugee camps are key concerns in Asia, Africa, and Central and South Americas, whereas single adults sleeping rough or in shelters, families living in temporary accommodation, and 'hidden' homeless groups 'doubling up' with friends and relatives are core issues in much of the developed world. While most identifiable homelessness is located within urban settings, there is a growing understanding of the particular dimensions of rural homelessness in countries as diverse as India, the United States, New Zealand, Spain, Ireland, and Finland.

There are clear patterns, at least within the developed world, of the characteristics of the people most vulnerable to 'literal homelessness'. This group tends to be male, single, middle-aged, unemployed, or disabled, with a strong overrepresentation of ethnic minorities and recent migrants. Men leaving institutional settings – such as prison and the armed forces – are often at particular risk of street homelessness. However, the broader one's definition of homelessness, the more 'feminised' it becomes, with women and children predominating among refugees and internally displaced people in the developing world.

Understandings of homelessness, like meanings of 'home', have benefited from multidisciplinary scholarship, though major challenges remain in integrating the varying perspectives that these different disciplines offer. Economists tend to focus on aggregates and macroexplanatory levels, often giving overwhelming importance to housing market conditions in explaining homelessness, whereas applied social psychologists, for example, focus on the ways in which homeless people's self-identity influences their propensity to engage with housing and support services. Added to this rich intellectual mix are distinctive theoretical and methodological approaches, which cut across disciplinary boundaries. Social constructionist perspectives have explored the meanings attached to homelessness by various actors, and the impacts that these representations can have on policy responses. Ethnographers provide rich and culturally sensitive details on the lives of marginalised people, such as homeless people, that enable their perspectives to be 'included' in debate and policy formulation. Explanatory frameworks have been offered from a 'critical realist' perspective, which contends that complex causal mechanisms operate across a wide range of social strata, and no single factor is likely to be 'necessary' or 'sufficient' for the generation of homelessness. As with scholarship on 'home', feminist perspectives have been influential, and have gained in sophistication and subtlety over time.

At its core, the study of homelessness reflects a concern with human suffering and exclusion and a desire to prevent and resolve it, with an increasing emphasis on commitments to 'end homelessness' by governments and NGOs across the developed world. Demands for 'rights-based' approaches have come to dominate political discourse in recent years, although there are also counter voices arguing for less adversarial 'social partnership' models. Another key schism is between those who advocate 'continuum of care' models, whereby homeless people move through a series of accommodation and support 'steps' to render them 'housing ready' before accessing mainstream accommodation, and the 'Housing First' model, rapidly gaining ground across the developed world, whereby ordinary housing is provided immediately with support services configured around this permanent accommodation. There is encouraging evidence from a range of countries on improved specialist responses to diverse homeless groups – including young people, older people, people with mental health, drug or alcohol problems, and women fleeing domestic violence – but these targeted programmes sometimes attempt to compensate for the absence, or retrenchment, of mainstream welfare protection. Another cause for concern in many quarters is the 'criminalisation' of homelessness in nations as diverse as India, Australia, Brazil, Japan, England, Hungary, and Rwanda.

Future scholarship on homelessness will doubtless be informed by intellectual trends across the academic world, as with other areas of study, but two important practical points stand out.

First, improved quantitative data on homelessness are required. The availability of robust statistical evidence on homelessness is extremely patchy, even if one confines oneself to the developed world. The United States has by far the best quantitative research, based on large sample sizes and robust methodologies, including the use of longitudinal and control/comparison group techniques to assess rigorously the effectiveness of specific homelessness programmes. Elsewhere, there is a dearth of quantitative research on homelessness, aside from basic, descriptive work on the characteristics of homeless people. Cost–benefit analysis and associated economic techniques designed to demonstrate the efficient use of public resources are a key concern in this regard. These types of economic analyses are relatively well developed within the homelessness sector in only Australia and the United States at the moment, but it seems inevitable that their importance will grow in the coming years, especially given ongoing downward pressures on public expenditure following the global economic crisis.

Second, there is a clear need for international comparative research on homelessness (both qualitative and quantitative). Key research questions on, for example, the impact of structural contexts on the scale and nature of homelessness cannot be answered without such evidence. Conducting cross-country empirical research on homelessness requires significant resources which are rarely made available, and there are also considerable methodological challenges to overcome with respect to conceptual equivalence, data harmonisation, and, perhaps most profoundly, institutional divergence in responses. However, there are many other areas of housing studies where such barriers are, if not overcome, at least worked around in order to deliver useful comparative findings. There is, in principle, no reason why similar progress cannot be made in the homelessness field.

R Dowling and S Fitzpatrick

INSTITUTIONS

The Purpose and Place of Housing Institutions

While housing is a basic human need that can be provided at a rudimentary level of shelter, and the home is a quintessentially personal realm where intimacy and privacy is realised, the provision and consumption of homes has become a highly regulated practice, mediated by various institutions and agencies. Housing agents and organisations are, especially in developed societies, regulated by the state or even civil sector organisations run on a nonprofit basis. At the same time, private enterprises concerned with housing have increasingly organised themselves into larger units in order to represent their own interests, often in tandem with the institutional and legislative mobilisation of governments. This section of the encyclopedia addresses the diversity and complexity of institutions and institutional relationships in the realisation of housing.

One conventional understanding of housing institutions is focused on the social organisations that support the specific housing and housing-related needs of society. Other approaches emphasise the need to see institutions more broadly as the norms, rules, and regulations – the entire body of mechanisms and structures of social order and cooperation – that govern the behaviour of a set of individuals. From this perspective, housing institutions encompass the norms and rules that enable a society to fulfil its need for adequate housing, including the complex interactions of housing supply and demand, and housing needs. 'Institutions' may thus refer to organisations that perform specific tasks within society, the laws and regulations formulated at different levels of government, and informal values and norms concerning how housing is used and circulated.

In order to be as inclusive and comprehensive as possible, we have assumed a broad definition of institutions in this volume. The literature on institutions within housing studies has usually taken the existence of 'typical' institutional entities and practices as givens, and thus become a normative force that has inadequately questioned the nature and role of housing institutions. Indeed, examples of housing practices in places like Africa, Latin America, and East Asia as set out in this section illustrate considerable complexity and diversity in institutional arrangements concerning the home and processes of housing.

Approaches

Understanding institutions in housing is a formidable task that requires, on the one hand, considerable sensitivity to social and cultural variations, and on the other hand, appreciation of the growing influence of global economic and regulatory forces. Recently, the changing institutional relationships around housing markets have heightened the 'interconnectedness' of households to an international institutional network, subjugating the 'micro' phenomenon of 'home', and the security and orientation of the family within the home, to the influence of multiscalar flows of capital and finance. This became particularly evident in the international property price bubble that emerged at the beginning of the twenty-first century, which helped to stimulate irresponsible lending and borrowing, especially in subprime mortgage sectors, and which was followed by the credit crunch and a global recession that has spread far beyond housing markets and mortgage finance. Housing institutions, regulators, and agencies not only triggered the unfolding of the latest financial crisis; their alignment around a particular mode of market housing provision, and commodity consumption, albeit manifest differently in each local context, helped reconfigure housing processes on a global scale while at the same time reconstituting the very meaning and experience of home at the individual level.

This is not to say that institutional relationships in each society have converged in line with neoliberal forms of capitalism. Indeed, the meaning and nature of housing and home in each culture or community reflects the complexity and idiosyncrasy of housing systems, which are locally and historically contingent and demonstrate considerable path dependency.

The articles collected in this volume attempt to capture the diversity of institutions that intersect with housing as well as differences in the formation and development of institutional constellations in different countries. As researches on, for example, welfare regimes and varieties of capitalism have demonstrated, institutions and institutional frameworks both shape the interaction of political, economic, and social dimensions and are shaped by the context with which they arise and evolve. Consequently, there is a particularly comparative focus to this volume with a number of articles and clusterings of articles that address comparable institutional phenomena in different societies and regions of the world. On the one hand, this helps demonstrate local institutional relations and their impact on housing markets, policies, and practices, as well as change and development over time. On the other hand, it illustrates how much the impact of individual agency, political intervention, and global forces is contingent on historic frameworks of organisational formations and relations. What is apparent across the articles here is how often relatively similar housing policy developments are mediated by different institutional structures and networks, leading to highly variegated social and market outcomes.

While the geographic separation of countries and regions provides one way to approach this text, it is also possible to consider different institutional dimensions. In terms of scale, the range runs from international and state agencies to neighbourhood associations to individual professionals. In terms of institutions as regulations, or rules of the game, there is also considerable variety, from the laws that define rights of ownership and access to housing, to the means by which management decisions are made, and to the cultural norms that regulate the exchange of shelter and housing wealth within the family or household unit. This volume also touches on important social issues such as ageing, gender, and race and how different institutional relations and practices affect these. There are also the more familiar topics concerning housing supply and demand, housing markets, and public policy.

Themes and Issues

More theoretically or conceptually driven approaches to scientific collections like this one can often impose frameworks for understanding the phenomena and the nature of relationships between them. However, in compiling this section we have considered eclecticism a merit, and the diversity of topics and approaches as an opportunity to re-engage with the dynamism and complexity of housing relations. One of the distinctive contributions offered by a focus on 'institutions' of housing and home within the framework of an encyclopedia is considerable freedom to move between topics and thereby make unanticipated connections and associations between ideas, practices, and places. It is useful, nonetheless, to highlight a number of key themes and issues, as well as make some illustrative links between topics.

The contributions in this section essentially explore differences in housing regimes and housing institutions. Housing institutions are viewed as culturally embedded in the overall process of economic, social, and political transformation, while recognising the power of specific local imperatives and market pressures to shape their response. The main argument is that housing institutions have differential capacities to direct these processes of change, leading to divergent responses in the housing provision system. The section explores these differences as well as the institutional relationships in four principal domains: (1) housing tenure and housing rights; (2) housing institutions providing affordable housing; (3) institutions for the supply of housing; and (4) housing markets and the myriad of formal and informal institutions involved in the provision of housing. While the articles themselves reveal the complexities of housing institutions, it is possible to identify some of the most significant issues addressed in relation to each of these domains. These issues are likely to dominate the discourse in the housing literature for years to come.

Institutional Perspectives on Housing Rights and Housing Tenure

Housing tenure is one of the central social institutions in the field of housing. Tenures provide users with rights and burden them with responsibilities related to the consumption of housing. Several articles provide comparative perspectives on a variety of housing tenures, their evolution, and specific forms. Types of tenure are constructed by abstracting from the variety of empirically and historically existing forms – owner-occupation and renting – with major differences in terms of user rights, control, and disposition provided to the resident. Tenure differences are qualified by specific institutional arrangements in different societies with a particular emphasis on provisions ensuring the right to housing for marginalised groups in society as well as housing challenges in postconflict situations.

Housing Institutions Providing Affordable Housing

Meeting the growing need for affordable housing is one of the biggest challenges in both developed and developing countries. A number of articles explore the institutional context and the myriad of arrangements to finance, provide, allocate, and manage affordable housing through public and nongovernment models. They review a variety of approaches that have been adopted as well as the roles and contributions of different institutions across the housing system – governments, private agencies, not-for-profit organisations, and market intermediaries. Characteristics of the historic and contemporary contributions of these institutions to the provision of affordable housing highlight divergent pathways in different countries and regions. The policy debate centres on policy instruments – fiscal, financial, and regulatory – supporting the production (supply side) or the consumption (demand side) of housing. Strategies to promote, produce, and manage affordable housing are also differentiated by tenure – renting versus homeownership – and classified by the degree of targeting and efficiency.

Institutions for Housing Supply

National systems of housing supply involve dynamic public, private, and not-for-profit institutions. Although their relationships are influenced by the country (or regional) context, historic tenure mix, the place of housing in the welfare system, and local structures of housing provision, converging trends are evident. Several articles highlight a broad shift away from direct provision of affordable housing by public agencies in favour of approaches involving the private and not-for-profit sectors, either separately or in partnership. This has resulted in a complex landscape of housing finance, ownership, and management. The growth of new institutions, coupled with the more general emphasis on competitive supply by market agents (landowners, developers, house-builders, managers), has led to new forms of housing provision and 'hybrid' organisations. The contributions explore several major forms of new housing supply, including public/private partnerships, speculative house building, self-help, and informal housing. They review regional patterns and country-specific trends and relationships among key institutions related to the promotion, production, allocation, and consumption of housing.

Housing Markets: Informal and Formal Institutions

Housing markets are culturally embedded in society and the efficiency of their institutions is critical for the provision of adequate and affordable housing. Several articles explore housing market institutions in developing countries, highlighting the importance of informality and difference. Major activities – access to housing, maintenance, services (water, sanitation, access roads), tenure security (to prevent eviction), finance for construction, purchase, or renting – occur through a combination of more or less formal processes. Depending on the social, economic, political, and legal context, some of these activities have been institutionalised over time into more permanent norms and rules implemented with varying degrees of formality by agencies or organisations of the state, market, or civil society. Such informality is very much part of the institutional transformation of post-socialist housing markets and is likely to distinguish them from some of their more mature, well-established European counterparts.

Concluding Remarks

Despite the common challenges facing housing systems in different countries, there are historical and deeply embedded differences in the nature of their housing institutions. There are also significant differences in the political, economic, and social drivers affecting housing policy reforms and the transformation of these institutions, which challenge the idea of convergence. The volume examines the range of strategies used in contemporary societies to protect housing rights, to improve housing quality and affordability, and to enhance the efficiency of housing markets through the lens of housing institutions. This approach brings into focus the role and respective contributions of government, private sectors, and not-for-profit agencies in the provision of housing. In 83 articles, this section addresses the diversity of institutions that have developed around the financing, production, and consumption of housing, accounting for differences between countries and institutional transformation. While capturing diversity is an exhaustive task beyond the scope of this work, this section, nonetheless, illustrates core differences in institutional configurations and relationships regarding housing markets, housing management, construction, planning, tenure, and housing rights.

R Ronald and S Tsenkova

POLICY

Aims and Structure

The aim of this section is to provide a global overview of housing policies and to engage with academic and practitioner audiences. A well-functioning housing market that provides shelter for all regardless of income is of key importance in societies all over the world, and therefore a primary objective of housing policy. During the global financial crisis, we learned that low incomes, subprime loans, and a global financial market proved to be an explosive combination. As a consequence, housing policies and financial policies are being reconsidered as is evident from several articles in this and in other sections. This section of the encyclopedia focuses upon various aspects of housing policy in developed, developing, and transitional economies, collectively reflecting the evolution of housing policy formulation and implementation in a variety of economic, political, and social contexts.

This section comprises 58 core articles and 7 longer overview essays written by recognised experts in the field, providing a comprehensive guide to a wide range of policy topics. Together, the articles are organised around the following seven key themes.

Housing Policy Development

Two essays by John Doling and Peter Ward provide a comprehensive overview of the evolution of housing policy in advanced, transitional and developing economies. Doling suggests a framework that emphasises processes of convergence and divergence with respect to broad historical trends in housing policy (Housing Policy Trends). He shows that over time, with economic development and urbanisation, countries' housing policies are characterised by increased state intervention in housing, but over the course of the last half century, they have relied more on market processes, with an increasing emphasis on homeownership. While Doling's primary focus is on the advanced economies, he also considers transition and developing countries.

Ward, in contrast, provides an overview of housing policies in developing countries. Detailing the evolution of housing policies from the 1950s onwards, Ward argues that housing policies and their implementation are shaped by broader economic and political ideologies, levels of development and urbanisation, and rates of urban growth. Exploring this in relation to changing development paradigms ranging from modernisation to neoliberalism, he charts the changing nature of state intervention in the housing arena from the very direct role played by governments in various sites and service schemes in the 1980s to the subsequent rolling back of the state associated with neoliberal economics and politics. The latter era has been marked by an emphasis on decentralisation, good governance, urban sustainability, and greater efficiency of urban management and city planning.

Self-Help

Articles by Richard Harris (Self-Help: Policy Assistance) and Diana Mitlin (Housing Policies in Developing Countries: Sites-and-Services and Aided Self-Help) both focus on one of the most prominent housing initiatives across the developing world, namely aided self-help or site and service schemes. Harris's article provides a rare insight into the evolution of self-help policies which he traces back to the early years of the twentieth century when a number of European nations (including Germany, Scandinavia, Austria, and Canada) began to help those on low incomes to construct their own housing. Articulated in the writings of Crane in the 1940s and Turner in the 1960s, the key principles of self-help were to afford poorer individuals and households the 'freedom to build' and for the state to facilitate this through the (varied) provision of serviced land, advice, finance, building materials, and training in management and construction.

These arguments are further developed in Mitlin's article which concentrates on the experience of developing countries from the 1970s onwards. She attributes the growing popularity of site and service programmes among both international agencies (such as the United Nations and the World Bank) and national governments to rapidly expanding urban populations as well as an urbanisation of poverty. Within this context, self-help housing initiatives provided a viable alternative in relation to previous (failed) interventions including squatter eviction and relocation as well as publically provided housing. This said, drawing upon a range of examples, both Harris and Mitlin identify the limitations of site and service programmes including the limited scale of many programmes, speculative investment, downward raiding by the rich and powerful, and demanding building standards. On a more ideological note, site and service programmes have also been criticised for shifting the responsibility of housing provision from the state to vulnerable individuals and households and for depressing wage levels. The article by David Satterthwaite on upgrading presents a type of self-help initiative undertaken by poor urban populations living in 'slum' or informal settlements to improve their housing.

Access and Affordability

Judith Yates and Vivienne Milligan provide an overview of policies that promote access to housing opportunities and the affordability of housing. They explain a rationale for policies that improve access and affordability, which highlights their impact on individual households and on the economy as a whole. A taxonomy of policies is proposed that gives insight into the diverse range of direct and indirect forms of assistance that can be provided. The authors highlight the importance of evaluating these policies against a broad rather than narrow range of objectives. The group of articles addressing access and affordability issues includes programmes that aim to directly alleviate housing costs burdens (Peter Kemp writes on housing allowances, and Marion Steele on housing vouchers). Marietta Haffner, Marja Elsinga and Jap Hockstra examine private renting, Hugo Priemus writes on administered rents in public housing, Jenny Schuetz and Rebecca Meltzer address inclusionary zones, and Hans Lint reviews the legislation on security of tenure. In more recent times, state intervention in the form of regulatory controls has been relaxed and direct provision via social housing has contracted. Innovative attempts to improve low-income households' access to housing opportunities are tackled in two articles (Intermediate Housing Tenures by Marja Elsinga and Social Housing: Measures to Attract Private Finance by Peter Phibbs). As John Doling, (mentioned above), points out, advanced countries have increasingly concentrated on expanding homeownership. Government policies to improve access for first-time home-buyers are reviewed in two articles (Contract Saving Schemes by Richard Ronald and First Home-Owner Grants by Tony Dalton), while measures to improve access to private rental housing are discussed in one article (Deposit Assistance Schemes for Private Rental in the United Kingdom by Julie Rugg). Finally, there is an article on schemes in developing countries that aim to improve access to housing loans. The programmes reviewed by Peer Smets (Housing Policies in Developing Countries: Microfinance) usually consist of small loans obtained for a short period of time and are suited to the ways in which poorer households manage their finances, as well as the ways in which they build their housing – incrementally and progressively.

Taxation and Housing

Housing and the land that housing is built on are an important source of tax revenue to most governments. A broad range of taxes are applied to housing and land. They can significantly shape how land is used, the structures that are built, and the cost of housing to the tenant or home-buyer. In most countries, the taxation of housing poses difficult challenges for policy-makers. The key policy issues are outlined by Miranda Stewart (Taxation Policy and Housing), an overview article that also describes the wide range of transaction, income, and wealth tax measures applied to housing. From this article, we learn that taxes can impact on market efficiency by influencing the allocation of resources between different housing tenures, as well as being an important determinant of housing affordability. A key feature of the taxation of housing is homeowner tax expenditures that are departures from the benchmark tax treatment of income, assets, or transactions benefiting homeowners. These have tended to attract critical attention from policy analysts (see Steven Bourassa's article on this theme). Local governments frequently derive much of their tax revenue from local government property taxes (see the article Local Government Property Taxes by Gavin Wood and Rachel Ong) that are commonly levied on the unimproved capital value of buildings, including housing. These taxes are the subject of a large literature that addresses a wide range of housing-related issues, but which also tackles impacts on neighbourhoods and residential segregation. Policy-makers have periodically considered the lift in land values accompanying changes in zoning or the grant of planning permission as an 'unearned' income that should be subject to tax. In some countries, they will be captured by a capital gains tax; but where this is not the case, a development land tax (as discussed by Michael Oxley) is commonly advocated.

Housing Supply and Neighbourhoods

Access to housing opportunities and the affordability of dwellings in market-driven housing systems will in part depend upon an ample supply of housing that is also responsive to changing market conditions. Policies that address these housing supply issues are overviewed in Kerry Vandell's article on housing supply. Extreme supply shortages that follow severely disruptive events such as wars commonly motivate programmes of investment in social housing to support housing supply (see Michael Berry's entry). But in more normal circumstances, supply responses from private developers and builders can be stimulated by supply-side subsidies (as discussed by Melek Cigdem); the competitiveness of the developer and construction industries will help shape the efficiency of housing supply, and this is addressed by governments through competition policy and regulation (as explained by David Hayward). Urban planning is a key influence on the size, location, and design of housing supply. Three articles by, respectively, Kyung-Hwan Kim, Michael Buxton and Lucy Groenhart, and Timothy Dixon, describe how governments use green belts, urban growth boundaries, and brownfield development to influence where housing is built and supplied. The location of housing and its size help shape a city's 'carbon footprint'; this important subject is explored in the article by Anthony Yezer. Finally, government approaches to the design and enforcement of residential building standards are described by Henk Visscher.

Housing also has a critically important role in driving neighbourhood dynamics, and, as a consequence, housing programmes are a component of policies addressing neighbourhood decline. Urban regeneration policies are reviewed by Ronan Paddison, while Reinout Kleinhans explains how housing programs are integrated into urban regeneration policies. There are also individual articles in this section that address issues with a strong neighbourhood dimension

(Exclusionary Zoning by Alan Mallach), and others that are focused on specific housing programmes with a strong spatial focus (HOPE VI by Diane Levy).

Labour Markets and Mortgage Markets

Housing systems are vital to the efficient functioning of economies, and the interrelationships between housing, labour markets, and the finance sector are vital in this respect. Labour market issues that have attracted concern among housing policy-makers are overviewed by Paul Flatau (in a piece on Housing and Labour Markets). Individual articles explore the following: policy responses to the efficiency and equity consequences of spatial mismatch between the residential location of workers and job sites: (Donald Houston considers the general policy response); policies that aim to retain key workers (e.g., teachers and firefighters) in regions where housing costs are high are set out by Nicola Morrison; housing subsidy programmes and incentives to work are discussed by Mark Shroder; the use of housing programmes to encourage mobility among disadvantaged subgroups are illustrated in the 'Moving to Opportunity' Programme introduced by William Clark; and finally, the relationship between social housing and employment outcomes is discussed by Kath Hulse.

Housing systems are a major sector of the national economy and are closely linked to the finance sector through mortgage markets. Housing and macroeconomic policy is discussed by Stephen Whelan and regulation and intervention in mortgage markets is addressed by Martin Flanagan; more specific regulatory instruments are described in articles dealing with mortgage guarantees by Robert Van Order, deposit guarantees for housing finance institutions by James Barth and Harris Hollans, and mortgage interest rate regulation by Ian Harper and Lachlan Smirl. The importance of housing finance and housing equity in personal wealth portfolios has meant that housing asset values and mortgage debt are an important consideration in the application of monetary policy, as discussed by John Muellbauer (Monetary Policy, Wealth Effects, and Housing).

Choice and Discrimination

We have witnessed a transformation in the role of governments in housing policy over the last few decades with an increasing emphasis on market-based solutions to housing problems. These trends and the policies that use market mechanisms to increase choice and promote individual responsibility are examined in Melek Cigdem and Gavin Wood's overview article (Choice and Government Intervention in Housing Markets). One of the first and most important policy initiatives of this kind was the sale and transfer of public housing (Privatisation of Social Housing by Manuel Aalbers); other market-based policy initiatives reviewed in this section include articles by Andrew Caplin (Shared Equity), Ray Struyk (Access and Affordability: House Purchase Certificates), and Freidman Roy and Richard Ronald (Contract Saving Schemes). Policies in transition countries are reviewed in Martin Lux's article (Policies to Promote Housing Choice in Transition Countries). The enthusiasm for neoliberal market-oriented housing policies is tempered by market imperfections that can impede choice among disadvantaged groups. Policies to address discrimination in housing markets, to tackle redlining, and to provide education programmes for home buyers and tenants have been motivated by these concerns. They are discussed here by Dag Einar Sommervoll, Manuel Aalberts, and Anitra Nelson, respectively. Finally, Val Colic-Peisker's article on immigration and housing policy is especially pertinent given the importance of migration in a globalising world.

The *International Encyclopedia of Housing and Home* has a separate section on 'Policy' because housing is a basic need and a substantial sector of the economy. Housing policy is therefore of a key concern for governments all over the world. The 65 articles in this section aim to provide the reader with an overview of the diverse housing policies in different parts of the world.

G Wood and K Datta

WELFARE AND WELL-BEING

Why Well-Being?

The *International Encyclopedia of Housing and Home* would not be complete without a set of articles which very directly tackles issues of human welfare and well-being. Of course, this theme appears, tacitly or more explicitly, in a very wide range of essays across all the main sections. Nevertheless, a central aim of very many areas of housing studies has been to engage with the importance of housing systems not only in reflecting wider patterns of exclusion and inequality but also as way of documenting and intervening in processes of discrimination, exclusion, and impoverishment. Many of the contributions in this section of the encyclopedia aim to profile such matters.

The entire encyclopedia, in its aim to appeal internationally, is challenged by the variety of meanings and implications attached in politics, policy, and practice to certain key words. There are, however, few concepts that introduce more confusion than those used to describe welfare and well-being. In the United Kingdom, and in many other European countries, for example, the term 'welfare' has a very broad meaning, which includes individuals' material conditions as well as the range of services and policy instruments that aim to secure certain levels of welfare across the population. In this sense, improving human welfare and securing well-being have very similar connotations. In addition, many, if not most, developed countries have forms of social welfare policy which commonly include housing policy, and there are extensive debates about the nature, variety, and direction of what are often termed 'welfare state regimes'. While the scope and scale of social housing provision and subsidy has frequently been scaled back or privatised in recent decades, the legacy and extent of social housing is still important in many countries; for example, see articles on social housing and the welfare state in Western Europe by Peter Boelhouwer, on social housing in the United States by Rachel Bratt, on housing finance and welfare by Peter King, and on privatization by Peter Malpass. Thus, welfare in this context is equally an individual or collective state, an ideal, and a set of policy instruments. In the United States and elsewhere, by contrast, the term 'welfare' carries the baggage of formal social welfare programmes which have in some contexts a variety of derogatory connotations, as well as limited applicability in many developing countries. Hence, our choice of the terms 'welfare' and 'well-being' to try to embrace the variety of different understandings involved.

The 62 articles in this section gathered under the collective heading of 'Welfare and Well-Being' make an important statement. Housing and home lie at the centre of many issues concerning individual and social welfare and well-being in the broadest sense, which impact on the quality of life that people experience through housing across the life course. So while some researchers and policy-makers examine housing in the context of structure, tenure, location, asset values, affordability, and accessibility, and while others consider patterns of residential and social segmentation, and the opportunities they contain for social and political mobilization, the articles in this section also look to other possibilities for the meanings of housing and home, in particular, their role in securing a better quality of life for individuals, households, and communities.

It is important, finally, to note that the section 'Welfare and Well-Being' for the purpose of the encyclopedia refers neither to the subjective measures that have become popular in health studies, nor to the 'happiness benchmark' that has come into vogue as a policy goal. It is a treated as material condition as well as a meaningful experience, and the articles are concerned as much with what produces its absence – what strips households of well-being – as with what guarantees its presence. So there are articles on housing and the state in a variety of countries, on housing wealth and quality of life, and on the reciprocal link between housing and health that is shaped by environments, policies, and institutions.

At Home with Well-Being

Several decades ago, Lee Rainwater (1966) wrote a paper entitled *Fear and the House-as-Haven in the Lower Class* in which he analysed the value and significance of the home as a refuge from human and non-human threats. Whether a single family dwelling, a self-built squatter home, a terraced cottage, or a high-rise flat, the idea is that home can be a haven – a space that is both defensible and secure. Although feminist scholarship over the years has questioned such visions (showing that for many women, home is anything but refuge (see Gender and Urban Housing in the Global South by Sylvia Chant)), the articles in this section do encourage us to think about the complex role of housing in relation to well-being: in terms of physical and economic security (or insecurity); a place to relax and have fun, or to simply get by and survive; a place of quiet and privacy (or noise and intrusion); and an asset that can be used to meet needs, now, in older age, or for children (see Asset-Based Well-Being: Use Versus Exchange Value by Beverley Searle). Housing generally, and the home in particular, has multiple significances at the individual level and this applies in both developed and less developed worlds.

In Latin American squatter and informal settlements, young households embrace the risks and social costs of living in neighbourhoods without services or secure tenure, and face having to self-build their homes, because such settlements offer a space for family life, a place to live hassle free (*vivir tranquilo*), and the eventual prospect of leaving a legacy to children (*tener un patrimonio para los hijos*). Several articles in this section examine these processes of settlement and home creation, and elsewhere there are reflections on the meanings of the home for those that live out that experience.

Interestingly, too, a high proportion of original homeowners who settled peripheral unserviced land informally some 30 or more years ago continue to live on those same lots, in dwellings that are today fully consolidated, serviced, and located in the intermediate ring of the city (see Urban Regeneration in Latin America by Peter Ward). Physical immobility appears to be the order of the day – at least among low-income homeowners. It seems likely that the meaning of those homes and the significance of their sacrifices have changed over time as people consolidated and expanded the physical space of their dwellings. For many of their (now adult) children, the home is already a patrimony, since they continue to live on the lot with their own families and fully expect to continue to do so once their parents die. How second and even third generations perceive and construct meanings about the family home is only now beginning to be researched.

In developed countries, housing markets operate to allow households to adjust home and housing to needs through residential mobility: moving out or moving inwards; building assets or drawing down on equity; upsizing or downsizing; moving into school catchment areas; and searching for amenity of one sort or other. Here the constraints are largely market based – affordability – although ethnicity and race may also be important, as are national and subnational housing policies. Nevertheless, the wider point is that housing is more than an artefact, or an asset, or a space in which to live; it carries meanings and significance which change in the life course and which are likely to be shaped or constructed by class, ethnicity, social trends and fads, advertising and real estate promotions, national ideology, and so forth. As the articles in this section show, this all has a bearing on both welfare and well-being.

Scales of Welfare and Well-Being

Whether in the developed or emerging world, the articles in this section identify a range of scales at which welfare and well-being can be considered, from the macro to the micro.

At the 'macroscale', as we have clearly seen with the recent financial crisis, housing is important in terms of the role it plays in the economy (especially in the developed world) through housing-related construction and spending, in the growth of mortgage debt, and in national economic policy. The inflation of a home price and mortgage lending bubble is implicated in the financial turmoil precipitated by subprime mortgage lending and by mortgage heavy-credit derivatives which proved unsustainable. The subsequent credit crisis, with sharp contractions in mortgage lending, sudden illiquidity in housing markets, dips in price, and a rise in repossessions, particularly in the United States, dealt a major blow to households who are vulnerable to the social and financial consequences of negative equity, bankruptcy, and homelessness. In a number of cities, particularly in the United States, the level of repossessions has led to stagnant or cratering housing markets, which are associated with high levels of vacancies and abandonment and a variety of consequent social and economic problems. While many of these issues are, appropriately, explored in the section 'Economics and Finance', their implications for the financial and wider welfare of home-buyers are drawn out in several of the articles of this section, including those of Lucy Delgadillo and Dan Immergluck.

As a result of recession, which has destabilised the economies and finances of a number of countries, including the United States, the United Kingdom, Spain, and Ireland, all of which had major housing booms, many governments have now embarked on austerity policies in order to try to rein in their national debt. This in turn has created problems in terms of rising unemployment and falling incomes and welfare cuts. There are also cuts in housing-related expenditures and subsidies which have increased housing costs and added to problems of affordability. And, as mentioned earlier, housing is also important as an asset whose erosion can undermine the well-being of homeowners, particularly older homeowners who may rely on live-in adult children to care for them in old age (as in Latin America) or who seek to trade down and release equity for retirement (increasingly the case in developed nations). These issues are explored in articles by Laurence Murphy (Asset-Based Welfare), Beverley Searle (Asset-Based Well-Being: Use Versus Exchange Value), and Hal Kendig (Older People: Well-Being, Housing and Neighbourhoods).

In short, at a macroeconomic level, housing is of importance for social well-being across the board. This is clear even when it is examined from a variety of perspectives, ranging from free-market economics to welfare state regime theory.

Moving to the 'urban scale', housing has a bearing on well-being, in particular, through its role in mediating the practice of segregation between different social and income groups. As is well known, this operates in a variety of different ways in both developed and developing countries. It includes the concentration of low-income groups into low-price, low-quality housing in inner cities or in peripheral social housing estates and irregular settlements; the flight of some higher-income households to suburban or periurban areas; and the creation of segregated housing in inner cities based upon race, class, and ethnicity. The concentration of different income and ethnic groups in different segments of the housing market can generate major differences in social conditions and quality of life: at one extreme, deprived groups are segregated within the poorest housing enclaves, and at the other extreme, highly privileged groups lock themselves away in gated communities. These themes are picked up in several articles, including those of James De Filippis (Social Movements and Housing), Anthony Lemon (Residential Segregation: Apartheid), William Wilson (Residential Segregation: Experiences of African Americans), Edward Geotz (Slum Clearance), Nora Libertun de Duren (Gated Communities: Global South), and Elena Vesselinov (Gated Communities: Developed Countries). These authors also indicate the extent to which such housing issues are tied to political struggles and campaigns. Examples include low-income self-builders mobilizing for legal recognition and for basic services, renters demonstrating to resist eviction, and sometimes – as in Mugabe's Zimbabwe – struggles over blatant ethnic cleansing. Commonplace, too, are protests to challenge rent hikes or threats of gentrification and displacement. In all of these cases, housing and neighbourhoods are the medium through which affected groups attempt to influence or change central or local government policy or to halt new developments which are seen as prejudicial to neighbourhood quality or residents rights (see the articles by Roger Zetter (Shelter and Settlement for Forcibly Displaced People), James DeFilippis (Social Movements and Housing) and others). All this engages with well-being in the broader sense.

At the 'neighbourhood level', processes such as housing abandonment, clearance and redevelopment, gentrification, condominium conversion, and the sale of social housing can contribute to changes in both the availability and the quality and affordability of the housing stock, in ways that adversely affect well-being (see articles by Alan Morris (Social Housing and Social Problems), Alan Smart (Squatter Settlement Clearance), Peter Malpass (Privatisation of Housing: Implications for Well-Being), and others). The form of housing and the environment in which it is located are also important for social interaction and quality of life. There are major differences between homes with gardens in green, communal areas, and life in high-rise blocks in a depressing environment where residents may live in fear or in a state of virtual imprisonment. Housing and home are also important for specific social groups in terms of availability, access, and exclusion. While some groups, particularly the more affluent and able bodied, have relatively few problems in finding appropriate housing, others, such as travellers, refugees, and asylum seekers in the United Kingdom, have difficulties in finding affordable homes that meet their needs. In developing countries, of course, the majority of city populations struggle to find affordable housing at all, and can only do so through informal mechanisms of self-help. It is sobering to note, nevertheless, that self-help and self-managed housing is increasingly observed as a means to homeownership among low-income groups in the United States (see articles by Richard Harris (Self-Help and Informal Sector Housing in the United States and Canada), and Vinit Mukhija (Informal Housing: Colonias in the United States)).

Everywhere there is evidence that older people, and those suffering from various health conditions and disabilities, experience difficulty in finding appropriate, accessible, enabling housing which enhances quality of life. The design and layout of housing, environmental quality, and other features of dwelling that are linked to physical and mental health are dealt with in the articles by Philippa Howden-Chapman (Health, Well-Being, and Housing), Mary Godfrey (Supported ousing), Rita Jacinto (Disability and Enablement), Diana Olsberg (Older People: Well-Being), Jason Prior (Health, Well-Being and Vulnerable Populations), and others. There are links here, too, to the articles in the section 'Environment'.

As mentioned at the outset, at the individual household level, housing is significant in terms of its role in social reproduction. Homes provide the locale for a great deal of day-to-day life, from cooking and eating to sleeping and a host of other activities, such as school homework, all of which require adequate and appropriate spaces. Some households are fortunate in having sufficient spaces for these activities, while others may be overcrowded and lack appropriate space or facilities. At the most basic level, homes are where occupants can express individuality in the way they personalise and use space. Some types of housing and environments permit this much more easily than others.

Similarly, the scope to remodel or revamp one's housing at the individual level varies. Renters, by and large, have little opportunity or incentive to undertake major remodels or retrofits (although some tenants in low-rent settings may find redecorating or housing improvement investment worthwhile). But most households do take the opportunity to redecorate, improve, or extend their homes, particularly where they have become invested in the neighbourhood, and where the home and actual dwelling itself is imbued with a special significance. Whether through contracting out, or through do-it-yourself (DIY), or through self-building and mutual aid, the housing stock generally, and the home specifically, may be refurbished over time.

Sustainable Well-Being?

'Greening' the home is a contemporary arena for physical improvements. Energy-efficient homes are on the increase and many householders are retrofitting their homes to add solar panels, improve insulation, install more energy-efficient appliances, and engage in rainwater harvesting, garbage, and other recycling, as well as undertaking garden/yard microenvironmental improvements and uses. While sustainable housing applications have traditionally been the preserve of middle-income and better-off groups, the challenge in developing countries especially will be to extend participation in sustainable housing practices to working and lower-income homeowners.

In the United States, 'weatherization' campaigns for homes using resources of the American Reinvestment and Recovery Act has targeted poorer and working-class households, and in countries such as Brazil and Mexico, one observes a quickening of interest in applying green technologies to new housing and to retrofitting older homes in working-class neighbourhoods. Indeed, the savings from making homes more energy efficient and sustainable form a much larger proportion of income among the poor than the rich. We expect interest in sustainable home buildings and retrofits to become more widespread in the future. As such, they are likely to add significant new (green) 'meanings' to housing and the home, especially among younger generations.

In the same vein, cutting across many of these scales are issues of housing rights and social justice. Such issues are rarely simple, as the current 'right to the city' debates illustrated in the article by Edesio Fernandes. While the 'right to the city' is a powerful political slogan, it tends to gloss over the crucial questions of rights for whom, and rights to what. Do landlords and developers have rights to the city or rights to housing, and if so, what form do they take and how are they to be evaluated against the rights of the overcrowded or the homeless? Equally, issues of rights for refugees or rights for travellers need to be evaluated against the rights of long-term residents in an area who may feel that their rights are being ignored or pushed to one side. In this respect, housing, whether viewed as an economic good, an individual possession, or a social right, is at the heart of wider economic, social, and political debates about the structure of society and the pursuit of social well-being.

C Hamnett and P Ward

References

Rainwater L (1966) Fear and the house-as-haven in the lower class. *Journal of the American Institute of Planners* 32: 23–31.

CONTENTS OF VOLUME 3

Homeless Families: United Kingdom	S Fitzpatrick	1
Homeless Families: United States	VA Fusaro, EL Bassuk, M Grandin, L Guilderson and M Hayes	8
Overview Article		
Homelessness: Causation	S Fitzpatrick	15
Overview Article		
Homelessness: Definitions	D MacKenzie	25
Homelessness: Measurement Questions	C Chamberlain	36
Homelessness: Prevention in the United States	J Apicello, W McAllister and B O'Flaherty	42
Homeless People: African Americans in the United States	RA Johnson	50
Homeless People: Care Leavers	P Mendes and G Johnson	57
Homeless People: Care Leavers in the United Kingdom	C Baker and S Baxter	62
Homeless People: Disasters and Displacement	S Breau	68
Homeless People: Economic Migrants in Southern Europe	A Tosi	74
Homeless People: Ex-Prisoners in England and Wales	A Jones	80
Homeless People: Ex-Service Personnel/Veterans in the United Kingdom	S Johnsen	86
Homeless People in China/East Asia	P Kennett, H-G Jeon and T Mizuuchi	90
Homeless People: Indigenous/Aboriginal	P Memmott and C Chambers	97
Homeless People: Older People	M Crane and AM Warnes	104
Homeless People: Polish Migrants in the United Kingdom	C McNaughton Nicholls	111
Homeless People: Refugees and Asylum Seekers	JA Sweeney	116
Homeless People: Single Men in Japan	Y Okamoto and J Bretherton	122
Homeless People: Street Children in Africa	L Van Blerk	127
Homeless People: Street Children in Asia	DOB Lam and FC Cheng	132
Homeless People: Street Children in Mexico	GA Jones and S Thomas de Benítez	138
Homeless People: Street Children in the United Kingdom	E Smeaton	145
Homeless People: Youth in Australia	G Johnson	151
Homeless People: Youth in the United Kingdom	D Quilgars	156
Homeowners' Associations in Post-Socialist Countries	J Hegedüs	161
Homestead and Other Legal Protections	DB Barros	167
HOPE VI	DK Levy	172
House Biographies	H Jarvis	176
House Building Industries: Africa	DCI Okpala	182
House Building Industries: Asia Pacific	Y Yau	187
House Building Industries: Latin America	A de Castro	195
House Building Industries: Post-Socialist	S Tsenkova	203

House Building Industries: Western Europe and North America	C Moore and D Adams	211
Household Organisation and Survival in Developing Countries	S Chant	217
Households and Families	R Simpson	227
Household Waste Recycling	M Watson	234
House Price Expectations	R Martin	239
Overview Article House Price Indexes	SC Bourassa	247
House Price Indexes: Methodologies	NE Coulson	252
House Prices and Quality of Life: An Economic Analysis	JF McDonald	258
Housing Agents and Housing Submarkets	C Donner	265
Overview Article Housing and Labour Markets	P Flatau	273
Housing and Neighbourhood Quality: Home Improvement Grants	P Leather	281
Housing and Neighbourhood Quality: Urban Regeneration	R Paddison	288
Housing and Sustainable Transport	E Holden and K Linnerud	294
Overview Article Housing and the Macroeconomy	J Muellbauer	301
Housing and the State in Australasia	B Badcock	315
Housing and the State in China	F Wu	323
Housing and the State in Latin America	C Zanetta	330
Housing and the State in South Africa	C Lemanski	337
Housing and the State in South Asia	S Kumar	340
Housing and the State in the Middle East	AM Soliman	346
Housing and the State in the Soviet Union and Eastern Europe	I Tosics	355
Overview Article Housing and the State in Western Europe	P Boelhouwer and J Hoekstra	363
Housing and Wealth Portfolios	M Flavin	374
Housing Auctions	D Brounen	380
Housing Careers	M Abramsson	385
Housing Classes and Consumption Cleavages	SG Lowe	390
Housing Construction Industry, Competition and Regulation	D Hayward	395
Housing Demand	S Malpezzi and SM Wachter	404
Housing Developers and Sustainability	A Congreve	408
Housing Developers: Developed World	W Amann and A Mundt	415
Housing Developers: Developing World	C Acioly Jr. and M French	422
Overview Article Housing Dynamics: Environmental Aspects	G Powells	429
Housing Equity Withdrawal in the United Kingdom	A Holmans	436
Housing Estates	F Wassenberg	444
Housing Finance: Deposit Guarantees	JR Barth and H Hollans	450
Overview Article Housing Finance: Global South	K Datta	456
Housing Finance: Mexico	M Lea	463

Housing Finance Institutions: Africa	F Roy	470
Housing Finance Institutions: Asia	H Zhu	480
Housing Finance Institutions: Latin America	WB Gwinner	486
Housing Finance Institutions: Transition Societies	W Amann and E Springler	491
Housing Governance	A Beer	497
Housing Indicators	J Flood	502
Overview Article Housing Institutions in Developing Countries	A Pal and W Van Vliet	509
Housing Market Search	WAV Clark	518
Housing Markets and Macroeconomic Policy	S Whelan	523
Overview Article Housing Market Institutions	K Hawtrey	528
Housing Need in the United Kingdom	A Clarke	538
Housing Paradigms	T Iglesias	544
Housing Pathology	A Thomsen	550
Overview Article Housing Policies in Developing Countries	PM Ward	559
Housing Policies in Developing Countries: Microfinance	P Smets	573
Housing Policies in Developing Countries: Sites-and-Services and Aided Self-Help	D Mitlin	579
Overview Article Housing Policy: Agents and Regulators	P Boelhouwer and J Hoekstra	585
Housing Policy and Regeneration	RJ Kleinhans	590
Overview Article Housing Policy Trends	J Doling	596
Housing Preferences	HCCH Coolen and SJT Jansen	606
Housing Standards: Regulation	HJ Visscher, FM Meijer and JP Branco	613
Housing Statistics	M Steele	620
Housing Subsidies and Welfare	P King	627
Housing Subsidies and Work Incentives	M Shroder	632
Housing Subsidies in the Developing World	A Gilbert	638
Overview Article Housing Supply	KD Vandell	644
Housing Supply: Green Belts	K-H Kim	659
Housing Supply: Urban Growth Boundaries	M Buxton and L Groenhart	664
Housing Trust Funds	KE Larsen	668
Housing Wealth and Consumption	M Iacoviello	673
Housing Wealth and Inheritance in the United Kingdom	C Hamnett	679
Housing Wealth as Precautionary Savings	R Martin	685
Housing Wealth Distribution in the United Kingdom	G Pryce	691
Housing Wealth over the Life Course	T Davidoff	697
Human Rights and Housing	P Kenna	703
Ideal Homes	T Chapman	709
Illicit Drug Use and Homelessness	J Neale	714

Homeless Families: United Kingdom

S Fitzpatrick, University of York, York, UK

© 2012 Elsevier Ltd. All rights reserved.

Glossary

Accepted as homeless Accepted by a local authority as eligible for assistance, unintentionally homeless and in priority need, and therefore owed the main homelessness duty.

Homeless families Homeless households containing dependent children (under age 18) or a pregnant woman.

Homelessness Persons without any accommodation in the United Kingdom who have a legal right to occupy, together with their whole household, are legally 'homeless' in England. Those who cannot gain access to their accommodation, or cannot reasonably be expected to live in it (e.g., because of a risk of violence), are also homeless.

Main homelessness duty To ensure that suitable temporary accommodation is available for qualifying households until settled housing becomes available for their use.

Settled accommodation Long-term accommodation offered to someone accepted as homeless that discharges the local authority duty to them under the homelessness legislation.

Social exclusion A situation experienced by individuals and households whose disadvantage is not merely financial (i.e., a current low income), but is also sustained and multidimensional such that they are marginalised in the labour market, experience poor health, low educational attainment, have weak or restricted social support networks, and so on. 'Deep social exclusion' is sometimes used to denote the most extreme forms of such exclusion, for example, that associated with rough sleeping, chaotic alcohol or drugs misuse, severe mental health problems, involvement with the criminal justice system and/or antisocial behaviour, street prostitution, and so on.

Statutory homelessness This denotes the experience of households which have been assessed by a local authority as fulfilling all of the statutory criteria to be owed the main homelessness duty.

Temporary accommodation Accommodation secured by a local authority for a household accepted as homeless until settled accommodation becomes available for them.

Worklessness This characterises the situation where no members of a household are engaged in paid employment.

Introduction

Despite the longstanding recognition of family homelessness as a major social problem in England and the wider United Kingdom, until recently far less was known about it than about single or youth homelessness (Grimshaw, 2008). The relatively limited amount of research conducted on family homelessness in England tended to be qualitative and small scale, and was often very narrow in scope. However, a recent nationally representative survey of 2500 homeless families in England represents a major step forward in our understanding of this phenomenon (Pleace et al., 2008). The main aim of this survey (hereinafter referred to as 'the English family homelessness survey') was to provide robust statistical evidence on families with children accepted as homeless by English local authorities. The nationally representative data generated by this survey challenge a number of 'myths' about homeless families which had taken root in the absence of a reliable evidential base. It must be borne in mind that this survey was confined to those families who approached a local authority for help and were assessed as fulfilling all of the necessary statutory criteria to be owed the 'main homelessness duty' (see below). Nonetheless, it represents by far the most robust statistical data currently available on homeless families in England, and includes a far wider spectrum of experience than any previous studies. This article begins by outlining the statutory homelessness framework in England (there are similar but not identical statutory frameworks in other parts of the United Kingdom), as it is necessary to understand this framework in order to appreciate the nature of the group of homeless families with whom the article is concerned.

The Legislative Framework in England

The Housing (Homeless Persons) Act of 1977 first established a statutory safety net for certain groups of homeless people in Great Britain (this legislation was extended to Northern Ireland in 1989). This legislation provides that local authorities are required to secure 'temporary accommodation' for qualifying homeless households until suitable 'settled housing' becomes available for them (this is known as the 'main homelessness duty'). In practice, this settled housing is almost always secured by the local authority that owes the homelessness duty, and in the great majority of cases it is a social rented tenancy that is secured (though attempts are increasingly being made to 'discharge' the main homelessness duty via private sector tenancies).

It is important to appreciate that the legal definition of homelessness that underpins these local authority duties in England (and the wider United Kingdom) is a very wide one:

> Broadly speaking, somebody is statutorily homeless if they do not have accommodation that they have a legal right to occupy, which is accessible and physically available to them (and their household) and which it would be reasonable for them to continue to live in. It would not be reasonable for someone to continue to live in their home, for example, if that was likely to lead to violence against them (or a member of their family). (Department for Communities and Local Government (DCLG), Department for Education & Science (DfES), Department of Health (DoH), 2006: 10)

However, while the legal definition of homelessness in England is a broad one, the main homelessness duty of local authorities is owed only to those 'homeless' applicants who are also 'eligible' for assistance (some persons from abroad, including asylum seekers, are ineligible for assistance under the homelessness legislation), in a 'priority need' group (the priority need groups include households which contain a pregnant women, dependent children, 16- and 17-year-olds (or 18- to 20-year-olds previously in local authority care), and adults who are vulnerable because of age, disability, an institutional care background, fleeing violence, or some other particular reason; they also include any person who has lost his/her accommodation as a result of an emergency, such as flood or fire), and 'not intentionally homeless' (i.e., they have not brought about their homelessness through their own actions or inaction). As is the common convention in England, the term 'statutory homelessness' is used in this article to denote legally homeless households who also fulfil all of these additional statutory criteria.

Ever since the homelessness legislation came into force in 1978, families containing dependent children or a pregnant woman have comprised a clear majority of all households accepted as statutorily homeless in England (though they constitute only about one-third of statutorily homeless households in Scotland and about half in Wales and Northern Ireland). The remainder of this article draws upon the English family homelessness survey to review the characteristics and support needs of these families, the causes of their homelessness, their experience of temporary accommodation, and, finally, the impact of the statutory homeless system on their well-being.

The Characteristics and Support Needs of Homeless Families

For a long time there appeared to be an implicit assumption on the part of both policy-makers and researchers that the needs of homeless families were fully met once they gained access to settled housing through the statutory homelessness system. However, the extensive research that has been conducted into youth homelessness, single homelessness, and rough sleeping has contributed to the now widespread view in England (and the wider United Kingdom) that these are social problems that require 'more than a roof' solutions (Office of the Deputy Prime Minister, 2002). The support needs that have been identified in these various homeless populations, and among rough sleepers, in particular, include mental health, drug, and alcohol problems, often related to severely disrupted and traumatic childhoods as well as to unsettled adult lives, with experience of institutional settings, such as local authority care and prison, also frequently mentioned.

These findings on other homeless groups led some commentators to wonder whether similar support needs may also be prevalent among homeless families, and this concern was reinforced by qualitative evaluations of support services for vulnerable homeless families which emphasised these families' need for intensive interpersonal support (Dillane et al., 2001; Jones et al., 2002). A government-funded study subsequently suggested that homeless parents with dependent children may have support needs associated with the following (Randall and Brown, 2003):

- Social isolation
- Domestic violence
- Antisocial behaviour (as victims and/or perpetrators)
- Drug and alcohol, mental health, and physical health care needs
- Poverty, debt, and unemployment
- Childhood histories of abuse and local authority care
- A history of unsettled accommodation and repeated homelessness
- Poor literacy and employability
- Behavioural, educational, and health problems among their children
- Multiple needs combining two or more of the above.

However, this study was not designed to estimate the overall prevalence of such support needs among homeless families, and the breadth of these families' experiences, needs, and characteristics had not been captured until the English family homelessness survey attempted to do just this (Pleace et al., 2008).

The family homelessness survey revealed that, as expected, most statutorily homeless families were headed by a lone woman parent (65%), and that they were generally small families with one or two young children. Statutorily homeless families were poor: two-thirds (64%) were 'workless' (this high level of worklessness (where no-one in the household is in paid employment) was partly but not fully explained by the large proportion of lone mothers with young children among statutorily homeless families) and almost all were dependent on means-tested benefits or tax credits. While the great majority of adult respondents (an 'adult respondent' was purposively selected in each family as the person best placed to comment on the circumstances and experiences of the whole family (usually this was the mother)) in these families were White (76%), those with a Black/Black British background (at 12%) were overrepresented as compared with parents in the wider population. Perhaps a more surprising finding was that 1 in 10 (11%) of all adult respondents had, at some point, sought asylum in the United Kingdom (these were 'former asylum seekers' – current asylum seekers are ineligible for assistance under the homelessness legislation). Both ethnic minority adult respondents and former asylum seekers were heavily concentrated in London.

The majority of adult respondents in statutorily homeless families had experienced some form of family or educational disruption in childhood. For example, 45% reported parental divorce when they were a child, and one-quarter (24%) had been suspended or excluded from school. However, only 7% reported experience of homelessness as a child. This finding suggests that fears that family homelessness may be largely intergenerational are misplaced.

Figure 1 shows the reported prevalence of a range of experiences (in adulthood) among adult respondents in statutorily homeless families. Half of all adult respondents (52%) said that they had experienced anxiety, depression, or other mental health problems at one time or another (note that this is a broad self-reported definition of mental health problems and does not require that they be severe). However, the proportion reporting current mental health problems at point of survey was much lower (27%). While this is somewhat higher than the general population (at 18% (comparison is to Health Survey for England (2005) (age 16–54 years))), this difference was partly attributable to the predominance of women among adult respondents, who are generally more likely than men to report mental health problems.

Two in five (41%) of all adult respondents (almost all women) reported having been a victim of violence from a partner as an adult; this is considerably higher than the rate of domestic violence in the general population, as it is estimated that one in four women in Britain will experience domestic violence during their lifetime (British Crime Survey (2005/06), Home Office, p. 23).

In total, one-quarter (25%) of all adult respondents reported that they had never had a 'settled home' as an adult (this was mainly the younger respondents). The number who had slept rough was very much smaller (4%). Thirteen percent had made a previous homelessness application.

The sort of 'deep social exclusion' identified among other homeless groups was confined to a relatively small proportion of adult respondents in homeless families. Thus only about 1 in 10 (11%) self-reported ever having had a drug or alcohol problem, and those who reported a current substance misuse problem at point of survey was very low (3%). Adult respondents were also very unlikely to report having spent time in prison or a young offenders' institution (4%) and, while they were somewhat more likely to have been involved in crime or antisocial behaviour, this was still reported by only around 1 in 10 (9%). Involvement in prostitution (defined in the survey as exchanging sex for money, food, or shelter) was reported by 2% of all adult respondents.

Consistent with these findings, a relatively small proportion of adult respondents (16%) said that they had received help with 'personal support' needs since acceptance as homeless, such as with mental health or substance misuse problems or with parenting skills. Only 4% reported an unmet personal support need. On the other hand, one-third of all adult respondents (35%) reported at least one current unmet need for practical support; this was most commonly practical or financial help with getting furniture or with money management.

We concluded on the basis of this evidence that, while they were clearly a relatively disadvantaged group in a number of social and economic respects, these statutorily homeless families were not in the main very vulnerable or chaotic. It seems that perceptions derived largely or entirely from qualitative studies, which have tended to focus on the neediest groups with high levels of service intervention, may have previously led to an exaggerated sense of the extent of support needs among homeless families.

The Causes of Family Homelessness

There is a longstanding and complex academic debate about the 'causes' of homelessness. Very briefly, this debate centres on whether homelessness is fundamentally driven by 'structural factors' (such as housing supply, poverty, unemployment, etc.) or by individuals' (and households') behaviour, vulnerability, and support needs (such as those related to trauma, mental ill-health, drug

4 Homeless Families: United Kingdom

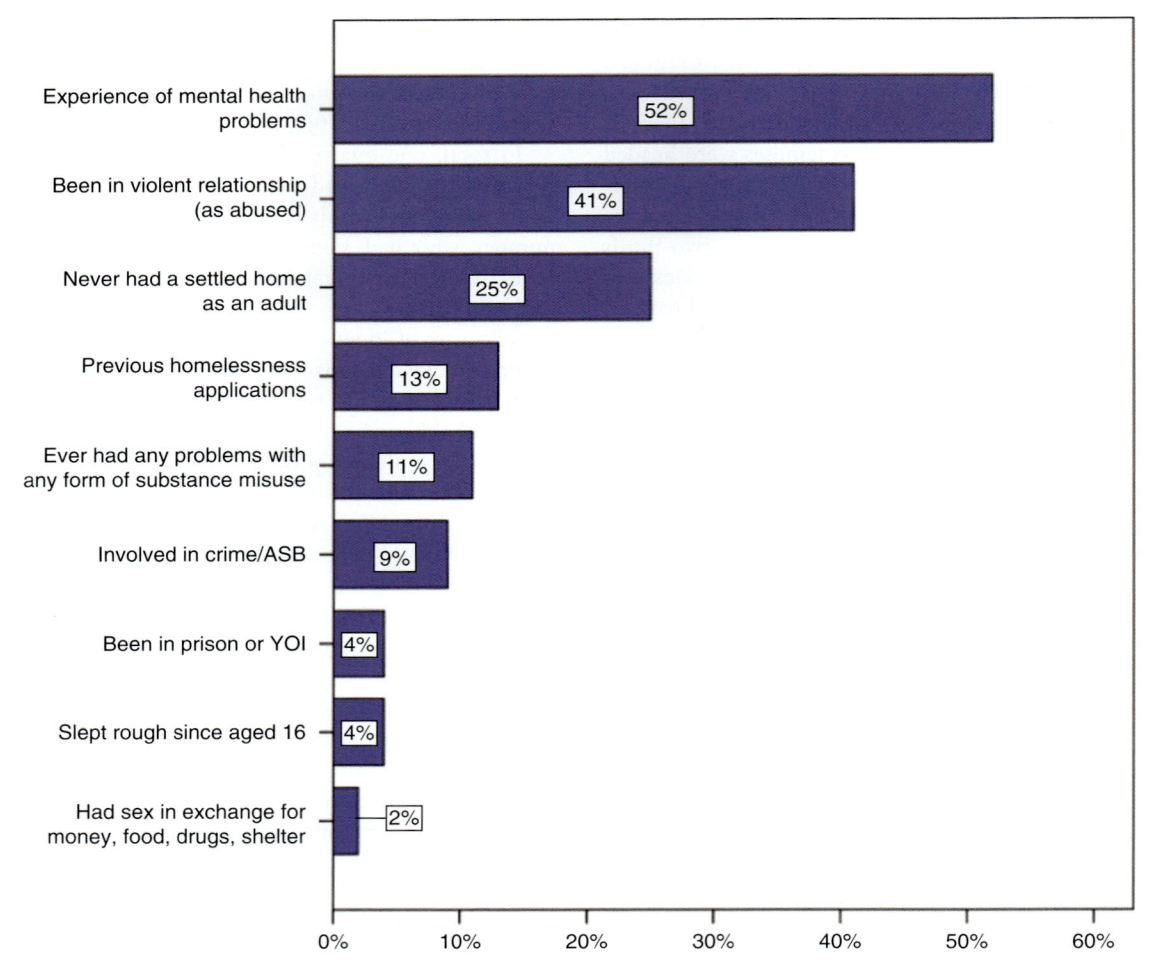

Figure 1 Experiences reported by adult respondents in statutorily homeless families. Base: 2053 adult respondents. Multiple responses were possible.
Source: Pleace N, Fitzpatrick S, Johnsen S, Quilgars D, and Sanderson D (2008) *Statutory Homelessness in England: The Experience of Families and 16-17 Year Olds*. London: Communities and Local Government.

and alcohol problems, etc.). In the United States, for example, there has been a clear shift from an emphasis on individual explanations of family homelessness, which dominated thinking until the 1990s, to explanations focused on structural factors, particularly housing market conditions (Fitzpatrick and Christian, 2006). In the United Kingdom, there was traditionally a stronger focus on housing- and poverty-based explanations for family homelessness, but, as noted above, this began to be questioned in the 1990s as evidence of high levels of support needs among single homeless people, as well as among some homeless families, began to emerge.

However, the English family homelessness survey provides a powerful corrective to any significant shift in the direction of attributing homelessness among families with children to unmet personal support needs. While there is a group of families for whom there are clearly complex support issues relating to drugs, alcohol, and mental health, they are firmly in the minority and cannot account for the majority of statutory homelessness among families.

Figure 2 depicts the 'immediate reasons' (triggers) for applying as homeless given by the adult respondents in statutorily homeless families. As can be seen, the most prevalent reason for applying as homeless, cited by 38% of adult respondents, was relationship breakdown (usually with a partner or, less commonly, with a parent(s)). The other major reasons that adult respondents gave for applying as homeless were eviction or being threatened with eviction (usually because of the end of a fixed-term tenancy) (26%), overcrowding (24%), and 'outstaying their welcome/could no longer be accommodated (20%) (however, it should be noted that both overcrowding and overstaying welcome as reasons for applying as homeless sometimes seemed to reflect the breakdown or expiry of informal 'emergency' arrangements with friends or relatives, rather than the 'original' cause of homelessness). All of the other potential reasons, including those

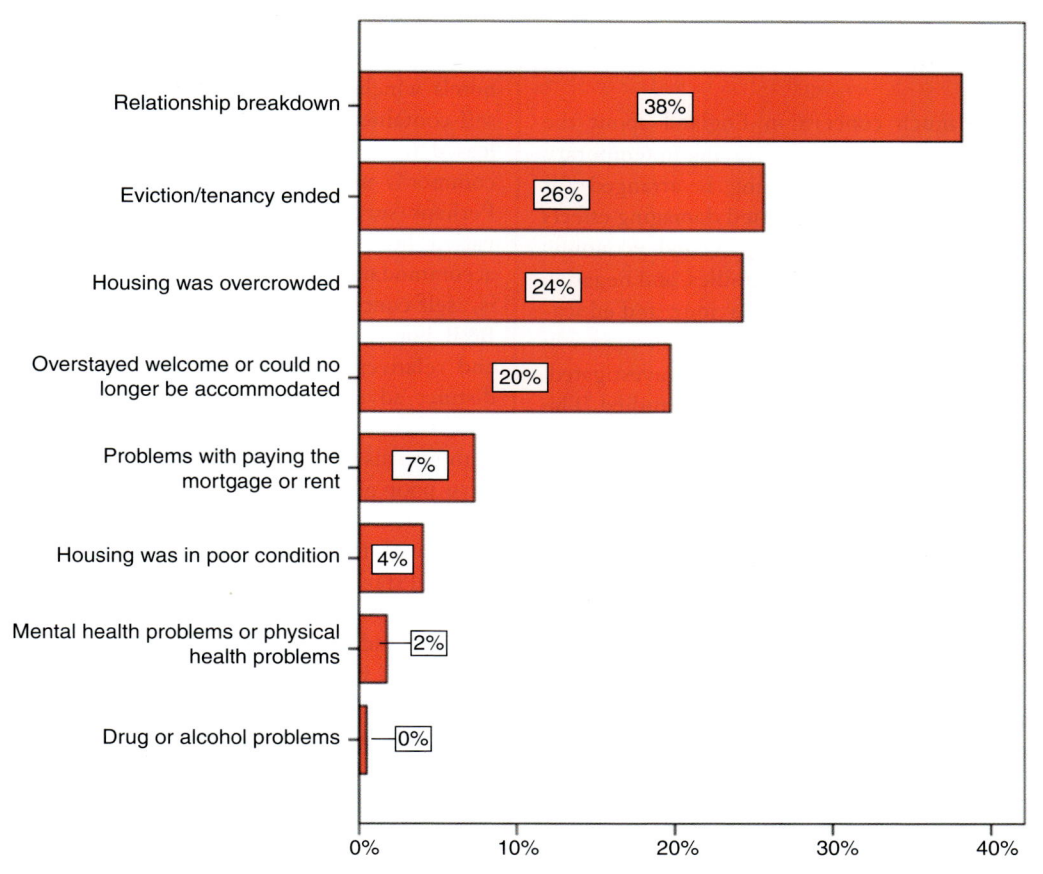

Figure 2 Reasons for applying as homeless. Base: 2053 respondents. Multiple responses were possible.
Source: Pleace N, Fitzpatrick S, Johnsen S, Quilgars D, and Sanderson D (2008) *Statutory Homelessness in England: The Experience of Families and 16-17 Year Olds.* London: Communities and Local Government.

Reason	%
Relationship breakdown	38%
Eviction/tenancy ended	26%
Housing was overcrowded	24%
Overstayed welcome or could no longer be accommodated	20%
Problems with paying the mortgage or rent	7%
Housing was in poor condition	4%
Mental health problems or physical health problems	2%
Drug or alcohol problems	0%

relating to 'individual' personal problems such as drug, alcohol, or mental health problems (2% in total), and inability to pay the mortgage or rent (7%), were rarely mentioned.

We had anticipated that financial or housing-related reasons for applying as homeless, such as mortgage/rent arrears or the end of a fixed-term tenancy, might be more prevalent in 'tight' housing market areas, whereas personal support needs and relationship breakdown, for example, might be proportionately more important in 'slack' housing market areas. There was some evidence of this in the English family homelessness survey, but it was a case of modest rather than pronounced geographical patterns. Thus, adult respondents accepted as homeless in areas of higher housing stress were likelier to report eviction as a cause of homelessness (31%) than those living in areas of lower housing stress (21%). Conversely, adult respondents accepted as homeless within the more affordable areas were likelier to report relationship breakdown as a cause of their homelessness (43%) than those living in less affordable areas (32%). No other geographical patterns were identified: in particular, no distinctions were found between different parts of England with respect to the contribution of personal support needs, or mortgage/rent arrears, to reasons for applying as homeless.

While it appears, then, that structural contexts, and in particular housing market conditions, have only a modest effect on the balance between the different 'routes in' to homelessness among families, they do impact on aggregate levels of statutory homelessness. This has been demonstrated by time series data which show that, at least until the recent vigorous push on homelessness prevention in England, statutory homelessness figures tended to move in parallel with affordability trends in the homeownership sector (Pawson, 2007). Thus, it seems that housing market conditions affect not so much the reasons why people lose their last settled accommodation (notwithstanding the modest impact on the relative importance of eviction and relationship breakdown with partners), but rather their ability, if they are on a low income, to find an alternative without resorting to the statutory system.

The Experience of Temporary Accommodation

There has been much concern in England about the impacts on families with children of staying in temporary accommodation until settled housing is arranged for them. A range of studies have suggested damaging effects on the health, social support networks, and economic position of parents within homeless families, and negative impacts on their children's health, behaviour, and education. However, this research has usually been narrowly focused with regards to the type of impacts investigated, and the forms of temporary accommodation studied. The English family homelessness survey systematically investigated families' experiences across the full range of forms of temporary accommodation now used and revealed a number of findings that run counter to received wisdom in this area.

We found that families' experience of temporary accommodation was largely determined by 'where' they were accepted as homeless. Families in the North and Midlands typically experienced a relatively short (or no) stay in temporary accommodation (very often temporary arrangements with parents, friends, or (other) relatives), before being moved on to settled housing. Families accepted in London, and to a lesser extent in the South, were likely to experience prolonged stays in temporary accommodation, and to spend most of their time in 'self-contained temporary accommodation' (i.e., ordinary flats and houses in the social or private rented sectors used as temporary accommodation by local authorities). Extended stays in temporary accommodation were heavily concentrated in London – 81% of families in temporary accommodation for over 1 year had been accepted as homeless in the capital – and were a source of considerable frustration for the families involved.

While there has been a great deal of anxiety about the instability wreaked on homeless families by multiple moves between temporary accommodation addresses, we found that such multiple moves were in fact relatively rare: only 35% of families had made any moves at all between temporary accommodation addresses by point of survey (interviews were conducted, on average, 9 months after families had been accepted as homeless), and only 8% had moved more than once (though multiple moves were far commoner among those who had been in temporary accommodation for over a year). The purpose of most of these moves appeared to be to relocate families from 'shared' forms of provision into self-contained settings whenever it became apparent that they were likely to spend an extended period in temporary accommodation, and there was no evidence that these moves had deleterious effects on families.

With respect to conditions in temporary accommodation, much concern has focused on the poor quality B&B hotels which once dominated temporary provision, but self-contained temporary accommodation (much of it leased from the private rented sector) is now far more commonly used, particularly in London and the South. Perhaps surprisingly, the overall levels of satisfaction varied little between the various types of temporary accommodation now employed by local authorities, that is, self-contained temporary accommodation, hostels, B&B hotels, and temporary arrangements with friends and relatives. Instead, each type was reported to have distinct advantages and disadvantages. Thus, self-contained temporary accommodation was rated most highly with regards to space standards, but was often reported to have poor physical standards, particularly in relation to damp, decor, and state of repair. Temporary arrangements with friends and relatives offered families the best physical standards and access to amenities, but were often very cramped. Access to household amenities (including kitchens and living rooms) was often more restricted in hostels and B&B hotels than in other forms of temporary accommodation.

Despite satisfaction with the accommodation itself being no higher in self-contained provision than in other forms of temporary accommodation, quality of life (e.g., with respect to the overall levels of happiness, worrying about the future, etc.) was consistently reported as highest in this type of provision. Thus, the efforts of local authorities to move families from shared into self-contained temporary accommodation (see above) seem well judged.

The Impact of the Statutory Homelessness System

Perhaps the most important overall finding of the English family homelessness survey was that the provision of statutory homelessness assistance seemed to have secured a substantial (net) improvement in homeless families' quality of life. Thus, those parents who reported that life was now better than in their 'last settled accommodation' (parents were asked about a range of their family's circumstances in their 'last settled accommodation' prior to acceptance as homeless, as a means of investigating whether there was evidence of changes that could be associated with the experience of homelessness and temporary accommodation) heavily outnumbered those for whom it was perceived to be worse (57% as compared with 19%). Likewise, they were far likelier to report an improvement (57%) than a decline (12%) in their child(ren)'s overall quality of life. As one might expect, the reported (net) improvement in overall quality of life was greatest for those families living in settled housing by point of interview, but there was nonetheless a substantial net improvement for those still in temporary accommodation.

Moreover, contrary to the suggestions in earlier research, the (net) impacts of statutory homelessness on the health and social support networks of parents in these families appeared to be largely negligible, or even marginally positive. Similarly, the children in families accepted as homeless generally appeared happy at school and at home, and their health profile, as reported by their parents, broadly reflected that of children in the general population. The majority (77%) of all child respondents reported being very or fairly happy with life. Furthermore, some positive (net) changes were reported for children since leaving their last settled accommodation, particularly with regards to their school performance and in their relationship with their parents. At the same time, some negative (net) changes were also apparent in relation to increased levels of loneliness and reduced participation in clubs/activities. One-third of school-aged children had changed school as a direct result of homelessness, and, perhaps surprisingly, this could have powerful positive as well as negative effects on outcomes for these children.

In contrast to these generally positive, or at least mixed, findings with regards to the 'social' impacts of the statutory homelessness system, there was a clear negative 'economic' effect of statutory homelessness on families. Thus, there was a net increase of 15 percentage points in levels of 'worklessness' since families left their last settled accommodation (this was not explained by relationship breakdown and departure of a working adult from the household), and almost half (47%) of adult respondents reported that they were now finding it more difficult to manage financially (only 18% said their financial situation had improved).

Conclusions

This article has drawn on a major survey of statutorily homeless families in England to review these families' characteristics and support needs, the causes of their homelessness, and their experience of temporary accommodation and the statutory homelessness system. The findings suggest that previous reliance on small-scale qualitative research on particular (exceptionally needy) subgroups of homeless families, together with the influence of the more extensive literature on single and youth homelessness, had led many commentators (including the present author) to develop an exaggerated sense of the scale of support needs among homeless families. The survey indicates that the causes of statutory homelessness among families appear in the main not to be associated with extreme vulnerability. Rather, they relate to the inability of low-income families to secure alternative housing, especially in tight housing market conditions, when they are confronted with a crisis such as relationship breakdown or eviction which causes them to lose their last settled accommodation. Very encouragingly, the provision of statutory homelessness assistance seemed to have secured a substantial overall net improvement in the quality of life for both adults and children in these families. However, the long waits for settled housing in London were a source of considerable frustration. Another note of concern was the apparent negative impact of homelessness on families' already weak economic position.

See also: Homeless Families: United States; Homelessness: Causation; Policies to Address Homelessness: Prevention in the United Kingdom.

References

Department for Communities and Local Government, Department of Health, and Department for Education and Skills (2006) *Homelessness Code of Guidance for Local Authorities*. London: DCLG, DoH, DfES.

Dillane J, Hill M, Bannister J, and Scott S (2001) *An Evaluation of the Dundee Families Project*. Edinburgh, UK: Scottish Executive.

Fitzpatrick S and Christian J (2006) Comparing research on homelessness in the United Kingdom and United States: What lessons can be learned? *European Journal of Housing Policy* 6(3): 313–333.

Grimshaw JM (2008) *Family Homelessness: Causes, Consequences and the Policy Response in England*. London: The British Library.

Jones A, Pleace N, and Quilgars D (2002) *Firm Foundations: An Evaluation of the Shelter Homeless to Home Service*. London: Shelter.

Office of the Deputy Prime Minister (ODPM) (2002) *More than a Roof: A Report into Tackling Homelessness*. London: ODPM.

Pawson H (2007) Local authority homelessness prevention in England: Empowering consumers or denying rights. *Housing Studies* 22(6): 867–883.

Pleace N, Fitzpatrick S, Johnsen S, Quilgars D, and Sanderson D (2008) *Statutory Homelessness in England: The Experience of Families and 16–17 Year Olds*. London: Communities and Local Government.

Randall G and Brown S (2003) *The Support Needs of Homeless People and Their Families*. London: ODPM.

Homeless Families: United States

VA Fusaro, EL Bassuk, M Grandin, L Guilderson and M Hayes, The National Center on Family Homelessness, Newton Center, MA, USA

© 2012 Elsevier Ltd. All rights reserved.

Glossary

Child welfare Refers to those public agencies that are charged with responsibility for child protection and foster care systems.

Doubled up A form of homelessness wherein families involuntarily live in tenuous and temporary conditions in the homes of friends or families.

Family reunification A term used in child welfare. It refers to the process that supports the return of children to their biological families after removal for child protection concerns.

Family separation When members of a family do not live together, either voluntarily or involuntarily.

Traumatic event An occurrence that threatens an individual's sense of physical and psychological well-being. In extreme or repeated conditions, impaired functioning in multiple life domains may result.

Introduction

Family homelessness in the United States is a multifaceted issue, requiring an examination of both macrolevel systemic factors and the individual-level needs and experiences of homeless families. This article begins by discussing the scope and causes of family homelessness, followed by a brief history of the problem in the United States. A demographic overview is then provided. Next, the needs and characteristics of US homeless families and the children of homeless families are examined. Finally, key elements of the US policy response to family homelessness are outlined, followed by a brief discussion of possible steps to strengthen the policy response.

Extent and Causes of Family Homelessness in the United States

Families comprise 34–40% of Americans experiencing homelessness, with approximately 1.8% of American families experiencing homelessness during a given year (Burt et al., 1999; U.S. Conference of Mayors, 1998). Family homelessness in the United States is largely a result of structural factors. The United States has an insufficient supply of affordable housing, which affects the ability of families living in poverty to access housing. They have insufficient income to afford market-rate housing, which, combined with the lack of affordable housing, places them at risk for homelessness. Demographic trends also influence family homelessness – an increase in the number of female-headed households in the United States has increased family susceptibility to poverty and, by extension, homelessness. Public supports critical to the prevention of homelessness are limited, with the country's most important housing assistance programme (Section 8) underfunded and its primary income assistance programme (Temporary Assistance to Needy Families (TANF)) providing families with limited opportunity to escape poverty. These factors combine to put American families at risk for experiencing homelessness.

The primary cause of family homelessness is a lack of affordable housing. There are simply not enough affordable units for all who might need one. During the late 1970s and through the 1980s, 2.2 million low-rent housing units were removed from the market in the United States. At the same time, the number of people requiring low rent to afford a dwelling increased by 4.7 million, creating an imbalance between the supply of and the need for affordable housing (Daskal, 1998). Without enough affordable housing units, some group of American must go without a home. Unfortunately, this group frequently includes families.

Families living in poverty have insufficient income from wages to cover market-rate housing. Among the nation's working families, 10 million are poor or nearly poor, and one in five jobs in the United States does not provide a wage sufficient to keep a family out of poverty. In 2006, 17.7 million households were using more than half of their incomes to pay for housing. This amount far exceeds the general recommendation of allocating one-third of a family's income to housing costs (Joint Center for Housing Studies of Harvard University, 2006). Demographic changes thrust more American families into poverty in the latter half of the twentieth century, which saw an increase in the number of female-headed households. Female-headed households have much lower incomes than other households. As more American families were headed by a single female, more families found themselves living in poverty and unable to afford housing – the genesis of modern American family homelessness.

Further contributing to family poverty and homelessness in the United States is the insufficient aid provided by assistance programmes. The federal Section 8 programme (for further discussion see section US Policy Response to Family Homelessness), for example, is widely recognised as critical to helping low-income families afford market-rate housing. The funding for the Section 8 programme, however, does not provide enough vouchers for everyone who qualifies. Long waiting lists are common. Income assistance programmes are similarly inadequate. Receiving aid still leaves families in poverty, making the acquisition of stable housing a significant challenge. Changes to these programmes have also reduced the amount and type of assistance available. In 1996, the established Aid to Families with Dependent Children (AFDC) programme was abandoned to implement a new approach, TANF. Unlike the AFDC programme, TANF is a federal block grant administered by each state, which allows great interstate variation in assistance provided to poor families. TANF also imposed time limits on benefits and enforced sanctions for programme noncompliance, reducing poor families' eligibility to receive aid. With insufficient support to either overcome poverty or afford housing, families are at risk of homelessness.

History of Family Homelessness in the United States

Family homelessness has not always been a pressing social issue in the United States. Mention is made of 'tramp families' in the literature of the early 1900s, but these discussions are few. Families most visibly lost their homes during the Great Depression, which saw extremely high unemployment and poverty across the nation. Concurrently, the 'Dust Bowl', a period of extreme dust storms in the North American prairie, devastated agriculture in Texas, Oklahoma, and the surrounding regions. Families, famously called 'Okies', were uprooted from their farms and travelled to other states in search of economic opportunity. With the exception of the Great Depression and other periods of serious economic recession, however, family homelessness was largely invisible through much of the twentieth century. It gained modern public attention only in the 1980s, when the previously described shortage of affordable housing and changing family demographics led many low-income families to become homeless.

It is likely that the economic downturn and housing foreclosure crisis of the latter half of the first decade of the twenty-first century will have an adverse impact on American families. High unemployment rates, foreclosures that impact both owners and renters, and other factors associated with the downturn are likely to further increase the ranks of homeless families and put formerly stably housed families at risk of homelessness.

Demographics of US Homeless Families

Today, the typical homeless family in the United States consists of a mother in her late 20s with two children. Some homeless families are two-parent or male-headed, with some geographic variation in family composition. Families of colour are disproportionately represented among the homeless population. Nationally, 43% of families experiencing homelessness are African American, 38% are White, non-Hispanic, 15% Hispanic, and 3% are Native American. These statistics differ sharply from those of the general US population. According to 2000 Census data, 75% of Americans are White, 12% African American, and 1% Native American. Thirteen per cent identified themselves as Hispanic.

Characteristics of Homelessness Episodes

The families described above may dwell in any number of places, including on the streets, in shelters, in automobiles, or other places not intended for human habitation. Episodes of homelessness may last for varying lengths of time. However, various patterns of homelessness are common to many families. Homeless families typically experience a high degree of residential instability before turning to emergency shelters or the streets. They move from place to place and housing situation to housing situation. A family may live in a shelter for a short time, move to a permanent apartment, live on the streets, and go back to a shelter, all in succession. Frequently, a homeless family will dwell in the home of a relative or friend, a situation commonly termed 'doubled up' (Rog and Buckner, 2007). According to one study, patterns of emergency shelter use vary among homeless families, but include single, short stays (139 days or less), multiple short stays, and single, more prolonged stays. Among these families, a majority appear to fall into the single, short stay category (Culhane et al., 2007).

Needs and Characteristics of US Homeless Families

Homeless families and the heads of those families have an array of social and psychological needs that extend beyond housing. They have economic needs that directly relate to poverty. In addition to economic factors, homeless mothers and families are frequently exposed to violence and other traumatic stress, resulting in high rates of post-traumatic stress disorder (PTSD). Depression, anxiety, other mental health issues, and substance abuse follow. Finally, the members of homeless families are frequently separated from one another, creating additional stress on the family as a unit.

Economic Needs

Extreme poverty, combined with lack of housing, is the hallmark of family homelessness. In the mid-1990s, the median income for a homeless family was less than half of the Federal Poverty Level (Burt et al., 1999). The Federal Poverty Level itself is only approximately half of what a family typically needs to meet basic needs, meaning that homeless families are unable to afford food, shelter, and other necessities. Contributing to this extreme poverty, homeless mothers often have limited educational attainment and work histories. Though these education and employment factors may not be substantially different from poor-but-housed mothers, they present additional barriers to mothers seeking a path out of homelessness (Rog and Buckner, 2007).

Psychosocial Needs

The psychosocial needs of homeless mothers and families are inextricably linked to traumatic stress. Homeless mothers have often been exposed to multiple traumatic events as both adults and children. Many of these mothers were not stably housed while growing up themselves. They may have been separated from their families and placed in foster care. Most notably, they are frequently victims of physical and sexual abuse. As a result, they suffer from PTSD at three times the rate of the general female population (Bassuk et al., 1996; Rog and Buckner, 2007). Exposure to traumatic events has other impacts. There is evidence, for example, that mothers exposed to violence and sexual assault as children are more likely to be homeless multiple times as adults (Bassuk et al., 2001). Exposure to traumatic stress can also negatively affect one's ability to parent; the child(ren)'s well-being is then impacted.

Perhaps also a result of exposure to traumatic events, many homeless mothers are affected by mental health disorders such as depression and anxiety disorders, which can then impact their children. Homeless mothers are not dissimilar from low-income housed women in this regard, but both groups have much higher rates of depression and PTSD than the general US population (Bassuk et al., 1998). Substance use is also common, and may be an attempt to self-medicate to reduce the impact of traumatic events. Within a family, the mental health of the mother can have an impact on the children, perhaps because of the lack of emotional availability necessary for healthy development. For example, children of parents with depression are therefore themselves more susceptible to psychological problems (Beardslee et al., 1996). They may also be more prone to developmental delays, poor academic outcomes, and difficulty with interpersonal relationships (Barocas et al., 1985; Sameroff and Seifer, 1983; Weintraub and Neal, 1984). In some, mothers experiencing homelessness are more prone to suffer from conditions such as depression; the children of these mothers are then at greater risk for a range of poor outcomes.

Homeless families as a unit face additional stresses due to family separation – that is, parent(s) and child(ren) are not living together. Although 60% of homeless women have children, only 65% of homeless mothers live with their children (Burt et al., 1999). Some separations are voluntary. For example, a parent may not want her child living in a shelter environment and so might send him/her to live with relatives. Other separations may be forced, brought about by shelter rules that exclude adolescent males from the facility. Such shelter rules may also impact fathers in two-parent homeless families, who may have to dwell elsewhere while the rest of the family lives in a shelter.

The child welfare system may also separate parents and their children involuntarily. Some researchers have hypothesised that, merely by being homeless, families are at greater risk for separation because they are under greater scrutiny by multiple systems, including shelter staff. It is then more likely that the family will be reported to a child welfare agency, resulting in separation. Regardless of the immediate cause of separation, however, experiencing homelessness can result in a potentially traumatic breakdown in the family unit (Cowal et al., 2002; Park et al., 2004; Rog and Buckner, 2007).

Further exacerbating the separation between homeless parents and their children, the state of being homeless makes eventual reunification more difficult (Rog and Buckner, 2007). For example, a mother may be separated from her child. She may then dwell in a shelter designed for single adults. Because the shelter is not intended for families, reunification in this environment is unlikely.

Needs and Characteristics of Children in Homeless Families

On any given day in America, an estimated 1 in 50 children have no home (NCFH, 2009). The children of homeless families tend to be young, with 42% of children experiencing homelessness being under the age of 6 years

(Burt et al., 1999). The children of homeless families have a set of psychosocial needs that, like those of their parents, extend beyond housing. These areas of need can be divided into the following categories: health, behavioural and emotional issues, and education. In some categories, research clearly indicates that homeless children differ from their peers, whereas in other domains the evidence is mixed.

Homeless children are at higher risk for many health maladies than their housed peers (Weinreb et al., 1998). Compared to other children, homeless children have four times as many respiratory infections, twice as many ear infections, five times more gastrointestinal problems, and are four times more likely to have asthma. Correlated with the extreme poverty of their families, homeless children are also at high risk for food insecurity. They go hungry twice as often as other children and, owing to the poor nutritional quality of the food they can access, have high rates of obesity (NCFH, 1999). These health issues are exacerbated by a lack of access to regular medical care.

The research is equivocal about whether the children of homeless families have higher rates of emotional and behavioural issues compared to other low-income children. Both groups have higher prevalence rates than children representative of the general population (Shaffer et al., 1996). Among those studies that have found more emotional and behavioural needs among homeless children than among low-income housed children, there is additional variation depending on the child's age. Preschool-age homeless children seem more prone to 'externalizing' behaviours, such as acting aggressively, compared to housed children (Bassuk et al., 1997). School-age homeless children, meanwhile, are more prone to 'internalizing' problem behaviours, such as acting withdrawn, depressed, or anxious (Buckner et al., 1999).

Homeless children may suffer from developmental delays with greater frequency than other children, though again the research is mixed. Two studies in the early 1990s, for example, found that homeless preschool children had more developmental delays than housed, low-income preschool children (Bassuk and Rosenberg, 1990; Wood et al., 1990). A later study, however, showed few differences between low-income housed and homeless infants and toddlers (Garcia Coll et al., 1998). These findings may indicate that the multiple stressors of homelessness have an impact as children age.

Homeless children are faced with a range of educational challenges. As many as 36% will repeat a grade, and graduation rates are lower than for the population as a whole (NCFH, 2009). Throughout the 1980s and into the 1990s, homeless children faced immense barriers to educational stability. For example, residency requirements disallowed them from attending their local public school. Without a permanent address, they could not be considered 'residents' (Rafferty, 1995). Such issues have begun to be ameliorated by the McKinney-Vento Homeless Education Assistance Improvements Act (for further discussion on this topic, see section US Policy Response to Family Homelessness), which seeks to ensure that homeless children have access to 'free and appropriate public education'. However, many homeless children still face barriers such as transportation to and from school and lack of immunisation records, which make it difficult to obtain an education similar to that of housed children. Homeless children also experience the educational difficulties faced by all children who live in poverty. Many school districts serving low-income children are underfunded, with limited or nonexistent resources to provide an adequate education. The crime, poor housing, and unemployment associated with low-income neighbourhoods create an adverse learning environment. Children living in poverty are less likely to have books at home. Finally, they may engage in more risky behaviours that interfere with learning, such as alcohol and drug use, than their higher-income peers (NCFH, 2009). The combination of barriers related to homelessness and poverty results in homeless children receiving a lesser education than other children.

US Policy Response to Family Homelessness

The US policy response specifically to family homelessness has been limited. Some policy efforts do, however, support homeless families, even if they are not the primary target of these initiatives. Many homeless families are eligible for programmes intended to aid low-income families more generally, such as the Supplemental Nutrition Assistance Program (SNAP, formerly the Food Stamp Program) and the aforementioned TANF. Examples of policy efforts directed specifically at homelessness are provided below. They include planning efforts (state and local 10-year plans to end homelessness), homelessness prevention (Emergency Shelter Grant), housing supports (Section 8, National Housing Trust Fund), and legislation to develop equality between homeless and housed children in the education system (McKinney-Vento Homeless Education Assistance Improvements Act). These examples are not intended to list all US policies related to family homelessness. Rather, they briefly describe some of the major initiatives presently in place.

Planning Efforts: 10-Year Plans to End Homelessness

A key element of US planning to address homelessness is the creation of 10-year plans to end homelessness by some state, territorial, and local governments. With the support of the United States Interagency Council on Homelessness, the primary focus of 10-year plans is ending chronic homelessness. Some of these plans, however, are aimed at all experiencing homelessness, including families. A small portion of these plans include specific subplans to address family or youth homelessness. Though each 10-year plan is different, common goals that impact families include

- increasing access to affordable housing
- increasing supportive housing options
- coordinating homeless services
- increasing employment training options
- increasing employment opportunities
- reducing out-of-home placements for low-income children
- developing family reunification strategies
- improving discharge planning for individuals residing in institutional settings
- enhancing services for families and individuals experiencing homelessness
- educating the public about homelessness
- improving data collection efforts around homelessness in the state
- supporting local communities in their efforts to develop 10-year plans

While a potentially powerful tool to combat homelessness, the status and quality of 10-year plans varies widely across jurisdictions. Additionally, as of 2008, only 22 of 50 states had created a plan (NCFH, 2009).

Homelessness Prevention: Emergency Shelter Grant

Emergency Shelter Grants are grants provided by the federal government to the state governments, counties, and US territorial governments for the purpose of providing shelter and services to people experiencing homelessness. These funds are regranted to local governments and social service agencies to build or renovate emergency shelters, and may also fund services to ease the burdens of homelessness such as case management, health, mental health, or substance-abuse services, and – vitally for families – child care. Funds may also be used for homelessness prevention efforts, including limited financial assistance, mediation with landlords, and eviction prevention. The American Recovery and Reinvestment Act of 2009, a major federal response to the economic crisis of 2008–09, includes funds dedicated to providing additional monies to programmes supported by the Emergency Shelter Grants.

Housing Supports: Section 8 and The National Housing Trust Fund

The hallmark federal programme for helping families afford housing is Section 8. The programme comes in two forms: tenant-based and project-based rental assistance. Under the tenant-based programme (the Housing Choice Voucher Program), a government entity administers a voucher that pays for a portion of a tenant's rent in a privately owned unit. It currently assists approximately 2 million households in affording rent. The amount paid to the landlord by the programme is based on a predetermined standard rental amount for the area, and is equal to this standard minus 30% of the tenant's income. The tenant is expected to pay the remainder of the rent. Unfortunately, a family who receives a Section 8 voucher is not guaranteed housing. The family must find a landlord who will rent to them, which may be complicated by prior evictions records or a poor credit rating. In addition to the voucher programme, Section 8 also provides for 1.2 million 'project-based' rental units. These are specific units funded by Section 8, and do not require the use of a voucher. The same income calculation as the voucher programme is used to determine rent.

In addition to Section 8, the recently created National Housing Trust Fund, established via the Housing and Economic Recovery Act of 2008, also provides support with housing. Unlike Section 8, which improves housing affordability, the Trust Fund increases housing supply. It is intended to create 1.5 million units of affordable housing, with approximately 90% of housing resources provided in the form of rental units. Priority would be given to households with extremely low incomes. The Trust Fund is funded via monies set aside annually by the Federal National Mortgage Association (Fannie Mae) and the Federal Home Loan Mortgage Corporation (Freddie Mac).

Ensuring Educational Equality: McKinney-Vento Homeless Education Assistance Improvements Act

The McKinney-Vento Homeless Assistance Act, signed into law in 1987 as the first major federal response specifically to homelessness, addressed multiple needs of those experiencing homelessness (funding, for example, emergency shelter, transitional housing, and job training). Among the elements of the Act most important to homeless families are its education provisions, which were reauthorized as part of the No Child Left Behind programme in 2001 as the McKinney-Vento Homeless Education Assistance Improvements Act. The primary purpose of this legislation is to ensure that homeless children have the same access to education as their housed peers. It requires each state to create an Office of Coordinator for Education of Homeless Children to execute this mission. Additionally, every Local Education Agency (LEA – generally a school district) is required to have a 'homeless liaison' to identify students who are homeless and ensure they are able to overcome barriers to school enrolment and success. Homeless students, for example, may have difficulty accessing transportation to get to school; the LEA is supposed to remove this barrier by providing transportation. Segregation of homeless students based solely on their homelessness is prohibited. For example, a school system cannot create a school specifically for homeless students – they are to be educated in the same classrooms as housed students.

Next Steps for US Social Policy

As the above discussion indicates, there are large gaps between the needs of US homeless families and the American policy response to family homelessness. Possible future directions in social policy might better address family homelessness in the United States by, helping families afford housing, increasing the supply of affordable housing and increasing the availability and accessibility of services. This approach addresses the imbalance between supply of and need for affordable housing that underlies family homelessness while providing support to ensure housing stability. One key area for future policy is to increase the number of available Section 8 Housing Choice Voucher Program vouchers. These vouchers have proven critical to stabilising homeless and at-risk families, yet their supply is limited and families often face extensive waiting lists when attempting to obtain a voucher. The National Housing Trust fund must also continue to grow. Through its resources, new affordable housing can be built and existing affordable units upgraded to modern standards. Though neither approach overcomes all challenges faced by families experiencing homelessness, they would help families obtain and maintain stable, affordable housing and ensure that fewer are at risk for homelessness.

See also: Access and Affordability: Developed Countries; Access and Affordability: Housing Vouchers; Affordable Housing Strategies; Domestic Violence; Health, Well-Being and Housing; Hidden Homelessness; Home and Homelessness; Homeless People: African Americans in the United States; Homelessness: Causation; Homelessness: Prevention in the United States; HOPE VI; Mental Health and Homelessness; Policies to Address Homelessness: Housing First Approaches; Policies to Support Access and Affordability of Housing; Social Justice; Social Psychological Perspectives on Homelessness; Urbanisation and Housing the Poor: Overview.

References

Barocas R, Seifer R, and Sameroff AJ (1985) Defining environmental risk: Multiple dimensions of psychological vulnerability. *American Journal of Community Psychology* 13: 433–447.

Bassuk EL, Buckner JC, Perloff J, and Bassuk SS (1998) Prevalence of mental health and substance use disorders among homeless and low-income housed mothers. *American Journal of Psychiatry* 155: 1561–1564.

Bassuk EL, Buckner JC, Weinreb L, et al. (1997) Homelessness in female-headed families: Childhood and adult risk and protective factors. *American Journal of Public Health* 87: 241–248.

Bassuk EL, Perloff J, and Dawson R (2001) Multiply homeless families: The insidious impact of violence. *Housing Policy Debate* 12: 299–320.

Bassuk EL and Rosenberg L (1990) Psychosocial characteristics of homeless children and children with homes. *Pediatrics* 85: 257–261.

Bassuk EL, Weinreb L, Buckner J, Browne A, Salomon A, and Bassuk S (1996) The characteristics and needs of sheltered homeless and low-income housed mothers. *Journal of the American Medical Association* 276: 640–646.

Beardslee WR, Keller MB, Seifer R, et al. (1996) Prediction of adolescent affective disorder: Effects of prior parental affective disorders and child psychopathology. *Journal of the American Academy of Child and Adolescent Psychiatry* 35: 279–288.

Buckner J, Bassuk E, Weinreb L, and Brooks M (1999) Homelessness and its relation to the mental health and behavior of low-income housed children. *Journal of School Psychology* 39: 45–69.

Burt M and Aron L (2000) *America's Homeless II: Populations and Services*. Washington, DC: The Urban Institute.

Burt M, Aron L, Douglas T, Valente J, Lee E, and Iwen B (1999) *Homelessness: Programs and the People They Serve. Findings of the National Survey of Homeless Assistance Providers and Clients*. Washington, DC: The Urban Institute.

Cowal K, Shinn M, Weitzman B, Stojanovic D, and Labay L (2002) Mother–child separations among homeless and housed families receiving public assistance in New York City. *American Journal of Community Psychology* 30: 711–730.

Culhane D, Metraux S, Park J, Schretzman M, and Valente J (2007) Testing a typology of family homelessness based on patterns of public shelter utilization in four U.S. jurisdictions: Implications for policy and program planning. *Housing Policy Debate* 18: 1–28.

Daskal J (1998) *In Search of Shelter: The Growing Shortage of Affordable Rental Housing*. Washington, DC: Center on Budget and Policy Priorities.

Garcia Coll C, Buckner J, Brooks M, Weinreb L, and Bassuk E (1998) The developmental status and adaptive behavior of homeless and low-income housed infants and toddlers. *American Journal of Public Health* 88: 1371–1374.

Joint Center for Housing Studies of Harvard University (2006) *America's Rental Housing: Homes for a Diverse Nation*. Cambridge, MA: Author.

Lu H and Kobal H (2003) *The Changing Demographics of Low-Income Families and Their Children: Living on the Edge Research Brief #2*. New York: National Center for Children and Poverty.

National Center on Family Homelessness (NCFH) (1999) *Homeless Children: America's New Outcasts*. Newton, MA: Author.

National Center on Family Homelessness (NCFH) (2009) *America's Youngest Outcasts: State Report Card on Child Homelessness*. Newton, MA: Author.

Park J, Metraux S, Brodbar G, and Culhane D (2004) Child welfare involvement among children in homeless families. *Child Welfare* 83: 423–436.

Rafferty Y (1995) The legal rights and educational problems of homeless children and youth. *Educational Evaluation and Policy Analysis* 17: 39–61.

Rog D and Buckner J (2007) Homeless families and children. In: Dennis D, Locke G, and Khadduri J (eds.) *Toward Understanding Homelessness: The 2007 National Symposium on Homelessness Research*, pp. 5:1–5:33. Washington, DC: U.S. Department of Health and Human Services, U.S. Department of Housing and Urban Development.

Sameroff AJ and Seifer R (1983) Familial risk and child competence. *Child Development* 54: 1254–1268.
Shaffer D, Fisher P, Dulcan M, et al. (1996) The NIMH Diagnostic Interview Schedule for Children Version 2.3 (DISC-2.3): Description, acceptability, prevalence rates, and performance in the MECA study. *Journal of the American Academy of Child and Adolescent Psychiatry* 35: 865–877.
U.S. Conference of Mayors (1998) *A Status Report on Hunger and Homelessness in America's Cities*. Washington, DC: U.S. Conference of Mayors.
Weinreb L, Goldberg R, Bassuk E, and Perloff J (1998) Determinants of health and service use patterns in homeless and low-income housed children. *Pediatrics* 102: 554–562.
Weintraub S and Neal JM (1984) Social behavior of children at risk for schizophrenia. In: Watt N, Anthony EJ, Wynne LC, and Rolf JE (eds.) *Children at Risk for Schizophrenia: A Longitudinal Perspective*, pp. 243–263. New York: Cambridge University Press.
Wood D, Valdez R, Hayashi T, and Shen A (1990) Health of homeless children and housed, poor children. *Pediatrics* 86: 858–866.

Relevant Websites

www.homelesschildrenamerica.org – America's Youngest Outcasts
www.familyhomelessness.org – The National Center on Family Homelessness
www.homeless.samhsa.gov – Homelessness Resource Center
www.serve.org/nche – National Center for Homeless Education

Homelessness: Causation

S Fitzpatrick, University of York, York, UK

Published by Elsevier Ltd.

Glossary

Critical realism An ontological theory that asserts that the social world has an existence independent of our perception of it, and is structured, open, and complex. Critical realists regard 'real' causal powers as 'necessary tendencies' of social objects and structures which may or may not be activated (and produce 'actual' effects) depending on 'contingent conditions'.

ETHOS A typology of homelessness definitions that encompasses a wide range of situations from 'literal homelessness' through to wider forms of housing exclusion, such as living in accommodation that is insecure or inadequate. This typology was developed by the European Federation of National Organisations Working with the Homeless as a means of improving understanding and measurement of homelessness in Europe, and to provide a common framework for transnational exchanges on homelessness.

Feminist approaches Theories and analysis that foreground gender inequalities and patriarchal structures in explaining social phenomena such as homelessness.

Individual causes of homelessness The antecedents to homelessness associated with the personal characteristics and behaviours of homeless people.

Literal homelessness A narrow conception of homelessness limited to those sleeping rough or living in emergency shelters or other accommodation for homeless people.

Positivism A theoretical perspective that assumes an objective social reality and focuses on empirical regularities in explaining and predicting social life.

Social constructionism A theoretical perspective primarily concerned with understanding the 'meanings' people attach to social situations, with some social constructionists arguing that human actions are not governed by 'cause' and 'effect' at all, but rather by the rules that we use to interpret the social world.

Structural causes of homelessness Social and economic structures that may drive homelessness, such as adverse housing and labour market conditions and limited social welfare protection.

Theory A statement, or group of statements, purporting to describe how a part of the world works.

Introduction

It is an extremely complex matter, in both theoretical and empirical terms, to analyse the causes of homelessness, particularly when one attempts to do so across countries. To start with, as countries vary so much in the definitions of homelessness that they employ, they are focusing to some extent on explanations of different phenomena. Moreover, the interpretation of causes may well be influenced by the dominant research traditions and ideological assumptions in different national contexts, as much as by the varying 'realities' of homelessness (Fitzpatrick and Christian, 2006).

Bearing these caveats in mind, this article attempts to summarise existing knowledge on the causes of homelessness in the developed world. It focuses in particular on the United Kingdom, but also makes reference to evidence from elsewhere in the European Union and from the United States, Canada, Australia, and Japan. After setting out some key issues with respect to definitions of homelessness, it considers the relatively straightforward issue of the immediate causes ('triggers') for homelessness, which display a remarkable degree of consistency across developed countries. It then moves onto the far trickier territory of the more fundamental ('underlying') causes of homelessness. It summarises traditional and 'orthodox' explanations of homelessness, which attempt to integrate both 'individual' and 'structural' causes, before examining more theoretically grounded approaches to understanding homelessness. The main theoretical positions considered are positivism, social constructionism, feminism, and critical realism.

Definitions of Homelessness

Countries across the developed world vary very widely in the definitions of homelessness that they employ. Many developed countries – including the United States, Canada, France, Spain, the Netherlands, and Central and Eastern European countries – use a narrow definition that has often been termed 'literal homelessness' (Fitzpatrick and Stephens, 2007). This definition is limited to: people sleeping rough; and people using emergency shelters or other accommodation for homeless people.

However, other countries such as Australia, Germany, Sweden, and the United Kingdom use wider definitions of homelessness in generating at least some of their published statistics and research. In Sweden, for example, the definition used in national surveys includes the 'houseless' living in various institutional settings, as well as some of those living temporarily with friends or relatives. The United Kingdom's definition of 'statutory' homelessness is exceptionally wide, including as it does all persons who do not have 'reasonable' accommodation within which they can live with their family:

> Broadly speaking, somebody is statutorily homeless if they do not have accommodation that they have a legal right to occupy, which is accessible and physically available to them (and their household) and which it would be reasonable for them to continue to live in. It would not be reasonable for someone to continue to live in their home, for example, if that was likely to lead to violence against them (or a member of their family). (Department for Communities and Local Government, Department of Health, Department for Education and Skills, 2006: 10)

In order to facilitate cross-country comparisons of homelessness, the European Federation of National Organisations Working with the Homeless developed the 'ETHOS' typology in 2005 as a common definitional framework. As can be seen in **Table 1**, 'literal homelessness' is captured in ETHOS categories 1–3, but a range of wider aspects of housing exclusion are also defined as potentially constituting homelessness. Even in those countries with the narrowest homelessness definitions, wider ETHOS categories are increasingly being recognised as relevant to homelessness prevention (Stephens et al., 2010).

Triggers to Homelessness

A range of research evidence indicates that the main triggers to homelessness – that is, the 'immediate' or 'proximate' reasons why homeless people lost their last-settled housing – are largely consistent across developed countries (Fitzpatrick and Stephens, 2007). The key direct causes are:

- eviction,
- relationship breakdown, and
- to a lesser extent, loss of employment.

Eviction is often cited as the largest direct cause of homelessness in developed countries, with most of these evictions prompted by rent arrears. The United Kingdom is, however, an exception, with rent arrears a relatively minor homelessness trigger (most probably because of the Housing Benefit system which pays up to 100% of eligible rent for low-income households). Mortgage repossession remains a minor cause of homelessness in the United Kingdom and wider European Union, even after the 'credit crunch' and subsequent recession (Stephens et al., 2010), but appears more significant as a driver of homelessness in the United States.

Relationship breakdown is very prominent as a cause of homelessness in all developed countries and most commonly involves relationship breakdown between spouses or partners (both violent and nonviolent) or exclusion by parents. However, while the 'exhaustion' of family relationships (both sudden and gradual) is a widespread trigger to homelessness, evidence from a range of developed countries indicates that most homeless people have some ongoing contact with family members (Toro, 2007).

Homelessness (particularly among men) is sometimes attributed directly to the loss of a job or other sharp decreases in income, such as those attributable to severe

Table 1 ETHOS: European typology on homelessness and housing exclusion

Roofless	1	People living rough
	2	People staying in a night shelter
Houseless	3	People in accommodation for homeless people
	4	People in women's shelters
	5	People in accommodation for immigrants
	6	People due to be released from institutions
	7	People receiving support (due to homelessness)
Insecure	8	People living in insecure accommodation
	9	People living under threat of eviction
	10	People living under threat of violence
Inadequate	11	People living in temporary/nonstandard structures
	12	People living in unfit housing
	13	People living in extreme overcrowding

Source: Edgar W, Harrison M, Watson P, and Busch-Geertsema V (2007) *Measurement of Homelessness at European Union Level*. Brussels: European Commission. http://ec.europa.eu/employment_social/social_inclusion/docs/2007/study_homelessness_en.pdf.

health problems when they compromise earning potential in the context of weak social protection. Loss of paid work certainly seems to be the overwhelming immediate cause of homelessness in Japan, for example, reflecting the close link between employment and housing via 'tied' or 'company' housing, with mainly older men affected (Okamoto, 2007). But persistent poverty or long-term worklessness seems more often to be the key issue in developed countries, rather than the loss of a particular job (Stephens et al., 2010), placing these issues in the category of more fundamental rather than proximate causes of homelessness (see below).

In some countries, particularly those which focus on narrow definitions of literal homelessness, drug, alcohol, and mental health problems, and leaving institutions such as prison or hospital, are often identified as key direct causes of homelessness (Stephens et al., 2010). For specific groups of homeless people, such as older homeless people, bereavement and other less common triggers may be especially important (Crane, 1999).

Traditional Explanations of Homelessness and the Emergence of the 'New Orthodoxy'

Looking now at the longer-term 'fundamental' causes of homelessness, a much more complex and contested picture emerges. Academic explanations of homelessness in the United Kingdom and elsewhere in the developed world have traditionally been divided into two broad categories: 'individual' and 'structural'. Individual explanations focus on the personal characteristics and, especially, behaviours of homeless people. Structural explanations, on the other hand, locate the causes of homelessness in broader social and economic structures, such as adverse housing and labour market conditions and weak welfare protection. These underlying causes of homelessness have been much discussed within the literature, but the debate has been hampered by a lack of conceptual and theoretical clarity (Neale, 1997) and by the adoption of polarised positions whereby some commentators assume that the causes are entirely 'structural' in origin, and others that they are entirely 'individual' (Fitzpatrick, 2005).

From an international perspective, it is clear that homelessness in some countries is interpreted as essentially an individual problem, whereas in others it is viewed as mainly a structural problem. For example, in recent comparative research across a number of EU countries, there was a consensus among service providers in both the Netherlands and Sweden that: "there are no economic homeless people" and "people who become homeless always have more than only financial problems" (Stephens et al., 2010: 210). In the Netherlands in particular, it was consistently reported that homelessness was always the result of an accumulation of personal or social problems. In Sweden, likewise, there was a strong emphasis on 'social' reasons for homelessness, such as drug addiction or mental health problems.

This was in contrast to the position reported by service providers in Germany and the United Kingdom in this study, who tended to offer a far more structural analysis of homelessness. While the resolution of the more extreme forms of homelessness – literal homelessness – was acknowledged to require 'more than a roof' solutions in both of these countries, broader forms of homelessness were usually interpreted as mainly a housing market problem. Thus, in the United Kingdom, housing affordability factors were viewed as central to the underlying causation of statutory homelessness, with trends in 'statutory' homelessness generally following the housing market cycle (at least until a recent strong emphasis on homelessness prevention, especially in England). In the German case, there had been a very sharp reduction in homelessness in recent years. Reduced immigration, especially by ethnic Germans from Central and Eastern Europe since the mid-1990s, was seen as one of the major drivers for this positive trend. But even this aside, there had still been a major decline in homelessness attributed to:

> ... a mix of demographic factors and the development of the housing markets, which ... is expected to continue influencing the [reduced] number of the homeless strongly ... The housing markets in many regions are still very relaxed, so that in these regions it has become easier to find a new home after the old home has been lost for whatever reasons. (NGO representative, quoted in Stephens et al., 2010: 210)

Various authors from the United States and Europe have attempted to explain these divergent national perspectives on the causation of homelessness by arguing that countries with benign social and economic conditions – well-functioning housing and labour markets, relatively low levels of poverty and inequality, and generous social security policies – are likely to have a low overall prevalence of homelessness, but that a high proportion of their small homeless populations will have complex personal problems (Shinn, 2007; Stephens and Fitzpatrick, 2007). The Netherlands and Sweden could be viewed as archetypical of these types of countries. The same authors have posited that the reverse will hold true (high prevalence/ low proportion with support needs) in countries with a more difficult structural context (e.g., high levels of poverty and inequality). The United Kingdom and Germany would come into this category, and so too would other developed countries considered in this article, such as the United States and Canada. While the international research evidence is not sufficient to test this hypothesis in a rigorous manner, existing knowledge does fit this broad hypothesis. For example, Milburn et al.'s (2007) cross-national comparison of risk-taking behaviours among homeless young people in the United States and Australia set out explicitly to test this thesis, and found that, consistent with it, homeless young people in Australia (a relatively benign structural context) were on average more 'risk-taking' than homeless young people in the United States (with a more difficult structural context).

As well as varying between countries, explanations of homelessness also change over time. Thus, traditional accounts of homelessness in the United States have been shaped by community and clinical psychology, leading to a strong emphasis on social disaffiliation and mental disorders (Fitzpatrick and Christian, 2006). This emphasis was also linked to the classic US sociological research on homelessness, which depicted homeless people as older men, often transient workers, who had poor relationships with family. Another factor contributing to this focus was the apparent coincidence between sharp increases in homelessness and deinstitutionalisation policies, with a resultant interest in understanding homelessness among those with mental health problems. However, from the late 1980s, increased attention was paid in the United States to the potential contribution of structural factors in the generation of homelessness, with some medical as well as social researchers criticising the emphasis on 'individual pathology' in traditional sociological and psychological accounts. Most recently, explanations related to housing supply and affordability have emerged strongly in the US literature. For example, research which employed statistical modelling techniques to investigate the relationship between the incidence of homelessness and housing market variables in urban areas of the United States concluded that

> ... rather straightforward conditions in US housing markets – not complex social pathologies, drug usage, or deficiencies in mental health treatments – are largely responsible for variations in rates of homelessness. (Quigley and Raphael, 2001: 324).

Similarly, Shinn et al.'s (1998) 5-year longitudinal study carried out in New York City found that receipt of subsidised housing was the primary predictor of long-term residential stability among formerly homeless families. Individual-level attributes – including mental health, substance abuse, size and quality of social networks, and work histories – were insignificant.

In the immediate postwar period, analyses of homelessness in the United Kingdom also tended to take an individual pathology approach – focusing on the ill health and substance dependencies of homeless people (Neale, 1997). This began to change in the mid-1960s as housing pressure groups and academic studies increasingly argued that homelessness was the result of housing market failures rather than individual choice or family failings. Structural, housing market-based accounts of homelessness then dominated until the 1980s, but came under growing pressure towards the end of that decade as research studies repeatedly identified high levels of health and social support needs among 'single' homeless people (homeless households without dependent children), particularly those sleeping rough (Pleace, 1998). As a result, UK researchers were obliged to take account of individual factors in their explanations of homelessness. However, most of them continued to assert the overall primacy of structural causes (Fitzpatrick et al., 2000). This led them to a position once described by Pleace (2000) as the 'new orthodoxy'. The key assertions of this (now well established) orthodoxy are as follows:

- structural factors create the conditions within which homelessness will occur; and
- people with personal problems are more vulnerable to these adverse social and economic trends than others; therefore
- the high concentration of people with personal problems in the homeless population can be explained by their susceptibility to macrostructural forces, rather than necessitating an individual explanation of homelessness.

An integration of individual and structural factors, similar to that of the British new orthodoxy, has also taken shape in understandings of homelessness in the United States. For example, Metraux and Culhane (1999) argued that from initially polarised accounts

> ... there has emerged a more moderate position that incorporates both structural issues and individual characteristics and circumstances. This position outlines a process in which structural factors such as poverty, the declining availability of affordable housing, and lack of employment have left growing numbers of persons and households facing considerable difficulty in maintaining their housing arrangements and who are at risk of experiencing episodes of literal homelessness. From this group, certain persons and households, because of individual factors – disabilities, family dynamics, misfortune or some other circumstances – are particularly vulnerable to experiencing homelessness and account for the unusually high prevalence of these individual factors in the homeless population. (p. 372)

This new orthodoxy provides a far more 'practically adequate' explanation of homelessness than the individual and structural accounts that preceded it. It is, however, clearly unsatisfying from a deeper, conceptual point of view for at least four reasons.

First, it fails to convincingly accommodate a whole range of factors that might plausibly contribute to homelessness, particularly where, as is often the case, they are restricted to 'macro' level social and economic forces at one extreme, and personal behaviours of the homeless person on the other. For example, having suffered childhood abuse would not normally be considered a macrostructural factor, and yet is hardly a behavioural factor in the sense of being within the control of the homeless person themselves. Relationship breakdown is one of a great many examples which could be interpreted as operating at either a structural or an individual level – should the breakdown in a homeless person's marriage be considered a personal problem or the result of a societal trend towards growing family fragmentation?

Second, the new orthodoxy cannot take account of those cases of homelessness arising from acute personal crises where structural factors can seem virtually absent, as Crane (1999), for example, has argued is often the case with older homeless people.

Third, the overwhelming importance attributed (a priori) to structural factors by many scholars means that the individual attributes, choices, and actions of homeless people have been neglected. This unwillingness to engage with the 'agency' of those directly affected may be because researchers do not want to be accused of adding to a stigmatising pathology of homelessness. But by 'writing agency out' of accounts of homelessness, people who face this experience are treated as wholly passive, and accounts of causation are potentially misleading (McNaughton-Nicholls, 2009).

Fourth, and most profoundly, it lacks any clear conceptualisation of causation. Such recurrent patterns of precursors to homelessness as are evident in the homeless population are often reconceptualised as 'risk factors' rather than 'causes' (with causation it seems felt to be an uncomfortable, unfathomable, or unsound concept). But, if we have dispensed with the concept of causation, what is it about these structural and individual 'factors' that can be said to generate an increased risk of homelessness? And, what is the conceptual basis for combining factors of such a very different order as, say, mental ill health and housing shortages, in the same explanatory framework as 'risk factors' in homelessness?

We therefore now consider a range of theoretical approaches to conceptualising causation in the social world, and assess their relative strengths and weaknesses with respect to explaining homelessness.

Positivist Explanations of Homelessness

Positivists adopt Hume's 'constant conjunctions' theory of causality which in practical terms translates into the search for statistically significant correlations between 'variables'. Most explanations of homelessness in the United Kingdom have implicitly employed this 'empirical regularity' notion of causation. One of the clearest examples is work by Randall and Brown (1999) who comment as follows:

> Housing shortages, poverty, unemployment, personal difficulties such as mental health, drug or alcohol problems are sometimes said to be the causes of rough sleeping. However, there are continuing problems of rough sleeping in areas with no housing shortage. Equally, the great majority of people in poverty or with mental health, or substance abuse problems, do not sleep rough. ... It follows that housing shortages, poverty, mental health and substance misuse problems cannot be said to cause rough sleeping. (p. 5)

There is a clear assumption here that the factors associated with homelessness can only possess causal force if there is a perfect match between their presence and homelessness resulting. This is a very strong version of the empirical regularities notion of causation – demanding not only statistically significant associations between proposed causal factors and homelessness, but also 100% correlations. Pleace's (1998) analysis also appears to be underpinned by a positivist conception of causation:

> Single homelessness and rough sleeping are never one thing or another, sometimes the structural factors seem all-important, sometimes it is relationships breaking down, loss of a job or a host of other factors that seem almost to be unique to each individual who experiences homelessness ... Instead of being confronted by patterns, clear relationships and shared characteristics, there is the impression of variation above all else, rather than a central tendency ... none provides a satisfactory explanation of all forms of homelessness or what is known about single homelessness on a case by case basis. (p. 56)

In fact, the research evidence in the United Kingdom and elsewhere demonstrates a recurring pattern of life events and circumstances implicated in 'pathways' into homelessness (Fitzpatrick et al., 2000), although the precise combination of these factors differs from person to person. As with policy-orientated advocates of the 'new orthodoxy', positivist-influenced researchers tend to reconceptualise these recurring factors as contributing towards 'increased risks' (rather than causes) of homelessness. Such an 'increased risk' approach has considerable value at the descriptive level in that it appears to be empirically well grounded, and is thus practically useful in enabling 'micro-level' prevention measures to be targeted appropriately. But it is clearly unsatisfactory at an explanatory level: if we have dispensed with the concept of causation, how can we understand why these factors lead to an increased risk of homelessness?

Social Constructionist Explanations of Homelessness

The main challenge to positivist analyses of homelessness has come from 'social constructionism' within the interpretivist tradition (Clapham, 2005). Social constructionists are primarily concerned with the 'meanings' people attach to social situations, with some arguing that human actions are not governed by 'cause' and 'effect' at all, but rather by rules that we use to interpret the social world (Williams and May, 1996). Hutson and Liddiard (1994) were among the first UK authors in the homelessness field to take this approach. They explored the diverse ways in which youth homelessness is interpreted and presented by a range of key actors – the media, homelessness agencies, politicians, and young homeless people themselves – and argued that:

> No longer should we simply aim to observe and measure aspects of society, such as crime or homelessness, as if they were objective facts. Instead we should concentrate on understanding the meanings and interpretations that people apply to the social world and to social phenomena, such as youth homelessness. (Hutson and Liddiard, 1994: 24)

The main question that this sort of statement begs is whether social constructionists believe that there is an underlying (social and/or material) reality which is being mediated through these social and cultural processes (the 'weak' constructionist approach), or whether all reality is simply the product of 'ways of seeing' (the 'strong' constructionist approach) (Lupton, 1999). In other words, is an exploration of the 'meanings' attached to homelessness by the range of social actors an alternative or additional exercise to investigating its 'real' causes?

A later, and more developed, contribution from the constructionist school of thought has been made by Jacobs et al. (1999). They focused on the contested nature of the definition of homelessness, arguing that:

> ... the struggle by different vested interests to impose a particular definition of homelessness on the policy agenda is critical to the way in which homelessness is treated as a social problem. (p. 11)

Jacobs et al. conceptualise the key ideological battle as between those who treat homelessness as a structural problem requiring broad welfare measures and those with a minimalist definition who view homelessness as resulting from individual fecklessness (a conceptualisation which mirrors the structure vs. agency debate discussed above). When compared with Hutson and Liddiard, they take a more explicitly 'critical' (yet orthodox) approach, arguing that those in positions of power use their resources to establish a dominant discourse through which social 'problems' are defined and dealt with. The authors imply at several points that they (unlike strong constructionists) recognise an underlying reality beneath these competing social constructions of homelessness, commenting, for example, that "... the structure of a society does provide the basis for the emergence of certain kinds of 'problems'" (p. 13).

More recently, Clapham (2005) has taken a social constructionist approach to examining the housing 'pathways' of homeless people, illuminating the ways in which people interpret and understand their homeless and other housing experiences, foregrounding "meaning, identity and lifestyle" (p. 237). As compared with Jacobs et al., Clapham seems to be a weak rather than strong constructionist, and certainly he appears to acknowledge the existence of 'real' social structures in his argument that the housing pathways approach enables one to examine "... the interaction between households and the structures that influence the opportunities and constraints they face" (p. 239).

These social constructionists' analyses made a major contribution to analyses of homelessness in at least two ways. First, they reinforced the importance of focusing on the perceptions and priorities of homeless people themselves in understanding the experiences and impacts associated with homelessness. Second, they furthered understanding of how homelessness is perceived by key social actors and the impact that these perceptions have on the types of policy interventions that are pursued. However, social constructionists do not generally acknowledge the limitations of their approach in providing explanations of social phenomena like homelessness, but rather tend to make assertions relating to the underlying causes of homelessness without offering substantiating evidence (e.g., "... the fewer resources that are committed to an area like housing, the more homelessness there is likely to be" (Jacobs et al., 1999: p. 13)). This is clearly less than satisfactory from an explanatory perspective.

Feminist Explanations of Homelessness

Feminist academics have launched a sustained critique of mainstream analyses of housing and homelessness over many years (Watson and Austerberry, 1986; Wardhaugh, 2001). Women, they argue, are often powerless to define their own housing needs or to house themselves independently from a man because of their weak economic position and the patriarchal assumptions embedded in housing policy and practice. These factors, together with women's vulnerability to domestic abuse and violence, have led numerous mainstream as well as feminist authors to identify being female as a particular risk factor predisposing a person to homelessness (Edgar and Doherty, 2001).

However, these attempts to establish the special vulnerability of women to homelessness do not always stand up to empirical scrutiny. In fact, consistent evidence from across the developed world indicates that single homeless men far outnumber single homeless women (Stephens et al., 2010). Many commentators have dealt with these awkward statistics by suggesting that female homelessness tends to take 'hidden' forms, with women more likely than men to stay with friends and relatives rather than approach homelessness agencies for help (Watson and Austerberry, 1986; Edgar and Doherty, 2001). However, the (limited) UK evidence on gender and homelessness (as opposed to women and homelessness) indicates that women are in fact more likely than men to approach local authorities and housing associations when they find themselves homeless, and to be treated more sympathetically by these agencies, than their male counterparts (Cramer and Carter, 2001). This suggests that, if anything, female homelessness rather than male homelessness is most likely to be 'visible' in the official statistics.

Moreover, an important point seldom acknowledged in the homelessness literature is that some gendered factors associated with homelessness almost certainly disproportionately affect men. For example, lack of social support is a key factor which can precipitate homelessness and we know that women tend to build up stronger kinship and other social relationships than men (Finch, 1989). It may also be that domestic training from an early age enables most women to manage independent living and domestic crises more effectively.

All of that said, if one takes a relatively broad definition of homelessness, it is likely that the gender imbalance in the single homeless population is more than compensated for by the very high vulnerability of lone parent families to homelessness, the great majority of whom are headed by women (Pleace et al., 2008). This gender distinction in household type is probably far more fundamental to understanding the difference between the male and female homeless experience that any notion of 'hiddenness' – quite simply, most homeless women are caring for dependent children and most homeless men are not.

Feminist frameworks have therefore been especially important in highlighting the complexities and dynamics of family homelessness as well as in furthering our understanding of particular vulnerability of the small minority of homeless women who sleep rough or find themselves in emergency shelters or in other homeless accommodation dominated by men. They have also been crucial in analysing (the very considerable proportion of) female homelessness associated with escaping domestic violence and abuse. But gendered and patriarchal social relationships are only one set of social structures which can contribute to homelessness. A more comprehensive theory of causation is required, which takes account of other potential explanatory factors.

Critical Realism: A Helpful Way Forward in Explaining Homelessness?

It has been argued by Fitzpatrick (2005) that critical realism provides a particularly useful theoretical framework for analysing the causation of social phenomena such as homelessness because of its emphasis on underlying generative mechanisms. Realists regard 'real' causal powers as necessary tendencies of social objects and structures which may or may not be activated (and produce 'actual' effects) depending on contingent conditions (Sayer, 1992).

According to realists, the 'open' nature of social systems means that different causal mechanisms are 'externally' related to each other in ways that are often unpredictable. Realist explanations of actual social events and phenomena are therefore not 'mono causal' and deterministic, but rather contingent, and also 'complex', with intricate feedback loops linking multiple (and multidirectional) causal mechanisms. They may also involve 'nonlinear dynamics', meaning that small changes can potentially result in dramatically varying outcomes (Byrne, 1998). Realism also places a great emphasis on 'emergence': from this complexity, new phenomena emerge which have a reality over and above any individual component, carrying causal powers which cannot be deduced from taking these components separately (Williams, 2001).

Realists would argue that the presence (or absence) of empirical regularities is not a reliable guide to the (non-)existence of causal powers as the presence of other causal mechanisms may often – or even always – prevent correspondence between cause and effect. Instead, they contend that potential causal mechanisms should be 'abducted' from the 'concrete' case in order to facilitate 'qualitative' examination – that is, close scrutiny of what it is about this mechanism that may tend to cause the relevant phenomena. Given this, and their preoccupation with causation rather than prediction in the social world, they tend to lay little emphasis on investigations of statistical associations, although there is an acceptance among realists that quantitative patterns can draw attention to potential causal mechanisms.

Perhaps the most important characteristic of realist ontology with respect to our present purposes is its positing of a layered (social as well as physical) reality (Pawson and Tilley, 1997). The central ontological assumption of realists is that the world is structured, differentiated, and stratified, and no one stratum is assumed to be logically prior to any other. This is a crucial point with respect to the causation of homelessness whereby the current orthodox position tends to assume that structural causes are somehow more 'fundamental' than more personal or individual ones (see above). In contrast, a realist ontology allows for causal factors operating at a range of different levels to be explored in an open-minded way, without assuming that any one level necessarily 'trumps' another. To be clear, while it may be that, in fact, factors operating at a macrostructural level are more important (in scale) and/or powerful (in predictive strength) in the generation of homelessness than those operating at a lower (micro) level, this is a matter for empirical investigation rather than a priori reasoning.

Drawing on a critical realist framework, Fitzpatrick (2005) has hypothesised that causal mechanisms related to homelessness could exist on several levels: economic and housing structures (macro level); interpersonal structures (meso level); and individual attributes and actions (micro level). Edgar (2009) proposes a very similar analytical framework, but adds 'institutional' structures (availability of services and institutional procedures) as a separate stratum. However one defines them, the interrelationship between these strata is likely to be fiendishly complicated, as now discussed.

Inadequate housing supply is probably the clear-cut example of a macrostructural factor: there is very little an individual can do to influence that. However, some other 'structural' factors – such as sustained poverty and labour market marginalisation on the part of particular individuals – may be considered to have some (variable) element of agency. At the other end of the extremes, while substance misuse may be viewed as the clearest example of what are thought of as individual causes and there is clearly a degree of agency involved in the sense of voluntary risk taking or 'edge working' (Lyng, 2005), the development of addictions can also be strongly linked to structural forces (poverty, social exclusion, and concentrated deprivation) (Buchanan, 2004). Mental health problems can involve personal 'transgression' (though not necessarily voluntary risk taking) (Jenks, 2003), and are 'individual' in that sense, but again there are often strong structural contextual factors implicated in their generation and persistence. It is also worth bearing in mind that, as noted above, many potential causes of homelessness usually considered to be 'individual' in nature are in fact interpersonal – such as experience of domestic violence or local authority care – involving little or no agency on the part of the homeless person themselves.

Central to this complexity is the likelihood of 'feedback loops' and causal interrelationships between several of these potential causal factors. Drug use, for example, is 'externally' related to persistent labour market marginalisation (i.e., one can exist without the other). But they can contingently interact in a bi-directional causal relationship (i.e., each can make the other more likely). There are also likely to be multidirectional causal relationships between homelessness and several potential precursors, including substance misuse and mental health (Johnson et al., 1997).

From the complex system of 'nested possibilities' created by these interacting causal mechanisms, the clustering of particular experiences and characteristics in any one individual increases the probability of homelessness resulting. Thus, long-term risk factors – both 'structural', such as sustained poverty, and 'individual', such as mental health problems – are 'causal', in that they have emergent powers which may make homelessness substantially more likely, but this is not determined (i.e., inevitable). Clearly, if an individual experiences an array of these long-term risk factors, then the 'weight of the weighted possibility' of homelessness starts to increase. However, the dynamics are also, at least potentially, nonlinear, meaning that a relatively small change in complex relationships (such as deterioration in mental health), can have dramatic consequences. The 'triggers' associated with homelessness may be understood as an example of such nonlinear dynamics (Fitzpatrick, 2005).

Two overarching points emerge from this discussion. First, there is no single 'cause' of homelessness and the search for any such 'silver bullet' is a vain endeavour. Rather, there are a series of more and less macro (or micro) causes and more or less proximate (or long-term) causes of homelessness. This is almost certainly true at the collective level and, most probably, at the level of any one homeless individual. The fact that a relevant factor is long term rather than a proximate feature of a homeless person's life does not make it 'noncausal', and the fact that a relevant factor is at the individual rather than structural end of that continuum does not necessarily make it subordinate.

Second, neither 'necessity' (in the sense of having to be present) nor 'sufficiency' (in terms of inevitably leading to homelessness) is assumed about any of these causal factors. Homelessness is an emergent condition which arises from the interaction of an array of distinct causal mechanisms – each implicated in multiple, often multidirectional causal relationships with other causal mechanisms – none of which are determinants. The challenge with respect to explaining any particular homeless groups or phenomena is to seek identifiable patterns ('deep simplicity' if possible; see Gribben, 2004) in this complexity.

Finally, to return to the opening discussion regarding the definition of homelessness, it is worth noting that a central distinguishing feature of critical realist approaches to social science is the close attention paid to conceptual validity and clarity, particularly with regards to the 'qualitative nature' of the social object under scrutiny. In this spirit, Williams (2001) has mounted an important challenge to the assumption that homelessness is a 'realistic category' amenable to causal analysis:

> ... there is no such thing as homelessness, but instead a range of heterogeneous characteristics that give rise to a wide range of symptoms that we term 'homelessness'. (p. 1)

The crux of his argument is that homelessness is a 'bad abstraction' (or 'chaotic conception') meaning that it "... arbitrarily divides the indivisible and/or lumps together the unrelated and the inessential" (Sayer, 1992: p. 138). One could indeed argue that a focus on more internally homogeneous subgroups within the 'homeless' population would yield better explanations of the social problems associated with 'suboptimal' housing circumstances. So, if, for example, single people sleeping rough and living in hostels shared many similar experiences (especially if there was extensive movement between these 'types' of homelessness) and exhibited similar health and other impacts of their experience of homelessness, they may constitute a 'real' category which could, for instance, be entirely separate from that of families living in bed-and-breakfast hotels. Systematic investigation of this point would require, as Williams has argued, empirically informed theorising about meaningful categorisations within the homeless experience, and a re-analysis of existing empirical material with this critical realist framework in mind. That said, as noted above, there is already sufficient evidence of similar life histories and recurring characteristics among at least some groups of homeless people to conclude that, contrary to Williams' speculative contention, such a realist conceptual interrogation would be unlikely to find that the reference category had to be reduced to the single case to be meaningful.

Conclusion

The causes of homelessness have been extensively debated, with a division usually drawn between 'individual' and 'structural' causes. While the balance between individual and structural explanations of homelessness varies between countries and over time, in recent years a 'new orthodoxy' has developed which seeks to integrate individual and structural factors into a unified explanatory framework. It has been argued that this new orthodoxy is useful at a descriptive and policy level, but unsatisfactory at a more profound conceptual level. Various attempts to provide more theoretically informed explanations of homelessness – including positivist, social constructionist, feminist, and critical realist – were examined. Each was found to have made important contributions to furthering our understanding of aspects of homelessness. However, it was suggested that critical realism is the most promising theoretical approach of those reviewed because it allows account to be taken of the full range of potential causal factors in homelessness without assuming the logical priority of any one type of factor, and provides a robust framework for understanding their complex interrelationships.

Acknowledgement

Parts of this entry draw heavily upon a previous paper published by the author (Fitzpatrick S (2005) Explaining homelessness: a critical realist perspective. *Housing, Theory & Society* 22(1): 1–17). The author wishes to thank Routledge/Taylor & Francis for permission to use material from this earlier publication.

See also: Homelessness: Definitions.

References

Buchanan J (2004) Tackling problem drug use: A new conceptual framework. *Social Work in Mental Health* 2(3): 117–138.
Byrne DS (1998) *Complexity Theory and the Social Sciences*. London: Routledge.
Clapham D (2005) *The Meaning of Housing: A Pathways Approach*. Bristol, UK: Policy Press.
Cramer H and Carter M (2001) *Homelessness: What's Gender Got to Do with It?* London: Shelter.
Crane M (1999) *Understanding Older Homeless People*. Buckingham, UK: Open University Press.
Department for Communities, Local Government, Department of Health, and Department for Education and Skills (2006) *Homelessness Code of Guidance for Local Authorities*. London: DCLG, DoH, DfES.
Edgar W (2009) *European Review of Statistics on Homelessness*. Brussels: FEANTSA.
Edgar B and Doherty J (2001) *Women and Homelessness in Europe*. Bristol, UK: The Policy Press.
Edgar W, Harrison M, Watson P, and Busch-Geertsema V (2007) *Measurement of Homelessness at European Union Level*. Brussels: European Commission. http://ec.europa.eu/employment_social/social_inclusion/docs/2007/study_homelessness_en.pdf (accessed 1 August 2011)
Finch J (1989) *Family Obligations and Social Change*. Cambridge, UK: Polity Press.
Fitzpatrick S (2005) Explaining homelessness: A critical realist perspective. *Housing, Theory and Society* 22(1): 1–17.
Fitzpatrick S and Christian J (2006) Comparing research on homelessness in the United Kingdom and United States: What lessons can be learned? *European Journal of Housing Policy* 6(3): 313–333.
Fitzpatrick S and Stephens M (2007) *An International Review of Homelessness and Social Housing Policy*. London: Communities and Local Government.
Fitzpatrick S, Kemp PA, and Klinker S (2000) *Single Homelessness: An Overview of Research in Britain*. Bristol, UK: The Policy Press.
Gribben J (2004) *Deep Simplicity: Chaos, Complexity and the Emergence of Life*. London: Allen Lane.
Hutson S and Liddiard M (1994) *Youth Homelessness: The Construction of a Social Issue*. Basingstoke, UK: Macmillan.
Jacobs K, Kemeny J, and Manzi T (1999) The struggle to define homelessness: A constructivist approach. In: Hutson S and Clapham D (eds.) *Homelessness: Public Policies and Private Troubles*, pp. 11–28. London: Cassell.
Jenks C (2003) *Transgression*. London: Routledge.

Johnson TP, Freels SA, Parsons JA, and Vangeest JB (1997) Substance misuse and homelessness: Social selection or social adaptation. *Addiction* 92(4): 437–445.

Lupton D (1999) *Risk*. London: Routledge.

Lyng S (2005) *Edgework: The Sociology of Risk Taking*. London: Routledge.

McNaughton-Nicholls C (2009) Agency, transgression and the causation of homelessness: A contextualised rational action analysis. *European Journal of Housing Policy* 9(1): 69–84.

Metraux S and Culhane DP (1999) Family dynamics, housing, and recurring homelessness among women in New York City homeless shelters. *Journal of Family Issues* 20: 371–396.

Milburn NG, Stein JA, Rice E, et al. (2007) AIDS risk behaviours among American and Australian homeless youth. *Journal of Social Issues* 63(3): 543–566.

Neale J (1997) Theorising homelessness: Contemporary sociological and feminist perspectives. In: Burrows R, Pleace N, and Quilgars D (eds.) *Homelessness and Social Policy*, pp. 35–39. London: Routledge.

Okamoto Y (2007) A comparative study of homelessness in the United Kingdom and Japan. *Journal of Social Issues* 63(3): 525–542.

Pawson R and Tilley N (1997) *Realistic Evaluation*. London: Sage.

Pleace N (1998) Single homelessness as social exclusion: The unique and the extreme. *Social Policy and Administration* 32(1): 46–59.

Pleace N (2000) The new consensus, the old consensus and the provision of services for people sleeping rough. *Housing Studies* 15(4): 581–594.

Pleace N, Fitzpatrick S, Johnsen S, Quilgars D, and Sanderson D (2008) *Statutory Homelessness in England: The Experience of Families and 16–17 Year Olds*. London: Communities and Local Government.

Quigley JM and Raphael S (2001) The economics of homelessness: The evidence from North America. *European Journal of Housing Policy* 1: 323–336.

Randall G and Brown S (1999) *Prevention Is Better Than Cure*. London: Crisis.

Sayer A (1992) *Method in Social Science: A Realist Approach*. London: Routledge.

Shinn M (2007) International homelessness: Policy, socio-cultural, and individual perspectives. *Journal of Social Issues* 63(3): 657–677.

Shinn M, Weitzman BC, Stojanovic D, et al. (1998) Predictors of homelessness among families in New York City: From shelter request to housing stability. *American Journal of Public Health* 88: 1651–1657.

Stephens M and Fitzpatrick S (2007) Welfare regimes, housing systems and homelessness: How are they linked? *European Journal of Homelessness* 1: 201–212.

Stephens M, Fitzpatrick S, Elsinga M, Steen GV, and Chzhen Y (2010) *Study on Housing Exclusion: Welfare policies, Labour Market and Housing Provision*. Brussels: European Commission.

Toro PA (2007) Toward an international understanding of homelessness. *Journal of Social Issues* 63(3): 461–481.

Wardhaugh J (2001) The unaccommodated woman: Home, homelessness and identity. *The Sociological Review* 47(1): 91–109.

Watson S and Austerberry H (1986) *Housing and Homelessness: A Feminist Perspective*. London: Routledge and Kegan Paul.

Williams M (2001) Complexity, probability and causation: Implications for homelessness research. *Journal of Social Issues*. http://www.whb.co.uk/socialissues/mv.htm (accessed 1 August 2011)

Williams M and May T (1996) *Introduction to the Philosophy of Social Research*. London: UCL Press.

Homelessness: Definitions

D MacKenzie, Swinburne University, Melbourne, VIC, Australia

© 2012 Elsevier Ltd. All rights reserved.

Glossary

Cultural definition of homelessness A social constructionist approach to defining 'homelessness' in terms of living situations below the minimum community cultural standards for habitation in a particular country.

ETHOS typology of homelessness A conceptual framework of categories of homelessness and housing exclusion categories with operational definitions developed under the auspice of FEANTSA for use across the European Union.

HEARTH Act (2009) Legislation in the United States that authorises federal homeless assistance funding across a number of specific programmes.

Literal homelessness People without access to conventional accommodation or staying in shelters for the homeless.

Rooflessness People sleeping rough, in cars, train carriages, or in other unsheltered situations.

UK Homelessness Act Legislation enacted in 2002 that lays down the legal duty of local authorities to respond to homelessness. This Act supercedes the 1996 Housing Act and the Housing (Homeless Persons) Act of 1977.

Introduction

A definitional debate about 'homelessness' continues and the first section outlines the core issues in the debate. The next section on homelessness as a social problem discusses how definitions of homelessness have implications for who is classified as 'homeless', thus determining the size of the homeless population, and whether homelessness can be argued to be a 'big' problem deserving of a high public policy priority or not. Definitions and their associated typifications shape how social problems such as homelessness are addressed in policy and social programmes. The section on official definitions looks at how homelessness is represented in policy and programmes. The United Kingdom, Australia, and the United States are contrasting case studies of definitions in different legislative contexts. The section on conceptual issues focuses on the development of the European ETHOS typology of categories of housing exclusion and homelessness and the cultural definition of homelessness from Australia that theorises homelessness as a social constructed concept. Both projects work with a continuum of situations that can be operationalised for measurement. Finally, the problems of the effort to advance a 'universal' definition of homelessness are discussed.

The Debate about Definition

Homelessness is recognised as a major social policy issue in many Western countries and a feature of extreme poverty throughout the developing world. However, homelessness can happen dramatically as a result of war or natural disasters. Conflicts around the globe produce large numbers of displaced peoples or natural disasters such as the Indian Ocean Tsunami in 2004, the cyclonic inundation of New Orleans by 'Katrina' in the United States in 2005, or the 'Black Saturday' bushfires in Australia in 2009, cause homelessness on a large scale. The Tsunami in 2004 was responsible for 227 898 deaths and 1.69 million displaced people. In New Orleans, more than a million people were evacuated, tens of thousands in the city had to be rescued, and some 1500 people lost their lives. In February 2009, over 1000 homes were destroyed, 173 people lost their lives, and 414 people were injured when the 'Black Saturday' bushfires raged around Melbourne, Australia. Some 5000 people were rendered homeless.

Under these circumstances, there is no debate about what caused people to become homeless. They are literally without shelter or sheltering in public buildings waiting for relief. Homelessness in these examples is not a social problem with a socioeconomic cultural aetiology, but the consequence of 'acts of god' or natural events. The typical responses to such disasters are public appeals, and government funds to meet the immediate needs of the people affected and to reestablish their housing and livelihoods as quickly as possible. But, where homelessness has been an outcome of social change or the unintended consequence of social reforms, in Western countries where the vast majority of the population have a first world standard of living, homelessness has become a 'social problem' in the public policy arena.

At one level, everyone readily agrees that people without conventional forms of accommodation (sleeping rough, in cars, or railway carriages, etc.) are homeless; this is the everyday 'common-sense' view of homelessness understood by the general public, and it is the visible homelessness captured most often in media images. The use of a literal definition of homelessness as in the United States and some European countries holds closest to this common-sense public conception of homelessness. However, a broader conception is strongly evident in the international research literature and in conceptual definitions such as the European Federation of National Organisations working with the Homeless (FEANTSA) ETHOS typology in Europe, the Australian cultural definition, and NGO documentation in the United Kingdom and United States.

A feature of the debate over many years has been an element of conceptual despair. As Brandon (1974) commented: "How can the researcher begin to define it (homelessness) ... writers have used it in almost every conceivable way – from meaning complete shelterlessness to simply having serious accommodation difficulties, from having no fixed abode to living in a hostel or lodging house" (p. 5). Hutson and Liddiard (1994) discussed the issue of young people sleeping rough who may subjectively not define themselves as homelessness, and concluded that: "the definition of homelessness is thus largely irresolvable. If there cannot even be agreement about whether or not sleeping rough constitutes homelessness, so there can evidently be no overall agreement about how homelessness as a whole can be defined" (p. 29).

According to Watson (1984) "there has been remarkably little consensus among policy-makers, researchers, local authorities, and voluntary housing organisations as to how to define the term 'homelessness'" (p. 60) and she concludes that "the concept of homelessness is not a useful one, and should be rethought or abandoned. To a large extent the difficulties inherent derive from the notion of a 'home' and what that means ... the range of meanings attributed to the home and too homelessness is both too vast and too complicated to have any explanatory or prescriptive use ... (and) ... there is no obvious place to draw the line, since so many aspects of the dwelling are of relevance, and these change according to the household involved, the current economic and social climate" (p. 70).

Because human societies and cultures are historied, concepts such as homelessness are socially constructed, as social life and the behaviour and attitudes of human beings change. Also, homelessness is a social problem and the definitional debates and decision-making take place in the real world of politics and policy-making. Social researchers play a part in that debate and in the policy processes, but as one among many stakeholders, including the major service agencies, advocacy and lobby groups, government bureaucracies, political parties, and politicians.

From a programme delivery perspective, definitions are required to identify who is eligible to receive assistance for homeless people; from a research perspective, definitions are required to determine who will be counted as homeless when estimating the size of the homeless population or for other research purposes; and from a policy and planning perspective, definitions are framed to 'target groups' authorised as a focus for planning and programme delivery. Apart from debate about the concept of homelessness, for all practical purposes, different operational definitions are required for a range of purposes.

Homelessness as a Social Problem

Certain conditions experienced by people become framed as 'social problems' by a process of claims-making by individuals and groups concerned about these conditions. Homelessness is a real social condition but how the problem of homelessness is represented and defined is subjective and established through social discourse – discussions, representations to politicians, press articles and media, as well as academic research and the process whereby social conditions become social problems is referred to as a 'social construction' perspective (Jacobs, 1999).

Much of the time homelessness is treated as a self-evident phenomenon, though people may differ on their views about the issue and what they think should be done. However, typically and routinely, homeless agencies work with policies and definitions framed by governments that fund the programmes and services for the homeless.

Homelessness implies 'lack of home', but it has been framed or conceptualised in somewhat different ways (Mallett, 2004). During the 1950s, 1960s, and early 1970s, homelessness was often characterised in terms of the disabilities of certain individuals with alcohol problems. Alternatively, structural factors have been highlighted as the primary driver of increased homelessness during the 1980s and 1990s. Terms such as 'youth homelessness' and 'family homelessness' focus on particular subgroups in the homeless population.

The media plays an important role in building public support for action on homelessness (Best, 1989). The film *Cathy Come Home* on the plight of a young couple in the United Kingdom forced to squat in empty houses and stay in shelters was influential in raising public awareness, in getting media attention and government action to address the housing crisis. In Australia, media associated with the 1989 Human Rights and Equal Opportunity Commission (HREOC) Inquiry into Youth Homelessness was associated with the making of a two-part documentary *Nobodies Children*. More recently, in 2008, the film *The Oasis* was broadcast on ABC National TV to an audience of 1.1 million Australians in association with the release of an independent National Youth Commission (NYC) report, *Australia's Homeless Youth*.

Statistics are important as claims-makers attempt to describe the size of the problem of homelessness and its dimensions. In the absence of accurate data that measure the problem, claims are couched as estimates. Guesstimates become facts when repeated in the media. US homeless advocate Mitch Snyder produced an estimate of 3 million homeless Americans, and in the absence of any other more grounded statistics, that estimate was repeated many times until it became an 'established fact'. The number of homeless has power as political rhetoric regardless of technical issues about what definition has been applied and how well the enumeration has been undertaken. In 2009, HUD reported a point in time figure of 643 000 for sheltered and unsheltered homeless persons. In Australia, using the broader cultural definition the total homeless population was estimated to be 105 000 on a given night (Chamberlain and MacKenzie, 2006).

A broadly social constructionist perspective on social problems allows for different claims about definition and provides a role for values and subjectivity in a real-world complex political and policy process. The political sensitivity of issues such as homelessness can be recognised as the reality process through which governments and advocates may seek to represent problems differently in the processes through which new policy emerges (Jacobs, 1999).

Official Definitions of Homelessness

Official definitions are formulated as governments begin to respond to the problem, but there are various levels of 'official' definitions: statistical reports from statutory authorities carry a degree of 'official' legitimacy, but Government White Papers are policy declarations for action, and legislation carries with it legal obligations linked to funding. At the level of deciding eligibility, the operational details of definitions are usually in agreements/instructions about what is allowable under legislation or policy.

Across the European Union, many countries do not have an official definition, but a range of definitions are used to collect statistics on homelessness. In France, there is a definition of 'sans domicile' used for statistical purposes. Germany has no official definition, but there is a widespread consensus that homeless people are those excluded from a rental tenancy who need help to gain more secure housing. In other countries, the issue has been given varying priorities, but on 16 December 2010, the European Parliament declared for an EU Homelessness Strategy to support the efforts of member states to deal with homelessness. This followed many years of work on the issue culminating in a European Consensus Conference on Homelessness on 9 and 10 December 2010.

The United Kingdom, the United States, and Australia do have 'official' definitions of homelessness embodied in legislation that frame how public funds for homelessness will be expended and the eligibility for homelessness assistance.

United Kingdom: The Homelessness Acts, 1977, 1996, and 2002

A legislative framework for homelessness has been in place in the United Kingdom since the late 1970s, beginning with the Housing (Homeless Persons) Act of 1977 followed by further legislative amendments in the Housing Act of 1985 and the Housing and Planning Act of 1986, and the Homelessness Acts of 1996 and 2002. Under the Act, there is a legal duty on local authorities to find accommodation for people who are homeless. To be accepted as homeless under the Act, households had to be homeless in the sense of having no right to access secure accommodation for the night, without a tenancy over a rental property or ownership of a property or face eviction from a property within 28 days. Second, applicants had to belong to a defined priority need group – a household with dependent children, a pregnant woman, a vulnerable person due to old age, mental illness, or a disability. A third condition was that a homeless household must not be intentionally homeless – that is, lose their accommodation by not paying rent or their mortgage when they could afford to do so. Finally, applicants were asked whether they had a 'local connection' or not, and if there was no local connection, their case could be transferred to an area where the applicant did have a local connection. The above criteria were applied as a decision tree to decide whether applicants will be provided with housing assistance.

The 1996 Housing Act reduced the statutory rights of homeless applicants from the right to be housed in secure permanent housing to temporary housing for a period of 2 years. However, the definition of homelessness embodied in the Act remained and was expanded somewhat with the inclusion of 'domestic violence' as a statutory duty, as well as people occupying caravans or boats with a permanent site. An incoming Labour Government in 1997 restored the statutory duty of local authorities to house homeless persons in priority need.

The 2002 Homelessness Act introduced several new duties by requiring local authorities to conduct homelessness reviews, to formulate a strategy for responding to homelessness, and build partnerships with community agencies to increasingly prevent homelessness. The duty to provide temporary accommodation for 2 years was replaced by a duty to provide assistance until a household obtained secure permanent housing. Priority need was expanded to include homeless 16- and 17-year-olds; young people aged 18, 19, and 20 years of age leaving care; persons leaving the armed forces, prison, or custody; and people vulnerable because of violence.

The definition embodied in the Act remains broad, including people staying in temporary accommodation with insecure housing, people sleeping rough, as well as people vulnerable for a number of reasons. However, only people who pass the eligibility tests under the Act would be accepted by local authorities for housing and be classified as 'statutory homeless'. A significant number of people in situations of homelessness may have applied to local authorities but not been accepted for housing assistance because they are not in a priority need group – a single homeless person in a hostel, shelter or bed and breakfast, or staying in a 'concealed household' – a section of the homeless population referred to as the 'nonstatutory homeless'. As well, there would be homeless people who have not sought assistance who may be sleeping rough or in a squat.

Australia: Supported Accommodation and Assistance Act (1994)

In Australia, the development of the Supported Accommodation and Assistance Programme (SAAP) was eventually ascribed in the SAA Act (1994). This Act provided the legislative framework for funding the joint Commonwealth-State special purpose programme that deployed supported accommodation and homelessness assistance programme around the country.

Definition of homeless The Act contains a broad definition of homelessness:

(1) For the purposes of this Act, a person is homeless if, and only if, he or she has inadequate access to safe and secure housing. Inadequate access to safe and secure housing

(2) For the purposes of this Act, a person is taken to have inadequate access to safe and secure housing if the only housing to which the person has access:

   (a) damages, or is likely to damage, the person's health; or
   (b) threatens the person's safety; or
   (c) marginalises the person through failing to provide access to:
      (i) adequate personal amenities; or
      (ii) the economic and social supports that a home normally affords; or
   (d) places the person in circumstances which threaten or adversely affect the adequacy, safety, security, and affordability of that housing.

Person living in SAAP accommodation

(3) For the purposes of this Act, a person is taken to have inadequate access to safe and secure housing if:

   (a) the person is living in accommodation provided under SAAP; and
   (b) the assessment of the person's eligibility for that accommodation was based on the application of subsection (1) or (2) (ignoring the effect of this subsection).

Generality of subsection (1)

(4) Subsections (2) and (3) do not limit the generality of subsection (1).

Legislation that included a definition of homelessness was developed to support the funding and administration of the SAAP, which applied to services funded under SAAP and to specialist homelessness services.

From 2009 onwards, the SAA Act (1994) has become redundant as funding for SAAP ceased, replaced by funding under a National Affordable Housing Agreement, with homelessness subsumed in the broader agreement, and under that framework there were associated bilateral agreements with state and territory jurisdictions (National Partnership Agreements). However, in December 2008, the Australian Government White Paper, *The Road Home: A National Approach to Reducing Homelessness*, stated a commitment that "a strong legislative base must remain in place to underpin the national homelessness response, set standards and deliver the best quality services possible for people who are homeless" (p. 38).

An Inquiry by the House of Representatives Standing Committee on Family, Community, Housing, and Youth found there was strong support for legislation on homelessness and the retention of a broad definition, but concerns were expressed about what kind of legislation that could be under the new funding arrangements between the Commonwealth and the states/territories. The Inquiry report (2009) recommended "a broad definition of homelessness in new homelessness legislation based on an extended version of the definition in the Supported Accommodation Assistance Act 1994. The revised definition of homelessness should be consistent with and complement the cultural definition as used by the Australian Bureau of Statistics, including recognition of primary, secondary and tertiary categories of Homelessness" (p. 38). While the legislative position in Australia has changed because the SAA Act has been retired, there was an expressed intention to retain the *status quo* of the former SAA Act definition and the cultural definition of homelessness. However, since 2010 a public debate and controversy about the nature and scope of the official homelessness definition has commenced.

United States: From the McKinney–Vento Act (1987) to the HEARTH Act (2009)

In the United States, the Stewart B. McKinney Homelessness Assistance Act of 1987, later renamed the McKinney–Vento Assistance Act under the President Clinton, was the first comprehensive law to authorise assistance for the homeless. In 2009, this long-standing legislation was superceded by the Homeless Emergency Assistance and Rapid Transition to Housing Act (HEARTH Act). The McKinney–Vento Act defined homeless persons as:

> ... the term "homeless" or "homeless individual or homeless person" includes:
>
> (1) an individual who lacks a fixed, regular, and adequate night-time residence; and
> (2) an individual who has a primary night-time residence, that is:
>
>   (a) a supervised publicly or privately operated shelter designed to provide temporary living accommodations (including welfare hotels, congregate shelters, and transitional housing for the mentally ill);
>   (b) an institution that provides a temporary residence for individuals intended to be institutionalised; or
>   (c) a public or private place not designed for, or ordinarily used as, a regular sleeping accommodation for human beings.

This definition is referred to as a 'literal definition' of homelessness, since it identifies as homeless, people without access to conventional accommodation (sleeping rough, etc.) or in people in shelters for the homeless.

The new HEARTH Act (2009) provides for four categories of homeless and is somewhat broader than its predecessor. The first is basically the same as above except that people will be considered homeless if they are exiting an institution where they have been for 90 days (previously it was 30 days) and they were homeless when entering the institution. The provision to assist people escaping domestic violence has been broadened somewhat to a wider set of violence. People losing their primary night-time residence, which may include a motel, hotel, or doubled up situation with 14 days (previously 7 days) and cannot obtain accommodation. The new category relates to "unaccompanied youth and homeless families with children and youth who are defined as homeless under other federal statutes who do not otherwise qualify as homeless" who have been "experiencing a long-term period without living independently in permanent housing, having experienced persistent instability as measured by frequent moves over such a period" and where this situation is "expected to continue in such status for an extended period of time" (HUD, 2010).

The process of reauthorising the McKinney–Vento Homelessness Assistance Act revivified a debate about the definition of homelessness. For many years advocates had raised issues about people defined as homeless under other Federal statutes, but not recognised under the McKinney–Vento Act, such as homeless young people staying with the families of friends. But, there were concerns among some advocates that expanding the scope of the definition in the Act to include people staying temporarily with other people or whose accommodation is persistently unstable would dilute the pool of available funding for homelessness assistance. Martha Burt from the Urban Institute in her testimony before the US House of Representatives hearing on these matters expressed a concern to retain the existing definition and that "pressure from a coalition of advocacy groups to expand them to include many more people and household are resisted". However, Burt's concern about broadening the scope of the definition was not conceptual but a pragmatic policy concern – that limited funds should be well targeted to those who most need assistance. Other testimony contributed to the various arguments in this debate. Since official definitions are used to determine how funding can be spent or who is eligible for homelessness assistance, the definitional debate was more about what might happen in the policy and programmes space as conceptual clarity.

For a long time, the United States has operated with a literal definition of homelessness and the statistical reports to the Federal Government have provided counts of sheltered and unsheltered residents. The HEARTH Act (2009) has widened the scope of the official definition somewhat in the direction the broader definitions used in other countries, and policy and programmes for prevention are being developed to supplement the well-established efforts to reduce chronic homelessness.

Conceptual Definitions of Homelessness

Postwar homelessness in Western countries was the subject of a considerable body of research during the 1960s and 1970s, particularly in the United States (Henslin, 1993). In theoretical terms, sociologists Howard Bahr and Theodore Caplow conceptualised homelessness as "a condition of detachment from society characterised by the absence or attenuation of affiliated bonds that link settled persons to a network of interconnected social structures" (Caplow et al., 1968: 494–499). This theory of homelessness was an application of Merton's middle-range functionalist theorising of social phenomena. People became homelessness due to a retreat from an integrated role in social life.

The operational definition of homelessness in the 1960s and early 1970s was an identifiable subpopulation of people living in the run down 'skid row' districts of large cities such as the Bowery in New York or West Madison Street in Chicago. Bahr described this as a 'spatial' perspective. In these areas, the cost of subsistence living was lowest and there were some welfare support programmes as well as mutual aid among individuals in a shared predicament. Caplow described the 'skid row' residents as:

> ... predominately male, predominately adult population made up of several distinct elements: (1) vagrants, wanderers and seasonal laborers-hobos, in the now obsolete term; (2) chronic inebriates, some partly employed and

others unemployable; (3) old men retired from manual employment and living on meagre pensions or savings; (4) steadily employed men without family or community affiliations.

While some of the 'skid row' residents slept on the streets, many took rooms overnight in cheap SRO hotels and many engaged in day labour in low-skilled employment. Disaffiliation was a theoretical explanation and conceptual underpinning of homelessness consistent with the dominant functionalist sociological perspective of the time, but it seemed conceptually persuasive given that certain persons were homeless despite near full employment.

Increasingly, as new groups such as families, young people, or women escaping domestic violence became homeless during the 1980s, the disaffiliation concept seemed less a general conceptual theory for defining homelessness and more like a contextualised explanation for a particular group of single persons.

European Union

There is no legislated or official definition of homelessness across the European Union. However, under the Strategy to Combat Poverty and Promote Social Inclusion, it was recommended that the European Commission "examine different approaches to the definition and measurement of homelessness and precarious housing in a comparable way across member states". This work has been undertaken by the European Observatory on Homelessness and the FEATSA Working Group on Data Collection and Homelessness Statistics.

A considerable body of systematic work has been done over more than a decade to develop a European definition of homelessness that can be used for statistical purposes.

In November 1998, a working group on income, poverty, and social inclusion statistics was approved and an expert group formed in 2001 to look at the statistics on homelessness. The draft definition that framed the early work is given in **Figure 1**.

FEANTSA has provided a major European forum for development work on a conceptual framework around a consistent set of operational definitions. The ETHOS typology of homelessness is the result. The concept of homelessness and housing exclusion is analysed across three domains – having a home that is adequate to meet the needs of the individual or family (physical domain), having privacy and adequate opportunity for social relations (social domain), and having exclusive possession, security of occupation, and legal title (legal domain) (**Table 1**).

A 2006 report from the UNECE/EUROSTAT Conference of European Statisticians made suggestions for the measurement of homelessness in part following the Australian approach. The Conference of European Statisticians (CES) identifies homeless persons in two broad groups:

(1) *Primary homelessness (or rooflessness)*. This category includes persons living in the streets without a shelter that would fall within the scope of living quarters.
(2) *Secondary homelessness*. This category may include persons with no place of usual residence who move frequently between various types of accommodations (including dwellings, shelters, institutions for the homeless, or other living quarters). This category includes persons living in private dwellings but reporting 'no usual address' on their census form.

It was acknowledged that this was not a comprehensive definition of homelessness. The ETHOS typology provides a wider range of categories of homelessness and

---

Part 1
A homeless person is someone who does not have access to accommodation, which they can reasonably occupy, whether this accommodation is legally their own property or whether the property is rented; provided by institutions; provided by employers; or occupied rent free under some contractual or other arrangement.

Part 2
In consequence they are obliged to sleep either:
  (a) outdoors;
  (b) in buildings which do not meet commonly agreed criteria for human habitation (e.g., privacy, hygiene; space);
  (c) in night-time emergency hostel accommodation provided by public sector or charitable organisations;
  (d) in longer-staying hostels provided by public sector or charitable organisations (e.g., Non-emergency centres, refuges for battered women, deportation centres for asylum seekers and illegal immigrants);
  (e) in Bed & Breakfast accommodation;
  (f) in other short stay accommodation (duration less than one month);
  (g) in the homes of friends or relatives;
  (h) in registered squats.

Figure 1 Eurostat Expert Group Statistics on Homelessness: Definition.

Table 1 ETHOS – European typology of homelessness and housing exclusion

Conceptual category	Operational category		Living situation	Generic definition
Roofless				
1	People living rough	1.1	Public space or external space	Living in the streets or public spaces, without shelter that can be defined as living quarters
2	People in emergency accommodation	2.1	Night shelter	People with no usual place of residence who make use of overnight shelter, low threshold shelter
Houseless				
3	People in accommodation for the homeless	3.1	Homeless hostel	Where the period of stay is intended to be short term
		3.2	Temporary accommodation	
		3.3	Transitional supported accommodation	
4	People in a women's shelter	4.1	Women's shelter accommodation	Women accommodated due to experience of domestic violence and where the period of stay is intended to be short term
5	People in accommodation for immigrants	5.1	Temporary accommodation/ reception centres	Immigrants in reception or short-term accommodation due to their immigrant status
		5.2	Migrant workers accommodation	
6	People due to be released from institutions	6.1	Penal institutions	No housing available prior to release
		6.2	Medical institutions	Stay longer than needed due to a lack of housing
		6.3	Children's institutions/homes	No housing identified (e.g., by 18th birthday)
7	People receiving longer-term support (due to homelessness)	7.1	Residential care for older homeless people	Long-stay accommodation with care for formerly homeless people (normally more than 1 year)
		7.2	Supported accommodation for formerly homeless people	
Insecure				
8	People living in insecure accommodation	8.1	Temporarily with family/friends	Living in conventional housing but not the usual place of residence due to lack of housing
		8.2	No legal (sub)tenancy	Occupation of a dwelling with no legal tenancy; illegal occupation of a dwelling
		8.3	Illegal occupation of land	Occupation of land with no legal rights
9	People living under threat of eviction	9.1	Legal orders enforced (rented)	Where orders for eviction are operative
		9.2	Re-possession orders (owned)	Where mortgagee has legal order to repossess
10	People living under threat of violence	10.1	Police recorded incidents	Where police action is taken to ensure place of safety for victims of domestic violence
Inadequate				
11	People living in temporary/non-conventional structures	11.1	Mobile homes	Not intended as place of usual residence
		11.2	Non-conventional building	Makeshift shelter, shack or shanty
		11.3	Temporary structure	Semi-permanent structure, hut or cabin
12	People living in unfit housing	12.1	Occupied dwellings unfit for habitation	Defined as unfit for habitation by national legislation or building regulations
13	People living in extreme overcrowding	13.1	Highest national norm of overcrowding	Defined as exceeding national density standard for floor space or useable rooms

Note: Short stay is defined operationally as normally less than 1 year; Long stay is defined as more than 1 year. This definition is compatible with Census definitions as recommended by the UNECE/EUROSTAT report (2006).
Source: ETHOS typology developed by FEANTSA (http://www.feantsa.org/code/en/pg.asp?page=484).

housing exclusion. The key operational item in census data collections for identifying hidden homelessness is 'no usual address' (Edgar et al., 2007).

While there has been significant interplay between the development of the ETHOS typology and the Eurostat recommendations, there are some differences. In the ETHOS typology, people living in insecure accommodation are categorised as 'insecure', whereas in the Eurostat definition is it placed under homelessness. The achievement of the ETHOS project is that it has produced categorical continuum of housing and homelessness situations with consistent operational definitions for the purpose of measurement, thus allowing comparison across the Eurozone. Development of the ETHOS tool is ongoing and substantial conceptual progress has been achieved. However, Marpsat (2005) has cautioned that the simple translation of the various terms used in different European languages for living situations is problematic culturally, because "not all countries really have an equivalent or even approximate concept to that of hidden homelessness, and the extended concept of homelessness is formed in those countries along different rationales that are tied to how the central concept itself is formed". The differences between ETHOS and the EUROSTAT statisticians appear to reflect this concern. However, underpinning the broader homelessness/housing exclusion approach is a continuum of categories and operational criteria and strong conceptual work has produced a framework to which member states can refer.

Australia: The Cultural Definition of Homelessness

In Australia, in the early 1990s the focus on 'youth homelessness' via the Human Rights and Equal Opportunity (HREOC) Inquiry into youth homelessness stimulated policy development and some new programme initiatives, but also renewed interest in research. MacKenzie and Chamberlain attempted to theorise homelessness by recognising that notions of homelessness and inadequate housing are socially constructed cultural concepts located in time and in certain social and cultural contexts. The concepts are socially relative in the sense that they refer to realities that change over time, but not absolutely relative or arbitrary in a philosophical sense. Homelessness in this line of argument is similar to the sociological concept of poverty (Townsend, 1979). Chamberlain and MacKenzie argue that homelessness is "a relative concept that acquires meaning in relation to the housing conventions in a particular culture" or community or society. A similar argument was advanced by Watson (1986: 10) who observed that when most people in a community live in mud huts then the community standard and accepted norm will be that mud huts constitute adequate accommodation.

Using this perspective, the problem of defining homelessness devolves to identifying the community cultural standards about the minimum acceptable housing that people have in order to live according to the norms and conventions and expectations of a particular culture or community. Cultural standards or norms are taken-for-granted cultural concepts that are embedded in people's thinking despite individual differences of opinion.

MacKenzie and Chamberlain argue that in Australia and possibly other comparable Western countries, the prevailing norm is people living in houses or apartments that they own or rent. At the lowest end of the scale of rented apartments is a small bedsit apartment with a kitchenette and bathroom facilities. That one room contains the kitchenette and the bathroom is usually a small separate room within the apartment. The residents would normally have a lease over the apartment.

A cultural bottom-line is used to decide how to frame the category of homelessness. The cultural standard will not be precisely specified in formal regulations although the minimum housing standard provides a close approximation. This benchmark is embedded in the housing practices of a particular society or culture. But, there is a whole continuum of housing and living situations in which people are living or staying that are below the cultural norm of acceptable housing circumstances and living arrangements. A population, defined by a range of objective living situations and housing circumstances, can be categorised as 'homeless' independently of the extent that the homeless are able to access services (**Table 2**).

The original empirical research from which the cultural definition was first derived was done in 1990 and 1991 at a youth drop-in centre (The Deli) at Flinders Street Station in Melbourne. The case notes on the large number of clients contained a great deal of information about the client, and if they had come in many times, then there was a record of their living situations over time. Typically homeless young people spent time in various situations including staying temporarily with friends, relatives, and acquaintances. Conceptually, it made little sense to call someone homeless when they slept rough or were staying in a refuge but not when they were temporarily sheltered 'couch-surfing' at an acquaintance's flat before returning to an agency for further help.

The inclusion of a 'no usual address' identifier in the 1996 Census allowed for the possibility that an estimate of the overall homeless population could be constructed including hidden homelessness where people were not necessarily in contact with homeless services but temporarily sheltered in private dwellings somewhere.

The cultural definition was adopted by the Australian Bureau of Statistics (ABS) because it potentially provided a way to enumerate the homeless population, if the housing situations under each category could be reasonably

Table 2 Australian cultural definition of homelessness: A revised model of homelessness based on shared community cultural standards embodied in housing practices

Categories	Living situations	Operational definitions
Marginal housing	Living situations close to the margin of the minimum community cultural standard for housing and living arrangements in Australia	A highly overcrowded household
		Living in improvised dwellings on land the resident owns or is purchasing
		Renting a dwelling not meeting regulations for a habitable dwelling
		Living permanently in a caravan park
Tertiary homelessness	People living in single rooms in private boarding houses – without a bathroom or kitchen and without security of tenure	Living in a boarding/rooming house with shared facilities and no security of tenure
		Permanent/semipermanent household (no members employed) renting in a caravan park
Secondary homelessness	People moving between or living in various forms of temporary shelter including with friends and relatives with no where to live, emergency accommodation, crisis accommodation, hostels, boarding houses used as crisis accommodation, or caravan parks used as crisis accommodation	Transitional accommodation while waiting for access to affordable housing
		Temporary rent-free occupation of house or flat by a person(s) with no other usual address
		Temporary accommodation with friends/relatives/acquaintances – 'couch-surfing'
		Emergency accommodation in hotel/motel or caravan park with a voucher from homeless agency
		Homeless crisis accommodation or night shelter
Primary homelessness	People without conventional accommodation living on the streets, in squats, railway carriages, in cars, under bridges, or in parks	Occupation of temporary improvised dwelling by a person with no usual address
		Sleeping in a disused building/railway carriage, and so on
		Sleeping in a car or van
		Sleeping rough in parks, on the street, or under bridges

identified. In 2001 and 2006, estimates of the homeless population were produced using the cultural definition (Chamberlain and MacKenzie, 2001, 2006).

One limitation of the original definitional model was that living in caravan parks was not explicitly described. Particularly in rural areas, homeless services place people in caravan parks as an emergency accommodation measure. Scattered throughout rural Australia, in many towns, are small usually rundown caravan parks with permanent or semi-permanent residents who cannot afford to live anywhere else. Chamberlain and MacKenzie have described these situations as the 'boarding houses' of rural Australia. Chronically, homeless people may spend long periods of time in the boarding house sector (like SROs in the United States) but then require assistance from agencies or sleep rough. Temporary accommodation with friends/relatives or acquaintances is more prevalent during the earlier stages of homelessness.

A Universal Definition of Homelessness

The UN charter and the field of international development provide a practical imperative for attempting to reach an agreed 'universal' definition of homelessness in order to monitor progress against benchmark standards for housing and human settlements internationally. The right to adequate shelter and other basic human needs is embodied in the Universal Declaration of Human Rights:

> Everyone has the right to a standard of living adequate for the health and well-being of himself and his family,

including food, clothing, housing and medical care and necessary social services, and the right to security in the event of unemployment, sickness, disability, widowhood, old age or other lack of livelihood in circumstances beyond his control (Article 25, UN Declaration of Human Rights, December 1948).

In the Global Report on Human Settlements 1996, there was explicit discussion of the different homelessness definitions used in the developed countries, and the lack of adequate and comparable statistical information on housing and homelessness in the developing world.

The United Nations, in its 1996 Global Report on Human Settlements, estimated the number of homeless people worldwide at anywhere from 100 million to 1 billion, depending on how homelessness is defined. The estimate of 100 million would apply to those who have no shelter at all, including those who sleep outside (on pavements, in shop doorways, in parks, or under bridges) or in public buildings (in railway, bus, or metro stations) or in night shelters set up to provide homeless people with a bed. The higher estimate of 1 billion homeless would include people in very insecure or temporary accommodation, squatters under constant threat of eviction, people in refugee camps, and people in temporary shelters such as in India, China, and parts of Africa. If people in dwellings with insecure tenure or a lack of basic facilities were included, then the number would be even higher.

Springer (2000) observed that: "different definitions of the minimum housing standard, varying by region, make it difficult to find a global agreement on which housing situations should be included in the definition of homeless" (p. 477). The differences reflect different levels of social and economic development as well as cross-cultural differences in how people are accustomed to live. Springer's objective was for an internationally comparative definition that could be used for statistical data comparison between countries under the UN development agenda. The term 'houseless' was preferred to 'homelessness' while accepting that the adjunct concept of 'inadequate shelter' would have to be defined on a regional basis according to varying regional housing standards.

Tipple and Speak (2005, 2006) conducted a comparative study on the causes, scale, and nature of homelessness in nine developing countries – Bangladesh, China, India, Indonesia, Egypt, Ghana, South Africa, Zimbabwe, and Peru. People living in the streets or in improvised dwellings in and around major cities cannot be assumed to be entirely similar to rough sleepers in developed countries. Many such people in developing countries have migrated from rural areas in search of work and may have employment. Sometimes men work in the cities and live in very inadequate circumstances while supporting families elsewhere. In India, entire families may live in makeshift shelters while collecting refuse for resale and recycling. Throughout the developing world there are large-scale squatter settlements where hundreds of thousands of people live in dilapidated dwellings. From a development perspective, Speak (2004) observed that for many people in the developing world "housing may not be their primary concern" because some would return to their homes elsewhere given some form of economic assistance, while for those who cannot return home, services to the squatter areas and *in situ* improvement of the squatter settlements is a policy option.

Tipple and Speak (2006) concluded on the basis of their nine country comparative study, that "being able to argue for a plausible threshold between homelessness and housing that is inadequate but acceptable for the time being, is a useful tool in targeting any subsidies to those in need" but with the caveat that "internationally, it is difficult to draw firm thresholds ... we have shown there to be real differences between street-homeless people and people in informal settlements ... (but) ... they present a fuzzy and chimerical margin rather than the 'clear water' implied in Springer's diagram" (p. 80). More-over, they do not support referring to 'houseless' rather than homelessness, which would represent a narrowing of scope in the definition, but suggest that the objective of a single definition may not be appropriate. This position would uphold a basis for comparison between literal or absolute or primary homelessness in the developed as well as the developing countries, not withstanding the widely varying housing standards in different countries and cultures.

The United Nations relies on reports from its member countries, so the standing operational definition of a 'homeless household' in census enumeration remains:

> ... those households without a shelter that would fall within the scope of living quarters. They carry their few possessions with them, sleeping in the streets, in doorways or on piers, or in any other space, on a more or less random basis (UN Demographic Yearbook Review, 2004: 23).

Depending on how it is applied, this definition will enumerate people without shelter but exclude many in the developing countries in highly improvised shelters in public places, who would be classified as people without conventional accommodation or literally homeless in a Western countries such as Europe, the United States, or Australia.

Debates on human rights, including the 'right to housing', adequate housing standards, and the setting of international benchmarks on housing and health issues will and can continue in UN forums without the realistic possibility a universal definition of homelessness.

Summary and Conclusions

The meaning of 'home' is the reference point for the conceptual debate about the meaning of homelessness. However, 'homelessness' is a concept that inhabits the real world of social problems claims-making, policy debate, and social policy. There is a wide acceptance among researchers and NGOs that homelessness is broader than 'rooflessness' or 'literal homelessness'. Broad definitions and data collected on people at the earliest stages of homelessness inform 'early intervention' and 'prevention' measures. Whereas, a focus on rough sleepers leads to a policy directed to dealing with chronic homelessness. Internationally, homelessness policy is shifting to incorporate prevention and early intervention alongside responses to people once they become homeless or the chronically homeless.

The ETHOS typology provides a logical matrix of categories of homelessness and social exclusion designed to provide operational definitions of homelessness and housing exclusion situations that can be used for data collection and comparative policy purposes. The cultural definition used in Australia takes the minimum community cultural standard of housing as its benchmark and the operational definitions applying to different situations have been developed through the Counting the Homeless project. While progress is underway to better count the homeless using census data, issues about duration and the needs of subgroups in the homeless population require inferences from other data sets. Longitudinal and pathways research is beginning to accumulate evidence about different groups that will bear on future revisions of the operational definitions – particularly the time spent in various circumstances of homelessness housing exclusion.

The notion of a universal definition of homelessness remains elusive because 'homelessness' is a socially constructed concept, which implies that in different cultural and national contexts, the official and everyday understandings will also be different. Therefore, an universally accepted and applied definition is an unlikely prospect.

See also: Criminological Perspectives on Homelessness; Home and Homelessness; Homelessness: Causation; Homelessness: Measurement Questions; Representations of Homelessness.

References

Best J (1989) *Images of Issues: Typifying Contemporary Social Problems*. New York: Aldine de Gruyter.

Caplow T, Bahr H, and Sternberg D (1968) Homelessness. In: *International Encyclopedia of the Social Sciences,?* (Sills D (ed.) *International Encyclopedia of the Social Sciences,* vol. 6, pp. 494–499. New York: Macmillan and Free Press.

Chamberlain C and MacKenzie D (2001) Understanding contemporary homelessness: Issues of definition and meaning. *Australian Journal of Social Issues* 27(4): 274–297.

Chamberlain C and MacKenzie D (2006) *Counting the Homeless 2006: Australia*. Canberra: Australian Bureau of Statistics.

Department of Housing and Urban Development (HUD) (2010) Homelessness emergency assistance and rapid transition to housing: Defining homelessness. *Federal Register* 75(75): 20541–20544.

Edgar W, Harrison M, Watson P, and Busch-Geertsema V (2007) *Measurement of Homelessness at European Union Level*. Brussels: European Commission, Employment, Social Affairs and Equal Opportunities DG.

Hutson S and Liddiard M (1994) *Youth Homelessness: The Construction of a Social Issue*. London: Macmillan.

Jacobs K (1999) The struggle to define homelessness: A constructionist approach. In: Hutson S and Clapham D (eds.) *Homelessness; Public Policies and Private Troubles*, pp. 11–28. London: Cassell.

Mallett S (2004) Understanding home: A critical review of the literature. *The Sociological Review* 52(1): 62–89.

Marpsat M (2005) The problem of definitions: Points of similarity and difference. *Paper Presented at the CUHP Thematic Network Conference*, Brussels, 3–4 November 2005.

Speak S (2004) Degrees of destitution: A typology of homelessness on developing countries. *Housing Studies* 19(3): 465–482.

Springer S (2000) Homelessness: A proposal for a global definition and classification. *Habitat International* 24: 475–484.

Tipple G and Speak S (2005) Definitions of homelessness in developing countries. *Habitat International* 29(2): 337–352.

Tipple G and Speak S (2006) Who is homeless in developing countries? Differentiating between inadequate housed and homeless people. *International Development Planning Review* 28(1): 57–84.

Watson S (1984) Definitions of homelessness: A feminist perspective. *Critical Social Policy* 4(11): 60–73.

Further Reading

Bailey-Salisbury A, Deering-Soth L, and Altshuler S (2007) Has the McKinney Act helped to create a universal definition of homelessness? *Journal of Social Distress and the Homeless* 16(1): 1–21.

Chamberlain C and MacKenzie D (1998) *Youth Homelessness: Early Intervention and Prevention*. Sydney: Australian Centre for Equity in Education.

Edgar W (2009) *European Review of Statistics on Homelessness*. Brussels: FEANTSA, European Observatory on Homelessness.

Fitzpatrick S (1998) Homelessness in the European Union. In: Kleinman M and Stephens M (eds.) *European Integration and Housing Policy*. London: Routledge.

Fitzpatrick S and Christian J (2006) Comparing homelessness research in the US and Britain. *European Journal of Housing Policy* 6(3): 313–333.

Fitzpatrick S, Quilgar D, and Pleace N (eds.) (2009) *Homelessness in the UK: Problems and Solutions*. Coventry: Chartered Institute for Housing.

Hopper K (1991) Homelessness old and new: The matter of definition. *Housing Policy Debate* 2(3): 757–813.

Pawson H and Davidson E (2006) Fit for purpose? Official measures of homelessness in the era of the activist state. *Radical Statistics* 93: 7–29.

Smith J (2003) *Defining Homelessness: The Impact of Legislation on the Definition of Homelessness and on Research into Homelessness in the UK*. London: Centre for Housing and Community Research, Cities Institute.

Williams M (2001) Complexity, probability and causation: Implications for homelessness research. *Social Issues* 1(2). Available at http://www.whb.co.uk/socialissues/mv.htm (retrieved 1 June 2011).

Homelessness: Measurement Questions

C Chamberlain, RMIT University, Melbourne, VIC, Australia

© 2012 Elsevier Ltd. All rights reserved.

Glossary

Annual count The number of homeless people over a year.
Census count The number of homeless people on a given night. Also referred to as a 'point prevalence' count (United States); the 'stock of homelessness' (Britain); or a 'point-in-time' count (Australia).
Cultural definition The definition used by the Australian Bureau of Statistics to enumerate homeless people. It distinguishes between 'primary', 'secondary', and 'tertiary' homelessness.
FEANTSA definition A broad definition of homelessness used by the European Observatory on Homelessness. The definition has 13 operational categories.
Literal definition People in emergency accommodation (shelters) or without accommodation ('street people' or 'rough sleepers').
Period prevalence count The number of homeless people over a given period of time.

Introduction

When people become homeless in Western countries, they typically move from one form of temporary shelter to another. Most people do not immediately become 'street people' or what the British term 'rough sleepers'. Homeless people often stay temporarily with friends or relatives when they lose their accommodation. Others move frequently from one set of friends to another, as they wear out their welcome with different households. Some homeless people stay in emergency accommodation such as shelters, refuges, and hostels. It is also common to find homeless people in what the Americans term 'single room occupancy' hotels (SROs), or what the British term 'bed and breakfast' hotels. Homeless people rarely sleep in public places or in derelict buildings unless they have exhausted all other possible accommodation options. This is called 'visible homelessness'.

In the late 1970s, homelessness began to emerge as a major issue in the United States, with increased numbers of people sleeping in public places. Many of the visibly homeless carried their meagre possessions in shopping bags, and there was a marked increase in public begging. Others established crude improvised dwellings under freeways or in other public places. In 1990, an opinion poll in the *New York Times* reported that 68% of urban Americans saw homeless people in their daily routine (Blau, 1992: 3).

In the 1980s, there was also an increase in visible homelessness in Western European countries, particularly Britain, France, and Germany (Fitzpatrick, 1998: 200). Craig and Schwarz (1984) retraced George Orwell's journey through the streets of London and Paris, where Orwell had been homeless in the 1930s. Craig and Schwarz reported more young people, including a significant minority of women, in the homeless population than in the past. Homelessness has also increased in Eastern Europe, particularly following the collapse of communism in the early 1990s.

In many countries, homelessness became a political issue in the 1980s and 1990s and 'legislators and journalists began asking for numbers' (Jencks, 1994). Advocates need numbers to press governments to take action. Governments need numbers to develop appropriate policy responses. Governments typically want information on the number of homeless people in different age groups, the number of homeless families with children, the length of time that people remain homeless, and so on. Most importantly, governments need information on the geographical distribution of homeless people to plan the location of services.

Issues of Definition and Counting

In order to count the homeless population, one has to have a realistic definition of homelessness. However, this has proved an intractable issue. According to Toro,

> defining homelessness should be a straightforward task. However, this is far from the case in the United States... Advocates for the homeless, policy makers, and researchers in the United States vary in what definitions they prefer.... (Toro, 2007: 462–463).

The situation is no better in the European Union:

> There is a wide range of official and unofficial definitions of homelessness employed within the European Union, reflecting different national perspectives on the issue, and the views of various commentators whose interests are served by either minimising or maximising the scale of the problem.... (Fitzpatrick, 1998: 197)

This article outlines three definitions that have been influential in debates about the measurement of homelessness. The first account is the literal definition of homelessness that has been used to estimate the homeless population in the United States. The second definition is that proposed by the European Observatory on Homelessness, commonly known as the FEANTSA (Federation Europeenne d' Associations Nationales Travaillant avec les Sans-Abri) definition. The third approach is the cultural definition of homelessness, which the Australian Bureau of Statistics (ABS) uses to count homeless people on census night.

There are two ways of counting the homeless population, and it is critical to understand the relationship between them. The first approach is a census count that gives the number of homeless people on a given night. These are known as 'point-in-time' counts or, in the American literature, as 'point prevalence counts'. In the British literature, point-in-time counts are referred to as the 'stock of homelessness'.

The second method of counting the homeless population examines the number of people who become homeless over a given period of time. These are called 'period prevalence' counts or 'annual counts', if they refer to the number of people who become homeless over a year. Welfare agencies often gather data over a 12-month period, but period prevalence counts can refer to other lengths of time.

An annual count will be many times larger than a census count if most people are homeless for a short period of time. For example, if 3.6 million Americans experience homelessness each year, and all of them are homeless for 1 month, then a point-in-time count will record about 300 000 homeless people (3 600 000 × 1/12 = 300 000). Advocates often cite annual figures because they assume that a higher figure puts more pressure on those in power to provide additional resources. However, when the annual figure is much higher than the census figure, there is a sense in which homelessness is less serious. Two examples will illustrate this point.

Let us suppose that 60 000 people become homeless this year, and all of them are homeless for 12 months. The annual count will be 60 000, and the census count will be 60 000 (60 000 × 12/12 = 60 000). This is a desperate situation where there are 60 000 chronically homeless people, who are part of an underclass from which they have little chance of escaping.

Now let us suppose that 240 000 people become homeless this year, but each one returns to secure accommodation after 1 month. The annual count will be 240 000, and the census count will be 20 000 (240 000 × 1/12 = 20 000). On a typical night, there will be fewer people requiring assistance than in the previous example (20 000 compared with 60 000), and it will be easier to help them because no one has an intractable problem.

From the point of view of policymakers, the critical figure is the census count because it indicates the demand for services on a typical night. Next census estimates in the United States are examined.

United States

When visible homelessness began to increase in the United States, journalists began clamouring for numbers. Hombs and Snyder (1982) estimated that there were between 2 and 3 million homeless Americans. It was not clear how 'homelessness' was defined or how the estimate was arrived at. Despite this, the 2–3 million figure was quoted in the American literature for the next 20 years. The estimate became "so familiar that many people treated it as an established fact" (Jencks, 1994: 1).

The Reagan administration was sceptical of the 2–3 million estimate. This stimulated the first systematic attempt to enumerate the homeless population in the United States. In the winter of 1984, the US Department of Housing and Urban Development (HUD) attempted to enumerate the homeless population at a point in time (Peroff, 1987). For the purpose of the research, a person was defined as homeless if his or her night time residence was in a public or private emergency shelter, or if they were literally homeless (streets, squats, subways, bus terminals, train stations, under bridges, etc.). This subsequently became known as the 'literal' or 'minimalist' definition of homelessness and this definition was incorporated into the McKinney–Vento Homeless Assistance Act of 1987.

The HUD study interviewed 500 'knowledgeable observers' in 60 large American cities and asked them to estimate the number of homeless people in their community. The interviews included shelter operators and local activists, gathered through a 'snowball' technique. HUD attempted to interview all the experts in a given area and then came up with an average figure on the basis of local knowledge. HUD came up with a best estimate of between 250 000 and 350 000 homeless people.

The 20 largest areas had a population of 78 million people (Appelbaum, 1990), so it is unlikely that local experts would have known how many were homeless in these huge conurbations. According to Appelbaum (1990), local experts often estimated the homeless population in the main city, but HUD applied these estimates to surrounding geographical areas. For example, in Boston (population 563 000), local experts estimated 2800 homeless people, but HUD applied this number to an area with a population of 3.7 million. Some concluded that HUD's figures were a "thinly veiled attempt by a conservative administration to minimize the seriousness of the homelessness problem" (Wright and Devine, 1992: 356). There was a huge furore, with many people critical of HUD's approach.

The next attempt to quantify homelessness in the United States was conducted by Martha Burt and Barbara Cohen (1989) of the Urban Institute. Burt and Cohen carried out a survey of shelter and soup kitchen users in a random sample of cities that had a population of over 100 000. People were defined as homeless if they met any of the following criteria:

1. They reported no permanent place to live.
2. Their home was a shelter, or a hotel room paid for by a voucher for the homeless, or a place not intended for sleeping.
3. They were staying in someone else's home, but could not live there for 5 days or longer.

The study involved a probability-based three-stage random sample of 1704 homeless service users in 20 cities. Homeless respondents were randomly selected from cooperating service providers with an interview completion rate of 88%.

The findings were weighted to represent all homeless service using adults in the 178 American cities with a population of 100 000 or more. The 7-day probability estimate of the homeless population was 229 000. An estimate was then made of the national homeless population. This was based on various assumptions, including a significantly lower rate of homelessness outside of the major urban areas. The best estimate was 500 000–600 000 homeless people across the United States. This became the generally accepted figure for the late 1980s and early 1990s.

Throughout the numbers controversy in the United States, it was known that the federal census of 1990 would attempt to enumerate homeless people. The census used the literal definition of homelessness that HUD had used. Between 6 p.m. and midnight on 20 March 1990, census collectors entered all known shelters for the homeless to count homeless people sleeping or staying indoors. This was a reasonable strategy, and it is likely that their number of shelter dwellers was realistic.

However, their attempt to count street people was sadly deficient. From 2 to 4 a.m. the next morning, census collectors attempted to count homeless people on the streets. It is difficult to count homeless people sleeping rough because they often hide away. Some are scared of being robbed; others are fearful for their personal safety; and some hide away to escape the cold. It was unrealistic to expect that census collectors could achieve a reliable count in the middle of the night.

The census counted 228 621 homeless people, less than half the figure of 500 000–600 000 that was widely accepted around that time. Once again, a storm of criticism broke out. Many people were scathing in their condemnation of the census methodology. The Bureau of the Census quickly backtracked, claiming that they had not intended to produce a count of homeless people.

In 1996, the US Interagency Council on Homelessness contracted the Urban Institute to conduct another national count of homeless people. The National Survey of Homeless Assistance Providers and Clients counted people at soup kitchens, shelters, and other centres for homeless service. As in 1987, national estimates of the homeless population were based on a series of assumptions built upon a fairly modest database. This time the Urban Institute estimated 440 000 homeless people in October and 842 000 in February. Burt and her colleagues also estimated the annual homeless population at between 2.3 and 3.5 million people, but this was an informed guess rather than a 'scientific' estimate.

It was another 10 years before the next attempt to estimate the homeless population using empirical data. In 2007, the National Alliance to End Homelessness (NAEH) attempted to collate local point-in-time counts of homeless people taken in 2005. By this time, HUD required local bodies coordinating homeless services to conduct point-in-time counts every 2 years. The counts used the literal definition of homelessness. The quality of the counts was 'uneven', with 'some jurisdictions using more rigorous methods than others' (NAEH, 2007: 9). The NAEH reported 744 313 homeless people in January 2005, of whom 56% were in emergency shelters and 44% were street people.

In 2008, HUD released data based on its nationwide Homeless Management Information System. Nearly 1.6 million people used emergency or transitional shelters between 1 October 2006 and 30 September 2007. On a single night in January 2007, 671 888 were estimated to be homeless. Nearly 60% were in emergency shelters or transitional housing and the remainder were in places not intended for human habitation.

Six attempts to estimate the homeless population in the United States have been reviewed. The HUD study (1983) suggested 250 000–350 000 homeless people on a typical night. The Urban Institute (1987) estimated 500 000–600 000, and the 1990 census reported 228 000 homeless people. A study by the US Interagency Council on Homelessness in 1996 reported 842 000 homeless people in October and 440 000 in February. The 2005 study by the NAEH reported 744 000 homeless people and the 2008 HUD research estimated 672 000.

There is a lot of variation between the different estimates, and it is difficult to draw firm conclusions about the number of homeless people in the United States, or whether homelessness has been increasing or decreasing. There is also the difficult issue of definition. As we know, most homeless people move around from one form of temporary accommodation to another. On census night, homeless people may be staying temporarily with friends or relatives, in SROs, as well as in various types of emergency accommodation, or sleeping rough. The studies described earlier used the literal definition of homelessness, which excludes people from the census count if they are staying with other households or in single rooms.

European Union

There are many definitions of homelessness in the countries of the European Union, as well as different understandings of how homeless people should be counted. Definitions of homelessness are often embedded in legislation specifying who is eligible for services. It is also common for welfare agencies and advocacy groups to promote broad definitions of homelessness that increase the size of the population, whereas official definitions tend to be narrower and reduce estimates.

Fitzpatrick and Stephens (2007) have pointed out that official agencies in France, Spain, and the Netherlands tend to use narrower definitions that are similar to the literal definition of homelessness used in the United States. On the other hand, official agencies in the United Kingdom, Germany, and Sweden tend to use more inclusive definitions.

Despite these variations, most people are agreed that statistical data collections on the homeless population are rudimentary in almost all European countries. In a major review of *Statistics on Homelessness in Europe*, Bill Edgar and Henk Meert (2006: 10) conclude,

> This overview demonstrates that very few countries collect and publish national level data on a systematic and regular basis on even the narrowest definition of homelessness – sleeping rough. It highlights the patchwork quilt of information available within countries between national, regional and municipal levels of government. Finally, it highlights the fact that data related to different operational categories of homelessness are collected by different methods.

Similarly, in a report of homelessness prepared for the European Commission, Brousse (2004: 89) has concluded that data on homeless people in the European Union is 'very patchy'. A study entitled 'Mutual Progress on Homelessness through Advancing and Strengthening Information Systems' (MPHASIS) is underway in Europe.

One attempt to solve the debate about definition has been put forward by the European Observatory on Homelessness who have proposed the FEANTSA definition of homelessness (also known as the 'ETHOS' typology) (**Table 1**). This is a broad definition of homelessness which is designed to facilitate the enumeration of homelessness in all European countries.

The FEANTSA definition identifies three aspects of a home, and the absence of one or more of these characteristics is said to denote homelessness (Edgar and Meert, 2006). The first requirement of a home is that it provides a decent dwelling that meets the needs of the household (the 'physical domain'). The second requirement is that the dwelling enables the household to maintain privacy and enjoy social relations (the 'social dimension'). The third requirement of a home is that the household has exclusive possession of the dwelling, security of occupation, and legal title (the 'legal domain').

This framework gives rise to four conceptual categories that are referred to as rooflessness, houselessness, insecure accommodation, and inadequate accommodation (**Table 1**). The conceptual categories are divided into 13 operational categories, ranging from people living rough to people in overcrowded accommodation, and further subdivided into 24 living situations (LS).

The FEANTSA definition is important, but there are some conceptual weaknesses in the schema. First, the FEANTSA definition classifies people who are awaiting release from penal institutions as homeless (LS 9). Prisoners may be at risk of homelessness when they are released, but they are not homeless whilst they are incarcerated.

Second, we know that many homeless people stay temporarily with friends or relatives when they first lose their accommodation, often moving frequently from one household to another. However, the FEANTSA schema classifies these households as 'insecurely housed' (LS 14).

Third, persons living in derelict buildings ('squatting') are obviously homeless, as are persons living in huts and improvised dwellings. However, the FEANTSA schema categorises them as 'inadequately housed' (LS 21–23).

Finally, the FEANTSA definition classifies 'formerly homeless people' who are in 'long-term supported accommodation' (more than 1 year) as homeless (LS 12–13). Surely, they are now adequately housed?

The FEANTSA definition is important, but the schema is excessively complicated and internally inconsistent.

Australia

The ABS uses the cultural definition to enumerate the homeless population on census night (Chamberlain and MacKenzie, 2008). This definition closely reflects the experiences of homeless people, since it was developed

Table 1 FEANTSA definition of homelessness

Conceptual category		Operational category		Living situation (LS)
Roofless	1	People living rough	1	Public space
	2	Emergency accommodation	2	Night shelter
Houseless	3	Accommodation for homeless	3	Homeless hostel
			4	Temporary accommodation
			5	Transitional accommodation
	4	Women's shelter	6	Women's shelter
	5	Accommodation for immigrants	7	Reception centre
			8	Migrant accommodation
	6	Awaiting release from institution	9	Penal institution
			10	Medical institution
			11	Children's institution
	7	Long-term assistance (due to homelessness)	12	Residential care for older homeless
			13	Long-term supported accommodation for formerly homeless
Insecure	8	Insecure accommodation	14	Temporarily with friends or relatives
			15	No legal (sub)tenancy
			16	Illegal occupation of land
	9	Threat of eviction	17	Legal orders enforced (rented)
			18	Repossession order (owned)
	10	Threat of violence	19	Police recorded incident
Inadequate	11	Temporary or nonconventional structure	20	Mobile home
			21	Nonconventional building
			22	Temporary structure
	12	Unfit housing	23	Dwelling unfit for habitation
	13	Overcrowded accommodation	24	Defined by national criteria

Adapted with permission from Edger B and Meet H (2006) *Fifth Review of Statistics on Homelessness in Europe*, p. 52. Brussels: European Federation of National Organisations Working with the Homeless (FEANTSA)

in services that work with the homeless (Chamberlain and MacKenzie, 1992).

The cultural definition contends that 'homelessness' and 'inadequate housing' are cultural constructs that only make sense in a particular community at a given historical period. In a society, where the vast majority of people live in mud huts, the community standard will be that mud huts constitute adequate accommodation (Watson, 1986). Community standards are embedded in the housing practices of a society, and most people recognise them because they are part of everyday knowledge. Once this principle is recognised, then it becomes possible to define homelessness.

In Australia, as in other European countries, the vast majority of people live in houses or self-contained flats, and the minimum that they can expect if they rent in the private market is a small self-contained flat, with their own kitchen, bathroom, and an element of security of tenure. This benchmark leads to the identification of 'primary', 'secondary', and 'tertiary' homelessness on census night.

Primary homelessness includes all people without conventional accommodation such as people living on the streets, sleeping in parks, squatting in derelict buildings, or using cars or railway carriages for temporary shelter. In Australia, primary homelessness is operationalised using the census category 'improvised homes, tents, and sleepers out', and this category also includes people in sheds, garages, and other improvised dwellings. There were 16 375 people in this category on census night, 2006.

Secondary homelessness includes people who are staying in any form of temporary accommodation because they have no home of their own. When people lose their accommodation in Western countries, they usually begin by staying temporarily with other households. The Australian census asks all persons to record their 'usual address' on census night; and people with 'no usual address' are instructed to write this on their census form. There were 46 856 people staying with other households on census night who reported 'no usual address'.

Secondary homelessness also includes people staying in crisis and transitional accommodation for homeless people provided under Australia's National Affordable Housing Agreement (NAHA). The starting point for identifying people in emergency and transitional accommodation is the census category 'hostels for the homeless, night shelters and refuges'. The number of persons in emergency and transitional accommodation was 19 849 on census night, 2006.

Tertiary homelessness refers to people who live in boarding houses (SROs). Residents of private boarding houses do not have separate bedrooms and living rooms;

they do not have kitchen and bathroom facilities of their own; their accommodation is not self-contained; and they do not have security of tenure provided by a lease. They are homeless because their accommodation does not have the characteristics identified in the minimum community standard. There were 21 596 people in boarding houses on census night.

Overall, the 2006 Australian census identified 104 676 homeless people, and this figure has been widely accepted by advocacy groups and policymakers. In December 2008, the Australian government released a white paper on homelessness that proposed two ambitious goals: to halve homelessness by 2020 and to provide accommodation to all rough sleepers who need it (Homelessness Taskforce, 2008).

The white paper was accompanied by a significant financial commitment of A$1200 million over 5 years, with $800 million allocated for prevention and early intervention services and $400 million to increase the supply of supported housing. Since the white paper, the government has announced a further A$6600 million to be spent on the construction of 20 000 homes for public housing, the largest expansion of public housing for many years. These initiatives were underpinned by widespread acceptance of the census data.

Conclusion

Debate about the definition of homelessness continues in many Western countries with little agreement on fundamental issues (Avramov, 1995; Chamberlain and Johnson, 2001; Hopper, 1997). One consequence of this continuing argument is that in most countries there is inadequate information on the number of homeless people, because there is no agreement about who should be counted. Homelessness is a serious issue, but governments are reticent to expend large amounts of money when there is no reliable information on the number of homeless people.

The obvious way to try to enumerate the homeless population is to use the census of population and housing that is carried out in many countries every 5 or 10 years. If there is an agreed definition of homelessness that can be operationalised using census data, then there is a reasonable chance of persuading governments that more ought to be done.

See also: Hidden Homelessness; Homelessness: Causation; Homelessness: Definitions; Homeless People in China/East Asia; Meanings of Home; Representations of Homelessness; Squatting: Developing World; Squatting: United Kingdom.

References

Appelbaum R (1990) Counting the homeless. In: Momeni J (ed.) *Homelessness in the United States: Data and Issues*, pp. 1–16. New York: Praeger.

Avramov D (1995) *Homeless in the European Union*. Brussels: FEANTSA.

Blau J (1992) *The Visible Poor: Homelessness in the United States*. New York: Oxford University Press.

Brousse C (2004) *The Production of Data on Homelessness and Housing Deprivation in the European Union: Survey and Proposals*. Luxembourg: European Commission.

Burt M and Cohen BE (1989) *America's Homeless: Numbers, Characteristics and the Programs that Serve Them*. Washington, DC: Urban Institute Press.

Chamberlain C and Johnson G (2001) The debate about homelessness. *Australian Journal of Social Issues* 36(1): 35–50.

Chamberlain C and MacKenzie D (1992) Understanding contemporary homelessness: Issues of definition and meaning. *Australian Journal of Social Issues* 27(4): 274–297.

Chamberlain C and MacKenzie D (2008) *Counting the Homeless 2006*. Canberra, ACT: Australian Bureau of Statistics, Catalogue No. 2050.0.

Craig S and Schwarz C (1984) *Down and Out: Orwell's Paris and London Revisited*. London; New York: Penguin Books.

Edgar B and Meert H (2006) *Fifth Review of Statistics on Homelessness in Europe*. Brussels: European Federation of National Organisations Working with the Homeless (FEANTSA).

Fitzpatrick S (1998) Homelessness in the European Union. In: Kleinman M, Matznetter W, and Stephens M (eds.) *European Integration and Housing Policy*, pp. 197–214. London; New York: Routledge.

Fitzpatrick S and Stephens M (2007) *An International Review of Homelessness and Social Housing Policy*. London: Department for Communities and Local Government.

Hombs ME and Snyder M (1982) *Homelessness in America: A Forced March to Nowhere*. Washington, DC: Community for Creative Non-Violence.

Homelessness Taskforce (2008) *The Road Home: A National Approach to Reducing Homelessness*. Canberra, ACT: Commonwealth of Australia.

Hopper K (1997) Homelessness old and new: The matter of definition. In: Culhane D and Hornburg S (eds.) *Understanding Homelessness: New Policy and Research Perspectives*, pp. 9–67. Washington, DC: Fannie Mae Foundation.

Jencks C (1994) *The Homeless*. Cambridge, MA: Harvard University Press.

National Alliance to End Homelessness (NAEH) (2007) *Homelessness Counts*. Washington, DC: National Alliance to End Homelessness.

Peroff K (1987) Who are the homeless and how many are there? In: Bingham RD, Green RE, and White SB (eds.) *The Homeless in Contemporary Society*, pp. 33–45. Newbury Park, CA: Sage Publications.

Toro P (2007) Towards an international understanding of homelessness. *Journal of Social Issues* 63(3): 461–481.

Watson S (with Austerberry H) (1986) *Housing and Homelessness: A Feminist Perspective*. London: Routledge; Kegan Paul.

Wright JD and Devine JA (1992) Counting the homeless: The census bureau's 'S-Night' in five U.S. cities. *Evaluation Review* 16(4): 355–364.

Homelessness: Prevention in the United States

J Apicello, W McAllister, and B O'Flaherty, Columbia University, New York, NY, USA

© 2012 Elsevier Ltd. All rights reserved.

Glossary

Affordable housing Rent or mortgage that costs no more than 30% of a household's income.
At-risk People who have conditions (e.g., mental illness) or histories (e.g., foster care) that make them more likely than others to incur a problem, such as homelessness.
Housing market Economic characteristics of buying and selling housing in a locale, for example, supply, demand, price, and so forth.
Housing subsidies Government payments to people or households targeted at defraying the cost of housing.
Incidence Measure of the risk in a population of developing a problem, usually measured as a rate, for example, the rate of homelessness in a city.
Low-income households Households whose incomes are below a certain threshold, set by law usually in relation to locale and the number of people in the household.
Minimum wage Hourly salary employers are legally obligated to pay their employees.
Population Collection of all people sharing a relevant, defining trait, for example, the population of all homeless people.
States Governing units in the United States that comprise the United States, for example, California.
Zoning Legal requirements for the siting and physical character of buildings.

Introduction

In thinking about homelessness prevention and in creating prevention policies, it is useful to distinguish between two different aspects of the problem: who becomes homeless and the rate of homelessness. We explain how two different kinds of prevention, individual and structural, aim at these different aspects, and review other ways of thinking about homelessness prevention. We then use a commonly made distinction between universalist and particularist policy-making to describe how individual and structural preventions get translated into policies and programmes, show how these other ways of thinking about prevention relate to individual and structural prevention, and categorise past and current initiatives in the United States aimed expressly or indirectly at preventing homelessness.

Conceptualising Homelessness Prevention

Individual/Structural Prevention

Homelessness can be prevented in one of two ways – individually or structurally. The first focuses on the causes of where particular people fall in the distribution of homelessness; the second focuses on the causes of the distribution of homelessness itself. For example, if some people are homeless because they suffer from mental illness, individual prevention focuses on improving their mental health functioning; if a city has high rates of homelessness because housing is scarce, structural prevention focuses on reducing the price of housing.

It may seem that both kinds of prevention are addressing the same thing. They are not. A common argument, for example, is that if we know homeless people are more likely than the general population to have, say, histories of mental illness, substance and alcohol use, and contact with the criminal justice system, then we can treat these problems to reduce homelessness. By successfully treating these problems, we will remove these kinds of people from homelessness. The problem of homelessness, however, will remain.

To see why this is so, suppose cities differ in the price of housing and in the proportion of their population that is poor. People are poor when their incomes are below some level P, the same level for every city (e.g., using a national government definition of poverty). People are homeless in city c when their incomes are below some level $H(c)$, which differs among cities because the price of housing differs among cities. Then variations in the proportion of the population between P and $H(c)$ will affect the size of the poverty population but not homelessness, and variation in housing prices and in the distribution of the poverty population below and above $H(c)$ will affect homelessness but not the size of the poverty population. Since almost all the poverty population is between P and $H(c)$, almost none of the variation in the poverty population is associated with variation in homelessness. Thus, in this model, an individual's being poor will be a strong predictor of homelessness, but in the cross-section, variation in the size of the poverty population will explain very little of the variation in the size of the homeless population. What this model shows is that it is possible for homelessness to be closely associated with demographic and other traits of an individual, but for the incidence of those traits to explain very little about the volume of homelessness.

In sum, individual prevention aims at people's characteristics that cause them to become homeless. Structural prevention aims at what produces the incidence of homelessness in a population.

Other Conceptualisations of Prevention

Individual and structural preventions exhaustively subsume other conceptualisations of homelessness prevention. The distinction we make clarifies whether prevention aims at the causes of who becomes homeless or at the causes of homelessness itself. Unlike other conceptualisations, it does not distinguish between different affected populations.

A traditional public health (PH) conceptualisation identifies three kinds of individual-level initiatives based on the timing of prevention: (1) 'primary prevention' aims at homelessness before risk factors appear; (2) 'secondary prevention' prizes early risk-detection and treatment of homelessness; and (3) 'tertiary prevention' aims to reduce homelessness among those already homeless. All three are different kinds of individual-level prevention because they effectively focus on different aggregates of individuals and aim at directly changing the behaviour of individuals, ignoring the underlying policy and economic conditions of people's lives. Some researchers have used this categorisation to describe programmes targeting housed people, those at the beginning of a homeless episode, and longer-term homeless people.

Similarly, but more overtly, the Institute of Medicine (IOM) conceptualises prevention for three populations of individuals: (1) 'universal prevention' targets an entire population, homeless and nonhomeless; (2) 'selected prevention' targets people in a social group linked to homelessness, for example, an age-defined group or a particular sex or race; and (3) 'indicated prevention' targets people with an assessed trait linked to homelessness, for example, mental illness or substance abuse. Some researchers have used this categorisation to describe housing programmes aimed at an entire population, at poorer people, and at people facing eviction.

A last conceptualisation, from social epidemiology (SE), is based on the causes of the outcome of interest. This distinguishes between causes of homelessness in a general population and those for high-risk individuals. The latter focuses on what causes people to be most likely to experience homelessness, akin to individual, secondary/tertiary, and selected/indicated prevention. The former focuses on conditions or behaviours in a population as a whole that cause homelessness. When such prevention focuses on behaviour, it is akin to primary and universal prevention; when it focuses on social, policy, and economic conditions, it is akin to structural prevention, as it aims not at the behaviour of people but at the conditions in which they live.

Prevention Policies and Programmes

To be concrete in the lives of homeless people, these conceptualisations are translated into general policies or specific programmes. In a commonly made distinction, policies or programmes are thought to be particularist or universalist. Particularist references efforts that are expressly directed at particular subpopulations, for example, income transfers through Medicaid, the US health insurance programme for people in poverty. Universalist references initiatives that are directed equally at an entire population, for example, income transfers to everyone in the United States through its old age insurance programme, Social Security. Combining this distinction with individual/structural prevention, **Table 1** relates the different conceptualisations of prevention. The empty cell indicates that the reviewed conceptualisations do not allow for this approach, not that the approach does not exist.

Table 1 Relationship between individual/structural prevention and universalist/particularist policies and programmes

		Prevention Level	
		Structural	Individual
Kind of Policies and Programmes	*Universalist*	• Population (SE)	• Primary (PH) • Universal (IOM) • Population (SE)
	Particularist		• Secondary/Tertiary (PH) • Selected/Indicated (IOM) • High-risk (SE)

The table also better specifies how individual and structural prevention happens. Individual prevention can occur through universalist efforts encompassing an entire population (e.g., money management classes for all students) or particularist efforts targeting would-be or currently homeless people (e.g., emergency help for at-risk people). In addition, structural prevention can occur through universalist action (e.g., lowering the cost of housing) or action targeted at would-be or currently homeless people (e.g., subsidised housing for mentally ill homeless). We note that, like all such simplifying tables, dimensions are more continuous and cell boundaries more porous than the table allows. For example, some specific policies and programmes could fall into different cells depending on what other policies and programmes are in place.

We can use this table to describe prevention approaches in the United States that are described in the homelessness prevention literature or found among existing US community prevention programmes as follows:

- Structural/Universalist Approaches
  1. Reducing housing market regulatory stringency
  2. Developing and rehabilitating housing
  3. Policies targeting labour markets

- Structural/Particularist Approaches
  1. Subsidised housing
  2. Increasing the reach of income support programmes
  3. Developing supportive housing for high-risk populations

- Individual/Particularist Approaches
  1. Emergency prevention interventions
  2. Systems prevention interventions
  3. Targeted supportive housing and service programmes
  4. Further targeted housing subsidies.

Our review of the literature and of existing programmes found no individual/universalist efforts.

Structural/Universalist Approaches
Reducing housing market regulatory stringency
A major argument is that high housing costs induce homelessness by, for example, forcing poorer households to choose food, clothing, or other necessities over housing. Higher housing costs are thought to be produced in different ways. One way is through local housing regulations, for example, habitation standards, density and quality zoning, and so forth. These regulations are thought to impact housing costs by increasing production costs, restricting housing supply, and increasing housing demand. A study using a state-level index of housing regulation finds a positive relationship between regulation and homelessness, suggesting policies that loosen local regulations may be a useful way to lower the incidence of homelessness. Of course, such policies would have to maintain housing quality and other conditions thought important for human habitation. Most of the policies in the state-level regulatory index used in this research are not tied to basic requirements for human habitation; they concern, for instance, large-lot zoning and long delays in permitting.

Developing and rehabilitating housing
Advocates, researchers, and consumers have argued that developing and rehabilitating low-cost housing is an important way to prevent homelessness. The key expectations are that by adding to the available housing stock, the price of housing is reduced, making housing more affordable and thereby reducing the rate of homelessness.

The US federal government has contributed to the construction of 1.4 million units of low-cost housing since 1937, but only about 5% of these units have been built since 1985. Government policies have shifted away from emphasising the supply of low-cost housing to increasing the demand for housing. In recent years, however, programmes have been developed to create incentives for constructing or rehabilitating low-cost housing: tax-exempt bond financing; the federal Low Income Housing Tax Credit (tax benefits for private equity to develop affordable housing); the federal HOME programme (funds for state and local governments for activities that build, buy, and/or rehabilitate housing for or provide direct rental assistance to low-income people); and, most recently, the National Housing Trust Fund, which establishes permanent, ongoing sources of revenue to build, rehabilitate, and preserve 1.5 million housing units, primarily rental housing.

Efforts to expand the supply of low-cost housing also occur at the local level. Besides changing local regulations, local grants, low-interest loans, or housing trust funds can support building or rehabilitating low-cost rental housing in the same fashion as federal efforts.

Despite the implementation of these strategies, no empirical research has directly investigated the hypothesised link between building and preserving housing and preventing homelessness. Much housing economics research suggests little effect of subsidised construction on housing stock. Subsidised housing crowds out production of nonsubsidised units, resulting in a small or no net addition to housing stock. One study found, for instance, that public housing had almost no effect on the total number of housing units. Also, cost–benefit analyses of subsidised construction show only a relatively low ratio of about 50 cents of benefit for each dollar spent. All this suggests that building subsidised housing is likely to have very small and overly costly effects on homelessness, if any.

Policies targeting labour markets

By increasing the income people have available to pay for housing, strategies aimed at labour market wages expect to reduce the rate of homelessness. Numerous studies and reports have shown that individuals in a full-time job at minimum wage cannot afford to live alone in a one-bedroom apartment anywhere in the United States without spending over 30% of their income on housing. However, no evidence yet links higher minimum wages with preventing homelessness, nor even, perhaps, with reducing poverty – a crucial link in the argument for hypothesised effects on homelessness.

Researchers have demonstrated that growing income inequality has coincided with increased homelessness. A summary of international papers addressing causes of homelessness in the developed world pointed out that nations with lower income inequality have less homelessness. However, the effect of policies to reduce income disparities on US homelessness has not been studied.

Structural/Particularist Approaches

Subsidised housing

The principle of this approach is that providing benefits specifically for housing to subpopulations below certain income thresholds makes the cost of housing more affordable. Some research has suggested, for example, that the rate of homelessness might be reduced by providing subsidies to offset the number of households that might otherwise 'choose' homelessness to eliminate an unaffordable rent burden. And other research points to housing subsidies as an evidence-based method for preventing and ending homelessness.

Several recent studies have found that existing and conceivable housing subsidy programmes show promise for improving housing stability or preventing homelessness. To take one example, a rigorously controlled experiment of a Housing Choice Voucher (HCV) demonstration project, conducted from 1999 to 2006, studied the effects of housing vouchers on families making the transition from welfare to work (also called Section 8, this programme allows households to choose privately owned rental housing and to spend no more than 30% of their income on that housing). Among virtually all types of families receiving demonstration vouchers, the evaluation found a substantial reduction in homelessness, an increase in independent housing, and a decrease in doubled-up situations. (Independent housing refers to housing where individuals live in their own home or apartment without any on-site social or health-related services.) The study suggests that housing vouchers eliminated much of the homelessness that families receiving welfare would have faced without the subsidy.

Studies have shown that receipt of subsidised housing can prevent recurrent episodes of homelessness and allow families to avoid seeking shelter in the first place. A New York City study found that receiving housing subsidies was the only significant predictor of staying housed among formerly homeless families.

Availability of subsidised housing is limited, however, and does not reach all households that are at the lowest rungs of the income distribution. Research has shown that only one-quarter to one-third of families receiving public assistance, Supplemental Security Income (SSI, which provides cash to aged, blind, and disabled people in the United States for their food, clothing, and shelter needs) or Temporary Assistance to Needy Families (TANF, which provides cash to indigent US families with dependent children), also receive any kind of housing assistance. Currently, federal Section 8 vouchers provide thousands of individuals and families with rental subsidies, but still leave thousands of households wait-listed in cities across the country. Furthermore, while housing subsidies do allow poor people to compete in the housing market, they work efficiently to prevent homelessness only if the affordable housing stock is sufficiently expanded to incorporate the number of subsidies issued.

More deeply, subsidies affect the rate at which housing filters to poorer people. Theoretical work and research on the Experimental Housing Assistance Program, which provided housing vouchers to indigent households, indicate that subsidies can provide more housing units to poor people without having major effects on the price of housing. This suggests that the indirect effects of subsidy may not be increasing homelessness. However, more recent work has raised issue about this argument, leaving the issue unsettled.

Studies on housing markets also suggest subsidised housing's impact on preventing homelessness. One study combined empirical data from the Survey of Income and Program Participation with the National Survey of Homeless Assistance Providers and Clients to estimate a probability model for homelessness. It estimated that between 3.8 and 5.0% of households receiving subsidies would have been homeless absent a housing subsidy. Using a general equilibrium simulation model and data from the 1990 decennial census, another study explored conceivable, expanded housing subsidy programmes and their effects on the prevalence of homelessness. They modelled a programme that would extend subsidies to all low-income households in the four largest metropolitan areas in California, and found that such a programme would result in reductions in homelessness of between 25 and 33%, and that subsidising landlords directly could reduce the rate of homelessness by 6–12%.

Another example of a subsidy programme is 'shallow' rent subsidies. 'Deep' subsidies pay an adjusted amount so that the tenants' housing costs are set at 30% of their income (e.g., Section 8 vouchers). 'Shallow' subsidies pay an amount that may mean families and individuals spend more than 30% of their income on housing, leaving some recipients rent-burdened, but less burdened than they otherwise would have been. Considering the severe shortage of vouchers and rental subsidies in cities that lack affordable housing options, shallow subsidies could prevent homelessness if targeted and distributed appropriately. For example, a quasi-experimental evaluation of a shallow rent programme in California found that 96% of households receiving rental support were still housed 2 years after subsidy-receipt, compared to 10% of comparison group clients (adjusting for necessary covariates). This suggests modest subsidies can perhaps prevent homelessness, though their effects on the incidence of homelessness are not known.

Increasing the reach of income support programmes

It is theorised that more relaxed or inclusive eligibility requirements for these types of income support programmes could help prevent homelessness among those receiving assistance, perhaps thereby lowering the incidence of homelessness. A number of federal safety net programmes have been designed to provide income support to very poor people, but barriers to obtaining benefits, coupled with strict eligibility criteria and limited resources, restrict the reach and preventive possibilities of these programmes.

For example, US federal programmes that we alluded to earlier provide direct cash. But these are available only to poor families with children (e.g., TANF) or to aged, blind, or disabled individuals (e.g., SSI and its similar sister programme Social Security Disability Insurance, SSDI). There is no empirical evidence for the hypothesised effect on homelessness, however. Researchers have analysed different kinds of public assistance without finding any effects on the rate of shelter use.

Research has been carried out on the effect of the 1996 US welfare reforms on housing stability in general and on homelessness in particular. One study synthesised key findings from 15 studies, looking at the impact on housing for families leaving welfare rolls voluntarily or sanctioned with services cutoff. It found that at least 25% of such families experienced trouble paying rent or utilities once they left welfare. However, using a time series analysis, another study did not find any effects of these reforms on Philadelphia's shelter population.

Research on TANF and on SSI as a homelessness prevention strategy among individuals with substance use disorders provides evidence for the importance of current safety net programmes on preventing homelessness. These suggest that diversifying the use of mainstream funding to include housing assistance can be one strategy for increasing the affordability of housing for low-income populations and thereby preventing homelessness.

SSI approvals are thought to lead to increased access to housing and, thus, to reduced episodes of homelessness. But gaining access to available benefits is a major barrier for many people experiencing homelessness. Perhaps 11% of homeless people receive SSI, even though rampant ill-health among homeless people suggests greater eligibility. The SSI/SSDI Outreach, Access and Recovery (SOAR) programme helps homeless people navigate the SSI/SSDI application process. Its goals are to increase overall application volume and approval rates on initial determinations and decrease time to initial decision. An evaluation of preliminary outcomes in 11 states (16 programmes) participating in the initial round of the SOAR Technical Assistance Initiative reported improvements in application approvals and reductions in wait times for initial decisions, but their impact on homelessness is unknown.

Supportive housing for high-risk individuals

Some communities have taken an integrated approach to housing development. In 'new-build' projects containing market-rate and affordable housing units, they set aside a percentage of affordable, supportive housing units (supportive housing refers to any subsidised housing-based programmes that offer on- or off-site supportive services). For example, a large, publicly funded project of New York City and State (New York/New York Agreement) has committed to building over 12 000 units of supportive housing for individuals with mental illness or with other special needs. Similar supportive unit construction and preservation projects are occurring across the country. Because these projects contribute to the supply of housing, albeit targeted to special needs households, they are expected to reduce the overall incidence of homelessness.

Individual/Particularist Approaches

Emergency prevention interventions

Individual-level prevention strategies target particular kinds of people to help them avoid homelessness. Strategies targeted at those at imminent risk of eviction or homelessness have been recommended by researchers and advocates for years, and the American Recovery and Reinvestment Act of 2009 allotted $1.5 billion for such strategies in its Homelessness Prevention and Rapid Re-Housing Program. The most common strategies include short-term financial assistance, tenant–landlord mediation, rapid-exit screening at shelters, comprehensive place-based prevention centres, and rapid-rehousing. We discuss each in turn.

Short-term financial assistance is offered in several forms to at-risk households: back rent and utility payments, security deposits or first month's rent to obtain new housing for people about to be displaced, and payments or loans to households facing foreclosures on mortgages. One review of community-based prevention strategies noted the dearth of systematic data collection and evaluation among many local programmes, but reported on several community-based, short-term financial assistance prevention efforts. For example, in counties in the states of Minnesota, Maryland, and Missouri, only 2–5% of families receiving short-term financial assistance entered a homeless shelter in the year after receiving assistance. However, with no comparison group, we do not know what percentage of the 95–98% of families who avoided homelessness would have become homeless without an intervention. An evaluation of prevention efforts in Massachusetts in 2007 also suggests positive outcomes for short-term financial assistance programmes. None of these studies, however, let us know whether or not those receiving assistance would have become homeless without the assistance.

Rapid-exit screening strategies ensure that people just entering shelter leave quickly and remain housed. This screening process assesses a family's housing barriers and refers it for tailored prevention services to help the family remain housed. Hennepin County, Minnesota, has used this strategy since 2001. Here, families who seek shelter and who do not have any other alternatives receive a voucher for shelter and are referred for screening to a rapid-exit coordinator. Evaluators report that 12% of families that rapidly exited from shelter returned to shelter within 12 months. Compared to shelter readmission rates from Philadelphia and New York City, this represents at least one-third fewer families returning to shelter.

Place-based prevention strategies target prevention efforts in neighbourhoods where a disproportionate number of people seeking shelter come from. For instance, HomeBase, a neighbourhood-based, city-wide programme in New York City serves community residents at risk of becoming homeless. According to City data, the initial six neighbourhoods where HomeBase programmes were located experienced fewer shelter entries than the rest of the city. Of the 7400 households served by the programme, 93% did not enter a shelter 18 months after programme entrance. It is unknown, however, how many of these households would have become homeless had they not received an intervention. Several evaluations attempting to answer this crucial question are now underway. Some answers may be available in 2011.

Rapid rehousing efforts operate under the 'housing first' philosophy: permanently house a homeless household quickly rather than require it to go through a series of shelter and services steps that comprise a standard 'continuum-of-care'. This latter approach often left people in emergency and transitional shelters for months or years.

Systems prevention interventions

Research has shown that many homeless and at-risk people move repeatedly through mainstream systems and institutions, such as jails and prisons, state psychiatric hospitals, drug treatment programmes, foster care, and homeless shelters. This link has encouraged the development of prevention strategies targeting this 'institutional circuit' which serves as de facto shelter in place of stable living situations. The most widely cited way to target this circuit is through discharge planning efforts, increasingly referred to as 'systems prevention' interventions. The main goal of such planning in homelessness prevention is to ensure that people leaving an institution are not sent to a homeless shelter or onto the street or to any other place not meant for human habitation, and that their placements are stable enough to prevent future homelessness. Recent system prevention strategies include those that encourage community-based organisations to assist in navigating the system and in transitioning from institutions (e.g., from prisons and jails or health care facilities). Other strategies mandate housing subsidy distribution through legislation (e.g., targeting transitions from foster care or through the military).

A review of homelessness prevention was sceptical of discharge planning's ability to prevent homelessness. They argued that although concentrating efforts on improving discharge planning is logical, we lack empirical evidence of its efficacy in preventing homelessness, particularly in the long term. A 2005 analysis of the ability to evaluate implemented discharge planning programmes relative to homelessness prevention, and a recent study looking at single-adult shelter admissions in New York City came to a similar conclusion. And, as with all individual/particularist efforts, effective systems prevention strategies may prevent homelessness among those discharged, but will not reduce the incidence of homelessness if those discharged simply replace others in existing units.

Targeted supportive housing and service programmes

Programmes that increase housing options for high-risk groups in the form of supportive housing are thought to prevent homelessness among those who receive it. Recently, these strategies have targeted people who qualify as 'chronically' homeless – those homeless for an extended period of time who are most often diagnosed with a disability. Several programmes also target individuals with recurrent episodes of homelessness. Supportive housing has a broad range of models, with varying degrees of evidence of their effectiveness. Little evidence exists that 'transitional' (i.e., time-limited subsidies) supportive housing programmes prevent homelessness or improve housing stability. Some evidence shows that 'permanent' (i.e., no time limit to subsidies) supportive housing improves residential stability and reduces shelter use, even among chronically homeless adults with severe mental illness and substance-use disorders.

Supportive services are thought to help individuals and families retain housing once they receive it. However, empirical evidence or consensus in the field about which services work best for which subpopulation is limited. In some housing programmes, clients receive standard case management, which has been found to improve residential stability. Other programmes have employed either of the two evidence-based service interventions found to be successful in promoting housing stability and in preventing recurrent homelessness: critical time intervention and assertive community treatment. Rigorous research is critically needed to determine when and how to implement or adapt such services and to decide which services are most appropriate for preventing homelessness.

Further targeted housing subsidies

The best predictor of whether a person or household will be homeless is whether or not a person or household is homeless today. Thus, housing subsidies for individuals and families who have become homeless avoid the problem of targeting that accompanies many prevention programmes. Although it is tempting to target these households as highest-risk or most-in-need of subsidised housing, policies must dance a fine line to avoid creating incentives to enter shelters or to remain sheltered to gain priority access to subsidies. For instance, until 2007, this was a potential problem in New York City, where families remaining in shelters were moved to the top of the Section 8 voucher waiting list. The potential problem may not have been realised, however, as one study found that subsidising 100 homeless households reduced shelter population by about 30, while subsidising 100 poor households is generally found to reduce shelter population by about 3–8.

This programme, however, and others targeting scarce housing resources to those currently homeless are unlikely to have an impact on the overall rate of homelessness. However, they could prevent recurrent or long-term homelessness among individual cases of homeless households.

Conclusion

Thinking about and creating policies for preventing homelessness can distinguish between the causes of who becomes homeless and the causes of the rate of homelessness. On this basis, we can conceptualise individual prevention, aimed at the former set of causes, and structural prevention, aimed at the latter. Each kind of prevention gets translated into programmes through particularist and universalist policies. Relating these two kinds of prevention and two kinds of policies allows us to see United States policies and programmes in terms of their causal nature and the generality of their effects. It shows, for example, how most prevailing ways of preventing homelessness focus on the causes of the specific kind of people who become homeless, that is, individual prevention.

It is important to note that we have identified major kinds of policies and programmes in the United States that address homelessness prevention. We have not tried to be exhaustive. Other kinds are also identified in the research literature or have been implemented. These too can be understood as one of the four types of prevention we described, with attendant expectations for effects on the rate of homelessness or on who becomes homeless and for how effects are brought about, by affecting an entire population (e.g., housing costs) or by targeting (e.g., those mentally ill).

See also: Economic Perspectives on Homelessness; Economics of Social Housing; Ethnographies of Home and Homelessness; Health, Well-Being and Vulnerable Populations; Homeless Families: United Kingdom; Homeless People: African Americans in the United States; Material Cultures of Domestic Interiors: India; Mental Health and Homelessness; Policies to Address Homelessness: Housing First Approaches; Shelter and Development; Social Psychological Perspectives on Homelessness.

Further Reading

Abt Associates Inc (2006) *Effects of Housing Vouchers on Welfare Families*. Washington, DC: U.S. Department of Housing and Urban Development, Office of Policy Development and Research.

Apicello J (2009) *Applying the Population and High-Risk Framework to Preventing Homelessness: A Review of the Literature and Practice*. Rockville, MD: Substance Abuse and Mental Health Services Administration.

Burt M, Pearson C, and Montgomery AE (2005) *Strategies for Preventing Homelessness*. Washington, DC: U.S. Department of Housing and Urban Development.

Herman DB, Conover S, Felix A, Nakagawa A, and Mills D (2007) Critical time intervention: An empirically supported model for preventing homelessness in high risk groups. *The Journal of Primary Prevention* 28: 295–312.

Hopper K and Barrow SM (2003) Two genealogies of supported housing and their implications for outcome assessment. *Psychiatric Services* 54: 50–54.

Ingrid E and O'Flaherty B (eds.) (2010) *How to House the Homeless*. New York: Russell Sage.

McAllister W, Lennon MC, and Çelimli I (2008) Prevention strategies and public health: Individual and structural prevention. In: Colgrove J, Rosner D, and Markowitz J (eds.) *The Contested Boundaries of American Public Health*, pp. 127–159. New Brunswick, NJ: Rutgers University Press.

Norris J, Scott R, Speiglman R, and Green R (2003) Homelessness, hunger and material hardship among those who lost SSI. *Contemporary Drug Problems* 30: 241–273.

O'Flaherty B and Wu LT (2006) Fewer subsidized exits and a recession: How New York City's family homeless shelter population became immense. *Journal of Housing Economics* 15: 99–125.

Quigley JM, Raphael S, and Smolensky E (2001) *The Links between Income Inequality, Housing Markets, and Homelessness in California*. San Francisco, CA: Public Policy Institute of California.

Rog DJ (2004) The evidence on supported housing. *Psychiatric Rehabilitation Journal* 27: 334–344.

Rose G (1992) *The Strategy of Preventive Medicine*. New York: Oxford University Press.

Shinn M, Baumohl J, and Hopper K (2001) The prevention of homelessness revisited. *Analyses of Social Issues and Public Policy* 1: 95–127.

Sinai T and Waldfogel J (2005) Do low-income housing subsidies increase housing consumption? *Journal of Public Economics* 89: 2137–2164.

Susin S (2005) Longitudinal outcomes of subsidized housing recipients in matched survey and administrative data. *Cityscape* 8: 189–218.

Homeless People: African Americans in the United States

RA Johnson, University of San Francisco, San Francisco, CA, USA

© 2012 Published by Elsevier Ltd.

Glossary

Crack cocaine In the United States in the mid-1980s, affordable cocaine became available in the form of crack cocaine. Baking soda is often used as a base for crack cocaine and it was called crack because of the sound made during its manufacture. While crack produced a shorter high than powder cocaine, it was also dramatically cheaper. It could be purchased for three to ten dollars for a single hit of the drug. Crack continues to be widely used in American urban areas and is considered a substance that has serious abuse problems.

Freedmen's Bureau The Freedmen's Bureau was a government agency created at the end of the Civil War by the US Congress to help the millions of newly emancipated slaves. Its agenda was initiated after Congress saw the partial success the Union army had in building work camps of freed blacks during the war. Through the Freedmen's Bureau, President Lincoln made an effort to distribute land to freed blacks by ordering that in the tax sales of land that had been owned by Southern whites, some land should be offered at affordable prices and in small quantities to blacks. The effort was limited under President Lincoln and then thwarted by his successor President Andrew Johnson. The goal of selling small parcels of land to significant numbers of blacks was never accomplished.

Legally binding slavery While slavery in the colonies began as a practice without legal foundation, it soon changed. The colony of Virginia was the first to make slavery hereditary by legally establishing that the status of a child should be determined by that of the mother. And, in 1705, a Virginia law provided for a slave being inventoried as real estate. As property, there was nothing to prevent slaves from being separated from their families. Before the law slaves were no longer considered persons, they were considered things.

New deal The term refers to the period between 1933 and 1940 in the United States and it also refers to the policies pursued during that period by President Franklin D. Roosevelt and his administration. The New Deal legislative programmes included government assistance and government-funded work projects; the policies were designed to bring reform to a broken economy and to provide relief from the trauma of a deep economic depression, referred to as the Great Depression.

Reconstruction After the American Civil War ended, during the period between 1865 and 1877, the United States underwent Reconstruction. During Reconstruction, the federal government controlled the Southern states that made up the former confederacy and the federal government tried to modify the political and social institutions of the South as a prerequisite for the Southern states being readmitted to the Union.

Skid row The term refers to a section of a city where hobos and bums congregate and where businesses cater to the needs of the poor and marginalised. The area usually had cheap hotels and flop houses, places to find employment, cheap restaurants, and taverns. The term originated in an area in Seattle Washington bordering the downhill slopes where logs were regularly 'skidded down the hill' on the way to being processed. By the twentieth century, all large cities had skid rows.

Underground railroad The term refers to the track of safe places used by runaway slaves as they escaped slavery and travelled north. The origin of the term underground railroad is purported to be the following: A slave named Tice Davids escaped from his owner in Ripley Ohio, and immediately disappeared. The master searched the vicinity as thoroughly as he could but found no trace of his runaway slave. The slave owner concluded ruefully, "He must have gotten away by an underground road." From the term road to the term railroad was a simple transition and it caught on because the terminology of railroading afforded names to mask a range of illegal activities. For example, the underground railroad had conductors and passengers and stations and station keepers.

Urban renewal In the United States, urban renewal policies were most vigorously pursued in the 1960s. They were federally funded programmes designed to remove slum areas in inner cities and replace them with newer more beautiful buildings including modern housing units and shopping malls. Most residents who were displaced by urban renewal were poor, and urban renewal did not provide most of them new dwellings.

Introduction: Black Homelessness in the United States

The usual story of homelessness in America has not always included descriptions of the experience of black Americans. The following narrative focuses exclusively on them. As will be shown, sometimes black homeless Americans were not categorised properly – for example, runaway slaves have not normally been seen as homeless, but they were. Sometimes black homeless Americans were not noticed or counted properly – for example, during the nineteenth and early twentieth centuries, there were black cowboys and black tramps but they were ignored, unrecognised, or undercounted by their contemporaries and by historians.

Furthermore, as will be shown, focusing exclusively on black homelessness can expose how some of their homelessness has been caused by official US policy. For example, the 1930s New Deal agricultural policy caused black homelessness in the South, and the 1950s and 1960s policy of urban renewal caused black homelessness in major American cities. This article will explore all of this in depth. In addition, it will explain why in recent decades the proportion of American homeless people who are black has grown so large.

Homeless People

Through the centuries, the American definition of people who are homeless has included those without family, those who have no access to private space, those who have no fixed address, and those who sleep in places not intended for human habitation. Those who currently sleep in public shelters, or during centuries past those who slept in an almshouse or poorhouse, have also been considered homeless. In this article the use of the term 'homeless' will reflect these various definitions.

Describing black homelessness in an historic context is especially difficult for two reasons. The first reason is that black people who were homeless were not always recognised by mainstream observers as being homeless. The second reason is that even when blacks were recognised as homeless, they were not always counted accurately. In fact, blacks are absent or underrepresented in almost all historic accounts of American homelessness (Baum and Burnes, 1993: ch. 6; Jencks, 1994: ch. 6; Rossi, 1989: ch. 2). This article begins to address this absence. We rewrite history starting from the colonies up to the present.

The Colonies

By the mid-seventeenth century, as the slave trade expanded, slavery became a legally binding arrangement in the American colonies. Black slaves lived in dilapidated, windowless, uncomfortable huts that were hardly adequate for human habitation (Franklin and Moss, 1994). But while their living conditions were deficient, because white people considered slaves 'sheltered' and part of the 'community', slaves were not considered homeless.

Population records show that slaves were primarily in the Southern colonies and that their numbers rose steadily. By 1850, 2.8 million slaves worked on farms and plantations; another 400 000 slaves lived in urban settings (Hopper and Milburn, 1996: 126).

The brutal slave system caused many slaves to commit suicide and, in increasing numbers, many slaves ran away. But textbooks describing the history of American homeless do not include runaway slaves as homeless – yet they were. Runaway slaves lived in the forests, mountains, and swamps of the South (Franklin and Moss, 1994: 143). Northern antislavery groups helped the homeless runaway slaves travel north by creating what was called an underground railroad (Strother, 1962: 5), and during this period, Native Americans also often provided a safe haven for homeless blacks who fled to the frontier to escape slavery or oppressive laws (*Editors of Ebony*, 1971). As many as 100 000 slaves ran away during the early nineteenth century.

As evidence that runway slaves were considered by their contemporaries to be 'homeless', the earliest New York City poorhouses, the places that housed the white homeless in the mid-eighteenth century, also housed the runaway slave (Mary Booth, *History of the City of New York*, 1859: 347 in Hopper and Milburn, 1996: 124).

The Civil War

The American Civil War not only promised freedom but it also caused great suffering and created an enormous problem of black homelessness. While the war was on, hundreds of thousands of African Americans sought refuge, protection, and help from the Union troops; but the Union soldiers were able to help just a small fraction of them.

Orders issued by General Ulysses S. Grant enabled runaway slaves to be put to work by the Army and to be provided shelter and food. But the Army could not accommodate the demand. Homeless camps of former slaves exploded throughout the Union lines (Slaughter, 1969: 35).

By the end of the war, most newly freed slaves were basically homeless. Their near starvation and miserable plight were described as 'hopeless' and 'lamentable'. They were perishing from lack of shelter as they crowded into Southern cities and former army camps (Slaughter, 1969: 91). At this time, estimates of the number of homeless black Americans scattered all throughout the South ranged from one million to four million (p. 92).

The Freedmen's Bureau, a government tool of the Reconstruction period, failed to bring employment and family-owned farms to former slaves. The newly freed blacks were left without means and were forced into contracts, usually with their former slave masters, to work the land as they had before. But their contracts provided no guarantee of shelter or health provisions and many of them remained homeless (Wharton in Foner, 1970: 208).

During this crucial period, the foundation of African American economic dependence as tenant farmers and day laborers was established (Mandel, 1992: 33, 39). In fact, the post Civil War period set the groundwork for creating a permanent class of black homeless migrant workers who emerged during the 1930s Great Depression.

Cowboys and Tramps

Tales of American cowboys may seem lofty and legendary, but cowboys are also considered part of America's vagabond and homeless history (Baum and Burnes 1993: 94; Miller, 1991: ch. 2). Black cowboys have usually been left out of the American cowboy narrative, but during and just after the Civil War, thousands of African American men, slave and free, left their communities for the homeless life of the cowboy. They came from many Southern states, but most came from Texas. Durham and Jones say that black cowboys may have numbered as many as 5000 (1965: 117).

Black cowboys drove millions of herds of cattle and they lived a dangerous life (p. 1), driving through the unmapped lands and the rough terrains of the developing states. Black cowboys rode the trails along with Mexicans and Native Americans but they also joined white cowboys to ride into the brush to hunt for wild cattle (p. 25).

The decades between the Civil War and the First World War mark the period of 'men on the tramp'. Blacks also participated in the American tramping experience, although they are usually left out of its historic descriptions. It was the heyday for the movements of millions of rootless and homeless male transient and seasonal workers. The new term 'tramp' was first used after the Civil War to refer to men who were without home and without family.

Mostly, tramps were on the road in search of work and their numbers were astounding – at one time tramps represented 7% of the entire American population. "In 1873–1874 the American population was about 40 million people, three million of these people were thought to be tramps" (Ringenbach, 1973: 11). The country's expansion and growth had "created a need for men – all kinds of men; men to work the mines, and log, and punch cows, and reap crops, and build railroads – 200,000 miles of railroads" (Miller, 1991: xix).

Winter brought many homeless tramping men into the cities. By the turn of the century, every city had a well-established area where its homeless men congregated, ate, and slept. These areas were sometimes referred to as 'skid rows' (the term derived from Seattle's skid road), but tramps more commonly referred to them as 'the main stem' (Schneider, 1986: 169–173).

According to Hopper and Milburn, "in the late 19th-century... available records show that African Americans were a significant presence among arrested tramps, lodging house residents, and transients in cities as diverse as Philadelphia, Kansas City, and Washington D.C." (p. 124). Furthermore, "African American men make frequent appearances in road memoirs of this period..." (p. 124). In general, however, historians have tended to overlook black tramps when writing about this period.

We do know that it was harder for African American tramps to survive, because even in this context they were less socially accepted (Ringenbach, 1973). Black tramps found it more difficult to find lodging in the few areas that would accommodate tramps, and it was harder for black men to get assistance from passersby by begging. Nevertheless, it appears that blacks were tramping in sizable numbers. A great many tramps ended up in New York City where there were as many as "450,000 [homeless] people lodged by the police station houses during the winter of 1874 to 1875". Because New York attracted so many homeless African Americans, New York City was sometimes referred to as the 'Black Hole of Calcutta'.

The Migration North

Southern black Americans started moving to the north in the aftermath of the Civil War. Sixty thousand migrated north between 1870 and 1880, 70 000 the following decade, and 168 000 between 1890 and 1900 (Mandel, 1992: 26). Many more followed.

Black migrants sought agricultural work in New Jersey and the state "received more of those migrants than any other state" (p. 33). So many African Americans migrated to New Jersey, the state was called the 'Georgia of the North'. The city of Chicago also received large numbers of black migrants. Chicago meat packers had actively recruited Southern blacks and Chicago's 'Southside' was called 'North Mississippi'. By 1970, seven million African Americans had moved from the rural South to cities in the North.

Two factors – scarcity and location – made finding shelter difficult for the newly arriving blacks. In terms of scarcity, blacks competed with the thousands of European immigrants who were also putting pressure on the housing supply. But the housing stock was further reduced for the Southern migrants because they were black. Due to residential segregation, available housing was even scarcer (Massey and Denton, 1993).

A second factor that had an impact on available shelter and caused overcrowding was location. The black migrants usually needed to live close to the center of the town because the new arrivals provided services to the rich in the central core. Philadelphia is a good example. The work most African-Americans did, according to W.E.B. Du Bois, was as "purveyors to the rich – working in private houses, in hotels, large stores, etc." (1973: 296). In Philadelphia's seventh ward, where approximately one quarter of all the blacks in the city lived (p. 58), there was so much overcrowding that as many as 10 persons were living in a single room.

Limited supply of available housing for blacks drove prices up. By 1910, 40 000 black people lived in Philadelphia and their rent for housing sometimes represented three-fourths of the family's total income. For many, the solution was to sublet or create boarding house-type arrangements (Du Bois, 1973; ch. xv). That is how about half of those living in Philadelphia's black seventh ward were able to pay a low $10 or less for rent per month.

In Chicago, scarcity also affected housing options. According to city records, on a single day in 1918, there were 664 African-American applications submitted for only 55 housing units. At that time, there were places in Chicago where up to six black families lived in apartment units designed for only one family. The African-American homeless male transients in Chicago were also restricted to segregated "colored men's hotels" (Hopper, Milburn, 1996: 124).

This housing situation was a recipe for widespread homelessness. It caused many of the black migrants to become what is currently referred to as 'protohomeless' (Wolch and Dear, 1993: Introduction). But although they were on the verge of homelessness, it appears that black homelessness even under these conditions was proportionately low.

In Philadelphia, for example, while the total annual number of transients applying to sleep in the police station house more than tripled between 1891 and 1896 (rising from nearly 14 000 to 46 000), the percentages of homeless black applicants during the same period only doubled from 2.7 to 5% (Du Bois, 1973: 271). As for those arrested for vagrancy (homelessness) in Philadelphia between 1887 and 1896 (600 per year), the percentage of black arrests stayed at under 10% of the total (p. 271). Albeit blacks were only 3.76% of Philadelphia's population, but fewer than 10% vagrancy arrest rate should be considered low because blacks were more likely to be arrested for vagrancy than whites.

Affordable housing was scarce and blacks competed for their limited supply. What today is called 'doubling up' and 'tripling up' was the rule not the exception. What is surprising is not that there was black homelessness at that time, but that there was so little of it considering the challenges these migrants faced.

Using data from Philadelphia's seventh ward during the 1890s, Du Bois noted that Negroes were 4% of the population but furnished 8% of the very poor. He commented on this disparity by suggesting that "[c]onsidering the economic difficulties of the Negro" one would expect an even higher percentage of people who were in need and asking for help (Du Bois, 1973: 273). Although they were stressed and challenged, this data reflects the resiliency of these black Americans.

The Depression Years and the New Deal

Blacks were hit earliest and most severely by the economic collapse of the Great Depression which produced widespread hardship and homelessness. In many Northern cities, there were a substantial number of blacks who were homeless. "By the winter of 1932–1933, nearly one-quarter of Philadelphia's homeless transients were black, as were one-tenth of Chicago's sheltered men, one-fifth of Buffalo's [non-seaman]... transients, and one-sixth of New York City's public shelter clientele" (Hopper and Milburn, 1996: 124). In all these cities, the percentage of black homeless was higher than the percentage of blacks in the population as a whole, although not by much in the case of Chicago. (According to census data, in 1930, in Philadelphia, blacks were 11% of the population; in Chicago, blacks were 6.9% of the population; in Buffalo, blacks were 2% of the population; and in New York City, they comprised 4.7%.)

During the Depression, African-Americans suffered because they were poorly paid marginal workers, because they were unemployed, and also because they were discriminated against in public and private assistance. Blacks were excluded from many privately run soup kitchens, and unemployed black families received less assistance than whites (Foner, 1970: 388). New Deal programmes also discriminated against blacks in employment practices and in their services and benefits. Examples of discriminatory practices include the National Recovery Act (NRA), the Tennessee Valley Authority (TVA), and the Works Project Administration (WPA).

The New Deal's Agricultural Adjustment Act (AAA) programme had a unique impact directly causing black tenants to become homeless. The AAA authorised payments to farm owners who pledged to plant less, thus raising the price of their produce. Less produce, however, required fewer workers and that forced tenant farmers off the land to become migrant workers and day labourers. During the 1930s, fully 192 000 fully farm tenant workers were displaced (p. 79).

Many black tenant farmers were literally homeless; a roof meant just a sheet of tin or metal, or even just a large tree. Some relief officials rationalised black homelessness as acceptable because they felt that blacks should feel comfortable living outdoors (Franklin, 1985). Day labourers became cheap temporary workers, and some were forced into moving for seasonal work.

In Georgia, during the 1930s, after thousands of their poor black tenant farmers and farm labourers were evicted and unemployed, having few options, many were pressured to migrate to Florida and New Jersey as seasonal farmworkers who were paid as low as three cents per field bag (Hahamovitch, 1997: 134).

Thousands from Georgia migrated year-round. They were homeless: they were "permanent transients who had no sharecrop arrangement to return to, no state of residence, and no home to speak of" (pp. 114, 115). According to the Florida Industrial Commission, by 1940, 40 000–60 000 of these homeless farm labour migrants were coming to Florida annually (p. 125).

During the Depression, the combination of evictions from land and home, seasonal, unreliable, underpaid work, and local white control of any possible federal relief made the rural black American vulnerable to starvation and homelessness. During the Depression, while Northern cities at least provided some public shelter for many of their impoverished black citizens, the rural South seemed to make no such commitment.

Urban Renewal

The mid-twentieth-century Urban Renewal policy contributed to black homelessness by design. Its underlying goal was to beautify cities and remove urban blight which would presumably improve housing. Ironically, although Urban Renewal was presented as a pillar of the War on Poverty, it was in many ways a war on the poor.

The process of urban renewal contributed to black homelessness by reducing the number of affordable housing units available to them. Almost two-thirds of the slum units that were removed were occupied by blacks; once cleared out, shopping malls, highways, and downtown luxury high-rise apartments replaced those units and blacks were forced to double up in housing units in the remaining slum areas (Bellush and Hausknecht, 1967: 467). A 1961 study of urban renewal projects in 41 cities showed that 60% of the dispossessed tenants were moved into other slums (p. 467). Urban renewal occasionally even created new ghettoes – when too many tenants crowded into one area and the buildings and the area deteriorated rapidly.

Only one-half of 1% of all federal expenditures for urban renewal between 1949 and 1964 was spent on relocation of families and individuals (p. 468). Because African Americans were hit hardest in urban renewal, many blacks nicknamed urban renewal 'Negro Clearance'.

By 1967, urban renewal had destroyed 404 000 housing units, most of which had been occupied by poor families. Only a small fraction, 41 580 housing units, was built and provided as replacements (Friedland in Squires, 1994: 100). African Americans who lost their homes were not only not able to afford the fancy luxury apartments that replaced them, but they were also not able to buy moderately priced homes in the suburbs.

Segregation policy prevented blacks from taking advantage of the Federal Housing Administration (FHA) and Veterans Administration (VA) loan financing. The suburbs were white and it was post-Second World War policy, articulated in the 1950s, that property should be occupied by the same racial and social classes. In fact, the FHA issued a warning prohibiting housing "inharmonious racial groups or nationality groups" (Jackson, 1985: 208 in Squires, 1994: 101). This blatant segregationist policy was applied at a crucial time for home ownership when there was suburban affordable housing being developed. These lending policies made it difficult for African Americans to become property owners in significant numbers.

Urban renewal, by reducing available affordable housing for African Americans, increased the number of African Americans who were precariously doubled up and tripled up in crowded apartments. While mid-twentieth century was a period of general economic prosperity, the number of African Americans on skid rows increased.

Skid row-type areas emerged at the turn of the century during the tramping years as places of residence for homeless and nearly homeless men. During the post-Second World War period, there was an increase of African American men present in these areas. Their proportion ranged from 9 to 40%. Although race-specific data are not always available, field workers in the New York's skid row area, the Bowery, did report a substantial number of African American men to be present on the Bowery in 1964 (29%), and even more in 1968 (33%) (pp. 124, 125).

As high as these numbers may seem, blacks were generally present in smaller proportions than poverty and unemployment figures would predict (Bahr, 1973: 105). For researchers, the discrepancy is attributable to the "robust networks of support (both kin-based and neighborhood-based) that had long characterized black communities in Northern cities" (Hopper and Milburn in Baumohl, 1996: 124). Du Bois, already referenced, also commented on the resilience of the black community during the Northern migration.

Deindustrialisation of the Economy

Starting in the 1970s, the United States began to lose its strong industrial base. Factories closed or moved to foreign shores because of changes in international finance and trade and due to cheap imports that reduced demand for more expensive American-made products.

Jennifer Wolch and Michael Dear described the effects of these economic changes especially on the blue-collar worker. "The declining fortunes of the traditional manufacturing sector", they wrote, "involved wave after wave of plant closures.... Over 10 million jobs were lost nationally because of closures or decreased product demand between 1979 and 1985...and well over one million jobs *net* were lost in the manufacturing sector during the Reagan presidency alone" (1993: 4). Blacks were a significant part of the industrial-based blue-collar sector. In 1969, 43% of blacks were blue-collar workers as compared to 35.5% of whites (U.S. Bureau of the Census, *Statistical Abstract of the United States 91*, 1970: 226).

America's industrial economy had been based on factory assembly line production called 'Fordism'. The industrial economy was able to offer secure jobs, good salaries, and union protection to millions of noncollege graduates. But the industrial-based economy was now being replaced with a growing service economy (post-Fordism).

This economic transformation from industrial to service was directly linked to the dramatic rise in American homelessness (Wolch and Dear, 1993: Introduction). When the manufacturing sector gave way to the service economy, while many at the top end of the service economy were paid handsomely, the majority of service sector jobs were poorly paid. In fact, "[b]etween 1979 and 1984, 44 percent of the net new jobs created paid poverty-level wages" and "[o]ver three-quarters of the new jobs created during the 1980s were at minimum-wage levels" (p. 7).

But the shift to post-Fordism was not only a shift to a service economy. It marked a change in the way business did business. "Firms in both manufacturing and services reorganized their employment practices, hiring part-time workers to avoid paying fringe benefits and taxes, [and] categorizing jobs as temporary to forestall claims on seniority ..." (p. 5). These changes were among the important factors that contributed to rates of long-term joblessness among traditional blue-collar workers, especially African American males (US Department of Housing and Urban Development 1994: 27; Wolch and Dear, 1993: 6).

In sum, American economic restructuring significantly reduced the number of well-paid blue-collar jobs. It also significantly reduced job security and wage protection. The African American community was especially vulnerable to feeling the effects of these shifts. These changes followed, after all, on the heels of decades of Urban Renewal policies that significantly reduced the numbers of affordable and available housing units. Because of deindustrialisation, good jobs were scarcer, and because of urban renewal, so were apartments. Then came crack cocaine.

Crack Cocaine

Crack cocaine "made its debut in the New York area in 1984...soon spread across the country, becoming a major substance of abuse within the general population..." (Shaw et al., 1999). But the numbers of homeless African Americans were rising before crack cocaine hit the streets of the inner cities. By the early 1980s (before crack), black men made up the majority of the residents in New York City's public shelters. Other cities reflected the same trend. It was also reported in 1982 (before crack) that "[i]n 17 studies of homeless *women* (mostly in shelters), at least half were minority women, most of whom were mothers with an average of two children" (Hopper and Milburn, 1996).

By the mid-1980s, because the use of crack cocaine was becoming prevalent as the number of homeless people escalated, crack cocaine has been considered another contributor to homelessness. Heavy drug use can cause people to be homeless if it makes "marginally employable adults even less employable, eats up money that would otherwise be available to pay rent, and makes... friends and relatives less willing to shelter" a drug user (Jencks, 1994: 44).

In interviews, even the homeless themselves have suggested the link between crack cocaine and homelessness (Chitwood et al., 1996: 107). The dysfunctionality of drug users continually tested the black extended family and kinship networks; the drug-related ancillary problems concerning health, crime, and incarceration stretched the resilience of an already taxed black community.

Conclusion

As we have seen, through the many decades of American history, blacks have been poor and they have been challenged by very difficult circumstances. Nevertheless, after the Civil War, while some blacks were homeless, there were not usually the large numbers of black homeless that one might expect given the challenges they faced. The resilience of the community seemed to keep them connected. An unfortunate confluence of factors would change this.

In the 1950s and 1960s, urban renewal reduced the number of affordable housing units for the poor and especially for blacks. Then, starting in the 1970s, America's industrial base was eroded and instead of well-paid union jobs, an emerging service economy was producing mostly unprotected part-time and low-paying jobs. This economic transformation had a disproportionate impact on blacks. Add to all of this the introduction of crack cocaine in the mid-1980s and you have the perfect storm creating a dramatic rise in black homelessness. Today, approximately half of all homeless people in America are black (Kwateng 2007: 5A; US Department of Housing and Urban Development, 2007: 31).

See also: Ghetto; Home and Homelessness; Policies to Address Redlining; Residential Segregation; Residential Segregation: Apartheid; Slums.

References

Bahr H (1973) *Skid Row: An Introduction to Disaffiliation*. Oxford: University Press.

Baum A and Burnes D (1993) *A Nation in Denial*. Boulder, CO: Westview Press.

Baumohl J (ed.) (1996) *Homelessness in America* (for the National Coalition for the Homeless). Phoenix, AZ: Oryx Press.

Bellush J and Hausknecht M (1967) *Urban Renewal: People, Politics, and Planning*. Garden City, NY: Anchor Books.

Chitwood DD, Rivers JE, and Inciardi JA, and The South Florida AIDS Research Consortium (1996) *The American Pipe Dream: Crack Cocaine and the Inner City*, pp. 104–114. Fort Worth, TX: Harcourt Brace College Publishers.

Du Bois WEB (1973) *The Philadelphia Negro*. Millwood, NY: Kraus Thomson Organization Limited.

Durham P and Jones E (1965) *The Negro Cowboys*. New York: Dodd, Mead, & Company.

Editors of Ebony (1971) *Ebony Pictorial History of Black America, Vol 1: African Past to Civil War*. Chicago, IL: Johnson Publishing Company.

Franklin JH and Moss AA (1994) *From Slavery to Freedom, a History of African Americans*. New York: McGraw-Hill Inc.

Franklin M (1985) *Organizing for Survival and Change: Rural Southern Blacks & the Works Progress Administration 1935–1939*. Hampshire College, Division III Independent Study, School of Social Science (unpublished).

Foner E (1970) *'Black Reconstruction' America's Black Past*. New York: Harper and Row.

Hahamovitch C (1997) *The Fruits of Their Labor: Atlantic Coast Farmworkers and the Making of Migrant Poverty, 1870–1945*. Chapel Hill, NC: The University of North Carolina Press.

Hopper K and Milburn NG (1996) Homelessness among African-Americans: A historical and contemporary perspective. In: Baumohl J (ed.) *Homelessness in America*, pp. 123–131. Phoenix, AZ: Oryx Press.

Jencks C (1994) *The Homeless*. Cambridge, MA: Harvard University Press.

Kwateng D (2007) Blacks make up large amount of U.S. homeless population. *Miami Times* 84(23): 5A.

Mandel J (1992) *Not Slave, Not Free: The African American Economic Experience Since the Civil War*. Durham, NC: Duke University Press.

Massey DS and Denton NA (1993) *American Apartheid: Segregation and the Making of the Underclass*. Cambridge, MA: Harvard University Press.

Miller H (1991) *On the Fringe: The Dispossessed in America*. Lexington, MA: Lexington Books.

Ringenbach P (1973) *Tramps and Reformers 1873–1916: The Discovery of Unemployment in New York*. Westport, CT: Greenwood Press.

Rossi P (1989) *Down and Out in America*. Chicago, IL: University of Chicago Press.

Schneider J (1986) Skid row as an urban neighborhood: 1880–1960. In: Erickson J and Wilhelmer C (eds.) *Housing the Homeless*, pp. 167–189. New Brunswick, NJ: Center for Urban Policy Research.

Shaw VN, Hser Y-I, Anglin MD, and Boyle K (1999) Sequence of powder cocaine and crack use among arrestees in Los Angeles County. *American Journal of Drug and Alcohol Abuse* 25(1): 47–66.

Slaughter L (1969) *The Freedom of the South*. Cincinnati. Ohio: Elm Street Printing Co.

Squires G (1994) *Capital and Communities in Black and White: The Intersections of Race, Class, and Uneven Development*. Albany, NY: State University of New York Press.

Strother HT (1962) *The Underground Railroad in Connecticut*. Middletown, CT: Wesleyan University Press.

US Bureau of the Census (1970) *Statistical Abstract of the United States*, 91st annual edn.

US Department of Housing and Urban Development (1994) *Priority: Home! the Federal Plan to Break the Cycle of Homelessness*.May. [HUD-1454-CPD (1)]

US Department of Housing and Urban Development (2007) *The Annual Homeless Assessment Report to Congress*.

Wolch J and Dear M (1993) *Malign Neglect: Homelessness in an American City*. San Francisco, CA: Jossey-Bass Publishers.

Homeless People: Care Leavers

P Mendes, Monash University, Clayton, VIC, Australia
G Johnson, RMIT University, Melbourne, VIC, Australia

© 2012 Elsevier Ltd. All rights reserved.

Glossary

Corporate parent State-provided high-quality parenting to nurture and support children in care by providing stability and promoting resilience.
Foster care Where children are placed with appropriate care givers in their home. Foster care is available to children from birth to age 18.
Leaving care The cessation of legal responsibility by the state for young people living in out-of-home care.
Out-of-home care Where the state assumes a statutory responsibility for young people at risk of abuse or neglect in the family home.
Post-care support Services provided to care leavers who require assistance with their housing, health, education, employment, and social needs.
Transition to Independent Living Allowance (TILA) One-off financial payment of $1500 to disadvantaged care leavers making a transition to independent living.
Transitional accommodation Supported accommodation provided to young people for a period of up to 12 months.

Introduction

In Australia, 31 166 young people were in out-of-home care on 30 June 2008 (Australian Institute of Health and Welfare, 2009), an increase of nearly 10% from the previous year and more than double the number from a decade ago. The majority of children and young people are accommodated in foster care (53%) with 41% in relative or kinship care. The rest are in residential care. In recent years the number of children in kinship care has increased and there has been a marked reduction in the use of residential care (Australian Institute of Health and Welfare, 2009). The estimated recurrent expenditure on child protection and out-of-home care in Australia was $2 billion in 2007/2008, an increase of 13.5% from the previous year (Council of Australian Governments, 2009: 6, fn2).

About 1700 young people aged 15–17 years exit the Australian out-of-home care system each year (Australian Institute of Health and Welfare, 2009). While some return to the family home and others move into independent living, Australian research consistently depicts care leavers as being particularly disadvantaged and as having significantly reduced life chances. Compared to most young people, they face particular difficulties in accessing educational, employment, housing, and other developmental opportunities. Care leavers have been found to experience significant health, social, and educational deficits including homelessness, involvement in juvenile crime and prostitution, mental and physical health problems, poor educational and employment outcomes, inadequate social support systems, and early parenthood.

This is not to suggest that there is a simple causal relationship between any experiences of state care and poor future outcomes. Care leavers are a heterogeneous group and they have varied backgrounds and experiences in terms of the type and extent of abuse or neglect, the age they enter care, their cultural and ethnic backgrounds, their in-care experiences, their developmental stage and needs when exiting care, and the quantity and quality of supports available to them. However, it is the structural disadvantages experienced by care leavers compared to other young people that leave them more vulnerable to poor outcomes. Three factors in particular stand out.

First, many have experienced and are still recovering from considerable physical, sexual, or emotional abuse or neglect prior to entering care including exposure to substance abuse, family violence, and mental illness. These experiences are highly traumatic, and may contribute to ongoing social and emotional disturbances, developmental delay, and significant behavioural difficulties compared to children and young people from a supportive family background.

Second, many young people have experienced inadequacies in state care including poor-quality caregivers and constant shifts of placement, carers, schools, and workers. Some have also experienced overt abuse including sexual and physical assault and emotional maltreatment. This lack of stability, continuity, and consistency undermines their social and educational/training opportunities, and hinders their capacity to make a successful transition towards independence following their discharge from care. The issue of emotional security, or what Cashmore and Paxman (2006) term "felt security," is one of the most significant indicators of how well young people fare after they leave care. They found that while stability and the number of placements were significant, "felt security in care was a more significant predictor of long-term outcomes" (p. 21). Children who experience supportive and stable placements including an ongoing positive relationship with social workers and significant others are far more likely to overcome the adversities resulting from their pre-care and in-care experiences and prosper when they leave care.

Third, many care leavers can call on little, if any, direct family support or other community networks to ease their involvement into independent living (Johnson et al., 2010). In addition to these disadvantages, many young people experience an abrupt end to the formal support networks of state care between 16–18 years of age. Care leavers are expected to transition directly from childhood dependence to adult self-sufficiency. In contrast, these days most young people experience a delayed adulthood whereby they continue to live with their parents until their mid-20s, often after several attempts to leave the family home. This highlights the point that young people's transition to independent living has changed. No longer is leaving home a linear process, but one that is more effectively understood as a process of achieving interdependence that takes place over time and within "the context of larger interdependent social networks, connection, [and] collaboration" (Green et al., 2007: 63). In this context, the state as a corporate parent often fails to provide the ongoing financial, social, and emotional support and nurturing offered by most families of origin. The ending of support crucially coincides with either the final years of schooling or the beginning of attempts to gain employment.

While the cost to individual care leavers is high, so are the costs to the community. A recent study by the Department of Families, Housing, Community Services and Indigenous Affairs suggested that just over half of all care leavers go on to be heavy service users throughout their lives (Morgan Disney Associates and Applied Economics, 2006). They estimate the additional lifetime costs to the community of a cohort of 1150 people who have left care to be around $2 billion or $46 million per annum. In contrast, the equivalent costs for the same number of people in the general community are estimated to be $3.3 million per annum.

Housing is a particularly important dimension in the experiences of care leavers and policy responses to their needs. The provision of safe, secure, and affordable accommodation is a crucial component of any successful transition from care to independent living, and is closely linked to positive outcomes in health, social connections, education, and employment. For care leavers accessing and maintaining accommodation is one of the most challenging tasks they confront and in Australia there are few housing options available for care leavers. As a result, many care leavers experience housing instability and homelessness that is linked to other negative outcomes such as drug and alcohol abuse, poor mental and physical health, involvement in the youth justice system, and educational and employment deficits.

Housing Instability, Homelessness, and State Care

Numerous studies in Australia have found a high correlation between state care and later housing instability, transience, and homelessness. The Human Rights and Equal Opportunity Commission's report *Our Homeless Children* was one of the first to identify that a large number of homeless young people came from state care backgrounds (Human Rights and Equal Opportunity Commission, 1989). Since then research has repeatedly confirmed the strong link between state care experiences and poor housing outcomes, including homelessness (Cashmore and Paxman, 2007; Hirst, 1989; Johnson and Chamberlain, 2008; National Youth Commission, 2008; Taylor, 1990). The Federal Government's white paper on homelessness, *The Road Home* (FaHCSIA, 2008), acknowledged that care leavers were a particularly vulnerable group due to the lack of support provided during their transition from care to independent living. Researchers and NGOs have urged both State and Federal Governments to introduce a universal needs-based leaving care entitlement up to the age of 24 in order to support care leavers to maintain their accommodation, prevent homelessness, and improve their opportunities to participate in mainstream life.

Factors that Contribute to these Poor Outcomes

A number of factors are thought to contribute to care leavers' poor outcomes. The high mobility of many young people while in care is closely associated with instability after care. Also linked to poor outcomes are the unplanned and unprepared nature of many departures from state care, unsuccessful attempts at reunification with the family of origin, the absence of sufficient personal and social skills such as shopping, cooking, and budgeting required to live independently, experiences of loneliness and social isolation, minimal education, and poor employment opportunities. In addition, care leavers often experience relationship breakdowns with their partners or friends, exposure to violence or harassment, eviction, poor-quality accommodation or living in an unsafe area, involvement in offending or substance abuse, mental health problems, and the lack of an option to "return home" or "backtrack" if the initial independent living arrangements do not work out (Cashmore and Paxman, 1996, 2007).

In Australia, there are limited accommodation options for care leavers. Cashmore and Paxman (1996) found that the most common arrangement care leavers 'exited' to was shared accommodation followed by living with siblings or friends on a temporary basis. They also found that the largest single reason for instability (accounting for nearly half of all housing breakdowns) occurred as a result of conflict between tenants.

Affordability problems also influence the housing choices that are available when young people leave care. Due to a shortage of affordable accommodation, many care leavers are forced to accept poor-quality permanent accommodation. Poor-quality accommodation is linked to a range of negative outcomes including poor health, lower self-esteem, diminished social networks, and housing instability (Biehal and Wade, 1999; Walker et al., 2002). Care leavers are often forced to accept accommodation in areas where they have few connections and that are removed from transport, shopping, and employment opportunities. Moving to a new area may provide some young people with a 'fresh start' (Walker et al., 2002: 182). However, in general, moving to a new area presents difficulties in "building up support" networks and more often than not, young people are at greater risk of housing instability when they are "dislocated from their home area" (p. 182).

Specific concern has also been expressed that care leavers are expected to rely on inappropriate accommodation programmes that were actually designed as short- to medium-term transitional housing programmes, with a significant component for those who are already homeless or escaping from domestic violence. For example, the Australian Institute of Health and Welfare (2003) found that 200 young Victorians aged 12–17 years, who were using homelessness services, had a Guardianship Order either at the beginning or end of their support period. In short, care leavers may transition directly from state out-of-home care into homelessness.

These concerns have been recognised by most States and Territories that have introduced specialist leaving care and after-care programmes and supports including some housing programmes. It was also directly recognized in the Labour Government's white paper on homelessness. *The Road Home* specifically identifies the prevention of young people leaving custodial and statutory care exiting into homelessness as a key goal (FaHCSIA, 2008). This commitment was reinforced in the COAG Child Protection Framework (Council of Australian Governments, 2009: 27), but the proposed targets seem to bear little resemblance to the number of young people who leave care each year.

Potential Reforms/Models that Would Contribute to Better Outcomes

Care leavers require a range of accommodation options to meet their differing needs that vary according to their care experiences, ethnicity, gender, contact with their families, degree of preparedness for independence, and any forms of disability (Frost and Stein, 1995).

UK authors argue that planning for better accommodation and support should include a thorough needs assessment given that some young people are not suited to living alone while others are not suited to sharing. In addition, offering young people a choice in the type and location of accommodation, preparing a contingency plan in case the proposed accommodation breaks down, and providing flexible financial and other supports are also viewed as critical elements in any effort to improve care leavers' outcomes (Broad, 2005; Stein and Wade, 2000; Wade and Dixon, 2006).

Australian authors recommend that public housing is made available on a priority basis to care leavers, establishing separate transitional units available only for care leavers, providing a housing subsidy to ensure care leavers pay no more than 25% of their income on housing, and providing assistance with the rental bond and establishment costs for setting up including the purchase of essentials such as bed, bedding, furniture, and a refrigerator and washing machine (Cashmore and Paxman, 2007; Centre for Excellence in Child and Family Welfare, 2006: 16; Johnson et al., 2010).

Given that 95% of the Australian children in care reside in home-based care – either foster care or kinship care – one obvious option would be to provide continuing financial support to maintain these placements. Where this is not possible, care leavers should be offered specific accommodation designed to meet their needs.

Recent Studies

Two recent Australian studies suggest some potential best practice support models. One study involved an evaluation of the St Luke's Anglicare Leaving Care and After Care Support Service (LCACSS) in rural Victoria which places a particularly strong emphasis on providing 'secure and safe housing' as a key component of their service. St Luke's was able to facilitate access for care leavers to a number of housing options including transitional units, public housing, private rental, private board arrangements, and head leased properties.

The evaluation was based primarily on individual interviews with 18 young people who were receiving support from the service. Most of the young people reported that they had been successful in attaining secure and stable accommodation. Some of the current housing arrangements include a student share house, boarding with ex-foster carers, renting a room in a private house, sharing with friends, owning accommodation with shared facilities, living with partners in private rental, living alone in a unit or apartment that can be associated with social isolation, and living with a parent or grandparent. However, a minority had experienced some housing problems. A few young people were residing in temporary accommodation and appeared to be quite transient. Nonetheless, the housing programme appears to have been instrumental in ensuring that most care leavers in Bendigo are able to access and maintain some form of stable housing (Mendes, 2009).

The other study interviewed 77 people aged between 18 and 25 who had left the out-of-home care system (Johnson et al., 2010). The study focused on their housing experiences since leaving care with the aim of identifying ways that care leavers' housing outcomes could be improved. The study found that those who left care at 18 had a smoother pathway into stable housing from care. Care leavers who graduate from care at a later age typically had fewer placements in care, were less likely to have substance abuse or mental health problems, were less likely to have experienced physical or sexual abuse prior to or while in care, and were more likely to have some reliable and consistent social relationships. However, the research found that over three quarters of the care leavers did not have a smooth transition from care with most experiencing acute residential instability and often homelessness. Many had secured accommodation at some stage since leaving care, but with limited social and economic resources the accommodation was often of poor quality and inappropriately located. Many of the young people who experienced a 'volatile' transition from care had left care early, in crisis and with little planning (Johnson et al., 2010).

The importance of leaving care planning has been highlighted in other studies as well. McDowall (2008: 43) found that while all states in Australia have articulated approaches to leaving care planning (albeit in slightly different ways), the way legislation has been implemented in each state has been uneven. For instance, McDowell found that 58% of the young people in their sample who had left care ($N=77$) "reported they did not have such a plan". Worse still, McDowell found that nearly two-thirds of those still in care but approaching discharge ($N=87$) "did not know of the existence of any leaving care plan" (McDowall, 2008: 43). The importance of leaving care plans was highlighted in Forbes, Inder, and Raman's (2006) study of 60 care leavers. They found that having a case plan was significantly associated with stable housing on leaving care. Young people with such a plan were twice as likely to be in stable housing, three times more likely to be employed and reported that receiving a range of advice and support "significantly improved outcomes" (p. 28).

Conclusion

For most young people the transition to adulthood is a process that takes place over time. The majority of young people are supported through this process by their family and friends. For many young people it is a time when relationships with their family start to change. Many young people seek greater independence and autonomy from their families, but families remain important nevertheless.

Research demonstrates that the age young people leave the family home has steadily increased over the last two decades. By staying in the family home, young people benefit from ongoing financial and emotional support in addition to enjoying the benefits of a stable, secure home. It has been estimated that up to two-thirds of young people return home at least once to save money or if things don't work out.

In contrast, leaving the care of the state is a 'final event' (Stein, 2006: 274). Young people leaving care often do so in an unplanned way and this can result in a sense of abandonment. This is particularly so for those aged between 15 and 17 years. While many people under the age of 15 return to the family home when they leave care, for those aged between 15 and 17 and who are still in the out-of-home care system, there is often no family home to return to. Not only do young people leaving care often have little family support, they typically have few financial resources to draw upon, have minimal life skills, and lower educational attainment; they often suffer from low self-esteem and have to deal with the emotional trauma of abuse or neglect. What is a difficult period for most young people is doubly so for many care leavers. As Stein (2006: 274) notes:

> Care leavers are expected to undertake the journey to adulthood, from restricted to full citizenship, far younger and in far less time than their peers.

For care leavers the provision of appropriate affordable housing is critical. Without good housing, the risk of becoming homeless is high. When care leavers become homeless their situation often gets far worse and more complex and costly to resolve. Post-care support systems that include housing are essential to prevent this happening.

See also: Homeless People: Care Leavers in the United Kingdom.

References

Australian Institute of Health and Welfare (2003) *Young Homeless People in Australia 2001–02*. Canberra, ACT: AIHW.

Australian Institute of Health and Welfare (2009) *Child Protection Australia 2007–2008*. Canberra, ACT: AIHW. Cat No. CWS 33.

Biehal N and Wade J (1999) I thought it would be easier: The early housing careers of young people leaving care. In: Rugg J (ed.) *Young People, Housing and Social Policy*, pp. 79–92. London: Routledge.

Broad B (2005) *Improving the Health and Well Being of Young People Leaving Care*. Dorset: Russell House Publishing.

Cashmore J and Paxman M (1996) *Longitudinal Study of Wards Leaving Care*. Sydney: University of New South Wales, Social Policy Research Centre.

Cashmore J and Paxman M (2006) Predicting after-care outcomes: The importance of 'felt' security. *Child and Family Social Work* 11: 232–241.

Cashmore J and Paxman M (2007) *Longitudinal Study of Wards Leaving Care: Four to Five Years on*. Sydney, NSW: Social Policy Research Centre.

Centre for Excellence in Child and Family Welfare (2006) *Leaving Care: A Model for Victoria*. Melbourne, VIC: CECFW.

Council of Australian Governments (2009) *Protecting Children is Everyone's Business*. Canberra, ACT: Commonwealth of Australia.

FaHCSIA (2008) *The Road Home: A National Approach to Reducing Homelessness*. Canberra, ACT: Department of Families, Housing, Community Services and Indigenous Affairs.

Forbes C, Inder B, and Raman S (2006) Measuring the cost of leaving care in Victoria. *Children Australia* 31(3): 26–33.

Frost N and Stein M (1995) *Working with Young People Leaving Care*. London: HMSO.

Green M, Brueckner M, and Saggers S (2007) *Moving in and Moving on? Young People's Transition from Homelessness to Independent Living*. Centre for Social Research; Edith Cowan University.

Hirst C (1989) *Forced Exit: A Profile of the Young and Homeless in Inner Urban Melbourne*. Melbourne, VIC: The Salvation Army.

Human Rights and Equal Opportunity Commission (1989) *Our Homeless Children*. Canberra, ACT: Australian Government Publishing Service.

Johnson G and Chamberlain C (2008) From youth to adult homelessness. *Australian Journal of Social Issues* 43(4): 563–582.

Johnson G, Natalier N, Thoresen S, et al. (2010) *Housing Pathways from Care*. Melbourne, VIC: Australian Housing and Urban Research Institute.

McDowall J (2008) *Report Card: Transitioning from Care*. Sydney, NSW: Create Foundation.

Mendes P (2009) Moving from dependence to independence: A study of the experiences of 18 care leavers in a leaving care and after care support service in rural Victoria. Paper Presented to Asia Pacific Regional Conference on Child Abuse and Neglect. Perth, WA, 17 November.

Morgan Disney Associates and Applied Economics (2006) *Transition from Care: Avoidable Costs to Governments of Alternative Pathways of Young People Exiting the Formal Child Protection Care System in Australia, Vol. 1: Summary Report*. Canberra: Department of Family and Community Services and Indigenous Affairs.

National Youth Commission (2008) *Australia's Homeless Youth*. Melbourne, VIC: National Youth Commission.

Stein M (2006) Research review: Young people leaving care. *Child and Family Social Work* 11(3): 273–279.

Stein M and Wade J (2000) *Helping Care Leavers: Problems and Strategic Responses*. London: Department of Health.

Taylor J (1990) *Leaving Care and Homelessness*. Melbourne, VIC: Brotherhood of St Laurence.

Wade J and Dixon J (2006) Making a home, finding a job: Investigating early housing and employment outcomes for young people leaving care. *Child and Family Social Work* 11: 199–208.

Walker M, Hill M, and Triseliotis J (2002) *Testing the Limits of Foster Care: Fostering as an Alternative to Secure Accommodation*. London: British Association for Adoption and Fostering.

Further Reading

Cashmore J and Mendes P (2008) Australia. In: Stein M and Munro E (eds.) *Young People's Transitions from Care to Adulthood: International Research and Practice*, pp. 23–35. London: Jessica Kingsley Publishers.

Frederick J and Goddard C (2006) Pathways to and from state care: The experiences of eight young people. *Children Australia* 31(3): 34–41.

Green S and Jones A (1999) Improving outcomes for young people leaving care: Which way forward? *Children Australia* 24(4): 64–68.

House of Representatives (1995) *A Report on Aspects of Youth Homelessness*. Canberra, ACT: Australian Government Publishing Service.

Johnson G, Natalier K, Bailey N, et al. (2009) *Improving Housing Outcomes for Young People Leaving State Care*. Melbourne, VIC: Australian Housing and Urban Research Institute.

Maunders D, Liddell M, Liddell M, and Green S (1999) *Young People Leaving Care and Protection*. Hobart, TAS: National Youth Affairs Research Scheme.

Mendes P (2005) Graduating from the child welfare system. *Journal of Social Work* 5(2): 155–171.

Mendes P and Moslehuddin B (2004) Graduating from the child welfare system: A comparison of the UK and Australian leaving care debates. *International Journal of Social Welfare* 13: 332–339.

Moslehuddin B and Mendes P (2006) Young people's journey to independence: Towards a better future for young people leaving state care in Victoria. *Children Australia* 3(3): 47–54.

Reid C (2007) The transition from state care to adulthood: International examples of best practices. *New Directions for Youth Development* Spring(113): 33–49.

Tweddle A (2007) Youth leaving care: How do they fare? *New Directions for Youth Development* Spring(113): 15–31.

Homeless People: Care Leavers in the United Kingdom

C Baker and S Baxter, National Care Advisory Service, London, UK

© 2012 Elsevier Ltd. All rights reserved.

Glossary

Care leaver In England, under the Children (Leaving Care) Act 2000, a care leaver is a young person who was in care for at least 13 weeks after their fourteenth birthday including at least 1 day between 16 and 18.

Eligible child Child aged 16 or 17 who has been looked after for at least 13 weeks since the age of 14 and who is still looked after – applies in England under the Children (Leaving Care) Act 2000.

Relevant child Child aged 16 or 17 who has been looked after for at least 13 weeks since the age of 14 and who has left care after – applies in England under the Children (Leaving Care) Act 2000.

Former relevant child Young person aged 18–21 (or until the end of agreed programme of education or training) who were previously 'eligible' or 'relevant' after – applies in England under the Children (Leaving Care) Act 2000.

Qualifying child Any young person under 21 (or 24 if in education or training) who ceases to be looked after or accommodated in a variety of other settings, or privately fostered, after the age of 16 after – applies in England under the Children (Leaving Care) Act 2000.

Unaccompanied asylum-seeking child Children under the age of 18 who arrive in the United Kingdom seeking asylum and arrive unaccompanied/without a responsible adult to care for them.

Introduction

This article describes the current arrangements for supporting care leavers in the United Kingdom. It examines the main accommodation pathways taken by young people as they make the transition from care, outlines local authority responsibilities, and highlights problems with the current arrangements. In conclusion, the article will reflect on what could improve young people's ability to secure and maintain appropriate accommodation.

Children in and Leaving Care in the United Kingdom

In the United Kingdom the latest figures (2008) show there are around 81 500 young people in the care of their respective local authorities at any one time. England is the largest country and has the largest actual number of children in care. Scotland has the highest rate of children in care, in part explained by the Scottish practice of including in the statistics children who are on supervision orders but placed at home with their parents (these children would not be counted as looked after in the rest of the United Kingdom). In all four countries the policy is to keep to a minimum the number of young people entering care and to limit the time they spend in care. If young people do need to remain in the care system then the aim is to provide them with stability and help those who leave the system in their transition to adulthood.

Information on England (2008) shows that the majority of the 59 500 young people in care entered the system due to reasons of abuse or neglect (62%); others for reasons of family dysfunction (11%), family in acute stress (8%), or the child's disability (4%) – the percentages have changed little over the last 5 years. Most children and young people live in foster care (71%) with a much smaller proportion (14%) in residential care and less than one in ten (8%) placed at home with parents. The most common point at which children become looked after (39%) is between the ages of 10 and 15; compared with around a fifth (19%) entering aged 1–4 or under 1, 15% aged 5–9, and 10% aged 16 or over.

Many children enter care for short periods of time: One study showed that nearly a third of those who ceased to be looked after in a year had spent less than a month in care and just under half leave the care system within a year of arrival. Once a child has been looked after for a year or more, the chance of leaving within the next year is low.

In England, the care population contains a group of (3500 in 2008) unaccompanied asylum-seeking children (UASC) who represent 6% of the total number. These young people tend to be concentrated in local authorities in London and the southeast of England. As a group they are mostly male, older, and unlikely to exit the care system for the reasons others leave, such as return to family or adoption, and so as a group they are likely to become care leavers. UASC are entitled to services from their local authority under the leaving care legislation after they are 18. Many UASC, however, face the uncertainty of not knowing what decision will be made about their immigration status, which leads to difficulties in accessing appropriate accommodation and other support.

Every year in the United Kingdom approximately 10 500 leave care aged 16 or over to live independently: 8300 in England; 477 in Wales; 306 in Northern Ireland; and 1486 in Scotland (those who were beyond minimum school-leaving age) (2008). For young people who have been in care for a specified amount of time (see glossary for definition of care leaver), there is a duty on the local authority to support and prepare them for the transition to adult life and a legislative framework to support this.

Legal and Policy Framework

The legislative base for leaving care differs across the United Kingdom. The Children Act 1989 remains the general legal framework for young people in and leaving care in England and Wales. In Northern Ireland the Children (Northern Ireland) Order 1995 and in Scotland the Children (Scotland) Act 1995 brought in similar changes. In England the main leaving care provisions were enshrined in Section 24 of the Children Act 1989 and its associated guidance (1991). Local authorities were given a duty to prepare young people for the time when they stop being in care. Some authorities used Section 24 funds to develop specialist leaving care schemes; evidence from inspections suggested that such developments were uneven with considerable variation in services both within and between local authorities.

Subsequently, the Children Act 1989 has been amended and supplemented by the Children (Leaving Care) Act 2000 and associated regulation and guidance. This legislation in England and Wales provided important new entitlements and extended the age range for support: up to 21 and beyond if the young person is in higher or residential further education. The main aims were to delay young people's transitions from care, improve preparation and planning, and strengthen the arrangements for financial assistance from the local authority (the act removed access to social security benefits from young people leaving care aged 16 and 17).

Young people are entitled to support under the act if they have been looked after for at least 13 weeks since the age of 14 with at least a day aged 16 years or over. The exact levels of support young people receive under the act depends on their 'eligible', 'relevant', or 'former relevant' status as care leavers and is related to their age. Generally, local authorities have to maintain contact, provide support through a personal adviser, and assist with education, employment, and training. All care leavers must have a pathway plan which is reviewed and maintained: the plan must identify how the local authority will support the young person's transition to adulthood and it covers many aspects of a young person's life including arrangements for accommodation and appropriate support.

The provisions of the act ensure if a young person is aged 16 or 17 there is a duty on children's services to provide and maintain them in 'suitable accommodation'. The mandatory guidance that accompanies the act states that although regulation does not prohibit certain types of accommodation, it would not be appropriate for 16- and 17-year-old care leavers to live completely independently. It identifies that bed and breakfast accommodation should not be considered for anything but very occasional short-term use. The regulations and guidance also stipulates that local authorities should take steps to make sure that young people have the best chance to succeed in their accommodation. They should:

1. avoid moving young people who are settled;
2. assess young people's needs and prepare them for any move;
3. ensure that the accommodation meets any needs relating to impairment;
4. where practicable offer a choice of accommodation;
5. set up a package of support to go with the accommodation;
6. develop a clear financial plan for the accommodation and have a contingency plan.

When a young person is over the age of 18, a local authority only has a duty to provide advice and support and to assist care leavers with accommodation and support to the extent that their welfare requires it (although those in full-time higher or residential accommodation are entitled to vacation accommodation).

The ongoing support through the implementation of a young person's pathway plan should ensure that young people who have left care avoid homelessness; where such arrangements break down the homelessness legislation provides an essential safety net. In England the local authority has a statutory duty under the Housing Act 1996 to make available suitable accommodation for those who are assessed as eligible for assistance, unintentionally homeless, and in priority need of accommodation. The subsequent Homelessness Act 2002 has strengthened the extension of priority need categories to include homeless 18–20-year-olds who were in care at 16 or 17 and those who are homeless over the age of 21 and are vulnerable as a result of being in care in the past. Similar protection is in place in Wales and Scotland (with Northern Ireland to follow).

Early Transitions and Preparation for Leaving Care

Over recent decades, in the general population there has been a tendency for young people to experience extended transitions. The average age for young people who are not in care to leave their parental home is in their mid-twenties. In contrast a consistent finding from studies of care leavers is that the majority who move to semi-independent or independent living are aged between 16 and 18. For most young people leaving home is a gradual process with the opportunity to return for short or longer periods of time. But for most young people in care this is not their experience: their transition is driven by age, not by readiness, and as a result it can be abrupt with little or no chance of returning.

In recent years, there have been improvements in delaying the age at which young people leave care. For example, in England there has been a drop in the percentage of young people leaving care at 16 from 30% in 2004 to 24% in 2008. These developments are to be welcomed as studies suggest that those young people who leave care later (at 18 and over) tend to have better outcomes than those who leave at an earlier age (at 16 or 17). Young people who do leave care early usually have come into care at a later juncture in their childhood and consequently had less time to settle in their care environments. These young people are likely to exhibit challenging behaviours (such as offending, running away, and substance misuse), which are also risk factors for social exclusion and homelessness.

Given that the majority of young people who leave care are under 18 years of age it is essential to prepare young people for this transition. Young people usually receive this guidance and support from their parents and or family. For young people leaving care it is the responsibility of the local authority as their corporate parent to prepare the young person to leave their care placement. However, research has shown that the planning and preparation young people receive can be inadequate and as a result many move before they feel ready. In studies documenting care leavers' experiences, young people continue to say that they were not prepared for the reality of leaving care. Young people have said that the preparation they do receive for leaving care has focused far too strongly on practical skills like do it yourself (DIY), cooking, and budgeting and had not responded to all the emotional resilience issues they faced such as how to cope with loneliness, low self-esteem, and lack of identity. This is despite the fact that evidence from Scottish research shows a significant association between good preparation before leaving care and young people's ability to 'cope' after care.

Pathways from Care

Leaving care is a process and not a single event. It entails care leavers making a series of crucial transitions – leaving their care placement, setting up and managing a home, obtaining work, or moving into further education – they face these at both an earlier age and within a much shorter period of time. As a result many care leavers experience 'accelerated and compressed transitions' to adulthood.

Young people who have spent time in care tend to have poorer outcomes than their peers and as a group are overrepresented in indicators of social exclusion. They are more likely to have low educational performance, contact with the criminal justice system, poorer health, and be vulnerable to homelessness and unemployment.

A review of research studies on care leavers suggested young people leaving care fall into one of three groups:

1. Young people who successfully 'move on' from care – as a group these young people tend to have experienced stability and continuity in their lives; they have had gradual preparation and they leave care later and in a planned way.
2. Young people who 'survive' – this group have experienced more instability and movement whilst in care; they leave earlier but they tend to make use of support networks and draw on their own resilience to try to help them overcome their poor starting points.
3. Young people who 'struggle' as they make the transition from care – this group of care leavers have had the most damaged past experiences compounded by a large number of moves whilst in care and as a result tend to fare badly after leaving care.

The pathways from care young people take are influenced by their pre-care experiences, the quality of care they received whilst in care, the nature of their transitions, and the post-care support they receive.

There are four basic pathways young people leaving their care placement can take:

1. *Extending Arrangements Beyond 18*

Young people cannot legally be 'in care' beyond their eighteenth birthday. However, some young people do stay in their former care placements under a variety of arrangements. This is more common for young people in foster care where the usual course of action is to convert the arrangement from a foster placement to a 'supported lodgings' arrangement. It is rarer that a young person is able to continue in a residential unit after the age of 18; this may be due to prohibitive factors such as cost or adherence to registration criteria for a 'children's home'.

2. *Supported Accommodation*

Supported accommodation is an umbrella term, which is applied to a whole range of housing-based solutions for vulnerable people. It usually refers to an accommodation project where people live in a specifically designated property to receive support services. This type of provision traditionally comprised shared housing environments often referred to as hostels or group homes. In more recent years, provision has included self-contained properties and housing-related support services (often referred to as floating support) that are delivered to people irrespective of where they live.

Some local authorities children's services departments provide their own supported accommodation, for example in the form of supported lodgings or training flats, that allow young people to try independent living before they move into their own flat.

However, in England and other parts of the United Kingdom the majority of housing support services are commissioned by the local authority utilising their Supporting People grant from central government. The conditions of the grant mean that it is currently not available directly for those leaving care under the age of 18. Although care leavers aged 16 or 17 can access Supporting People funded services, children's services are expected to pay for the cost of the accommodation and support. Recent statistics in England indicate that over 1000 care leavers accessed Supporting People services in 2007–08: around four in ten (43%) received a floating support service or were living in some form of shared or self-contained supported housing (40%). Overall, care leavers represent only a tiny fraction (around 1%) of Supporting People users.

3. *Birth Family and Friends*

Young people leaving care are often part of extensive family and friends networks. The majority (around 80%) of young people when they leave care will have contact with some of these members and a small number of young people leave care and return to live with their families. At present, very little is known about the nature, quality, and impact on young people of returning to live with family or friends. The government (England) identify that 12% of care leavers are living with their family or friends at age 19.

Returning to live with family can affect a young person's eligibility for Children (Leaving Care) Act services. If a young person aged 16 or 17 returns home successfully to a parent or someone with parental responsibility for a continuous period of 6 months, then they will no longer be treated as a 'relevant child'. A review should take place at least 6 months after the return and this will judge if the return is successful and if so the young person's status would change and they would become a 'qualifying child'. There would not be any statutory duty to maintain the pathway plan but a local authority does have a power to advise and assist. If a child returns home but is still on a care order the child remains an 'eligible' child until the care order is discharged by a court.

4. *Independent Living*

Government statistics show that by far the largest cohort of those leaving care are independent living (e.g., independent tenancy of flat, house, or bedsit, including local authority or housing association tenancy) by age 19 (42%, England). There are four main types of independent living accommodation: local authority housing, housing association properties, private rented sector properties, and owning the whole or part of a property. In England 70% of people are owner-occupiers, 18% live in some type of social housing (local authority housing or housing association properties), and 12% in the private rented sector. As a group, care leavers are most likely to be independent living in social housing when they leave care.

The independent accommodation options available to care leavers will depend on a range of factors, including the availability of the different types of accommodation within the young person's local authority or the area where the young person wants to live; the needs and aspirations of the young person; the circumstances of the young person (e.g., their previous housing experiences); and the policies and procedures of housing providers.

Care Leaver's Experience of Housing and Homelessness

On leaving care, young people take various routes to living more independently in a variety of accommodation provision. Statistics from England (see **Table 1**) show that at age 19 the largest group were in independent living (42%); followed by a fifth (20%) in some form of supported accommodation, with formal support organised as part of the accommodation (semi-independent accommodation, supported lodgings, or foyer), and around one in ten with parents or relatives (12%).

In addition to recording the accommodation type where the young person lives, the local authority is asked to make a subjective assessment as to its suitability. Of those young people who were in touch with their local authority at age 19 only 11.6% were in accommodation that was regarded to be unsuitable by the local authority. This assessment by local authorities is not necessarily reflected in studies documenting care leavers experiences of housing and their own views on the suitability of their accommodation.

There are limits to research data which at best can usually only offer a snapshot picture and do not usually capture the movement of young people between types of accommodation and the varying success young people have in the different pathways from care that they take. There are a range of 'risk factors' that heighten a young person's likelihood of experiencing homelessness. These include the following:

- family disruption;
- difficulty getting on with parents;
- witnessed or experienced violence within the family home;
- lived in a family that experienced financial difficulties;
- run away from home;
- spent time in care;

Table 1 All children now aged 19 years who were looked after on 1 April 2005 then aged 16 years

	n[a]	%[a]
Accommodation	5800	100
With parents or relatives	700	12
Community home	280	5
Semi-independent, transitional accommodation	550	9
Supported lodgings	520	9
Ordinary lodgings	280	5
Foyers	90	2
Independent living	2400	42
Emergency accommodation	40	1
Bed and breakfast	50	1
In custody	180	3
Other accommodation	340	6
Not in touch	380	6

[a]Numbers and percentages do not equal due to rounding of figures.

- been involved in crime or antisocial behaviour;
- had their education severely disrupted (e.g., been suspended or excluded from school).

Care leavers are likely to experience a greater number of these factors and on more than one occasion. It is therefore not surprising that as a group they are overrepresented in the population of young homeless people reflected in both official statistics and research studies.

In the year 2006–07 just over 2000 young people were accepted as homeless because they were care leavers (aged 18–20) or at risk of exploitation in England, Scotland, and Wales. In Scotland, there are broader criteria that can place 18–20-year-olds in priority need and results in higher annual numbers of acceptances than are found in England or Wales. There is no equivalent data available for Northern Ireland as it currently does not have equivalent priority need groups.

However, statistics of statutory acceptances of homelessness do not capture the full picture. Some care leavers are too old to qualify for priority need status, others will not be accepted due to being considered 'intentionally homeless' and a number of care leavers do not approach official agencies for assistance under the legislation.

Research describing young people's experience after leaving care from across the United Kingdom demonstrates a higher proportion experiencing homelessness both in the short time immediately after leaving care and during their housing careers. Estimates from a number of studies in England and Scotland suggest that a high proportion of young people leaving care experience periods of homelessness. In these studies, homelessness tended to be self-defined by young people and workers. It included young people staying temporarily in hostels, with friends or family as well as those who were roofless. Going by this definition, around a third of the young people had experienced homelessness at some time in the year after leaving care.

There is also evidence that there is a longer-term impact of being in care as surveys of people using hostels have also highlighted the overrepresentation of people with care experience in their samples as has data on the background of rough sleepers.

Supporting Transitions from Care

The transition from being looked after to leaving care is one of the most significant changes for young people. One of the essential components of pathway planning is identifying appropriate accommodation for that young person and the skills they require to manage it. Adequate planning is required so that young people are provided with opportunities to develop the necessary skills before they are expected to live independently. The more prepared young people are for living more independently, the less likely it is that their initial housing will break down, triggering them on a downward spiral of increasingly inappropriate accommodation.

In order to support young people's transitions from care, local authorities must be able to provide a range of accommodation options to meet the diverse levels of support needs amongst young people leaving care. Currently, local authorities report mixed success in meeting the needs of their young people. This can be explained in part by local housing shortages and the local market. However, it is also caused by inconsistent planning and the quality of cooperation between children's services and local housing authorities.

Improving outcomes for all young people leaving care requires comprehensive resources including targeted support at groups who are particularly vulnerable to difficulties when leaving care: young people with mental health problems; disabled young people; those with persistent offending or substance misuse problems. Young people with a history of such difficulties are at greater risk of housing breakdown compared to others. Currently, local authorities struggle to find suitable accommodation for the small number of young people leaving care with these challenging needs who wish to live independently but are not equipped to manage. Such problems can be exasperated when young people live outside of their local authority as there can be difficulty negotiating access to accommodation in other areas.

At present, local authorities have a varied approach to how they support young people to stay in care longer, to acquire the skills they need to live independently, to access suitable accommodation, and how their approach links with the planning process. The extent to which young people feel in control, engaged, and informed will depend on the commitment and resources the local authority has invested in this process.

It is important to local authorities to get this process right: assisting young people leaving care with accommodation can make a difference to their lives in the long term. Research suggests that how well young people fare in housing is not particularly associated with past events in their lives such as length of time in care or number of placement moves, but is more closely linked to events after leaving care. Support with housing is therefore an arena where leaving care can make a real difference. Addressing housing needs often leads to improvements in other life areas such as employment, education, and overall well-being. The effects of brief periods of homelessness can be overcome provided support is available to help young people back into suitable accommodation.

Conclusion

For most young people leaving home is usually a gradual process with the opportunity to return for short or longer periods of time. However, for the 10 000 young people who leave care every year in the United Kingdom, this is not necessarily their experience and their transition is often driven by age and not by readiness. There is a legislative and policy framework that is designed to ensure that those leaving local authority care find appropriate accommodation. However, both young people and the local authorities who support them report mixed success in this area and as a result research continues to show many care leavers experience homelessness and problems finding and sustaining suitable accommodation.

See also: Home and Homelessness; Homeless People: Care Leavers; Homeless People: Youth in the United Kingdom.

Further Reading

Biehel N, Clayden J, Stein M, and Wade J (1995) *Moving On: Young People and Leaving Care Schemes*. London: HMSO.

Department for Children, Schools and Families (2007) *Care Matters: Time for Change*. London: TSO.

Dixon J and Stein M (2005) *Leaving Care: Throughcare and Aftercare in Scotland*. London: Jessica Kingsley Publisher.

Gibbs I, Sinclair I, and Stein M (2005) Children and young people in and leaving care. In: Bradshaw J and Mayhew E (eds.) *The Well-Being of Children in the UK*, pp. 202–220. London: Save the Children.

Quilgars D, Johnsen S, and Pleace N (2008) *Youth Homelessness in the UK: A Decade of Progress?* York: Joseph Rowntree Foundation.

Pleace N, Fitzpatrick S, Johnsen S, Quilgars D, and Sanderson D (2008) *Statutory Homelessness in England: The Experience of Families and 16–17 Year Olds*. London: Department for Communities and Local Government.

Sinclair I, Baker C, Lee J, and Gibbs I (2007) *The Pursuit of Permanence: a Study of the English Care System*. Quality Matters in Children's Services Series. London: Jessica Kingsley Publishers.

Sinclair I, Baker C, Wilson K, and Gibbs I (2005) *Foster Children: Where They Go and How They Get On*. London: Jessica Kingsley Publishers.

Stein M (2004) *What Works for Young People Leaving Care?* Ilford: Barnardos.

Wade J and Dixon J (2006) Making a home, finding a job: Investigating early housing and employment outcomes for young people leaving care. *Child and Family Social Work* 11(3): 199–208.

Relevant Websites

www.leavingcare.org – The website has been developed and is maintained by the National Care Advisory Service in England – it provides a range of free resources and a comprehensive overview of issues facing young people making the transition from care.

Homeless People: Disasters and Displacement

S Breau, Flinders Law School, Adelaide, SA, Australia

© 2012 Elsevier Ltd. All rights reserved.

Glossary

Disasters Situations or events, which overwhelm local capacity, necessitating a request at national or international level for external assistance; unforeseen and often sudden events that cause great damage, destruction, and human suffering.

Displacement Being forced or obliged to flee or to leave one's homes or places of habitual residence, in particular as a result of or in order to avoid the effects of armed conflict, situations of generalised violence, violations of human rights, or natural or man-made disasters.

Homeless people Individuals who (1) lack a fixed, regular, and adequate nighttime residence and (2) have a primary nighttime residence that is (a) a supervised, publicly or privately operated shelter designed to provide temporary living accommodations (including welfare hotels, congregate shelters, and transitional housing for the mentally ill), (b) an institution that provides a temporary residence for individuals intended to be institutionalised, or (c) a public or private place not designed for or ordinarily used as a regular sleeping accommodation for human beings.

International Human Rights Laws This is a system of international laws consisting of treaties and customs that protect individual human rights.

International Humanitarian Law These are the international treaties and customs which apply during international armed conflict and civil wars.

Introduction

For a discussion on the legal regime that might apply to homeless persons displaced by disasters, it is essential to discuss definitions to each of these terms: homeless people, displaced peoples, and disasters. Once the definitions are established, the legal and political debate is whether there is a responsibility to intervene in situations of mass displacement of persons to ensure that these persons are returned to their habitual residences. This analysis focuses on the customary and treaty-based international human rights and international humanitarian law and finds that the right to return to home only exists within the paradigm of armed conflict. A possible framework for such a right is the development of a new political and perhaps legal obligation 'the responsibility to protect', which might mandate that the international community intervene in situations of natural and man-made disasters to ensure that victims are allowed to return home as soon as practicable.

Homeless People

A suitable definition of homeless people can be found in the Stewart B. McKinney Homeless Assistance Act enacted by the US Congress in 1987. It defines a homeless person as an individual who

(1) lacks a fixed, regular, and adequate nighttime residence and
(2) has a primary nighttime residence that is

  (a) a supervised, publicly or privately operated shelter designed to provide temporary living accommodations (including welfare hotels, congregate shelters, and transitional housing for the mentally ill),
  (b) an institution that provides a temporary residence for individuals intended to be institutionalised, or
  (c) a public or private place not designed for or ordinarily used as a regular sleeping accommodation for human beings (McKinney Act (P.L. 100-77, sec 103(2)(1), 101 sat. 485 (NB: Although this is a definition from a US source, the McKinney-Vento Act is suitable for those persons at the most desperate and extreme end of homelessness – the subject of this article.))).

Displaced Peoples

There is no agreed definition of internally displaced persons. Phoung proposes that the root causes of displacement vary, including natural disasters, interstate conflicts, intrastate conflicts, human rights violations, development projects, and internal strife. Internally displaced persons are those who have fled their residence due to one of the above causes and by implication are also homeless persons. The

Guiding Principles on internally displaced persons propose a definition suitable for this article which is

> internally displaced persons are persons or groups of persons who have been forced or obliged to flee or to leave their homes or places of habitual residence, in particular as a result of or in order to avoid the effects of armed conflict, situations of generalized violence, violations of human rights or natural or human-made disasters and who have not crossed an internationally recognized State border

In the case of this article, we are discussing all of those persons defined in the Guiding Principles.

Disasters

The Centre for Research on the Epidemiology of Disasters defines a disaster as a "situation or event, which overwhelms local capacity, necessitating a request to national or international level for external assistance; an unforeseen and often sudden event that causes great damage, destruction and human suffering". For a disaster to be entered into the Centre's Emergency Events Database (EM-DAT), at least one of the following criteria must be fulfilled:

- Ten or more people must be reported killed.
- One hundred people must be reported affected.
- There must be a declaration of a state of emergency.
- There must be a call for international assistance.

Macalister-Smith describes a disaster in more general terms as emergency situations in which there is an urgent need for international assistance to relieve human suffering. The distinction between man-made and natural disasters may be difficult as when authorities in a natural disaster fail to acknowledge the problem or the international community fails to respond with the aid needed. Sometimes these disasters rise to the level of catastrophes defined by Fidler as a large-scale, sudden, disastrous event that causes widespread death, destruction, and suffering.

It is evident that in many natural or man-made disasters peoples are rendered homeless and thus require assistance to either return to their homes or to find new accommodation. Examples of natural disasters would include Cyclone Nargis that devastated Burma or the Tsunami of December 2004 that killed 300 000 and injured 500 000 and left over 1 million persons internally displaced. Examples of recent man-made disasters were the displacement of peoples as a result of civil wars in Darfur (4.9 million), Sri Lanka (495 000), and recently in the Swat valley of Pakistan where an estimated 3 million Pakistanis were displaced when the government commenced operations against the Talibans who controlled that area (figures provided by the Internal Displacement Monitoring Centre, August 2009). All of these examples comply with the criteria set out by EM-DAT.

Humanitarian assistance can be offered by a wide variety of nations and can constitute assistance in kind, financial aid, or the provision of trained personnel. There are many governmental and nongovernmental organisations that operate in situations of natural or man-made disasters. Leading among these are the International Committee of the Red Cross, the World Food Programme, and the United Nations High Commissioner for Refugees. Other organisations involved are the United Nations Children's Fund, the United Nations Development Programme, the World Health Organization, and the International Organization for Migration. Within the United Nations system, the office of the Emergency Relief Coordinator undertakes the task of coordination of relief efforts between these organisations and a large number of nongovernmental organisations such as Oxfam, Medécins Sans Frontiers, and Care.

Legal Regimes Governing Homelessness and Displacement

Human Rights

A key question is whether a displaced person has a legal right to return to his/her home and homeland. Is there a right to return within existing international conventions? The rights that can be derived from both human rights law and humanitarian law include: (1) protection from arbitrary displacement in the first instance; (2) protection and assistance after displacement has taken place; and (3) assistance with safe and voluntary return or resettlement and rehabilitation.

The Universal Declaration of Human Rights of 1948 (UDHR) – a resolution of the General Assembly which has arguably become part of the corpus of customary international law – has two articles concerning the right to shelter and homelessness. Article 25 of the UDHR states that everyone has the right to a standard of living adequate for the health and well-being of himself/herself and his/her family, including food, clothing, housing and medical care, and the necessary social services. Article 17 states that everyone has the right to own property alone as well as in association with others and that no one shall be arbitrarily deprived of his property.

The primary human rights treaty with a large number of ratifications dealing with a right to a home is the International Covenant on Economic, Social and Cultural Rights of 1966 which in Article 11 states that there is a "right of everyone to an adequate standard of living for himself and his family, including adequate food, clothing and housing, and to continuous improvement of living conditions". This is a positive right and includes the obligation on States Parties to provide their citizens with an adequate standard of housing. The General Comment on the housing part of this article indicates that this is an international obligation and that "States parties, both recipients and providers, should ensure that a substantial proportion of financing is devoted to creating conditions leading to a higher number of persons being adequately housed." Other treaties containing rights to a home are the Convention on the Elimination of All Forms of Discrimination Against Women (1979) which in Article 14 indicates that women in rural areas have the right to enjoy adequate living conditions, particularly in relation to housing, sanitation, electricity and water supply, transport, and communications. In the International Covenant on the Elimination of All Forms of Racial Discrimination (1965), Article 5, States Parties undertake to prohibit racial discrimination and guarantee the right of everyone without distinction as to race, colour, or ethnicity to equality before the law in the enjoyment of the right to housing. In the almost universally ratified Convention on the Rights of the Child (1989), Article 27 specifies that States Parties shall take appropriate measures to assist parents and others responsible for children in cases of need to provide material assistance and support, particularly with regard to nutrition, clothing, and housing. The Convention Relating to the Status of Refugees has a specific article with respect to housing. Article 21 mandates that as regards housing States shall accord to refugees as favourable as possible treatment and in any event not less favourable than that accorded to aliens generally in the same circumstances.

None of the human rights treaties contain a right to return to property that a person has had to leave as a result of a man-made or natural disaster. The free-standing right to property with respect to either ownership or tenancy has not been included in international treaties – only the right to shelter is unequivocally stated. The only body of law that contains such a right is international humanitarian law.

Humanitarian Law

International humanitarian law only applies if a disaster resulting in displacement results from an international or noninternational armed conflict. There are extensive treaty provisions with respect to housing and displacement. The Fourth Geneva Convention Relative to the Protection of Civilian Persons in Time of War in Article 55 mandates that an occupying power has the duty to the extent of the resources available to provide foodstuffs and medical supplies but the provision did not include providing shelter. Additional Protocol I of 1977 widens that obligation to include the provision of shelter. Article 49 of Geneva Convention IV prohibits individual or mass forcible transfers, as well as deportations of protected persons from occupied territory to the territory of the Occupying Power or to that of any other country, occupied or not. However, that protection is not absolute. The Occupying Power may undertake total or partial evacuation of a given area if the security of the population or imperative military reasons so demand. Such evacuations may not involve the displacement of protected persons outside the bounds of the occupied territory except when, for material reasons, it is impossible to avoid such displacement. However, Article 49 states that persons evacuated shall be transferred back to their homes as soon as hostilities in the area in question have ceased. Article 53 of the Fourth Geneva Convention prohibits the destruction by the Occupying Power of real or personal property belonging individually or collectively to private persons, or to the State, or to other public authorities, or to social or cooperative organisations, except where such destruction is rendered absolutely necessary by military operations.

The International Committee of the Red Cross undertook an important study of customary international humanitarian law, which contains rules respecting property rights and displacement. Rule 51 states that in occupied territory: (a) movable public property that can be used for military operations may be confiscated; (b) immovable public property must be administered according to the rule of usufruct; and (c) private property must be respected and may not be confiscated – except where destruction or seizure of such property is required by imperative military necessity. This is applicable only in international armed conflict. The rules have a separated section on displacement and displaced persons. Rule 129 specifies that parties to an international armed conflict may not deport or forcibly transfer the civilian population of an occupied territory, in whole or in part, unless the security of the civilians involved or imperative military reasons so demand. It also delineates in part B that parties to a noninternational armed conflict may not order the displacement of the civilian population, in whole or in part, for reasons related to the conflict, unless the security of the civilians involved or imperative military reasons so demand. Rule 131 states that in the case of displacement, all possible measures must be taken in order that the civilians concerned are received under satisfactory conditions of shelter, hygiene, health, safety, and nutrition, and that members of the same family are not separated. Most importantly, Rule 132 sets out that displaced persons have a right to voluntary return in safety to their homes or places of habitual residence as soon as the reasons for their displacement cease to exist. This rule applies in both international and noninternational armed conflict. Finally, Rule 133 mandates that the property rights of displaced persons must be respected.

Taken together international humanitarian law is the most comprehensive regime providing for protection of property, prohibitions against forced displacement, and return to habitual residence.

Do Homeless Displaced Persons have a Right to Return to their Homes or Homeland?

It is evident from the above analysis that there is not a clear right for displaced persons to return to their home or homeland in a situation of natural or man-made disaster that does not rise to the level of an armed conflict. There is one instrument that attempts to secure that right, the Guiding Principles on Internal Displacement developed in 1988 by the Representative of the Secretary-General on Internally Displaced Persons. These Guiding Principles compile and restate the various relevant norms of international human rights and humanitarian law and apply these to situations of internal displacement. In The Principles on Internally Displaced Persons which at this point may be not international law but rather 'soft law', state in Principle 18 that competent authorities shall provide internally displaced persons with and ensure safe access to basic shelter and housing. Critically Principle 28 indicates that competent authorities have the primary duty and responsibility to establish conditions and means to allow internally displaced persons to return to their homes or places of habitual residence. The UN Security Council in situations of displacement due to internal armed conflict has on several occasions called on governments and the international community to facilitate the return of internally displaced persons to their former homes (SC Resolutions, Bosnia 820 (1993), Croatia 1009 (1995), Georgia 876 (1993), Georgia 1781 (2007), and Kosovo 144 (1999)). It may well be the case that these principles do become part of customary international law if they are not incorporated into a treaty provision.

International Legal Obligations on Other States

Although there are clearly national obligations to protect one's own citizens, the key legal and political question for this article is whether there is an international legal obligation on other States to come to the aid of homeless persons, who are displaced as a result of a disaster. It can be asserted that this international legal obligation exists firstly within the Charter of the United Nations, which in Article 1(3) sets out that part of the goals of the United Nations is to achieve international cooperation in solving international problems of an economic, social, cultural, or humanitarian character.

With regard to international armed conflicts, Articles 55 and 81 of the Fourth Geneva Convention Relative to the Protection of Civilian Persons in Time of War of 1949 mandate that States have the duty to provide humanitarian aid to the civilian population under their control (nonnationals, whether free or detained, and the population of occupied territories) of the adverse party and, if the State is unable to do so, it is bound to accept the offer of third parties to provide the required aid. However, the duty of States to provide humanitarian assistance and to allow others to do so for their own nationals is not expressly laid down in this instrument. The right of the nationals of neutral States to humanitarian aid is not provided for in it either, although it was later included in Article 50 of the Additional Protocol I to the Geneva Conventions of 1977. In noninternational armed conflict, Article 18 of Additional Protocol II imposes on the parties to conflict the obligation to accept humanitarian aid essential to the survival of the population. None of these treaty provisions bind the occupying party to provide appropriate housing as part of the provision of humanitarian aid.

The Millennium Declaration is another 'soft law' instrument confirming collective responsibility binding States to provide for all peoples by stating:

> We recognise that, in addition to our separate responsibilities to our individual societies, we have a collective responsibility to uphold the principles of human dignity, equality and equity at the global level. As leaders, we have a duty therefore to all the world's people, especially the most vulnerable and, in particular the children of the world, to whom the future belongs.

In the Millennium Development goals under 'Protecting Our Common Environment' is a statement resolving "to adopt in all our environmental action a new ethic of conservation and stewardship and, as first steps, resolves ... to intensify cooperation to reduce the number and effects of natural and man-made disasters".

The idea of shared responsibility was also endorsed in the Outcome document of the 60th anniversary summit. The nations at the summit emphasise the need for continued, coordinated, and effective international support for achieving the development goals in countries emerging from conflict and in those recovering from natural disasters.

However, most international statements and documents do not tie housing into any plan for humanitarian assistance. This is challenged by Harroff-Tavel, a political advisor to the ICRC, who argues that access to land, its use, its management, its ownership, and its transfer are key political issues in many armed conflicts, in particular when forced displacement is a wartime strategy. She asserts that land is also at the heart of humanitarian activities as farming can be a way for communities affected by the fighting to recover long-term economic security.

The Responsibility to Protect and Disasters

At the 60th Anniversary General Assembly Summit, the international community endorsed that in the event of a national government failing in their primary responsibility to protect their populations from genocide, war crimes, ethnic cleansing, and crimes against humanity that responsibility should move to the international community acting through the United Nations. However, on the face of it, this did not include an international obligation to prevent internal displacement or protect persons who have been displaced due to natural or man-made disasters. Barbour and Gorkick argue that the Responsibility to Protect should be interpreted as a positive obligation on States to take steps to prevent victimisation, reduce statelessness, and redress the dire circumstances for those who have no human rights protection. This idea certainly could be extended to victims of disasters when their home nations are unwilling or unable to address the displacement issues. Wong argues that the doctrine should authorise the international community to react when a government demonstrates a 'criminal failure' to protect its people based on omissions that are arguably crimes against humanity.

The case study to support the Responsibility to Protect and its applicability to disaster and displacement is the situation in Myanmar in 2008. This controversy erupted in May 2008 as a result of the Cyclone Nargis when the Myanmar regime refused to allow delivery of aid. French Foreign Minister Kouchner called on the Security Council to impose the international delivery of aid on the Myanmar government. It was noted by Wong that the threshold for the international responsibility was not the disaster itself but a state's failure to protect its citizens in the aftermath of the disaster. The inaction would have to be deliberate to amount to a crime against humanity under international law. This interpretation met with favour by the Co-Chair of the International Commission on Intervention and State Sovereignty (the commission who introduced the responsibility to protect), who argued that if the generals were "in effect denying relief to hundreds of thousands of people at real and immediate risk of death", this could be "characterised as a crime against humanity, then the responsibility to protect principle does indeed cut in". These arguments could be called a 'constructive interpretation' of the Responsibility to Protect grounded in international criminal jurisprudence that an omission may be the basis of a finding of a crime against humanity.

Furthermore, Barber argues that the Security Council is competent to declare a humanitarian crisis to be a threat to international peace and security, and thus exercises its Chapter VII powers to authorise the use of force. She argues that this competence has been so widely accepted that it may reasonably be said to have found a place within customary international law. This may stretch the interpretation of actions in Kosovo and Somalia as these situations were clearly noninternational armed conflicts and not situations of natural disasters resulting in homelessness and displacement.

Nevertheless, the Responsibility to Protect in itself is a very new concept that emerged only in 1999 (in a Dutch report entitled 'Humanitarian Intervention'), and it may not yet be a doctrine of international law. To call on international responsibility at this juncture may only be a political tool rather than a legal obligation. In any event as a result of intensive diplomatic efforts, perhaps with the threat of international intervention, the regime in Myanmar allowed limited relief efforts. Action in a situation such as in Myanmar would have confirmed the extension of the doctrine of collective security, which cannot be said to have happened as a result of the peaceful resolution to the humanitarian disaster. Nevertheless, the door has been opened to the use of the Responsibility to Protect ideal in humanitarian emergencies.

Conclusion

A key difficulty in the legal regime to deal with homelessness and displacement resulting from disaster is the lack of legal effect of the Guiding Principles on Internal Displacement. Even though the principles are widely accepted as an important tool and standard for addressing situations of internal displacement, and are being used around the world by Governments, the United Nations, regional organisations, NGOs, and other actors concerned with internal displacement, they do not have the status of an international treaty and are not enforceable against any state. Nevertheless, the examples of the customary law status of international humanitarian law principles may well extend to principles for the return of displaced persons after humanitarian emergencies. The debate with respect to the Responsibility to Protect only adds pressure to ensure that victims of natural or man-made disasters are able to return to their homes.

See also: Homeless People: Refugees and Asylum Seekers; Human Rights and Housing; Policies to Address Homelessness: Prevention in the United Kingdom; Post-Conflict Housing Restitutions.

Further Reading

Barber R (2009) The responsibility to protect the survivors of natural disaster: Cyclone Nargis. A case study. *Journal of Conflict and Security Law* 14(1): 3–34.

Cohen R and Deng FM (1998) *Masses in Flight: The Global Crisis of Internal Displacement*. Washington, DC: The Brookings Institution.

Fidler DP (2007) Governing catastrophes: Security, health and humanitarian assistance. *International Review of the Red Cross* 89: 247–270.

Guiding Principles on Internal Displacement (1998) UN Doc. E/CN.4/1998/53/Add.2, http://www.unhchr.ch/html/menu2/7/b/principles.htm.

Henckaerts J-M and Doswald-Beck L (2005) *Customary International Humanitarian Law, Vol. 1: Rules*. Cambridge, UK: Cambridge University Press.

Institute of Medicine (1988) *Homelessness, Health and Human Needs*. Washington, DC: National Academy Press.

Leckie S (2007) *Housing, Land, and Property Restitution Rights of Refugees and Displaced Persons*. Cambridge, UK: Cambridge University Press.

Macalister-Smith P (1985) *International Humanitarian Assistance: Disaster Relief Actions in International Law and Organization*. Dordrecht, The Netherlands: Martinus Nijhoff.

Phuong C (2004) *The International Protection of Internally Displaced Persons*. Cambridge, UK: Cambridge University Press.

Piotrowicz R (2007) Displacement and displaced persons. In: Wilmshurst E and Breau S (eds.) *Perspectives on the ICRC Study on Customary International Humanitarian Law*. Cambridge, UK: Cambridge University Press.

Stoffels RA (2004) Legal regulation of humanitarian assistance in armed conflict: Achievements and gaps. *International Review of the Red Cross* 86: 515–545.

Wong J (2009) Reconstructing the responsibility to protect in the wake of cyclones and separatism. *Tulane Law Review* 84 SSRN: http://ssrn.com/abstract=1446364.

Homeless People: Economic Migrants in Southern Europe

A Tosi, Polytechnic of Milan, Milan, Italy

© 2012 Elsevier Ltd. All rights reserved.

Glossary

Economic migrant A person who moves to another country in search of work and better economic prospects.
Immigrant A person who leaves their native land and goes to another country as a permanent resident, for the purpose of work or to escape persecution or for personal reasons, based on a relationship, such as in family reunification.
Informal housing Accommodation outside the established channels of provision (the market and the state), among friends and relatives, in informal shelters and in charitable hostels. Coping strategies are based on community and family networks.
Informal/illegal settlement A group of unplanned shelters created by squatting in abandoned buildings or by building shanty huts on uncultivated land, where the occupants generally live without water, heating, electricity, and sanitary facilities.
Rooflessness The most visible forms of homelessness: people living in the streets or public spaces, and people with no usual place of residence who make use of night shelters/low threshold shelters.

Introduction: The Scale and Pattern of the Problem

Immigrants currently represent around half of the homeless population in southern European countries (i.e., Spain, Italy, Greece, and Portugal). For the past 10 years surveys of roofless people in Italy have indicated an immigrant presence of around 50%. The proportion of immigrants is higher in large cities and includes, for example, 60% of the roofless in Milan. An investigation in Spain in 2005 estimated that immigrants accounted for 48% of the homeless population. On the basis of a count made in February 2008, this figure rises to 53% in Madrid and to 62% in Barcelona. Immigrants also form a large and growing share of the users of services for the homeless in southern Europe. In Spain, this can sometimes amount to 70% of all service users. The percentage may be a little lower in Portugal. Estimates for Lisbon indicated that immigrants comprised between 25 and 35% of the homeless population in 2004. The presence of immigrants is most pronounced in Greece. Workers in the field there estimate that immigrants (including refugees) make up two-thirds of the homeless population (Cabrera et al., 2008; Rodrigues, 2005; Sapounakis, 2003; Tosi, 2003).

These data would suggest, particularly when considered alongside the rapid increase in the overall immigrant population, that the numbers of homeless immigrants are rising sharply in southern Europe. Certainly, the percentage of immigrants among the homeless is thought to have roughly doubled over the past decade in Spain. Nevertheless, it is not easy to make a precise quantitative estimate of this increase across southern Europe, nor of the absolute size of the phenomenon of homeless immigrants in this part of the world. Even if one assumes, based on current indications, that the size of the immigrant homeless population is higher in southern than in other European countries, quantification brings problems of definition into play and would require a detailed examination of the different forms of homelessness. While there tends to be a relatively low percentage of immigrants reported to be roofless in southern Europe (around 2–3% of the total immigrant population), they are much more numerous in other homeless situations, such as living temporarily in the homes of other immigrants, staying in shanty towns, or in the many forms of squatting. This particular pattern with respect to the informal housing of immigrants forms part of the specificity of homelessness in these southern European countries.

Highly relevant here are the specificities of immigration in these southern European countries and their types of welfare regime. The implications of the 'Mediterranean model of immigration', a model that has shaped the migratory history of the last 20 years in southern European countries, can be seen in the vulnerability of immigrants to homelessness. This model is characterised, to a greater or lesser extent in each country, by a substantial undocumented component of immigration and a large informal sector in the national economy, which acts as a pull factor for migrants. A significant proportion of immigrants find work in the 'hidden economy', and this is one of the main factors generating illegal immigration.

Furthermore, homelessness amongst migrants has clearly been affected by the immigration, welfare, and housing policies implemented over the past few decades.

While considerable progress has been made at a local level, usually by municipalities and/or non-governmental organisations (NGOs), national integration policies have often been relatively weak and fragmented. Generally speaking, social policies are shaped by the traditions of the welfare regimes in these southern European countries (variously defined as 'formative welfare states' or 'Mediterranean welfare regimes'): a strong role is played by civil society accompanied by modest state involvement in social protection and, generally speaking, a relative weakness or limited coverage of social protection systems.

Consistent with this tradition, housing policies in southern Europe have, as a whole, been fairly ineffective in assisting lower income groups. A lack of initiative by the public sector (whose investment in welfare progressively reduced in the 1980s and 1990s) has consistently been allied with an approach that has promoted home ownership. Today, all these southern European countries have rates of home ownership that are amongst the highest in Europe (around 80% of all households) and rates of social housing which are among the lowest (between 1 and 4% of households). All of these countries have been affected by a progressive decline of the private rented sector and by a substantial increase in house prices and rents: a particularly difficult combination for immigrants seeking housing.

Vulnerability to Homelessness

Irregular legal status, low income and weak labour market position, lack of support networks, and (racial) discrimination are the most important factors which determine the vulnerability of immigrants to homelessness according to international research. These factors can combine together to establish a 'hierarchy of vulnerability', which gives rise to different degrees of social and housing marginality: "Legal status combined with weak economic position are the key factors creating access barriers to decent/affordable housing", with these structural factors being "exacerbated by discrimination" (Edgar, 2004: 36).

Taken together, these factors explain the scale of immigrant homelessness in the countries of southern Europe, as they do elsewhere in the world (Sánchez Morales and Tezanos Vázquez, 2005). Nevertheless, there are important elements of specificity within countries which give rise to particular configurations within hierarchies of vulnerability. These relate to the links between the determinants of homelessness on the one hand, and the immigration policies and the policies that govern access to housing, to the labour market, and to citizenship rights on the other hand.

The first and most important factor is legal status. As is obvious, being without proper documents makes it virtually impossible to gain access to even the most basic of rights and drastically reduces access to the resources upon which settlement in a new community depends. Given the illegality of their presence, and their economic weakness, undocumented immigrants constitute a particularly vulnerable group in the housing market. The accommodation to which they do have access is generally in a much worse condition than that which local people and legal migrants are able to find. Undocumented migrants are not only excluded from social housing, but their lack of documents also weakens their bargaining position in the private market: they are not allowed to conclude a contract for renting a house and their situation of irregularity prevents them from enforcing their rights against the owners of their accommodation. Thus their exclusion from social housing and normal rental contracts means that the private market is accessible to them only under very exploitative conditions, and they must often turn to the informal housing sector.

A second key factor is institutional barriers. The rapid growth of immigrants as users of services for the homeless, and of homeless shelters in particular, should not be taken to indicate that they do not encounter problems in using these services. Once again, barriers are greatest for undocumented immigrants as, generally speaking, state shelters won't help undocumented people. The role played by NGOs in providing emergency assistance is therefore crucial. However, both documented and undocumented migrants can encounter access difficulties even in this sector. NGOs may be unable to cope with the quantity of demand for their services. Furthermore, there may be resistance on the part of NGO service providers to admitting immigrants. Homeless organisations are mainly highly specialist in the problems of their indigenous homeless population, whom they assist by reintegrating into society and through 'resocialization projects'. The workers in shelters often lack the capacity and skills to properly assist migrants, whose needs and reasons for homelessness are usually quite different to those of the indigenous homeless population (Van Parys and Verbruggen, 2004: 34, 42). As also happens in other European countries, many associations and services in southern Europe call for the creation of separate services for homeless immigrants. A key problem, however, is the potential fragility of a specialist system of emergency accommodation for immigrants in these countries, as this risks reproducing the situation of housing instability which they already face. Recent research in Spain indicates that a large majority of shelter users are unable to sleep in them on a regular basis, so they must alternate nights in shelters with nights in parks, on benches, squatting in buildings, and so on:

> If we consider that the vast majority of places in the emergency accommodation network are found in shelters (81 percent), we must conclude that as a whole, the supply of this accommodation that is available in Spain is unstable and precarious. And that is precisely what it is intended to combat (Cabrera et al., 2008: 52).

Finally, a third key factor is the precariousness of work. Most immigrants work, but for large proportions of them – particularly in certain regions – this work is highly insecure and is often irregular and found in the informal economy. One issue that has received much attention in the press in Italy and in Spain is the situation of seasonal agricultural workers:

> In Spanish rural areas there is a tendency to live under very precarious conditions, next to farming fields, which do not meet the minimum conditions of habitability. They [immigrants] are employed only while the work lasts or during the harvest season, thus condemning workers to itinerancy which enhances their sense of being uprooted and forces them to resort to shelters and support institutions during periods of unemployment (Edgar et al., 2004: 77).

The position of seasonal workers in the regions of southern Italy illustrates the extreme vulnerability of those affected by illegal status, combined with working in the informal economy and accommodation in the informal housing sector. Black market labour in these regions – which means exploitation of workers under conditions which in many cases are close to slavery – and accommodation in terrible conditions constitute the everyday reality for many seasonal workers, many of whom are without documents. And in addition to the immediate material impact on these workers, this insecure form of employment prevents them from meeting the conditions required to attain proper legal status (Alisei et al., 2007: 52).

If the prevalence of precarious employment, the consequences of irregular legal status, and the barriers to accommodation are considered together, then it is easy to understand why the figure of the homeless immigrant worker is a particularly common one in southern Europe. However, it is also worth noting that, while undocumented migrants working in the informal economy are especially vulnerable, quite often it is also legal immigrants in permanent jobs that are hit by homelessness.

These key factors set out above are reflected in the diversity of the individual case histories of homeless immigrants when compared to those of the nonimmigrant homeless. This has been an important aspect of the debate in Italy. Research on the pathways into/out of homelessness confirms that, for immigrants in Italy, there is a higher probability of housing exclusion occurring without the strong elements of marginalisation and, even more frequently, without those traits of shattered personalities, which characterise the Italian *no abode* (Tosi, 2003: 22–23). For most immigrants, homelessness is nothing more than a phase on the path to settlement in society: in fact it is found above all during the initial phases of the migratory path, on arrival in the country of destination.

Nevertheless, homelessness is a condition that can be prolonged or can recur, even after the initial stages of migration. Similar observations have been made for Spain (Cabrera et al., 2008).

That homelessness may be a stage in the integration process, as well as reflecting a possible failure of integration, is a commonly made observation in research on immigration. However, in the case of southern European countries, given what has been said about the relative weakness of their welfare and immigration policies, an important policy issue relates to the extent to which the homelessness and housing careers of immigrants in these countries lead (eventually) to an improvement in their situation and whether integration policies assist in this process (Edgar et al., 2004: 95, 117). The scale of immigrant homelessness, and the considerable length of time over which homelessness persists for a significant proportion of immigrants, raises important questions about the weakness of integration and welfare policies in these countries.

The Impact of Housing Markets

Even if the housing conditions of immigrants are very varied, the overall picture is clearly that of large numbers of immigrants suffering housing hardships in southern Europe. Along with the high proportion of immigrants found amongst the homeless population – albeit that rooflessness affects a relatively low percentage of the total immigrant population – the widespread existence of conditions bordering on homelessness provides evidence of the risk factors and of the pathways that may lead to homelessness for this group.

Systematic data on the housing tenure of immigrants are available for Spain and Italy. In these countries rented housing (almost all of it in the private sector market) is the prevalent form of tenure, accounting for between 70 and 80% of immigrant occupation. In most cases this is shared renting or subletting (a form of tenure which accounts for 47% of the immigrant population in Spain). Little more than 10% of immigrants live in properties that they own. More or less the same proportion live in very precarious circumstances: at the workplace or in extreme conditions such as sleeping rough, or stay temporarily with relatives or friends, in shelters and hostels, and so on (Censis, 2006; Pereda et al., 2005: 201–205).

Situations vary greatly according to the region, especially with regard to the proportion of immigrants living in the most precarious conditions. In some areas of southern Italy, one out of three immigrants live in extremely precarious situations, with 20% having access to only a bed space. In the Naples area, 10% of immigrants live in makeshift accommodation. Almost half of immigrants in rented accommodation in southern Italy have no rent contract or a contract that is not fully valid. In the areas where seasonal employment is available, most immigrants live in squats (Alisei et al., 2007; Coppola and Amato, 2005).

The pattern of accommodation types also varies according to the length of time immigrants have been present in their country of destination. Typical paths can be identified which reflect the progression over time in integration opportunities: better work, proper legal status, the arrival of family members from the country of origin, or the creation of a new family. The relationship, however, is not linear: factors such as the availability of support networks, legal status, and the type and stability of work can positively or negatively deflect the paths of many immigrants from the average course (Pereda et al., 2005: 205–206).

The severe housing problems that many immigrants encounter are due in large part to their need to resort to rented housing in countries in which private rented provision is scarce, and social rented housing extremely scarce. To make matters worse, the arrival of immigrants in these countries coincided with a tightening of the private rental market, affected in recent decades by a contraction in supply. This scarcity of private tenancies helped to drive rents up, weakening the bargaining power of potential tenants and reducing their chances of finding adequate housing. If we add to these contextual constraints the specific disadvantages immigrants suffer, it is easy to understand why their experience of rental accommodation is characterised by considerable hardship. In many cases, their tenancy contract is precarious, the rents they have to pay are exorbitant, and their housing conditions are very poor (Da Costa and Baptista, 2003; Pereda et al., 2005; Sapounakis 2003; Tosi, 2003).

The obstacle presented by the low incomes of immigrants is exacerbated by the resistance of many landlords to renting to immigrants, for fear that their accommodation will be mistreated and deteriorate and that there will be friction with neighbours, or that the value of the property will depreciate. Some landlords simply refuse to rent to immigrants, while others charge a higher rent. A 'special rent for immigrants' has been recorded in all of these southern European countries. Paying a higher price for accommodation of the same (or even lower) quality is a clear indicator of the existence of discriminatory practices towards a part of the population. But a high level of racial prejudice is not necessary for there to be discrimination towards immigrants. It is a phenomenon inherent to the rental market in these countries, as a consequence of the imbalance between supply and demand outlined above. And in some ways these exploitative practices fit with the needs of immigrants who are willing to allow sharing because of ethnic solidarity or friendship, and who also need to keep costs down and to conceal undocumented persons.

The widespread resort by immigrants to substandard housing extends to include genuinely uninhabitable housing stock, well below the minimum criteria that culturally define habitability in a country: thus otherwise unmarketable housing stock is brought back into use, constituting a specific market segment (Tosi, 2003: 13–14). The distinguishing traits of this informal market are rent calculated on a number of beds basis (renting many beds in a flat or the same bed for different hours of the day or night: what in Spain has been named 'camas calientes' – warm beds); subletting; and operation according to extremely exploitative black market rules, including sometimes the presence of genuine 'rackets'.

Informal housing – whether it arises from the intervention of community networks and reciprocal arrangements in providing a place to live, or is accommodation let within 'unregulated' segments of marginal housing markets – is not specific to southern European countries nor even to immigrants. In these countries, however, informal housing is a particularly significant phenomenon, with aspects of civil society and reciprocity especially pronounced, and in many cases they assume the most dramatic forms, particularly when informal housing, irregular legal status, and employment in the informal economy come together. These processes entail a variety of forms of homelessness, including illegal/informal settlements, encampments and shanty towns, as well as the many forms of squatting.

Illegal settlements have played an important role in immigrant housing strategies in the cities of southern Europe (Edgar et al., 2004: 76–78). In Italy, they have been on the increase in all the main cities. In Milan, in 2005, it was estimated that there were some 6000 persons in illegal settlements, created by squatting in abandoned buildings or by building shanty huts on uncultivated land or in the country, where the occupants generally live without water, heating, electricity, and sanitary facilities. The majority of the inhabitants are the victims of the 'vicious circle of irregularity': the combination of illegal status, illegal labour, and precarious residence in the informal sector forces them into a condition of absolute marginalisation from which it is difficult to emerge, and which reduces the probability of successful outcomes for their migration plans. Nevertheless, persons with work and an income are also to be found in these settlements. Often these people do have documents. For many, living in a shanty town is a consequence of a lack of alternative affordable accommodation. Even if in some cases living in these settlements forms part of a migration strategy (short-term migration and extreme economising in housing expenses), essentially, these settlements are signs of major faults in policies – immigration, housing, and welfare policies.

Conclusion: Looking Forward

The path from social and housing precariousness to a more or less successful inclusion has been the norm for immigrants in southern Europe as elsewhere. This confirms that integration processes – which are in fact often supported by interventions by local authorities and NGOs – are operating in these countries. Nevertheless, the persistence of situations of great precariousness (of which homelessness is the most visible expression) suggests that we are in the presence of contradictory trends: alongside the majority of immigrants who in time find some sort of permanent settlement in their new countries, a dimension of vulnerability persists and is perhaps growing, experienced by the weakest group of immigrants, and not just by those at the start of their migration path.

The underlying reasons for the persistence of homelessness are clear in the (many) cases which diverge from the 'normal' paths to settlement: the fragility of the persons involved, constraints imposed by the system of opportunities offered, and also the specific strategies of some migrants. These are all factors which relate to the specific 'hierarchies of vulnerability' in these countries and they call into question the important role played by policies that govern the chances for integration. This precarious component of immigration seems irreducible if current welfare, housing, and integration policies and the present construction of the question of immigration persists.

Current trends may be increasing the risk of precariousness for immigrants. One risk factor is the higher level of vulnerability amongst many immigrants that compose the 'new wave' of migration. The most recent arrivals – often equipped with more modest resources (motivational and educational) compared to those of the previous phases, and increasingly oriented to short-term plans and involved in irregular migratory flows – seem to be disproportionately subject to the negative effects of political, social, and economic changes.

From another perspective, risks are presented by changes in the policy and political framework in which the question of immigration is constructed. The current economic and financial crisis and its recent worsening, together with an upsurge of xenophobic attitudes and restrictive political agendas, may cause the situation of immigrants to deteriorate further. The growing insecurity of broad segments of the labour market may extend the area of informal work and encourage the drift of immigrants into that part of the labour market. The 2008 ENAR report (Bencini and Cerretelli, 2008) signalled an increase in immigrants working in the hidden economy in Italy. That same year, a report by a UN agency predicted a 'risk of favelas' for Europe (Salis, 2008; United Nations, 2008), as a consequence of the economic crisis compounded by the continuing inflow of migrants, the lack of effective social housing policies, and growing poverty. Immigrants are likely to be the main victims and Spain and Italy are the two countries where the risk is highest.

For their part, restrictive immigration control ideologies reinforce hostility towards immigrants and reduce the space for integration policies. The rejection of undocumented immigrants may have serious consequences in countries where to date the lack of documents has been experienced as a transitory circumstance ("a sort of toll or price to pay to reside in the country" (Pereda et al., 2005: 209)), an experience that until now has been confirmed by repeated measures to grant papers to undocumented immigrants under regularisation programmes. The combination of economic crisis and the upsurge of restrictive political agendas enormously increases the risk, already reported long ago, of a "growing polarisation" between "residents with full rights of citizenship and a marginalised class of aliens compelled to work on the periphery, within a shadow economy", "confined to menial jobs and relegated to the worst housing" (Daly, 1996: 11).

See also: Ethnic Minorities and Housing; Migration: Ethnicity, Race and Mobility; Temporary Housing.

References

Alisei C, Cipac C, and Promidea S (2007) *Sotto la soglia. Indagine conoscitiva sul disagio abitativo degli immigrati presenti nell'Italia Meridionale*. Roma: Ministero della Solidarietà sociale.

Bencini C and Cerretelli S (2008) *ENAR Shadow Report 2007: Racism in Italy*. Bruxelles: European Network Against Racism.

Cabrera P, Rubio MJ, and Blasco J (2008) Quién duerme en la calle? Una investigación social y ciudadana sobre las personas sin techo. *Observatorio de la inclusión social*. Barcelona: Caixa Catalunya Obra Social.

Censis (Centro Studi Investimenti Sociali) (2006) *Quarantesimo Rapporto sulla situazione sociale del paese 2006*. Milano: Franco Angeli.

Coppola P and Amato F (2005) Gli spazi insediativi degli stranieri nell'area metropolitana di Napoli. *Dipartimento di Scienze Sociali*. Napoli: Università degli Studi di Napoli L'Orientale.

Da Costa B and Baptista I (2003) Immigration and homelessness in Portugal. *Report for the European Observatory on Homelessness*. Brussels: FEANTSA.

Daly G (1996) Migrants and gatekeepers: The link between immigration and homelessness in Western Europe. *Cities* 13(1): 11–23.

Edgar B (2004) *Policy Measures to Ensure Access to Decent Housing for Migrants and Ethnic Minorities*. Dundee and St Andrews: Joint Centre for Scottish Housing Research (JCSHR).

Edgar B, Doherty J, and Meert H (2004) *Immigration and Homelessness in Europe*. Bristol: Policy Press.

Pereda C, Actis W, and de Prada MÁ (2005) *Inmigración y vivienda en España*. Madrid: Ministerio de Trabajo y Asuntos Sociales e Colectivo Ioé.

Rodrigues C (2005) The changing profile of rough sleepers: Immigrants from Eastern Europe sleeping rough in Lisbon. *Homeless in Europe Winter*: 18–20.

Salis G (2008) Favelas in Europa? *LaVoce*. www.voceditalia.it.

Sánchez Morales R and Tezanos Vázquez S (2005) Los inmigrantes 'sin hogar' en España: un caso extremo de exclusión social. *Revista del Ministerio de Trabajo y Asuntos sociales* 55: 45–63.

Sapounakis A (2003) Immigration and homelessness in Greece. *Report for the European Observatory on Homelessness*. Brussels: FEANTSA.

Tosi A (2003) Immigration and homelessness in Italy. *Report for the European Observatory on Homelessness*. Brussels: FEANTSA.

United Nations (2008) *Press Conference by Special Rapporteur on Adequate Housing*. New York: United Nations Department of Public Information.

Van Parys R and Verbruggen N (2004) *Report on the Housing Situation of Undocumented Migrants in Six European Countries: Austria, Belgium, Germany, Italy, the Netherlands and Spain*. Bruxelles: PICUM (Platform for International Cooperation on Undocumented Migrants).

Further Reading

Cabrera P and Malgesini G (2003) Immigration and homelessness in Spain. *Report for the European Observatory on Homelessness*. Brussels: FEANTSA.

Calavita K (2005) *Immigrants at the Margins*. New York: Cambridge University Press.

Czischke D (ed.) (2007) *Social Housing and Integration of Immigrants in the European Union*. Brussels: CECODHAS.

Malcata Rebelo EM and Tiago Paiva L (2006) *Planeamento urbano para a integraçao de imigrantes*. Lisbon: Alto-Comisariado para a Imigraçao e Minorias etnicas.

Meert H, Morel E, Wolf J, et al. (2003) *The Changing Profiles of the Homeless People. Macro Social Context and Recent Trends*. Brussels: FEANTSA.

Natale L (2003) Immigrati stranieri regolari e irregolari: quale condizione abitativa? In: Acocella N and Sonnino E (eds.) *Movimenti di persone e movimenti di capitale in Europa*, Bologna: Il Mulino. pp. 181–206.

Sapounakis A (2002) Migration and access to housing in Greece. *Homeless in Europe* Winter. 13–14.

Shashati A and Mardaki A (2008) *Racism in Greece. ENAR Shadow Report 2007*. Bruxelles: European Network Against Racism.

Homeless People: Ex-Prisoners in England and Wales

A Jones, University of York, York, UK

© 2012 Elsevier Ltd. All rights reserved.

Glossary

Ex-prisoner Anyone who has spent time in prison either as part of a sentence or on remand (whether convicted of a crime or not).

Homeless and in priority need In England and Wales the homelessness legislation (Part 7 of the Housing Act, 1996) places a range of duties and powers on local authorities to assist people who are homeless or likely to become homeless within 28 days. Local authorities have a duty to secure accommodation for households who are eligible for assistance, homeless through no fault of their own, and have a priority need for accommodation.

Persons who are 'found to be vulnerable' as a result of having spent time in prison are deemed to be in priority need. Where a local authority finds an applicant eligible, homeless, but not in priority need, the authority must ensure that the applicant receives advice and assistance to help the applicant find accommodation for himself or herself.

Local prisons A local prison is a type of prison where a person is detained before a trial (on remand), before sentencing, or, directly after a conviction. Adult males and young offenders start their sentence in a prison local to the court where they were sentenced. If the sentence is short then it may be carried out at the local prison; otherwise longer-term prisoners are transferred soon after starting their sentence. As there are far fewer women's prisons, women are likely to be imprisoned some distance from their homes.

NOMS The National Offender Management Service is an executive agency of the Ministry of Justice and brings together HM Prison Service and the Probation Service to enable a more effective delivery of their services. NOMS is responsible for commissioning and delivering offender management services in custody and in the community helping to deliver punishments and reparation and coordinate rehabilitative, health, educational, employment, and housing opportunities for offenders to reduce reoffending as well as overseeing the contracts of privately run prisons, managing probation performance, and creating probation trusts.

Parole The parole system allows prisoners serving more than 4 years to be released before they have served their full sentence. The decision to grant or not grant parole depends on the nature of a prisoner's offences, their home circumstances, their plans for release, and their behaviour in prison.

Probation Convicted criminals are likely to be put on probation when a judge or magistrate gives them a community sentence or the Parole Board decides that they can be released early from their prison sentence. Any breach of probation conditions can result in offenders being sent, or returned, to prison.

Probation service The National Probation Service for England and Wales is a statutory criminal justice service, mainly responsible for the supervision of offenders in the community and the provision of reports to the criminal courts to assist them in their sentencing duties. It also offers some prisoners help during their sentence and as they prepare for release.

Introduction

The United Kingdom has one of the highest rates of imprisonment in Europe. Criminal justice data for the European Union indicate that the highest rates of imprisonment are found in England and Wales (139 per 100 000) compared with the EU average (98 per 100 000) (EU, 2006). Although crime rates have fallen over recent years, more people are imprisoned every year and the prison population has been rising steadily, increasing from 41 600 to 85 200 in March 2010 (80 900 men and 4300 women). Prison overcrowding in England and Wales has been a concern for successive governments; the reported occupancy rates, based on official capacity, have consistently been more than 100%. According to the Prison Reform Trust (*The Guardian*, 2009) two-thirds of prisons in England and Wales were overcrowded in 2009. Overcrowding has a negative impact both on the well-being of prisoners who often have to share accommodation intended for single use and find themselves confined to their cells for most of the day and on rehabilitation services within prisons which aim to prepare prisoners for release through various purposeful activities such as work, education, training and offending behaviour programmes, as well as housing advice and support.

Homelessness among Ex-Prisoners

Research conducted in England and Wales found that around half of prisoners had housing problems prior to imprisonment; of these prisoners, almost a third were not living in permanent accommodation, and 5% were sleeping rough before being imprisoned. A third of prisoners lose their accommodation while in prison and a quarter of all prisoners leave prison without accommodation (Home Office, 2003). Women prisoners (40%) are particularly unlikely to have accommodation for their release and one study found that almost half (49%) of prisoners with mental health problems had no fixed address on leaving prison.

Prisoners lose their accommodation for a variety of reasons including rent or mortgage arrears because they are unable to meet payments whilst in custody. In the case of tenants, arrears often accrue due to a loss of entitlement to housing benefits (which covers part or all of the rent). Relationship breakdown and/or loss of contact with family, following imprisonment, are also significant factors.

Studies in a number of countries have highlighted the difficulties ex-prisoners face in securing suitable accommodation on release (see, for example, Nelson et al., 1999). The problems faced by ex-offenders on release include:

- a shortage of social housing;
- a lack of suitable accommodation, for example, supported housing for offenders with specialist needs such as substance misuse or mental health problems;
- previous/existing tenancy problems such as rent arrears or antisocial behaviour;
- difficulties in accessing private rented accommodation because of a lack of resources and delays in obtaining welfare benefits (most, though not all, prisoners are given a discharge grant which is intended to meet their immediate needs on release; the discharge grant was never intended to cover accommodation costs); and
- social and private landlords' perception of offenders as risky or undesirable tenants, particularly if they have histories of sexual and violent offending and/or arson.

Accommodation options are further constrained because prisoners often do not wish to be accommodated in hostels where substance misuse is rife, or in areas where they are likely to come into contact with former associates, drug dealers or users, pimps, or violent ex-partners.

> I really didn't want to be there as I had family what died in there because of drugs ... and the place is riddled with drugs ... Everyone there is drinking or on drugs, you have to step over drunks outside, people are knocking on your door asking you if you want to chip in with them ...

I did lapse a bit but not in a big way and I did manage [with the help of support worker] to get out of there in time. (Service user)

Homelessness and Reoffending

There is now a body of evidence to suggest that not having a settled place to live or being in poor or unsatisfactory accommodation can increase the likelihood of reoffending (ODPM and Home Office, 2005). Those who have served a custodial sentence and are released homeless are more than twice as likely to reoffend. A Home Office research study found that less than a third of released prisoners who had homes to go to were reconvicted, compared to over two-thirds of prisoners who had no home to go to (Home Office, 1999). A more recent study (May et al., 2008) of factors linked to reoffending builds on the existing evidence by showing that accommodation and employment were significantly associated with an increased likelihood of reoffending when a prisoner had problems with both of these on release. Ex-prisoners with an address to go to on release are three times more likely to have employment than those who had no accommodation arranged. Having accommodation and appropriate support is thought to help offenders embark upon more stable lives and access the support services they need (NOMS, 2005).

Preventing homelessness among ex-prisoners has been a key element of recent government homelessness policies and is an important part of government strategies to reduce reoffending. Under the homelessness legislation, vulnerable ex-prisoners are deemed a priority group and local authorities therefore have a duty to secure accommodation for them. (The key test of vulnerability is set out in the case of *R v. Camden LBC ex-parte Pereira* [1998] 30 HLR 317: "Whether the applicant when homeless is less likely to fend for himself than an ordinary homeless person so that injury or detriment to him will result when a less vulnerable person would be able to cope without harmful effect." In Wales all ex-prisoners are considered vulnerable and in priority need.) However, it is difficult to prove vulnerability and few ex-prisoners have been accepted as homeless under the legislation, although, as will be seen, many ex-prisoners have extremely high support needs. There is also evidence that some local authorities intentionally avoid rehousing ex-prisoners (House of Commons Library, 2010). (Someone can be found to be intentionally homeless if the person deliberately does or fails to do anything in consequence of which the person ceases to occupy accommodation (or the likely result of which is that the person will be forced to leave accommodation). In the case of prisoners this can include committing a crime which results in imprisonment.) Government guidance states that local authorities and social landlords should not discriminate and impose blanket exclusions for any group. However, some homelessness charities have claimed that many social landlords operate such allocation policies in practice.

Support Needs of Ex-Prisoners

A report by the government's Social Exclusion Unit (SEU, 2002) shows that many prisoners have experienced a lifetime of social exclusion. In addition to their housing problems, many prisoners have poor basic skills, little or no experience of work, and few positive social networks. All of this is often severely complicated by substance misuse and mental health problems. Compared with the general population, prisoners are 13 times as likely to have been in the care of the local authority as a child, 13 times as likely to be unemployed, 10 times as likely to have been a regular truant, and 2.5 times as likely to have had a family member convicted of a criminal offence. Many prisoners' basic skills are very poor: 80% have writing skills, 65% numeracy skills, and 50% reading skills at or below the level of an 11-year-old child. Offenders also have high levels of need: over 70% suffer from at least two mental health disorders and 20% of male and 37% of female sentenced prisoners have attempted suicide in the past. The position is even worse for young offenders (aged 18–20), whose basic skills, unemployment rate, and school exclusion background are all over a third worse than those for older prisoners. Despite these high levels of need, many offenders have effectively been excluded from access to services in the past. It is estimated that around half of prisoners had no GP before they came into custody; prisoners are over 20 times more likely than the general population to have been excluded from school; and one prison drugs project found that although 70% of those entering the prison had a drug misuse problem, 80% of these had not received any support for their drug misuse before entering custody.

Women offenders have higher levels of need than male offenders. Whilst drug addiction plays a huge part in all offending, this is disproportionately the case with women and drug dependency is more prevalent amongst women (in particular white women) than amongst men (Ramsay, 2003). The likelihood of women prisoners having mental health problems is higher as compared to male prisoners or the general population. A study in a women's prison found that 65% of the prisoners had both mental health problems and drug dependency. Outside prison, men are more likely to commit suicide than women but the position is reversed inside the prison. Self-harm in prison is a huge problem but, again, is more prevalent in women's prisons (Home Office, 2007).

Support for Ex-Prisoners

The problem of homelessness among ex-prisoners has prompted policy development in various countries and a range of initiatives designed to prepare prisoners for release (see, for example, Penfold et al., 2009). In the United Kingdom, recent years have seen increased provision of housing advice and assistance targeted at prisoners before release. Whilst housing advice is provided by statutory agencies, including local authority housing departments, which provide outreach services in some prisons, and the Prison Service itself, many housing advice and accommodation support services are provided by voluntary agencies, charities, and organisations working within prisons, often in conjunction with Prison Service staff. Since April 2005, all local prisons have been required to carry out a housing needs assessment of new prisoners, including those serving short sentences (prisons must now complete a Housing Needs Initial Assessment (HNIA) for 90% of new receptions within 4 days of the prisoner's arrival). However, research suggests that housing advice and support is not routinely provided to prisoners even where a need is identified (Hartfree et al., 2008).

Prisoners serving sentences of more than 12 months are subject to statutory supervision and are supported, amongst other things, to find appropriate accommodation both before and after release. Short-term prisoners (defined as prisoners sentenced to less than 12 months in prison) are usually released without statutory supervision and there is currently no prison rehabilitation regime specifically designed to meet their needs. This has been justified on the grounds that there is insufficient time for rehabilitation services to make a difference. Short-term prisoners constitute the majority of those imprisoned each year. In 2003, 64% of all adult males sent to prison were sentenced to less than 12 months whilst three-quarters of female prisoners served short-term sentences. In 2002, 95 000 people were sentenced to prison and, of those, 53 000 were sentenced to 6 months or less. This group has both a high level of social need and the highest reconviction rate of released adult prisoners. They are also the most likely to have no accommodation on release. Many receive inadequate provision in relation to housing, health, and employment, and, given the length of their sentences served in custody (which can be as little as a few weeks), the opportunity for this group to engage in offending behaviour programmes and prerelease services is limited (House of Commons, 2004). (If the sentence is less than 12 months the prisoner gets Automatic Unconditional Release and serves only half their sentence in prison (as long as they have not broken any prison rules and been given additional days in prison). Time spent on remand is deducted from the time spent in prison.)

It has been argued that the lack of attention paid to short-term prisoners during their stay in prison, combined with the lack of resettlement services or social support following their release, helps to create a 'revolving door' pattern of those prisoners returning to homelessness or becoming homeless on release, reoffending and returning to prison within a short space of time after release. US studies have highlighted the importance of prerelease support:

> While the time after release is fraught with problems, it also offers an opportunity to capitalize on most people's strong desire to turn their lives around. But to take advantage of this considerable momentum, people need to be better prepared before release. (Nelson et al., 1999: i)

Adding to the difficulties described above is the operation of policies and practices designed to address prison overcrowding in England and Wales. Prisoners are transferred to prisons often located many miles away from their homes in order to free up spaces in local prisons. This reduces the likelihood of advisers having local housing knowledge or contacts. These moves can also jeopardise family relationships and the chances of successful reintegration back into the community on release, both important factors in reducing reoffending and accommodation outcomes. This is a particular problem for women prisoners as there are only 14 women's prisons in England (there are none in Wales), so many women prisoners are imprisoned some distance from their home area. Attempts to address prison overcrowding have included the introduction of various early release schemes such as the End of Custody Licence (ECL) scheme, under which certain categories of prisoners can be released 18 days early, often with little notice (this is an early release scheme designed to ease prison overcrowding, under which eligible prisoners are released from prison under temporary licence up to 18 days earlier than would otherwise be the case). (For more detail of various types of early release schemes, refer to Relevant Websites.) Prisoners released on ECL should have an address to go to but research suggests that prison services rarely undertake checks. Where arrangements have been made for release then ECL often disrupts these. As one ex-prisoner explained, he was released early and became homeless, which he felt placed him at an increased risk of reoffending (Jones and Quilgars, 2010).

> The day I got released, they are giving me my methadone that morning but no appointment to go and see nobody, so I am released with my discharge grant and no fucking medication so I'm going to start using again and shoplifting aren't I? Obviously when you're released homeless you go back to your old haunts ... I got early release and [support worker] should have known. (Service user)

While many ex-prisoners return to the family home and require little immediate support or advice, for others support with gaining stable and affordable housing is a critical need in the period immediately following release. For some of the most vulnerable ex-prisoners, being unsupported in their efforts to find accommodation forces them into situations where the chance of them reoffending or reengaging in substance misuse, and ultimately returning to prison, is high (Hartfree et al., 2008: 87).

Housing Advice and Interventions to Prevent Homelessness amongst Ex-Prisoners

Housing advice services within prisons have two main aims: to help prisoners who have accommodation maintain their housing and to arrange appropriate accommodation for those who would otherwise be homeless on release.

Although support to address problems such as rent arrears and housing benefit payments and the provision of housing advice can be helpful, it is often difficult to arrange accommodation before release. For example, not all local authorities assess cases before release, which reduces the chances of prisoners securing some form of temporary accommodation through the provisions of the homelessness legislation. The process of seeking and securing accommodation provided by other social landlords can be lengthy and complex, involving the completion of several detailed applications to a number of providers. This often means that despite the best efforts of support services, prisoners are discharged without accommodation and have to present at the homeless person's unit on the day of release.

The immediate moment of release from prison has been identified by researchers in the United States as a critical point in the reintegration process. Ultimately, individuals have to choose among competing courses of action, but the release process itself can influence the decision (Nelson et al., 1999). In England and Wales the importance of 'meet at the gate' services such as those provided by Shelter and St Giles Trust has been increasingly recognised. (For more information, refer to Relevant Websites.) Here support workers arrange to meet the prisoner immediately after release and accompany him or her to their accommodation, or, where no accommodation has been arranged, to the local housing department where they advocate for the client. Recent studies in the United Kingdom (see, for example, Jones and Quilgars, 2009, 2010) have also found that support and advocacy in the immediate postrelease period is crucial:

You lose your children, you lose your home... You come out and you have to go to the Homeless Persons' Unit and then benefits take forever... You end up somewhere that you don't know... It is not easy and if you are all on your own trying to sort everything – let's say if you are into drugs or drink then you are more likely to take drugs and drink again because you are so fed up and then you might end up in a bad way again... so it is really important that people have support. (Service user)

The Provision of Continuing Support

There is now a great deal of evidence in the general homelessness literature about the importance of resettlement support for formerly homeless and/or insecurely housed people. (In general homelessness literature the term 'resettlement' is used to describe the process of reintegrating into the community following a period of homelessness whilst in criminology literature and within the prison service 'resettlement' usually refers to preparation for release undertaken in custody.) As noted earlier, many ex-prisoners are amongst the most vulnerable in society and have often led disrupted lives and require a great deal of support if they are to resettle successfully in communities and engage with the necessary mainstream support services they require, particularly when, as Dutreix has noted, some have never led settled lives before:

> Reintegration back into society assumes that one was integrated into society at some previous time. In the author's experience it has been found that many women in prison and released from prison have never felt part of society. They were never integrated in the first place. Thus, rather than reintegration, support may need to assist a woman to enter society for the first time. (Dutreix, 2003: 12)

Although ex-prisoners often value support, many disengage with services before their support plan is completed (as many as two-thirds working with one 'through the gate' service; Jones and Quilgars, 2009). The reasons for this are unclear and it may be that some individuals disengage because they feel they have received all the support they required. However, it is likely that some continue to experience problems with substance misuse and/or reoffend. Further, ex-prisoners, like other vulnerable groups, often find it difficult to engage with the mainstream services on which they have to rely for ongoing support.

Conclusion

It has been seen that ex-prisoners share the same social disadvantages as many others in the homeless population and are often extremely vulnerable and at risk of reoffending. Whilst the importance of meeting the accommodation needs of ex-prisoners has been recognised for some time, many individuals continue to leave prison without accommodation or are released to unsuitable accommodation and/or inappropriate areas. Even where support services are successful in finding accommodation for their clients, many lose contact with services or fail to engage with mainstream support services. The reasons for this are unclear and further longitudinal research is required to understand the longer-term needs of ex-prisoners as well as the longer-term outcomes for those who appear to have been successfully accommodated immediately after release.

See also: Criminological Perspectives on Homelessness; Homeless People: Care Leavers; Homeless People: Care Leavers in the United Kingdom; Homeless People: Ex-Service Personnel/Veterans in the United Kingdom; Housing Need in the United Kingdom; Illicit Drug Use and Homelessness; Mental Health and Homelessness; Supported Housing.

References

Dutreix C (2003) *Homelessness and women exiting prison*. Parity 16(5): 11–13

EU (2006) *European Sourcebook of Crime and Criminal Justice Statistics*. Available at: http://www.europeansourcebook.org/ (accessed 25 January 2010).

Hartfree Y, Dearden C, and Pound E (2008) High hopes: Supporting ex-prisoners in their lives after prison. *DWP Research Report No. 509*. London: Department for Work and Pensions.

Home Office (1999) Explaining reconviction following a community sentence: The role of social factors. *Home Office Research Study 192*. London: Home Office.

Home Office (2003) *The resettlement of short-term prisoners: An evaluation of seven pathfinder programmes, findings 200*. London: Home Office.

Home Office (2007) The Corston Report, London: Home Office. Available at: http://www.homeoffice.gov.uk/documents/corston-report/ (accessed 25 January 2010).

House of Commons (2004) Home affairs first report session 2004–2005. Available at: http://www.publications.parliament.uk/pa/cm200405/cmselect/cmhaff/193/19302.htm (accessed 25 January 2010).

House of Commons Library (2010) Housing ex-offenders, Standard Note SN/SP/2989.

Jones A and Quilgars D (2009) Evaluation of the Shelter London prisons project: Resettling women prisoners from HMP Holloway, Unpublished.

Jones A and Quilgars D (2010) Supporting short-term prisoners leaving HMP Leeds, Unpublished interim report on the evaluation of the Shelter Prisoners Advocacy Release Team.

May C, Sharma N, and Stewart D (2008) Factors linked to reoffending: A one-year follow-up of prisoners who took part in the resettlement surveys 2001, 2003 and 2004, *Research Summary 5, Ministry of Justice*. http://www.justice.gov.uk/publications/docs/research-factors-reoffending.pdf (accessed 25 January 2010).

Nelson M, Deess P, and Allen C (1999) *The First Month Out: Post-Incarceration Experiences in New York City*. New York: Vera Institute of Justice.

NOMS (2005) The government's national reducing re-offending plan. London: Home Office. Available at: http://noms.justice.gov.uk/news-publications-events/publications/strategy/reducing-reoffend-delivery-plan/ reducing-reoffend-delivery-sum?view=Binary (accessed 25 January 2010).

ODPM and Home Office (2005) *Guide to Housing and Housing Related Support Options for Offenders and People at Risk of Offending*. London: ODPM/Home Office.

Penfold C, Day N, Nixon J, and Webster Swith Jones A and Thomas S (2009) *Homelessness Prevention and Meeting Housing Need for (Ex)Offenders*. London: Communities and Local Government.

Ramsay M (ed.) (2003) *Prisoners' Drug Use and Treatment: Seven Research Studies: Home Office Research Study 267*. London: Home Office.

SEU (2002) *Reducing Re-Offending by Ex-Prisoners*, Social Exclusion Unit London: ODPM.

Further Reading

House of Commons Home Affairs Committee (2004–2005) Rehabilitation of prisoners. *First Report of Session 2004–2005*, Vol. 1. London: The Stationery Office.

James K, Curtis S, and Griffiths S (2004) *Just Surviving: The Housing and Support Needs of People on the Fringes of Homelessness and/or the Criminal Justice System in West Yorkshire*. Leeds, UK: Leeds Supporting People Team.

La Vigne N, Shollenberger T, and Debus S (2009) One year out: Tracking the experiences of male prisoners returning to Houston, Texas, Urban Institute Justice Policy Center. Available at: http://www.urban.org/UploadedPDF/411911_male_prisoners_houston.pdf (accessed 25 January 2010).

Niven S and Stewart D (2005) Home Office Findings 248. *Resettlement outcomes on release from prison*. London: Home Office.

Home Office (2006) Five Year Strategy for Protecting the Public and Reducing Re-Offending. London: Home Office.

ODPM *Sustainable Communities: Settled Homes; Changing Lives*. London: ODPM.

Pleace N and Minton J (2009) Delivering better housing and employment outcomes for offenders on probation. *DWP Research Report No. 610*. London: Department for Work and Pensions.

Social Exclusion Task Force (2009) *Short Study on Women Offenders*. London: Cabinet Office & Ministry of Justice.

Willis M (2004) Ex-prisoners, SAAP, housing and homelessness in Australia: Final report to the national SAAP coordination and development committee. Canberra, Australia: Australian Institute of Criminology.

Relevant Websites

www.parliament.uk – UK Parliament.
www.stgilestrust.org.uk – St. Giles Trust.

Homeless People: Ex-Service Personnel/Veterans in the United Kingdom

S Johnsen, Heriot-Watt University, Edinburgh, UK

© 2012 Elsevier Ltd. All rights reserved.

Glossary

Active service Engagement in operations against the enemy, in the protection of life or property, or military occupation of a foreign country.

Early service leavers Personnel who leave the armed forces with less than 4 years' service or as a result of compulsory discharge.

Ex-service personnel/veterans Individuals who have served in Britain's Army, Royal Navy, or Royal Air Force (whether or not they have engaged in active service), or in the merchant navy in a war zone.

Nonstatutory (or 'single') homeless people Individuals sleeping rough, living in a hostel, living in a bed and breakfast hotel, or staying with friends or family because they have no home of their own.

Service leavers Personnel discharged from the armed forces.

Statutory homeless households Households (usually families) accepted by a local authority as homeless and in priority need of rehousing.

Introduction

Research in the mid- to late 1990s suggested that approximately one-quarter of homeless people in Britain had served in the armed forces (Gunner and Knott, 1997; Randall and Brown, 1994). This also indicated that homeless ex-service personnel tended to be more disadvantaged than other homeless people: they were older on average, and were more likely to have slept rough, to have suffered from physical health or alcohol problems, and/or to have been homeless for prolonged periods. These findings echo those from research in the United States, where veterans account for 23% of all homeless people, and many suffer from mental illness or substance abuse problems (National Coalition for the Homeless, 2009).

A number of measures were therefore put in place by central government departments in the United Kingdom in an attempt to reduce the incidence of homelessness amongst ex-service personnel. Most notably, the Ministry of Defence (MoD) expanded its predischarge resettlement service to ensure that most service leavers are given time and resources to undertake a variety of management and vocational training courses, as well as opportunities to attend briefings on housing and financial matters. In addition, in 2002 the categories of homeless applicants who have a priority need for accommodation from local authorities were extended to include those deemed vulnerable as a result of having been a member of the armed forces. Moreover, the Joint Services Housing Advice Organisation (JSHAO) was set up in 1994 to provide service personnel and their families with information and advice on housing options during and after their time in the armed forces.

However, in London, in particular, concerns about the welfare of homeless ex-service personnel and the apparent scale of the problem prompted the formation of the Ex-Service Action Group on Homelessness (ESAG) in 1997. ESAG was very proactive in implementing several service initiatives in the capital. They also commissioned an independent study which examined the effectiveness of these initiatives in counteracting homelessness amongst ex-service personnel in London (Johnsen et al., 2008). The research was funded by the Veterans Minister's Challenge Fund and The Royal British Legion.

The London study comprised a review of existing statistics, and interviews with managers and frontline staff in ex-service-specific and 'mainstream' services working with homeless ex-service personnel, as well as representatives of central government departments and national homelessness umbrella bodies. It also involved in-depth interviews with a total of 59 ex-service personnel, 32 of whom were homeless at the point of initial interview and 27 of whom had recent experience of homelessness but had been rehoused successfully. The study included a longitudinal element, tracing the support service use and experiences of the 32 currently homeless ex-service personnel over the course of 1 year. These data provide the most up-to-date evidence on the experiences of homelessness amongst ex-service personnel in the United Kingdom.

The Number and Characteristics of Homeless Ex-Service Personnel in London

By 2007, an estimated 6% of London's current nonstatutory ('single') homeless population had served in the armed forces. This represented a substantial drop from the proportion (approximately one-quarter) reported in the mid-1990s. Numbers did, however, remain significant: an estimated 1100 single homeless ex-service personnel (predominantly hostel residents, but including some rough sleepers) and approximately 2500 ex-service personnel in statutorily homeless households (accepted for rehousing by local authorities) were living in London on any given night. At the time of writing it remains unclear what, if any, impact ongoing conflicts in Iraq and Afghanistan might have on the scale of ex-service homelessness in the United Kingdom.

Demographically, the homeless ex-service personnel in London were almost exclusively male, most were of White ethnic background, and they had an older age profile than the wider nonstatutory homeless population. The vulnerabilities and support needs of homeless ex-service personnel were, on the whole, very similar in nature to those of other nonstatutory homeless people, but a greater proportion of ex-service personnel had alcohol, physical, and/or mental health problems.

Only a small minority reported vulnerabilities and support needs that were unique to people with a history of the armed forces, such as combat-related posttraumatic stress disorder. Some homeless ex-service interviewees with mental health problems attributed these to events during military life – typically, but not exclusively, active service. For a greater number, however, poor mental health was reported to be symptomatic of problems beginning in childhood, or traumatic events after leaving the armed forces (e.g., bereavement).

Pathways into Homelessness

It was possible to identify four main life history trajectories amongst the current and former homeless ex-service personnel interviewed in London:

- First, there were those who carried vulnerabilities deriving from childhood or adolescence – such as having been 'looked after' by the state (because of parental abuse or neglect), problematic drinking, and/or involvement in criminal activity – into the armed forces and later civilian life. For many of these individuals, their time in the armed forces was something of a period of 'suspended animation', with earlier problems remaining unresolved at the point of discharge.
- The second group comprised those who encountered difficulties within the armed forces, such as the onset of alcohol or mental health problems, which continued to affect them after discharge. The nature of these problems varied. For some they were the outcome of bullying or traumatic incidents during active service; for others, they were the apparent consequence of the drinking culture associated with the armed forces and/or failure to adhere to behavioural protocols.
- The third group included those who had a successful career in the armed forces but found adjustment to civilian life very difficult. These difficulties often revolved around problems settling into stable employment and/or adjusting to 'normal' family life on 'civvy street' (i.e., in civilian society).
- Fourth, there were others who had a successful career in the armed forces and did not encounter difficulties until a trauma later in life – such as relationship breakdown, bereavement, or financial crisis. Such crises commonly occurred many years after discharge, and were usually considered by interviewees to be entirely unrelated to their service history.

Of these experiences, the third trajectory was the least common, and the fourth the most widespread. This finding adds weight to claims that the incidence of homelessness amongst ex-service personnel is not necessarily closely related to either the 'institutionalisation' of armed forces personnel or their exposure to military combat, as is often presumed (Rosenheck et al., 1997).

The Experience of Homelessness

Whilst many of the triggers for homelessness amongst ex-service personnel were similar to those commonly reported by other homeless people, it was clear that a military background influences – and often quite profoundly – 'how' ex-service personnel experience homelessness. Given their alleged adaptability to physical discomfort, most considered themselves better equipped to endure, and were less fearful of, the hardships of street life than the wider homeless population generally.

They were also less inclined to seek or accept help given their tendency to elevate the perceived 'shame' of their situation – a phenomenon often attributed to the reportedly stoic pride and independence of armed forces personnel. The elevation of shame, and reluctance to seek assistance from ex-service welfare charities, was especially acute when interviewees had been discharged dishonourably – for going absent without leave ('awol'), for example.

These factors, together with their greater propensity to drink heavily – which many claim was initiated or exacerbated by the military lifestyle – combined to make ex-service personnel more susceptible to sustained or repeat homelessness. Some had resisted the attempts of support agencies to move them from the streets into accommodation for many years.

The Effectiveness of Provision for Homeless Ex-Service Personnel

A key finding of the London study was that a greater range of support options was available to homeless ex-service personnel than most other members of the homeless population. In addition to mainstream homelessness services, they were eligible for specialist ex-forces hostels, resettlement support, settled housing schemes, and employment initiatives. Some ex-service personnel preferred ex-service-specific provision because they enjoyed the company of people with shared experiences and appreciated the way staff valued and 'understood' their service history. Others, however, would not utilise dedicated ex-service projects given their dislike of the dynamics in such provision, elevated feelings of perceived 'shame', and/or negative feelings towards the armed forces.

The reduction in the proportion of London's homeless population with a history of the services and successful resettlement of many homeless ex-service personnel indicated that the strengthened service network was leading to positive outcomes. Most notably, the ex-service 'route' provided quicker access to emergency accommodation than did generic provision, and the specialist settled accommodation was regarded to be of high quality.

The study also noted, however, a number of weaknesses in the service network for homeless ex-service personnel in London. Awareness of services amongst potential clientele and mainstream homelessness agencies regarding specialist ex-services initiatives was generally poor. Recent service leavers were more aware of such provisions than their older counterparts were, suggesting that the influence of ESAG and enhanced predischarge resettlement package offered by the MoD may have a preventative impact in the long term. There was nevertheless a cohort of older ex-service personnel who had not had the benefit of this information and advice.

The resettlement of homeless ex-service personnel and other homeless people was impeded by a shortage of settled housing in London. Support provided in the lead-up to, and period following, rehousing was greatly valued by ex-service personnel but was often provided in an unstructured and potentially unsustainable manner – particularly to those rehoused in independent social tenancies. The quality of life of a significant number of formerly homeless ex-service personnel was severely compromised by social isolation and loneliness, as is often the case with other nonstatutory homeless people.

Also, provision for homeless ex-service personnel with mental health problems – particularly 'low-level' conditions such as depression and anxiety – was considered insufficient to meet levels of demand.

Conclusions

Literature on homeless ex-service personnel in the United Kingdom has suggested that the numbers affected were relatively large and that they were a particularly vulnerable group. However, a recent London study demonstrated that interventions by both the government and voluntary agencies had successfully reduced the numbers in the capital and provided ex-service personnel with more options than those available to other single homeless people. One should not assume, however, that these findings would be replicated elsewhere in the United Kingdom where similar research has not as yet been carried out.

A number of recommendations arose from the study, including the need to enhance the armed forces' resettlement and postdischarge support programmes by considering ways of breaking down the 'shame' barrier that inhibits ex-service personnel from accepting help; promoting the value of the housing and financial briefings available within resettlement programmes; training commanding officers and resettlement staff in the detection of risk factors for homelessness and social exclusion (particularly amongst early service leavers); and more proactively monitoring the well-being of ex-service personnel after discharge.

Whilst the overwhelming majority of ex-service personnel make a successful transition to civilian life and only a very small minority experience homelessness, the characteristics and experiences of those who do dictate that a particularly proactive and coordinated response is required.

See also: Health, Well-Being and Vulnerable Populations; Homelessness: Causation; Homelessness: Definitions; Homelessness: Prevention in the United States; Policies to Address Homelessness: Prevention in the United Kingdom; Policies to Address Homelessness: Rights-Based Approaches.

References

Gunner G and Knott H (1997) *Homeless on Civvy Street: Survey of Homelessness amongst Ex-Servicemen, 1997*. London: Ex-Service Action Group.

Johnsen S, Jones A, and Rugg J (2008) *The Experiences of Homeless Ex-Service Personnel in London*. York, UK: Centre for Housing Policy.

National Coalition for the Homeless (2009) *Homeless Veterans*. Washington, DC: National Coalition for the Homeless.

Randall G and Brown S (1994) *Falling Out: A Research Study of Homeless Ex-Service People*. London: Crisis.

Rosenheck R, Frisman L, Fontana A, and Leda C (1997) Combat exposure and PTSD among homeless veterans of three wars. In: Fullerton CS and Ursano RJ (eds.) *Posttraumatic Stress Disorder:Acute and Long-Term Response to Trauma and Disaster*, pp. 191–207. Washington, DC: American Psychiatric Association.

Further Reading

Ballintyne S and Hanks S (2000) *Lest We Forget: Ex-Servicemen and Homelessness*. London: Crisis.

Higate PR (1997) Soldiering on? Theorizing homelessness amongst ex-servicemen. In: Burrows R, Pleace N, and Quilgars D (eds.) *Homelessness and Social Policy*, pp. 109–122. London: Routledge.

Higate PR (2000) Ex-servicemen on the road: Travel and homelessness. *Sociological Review* 48: 331–348.

Higate PR (2000) Tough bodies and rough sleeping: Embodying homelessness amongst ex-servicemen. *Housing Theory and Society* 17(3): 97–108.

Higate PR (2001) Theorizing continuity: From military to civilian life. *Armed Forces and Society* 27(3): 443–460.

Homeless People in China/East Asia

P Kennett, University of Bristol, Bristol, UK
H-G Jeon and T Mizuuchi, Osaka City University, Osaka, Japan

© 2012 Elsevier Ltd. All rights reserved.

Glossary

Financial tsunami Term used in East Asia to refer to the global economic crisis.
Jahwal ŭi jib Private, transitional housing units available to homeless people leaving shelters in Korea.
Jjogbang (Often illegal) rental hostels mainly used by daily labourers and low-income people in Korean cities.
Purangja Traditional and derogative term for the homeless in Korea referring to vagrants or bums.
Vinyl houses Substandard and squatter housing in Korea for low-income residents, most of whom have been forcibly evicted from housing renewal areas. These are illegally constructed using thin wood board layers and vinyl covering, which began in 2008.
Yoseba Districts and communities in Japanese cities for day labourers and the able-bodied poor in which to seek manual labour and accommodation in the cheap hostels, dormitories, and flophouses (doya).

Introduction

This article will explore the nature, extent, and dynamics of homelessness in East Asia. It will also consider the institutional and policy responses to the phenomenon. The article will discuss developments in mainland China (hereafter China), Hong Kong SAR (hereafter Hong Kong), Japan, and South Korea (hereafter Korea). These societies represent some of the fastest growing economies during the last 40 years, all of which have also experienced a substantial rise in the standard of living. However, not all have benefited from the rapid and dynamic growth, and increasing wealth has been accompanied by widening levels of inequality and new forms of stratification and exclusion. Globalisation, neoliberalism, as well as structural and social change have increased individual risk of homelessness. This article will highlight the dynamics of homelessness and the institutional and policy responses in each society. It will outline current and emerging fissures of stratification, inequality, and insecurity, and consider their relationship with homelessness.

The Context and Concept of Homelessness in East Asia

Prior to the 1990s in the newly industrialising economies of Hong Kong, Japan, and Korea, the homeless were invisible to mainstream society and policy makers, and were characterised as ageing, aberrant, and morally deficient individuals. The bursting of the bubble economy and the Asian Financial Crisis in 1997 was followed by the SARS epidemic in 2003 and, in combination, contributed to a severe economic downturn, massive unemployment and wage cuts, rising poverty, and an increase in those inadequately housed, visibly homeless, and destitute.

In China, until the 1990s, poverty was regarded as a rural phenomenon. In urban areas of this state socialist society, the work unit system provided the institutional framework for the range of state provided social welfare. Social division was constructed around political background and urban–rural residence but, in general, it was a society of low-income equality. However, by the 1990s, fundamental transformation through an extensive economic reform programme emphasising global integration, marketisation, privatisation, and competitiveness saw the emergence of a 'socialist market economy', the dismantling and reconstruction of state-owned enterprises and rural communes, the removal of employment guarantees, and the emergence of a 'floating population' of migrants in urban areas largely excluded from social rights. Whilst for some the Chinese city has become a place of opportunity, wealth accumulation, and social mobility, for many others it has become a space of insecurity, unemployment, poverty, discrimination, and exclusion.

In Hong Kong, Japan, and Korea, the painful recovery following the Financial Crisis, institutional and policy responses from governments, and the extensive intervention, support, and lobbying from nongovernmental organisations (NGOs) and grassroots organisations working with the homeless did bring about a reduction in the numbers of people sleeping on the streets. However, what has become clear is that the problem is far from 'solved'.

Whilst the risk of homelessness is clearly greater during periods of economic downturn (as suggested by the current upward trajectory of homelessness in the context of the global 'financial tsunami'), the homelessness dynamic is more complex and multidimensional and linked to structural and social change within societies. This has contributed to increasing income disparities between high-income and low-income earners as the wage gap between skilled/well-educated and unskilled/less well-educated workers has consistently widened, job insecurity with the deterioration of employment conditions and the expansion of contract and part-time work, and welfare systems that are unable to adequately provide for the new conditions of insecurity and risk.

As the context and dynamics of homelessness have been transformed in East Asian societies, the homeless population has increasingly included younger, better educated, and able-bodied men and women. Whilst there has been a growing recognition of the role of socioeconomic and structural factors in the homelessness dynamic and increasing diversity amongst the homeless population, there nevertheless continues to be an identification of homelessness with the narrowest and most visible forms of destitution such as street sleeping, tent dwellers, or vagrants. Accordingly, for the most part the phenomenon continues to be characterised as 'male' and homeless people subjected to social discrimination, stigma, coercion, and moral subordination. As De Venanzi (2007) argues "the homeless find themselves at the unfavourable end of two powerful classifying systems: Pollution-stigmatization, which have the function to preserve a sense of order, clarity, and continuity in 'normal' peoples lives ... The homeless become stigmatized due to supposed blemishes in their individual character that presumably explain their deviant way of life" (De Venanzi, 2007: 134).

The exact number of homeless people in a country is notoriously difficult to quantify given the different definitions and methodologies applied, as well as the transient and hidden nature of the phenomenon. In Hong Kong, a Street Sleepers Registry has been established to officially capture the number of street sleepers. This shows that the number of street sleepers has gradually declined from its peak of 1399 in February 2001 to 785 in December 2002 and 335 in 2007. However, during 2008 and 2009 numbers have again started to rise with the average number of registered street sleepers per month from February 2008 to January 2009 estimated to be 358, showing an increase of 23 people over the average figure for the previous year. The figures do not include residents of the seven street sleeper hostels operated by NGOs on a self-financing basis, nor the five hostels and temporary shelters operated by NGOs and funded by the Social Welfare Department. In addition, official figures indicate that just over 53 000 domestic household members were living in cubicles and bedspaces, whilst the Society for Community Organisation (SoCo) suggests that there are still some 100 000 people living in cage homes, or in flats divided into cubicles often with no more than 133/4 sq. ft. of space, particularly in poor parts of Kowloon such as Sham Shui Po and Tai Kok Tsui. Conditions are often little better than living on the streets but locations are convenient and rents cheap, at a time when rents for small units with a saleable area less than 430 sq. ft. have increased year on year, by 11% in 2005, 10% in 2006, and 13% in 2007.

In Japan a nationwide survey conducted in 1999 revealed a total of 17 172 rough sleepers in the five Japanese cities of Yokohama, Kawasaki, Nagoya, Tokyo, and Osaka. According to the most recent Government survey in 2008, there are now approximately 16 000 rough sleepers in Japan. However, if those living in temporary shelters, transitory housing, internet cafes, hostels, and other insecure housing are taken into account the number of homeless in Japan could well exceed 35 000 people (Obinger, 2009).

In Korea, government statistics include 'those in shelters' and 'those sleeping on the street' and, as **Table 1** indicates, the number of homeless nationally is approximately 5000, of whom just over 3500 are shelter entrants and just over 1000 are sleeping on the street.

However, if the approximately 6000 residents of *jjogbang* (rental hostels) are included, the total number of people exceeds 10 000. As **Figure 1** highlights street sleepers are concentrated in Seoul. In recent years, around 3200 street sleepers have been counted in that city, representing 60% of the total.

In China, the homeless population is particularly difficult to quantify. As well as beggars and long-term street sleepers, rural–urban migrant workers without the required registration documents, the urban poor and laid-off workers, forced evictees, and children on the streets fall into the official category of 'vagrants and beggars'. In 2009 there were more than 230 million migrant workers in China, with numbers of jobless migrants at around 20–30

Table 1 Homeless statistics in South Korea according to the health and welfare ministry 2000–2006

	2000	2001	2002	2003	2004	2005	2006
In shelters	4601	4321	3569	3612	3497	3763	3563
On the streets	445	517	670	928	969	959	1293
Total	5046	4838	4439	4540	4466	4722	4856

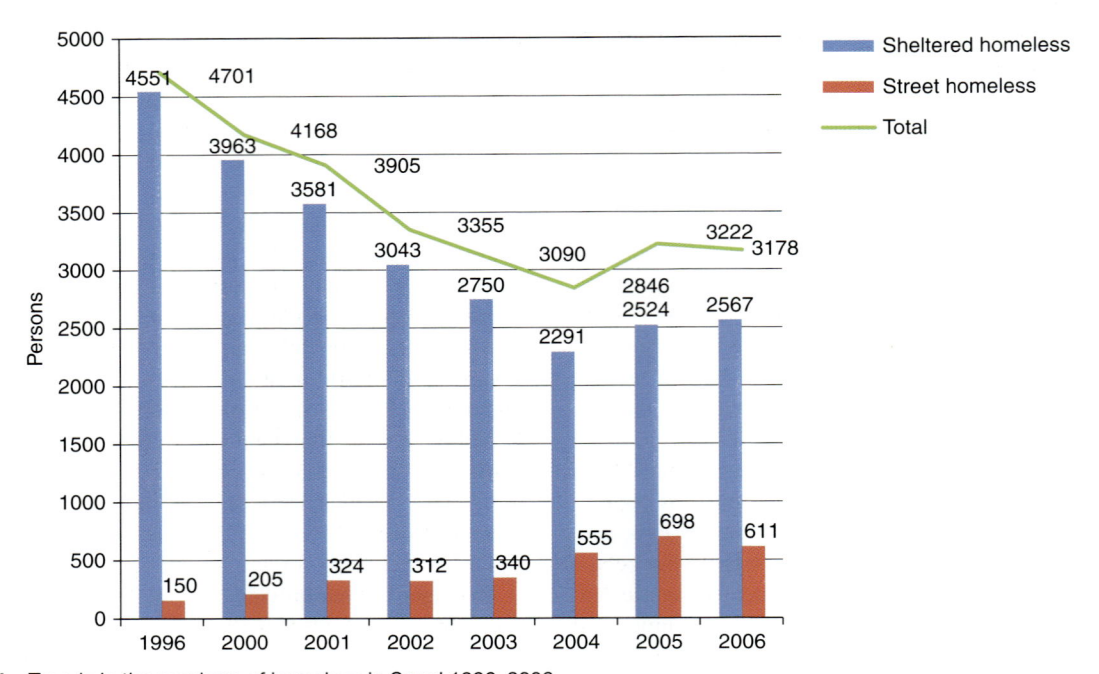

Figure 1 Trends in the numbers of homeless in Seoul 1996–2006.
Courtesy of Seoul Homeless Rehabilitation Aid Groups (changes in the number of homeless from 1998 to 2006; for 1999–2005, as of the end of January; for 2006, as of the end of December).

million. The rising numbers of jobless migrants intensify the competition for work, creating the conditions for even lower pay, poorer conditions, and homelessness.

In China, a 2006 National Survey by the National Working Committee on Women and Children indicated that there were at least 1 million vagrant and begging minors in China. The number of urban street children, based on the number of children passing through protection centres is, according to the Ministry of Civil affairs, around 150 000, having increased significantly in urban areas in China over the last two decades. In addition, an estimated 100 000 Chinese children are abandoned each year, most of them disabled and girls, and are cared for in China's Child Welfare Institutes (CWIs).

Institutional and Policy Support for the Homeless

Hong Kong

Homeless people in Hong Kong are eligible to receive temporary, emergency cash grants, and can apply for Comprehensive Social Security Allowance (CSSA), and public housing (which in Hong Kong is extensive and relatively nonstigmatised, accommodating almost a third of the population), providing they meet the criteria for the latter in relation to residence, income and assets, ability to and actively seeking work, and willingness to participate in the support for self-reliance scheme. New arrivals from China, for example, are ineligible to apply for CSSA and public housing until they have been resident in Hong Kong for 7 years (except in very exceptional circumstances). This is a group of people subject to institutional and individual discrimination and particularly vulnerable to insecurity and homelessness. The majority of new arrivals have nonexistent or limited social networks, relatively low educational attainment and work experience, and the unemployment rate for new arrivals is disproportionately high.

Research in 2002 showed that 66% of street sleepers were between 20 and 49 years of age and were able bodied, whilst 30% were on CSSA. Of the non-CSSA receiving street sleepers 10% worked full-time, 20% took odd jobs, 10% lived on the streets, and the rest relied on loans or financial support from friends and relatives. 28.5% of the street sleepers were drug misusers (Wong, 2001).

In Hong Kong, in 2001, a three-year action plan to help street sleepers was implemented as a response to the rising number of people living on the street and concern that the homeless population was getting younger, fitter, and more short term. NGOs, funded by the government, have been encouraged to play a central role in providing hostel accommodation and integrated services such as counselling, assistance with accommodation, advice on employment, arrangement of job placement, and assistance with applying to the emergency fund. There are seven street sleeper temporary shelters operated on a self-financing basis, with a period of stay not exceeding 6 weeks, and five urban hostels and a temporary shelter operated by NGOs (and funded by the Social Welfare Department), with a period of stay normally up to

6 months, as well as Social Welfare Department rough sleepers outreach teams and emergency shelters. Whilst shelter provision and services have increased over the years, these are services directed at homeless men. Women's homelessness is invisible in Hong Kong as in other East Asian societies, but what is evident is that as domestic violence has increased, with 3412 cases newly reported representing an increase of 37.1% for the same period in 2005, women's refuge centres have been unable to meet the demand with places increasing from 152 to 180 between 2006 and 2007.

China

With the deterioration and dismantling of the enterprise-based schemes, and the near complete privatisation of public housing in 1998, the cornerstones of social protection in urban China have all but disappeared. In its place is a multitier social security framework based on contributory social insurance programmes introduced in 1986 and the Minimum Standard of Living Scheme (MLSS) providing social assistance. Since 1990 the latter has been extended substantially in terms of the number of beneficiaries and the level and scope of support, but it remains underresourced, underregulated, and the homeless and unregistered migrants have virtually no entitlements.

In China traditional forms of poverty have been associated with households with the 3 nos – no stable income, no capacity to work, and no family support. More recently, rapid social and economic transformation, urbanisation, and the rise in insecure employment, underemployment, and unemployment have created new dynamics of risk, insecurity, and poverty. From the mid-1990s to early 2000s more than 20 million workers were made redundant with only 15% of laid-off urban workers able to find new jobs. Underemployment in rural areas and the rapid economic development of cities and regions, particularly along the eastern coastal region, has generated enormous rural-to-urban migration in China. Migrants have been largely excluded from access to social rights, with rural- and urban-registered citizens being governed by institutionally separate policy regimes (via *hukou* or the household registration system) (Davies and Ramia, 2008). The household registration system requires each person to register in either a rural or an urban area and was a key element of government control of population movement in the 1950s. It still survives today but, in general, is enforced with a little less vigour and more flexibility. However, lacking an urban resident permit and in the absence of policies to support rural migrants, their security of tenure to shelter in the city is tenuous.

In China in 2003 the former Measures for Internment and Deportation of Urban Vagrants and Beggars was replaced by the Measures for the Assistance and Administration of Persons Without Assured Living Sources in Cities. This reform represented the abolition of a 20-year-old regulation that allowed police to round up beggars, homeless people, and those without identification cards at will and incarcerate them before returning them to their place of origin. It indicated a change in approach from one that coerced and criminalised homeless people and called on security officers to punish activities of 'hooliganism' that disrupted public order, such as begging and camping in the open, to one that emphasised the 'voluntary' basis of the new relief system. Since 2003 responsibility has transferred from the Ministry of Public Security to Civil Affairs and is an indication of a change in approach to one of relief management for urban indigent vagrants and beggars. Custody and repatriation centres which detained millions of people annually in the late 1990s have been converted into aid centres for homeless people. The new centres offer shelter for a limited period and limited amounts of food. Under the new regulation, vagrants can receive help from these aid stations if they are unable to feed themselves, have no relatives or friends with whom they can seek refuge, and if they receive no minimum living allowance.

The reform of regulation for homeless people and the 'floating population' has been hailed by many in China as a major civil rights victory, a curb on police powers, and an indication of the loosening of the *hukou* system. The key goal of the authorities remains the same and that is to repatriate individuals to their place of previous residence or registration, rather than to provide long-term, affordable accommodation and welfare provision.

Until 2001 street children were treated in the same way as adult vagrants, gathered and sent back by relief and administrative stations. More recently a series of laws and regulation including the Law on the Protection of Minors and the Law on the Prevention of Crimes by Minors have been introduced. The introduction of special protection centres providing short-term protection and education and the administration by the Social Welfare and Social Affairs Department of the Ministry of Civil Affairs now demonstrates the separation of street children from adults in terms of public assistance. By 2003, the Chinese government had spent more than 120 million yuan (14.46 million US dollars) to establish more than 130 special protection centres. The street children also have access to food and accommodation in relief stations, which also provide assistance for adult homeless people. The Ministry of Civil Affairs plans to add 30 000 beds in shelters across the country by 2010 to help about 1.5 million homeless people.

Japan

In Japan, the first official use of the term 'homeless' in the policy arena was in the Special Measures Law

Concerning Assistance for the Rehabilitation of the Homeless enacted in 2002. This represented open and legal recognition of homelessness as a 'new' social problem and the inability of the government to ignore the issue or the voices of NGOs and activists supporting the homeless. However, homelessness is not a new phenomenon in Japan. 'Sleeping rough' in Japan is something that historically has been linked to the casual labour hiring sites (*yoseba*) where male day labourers would congregate. Most of the day labourers lived in *doya*, rude lodgings or flophouses. Since most of them had no residency papers they were considered a problem of poor people with no fixed abode and were shunted into the particular local areas around *yoseba* hiring sites and dealt with according to the few policies that pertained only to those districts. In the first nationwide survey of rough sleepers made in 2002, 36.2% of the national total of 25 296 had experience of working and living at *yoseba* hiring sites.

In the 2002 national survey, the nine largest cities, beginning with Tokyo and Osaka, had 65.9% of the total number of homeless people nationwide, while at the same time homelessness had become a visible phenomenon in regional cities as well. Routes leading to homelessness were no longer limited to *yoseba* hiring sites with over 60% of the total having no experience of the *yoseba*. Subsequent nationwide surveys conducted in 2007 and 2009 showed that the total number of homeless had declined by 6732 to 18 564, and by a further 2805 people to 15 759 in the later study.

The social security system in Japan provides a distinct and highly stigmatised tier of means tested, special programmes for those excluded from the mainstream labour market (Kennett and Iwata, 2003). Eligibility criteria are harsh and, as in many societies, require a fixed address. Nevertheless, welfare benefits, health-care programmes, and low-rent recovery assistance lodgings (transitional housing) have provided routes off the street for homeless people in Japan, particularly when combined with support from the NGOs who have provided the 'fixed abode' and rehabilitation support. Publicly provided homeless rehabilitation aid centres, prescribed under the Homeless Assistance Law, are mainly in the largest cities and have a capacity of 2025 people. In addition, there are shelters at 11 locations with a capacity of 1953 people. Evidence suggests that they have done little to aid people in escaping homelessness as the number of people who repeatedly enter and leave these transitional facilities for the homeless is increasing.

Since 2002, the rise of insecure employment and the new phenomenon of housing poor and vulnerable people, such as 'freeters' (unskilled part-time workers who frequently change jobs or only work casually), internet cafe refugees, homeless young people mainly in their 20s and 30s who are unable to afford accommodation, people laid off from companies, and exprisoners, have become particularly evident. Approximately one-third of the total workforce is engaged in nonregular employment, whilst the number of working poor has also been rising, reaching more than 10 million in 2006, an increase of 30% over the last decade. The issue for the Japanese society and government is to recognise the need for the construction of mechanisms for aiding the homeless in the broadest sense and ensuring an effective safety net.

Korea

In Korea, the homeless population is roughly classified into two groups: the older term *purangja* (vagrants or bums) and a newer group identified as the 'street sleepers' who increased in number at the time of the financial crisis of the late 1990s. The demographic profile of the homeless is overwhelmingly adult males, over 90%, with the largest number in their 40s. The next largest age cohort are in their 50s. This is consistent with the fact that the largest number were in their 30s when homeless assistance policies began 10 years ago. On the other hand, the number of female homeless has been gradually increasing in comparison with the late 1990s. The average period of homelessness has lengthened somewhat compared to the late 1990s, and the proportion of repeat shelter entrants has become higher than the number who are entering shelters for the first time. Additionally, the recent influx of young people with debt or credit problems is also increasing.

Whilst the *purangja* have been subject to social welfare project laws, up until 2003 street sleepers had no legal recognition. However, since 2003 a systematic legal base for dealing with street sleepers has been established. For example, in section 2 of the revised regulations of the Social Welfare Projects Law of July 2003, a clause for 'street sleepers' was inserted into the range of social welfare projects, and on 5 January 2005 the existing Regulations for Establishing and Operating Vagrant (*Purangja*) Welfare Facilities were revised as Regulations for Establishing and Operating Street Sleeper and Vagrant Protection Facilities (referred to below as 'the regulations'). Nevertheless, both terms are used interchangeably, and confusion remains since the meaning of neither term has been defined precisely.

It was after the publication of the General Assistance Measures for the Urban Homeless by the Health and Welfare Ministry on 7 June 1998 that the government began to address seriously assistance for the homeless whose number had drastically increased around Seoul Station. Subsequently, in July of the same year in Seoul, the Seoul Homelessness Measures Association was organised, composed of citizen groups, government officials, and academics, and assistance projects began through a public–private partnership. In the early period of countermeasures implementation, immediate shelter was the main emphasis, and securing places for people to sleep was at the top of the agenda. Thereafter, the emphasis shifted to rehabilitation assistance in order to assist the homeless off the streets. In 2002 'roadside clinics' were established, as well as 'drop-in centers' for those living in shelters, on the streets or in *jjogbang* (illegal hostel rentals). Additionally, the *jahwal ŭi jip* (transitory housing) programme has been launched as medium-term housing for those leaving the shelters. These are private rental housing units that have been leased out and where those transitioning from homelessness may stay for up to a maximum of 4 years. Also, although there has not yet been a great response, Rental Assistance Projects where 50% of housing rent is subsidised have also been introduced.

In recent years, for those inhabitants of substandard dwelling spaces, such as *jjogbang* and vinyl houses, a Purchased Rental Housing Project for Single Householders has been put in place whereby private groups can buy or lease rental housing and then make it available to particular groups of people. In addition, homeless assistance groups may actually provide aid to assist homeless people move into *jjogbang* using private funds, from where livelihood assistance welfare payments can then be applied for and received.

At the end of 2002, the Korean government announced that the housing supply availability level had exceeded 100%. So the housing problem is no longer one of an inadequate number of units available. However, it was reported in 2000 that 3 300 000 households, or 23% of all households, were living in housing that fell below the 'minimum housing standard'. This is a cutaway view of low-income people's housing, which is hidden from view in the age of 100% housing supply availability. If we dig deeper, the dark shadows of the era of 100% housing supply come more vividly into view. First of all, there is the problem of rising housing costs due to urban renewal and an inadequate supply of smaller, low-rent dwellings. After the Smaller Dwelling Mandatory Construction System was abolished in 1998, the proportion of smaller dwellings within the overall housing supply gradually diminished, the purchase prices and rental fees for smaller dwellings escalated, and this brought about an increase in the burden of housing expenses for low-income people. The housing cost burden for low-income people is particularly heavy. The Rent to Income Ratio (RIR) is inverse to income, and the lower the income of people living in substandard housing, the more the housing cost burden increases. The RIR for people in the lowest 10% income level is 28.6%, but for people in the highest 20% income levels it is no more than 11.7%. The problems of insecure housing and substandard housing as represented by underground rental housing, vinyl house encampments, and *jjogbang* (illegal hostel rentals) have yet to be resolved.

Conclusions

In China, Hong Kong, Japan, and Korea, shelter provision and rehabilitation services for the homeless have increased substantially in recent years. Whilst there has been a reduction in the numbers of street sleepers there has been only limited response to the growing recognition that routes into homelessness are increasingly associated with broader social and economic change and are impacting on a wider spectrum of society. A greater focus on preventative measures as well as a broader understanding of the dynamics and definitions of homelessness in the formulation of policy might contribute to a reduction of insecurity and homelessness.

Acknowledgments

This article was written whilst the author (PK) was a visiting fellow in the Department of Applied Social Sciences, at The Hong Kong Polytechnic University, Hong Kong, China.

See also: Ethnographies of Home and Homelessness; Government/Public Lending Institutions: Asia-Pacific; Homelessness: Measurement Questions; Homeless People: Single Men in Japan; Housing and the State in China; Housing Finance Institutions: Asia; Slum Clearance.

References

Davies G and Ramia G (2008) Governance reform towards 'Serving Migrant Workers': The local implementation of central government regulation. *China Quarterly* 193: 140–149.

De Venanzi A (2007) The institutional dynamics of homelessness. The United States of America and Japan compared. *International Journal of Sociology and Social Policy* 28(3/4): 129–145.

Kennett P and Iwata M (2003) Precariousness in everyday life: Homelessness in Japan. *International Journal of Urban and Regional Research* 27(1): 62–74.

Obinger U (2009) Working on the margins. Japans *Precariat* and Working Poor, *Electronic Journal of Contemporary Japanese Studies*, Discussion Paper 1.

Wong H (2001) Evaluation Research for Pilot and Existing Services for Homeless People in Hong Kong, City University, HKSAR and Social Welfare Department, HKSAR.

Further Reading

Jeon HG (2005) *Housing Rights of the Homeless, The Human Rights Condition of the Homeless in Korea*, pp.237–286. National Seoul: Human Rights Commission of Korea. (in Korean).

Kornatowski G (2008) The reconceptualization of homeless policy and the social welfare response of non-governmental organizations in Hong Kong, *Japanese Journal of Human Geography* 60(6): 53–76.

Kornatowski G and Mizuuchi T (2009) Reinventing Public Service Provision for the Socially-Excluded in the City: The Recent Transformation of Homelessness Support and Different Paths toward Self-dependence for the Homeless in Japan. *URP GCOE Working Paper Series No. 6*, May, pp. 1–12.

Homeless People: Indigenous/Aboriginal

P Memmott and C Chambers, University of Queensland, Brisbane, QLD, Australia

© 2012 Elsevier Ltd. All rights reserved.

Glossary

Indigenous public place dwellers Indigenous 'public place dwellers' live in a mix of public or semipublic places, for example, parks, churches, verandahs, carparks, beaches, drains, riverbanks, vacant lots, and dilapidated buildings. They can be further characterised as people who do not usually pay for their accommodation and have a high public profile (sheltering, drinking, rejoicing, partying, arguing, and fighting in public). They have low incomes of which a substantial part is often spent on alcohol, have generally few possessions (minimal clothes and bedding), and usually prefer a beat of places where they camp and socialise.

Indigenous at risk of homelessness Indigenous people to whom the phrase 'at risk of homelessness' applies and who reside in some form of housing but are at risk of losing it or its amenity. They can also be divided into four distinct subcategories (albeit not mutually exclusive ones), which include (1) people lacking secure tenure over their houses or accommodation; (2) people whose housing is architecturally substandard rendering it unsafe or unhealthy; (3) people experiencing crowded housing; and (4) dysfunctionally mobile persons being in a state of continual or intermittent residential mobility. This overarching category is sometimes referred to as 'hidden homelessness'.

Native title Indigenous land title that existed at the time of Australian sovereignty and which, since 1993, has been protected by and claimable under Australian statutory law as coexisting with certain other forms of land title (excluding freehold).

Spiritual homelessness 'Spiritual homelessness' is a state arising from the separation of Indigenous people from their traditional land and/or family and kinship networks, and involves a crisis of personal identity wherein their understanding or knowledge of how to relate to country, family, and Aboriginal identity systems is confused or lacking.

Traditional owners Aboriginal people who own their land under the classical Aboriginal land (and sea) tenure system that operated prior to the commencement of European colonisation in 1788, and the variants of that system, which continued to exist into the early twenty-first century.

Introduction

Increasingly, since 2000, definitions of Australian Indigenous homelessness in the social science literature have become culturally specific. Pathways into homelessness for contemporary Indigenous Australians can involve longitudinal factors, including those having an impact from early childhood in Indigenous settlements and communities that have institutionalised and marginalised histories. They can also involve situational factors acting upon the lives of certain individuals, but which also arise from colonial contact histories and directed cultural change. To comprehend the definitions and pathways into homelessness some understanding of the cultural and historical backgrounds of Aboriginal and Torres Strait Islander peoples is necessary; thus a brief overview follows.

Historical and Cultural Context to Indigenous Homelessness in Australia

Approximately 300 000 Indigenous people occupied the entire Australian continent when British colonisation was imposed in 1788. The most common local Aboriginal land-holding group (also referred to as a 'traditional owner' group) was the patriclan, which held religious, hunting, and food-collecting rights over its estate. Such localised groups were organised into larger regional groupings whose members intermarried according to strict rules, and shared some aspects of social organisation, beliefs, and customs. Altogether there were about 200 different languages spoken on the continent, many having numerous dialects. Religion, social organisation, and language were three of the more elaborate cognitive domains of Aboriginal cultures (Memmott 2007).

Groups of Aborigines were nomadic in the sense that they moved between a number of contiguous ecological systems to effectively exploit seasonal foods and resources; their territory was most often restricted by various protective rules as well as by the need for individuals to meet local religious obligations at sacred sites in their land estate (and on the coast and sea estate), and sometimes those of their grandparents and spouse(s). So, according to the season, small local groups or bands were scattered throughout their respective countries, engaged in hunting, gathering, and fishing, as well as in social and ritual activities. People were conscious of their place within their own local territory, intimate with its geography, and spiritually attached to its sacred sites and sacred histories.

From the commencement of colonisation in the late eighteenth century until the 1890s, the inwardly moving frontier was largely characterised by the wholesale slaughter of Aboriginal people and the taking of their land and water holes – being met with sporadic guerrilla warfare in many regions. The British colony expanded slowly inland for 150 years having widespread impact on Aboriginal cultures. Many of the unique, ecologically adaptive lifestyles of the Aboriginal language groups were lost.

By the beginning of the twentieth century, traditional styles of Aboriginal camping and land use were no longer found in the eastern and southern parts of the continent. Within its interior, displaced tribespeople camped near newly formed towns and pastoral stations in makeshift shelters. Here the devastation to life and culture continued through alcoholism, prostitution, disease, rape, economic exploitation, and further violence. A collapse of the Indigenous population occurred, the number falling to about 31 000. They were spoken of as a 'doomed race', which would inevitably become extinct.

This destruction culminated in the enactment of various pieces of Aboriginal protection legislation between 1897 and 1915 in each state of Australia, which empowered government officials and police to control the movements of Indigenous individuals, families, and whole communities within and between settlements on newly established Aboriginal and Islander reserves. However, this directed movement of people was as often enforced for punitive as for protection reasons. Many people became disconnected from both their land and their kin resulting in loss of social, psychological, and spiritual well-being. This was exacerbated by the implementation of an assimilation policy in the middle decades of the twentieth century, which was not abandoned until the mid-1970s. Only then were most Indigenous people able to travel of their own free will again.

By the 1980s, small groups of Indigenous people had come to live in public places in the regional towns and metropolitan cities of Australia, residing in these places despite, in many cases, the existence of formal Indigenous town camps and an increasing range of other Indigenous housing options. Their numbers gradually increased in the 1990s and early 2000s. Although these people were often categorised as homeless, a number of them saw themselves as being both placed and homed, and preferred instead to refer to themselves by such names as parkies, goomies, ditchies, long grassers, or river campers. However, they and their camps were largely seen by local government authorities, politicians, and members of various business communities as a public eyesore and nuisance. The people were stereotyped as displaying antisocial behaviour and discouraging tourism and general town trading (Memmott 2007).

Demographic Extent of Indigenous Homelessness

According to the 2006 census, some 105 000 Australian people were identified as homeless, of whom at least 16 000 were categorised as rough sleepers or experiencing primary homelessness. The remainder were described as experiencing secondary or tertiary homelessness, meaning respectively that they moved frequently between temporary forms of shelter, or lived in boarding houses for periods of 3 months or more. Indigenous people, who formed 2.3% of the total Australian population in the 2006 Census (455 028 in 20.7 million), were overrepresented in these homelessness figures, making up 9% of the homeless population according to the census enumeration (FaHCSIA 2008:4–6). Nevertheless, the Australian Bureau of Statistics which conducts the triennial census has conceded that there was a likely undercount of the number of Indigenous homeless people because of difficulties in locating them, particularly those in the rough sleeper category (ABS 2005:47). This undercount, which results from the mobility of people camping in public places as well as their hiding from census collectors, has been confirmed by independent field researchers.

Defining Indigenous Homelessness

One of the problems with categorisation is that when certain mainstream definitions of homelessness are applied, the composition of Indigenous groups dwelling in public spaces are oversimplified, and their needs may be at best misunderstood and minimally serviced, or at worst overlooked entirely. While government policy statements during the late twentieth century frequently recognised that many structural factors can cause and perpetuate homelessness, they largely adopted a limited or narrow definition of homelessness, one based on a lack of housing and accommodation. The result being that responses to Indigenous homelessness focused on finding accommodation as a pivotal intervention, to which other interventions were subordinate. However, for many Indigenous homeless people, finding accommodation was not necessarily their most crucial support need. Homelessness was not always simply created by a lack of housing, nor simply addressed by its provision. This was particularly true of many Aboriginal public place dwellers who had chosen to sleep out in the open, but who did not see themselves as homeless. The way Indigenous homelessness has been defined or categorised has thus influenced the types of response strategies that have been implemented by Indigenous organisations, and government and nongovernment agencies.

This realisation has prompted a more refined set of definitions of Indigenous homeless people in Australia to be created. Three useful, broad categories can be identified from the limited empirical and literature research available on the subject: (1) public place dwellers, (2) housed people who are nevertheless at risk of homelessness, and (3) spiritually homeless people. These can be further divided into subcategories. Each will be described in turn (Memmott et al. 2004).

Public place dwellers live in a mix of public or semi-public places (including some private places that are entered illegally to gain shelter overnight), for example, parks, churches, verandahs, car parks, beaches, drains, riverbanks, vacant lots, dilapidated buildings, and even under vehicles in car sale yards on rainy nights. Public place dwellers can be further characterised as people who do not usually pay for their accommodation, are highly visible in a public setting (sheltering, drinking, rejoicing, arguing, partying, and fighting in public), have low incomes of which a substantial part is often spent on alcohol, have generally few possessions (minimal clothes and bedding), and usually frequent a beat of places where they camp and socialise. Because Aboriginal people have a tradition of open-air camping, it is not necessarily stressful for them to adopt this style of living for a while, particularly in towns with mild climates. So the customary Aboriginal practice of camping without any roofed shelters in fine weather contributes to the ease with which such people can readily fall into a public place dwelling lifestyle in regional centres. Although such a lifestyle may be acceptable to more tolerant citizens, such broad-mindedness may be quickly eroded by regular alcohol consumption, subsequent intoxication, and other antisocial behaviour.

Four subcategories of public place dwellers have been defined, although they are not mutually exclusive and one often provides a pathway into the next. The first includes those who are voluntary and short-term intermittent public place dwellers. They often comprise visitors who have come to town from rural or remote communities to enjoy themselves socialising and drinking, but who intend to return home at some time. These people are relative newcomers who do not have a strong sense of attachment to the town, and include individuals who stay in conventional accommodation (such as a relative's house) and have their own residence in a rural or remote settlement, but who socialise in public urban places, and may or may not decide to camp out overnight, usually with others, despite the availability of accommodation. The second subcategory of public place dwellers are those who voluntarily adopt a homeless lifestyle over the medium term, residing continually in public places (including overnight) without having other accommodation. They acknowledge that they have another place of residence in a home community, but are uncertain if and when they will return. They have usually been pursuing this lifestyle for quite some months or years. The third subcategory of public place dwellers contains those who voluntarily adopt a homeless lifestyle over the long term. They live a permanent public place dwelling lifestyle. Having cut off their ties with their home community many years previously, they accept that their homeless lifestyle will persist and retain a sense of belonging to the town and to their group. It is unclear whether a reconciliation between such individuals and their home community and family is possible for a range of reasons. They have come to regard a beat of public places as their home. This category corresponds with the definition of long-term or chronic homelessness, whereby homelessness has ceased to be a crisis event and has become an accepted way of life (Coleman 2001). The fourth subcategory of public place dwellers includes those who are reluctantly homeless but living as they do out of necessity. Although residing continually in public places, they wish to return to their home community where they may well have a house, but are obligated to remain in an urban area because they have a service need that can only be met in that location, or because they support a hospitalised relative or friend. Or they may wish to return home but have no funds for travel and/or the capacity to organise it. They may also be on a waiting list for public rental housing elsewhere in the city.

The second broad category of Indigenous homeless people encompasses those at risk of homelessness. They reside in some sort of housing but are at risk of losing it or its amenity. This category is sometimes referred to as hidden homelessness. They can also be broken down into four distinct subcategories (again, not mutually exclusive ones). The first subcategory is that of insecurely housed people, or those residing in adequate housing but under threat of losing it, through a lack of secure tenure or due to circumstances of poverty. A second subcategory includes people whose housing is architecturally substandard, making it unsafe or unhealthy. However, what constitutes an acceptable quality of building needs to be carefully defined as there are issues of cross-cultural variation in such standards. The third subcategory is that of people experiencing crowded housing; however, again it needs to be noted that the construct of crowding also varies culturally. It should be defined as a level of proximity between dwelling occupants that causes considerable stress and not be ascertained by density measures alone. The fourth subcategory of at-risk homelessness includes dysfunctionally mobile persons, those in a state of continual or intermittent residential mobility including temporary residence (e.g., crisis accommodation) that is a result of personal and/or social problems (e.g., violence, alcohol and substance abuse, lack of safety or security in a social sense, personality or identity crisis, lack of emotional support and security). The demographic research on Indigenous people in Australia has thus focused in recent years on their relatively high circular mobility as a dominant trait, in contrast to the mainstream migration patterns.

A third broad category of Indigenous homelessness has been identified as spiritual homelessness, a state arising from separation from traditional land, and from family and kinship networks (noted earlier as a result of historical governmental policies), and involving a crisis of personal identity wherein a person's understanding or knowledge of how they relate to country, family, and Aboriginal identity systems is confused or lacking. Such feelings add to the already depressed emotional state in which Aboriginal people, either public place dwellers or those at risk of homelessness, find themselves. The separation from family and community connections that these individuals experience can have serious effects on their mental health, sometimes resulting in suicide, the rates of which are disproportionately high among the Australian Indigenous population. The importance of feeling a connection to related people also explains why Indigenous Australians from a common cultural region congregate together in public places. The two basic points of introduction for a newly arrived Indigenous person are where they come from and to which 'mob' they belong. People thus tend to join public place dwelling groups to be near people who are known to them and to feel secure.

The three broad categories of Indigenous homelessness outlined above are not mutually exclusive. Those categorised as at risk of homelessness may experience a number of episodes of living on the streets, in rental housing, and insecure accommodation, moving back and forth between insecure housing circumstances and public place dwelling. In either case, individuals may be suffering from spiritual homelessness.

Case study: Public Place Dwellers in Inner Sydney

Field research conducted in 2004 revealed that approximately six distinct Aboriginal homeless groups or mobs operated in the public and semipublic places of the inner city area (CBD) of Sydney. The majority of these public place dwellers were male and aged between 25 and 45 years. Most mobs comprised a network of individuals who shared a common rural region of origin in New South Wales. Some were from elsewhere in Australia. The members of each mob frequently moved between a set of regularly visited places, but despite their local mobility, each mob largely operated within a clearly designated territory of up to 2 square kilometres. These individual groups often functioned like a family unit, looking after one another's safety and personal possessions. Each individual identified strongly with his or her mob, conforming to its political norms of membership rights, leadership loyalty, and resource sharing. Certain protocols had to be observed when entering or engaging with the different groups (Memmott and Chambers 2008).

As a destination for these people, Sydney was thought to provide better chances for employment and education, but people also left their home community seeking the excitement of Australia's largest metropolis. Some were escaping the turmoil being experienced in their home communities and the spiritual void being created by elders dying without anyone succeeding to their cultural roles and duties. Other attractions of the inner city included the existing homeless population with their valuable advice for newcomers, an array of places in which to obtain immediate shelter, and the availability of a range of services compared to other areas. A significant majority of those interviewed preferred to remain in Sydney.

The Sydney study also included interviews with Aboriginal people in the at-risk-of-homelessness category, and demonstrated that the issues of insecure tenure, overcrowded and substandard housing stock, and dysfunctional household mobility were intertwined; they interacted with one another over the course of people's lives. These factors combined with the other symptoms of disadvantage such as poor physical and mental health, drug and alcohol abuse, and involvement with the criminal justice system to keep people teetering on the edge of a life of public place dwelling, and moving from one vulnerable residential circumstance to another. Many of the insecurely housed interviewees were living as boarders, a circumstance inherently prone to change. Their security relies on the behaviour of the head tenant, visitors, and other boarders, and on the actions of the landlord. And given the Aboriginal cultural preference for hosting larger numbers of related visitors for longer periods than the general Australian population, the actions of such visitors are often less subject to control. These people can also overburden domestic facilities such as toilets that were not designed for such high loads.

A number of factors were found to have led the Sydney interviewees into homelessness and prevented them from being able to readily change their circumstances, particularly mental and physical illness, abuse of alcohol and drugs, violence and crime, racism, intergenerational effects, and spiritual pain. Some were drawn to inner city Sydney by positive factors, because of a desire to better themselves through education or improved employment opportunities, or because of an ambition to live in a more exciting place. Other people left their home communities for negative reasons such as the lack of opportunities and services, or the levels of violence and social upheaval being experienced there. Once in Sydney they then found their housing situation tenuous for a number of reasons. Sometimes a lack of preplanning was involved, or racism within the rental market. Aboriginal people experienced more discrimination from housing providers than the general Australian population, and were further disadvantaged by their lower levels of literacy and numeracy. And when congregating in inner suburbs where problems such as drug and alcohol abuse were severe, people found themselves drawn into these lifestyles, many becoming addicted to heroin.

Once heavily engaged in substance abuse, people found it very difficult to extricate themselves and a host of physical and mental ailments ensued. All the interviewees suffering from a mental illness endured their conditions without medication or ongoing treatment. As people spent longer abusing alcohol or drugs and living rough with untreated physical and mental illnesses, it became more and more difficult to find a way out of their predicament. Mental illness clearly drove people into homelessness as it severely destabilised families and lives. Domestic and family violence was another factor that directly brought women and children into homelessness. The majority of women interviewed were on the streets either because of domestic violence or because of sexual abuse from a family member. And once engaged in a public place dwelling lifestyle, Aboriginal females became the continual victims of sexual and physical abuse at the hands of male transients. Interviews revealed that this was a common pattern of how homeless women were treated. Unsupported prison release was another factor making Indigenous people homeless.

It was found in Sydney that homelessness and the social problems that helped produce and perpetuate it were transmitted across generations. For example, not only did parents pass their drug habits onto their children but the example they set as drug dealers had a profound effect. Where relatives cared for such children, there was the potential for them to slide into dysfunctional mobility if those relatives were not properly supported. Another example was parents with mental illness significantly compounding the instability of their children's living arrangements, which in turn became a factor in their homelessness.

Practice Responses to Indigenous Public Place Dwelling and Homelessness

Although there is an increasing comprehension of the need to ally housing responses with other policy areas such as health, welfare, and the justice system, previously unrelated policy areas such as Indigenous governance, education, regional and urban planning, and native title can also be significant in addressing the full spectrum of needs presented by homeless Indigenous Australians. The term response types refers to a broad range of initiatives including philosophies, policies, programs, services, strategies, methodologies, legislations, and activities that are aimed at addressing the needs of Indigenous people who are homeless and/or residing in public places. Four practice response categories that have emerged as having culturally distinct ramifications in relation to Indigenous people will be briefly described.

Legislative Approaches

The law-and-order approach employs reactive policing, supported by various forms of legislation, in order to forcefully remove Indigenous people from public places. Experience in a number of urban centres demonstrates that such law-and-order approaches may only be partly successful and even totally unsuccessful in eliminating Indigenous public place dwelling. They are likely to result in temporary or local displacement, whilst overall cycles of incarceration, alcohol abuse, and public place dwelling continue, and also risk breaching antidiscrimination legislation. Forced physical removal to distant remote settlements is also equally repugnant and a violation of civil liberties. As a general principle, any movement of Indigenous people from the public spaces they occupy due to conflicting public needs should be carried out through a process of negotiation no matter how protracted, and supported by a planned set of alternate accommodation and servicing options acceptable to all parties (Memmott 2006).

Implementation of such a law-and-order approach has often been the result of a law-and-order crisis as perceived by politicians and the local press. However, a key finding of several studies is that the blame for such a crisis has at times been erroneously directed at Aboriginal public place dwellers. When people, whose codes of behaviour are little understood by the general public, are leading a culturally different lifestyle, and simultaneously enacting some visible antisocial behaviour, they are only too readily made the scapegoats for all local crime. Many Anglo Australians believe people camping in public places is unacceptable behaviour and seem to have forgotten, or do not know of, the Great Depression of the 1930s when the drastic economic downturn of the period forced many white Australian people to camp in public places while searching for work in whatever location they could find it (Coleman 2001: 166; Eastgate 2001; Memmott 2006).

A key finding of recent research is that social problems impact differently on a range of cultural and urban sectors and require analysis and solutions that incorporate the social values of all groups. Cross-culturally, Aboriginal and non-Aboriginal groups are likely to see one another's positions quite differently and a problem definition, if it is to be complete, must incorporate both perspectives.

Similarly, if there is to be a solution to the problem, it must be articulated from opposite sides incorporating values that are at least tolerable to both. Not to take such a cross-cultural position in approaching social problems is likely to fuel already existing racial tensions.

Patrols and Outreach Services

In the mid-1980s a Central Australian Indigenous community initiated the night patrol, where a group of responsible volunteer community members drove around their city intervening in alcohol-fuelled situations and caring for at-risk people. The concept quickly spread across the continent and today there are a range of night patrols, wardens, and outreach workers operating, although the precise nature of their services varies. The functions of Aboriginal night patrols have included intervention in situations of substance abuse (especially alcohol) and violence, mediation and dispute resolution between people in conflict, and the removal of disruptive or potentially violent persons from public or private social environments. Outreach workers tend to take a stronger 'case file' approach, attempting to establish links to relevant service agencies in response to the needs of their clients. Night patrols take intoxicated, and possibly aggressive or otherwise at-risk, persons and place them in managed accommodation until they can become sober, and have a sleep and meal. The service aims to keep at-risk, intoxicated individuals out of the watch-house (where they may be susceptible to suicide). The managed accommodation to which they are taken may be a relative's house, a sobering-up shelter, a refuge, or other such facility. A variety of complementary strategies can be incorporated into this service, including follow-up 'shaming' sessions between offenders and aggrieved members of the community, the use of a detox centre within a residential alcohol treatment centre, and a day centre providing diversionary recreational or entertainment facilities.

Addressing Antisocial Behaviour

Local Indigenous traditional owners may take exception to the antisocial behaviour of certain public place dwellers (intoxication, begging, violence, etc.), seeing it as 'shaming' their own people as well as their law and custom, and they may be adamant about asserting their authority in an effort to prevent it. In the few places where this has been tried, an effective approach has emerged involving the establishment of models of appropriate versus antisocial behaviour (in terms of Aboriginal value systems) to be adhered to by public place dwellers, as well as territorial rules concerning where particular individuals or groups should camp. The public place dwelling people involved in these instances acknowledged their respect for Aboriginal law and native title. This approach also involves the empowerment of an Indigenous authority structure reflecting the need to create new, as well as to reaffirm old, standards of behaviour; to acculturate public place dwellers with new behavioural norms; and to somehow maintain these standards in an active process of social reform. One of the initial challenges has been finding the membership to form such an authority group, which would be respected and thereby legitimised and empowered by Aboriginal people to act in situations where antisocial behaviour was causing conflict.

A useful example to illustrate these points is that of the Four Corners Council of Elders, which was established in the early 1990s to address the offensive behaviour of public place dwellers in Alice Springs in Central Arrernte country. Aboriginal social authority in precontact Central Australia had been based in totemic geography – power being vested in a network of elders (Strehlow 1965). So the Four Corners Council was based on the sacred site of Emily Gap or Ntherrke, to which five groups of traveling Caterpillar Beings traveled from different directions in the Dreamtime, thus linking a large number of surrounding language groups in Central Australia. The name Four Corners symbolised pan-tribal unity founded in the geography of Aboriginal law. This construct gave the Council a capacity to communicate with elders from other tribes or language groups in the outer parts of the region, and to ask for their support and assistance, particularly in dealing with their own people when they came to Alice Springs. This capacity was increased by reciprocal behavioural responsibilities or obligations operating between the Central Arrernte and other surrounding tribes, which were based on ceremonial ties created through the travels of Dreamtime ancestors. The adherence to Aboriginal law and the recovery of influence over young men through the revitalisation of ceremony and initiation culture was one of a number of methods used by the Council to strengthen leadership and social cohesion.

Through the valuing of appropriate social behaviour as a distinct aspect of culture, the process of social reform can be characterised primarily as one of cultural maintenance and development and can thereby draw upon traditional Aboriginal concepts for application to contemporary problems.

Regional Strategies

Regional strategies must be founded in an understanding of the cultural blocs made up of multiple language or tribal groups relevant to the communities in question, and must examine Indigenous migration and residential mobility patterns in order to anticipate why people leave their home communities, and what prevents them from returning. They necessitate a common set of values being in place for the regional centre's service providers as well as the communities of the outer parts of the region, so as to facilitate shared decision-making in addressing client's needs. This in turn may be accompanied by a regional education programme concerning urban lifestyles and values, and what might be expected of Indigenous people when visiting large cities, both in terms of mainstream and Aboriginal laws, and behavioural values. The migration of Indigenous people to urban centres generates serious political questions concerning the quality of life in remote and rural Aboriginal communities, as well as the distribution and licensing of alcohol outlets throughout such a region. This response category has seldom been implemented in Australia.

In addition to the four responses or strategies outlined above, other more conventional approaches to Indigenous homelessness, which are embedded in mainstream Australian practice and reported in the literature, can prove useful. They include (1) alcohol and drug strategies including diversionary responses for intoxicated individuals, (2) accommodation strategies and options, (3) dedicated service centres and gathering places, (4) the design of public places to enhance public place dwelling, (5) public education strategies, (6) telephone information and help services, (7) skills and training for outreach workers, (8) intensive case management, (9) charismatic mentors, (10) philosophies of client interaction that involve empowerment of clients, and (11) partnerships between government and nongovernment agencies (Memmott et al. 2003).

Collectively these responses address a wide range of needs reflecting the complex circumstances of Indigenous public place dwellers and homeless people. Which combination of responses is relevant to a particular place or group will vary across the continent depending on the local environmental and socio-economic context, and the history of culture contact between Indigenous and non-Indigenous people. Holistic approaches to Indigenous homelessness combine a significant number of these response types and address both immediate problems and other underlying issues and causal factors, which may not necessarily be identified by the clients themselves. This involves reactive and proactive components that are both short and long term in their duration.

Conclusion

Holistic approaches to homelessness empower Aboriginal people with effective self-help strategies and problem-solving skills. A key component of any approach or strategy must be to promote a better style of drinking, if not complete abstinence, as alcohol consumption is a consistent factor in the antisocial behaviour of public place dwelling Indigenous people. Such projects also must involve the development of rules and norms concerning preferred behaviour and styles of occupying residences, sustained education between town and bush communities about such appropriate behaviours and lifestyles, development of leadership and support within communities, and the strengthening of the bonds between parts of the extended family to serve as a mechanism to enforce such norms.

See also: Hidden Homelessness; Social Psychological Perspectives on Homelessness.

References

Australian Bureau of Statistics (2005) *The Health and Welfare of Australia's Aboriginal and Torres Strait Islander Peoples, 2005*, p. 47. Canberra: Commonwealth of Australia, ABS Cat. No. 4704.0, http://www.abs.gov.au/AUSSTATS/abs@.nsf/DetailsPage/4704.02005?OpenDocument, accessed on 30 May 2009.

FaHCSIA (2008) Australia, department of families, housing, community services and indigenous affairs. *The Road Home: A National Approach to Reducing Homelessness*. Canberra: Commonwealth of Australia.

Coleman A (2001) *Five Star Motels: Spaces, Places and Homelessness in Fortitude Valley Brisbane*. Draft PhD Thesis, University of Queensland. St Lucia: School of Social Work and Social Policy.

Eastgate J (2001) Where do people go when there's nowhere to go? Brisbane city council's response to homelessness. *National Housing Action* 15(1): 39–44.

Memmott P (2006) Public-place dwelling indigenous people: Alternative strategies to the law and order approach. *Parity* 19(1): 71–73.

Memmott P (2007) *Gunyah, Goondie + Wurley: The Aboriginal Architecture of Australia*. St Lucia: University of Queensland Press.

Memmott P and Chambers C (2008) Homelessness amongst aboriginal people in Inner Sydney. *Paper Delivered at the 2nd Australasian Housing Researchers Conference, 20–22 July 2007*, Brisbane: Customs House. http://www.uq.edu.au/housingconference2007/refereed-papers-and-presentations, accessed on 18 June 2008.

Memmott P, Long S, and Chambers C (2003) Practice responses to indigenous public place dwelling and homelessness. *Parity* 16(9): 11–13.

Memmott P, Long S, Chambers C, and Spring F (2004) Re-thinking indigenous homelessness. *AHURI Research and Policy Bulletin* 42, May, Melbourne: Australian Housing and Urban Research Institute.

Strehlow TGH (1965) Culture, social structure and environment in aboriginal central Australia. In: Berndt R and Berndt C (eds.) *Aboriginal Man in Australia*, pp. 121–145. Melbourne: Angus & Robertson.

Homeless People: Older People

M Crane and AM Warnes, Sheffield Institute for Studies on Ageing, Sheffield, UK

© 2012 Elsevier Ltd. All rights reserved.

Glossary

Hostels In Great Britain, most hostels for homeless people are operated by voluntary sector homelessness organisations as temporary accommodation (although some older people have been resident for years). Some are exclusively for men or women, some accept people with various problems and needs, and others provide specialist help for people with problems such as drug or alcohol dependency. Most hostels now have single rooms and are open 24 hours (in the past, many provided only dormitory accommodation and the residents had to leave the premises during the day).

Shelters Shelters for homeless people provide temporary accommodation, often in dormitories. Some are similar to hostels (q.v.), but most expect clients to leave the premises during the day. In the United States, shelters for homeless people are more common than hostels. In Great Britain, there are still a few night shelters that require the users to leave during the day. Most are operated by voluntary or faith-based organisations.

Single homeless people A term used in Great Britain for homeless people without dependent children, so in most cases they are not eligible for priority housing arranged by a local authority and are not included in the local government homelessness statistics. They sleep rough or stay in hostels, with friends or in other temporary accommodation. There are no national figures for this group.

Sleeping rough A term (principally in Great Britain) for those whose primary night-time residence is on the streets, in doorways, railway stations, bus terminals, parks, vacant buildings, or abandoned cars. The equivalent term in North America is 'street living'.

The Bowery A street and neighbourhood on the lower east side of Manhattan, New York City, which in the early twentieth century was inhabited predominantly by homeless men who stayed in shelters (q.v.), single-room occupancy hotels, and lodging houses. At different times during the 1920s and 1930s, between 26 000 and 75 000 were resident. Since the 1990s, much of the area has been redeveloped and gentrified, with many high-rise condominiums.

Introduction

This article is about homelessness among older people. It describes the pathways into homelessness in later life, the risk factors and causes of the outcome, and the characteristics, problems, and needs of older homeless people. The final section examines the poor fit between the group's needs and mainstream homelessness and old-age care services, and describes the imaginative services that have been developed specifically for them. The article refers largely to Great Britain, the United States, and Australia, because we have investigated the issues closely in these three countries and evidence from elsewhere is scarce.

There is no consensus among policy makers, service providers, and researchers as to the age at which 'older' homelessness begins: various ages between 45 and 65 years have been applied. During the 1980s, Cohen and Sokolovsky conducted studies of older homeless men in New York City and argued for a threshold of 50 years, because many homeless people in their fifties have chronic health problems and disabilities normally associated with old age, and view their lives as over. The 50-years cut-off has been widely adopted by researchers and service providers.

Numbers

During the first half of the twentieth century, most single homeless people in Great Britain and the United States were middle-aged or older men: broadly, around two-thirds were over the age of 50 years, and one-quarter over 60 years. The profile of homeless people changed during the 1970s and 1980s, with more young adults and more women in the population. Nonetheless, older homeless people are still a large proportion of single homeless people in many developed countries, although in the current media and policy discourses, homelessness is more often associated with disadvantaged and troubled young people than those aged in their fifties and sixties.

There are no aggregate point-in-time or period statistics for all older homeless people in Great Britain, although some components of the homeless population are monitored. From 1997 to 2003 in England, around 4000 households were accepted each year by local authority housing departments as homeless and in 'priority need' of rehousing on the grounds of 'old age' (generally 60 years for women, and 65 years for men). In line with a fall in all priority housing acceptances, probably a consequence more of administrative than social changes, the number fell to 2530 in 2005 and 1540 in 2006. In Scotland in 2007–08, local authorities accepted 957 people of retirement age as homeless and in priority need of rehousing. In Wales in 2008, the respective figure was 132. Many older homeless people in Great Britain, however, sleep rough or stay in hostels and do not apply to local authorities for priority rehousing. In London, for example, 700 homeless people aged 50 or more years were in hostels on one night in 2000.

In the United States, surveys in 2007 in Baltimore City, Dallas County (Texas), Greater Los Angeles, Hillsborough County (Florida), and two California counties (Santa Clara and Sonoma) found that among homeless people on the streets and in shelters, 19–33% were aged more than 50 years, although less than 10% were over 60 years. Moreover, older homeless people are a rising percentage of the single homeless population. For example, in Greater Los Angeles, there were 745 homeless people aged 51 or more years in 2005, 24% of all homeless people. By 2007, the number had increased to 927 and the share of the total had increased to 29%. In Dallas County, Texas, homeless people aged 50 or more years were 25% of the homeless population in 2004, and 33% in 2007.

Australian and Canadian statistics show similar trends. The Australian Census enumerated 18 108 homeless people aged 55 or more years in 2006, compared to 13 878 older homeless people in 2001. In the 2006 Census, 10% of homeless people were aged 55–64 years, and 7% were 65 or more, but the equivalent percentages for 2001 were 8 and 6. In Metro Vancouver, British Columbia, there were 212 homeless people aged 55 years or over in 2008, compared to just 51 in 2002. Likewise, in Edmonton, Alberta, the number of homeless people aged 55 years or more increased from 81 in 2000 to 306 in 2008.

Studies

Although older people have been included in surveys and investigations of homeless people of all ages, few published studies have been dedicated to the age group. The first of substance, by Cohen and his colleagues in the United States during the 1980s, were of the circumstances, problems, and needs of older homeless men on The Bowery in New York City, and in 1990 they studied older homeless women in the city. During the mid-1980s, other researchers examined the characteristics of older homeless people in Chicago and Detroit and the reasons why they became homeless (Douglass et al., 1988; Keigher and Greenblatt, 1992; Kutza, 1987). The first British study was Crane's ethnography of older homeless people on the streets and in hostels during the early 1990s. Subsequently, reports about the problems and needs of older homeless people have been published in Australia and Canada (Hightower et al., 2003; Kavanagh, 1997; McDonald et al., 2006). During 2001–03, the authors organised a 'Tri-Nation Study' of the causes of homeless among 378 newly homeless older people in four English cities, Boston (Massachusetts), and Melbourne (Australia). This used the same life course and accommodation history questionnaire in all three countries and produced valuable comparative evidence (Crane et al., 2005).

Pathways Into and Causes of Homelessness

Some people who have been homeless for years reach old age while homeless, while other older homeless people became homeless for the first time in later life. While many older homeless men's histories include intermittent or long-term homelessness, older homeless women are more likely to have first become homeless after the age of 50 years. A number of pathways into homelessness characterise subgroups of older homeless people.

Long Trajectories of Homelessness

Some became homeless as teenagers or in early adulthood, after leaving disturbed, dysfunctional, or broken family homes, and having experienced various traumas, such as the death of one or both parents, physical or sexual abuse, or the disadvantage and damage that accrues from parental abuse and neglect. A second less common pathway among men begins when they are in their early twenties, following discharge from the army after serving just a few years. Most of this group report disturbed or broken childhood homes before enlisting – which some do to escape problems at home – and heavy drinking is common among them.

Distinctive pathways are also followed by those who become homeless for the first time when aged in their forties or early fifties. Some have previously always lived with their parents, never married or sustained employment, and have poor social and domestic skills – the term 'undersocialised' applies to many. Mental health problems are prevalent in this group. Characteristically, the parent(s) took responsibility for looking after the home and paying the bills. After the last parent's death, the surviving adult child takes over the home but fails to cope. Many different problems lead to eventual abandonment or eviction: low income, lack of understanding, and competence concerning rent, utility, and property-tax payments, and the inability to maintain a tenancy in reasonable order, resulting in squalor and complaints from neighbours.

Another subgroup are the men who became homeless in middle age after working for many years as merchant seamen or building labourers. Many were transient and generally stayed in missions, lodgings, or work camps. They relied on employers or lodgings for accommodation, and became accustomed to masculine communal settings in which they had few responsibilities. Many have long histories of heavy drinking and are estranged from their parental or nuptial families. When they can no longer find work or ill-health prevents them from working, they have no settled base or savings, are unaccustomed to living independently, and resort to hostels and homeless shelters.

Becoming Homeless in Later Life

Some older homeless people first lose a conventional home when aged in their fifties or older. Some previously had demanding jobs, were prosperous, and raised children successfully. After becoming widowed, some men volitionally give up their accommodation and sleep on the streets because they find it too painful and upsetting to stay at home, while some drink heavily, neglect themselves and their home, fail to pay bills, and are evicted for rent arrears. Marital breakdown is an important trigger to homelessness among older people (as at all ages). Some have been married for years, and associate the ending of the relationship with stresses and negative events concerning them or their spouse, such as retirement or redundancy, physical or mental health problems, heavy drinking, or infidelity.

There are connections between retirement or other work exits and later life homelessness. After stopping work, many experience a huge drop in income, particularly those who are too young for 'old-age' pensions or benefits. Some find their finances disrupted by delays in arranging benefit payments and are eventually evicted for rent arrears. A few of pension age fail to claim the state pension or other income support. Apart from the financial impacts, some that have only slender family support are greatly affected by the loss of the stability, structure, and support that a job provides. When they stop work, they become isolated, bored, depressed, and drink heavily, which leads to rent defaults and homelessness. There are also those who have worked abroad for years, and on retirement return to their country without family, friends, or accommodation. Others become homeless when they retire from a post that provided 'tied' (attached) accommodation. Examples include women who work as domestics and live in hospitals and hotels for years, and men who are residential porters or maintenance staff. They become accustomed to living in congregate settings and have poor daily living skills, and when they take on an independent home fail to cope.

Health problems, particularly the onset of a mental illness, can trigger homelessness among older people who live alone. Dementia and paraphrenia (late-onset schizophrenia) are sometimes present in later life but undetected, and affect a person's ability to cope at home. This can lead to squalid living conditions or rent arrears and eventually eviction, while some abandon their accommodation because they develop persecutory ideas about relatives or neighbours. Others who are confused or mentally disturbed drift into homelessness as they have simply wandered away from their homes.

Risk Factors and Causes

The pathways leading to homelessness for older people are therefore several and complex, which means that understanding the causes is not straightforward. The Tri-Nation Study (described earlier) tackled the question directly and found that the majority of cases arise through a combination of personal problems and incapacities, welfare policy gaps, and service delivery deficiencies. The study also suggested that the causes of homelessness should be understood as the outcome both of risk factors (or propensities) and of immediate precipitating events (or triggers). For example, low education, few job skills, and low or irregular income constitute a nexus of related risk factors for rent defaults and arrears. Many on marginal incomes get by until a negative event, such as bereavement or marital breakdown, creates a situation with which they cannot cope. Similarly, those with few daily living or social skills can live for decades in conventional accommodation with the support of a parent or partner, or in accommodation attached to a job, but if they lose their supporter, they may be unable to manage their domestic situation and eventually become homeless.

Among the Tri-Nation Study respondents, some lacked the skills, resources, or motivation to cope with the changes or stresses experienced in later life. At the same time, policy gaps and changes meant that some services and resources were unavailable for people in need, or that they were intentionally excluded, or that welfare services did not respond effectively to vulnerable people. In all three countries, recent changes in housing markets and housing management practices were implicated in many of the transitions to homelessness. Relatively low variability was found by country among the causal factors that are intrinsic to the human condition (e.g., bereavement and mental health problems), but relatively high variability characterised the social pathologies that are culturally influenced and time-specific. For example, gambling problems were an instrumental factor in homelessness among only the Melbourne respondents – electronic gaming machines were legalised in Victoria in 1992, and gambling problems in the state have since increased. In such cases, homelessness occurs among people who are weak and prone to addictive behaviour when social control is relaxed.

The Characteristics and Problems of Older Homeless People

People who become homeless are diverse, whether young, middle-aged, or older. At the same time, there are substantial differences between the characteristics of homeless people and the general population. On average, homeless people have lower education and fewer job skills, while a pervasive characteristic is that they have weak family and social networks – a strong, concerned, and supportive network generally prevents a person becoming homeless. The distinctive profiles of homeless people encourage stereotypes, which then mask the group's diversity. Among older homeless people, a few display exceptional and idiosyncratic behaviours that draw the attention of the media and imaginative writers, but most are unassertive and do not attract attention.

Many older homeless people stay in temporary accommodation such as hostels and shelters managed by voluntary sector and charitable organisations. Some have little or no contact with services and sleep on the streets or in secluded places such as derelict buildings, claim no welfare benefit entitlements, and survive by eating discarded food from litter bins. Many older homeless people are isolated, estranged from their relatives, and have no friends. Some have no living relatives or have had no family contact for more than 20 years and do not know if their parents or siblings are alive. For some, a family estrangement is the trigger for homelessness. Some men who become homeless after a marital breakdown deliberately sever family contacts because they are angry and feel rejected, and in other cases the family severs the contact. Some who abandon their homes on becoming widowed do not keep in touch with their family because they are ashamed of their circumstances and do not want to be a burden.

Health and Addiction Problems

Physical health problems are common among older homeless people, and are exacerbated by age, lack of treatment, and lifestyle. Those who sleep on the streets are exposed to dampness, extreme temperatures, and infections, and are susceptible to chronic respiratory disorders and gastrointestinal problems. Many have musculoskeletal and circulatory problems such as leg ulcers, oedema, and cellulitis, and injuries from accidents and assaults are common. Mental health problems are also prevalent, particularly among women. According to British and American studies, between one-third and two-thirds of older homeless people report being depressed, while many of the women and one-third of the men have a psychotic illness or severe memory problems. A study in London in 2000 found that three-quarters of homeless women aged 60 years and over in hostels and on the streets had mental health problems (Crane and Warnes, 2001).

About two-fifths of older homeless men and one-fifth of the women have alcohol problems. Some have been drinking heavily since early adulthood, and relate the behaviour to stresses and traumatic events before they became homeless, or to lifestyle influences such as habitual drinking in the merchant navy. Others associate heavy drinking with depression and stresses since becoming homeless. Many have serious physical illnesses related to years of heavy drinking, cognitive impairments, and nutritional deficiencies, and many neglect themselves. Up to one-quarter of older homeless men and one-tenth of the women have both mental health and alcohol problems.

The use of illegal drugs among older homeless people was rare during the 1980s and 1990s (affecting less than 5%). Although the prevalence of illegal drug use among the age group is lower than among young adults, it is increasing and coincides with a substantial rise in drug abuse and drug dependence problems among both the general and the homeless populations. A 2004 survey in London by St Mungo's of 365 homeless people aged 50 years or more found that 10% had a drug problem. Among the Tri-Nation Study respondents, 9% said that they used illegal drugs before they became homeless. For some, the behaviour dated back to early adulthood, but for others the onset occurred when they were in their forties or older.

Service Responses

Some older people are homeless briefly following a short-term financial, housing, or relationship crisis and are quickly identified by homelessness services, assisted, and rehoused. Others have persistent, multiple, and deep-seated problems and remain homeless for years, either because they do not make their needs known or refuse help, or because appropriate services are unavailable. Many who sleep on the streets, particularly older women, are alienated, suspicious, and hostile when approached and resist help. Many with alcohol problems find it impossible to break the cycle of heavy drinking, deteriorating health, and low morale. They have lost their family, job, and home, and have no motivation to stop drinking. Some are admitted to hospital or to a detoxification unit for a few weeks during which time they abstain, but when they are discharged they soon start drinking again.

The distinctive problems and needs of older homeless people become clearer when one examines the appropriateness for them of most homelessness services. Some hostels provide temporary accommodation and individual casework, with the aim of addressing the residents' problems and resettling them in permanent housing as soon as possible. Others do not provide intensive or personalised help, one result being that some unassertive older homeless people have lived in hostels for years without being rehoused. Many hostels and shelters accommodate homeless people of all ages and with various problems, and do not adequately meet the needs of those who require specialist help. The needs of a young person who became homeless when he or she left care differ from those of an elderly man who became homeless for the first time when his wife died. Moreover, many older homeless people are reluctant to use day centres and hostels for homeless people of all ages because they fear violence, threats, and intimidation from young users and from those desperate for drugs or alcohol.

A few organisations in Great Britain, the United States, and Australia have developed services exclusively for older homeless people, but we are aware of only two that formed for the specific purpose. Wintringham, in Melbourne, Australia, was founded in the late 1980s and provides more than 100 units of supported housing for older homeless people, and a nursing home with 60 beds. It also owns or manages 140 units of permanent housing for older people who have been homeless or at risk. Its accommodation has relatively high staffing levels and, more importantly, both the physical design and the management model encourage a degree of social control and individual responsibility among the residents. The second dedicated organisation is Hearth in Boston, Massachusetts. It was formed as the Committee to End Elder Homelessness in 1991, and adopted its current name in 2005. By 2008, it had 136 units of permanent supported housing in seven projects, an outreach service for older homeless people living in shelters, and integrated health and welfare programmes.

Some voluntary sector and charitable organisations working with homeless adults have developed day centres, hostels, and supported housing specifically for older clients. In the United States, there are day centres for older homeless people in Boston, New York City, Seattle, and Washington, DC. In New York City, for example, the Bowery Residents' Committee supports more than 100 older homeless people daily at its Senior Center. It also runs a Homebound Program that provides meals and support to older people living on the Bowery who are too frail to attend the centre. In Seattle, Washington State, the Catholic Community Services of Western Washington and the Archdiocesan Housing Authority run the Lazarus Day Center for older homeless people and the St Martin de Porres Shelter for older homeless men. The day centre is open seven days a week and is used by around 350 homeless and marginally housed older people each day. The shelter accommodates 212 men each night, and provides convalescent care during the day for those with medical needs.

A few organisations working with older people have also developed services for those who are homeless or at risk. For example, the Senior Community Centers of San Diego, California, provide services for low-income, at-risk older people, and have a Transitional Housing Program with 35 subsidised units of accommodation in a single-room occupancy hotel accompanied by assisted access to permanent housing. Likewise, Kit Clark Senior Services in Boston, Massachusetts, runs the Medeiros (Day) Center for Change for older homeless people. In 1998 in the United Kingdom, the national charity Help the Aged together with Crisis and the Housing Associations Charitable Trust formed the Older Homelessness Partnership Programme. It ran for 5 years and funded services nationwide for older homeless people. These included specialist workers at day centres for homeless people of all ages and resettlement and tenancy support workers. The UK Coalition on Older Homelessness was set up in 2000 to lobby for improved services for older homeless people.

Some older homeless people have problems and needs comparable to those of sick and frail older people: they require, accommodation that is 'sheltered' or provides personal care, and treatment for physical and mental health problems. Logically, it might appear more appropriate to tackle their problems through vulnerable older people's care services, but there are two practical (and structural) impediments. Firstly, in most countries budgets and services for 'elderly people' are available only for those of a stipulated age (often at least 60 or 65 years), and secondly, most 'elderly care' services are no more suited to the group than mainstream homelessness services. In Great Britain, for example, local authority social services fund places for vulnerable and impaired older people in residential 'care homes'. Increasingly, however, the budget is reserved for older people with severe physical and mental disabilities – a majority of the recipients are diagnosed with dementia. Moreover, the fees for care homes and their staffing levels are low, and their closely regulated *modus operandi* is to provide for basic needs (protection, nutrition, medication, and hygiene) and to minimise health and safety risks. A large majority of the residents are widowed women aged in their late seventies and older, and most are unassertive if not supine. Habitual drinkers who are disruptive or who behave inappropriately are definitely not welcome.

There are rare examples of imaginative uses of the 'age care' system to provide specialised protective and supportive accommodation for older homeless people. Wintringham has successfully garnered 'age care' funds to build and manage its supported independent living units and nursing home. In Great Britain, St Mungo's has taken a special interest in supporting older homeless people for more than two decades. It has established two registered care homes in London for 55 older homeless men and the places are funded by local authority adult services budgets. Likewise, a few other British organisations, including the Aberdeen Cyrenians, Framework, Midland Heart, Novas Scarman, the Talbot Association, and Thames Reach have established permanent supported housing or registered care homes for older people with long histories of homelessness, heavy drinking, and mental health problems.

Required Policy Responses

Research findings about the risk factors and causes of homelessness in old age have proved valuable for policy makers and service providers. As compared with 10 years ago, it is now possible to identify the kinds of interventions and services that are effective in either preventing homelessness or in providing care and support for those who have become homeless. Effective prevention requires attention to both the underlying risk factors, many of which are structural features (such as very low income), and to ways of quickly identifying cases of housing and personal stress. Some British social housing providers have successfully introduced 'early warning' systems when delays in rent payments occur. They make contact with the tenant, offer advice, and seek to agree a manageable repayment schedule. This has proved effective and circumvents later threats of legal action (which some vulnerable tenants find alarming and others ignore). Elsewhere, primary health-care nurses have taken a special interest in identifying older, socially isolated patients at risk of homelessness. As so often, it has been found that the timely exchange of information between housing and health-care providers is all that is required to identify highly vulnerable individuals.

As to providing more appropriate services for older homeless people, there are two fundamental requirements, not so much for change in the framework of 'age care' and 'housing with care/support' measures but for more flexible implementation. The perhaps inevitable tendency to adopt proven models of support and care as the universal design is not the way to meet the needs of older homeless people. As has been shown, the group is both diverse and distinctive from others. We examined the causes of homelessness among older people in Boston, Melbourne, and London, and in each city found agencies that had imaginatively used existing funding structures to devise accommodation and care models that meet the group's needs. Accepting a departure from the safe, proven model requires evidence and persuasion, and a good deal of the latter is required to achieve the second requirement, acceptance that higher than normal funding is justified.

See also: Homelessness: Causation; Mental Health and Homelessness.

References

Crane M, Byrne K, Fu R, et al. (2005) The causes of homelessness in later life: findings from a three-nation study. *Journal of Gerontology: Social Sciences* 60b(3): S152–S159.

Crane M and Warnes AM (2001) *Single Homeless People in London: Profiles of Service Users and Perceptions of Needs.* Sheffield: Sheffield Institute for Studies on Ageing, University of Sheffield.

Douglass R, Atchison B, Lofton W, Hodgkins BJ, Kotowski K, and Morris J (1988) *Aged, Adrift and Alone: Detroit's Elderly Homeless.* Ypsilanti, MI: Department of Associated Health Professions, Eastern Michigan University.

Hightower HC, Hightower J, and Smith MJG (2003) *Out of Sight, Out of Mind: The Plight of Seniors and Homelessness.* New Westminster, Vancouver, BC: Seniors' Housing Information Program.

Kavanagh K (1997) *The Battlers: Elderly People Residing in Insecure Housing.* Sydney, NSW: Mercy Family Centre.

Keigher SM and Greenblatt S (1992) Housing emergencies and the etiology of homelessness among the urban elderly. *The Gerontologist* 32(4): 457–465.

Kutza E (1987) *A Study of Undomiciled Elderly Persons in Chicago: A Final Report.* Chicago, IL: Retirement Research Foundation.

McDonald L, Donahue P, Janes J, and Cleghorn L (2006) *In from the Streets: The Health and Well-Being of Formerly Homeless Older Adults.* Toronto, ON: Institute for Life Course and Aging, University of Toronto.

Further Reading

Cohen CI and Sokolovsky J (1989) *Old Men of the Bowery: Strategies for Survival Among the Homeless.* New York: Guilford.

Crane M (1999) *Understanding Older Homeless People: Their Circumstances, Problems and Needs.* Buckingham: Open University Press.

Crane M and Warnes AM (2002) *Resettling Older Homeless People: A Longitudinal Study of Outcomes.* Sheffield: Sheffield Institute for Studies on Ageing, University of Sheffield.

Judd B, Kavanagh K, Morris A, and Naidoo Y (2003) *Housing Options and Independent Living: Sustainable Outcomes for Older People Who are Homeless.* Melbourne, VIC: Australian Housing and Urban Research Institute.

Keigher SM (ed.) (1991) *Housing Risk and Homelessness Among the Urban Elderly.* Binghamton, NY: Haworth.

Lipmann B (1995) *The Elderly Homeless: An Investigation into the Provision of Services for Frail, Elderly Homeless Men and Women in the United States of America, Britain, Sweden and Denmark.* Flemington, VIC: Wintringham.

Warnes AM and Crane M (2000) *Meeting Homeless People's Needs: Service Development and Practice for the Older Excluded.* London: The King's Fund.

Relevant Websites

http://www.hearth-home.org – Hearth
http://kitclark.org – Kit Clark Senior Services
http://www.mungos.org – St Mungo's
http://www.servingseniors.org – Senior Community Centers
http://www.olderhomelessness.org.uk – UK Coalition on Older Homelessness
http://www.wintringham.org.au – Wintringham

Homeless People: Polish Migrants in the United Kingdom

C McNaughton Nicholls, National Centre for Social Research, London, UK

© 2012 Elsevier Ltd. All rights reserved.

Glossary

A8 and A10 countries The eight Central and Eastern European countries that joined the European Union on 1 May 2004. These countries are the Czech Republic, Estonia, Hungary, Latvia, Lithuania, Poland, Slovakia, and Slovenia. On 1 January 2007, Romania and Bulgaria joined the European Union. Collectively, these countries are known as the A10.

Circular migration Movement between home country and host country rather than settlement in the host country.

Destitution Lacking the means to live; being totally impoverished.

Economic migrant Someone who moves from their country to another to obtain employment.

Frontline homelessness services Services providing emergency support for homeless people such as food, clothing, blankets, and advice.

Hidden homelessness This denotes those people who are homeless, in the sense of lacking secure accommodation but are not in contact with homelessness agencies or sleeping rough in a visible location.

Tied accommodation Accommodation provided alongside, and often in the same location as, employment. If employment ends, then this housing is no longer available.

Workers Registration Scheme (WRS) New migrants from the A8 countries are required to register to work in the United Kingdom and to reregister each time they change employment. There is a fee to pay for registration and some do not register.

Introduction

On 1 May 2004 eight Eastern and Central European countries – the Czech Republic, Estonia, Hungary, Latvia, Lithuania, Poland, Slovakia, and Slovenia – joined the European Union. Citizens of these countries obtained immediate rights to work in the United Kingdom, subject to their registering with the Home Office (a formality but a requirement), but had, during 'transitional arrangements' that were still in place at the time of writing, only limited rights to welfare benefits until they had completed 12 months of employment. Of these eight accession countries (collectively known as the A8) it was the accession of Poland that had the greatest impact in the United Kingdom, with over 600 000 Polish nationals registering to work in the United Kingdom between May 2004 and September 2008 (Home Office, 2008). Many postaccession Polish migrants found employment and accommodation with relative ease in the United Kingdom. Some, however, did not fare so well, with frontline homelessness agencies in London in particular reporting significant numbers of A8 nationals, predominantly Poles, amongst their service users (Homeless Link, 2006). This article will review the context for postaccession Polish migration to the United Kingdom, before summarising the evidence on the housing circumstances of these Polish migrants in the United Kingdom. It then considers the specific situation of homeless Poles in London and the causes of their homelessness, before reviewing service responses to this group, and, finally, the 'changing landscape' for homelessness and migration.

The Context for Migration

An individual's or household's decision to migrate will be influenced by both 'push' and 'pull' factors. Push factors will often include high unemployment at home, with employment opportunities in a host country frequently a powerful 'pull' factor. Economic migrants such as those moving from postaccession Poland (where unemployment was high) to the United Kingdom (where, until recently, the economy was booming) represented a migration flow directly influenced by political developments (entering the European Union) and economic factors (employment opportunities and relatively higher wages). However, additional, individual factors will also come into play and will influence both the decision to migrate and the choice of country to migrate to. These individual factors include existing social networks, such as relatives or friends who have already moved to a new host country; information about, and transport links to, a potential host country; and an individual's aspirations or personal goals. Furthermore, there may be marked differences between migrants who plan to settle in a host country long term and those engaged in 'circular migration', moving back and forth between their country of origin and host country. Circular migration is thought to be on the increase as the 'late modern' world is increasingly becoming a 'space of flows', influenced by globalisation, cheap travel, new technology and characterised by movement in search of capital (Castells, 2000).

The migratory process has been likened to a form of homelessness – a homelessness negotiated in the time between leaving one's country of origin and obtaining secure accommodation in a host country. Influencing this process of settlement will be the legal rights that migrants are afforded in the host country, which will in turn depend on their country of origin and reason for migration, and can change over time (e.g., if they marry a citizen of their host country). Differing levels of entitlement to social and legal protection place new migrants in a 'hierarchy of vulnerability' (Edgar et al., 2004). Postaccession Polish migrants in the United Kingdom had a degree of security in that they had the right to work in their host country; however, access to welfare services was restricted during a transitional period (up until May 2011), which introduced a significant element of vulnerability.

During this transitional period, postaccession A8 migrant workers in the United Kingdom had to be self-employed or in registered employment to be eligible for social housing or welfare benefits such as housing benefit. To be eligible for welfare benefits and housing when not working, they were required to have completed one year of continuous employment in the United Kingdom and to have been registered with the Workers Registration Scheme (WRS) throughout that time. Given that A8 migrants often worked in short-term contracts, many had not experienced continuous employment for a year. In addition, they had to pay to reregister on the WRS on entering new employment, and unsurprisingly, not all registered in the first place. After May 2011, A8 nationals may have access to welfare services in the United Kingdom on the same basis as other EU nationals.

However, with these transitional arrangements in place, Polish migrant workers faced destitution if something went wrong in the United Kingdom – if, for example, they lost their employment due to assault, injury, or illness. In these circumstances, A8 migrants were unable to claim either subsistence income benefits or housing benefit. The Audit Commission (2007: 24) explained the impact of this:

> *The few [migrant workers] who fail to find accommodation or work, or are made redundant, or become victims of domestic violence and leave their homes, may not be entitled to Housing Benefit. Because hostels often depend on this, they may not be able to accept 'such people (...) individuals can drift' into squatting, rough sleeping and street drinking.*

Polish Migrants to the United Kingdom and Housing

When people migrate to find work, they must find adequate shelter in their destination country. The postaccession entry of Polish nationals into the United Kingdom generated two contrasting concerns regarding their housing circumstances. On the one hand, there were widespread popular concerns that these migrants were absorbing a large proportion of new social tenancies in the United Kingdom, even though in reality less than 1% of social housing allocations in England and Wales in 2006–07 were to A8 nationals (Robinson, 2007).

On the other hand, there were persistent concerns about the poor housing conditions faced by new migrants, including, at the most extreme end, homelessness. Postaccession Polish migrants predominantly worked in low-paid employment – construction, catering, factories, and agriculture. Such low-paid new migrant groups in the United Kingdom (and postaccession Poles were among the lowest-paid migrant groups in the United Kingdom in 2007 (Sriskandarajah et al., 2007)) tend to rent accommodation at the bottom end of the private rented sector or live with friends or relatives when they first arrive (often also in private rented housing). This cheap private rented housing is often of poor quality, and overcrowding is common, with unrelated people sometimes sharing bedrooms.

In some cases, economic migrants' accommodation was 'tied' to employment. If this employment ended, then so did their access to housing. The type of employment that postaccession Poles took up in the United Kingdom often included that associated with tied accommodation, such as nannies living with a family, farmworkers living in caravans on farm sites, or kitchen staff accommodated in hotels where they worked.

However, many of these low-paid Polish workers did obtain adequate housing in the United Kingdom, and given that some Polish migrants were working in highly transient employment and regularly returning to Poland, the priority for a significant number may have been to find cheap and short-term accommodation, with less concern for its quality or security (Robinson et al., 2007). Living in poor or insecure conditions can constitute a conscious housing strategy on the part of economic migrants, purposefully employed to minimise rental costs and to ensure that as much surplus money as possible is available to save or send home.

Unusual for a new migrant group in the United Kingdom, postaccession Poles spread across the country rather than becoming concentrated in urban locations. A number of factors may explain this pattern. The availability of cheap travel options, particularly flights, arriving directly into locations across the United Kingdom from Poland meant that the main traditional urban point of entry – London – could be avoided. Employment in agriculture meant many travelled to find work in rural areas and may have encouraged friends or family to join them. Also, Polish migrants share the white ethnicity that predominates in rural locations throughout the United Kingdom. This may have led them to have a greater degree of comfort travelling outside of conurbations than migrants of other ethnicities. Nevertheless, it was in the capital – London – that reports of homelessness among Polish migrants were most prominent.

Homeless Poles in London

Almost a fifth of all street contacts made by frontline homelessness agencies in London in one week of 2007 were reported to be with A8 nationals, predominantly Polish men (Homeless Link, 2008). There may be a number of reasons why Poles became particularly evident amongst the users of homelessness services in London, despite Polish migrants being located throughout the United Kingdom.

First, the cost of accommodation in London is higher than any other area of the United Kingdom. Those in low-paid employment may not be able to afford even the most basic of accommodation. Given that London is a hub for economic migrants (both legal and illegal) from across the world, it may also be that there is greater competition for peripheral employment. Therefore, unskilled Polish migrants may have found it harder to find both employment and housing in London compared with elsewhere in the United Kingdom.

Second, it could also be that the capital draws those who have encountered difficulties elsewhere, as they try to change their luck in a new location. It has been found, for example, that Scottish rough sleepers in London have often travelled there to escape problems at home (Fitzpatrick et al., 2000). The lure and relative anonymity of large urban centres may lead those with existing vulnerabilities to seek refuge there.

Despite almost as many Polish women as men being registered on the WRS, women were largely absent from those reported to be homeless by frontline agencies in London. Then again, this is in keeping with patterns in the indigenous street homeless population in London where few women are found. Polish women experiencing homelessness in the United Kingdom may deal with it in a different way to those who make contact with frontline homelessness agencies or are visibly sleeping rough. They may, for example, be more likely than men to be able to stay with friends, given the perceived additional vulnerability of women on the streets. They may simply hide away to a greater extent, avoiding contact with service providers and finding places to sleep that are out of sight.

If it is the case, as is likely, that some homelessness experienced by Polish migrants in the United Kingdom is hidden, then it may also have occurred outside of London on a larger scale than is evidenced.

Causes of Homelessness amongst Polish Migrants in London

In the limited research conducted with homeless Poles in London, it was reported that poor command of English and an overall lack of preparation for life in the United Kingdom underpinned many of their difficulties (Broadway, 2007; Davis et al., 2007; Mills et al., 2007). Lack of preparation for life in the United Kingdom in general and in London in particular referred to matters such as being unaware of where to obtain employment and unrealistic expectations regarding housing costs.

Another recurring theme was that of individual trauma and misfortune affecting Polish migrants who were homeless in London. There were reports of Poles being robbed of their money and passport, on their arrival into the country, in the areas surrounding the main train and coach stations. Others became victims of violence or exploitation from other Poles, including those who had paid employment agencies in Poland before departing for the United Kingdom, only to discover, once they arrived, that no such agencies existed in the United Kingdom. Finally, those experiencing homelessness sometimes had their difficulties exacerbated by substance use, especially heavy drinking, or had poor mental or physical health. This affected their ability to find and maintain work. Whilst some reported that their substance misuse or health problems were consequent on the difficulties that they had encountered in the United Kingdom, others had long-standing needs and may have left Poland in an attempt at a 'new life'. It is worth noting here that, under the transitional arrangements, A8 nationals were unable to access secondary health care funded through the National Health Service (NHS), although they were entitled to primary health care. Therefore, Poles and other A8 nationals admitted to hospital due to chronic alcohol use would have to be released once they stabilised, with no access to rehabilitation services.

The overall picture that emerged was that of two 'types' of homeless Poles in London. There were, on the one hand, those who had long-standing vulnerabilities related to substance use (often alcohol), poor health, and experiences on institutionalisation. This group resembled the 'traditional' rough sleeping/street homeless population in the United Kingdom and required extensive support to overcome these problems. The second group were those who found themselves in difficulty on arrival into the United Kingdom due to a lack of knowledge, skills, or sheer misfortune. However, it is important to recognise that homelessness is often part of a dynamic 'trajectory' of increasing marginalisation and insecurity. When placed within the temporal span of an individual's life course, it can be seen that those with entrenched needs may, at one time, have entered homelessness in similar circumstances to those who have more recently become homeless for the first time and, currently at least, have less complex needs.

Street activity among Polish migrants (such as street drinking and begging) was identified in certain areas of London (with large established Polish communities) as a serious 'antisocial' issue. Therefore, in response to a growing number of destitute and excluded Poles attempting to access mainstream services for street homeless people, and amid concerns of growing antisocial activity amongst this group, some London homelessness agencies developed specifically tailored responses, as now discussed.

Service Responses to Homeless Poles in London

Emergency Shelters and Drop-in Services

Emergency shelters and drop-in services in London (often managed by faith-based organisations) experienced a particularly sharp rise in the uptake of their services from new Polish migrants in the period after accession. Drop-in services provide food, a place to spend time (and in some cases a bed over night), advice, washing facilities, and access to other services such as on-site health clinics. Mainstream hostels and other temporary forms of accommodation for homeless people in the United Kingdom are funded through housing benefit, which Polish and other A8 migrants were often ineligible for during the transitional arrangements. Faith-based emergency drop-in services were often the only source of help that new Polish migrants either could access or knew about, as networks of new migrants speaking the same language informed each other of the provision that was available, creating 'nodes' of service uptake.

The large number of Poles accessing some of these services could cause tensions. Some services reported having to turn people away and having to ration their services to Polish migrants. It was feared that long-term, indigenous users of these services resented newcomers, and also that some new migrants were using these services as a means to access cheap food and resources, such as washing machines, rather than because of actual destitution.

Repatriation

Another response that was made to the plight of homeless Poles in London was repatriation or, as it was more diplomatically termed, 'reconnection'. This process was formalised in a partnership between Hammersmith and Fulham London borough Council, Broadway, a large homeless service provider in London, and the BARKA Foundation, a Polish agency that worked with 'socially excluded' individuals in Poland. Two bilingual workers were funded to provide staffing at mainstream drop-in services in the borough. These workers made contact with Polish nationals accessing these services and offered them the opportunity to return to Poland and to access support there. Transport was arranged, and in the first six months that this partnership operated, 56 such 'reconnections' were made.

These reconnections returned those in difficulty to their country of origin, but did little to address the root of the problem, that is, the housing vulnerabilities migrants to the United Kingdom experienced. One agency that conducted research into homelessness and A8 migrants found that the migrants that they had had contact with did not want to return to their country of origin because, though they reported that their experience of living in the United Kingdom had been difficult, 'many participants reported that their quality of life was still better than in their home country' (Broadway, 2007: 40).

Specialist Sign Posting and Support Services

Some homelessness services attempted to be flexible in their response to new Polish migrants accessing their services. They developed targeted support and advice services at their drop-in services provided through bilingual advice workers or volunteers. These services provided advice to homeless A8 migrants on how to access employment, register on the WRS, and search for accommodation. Employment was viewed as the key route for migrants to access low-cost accommodation and to be self-sufficient. Thus the focus in these services was generally on obtaining employment, but additional support needs were also assessed and assistance in dealing with them was sought.

In relation to these additional support needs (and perhaps connected to the increase of Polish professionals also migrating to the United Kingdom with counselling and therapy skills) a Polish-speaking branch of Alcoholics Anonymous and a network of Polish psychologists providing therapy and support were set up. Individuals experiencing more complex difficulties could then be referred to these services.

Conclusion: Changing Landscapes of Migration

The 'influx' of postaccession migrants to the United Kingdom was well documented in the media. Clear discursive characters developed, such as the hardworking

'Polish plumber', alongside the narratives of those who had fallen on hard times. At the time of writing, amidst a global economic downshift felt acutely in the United Kingdom, migratory flows are changing, amidst reports that many A8 migrants are returning to their home countries.

Thus the problems associated with homeless Poles in London and the challenge of developing services appropriate to their needs may abate, especially once the transitional arrangements that limit their access to welfare benefits end. However, it is also likely that some of those in the greatest difficulties, entrenched in street cultures, will remain. In due course new waves of migrants will arrive, some with their own complex problems, and may feed into the street homeless population. It is indicative of globalisation that homelessness services (particularly in urban areas) increasingly have to respond to a multiethnic and multicultural set of excluded individuals, with ebbs and flows influenced by global affairs. The experience of postaccession Poles in the United Kingdom was just one example of this. It was perhaps due to their predominant characteristics (white, middle aged, male, often alcohol users) that some of those who found themselves in difficulty fitted in so quickly with the traditional street homelessness patterns in London and at one point appeared to account for almost one-fifth of those in contact with frontline homelessness agencies.

Migration and homelessness are interlinked in a number of ways. First, the homelessness experienced by migrants could be seen as politically constructed. Immigration laws and entitlements create the context and resources whereby an individual may or may not be able to negotiate access to housing successfully. Second, migrants are in transition. They have to obtain housing/shelter on arrival into their host countries. Housing transitions can be more or less risky depending on an individual's circumstances and the resources they have access to, and for some the chances of housing exclusion may be high. Third, homeless services operate within a politicised context. How and why they respond to new migrants' homelessness will have a direct influence on these homelessness experiences and pathways through it. As yet there appears to be little coordination or shared strategy between services with respect to responding to homeless migrants, and the migratory landscape within which these responses take place is a rapidly shifting one.

See also: Feminist Perspectives on Homelessness; Hidden Homelessness; Housing Careers; Migration and Population Mobility.

References

Audit Commission (2007) *Crossing Borders – Responding to the Local Challenges of Migrant Workers*. London: Audit Commission for Local Authorities and the National Health Service in England.

Broadway (2007) *Routes into London's Homelessness Services: The Experiences of A8 Nationals*. London: Broadway and the Ashden Trust.

Castells M (2000) *The Rise of the Network Society*. Oxford: Blackwell.

Davis F, Stankeviciute J, Ebbutt D, and Kagga R (2007) *The Ground of Justice: The Report of a Pastoral Research Enquiry into the Needs of Migrants in London's Catholic Community*. London: Van Hugel Institute.

Edgar B, Doherty J, and Meert H (2004) *Immigration and Homelessness in Europe*. Bristol: Policy Press.

Fitzpatrick S, Goodlad R, and Lynch E (2000) *Homeless Scots in London*. London: Borderline.

Home Office (2008) *Accession Monitoring Report May 2004–September 2008*. London: UK Border Agency.

Homeless Link (2006) *A8 Nationals in London Homelessness Services*. London: Homeless Link and the Housing Corporation.

Homeless Link (2008) *Central and East European Rough Sleepers in London: Baseline Survey*. London: Homeless Link.

Mills K, Knight T, and Green R (2007) *Beyond Boundaries: Offering Substance Misuse Services to New Migrants in London*. Hertfordshire: Centre for Community Research, University of Hertfordshire.

Robinson D (2007) European Union Accession State Migrants in Social Housing in England. *People, Place and Policy Online*, 1(3): 98–111.

Robinson D, Reeve K, and Casey R (2007) *The Housing Pathways of New Migrants*. York: JRF.

Sriskandarajah D, Cooley L, and Kornblatt T (2007) *Britains Immigrants: An Economic Profile*. London: Institute for Public Policy Research.

Further Reading

Castles S and Miller M (2003) *The Age of Migration: International Population Movements in the Modern World*. Basingstoke: Palgrave.

Shelter (2008) *Policy Briefing: Eastern European Migrant Workers and Housing*. www.shelter.org.uk/policy briefings

Spencer S, Ruhs M, Anderson B, and Rogaly B (2007) *Migrants' Lives Beyond the Workplace: The Experiences of Central and East Europeans in the UK*. York: JRF.

Robinson D and Reeves K (2006) *Neighbourhood Experiences of New Immigration: Reflections from the Evidence Base*. York: JRF.

Relevant Websites

www.shelter.org.uk
www.homelesslink.org.uk

Homeless People: Refugees and Asylum Seekers

JA Sweeney, Durham University, County Durham, UK

© 2012 Elsevier Ltd. All rights reserved.

Glossary

Asylum seeker A person seeking recognition as a refugee.
ECHR European Convention for the Protection of Human Rights and Fundamental Freedoms (1950).
ICCPR International Covenant on Civil and Political Rights (1966).
ICESCR International Covenant on Economic, Social and Cultural Rights (1966).
Internally displaced person A person who has been forced from their home by, for example, conflict, persecution, or natural disaster and who has not crossed a national boundary.
Refugee A person recognised as falling within the definition provided by the 1951 UN Refugee Convention.
UNHCR Office of the United Nations High Commissioner for Refugees.

Refugees, Asylum Seekers, and Displacement

Refugees and those seeking asylum are by definition displaced from their normal place of residence and the place with which they have had an established home connection. In their host state they are particularly vulnerable to homelessness and poor housing. Both international refugee law and international human rights law provide some housing rights for refugees and asylum seekers, but these instruments leave considerable discretion to states. In this article, we shall explore the differing circumstances of refugees in the developing and developed worlds and the protection of their rights under specialised international refugee law and general international human rights law.

Refugees in the Developing World

By the end of 2007, the office of the United Nations High Commissioner for Refugees (UNHCR) estimated that the global refugee population stood at 11.4 million, plus another 4.6 million Palestinian refugees (who are supported by the United Nations Relief and Works Agency for Palestine Refugees in the Near East (UNRWA)). Most refugees flee to neighbouring states and therefore remain within their region of origin. The 2007 UNHCR *Statistical Yearbook* estimates that the major refugee-generating regions host between 83% and 90% of 'their' refugees. For example, Afghanistan is currently the highest producer of refugees (3.1 million by the end of 2007), but 96% of them are hosted in Pakistan and Iran. Indeed Pakistan and Iran, in that order, are the top two states of asylum in the world. The implication of these figures is that the refugee crisis is more severe in the developing world that tends to produce them, and thus the vulnerability to homelessness and poor housing is more acute there also.

The nature of the homelessness problem for refugees in the developing world is closely tied to the resources available to the host state and the amount of international aid supplied by UNHCR. Whilst in the developed world refugees tend to arrive as individual applicants for asylum, the developing world also faces the sudden mass influx of refugees from neighbouring states. This can lead to serious problems with reception conditions, including situations where initially 'temporary' measures become *de facto* large and semi permanent refugee camps. It is often feared by governments that a temporary influx will become a permanent and burdensome population that would result in the exposure of refugees to poor treatment.

Most refugees in the developing world are 'housed' in organised camps or settlements. For example, some 14 000 Sudanese refugees are hosted at the Djabal camp in eastern Chad alone. In its *World Survey 2007*, the US Committee on Refugees and Immigrants estimated that 8.8 million people are housed in refugee camps for 5 years or longer. Confinement to a closed camp, particularly as a result of formal judicial or administrative processes, may be akin to detention. Access to clean water and adequate and nutritious food is of paramount importance in large refugee camps. The risk of overcrowding as camps become more established has a particularly deleterious effect on the quality of life for those living there.

Refugees in the Developed World

Refugees in the developed world tend to arrive not by mass influx but by individual applications for asylum.

According to the 2007 *UNHCR Statistical Yearbook*, Europe hosts approximately 14% of the world's refugee population, whilst the United States hosts approximately 2.5%. Nevertheless, policies towards refugees and asylum seekers have become marked by increasing suspicion, stringency, and legalisation. Such policies are designed to restrict illegal immigration and to protect national security.

To preemptively avoid such issues as housing asylum seekers, several governments have instituted policies designed to prevent their arrival in the first place. These include tough 'carrier sanctions' imposed upon those bringing people into states (be they migrants or asylum seekers) and a preference for extraterritorial processing of asylum claims. For example, the so-called 2001–07 'Pacific Solution' of the Australian government involved the removal of asylum seekers from Australia to third countries in the Pacific, where their claim for asylum in Australia would then be processed.

Whilst the rights of refugees are dictated by international law, the rights of asylum seekers tend to be exercised at the discretion of the host state and may hinge on domestic policy decisions concerning the quality of welfare provisions. States may choose to assimilate the support of asylum seekers with other forms of welfare support or may separate it completely. On arrival, states may also tightly restrict the liberty of asylum seekers, so that they are 'housed' in immigration detention centres (often former prisons). This raises issues not of the absence of accommodation but of its adequacy and appropriateness: particular concerns include overcrowding, unsanitary conditions, inadequate recreational space, and mixed-sex accommodation. States may also choose to adopt a mixture of assimilation, separation, and detention approaches.

The exposure to a risk of homelessness also hinges on policy decisions over whether asylum seekers should be allowed to undertake paid work either instead of or in addition to receiving welfare support from the state. If a state, like the United Kingdom, generally withholds permission to work from asylum seekers, then they are wholly reliant on public or private assistance and become particularly vulnerable to homelessness and poor housing. Such policies are usually justified as an attempt to remove incentives to people arriving to work illegally and to maintain the integrity of managed migration routes. To this end, in the United Kingdom asylum seekers are outside the mainstream benefit system, and where financial support is given, the level of support for asylum-seeking adults is calculated at only 70% of the income support level for non-asylum-seeking adults. Successful applicants have their support terminated after 28 days, a period which may not be long enough to find employment and alternative accommodation and which creates a further risk of destitution even amongst recognised refugees.

In a 2007 report, the Joint Committee on Human Rights of the House of Lords and House of Commons stated that it had been "persuaded by the evidence that the Government has indeed been practising a deliberate policy of destitution of this highly vulnerable group [viz. asylum seekers and failed asylum seekers], at all stages of asylum claim process". Although the UK Government rebutted this in their formal response to the report, the allegation continues to be made.

Policies towards the approximately 280 000 'failed' asylum seekers remaining in the United Kingdom have been identified as particularly problematic. If an application for recognition as a refugee fails, then financial support and accommodation are withheld after 21 days on the assumption that the failed applicant should leave the United Kingdom. A safeguard against destitution is said to apply, but a report by the Independent Asylum Commission in 2008 showed that less than 4% of failed asylum seekers receive support under it (9365 out of 283 500 people). The merits of this policy, and its success at encouraging 'voluntary' return, are hotly contested, but it clearly impacts on the risk of homelessness for displaced peoples.

A Brief Note on the Forms and Status of International Law

Most of the legal standards relating to refugees and their housing discussed below derive from international law.

There is no single international law-making body like a world parliament. Instead, international law is said to have several sources. The generally recognised authoritative statement of the sources of international law is contained in Article 38(1) of the Statute of the International Court of Justice:

a. international conventions, whether general or particular, establishing rules expressly recognized by [...] states;
b. international custom, as evidence of a general practice accepted as law;
c. the general principles of law recognized by civilized nations;
d. [...] judicial decisions and the teachings of the most highly qualified publicists of the various nations, as subsidiary means for the determination of rules of law.

It is generally understood that this list is hierarchical, so that agreements explicitly entered into in the form of treaties will take precedence over customary international law, and customary international law will take precedence over 'general principles of law' and the other auxiliary sources.

The effect of international treaties, such as the 1951 UN Convention on Refugees, on the domestic legal systems of its signatory states is a matter of national constitutional law. In 'monist' states, such as the Netherlands, the provisions of international treaties may take effect in the national legal order without further enactment and be relied upon in judicial proceedings. In 'dualist' states, such as the United Kingdom, the executive branch of the state (the Government) signs the treaty, but it may only take effect within the national legal order if the legislative branch (the Parliament) incorporates it by passing a legislative instrument such as an Act of Parliament. For example, the Human Rights Act 1998 incorporated the 1950 European Convention on Human Rights into UK law (albeit with some differences).

The UN Convention on Refugees: Definitions and Protection from Homelessness

The 1951 UN Convention Relating to the Status of Refugees was drafted in the immediate aftermath of World War II, and UNHCR began working in the same year to further its aims. A further agreement, the 1967 Protocol, extends the temporal scope of the 1951 Convention to cover refugee situations caused by events beyond the original cutoff date of 1 January 1951. The Convention, as amended, continues to elaborate the rights of refugees and the corresponding obligations of signatory states. The postwar historical context in which the Convention was drafted leaves it with some inherent weaknesses, particularly in terms of its definition of a 'refugee'.

The international legal definition of a refugee established by the 1951 UN Refugee Convention is limited to displaced individuals without protection from their state of nationality or habitual residence who have a well-founded fear of persecution for one of the reasons exhaustively specified in the Convention's first Article: race, religion, nationality, membership of a particular social group, or political opinion. States are under an obligation not to 'refoul' (return) refugees to a place where they have a well-founded fear of persecution. This is known as the obligation of 'non refoulement'.

Two features of this definition are relevant to the issue of homelessness. The first is that there is a necessary cross-border element to it – a refugee is outside their state of nationality or habitual residence. However, a great many displaced people, particularly in the developing world, are in a situation that is as tragic as that faced by Convention refugees, but have not crossed a national border. They are known as 'internally displaced people' or 'IDPs'. UNHCR estimated in 2007 that there were around 24.5 million IDPs in 52 states. Half of them are in Africa. The legal protection of IDPs is in the early stages of its evolution. The extent to which homeless and poorly housed IDPs may lay claim to housing rights derived from refugee law is thus moot.

The second relevant feature of this definition is the element of 'persecution' required – individuals fleeing poverty or a natural disaster will not normally be a 'refugee' for the purposes of the 1951 UN Refugee Convention (although states may, at their discretion, choose to offer protection on general humanitarian grounds). The persecution element is increasingly significant because the dynamics of forced migration are changing, and due to a reduction in the number of armed conflicts globally, natural disasters are now a far greater cause of displacement.

Housing Rights of Refugees under the 1951 UN Refugee Convention

Refugees gain some protection from homelessness under rights derived from the 1951 UN Refugee Convention.

Article 21 of the 1951 UN Refugee Convention states:

> As regards housing, the Contracting States, in so far as the matter is regulated by laws or regulations or is subject to the control of public authorities, shall accord to refugees lawfully staying in their territory treatment as favourable as possible and, in any event, not less favourable than that accorded to aliens generally in the same circumstances.

The standard of treatment in relation to housing ('as favourable as possible') is lower than the standard in relation to other elements of welfare support, where under Article 23 'public relief' for refugees must be assimilated with that provided to the general population. The leading refugee law scholar James Hathaway has criticised this for the apparent anomaly that states providing financial support to refugees are held to a higher standard than those that choose to provide accommodation directly (since only the latter would fall under Article 21).

It is also notable that the housing obligation under Article 21 is to treat refugees equally to 'aliens generally' and not to the nationalised population. Nevertheless, as Hathaway has identified, this terminology incorporates by reference the entitlements owed to aliens under international human rights treaties such as the 1966 International Covenant on Economic, Social and Cultural Rights (ICESCR) discussed below. In this way, the 1951 UN Refugee Convention affords some protection from homelessness to refugees.

Housing Rights of Asylum Seekers under the 1951 UN Refugee Convention

The 1951 UN Refugee Convention is rather ambiguous in terms of the economic, social, cultural, and other human rights of those who are not yet recognised as refugees. However, it is not permissible to treat an asylum seeker so poorly that they are compelled not to pursue their claim: this would amount to 'constructive refoulement' and is prohibited. Nevertheless, it is generally assumed that most of the substantive rights in the Convention apply only to those formally recognised as refugees. Thus, on its own, the 1951 UN Refugee Convention does little to protect asylum seekers from homelessness.

The Human Rights of Refugees and Asylum Seekers

Human rights abuses are not only a cause of displacement, but may also be an unfortunate consequence of seeking refugee status in another state. However, in addition to the rights gained by virtue of being a refugee, some of the human rights possessed by every person take on particular significance in relation to refugees and asylum seekers. Since these rights are possessed by everybody, the distinction between their applicability to asylum seekers and recognised refugees is not as rigid. The protection of refugees and asylum seekers from homelessness may thus be grounded in the identification of housing rights within international human rights law.

Human rights relating to housing and the home are contained in both the ICESCR and regional human rights instruments such as the European Convention for the Protection of Human Rights and Fundamental Freedoms (ECHR).

Economic, Social, and Cultural Rights of Refugees and Asylum Seekers

The right to housing in international law has its origins in Article 25(1) of the 1948 Universal Declaration of Human Rights. The 1966 ICESCR is now the most significant international human rights law applicable in this field. Under Article 2(2) ICESCR, States Parties agree to guarantee the rights contained within without discrimination on, amongst other grounds, 'national and social origin'. Thus states must guarantee the rights for non nationals such as refugees and asylum seekers.

Article 11 ICESCR requires that states recognise

> the right of everyone to an adequate standard of living for himself and his family, including adequate food, clothing and housing, and to the continuous improvement of living conditions.

Article 11 ICESCR is included within the rights owed to 'aliens generally' under Article 21 of the 1951 UN Refugee Convention and has been used to ensure that refugee accommodation is, for example, habitable and not impracticably remote.

The weakness of housing rights for refugees and asylum seekers derived from the ICESCR lies within the nature of the obligation that the Covenant places upon states. The notion of economic, social, and cultural rights is controversial in some quarters because they may be understood as insufficiently precise in scope and requiring an unrealistic amount of state expenditure. In the light of this, under Article 2(1) ICESCR each State Party undertakes

> to take steps, [...] to the maximum of its available resources [...], with a view to achieving progressively the full realisation of the rights recognised [...].

Much legal analysis has been devoted to clarifying the nature of this obligation. Significant practical and conceptual problems remain with economic, social, and cultural rights in general and with the obligations emanating from the ICESCR in particular. However, it is now generally understood by legal academics that under Article 2(1) ICESCR, States Parties are under an immediate duty to take steps to secure the rights contained in the Covenant, unless they can demonstrate that they do not have the resources to comply with even a 'minimum core obligation'. Moreover, in carrying out any actions relative to the right to housing, states are bound by the overarching principle of nondiscrimination.

In relation to refugees and asylum seekers, who by definition are non nationals of the state in which they seek refuge, it is significant that Article 2(3) ICESCR adds a further caveat:

> Developing countries, with due regard to human rights and their national economy, may determine to what extent they would guarantee the economic rights recognized in the present Covenant to non-nationals.

The UN Committee on Economic, Social and Cultural Rights has expressed its view of the obligations arising under the Covenant in its 'General Comment No. 3: The nature of States Parties obligations'. It has discussed the issue of housing specifically in its 'General Comment No. 4: The right to adequate housing'.

In General Comment No. 4, the UN Committee on Economic, Social and Cultural Rights has taken a broad interpretation of Article 11 ICESCR so that it encompasses not merely the provision of shelter, but 'the right to live somewhere in security, peace and dignity'. The right to housing has instrumental as well as inherent value, since it facilitates the protection of other rights.

Economic, social, and cultural rights in domestic law

This section explores some key examples of the way that economic, social, and cultural rights may be guaranteed in domestic constitutional law. The Irish and Indian constitutions are notable for the way that they enshrine economic, social, and cultural rights. However, in those states, economic, social, and cultural rights are seen as 'directive principles' that are not judicially enforceable. By contrast, the South African constitution makes economic, social, and cultural rights justiciable, but also incorporates the caveats of the ICESCR in relation to the availability of resources. The South African Supreme Court of Appeal has, however, held that withholding the right to work from asylum seekers whilst not providing any welfare support violated the constitutional right to dignity (in the 2004 case of *Minister for Home Affairs v Watchenuka*).

Other constitutions lacking express reference to economic, social, and cultural rights nevertheless imply their existence. In the 2002 case of *Gosselin v Quebec* the Canadian Supreme Court explored the relationship between acute poverty and the right to life. Likewise, the Indian Supreme Court held in the 1981 case of *Franic Caralie v Union of Territory of Delhi* that the right to life "includes the right to live with human dignity and all that goes along with it, namely, the bare necessaries of life such as adequate nutrition, clothing and shelter".

These examples demonstrate that, as well as by relying upon rights derived from international instruments, protection from homelessness may be achieved for refugees and asylum seekers through creative interpretation of national provisions on economic, social, and cultural rights.

Civil and Political Rights of Refugees and Asylum Seekers

The legal nature of civil and political rights has been less controversial: they tend to be more narrowly defined and often impose negative rather than positive obligations. Human rights treaties guaranteeing civil and political rights are consequently understood as imposing immediate rather than progressively realisable obligations.

The key international law in this field is the 1966 International Covenant on Civil and Political Rights (ICCPR). Like the ICESCR, the ICCPR applies to non-nationals such as refugees and asylum seekers. It can be argued that in severe cases the denial of certain economic, social, and cultural rights may amount to the consequent infringement of certain civil and political rights, including the right to life (Article 6(1) ICCPR) and the right not to be subjected to torture or to cruel, inhuman or degrading treatment or punishment (Article 7 ICCPR). However, it is in the regional jurisprudence of the European Court of Human Rights that the relevance of civil and political rights to the issue of housing and homelessness amongst refugees and asylum seekers has taken on particular importance.

Refugees, asylum seekers, and homelessness in the ECHR

Article 8 ECHR provides a right to respect for home, family, and private life. The European Court of Human Rights has developed the principle that the rights enshrined within the European Convention on Human Rights impose not only a negative duty upon states to refrain from violating the rights but also a positive obligation to guarantee their enjoyment. Thus the European Court observed in *Airey v Ireland* that some rights will have implications that are economic and social in nature. There was, it explained, no 'watertight division' separating the sphere of economic and social rights from the civil and political sphere. However, in the 2001 case of *Chapman v United Kingdom*, the European Court held that 'Article 8 does not in terms recognise a right to be provided with a home'. Instead, much of the case law has focussed on protection against interference with an established home. Obviously, for a homeless asylum seeker or refugee this is of little consolation.

Notwithstanding the limitations of the right to respect for home, in some important cases the relevance of the right to freedom from torture and inhuman or degrading treatment has been demonstrated. This line of reasoning has, in turn, been taken the furthest by the UK House of Lords, which, when it acts in its judicial capacity, is the United Kingdom's highest court (except in matters of Scottish criminal law).

The House of Lords and the destitution of asylum seekers in the United Kingdom

The Immigration and Asylum Act 1999 guaranteed that support provided nationally to asylum seekers would be completely separate from the regular entitlements of individuals to social security benefits. The Nationality, Immigration and Asylum Act 2002 then purported to exclude late-applying asylum seekers from that protection altogether.

In 2005 the UK House of Lords gave a groundbreaking judgment. In the case of *R (Limbuela and others) v Secretary of State for the Home Department*, the House of Lords held that by creating a statutory framework that coupled a prohibition upon work with disentitlement to state support, the UK Government was directly responsible for the considerable hardship, including rough sleeping, suffered by the applicants (Mr Limbuela and others). Moreover, they found that the statutory framework amounted to 'inhuman or degrading treatment', prohibited by Article 3 ECHR. In this way the civil and political right to freedom from torture and inhuman or degrading treatment was transformed into the source of housing rights for some asylum seekers. However, the House of Lords also held that a general duty to house the homeless or to provide for the destitute could not be derived from Article 3 ECHR.

The relevance of the decision in *Limbuela and Others* to the interpretation of the ICCPR has not yet been demonstrated. Likewise, the application of this judgment to the situation of destitute failed asylum seekers remains moot.

Conclusion

Immigration and asylum law and policy are hotly contested areas of political debate in both the developed and developing worlds. Many states seek to balance their responsibilities under international law against domestic policies designed to reduce 'pull factors' for asylum seekers and to discourage permanent settlement. It is argued that where pull factors such as the provision of housing are reduced, fewer unmeritorious applications for asylum are made and more resources can be spent on 'genuine' applications. This fundamentally misunderstands the decision-making process of forced migrants, who are overwhelmingly more concerned by the conditions in their home state ('push factors') than in their prospective host state. In the meantime, displaced people who are not covered by international law or who are unable to enforce it are left at the mercy of national policies whose chief addressee is not the displaced people themselves, but the national electorate.

See also: Homeless People: Disasters and Displacement; Human Rights and Housing; Rights, Citzenship, and Shelter.

Further Reading

Barber R (2008) Protecting the right to housing in the aftermath of natural disaster: standards in international human rights law. *International Journal of Refugee Law* 20: 432–468.

Cholewinski R (2000) Economic, social and cultural rights of refugees in Europe. *Georgetown Immigration Law Journal* 14: 709–755.

Clayton G (2006) *Textbook on Immigration and Asylum Law*, 2nd edn. Oxford: Oxford University Press.

Edwards A (2005) Human rights, refugees, and the right 'to enjoy' asylum. *International Journal of Refugee Law* 17: 293–330.

Edwards A (2008) The optional protocol to the convention against torture and the detention of refugees. *International and Comparative Law Quarterly* 57: 789–825.

Fredman S (2006) Human rights transformed: positive duties and positive rights. *Public Law* 498–520.

Goodwin Gill G and McAdam J (2007) *The Refugee in International Law*, 3rd edn. Oxford: Oxford University Press.

Hathaway JC (2005) *The Rights of Refugees in International Law*. Cambridge: Cambridge University Press.

Independent Asylum Commission (2008) *Second Report of Conclusions and Recommendations, Safe Return*. London: Independent Asylum Commission. http://www.independentasylumcommission.org.uk/

Joint Committee on Human Rights (2007a) *The Treatment of Asylum Seekers – Tenth Report Of Session 2006–2007*. London: The Stationary Office Limited.

Joint Committee on Human Rights (2007b) *Government Response to the Committee's Tenth Report of This Session: The Treatment of Asylum Seekers*. London: The Stationary Office Limited.

O'Cinneide C (2008) A modest proposal: destitution, state responsibility and the European Convention on Human Rights. *European Human Rights Law Review* 5: 583–605.

Sweeney J (2008) The human rights of failed asylum seekers in the UK. *Public Law* 277–301.

Ugarkovic B (2004) Comparative study of social and economic rights of asylum seekers and refugees. *Georgia Journal of International and Comparative Law* 32: 539–579.

UNHCR (1998) *Guiding Principles on Internal Displacement*, UN Doc. E/CN.4/1998/53/Add.2.

UNHCR (2007) *Q &A on Internally Displaced Peoples*. Geneva: UNHCR Media Relations and Public Information Service.

UNHCR (2008) *2007 Statistical Yearbook (Draft)*. Geneva: UNHCR.

US Committee on Refugees and Immigrants (2007) *World Refugee Survey 2007*. http://www.refugees.org/

York S and Fancott N (2008) Enforced destitution: impediments to return and access section 4 'hard cases' support. *Journal of Immigration and Nationality Law* 22(1): 5–26.

Homeless People: Single Men in Japan

Y Okamoto, Chukyo University, Nagoya, Japan
J Bretherton, University of York, York, UK

© 2012 Elsevier Ltd. All rights reserved.

Glossary

Latent homelessness The 'hidden' homeless residing in temporary accommodation usually tied to employment or in welfare institutions or hospitals.
Net café 24-h access Internet cafés.
Pachinko Japanese slot machine gaming parlours.
Yoseba These are a type of area where day workers gather seeking work and companies hire them as a buffer against business fluctuating by employing workers during a boom and dismissing them in a recession.

Introduction

Japan is one of the richest nations in the world. According to the United Nations Development Programme's 'Human Development Report 2007/2008' (United Nations Development Programme, 2007), Japan's GDP per capita was $31 267 in 2005, placing it seventeenth overall in the world. Its record on housing supply is also impressive: figures for 2006 indicate that the annual number of housing starts exceeded 1.2 million, and the number of houses (57 593 100) is more than the number of households (49 988 800) by 15% (figures for 2008). Nevertheless, there are around 16 000 homeless people (i.e., rough sleepers) in Japan, according to the latest government count of 2009 (Ministry of Health, Labour, and Welfare, 2009a). This 2009 national survey shows that these rough sleepers are almost all men (92%), and the vast majority are single (90%).

The traditional context for homelessness in Japan is Yosebas – areas where day workers gather seeking jobs – which have long been a crucial element in the Japanese economy. In a strong economy, these day workers are hired, and in a sluggish economy, they are laid off, and hence forced to sleep outside in and around the Yoseba area. Thus, Yosebas have functioned as a buffer against economic fluctuations and have supported companies – especially within the construction business – that require increased labour power at short notice. In addition, the lives of Japanese people have traditionally been supported by what could be considered supplements to the insufficient social welfare system from private companies, families, and local communities. Since the 1990s, the wider safety net that had supported many Japanese people collapsed, largely because of economic globalisation, with its accompanying free movement of capital and industry, and the issue of homelessness became a major social problem in Japan.

This article reviews the extent, nature, and background of homelessness in Japan. It employs a wider definition of homelessness than that used by the government, expanding the meaning to include a range of inappropriate housing situations alongside rough sleeping. Principal 'categories' of homeless people in Japan, taking into account typical causal patterns, are outlined first. This is followed by an overview of the characteristics and demographic profile of Japan's homeless. Recent government policies aimed at reducing the numbers of homeless people are then discussed before finally considering the likely future pattern of homelessness in Japan.

Defining Homelessness in Japan

The official and narrowest definition of homelessness in Japan was stipulated in Article 2 of the 'Special Measures Law Concerning Support for Self-Sustaining Living of the Homeless' in 2002. This definition of homelessness includes "people who live their daily lives at city parks, riversides, streets, railway stations, or at other public facilities". Only homeless people who are clearly visible because of their occupation of public space by setting up a tent or hut to sleep in a park, on a riverbank, and such, are included. Consequently, those that drift from one area of public space to the next without setting up a tent or hut are excluded from the definition, and hence the measures outlined in the 2002 legislation.

Also excluded are the homeless who use Internet cafés or other 24-h access facilities as bases for living, those persons who stay in welfare facilities or hospitals, or temporary workers who have tied accommodation.

These groups that are included in our broader definition of homelessness are discussed in more detail below.

Types and Causes of Homelessness in Japan

The reasons for, or causes of, homelessness in Japan can be attributed to structural changes in society, the economy, and the policy framework in combination with personal factors. Although the impact that any or all of these factors have on an individual may vary depending on the attributes of the homeless individuals themselves, several broad categories of homeless people in Japan can be identified.

The Homeless Who Use Yosebas as Bases for Living

Yosebas' function as a labourer supply service has declined dramatically in the context of economic globalisation. In an effort to reduce personnel costs, companies often now hire lower-paid workers, such as foreign workers and students, from places other than Yosebas. Furthermore, those who currently gather at Yosebas are primarily from the baby boom generation born between 1947 and 1949, are now over 60 years old, and are, consequently, not an attractive workforce for employers. Those workers who once worked at Yosebas but now cannot find employment there sleep outside in or around Yoseba areas. Traditionally, the number of homeless people at Yosebas has fluctuated along with the economic climate. However, since 1990, because of these structural changes, the numbers of homeless people at Yosebas have remained static (Shima, 2001).

The Homeless Outside of Yosebas Who Are Unemployed Because of the Restructuring of the Economy

As with the Yoseba homeless, other homeless populations have emerged because of globalisation. The collapse of the economic bubble that peaked around 1990, and the free movement of capital and the labour force resulting from the end of the Cold War, accelerated the need for companies to reduce personnel costs. This led to temporary employment instead of regular employment for young workers and often unemployment for middle-aged and elderly workers. Those workers who were dismissed suddenly and did not know of Yosebas began to spend their days at city centre railway stations, city parks, and other public spaces, where homelessness became an observable social phenomenon.

The Homeless Who Use Internet Cafés or Other 24-h Access Facilities as Bases for Living

The Internet has become widely used following the establishment of more stable communication networks in Japan subsequent to the Great Hanshin Awaji Earthquake (Kobe Earthquake) in 1995. Places where customers can use the Internet all day and night in a private room have now been opened nationwide. A recent phenomenon is for these Internet cafés to be popularised as a place to not only search for a job but also as a place to casually spend nights for about ¥2000 (£13 or $21) per night. Since the latter half of the 1990s, young people who could not get regular employment and middle-aged temporary workers who had lost regular employment have frequently used Internet cafés as a form of accommodation. They are forced into this position both because of their low-income status and because a guarantor is required to obtain a rental property in Japan.

These Net café homeless people are not covered by the official help offered under the homelessness legislation. Their lifestyles are irregular and unstable, on occasion sleeping outside, spending other nights at Internet cafés, taking naps at libraries or pachinko (Japanese slot machine gaming parlours), spending all night on a train, or staying overnight at 24-h bookstores (Kamagasaki Shien Kiko and Graduate School for Creative Cities, Osaka City University, 2008).

The Latent Homeless

This often refers to persons who stay in welfare facilities or hospitals or to temporary workers that have tied accommodation. This population can become homeless very suddenly and unexpectedly. First, there are increasing concerns about the rise in the number of people who may lose their right to stay in welfare or medical facilities or institutions as a result of a policy shift emphasising community-based care (as stipulated in the Ministry of Health, Labour and Welfare, 1995 White Paper). Thus as their eligibility to stay in social welfare or medical facilities is lost, so too is their place of residence, and homelessness is inevitable unless they find an alternative, stable place to stay.

Second, within this homeless 'category' are temporary workers whose housing is 'tied' to their employment; so they lose their place to stay when they lose their jobs. Because of the frequently unexpected nature of their dismissal, they often become homeless prior to eligibility for any homelessness assistance. This dismissal of employees who lived in dormitories and company residences became particularly noticeable after the autumn of 2008. This resulted in a large-scale increase in homeless individuals who had suddenly lost tied accommodation. According to the Ministry of Health, Labour, and Welfare

(2009b), the number of temporary workers who lost their jobs from October 2008 up to the end of September 2009 is anticipated to be more than 240 000. Many of these would have had tied accommodation. This reason for homelessness is primarily due to the recent dramatic events in the global economic climate.

Finally, there are others who may be regarded as homeless in a much broader sense. They presently live in a property, but their accommodation is inadequate, and, as a result, they are latently homeless. The Ministry of Land, Infrastructure, Transportation, and Tourism (2003) stipulates a minimum housing standard for every household in order to maintain a basic level of living. Below this minimum housing standard are those properties which are dilapidated, overcrowded, or without adequate amenities. This is defined as 'people living in conditions that must be immediately improved'. According to the Land/Housing Statistical Survey in 2003 (Ministry of Internal Affairs and Communications, 2003), the proportion of Japanese households that live under this minimum housing standard is 4.2%. There appears to be a correlation between the annual income of households and propensity to live under this housing standard: the percentage living under this minimum housing standard is 1.2% for households whose annual income is ¥15 million (£94 950 or $156 250) or more, while the percentage is 6.3% for those whose annual income is less than ¥2 million (£12 600 or $20 800).

Characteristics of the Homeless in Japan

Although the issue of homelessness has been around for a number of years in Japan, it is only relatively recently that the government has acknowledged it as such. Hence, in 2003 the first 'official' national homelessness survey was undertaken. This was followed by one in 2007 and the most recent in 2009. On the basis of these three national homelessness surveys and the August 2007 Net Café Survey by the Ministry of Health, Labour, and Welfare (that looked at people frequently using Internet cafés as places of accommodation), we can come to several conclusions about the characteristics of the homeless in Japan.

The first national homelessness survey of 2003 stated there were 25 296 homeless people nationwide. Although homeless people were concentrated in the big cities (6603 homeless people were in Osaka and 5927 in Tokyo), there was some level of homelessness identified in every municipality. Homeless people most commonly slept in city parks (48.9%), followed by riversides (17.5%), and streets (12.6%). The homeless population was overwhelmingly male. The average age was 55.9 years, and people who had been homeless for more than 5 years accounted for 24%, showing that almost a quarter had been homeless for a significant period of time. Almost two-thirds (64.7%) of the homeless engaged in work such as the collection of waste articles for recycling. About half (47.4%) complained of physical ailments, but more than two-thirds (68.4%) of these did not receive any treatment. The findings of the national survey demonstrated many had a strong desire for independence via work, as half (49.7%) selected the response 'I want to get regular employment and work.'

The second survey in 2007 revealed changes in the attributes of the homeless. First, there had been a decrease in the total number of homeless people to 18 564. Second, there had been an increase in the average age (to 57.5 years old). Third, a change in the patterns of sleeping place, with a movement from city parks (35.9% of total in 2007 compared with 48.9% in 2003) to riversides (31.8% of total in 2007 compared with 17.5% in 2003). Finally, there had been a decrease in the drive to achieve independence (only 35.9% said 'I want to get regular employment' in 2007). Although a breakdown of the exact demographic data is not yet available, the latest national survey in 2009 found that homelessness has further decreased to 15 759.

A major factor thought to underpin the changes revealed by these periodic national surveys, particularly the overall decrease in numbers, is thought to be the relative success of the independence through employment policies in helping some people to move out of homelessness. Another important factor is the increased eligibility of rough sleepers for Social Welfare Assistance to enable them to live in specially constructed accommodation facilities and thus outside of the rough sleeper count. Since the recognition of homelessness as a social issue in Japan, many such accommodation facilities have been built and run by NGOs or government social welfare agencies.

Turning to those who are in temporary or unstable housing but not regarded as officially homeless, a survey in 2007 estimated that overall 60 000 individuals were using Internet cafés on any one night across Japan. Of these, 21 000 persons had spent at least a continuous period of 3 days staying there. A further 5400 were using these places as a permanent form of accommodation.

More than 90% of all those using Net cafés as accommodation are male, and the age composition shows two peaks: in their 50s (26.3%) and in their 20s (26.5%). Among the 5400 people using Net cafés consistently, two-fifths (40%) had experienced life on the streets and lived chaotic lives, drifting from sleeping on the streets to staying in Internet cafés, fast food restaurants, saunas, or similar buildings that allow 24-h access. The average monthly income for these 5400 people is very low at ¥107 000 in Tokyo (£678 or $1114) and ¥83 000 in Osaka (£526 or $864), compared with the national average monthly income per Japanese household estimated to be

¥443 429 (£2808 or $4617) (Ministry of Internal Affairs and Communications, 2009). If we set this alongside average monthly rents in these two cities, ¥78 706 in Tokyo and ¥54 161 in Osaka, the difficulty they have in paying for rented accommodation is evident (Ministry of Internal Affairs and Communications, 2003).

Government Policy Aimed at Homelessness in Japan

The relevant government support measures are based on the 'Special Measures Law Concerning Support for Self-Sustaining Living of the Homeless' in 2002 and on the assumption that homeless people can best achieve independence through employment. The direction of this policy was developed from 'Immediate Countermeasures for the Homeless Issue' in 1999 (The Liaison Committee for Homelessness, 1999). Within this policy document, homeless people are classified into the following three categories:

1. people who are willing to work but cannot find a job;
2. people requiring support, such as medical care and welfare; and
3. people who refuse ordinary social life and wish to 'step out' of society.

The first group is the subject of the specialist support measures for the homeless and the second group is covered by the conventional social welfare system. The third group – those considered unwilling to live in mainstream society – are not within the remit of government support. This policy has been the basis of all subsequent measures that have been introduced to support the homeless in Japan.

With respect to the first of these groups, specialist measures to support independence through employment involve support in:

- 'shelters' – emergency temporary accommodation where people can stay for up to 6 months. As at March 2006, there were 10 facilities with a total capacity of 2200 persons, located in the big cities where homeless people are concentrated. Individuals may then move on to:
- 'centres for support for self-sustaining living of the homeless' where people again can stay for up to 6 months. Again, as at March 2006, there were 22 facilities, with a total capacity for 2060 persons. These facilities are designed to move people towards employment through counselling and training. Also, assistance with health care is often provided where needed. However, the quality of service and intensiveness of the support varies according to location.

In the regions where neither shelters (which are currently found in Kawasaki, Yokohama, Nagoya, and Osaka) nor centres for support for self-sustaining living of the homeless (which are currently found in Tokyo, Sendai, Yokohama, Kawasaki, Nagoya, Kyoto, Osaka, Sakai, and Kita-Kyushu) have as yet been established, outreach services are offered. This often includes staff from local authority social welfare offices visiting those living on the streets and directing them to appropriate support services.

Several points can be made about these measures aimed at supporting independent living among homeless people. First, the 2002 law is in effect for a limited period and measures to support independent living among homeless populations are often only short-term solutions. Second, the overall scale of interventions is small. To illustrate, although the official homeless population exceeded 25 000 in 2003, the total capacity of shelters and centres that provide support for independent living was just 4260 persons. Third, measures have different characteristics according to their regional location, with some of the larger cities having more comprehensive support. For instance, in Tokyo a rather radical intervention, under the 'Local Homeless Life Transition Support Program' and referred to as "Housing First', provides low-rent housing at ¥3000 (£19 or $31) per month, though again for only a short, 2-year period.

The Future of Homelessness in Japan

It is clear that much of the prevailing homelessness situation in Japan has been created by the Japanese socioeconomic system, through which people on the whole secure accommodation through their employment. The economic instability generated by globalisation has led many people, particularly older male workers, to lose their jobs, and therefore their homes. In Japan, securing a permanent residence requires a stable income, a relatively large sum of money at the outset for a deposit and rent in advance, and a guarantor. Moreover, a weakening of informal social support means that not only is it quite difficult to obtain the initial sum of money but the biggest issue for homeless people, many of whom no longer have close relationships with others, is to find the guarantor.

The global economic crisis that emanated from America in 2008 further dampened the activity and output of many Japanese companies, resulting in considerably more dismissals and unstable employment. This is likely to result in greater numbers of people in precarious housing situations unless a system is constructed to secure appropriate housing for all.

One observable trend is that housing subsidies that companies formerly provided to employees have been reduced following overall cost-reduction strategies. Furthermore, those employee dormitories and company residences that do still exist are not suitable for many employees and represent a substandard form of accommodation. Thus, unless other means of accommodation and more appropriate housing is offered by employers, the housing conditions of workers will decline further.

The notoriously expensive private housing market in Japan must be supplemented with public (social) housing for those who cannot afford accommodation in the private sector. However, construction of new public housing has been decreasing continuously over a long period in Japan, and only people within the 25% lowest-income bracket can apply for what already exists. Also, public tenants must be in family households, and the only single households eligible to take up public tenancies are the elderly or disabled. Moreover, urban renewal strategies have led to lower numbers of affordable properties because of gentrification. In combination, these factors mean that there is an acute shortfall in public sector lettings. The difficulty experienced in obtaining mortgages for home purchase has also increased because of the demise of a salary system based on seniority and lifelong employment. This suggests that in the future, there will be many more people unable to obtain permanent and suitable housing.

In response to such a difficult housing situation, NGOs are implementing measures to support homeless populations in various locations throughout Japan. Good examples include: Supported House, a cheap lodging house with an independent living support service in Kamagasaki, Osaka; Hot Pot (in Saitama), that aims to promote the independence of homeless people by using vacant private houses in the local region, acting as both guarantor and intermediary between the private landlord and formerly homeless tenant. Another good example is Kita-Kyushu Homeless Support Organisation, which takes care of the homeless in the community over the course of their lives, through close collaboration with the local government. Each of these organisations aims to create an integrated multiagency system to support homeless people with involvement from the wider community. Although these interventions are considered to be desirable models such projects must be more widely available from both NGOs and the government if the problem of homelessness in Japan is to be dealt with satisfactorily.

See also: Government/Public Lending Institutions: Asia-Pacific; Home and Homelessness; Home in Temporary Dwellings; Home: Paid Domestic Labour; Homelessness: Causation; Homelessness: Definitions; Homeless People in China/East Asia; Homeless People: Older People; Housing Finance Institutions: Asia; Post-Bubble Housing in Japan; Private Sector Housing Management: Asia Pacific; Social Housing Landlords: Asia Pacific; Squatting: United Kingdom.

References

Kamagasaki Shien Kiko and Graduate School for Creative Cities, Osaka City University (2008) Jyakunen Fuantei Shuurou, Fuantei Jukyosya Kikitori Chousa Houkokusyo. *Report of Interview Survey for Young People Who Are Employed in Unstable Jobs and Living in Unstable Accommodation.* Osaka, Japan.

Ministry of Health, Labour, and Welfare (2009a) National homelessness survey Press Release, 9. March 2009. http://www.mhlw.go.jp/bunya/seikatsuhogo/homeless09/index.html (accessed 26 March 2010).

Ministry of Health, Labour, and Welfare (2009b) Temporary Workers Unemployment Statistics Press Release, 1 May 2009. http://www.mhlw.go.jp/houdou/2009/05/h0501-1.html (accessed 26 March 2010).

Ministry of Internal Affairs and Communications (2003), 2003 Housing and Land Survey; Household Incomes http://www.e-stat.go.jp/SG1/estat/ListE.do?bid=000000050125&cycode=0 (accessed on 26 March 2010).

Ministry of Internal Affairs and Communications (2009) Family Income and Expenditure Survey http://www.stat.go.jp/english/data/kakei/156.htm (accessed on 02 May 2009).

Ministry of Land, Infrastructure, Transport and Tourism (Undated) Minimum Housing Standard. http://www.stat.go.jp/english/data/jyutaku/15022.htm (accessed on 26 March 2010).

Shima K (2001) Labour market of today's Kamagasaki and its transformation. *Studies in the Humanities* 53(3): 23–49.

The Liaison Committee for Homelessness (1999) Homuresu mondai ni taisuru toumen no taiousaku ni tsuite. http://www.jil.go.jp/jil/kisya/syokuan/990526_01_sy/990526_01_sy_betten.html (accessed 26 March 2010).

United Nations Development Programme (2007) Human Development Report, 2007/2008. http://hdr.undp.org/en/reports/global/hdr 2007-2008/chapters (accessed 26 March 2010).

Further Reading

Iwata M (2006) Social exclusion and homelessness. In: Hirayama Y and Ronald R (eds.) *Housing and Social Transition in Japan*, pp. 140–164. London: Routledge.

Okamoto Y (2007) A comparative study of homelessness in the United Kingdom and Japan. *Journal of Social Issues* 63(3): 525–542.

Sassen S (2001) *The Global City: New York, London, Tokyo.* Princeton, NJ: Princeton University Press.

Homeless People: Street Children in Africa

L Van Blerk, University of Dundee, Dundee, UK

© 2012 Elsevier Ltd. All rights reserved.

Glossary

Core places Particular niches in the city where young people carry out their daily activities. A group will use a particular core place for eating, sleeping, socialising, and sometimes working, begging, and stealing. These niches may also be temporally located, only used at particular times of the day or night.

Home In the context of street children's lives home is conceptualised as a fluid space made up of particular social relations that are both spatially and temporally connected, rather than a fixed physical space or house.

Street In the context of street children's/youth's lives, the street, in the widest sense of the word, encompasses all urban public spaces young people make use of and inhabit.

Street child/youth A young person who spends the majority of his or her time on the streets of large towns/cities and sleeps rough on the street all or part of the time. This particular term emerged from the NGO community to describe collectively those on the streets and is often not used by street children themselves as it can imply a lack of family or community connection. Homeless young people or children/youth living in street situations are generally preferred; however, the term 'street children' is used interchangeably in this instance for continuity between articles.

Street (sub)culture Identity markers in young people's lives that set them apart, classifying them as street children/youth. This usually includes some or all of the following: drug use, criminal activity and begging, sleeping rough, and a dishevelled appearance.

Surrogate/street family The term often used to refer to the supportive ties children and youth develop with a group of their peers on the street relating the connections they have to those of a family – sharing resources and information, working together, and caring for each other.

Introduction

This article explores the lives of young people living in street situations in African contexts. It focuses on homeless street children and youth and begins by discussing the various reasons for their presence in urban areas. The article then discusses the street as 'home' and the ways alternative spaces are appropriated by young people during their time on the streets. Day-to-day street life is produced by young people economically and socially in different ways. This is highlighted through examples that also indicate that street life does not take place in isolation but operates relationally. The article ends with a consideration of the temporality of street life and calls for a greater understanding of young people's life trajectories.

Living on the Street

In African cities, streets have historically played an important role in young people's lives. The street has often been viewed as an extension of the home, where leisure and playing take place because of lack of indoor space. In addition, young people sometimes work in the streets, often helping other family members to support the household. Despite this, the globalised notion of childhood transports the Western notion of the streets as unsafe for children around the globe, and this idea has been transposed onto the social welfare policies of many African countries. Hence, young people living on city streets are seen dualistically as out of place – as innocent and in need of protection from the harsh realities of the street and as deviant and criminal by virtue of being part of the street. In the late 1980s, street children were thrust to the forefront of public attention through the establishment of the International Convention on the Rights of the Child. Initially, researchers were concerned with the numbers of children on the streets, but attention quickly turned to examining their unique lifestyles. As Ennew and Swart-Kruger (2003: 3) note: "Morally-powerful social constructions of family, home, domesticity, and childhood could not exist without the construction of the other – the danger of the street, the amorality of street life and, above all, street children who are outside the domestic sphere and challenge the order of social existence." For this reason, an examination of young people living on the streets provides some interesting issues around the fluidity of home and homelessness.

There are numerous reasons why young people can be found living on urban streets; most often the reasons are attributed to microlevel poverty in families and communities, including lack of money to pay for food and schooling, the need to go and find work to support the family, alcohol and drug abuse, scarce resources shared among reconstituted families with some members favoured over others, and parental death. In the African context, several key structural reasons, including war, AIDS, structural adjustment, natural disaster, and political famine, can be identified for these homelife conditions. However, it is important to point out that these reasons can vary enormously from place to place and even from child to child. For example, South Africa has a number of unique characteristics that demonstrate this point. The unique situation of the apartheid system in South Africa and subsequent protests against this in the 1980s and the early 1990s resulted in a large influx of young people taking to the streets. More recently, gang culture and associated violence and drug and alcohol abuse in the township communities have been attributed to young people coming onto the streets. In addition, some children are there not because of any associated poverty or negative homelife situation but merely through accidental causes such as hanging out with and befriending those already on the streets. It is, therefore, important to acknowledge the complexity of young people's lives and their reasons for living on the streets.

The ways in which young people come to live on the streets also varies across the continent. For example, in countries where the majority of the population still live in rural areas and urban settlements remain small, children tend to migrate to the cities from rural locations. The reasons for this are many, including AIDS (Uganda, southern Africa) war (Northern Uganda), and famine (Ethiopia). In more urbanised settings, for example, in Kenya (Nairobi), Zimbabwe (Harare), or South Africa (Johannesburg, Cape Town, and Durban), young people mainly come to the streets from low-income impoverished (sub)urban neighbourhoods. In these cases, the stark contrasts between poverty and wealth are visible and the streets are seen as places of opportunity.

Home Spaces: Home Activities

The street takes on a new meaning for young people living there and particular public places become home. These niches have been identified as core places where young people live and carry out many of their daily activities that would normally be considered home activities such as eating, sleeping, and socialising. Core places are often located in busy central locations such as train stations or taxi (minibus) ranks and may be used by street children/youth at different times, for example, at night when the areas are less busy. Core places have also been found in hidden or marginal locations such as rubbish dumps, where young people lead their daily lives without being disturbed or moved away – they are hidden from the gaze of the police and the public. The use of core places can take on different meanings depending on their location and temporality. In Uganda, large groups of young people making use of highly visible locations such as the taxi park in central Kampala at night did so as an act of resistance to the dominant culture of the area during the day. They displayed their resistance through setting rubbish alight, drug-taking, and robbing unsuspecting members of the public who were isolated in the space after dark.

Alternative Homes: Institutions

Institutions play a key role in the lives of street children both on a daily basis and throughout their time on the streets. In the 1980s and the 1990s when the issue of street children became widely known, numerous nongovernmental organisations (NGOs) set up programmes to support them. Initially this took the form of an institutionalised model that sought to remove young people from the streets for their own protection and to rehabilitate them as respectable citizens. In practice, children and youth responded differently to their programmes and rarely returned to their communities successfully for extended periods of time. Instead, institutions were places for making new street friends and learning new ways of becoming absorbed into street life, such as through criminal activity or drug use. Some children who returned home as part of these programmes returned to the streets within months, sometimes weeks. Part of the institutionalisation process resulted in street children/youth periodically attending reformatories or juvenile (and sometimes adult) prisons. Again, this merely trained young people in criminal activity and better prepared them for a return to street life.

Later in the 1990s, many NGOs moved away from this form of provision, embarking on a street-based model of provision that offered not only education and training through drop-in centres but also eating and washing facilities. This enabled young people to access services as and when they wished on their terms and often through outreach workers coming to them. In some cases, this method of delivery of services was seen as encouraging children on to the streets to receive handouts.

The Production of Street Life

The ways in which children and youth experience street life is not uniform, and the production of street life occurs in many diverse ways, depending on young people's characteristics, such as age, gender, and ethnicity. The production of street life can also be economic (related to working or accessing money by legal and illegal means) and sociocultural (related to the display of street (sub)culture).

Economic Life on the Street: Age, Gender, and Ethnicity

The ability to access money is a key aspect of survival on the streets, be it shared with the group or street family or be it solely for the use of the earner. Street children engage in a variety of money-earning activities that depend on their individual and collective ability to hustle and are often related to their age (maturity), gender, and ethnicity.

Work on the streets is usually informal and can be both legal and illegal. Although some children may be well known for their expertise in one area, the majority engage opportunistically in several activities depending on the availability of work. Some young people engage in illegal activities – usually housebreaking, pickpocketing, robbing, and sometimes sex work – alongside begging and work such as shoe-shining, hawking, cleaning cars, portering, and rubbish collecting, which demonstrate their eclectic range of survival skills. These skills are usually developed over time, as newcomers to the street act as apprentices learning the tricks of the trade – such as looking poverty-stricken – from older, more established youth. In Uganda, older young people taught children to pickpocket and trained them to steal skilfully from a mousetrap without the trap springing. If the trap sprang, the apprentice would feel the effect on their fingers, the test representing a customer noticing their attempt to pickpocket. If the trap was not released, the apprentice was considered ready to work on the streets.

Mobility is key to many aspects of street children's/youth's ability to appropriate income. They become adept at moving around the city to benefit from spatial and temporal opportunities that exist in different places. For example, begging at churches and mosques can be lucrative on religious days and at festival or prayer times, while market work such as portering or rubbish collection may be best at the beginning and the end of the day. Similarly, shoe-shining, hawking, and cleaning cars are best undertaken in busy streets, catching people on their way to and from work. Sometimes, young people will move considerable distances to other towns or outlying areas on special occasions to engage in work-related opportunities. Where transport connections are good, young people regularly work while mobile. In South Africa, moving up and down on moving trains looking for begging or stealing opportunities was a lucrative business; however, this has recently slowed as increased security on the trains has reduced these possibilities.

The ways in which young people engage in the economic production of street life is also highly varied and relates to key markers of social difference. Age is one of the ways in which the production of work on the streets is diversified. Older (physically mature) youth are usually embarrassed to beg on the streets or scavenge rubbish and view these activities as shameful, while young (physically immature) children are able to draw on their size and childish appearance for increasing their earnings from begging or stealing. For example, young children are often used for begging or for criminal activity because they cannot be imprisoned if they are below the age of criminal responsibility.

Gender is a further marker of difference that results in diversification in the production of work on the streets. Girls are fewer in number and more likely to be hidden on the streets and sometimes drawn into sex work as a survival strategy, although it is worth acknowledging that boys can also engage in this type of work. As Abebe (2008: 271) illustrates with this quotation from Merlat (12), in Ethiopia girls are often excluded from the work that boys do, leaving them with little alternative for earning on the streets: "When we beg people for their kindness, they give us coins, but others don't give us any... When we want to carry things and make money, people prefer ... older children, or boys. They don't like girls." Hansson (2003) attributes the gender differences in the production of street life to the gendered dynamic present at home. She states that girls in southern Africa are more protected in the family with the gendered division of labour in the home generally resulting in girls employed in domestic tasks, while boys are sent out to generate income for the family. From her work in Cape Town, Hansson (2003) highlights that there are fewer girls on the streets (and they tend to be older) because opportunities for income earning are male dominated as was similarly stressed in the Ethiopian example. Selling sex is the only realistic option for girls, and this is a high-risk activity. The alternative is to have a boyfriend on the streets.

Finally, ethnicity is a further marker of difference that can influence the work done on the streets. Abebe (2008) notes that begging is a cultural taboo for the Ethiopian Gurghe tribe, and therefore those children are known for their industriousness and business-mindedness, engaging in informal work rather than criminal or begging activities.

Sociocultural Life on the Streets: (Sub)culture

It is not easy to separate the sociocultural lives of those living on the streets from their economic lives as street (sub)culture is highly related to survival strategies. Often the appearance projected by street children/youth aims at developing a collective identity that defines street children as poor, needy, requiring sympathy and yet at the same time wild, unruly, and to be feared – simultaneously representing the dual picture of children as different and childhood as a learning life phase, either as needing protection (angelic) or as needing correction (demonic). A dishevelled appearance such as that by wearing old, dirty, and tattered clothing is related to reaping the benefits from begging, while drug use in public, especially sniffing fuel/glue, which is known to enhance feelings of courage and strength, is related to inducing fear into members of the public when stealing. For girls taking on a boyish appearance, such as dressing like boys and having short hair, can act as a mechanism for self-defence against rape and abuse on the streets.

Street culture is also about developing a sense of belonging among street children and youth and creating a culture of solidarity, sharing, and family structure that can be hierarchical in nature. Hansson (2003) notes how groups/surrogate families in Cape Town were highly structured with each group having a leader and particular roles and ways of behaving. In many instances, newcomers to the streets had to go through rites of passage to become members of a street family or group through engaging in the groups' livelihood survival activities, drug-taking, fighting, or sexual initiation. In many ways, this can be similar to African notions of belonging to a community through initiation into adulthood.

Incidentally, through street (sub)culture, many of the issues young people sought to escape by coming to the streets are amplified. Drug-taking, crime, and abuse (especially physical and sexual abuse) are all part of the daily existence of groups on the street. In addition, being on the streets and displaying a homeless image can result in abuse from others. However, the protection, solidarity, and power street (sub)culture provides overshadow these negative aspects.

Family and Community Relations

Conceptualising home as a fluid space made up of particular social relations that are both spatially and temporally connected, rather than a fixed physical space or house, makes it possible to identify the ways in which homeless children and youth living on the streets develop family relationships and connections. Groups on the street have sometimes been referred to as 'surrogate families' or 'street families' as sharing resources and information, working, begging, and stealing together, and looking out for each other is considered vital to survival on the streets. Being in a group is also a means of support and care when a member is ill or injured. Yet, street children often have connections to others on the street that predate their homeless lives. For example, many join up with other children from their home communities or have friends, siblings, and relatives that they stay with on the street. This indicates that some relationships are stronger than others through long-established supportive ties. This is not to suggest that their social relationships are solely related to the street, and street children/youth can, and sometimes do, maintain connections to their families and communities. For some, these connections are purely memories, as they never really return home; for others, the links are tenuous, for example, when a relative is called upon to represent a young person in court. In some cases, these links can be strong, with children returning to their families periodically for visits or to live for a while before returning to the street, when circumstances of poverty or abuse make life difficult. Writing about Tanzania, Evans (2004) highlights that street children's narratives of home demonstrate this mix of positive associations and negative connotations, describing a number of incidences where street children mentioned beatings by relatives and neighbours. The example of Charles highlights this fluidity. He moved between his family home – where he enjoyed going to school – and the street in Arusha when he was beaten by his father for not helping in the fields, using the street as escapism from the harsh realities of rural life.

The degree of fluidity between street and family home is also connected to proximity of families to the city. In highly urbanised settings where young people come on to the streets from neighbouring impoverished communities, greater interaction between the home and the street can be noted. From work in South Africa, research investigating street children's family connections identified that street and family can be highly integrated. On working with boys from a local Cape Town township, it became clear that they were connected to their biological families in two ways – many had brothers or cousins with them on the street – and many visited their parents (mostly (single) mothers and stepfathers) at home almost on a daily basis walking between the town and the community. Although some would sleep at home some nights of the week, others merely visited because of problems of alcoholism and drug use and gangsterism in the families. Although the boys took drugs and alcohol on the streets, they did not want to return home for fear of being enlisted into gang activities (van Blerk, 2008a).

Lifecourse: The Fluidity of Street Life

A key theme that appears throughout this discussion of street life is its fluidity, both spatially and temporally, as young people living on the streets make use of the resources available to them during their time on the streets. The temporality of childhood/youth itself calls for greater understanding of the lifecourse trajectories of young people on the streets. The outcomes of street life are many and varied, depending mostly on the needs and desires of individual young people but also impacted upon by the social relations – from peers, practitioners, social workers, NGO workers, and criminals and gang members – they encounter while on the streets. Their adult lives can therefore be characterised by continuing life on the streets, and invariably also in prison, yet can also involve creating a home, having a family, and legal employment. There is, however, no dualistic division, and over the course of their lives, many children growing up on the streets will encounter several of these experiences as adults (van Blerk, 2008b).

Conclusion

The diverse and varied experiences of childhood and youth are evident among those living in street situations. This article has demonstrated that even within the African context the production of street life is both fluid and eclectic. The types of social and economic activities engaged in may be dependent on group dynamics as well as individual characteristics such as age or gender. However, street children's lives are also relational, situated within the wider context of families, communities, organisations, and peers.

See also: Children and Parenting; Homeless People: Street Children in Asia; Homeless People: Street Children in Mexico; Homeless People: Youth in Australia; Homeless People: Youth in the United Kingdom; Homelessness: Causation; Illicit Drug Use and Homelessness.

References

Abebe T (2008) Earning a living on the margins: Begging, street work and the socio-spatial experiences of children in Addis Ababa. *Geografiska Annaler Series B: Human Geography* 90(3): 271–284.

Ennew J and Swart-Kruger J (2003) Introduction: Homes, places and spaces in the construction of street children and street youth. *Children, Youth and Environments* 13(1): 1–21.

Evans R (2004) Tanzanian childhoods: Street children's narratives of 'home'. *Journal of Contemporary African Studies* 22(1): 69–92.

Hansson D (2003) 'Strolling' as a gendered experience: A feminist analysis of young females in Cape Town. *Children, Youth and Environments* 13(1): 1–28.

Van Blerk L (2008a) Constructing identities with Muizenberg street boys: Merging street and family life in Cape Town, South Africa. *Invited Paper Presented at the ESRC Workshop on Street Children's Identities, London School of Economics*, London, 29 February 2008.

Van Blerk L (2008b) Between the street and the prison cell: Youth negotiating identities within street/gang culture in Cape Town, South Africa. *AAG Annual International Conference*, Boston, MA, USA, 15–19 April.

Further Reading

Bourdillon M (2001) The children of our streets. *CYC-Online: Reading for Child and Youth Care Workers*, Vol. 35. http://www.cyc-net.org/cyc-online/cycol-1201-bourdillon-l.html (accessed 26 November 2009).

Evans R (2006) Negotiating social identities: The influence of gender, age and ethnicity on young people's 'street careers' in Tanzania. *Children's Geographies* 4(1): 109–128.

Nieuwenhuys O (2001) By the sweat of their brow? 'Street children', NGOs and children's rights in Addis Ababa. *Africa* 71(4): 539–557.

Rumbidzai R and Bourdillon M (2003) Girls: The less visible street children of Zimbabwe. *Children, Youth and Environments* 13(1): 1–25.

Swart J (1990) *Malunde: The Street Children of Hillbrow*. Johannesburg: Witwatersrand University Press.

Van Blerk L (2005) Negotiating spatial identities: Mobile perspectives on street life in Uganda. *Children's Geographies* 3(1): 5–21.

Young L (2003) The place of street children in Kampala, Uganda: Marginalisation, resistance and acceptance in the urban environment. *Environment and Planning D: Society and Space* 21(5): 607–628.

Young L (2004) Journeys to the street: The complex migration geographies of Ugandan street children. *Geoforum* 35(4): 471–488.

Homeless People: Street Children in Asia

DOB Lam, The University of Hong Kong, Hong Kong, China

FC Cheng, Shanghai Academy of Social Sciences, Shanghai, China

© 2012 Elsevier Ltd. All rights reserved.

Glossary

Child abuse This generally refers to harm being done to children on purpose. It may take the form of neglect or physical, psychological, or sexual abuse.

Institutional care It may be in the form of shelters, centres, or large-scale homes. For the children, such institutions provide food and lodging and sometimes educational programmes. Life is usually very structured.

Neglect This refers to inadequate care for children, which could be physical, emotional, or educational.

Physical abuse This refers to the physical harm done to a child intentionally. It may be inflicted by spanking, burning, choking, kicking, or any form of physical aggression. The distinction between physical abuse and child discipline relates to the cultural norms of a society.

Psychological abuse This refers to emotional harm caused to a child through shaming, belittling, scolding, or withholding of affection.

Sexual abuse Comprises any sexual act between an adult and a child, disregarding whether the child is willing or not, and is based on the presumed inability of a junior to judge what is right or wrong and to fight back. It could also be a sexual act between two children when the victim is forced into the act. All these forms of abuse may cause long-term psychological damage to a child.

Street children Children who spend most of their time in the public spaces of cities away from home, with little or even no supervision by responsible adults. They are mostly between 5 and 17 years old.

Street-cleansing campaign This refers to actions by public authorities to drive street children away from streets if they involve in economic activities which are illegal (as they are underage), beg, or simply rest in public areas.

Introduction

Street children spend most of their time in the public spaces of cities away from home, with little or even no supervision by responsible adults. Because of this, street children are very visible on the streets. Today, the phenomenon of street children is visible in nearly every country across the world, particularly Africa, Latin America, and Asia. There are no official statistics on street children, but an estimated 100 million children live on the streets around the world. This article describes the phenomenon of street children in Asia.

The Scale of the Street Children Population in Asia

Because of the mobile nature of street children's daily life, it is difficult to assess their real numbers. According to a report by United Nations Children's Fund (UNICEF) in 1998, there were ~25 million street children in Asia (cited in Casa Alianza, 2000). Published data on street children from Asian countries show that this number might have been a significant underestimation. In India alone, Alderfer (2002) reported that there might be 25 million street children. The Ministry of Civil Affairs (MCA) (2007) of the People's Republic of China estimates there are 1 to 1.5 million street children in China. West (2003) reports the estimates of 10 million in Pakistan, 0.22 million in Philippines, 30 000 in Nepal, and 50 000 in Vietnam. With the economic and political transformation in Central Asia, Kazakhstan, Kyrgyz Republic, Tajikistan, Uzbekistan, and other countries of the former Soviet Union, these areas of Asia have also seen a rapid increase in the number of street children over the last 20 years.

In 1986, UNICEF identified two categories of street children: 'children *on* the street' who work on the streets but keep connections with their families, and 'children *of* the street' who work and live on the streets with little or even no connection with their families. The latter are practically homeless. Previously, most were children on the streets, often returning home in the evening. For example, in the city of Indore in India, this category constituted about 70% of the street children in the city (Phillips, 1992). Yet, over the past 20 years, the ratio of children of the street has been increasing. Silva (1996) reported that in 1988, the proportion of children of the street in the overall street children population in the

Philippines was only 25%, and the number rose to 37.14% in 1993. According to Cheng's (2008) ethnographical study with street children in Shanghai (China), over 50% of the street children wander through the streets day and night. Because children of the street have even less supervision by responsible adults than those with a home to return to at night, it can be argued that the problem of street children is becoming more serious.

Street children in Asia include boys and girls, but the majority are boys. Among the 150 000 street children registered by the Chinese government, boys constituted 70% (105 000), with the number of street girls around 45 000 (MCA, 2003). The majority of street children in Pakistan are also boys (Ali et al., 2004). The ages of street children normally range from 6 to 18 years (Casa Alianza, 2000). In Afghanistan, Pakistan, and China, most of the street children are aged from 8 to 14 years (Ali et al., 2004; MCA, 2003; Tdh, 2002). These children should ideally be in school and under their parents' supervision. Yet they are excluded from education and most of them lead a homeless life.

The Causes of the Phenomenon of Street Children

The causes of the phenomenon of street children vary between different Asian countries and are multiple. Among all, the most common factors reported are uneven development in rural and urban areas, poverty, family dysfunction, and school problems.

Uneven Development and Rural to Urban Migration

The phenomenon of street children is a product of uneven social development. From a global perspective, this can be seen because of uneven development between the developed countries and the developing countries. Many developing countries get foreign loans to support their economic activities. Yet many of these countries rely on agriculture. Unfair trade has been an issue, with developed countries granting subsidies to their producers, thus weakening the competitive abilities of the developing countries. If these countries' repayment ability is lower than their debt level, their economic endeavours are futile. All income generated is just spent on repaying the loan. These countries have to spend large percentages of their national budgets to meet high debt service rates, with little left for the social welfare of their disadvantaged people. Poor people can rely only on their own means. They have to encourage their children to be more self-supporting, and this constitutes an underlying force driving the phenomenon of street children.

A more visible cause of the phenomenon of street children is the increasing polarisation between the development of urban and rural areas within particular countries. In most of the developing countries in Asia, more resources are invested in urban areas, while the countryside is given a low priority. As a result, the economic gap between urban and rural areas becomes larger. Many rural families and/or their children are attracted to the better life opportunities in urban areas and migrate to the city. This has been the situation for the past 30 years in China. Some children also become lone migrants to the big cities and can be found working or/and living on the streets. In India (Tiwari et al., 2002) and Pakistan (Ali et al., 2004), the connections between rural to urban migration and the phenomenon of street children have also been documented. As minors with little earning power, these children are often homeless.

Poverty

Clearly, poverty is the core contributing factor to the phenomenon of street children. Family poverty may compel parents to abandon their children or children to abandon their families. Silva (1996) found that in the Philippines, many children from poor families do not get basic necessities such as food and clothing from their parents. Consequently, many of them choose to or are forced to leave their families and participate in income-generating activities on the streets. Despite the fast growth in GNP, a similar situation exists in China, especially in the central and western parts of the country. For the family's survival, many parents ask their children to earn their own living or even to contribute financially. In Pakistan, child labour is of great significance for parents with low incomes. Evidence from Afghanistan, Nepal, and Indonesia reflect the same pattern. Some parents who cannot meet the needs of their families send their children to the street to gain more income. Some children simply generate their income by begging, as they often attract more sympathy than adults do. This scene is common in many Asian tourist spots that are unguarded by private agencies or the local police.

Family Dysfunction

Aside from social structural reasons leading to the street children phenomenon, child neglect and abuse by family members also contribute to children living on the streets. This could be a result of the children's failure to meet the expectations of parents, rejection by stepparents in reconstituted families, or other reasons. The causes are not totally clear. Some children disclosed that they just could not understand why they were treated badly. Their feelings of injustice were clear. Male descendents are often treasured in Asian countries, yet these boys are exceptions. Many children in China are 'pushed' to the streets because of their parents' physically or psychologically abusive behaviour. For these children, abandoning home actually reflects their dissatisfaction with their family lives and their aspiration for a better life. Inappropriate parenting has also been reported as one of the reasons for children living on the streets in countries such as Nepal and India.

School Problems

Not all street children have a miserable family life. Some come from families which provide them with all of life's necessities, care, and schooling. The driving force for such children to leave home was to avoid schooling, despite education being considered a right of children! The reasons could be interpersonal or institutional. Some students dislike schools because they have conflicts with teachers, or have been bullied at school. For others, school is a difficult world characterised by boring learning material, failure, and frustration. To avoid such unpleasant experiences, they choose to leave home and venture into the streets to find their freedom. While education is for the intellectual development of children, it often goes with examinations, which unfortunately could have some detrimental effects. For example, in China, students have to take part in a series of entrance examinations. Examination scores are the key determinant of their chance of admission to good secondary schools and, in the future, good universities; thus, many parents and schools are keen on getting students to improve their examination scores, neglecting their individual feelings and psychological needs. The adults may have goodwill, but the children may experience pressure. Children who do not perform satisfactorily may experience great frustration. Some detest studying or dislike people at the school, or both. They wish to rebel and choose to give up home to avoid schooling, thus becoming street children.

As mentioned earlier, these four general factors apart, there are also other significant issues depending on the specific circumstances of individual countries. For example, child trafficking (especially in Southeast Asia), war (e.g., Afghanistan, Sri Lanka, Indonesia, and Cambodia), drug trafficking (e.g., Thailand and Myanmar), and natural disasters have all been reported as playing a part in generating a population of street children. Whatever the specific reason, these children become homeless and face very harsh challenges in life.

The Daily Life of the Street Children

Away from the protection of family members, street children often suffer from a lack of basic necessities of life (e.g., food, shelter, and medical care) and exclusion from educational opportunities. Basically, they are unengaged round the clock, wandering and playing. Yet they have to find their own means of living, and they often experience hostilities from the rest of society. To survive the harsh street life, they display great resilience. These children have to be creative and flexible to make a living as well as develop their social support network.

Difficulties on the Streets

Getting the basic necessities of life is essential for survival. Street children do not have the necessary provision and protection from adults as normal children do. Because of their poor education and young age, it is difficult for them to find a job in the labour market. Consequently, they turn to low-paid informal economic and criminal activities. These activities cannot provide a stable income. They have to live in very poor conditions. Food, clothes, and shelter are their everyday concern. Physical injuries, tuberculosis, skin disease, dental problems, parasitic diseases, and sexual and reproductive health problems easily affect these children. Malnutrition and being seriously underweight and/or underheight are all too common.

In addition to their poor life conditions, street children face different kinds of hostility from the rest of the society. Many studies report that street children are trapped by stigmatisation and victimisation. In the eyes of many people, street children are dirty, lazy, highly impulsive and violent, and engage in drug abuse, prostitution, and theft, and they are often considered a contaminating virus. The public often complain that the street children are disturbing, and thus should be cleansed from the streets. In Indonesia, many street children are arrested, imprisoned, and sometimes even tortured (Beazley, 2002). Such a scenario is also apparent in China (Cheng, 2008) and Nepal (Southon and Dhakal, 2003).

Asian street children are widely reported to be abused in different ways by other street children and street people, the underworld, the public, and law enforcement officials. Street children, particularly girls, are subjected to sexual abuse. Xiang's (2002) study found some Chinese street girls were sexually exploited by street boys and other adult street people. Thapaliya (2005) found street boys in Nepal also suffered from sexual harassment. Boys are sometimes sodomised. In Cheng's (2008) study of Chinese street children, some boys 'accept' sexual activity with gay adults for monetary reward. Provision of a sleeping place is also used as a bait to solicit sexual favours.

The existence of child sex workers of both sexes in countries like Cambodia, Thailand, and Sri Lanka is well noted. To most people, law enforcement bodies are supposed to offer protection and security in our life. However, street children may not get equal treatment. In Nepal, Thapaliya (2005) found that street children were often beaten, harassed, and sometimes tortured by police. Some police even directly asked street girls for sexual favours. West's (2003) study revealed that some street children in the Kyrgyz Republic were forced to spend all their earnings bribing law enforcement officials in order to avoid detention or imprisonment.

Life Strategies

Street children are resourceful and resilient social actors and much more capable than people commonly assume. Their resilience is reflected in their survival strategies in handling life's threats and challenges.

On being excluded from the formal labour market because of their young age, street children resort to informal economic activities such as street vending, shoe shining, watching and washing cars, selling newspapers, handing out advertising cards, running errands, and scavenging. But they do not always get these jobs. Many street children also employ deviant methods such as petty theft and robbery to make a living. Sometimes, judicial protection for children gives them some leeway. In Shanghai, some street children turned to minor criminal activities with the awareness that they had low risk of being legally charged (Cheng, 2008). Street children learn to be flexible and resourceful as their life experience accumulates.

Social networking is an important resource supporting their survival. Many informal groups exist among street children. In the Philippines, these groups – usually named 'families' – not only provide companionship for the street children but also exist as a medium for learning ways to cope with street life. In China, street children also form small informal social networks for support. They share information and resources among themselves, cultivate their peer friendship, and establish supportive relationships with some adults who befriend them. Such social networking is significant in helping street children deal with social exclusion. Even if others reject them, they have their own groups to fall back on emotionally. A similar situation exists among street children in Yogyakarta, Java, and Indonesia (Beazley, 2003).

The world of street children is tough. Yet most of them are ready for the challenges. Some may be victimised, but most learn to be creative and find different ways to live. Despite their pitiful incomes and the discrimination they encounter, they survive. They experience starvation, fear, great frustration, illness, and pity, but they support each other and help one another overcome the difficult moments. They have their private fun time and gathering point in some deserted or inaccessible places. They learn to distinguish between 'friends' and 'nonfriends'. They show their ability as social agents and are not just passive or vulnerable.

Policy Interventions

All governments are aware of the worth of investment in the development of children as they are a nation's future pillars. Yet street children are obviously not provided with decent opportunities for development. In reaction to the problem of street children, many governments have come up with some social service provision. There is much variation in the policy interventions in different subregions of Asia due to the different social and political environments. In South and Southeast Asia, most governments provide huge room for nongovernmental organisations (NGOs) to help street children, while they themselves play a small role. In the Philippines, India, and Thailand, NGOs have developed a good range of intervention programmes for street children, including outreach services, shelters, and different kinds of educational and career-training programmes. These services provide emergency help as well as more long-term services for street children's development. Some of the programmes place strong emphasis on the street children's preferences and participation. Street children not only can choose services according to their own preferences but are also encouraged to participate actively in helping other street children. As reported by UNESCO (International Catholic Child Bureau, 1995), in the Philippines, welfare programmes invite street children to teach, to help, and to do research on street children. It seems that in this subregion of Asia, mainstream society has acknowledged, rather than denied, the existence of street children. Few street-cleansing campaigns are conducted to clear the children from the streets, and less emphasis has been laid on institutional care. However, efforts by civil society alone would not be adequate to rid the problem of street children, as poverty is still a root cause.

In contrast to the situation in South and Southeast Asian countries, governments in East and Central Asia assume a more active role in dealing with the street children problem. NGOs and civil society play a relatively smaller part. These governments tend to take children away from the streets forcefully in the name of protecting the children and in their best interests. Institutional care in the form of shelters for street children or child protection centres is developed in these countries. Children wandering through the streets are often transferred to such institutions. Some of them are sent back to their home afterwards; some just stay there to become adults. In China, child protection centres mainly provide temporary care. Street children are often locked up while waiting for an arrangement to be sent home, and there are few developmental services. There is also little effort towards helping improve the street children's family situation before sending them home. In Shanghai, many street children refuse to stay in these centres. Some return to the city after being sent home (Lam and Cheng, 2008). Policy interventions of this kind, therefore, also fail to help street children effectively. Such policies can at best temporarily alleviate the risk to children on the streets.

Despite the inadequacies of the various policy interventions, the problem has been getting increasing attention in Asian countries. In China, for example, some NGOs are involved in the development of relevant services and overseas experiences are brought in. With help from UNICEF, a voluntary foster care service for street children has been developed in Zhengzhou. Some local governments have set out to develop different models of institutions for these children (e.g., semi-family in Zhengzhou and Big House in Changsha). These two programmes are more familylike, and they have been well received by the street children. In Nepal, policymakers have tried to employ more integrated and sustainable measures to help children on the streets. In Cambodia, international NGOs are also offering some support.

Looking to the Future

In the last few decades, South and Southeast Asia have experienced some economic growth. Yet the problem of street children has not improved. Countries like Indonesia and India have in fact experienced a rapid growth in the number of street children. Meanwhile, in East and Central Asia, the phenomenon of street children is emerging as a major social problem. It is related to a country's political situation, economic development, and social welfare development. Effective measures have to be mapped out at the preventive, developmental, and remedial levels. Rural development may help reduce the drive among poor children to leave home for the city's glamour. Social support and assistance may help dysfunctional families raise their children properly. Yet, for developing countries with limited socioeconomic resources, development of preventive intervention may be difficult. In the near future, strategies may remain at the remedial level. More efforts may be directed towards child protection and improvement of developmental programmes for those children who have already migrated to the streets. To maximise resources, it would be most favourable if NGOs, civil society, and the government could all be involved.

See also: Children and Parenting; Homeless People: Street Children in Africa; Homelessness: Causation; Homeless People: Street Children in Mexico; Migration and Population Mobility; Policies to Address Homelessness; Policies to Address Homelessness: Rights-Based Approaches.

References

Alderfer WH (2002) *Street Children in Delhi, India: Their Lives Today, Their Hopes for Tomorrow.* Unpublished Doctoral Dissertation, The Union Institute and University, Cincinnati, OH.

Ali M, Shahab S, Ushijima H, and Muynck A (2004) Street children in Pakistan: A situational analysis of social conditions and nutritional status. *Social Science & Medicine* 59: 1707–1717.

Beazley H (2002) 'Vagrants wearing make-up': Negotiating spaces on the streets of Yogyakarta, Indonesia. *Urban Studies* 39(9): 1665–1683.

Beazley H (2003) Voices from the margins: Street children's subcultures in Indonesia. *Children's Geographies* 1(2): 181–200.

Casa Alianza (2000) Exploitation of Children – A Worldwide Outrage. http://www.hiltonfoundation.org/press/16-pdf3.pdf (accessed 1 August 2009).

Cheng FC (2008) *Negotiating Exclusion: An Ethnographic Study of the Street Children in Shanghai, China.* Unpublished Doctoral Dissertation, The University of Hong Kong, Hong Kong.

International Catholic Child Bureau (1995) *Working with Street Children: Selected Case-Studies from Africa, Asia, and Latin America.* Paris: UNESCO.

Lam D and Cheng F (2008) Chinese policy reaction to the problem of street children: An analysis from the perspective of street children. *Children and Youth Services Review* 30(5): 575–584.

MCA (2003) *A Report of Working with Street Children* (in Chinese). http://www.mca.gov.cn/artical/content/WTG_YWJS/200443185205.HTML (accessed 11 June 2004).

MCA (2007) *The Development Plan of Working with Street Children in the Eleventh Five-Year* (in Chinese). http://fss.mca.gov.cn/article/jhgh/200712/20071200008828.shtml (accessed 1 July 2008).

Phillips W (1992) *Street Children of Indore.* Noida, India: National Labour Institute.

Silva T (1996) Poverty and uneven development: Reflections from a street children project in the Philippines. *Childhood* 3: 279–282.

Southon J and Dhakal P (2003) *A Life Without Basic Service: 'Street Children Say'.* Kathmandu, Nepal: Sath-Sath and Save the Children UK. http://www.savethechildren.net/nepal/key-work/street-children.htm, accessed 29 September 2009.

Tdh (2002, July) *Needs Assessment of Children Working in the Streets of Kabul.* Swiss Foundation of Terre des hommes; ASCHIANA Street Children Project; Central Statistics Office of Afghanistan. http://www.reliefweb.int/library/documents/2002/tdh-afg-08jul.pdf, accessed 2 September 2009.

Thapaliya B (2005) *The Pathetic Reality of Street Children in Nepal.* http://www.globalpolitician.com/21288-nepal (accessed 1 September 2009).

Tiwari PA, Gulati N, Sethi GR, and Mehra M (2002) Why do some boys run away from home? *Indian Journal of Pediatrics* 69(5): 397–399.

UNICEF (1986) *Exploitation of working children and street children.* Executive Board Document E No. ICEF/1986/CRP.3. New York: UNICEF.

West A (2003) *At the Margins: Street Children in Asia and the Pacific.* Manila: Asian Development Bank (Publication Stock No. 100103). http://www.adb.org/Documents/papers/Street-children-Asia-Pacific/default.asp, accessed 2 September 2009.

Xiang R (2002) A study of street children. In: Zhang HQ, Xiang R, and Gao WH (eds.) *Voices of the Disadvantaged Group and the Interventions of Social Work* (in Chinese), pp. 18–170. Beijing: Chinese Financial and Economic Publishing House.

Further Reading

Ferguson KM, Dabir N, Dortzbach K, Dyrness G, and Spruijt-Metz D (2006) Comparative analysis of faith-based programs serving homeless and street-living youth in Los Angeles, Mumbai and Nairobi. *Children and Youth Services Review* 28(12): 1512–1527.

Hixon A (1993) Social correlates of malnutrition among Filipino street children. *Connecting Medicine* 57(6): 373–376.

Khir S (2001) Street children in conflict with the law: The Bangladesh experience. *Asia Pacific Journal on Human Rights and the Law* 2(1): 55–76.

Kidd SA (2003) Street youth: Coping and interventions. *Child and Adolescent Social Work Journal* 20(4): 235–261.

Nahar N, Ahammed I, Milkey SA, Chowdhury SM, and Islam ST (2000) The status of street children of Dhaka metropolitan area and their vulnerability to STD/HIV/AIDS. *Abstracts of XIII International Conference on AIDS (Abstract No. WePeC4401), Durban, South Africa, 9–14 July.*

Nigam S (1994) Street children of India: A glimpse. *Journal of Health Management* 7(1): 63–67.

Pradhan G (1990) Street children in Kathmandu. *Lost Childhood* 6: 1–18.

Roux JI and Smith CS (1998) Causes and characteristics of the street child phenomenon: A global perspective. *Adolescence* 33(131): 683–688.

Seth R, Kotwal A, and Ganguly K (2005) Street and working children of Delhi, India, misusing toluene: An ethnographic exploration. *Substance Use and Misuse* 40(11): 1659–1679.

UNICEF (2005) *The State of the World's Children 2006: Excluded and Invisible*. New York: UNICEF.

WHO (2000) *Working with Street Children: A Training Package on Substance Use, Sexual and Reproductive Health Including HIV/AIDS*. http://www.who.int/substance_abuse/publications/vulnerable_pop/en, accessed 2 September 2009.

Homeless People: Street Children in Mexico

GA Jones and S Thomas de Benítez, The London School of Economics and Political Science, London, UK

© 2012 Elsevier Ltd. All rights reserved.

Glossary

Banda Popularly synonymous with gang, banda literally means 'ring' and more generally means a group of young people who meet regularly to hang out. In the context of 'street children', banda is one preferred term to self-identify positively as a group and affords a sense of agency over the classifications of government agencies or NGOs.

De la Calle a la Vida (from the street to life) Launched by President Vicente Fox, De la Calle operated from 2000 to 2006 as Mexico's federal social programme for street children. De la Calle depended for its finance on a pledge to manage contributions from the public and the private sector and to match with government funds. In practice, the appeal was unsuccessful and the programme dispersed only very limited funds to NGOs through the State welfare agencies.

Programa de Acción 2002–2010 Un México apropiado para la infancia y la adolescencia – the Programme of Action for Children was the social programme for children set up by President Fox. In principle, the programme had children's rights at its centre, although in practice the emphasis was on child welfare and coordination of government agencies.

SNDIF Sistema Nacional para el Desarrollo Integral de la Familia – the National System for Integrated Development of the Family is the Federal Welfare Department, a decentralised department within the Federal Health Ministry. In practice, the SNDIF has operated programmes for distribution of free milk, provision of school meals, and basic health care, as well as run campaigns on family and child health, and is responsible for promoting the rights of the child.

UNICEF The United Nations Children's Fund is charged with improving the welfare of children, a task that it does mostly through promotion of education and health. In 1989, UNICEF famously estimated that there might be 100 million street children worldwide, an assessment which has been widely ridiculed. The lead UN agency in support of the Convention on the Rights of the Child, UNICEF, has sometimes been criticised for its seemingly limited enthusiasm for implementing the rights agenda, a position often interpreted as the result of successive appointments of executive directors from the United States, which has not ratified the Convention.

Introduction

Researchers and policy-makers have agonised over the adjectival accuracy of the word 'street' in the term 'street children', debating young peoples' relations with the 'street'. In the 1980s, UNICEF promoted the distinction between children 'of' the street, associated with children who slept in public spaces, and children 'on' the street, who would work on the streets but return to a family to sleep. In the years since this distinction was made, others have been suggested, for example, street based and street involved. All suggestions rely on a distinction of where young people sleep and the bond with a family away from the streets. Research, however, has almost exclusively focused on what happens to these people on the streets. Far less attention has been afforded to these young peoples' ideas of and relations with home. This article draws on an ethnography of young people in Mexico to consider how they construct ideas of home, usually rejecting the clear distinctions adopted by policy-makers, and how they define themselves in the process.

Homelessness and the Street Child

A UNICEF leaflet dropped through the letter box last month captured a familiar trope of the street child. Under the caption 'Please Pick Up', a small child huddled pitifully under an over-sized shirt, lying on a cold grey pavement against a dirty concrete wall. The accompanying text called on the reader to "imagine what it is like for a child forced to live on the pavement in one of the poorest countries in the world". While in the developed world, the leaflet claimed, "the thought of children just playing on the street can be alarming," UNICEF reminds us that there are "millions of children living alone and unprotected on city streets ... hungry, thirsty, cold and unwashed [as] part of their daily life ... exposed to all kinds of exploitation, including physical violence, child labour and trafficking". This situation – UNICEF points out – violates the children's rights.

To most readers, the leaflet's image and accompanying message elicit immediate recognition. The street child portrait is a staple of magazine articles and Sunday broadsheets, of novels from Dickens' *Oliver Twist* through

Conan Doyle's *Sherlock Holmes* stories to Makkawi Said's *Cairo Swan Song*, and movies such as *Salaam Bombay*, *Malunde*, and *Slumdog Millionaire*. According to some observers, the street child has become widely recognised, thanks to successful advocacy by nongovernmental organisations (NGOs) since the late 1980s, dominating the international child rights agenda possibly to the detriment of issues concerning the lives of young people more numerous and more vulnerable (Ennew, 2000). As a development icon of children in poverty, 'street children' may be on the wane, supplanted by other child-related 'hot topics' on the international policy-maker agenda, including HIV/AIDS, violence, and trafficking. Nevertheless, UNICEF's representation of a street child forced by circumstance from the safe world of Rousseauian innocence into one of vulnerability and risk on the streets still has considerable popular – if essentially negative – appeal. Street children are seen by some as ill-prepared for survival: They are the victims or socially excluded for whom welfare agendas motivated by needs to 'rescue' and 'protect' have segued in recent decades with discourses around rights. For others, street children are antisocial, disruptive, and ungrateful, their dirty, gaunt features and attitude indicators of drug use; their survival a sign of wily criminal endeavour rather than resilience.

Street Children in Mexico: Stereotype and Archetype

The last perspective is provided by an important film about street children in Mexico: *De la Calle* (On the Street) released in 2000. Written by Jesús González Dávila, one of Mexico's foremost playwrights specialising in gritty dramas, *De la Calle* depicts Rufino, an adolescent boy, subsisting in a tough Mexico City barrio, navigating between life on the rooftops and sleeping in the sewer, running errands, and petty crime. Finding a bag of cocaine after a deal gone wrong, Rufino decides this is his chance to make quick money and, with his girlfriend Xóchitl, to leave the street behind, not realising the drugs belong to El Ochoa, a corrupt police officer who pursues Rufino. *De la Calle* depicts street life as brutally violent and short, the intense social relationships providing insufficient protection from betrayal, while memories of family and loved ones add to the melancholia.

Shortly after the film was released, Mexican President Vicente Fox on his first day in office flamboyantly launched a new street child welfare programme. Run by a department in the Health Ministry called Sistema Nacional Desarrollo Integral de la Familia (Family Welfare Agency, SNDIF), El Programa de Prevención y Atención a Niñas, Niños y Jóvenes en Situación de Calle 'De la Calle a la Vida' (Programme for the Prevention and Treatment of Girls, Boys, and Youth in Street Situations 'From the Street to Life'), widely known as 'De la Calle', aimed to involve welfare agencies at the national, regional, and local levels with NGOs in order to provide street children with access to education, health, and rehabilitation services. Such access was a street child's right – as it was the right of all children – according to Fox's Programa de Acción 2002–2010: Un México apropiado para la infancia y la adolescencia (Action Programme for Children 2002–2010: A Mexico appropriate for childhood and adolescence) which identified street children as one of 13 priority groups for targeted support. In reality, despite its high-profile start, De la Calle received almost no public or private funding – marking, at best, an effort to improve coordination between government and civil society.

De la Calle, the film, and De la Calle, the government programme, share both a common title and a normative appeal. In the film, the lead characters are shown as streetwise yet emotionally damaged kids whose resistance to the violence and predations of the street lead inevitably to their demise. In the sewers, street children ward off hunger, cold, and emotional detachment through drugs and bond desperately with any figure of affection and care. 'Home' is a bundle of rags and cardboard amidst detritus; 'shelter' is the feeling of home as a place of safety and love provided through fleeting and unstable human attachments. For De la Calle, the government programme, however, 'home' is a normatively constructed space that is not the street. In line with broader government ideology, home is synonymous with family, and the stronger the family the stronger is the society. Hence, while SNDIF and NGO facilities are better than the street, they are second best to children returning to their family 'homes'.

This general view of home as equivalent to family, and of homeless children, therefore, as being 'away' from home, predates the 2000–06 Fox administration and is shared by the current government led by Felipe Calderón as evidenced in Mexico's 2007–12 Plan Nacional de Desarrollo (National Development Plan). Children on the streets have therefore been a sensitive political issue for some time. In the 1970s, media claims that Mexican cities were swamped with street children and that Mexico City alone might have 200 000 children 'roaming the streets' were largely dismissed by the national authorities, and NGO programmes for such children were quietly discouraged. By the mid-1980s, in line with wild estimates made by UNICEF of as many as 100 million street children worldwide, some claimed that there could be more than 1.5 million street children in Mexico alone. In 1985, President Miguel de la Madrid's government conceded that children were living on Mexico's streets, leading to the establishment of the first Menores En Situación Extraordinaria Programme

(Children in Extraordinary Situations) in 1987 and to a flourishing of NGO programmes in major cities. By 1993, 80 NGOs provided services for vulnerable children in Mexico City alone, 15 of which focused on street children and 11 of these exclusively targeted children living on the streets (Thomas de Benítez, 2008). In the absence of comprehensive data, local authorities and NGOs occasionally provided insights into children in the streets of the cities where they worked, while the few attempts at developing a national picture were limited by the use of extremely vague methodologies and very loose definitions of who might be a street child; numerical results were extrapolations from partial headcounts.

In 1997, the government sought to provide a more systematic account of street children. SNDIF and UNICEF adopted a more rigorous definition of street children and conducted a survey in Mexico's 100 largest cities, excluding the Federal District of Mexico City. A headcount was conducted at three different times of day during 1 week and a questionnaire applied to a stratified random sample of working children plus a complete sample of street-living children. Unlike the definition adopted by SNDIF hitherto that street-living children were people under 18 who had "broken the family link either permanently or temporarily, and sleep in the public thoroughfare", the new definition simply emphasised sleeping in public space:

> those for whom the street forms their daily habitat, and who sleep in wasteland, bus terminals, sewers, markets or hiding places in tourist and commercial areas [...] what defines their category is the fact of living in the street.
> (SNDIF 1997: 14, cited in Thomas de Benítez, 2008)

No mention was made of family relations in the formulation of this definition or in the subsequent questionnaire which contained no questions on continued family contact or support. Street-working children, by contrast, were understood to sleep in a 'home' environment. Nevertheless, the survey adopted an innovative understanding of street-working children. It identified working girls, boys, and adolescents in street situations (trabajadores en situación de calle) as both children who worked for money in the streets or other public spaces and young people who work in public spaces such as "markets, supermarkets, wholesale markets, bus terminals, cemeteries, entertainment centres" (SNDIF 1997: 14, cited in Thomas de Benítez, 2008). Introducing 'supermarkets' as a form of public space and differentiating streets from other public spaces were interesting new dimensions.

The 1997 survey concluded that there were 114 497 working children in Mexico outside the capital city, of whom just under 2300 were living on the streets. Puebla, Mexico's fourth largest city and the site of our field research, was reported as having 1968 working children in 1997, although the number of street-living children was not provided. In 2002–03, the survey was repeated, using approximately the same methodology (SNDIF, 2004). This time, the data showed 94 795 working children in Mexico's provincial cities, of whom 1517 were identified as street-living children; 2952 children were reported as working and 67 living on Puebla City's streets. The inclusion of children working in supermarkets as part of the definition of children working in public spaces, however, meant that of the age group 6–17, almost 40% were classified as 'empacadores' (packers) (see **Table 1**).

Despite their improvements on previous 'estimates' and research instruments, both '100 Cities' surveys possess a number of shortcomings. Conducting headcounts of children, particularly when living on the streets, is notoriously difficult: Activities are often conducted in the late evening or at night; children avoid detection; mobility within the city and across Mexico can be high; and, not least, children can spend long periods in detention centres, NGO facilities, and addiction rehabilitation centres (Thomas de Benítez, 2008). Although both surveys were supported by questionnaires with all identified as street living, the primary identification of whether a child is street working or street living can be very elusive: One may work and only occasionally sleep on the 'street'; another may sleep habitually on the street and only work there at other times. Moreover, faced with questions by strangers, most will obscure their status, resisting even provision of date and place of birth, schooling, and residence. It is no surprise therefore to note that the 2002–03 data reveal some strange results. For example, only 21 of 32 street-living children aged 6–17 admitted to using

Table 1 Street children in Mexico

	1997 Survey		2002–3 Survey	
	Number	%	Number	%
Children working on the street	80 491	70.3	56 403	59.5
Children working in self-service shops or supermarkets (empacadores)	31 716	27.7	36 875	38.9
Children living on the street	2 290	2.0	1 517	1.6
Total population	114 497	100	94 795	100

Author calculations based on SNDIF (2004).

drugs or alcohol and 10 claimed never to have done so; although very young children might not use drugs, unless administered by an adult, almost all in this age group will have had some experience with drugs.

The Street, Homes, and Mobilities

Attempts to quantify street children in Mexico reveal how the idea of a social reality becomes part of social reality itself. This is not to deny that many young people in Mexico spend time on the streets, a phenomenon recorded as far back as the mid-nineteenth century and long before the term 'street child' came into policy usage in the early 1970s internationally and in Mexico. Outside of education, such children have been considered as vagabonds, delinquents, abandoned, runaways, and orphans. But from the 1970s they became 'street children' (niños de la calle), and with the distinctions promoted by UNICEF during the 1980s between street living and working, the former became 'of' the street and the latter 'on' the street as they were further divided into niños de la calle and niños en la calle. Together they might be referred to as niños en situación de calle (children in street situations). This labelling and relabelling, in large part due to the imperatives of different policy perspectives rather than due to changing circumstances in the lives of children themselves, supports arguments that 'street children' are a subject constructed through discourse, devised to further advocacy or particular policy positions, rather than usefully to capture key characteristics of young peoples' lives (Lucchini, 1997).

An important feature used to distinguish street living from street working is the link to a home. The conventional notion that street-living children are homeless is widely dismissed in the literature. Unlike the UNICEF leaflet's provocation, few children sleep literally on the street but seek out some form of shelter, from the elements, predatory adults and other children, the police, social services, and vermin. 'Street children' have been shown to acquire homes in a variety of spaces, including squats in disused shops and houses, rooftops, drainage ducts, and public toilets (see also Beazley, 2002; Hecht, 1998). In Mexico City, abandoned buildings after the 1985 earthquakes provided for a time a large supply of vacant plots and empty structures (Gigengack, 2011). Subsequent movement of offices from the city centre and gradual redevelopment of these sites, and of small warehouses and workshops, provided another tranche of properties to be occupied.

In Puebla, street children used to frequent the city bus depot, taking advantage of the relative warmth, food stalls, and income opportunities from running errands, carrying bags, and opening taxi doors, to petty theft. An empty water tank alongside the depot and adjacent to a busy market was the home of one group until local traders filled the tank with water, threatening that next time they would not wait for the kids to vacate. Others slept wrapped in carpet on a restaurant roof protected by a billboard, yet more used a half-built house as home. Another large group would congregate under the concrete stanchions of a freeway, even dragging two sofas into the space. In the mid-1990s, NGOs in the city put the number of young people sleeping in these circumstances in the hundreds (Jones, 1997). Some would be classified as 'permanentes', those unlikely to leave the street having walked out of programmes and half-way houses. For those who do enter institutional 'homes' and especially rehab programmes, the order and ritual can be disturbing (Herrera et al., 2009). In some cases, it can be a great deal worse. As the former director of Puebla's municipal street child programme described one intervention:

> One day, we went to the rescue – that's what we call it – of some [street] youngsters who had been shut away in an Alcoholics Anonymous [residential programme] and we knew that there they tortured the youngsters as part of the therapeutic process – it's not a story, it's perfectly documented. When we took out those who allowed us to get them out, some 11 people, they went straight to hospital. In 2 cases, they were close to amputating their legs because, as drug addicts, the punishments had been terrible. There were infections; there was torture – literally torture. So then there was a reaction by the people in charge of the Annex, who went armed to the Welfare Department in search of us.

It is little wonder that many young people spoke about sleeping in vacant buildings as a safer option, or that the houses we visited were presented with pride and carefully looked after – however rudimentary their structure and contents, however chaotic and destructive the young peoples' daily lives seemed to be.

Research also shows that street children move back and forth between their families and the street. According to Lucchini (1997), movements may be frequent and numerous; a complete divorce from all family members is the exception, not the rule. For researchers who have followed children between street living, occupancy of NGO facilities, state institutions, and family return, it may be useful to think of mobilities as 'street life paths' or as 'careers' (van Blerk, 2005). These are not necessarily well-thought-out strategies. In their account of the *Tunnel Kids*, Taylor and Hickey (2001) describe members of the Barrio Libre, a loose assemblage of young people who live in the border city of Nogales, occasionally passing to the US side through a storm tunnel. The group is in a seemingly constant flux between Nogales and their ranchos, villages and cities of origin, or last known familial address. Chito describes going back to his mother in the city of

Navajoa, 500 km to the south to give her money; a number of others go 'home' to Guadalajara and other cities; and the authors drive Jesús to see his mother and siblings in Guaymas, a small city on the Sonora coast, after she had visited him earlier in Nogales. The reunion in Guaymas being a disaster, they return to Nogales. Flor takes the researchers to visit her father and sister in a neighbourhood not far from where she hangs out, alternating between a row of shacks, abandoned buildings, and a day centre. Later, Flor provides a tour of places where she has slept in the past, offering a "house tour worthy of Century 21" (Taylor and Hickey 2001: 125). Her request to visit her birthplace on the coast however elicits near indifference when she arrives and meets aunts and cousins. Later, when she discovers that other family members live near Nogales, Flor shows little interest in keeping in contact with them. Having gone some considerable way to working through her past and dealing with her present, including the loss of a child to her sister in adoption, and seeming to take seriously the possibility of schooling, Tunnel Kids ends with Flor suddenly announcing that she, Jesús, and others are off to Tijuana.

The mobilities of young people in Puebla are similarly diverse and unpredictable. In the early 1990s, migration accounts were of young people from rural areas or smaller towns and cities moving to Puebla City (Jones, 1997). Trips back to visit relatives were frequent and interspersed with seasonal journeys to coastal cities such as Veracruz or Acapulco, before return to Puebla. These trips remain a fundamental part of street life for young people we have known for several years. In 2005, 32-year-old Edmundo described how he regularly went back to the inner-city barrio of Tepito in Mexico City where his parents and seven brothers and sisters lived, despite having arrived in Puebla aged 12. As he explained, "yeah, every now and again I go to see my mum. . . . Umm, every month . . . I've always kept close and I get on well with my mum" (cited in Thomas de Benítez, 2008). Three years on, still working on the street, little appeared to have changed. For Edmundo and many others, going away remained an important release from the emotional and physical pressures of being on the streets. By the early 2000s, however, a more complicated picture was emerging of young people moving to cities on the US border. The 2004 SNDIF survey suggested northern Baja California received almost half as many young child workers again as the central State of Mexico, with border states Tamaulipas and Chihuahua, the third- and fifth-ranked states for recipient numbers. The report noted that street children were moving to Tijuana, Ciudad Juarez, Reynosa, and Nuevo Laredo – just like many other young Mexicans in recent decades. For many of the young people with whom we spent time in Puebla, however, reaching the border was a frustrating process; many claimed to have been to the United States, but others recalled turning back. The 'idea' of going home or getting away – increasingly meaning to the United States – filtered frequently into our conversations (Jones and Thomas de Benítez, 2009). It tells us that whatever their attachments to homes set up in abandoned buildings, or to hostels or brick structures in marginal neighbourhoods, there were competing notions of 'home' with family or further along – imagined in the future as someplace else.

We have shown in a case study of two young men who experienced living on the streets from a very young age that multiple moves across the country and eventually abroad are not inconsistent with understandings of 'home' (Jones and Thomas de Benítez, 2009). Indeed, family reunification in one case meant moving to the United States to link up with a sibling and father, and earning sufficient money to contemplate an eventual return to Mexico to build a home for himself and partner. En route, as it were, younger siblings who had been placed into different Pueblan institutions as children were tracked down, brought up to the United States, and motivated to follow the same 'path' of earning and saving money to return 'home' to Puebla. In the other example, subsistence on the streets of a red-light district in the southern state of Oaxaca, followed by moves through institutions and public spaces in Puebla, transformed into a route to university in Spain, a marriage proposal on the Seine, and setting up home in the city of Veracruz with his new wife as a young lawyer and associate lecturer at the local university.

Rethinking the Labels

In his ethnography of young people in central Mexico City, Gigengack (2000) explores how young people organise into groups, maintaining links with family and relationships with residents and institutions of their local communities. Again, these relations are fluid. The González family are living in two rooms in an encampment near Garibaldi Square in downtown Mexico City, variously splitting up and reforming as tensions between mother, stepfather, and children played out (Gigengack, 2000). Sixteen-year-old David had spent time on the street, sniffing solvent, participating in muggings, and selling coffee to nightclubbers. As Gigengack observes, "David had been a child 'of' the street, a working child 'on' the street, as well as school child on a part-time basis" (2000: 76). Another young person, Rat, is a hard-core sniffer and juvenile delinquent but, having expected to find the kid's home full of 'child abusers and drug takers', Gigengack is surprised to discover a 'loving family' making do in a one-bedroom apartment in which mother, aunt, sister, brother-in-law, three nephews, two brothers, and Rat all sleep. As Gigengack explores at length, the distinctions between categories of street children as adopted in the policy and research literatures are highly contested. The young people described in his research would fall variously into different categories. Being homeless, in the sense of not having a house that equates with societal expectations of a 'casa', should not imply being without family. In most respects, street children are more similar than they are different to other poor people, to what in Mexico is referred to as the 'populacho'; the principal distinction being not home or family but immersion in a self-destructive street culture.

In Puebla, the young people we worked with never referred to themselves as 'street children' – neither as niños de la calle nor as niños callejeros. When we showed the *De la Calle* film to three children, two with considerable experience of street living, it was watched with close fascination but at the end dismissed as inaccurate. On the streets they avoided use of any collective noun or adjectival addition to child or youth. Most commonly, and usually in general reference to others like themselves, they might use 'chamaco' (lad). While rejecting the street child label and recognising their heavy use of drugs and different lifestyles, they would react strongly to the suggestion made by some NGO workers that they were gang members or delinquents.

A similar observation is made by Taylor and Hickey (2001) who are keen to point out that the young people of Barrio Libre in Nogales are not a gang, despite having many apparent gang attributes such as dress codes, hand signal (señas), drug taking, and involvement in crime – in their case the mugging of people (pollos) who use storm drains to access the United States. Writing about Mexico City, Gigengack (2011) argues that the street children of his study refer to themselves and others as 'banda' and non-banda, terms that translate literally as 'ring' but which are more usefully defined as group. To be banda offers connections with youth cultures generally, without the limitations implied by an idea of street child. Importantly, banda opposes the synonym of gang which is often the implicit meaning of the term in the media (Jones and Thomas de Benítez, 2012). Rather, as we have explored at some length, being on the street as a young person is an arduous process of constructing and reconstructing identities, of a performativity of 'street child' to the expectations of others while nourishing the needs of the self (Herrera et al., 2009).

Conclusion

Young people on Mexico's streets construct nuanced ideas of 'home' to describe a variety of affective and spatial environments, both transitory and more permanent, which reflect their mobility and fluctuating living circumstances. They do not consider themselves 'homeless', since they may simultaneously share a temporary 'home' with street-based peers; return 'home' periodically to stay with one or more parent, siblings, and/or other relatives; live at times in NGO or governmental 'homes' to which they are emotionally attached. Our findings, which resonate with other street-ethnographic accounts within Mexico and beyond, challenge the clear distinctions used in policy formulation of 'home' as off-street and nuclear family-oriented, and of 'homeless' as on-street and abandoned by family. Such conceptual differences, with their implications for understandings of identity, shed some light on why homes established for 'homeless street children' so often fail to engage the very young people they are designed to attract.

See also: Children and Parenting; Ethnographies of Home and Homelessness; Hidden Homelessness; Homeless People: Street Children in Africa; Homeless People: Street Children in Asia; Homeless People: Youth in Australia; Homeless People: Youth in the United Kingdom.

References

Beazley H (2002) 'Vagrants wearing make-up': Negotiating spaces on the streets of Yogyakarta, Indonesia. *Urban Studies* 39(9): 1665–1684.

Ennew J (2000) Why the Convention is not about street children. In: Fottrell D (ed.) *Revisiting Children's Rights: 10 Years of the UN Convention on the Rights of the Child*, pp. 169–182. Dordrecht, the Netherlands: Kluwer.

Gigengack R (2000) Populacho and Callejeros: Stories about street children and other urban poor in Mexico City. *Medische Antopologie* 12(1): 71–102.

Gigengack R (2011) *Young, Damned and Banda. The World of Young Street People in Mexico City, 1990–1997*. Amsterdam: CEDLA.

Hecht T (1998) *At Home in the Street: Street Children of Northeast Brazil*. Cambridge, UK: Cambridge University Press.

Herrera E, Jones GA, and Thomas de Benítez S (2009) Bodies on the line: Identity markers among Mexican street youth. *Children's Geographies* 7(1): 67–81.

Jones GA (1997) Junto con los niños: Street children and NGOs in a Mexican city. *Development in Practice* 7(1): 39–49.

Jones GA and Thomas de Benítez S (2009) Tales of two or many worlds? When 'street' kids go global. In: Wetherell M (ed.) *Theorising Identities and Social Action*, pp. 75–92. Basingstoke, UK: Macmillan-Palgrave.

Jones GA and Thomas de Benítez S (2012) *Street Corners in a Global World: Everyday Life and Identities of Mexican Street Youth*. Philadelphia, PA: Temple University Press.

Lucchini R (1997) *Deviance and Street Children in Latin America: The Limits of a Functionalist Approach*. Fribourg, Switzerland: University of Fribourg Press.

SNDIF (1997) *Yo tambier cuento! Estudio de ninas, ninos y adolescentes trabajados en 100 ciudades*. Mexico City: SNDIF.

SNDIF (2004) *Informe ejecutivo: Segundo estudio de niñas, niños y adolescentes trabajadores en 100 ciudades 2002–2003*. Mexico City: SNDIF-UNICEF.

Taylor L and Hickey M (2001) *Tunnel Kids*. Tuscon, AZ: University of Arizona Press.

Thomas de Benítez S (2008) *Square Holes for Round Pegs: 'Street' Children's Experiences of Social Policy Processes 2002–2005 in Puebla City*. Mexico: Unpublished PhD Thesis, LSE.

Van Blerk L (2005) Negotiating spatial identities: Mobile perspectives on street life in Uganda. *Children's Geographies* 3(1): 5–21.

Relevant Website

www.streetchildren.org.uk – Consortium for Street Children.

www.juconi.org.mx – Junto con los niños (JUCONI).
www.unicef.org – United Nations Children's Fund (UNICEF).
www.un.org/youth – United Nations Programme on Youth, especially Briefing Paper 3, *Youth on the Streets* prepared by S. Thomas de Benítez and G.A. Jones.

Homeless People: Street Children in the United Kingdom

E Smeaton, York, UK

© 2012 Elsevier Ltd. All rights reserved.

Glossary

Blagging To gain something through confidence or cheekiness.

Disorganised attachment The inability to form attachments to primary caregivers in early childhood that can negatively affect a child's development.

Football firms A gang formed to fight with supporters from other football clubs.

Gang A named group who see themselves, and are seen by others, as affiliates of the group with structure and territory.

Sexual exploitation Any activity containing or suggesting a sexual component but that a person is not consenting to freely. It contains varying degrees of coercion from gentle persuasion to force. Sexual exploitation can also include the concept of exchange for both tangible (i.e., money, drink, drugs) and intangible (i.e., shelter, protection, coercion) forms of payment. Sexual exploitation is often present where children have needs that compromise their ability to provide any form of informed consent to sexual activity.

Introduction

Presentations of children on the streets commonly conjure images of, for example, children on the train stations in India, street boys hovering around the bus terminus in Nairobi, or the many children on the streets in Brazil at risk from death squads. However, recent research (Smeaton, 2009) carried out by the author identifies how children also live on the streets in the United Kingdom with no support from family or statutory agencies, despite a range of policy and practice commitments and initiatives to meet the needs of vulnerable children. This article highlights key findings from this relationship focusing upon children's experiences of family and home, violence, gangs, experiences of the streets, and survival strategies. The lack of agency intervention in their lives is identified as are their identities, behaviours, and states of being. The article moves on to discussing the extent of exploring how children on the streets have strengths and concludes that normalisation, disassociation, and denial are prevalent and that there is conflict between perceptions of childhood in the United Kingdom and realities of children who live on the streets.

Family and Home

The families of children who spend time on the streets in the United Kingdom are particularly complex. Intergenerational issues are often embedded in family relationships and patterns. Experiences and issues within the family are often reinforced by similar patterns among others that children know. There is often a sense of acceptance and a process of normalisation that prevents both adults and children from seeking support to address their own issues and problems and those of other family members. Many children have been forced to deal with a range of difficult events and circumstances within their family, such as the violent death of a parent, not knowing a parent or being abandoned by a parent, and have been left to navigate their way through them with no support to understand the behaviour of the adults around them and their own emotions:

> He was murdered, basically ... The worst thing that happened to me was that my dad was taken away from me ... and my mum just lost it, started drinking and getting depressed and hitting me. ... (It) really did a lot of damage (Smeaton, 2009: 40).

Many have parents who are not able to show love and care because of their own experiences of being parented and being lost in a world of substance misuse, mental health issues, and domestic violence that leaves no room for meeting children's needs. Emotional abuse, physical abuse, sexual abuse, and neglect are common, and many children's development has been adversely affected by disorganised attachment that stems from early childhood experiences.

Violence

Violence is frequently part of life for children who live on the streets in the United Kingdom. Many experience extreme violence at the hands of family members:

> He (father) used to beat me and he tried to stab me. ... He wrapped the telephone cord around my neck, pulled

it so hard he thought I wasn't breathing and put me in a cold bath so I'd start breathing again. . . . And my daddy broke two of my fingers (Smeaton, 2009: 30).

Some children witness violent acts where their parent is the victim through domestic violence directed towards both mothers and fathers or where a parent has been assaulted or murdered. Some experience violence from carers in residential care and foster placements. Threats and intimidation are a common experience while living with family and on the streets. Many children move on to experience or perpetuate domestic violence in their own relationships. Some young people, both males and females, have experienced sexual violence at home and on the streets, including being gang-raped.

Violence on the Streets

Accounts of life on the streets reveal an overwhelming sense of violence being ever-present. Being involved in fights was common among young males and sometimes experienced by young females also. Substance use is often at the core of violent acts towards others and also perpetrated when a child is in the pursuit of money to buy drugs. Most young males feel that it is important that they are able to physically take care of themselves and some go to extreme lengths to prove this so that reputation and past acts of violence ensure that others leave them alone. Many children are victims of violence while on the streets. Some respond with violence when finding themselves the target of assault. Some children who have been victims of violence on the streets become perpetrators of violence, although this is not inevitable. Some children have been attacked by children and adults wielding weapons. Such an experience is often the trigger for young males to start carrying a weapon. Many young males prefer not to carry or use weapons but do so because others do and carrying a knife is common among young males on the streets. There is a limited gun culture among children on the streets among those who have to consider that others may carry firearms and carry a gun for protection.

To understand why children commit violent acts and exhibit damaging behaviour is to understand what has happened in their past and to recognise that they developed in the only way they knew to adapt and manage their circumstances. The normalisation of violence, alongside the need for self-preservation in often violent environments, explains the process by which many children on the streets in the United Kingdom find themselves embroiled in a world of violence.

Gangs

Gang culture features significantly among children on the streets in the United Kingdom with many males identifying as belonging to a gang. Many children believe that life has become more dangerous for them and being part of a gang affords some protection from other gangs and individuals. When a child is on the streets, the potential of risk and harm increases and becoming part of a gang is an important survival strategy. Females also identify as belonging to gangs consisting of those from the homeless population who come together to manage being on the streets.

There is some diversity in the gangs that children on the streets belong to. Some are members of a football firm which can be differentiated from a gang because, whereas gang allegiance is expected to be complete, members of football firms live separate lives for most of the week, only coming together for football matches and organised fights around football events. A few children are involved in criminal business organisations that are well-established and highly organised, with a hierarchical order and trade in guns, drugs, and other criminal activities. However, the majority of children on the streets belong to gangs of children who spend time together, perhaps share a similar identity and are involved in fights with other gangs of a similar ilk.

For those without family, with a weak bond or negative experiences of family, a gang provides an alternative family, and sometimes young males left their birth family with all their complexities and conflict to be with their other family: their brothers. Having this alternative family eases leaving home for some children as the gang will keep them protected; sometimes being part of a gang gives a child confidence to leave. For those children who are thrown out of home by parents or carers, there is also the security offered by the gang: they are not going to be on their own with all the vulnerabilities of the isolated.

The Streets

Many children start to spend time on the streets while still living with parents and carers. Some of the allure of the streets stems from the friendships, comfort, and company that can be found on the streets. Many children have parents and carers who spend significant amounts of time away from home or do not pay attention to the whereabouts of their children. Many children turn to the streets while still living with parents and carers to escape abuse in the home and because they are unhappy with home life:

> There was nothing for me at home: no love, no food. I stayed out with my mates having a laugh and that (Smeaton, 2009: 71).

Children can find themselves on the streets via a number of different routes: some are thrown out of home by parents or carers, some run away, and some gradually drift away from home after spending more and more time on the streets. For children who spend time on the streets while still living at home, it is a natural progression to turn to the streets when they cease to live at home. Once permanently on the streets, life becomes uncertain and inconsistent. Some days there will be plenty of opportunities to make money and offers of somewhere to stay; other days there will be nothing. Sometimes, the streets provide warmth and shelter, other times hostility and anger.

Living on the streets in the United Kingdom can be very dangerous for children who experience both sexual and physical violence. Some children are very frightened while on the streets and describe a number of negatives such as being cold and hungry, lonely, and frightened. Some children acknowledge that while they have fun, there is a darker side to being on the streets. Despite this, some children prefer to risk the dangers of living on the streets because home life is also dangerous and living on the streets offers freedom and opportunities that are not available elsewhere. There are also a number of positive factors of being on the streets such as the possibility of adventure and excitement. Other children view being on the streets as having been beneficial for them in terms of their own maturity and ability to handle certain situations.

An inherent assumption exists among many children that being on the streets is a natural progression in their lives and there is an acceptance that this is how their life is and they reveal no desire to change their life or any awareness that there is an alternative to the pattern of their life.

Integration with the Homeless Population

Integration of the homeless population and nonhomeless population sometimes plays a part in how a child finds themselves on the streets after children become involved with the homeless population while still living at home or care. Because of the contact between homeless and nonhomeless groups, the transition from nonhomeless and homeless can take place very quickly. For example, a child with contacts in the homeless population who is experiencing difficulties at home may take to the streets in a quicker timeframe than a child who has no contacts on the streets and no knowledge of street life. Where children have previously established relationships of different kinds, they are able to draw upon these relationships as a survival strategy and become part of an established network. This brings about both positive and negative consequences. For example, homeless adults may provide support for others on the streets, especially those who are young. However, the homeless community can also be subject to petty jealousies and conflict that may have negative impacts for children who can experience both support and harm from others on the streets.

Survival Strategies

Children in the United Kingdom employ a range of survival strategies to manage living on the streets including shoplifting, burglary, stealing cars, involvement in selling drugs, selling sex, begging, and blagging:

> I was begging or shoplifting; whatever I could really ... I have, like slept with people to get money and that as well (Smeaton, 2009: 75).

Some children become involved in organised crime through gaining a reputation as being skilled at committing crimes such as stealing cars or burglary and are sought by more organised and professional criminals. Meeting others on the streets and spending time with them is also a crucial survival strategy for children who would otherwise be very isolated and at particular risk. Children also seek and identify safe places. Some feel safer in city centres, while others prefer to keep away from urban centres and find a quiet place.

Other survival strategies involve children adopting and adapting attitudes and behaviours to minimise danger and match what is required to survive on the streets; the streets can shape attitudes, behaviours, and actions. Some children stop acting in certain ways because they do not match the nature of the streets. Some children do not feel at risk or frightened on the streets in the United Kingdom because they prepare themselves not to and this enables them to cope with being on the streets. Some express a clear moral code that guides their own conduct and how they perceive others' actions.

Lack of Agency Support and Intervention

The government's aim, outlined in its Every Child Matters agenda (see Relevant Website), is for every child, whatever their background or circumstances, to have the support they need to:

- be healthy
- stay safe
- enjoy and achieve
- make a positive contribution
- achieve economic well-being.

Despite this policy agenda and the legal duty of local authorities to safeguard and promote the welfare of children at risk and in need who are known to Social Services, many children who live on the streets do not receive interventions to address problematic issues in their lives both prior to living on the streets and once on the streets. The majority of children who live on the streets do not enjoy school and left before the age of 16 with no qualifications, sometimes because it was difficult for them to attend school and often because they preferred the culture and company on the streets.

Some children identify barriers to seeking support such as not knowing where to go for help. Many children do not attempt to seek formal support because they did not realise that there were problems as their experiences had become normalised and reinforced by the lives of others around them that were similar; most know other children who live in similar circumstances and some children have siblings who have also left home before the age of 16. For those children that simply drifted away from home, it was sometimes difficult to pinpoint when they had actually left home and when a way of living becomes problematic; some children live a particular lifestyle for a long time before it feels difficult, uncomfortable, or problematic. Other children are happy with their lives on the streets or just accept that this is how it is and do not want to seek change until their coping mechanisms break down or suppressed reactions and emotions related to past events and experiences come to the fore and are impossible to ignore. Many children on the streets have very few expectations: that life could have dealt them anything but the harsh hand they experience; that their life could be different; and that they deserve a safe and protected childhood where they can develop to meet their potential and have access to support and opportunities. A few children have some understanding that certain things should not be happening to them, that others should not be acting in various ways, and that they should not be on the streets. Some children do not want any other support than that offered by their friends. Others feel that they are managing adequately without additional support and some just find it easier and safer to be self-reliant.

Identities, Behaviours, and States of Being

Identities, behaviours, and states of being are too often a consequence of damaging experiences from early childhood that are reinforced as a child grows older. Substance use is rife among children on the streets, often starting at a young age while still living at home or in care, and linked to fun, escapism, and coping with emotional feelings that are difficult to manage. The normalisation of substance use partly accounts for why children who use drugs and substance use often escalates when a child lives on the streets. Polydrug use is common and some children and young people become heavy users of drugs such as heroin and cocaine. There is a close relationship between substance use and crime. Many of the children and young people have experienced depression, and other mental health issues, and have not received support to address the trauma behind their depression:

> I've been depressed plenty of times and I've self-harmed as well. I used to slice me wrists ... when I was about thirteen. I used to burn myself with lighters as well (Smeaton, 2009: 101).

Children on the streets in the United Kingdom experience sexual exploitation in different forms including sexual relationships with older adults and selling sex. There are some differences between males and females in relation to sexual exploitation. Males tended to self-present as 'having a good time', enjoying themselves and taking 'older' men for a ride, thereby blurring the boundaries between exploiting and being exploited. Females perceived their involvement with older men as a relationship and these men as their boyfriends. There is often a power imbalance when a male or female has an older 'boyfriend' or 'girlfriend', making it very difficult for the child or young person to resist their demands and express their own wishes (Barnardo's, 2008). Many relationships between young females on the streets and older men are abusive in ways other than being sexual abusive as domestic violence, physical abuse, emotional abuse, isolation, and control have been features between young females on the streets and older men.

Children on the streets in the United Kingdom sometimes reveal the ability to manage risk and cope with a range of damaging and dangerous experiences, environments, and possibilities. In addition, individual children react differently to similar experiences, some managing to cope in ways that others do not, and to protect themselves in different ways. It is appropriate to consider resilience as a key concept in understanding the experiences of children on the streets in the United Kingdom. Resilience is acquired in two ways: through genes and through social experience (Gilligan, 2009) and there are a number of protective factors that influence resilience of many children on the streets, yet some are clearly resilient.

The concepts of attachment and detachment are relevant, especially in relation to the importance of attachment and children's experiences of being parented and the likelihood of disorganised attachment (Howe, 2005). In addition, the extent of children and young people's attachment to other people and behaviours played an important part in their experiences. For example, children become attached to other people, to their gang or group, to substances, certain behaviours, and to the streets, often finding it difficult to leave the streets. It appears that many children who live on the streets in the United Kingdom have parents who are emotionally or physically detached from them. Thus, parental detachment plays a part in children becoming detached from parents, carers, and key societal institutions and living on the streets.

Risk

Children on the streets are often at risk through others' actions but also because of their actions and, for example, placing themselves in situations that are inherently dangerous or that they do not possess the maturity to manage. Children are also at risk because they do not receive appropriate support to address their issues. For example, the extent of depression experienced by children and young people has potential for the longer-term impacts and also affects children's enjoyment of childhood and youth and their ability to make decisions.

Children are not always aware of potential risks when engaging in certain activities or making decisions about what form of action to take. Children's perceptions of risk influence their decisions. For example, some children feel that becoming reliant on others is a risk that they cannot take because if they cease to be able to cope on their own and support is subsequently pulled away, there is concern that they will not be able to manage. The choices available to children are also linked to risk. While some of their actions may be viewed as risky from the perspectives of others, the child may view available alternatives as riskier. In addition, lack of alternatives may also compel a child to contemplate a course of action that is inherently risky.

There are some mixed messages relating to others for children who live on the streets in the United Kingdom. Many have not been protected from harm by adults that are supposed to protect them, by their parents, and by support agencies, and others have been subjected to harm by the very people who should have their welfare at heart. Many children have witnessed prevention of risk, as far as possible, by the very people often presented as a potential source of risk. For example, the adult homeless population and those involved in selling sex. It is also possible that the same person may be both the protector/provider and exploiter and a child may decide that the protective element takes priority.

There are often risks related to sexual behaviours and attitudes towards sex. Sometimes, females are at risk from how males use sex to express emotions that have little to do with sexuality but are dominated by power and anger issues (Groth et al., 1977). There are a number of factors that are likely to decrease the likelihood of practising safe sex including drug-related sex, being desperate for money, and being sexually exploited by those who have no concern for the child's welfare. Therefore, there is heightened risk of becoming infected, and infecting others, with HIV/AIDS and sexually transmitted diseases (STDs).

Recognising That Children on the Streets Have Strengths

The experiences of children on the streets in the United Kingdom reveal how many have developed coping strategies to manage a range of difficult and disturbing events and circumstances. While many have not completed secondary education, alternative education has often taken place, teaching children what they need to know to survive in the world they inhabit that sits at odds with formalised education. Despite the odds, a few of the children and young people have arrived at a place in their lives where they have changed a number of their behaviours and attitudes, choosing to forego crime, substance use and social networks where drugs and crime are common, and are ready to become a part of the more formal world of education, training, and work and all that entails. Whether or not children are ready to leave the streets, they still share the same general hopes for the future as most people relating to a home, a family, and a safe and secure existence. Sometimes, children want their lives to change but are at a loss to know where to begin.

Normalisation, Disassociation, and Denial

The term 'normalisation' has been used to offer some explanation of, for example, how children accept being harmed and inflict harm upon others, their involvement in substance use, and their acceptance that part of their life is lived on the streets. Normalisation also offers some explanation of why many children on the streets do not seek support. To further understand processes of normalisation, it may be useful to consider other options available to children who live on the streets. One such option could be to disassociate from what happened to them and took place around them. While some children have taken this option, events often spiralled to the point where it was no longer possible for a child to disassociate because something happened externally or internally to the child and they are forced to react. A second option could be to deny that which is taking place. This can be seen in children's presentations of, for example, their sexual relationships with older adults. However, it is argued that normalisation can contribute to both disassociation and denial and that all three are interlinked to differing degrees at different stages in a child's life and form part of a process. Normalisation, disassociation, and denial are also seen in children's parents' and carers' behaviours and responses.

Conflict between Perceptions of Childhood and Realities of the Lives of Children on the Streets in the United Kingdom

The experiences of children who live on the streets do not always fit with public perceptions and other portrayals of childhood which ignores that there are many experiences of childhood. There is also tension between perceptions of what childhood is and failing to meet the needs of children who are forced to adopt adult behaviours to manage their circumstances, and simultaneously expected to fit into preconceived moulds of childhood.

Conclusion

Despite a range of legislative measures, guidance, and policy commitments, there are children and young people in the United Kingdom who do not receive the support and care they are entitled to. If a society does not want children to be on the streets, it has to provide alternatives to the streets and needs to protect children from harm both in the home and on the streets. If children on the streets are expected to change their behaviours, there needs to be some alternative opportunities, alternative support mechanisms, and alternative ways of engaging and including vulnerable and marginalised children. Only by understanding the realities of children on the streets will it become possible to meet children's needs and prevent other children from living on the streets in the United Kingdom.

See also: Homeless People: Street Children in Africa; Homeless People: Street Children in Asia; Homeless People: Street Children in Mexico.

References

Barnardo's (2008) *Whose Daughter Next?* Barkingside, UK: Barnardo's.
Gilligan R (2009) *Promoting Resilience: Supporting Children and Young People Who Are In Care, Adopted or In Need*. London: British Association for Adoption and Fostering.
Groth A, Burgess W, and Holmstrom L (1977) Power, anger and sexuality. *American Journal of Psychiatry* 134: 1239–1243.
Howe D (2005) *Child Abuse and Neglect: Attachment, Development and Intervention*. Basingstoke, UK: Palgrave Macmillan.
Smeaton E (2009) *Off the Radar: Children and Young People on the Streets in the UK*. Sandbach, UK: Railway Children.

Relevant Website

http://www.education.gov.uk/consultations/downloadableDocs/EveryChildMatters.pdf – White paper presented to Parliament by the Chief Secretary to the Treasury by Command of Her Majesty, September 2003.

Homeless People: Youth in Australia

G Johnson, RMIT University, Melbourne, VIC, Australia

© 2012 Elsevier Ltd. All rights reserved.

Glossary

Chronic homelessness Occurs when people remain homeless for long periods of time. It is common to find disproportionate rates of mental and physical health problems, substance abuse, and social isolation among the chronically homeless.
Early intervention Policy approaches designed to intervene at the start or early on in a young person's experience of homelessness.
Episodic homelessness Refers to the pattern of repeated movement in and out of homelessness. Each experience is referred to as an episode.
Youth homeless career This concept highlights the processes and stages young people pass through before they develop a self-identity as a homeless person.
Homeless subculture A patterned set of behaviours, routines, and orientations that are adaptive responses to the predicament of homelessness.
Street kids A term used to describe young people who live on the streets or in squats.

Introduction

Youth homelessness is a serious issue in Australia, although this had not always been the case. Until the mid-1970s homelessness was typically confined to older, single males in the inner cities. Then, the appearance of homeless adolescents signalled that the homeless population was becoming more diverse. In the mid-1980s advocates and service providers reported increasing numbers of young people seeking assistance. In 1982 the Australian Federal government responded to these concerns in the Senate's *Report on Youth Homelessness*. The report resulted in the development of the national Supported Accommodation Assistance Program (SAAP) in 1985, which explicitly identified youth homelessness as a priority area. One year later the Federal government implemented the Youth Homeless Allowance in recognition of the specific financial difficulties faced by homeless young people.

However, it was the release of the report *Our Homeless Children* (Human Rights and Equal Opportunity Commission, 1989) that brought youth homelessness onto the community agenda. The 'Burdekin Report' received extensive media coverage and commentary and generated widespread public debate over youth homelessness. Since the release of the Burdekin Report, policy makers and researchers in Australia have identified a range of strategies and dedicated significant resources to address the problem of youth homelessness. Despite these efforts, youth homelessness remains a persistent feature on Australia's social landscape.

This article examines four issues. The first focuses on the number of homeless young people in Australia. The second deals with three competing explanations for youth homelessness. The third focuses on youth homelessness as a process of adaptation and exclusion. The final section examines contemporary policy responses to youth homelessness in Australia.

How Many Young People Are Homeless?

There has been some debate in Australia over what constitutes 'youth', but it is generally accepted that youth includes anyone between the ages of 12 and 24. While there is little doubt that Australia has a significant problem with youth homelessness, estimating the number of homeless young people is difficult for three reasons. First, without a clear definition of homelessness it is difficult to establish who is homeless and consequently how many people are homeless. Second, there are obvious methodological difficulties trying to count a highly mobile population that in many cases does not want to be identified. Third, researchers use two different approaches to count homeless people. Point-in-time estimates tell us how many people are homeless on a given night, while the annual estimates tell us how many people experience homelessness over 1 year. Each approach produces different estimates.

Although disagreement exists about the most appropriate way to define homelessness, policy makers, advocates, and researchers generally opt for one of two approaches. The first is based on the theoretical arguments of Chamberlain and Mackenzie (1992) and is known as the 'cultural definition' of homelessness. The cultural definition contends that homelessness should be measured in relation to minimum community housing standards and includes the following people as homeless: people without conventional accommodation (streets, squats, etc.); people staying temporarily with other households (because they have no usual address); people in emergency accommodation (refuges, shelters, etc.); and people in boarding houses. This approach is used by the Australian Bureau of Statistics (ABS) to enumerate homeless people.

Every 5 years the ABS conducts a census of the Australian population. As part of the census, the ABS carries out a special strategy to enumerate the number of people who are homeless on census night. This is a point-in-time count. On census night 2001 the ABS estimated that 99 900 Australians were homeless and that 36 173 (or 36%) were aged between 12 and 24. In 2006 the ABS reported that 104 676 people were homeless on census night. Of these 32 444 (or 31%) were aged between 12 and 24 (Chamberlain and Mackenzie, 2008). This represents a 10% decrease over 5 years.

The second definition is contained in the SAAP Act 1994. It contends that homelessness occurs when people have inadequate access to safe and secure housing. This approach is used by welfare services to allocate resources to people seeking assistance. Using this definition, agencies collect data on the number of people who use their services over the course of 1 year (an annual count). In 2006–07 there were 187 900 people who received assistance from a SAAP agency. Of this group 118 800 were 15 years of age or older (the remainder being accompanying children). SAAP data show that of these 118 800 people, 39 300 (or 33%) were between the ages of 15 and 24. Most were born in Australia, the majority are single and unemployed, and few actively participate in education. According to SAAP statistics the number of young people seeking assistance has increased by 21% over the last 5 years (see Australian Institute of Health and Welfare, 2008), although as a proportion of SAAP clients, the rate has remained relatively constant.

Explaining the Causes of Youth Homelessness

Since youth homelessness emerged as a public and policy concern in the mid-1980s, considerable scholarly, policy, and public attention has been focused on identifying the causes of it. As is the case in the broader literature on homelessness, youth homelessness is often explained in terms of individual, structural, or situational factors. Individual explanations are often favoured by the Australian public and media. This approach suggests young people are responsible for their situation because of various personal deficits and inadequacies such as drug use, indolence, deviant behaviour, and mental illness. In Australia a common perception is that young people choose to be homeless. While the Burdekin Report emphasised the structural causes of youth homelessness, the media ignored this and focused on individual explanations. For instance, on the release of the Burdekin Report the *Sydney Morning Herald* proclaimed that in the 'eastern suburbs a vast majority have homes to go to; they are often children of middle class parents... The children choose to live on the streets'. The notion of choice invokes a particular morality in which the young person must accept responsibility for any problems they experience. This approach has been criticised for blaming young people for their circumstances.

However, accounts that explain youth homelessness as a result of individual behaviour often ignore the structural context in which these issues occur. Structural explanations locate the reasons for the emergence of youth homelessness beyond the individual and in wider social and economic conditions. The argument is that changing structural conditions give rise to new forms of disadvantages that increase the susceptibility, or risk levels, of some young people to homelessness. This approach focuses on young people living in households experiencing poverty and on the lack of affordable housing and/or the shortage of reliable employment. In the 1950s, 60s, and early 70s, if young people had problems at home they could find work and alternative accommodation with relative ease. Since the mid-1980s unemployment rates among young people have remained significantly higher than unemployment rates among adults, and changes to the housing market have compounded the problems experienced by young people. Whereas in the 1960s and 70s rental housing was relatively easy to come by, over the last two decades vacancy rates in private rental markets across Australia have been at record lows. In addition, young people often experience discrimination while trying to get access to private rental housing because of their age, their lack of a rental history, and a perception that young people lack a stable income. The reduction in, and residualisation of, public housing stock has further decreased the housing choices available to young people.

While structural changes in the housing and labour markets have contributed to the number of young people at risk of homelessness, a range of situational factors have also been linked to youth homelessness. Situational causes include such factors in the young person's immediate environment as conflict within the family (Pinkney and Ewing, 1997). While a minority of young people might be attracted by the 'excitement' and 'freedom' of the streets, young people are often running from dysfunctional and abusive families. This point is repeatedly confirmed by

Australian studies. The Burdekin Report (1989: 88) noted that family conflict 'features strongly in most studies of young people leaving home', and the National Committee for the Evaluation of the Youth Services Support Scheme (1983) found that 78% of young people had experienced some form of conflict prior to leaving home, with the rate increasing to over 85% for those who left home before they were 16. More recent research confirms that family conflict remains a root cause of youth homelessness (Johnson et al., 2008; Rosenthal et al., 2006). Family conflict has been used to describe a range of issues: young people leave home because of problems at school, cultural conflict, their sexual activity or preferences, or traumatic life events such as abuse or neglect.

Other situational factors include young people who have been in the care of child protection authorities. The number of young people who have been in State care and who also experience homelessness is difficult to quantify, but estimates suggest the number to be in the range of 20–40%. Similarly, empirical evidence indicates that young people who have been involved in the juvenile justice system are also at an increased risk of homelessness. Other situational factors include a lack of support for young people with mental health problems (see Rosenthal et al., 2006).

The debate over structure and agency is important, but the reality is that there is rarely a single cause of homelessness; instead it is often a combination of structural, situational, and individual factors that results in homelessness for young people.

Homelessness as a Process

Identifying the causes of youth homelessness is important, particularly in terms of prevention, although the heavy emphasis on the 'causes' of youth homelessness contributed to the perception of homelessness as a state into which people fall and remain. In the early 1990s researchers found that people's experience of homelessness was highly differentiated, and consequently, more attention was given to the experience of homelessness itself (see Neil and Fopp, 1993). A result was that the traditional view of homelessness as a sudden crisis started to give way to the recognition that homelessness is best understood as a process of adaptation and exclusion that affects young people in different ways with different consequences.

The notion of homelessness as a dual process of adaptation and exclusion led to the development of the 'youth homeless career'. In Australia this approach was first articulated by Chamberlain and Mackenzie (1998) who created an 'ideal-type' model of the youth homeless career. Chamberlain and Mackenzie developed the idea of a youth homeless career after analysing administrative data from a youth agency which alerted them to the fact that many young people first experience homelessness at school. They explored this further in a national census of homeless school students in 1994 and developed a descriptive model that identifies various stages young people move through before they develop an identity as homeless. The youth homeless career model draws attention to the fact that young people go through a series of biographical transitions if they remain in the homeless population, culminating in the development of a self-identity as a homeless person. This argument centres on the idea that if young people become immersed in the homeless subculture, they are likely to become acculturated, or adapt to a homeless way of life.

Chamberlain and Mackenzie argue that young people often make a tentative break when they first leave the family home. This 'in and out' phase can be quite short, and the young person may move back home or may move onto independent living. However, the permanent break, 'the next biographical transition ... signifies that the young person no longer thinks of himself or herself as belonging to the family unit' (Chamberlain and Mackenzie, 1998: 71). At this stage in their 'career', young people are likely to become involved with other homeless people (the homeless subculture). It is the next biographical transition that is crucial, for it denotes that they have made the 'transition to chronicity', or chronic homelessness. This model was critical in promoting early intervention as the most appropriate policy response, and as indicated in **Figure 1** (below), Chamberlain and

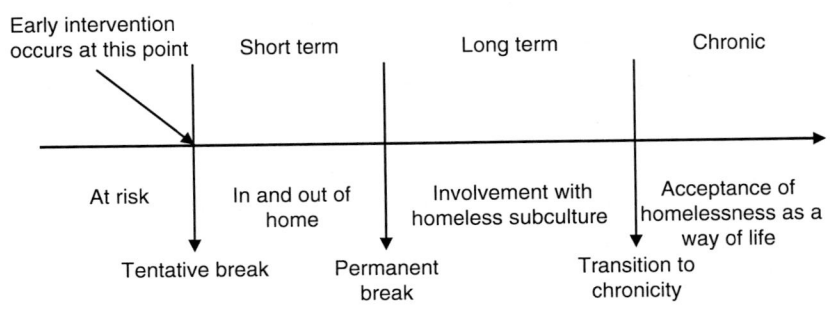

Figure 1 Ideal typical model of the youth homeless career. Taken from Chamberlain and Mackenzie 1998:71.

Mackenzie use the point of leaving home to identify when and where early intervention should start.

Chamberlain and Mackenzie's interest in the early stages of homelessness led to the identification of schools as an important site where early intervention strategies for young people at risk of, and those already experiencing homelessness, could be based. Their argument is that if young people stay at school, they are unlikely, or at least less likely, to get involved with the homeless subculture. If young people fall out of school, they begin the transition to chronic homelessness, and once this happens, the opportunity for early intervention is over.

Australian researchers have made two criticisms of Chamberlain and Mackenzie's work. The first criticism is that their model fails to explain why young people, even though they generally come from similar economic backgrounds, experience homelessness for varying periods of time. The second criticism is directed towards the idea that young people who remain homeless self-identify and accept homelessness as a way of life. Although researchers generally agree that the longer people are homeless the more likely they are to adapt in response to the contingencies of day-to-day life, the acceptance of a homeless identity is a contentious issue. To address these concerns there has been a move away from the idea of a single youth homeless career and more attention given to the different pathways young people travel into, through, and out of homelessness (Johnson et al., 2008; Mallett et al., 2005). Using the pathways approach, researchers have explored the interaction between different social structures and individuals on different pathways as well as the link between young people's experiences prior to becoming homeless and their experiences of homelessness. The empirical foundation for this approach came from overseas, in particular the United States and the United Kingdom, where studies indicate that certain adverse childhood experiences such as abuse, neglect, or trauma are powerful predictors of adult homelessness.

While there is considerable variation in young people's experience of homelessness, Johnson et al. (2008) argue there are two distinct pathways into youth homelessness. The first pathway is where young people leave home because of fights with their parents, resistance to parental control, and/or a desire for independence. They refer to this group as 'dissenters'. Dissenters often maintain a connection to the mainstream, typically through their ongoing involvement at school, and they generally have a short experience of homelessness.

The second pathway is where young people leave home because of abuse, neglect, or trauma. They refer to this group as 'escapers'. Escapers often become homeless at a younger age, leave school earlier (and consequently have lower education levels), and typically have little, if any, social, economic, or cultural capital available to them when problems occur. Without these resources escapers face significant barriers getting out of homelessness, and they often end up chronically homeless as a result. Other studies have noted that young people who have been abused or neglected (and who have often been in the care of the State) are disproportionately represented among the long-term homeless population.

Although family conflicts come in many different forms, the two pathways highlight the point that the nature or severity of family conflict influences the way young people respond to homelessness. The experiences of the dissenters and escapers emphasise how young people's life histories (or biographies) have important implications in terms of how they respond to homelessness and the length of time they are likely to remain homeless. Three important points emerge from this.

First, involvement in the homeless subculture is often influenced by the social and economic resources young people have available to them and the stigma they attach to homelessness. In the broader community, homelessness is a highly stigmatised identity. Dissenters recognise this, and they typically try to maintain existing friendships and often distance themselves from other homeless people. A result is that they often avoid becoming involved in the homeless subculture. By way of contrast, escapers are more likely to engage with other homeless people. These young people often invert the stigma of homelessness as a way of connecting with others in similar circumstances. Local and international research show that engaging with other homeless people can create a sense of belonging that is frequently missing from their lives.

Second, involvement in the homeless subculture is, however, a double-edged sword. Over time as young people overcome their initial anxiety and disorientation, they start to develop survival strategies that enable them to get by in an often harsh, chaotic, and materially deprived world. The longer young people remain homeless the more heavily they rely on these survival strategies, as well as other social practices they learn from homeless people. Over time new social networks involving other homeless people form, and these networks have a strong influence on their day-to-day activities. This often creates additional problems which can make extrication more difficult. There is clear evidence that, when compared with their peers, young homeless people are more likely to suffer from mental health problems, have poorer physical health, higher rates of substance abuse, and higher rates of offending behaviours. These problems are often presumed to be the cause(s) of homelessness, but for many homeless young people, and for escapers in particular, problems like substance abuse and mental illness emerge as a consequence of prolonged exposure to homelessness (Johnson and Chamberlain, 2008; Martijn and Sharpe, 2006).

Finally, the career idea implies that chronic homelessness is the end point of a linear process, and at the final stage, young people identify with a homeless way of life. Research shows, however, that many chronically homeless adults first become homeless as young people and often cycle in and out of the homeless population over long periods of time (see Johnson and Chamberlain, 2008). This pattern of episodic homelessness questions the extent to which long-term homeless people normatively accept homelessness as a 'way of life'. Most people who have a long-term problem do not endorse homelessness as a preferred lifestyle. On the contrary, they frequently try to get out of the homeless population, but they often struggle to remain housed.

Policy Responses

In Australia most States have developed strategies to address the issues facing young homeless people. During the 1990s and early part of this century, the emphasis was on school-based early intervention and family reconciliation programmes. While the primary focus of these strategies is to prevent homelessness or intervene as early as possible, the design of these programmes limited their application to young people still at school or for those whom family reconciliation is a possibility. When the Rudd government was elected in 2007 it highlighted homelessness as a 'national disgrace' and signalled its intention to reduce homelessness by half by 2020. In its white paper on homelessness, 'The Road Home' (FaHCSIA, 2008), the importance of early intervention is clearly highlighted, and a significant amount of funding is targeted at expanding the existing capacity of services that work with young homeless people. However, there is now a much stronger recognition in policy circles that for young people leaving the care of the State, those exiting from juvenile justice facilities, and those who have experienced abuse, school-based early intervention and/or family reconciliation services are inappropriate. This has prompted policy makers to turn their attention to preventative strategies that minimise the possibility young people leaving care or custody will exit into homelessness. While gaps still remain in policy interventions designed for homeless youth, there is now a greater recognition that young homeless people are a diverse group and that their experiences prior to becoming homeless provide crucial insights into the different services they require.

Conclusion

In Australia there is a strong recognition that assisting young people early is not only a cost-effective strategy, but also a morally appropriate one – when young people remain in the homeless population for long periods of time their situation often becomes far more complex and ultimately more difficult and costly to resolve.

See also: Children and Parenting; Homeless People: Indigenous/Aboriginal; Homeless People: Youth in the United Kingdom; Policies to Address Homelessness.

References

Australian Institute of Health and Welfare (2008) *Homeless People in SAAP: SAAP National Data Collection 2006–2007 Australia*. Canberra: Australian Institute of Health and Welfare.

Chamberlain C and Mackenzie D (1992) Understanding contemporary homelessness: Issues of definition and meaning. *Australian Journal of Social Issues* 27(4): 274–297.

Chamberlain C and Mackenzie D (1998) *Youth Homelessness: Early Intervention and Prevention*. Sydney: Australian Centre for Equity through Education.

Chamberlain C and Mackenzie D (2008) *Counting the Homeless 2006*. Canberra: Australian Bureau of Statistics.

FaHCSIA (2008) *The Road Home: A National Approach to Reducing Homelessness*. Canberra: Department of Families, Housing, Community Services and Indigenous Affairs.

Human Rights and Equal Opportunity Commission (1989) *Our Homeless Children*. Canberra: Australian Government Publishing Service.

Johnson G and Chamberlain C (2008) From youth to adult homelessness. *Australian Journal of Social Issues* 43(4): 563–582.

Johnson G, Gronda H, and Coutts S (2008) *On the Outside: Pathways in and Out of Homelessness*. Melbourne: Australian Scholarly Press.

Mallett S, Rosenthal D, and Keys D (2005) Young people, drug use and family conflict: Pathways into homelessness. *Journal of Adolescence* 28: 185–199.

Martijn C and Sharpe L (2006) Pathways to youth homelessness. *Social Science and Medicine* 62: 1–12.

National Committee for the Evaluation of the Youth Services Support Scheme (1983) *One Step Forward: Youth Homelessness and Emergency Accommodation Services*. Canberra: Australian Government Publishing Services.

Neil C and Fopp R (1993) *Homelessness in Australia: Causes and Consequences*. Melbourne: CSIRO.

Pinkney S and Ewing S (1997) *Responding to Youth Homelessness: The Economic Costs and Benefits of School-Based Early Intervention*. Melbourne: Centre for Youth Affairs Research and Development in Association with the Queens Trust for Young Australians.

Rosenthal D, Mallett S, and Myers P (2006) Why do young people leave home? *Australian and New Zealand Journal of Public Health* 30(3): 281–285.

Further Reading

Milburn N, Rosenthal D, Rotheram-Borus MJ, et al. (2007) Newly homeless youth typically return home. *Journal of Adolescent Health* 40: 574–576.

Senate Standing Committee on Social Welfare (1982) *Report on Youth Homelessness*. Canberra: Australian Government Printing Service.

Homeless People: Youth in the United Kingdom

D Quilgars, University of York, York, UK

© 2012 Elsevier Ltd. All rights reserved.

Glossary

Floating support services Services delivered by visiting workers to young people (and other types of households) living in their own homes. Floating support services are primarily designed to support households with maintaining their accommodation through helping people to budget, pay bills, be good neighbours, and so on.

Hidden homeless People who have not been accepted as statutorily homeless by a local authority and are also not utilising formal provision such as hostels for young people. People staying with friends or relatives on a temporary basis, often sleeping on the sofa or floor and frequently moving between different addresses ('sofa surfing').

Homeless and in priority need ('statutorily homeless') Across the United Kingdom, homelessness legislation (Part 7 of the Housing Act 1996, England and Wales; Homelessness Etc. Act 2003, Scotland) places a range of duties and powers on local authorities to assist people who are homeless or likely to become homeless within 28 days. Local authorities have a duty to secure accommodation for households who are eligible for assistance, homeless through no fault of their own, and have a priority need for accommodation. Young people aged 16–17 years (and care leavers aged 18–20 years) are a priority need group in England, Scotland, and Wales; this also includes young people at risk of financial or sexual exploitation (Scotland, Wales, Northern Ireland) and 18–20-year-olds involved in substance misuse (Scotland).

Housing options 'Housing options' services is a term used to describe a general, nonstatutory service which many local authorities provide to assist people seeking help with accommodation. Housing options services will often include services to prevent homelessness. In many local authorities, duties under the homelessness legislation are delivered as part of a housing options service.

Private rented sector Any residential accommodation provided at a market rent by a private landlord (individual or organisation).

Social housing Publicly subsidised housing usually provided at submarket rent levels under, for example, a secure tenancy provided by a local authority or an assured tenancy provided by a registered social landlord/housing association.

Temporary accommodation This term is often used to refer to accommodation provided under the homelessness legislation which is not settled accommodation. The term 'temporary accommodation' also has a more general meaning, and can include bed-and-breakfast accommodation, hostels, or other forms of accommodation intended to be temporary or short term.

Introduction

The article reviews the cases of 16–24-year-olds (single people, couples, and families with children) who experience, or are at risk of experiencing, homelessness in the United Kingdom. In this article, homelessness is defined as the condition of those who are without any shelter ('roofless'), as well as those without a settled place to stay (including those living in temporary provision such as hostels and unsuitable or insecure accommodation (e.g., squats), and those staying temporarily with friends or relatives, 'the hidden homeless').

This article draws heavily upon a recent review conducted by the voluntary organisation, Centrepoint, and funded by the Joseph Rowntree Foundation. The review was coauthored with Sarah Johnsen and Nicholas Pleace.

The Scale of Youth Homelessness

As is the case with the homeless population generally, data on youth homelessness are partial and limited. Estimates of the scale of youth homelessness are based on the numbers of young people utilising certain formal services and/or approaching the local authority as homeless. They do not include the 'hidden homeless' such as young people staying temporarily with friends or relatives.

A recent UK-wide review estimated that at least 75 000 young people experienced homelessness in the United Kingdom in 2006/2007 (Quilgars et al., 2008). This figure comprised:

- 43 000 people aged 16–24 years who were accepted under the homelessness legislation (across the whole of the United Kingdom);

- 31 000 people aged 16–24 years using other homelessness services including hostels and floating support services under the Supporting People Programme. The Supporting People Programme ran from 2003 to 2011. Local administrative authorities, via a central government grant, funded accommodation and housing-related support for a range of vulnerable households. This grant is now part of local authorities Area Based Grant (England, Scotland, and Wales only);
- 2400 single homeless 16–24-year-olds rehoused by housing associations (this figure overlaps to a degree with the Supporting People statistics); and
- at least several hundred others experiencing rough sleeping during the course of a year (this figure is also likely to overlap with other statistics).

The prevalence of youth homelessness varies across the United Kingdom. Table 1 depicts the proportion of young people accepted as statutorily homeless in 2006/07 per 1000 people in the same age bracket in the general population, indicating that rates were highest in Scotland (at 15.1 per thousand 16–24-year-olds), followed by Wales (8.2), with lower levels in England (4.9) and Northern Ireland (4.8).

The number of young people accepted as statutorily homeless in the United Kingdom has changed significantly over the past decade, as shown in Table 2. The expansion of age-related priority need groups (most notably inclusion of 16- and 17-year-olds in England, Scotland, and Wales) led to an increase in the number of young people accepted as statutorily homeless in the early 2000s. Levels subsequently dropped in England and Wales – with these trends generally being attributed to the impact of preventative initiatives (see below). Levels of statutory youth homelessness have not altered notably in either Scotland or Northern Ireland.

Who is Young and Homeless?

Homelessness statistics reveal that young women continue to outnumber young men in statutory homelessness acceptances, while young men (over the

Table 1 Annual statutory youth homelessness during 2006–07 relative to mid-2006 estimates of total populations of young people (United Kingdom)

	England	Scotland	Wales	Northern Ireland[a]	United Kingdom
Acceptances 16–17-year-olds	5652	1871	686	182	8391
Population	1 322 800	128 400	79 700	51 900	1 582 800
Rate per thousand	4.27	14.57	8.6	3.5	5.3
Acceptances of young people aged 16–24 years	29 937	9132	2927	1079	43 075
Population	6 028 800	602 100	358 100	254 700	7 243 700
Rate per thousand	4.9	15.1	8.2	4.8	5.7

[a]Figures are for 16–24-year-olds for England, Wales, and Scotland, but are for 16–25-year-olds for Northern Ireland.
Source: Reported and Grossed P1E Statistics (England), HL1 statistics (Scotland), WHO-12 statistics (Wales), Northern Ireland Housing Executive and Office for National Statistics mid-2006 population estimates for England, Scotland, Wales, and Northern Ireland. Quilgars D, Johnsen S, and Pleace N (2008) Youth Homelessness in the UK: A Decade of Progress? p. 14. York: Joseph Rowntree Foundation.

Table 2 Annual numbers of households accepted as unintentionally statutorily homeless in which the applicant was a young person (United Kingdom)

Year	England	Scotland	Wales	Northern Ireland	United Kingdom
1997/98	35 972[a]	5400[a]	1636[a]	770	43 778[a]
1998/99	36 704[a]	5800[a]	1733[a]	818	45 055[a]
1999/00	37 232[a]	6500[a]	1460[a]	653	45 845[a]
2000/01	40 868[a]	6700[a]	1756[a]	824	50 148[a]
2001/02	**41 664**[a]	**8500**[a]	**2133**[a]	1002	**53 299**[a]
2002/03	**51 416**[a]	**8684**	**2772**	1096	**63 968**[a]
2003/04	**54 172**[a]	**8998**	**3732**	1170	**68 072**[a]
2004/05	**48 344**[a]	**9044**	**3982**	1073	**62 443**[a]
2005/06	**36 765**	**9447**	**3203**	1052	**50 467**
2006/07	**29 937**	**9132**	**2927**	1079	**43 075**[a]

[a]Estimated based on available data. Figures for Northern Ireland are for 16–25-year-olds.
Bold figures indicate period following homelessness legislative change.
Source: Reported and Grossed P1E returns, HL1 returns, WHO-2 returns, Northern Ireland Housing Statistics. Quilgars D, Johnsen S, and Pleace N (2008) Youth Homelessness in the UK: A Decade of Progress? p. 29. York: Joseph Rowntree Foundation.

age of 18) are more likely to be nonstatutorily homeless. With regard to ethnicity, statutory homeless households headed by a 16–24-year-old are very unlikely to be a minority ethnic household in Scotland, Wales, or Northern Ireland. Ethnic minority households, particularly black/black British or mixed households, are however significantly overrepresented among homeless people in England, especially London.

Youth homelessness has traditionally been thought of as involving lone teenagers and young people in their early twenties. This group remains significant, but many statutorily homeless young people, especially those in the 18-and-over age bracket, have dependent children. A recent nationally representative survey of more than 3000 statutorily homeless families in England revealed that nearly one-third (32%) were headed by someone under the age of 25 years (Pleace et al., 2008b).

Reasons for Youth Homelessness

It is generally accepted that youth homelessness is a result of a complex interaction between structural factors and individual circumstances. Economic and social changes including the withdrawal of income support from 16- and 17-year-olds, reductions in social housing stock, as well as increases in family breakdowns in society were considered central to the overall growth of homelessness among young people in the late 1980s and early 1990s (Carlen, 1996; Evans, 1996). Difficulties in accessing affordable housing, particularly given the competition for limited social housing stock and barriers to accessing accommodation in the private rented sector, are commonly identified as ongoing contributory factors to youth homelessness (Quilgars et al., 2008).

Within this context, the main immediate reason for homelessness among young people is relationship breakdown with parents or carers – this being the case for 65% of the respondents in a recent survey of young people accepted as statutorily homeless 16–17-year-olds in England (Pleace et al., 2008). Research has also identified specific characteristics or 'risk factors' that are considered to heighten a young person's likelihood of experiencing homelessness (e.g., Randall and Brown, 2002; Smith, 2003) including:

- family disruption (due to parental separation or divorce and/or the arrival of a stepparent);
- difficulty getting on with parents or stepparents;
- witnessing or experiencing violence within the family home;
- living in a family experiencing financial difficulties;
- running away from home;
- spending time in care;
- being involved in crime or antisocial behaviour; and
- having their education severely disrupted (e.g., been suspended or excluded from school).

Impact of Homelessness

Homelessness often compounds the already very difficult circumstances of young people coming from disadvantaged backgrounds. Although the cause and the effect are difficult to ascertain, homelessness has been shown to impact negatively on people's health, drug use, education and employment outcomes, involvement in illegal and dangerous activities, and motivation and confidence levels:

- One-third of statutorily homeless 16–17-year-olds reported that they suffered from depression, anxiety, or other mental health problems – a rate approximately three times that of the general population the same age (Pleace et al., 2008a).
- The onset of drug use, and/or increased consumption of illicit substances, has been associated with the experience of homelessness (Wincup et al., 2003).
- Young people are vulnerable to sexual assault, violence, and crime if they spend time on the street (Raws, 2001). People may also commit crimes in order to survive, ranging from petty theft to involvement in the illegal sex industry (Wardhaugh, 2000).
- Fifty-seven percent of statutorily homeless 16–17-year-olds were not in education, employment, or training, including a third of those who had discontinued their participation in education, employment, or training since leaving their last home (Pleace et al., 2008b).
- Young people's social networks may be fractured as they often have to move away from their previous home area to access support services (Lemos and Durkacz, 2002).
- Many report feeling that their lives are 'on hold' when living in temporary accommodation and negotiating their way through the homeless 'system' (Pleace et al., 2008b).

Research also shows that homeless services can have positive impacts on young people including:

- Temporary accommodation may be associated with increased feelings of safety as young people are distanced from abusive relationships (Pleace et al., 2008).
- Some young people report an improvement in their access to social support after leaving home, often due to the involvement of professional support workers (Pleace et al., 2008b).

Responses to Youth Homelessness

A Strengthened Safety Net and a Focus on Preventing Homelessness

As outlined above, in recent years, the housing safety net for vulnerable young people has been strengthened via the expansion of homeless priority need groups in three of the four UK countries. However, evidence suggests that young people continue to find the experience of homelessness assessment intimidating, and commonly report feeling confused, misunderstood, and/or powerless when navigating the homelessness 'system'. Agencies and young people have called for more widespread provision of dedicated housing officers for young people (Quilgars et al., 2008).

In addition, policies to prevent homelessness have been strongly promoted across the United Kingdom, particularly in England. This has resulted in a significant shift in responses to youth homelessness, with a greater focus on prevention and helping young people before they need to present as homeless under the legislation via a 'housing options' approach. This shift has generally been welcomed although there have been some concerns that some young people might be encouraged (or forced) to remain or return home when it was not safe for them to do so.

The prevention agenda had led to an expansion in initiatives that focus on making early interventions, especially family mediation schemes which attempt to improve parent–child relationships enabling young people to return home (or at least gain support in independent living). Research has suggested that the prevention agenda should be pushed further via a greater focus on supporting the parents of young people and recognition that conflict in the home can predate the young person leaving by many years, while also recognising that preventative initiatives are not suitable for young people experiencing severe family conflict and/or violence. It is also commonly argued that effective prevention should include the creation of affordable housing pathways for young people (Quilgars et al., 2008).

Supported Accommodation Models

A range of models of temporary accommodation for young people exists in most (urban) areas. Humphreys et al. (2007) identified no less than a total of 21 models available to young people in the United Kingdom, differentiated by stated aims, length of stay, level of support, and type of accommodation (e.g., whether dispersed or single site). Foyers for young people are an established form of provision that offer both temporary accommodation and access to support with employment, training, and education. A range of different short-term hostels and medium-term supported accommodation is also provided across the United Kingdom. Supporting lodging schemes, where young people stay with a trained host household, are a relatively recent model for young homeless people in the United Kingdom.

There is, however, a lack of clarity regarding whether accommodation for young people should be viewed as 'temporary' (aiming to move them on as soon as possible), or more deliberately 'transitional' (offering a more settled environment in which young people can gain life skills). Generally, there seemed to be more support from providers and young people for specialist transitional accommodation for younger age groups without dependents, particularly teenagers. In contrast, extended stays in temporary accommodation for older age groups were often experienced as problematic (Quilgars et al., 2008).

Gaps in emergency accommodation provision have been identified in some areas of the United Kingdom, especially for young people with complex needs. While the incidence of long-term rough sleeping among young people has diminished dramatically since the 1990s, there is some evidence that a significant minority of young people continue to experience short periods of rooflessness before accessing accommodation either because young people lack information on options or because emergency accommodation was not available in their local area.

While some supported housing models have been evaluated, there remains a significant gap in the evidence base of 'what works well' for young homeless people.

Longer-Term Accommodation and Support

Shortages of available longer-term housing have meant that young people often stay in temporary accommodation for many months or years. Young people without children are a low priority for social housing. Support providers often try to facilitate young people's access to the private rented sector, although high rents, lack of deposits, limited benefits (particularly the 'single room rent restrictions' where single young people can usually only claim benefits for one room), and limited security of tenure are often seen as problems of access and sustainability.

For young people who had moved on into settled housing, research has indicated that floating support services are generally effective in improving levels of tenancy sustainment. Providers increasingly seek to complement these by (re)building young people's social support networks, for example, via mentoring and befriending schemes. Supporting young people into education, employment, and training is also a key priority, although the welfare benefit system often creates financial barriers to studying or working full-time.

The recent UK-wide review indicated that there have been significant improvements in operational joint working across different sectors at the local level in the last decade (Quilgars et al., 2008). There have been particular successes in coordinating services for 16–17-year-olds and young people who had been looked after. However, concerns remained for those aged 18 and over (without children) who had little priority under the homelessness legislation.

Conclusion

There have been considerable improvements in youth homelessness policy and provision in the United Kingdom over the last decade, including reductions in the numbers of young people experiencing homelessness. However, youth homelessness continues to exist on a significant scale and young homeless people remain a highly vulnerable group. Within this, the diversity of needs and circumstances of young people need to be recognised, focusing on the very young, other single people as well as young families. A range of supported housing provision has been developed for this group, but greater attention is needed on the role of any transitional accommodation. Fundamentally, a challenge remains as to how to create more affordable housing pathways for young people. This challenge is likely to continue into the future with public spending cuts and a further shift away from social housing under the current new coalition government.

See also: Homeless People: Care Leavers; Homeless People: Care Leavers in the United Kingdom; Homeless People: Youth in Australia.

References

Carlen P (1996) *Jigsaw: A Political Criminology of Youth Homelessness*. Buckingham, UK: Open University Press.
Evans A (1996) *'We Don't Choose to be Homeless – The Inquiry into Preventing Youth Homelessness'*. London: CHAR.
Humphreys C, Stirling T, Inkson S, and Delaney A (2007) *A Study of Models of Accommodation and Support for Young Single Homeless People*. Cardiff, UK: WAG.
Lemos G and Durkacz S (2002) *Dreams Deferred: The Families and Friends of Homeless and Vulnerable People*. London: Lemos and Crane.
Pleace N, Fitzpatrick S, Johnson S, Quilgars D, and Sanderson D (2008a) *Family Homelessness in England*. London: Communities and Local Government.
Pleace N, Fitzpatrick S, Johnsen S, Quilgars D, and Sanderson D (2008b) *Statutorily Homelessness in England: The Experiences of Families and 16–17 Year Olds*. London: CLG.
Quilgars D, Johnsen S, and Pleace N (2008) *Youth Homelessness in the UK: A Decade of Progress?* York, UK: Joseph Rowntree Foundation.
Randall G and Brown S (2002) *Trouble at Home: Family Conflict, Young People and Homelessness*. London: Crisis.
Raws P (2001) *Lost Youth: Young Runaways in Northern Ireland*. Belfast, UK: Children's Society.
Smith J (2003) *Who is at Risk of Homelessness in North Staffordshire? A Study of Young Homeless People and their Pasts*. Stoke-on-Trent, UK: Centre for Housing and Community Research, Staffordshire University.
Wardhaugh J (2000) *Sub City: Young People, Homelessness and Crime*. Aldershot, UK: Ashgate.
Wincup E, Buckland G, and Bayliss R (2003) *Youth Homelessness and Substance Use: Report to the Drugs and Alcohol Research Unit*. London: Home Office.

Further Reading

Communities and Local Government (2007) *Tackling Youth Homelessness – Policy Briefing 18*. London: Communities and Local Government.
Fitzpatrick S (2000) *Young Homeless People*. Basingstoke, UK: Macmillan.
Heath S (2008) *Housing Choices and Issues for Young People in the UK*. York, UK: Joseph Rowntree Foundation.
Pawson H, Netto G, and Jones C (2006) *Homelessness Prevention: A Guide to Good Practice*. London: DCLG.
Smith J, Gilford S, and O'Sullivan A (1998) *The Family Background of Homeless Young People*. London: Family Policy Studies Centre.

Homeowners' Associations in Post-Socialist Countries

J Hegedüs, Metropolitan Research Institute, Budapest, Hungary

© 2012 Elsevier Ltd. All rights reserved.

Glossary

Condominium A unit in a multiunit building where the owner, usually the occupant, has the right, along with other owners, to use the common areas. Elements such as exterior walls, floors, or structural systems are owned by condominium associations. There are usually association fees for upkeep and maintenance, taxes and insurance, and reserves for improvements.

Homeowners' associations Legal entities created to maintain common areas, where membership is typically mandatory for property owners. Associations are also responsible for maintenance and enforcing standards in accordance with national law.

Housing cooperatives Collective housing organisations in which members (or shareholders) participate in the governance of the property. Such organisations typically run on a not-for-profit basis in order to provide goods and services for members at the lowest practical cost.

Housing privatisation Housing privatisation in transition societies meant the sale of public rental housing units to sitting tenants at favourable prices. In some countries, privatisation was supported by right-to-buy legislation (e.g., in Hungary) or under the discretion of municipalities, the typical owner of public housing stock (e.g., the Czech Republic).

Quorum In the case of housing/condominium associations, a minimum number of owners is necessary to make management decisions related to the maintenance and renewal. Various types of quorum are needed for different kinds of decisions (ordinary maintenance, fee structure, property rights, etc.) according to each national legal structure.

Transition society A society which is changing from a centrally planned economy to a free market one. Transition societies undergo economic liberalisation, where market forces set prices rather than being centrally planned, trade barriers are removed, government-owned enterprises and resources are privatised, and a multiparty political system is created.

Introduction

As a consequence of urbanisation in the nineteenth and twentieth centuries, high density became a determining factor of construction policies as land became scarce and expensive. The typical building type in most contexts was the multistorey tenement house with rental apartments owned by the developers and/or by investors. The regulatory foundations of multiunit buildings were very sketchy in the first decades of the twentieth century, and a new legal structure for coownership was needed for housing investment in cities in order to manage the problem of common ownership. Individual owners typically had exclusive property rights to their apartment but had to share ownership (rights and responsibilities) of common parts of the buildings with other owners. The legal structure has had to provide for easy and flexible entrance into the building, to regulate the decisions related to the common parts, to reasonably limit the property rights of individual owners, and to manage conflicts among owners over decisions about the level of maintenance, use of the common areas, and so on.

In developed countries, two major types of legal forms emerged: 'cooperative arrangements' and 'condominium arrangements'. The basic difference between these types is that the cooperative is the legal entity and individual rights are more limited. In the case of condominiums, each owner holds an individual title to their condominium unit while sharing ownership of common facilities. Housing cooperatives are typically organisations owned and controlled by member-users for the benefit of members, usually on a not-for-profit basis, in order to provide necessary goods and services at the lowest practical cost. Housing/apartment cooperatives and condominium management may differ in terms of taxation as well depending on the legal and fiscal system of the given country. Generally, cooperatives are nonprofit organisations, which may enjoy tax advantages, although in some systems condominiums have the same tax positions. One of the most important elements of the regulation is how decisions are made on the maintenance and development of common parts of the property and how possible conflicts among owners are managed.

In the context of transition societies, the development of homeowners' associations has been complicated first by the appropriation of much of the housing stock during the communist period and second by the privatisation of urban housing estates during the postsocialist transition. Many countries experienced a rapid shift from mass state ownership to more than 90% of the housing stock becoming privately owned. The transfer of management from public authorities to different forms of homeowner associations (condominiums, housing cooperatives, etc.) has generated numerous social and management problems and is the focus of the rest of this article.

Multiunit Buildings in the Eastern European Housing Model

After the Second World War, the existing urban housing stock was typically nationalised and transferred into state or municipal ownership in most socialist countries. Nonetheless, regulation varied, and not all existing multiunit buildings were nationalised after the communist takeover. In some countries, for example, in Bulgaria and East Germany, nationalisation was limited but control over the property rights of private owners was strictly regulated through allocation and price/rent control. In Hungary, only buildings with more than six units were nationalised, although the private rental sector was placed under the control of council authorities. Consequently, in the socialist period, two main types of multiunit buildings can be differentiated: the inner city tenement housing built before the Second World War and the 'new' apartment buildings built on housing estates. However, various forms of joint ownership that have persisted are partial remnants of the presocialist period. For example, condominiums (which were a legal form of multiunit building from the 1920s) in Hungary were reintroduced and became an important form of private housing investment in cities (**Table 1**).

In socialist housing systems, new urban housing investments were dominated by multiunit high-rise buildings in housing estates located, typically, in the outer rings of cities. By the end of the 1960s, prefabricated construction technology had become standard and remained the most popular form of urban housing development until the end of the 1980s (even though prefabricated housing construction in other developed countries had ceased by the middle of the 1970s). As a consequence, in a typical socialist city, this type of building accounted for 60% of the urban stock by the end of the communist period. The legal forms of new construction varied across countries: public (state, municipal, and enterprise) housing, different versions of 'cooperative' housing, or even condominiums. Multiunit buildings were managed by state-owned companies or housing cooperatives, which operated in very similar ways to state companies. Tenants and owners had very little influence on the decision-making of management companies (e.g., about the level of maintenance and renewal), but as a consequence of the socialist housing system, housing costs were kept very low.

The quality of the high-rise prefab housing estates built between 1960 and 1980 varies greatly between different postsocialist countries. Broadly speaking, the former Yugoslavia, Hungary, and Czechoslovakia represent countries with higher-quality buildings, while Moldova, Russia, and Bulgaria constitute the other end of the spectrum. One extreme case is the five-storey apartment buildings in Russia known as 'khrushchevki'. These were built in the 1960s with minimum construction expenses and low-quality thresholds. Apartments were small and had very low ceilings (the norm was a two-room apartment of 40–45 m^2 and 2.2 m in height). The other extreme was the housing estates in ex-Yugoslavia, which represent the highest standard among the socialist countries in respect of housing estates. Quality also fluctuated even within each country. For instance, the housing estates built in Hungary in the 1970s had lower standards than housing estates built in the 1980s. Generally speaking, high-rise, prefab housing estates have come to represent the deteriorated parts of the urban housing stock. Moreover, housing has long been neglected and much is now in urgent need of repair. Management companies have particularly neglected stock maintenance on 'new' housing estates, and in some cases no

Table 1 Share of dwellings in multifamily and single-family buildings (around 2000)

	Total	Multifamily	Single family	Year
Czech Republic	3828	2196	1632	2000
Estonia	626	567	59	2004
Hungary	4043	1674	2369	2001
Latvia	1042	744	298	2009
Romania	7659	3417	4242	2000
Slovakia	1665	845	820	2000
Slovenia	777	416	361	2000
Croatia	1419	652	767	2001

Source: Housing Statistics in the European Union (2010).
For Romania Country Profile (UNECE), Croatia: Census 2001.

Table 2 Estimated proportion of dwellings in central and eastern Europe located in large housing estates (in %)

Country	Built between 1960 and 1990	Percentage of all existing dwellings, 1990
Bulgaria	55	27
GDR	48	18
Poland	61	35
Romania	49	26
CSSR	64	56
Hungary	52	29

Source: Knorr-Siedow T (1996) Present and future outlook for large housing estates. European Academy of the Urban Environment and Institute for Regional Development and Structural Planning. Available at URL: http://www.eaue.de/Housing/housfut.htm

maintenance has been provided for condominium buildings since the very beginning of their existence, since they have continued to be regarded as new stock. The other general characteristic of the communist period housing was the low level of energy efficiency.

Urban housing estates occupied a special status in the socialist housing system (**Table 2**). They were well located, typically had a high level of infrastructure (roads, schools, health institutions, etc.), and were well connected by transportation. However, the quality of the housing was poor, largely because of the application of prefab technology. While there has been a danger of fast downgrading both in technical and social terms, it has not taken place because these housing estates have often maintained their relatively good image and social mix even after two decades of transition.

Mass Privatisation and Its Consequences

After the collapse of the socialist system in 1989 and 1990, a relatively universal mass privatisation (and restitution) programme took place. More than 80% of the public housing stock was privatised, typically at a low price (giveaway privatisation), which created a new situation with regard to the management of multiunit buildings. The privatisation of the public housing stock was not always accompanied with proper change in the regulatory framework for new condominiums. The poorly regulated privatisation was also responsible for disputes concerning land ownership and the proprietary rights of the different facilities attached to the condominium. There were different solutions. The worst cases were where individual units were privatised but the common property remained in state ownership, for example, in Albania, Georgia, and Serbia. In other countries, even if a legal framework for coownership existed, either the setup of condominiums or the membership for housing associations was not compulsory, which led to conflicts over the maintenance of common areas, for example, in Moldova, Lithuania, and Romania. In other countries, a legal framework for condominium ownership had already existed; however, it did not guarantee their smooth operation due to the lack of means to enforce the law. In the past 20 years, almost every transition country has introduced important changes for the regulation of condominiums.

The legislation of the Russian Federation illustrates the dynamics of such changes. Condominium (homeowners') associations were created by law in 1996, but membership was voluntary, as the Russian Federation Constitutional Court deemed compulsory membership a violation of the right to free association. The new Housing Code implemented in 2005 made membership obligatory for all apartment owners, in order to improve the self-organisation of management and maintenance of multifamily buildings. Consequently, condominium associations started to become a more common type of housing management. For example, according to St. Petersburg's Housing Committee, 25% of the city's housing stock was managed by homeowners' associations by the spring of 2006.

However, the management of multiunit buildings has changed not only because of privatisation but also because of the transformation of management companies. In most countries, a process of 'management privatisation' started where control over the common facilities and infrastructure of multiunit buildings (common parts like elevators, staircase, etc.) has been devolved from local governments to tenants organised in condominium-like homeowners' associations.

Social and Economic Issues in the Management of Housing Associations

As a consequence of privatisation and the transformation of property management after the transition, the owners of apartments – having different financial and cultural backgrounds and different aspirations – faced new challenges in how to manage buildings (how to make plans, set up budgets, allocate the costs, collect the fees, etc.). Other issues concerned how to build cooperation among owners in the area of maintenance, renovation, and common use and how to organise community-based decision-making.

These activities were unknown during the socialist period, and the new owners – who typically lacked knowledge and experience in property management – had to develop the capacity to deal with these issues within emerging legal and institutional frameworks. In many transitional countries, after privatisation, many new owners were able to operate homeowners' associations efficiently, but improvement was very slow due to ineffective legal regulations, lack of effective support or incentives, and, in some cases, the voluntary nature of such associations. The social conflicts generated by the transition can be broadly grouped under three headings: rules of decision-making processes, organisation of the management, and financing operation and renovation.

Decision-Making (Representing Owners' Interests)

The good management of the multiunit condominium buildings requires clear and reasonable rules. One of the most important elements of the condominium legal framework is the regulation of the voting system with regard to the different types of decisions related to the property. The voting system has to guarantee the participation of all owners in all relevant decisions concerning the property and its administration. There are different views on the efficiency of various solutions. The requirement of unanimous support for decisions concerning major renovations (including energy-saving investments) could easily block important investments required for proper maintenance and renovation. There are many different rules about majority voting – simple or qualified (two-thirds, three-quarters, etc.), which may also involve certain risks. For instance, the simple majority rule may cause hardship for low-income owners and may force them out of the condominium, because they cannot afford higher maintenance fees.

The minimum requirements necessary to form a quorum in assembly meetings also play an important role in the regulation of condominiums. One dilemma that presents itself is that, in the case of high quorum requirements, it is difficult to make decisions, whereas with low level of quorum requirements, there is a danger that minority interests are not respected. Another important issue concerns the everyday decisions made by the executive committee of the board of owners. How much power the board has and how the activity of the board is controlled by the assembly can become a sensitive political issue.

Management of Condominiums

The management of multiunit buildings was broadly restructured after transition, but different countries followed different paths. At one extreme (e.g., in Russia and Serbia), state management companies continued to have a monopoly on managing buildings in housing estates, which typically led to under-maintenance and huge dissatisfaction among residents. Gradually, owners of new condominiums have asserted their right to organise maintenance, but they have to compete with public companies. At the other end of the scale (e.g., Romania and Hungary), the new condominium buyers, through the elected board of owners, have the right and responsibility to organise the management of the buildings, and therefore, public companies have lost their monopoly on management. This solution has also led to under-maintenance because of the lack of professional knowledge and shortsighted interests in decreasing maintenance fees. It is not rare that condominiums are managed by individual owners that underuse professional service providers. Modifications in the legislation of condominiums have tended to address this problem by prescribing the mandatory use of professionals, and there have been different programmes to increase the management capacity of new condominium managers: typically by offering them training, licensing administrators, and so on.

Renovation of High-Rise Housing Estates and Mortgages for Condominiums

As a result of transformations in the management and maintenance of condominiums, the existing multiunit housing stock has been rapidly deteriorating in the last two decades, calling for urgent investment in, or even a complete overhaul of, elevators, installations, roofs, and facades. However, most renovation has primarily aimed at energy saving, with thermal refurbishment becoming a particularly important issue in transitional countries. In many societies, current legal arrangements for ownership of common housing assets do not provide adequate incentives and enforcement for households to invest in their property in this way.

As a consequence of privatisation, many new owners were poor and thus unable to pay the cost of required renovations. In this respect, even a well-designed regulatory framework for condominiums could not have prevented this housing stock from major deterioration without state intervention. Realising the social importance of the efficient operation of housing estates, subsidy programmes were initiated. In Estonia, for example, in 2003, Kredex (state bank) started a programme supporting the thermal rehabilitation of multiunit buildings. Lending for housing cooperatives and associations has also been supported by municipalities (e.g., in Tallinn, Paide, and Rakvere). Similar programmes were implemented in Hungary and Romania.

Opportunity and access to mortgage finance is a crucial condition majoring the rehabilitation of housing estates. For major repairs, condominium owners need to take out loans, but typically mortgage collateral can only be used for individual units. Furthermore, in a typical case, owners are not collectively willing to pledge their individual properties as collateral on a loan, which blocks the renovation of the housing stock. The proper regulation of the financial operation of condominiums in some contexts makes it possible to take loans against the cash flow of the condominium, but in this case there need to be clear and effective procedures to prevent nonpayments. This approach is used in Estonia and Hungary.

Affordability and Enforcement Issues

Affordability (ability to pay housing costs) has become one of the most critical issues in postsocialist transition countries. Because of price liberalisation, the average cost of housing has increased significantly resulting in hardship for most households (10–20% of households in transition economies currently struggle with problems of payment arrears). The household adjustment to the increased housing cost has been even more problematic in the case of multiunit buildings, where the cost level is determined by the assembly of the owners, and individual owners have limited room to manoeuvre when trying to decrease costs. Mass privatisation enhanced this problem because many poor households (who had cheap rents and no maintenance costs) became homeowners and have had to face increasing expenses. The problem of free riding has also appeared due to both the lack of financial resources among homeowners and also the reluctance of many individuals to pay collective costs, causing tension between condominium members.

Energy costs have been a particular source of contention as many multiunit condominium buildings inherited collective heating systems from the socialist construction era. District heating systems are normally highly inefficient and expensive, and many poor owners have difficulty paying these costs. Many condominium owners' associations have sought alternative solutions to collective heating systems, that is, separating the building's (or the individual apartment's) heating from the common system. Service providers have also had difficulty enforcing payments. Generally speaking, with enforcement being inadequate, both condominium associations and service providers have had to develop solutions in order to reach financial sustainability. Innovations in legal regulations have made it possible for some condominiums to enforce the collection of payments by putting a loan on the property of an indebted owner (in Hungary) or selling the unit of an indebted owner through a compulsory sale in order to cover the unpaid costs (former East Germany). However, these options are not always viable if too many owners are in debt. Service providers (district heating, water and sewage, and garbage collection) can disconnect or discontinue services in case of arrears. However, they do so not only for the nonpaying owner but for the whole condominium block. This may well force the community of owners to solve the problem of nonpayment.

Conclusions

Regulation and management of multiunit buildings became a critical element of the housing system in transitional societies. This was largely because of inadequate maintenance in the socialist period and the financial/legal problems emerging in the transition process. Due to the lack of a clear legal framework, proper financial incentives, and enforcement of the laws, the future of the housing estates has become one of the most important issues of the housing system. The quality of apartments has become quite poor in many cases. Nevertheless, because of their good location and high level of housing services offered, a general mass deterioration has not taken place. It is hoped that the improvement of the management, the opening up of affordable finance possibilities, and the improved legal framework will provide an opportunity for mass renovation of this special stock.

See also: Cooperative Housing/Ownership; Maintenance and Repair.

Further Reading

Bank C, O'Leary S, and Rabenhorst C (1996) Privatized Housing and the Development of Condominiums in Central and Eastern Europe: The Cases of Poland, Hungary, Slovakia, and Romania. *Review of Urban & Regional Development Studies* 8(2): 137–155.

Economic Commission for Europe, United Nations (2003) *Guidelines on Condominium Ownership of Housing for Countries in Transition*. New York and Geneva: UNECE.

Gruis V, Tsenkova S, and Nieboer N (eds.) (2009) *Management of Privatised Social Housing: International Policies and Practice*. Wiley-Blackwell.

Hegedüs J and Teller N (2003) *Management of the Housing Stock in South-Eastern Europe Prepared for the Joint Programme Council of Europe – Council of Europe Development Bank to the preparation of a High Level Conference on Housing in Southern Europe MRI*.

Knorr-Siedow T (1996) *Present and future outlook for large housing estates*. European Academy of the Urban Environment and Institute for Regional Development and Structural Planning. Available at URL: http://www.eaue.de/Housing/housfut.htm (accessed 30 October 2011).

Lujanen M (2011) Legal challenges in managing privatized apartment buildings. Ministry of the Environment, Finland, June 3, 2009. Downloaded 9/1/2011. Available at URL: http://www.soc.cas.cz/download/896/paper_lujanen_17.pdf (accessed 30 October 2011).

Mais V (2004) Housing policy in Armenia. *Condominium Activity Working Paper No. 04/10*. Local Government Program USAID/Urban Institute.

Rabenhorst C., Ignatova SI (2009) Condominium housing and mortgage lending in emerging markets – Constraints and opportunities. *IDG Working Paper No. 2009-04 June*.

Roerup K (1998) Homeowners' associations – A new framework for housing in Lithuania. *Facilities* 16(11): 302–305.

Relevant Websites

http://en.wikipedia.org/wiki/Housing_cooperative – A housing cooperative is a legal entity

http://en.wikipedia.org/wiki/Homeowner_association – A site about homeowner associations

http://en.wikipedia.org/wiki/Condominium – A site about the form of housing

http://en.wikipedia.org/wiki/List_of_house_types – A site on the list of house types

http://unece.org/hlm/welcome.html – United Nations Economic Commission for Europe

Homestead and Other Legal Protections

DB Barros, Widener University School of Law, Harrisburg, PA, USA

© 2012 Elsevier Ltd. All rights reserved.

Glossary

Eminent domain The governmental power to expropriate property; many legal systems require that fair compensation be paid to the property owner for the loss of their property.

Expropriation A seizure of property, typically by a governmental actor.

Lien A type of security interest.

Security interest An interest in property used to secure an obligation. Typically, a security interest is granted (sometimes voluntarily and sometimes involuntarily) by a debtor to a creditor. If the debtor defaults on her obligations, the creditor may use the security interest to access the debtor's property to satisfy the debt.

Tenancy by the entirety A form of property ownership found in some common-law jurisdictions. Only married people can hold property by the entirety. In some jurisdictions, the practical effect of the tenancy by the entirety is that a creditor of one spouse cannot reach property held by the entirety to satisfy a debt.

Introduction

In many legal contexts, homes are given more legal protection than other types of property. This additional protection can be divided into three categories. First, possessory rights in a home might be given more protection than possessory rights in another kind of property. For example, a legal system might make it more difficult for a creditor to force the sale of a home to satisfy a debt than it would be for the creditor to force the sale of another type of property (say, a commercial office building) to satisfy that same debt. Second, a legal system might economically favour ownership or possession of a home over ownership or possession of another type of property. For example, ownership of a home might be subsidised where ownership of other types of property is not. Third, a home might be given special treatment when issues of privacy, freedom, or security are at stake. For example, a legal system might require the government to have a stronger justification for searching a home than is required for searching a commercial property.

This article focuses on the first category – those legal protections that give special protection to possessory rights in a home. It first elaborates on the distinction between rules favouring possession and the other two types of special legal protections given to homes. It then discusses various types of legal rules that give additional protection to possession of a home, including homestead rules favouring homeowners over creditors and tenure rules favouring renters over their landlords. Finally, it discusses theoretical issues related to the protection of possessory rights in homes, and considers open questions about whether this special protection is justified.

Possession, Subsidy, and Security Distinguished

The rules favouring possession discussed in this article focus on a person's entitlement to live in a particular home in a particular place. These rules may assist a resident in resisting efforts by another party to displace the resident from her home. Other types of legal rules may protect homeowners in different ways.

Legal systems may include subsidies for homeownership or home rental that are not available for other types of property. Some subsidies, such as direct payments made to support rent payments, are easy to see. Others are more subtle. Beneficial tax treatment, for example, could be given to landlords who rent to low-income people. In the United States, homeownership is subsidised through the mortgage interest tax deduction, which allows a homeowner to subtract the interest paid on a home purchase loan from her tax liabilities. These subsidies are indirectly related to possession, in that without them a resident may not be financially able to possess their home. They are distinguishable from the possessory category of rules, however, because they do not directly affect the legal right to possession.

Legal systems may also include special rules that protect privacy, liberty, or security interests in the home. Legal rules in some jurisdictions make it harder for the government to conduct a search of a home than of another type of property. Other legal rules might impose a higher penalty in criminal law for an invasion of a home than for an invasion of another type of building. In many common-law countries, these special protections are encapsulated in the maxim that 'a man's home is his castle.' The spirit of the castle doctrine is followed more extensively in some common law jurisdictions than in others. In the United States, the special role of the home as a source of individual autonomy is reflected in the Fourth Amendment to the United States Constitution ('The right of the people to be secure in their persons, houses, papers, and effects, against unreasonable searches and seizures, shall not be violated ...') and in a wide range of court decisions. The Singapore legal system, in contrast, tends not to follow the castle doctrine in legal issues surrounding the home. To the extent that they are present in a given legal system, these rules favouring autonomy and security in the home involve the ability of the resident to exclude others from the home, rather than a legal entitlement to possess a particular home.

Homestead and Other Rules Protecting Possession

Rules favouring possessory interests protect a resident's ability to remain in a particular home in a particular place. The resident's possessory interest, of course, often comes into conflict with other legitimate legal interests. The nature of these competing interests can shape the form of the legal rules favouring possession. This section considers the operation of rules favouring possession in four specific contexts, each of which presents a different set of competing interests. These contexts are (1) disputes between creditors and homeowners, (2) disputes between renters and landlords, (3) disputes over possession of a home in family law, and (4) disputes arising out of government expropriation of homes.

Creditors and Homeowners

A homeowner's possessory interest comes into conflict with a creditor's interests when the creditor seeks to have the home sold and the proceeds used to satisfy a debt. The larger category of creditors can be divided into two subparts, each presenting a different set of issues when in conflict with a homeowner.

First, a consensual, or secured, creditor obtains a security interest in the home that is voluntarily granted by the homeowner. For example, if a financial institution lends the homeowner a sum of money to be used to purchase the home, the homeowner typically grants the financial institution a security interest in the home. The express purpose of the security interest is to secure payment of the debt. If the homeowner fails to pay the debt, the creditor may exercise the security interest, often by invoking a judicial process to have the home sold.

Second, a nonconsensual, or unsecured, creditor initially has no security interest in the home, but may later obtain a lien through a judicial process if the homeowner fails to satisfy the debt. The relevant consent here is to the creditor's acquisition of the lien, not the debt itself. The homeowner might voluntarily incur consumer debt, or might instead involuntarily incur a debt, for example, by incurring liability to another person for causing an automobile accident. In either case, if the homeowner fails to repay the debt, the creditor may try to obtain an involuntary lien in the home, or otherwise use the value of the home to satisfy the debt.

Legal systems often have rules that safeguard the homeowner's possessory interest against both consensual and nonconsensual creditors. Of the two, however, consensual creditors typically have a much easier time in using the home to satisfy the unpaid debt. Consensual creditors are favoured in this context because the security interest is consensual and because protecting lenders' interests is important to the maintenance of a fully functioning housing market. Protections given to homeowners from consensual creditors are often procedural, and aimed at giving the homeowner an opportunity to pay off the debt before the home is sold in an involuntary proceeding. (These protections are often given to owners of other types of property, and are not unique to the homeownership context.) In times of widespread housing market crisis, legal systems may impose rules that temporarily or permanently give homeowners additional protection from consensual creditors.

Legal protections of homeowners from nonconsensual creditors are often more substantial. Many common-law jurisdictions have homestead laws that limit nonconsensual creditors' ability to gain access to a home to satisfy a debt. In some jurisdictions, homestead laws prevent nonconsensual creditors outright from reaching the home. In other jurisdictions, homestead laws protect a certain portion of a home's value from the creditor. Similar protections are created in some jurisdictions through legal mechanisms other than homestead legislation. For example, many jurisdictions in the United States that do not have express homestead legislation achieve a similar result in many circumstances through the recognition of an ownership status called tenancy by the entirety. Only married spouses may own property in tenancy by the entirety. In some jurisdictions that recognise the tenancy by the entirety, the home cannot be used to satisfy the debts of only one spouse. For example, if one spouse incurs a large credit card debt, or incurs substantial liability through some sort of wrongful conduct, the creditor will not be able to access a home held in tenancy by the entirety to satisfy the debt.

Homestead laws are often justified in terms of protecting the family home. Some homestead laws, like New Zealand's, are limited to homes owned by married spouses. Others, such as those enacted in Ireland and in various Canadian provinces, are further limited to protecting the marital home from debts unilaterally incurred by one spouse. These statutes operate in the same way as the tenancy by the entirety, and are motivated by a similar concern – the desire to protect the innocent spouse and the family home from the debts incurred by one irresponsible spouse. This protection, of course, comes at the costs of the creditor, who in some circumstances may be the most innocent party involved.

Landlords and Renters

A rented home is a home nonetheless. Like homeowners, renters often have a strong interest in remaining in their homes. The inherently limited duration of the rental relationship, of course, shapes the legal relationship between the renter and the landlord. It also influences the expectations of both parties. Absent a contractual agreement to the contrary, a renter's legal right to occupy a rented home will expire at the end of the rental term. A renter, however, may wish to remain in the home when the rental term expires. If the landlord objects, then a conflict arises between the interests of the renter and the landlord.

Some legal systems protect renters' possessory interest in their homes by requiring landlords, in at least some circumstances, to allow the renter to remain in possession for successive rental terms. These legal protections can have two distinct components. First, tenure rights give renters the power to remain in their homes for successive periods. Second, rent control or stabilisation provisions limit landlords' ability to raise the amount of rental payments when rental arrangements are renewed for a new term. These two components work in concert – tenure rights often will not help a renter if the landlord has the ability to raise rent to a level that the renter cannot afford. This is not to say that tenure rights are valueless to renters if not accompanied by some limitation on the landlord's ability to raise rent. Tenure rights may protect renters from the loss of their home if the landlord does not want to renew the rental relationship for some reason not related to finances, such as personal animus towards the renter. Depending on their scope, tenure rights may also protect renters when a landlord wishes to convert a building from rented housing to owned housing.

Minor Children and Allocation of a Home in Divorce

Allocation of the marital home in divorce at a minimum presents a conflict between two residents, at least one of which will lose their home. Decisions about which of the two divorcing spouses will keep a home may or may not involve consideration of fault and assessment of responsibility for the termination of the marriage. Regardless of culpability on the part of the spouses, minor children living at home are typically faultless. Many legal systems protect the possessory interests of innocent minor children by allocating the marital home to the spouse who receives primary custody of the children. The strength of this protection varies between jurisdictions, with some recognising a categorical rule allocating the marital home to the custodial spouse while others treat the interests of the minor children as one, typically very important, factor to be considered.

In some jurisdictions, however, the possessory interests of minor children play no role in the allocation of the marital home. For example, some jurisdictions have mechanical rules that require the equal distribution of marital property. The application of these mechanical rules often leads, as a practical matter, to the sale of the marital home. As a result, mechanical equal division rules have been criticised for failing to protect minor children's possessory interest in their homes.

Government Expropriation of Homes

Government projects often involve the expropriation of homes. Such expropriations are often achieved through an exercise of the power of eminent domain. The extension of a roadway may require some homes to be taken and demolished. Blighted homes might be taken as part of a slum-clearance programme. An entire neighbourhood might be demolished as part of an urban renewal project. Regardless of the specific context, the expropriation of a home presents a clear conflict between the interests of the government (ideally representing the interests of the larger community) and the homeowner.

The particular protections offered to homeowners vary widely between legal systems. They may also vary widely in particular within legal systems depending on the particular context. In many legal systems, homeowners are not given any more protection from expropriation than any other sort of property owner. Legal systems may, however, provide additional procedural or substantive protections for homeowners facing the expropriation of their homes. For example, a legal system might permit a government entity to take a home only on a showing that there is no other reasonable alternative way to meet the government's objective. A legal system could also require extra compensation for the expropriation of a home, or require that homeowners be given financial relocation assistance. Strategies that lead to higher compensation rates for homes as compared to other types of property indirectly protect homeowner's possessory interest by making homes comparatively more expensive to expropriate.

Theoretical Dimensions: Should Possession of Homes Be Given Special Protection?

Legal systems tend to give more protection to possessory interests in homes than they do possessory interests in other types of property. This phenomenon seems to reflect a widely held belief that people have special relationships with their homes, and that these special relationships are worth protecting.

This belief is reflected in the personhood theory of property developed by Margaret Jane Radin, which has been particularly influential on academic commentary on issues related to the home. Radin's theory is based on the intuition that people become personally connected with certain types of property – for example, family photographs, wedding rings, heirlooms, and homes. Building on this intuition, Radin divided property into two categories, personal and fungible. Personal property in this context is property that has more than market value to its owner. Fungible property, in contrast, has only market value to its owner. Radin's best illustration of the distinction involves a wedding ring. A jeweller should not care whether she has a particular wedding ring, another ring of the same value, or the cash equivalent. A wedding ring is therefore fungible property for a jeweller. Once a wedding ring has been exchanged with a spouse, however, we would expect that its owner would not be willing to freely exchange the ring for mere market value. A wedding ring is therefore personal property to a recipient spouse. Radin argued that legal systems should favour personal interests over fungible interests. In the housing context, Radin therefore argued that the personal interest of a homeowner should be favoured over the fungible interest of a creditor, and that the personal interest of a renter should be favoured over the fungible interests of a landlord.

Radin's position is expressly based on an intuitive notion about people's relationships with their homes. Legal rules giving special protection to homes are likely based on similar widely held intuitions about people's personal interests in their homes. Intuitions, however, can be wrong or misleading, and therefore form a risky basis for legal policy. There is some support in the literature on the psychology of home that supports, at least to a degree, the idea that people become personally connected with their homes. Many open questions remain, however, as to the strength and nature of this personal connection, and as to the degree to which legal systems should favour this personal connection against legitimate competing interests.

Is There a Personal Connection to the Home?

Critics of Radin's theoretical position, or of particular legal doctrines giving special protection to possession of a home, tend to question the strength and nature of the personal connection to the home. Some legal scholars have expressed doubts about the very existence of a personal connection to the home, and have broadly questioned the justification of special legal protection of the home.

Psychological studies do show that homes can be important sources of psychological feeling of rootedness, belonging, continuity, stability, and permanence. All of these feelings would be undermined if a person is dispossessed from a home. There are reasons to think, however, that unexamined intuitions might overstate the strength of the personal connection to the home. As suggested above in the context of the category of legal protections that fall under the umbrella of the castle doctrine, homes are important when issues of freedom, privacy, and security are at stake. Unsurprisingly, the psychological literature suggests that homes are important sources of feelings of freedom, privacy, and safety. These feelings, however, may not be tied to a particular home in a particular place. If a person moves to a new home of roughly equal quality to her old home, the new home should provide feelings of freedom, privacy, and safety similar to those provided by the old home. If a person's general feelings about her home mix both feelings that are tied to possession and feelings that are movable, then unexamined intuition will tend to overstate the psychological connection to a particular home in a particular place.

On this and other issues, the existing literature on the psychology of home is not sufficiently robust and fine-grained to lend strong support to particular legal positions. Presuming that people do have some personal connection to their home, it is unclear whether this connection is based on a tie between the person and the physical home or is based on other factors such as social networks. A home locates a person physically within a community, and it may be that it is relationships with other people nearby, rather than the physical home itself, that leads to important psychological feelings about the home. It also may be that both the physical home and personal relationships are important. Whatever the answer, resolution of this issue is important in resolving contested legal issues relating to the possession of homes. For example, if social networks are more important than physical space, then displacement of a person from a home in a neighbourhood should not have a major negative impact on that person if she can get another home in the same neighbourhood, and thereby maintain her social networks. If, on the other hand, the physical home is important, then displacement would have a negative impact on the person even if another nearby home is available to her.

Should Legal Systems Give Special Protection to Possession of a Home?

Legal rules that protect the possession of homes are not costless. In any given scenario, legitimate competing interests typically are at stake. These competing interests may be broader than they initially appear. When homeowners face the loss of a home because of loan defaults, the immediate competing interests are those of the lenders. If lenders are unable to reach homes to satisfy the debts, however, the costs of borrowing for the general public are likely to increase. Similarly, if restrictions on the eviction of renters are made too strong, the overall costs of renting are likely to increase. If residents are given too much power to resist the expropriation of their homes by the government, the legitimate goals of the government (presumably acting for the public benefit) will suffer.

The desirability of special legal protections for possession of the home therefore turns on a balance between the strength of the personal possessory interest in the home and the strength of competing interests. Some legal rules protecting home possession come at a relatively modest price. For example, a rule giving a renter tenure rights in a home so long as the renter is willing to pay market value in rent would protect possession while having a minimal impact on the landlord's interests. Similarly, rules that require governments to take additional procedural steps before they expropriate a home may provide important protection at a minimal cost.

Other rules, however, may impose too high a cost for the benefit they convey. Homestead laws that provide absolute protection of a home from creditors may be an example. Consider a person who has been a victim of fraudulent conduct by a homeowner, and who as a result has obtained a court judgement for money damages against the homeowner. The strongest homestead laws would prevent this creditor from using the value of the home to satisfy the debt. Providing some protection for homeowners against creditors may have merit in many contexts. Giving wrongdoers absolute protection against innocent creditors simply because the asset involved is a home, however, may be excessive, even when the interests of innocent members of the homeowner's family are taken into account.

See also: Rights to Housing Tenure.

Further Reading

Barros DB (2006) Home as a legal concept. *Santa Clara Law Review* 46: 255–306.
Barros DB (2009) Legal questions for the psychology of home. *Tulane Law Review* 83: 645–660.
Fox L (2007) *Conceptualizing Home: Theories, Laws and Policies.* Oxford, UK: Hart Publishing.
Radin MJ (1982) Property and personhood. *Stanford Law Review* 34: 957–1015.
Radin MJ (1986) Residential rent control. *Philosophy and Public Affairs* 15: 350–380.
Stern S (2009) Residential protectionism and the legal mythology of home. *Michigan Law Review* 107: 1093–1144.
Tang HW (2007) The legal representation of the Singaporean home and the influence of the common law. *Hong Kong Law Journal* 37: 81–102.

HOPE VI

DK Levy, Urban Institute, Washington, DC, USA

© 2012 Elsevier Ltd. All rights reserved.

HOPE VI Programme Overview

The United States Department of Housing and Urban Development (HUD) provides competitive grants to local housing authorities through the HOPE VI programme. The majority of HOPE VI grants provide funds for the redevelopment of distressed public housing developments, though the programme also offered planning grants (discontinued in 1996), which were used to support housing authorities' efforts to prepare a development for demolition or revitalisation activities, and grants for demolition alone. This article focuses on the revitalisation component of the programme.

In response to a study that found approximately 8% of the public housing stock was deteriorated, Congress established the National Commission on Severely Distressed Public Housing in 1989. The commission was charged with identifying developments in severe distress, identifying strategies for addressing the problems found, and developing a plan of action to eliminate the poor conditions by the year 2000. The resulting report estimated that about 86 000 public housing units met the established criteria of severe distress, which included families living in distress, high rates of serious crime in the development or surrounding area, management difficulties, and physical deterioration of the public housing buildings.

Based on the commission's findings and recommendations to improve severely distressed developments' physical environment, advance public housing authority management practices and provide social services to residents in distress, Congress appropriated $300 million in 1992 to finance the sixth programme rolled out under the moniker Homeownership and Opportunity for People Everywhere. Through HOPE VI, initially known as the Urban Revitalization Demonstration, HUD awarded the first round of redevelopment grants to local public housing authorities in 1993.

Over time HOPE VI has become a mixed-finance, -income, and -tenure programme. When it began, the programme awarded grants as large as $50 million to public housing authorities to demolish and redevelop, or rehabilitate existing structures for public housing tenants. A portion of the grant could be used to provide supportive services. The programme evolved through changes in the yearly Notice of Funding Availability (NOFA). Grants were reduced to between $20 and $35 million, necessitating greater financial leverage to cover redevelopment costs. Redevelopment financing has become more complex as housing authorities leverage funds from multiple public and private sources, each with different requirements and timelines. These new financial partnerships and a growing awareness of the detrimental effects of spatially concentrated poverty supported the shift towards redeveloping public housing developments into mixed-income and, in some cases, mixed-tenure developments. These changes were also accompanied by a move towards private ownership and/or management of the redeveloped properties.

When it began, HOPE VI targeted 86 000 units of public housing for redevelopment. As of September 2008, over 96 000 public housing units had been or were planned to be demolished and replaced with approximately 111 000 new and rehabilitated rental and homeownership units, slightly more than half of which will be deeply subsidised public housing units. Since the first grants were issued in 1993, 254 HOPE VI Revitalization grants valued at more than $6.1 billion have been awarded to 132 public housing authorities as of August 2010.

The growing mixed-tenure, mixed-income emphasis in the programme has been criticised by housing advocates for reducing the number of public housing units available to very-low-income households, and for the increased reliance on Housing Choice Vouchers to address the housing needs of severely disadvantaged persons, a not insignificant number of whom have multiple challenges, including very poor physical and mental health. There has been considerable concern that relocation itself and the reduction in public housing opportunities would lead to homelessness for some of the most disadvantaged residents (see article Homelessness: Causation). The programme has also been cited as a factor speeding the gentrification of desirable areas of cities, thereby increasing the difficulty disadvantaged households face in locating decent, affordable housing, and for allowing screening criteria that preclude many former residents from returning to redeveloped sites. Some policy analysts and commentators have criticised the slow pace of redevelopment activities. Others have argued that HOPE VI has directed public funds to projects that benefit private developers, and relatively higher-income households that move into the new mixed-income developments, more than it has helped displaced residents of the distressed public housing developments.

The programme has faced periodic threats of elimination since the mid-2000s in part due to arguments that the original goals of replacing the distressed public housing developments, as identified by the National Commission, have been met. To date, the programme, popular with state and local government leaders, has survived and continues to award revitalisation grants. HOPE VI forms the core of the Obama Administration's Choice Neighborhoods programme. This new initiative expands the HOPE VI model from the redevelopment of public housing developments to revitalisation of neighbourhoods (see article Housing and Neighbourhood Quality: Urban Regeneration). Under Choice Neighborhoods, HUD will award grants to support comprehensive community development efforts that include the redevelopment of publicly assisted housing located in the target area. Choice Neighborhoods grants can be made to public housing agencies, nonprofit organisations, private companies, or local governments. It is expected that the initial pilot grants will be awarded in 2011. Whether HOPE VI will continue as a separate programme is unclear.

Programme Goals

The objectives of the HOPE VI programme, in accordance with Section 24(a) of the United States Housing Act of 1937, are to:

- improve the living environment for residents of severely distressed public housing through the demolition, rehabilitation, reconfiguration, or replacement of obsolete projects (or portions thereof);
- revitalise sites on which such public housing projects are located and contribute to improvement of the surrounding neighbourhood;
- provide housing that will avoid or decrease the concentration of very-low-income families; and
- build sustainable communities.

The objectives also include supporting the growth of economic self-sufficiency among low-income residents.

An initial justification for the programme was arguments put forwards by William Julius Wilson and others about the deleterious effects on adults and children from living in areas with high rates of poverty and its attendant ills, including a lack of services and amenities, high rates of crime, and seemingly few ways out (see article Policies to Address Social Mix in Communities). The HOPE VI model of redevelopment offered one path for deconcentrating poor families through the demolition of public housing and construction of mixed-income developments. Though mechanisms of influence were not explicitly theorised, researchers have since identified four hypotheses following analyses of mixed-income's impact on poverty and poor households. Mixed-income environments are hypothesised to: (1) improve the social networks of poor people that could lead to employment prospects; (2) promote increased social control due to higher-income residents' expectations with respect to accountability and norms of behaviour; (3) have peer group effects due to higher-income residents' modelling of presumably preferable lifestyles and norms, which will lead to behaviour change among low-income residents; and (4) lead to effective political pressure from higher-income residents that will result in better services for all residents in the area.

These hypotheses assume effective, instrumental interactions will occur between residents belonging to different income groups such that benefits will flow from those with higher income to those with less. They also assume the higher-income residents will be engaged both within and beyond the redevelopment to ensure rules are enforced, and the broader area gets the attention and services it should receive.

Hypotheses about the mechanisms of influence have been modified over time such that fewer benefits are now expected to result from interactions across class lines. Instead, lower-income residents are expected to benefit from living in safer and relatively resource-rich environments.

Research on HOPE VI

There is a considerable body of research on numerous aspects of HOPE VI, the findings from which can be divided into the two broad strands of people and place. Much of the research has been carried out in one or a small number of redeveloped sites, though multisite studies have been conducted as well.

Researchers have thoroughly documented the poor health of pre-HOPE VI public housing residents in the grant sites. Rates of asthma, high blood pressure, arthritis, obesity, and other physical health problems are very high, as are levels of stress and depression. Studies that have followed residents after relocation have found some reduction in indicators of poor mental health, but little to no reduction in other health problems. Poor health is strongly correlated with low employment rates, which indicates that the HOPE VI goal of improved self-sufficiency is unlikely to be met without efforts to improve health conditions. In addition to low rates of employment, studies have found high rates of job cycling, with heads of households moving into and out of employment. Low educational attainment has also been found to inversely correlate with employment as does having a young child in the home – both characteristics are typical among HOPE VI residents.

By and large, most residents of the public housing developments have not returned to the sites post-redevelopment. Many people relocate to other traditional public housing developments or move to private market housing with the assistance of a Housing Choice Voucher (see article Access and Affordability: Housing Vouchers). In some instances, the former residents now feel settled and do not want to move again while in others, screening criteria prevent residents from returning, or residents think they would no longer feel at home in the mixed-income environments.

Multisite studies have found that on average, households are doing relatively well post-relocation. The concern that many families would become homeless as a result of the HOPE VI programme has not been borne out so far (see article Homeless Families: United States). However, some households living in private market rental units have experienced food hardship as they first strive to cover housing-related costs, and at times have insufficient funds to cover other basic needs.

Redeveloped sites have been able to attract residents from different income groups. Studies of the community within the sites have found little cross-class interaction and some evidence of tensions among residents based on perceived or real differences. Some property managers are also concerned about community governance structures that can create barriers to resident interactions across housing tenure. Redevelopments with owner-occupied units have homeowner associations, which provide a forum for owners to address any concerns, as well as a space within which to form social ties. Renters can participate in tenants' associations but many sites do not have a development-wide, cross-tenure organisation that could support site governance interactions among all residents.

Place-focused research has shown considerable variation across HOPE VI sites. An ideal percentage mix of subsidised and nonsubsidised housing units has yet to be determined, so the percent affordable and market rate, and the definition of 'affordable' can vary by development. Redeveloped sites also vary in layout. Some sites integrate affordable and market units on each block and in multiunit buildings while other sites separate housing by income tier. Housing does tend to be less dense than the stock it replaces, whether due to a reduction in the total number of units or to expansion of a development's footprint, which can allow construction of the same or a greater number of units spread over a larger area. There is variation as well in the degree of development that takes place around the HOPE VI footprint. Some redeveloped sites located in areas considered to have broader development potential tend to see public and private investments supporting area infrastructure and business development, as well as additional privately developed housing units.

There is growing interest in whether mixed-income redevelopments are viable over time. Exploratory research suggests that the time it can take to turnover subsidised units, maintenance costs, and possible reductions in HUD operating subsidies all could negatively affect the financial health of a site. Depending on contractual arrangements between project partners, including the local public housing authority, redevelopments owned and managed by private development companies can begin a process termed 'transformation' in the event expenses exceed revenues, and operating-reserve account balances diminish below a contractually allowable floor for a specified period of time. Transformation allows the original contractual arrangements between housing authorities and owners to be altered. Remedy options vary by development but an early study found options to include replenishing operating reserves by the housing authority, modifying the mix of affordable and market rate units, converting all affordable units to market rate, and returning ownership of the property to the local public housing authority.

Research has also examined the neighbourhoods into which relocated public housing residents have moved. Multisite studies have found that, on average, former relocatees have moved to relatively safer areas that are less poor than the developments from which they came. Because of the high percentage of people who move either to other public housing developments or to rent with a voucher, and because not all HOPE VI efforts include enhanced mobility services that help people search for housing in low-poverty areas, many people still reside in poor areas that, while safer, are not necessarily low crime. Researchers are also examining whether disorder associated with the disadvantaged public housing developments follows households when they relocate to other areas.

Key Issues Moving Forwards

Whether HOPE VI continues as a separate programme or not, the model of public housing redevelopment it has introduced has been influential in the United States and internationally. Based on the HOPE VI experience so far, key issues to pay attention to now and into the future include those related to the most disadvantaged households affected by redevelopment and to the redeveloped sites themselves.

There is concern that the most distressed households will move, either on their own or with a housing voucher, and settle in other distressed neighbourhoods. Households for which this is the case could be no better off due to HOPE VI and even worse off once they no longer have whatever supports they might have had access to through the public housing development. These so-called reconcentrations of poor households will further entrench the poverty of the receiving areas.

Questions remain about how best to serve disadvantaged people once they are dispersed.

For poor residents who return to the redeveloped site, questions remain about the benefits they might gain as a result of living among higher-income households and in an improved physical environment. So far research has shown little or no improvements in economic self-sufficiency of the most disadvantaged residents and little or no improvements in their physical health. How best to reach programme objectives for these residents is yet to be settled.

There is growing evidence of the challenges involved in creating community within the redeveloped sites. Models and mechanisms for supporting positive resident interactions and addressing problematic relations need to be examined, both for the good of the residents and for the health of the redevelopment itself.

The HOPE VI model for redevelopment of distressed public housing has grown to depend on private market financing. The extended and deep recession that began in the mid-2000s has raised questions about how to build and maintain redeveloped sites when private sources of funds constrict.

Related to most of these issues is the question of how redevelopments will fare over time. The roles that project revenue and expenses, community life, and broader economic forces play in viability are not yet well documented or understood.

See also: Access and Affordability: Housing Vouchers; Homeless Families: United States; Homelessness: Causation; Housing and Neighbourhood Quality: Urban Regeneration; Policies to Address Social Mix in Communities.

Further Reading

Joseph M, Chaskin RJ, and Webber HS (2007) The theoretical basis for addressing poverty through mixed-income development. *Urban Affairs Review* 42(3): 369–409.

National Commission on Severely Distressed Public Housing (1992) *The Final Report of the National Commission on Severely Distressed Public Housing: A Report to the Congress and the Secretary of Housing and Urban Development*. Washington, DC: The Commission.

Popkin SJ, Bajaj B, Buron L, Comey J, Cove E, Gallagher M, Guernsey E, Levy DK, Manjarrez C, McInnis D, and Woolley M. *Hope VI: Where Do We Go From Here?* (a series of policy briefs based on a panel study of relocated public housing residents). Urban Institute. http://www.urban.org/projects/hopevi (accessed 30 November 2010).

Wexler HJ (2001) HOPE VI: Market means/public ends: The goals, strategies, and midterm lesson of HUD's urban revitalization demonstration program. *Journal of Affordable Housing and Community Development Law* 10(3): 195–210.

House Biographies

H Jarvis, Newcastle University, Newcastle upon Tyne, UK

© 2012 Elsevier Ltd. All rights reserved.

Glossary

Biography A (usually written) record, account, or narrative description of a series of events making up the life of a person (or thing). A biography is usually framed chronologically (from cradle to grave or from construction to demolition) but it may focus on particular events, transitions, or memories.

Biographical disruption A concept usually applied in the context of a health crisis whereby the onset of chronic illness or disability can be viewed as a disruption to a previously anticipated biography. Housing conditions are implicated in the sense that a house move may become necessary, or an anticipated move may be abandoned, because of a long-term change to health or mobility.

Household A coresident group sharing a range of domestic facilities associated with cooking, eating, and sleeping. Whereas a family comprises a group of two or more people who live together and are related by birth, marriage, cohabitation, or adoption, a household may comprise a family, one person living alone, or a group of unrelated people who choose to live together in a shared house.

Housing career The concept of a housing 'career' is widely used in housing studies; it follows the same ordering logic of an employment career; it traces a series of transitions in housing consumption (tenure, price, location, quality, size) and household structure (composition, employment and income, and stage in the life course). Housing careers are socially constructed in the sense that a 'normal' housing career is typically expected to involve 'trading up' (in size, investment, and amenity) over the life course. Use of the term can be problematic because of this assumption of a progression to better and more secure housing options. Alternative terms include 'pathway', 'trajectory', or reference to a series of transitions.

Life course This term describes an individual's passage through life, analysed as a sequence of significant life events, including birth, marriage, parenthood, divorce, and retirement. The term life course has tended to replace the term life cycle in analysing these sequences of events, because the former allows for the reality of many varied trajectories rather than an assumed 'normal' cycle of events.

Narrative analysis A description or account that communicates the details (including feelings, metaphors, and associations) of a course of events. It usually takes the form of a chronologically told 'story' explaining why some events or aspects of experience are perceived as more significant than others. As a method, narrative analysis is generally considered to be richer in depth of detail (on aspects of identity and emotional attachment for instance) than a traditional attitude survey.

Transition The concept of 'transition' is used as a temporal framework to the anticipated sequence and timing of events. For example, the transition to adulthood is anticipated by a culturally constructed 'coming of age' and associated expectations of leaving the parental home and attaining financial independence. While these transitions may be anticipated, they are not inevitable or uniform.

Triangulation (of data) All methods have their strengths and weaknesses, so there is a strong argument for militating against the potential weaknesses of any one method by 'triangulating' observations from multiple methods, several time periods, and a variety of data sources.

Vintage A term used to describe the age of construction of a property. For example, British 'interwar' housing can be identified by certain characteristics associated with the materials and mode of construction used in the 1920s and 1930s. Housing vintage is one of the aspects (of character and aesthetic) that people may consider when choosing a home to live in.

Introduction: Intersecting Life Stories

Associated with every individual, house, street, place, and 'thing' are histories and intersecting accounts (biographies) of social and material aspects of the world. Just as the totality of 'life' is complex and varied, so too are biographies. Each biography is made up of several interdependent strands. From this it follows that in order to understand the choices and constraints that people face in their housing careers over the life course, more detailed information is needed than that usually gathered via questionnaire surveys on house location, tenure, and type. Just as relevant to decisions and events associated with housing choice, and a move from one neighbourhood to another, for instance, are decisions and events arising from relationship changes (marriage, childbirth, widowhood), time spent in training and employment, the accumulation and loss of wealth, biographical disruptions (such as to health), and transitions into and out of autonomy. In turn, these strands of life are shaped by intersecting aspects of identity (of gender, generation, class, race, ethnicity, and lifestyle) as well as formative experiences of home, security, and mobility.

Biographical research has become increasingly recognised in housing studies as a means of bringing together these interdependent strands of social and material life. Keith Halfacree and Paul Boyle (1993) suggest that, as a minimum, research on migration and residential mobility should consider a 'triple' biography linking elements of housing, employment, and personal life. Similarly, Adrian Bailey (2009) notes growing interest within population geography in the housing and household context of linked lives and time–space coordination, such as the routines entailed in chaperoning children to and from school or nursery. This focus on an integrated perspective parallels a similar shift in social policy towards 'joined up' thinking on issues of housing, employment, education, and transport.

Since the early 1990s, there has been growing recognition across the social sciences that people's opportunities, constraints, and experiences of the world are socially constructed rather than given, as a set of facts to be discovered. This shift, from a positivist (rational economic) model, to a culturally embedded understanding of social difference, has influenced the development and application of new methods and techniques of research and analysis. Among the new methods and techniques used are in-depth interviews, interpretative biographies, narrative analysis, life histories, respondent diaries, and photo elicitation. An important contribution to this development of a 'biographic turn' is the concept of a 'life story' model of identity whereby people are understood to conduct their lives and make sense of events by constructing and continually refining internal narratives of the self (McAdams, 1983).

Biographies of People and Things

A distinction has to be made between biographies of the house, as a 'thing', as a commodity (a dwelling valued for its living space properties or as a store of wealth), and household biographies through which information is gathered on the linked lives of individual household members. We are used to thinking about individual men, women, and children cultivating a personal biography, from cradle to grave, which can be observed by others and then represented through various forms of oral and written narratives. But what about inanimate, material, cultural artefacts, such as the house and all the possessions of a typical home; can the house be understood in terms of a discrete biography? A growing number of scholars believe it can be constructive to employ biographical methods and life-story metaphors to view the house as the subject and focus of research.

There is a precedent within material cultural studies for understanding human biographies through the lens of, and in relation to, possessions and artefacts. For example, Daniel Miller (2008) spent 17 months visiting the homes of residents living in a single South London street, talking to them (using semistructured ethnographic interviews) about the objects in their homes and the memories, feelings, and stories behind the possessions they had collected and how and where they had arranged these (such as pictures displayed on a mantelshelf). In his book *The Comfort of Things* he notes that although it was relatively easy to build up individual biographies of the things in people's homes, it was not possible from these fragments of life stories to represent a biography of the street or even of the house itself because "each portrait seems to be a separate encounter with a separate household" (Miller, 2008: 299). His approach sought to demonstrate how people could be understood through the medium of the material possessions they had accumulated over the course of their life.

The power of the biographical approach rests with the ease with which we as ethnographers, as the audience, can empathise with, and relate to, commonly held thoughts and feelings associated with the domestic living space. Everyone has to live somewhere and the intimate practices associated with daily life, however varied by income and geography, effectively create a common language of affect. A good example of this popular imagination at work can be illustrated in the case of Rachel Whiteread's temporary public art installation, *House* (**Figure 1**). For this sculpture the artist poured concrete into the rooms of a traditional Victorian terraced house (originally built to accommodate a low-income industrial working-class family) days before it was due to be demolished, as the last remaining house on an East London street cleared for urban renewal. Once the original brick structure had been discarded, the concrete cast that remained represented a ghostly inverse of a liveable space. Commentators observed how, as a solid and impenetrable block, the sculpture created a striking memorial to the idea of home which conjured forth contradictory thoughts, feelings, and memories of comfort, insecurity, nostalgia, and loss (Lingwood, 1995). The viewing public felt that they came to 'know' the Gale family, whom the local authority moved out of

Figure 1 Rachel Whiteread's sculpture 'House' (now destroyed) communicates intimate and familiar imaginations of domestic life. © 2012 Rachel Whiteread. Photographed by Sue Omerod.

the dwelling that eventually became the sculpture *House*, because they projected onto this impression of a house their own reflections and interpretations of an intimate and familiar social space. In this case, the vintage of the house chosen for the cast was significant: It communicated myriad mixed emotions of loss and renewal associated with changes taking place in the postindustrial landscape.

The Development of Biographical Methods in Housing Research

Biographical methods came to be applied increasingly widely in housing research from the mid-1990s. Development of these methods and techniques followed repeated calls for more in-depth ethnographic research and a general recognition of the limitations of secondary data analysis and traditional social surveys in situations where account needed to be taken of multiple and fluid social and cultural contexts. The development of biographical methods built on the seminal work of social anthropologists and early proponents of ethnographic methods across the social sciences, such as Sandra Wallman's (1984) *Eight London Households*, Peter Rossi's (1980) *Why Families Move*, Clare Wallace's (1987) *For Richer, For Poorer*, and Paul Willis's (1977) *Learning to Labour*. These 'classic' texts inspired a shift in the focus of housing studies: from the outside of the house and household, to the inside, to explore social interactions and cultural identities which could only be revealed through qualitative interview-based research.

Today, in-depth biographic research contributes significantly to both the development of theories and analyses of the house and home. Proponents argue that biographical narratives offer a richer tool for understanding the cultural milieu of the house and residential location compared with the traditional survey. Qualitative, ethnographic methods highlight real-life social relations in the context of real-life material circumstances. Divisions in understanding continue to exist between those scholars who advocate qualitative insight and those who pursue quantitative methods of secondary data analysis. Nevertheless, a strong argument can be made for mixing methods for the purpose of triangulating data from multiple sources and time frames. Biographic methods are frequently employed in a wide variety of research: exploring migration and residential mobility, considering the dilemmas facing dual-income couples commuting to work from one location or living apart together as a dual-location household, scrutinising the complex factors behind episodic homelessness, comparing the everyday lives of different types of household or the domestic arrangements of those living in particular communities or different parts of the world. Biographic methods offer social scientists a powerful tool (site and scale) of analysis and they offer policy makers a timely barometer of social and demographic change.

Biographic Time Frames

Time is a key constituent of any biography. The temporal dynamic may simply represent history (change over time), chronological sequence (events and transitions), historical vintage (the legacy of living with a particular type of house and construction), or a more complex cultural understanding of rhythm and pace beyond the calendar and clock. The temporal dimension of biography bears witness to intimate details and experiences of social and demographic change. The time frame of a biography may vary from the full span of human life, from cradle to grave, or it may focus on the sequence of events and characteristics of a particular transition, or it may explore a routine set of practices, such as with a 'day in the life' research, tracing all the points of coordination (in time and space) that join up the elements of home, work, and personal life.

The temporal dynamic that is built into a biographical approach differs from that produced through longitudinal, time-series or panel data. The data used to compile a biography are usually collected at a single sitting, via an in-depth ethnographic interview (or oral history), prompted perhaps by visual aides memoires such as photographs, props, or mind-mapping exercises. In some cases, there may be sufficient resources to conduct repeat interviews with the same subject or separate interviews with a number of residents living in the same house, where the benefits of data triangulation are made possible.

Much of the data sought from interview respondents in biographic research is retrospective in nature and therefore subject to problems of imperfect recall and the 'tidying up' of past events to fit with current opinions. These challenges are widely acknowledged and the potential limitations of human cognition and memory are continually being addressed by the development of increasingly sophisticated techniques of elicitation – such as via family photographs and other visual media. It is understood to be easier for interview respondents to remember biographic details by working backwards from the present and to relate changes in housing and employment to other life events, such as childbirth, which may have happened around the same time. Biographic interviews are usually loosely structured around the intersecting themes recognised to make up the biography, such as housing, employment, and personal (family) life.

Interviews tend to be conversational in style, conducted in such a way as to flesh out substantive themes (such as housing choice and attachment to place) in a flexible, non-linear manner to follow the train of thought of each respondent. This approach means that considerable work needs to be done by the analyst to split and splice fragments of intersecting strands of biography to reconstruct a chronology or build up evidence on a particular theme or metanarrative (Kitchen and Tate, 2000). The biographic approach seeks to generate a deeper explanation of the tensions and negotiations underpinning preferences and decisions in housing markets. This recognition of complexity, contradiction, compromise, and mixed feelings contrasts the biographic approach with neoclassical models of a unitary household assumed to make 'rational economic' decisions on the basis of utility maximisation.

Representing Biographies

There are different ways of communicating and representing the most salient features of house and household biographies. A limited selection of the different techniques of representation is illustrated in **Boxes 1–3**. One technique (shown in **Box 1**) is to provide a 'potted biography' which pieces together in a selective, linear fashion the details of key transitions and events. This can provide insight into the linked lives and intersecting pathways of housing, employment, gender, and generation. A popular means of representing biographic evidence is to include for discussion extracts of verbatim transcription from interviews with individuals or dialogue between respondents and the interviewer (as shown in **Box 2**). This method of representation allows the researcher to highlight the intersections between dynamic structures and feelings (lack of affordable housing and identification with an urban way of life) or how a particular story is told, what gets privileged and what is omitted from the story. Finally, there are techniques of composite vignettes that are employed as a means to succinctly convey the rich complexity of home–workplace–life intersections, while masking individual subject identities. The use of the vignette approach typically incorporates real situations and people but in composite form, based upon numerous observations, drawing on original household research together with additional secondary sources (as shown in **Box 3**).

While biographical methods are primarily used, as above, to explore and represent the processes behind

---

Box 1: Example of a potted biography indicating episodic homelessness over the housing career of a homeless subject 'Shaun' (age 22).

Brought up by his grandparents after his parents' divorce, Shaun left home at 16 unable to afford a flat of his own. After a period in two bed and breakfast 'hotels' he moved in with friends before being able to get enough money to secure a deposit on his own bedsit. At the end of the tenancy the landlord offered him a place in another bed and breakfast for a few weeks until Shaun was able to move into a new flat owned by the same landlord. Over the next few years Shaun moved through seven bedsits and flats, sometimes living on his own and sometimes with his girlfriend and interspersed by the occasional stay at his girlfriend's parents or with friends. With neither of them able to find any work, Shaun and his girlfriend eventually decided to move to the south of England, stopping on the way in London where Shaun had relatives. Reaching the coast they again found a private rented flat which they shared until their relationship ended and Shaun moved out. Still unemployed, for the next couple of months Shaun moved between different friends before finally running out of places to stay and, after a night on the street, came to the hostel where he was interviewed.

Source: May (2000: 628).

Box 2: Example of a narrative extract (verbatim quote from an interview with a couple, Irma and Paul, living in rented accommodation in San Francisco). This extract was the focus of further reflections on the intersections of home, work, and family life in the context of a lack of affordable housing in San Francisco in 2000.

Irma: It's sad because I like it here, it really is kind of, for me it's heartbreaking, it's not like, well yeah, let's leave, it's more like we are kind of, we are trying to make some realistic choices.

Paul: the only reason we consider moving out of the city now is just because, now we're stuck for housing. Our little boy is

> sleeping in a closet up there and as he gets bigger, this is a one bedroom (rented apartment), you can see like straight up there that's the bedroom up there, there's the bathroom there and he's next to it in a little, what was a walk-in closet.
>
> Irma: so we took the doors off, put up a curtain, painted it, it works for now but not that much longer.
>
> Source: Jarvis (2005: 94).

Box 3: Example of a fictitious/composite 'vignette' to highlight commonly overlooked daily-life issues.

Sue lives in a largely white, middle-class suburban neighbourhood in America's heartland. Like most people in her neighbourhood, she owns a house and partakes in much of the material culture of her neighbourhood (cars, clothes, furniture). She appears to be very much embedded in her neighbourhood – both a product of the neighbourhood and an agent in reproducing local consumer society by virtue of her participation in it. Yet, unlike many of her neighbours, she has a lawn covered with dandelions. Why doesn't she use chemicals to rid her lawn of weeds like most other people in the neighbourhood? When Sue moved into the area, she retained the open space between her house and her neighbour's houses, yet within just 3 years she had put up a privacy fence with an iron gate. Her front door features unique stained glass that she bought at a garage sale when she lived in another neighbourhood. She has a nice dog with a lot of character, although he is unattractive: he is a mutt from the pound – not like the pedigree dogs found at most other homes in the neighbourhood. She has an interesting weather vane on her house that is, however, dysfunctional (it was her mother's). Most people in the neighbourhood don't know Sue very well. She works outside the neighbourhood and doesn't socialise much.

Source: Ettlinger (2004: 22).

particular patterns of behaviour, they can also be used to identify new or unfamiliar patterns or 'types' of biography. In their study of student renting, for instance, Rugg et al. (2004: 28) identify five housing career 'pathways' (chaotic, unplanned, constrained, planned (nonstudent), and student (shared)), each predicated on three elements: the ability to plan the first move from the parental home; the operation of economic and housing market constraints; and the degree of family support. Similarly, in a study of two-parent working family households, Jarvis (2005) identified five composite biography types (career-egalitarian, resist the treadmill, keep a lid on the hours, all hands to the pump, the path of least resistance) based on preferences expressed and events mapping across the triple biographic strands of home, work, and family life. A key function of the lifestyle metanarratives pursued in each biography type relates to housing attributes, assets, and liabilities. This way a biographical approach can be used to make thematic observations between category 'types' (household, housing career, life-course stage, regional housing market) while at the same time highlighting unique characteristics that transcend these categories. By considering overlapping narratives, of similarity and difference, a biographical approach can be used to critically examine evidence and assumptions based on pattern-based survey or secondary data analysis alone.

See also: Ethnographies of Home and Homelessness; Housing Careers; Life Course; Memory and Nostalgia at Home; Qualitative Methods in Housing Research; Sustainable Housing Cultures.

References

Bailey AJ (2009) Population geography: Lifecourse matters. *Progress in Human Geography* 33.3: 407–418.
Ettlinger N (2004) Toward a critical theory of untidy geographies: The spatiality of emotions in consumption and production. *Feminist Economics* 10.3: 21–54.
Halfacree K and Boyle P (1993) The challenge facing migration research: The case for a biographical approach. *Progress in Human Geography* 17: 333–348.
Jarvis H (2005) *Work/Life City Limits: Comparative Household Perspectives*. Basingstoke: Palgrave Macmillan.
Kitchen R and Tate NJ (2000) *Conducting Research into Human Geography: Theory, Methodology and Practice*. Harlow: Prentice Hall.
Lingwood J (ed.) (1995) *Rachel Whiteread: House*. London: Phaidon Press Limited.
May J (2000) Housing histories and homeless careers: A biographical approach. *Housing Studies* 15.4: 613–638.
Miller D (2008) *The Comfort of Things*. Cambridge: Polity.
McAdams DP (1983) *The Stories We Live By: Personal Myths and the Making of the Self*. New York: Morrow.
Rossi PH (1980) *Why Families Move*, 2nd edn. London: Sage.
Rugg J, Ford J, and Burrows R (2004) Housing advantage? The role of student renting in the constitution of housing biographies in the United Kingdom. *Journal of Youth Studies* 7.1: 19–34.
Wallace C (1987) *For Richer, For Poorer: Growing Up In and Out of Work*. London: Routledge.
Wallman S (1984) *Eight London Households*. London: Tavistock.
Willis P (1977) *Learning to Labour: How Working Class Kids Get Working Class Jobs*. Basingstoke: Ashgate.

Further Reading

Chamberlayne P, Bornat J, and Wengraf T (2000) *The Turn to Biographical Methods in Social Science*. London: Routledge.
Denzin N (1989) *Interpretive Biography*. Newbury Park, CA: Sage.
Franklin A (1990) Ethnography and housing studies. *Housing Studies* 5.2: 92–111.
Gurney C (1997) 'Half of me was satisfied': Making sense of home through episodic ethnographies. *Women's Studies International Forum* 20.3: 373–386.
Miller D (ed.) (2001) *Home Possessions: Material Culture Behind Closed Doors*. Oxford: Berg.
Roberts B (2002) *Biographical Research*. Buckingham: Open University Press.

Relevant Websites

www.sussex.ac.uk – Centre for Life History and Life Writing Research, University of Sussex, UK www.sps.ed.ac.uk – Centre for Narrative and Auto/Biographical Studies, University of Edinburgh, UK

http://grandfamilies.org – Grandfamilies State Law and Policy Resource Centre (showing use of biographic analysis, vignettes, and stories in social policy)

http://ncb.anu.edu.au – National Centre of Biography, Australian National University

www.workinglives.org – Working Lives Research Institute, London Metropolitan University, UK

House Building Industries: Africa

DCI Okpala, Idoplin Ltd, Nairobi, Kenya

© 2012 Elsevier Ltd. All rights reserved.

Glossary
Conventional housing This refers to housing built according to all the existing statutory building codes, standards, and regulations.
Habitat agenda This comprehensive set of agreements on the principles, policies, and strategies for the promotion and management of human settlements development was adopted by the international community in Istanbul, Turkey, in 1996.
Housing deficit This refers to the number of housing units required to meet existing housing needs or demand.

Introduction: The Importance of Housing and House-Building Industries

The importance of housing as a basic need and as a component of the national economy cannot be overemphasised. The role of housing in economic development is well documented in the literature. It is estimated that on average, between 15 and 40% of the household monthly expenditure is spent on housing and housing services. The world invests anywhere between 3 and 15% of the Gross Domestic Product (GDP) annually on housing construction, and provides jobs for 5–16% of the work force in the construction and real-estate services sectors. Housing or real estate represents a major capital resource for many individuals and households. It constitutes an important form of personal wealth. A soundly financed housing sector can play a major role in national economic growth and economic stabilisation through the creation of jobs in construction and in building-materials production industries, and by creating the demand for new enterprises. It thus has an indirect impact through the expansion of subsidiary activities, including infrastructure installations, materials, furnishings, and services. Housing and related services account for upwards of 20% of the GDP in several countries. Indeed, statistics of monthly and annual housing starts is a key barometer or measure of the growth and health of the national economy.

Housing and homeownership is also a cornerstone of social and family stability. In Africa, households cling to housing as the best form of savings. It has been established, for example, that inflation-adjusted yields of housing are higher than those of financial savings such as pension, provident funds, and bank deposits. It is acknowledged that the household sector is a consistent net saver in the economy and that housing is the investment priority for almost all households.

Generally, the rapid growth in urban population in Africa has not been commensurately matched by increases in the provision of adequate housing for the population. The result is an acute shortage of decent and affordable urban housing. In Uganda, for example, by 2005–06, the additional national housing requirement was estimated to be 560 000 units. This included a housing deficit of about 420 000 units, 160 000 of which were in the urban areas. Kampala, the capital city, alone had a housing deficit of 100 000 units. This scenario of housing deficit repeats itself in many sub-Saharan African cities.

Only about 61% of the total households in sub-Saharan African countries live in so-called permanent dwellings, and only about 48.6% of these meet the standards of planning regulations. It is extremely difficult, indeed presumptuous, to attempt to put near-accurate figures on the quantum of housing deficit in African countries. As suggested by the United Nations Human Settlements Program (UN-Habitat, 2005: 4), "precision is not really important. What is critical is the order of magnitude." What can be plausibly said, therefore, is that the magnitude of housing deficit – quantitatively and qualitatively – is enormous in all African countries.

Institutional Modes of House Building in Africa

Institutions as used here refers to the specific configurations of organisations, which operate within the parameters of wider norms and practices to realise the identified goals and objectives. In this context, they are the institutional or organisational mechanisms that get houses built and delivered.

The institutional or organisational modes for house building and delivery in Africa comprise the following:

1. The government housing corporation or agency production mode is a relatively large-scale operation and is usually contractor-executed.
2. The formal, private, commercial, entrepreneurial, or real-estate developer mode builds standard and legal houses for renting, leasing, or for sale.
3. The informal house-building mode – in which an individual, family, or household organises their own house building – involves employing small contractors or various individual building technicians and artisans, sometimes with financial assistance from relatives, friends, or community or work associations.
4. There is also the cooperative or mutual-help organisational housing-promotion mode, in which groups or associations of people organise the acquisition of land. Houses are built cooperatively on this land. This ensures that the members get ownership of their housing units.

The private sector house-building operators comprise a number of subcategories: (i) The merchant builders are wealthy industrialists or syndicate groups, who take a single design and build many units to take advantage of economies of scale, and who dispose of these houses at prices that will allow them to recoup their investments quickly. (ii) There are the builder-investors, who are similar to the merchant builders, but who generally retain ownership of the houses they build. (iii) The third category is the most common – that of the on-site builders consisting essentially of individuals who build incrementally and as fast as their resources will permit. (iv) There are the prefabricator types, who take advantage of industrialised systems to mass-produce housing elements, thus maximising cost savings. (v) The last category includes the land developers and speculators, who acquire land and improve it with infrastructure and services, and then sell the same to builders.

Each of these modes makes contributions to house building and housing delivery in African countries, although they may vary in effectiveness. Housing has a characteristic unique among socially desirable goods and services: it is being provided by almost anyone, even by amateurs. The dividing line between these modes, therefore, is not always that distinct or sharp: it can be rather fluid.

The Government or Public Sector House-Building Mode

Out of public policy concern to address the acute shortages of housing created by growing urbanisation, many governments in Africa embark on the direct building and delivery of housing. They usually achieve this by creating government or parastatal housing corporations or agencies to execute housing schemes. It is commonly assumed that with a government agency at the forefront of the house-building scene, adequate quality housing will be made available, to take care of the growing needs and requirements of urban housing. It was initially thought that the government-sponsored production approach would hold great promise and prospects. Public sector housing would have the backing of the governmental authority, substantial resources available to them as funds, access to technical skills, the potential for adopting more organised, capital-intensive, contractor-execution approaches, and the capacity to employ industrialised and integrated building systems and associated technologies. Statutory approvals would be easier and quicker to process in this mode. Producing large numbers of housing units by this mode was envisaged to make the units cheaper and, therefore, more accessible and affordable to all socioeconomic groups, including the low-income segment of the population.

In a number of African countries, this mode of house building has made relatively significant contributions to housing production and delivery. Tunisia has been outstanding in this regard. So also has South Africa in more recent years. Algeria and Morocco have also had notable success with this mode. Botswana, Namibia, Kenya, and Cote D'Ivoire have also relatively succeeded in like manner. In Nigeria, the Lagos state government has been outstanding in this respect.

In these countries, government housing agencies have been able to build substantial numbers of housing units for delivery to the population.

Relative to the overall housing needs and requirements in most African countries, however, this mode of house building has had a limited impact on the urban housing problem. The output of this mode is too low and too highly priced. It has not been able to produce and deliver housing units in sufficient numbers or at sufficiently low prices, to make them affordable for the majority low-income segments of the population, who constitute 'the housing problem'. Acceptable, modern, contractor-built, low-cost housing cannot – obviously – be supplied at prices that the majority of urban dwellers can afford. The most effective government action for housing, therefore, would have to be an indirect one. Such action will have to concentrate more on providing access to the necessary resources and on providing infrastructure at levels and times that match users' preferences and demands.

Private Sector Entrepreneurial House Builders or Developers

In all African countries, there are organised, formal, and conventional private estate developers. They are represented either as individuals or firms, who build housing for lease, rent, or sale. Builders in this institutional mode include firms employing the latest construction technology to erect single-family houses or multiunit apartment buildings. Most of these firms are, however, small in size and may employ a flexible work force or contractor-builders.

This mode produces and delivers a significant proportion of overall conventional housing for the entire socioeconomic spectrum of the population. The beneficiaries are – more significantly – the lower-middle-income, and high-income strata of the population, which still constitute a relatively small proportion of the overall population.

The Informal/Nonconventional or 'Popular' (Including Self-Build) House-Building Mode

The informal house-building mode is informal in the sense that it involves building without statutorily approved building plans or permits. Consequently, this mode often does not fulfil statutory planning standards, building codes, and regulations. Builders following this mode are often considered illegal builders. This mode is usually neither capital-intensive nor does it use high technology. Instead, it usually mobilises and utilises building artisans and unskilled labour in construction. It exhibits great flexibility and resourcefulness in responding to local housing needs and demands, catering in the main to poorer households who have few other housing alternatives. This mode is the largest single producer of housing in African countries.

This mode integrates substantial construction economies through the utilisation of relatively inexpensive, locally available building materials. Through this mode, many households build or access their own housing, often incrementally and eventually progressively upgrading to quite acceptable modern space and construction standards. Many entrepreneurs in this category also build for renting.

This mode has contributed immensely to housing delivery in all African countries, accounting for the housing needs of the lower fiftieth percentile of the population at the very least. A report on Botswana, for example, states that the biggest provider of housing in urban areas is the self-help housing agent. This provider meets 45% of the housing needs, followed by the Botswana Housing Corporation at 28%, and others at 27%. This mode exhibits a less expensive system of house building and often utilises appropriate technologies. Housing output from this mode is, therefore, more accessible and affordable for low-income families than that from the other modes. This mode holds the greatest promise for supplying truly low-cost housing in the scale approximating the urgent needs in African countries for urban housing.

In the past, public policies in the various African countries have striven to eradicate or strictly constrain this mode of housing production. The rationale was that it often did not meet the statutory standards of safety, health, and other quality criteria. In recent years, however, this policy has recognised the efficacy of this mode in producing and delivering housing. It has consequently begun to progressively adopt the upgrading option for the output of this mode, rather than seeking its eradication.

The Cooperative or Mutual-Help Mode

A subcomponent of the private sector house-building industry organisation is the cooperative or mutual self-help housing mode. This is a more formally organised subsystem, in which groups or associations of people – in the spirit of mutual help – pool their resources together to access land for the housing, mobilise the finances, and organise the construction of the housing units. In this manner, members of the cooperative are enabled to own housing units. In this process, members of the cooperative contribute in agreed forms and proportions towards the realisation of the cooperative housing project. Sometimes, the cooperatives are able to access some credit or loans from financial institutions, governments, employer organisations, or even from bilateral or multilateral agencies.

The traditional form of organisation of housing cooperatives is based on affiliation to the same trade, profession, or work organisation. It can be said that the role of governments in housing cooperative development in some African countries has been pivotal. They have carried out promotional, advisory, supervisory, and auditing roles. Moreover, these governments have facilitated the allocation of land to the cooperatives or the obtaining of housing loans from financial institutions by guaranteeing them.

The cooperative mode of house building is at its more advanced stages of development in Egypt, where the government has set up the Egyptian Corporation of Cooperative Housing, which gives financial and technical assistance to housing cooperatives. This mode has also been actively promoted in Botswana, Ethiopia, Ghana, Lesotho, Kenya, Tanzania, and Tunisia. In more recent years, it has been massively promoted in South Africa.

The cooperative housing mode is known to produce housing that is more affordable by virtue of the elimination of the profit component. Its social nature has the advantage of potentially attracting government subsidies. Although the impact of the cooperative housing mode has been significant in a number of African countries as exemplified above, in the overall African housing scene, the impact of the mode is still relatively limited.

Impact of House-Building Institutional Modes to Housing Output or Delivery in African Countries

The vast majority – upwards of 75% – of housing units in most African countries are either self-built for own occupation or built by private individual entrepreneurs for renting. In Kenya, private developers – consisting of firms and individual builders – produce the bulk of formal housing in the urban centres. In Kenya, for example, the public sector (comprising direct government-built housing, parastatal-built housing, and local government council-built housing) accounted for only about 16% of all produced housing units. The private sector developers taken together (private construction companies, real-estate firms, individual entrepreneur-builders, self-build owner-occupation or rental units) accounted for about 84% of all housing units built. Of this, about 80% is accounted for by private individual entrepreneur-builders.

In Dar es Salaam, Tanzania, 67% of all housing in the formal sector is by the private individual entrepreneur-builders. These have been either directly constructed by owners (11%) or indirectly constructed using the services of various building artisans (*fundis*) (56%). The private sector informal house-building mode accounted for 85% of all housing in the informal sector, with 32% being owner-constructed and 53% constructed using various building artisan groups (*fundis*). The output of private housing construction companies or real-estate firms was not significant.

It bears emphasising that a substantial proportion of housing built by private individual entrepreneur-builders is in the formal sector. 'Formal' is used in the sense that, in many cases, the builders fulfil most of the design requirements or provisions and do obtain building permits or plan approvals from the relevant regulatory authorities before building. The informal housing component is equally substantial. All individual entrepreneur-built housing is not informal in the strict sense of the term. Many are regular formal apartment units or rooming housing.

Although the contributions of private construction companies and real-estate firms to house building in Africa have been increasing in recent years, their relative contributions to total housing output have remained relatively small. This contribution has been in the range of 2–5% and has largely impacted the middle-to-upper market housing segment. Indeed, most formal housing is still accounted for by private individual entrepreneur-builders (formal and informal) and not by construction companies or real-estate firms.

The contribution of the public or government sector accounts for less than 20% of the total houses built. Even at the height of the house building in Kenya in the 1970s, this source of housing provision was able to account for only a small proportion of the total housing units produced in the country.

Conclusions

House building in Africa is dependent on two broad categories of inputs – the principal inputs of house building namely, land, building materials, and finance and the institutional or organisational modes and mechanisms for the actual production of housing units. These include the public or government sector institutional mode, the private sector (formal or informal) institutional mode, and the cooperative or mutual-help institutional mode.

House-building industries in Africa are generally beset by the need to reconcile the dilemma between producing adequate housing for the rapidly growing urban population (which continues to outstrip available housing) and producing affordable quality housing (that meets acceptable standards of safety and health) for the majority low-to-middle income group of the population.

Different house-building institutional or organisational modes attempt to address these dilemmas with varying degrees of efficiency, success, and relative impacts on the objective problem, which is the provision of affordable housing that is acceptably healthy and safe.

On balance, contrary to hopes and expectations, it has proved difficult in most African countries, as in other developing countries, to credit the public or governmental house-building and delivery mode with being the most productive, efficient, and beneficial one. This is not strange, considering that corruption, political interference, inefficiency, inflexibility, unfair allocation, and extensive delays in house-building processes are the rule rather than the exception in this institutional mode. Most important, resources available for housing by this mode are seldom sufficient to make more than a token dent in the housing problem (UN-Habitat, 2003: 125).

The private sector (formal and informal) institutional house-building mode (including the private entrepreneur-self-builder) remains the dominant and most productive mode of house building and delivery in African countries.

In addition, therefore, to facilitating easier access to the major house-building inputs such as land and financing, other statutory measures play a part in further stimulating the house-building industry in Africa. These include the statutory approval, adoption, and promotion of the use of local building materials, as well as the simplification of building regulations, codes, and standards to deliver more affordable housing to a much broader socioeconomic spectrum of the population.

See also: Construction of Housing Knowledge; Households and Families; Housing Governance; Housing Preferences; Housing Statistics; Immigration and Housing Policy; People and the Built Form; Sustainable Urban Development; Welfare States and Housing.

References

UN-Habitat (2003) *The Challenge of Slums: Global Report on Human Settlements 2003*. Nairobi: Earthscan Publications Ltd.

UN-Habitat (2005) *Financing Urban Shelter: Global Report on Human Settlements, 2005*. London, Sterling, VA: Earthscan.

Further Reading

Government of Kenya (2007) *Proposed Housing Sector Incentives and Market-Engineering Measures*. Nairobi: Ministry of Housing.

McAuslan P (1985) *Urban Land and Shelter for the Poor*. London: Earthscan Paperback.

McCarthy S (1978) *Progress through Self-Help: Urban Housing in Botswana*. Monograph No. 3. Botswana: Institute of Development Management.

Renaud B (1984) *Housing and Financial Institutions in Developing Countries: An Overview*. The World Bank Staff Working Paper, No. 658. Washington, DC: World Bank.

Republic of Botswana (1997) *Review of the National Policy on Housing*. Gaborone: Ministry of Local Government, Lands and Housing.

Republic of Kenya (2004) *National Housing Policy for Kenya*. Sessional Paper No. 3, July. Nairobi: Ministry of Lands and Housing.

Shelterafrique (2005) Delivering affordable housing in Africa: Challenges, opportunities and strategies. *Proceedings of the Shelterafrique Annual Symposia, 1999–2004*. Nairobi, Kenya.

UNCHS (Habitat and International Cooperative Alliance) (2001) *Shelter Cooperatives in Eastern and Southern Africa*. Nairobi: International Co-operative Alliance.

UN-Habitat (2008) *Housing Finance System in South Africa*. Nairobi: UN-Habitat.

UN-Habitat/UNECA (2008) *The State of African Cities 2008: A Framework for Addressing Urban Challenges in Africa*. Nairobi: UN-Habitat.

United Nations (1988) *The Global Strategy for Shelter to the Year 2000*, Supplement 8 (A/43/8), 6 June. New York.

House Building Industries: Asia Pacific

Y Yau, City University of Hong Kong, Kowloon, Hong Kong

© 2012 Elsevier Ltd. All rights reserved.

Glossary

Asian financial crisis A period of financial crisis beginning in Thailand in July 1997 that adversely impacted the economy of many Asian countries, and slowed down economic growth in other parts of the world.

Bogeumjari plan A plan set out by South Korea's government in 2009 to build 1.5 million low-cost homes for low-income families who could not afford home purchase in the private sector by 2018.

Bumiputera Indigenous people of the Malay Archipelago.

Collective-owned construction enterprise An economic unit where the assets are owned collectively and which have been registered in accordance with the Regulations of the People's Republic of China on the Management of Registration of Corporate Enterprises.

Competitive bidding A project procurement process in which proposals or tenders to undertake a project are submitted by bidders with the winning bid selected on a competitive basis.

Gross domestic product (GDP) The market value of all goods and services produced within an economy in a given period.

Sale and purchase agreement A legally binding contract signed between purchaser and seller in a property transaction, containing terms regarding property particulars, purchase price, deposit arrangements, and obligations of the two parties.

State-owned construction enterprise A legal entity created and owned by a government to undertake construction business on behalf of the owner government.

Value added The difference between an entity's or industries' sales and its intermediate purchases of materials and services from other entities or industries.

Introduction

The house-building industry is characterised by three functional aspects of housing development, namely residential land development, housing production, and house marketing and sales. Owing to the high procurement costs and sale prices of the housing products, the prosperity of the industry depends very much on the availability of finance for house building and home purchase. Except for places such as Hong Kong, Singapore, and Japan, house-building industries in most parts of the Asia-Pacific region have a relatively short history as real estate markets in these countries have only become fully formed in the last 20 years or so, and, often, only in major cities. Compared with North America and Western Europe, house-building industries in the Asia-Pacific region have been developing very fast in the past two decades. The growth of these industries has given momentum to economic development in the region because of the economic activities opened for hundreds of upstream and downstream industries.

The Asian Financial Crisis in late 1997 and the outbreak of Severe Acute Respiratory Syndrome in 2003 severely hit the industry in the region. Afterwards, however, real estate and construction sectors recovered very strongly. Recent skyrocketing house prices point to an overheating in housing markets in various countries. For example, the ratio of the total house value to gross domestic product (GDP) in China in 2003 was about 2.3. It increased sharply to 3.3 in 2009. Over the period between 2002 and 2008, the average house price in South Korea increased by almost 60%. State interventions such as increased land supply and raised property tax were implemented to curb the problems associated with low housing affordability and proliferation of speculative activities in housing markets.

Historically speaking, the house-building industry contributed a great deal to the economic growth in Japan in the 1950s and 1960s. The 1980s and 1990s were the key periods for the sector's boom in South Korea and other South-East Asian countries like Thailand and Malaysia. As shown in **Table 1**, the construction industry's contribution to GDP in Asian countries generally decreased in the first decade of the twenty-first century, except for mainland China, Singapore, and Taiwan.

The infancy of some house-building industries and the closedness of the economies in the region mean that data and information are relatively limited in some countries.

Table 1 Contribution of the construction industry to local economic development by countries

	Contribution of the construction industry at local currency (proportion of the total GDP)					
Year	2003	2004	2005	2006	2007	2008
Japan (billion yen)	32 333 (6.6%)	32 954 (6.6%)	31 861 (6.4%)	31 849 (6.3%)	31 444 (6.1%)	30 924 (6.1%)
Hong Kong (million HK$)	44 910 (3.6%)	40 376 (3.1%)	38 538 (2.8%)	38 688 (2.6%)	40 153 (2.5%)	47 922 (2.9%)
Mainland China (billion yuan)	749.1 (5.5%)	869.4 (5.4%)	1036.7 (5.6%)	1240.9 (5.7%)	1529.7 (5.8%)	1874.3 (6.0%)
Malaysia (million ringgit)	15 200 (3.6%)	15 458 (3.3%)	15 680 (3.0%)	15 976 (2.8%)	18 177 (2.8%)	20 606 (2.8%)
Singapore (million SGD)	Data not available	Data not available	6275.3 (3.0%)	6542.1 (2.8%)	7898.2 (3.0%)	11 342.4 (4.1%)
South Korea (billion won)	54 818 (7.1%)	57 833 (7.0%)	59 285 (6.9%)	61 359 (6.8%)	64 979 (6.7%)	64 612 (6.3%)
Taiwan (billion NT$)	253.5 (2.4%)	288.1 (2.5%)	284.8 (2.4%)	332.4 (2.7%)	357.6 (2.8%)	363.3 (2.9%)
Thailand (billion baht)	174.7 (3.0%)	194.5 (3.0%)	214.0 (3.0%)	234.5 (2.9%)	249.3 (2.9%)	260.7 (2.7%)

On account of the varying availability of industry data, direct comparative analysis across countries is not possible. In the following sections, house-building industries will thus be viewed country by country. Nations specifically considered include Japan, South Korea, Singapore, China, Thailand, and Malaysia.

Japan

The most glorious era for the house-building industry in Japan was the years immediately before the burst of the asset-price bubble in the early 1990s. At that time, the investor's confidence in Japan's economy accelerated business expansion, increased corporate earnings, and boosted personal income pushing up the house prices. However, the country entered its 'Lost Decade' after the bubble burst, and the house-building industry was severely hit. The recession of the industry continued in the 2000s. Construction investment turned sluggish, and the share of construction industry in the GDP decreased gradually from 7.4% in 2000 to 6.1% in 2007. The value of housing construction contracts dropped from 2840 billion yen in 1995 to 2641 billion yen in 2000, and further to 2441 billion yen in 2007.

Similar declines were also experienced in the numbers of establishments and employees in the construction industry. The number of employees in the industry in 2008 was 5.4 million which is 17.8% less than in 2000, and the number of establishments also fell from 607 000 in 2001 to 549 000 in 2006. As shown in **Table 2**, housing construction started in 2009 amounted to 788 410 units or 72.5 million square metres. The market has been recently dominated by private-sector projects. Although reinforced concrete (with and without steel frames) gained popularity in the mid-2000s, wooden structures still remain the most common structural form for housing construction.

Given the downturn in the housing market, the construction business is highly competitive. Yet, the Japanese construction industry is still among the most developed in the world. The industry has been renowned for its innovative construction techniques and designs (e.g., earthquake-resistant and green building designs), uncompromising quality control, and zealous commitment to research and development. Owing to their experience and expertise, many large Japanese construction companies have been increasingly placed in the world spotlight. They have built houses in other fast-growing regions in different parts of the world, including Europe, the Middle-east, Southeast Asia, the United States, and Greater China.

South Korea

In spite of the Asian Financial Crisis in 1997, the housing bubble reinflated quickly in South Korea in the early 2000s. Generally speaking, there are two reasons underlying the price hike. First, housing development in South Korea has lagged economic development. The ever-increasing demand was not met by market supply, pushing up house prices. Second, housing construction in South Korea has been shaped, in the context of repressive government financial policy, by speculative investment practices. The more affluent have enthusiastically invested in the housing market, further stimulating housing demand.

The annual completion of private housing increased from 253 388 units in 1999 to 398 803 units in 2007, that is, a rise of 57.4%. However, the new supply of housing was retarded by the global financial turmoil in 2008. The private sector experienced a drop of 42.3% in new supply that year. During the housing boom, the Korean government took some initiatives to meet people's housing

Table 2 New dwelling construction started in Japan

Year		1999	2004	2005	2006	2007	2008	2009
Funding source (no. of units)	Private	677 037	952 839	1 044 946	1 146 888	960 938	984 392	690 058
	Public	537 564	236 210	191 229	143 503	99 803	109 093	98 352
	Housing Loan Corporation	454 981	161 182	114 691	67 389	33 960	43 593	39 897
Type of structure (no. of units)	Wooden	565 544	540 756	542 848	559 201	504 546	516 868	430 121
	Steel-frame reinforced concrete	96 507	46 351	28 466	31 158	21 282	18 714	5658
	Reinforced concrete	288 103	358 127	436 568	470 604	335 548	336 325	192 396
	Steel frame	262 316	240 122	225 057	226 991	197 394	219 519	158 298
	Concrete block	874	492	427	520	402	469	610
	Others	1257	3201	2809	1917	1569	1590	1327
Total (no. of units)		1 214 601	1 189 049	1 236 175	1 290 391	1 060 741	1 093 485	788 410
Floor area (million square metres)		125.4	112.3	113.6	115.5	95.9	96.4	72.5

demand and need. For example, in redevelopment projects, developers are required to provide a prescribed minimum amount of small-sized housing units. In the period between 2003 and 2012, a total of 1 million long-term public rental housing units were scheduled for construction in order to address the housing problems of lower-income people. Since 2009, however, housing policy under the *Bogeumjari* plan has been modified to also include a large portion of subsidised owner-occupied houses for middle-income households.

The number of general construction enterprises as of the end of 2009 was 10 894, which was only slightly fewer than the figure in 2004. As of July 2010, there were 1.8 million people working in the construction industry in South Korea. There was a gradual increase in the total domestic construction value from 148 267 billion won in 2004 to 186 901 billion won in 2009, or 26.1% (**Table 3**). The private sector remained the largest contributor to total domestic construction. Korean construction companies have also been looking overseas where the potential for growth has been far more significant. The overall value of the construction sector jumped by almost 540% in less than 5 years, reaching 30 119 billion won in 2009. This indicates that the export of services by the construction industry has been growing rapidly in recent years.

Singapore

Unlike many other jurisdictions in the region, the Singaporean government has heavily intervened in the local housing sector. The housing market has long been characterised by a large proportion of state-built housing constructed by the Housing and Development Board (HDB). About 81% of the resident population in the country lives in HDB flats (in 2009). In the financial year 2008/09, 1769 HDB flats were completed with another 31 058 units under construction. Compared with the level in 2003/04, the amount of HDB housing under construction in 2008/09 increased by 106%. Yet, as indicated in **Table 4**, the total value of building work contracts in the private residential sector started exceeding that of the public sector after 1999. **Table 4** illustrates the differences in public and private housing completions over the past 10 years.

Private housing development in Singapore has grown fast despite barriers to market entry. Private developers must hold a Housing Developer's License in order to carry out housing developments with more than four dwelling units, pursuant to the 'Housing Developers (Control and Licensing) Act'. To obtain the license, developers have to fulfil certain requirements, like provide a minimum paid-up capital of SGD100 000. Moreover, the Singaporean government prescribes sale and purchase agreements for new flat sales and exercises tight controls on developers' withdrawal of money from their project accounts. The proportion of the working force engaged in the construction industry dropped from 7.2% (around 109 000 out of 1.5 million people) in 1999 to 6.09% (around 113 800 out of 1.9 million people) in 2009. Overall, the construction industry contributed to about 3.5% of the country's GDP in the past decade.

Table 3 Statistics of the construction industry in South Korea

Year		2004	2005	2006	2007	2008	2009
New housing constructed (no. of units)	Public	123 991	140 978	143 694	156 989	141 160	168 300
	Private	339 809	322 663	325 809	398 803	230 125	213 487
	Total	463 800	463 641	469 503	555 792	371 285	381 787
No. of general construction enterprises		11 008	11 059	10 950	11 076	10 912	10 894
Domestic construction value (billion won)	Public	55 837	53 419	53 262	57 434	63 737	82 615
	Private	87 199	92 948	97 811	107 572	114 678	103 851
	Others	530	384	446	523	404	435
	Total	148 267	151 641	161 636	165 529	178 819	186 901
Overseas construction value (billion won)		4701	4890	10 117	16 139	32 736	30 119

Table 4 Statistics of the construction business in Singapore

Year		1999	2004	2005	2006	2007	2008	2009
Values of building work contracts (SGD million)	Public housing	2824	1277	1135	1163	1810	4677	2772
	Private housing	2115	2586	2589	4135	5551	6397	3526
Building plan approval for private housing (no. of units)		8290	10 038	5333	11 863	16 345	13 350	10 506
Building commencement for private housing (no. of units)		6806	4145	10 282	11 295	12 432	14 239	8603
Building completion for private housing (no. of units)		11 079	11 799	8697	6520	6513	10 122	10 488

Greater China

Mainland China

In comparison with the other well-developed economies discussed above, the house-building industry in mainland China has grown exceptionally fast in the past decade. The affluence of households, particularly those in cities, has swelled upon the economic expansion of the country, with improved household consumption power augmenting demand for private housing. The total floor space of commercialised housing sold rose by 3.6 times, from 130.0 million square metres in 1999 to 592.8 million square metres in 2008. The growth is estimated to be 7.6 times in terms of total revenue. As of 2008, there were 87 562 enterprises engaged in real estate development. More and more state-owned developers have turned into private enterprises. At the same time, owing to China's entry to the World Trade Organisation in 2001, barriers to foreign-funded companies entering China's real estate market have been reduced. This helps explain why Table 5 shows the number of foreign-funded real estate development enterprises in 2008 almost doubling since 2003.

In the 1980s, the Chinese construction industry was rather primitive. No building codes governed building product specification, design, and construction. Moreover, nearly all construction enterprises were directly supervised by the central ministries or municipal governments. Construction work projects were assigned by the authorities rather than being acquired through competitive bidding. That is why the construction industry in mainland China was regarded as a single large enterprise with a centralised hierarchical organisation where factors of production and other resources were almost exclusively realised through administrative channels. These conditions were not favourable for the development of the industry and represented a fundamental lack of market competition.

The picture has changed significantly along with reform of the industry in the 1990s and 2000s. Construction law was promulgated by the National People's Congress in 1997 to regulate various aspects of the industry such as the qualifications for operation, contracts among different parties, and quality of construction. The industry has since become more market-based. Table 5 indicates that the numbers of state-owned and collective-owned construction enterprises declined in the period between 1999 and 2008. The industry employed 33.1 million people, about 4.3% of the total labour force in 2008. The total gross output of the industry grew at an average annual rate of 50.7% in the period between 1999 and 2008. It amounted to 6203.6 billion yuan in 2008. The whole industry earned a profit of 220.2 billion yuan. The total housing investment completed increased from 263.8 billion yuan in 1999 to 2244.1 billion yuan in 2008, corresponding to an average annual growth of 83.4%. Throughout the country (except Hong Kong, Macau, and Taiwan), around 4.9 million housing units were completed in 2008.

The Hong Kong Special Administrative Region (Hong Kong)

In spite of the restricted geographical size of Hong Kong (about 1107 km^2), the local house-building industry is famous for its high productivity and efficiency. About half of the total population in the territory lives in the private housing sector. While there are thousands of companies engaged in the real estate development in the territory, the private house development sector has been dominated by several large property developers with a lot of political and financial power. Hong Kong

Table 5 Numbers of real estate development and construction enterprises in mainland China

Year		1999	2003	2004	2005	2006	2007	2008
Number of real estate development enterprises	Domestic-funded	21 422	33 107	53 495	50 957	53 268	56 965	81 282
	State-owned	7370	4558	4775	4145	3797	3617	3941
	Collective-owned	4127	2205	2390	1796	1586	1430	1520
	Funded from Hong Kong, Macao, and Taiwan	3167	2840	3639	3443	3519	3524	3916
	Foreign-funded	1173	1176	2108	1890	1923	2029	2364
	Total	25 762	37 123	59 242	56 290	58 710	6258	87 562
Number of construction enterprises	State-owned	9394	6638	6513	6007	5555	5319	5315
	Collective-owned	27 197	10 425	8959	8090	7051	6614	5843
	Funded from Hong Kong, Macao, and Taiwan	664	535	511	516	479	482	474
	Foreign-funded	341	287	386	388	370	365	363
	Others	9638	30 803	42 649	43 749	46 711	49 294	59 100
	Total	47 234	48 688	59 018	58 750	60 166	62 074	71 095

Table 6 Statistics of the house-building industry in Hong Kong

Year		1999	2003	2004	2005	2006	2007
Number of establishments	Construction	20 233	19 520	18 302	17 985	19 057	19 399
	Real estate development and leasing	3583	3084	3276	3351	3037	3134
	Real estate management and maintenance	465	431	292	367	543	581
	Real estate agency	1958	1496	1050	1220	1306	1411
	Total	26 239	24 531	22 920	22 923	23 943	24 525
Number of people directly engaged	Construction	157 685	124 933	122 007	122 870	135 337	114 294
	Real estate development and leasing	9464	8794	8900	9375	10 260	10 476
	Real estate management and maintenance	53 280	58 258	62 186	68 126	67 523	67 885
	Real estate agency	14 551	13 409	14 819	15 585	16 179	17 762
	Total	234 980	205 394	207 912	215 956	229 299	210 417
All private residential projects	Number of projects	286	213	159	127	131	140
	Total expenses (million HK$)	43 010	29 600	21 869	21 131	22 363	19 788
	Payments to contractors (million HK$)	28 287	22 981	16 365	14 308	16 352	13 939
	Building materials and fittings supplied (million HK$)	134	0[a]	0[a]	2	5	8
	Architectural design and technical consultancy fees (million HK$)	1441	1125	938	747	747	689
	Interest payments (million HK$)	10 686	2273	1143	2128	2966	3540
	Other project expenses (million HK$)	2462	3221	3423	3947	2294	1612

[a]Less than HK$0.5 million.

developers that deliver their product to the market at the right time can reap obscene profits.

Table 6 shows that 24 525 establishments worked in the industry at the end of 2007, engaging a total of 210 417 people. The numbers of establishments and people directly engaged have dropped compared with 1999. Similarly, the total number of active private residential projects decreased from 286 in 1999 to 140 in 2007, and the total expenses incurred experienced a drop by 54% in the same period. These decreasing trends are actually signs of the maturation of the industry in the local market and more and more housing developers have turned their attention to mainland China. Overall, the construction industry contributed around HK$40.2 billion to the region's GDP (2.5% of total GDP) in 2007.

Taiwan

Taiwan's housing market has been growing steadily since 2003 on account of the relaxation of the rules hindering foreign investment in the region and closer economic linkage between Taiwan and mainland China. The Taiwanese government put forward an ambitious 5-year property development plan worth NT$500 billion in 2003. The construction industry employed around 842 000 people in 2008, corresponding to 8.1% of the total labour force in Taiwan. However, the industry's contribution to the region's economy was relatively small. It only shared 2.9% of the total GDP, or NT$363.3 billion in 2008.

Thailand

Starting from the mid-1970s, the economy of Thailand grew very quickly until the Asian Financial Crisis in 1997. At that time, Thailand strived to become an industrialised country and a vast amount of construction works were taken on. In spite of the economic slump between 1997 and 2003, Thailand's construction industry has grown very quickly in recent years. The value of gross output or receipts of construction establishment amounted to 394 billion baht in 2008, increasing by 22.5% from 322 billion baht in 2003. In the same year, the intermediate consumption and value added were 276 and 118 billion baht, respectively. The respective rises were 21.8% and 24.3% in comparison with the figures in 2003. As shown in Table 7, the value of residential construction also increased continuously from 2001 to 2005. In 2006, permits were issued by the authority for construction of a total of 146 229 residential buildings throughout the country, resulting in the addition of 218 767 dwelling units or an increase in floor space of 45.6 million square metres.

In the 2009 Construction Industry Survey, the number of building companies in Thailand in 2008 was estimated at 29 360, constituting an increase of around 41.4% since 2003. The number of persons engaged in the construction

Table 7 Gross fixed capital formation contributed by residential construction in Thailand

Year	2001	2002	2003	2004	2005
Private housing (million baht)	78 549	104 063	130 997	167 806	194 665
Public housing (million baht)	11 333	8080	6751	14 451	30 244

industry increased from 234 925 in 2003 to 364 694 in 2008, representing a 55.2% rise. However, the survey results also indicate that the majority of construction establishments (83.1%) were small in scale, with not more than 10 persons. On the whole, there was a business concentration in a few large-scale listed construction companies. Apart from local projects, large Thai construction companies have also started working on construction projects in Bangladesh and other neighbouring countries like Laos in recent years. Compared with Asian counterparts, the Thai construction industry is still far from mature with a significant absence of professional skills and advanced technologies. In this light, there has been a call for the establishment of a national institution of construction to improve industry standards.

Malaysia

The house-building industry in Malaysia has been strongly influenced by sociopolitical forces and transformations in the country. For example, the May 13 incident in 1969, involving sectarian riots in Kuala Lumpur, revealed the socioeconomic imbalances between different ethnic groups. To encourage homeownership among *bumiputera* and promote greater interaction among the various ethnic groups living in Malaysia, the Malaysian government introduced the National Economic Policy in the 1970s. Under that policy, housing developers in Malaysia have been required to set aside at least 30% of the completed housing units for the *bumiputera* and offer a discount of 5–15% to them. In spite of its social objectives, this policy has resulted in large inefficiencies in the local housing delivery system. Nonetheless, the development industry is still a major contributor to the country's GDP even though the housing completion rate has decreased in recent years as shown in **Table 8**.

The Malaysian construction sector recorded strong growth between 2006 and 2008, with an 8.8% increase. As of December 2008, the loans made by commercial banks and merchant banks for construction of residential properties amounted to 7300.8 million ringgit in total. The progressive growth in the sector can be ascribed to the implementation of the construction-related activities under the Ninth Malaysia Plan and other fiscal stimulus packages. **Table 8** illustrates that the number of people engaged in the construction industry increased by 12.3% in the period between 2005 and 2009. However, the fast growth of the industry also resulted in a rise in business malpractices. Since the late 2000s, the Malaysian government has stepped up its control over the house-building industry. For example, over 1000 housing developers were blacklisted for having abandoned projects, defective works, or noncompliance with decisions of the Housing Tribunal and failure paying fines.

Concluding Remarks

It appears that the pace of development in home building industries in different Asian countries is quite dissimilar. While the construction industry's contribution to GDP in most jurisdictions in the region decreased over the period between 2003 and 2008, this does not necessarily represent a recession in the industry across the region. While high-speed economic development in the less developed countries has offered opportunities for intensive growth in house-building industries, challenges such as quality assurance and sustainable construction still need to be addressed.

Table 8 Statistics of the house-building industry in Malaysia

Year	2005	2006	2007	2008	2009
Building plan approval (no. of units)	161 657	154 703	141 002	115 874	78 336
Building commencement (no. of units)	152 892	153 268	133 948	108 012	86 549
Building completion (no. of units)	180 600	171 448	181 123	134 334	101 604
Number of persons engaged in construction (thousand persons)	904.4	908.9	992.5	998.0	1015.9
Number of persons engaged in real estate, renting, and business activities (thousand persons)	459.0	508.4	558.1	553.2	601.9

See also: Housing and the State in China; Housing and the State in South Asia.

Further Reading

Asian Development Bank (2010) *Key Indicators for Asia and the Pacific 2010*. Manila: Asian Development Bank.

Ball M (2003) Markets and the structure of the house-building industry: An international perspective. *Urban Studies* 40(5/6): 897–916.

Chiang YH, Anson M, and Raftery J (eds.) (2004) *The Construction Sector in Asian Economies*. Abingdon, UK: Spon.

Ganesan S (2000) *Employment, Technology and Construction Development: With Case Studies in Asia and China*. Aldershot, UK: Ashgate.

Guan K, Feng K, and Zeng SX (2001) Urban housing reform and development in China: China's construction industry in transition. *Building Research and Information* 29(4): 286–292.

Lu Y and Fox PW (2001) *The Construction Industry in China: Its Image, Employment Prospects and Skill Requirements*. Geneva: International Labour Office.

Raftery J, Pasadilla B, Chiang YH, Hui ECM, and Tang B (1998) Globalization and construction industry development: Implications of recent developments in the construction sector in Asia. *Construction Management and Economics* 16(6): 729–737.

Sparkes S and Howell S (eds.) (2003) *The House in Southeast Asia: A Changing Social, Economic and Political Domain*. London: RoutledgeCurzon.

Walker A and Flanagan R (eds.) (1991) *Property and Construction in Asia Pacific: Hong Kong, Japan and Singapore*. Oxford, UK: BSP Professional Books.

Relevant Websites

www.bca.gov.sg – Building and Construction Authority, Singapore.
www.censtatd.gov.hk – Census and Statistics Department, Hong Kong.
www.statistics.gov.my – Department of Statistics, Malaysia.
www.singstat.gov.sg – Department of Statistics, Singapore.
www.hdb.gov.sg – Housing and Development Board, Singapore.
www.mlit.go.jp – Ministry of Land, Infrastructure, Transport, and Tourism, Japan.
www.stats.gov.cn – National Bureau of Statistics of China.
www.stat.gov.tw – National Statistics, Taiwan.
http://web.nso.go.th – National Statistics Office, Thailand.
www.rvd.gov.hk – Rating and Valuation Department, Hong Kong.
www.stat.go.jp – Statistics Bureau, Japan.
http://kostat.go.kr – Statistics, Korea.
www.jpph.gov.my – Valuation and Property Services Department, Malaysia.

House Building Industries: Latin America

A de Castro, Columbia University, New York, USA

© 2012 Elsevier Ltd. All rights reserved.

Glossary

Housing deficit Quality-of-life indicator that reflects the number of inadequate houses and can be identified as (1) quantitative deficit (number of houses that should be built so that each family has one house) or (2) qualitative deficit (the number of houses that are in need to be repaired).

Slum dwellings Urban areas that lack basic infrastructures (such as water, sewage, or electricity) or secure tenement.

Third sector Economic sector formed by not-for-profit organisations. It excludes municipal, state, and federal public institutions and includes NGOs, community groups, and international organisations such as the Inter-American Development Bank (IDB).

Introduction

The house-building industry, an integral part of the construction industry, is formed by an array of actors that include providers of construction materials, developers, finance institutions, constructors, policy makers, engineering and design firms, and users. Housing production greatly depends on the role that private, public, and voluntary institutions play; each of them invests its financial resources in specific market segments, although cooperation across institutional sectors occurs. This article provides an overview of housing developments managed by the sectors identified above in a comparative perspective.

Historical Context

The formalisation of the public housing sector in Latin America dates back to the end of the nineteenth century. At that time, the modernisation and industrialisation of many urban areas increased their population. Population growth was not necessarily accompanied by a transformation in urban infrastructure, and therefore lower-income households often lived in overcrowded or illegal settlements – a famous example being the Morro da Providencia, the first favela to appear in Rio de Janeiro in 1898. In response, governmental and religious institutions resettled residents of informal settlements in social housing, which led to the development of long-term affordable housing programmes. The massive rural-to-urban migration within poor populations expanded in Latin America throughout the twentieth century. In the 1950s, approximately 330 000 people lived on the outskirts of Mexico City; by the early 1990s, this number had grown to approximately 9.5 million. In the absence of private housing developments for that population, governments in many Latin American countries created public housing corporations such as the Banco Nacional de Habitação (BNH) in Brazil or the Corporación de la Vivienda (CORVI) in Chile, which produced mass housing projects to alleviate national housing deficits.

During the past two decades, global trends of urbanisation, democratisation, decentralisation, and globalisation have driven the housing sector in Latin America. In this period, many governments shifted toward a market-based approach, which relies heavily on increased economic growth and on a more equal distribution of this growth. The facilitation of private market housing provision was intended to reduce planning regulations and controls, but failed to reach a greater number of poor people with a greater degree of efficiency. Macroeconomic stability and the growth of mortgage securitisation have substantially increased the availability of housing finance in the region and led to a wider range of financial instruments for housing provision as well as prompted a transformation in the role of governments from a housing provider to an enabler.

Demographic Context

Latin America is one of the most urbanised regions. In 2007 its urban population was 450 million, close to 80% of the region's total population. Causes for this process of urbanisation are twofold, the first being a massive rural-to-urban migration over the past 40 years and second the explosive population growth due to high birth rates and rapidly declining death rates. Over 61% of Latin America's current urban population lives in seven cities with population exceeding 5 million people: Mexico City, São Paulo, Buenos Aires, Rio de Janeiro, Lima, Bogotá, and Santiago. Accelerated urbanisation has led to concentrations of the poor in urban centres and has resulted in unbalanced national and regional human-settlement networks throughout Latin America.

Housing Context

Approximately 50% of the construction industry is involved in residential activities, whose revenue comprises approximately 5% of the national GDP of many Latin American countries. Between 5 and 7% of the national working population is employed in the construction sector, though its growth differs between countries (see **Figure 1**). Panama has the highest national growth rate (30.7%), while Colombia represents the lowest growth rate (1.7%). By contrast, some countries in the region are seeing their construction industries decline, such as El Salvador.

Latin America has a higher level of home ownership than most other regions of the world at 73% on average in 2007 (see **Figure 2**). Although the mortgage portfolio, outstanding loans as a share of GDP, is very small when compared with other world regions, in 2001 it represented $123 billion, while for North America the amount was $6087 billion and for Europe it was $3012 billion. At the national level, Panama is the country where the mortgage portfolio represents the greatest percentage (27%) of its national GDP; Venezuela is the country where mortgage portfolio represents the lowest percentage (0.2%) of GDP. In Latin America, less than a quarter of all housing is financed through formal mechanisms; and mortgages or loans for building or buying a home account for a small fraction of total credit. Lack of access to credit forces families to live and work in substandard housing. Housing quality, measured by access to piped water and sewer system, and quality of building materials are lower across the region, although variations exist (see **Figure 3**). Paraguay and Chile can be seen as extremes in this broad spectrum, with 8.6 and 82.5%, respectively, of housing with toilets connected to a sewerage system.

Public Housing Developments

Housing programmes represent the public sector's attempt at reducing the number of inadequate dwellings and the housing deficit for the low – and sometimes middle – income households. In 2007, around 45% of the total housing deficit in Latin America was quantitative, equalling approximately 24 million dwellings (see **Table 1**). Over the past 10 years, the annual housing demand in Latin America was estimated at 2.5 million dwellings, but only 1.5 million units are added to the housing stock annually. This deficit is mostly due to structural problems in the housing provision system, low purchasing power, insufficient public expenditures, and

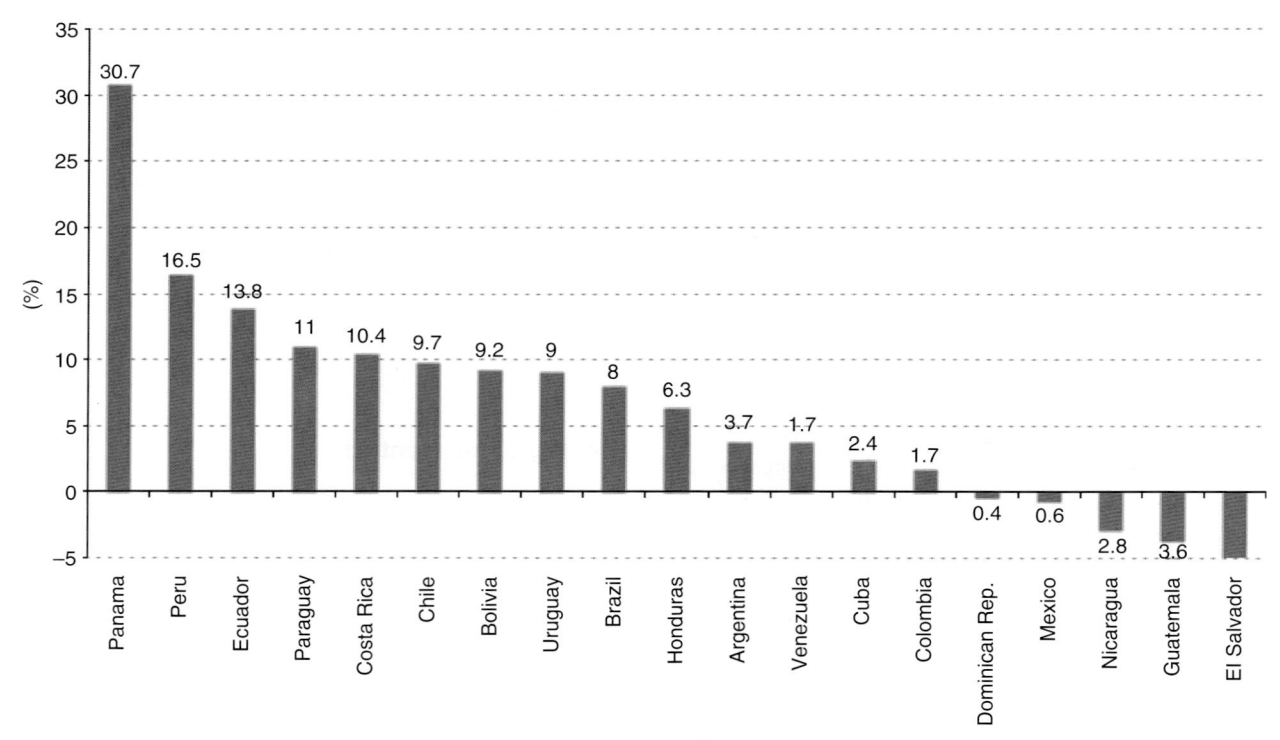

Figure 1 Growth rate of GDP for the construction sector in some Latin American countries (2008).
Source: Data from Centro de estudios de la construcción y el desarrollo urbano y regional (2010) Contexto sectorial Internacional: Colombia y América Latina. Bogotá, Colombia: CENAC (based on United Nations, Comisión Económica para América Latina).

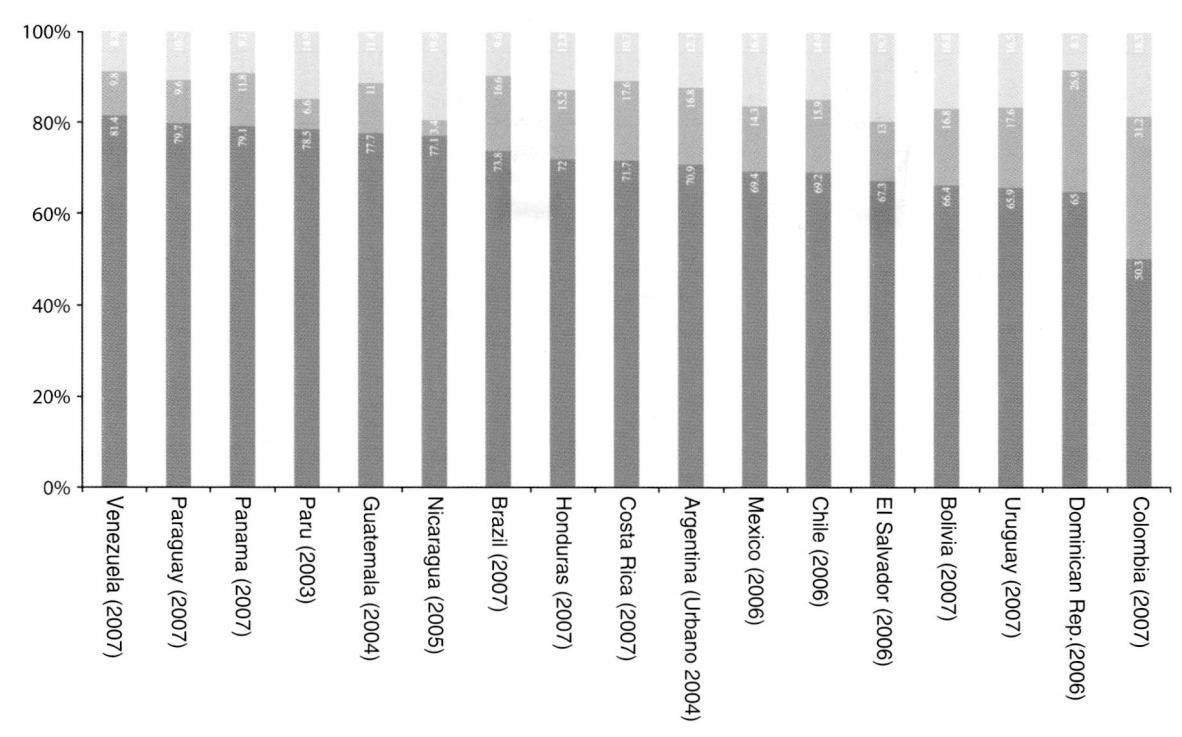

Figure 2 Home ownership by type and percentage in some Latin American countries.
Source: Data from Centro de estudios de la construcción y el desarrollo urbano y regional (2010) Contexto sectorial Internacional: Colombia y América Latina. Bogotá, Colombia: CENAC and UN-Habitat (with calculations based on United Nations, Comisión Económica para América Latina).

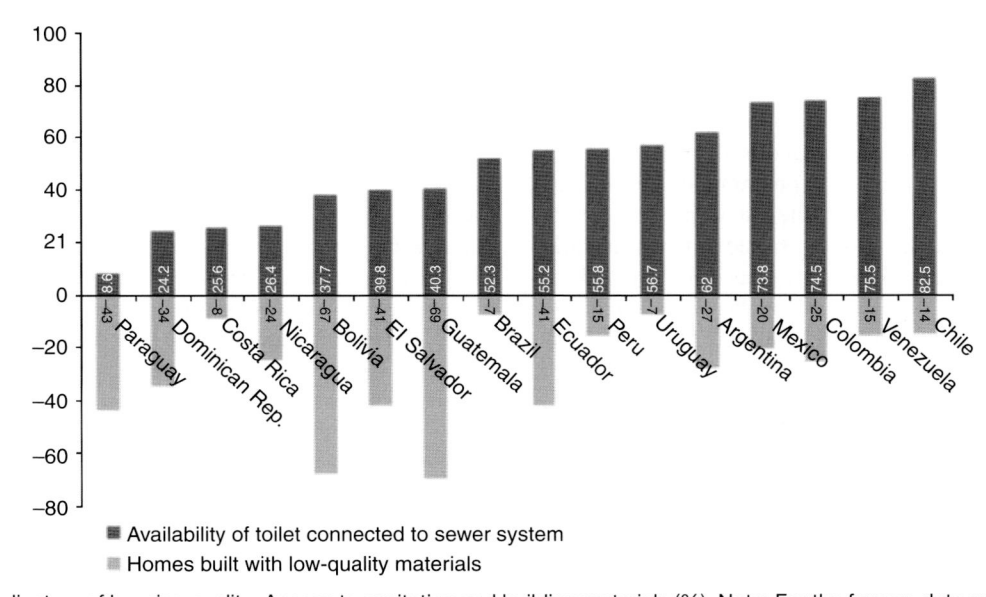

Figure 3 Indicators of housing quality: Access to sanitation and building materials (%). Note: For the former, data vary from 2006 to 2008. The latter shows housing quality differences between population within 20% of lowest and highest incomes.
Source: Data from Informe Regional solore Desarrello Humano para America Latina y el Caribe (2010) Contexto sectorial Internacional: Colombia y América Latina. Bogotá, Colombia: CENAC (data based on Gasparini et al. (2009a), SEDLAC (CEDLAS and World Bank), appeared at publications from UN Comisión Económica para América Latina and UNDP).

inadequate access to land. Common methods of increasing access to developable land by governments include redeveloping publicly owned land and acquiring private land through expropriation. This sometimes requires the eviction of informal residents, who are in many cases relocated in similar areas.

Table 1 Quantitative housing deficit in Latin American countries

Country (Year)	Houses (No.)	Housing deficit (No.)	Housing deficit (%)
Honduras (2001)	1 211 307	700 000	57.8
Nicaragua (2005)[a]	1 091 400	550 000	50.4
Bolivia (2007)[a]	2 457 000	855 000	34.8
El Salvador (2004)	1 626 036	545 000	33.5
Venezuela (2001)	5 261 202	1 600 000	30.4
Dominican Republic (2007)[a]	2 634 865	800 000	30.4
Argentina (2001)	10 073 625	3 000 000	29.8
Paraguay (2007)[a]	1 492 683	400 000	26.8
Guatemala (2002)	2 200 608	410 097	18.6
Costa Rica (2004)	1 055 075	189 261	17.9
Mexico (2005)	24 803 625	4 290 665	17.3
Peru (2003)[a]	6 050 227	1 010 878	16.7
Colombia (2005)	10 570 899	1 307 757	12.4
Brazil (2007)[a]	58 377 273	6 656 526	11.4
Chile (2005)	4 000 000	450 000	11.3

[a]The number of homes corresponds to an estimation based on total population and home average size.
Source: Data from United Nations-Habitat (2010) Estado de las Ciudades de América Latina y el Caribe. ONU Habitat (Data based from United Nations, Comisión Económica para América Latina).

In Latin America, a number of public policies are devoted to upgrading of informal areas. Public spending on housing programmes not only exceeds 2% of GDP in several countries – Bolivia, Nicaragua, Dominican Republic, and Cuba, but also tends to be less than 1% of the GDP in Columbia, Chile, and Uruguay. Common examples include subsidising construction, transferring property rights to residents, renovating inadequate housing units, and building new social housing targeted specifically at low-income households. In some countries, these policies support a significant amount of housing projects. In Chile, subsidised housing represents more than 50% of new housing stock; in Brazil, the programme Minha Casa, Minha Vida (My House, My Life) supports the construction of 1 million new, publicly subsidised housing units. Public institutions create privately owned real estate development companies (e.g., the Companhia Metropolitana de Habitação (COHAB) in São Paulo) and financial institutions (e.g., the Banco Nacional de Desenvolvimento (BNDES) in Brazil) that manage the production and mortgage portfolio of new units. While the housing deficit continues to increase exponentially within the lowest-income segment of the population, public housing programmes are often focused on income segments that can afford cost-recovery rent and/or mortgage costs.

Single-Family Housing

Detached and semi-detached single housing units are built either to provide quick supply of houses (such as in emergencies) or to urbanise large areas in empty, affordable lots. For this reason, houses need to incorporate essential infrastructure such as sewage, water, and electricity. These houses are predesigned and often hold patented construction systems. Standardisation of building processes also brings patenting companies the opportunity to lower construction costs, which has led to the experimentation with construction materials. For example, Venezuelan Petrocasas (Oil Houses) utilise oil subproducts moulded into lightweight concrete blocks. These blocks and insulating concrete forms (ICF) reduce construction labour and time, although they limit the flexibility to change the interior distribution of the house.

The massive construction of single-family houses ensures affordable housing supply with reasonable profit for the house-building industry. For this reason, they are used to urbanise large, remote areas, which often lack urban services and whose residents have long commutes. The houses built through the Programa de Fraccionamiento Popular at Ecatepec, or the Casas Geo (Geo Houses) in Mexico, are popular examples of these types of intervention. Public institutions also sponsor self-help housing projects, where the dweller can act as the developer, constructor, or designer of his or her own house. Designed in conjunction with architecture firms, the Quinta Monroy Project in Iquique (Chile) and the mutirões (Brazil) are examples of sponsored self-help housing.

Multifamily Housing

Multifamily social housing encompasses a great variety of typologies. Among them, the linear and the H-shaped blocks, most commonly seen in São Paulo, illustrate a mass housing solution and the ideal of a green city (see **Figure 4**). These buildings minimise their footprint and costs of building maintenance, while also maximising natural lighting, ventilation, and occupation density. For these reasons, public institutions have adopted the

Figure 4 Social housing blocks in São Francisco, São Paulo. Source: Author's photo.

'verticalisation' of social housing as an affordable option for housing large populations in relatively small lots. Typically, predesigned housing plans are used for public bidding, where mid-sized and large private companies compete on the basis of costs and time to complete construction. Recently, São Paulo and Rio de Janeiro have intensively looked for new housing solutions and asked architectural designers to design social housing projects in strategic urban areas. In some cases municipalities have called renowned architects to design specific housing projects such as Edson Elito in São Paulo and Jorge Mario Jáuregui in Rio de Janeiro. Additionally, municipalities and federal governments have launched national architectural competitions (e.g., Morar Carioca or Habitaçao Para Todos).

Corporate Private Housing Developments

The location of empty housing lots and the land use regulations that apply to them drive, among other factors, the actions of private housing developers. Their profit in low-income housing projects is mostly tied to the quantity of dwellings that are built, while the profit at middle and upper class developments relies more on the materials used for construction and finishing. The scarcity of available land in some cities in Latin America has pushed private investors to either use 'verticalisation' of housing in central urban areas or urbanise new residential areas on the outskirts. Gentrification processes have tied upscale private housing development to previously neglected urban centres of large Latin American cities, such as the

Figure 5 View of the favela of Paraisópolis, São Paulo. Source: Author's photo.

Table 2 Public housing programmes in Latin American countries

Subsidies for construction or acquisition of house

Bolivia	Financiamiento de vivienda (PFV)
	Subsidio directo a la vivienda
Brazil	Carta de Crédito Associativo
	Programa de Arrendamento Residencial (PAR)
	Crédito Solidário
	Minha casa, Minha vida[a]
Chile	Chile Barrio
	Vivienda Social Dinámica sin Deuda
	Fondo Concursable para proyectos habitacionales solidarios
	Sistema de subsidio habitacional DS 40
	Sistema de subsidio habitacional rural
Colombia	Subsidio Familiar de vivienda
	Sistema de Vivienda de Interés Social[a]
Costa Rica	Bono familiar de vivienda
	Bono familiar de vivienda mediante la aplicación del art 59 de la ley del SFNV.
	Ahorro – Bono – Crédito (ABC)
Dominican Republic	Subsidio habitacional
Cuba	Programa de Construcción y Rehabilitación de Viviendas[a]
Ecuador	Sistema de incentivos para vivienda urbana – Fideicomiso BEV
	Sistema de incentivos para vivienda rural y urbano marginal
	Sistema de incentivos – SIV Magisterio and Urbano
Guatemala	Subsidio directo para poblaciones desarraigadas y desmovilizadas
	Descentralización y desarrollo a la vivienda popular[a]
	Fortalecimiento a la demanda de vivienda popular[a]
Honduras	Convenio Asociación de municipios de Honduras – SOPTRAVI[a]
Mexico	Productos INFONAVIT
	Programa VIVAH
	Ahorro, subsidio y crédito para la vivienda progresiva 'Tu casa'
	HABITAT
Nicaragua	PRODEL
Panama	Apoyo Rápido para Viviendas de Interés Social
	Financiamiento Conjunto
	Fondo de Ahorro Habitacional
Paraguay	Redescuento de Créditos Hipotecarios
Uruguay	CREDIMATde créditos para materials
Venezuela	Nuevas urbanizaciones y viviendas de desarrollo progresivo

Upgrading of inadequate housing units

Argentina	Mejoramiento de Viviendas 'Mejor Vivir'
	Urbanización de Villas y Asentamientos Precarios[a]
Bolívia	Mejoramiento de viviendas en zonas endémicas de Chagas (Chagas)
Costa Rica	Reparaciones, ampliación., mejora y terminación de vivienda (RAMT)
Dominican Republic	Mejoramiento y/o reconstrucción de viviendas urbano y rural
Panamá	Mejoramiento Habitacional
	Fondo de Asistencia Habitacional[a]
Uruguay	Programa integrado de asentamientos irregulares (PIAI)[a]
Venezuela	Mejoramiento y ampliación de casas en barrios (Pr.)
	Rehabilitación de urbanizaciones populares
	Habilitación Física de las zonas de barrios[a]

Building of new social housing

Argentina	Fondo Nacional de Vivienda (FONAVI), Reactivación I, II
	Solidaridad Habitacional
	Emergencia Habitacional
	Urbanización de Villas y Asentamientos Precarios[a]
Bolivia	Vivienda Social y Solidaria (PVS)
	Prevención, mitigación de riesgos y atención de emergencias
Brazil	Habitar Brasil BID (HBB) – DI and UAS[a]
	Atendimento Habitacional através do Setor Público (PRÓ-MORADIA)[a]
	Subsídio à Habitação de Interesse Social (PSH)[a]
	Urbanização de Favelas (São Paulo)[a]

(Continued)

Table 2 (Continued)

	Minha casa, Minha vida[a]
Dominican Republic	Construcción de viviendas nuevas
	Construcción de viviendas nuevas de emergencia
Cuba	Programa de Construcción y Rehabilitación de Viviendas[a]
El Salvador	Casa para todos
Guatemala	Descentralización y desarrollo a la vivienda popular[a]
	Fortalecimiento a la demanda de vivienda popular[a]
Panama	Construcción de Viviendas
	Fondo de Asistencia Habitacional[a]
Paraguay	Cooperativas de Vivienda por Ayuda Mutua
Peru	Techo Propio con el Bono Familiar Habitacional
Uruguay	Cooperativas de vivienda por ayuda mutual
Venezuela	Habilitación Física de las zonas de barrios[a]
Urbanisation, Infrastructure, and Transference of Property Rights	
Argentina	Mejoramiento de Barrios (PROMEBA) (with BID)
	Urbanización de Villas y Asentamientos Precarios[a]
Brazil	Apoio à Melhoria das Condições de Habitabilidade de Assentamentos Precários
	Habitar Brasil BID (HBB) – DI and UAS[a]
	Atendimento Habitacional através do Setor Público (PRÓ-MORADIA)[a]
	Subsídio à Habitação de Interesse Social (PSH)[a]
	Urbanização de Favelas (São Paulo)[a]
	Favela-Bairro (Rio de Janeiro)
Colombia	Mejoramiento Integral de Barrios
Cuba	Programa de Construcción y Rehabilitación de Viviendas[a]
Nicaragua	Programa de Renovación urbana (PRU)
Uruguay	Programa integrado de asentamientos irregulares (PIAI)[a]
	Vivienda por ahorro previo
	MEVIR
	SIAV
Venezuela	Habilitación Física de las zonas de barrios[a]
	Nuevas urbanizaciones y viviendas regulares

[a]Programme is present in several groups.
Note: This list is not exhaustive and might represent programmes that have been adapted into new policies.

Punta Pacífica (Pacific Point) in Panama City and the Berrini area in São Paulo. Private developers have also built gated communities in an attempt to provide security and services to upper classes. These walled areas limit pedestrian and car access for residents and guests, have private services such as security and garbage collection, and sometimes also commercial malls, sport centres, or movie theatres. Gated communities represent an exclusionary urban model that elicits social inequality and insecurity. The Interlomas area of Mexico City and the Alphavilles communities in São Paulo are some of the most significant examples of luxury gated communities.

Mixed Public–Private Housing Developments

Public housing institutions have recently developed policy tools to share expenses and profits of social housing projects with private companies. Called public–private partnerships (PPP), these schemes allow both parties to negotiate the land use and master planning activities within a particular area. PPPs allow real estate and construction stakeholders to assume part of the expenses associated with the construction of physical infrastructure and social housing in an area. In return, these companies can use a percentage of the land to build and develop their own projects. Advocates of PPPs allege that this approach is socially sustainable and improves social inclusion through the creation of mixed-income housing areas. Urban areas already undergoing the process of gentrification, such as the port area in the centre of Rio de Janeiro, incentivise the development of PPPs. Currently, public discourse on PPPs is focused on how to avoid induced eviction in these areas.

Third Sector Housing Developments

Housing stock directly produced by nonprofit organisations is small when compared with public and private sectors. However, they have an important role in reaching population groups that fall out of existing public and private programmes and in promoting inclusive policies to integrate the poor into mainstream urban life. Some of these institutions advocate for the implementation of housing rights, while others provide housing-related infrastructure and unilateral or multilateral financing for low-income housing projects. Often, these organisations work within the frame of existing public programmes.

Individual Private Housing Developments

The construction of single-family houses built by homeowners can be considered either formal or informal depending on many factors, the most significant being the legal right of property ownership. Informal dwellers represent 30.8% of the population of Latin America, and this number has risen steadily during the second half of the twentieth century. In Mexico City, for example, the population living in self-constructed homes has increased from 14% in 1952 to an estimated 60% in 1990. Historically, governments that are unable to afford provision of formal sector housing or services encouraged or permitted land invasions for the development of informal settlements. In cities where the government took measures to prevent land invasions, formal housing units were subdivided as families rented rooms in other family's houses or constructed backyard shacks on plots of subleased land. The lack of access to loans by many households erodes housing affordability and perpetuates informal housing provision. This is caused by several factors, including (1) insufficient incomes, (2) lack of clear land title and ability to provide employment documentation need for the loans, and (3) difficulty of return guarantees from unfulfilled loans. Housing finance institutions intending to assist low-income people have often proved inaccessible to the majority of the poor, which highlights the importance of financing alternatives such as microloan programmes and noncommercial bank programmes.

Slum dwellings are often built in different construction stages. In a first stage, many of them rely on reused materials (such as wood, PVC, and lightweight panels). Later on, with economic or family growth, the dwellings gain additional floors constructed of brick and concrete. In Brazil, the consumption of cement in informal settlements exceeds the rate of formal construction activities. In addition, favelas like Paraisopolis (São Paulo) have developed their own informal real estate market (see **Figure 5**).

Further Reading

Centro de estudios de la construcción y el desarrollo urbano y regional (2010) Contexto sectorial Internacional: Colombia y América Latina. Bogotá, Colombia: CENAC.

Comisión Económica para América Latina (2006) Instrumentos Financieros para mejorar el acceso a la vivienda de los sectores de menores ingresos en América Latina y el Caribe. Santiago, Chile: Naciones Unidas.

Duncan J (2003) Causes of Inadequate Housing in Latin America and the Caribbean. Habitat for Humanity. http://www.habitat.org/lac_eng/pdf/causes.pdf (accessed 1 October 2011).

Gilbert A (2000) La Vivienda en América Latina. Washington, DC: INDES Documentos de Trabajo – n. I-7.

Jha AK (2005) Low Income Housing in Latin America and the Caribbean, En Breve, 101. The World Bank.

Lora E (Coord.), Powell A and Sanguinetti P (2008) Calidad de Vida Urbana, más que ladrillos y cemento. In: Calidad de Vida: más allá de los hechos. Banco Interamericano de Desarrollo (BID), Serie de Desarrollo en las Américas.

National Administrative Department of Statistics of Colombia – DANE (2001) Statistics on the Construction Sector. Santiago, Chile: Economic Commission for Latin America and the Caribbean (ECLAC).

Salas Serrano J (2001) Latinoamerica: Hambre de Vivienda, in Boletin del Instituto de Vivienda, vol. 17, numero 45. Santiago, Chile: Universidad de Chile (INVI-FAUUCH).

Simioni D and Szalachman R (2007) Primera Evaluación del Programa Regional de Vivienda Social y Asentamientos Humanos para América Latina y el Caribe. Santiago, Chile: United Nations.

Tapia Zarricueta R (2006) Programas Habitacionales en America Latina y su relación con programas que contemplan la evolutividad del habitat. Santiago, Chile: Biblioteca Digital INVI, http://www.invi.uchile.cl/documentos/tapia.pdf (accessed 1 October 2011).

The World Bank (2008) Latin America and the Caribbean Data Profile 2008.

United Nations Development Program – UNDP (2010) First Human Development Report for Latin America & the Caribbean. United Nations.

United Nations-Habitat (2010) Estado de las Ciudades de América Latina y el Caribe. ONU Habitat.

Winchester L (2005) Sustainable Human Settlements Development in Latin America and the Caribbean. Santiago: Chile: United Nations.

House Building Industries: Post-Socialist

S Tsenkova, University of Calgary, Calgary, AB, Canada

© 2012 Elsevier Ltd. All rights reserved.

Glossary

Commonwealth of Independent States
Commonwealth of Independent States, whose participating countries are former Soviet Republics, is a regional organisation with coordinating powers in trade, finance, lawmaking, and security.

Forms of housing provision Forms of housing provision are distinguished on the basis of processes and institutions related to the promotion, production, allocation, and consumption of housing.

Private housebuilders Private housebuilders have a strategic role in the provision of new housing and act as residential developers. They manage the entire development process from identification of the site, through planning negotiations, land provision, supply of building materials and equipment, labour contracts, marketing, financing, and the final sale of dwellings.

Speculative housebuilding Speculative housebuilding operates by linking investors with capital, land, building materials, equipment, or labour. The home is built with the intention of being sold at the end of the production cycle or presold in the case of multi-family housing.

The Socialist Legacy

The housing industry in postsocialist countries has gone through a dramatic process of restructuring in the last two decades. Housing construction in the socialist planned economy was dominated by the public sector with state and local governments acting as developers and state-owned construction enterprises as builders. Housing was allocated according to housing needs and was universally affordable due to bureaucratic regulation of prices. The production and investment in housing were centrally planned, and market mechanisms were excluded in the production of housing. Systemic similarities in the planning, organisation, and implementation of housing sector activities have resulted in a number of generic features common to all socialist countries. However, in each country there has been a different balance between the state and the private sphere in the provision system. New housing in the region was developed and financed by state enterprises, building cooperatives, and individuals through self-help. Despite the relative diversity of developers, the construction process was carried out exclusively by state construction enterprises with the exception of a smaller share of self-help/self-built housing in rural areas. Prices of land, building materials, labour, and the dwelling itself were regulated according to nationally set norms, with little to no variation related to location, city size, and actual production costs.

Data on new housing construction by type of developer at the start of the transition in 1990 indicate that in Central and South Eastern Europe close to half of the new housing was developed by the state or other public institutions. By contrast, Russia and most of the other countries in the former Soviet Union had 90% of the new housing developed by the public sector. The cooperative provision was significant in Poland, the Czech Republic, Slovakia, and Latvia, accounting for a third of new housing development. In Yugoslavia self-managing enterprises providing housing for their employees played a similar role. Private sector involvement was important, but choices for consumers were limited due to the centrally controlled production process by state enterprises. In reality, private ownership and market mechanisms were never excluded from the socialist housing systems. A reliance on limited, controlled, and 'encapsulated' market solutions, particularly in the self-help/self-built sector, always existed.

The Housing Industry in Transition

The economic adjustment and privatisation of state industries across the region has had a significant impact on the housing industry, with three important implications. First, the shift from state/publicly funded to privately developed housing was rapid. These programmes were eliminated in most countries due to budget deficits; in Hungary and Croatia the share of publicly funded housing was as low as 3–5% by the mid-1990s. Second, the restructuring of the industry (building material and construction enterprises) proceeded in line with economic reforms at different speed and consistency in each postsocialist country. The construction sector was subject to privatisation and open to foreign investors, mostly attracted to strategic suppliers of building materials. State construction enterprises specialised in panel housing production were closed down due to lack of demand for their product and limited state subsidies. Other unprofitable enterprises were subdivided, with parts transformed into private structures or privatised through employee buyouts. Third, the adjustment to new market realities – new subsidy regime, price policies, commercial financing, and responsiveness to housing demand – defined the emerging profile of the new housing industry in the context of transition. A wide range of organisations, varying by size, ownership, and expertise, has emerged. Indeed, within a decade the shift to private housebuilding has become almost universal in all postsocialist countries, with further restructuring driven by demand in the homeownership market. Private housebuilders acting as developers and constructors have emerged as the dominant players in most urban markets with significant housebuilding activity.

In the general absence of national/local data on the housebuilding industry, information on the construction firms in the region can be used to highlight major outcomes of the transformation process. Several characteristic features emerge. First, the share of private construction firms in 2000 increased to over 70% in the region. Second, employment in the construction sector contracted in the 1990s in all countries, with some notable increases since 2000 due to infrastructure and nonresidential investment. Third, there has been a phenomenal growth in the number of firms, particularly those with less than 20 employees. The process has had a dramatic impact in the Czech Republic, Poland, Romania, and Bulgaria as shown in **Table 1**, in which available data on construction firms grouped according to number of employees are presented. Time series data indicate that a fragmented industry has emerged in a short period of time. Small firms with less than 20 employees account for more than two-thirds of all firms in most countries and for 92% in the Russian Federation.

Private housebuilders have become the new agents in the homeownership market, with a strategic role in the provision of new housing. They manage the entire development process from identification of the site, through planning negotiations, land provision, supply of building materials and equipment, labour contracts, marketing, financing, and the final sale of dwellings. The existence of a large number of small firms in the housebuilding sector reflects the ease of entry into the industry, the fragmented nature of the development process, the demand for small, traditionally built housing, and the lack of economies of scale. In general, the industry is characterised by a large number of small firms building up to 25–30 houses and/or apartments per year and only a handful of larger firms building more than 100 housing units per year. Large builders play a more prominent role in selected large urban markets, including the capital cities. Those companies use their own resources for construction finance, and in some cases have established investment and development subsidiaries. Some housebuilding firms have started by spinning off from state construction enterprises; others as new business ventures driven by market demand.

Table 1 Construction firms by number of employees in the region

| | | | Percentage of firms in the following employee categories | | | |
Country	Year	Total number of firms	Up to 19	20–99	100–999	1000+
Albania	1995	1457	86.6	9.7	3.6	-
	1996	1789	88.8	8.2	3.0	-
Bulgaria	1991	923	4.3	35.2	58.0	2.5
	1992	4576	75.3	13.1	11.3	0.3
Croatia	1990	953	60.8	13.3	24.2	1.7
	1996	2144	78.0	16.0	5.6	0.3
Czech Republic	1991	392	-	-	91.6	8.4
	1996	90 527	97.4	2.0	0.6	-
Estonia	1990	967	0.1	86.0	13.2	0.6
	1996	2139	76.5	21.4	3.1	-
Hungary	1990	2132	47.7	37.1	12.6	2.5
	1996	22 367	96.3	3.3	0.4	-
Poland	1990	1997	8.5	28.1	56.2	7.2
	1996	146 532	96.9	2.3	0.7	-
Romania	1990	203	4.9	1.5	25.1	68.5
	1996	7046	68.1	20.2	11.1	0.7
Russian Federation	1994	124 973	84.2	16.4	-	-
	1996	134 620	92.9	4.3	2.9	-
Yugoslavia	1992	2631	76.1	8.5	14.1	1.3

Reproduced from Economic Commission for Europe, 1998.

Trends in New Housing Construction

The shift from publicly dominated housing supply in transition countries to a housing provision system based on demand and actual costs to consumers has affected new construction in the last 20 years. On the one hand, new actors and institutions have emerged, public–private partnerships have become more prominent, and a robust private sector has continued to be the main mechanism for the provision of housing services. On the other hand, rates of housing construction have reached historically low levels with considerable loss of residential capital due to subsidy cuts and macroeconomic adjustment. The provision of new housing across the postsocialist countries is dominated by private sector output and investment. Over 80% of new housing is produced by private housebuilders, with a growing share of single-family housing. For example, single-family homes account for 99% of new construction in Latvia and Bulgaria and for 68% in Slovenia. This change might reflect pent-up consumer demand as well as the resurgence in self-promoted/self-help housing.

Available data on new housing construction in select countries in the region are presented in **Figures 1** and **2**. Construction rates (dwellings per 1000 residents) indicate different subregional patterns. Housing construction is showing signs of recovery, particularly in Central European countries and the Baltic States, reflecting macroeconomic stability, rising consumer confidence, and availability of mortgage credit. In South Eastern Europe, the level of new production is around half of the level in the 1990s. Private developers continue to face financial difficulties, high inflation, and a lack of adequate credit supply. With a few exceptions, mortgage lenders have been reluctant to introduce alternative mortgage instruments more suitable to inflationary environments, although recent developments in Bulgaria and Romania suggest a rapid growth in mortgage lending and greater diversity of mortgage products.

The impact of the turbulent economic and social transition on housing output across the Commonwealth of Independent States (CIS) is equally significant. Lower GDP growth, persistently high inflation, and low level of public investment have reduced housing output to half of its level in the early 1990s. In Azerbaijan output in 2002 was 50% of the 1993 level, in Kazakhstan – 23%, in Ukraine – 35%, and in Georgia – 40%. Although systematic data on rates of housing construction are lacking, its volume has tripled since 2003, albeit from a very low level. For example, in Azerbaijan new housing construction increased from 560 000 square meters in 2001 to about 1.4 million square meters in 2005, with half of that concentrated in Baku. In Kazakhstan new housing construction in 2002 was 1.5 million square meters and reached 5 million in 2005, partly fuelled by some government programmes accounting for 25% of the output.

Forms of New Housing Provision

The radical change in relationship between the state and the market during the transition period has modified the forms of new housing provision and has set a new framework for the operation of key actors and institutions in

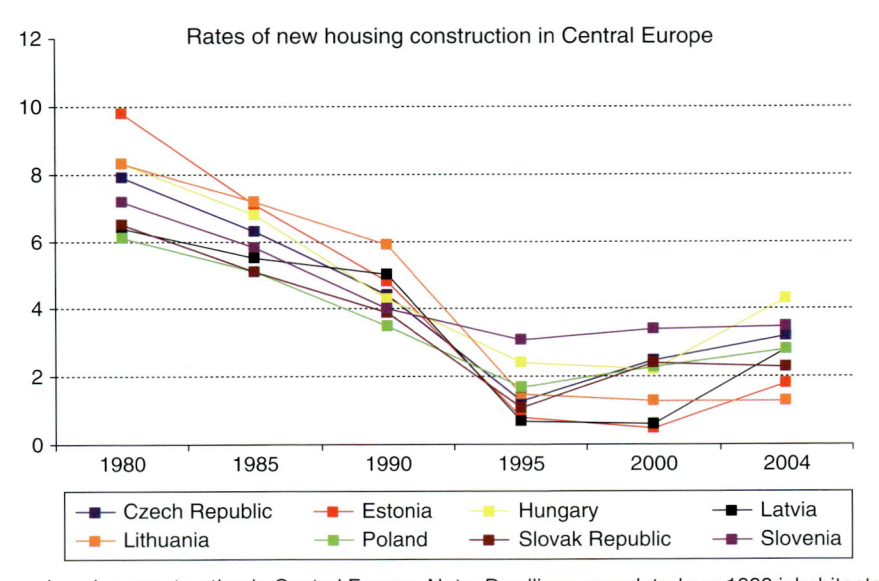

Figure 1 Rates of new housing construction in Central Europe. Note: Dwellings completed per 1000 inhabitants. Source: Author's estimates based on national statistics.

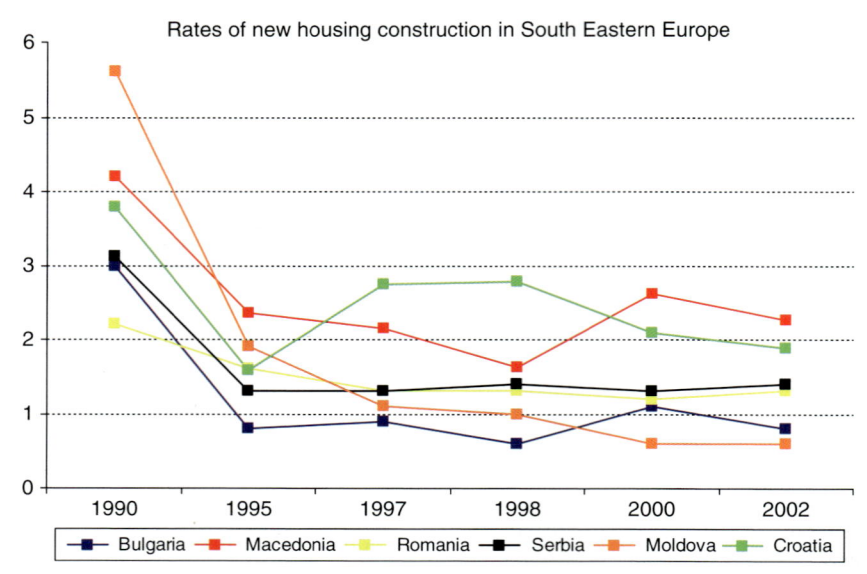

Figure 2 Rates of new housing construction in South Eastern Europe. Note: Dwellings completed per 1000 inhabitants. Source: Author's estimates based on national statistics.

postsocialist countries. Some can be regarded as successful and adaptable to the new political and economic reality; others can be expected to fade along with the transition period. On the basis of processes and institutions related to the promotion, production, allocation, and consumption of housing, the following major forms of new housing provision can be identified: public–private cooperation, speculative housebuilding, self-help housing, and informal housing. Forms also determine the level of participation of key public and/or private sector actors and institutions.

Public–Private Cooperation

In this model, local or national housing agencies initiate the majority of the housing schemes. Other developers are municipalities, nonprofit agencies, and public organisations. Land is often owned by municipalities or other public institutions. The construction process is carried out on a contract basis by private construction firms under regulated costs. Funding is provided proportionally by all parties in the project using different sources: loans, mortgages, enterprise funds, subsidies, and so on. Often those shared participation schemes have evolved as a strategy to overcome shortage of construction finance or to develop nonprofit housing. Allocation to each partner is according to its share of financed development costs. Municipalities and other public institutions, as landowners, often receive up to 20–25% of the units. More recently, the model has been implemented in several countries – Romania, Macedonia, Bosnia and Herzegovina, and Albania – to provide public rental housing, often with state-guaranteed loans.

Speculative Housebuilding

Speculative housebuilding is usually a small-scale undertaking which operates by linking investors with capital, land, building materials, equipment, or labour. In the case of condominiums, landowners acquire a share of the built units, though larger firms are often in a position to buy the land. Equity financing is the dominant source of funding for both multi-family and single-family housing, particularly in countries with underdeveloped markets for construction finance. Condominiums have become a significant part of the new housing market in urban areas (**Figure 3**). Costs are lowered through collective ownership of the land, common elements, and shared maintenance. The scale of some developments, however, creates difficulties in management of the production process and in coordination of financial contributions in the current financial crisis. There is a growing preference among speculative housebuilders to initiate single-family housing in attractive suburban areas. The small scale of development provides an opportunity to control and even reduce the investment risk through appropriate management of the construction process.

Self-Help Housing

This small-scale development is initiated by one or two households on privately owned land and has a long tradition in small towns and villages across the region. Future homeowners often control the promotion, financing, and production processes. Construction tends to be labour intensive and is carried out by a contractor with the help of the

Figure 3 A landmark residential building in Prague, architects Frank Gehry and Vlado Milunic. Client: ING Real Estate.

housebuilding in both rural and urban areas. However, the scale of these developments today is much more challenging and varied – from slums to luxury residences, from centrally located areas to suburbs, and from several small units to large settlements. Studies indicate that most of the new housing units are illegally constructed in Serbia, Montenegro, and Albania. This includes illegal, mostly single-family construction on both regulated and nonurbanised land. The construction process is heavily dependent on the availability of funds and remittances from family members. Land is often unserviced, without a clear title, but the construction is solid, with concrete frame and bricks (**Figure 4**). As both building and planning control are limited, the quality of construction varies and materials can be of poor quality. Some of the significant disadvantages are associated with the lack of infrastructure services – piped water, sewer, and transport. Informal construction is carried out by private housebuilders in many high-growth areas in the region (Tirana, Tbilisi, Sarajevo, Belgrade), but housing is legalised after its completion.

The Impact of Housing Policies on New Housing

Housing reforms in postsocialist countries in the past decade have promoted policies to reassert market forces and to reduce state intervention. Across the region, the changing demographic and social composition of the population, the growing social polarisation and income differentiation have influenced housing demand. On the one hand, these factors have led to a more diverse pattern of lifestyles and housing choices. People with more disposable income seek better

extended family for 4–5 years. Access to land is critical, housing construction costs are lower, and the quality varies.

Informal Housing

Informal housing has grown rapidly in the region since the early 1990s. In fact, authorities in the former Yugoslavia had a higher tolerance towards informal

Figure 4 Informal housing in Tirana, Albania, built in the 1990s.

living standards and move upmarket to more attractive environments. On the other hand, poverty manifests itself through the growing number of people on welfare, rising homelessness, and a general shortage of affordable housing, particularly in urban areas. Postsocialist housing policies have emphasised the importance of financial instruments – mortgage insurance, tax incentives, and demand assistance to target groups – to facilitate access and choice. However, due to price inflation and higher rates of homeownership, the gap between income and entry costs has continued to increase for low-income households, making affordable housing of decent quality more difficult to obtain. In postsocialist countries, rapid price increases in the 1990s, coupled with high unemployment and higher interest rates on mortgages, excluded more than 80% of new households from the housing market. The previous housing shortage has been replaced by a shortage of affordable housing, suggesting a deepening housing crisis. Under the new subsidy regime postsocialist countries devote less than 1% of their GDP to housing subsidies, predominantly focusing on mortgage interest tax relief and grants for homeowners (Russia, Croatia, the Czech Republic, Hungary, and Poland). Very few countries (Poland, the Czech Republic, and Slovakia) have initiated new social housing programmes in recognition of their importance for marginalised groups in society. In this context, it is not surprising that the housebuilding industry is targeting mostly the high end of the market and little capacity is being developed to produce affordable housing.

Quality and Costs in New Housing Provision

The opening up of housing markets to private construction activity and the reorganisation of the industry have resulted in significant changes in the size, quality, and type of new housing. Aggregate data indicate that in 2002 the average size of newly built housing had increased in all postsocialist countries. Increases were particularly significant in Moldova and Romania, where the average size nearly doubled compared with levels in 1990. The elimination of state/publicly funded housing construction programmes and the shift in construction methods is reflected in a growing share of single-family houses and the extensive use of traditional construction methods. Contrary to the uniform output of state construction enterprises during socialism, brick and concrete construction has improved dramatically the diversity of housing products, reflected in the design and variety of dwellings offered on the market. Private housebuilding has been very quick to adjust to the marketplace and to broaden consumer choices with respect to size, type of units, and architectural styles.

Notwithstanding these positive results, land and construction costs in new housing initiatives have increased significantly. The first comparative housing assessment in transition countries, carried out by the Metropolitan Research Institute in 1996, documented the widening differences in land and construction costs. These differences appear to have been sustained, although some convergence in land acquisition strategies and costs have also been observed. Average land costs defined as a percentage of the total house price in a typical new housing development vary between 20 and 25% in most countries. Access to serviced land continues to be problematic, particularly in high-growth areas of capital cities. Jurisdictional and titling problems are driving land prices upwards. Legal uncertainties about restitution claims, property titles, and inadequate land register systems further contribute to land shortages and the fragmented nature of land supply. In some CIS countries urban land is auctioned by municipalities, reportedly under procedures that are not very transparent. Furthermore, the supply of serviced residential land is also constrained by local governments' lack of capacity to finance necessary infrastructure. Typically, cash-constrained municipalities shift infrastructure costs to the housebuilder, adding a significant share to land acquisition and development costs.

Construction costs are difficult to forecast, and estimates do not remain valid for long. As time series data in **Table 2** indicate, there has been a considerable increase in construction costs since 2000, particularly in Slovenia and the Slovak Republic. The changes no doubt reflect inflationary processes, increases in the prices of building

Table 2 Construction cost index in residential buildings, 1995–2004

Country	1995	2000	2001	2002	2003	2004
Czech Republic	67.7	100	103.4	106	108.3	110.79
Estonia	136.3	100	105.7	109.9	113.7	119.73
Latvia	NA	100	97.9	98.9	105.1	NA
Lithuania	73.1	100	98.9	99.1	100.5	107.5
Slovak Republic	60	100	106.2	111.5	116.2	124.2
Slovenia	NA	100	106.5	112.1	118.6	130.9

Source: Author's estimates based on Eurostat data.
Note: 2000 = 100.

materials and in energy and transportation costs. In the context of general economic instability in the region, most firms adopted a US$ pricing strategy in 1994, and switched to EUR in 2003.

Housebuilders' Business Strategies

Housebuilders in postsocialist countries have been particularly resourceful in terms of developing business strategies to manage risks and to increase market share. Land acquisition strategies include a joint ownership with the landowner, purchase of building rights for a period up to 5 years, or direct acquisition. Larger developers prefer a wider selection of sites in their land portfolio to minimise risks; however, smaller firms tend to be specialised in niche markets, such as gated communities. Efficiency and higher profits are achieved through greater flexibility in the organisation of the production process itself. In general, firms attempt to maintain a steady flow of units in order to utilise their existing technological and labour capacity. Having a set of projects at different stages of the construction process enables them to streamline the supply of materials and to increase production efficiency. Another strategy available to volume housebuilders is to control the costs of building materials and labour. For example, MAGIC, the largest housebuilder in Moldova, owns building material enterprises, construction companies, and design firms, thus controlling all phases of the development process and internalising profits. Most of the small- and medium-size firms limit their full-time staff and contract 'brigadi' for bricklaying (semiskilled labour) and specialised labour for groundwork and insulation.

The strategies for mobilisation of funds are closely linked to sales. Housebuilders try to be independent from borrowing, and commercial banks in the region are reluctant to lend for new construction, even in larger, high-profile projects such as that illustrated in **Figure 5**. Through land barter (building rights in exchange for a share of the newly built housing) payment for the land is deferred, but builders need to cover the costs of project development, legal fees, and marketing upfront. The bulk of the capital is provided by prospective homebuyers. Equity financing (cash provided by future homeowners or investors) has given a lot more power to consumers in terms of influence over the design, size, and quality of dwellings, but has also created a number of problems. In larger projects the process is more difficult to manage; often shares held by buyers unable to keep up with the payments need to be resold. Inflation and changes in local labour markets further increase the risk. There are several implications for the organisation of the production process: (1) a shift towards small-scale, traditionally built housing, (2) low-tech solutions (cheaper labour and local materials), and (3) a longer construction period so that buyers can mobilise funds. Under unstable macroeconomic conditions longer construction periods paradoxically shelter the housebuilders from higher risk, since both sales and prices can be adjusted to surges in costs and exchange rates.

Conclusion

The transition from a centrally planned to a market-based housing system has created a very different environment for the provision of housing in postsocialist countries and

Figure 5 New residential development in Podgorica, Montenegro, integrating central government institutions and retail.

has increased the role and involvement of private institutions. A large number of private housebuilders produce new housing; the forms of provision have become very diverse to include speculative, self-help, and informal housing. These new actors compete in the marketplace to deliver better products and services. While new construction has reached historically low levels, patterns of recovery have emerged across different subregions, reflecting adjustments in the macroeconomic environment and changes in housing demand. Private housebuilders have delivered better products compared with the state-controlled system. The socialist state construction enterprises ('kombinats') were infamous for production delays, poor management of the construction process, and unfinished projects. The uniform, system-built apartments in high-rise estates were not attractive to residents and costly to maintain. Though new housing in the deregulated markets has become more expensive, housebuilders offer a diversity of types and styles as well as improved quality.

Growing affordability constraints are a major concern for the efficient operation of housing institutions in the market for new housing, as is the absence of a well-developed system for housing finance. Success in housebuilding in postsocialist countries depends on land deals, on more conservative organisation of production, and on equity financing. In the absence of comprehensive housing policies and limited support for housing, it is not surprising that housebuilders service mainly the upper end of the housing market and little capability is being developed to deliver affordable housing.

See also: House Building Industries: Western Europe and North America; Housing Developers: Developed World; Housing Market Institutions; Institutions for Housing Supply.

Further Reading

Colliers International (2007) *Residential Real Estate Market Report 2nd Half*. Prague: Colliers International.

Hegedüs J, Mayo S, and Tosics I (1996) Transition of the housing sector in the east central European countries. *Review of Urban & Regional Development Studies* 8: 101–136.

Hegedüs J and Struyk R (eds.) (2006) *Housing Finance: New and Old Models in Central Europe, Russia, and Kazakhstan*, pp. 43–62. Budapest: Open Society; Local Government and Public Service Reform Initiative.

International Finance Corporation (2006) *Central Asia Housing Finance Gap Analysis*. Washington, DC: IFC; World Bank Group.

Lux M, Sunega P, Mikeszová M, and Kostelecký T (2008) *Housing Standards 2007/2008. The Factors Behind the High Prices of Owner-Occupied Housing in Prague*. Prague: Institute of Sociology; Academy of Sciences of the Czech Republic.

Renaud B (1995) The real estate economy and the design of Russian housing reforms. *Urban Studies* 32(8): 1247–1264.

Tsenkova S (2000) *Housing in Transition and the Transition in Housing: The Experience of Central and Eastern Europe*. Sofia: Kapital Reklama.

Tsenkova S (2005) *Trends and Progress in Housing Reforms in South East Europe*. Paris: Council of Europe Development Bank.

Tsenkova S (2009) *Housing Reforms in Post-Socialist Europe. Lost in Transition*. Heidelberg: Springer-Verlag.

United Nations Economic Commission for Europe (2000) *Annual Bulletin of Housing and Building Statistics*. Geneva: United Nations Economic Commission for Europe.

Relevant Websites

www.globalpropertyguide.com – Globalpropertyguide: Residential Property Data

www.constructionrussia.com – Construction Portal for Russia

www.colliersmn.com – Colliers International

House Building Industries: Western Europe and North America

C Moore and D Adams, University of Glasgow, Glasgow, UK

© 2012 Elsevier Ltd. All rights reserved.

Glossary

Institutional structures Institutional structures can be understood as the broader social, political, economic, and juridical contexts within which housing production can take place. These tend to be country-specific, but distinct clusters of regime types can be identified that transcend national boundaries, particularly in relation to the role of the state in shaping the characteristics of national housing systems.

Models of housing production Models of housing production describe the different ways in which housing can be produced in different countries. This can include 'speculative' housing development, 'self-promotion' models, and 'restricted private profit' forms of production. Crucially, most forms may be undertaken alongside another to varying extents within a single institutional context or country.

Private housebuilders Private housebuilders play a primary role in the housing development process and usually act as residential developers. They typically manage the entire development process which can include the sourcing and acquiring of land, the negotiation of regulatory permissions, the management of the construction process, and the marketing and sale of the finished product.

Speculative housing development Speculative housing development is the process by which much new housing is produced. This process operates through the private market and typically involves land purchase and much or all of the building work is completed before there is any contact with the house-buyer.

International Differences in Housing Provision

The housebuilding industry plays a crucial role in the delivery of new housing in most countries. In the United Kingdom, for example, private housebuilders now dominate new housing production, accounting for approximately 90% of all new homes produced annually. In this sense, it plays a vital part in the key processes by which the housing stock changes and adapts to new economic, social, and cultural trends. Despite this, the way in which modern housebuilding industries are organised across Western European and North American countries tends to vary significantly.

Unlike in many other industries, there is a distinct lack of globalisation in housebuilding. While other forms of production have transcended national barriers in the global age, the way in which housing production is organised tends to be specific to individual countries. Thus, its characteristics as an industry and activity can vary and take on very different institutional forms between countries. This raises two important questions that will be the focus of this article: What are the key features of housebuilding industries in Western European and North American countries and in what ways do these characteristics differ? And why do such differences exist?

In looking at the features and differences of housebuilding industries, a focus will be placed upon the performance of these industries; the roles housebuilders occupy and the functions they undertake in the housing development process; and the structure and characteristics of different industries and of the firms that operate within them.

In explaining the distinctive nature of housing production, a key theme that emerges is the role of broader institutional structures, particularly the different relationships between the market and the state. Although these tend to be country-specific, it is important to ask whether we can identify broad groupings.

A useful distinction has been made between countries in terms of the market–state mix in their systems of housing provision, creating what has been termed 'distinct clusters of regime type' (see Barlow and Duncan, 1994). Essentially, this delineates countries in terms of the role afforded to the state in shaping the characteristics of national housing systems. This provides a way in which to conceptualise the broader contexts within which housing provision can take place. Three types of regimes provide a useful classification of the different types of housing provision systems in Western European and North American countries.

A 'liberal' regime could be seen as characterising housing systems with limited overt state intervention in housing production. State policy will tend to favour the market, and a more marketised system of housing provision will be apparent. The United States and

Canada can be seen as typical cases of this type of regime, while more recently, the United Kingdom can be included. A 'corporatist' regime, including countries such as Germany and France, can be characterised as holding less of an obsession with free markets and instead demonstrate more overt state support for housing. Finally, a 'social democratic' regime, characterised by widespread state intervention in the housing production process, includes Scandinavian countries and the Netherlands. For example, in Sweden, high levels of state intervention exist in housing production, with a markedly interventionist approach to land supply through public land banking and the taxation of profits on land sales. These classifications highlight broadly the different institutional contexts within which housing activity takes place, and provide an insight into how we can explain differences in housing production between countries.

Housebuilding Industry Performance

A key feature of housebuilding industries is their performance, and this can vary significantly between different countries. **Table 1** shows national variations in importance of housebuilding in terms of housing investment as a share of GDP between 1956 and 2000. It demonstrates that, for many countries, the average housing output usually hovers around 5% of GDP, and that the maximum amount of new housing investment that an economy can generally cope with is around 8% of GDP, even when faced with stark shortages. This is most likely due to the knock-on effects to other industries and highlights the difficulties in significantly increasing housing supply in the short term to meet sharp increases in demand, although some countries have demonstrated an exception to this. In Spain and Ireland, for example, housing booms at the end of the twentieth and into the twenty-first century saw record levels of housing production. In Spain, annualised housebuilding rates more than trebled in the 10-year period following 1996, while the housing boom in Ireland peaked in 2006 with output reaching 16% of GNP. The lack of housing investment in the United Kingdom might be explained in terms of the tight land supply in growth areas, while the relatively high rate of investment in Germany can be seen as a product of the postunification housing boom.

A common feature across all countries is the volatility of housing supply. Housebuilding is a cyclical industry, with variations in output and prices driven by cycles in the wider market. These cycles are an inevitable consequence of the nature of housing as a product, where the existing stocks of housing far outstrip the current level of output. For example, in the United Kingdom, current levels of production account for merely 1% of the existing stock, and typically around 10% of housing market transactions. As a result, small changes in the demand for housing as a whole result in much larger variations in demand for new housing. This means that housing markets are extremely volatile.

The extent to which this volatility is transmitted more to prices or levels of housing production depends upon 'elasticity', the ability and speed of the housing supply system to produce extra housing when prices rise. Thus, when looking at, and comparing, the performance of housebuilding industries, a useful way to do so might be to consider the level of housing production and housing prices (**Table 2**).

Levels of housebuilding across Europe and North America vary both between countries and with time. Compared with other countries, there has been relatively less new housing in the United Kingdom, which has seen a sustained decline in building rates over the past 35 years. Alongside this, the United Kingdom has also seen a long upward trend in real house prices. Although the experience of long-term real price inflation is not unique to the United Kingdom, the increases in many other European countries such as France, Germany, and Italy have been much lower. Similarly, volatility in house prices has been a key feature of the UK housing market and also evident in many other countries, such as the Netherlands and Italy, although less so in France and Germany.

These figures highlight how the ability of housing systems in different countries to respond to changes in demand can vary significantly, consequently impacting

Table 1 Housing investment as a share of GDP (1956–2000)

Country	Mean (% of GDP)	Max (% of GDP)
Germany	6.4	8.1
France	5.7	7.8
Netherlands	5.3	6.4
Canada	5.3	7.4
USA	4.4	5.7
UK	3.5	4.7

Source: Adapted from Ball M (2006) *Markets and Institutions in Real Estate and Construction*. Oxford, UK: Blackwell.

Table 2 Number of dwellings built per 100 000 persons

Country	1990	1992	1994	1996
France	5.4	4.7	5.1	4.7
Germany	4.1	4.8	7.0	7.2
Italy	4.5	4.9	4.9	4.6
Netherlands	6.5	5.7	5.7	5.7
Spain	7.2	5.3	5.6	6.5
UK	3.4	3.0	3.2	3.0
All EU 15	4.9	4.8	5.3	5.2
USA	5.2	4.5	5.2	5.3

Source: Adapted from Barlow J (2000) The private sector housebuilding industry: 21st century challenges. *Housing Finance* 48: 40–44.

on the level and price of housing output. For example, while the United Kingdom suffers from low levels of production, and volatility in prices in recent years, in Sweden, output levels were much higher and less subject to boom and slump. Indeed, the UK housebuilding industry is often considered relatively inefficient in comparison with its European counterparts. These differences in performance represent an important feature of housebuilding industries in Western Europe and North America, but they also serve to highlight how industry performance is largely a product of the way in which housing production is organised in each country, which can also be highly variable. Therefore, understanding the different ways in which the functional aspects of housing provision are organised within different countries becomes crucial in identifying and explaining the key features of housebuilding industries.

Models of Housing Production

Housebuilders are the main agents in the housing development process and they play a vital role in the provision of new housing. However, key distinctions can be made between countries in terms of the different models or forms of housing production that tend to be prominent. In many countries, such as the United Kingdom and the United States, most new housing is the product of 'speculative' development. In this model, a private firm initiates the housing development process, land for development is purchased, regulatory consents are gained, and construction is undertaken before there is contact with a purchaser. Risk is therefore a key feature of the speculative process, as firms operate between a range of input and output markets, such as land, labour, materials, finance, and housing, and within the context of regulatory regimes.

However, this model is different from others found elsewhere. Some countries make much more use of the 'self-promotion' model of development. In this model, individual households act as the initiators of the housing production process, typically purchasing preserviced plots and managing the construction process through subcontraction of labour, while also acting as the final consumer of the dwelling. In countries such as France and Germany, this form of production has traditionally constituted a significantly high proportion of new housing, for example, around 50% of new housing in France, with speculative housing much less prevalent. In this context, the private land development firms, who buy land and sell serviced plots for housing, play an important role in the system of housing provision.

In other countries, 'restricted private profit' forms of development have been historically important. In this model, development proceeds through the same stages as the speculative model, but regulatory rules reduce the ability of firms to make development gains. This model has been widely applied in social democratic regimes such as Sweden, while the speculative model is more common in liberal regimes, with the corporatist cluster typically being characterised by self-promotion.

Functional Organisation of Housing Production

The housing development process can be, in essence, broken down into a series of functional aspects. The development of residential land, where land is purchased, regulatory permissions gained, and infrastructure prepared, can be seen as the first. Second, the production of the housing product itself has to be undertaken, bringing together labour and materials. Finally, the completed dwellings need to be marketed and sold to the end-user. Crucially, however, different ways of organising these functional aspects of the development process exist across and within countries, and variations can be seen in the functions undertaken by, and the role of, housebuilding firms.

A major functional distinction can be seen between firms that undertake land assembly and development, others that focus their activities on housing construction, and those that combine both of these development and building roles. In some countries, such as the United States, there is a tendency for the separation of land and housing development, while in others, such as the United Kingdom, single firms tend to combine both functions. These different ways of organising housing production represent a useful way to highlight how the key features of housebuilding industries can vary between countries. Equally significant, however, is the question of what drives these different methods of organising production between countries. Three key drivers will be highlighted below, focusing first on the land development process and then on housing construction.

Direct State Intervention

In some countries, direct government intervention serves as a driver for the organisation of the housebuilding industry in terms of the roles of different types of firms. Common in liberal housing regimes, such as Sweden or the Netherlands, states can intervene directly in the development process through the creation of public or semipublic bodies charged with land development, taking over the functions of private land developers and thus creating a distinction between the roles of land developers and housing producers. In Sweden, for example, local authorities have historically played an important role in building up large public land banks for new housing with the aim of reducing land development cost. However, alongside these public bodies, significant numbers of private developers continue to exist, and in countries where direct intervention is absent, differences in the functional organisation of housing production still arise.

Land and Housing Markets and Their Regulatory Framework

For housebuilders, land is the essential lifeblood of their industry and is a central element in housing production. Therefore, differences in the operation of land markets and their regulatory frameworks have important implications for housebuilding industries.

In countries where land supply is tightly restricted as a result of planning or state regulations, such as the United Kingdom, the combination of both land development and housing production is common. This is because development gain represents a major source of profit for housebuilders. As a result of the high cost of land relative to the selling price of housing, the overriding concern for UK housebuilders is with the trading of land as a source of profit, rather than focusing on productivity gains in the construction of new housing. Gaining access to developable housing land and building up land banks become crucial and housebuilders devote considerable expense in this pursuit, and the housing construction process often becomes a secondary concern.

This market and regulatory context rationally leads firms to pursue short-term profits through development gain, but also, and crucially, provides housebuilders who own land with a degree of strategic advantage in local housing markets. Where land is tightly controlled as in much of the United Kingdom, firms with access to developable housing land are provided with a degree of certainty over the extent of competition in the local housing market and a considerable amount of influence. Thus, combining both land development and housing production allows firms to exert their influence in local housing markets and realise development gain profits.

In other contexts, however, the separation of land and housing development is more common. Where land is supplied more cheaply and markets are more competitive than in the United Kingdom, such as in North America or in many European countries, firms rely on production profits from the housebuilding process, in contrast to development gain. Value is created not through the trading of land, but rather through the construction of new housing and more focus is placed upon long-term productivity gains. It has been suggested that in countries such as the United States and Canada, the tendency for the separation of land development and housing production arises from the heightened project risk associated with individual developments. In Sweden, for example, competition takes place in the housing development process, and the scope for development gain is limited as credit for development is state subsidised, with public firms playing more active roles in land development. In France, specialist land assembly firms exist to provide serviced plots for self-promotion.

Employment Relations in the Housing Production Process

In the housing production process, an important factor that influences the organisation of production is the employment relationship. This relationship can vary between countries and is strongly related to labour laws and practices. The subcontracting of labour is common in the United Kingdom and the United States, and in other countries with flexible labour practices. In this model, the major aspects of the housing construction process are contracted out to builders and other specialists by housebuilding firms who hold a coordinating role and manage the process. This has the advantage of lowering overhead and management costs and allows for activity specialisation. Crucially, it enables firms to be flexible in the face of uncertain and often volatile demand. For example, in a period of low demand, firms are not burdened with having idle workers or the high costs of redundancies, but merely have to take on fewer contractors. In this sense, this form of organising production has been considered economically efficient as it potentially allows resources to be fully employed by other firms when a particular firm has insufficient work to maintain a steady flow of contracts. However, this model also encourages the standardisation of work tasks and the production methods used tend to be simple to avoid any skills difficulties. This can have an impact on innovation in both the processes and the products of housebuilding.

In some countries, the subcontracting model is forbidden and labour laws require housebuilding firms to employ their workforce directly. This is common in France and Germany. It has been speculated that this has significant consequences for housebuilding industries as firms are likely to be bigger in terms of employment size, while labour-related costs will be relatively higher than in the subcontracting model. As a result, these forms of employment relations are often considered more expensive and less efficient. Further still, the scope of firms, in terms of activities, might be broader than in the specialist subcontracting model to ensure a steady workload. However, in countries where there are strict labour relations, often these regulations tend not to apply for small firms, which might go some way in explaining why self-promotional forms of development are so prevalent in countries such as France and Germany.

Structure of the Housebuilding Industry

Industry Concentration

Typically, housebuilding is an industry in which there should be ease of entry into the industry by new firms. However, for many countries, the picture of an industry characterised by a large number of small firms operating locally has been replaced by one of a small number of large firms operating at a national level. Nonetheless, the extent to which this change has occurred is highly variable. In the United Kingdom, for example, a sustained period of concentration of housebuilding in the hands of a small number of large firms has been prevalent since the 1970s, and consequently a small number of very large firms have emerged as the main players in new housing production. In 1980, there were four 'volume' builders, each producing over 2000 dwellings per year. By 1990 there were 8, and by 2000 this figure had risen to 14. Indeed, in Sweden too, there is an exceptionally high level of concentration of output between the largest firms.

The share of market output of the largest firms in the United Kingdom is in stark contrast to the United States. The top 10 firms in the United Kingdom, in 2000, produced 44% of all new housing, while in the United States, the market share for the top 10 producers was only 15%. Indeed, the top 100 producers in the United Kingdom accounted for 70% of new housing, while the corresponding figure for the United States was 29%.

There has been considerable debate in the UK literature surrounding the drivers of industry concentration. In housebuilding, economies of scale provide an unconvincing explanation of this trend as the importance of scale benefits appears to be exhausted at levels of output significantly below those of the largest firms. Indeed, it has been argued that significant diseconomies of scale are introduced much more severely for housebuilding firms than in other types of production, which might explain the structure of the industry in the United States. So why then is the UK housebuilding industry increasingly concentrated with a small number of large firms dominating?

The regulatory regime in the United Kingdom might go some way to explaining the housebuilding industry structure. The tight control of land as a result of planning constraints has meant that mergers and acquisitions of firms, often between the largest housebuilders, have become a means of gaining access to developable land and building up strategic land banks. As a result, the industry has become increasingly concentrated in the hands of a very few large firms. In contrast, in the United States, where land is more readily available for development, the incentive for such strategy is diminished.

There has been concern with the potential impact on the competitiveness of the UK industry in the light of its high concentration. However, despite its structure, the housebuilding industry in the United Kingdom is still relatively competitive in that there is intense competition between firms for land and market share. Indeed, for the larger firms, as much competition takes place within firms as between them.

Firm Size and Organisation

Not only has the UK industry become more concentrated but the leading firms have themselves become significantly larger. This has required the largest companies in the United Kingdom to adapt their organisational structures to minimise scale diseconomies through strategies of regionalisation. Rather than functioning as a single business, the dominant housebuilding firms operate as a collection of a number of distinct regional divisions. This allows national management to identify the performance of each division and take action, such as shutting or scaling down poorly performing operations. Crucially, this strategy encourages a strong sense of internal competition within the firm. These larger firms that dominate are often very different from others in the UK industry, not simply in terms of the way they operate but also in terms of their ownership.

Firm Finance and Ownership

In the United Kingdom and the United States, firms tend to be primarily specialist housebuilders dedicated wholly to housebuilding, rather than being a subsidiary of larger groups. In contrast, in much of continental Europe, many of the large housebuilding firms are part of broader construction enterprises or subsidiaries of large conglomerates. Similarly, these large firms in the United Kingdom and the United States tend to be publicly listed on stock exchanges, and therefore rely on equity finance as well as bank borrowing. In contrast, in continental Europe, longer-term banking relationships are a more common source of finance. Indeed, by 2000, all but 2 of the top 15 housebuilding companies in the United Kingdom were specialist housebuilders with their own stock market quotation.

Product and Process of Housebuilding

The concentration of the UK industry has also raised concerns about the processes and products of the housebuilding industry. The standardisation of housing as a product is a key feature of the housebuilding industry in the United Kingdom in the sense that most housebuilders have a limited number of standard house types that are constructed using standard materials in a repetitive way in a range of different locations. This stands in contrast to customised, one-off designs for specific sites. While standardised products are common in the United Kingdom, their use becomes more prevalent among the larger firms that dominate housing production, and this link between industry concentration and standardisation of process and products of housebuilding has been widely explored in the literature.

By adopting standardised methods of production and housing products, firms can reduce design, supply, and construction costs and provide a greater degree of certainty about these costs. They can also tailor their output to designs that have sold well in the past and achieve blanket building regulation consents. However, more generally, design issues in housing production in the United Kingdom tend to take a less prevalent role than in many other European countries and the relative lack of innovative capacity in the UK housebuilding industry has been well documented.

While in the United Kingdom, corporate strategy focuses on land development gain, in other countries housebuilders pay more attention to generating profit by adding value directly to their product. In Sweden, for example, where competition takes place in the actual construction of housing, a greater emphasis on design and innovation in both process and product is necessary as there is less scope to make purely inflationary profits from land development.

Conclusion

It could be argued that a key feature of housebuilding industries in Western European and North American countries is their variability. In understanding this variability, a useful tool might be to conceptualise different countries in terms of clusters of regime types: constellations of state–market relations. Understanding the broader institutional and market contexts of housebuilding industries therefore becomes a key aspect in identifying and accounting for features of housebuilding industries and their diversity. Differences between states can also be seen in terms of the performance of housebuilding industries, the way in which these industries are structured and organised, and their role in the housing development process. A crucial determinant of these factors appears to be the different relationships between the public policy, the housebuilding companies, and the broader institutional and market contexts within which housebuilding activity takes place.

See also: Housing and the Macroeconomy; Housing Construction Industry, Competition and Regulation; Housing Developers: Developed World; Housing Markets and Macroeconomic Policy; Housing Policy: Agents and Regulators; Housing Policy Trends; Housing Supply; Institutions for Housing Supply; Planning Institutions: Canada/United States; Post-Conflict Housing Restitutions; Submarkets; Time and the Economic Analysis of Housing Systems.

References

Ball M (2006) *Markets and Institutions in Real Estate and Construction*. Oxford, UK: Blackwell.
Barlow J (2000) The private sector housebuilding industry: 21st century challenges. *Housing Finance* 48: 40–44.
Barlow J and Duncan S (1994) *Success and Failure in Housing Provision: European Systems Compared*. Oxford, UK: Pergamon.

Further Reading

Adams D and Watkins C (2002) *Greenfields, Brownfields and Housing Development*. Oxford, UK: Blackwell.
Ball M (1983) *Housing Policy and Economic Power*. London: Methuen.
Ball M (2003) Markets and the structure of housebuilding industry: An international perspective. *Urban Studies* 40(5–6): 897–916.
Ball M (2008) *Firm Size and Competition: A Comparison of the Housebuilding Industries in Australia, the UK and the USA, FiBRE Series*. London: RICS.
Ball M (2009) RICS European housing review 2009. *Royal Institution of Charter Surveyors Research Report*. London: RICS.
Barlow J (1999) From craft production to mass customisation. Innovation requirements for the UK housebuilding industry. *Housing Studies* 14(1): 23–42.
Barlow J and King A (1992) The state, the market, and competitive strategy: The housebuilding industry in the United Kingdom, France, and Sweden. *Environment and Planning A* 24: 381–400.
Buzzelli M (2004) Exploring regional firm size structure in Canadian housebuilding: Ontario, 1991 and 1996. *Urban Geography* 25(3): 241–263.
Callcutt J (2007) *The Calcutt Review of Housebuilding Delivery*. London: HMSO.
Gibb K (1999) Regional differentiation and the Scottish private housebuilding sector. *Housing Studies* 14(1): 43–56.
Nicol C and Hooper A (1999) Contemporary change and the housebuilding industry: Concentration and standardisation in production. *Housing Studies* 14(1): 57–76.
Wellings F (2006) *British Housebuilders: History and Analysis*. Oxford, UK: Blackwell.

Household Organisation and Survival in Developing Countries

S Chant, London School of Economics and Political Science, London, UK

© 2012 Elsevier Ltd. All rights reserved.

Glossary

Female-headed household Generally describes a domestic unit in which the senior adult female member does not have a coresident spouse or partner.

'Feminisation of poverty' Commonly refers to the growing incidence of poverty among women relative to men, with income or consumption privation being the primary (if implicit) referent.

Gender division of labour In the context of households refers to the normative and actual divisions in roles and responsibilities between women and men, and boys and girls.

Household Defined predominantly as a unit which generally comprises the sharing of residential space and of key reproductive functions such as cooking and eating.

Household headship A frequently vaguely defined concept, which is difficult to establish instrumentally on grounds of economic responsibility or decision-making power. Given the tendency towards a 'male bias' in most societies, headship often devolves on men. This happens even when two people are commonly responsible for the creation of a household (as in a parent–child household).

Household livelihood strategies Activities undertaken and resources mobilised by household members in the pursuit of everyday tasks of production and reproduction, subsistence, security, and socioeconomic mobility. They are also sometimes referred to as 'household survival strategies'.

Household structure Comprises both household composition (or membership) and household headship (see above).

'Intergenerational transmission of disadvantage' A phrase commonly used to describe the implications for younger generations growing-up in female-headed households.

Reproduction tax A tax falling on women in the form of disproportionate responsibilities for domestic and unpaid care work (UCW), which impacts their labour-force participation and earnings.

Structural adjustment programmes (SAPs) Macroeconomic policy instruments geared to restoring a country's fiscal balance, to maintain its loan-worthiness. They typically involve privatisation, deregulation, reductions in government subsidies on basic foodstuffs and services, and the lowering of trade barriers.

Household Organisation and Survival among the Urban Poor: Introduction and Overview

This article details the key features of household organisation and survival among low-income groups in the urban areas of the Global South. Notwithstanding variations across countries, the main focus is on which household member does what, in the context of household livelihood strategies. The article examines how the configuration of households – in respect of composition and headship – affects resource mobilisation and well-being. Particular attention is paid to female-headed households, as these represent an important and growing constituency in developing regions, and as they have attracted considerable debate on the implications for the well-being of women and children.

The first part of the article introduces key terms such as 'household', 'household organisation', and 'household survival'. In the second part, household organisation and survival are analysed with particular reference to the impact of the post-1980 neoliberal economic restructuring on household livelihood strategies. The third part considers the role of the household structure as a survival mechanism in its own right, whereas the final section considers the increasingly contested interrelationship between the 'feminisation' of household headship and the 'feminisation of poverty'.

What is a Household?

Considerable debate has taken place as to how to define households when their forms and nomenclature vary so widely among societies. Most censuses and international data sources, nevertheless, define households on the bases of 'space' and 'function'. These two criteria have been coined respectively in United Nations (UN) statistical documents as 'house-dwelling' and 'house-keeping'. The 'house-dwelling' concept refers to households as units, which occupy common residential space, whereas, the 'house-keeping' concept pertains to the collaboration of the household members in the basic productive and reproductive activities, and in consumption. These include, particularly, cooking and eating, as well as the raising and socialisation of children (see Chant and McIlwaine, 2009: 237).

The majority of households comprise members who are related by ties of blood or marriage. Despite this, the overlap between 'households' and 'families' does not imply synonymy (Moore, 1994). There are many cases, for instance, in which people do not live with kin, but reside alone, or with friends or workmates. As Kabeer (2007: 54) identifies: "... the boundaries of the household are not coterminous with the boundaries of the family". In turn, 'families' are generally bigger than households, insofar as they extend beyond the confines of shared living space and may be scattered over wide distances, including across national borders. 'Family' is also a more formally identifiable institution than 'household', subject to legislated norms regarding marriage, property, inheritance, the care and guardianship of minors, and so on. While most countries have a 'Family Code' or a 'Family' section in the Civil Code, there is no equivalent for 'households' (Chant and McIlwaine, 2009: 238). Having said this, the frequent crossover between households and families means that the former are often heavily influenced by familial norms and ideologies, and may well depend, at least in part, on ties with wider kin networks for survival (Kabeer, 2007). Indeed, even if households are residentially nuclear, they may be functionally extended (see Chant, 2007: 227, for discussion and references).

Household Organisation

Household organisation refers to two main features: (1) household structure and (2) divisions of labour. In respect of household structure, this term comprises household composition and household headship. In respect of family-based households, composition generally falls into one of two categories:

1. 'Simple' composition refers to households which are two-generational and which consist either of one or both parents and their immediate offspring.
2. 'Complex' or 'extended' composition refers to those households, which – in addition to containing a parent or parents and children – include one or more of other relatives such as in-laws, grandparents, cousins, and so on.

Complex composition can also refer to households whose members are not related by blood or marriage, as in 'nonfamily' or 'semifamily' households (see **Box 1**).

Box 1 Typology of household structures in the Global South

Household structure	Brief description
Nuclear household	This includes a couple and their biological children.
Female-headed household	This is a generic term for a household in which the senior woman or household head lacks a coresident male partner. Often, although not always, the household head is a lone mother.
Extended household	This is a household, which comprises – in addition to one or both parents and children – other blood relatives or in-laws. This may be a male-headed or female-headed household, a laterally or a vertically extended one, or a multigenerational one.
Nuclear-compound household	This refers to an arrangement in which two or more related households share the same living space (e.g., dwelling or land plot), but operate separate household budgets and daily reproductive functions such as cooking and eating.
Single-sex household	This is a household in which the senior members are of one sex only (as is common among the Ga and the Asante in Ghana, where the women live with female kin, daughters, and infant sons).
Nonfamily or nonkin household	This is a household in which the members are not related by blood or marriage (e.g., workmates sharing accommodation).
Semifamily household	This is a household that comprises related members as well as nonrelated members, as in situations where there are live-in domestic servants or apprentices.
Couple household	This is a household comprising a married or a coresident couple.
Lone or single-person household	This refers to a woman or a man living alone.
Grandmother-headed household	This comprises a grandmother and her grandchildren, but not the intermediate generation.
Blended or stepfamily household[a]	This is a household in which at least one partner in a couple is not the biological parent of at least one coresident child.
Child-headed household	These are households in which minors occupy positions of headship usually because they have been orphaned, the parents having died of AIDS or as a result of civil or military conflict.

[a]Also referred to in some sources as 'reconstituted household'.
Adapted from Chant S and McIlwaine C (2009) *Geographies of Development in the 21st Century: An Introduction to the Global South*, Box 9.1. Cheltenham, UK: Edward Elgar.

Despite the inherent dynamism of household units, their composition is relatively straightforward to identify at any point in time; however, this identification is arguably less easy in the case of household headship.

The concept of 'household head' is often regarded as having its roots in Judaeo-Christian societies, in which power historically devolved upon men at the household level (Harris, 1981). 'Household headship' encompasses the notion that one member is responsible for the rest and occupies a position of authority at the apex of the household unit. This idea was spread to several parts of the world during the colonisation process via religious and 'moral' teachings, and through bureaucratic procedures such as population surveys (Harris, 1981; also Folbre, 1991).

This Eurocentric construction of household headship has, nevertheless, come under attack on two main grounds: first, it makes no allowance for alternative ideologies and practices of household management; second, it undervalues and even renders invisible the roles of women. In relation to the latter, for example, disquiet has arisen over the fact that few censuses make their interpretations of 'household headship' explicit. Although some censuses specify instrumental criteria, such as primary financial provision or decision-making power, most rely on self-reporting or proxy-reporting. This aspect, given the male bias in most societies, means that adult men are usually accorded the status of head. Indeed, patriarchal norms are often so pervasive that even where women are not living with partners or husbands, they may name their eldest sons as heads. In most statistical classifications, however, households tend to be described as female-headed only when the adult woman has no partner in residence (Chant, 1997; see also **Box 1**).

As for the second main feature of household organisation – namely divisions of labour – gender, age, and relationship to the household head are often the key organising principles in the normative and actual allocation of duties and activities. In family-based households headed by men, for example, adult men tend to be mainly responsible for production and for the generation of income. In contrast, the main, if not exclusive, preserve of adult women comprises the category 'reproductive' activities: cooking, cleaning, and the care of the children, the elderly people, and the infirm. The latter responsibilities are not commonly paid for. Levying this heavy 'reproduction tax' (Palmer, in Afshar and Dennis, 1992) on women means that they have less time available to earn income than their male counterparts. That women also face more discrimination than men do when entering the labour force further implies a financial dependency that weakens their 'fall-back' position (the term ' fall-back' position being normally attributed to the economist Amartya Sen), as well as their decision-making power. In other words, women often face obstacles to leaving bad marriages or to setting up independent households, although, as we shall see, some possibilities do exist.

Household Survival and Livelihood Strategies

Many of the urban poor in developing countries draw on multiple activities and resources to get by. The ways in which people's diverse activities, capabilities, and assets (stores, resources, claims, and access) are mobilised in the interests of ensuring survival are referred to as 'livelihood strategies'. While there are slight variations in theoretical and policy approaches to livelihoods (such as the 'asset vulnerability' framework devised by Caroline Moser and the 'capital assets' framework developed by Carole Rakodi), all of them reflect an attempt to codify the multiple resources on which household livelihoods depend. As a 'livelihoods' approach concentrates on what the poor have rather than on what they do not have, there is more scope to appreciate in a more holistic and agentic way how the poor negotiate survival (Moser, 2009).

Carole Rakodi's (1999) exposition of the 'capital assets' approach to livelihoods lays stress on 'stocks of capital' of varying types (human, social, natural, physical, and financial), which can be stored, accumulated, exchanged, or activated to generate a flow of income or other benefits (see **Box 2**). Depending on the local environment, the social and cultural context, power relationships within the households, and so on, people may manage assets differently; although, on the whole "households aim at a livelihood which has high resilience and low sensitivity to shocks and stresses" (Rakodi, 1999: 318).

Household Survival in the Context of Neoliberal Economic Restructuring

Accepting that poverty has always called upon the poor to be resourceful, it is commonly argued that urban households in the last three decades have come under unprecedented strain owing to recession and neoliberal economic restructuring. Interest in this topic took off in the 1980s with the outbreak of the debt crisis and the implementation of the structural adjustment programmes (SAPs) across a wide range of countries, especially Latin America and sub-Saharan Africa. According to Elson (in Afshar and Dennis, 1992), the four main phenomena that affected households in the early stages of these SAPS were declining incomes, increased precarity in employment, rising prices of basic commodities, and downward shifts in public expenditure on the social sector.

> **Box 2** Capital assets of the poor
>
> *Human capital*
> - Vocational skills, knowledge, labour (access to or command over), health.
>
> *Social capital*
> - Relationships of trust, reciprocity, and exchanges that facilitate cooperation, and may provide for informal safety nets among the poor (Note: there can also be 'negative' social capital in the form of violence, mistrust, and so on).
>
> *Natural capital*
> - Natural resource stocks, such as trees, land, biodiversity.
>
> *Physical capital*
> - Basic infrastructure and producer goods, such as transport, shelter, water supply and sanitation, energy, and communication.
>
> *Financial capital*
> - Savings (whether in cash, livestock, or jewellery) and inflows of money, including earned income, pensions, remittances, and state transfers.
>
> Adapted from Rakodi C (1999) A capital assets framework for analysing household livelihood strategies: Implications for policy. *Development Policy Review* 17: 315–342.

Exploring how these changes have affected low-income people is inevitably complicated by variations in contextual factors such as local labour-market conditions, preexisting levels of national poverty, and specific measures adopted by different countries to restructure their economies. Nonetheless, the findings of case studies from different parts of the world indicate broadly similar patterns in terms of the effects on households of – and their responses to – recession and restructuring.

Rakodi (1999) posits four common strategies through the lens of the capital assets framework for livelihoods:

1. Strategies to increase resources by intensifying the use of natural, physical, or human capital include diversifying economic activities, starting businesses, migrating, renting out rooms, increasing subsistence production, and increasing 'occupational density'. The latter involves adopting multiple earning patterns by sending more members into the workforce, rather than relying on a single breadwinner. Many of these new workers are women who may have been economically inactive until then. This was certainly the case in countries like Mexico and Ecuador in the 1980s (see, for example, González de la Rocha, 1994; Moser, 2009).

2. Strategies to change the quantity of human capital involve the following activities. In some instances, it may be appropriate to increase the household size, especially if this entails incorporating new members. These members may work in remunerated activities themselves or take on domestic chores and childcare, to release wives and mothers into the labour force. Alternatively, households might opt for cutting consumption costs by lowering fertility, by engaging in emigration, or by shedding members who fail to make an adequate contribution to the household well-being. The latter option sometimes applies when men do not act in the interests of collective well-being and thus force women and children to establish households on their own.

3. Strategies involving drawing on stocks of social capital necessitate the strengthening of links beyond the household unit. The activities include borrowing, seeking charity, begging, and perhaps most importantly, strengthening people's extra-domestic links with kin and friends for securing and exchanging money, food, labour, and so on.

4. Strategies to mitigate or limit are aimed at achieving a decline in consumption. These encompass the avoidance of 'luxury' purchases or expenditure, the withdrawal of children from school, the scaling down of social engagements, the buying of cheaper or secondhand clothes, and the reduction of expenditure on food and drink. Although people normally try to protect food consumption above all else, studies from countries as diverse as Mexico, Ecuador, the Philippines, Zambia, Cuba, and Gambia indicate that recession and restructuring have led to the poor eating fewer meals per day and also to their cutting down substantially on expensive items such as meat, milk, and fresh fruit juice (see Afshar and Dennis, 1992; Chant, 2007; Moser, 2009, for discussions and references).

Rakodi's fourfold classification of strategies is underpinned by two main imperatives: to minimise consumption ('expenditure-conserving' or 'negative' strategies) and to maximise income ('income-generating' or 'positive' measures) (see also González de la Rocha, 1994). To a large degree it is conceded that these tactics enabled the poor to cushion themselves from the worst ravages of the post-1980 recession and restructuring. For example, between 1982 and 1985 in Guadalajara, Mexico, the increase in multiple-earning strategies and household extension in one low-income settlement resulted in a fall of only 11% in real per capita income, despite a decline of 30% in the wages of household heads (González de la Rocha, 1994).

Intersections between Household Structure and Survival

As intimated above, changes in household structure and headship can be important survival strategies in their own right. In respect of household composition, for example, it appears that large, extended units may be better able to withstand destitution than nuclear households. Despite the conventional wisdom that urbanisation is associated with a trend towards nuclearity, there is considerable evidence to suggest that extended households are far from a minority in the towns and cities of poor countries (see Chant and McIlwaine, 2009: Chapter 9). Even in highly urbanised regions such as Latin America and the Caribbean, for instance, a mere 36% of the households now conform to the model of male-headed nuclearity. Substantial evidence also suggests that among low-income urban populations extended households have actually increased in proportion over the last three decades, as people have struggled to cope with pressures brought about by recession, neoliberal economic restructuring, and globalisation. Adepoju and Mbugua (in Adepoju, 1997), for example, stress that one of the reasons why extended-family households have persisted in African cities is scarcity of employment. Household extension not only provides 'social insurance' for those without work, but can also be a means of allocating labour more efficiently between adults, of preventing the situation where children might need to be withdrawn from school, and of reducing people's vulnerability to destitution. The formation of extended households may also be an adjustment against housing shortages. In addition, extended households permit members to cope better with the daily domestic burdens that result from residing in unserviced periurban settlements. In this way, extended-household structures can represent a positive strategy for survival.

All the same, it is also important to recognise that households may not always function as unified entities. Gender disparities in respect of labour and incomes, for example, have led Bruce and Dwyer (in Dwyer and Bruce, 1993: 8) to propose that it might be more appropriate to conceive of households as comprising an 'uneasy aggregate of individual survival strategies'. Here it is vital to take on board the fragmentation of households associated with female headship.

The Formation of Women-Headed Households

One seemingly ubiquitous trend dating from the mid-twentieth century is a rise in women-headed households. On the basis of a weighted average derived from the overall total of 85 countries for which data are currently available, just over one-fifth of households worldwide are now headed by women (Varley, 2008; see also **Table 1**). Increases appear to be particularly marked in urban areas, as indicated by data from Latin America (**Table 2**).

Notwithstanding variations in levels and rates of increase in female household headship in different countries in the South, it is also important to acknowledge that there are differences in the composition of households headed by women, and in respect of routes to this status (see **Box 3**).

The incidence of female headship is often highest where there are few historical precedents for – or little societal emphasis on – legal marriage, and where there is growing acceptance of nonmarriage and marital dissolution. Such patterns have long existed in the Caribbean, and have – more recently – become apparent in parts of Latin America (see Chant, 1997; Safa, 1998). Alternatively, wherever formal marriage continues to be

Table 1 Percentage of households headed by women in developing regions, 1995–2003

	Percentage (weighted)	No. of countries for which data are available
Africa	23.8	37
Northern Africa	12.9	2
Southern Africa	42.2	3
Rest of sub-Saharan Africa	23.5	32
Asia and Oceania	13.4	27
Eastern Asia	20.0	5
Southeastern Asia	15.4	5
Southern Asia	9.6	5
Central Asia	27.6	5
Western Asia	10.8	2
Oceania	54.1	2
Latin America and the Caribbean	23.9	21
The Caribbean	33.5	7
Central America	21.2	6
South America	24.2	8

Adapted from Varley A (2008) Gender, families and households. In: Desai V and Potter R (eds.) *The Companion to Development Studies*, 2nd edn., pp. 346–351; Table 1. London: Hodder Arnold.

Table 2 Female-headed households as a proportion of all households in urban areas: selected Latin American countries, 1987–99

Country	Years	% of households headed by women	Percentage point change
Argentina	1990	21	
	1999	27	+6
Bolivia	1989	17	
	1999	21	+4
Chile	1990	21	
	1998	24	+3
Colombia	1991	24	
	1999	29	+5
Costa Rica	1990	23	
	1999	28	+5
Ecuador	1990	17	
	1999	20	+3
El Salvador	1995	31	
	1997	31	0
Guatemala	1987	20	
	1998	24	+4
Honduras	1990	27	
	1999	30	+3
Mexico	1989	16	
	1998	19	+3
Nicaragua	1993	35	
	1998	35	0
Panama	1991	26	
	1999	27	+1
Paraguay (Asunción)	1990	20	
	1999	27	+7
Uruguay	1990	25	
	1999	31	+6
Venezuela	1990	22	
	1999	27	+5

Adapted from Chant S and McIlwaine C (2009) *Geographies of Development in the 21st Century: An Introduction to the Global South*, Table 9.2. Cheltenham, UK: Edward Elgar. Based on data from the Economic Commission for Latin America and the Caribbean (www.eclac.org).

a dominant practice, as in many parts of South Asia, the Middle East, and North Africa, levels of female headship remain low. Here the majority of female heads are widows, although rising proportions of abandoned women are noted in places such as Southern India and Bangladesh. Men from these places have increasingly engaged in international labour emigration. Emigration is also a key factor in sub-Saharan Africa, which – along with war, civil conflict, and environmental disasters – has led to the fragmentation of households through population displacement and death (see Adepoju, 1997).

Numerous factors affect the levels of and trends in female household headship (see **Box 4**). However, some factors can be singled out as being particularly relevant to the widespread increases that have occurred in recent decades. First, it is generally agreed that women's mounting propensity to head households is due to the undermining of traditional economic and kinship structures by capitalist development and 'modernisation' (Folbre, 1991). Most rural-based developing societies were patriarchal in nature and allowed women only limited command over resources such as land, income, and labour. Urbanisation, industrialisation, and globalisation, by contrast, have often expanded women's opportunities for waged work. This has reduced their dependency on men and has correspondingly enhanced their own capacity to head households. This trend has been exacerbated by the decline in male employment, especially at the lower end of the occupational spectrum. Inability to fulfil the social expectations of being the family breadwinner appears to be making the men in some countries less likely to marry; this inability is also associated with rising rates of conjugal breakdown (see Chant, 2007; Moore, 1994). Other economic factors that have been implicated in the 'feminisation of household headship' include poverty, with particular emphasis being placed on post-1980 neoliberal economic restructuring. Cutbacks in

> **Box 3** Typology of female-headed households
>
> *Lone-mother households*
> This group comprising the mother and her coresident children constitutes the largest group of female-headed households in most parts of the world.
>
> *Female-headed extended households*
> Households are sometimes headed by a lone mother having coresident children *and* other relatives. Case studies from many countries – especially Latin America, the Caribbean, and sub-Saharan Africa – indicate that the extension of household units is more common under the headship of a woman than that of a man.
>
> *Lone-woman households*
> Less common in the South than in the North – but prevalent in countries such as India and Mexico – this type of household is most likely to consist of an elderly widow living alone.
>
> *Single-sex or women-only households*
> In Southeast Asian countries these usually consist of households comprising young women who work in the same factory or enterprise. In West Africa they are common among certain ethnic groups such as the Ga and the Asante, where women may follow the custom of maintaining separate residences from husbands. Single-sex households are also known in areas where polygamy[a] and polygyny[b] are practised.
>
> *'Female-dominant or female-predominant' households*
> These households are headed by women. Although men may be present, they are only juniors, with less power and authority than adult women.
>
> *Grandmother-headed households*
> This household consists of grandmothers and grandchildren, without the intermediate generation. It is found frequently in areas where child-fostering is common and where adult women need to migrate to find work, as in Sub-Saharan Africa and the Caribbean.
>
> *'Embedded' female-headed units*
> These are units generally comprising a mother and child(ren) – within other households. They are, hence, sometimes known as 'female-headed sub-families'.
>
> ---
>
> *Differentiating factors among female household heads*
> Marital status
> Age or life-course
> Class
> 'Race'
> Sexuality or sexual orientation
> De facto or de jure status[c]
> Child support
> Route into female headship, for example, as a result of widowhood, separation, or nonmarriage; 'forced' or 'voluntary'.
>
> Notes
> [a]This refers to a system where men are legally entitled to more than one wife. In Islamic societies, for instance, the notional maximum is four wives.
> [b]This refers to the practice of men engaging in intimate relationships, including having children, with more than one woman, although this may not be legally sanctioned.
> [c]De jure normally refers to situations where women are heads of household either by law or by virtue of their single status as widows or divorcées. De facto female heads are those whose partners are either absent (e.g., through labour emigration) or present but unable to provide for the household because of disability, sickness, long-term unemployment, and so on.
> Adapted from Chant S and McIlwaine C (2009) *Geographies of Development in the 21st Century: An Introduction to the Global South*, Box 9.2. Cheltenham, UK: Edward Elgar.

public services, the reduction or removal of government subsidies on basic foodstuffs, wage freezes, and so on have increased strains and separations within families. These events have also diminished the prospects for the reentry of women into the households of parents and male relatives following widowhood, divorce, or separation.

Female household headship has been linked with changes in the labour market, development, and globalisation. However, it has also resulted from increases in internal and international migration. As most migration streams have historically been gender-differentiated, this has led to localised imbalances in populations: where 'sex ratios' are strongly feminine, there is a greater likelihood that female household headship will prevail (see Chant, 1997). For example, men in sub-Saharan Africa have traditionally predominated in rural–urban migration, leaving the women to head the households in the countryside. In Latin America and Southeast Asia, by contrast, where selective urban movement by women has prevailed, female-headed households occur more frequently in urban than in rural areas (Chant, 1997). Increases in women's rights in the spheres of sexual and reproductive freedom,

> **Box 4** Factors affecting the formation of female-headed households in developing countries
>
> *I Demographic factors*
> 1. Uneven sex ratios
>   a. Gender-selective migration
>   b. Gender-differentiated life expectancy
>   c. War and disease
> 2. Urbanisation
> 3. Age at marriage
>   a. Women's age at marriage
>   b. Gender differentials in age at marriage
> 4. Fertility and birth control
>
> *II Economic factors*
> 1. Access to land and property
> 2. Production systems
> 3. Women's participation in the labour force
> 4. Economic restructuring and poverty
>
> *III Legal–institutional factors*
> 1. State attitudes and interventions
> 2. Family and divorce legislation
>   a. Divorce
>   b. Child custody
>   c. Enforcement of legal provisions
> 3. Welfare and benefit schemes
> 4. Women's movements
>
> *IV Sociocultural factors*
> 1. Culture
> 2. Religion
> 3. Gender roles, relations, and ideologies
> 4. Kinship and residence
> 5. Marriage practices, childbirth, and social identity
>   a. Polygamy
>   b. Arranged marriages
>   c. Consensual unions
>   d. Wifehood, motherhood, and social status
> 6. Morality and sexuality
>
> Adapted from Chant S and McIlwaine C (2009) *Geographies of Development in the 21st Century: An Introduction to the Global South*, Box 9.3. Cheltenham, UK: Edward Elgar.

access to divorce, and custody of children, have also led to increases in female headship. In many societies marriage is not the prerequisite for childbirth that it once was. Marital breakdown has increased, as the grounds for divorce have widened, as women have become freer to petition for divorce in their own right, and as their entitlements to conjugal property, maintenance payments, and child support have risen. In Thailand, for example, a rise in divorces by 50% during the 1980s meant that by the early 1990s, nearly 25% of the marriages ended up being formally dissolved. In Costa Rica, only one marriage in eleven was terminated through divorce in 1984, but by 2001 the proportion was four marriages in ten (see Chant, 2007: 294 for discussion and references).

Female-Headed Households and the 'Feminisation of Poverty'

The rise in female household headship has frequently met with concern, if not alarm, in public-policy circles. Growing numbers of female heads, especially those who are unmarried, divorced, or separated, are widely construed as symbolising a 'breakdown' in the family, especially wherever the patriarchal (male-headed) unit remains a normative ideal (Chant, 2007; Moore, 1994; Safa, 1998). Part of the anxiety around these processes stems from links drawn between rising levels of female headship and a putative 'feminisation of poverty'. Even if the 'feminisation of poverty' ought technically to imply a trend for women (not just female household heads) to become poorer over time, female-headed households are frequently typecast as the 'poorest of the poor'. 'Feminisation of poverty' is frequently confused with 'feminised poverty', which is merely a state in which women are poorer than men (see Medeiros and Costa, 2006). This typecasting of female household heads may have been based on their allegedly greater likelihood of being poorer, and of experiencing more pronounced degrees of indigence than male-headed units. These notions rest upon the facts that women's earnings are lower than those of men; that female heads are time-constrained and resource-constrained by their triple burdens of employment, housework, and childcare; and that in most countries in the South, female heads receive little transfer income through state welfare or child-maintenance payments from absent fathers (see Chant, 1997, 2007). Poverty also figures prominently in another conventional nugget of wisdom perniciously attached to female household headship, particularly lone motherhood. This is termed the 'intergenerational transmission of disadvantage', whereby children are regarded as suffering a setback as a result of being raised only by women (Chant, 1997). Alongside poverty, psychological problems are presumed to emanate from 'father absence', lack of time for maternal care, limited parental discipline, and so on. These are deemed to fuel a self-perpetuating and cumulatively downward spiral of insecurity, poverty, and family instability (Chant, 1997).

It cannot be denied that women suffer disproportionately from social and economic inequalities. Whether these disadvantages necessarily make female-headed households the 'poorest of the poor' is, however, less certain. Indeed, a mounting body of research has contested these unilaterally negative portrayals of female household headship. One critical challenge is posed by evidence from countries as diverse as Vietnam, Indonesia, Colombia, Panama, Zimbabwe, Guinea, and Morocco, which reveals that in income terms, female-headed units are not more likely to be poor than male-headed households (Chant, 2007; see also Medeiros and Costa, 2006; Sen, 2008). Part of the reason for this is that female-headed households constitute a diverse group in respect of the ages and relative dependencies of (or indeed, financial contributions from) offspring. Household composition, socioeconomic status, and access to resources from beyond the household unit (from absent fathers, kinship networks, state assistance, and the like) may also vary. A common finding from a range of countries, for example, is that female-headed households are more likely to be extended than male-headed units. If this extension involves the incorporation of other adults, the labour burden might be eased. This might boost the economic situation of female heads such that they benefit from lower dependency ratios and higher per capita incomes than their male counterparts. Detailed empirical studies at the microeconomic level have also found that expenditures in female-headed households tend to be dedicated more to the basic needs of the children and less to the personal consumption of the adult earners. In male-headed units, men may spend a significant proportion of their incomes on 'non-merit' items such as tobacco and alcohol. In contrast, female-headed households allocate more resources to food, health, and education, particularly that of daughters (see Bradshaw, 2002; Chant, 1997, 2007; Dwyer and Bruce, 1993; Kabeer, 2007). Contrary to prevailing conventional wisdoms, levels of nutrition and educational attainment may thus be higher among children in female-headed units, and less gender-differentiated (Chant, 2007; also Varley, 2008). These issues are important in deconstructing blanket stereotypes. 'Feminisation of poverty' may be broadened to include other dimensions of privation and inequality beyond incomes – such as inputs of labour, imbalances of power and privilege, and so on. If this were done, then greater bias against women and girls may actually be acknowledged to exist in male-headed households (see Chant, 2007). In situations where families are affected by violence or financial neglect by men, for example, female headship can represent an escape from privation; it can also enhance women's personal power and autonomy. As summarised by Gita Sen (2008: 6):

> It is clear now that, not only is the empirical generalisation inaccurate, but that a single-minded focus on female-headed households narrows which households we focus on and how we understand what goes on within them....Viewing poverty as a gendered experience allows us to broaden the scope of analysis to include all poor households however headed. It also directs us to a wider range of issues beyond simply asking whether women or men are poorer in income terms. These include the ways in which poverty is made a gendered experience by norms and values, divisions of assets, work and responsibility, and relations of power and control.

Negative generalisations about female-headed households remain largely unsubstantiated, and caution is needed to prevent concerns about gender disadvantage from falling further into a 'poverty trap' (Jackson, 1996). Nevertheless, it is obvious that female headship places women and children at risk in societies where two-parent households are a normative ideal, and where gender inequalities of varying types prevail. In such contexts, directing public assistance to female-headed households is arguably imperative.

Although there are programmes of assistance for female-headed households in a number of countries in the Global South, these are often limited in scope. One major fear is that targeting may produce 'perverse incentives' and encourage more 'family breakdowns' (Buvinic and Gupta, 1997; Chant, 1997). However, if the protection of the rights, well being, and security of children is the ultimate objective of social policy, as stressed by international organisations such as UNICEF, it is also important to adopt the spirit of the Beijing Platform for Action (BPFA) and to recognise and support household diversity. This implies abandoning the adherence to an arbitrary Eurocentric norm of family life. Social programmes in the South must be adapted to cater to the multiplicity of domestic contexts in which children are raised in the twenty-first century (Chant and McIlwaine, 2009: 252).

Future attempts to bolster household survival are possible only after acknowledging the fact that household strategies have been indispensable in coping with economic crises and restructuring; however, many individual members, especially women, have practised these strategies at the cost of unprecedented self-exploitation and self-denial. Indeed, one major worry is that the disproportionate burdens that have fallen on women have stretched their personal reserves to full capacity. It is possible that there will be no further 'slack' to be taken up (see also Elson in Afshar and Dennis, 1992; Chant, 2007; González de la Rocha, 2007; Moser, 2009). Moreover, there is considerable doubt that household efforts can withstand further onslaught from macroeconomic processes, which can disadvantage the poor. González de la Rocha (2007), for example, warns that persistent poverty in Mexico has effectively brought some segments of the population to their knees. The mobilisation of household, family, and community solidarity served as vital resources in the past. Nonetheless, there is undoubtedly a limit to the favours that people can call on from one another. The effectiveness of these exchanges in the face of huge structural impediments to well-being is limited (González de la Rocha, 2007). Indeed, given the disturbing evidence of weakened 'social capital' and solidarity in several developing countries in recent years, and in the wake of the current global financial crisis, it is advisable for states, international agencies, and other institutional providers to put their weight behind existing attempts by the poor to secure household livelihoods.

References

Adepoju A (ed.) (1997) *Family, Population and Development in Africa*. London: Zed.

Afshar H and Dennis C (eds.) (1992) *Women and Adjustment Policies in the Third World*. Basingstoke, UK: Macmillan.

Bradshaw S (2002) *Gendered Poverties and Power Relations: Looking Inside Communities and Households*. Managua, Nicaragua: ICD, Embajada de Holanda, Puntos de Encuentro.

Buvinic M and Gupta GR (1997) Female-headed households and female-maintained families: Are they worth targeting to reduce poverty in developing countries? *Economic Development and Cultural Change* 45(2): 259–280.

Chant S (1997) *Women-Headed Households: Diversity and Dynamics in the Developing World*. Houndmills, Basingstoke, UK: Macmillan.

Chant S (2007) *Gender, Generation and Poverty: Exploring the 'Feminisation of Poverty' in Africa, Asia and Latin America*. Cheltenham, UK: Edward Elgar.

Chant S and McIlwaine C (2009) *Geographies of Development in the 21st Century: An Introduction to the Global South*. Cheltenham, UK: Edward Elgar.

Dwyer D and Bruce J (eds.) (1993) *A Home Divided: Women and Income in the Third World*. Stanford, CA: Stanford University Press.

Folbre N (1991) Women on their own: Global patterns of female headship. In: Gallin RS and Ferguson A (eds.) *The Women and International Development Annual*, Vol. 2, pp. 69–126. Boulder, CO: Westview.

González de la Rocha M (1994) *The Resources of Poverty: Women and Survival in a Mexican City*. Oxford, UK: Blackwell.

González de la Rocha M (2007) The construction of the myth of survival. *Development and Change* 38(1): 45–66.

Harris O (1981) Households as natural units. In: Young K, Wolkowitz C, and McCullagh R (eds.) *Of Marriage and the Market*, pp. 48–67. London: CSE Books.

Jackson C (1996) Rescuing gender from the poverty trap. *World Development* 24(3): 489–504.

Kabeer N (2007) *Marriage, Motherhood and Masculinity in the Global Economy: Reconfigurations of Personal and Economic Life. Working Paper 290*. Sussex, UK: Institute of Development Studies. http://www.ids.ac.uk/ids/bookshop (accessed 12 December 2007).

Medeiros M and Costa J (2006) *Poverty among Women in Latin America: Feminisation or Over-Representation? Working Paper No.20*. Brasilia: International Poverty Centre. http://www.undp-povertycentre.org (accessed).

Moore H (1994) Is there a crisis in the family? *World Summit for Social Development, Occasional Research Paper 3*. Geneva: United Nations Research Institute for Social Development. http://www.unrisd.org (accessed).

Moser C (2009) *Ordinary Families, Extraordinary Lives: Assets and Poverty Reduction in Guayaquil, 1978–2004*. Washington, DC: Brookings Institute Press.

Rakodi C (1999) A capital assets framework for analysing household livelihood strategies: Implications for policy. *Development Policy Review* 17: 315–342.

Safa H (1998) Female-headed households in the Caribbean: Sign of pathology or alternative form of family organisation? *The Brown Journal of World Affairs* 5(2): 203–214.

Sen G (2008) Poverty as a gendered experience: The policy implications. Poverty in Focus 13: 6–7. http://www.undp-povertycentre.org/pub/IPCPovertyInFocus13.pdf (accessed 15 January 2008).

Varley A (2008) Gender, families and households. In: Desai V and Potter R (eds.) *The Companion to Development Studies*, 2nd edn., pp. 346–351. London: Hodder Arnold.

Relevant Websites

www.un.org – UN website on families.
www.unicef.org – United Nations Children's Fund.
www.unrisd.org – UN Research Institute for Social Development.
www.uk.youtube.com/watch?v=bPuNXO7_tno – IRIN Slum Survivors Part 1 (a woman's struggle for survival in the low-income settlement of Kibera, Nairobi) (5 min).

Households and Families

R Simpson, University of Edinburgh, Edinburgh, UK

© 2012 Elsevier Ltd. All rights reserved.

Glossary

Average household size This is calculated as the ratio between the number of people (adult and children) living in private households and the number of households of each different category.

Family unit/family nucleus This comprises either a single person, or a married/cohabiting couple, or a married/cohabiting couple and their never-married (adopted) children who have no children of their own living with them, or a lone parent with such children. Family units may include nondependent adult children, provided they have never married and have no children of their own living with them.

Head of household In a household where there is one adult only, that adult is the head of the household. If there are two adults of the opposite sex living together as a married or cohabiting couple, the husband/male partner is the household head. Otherwise, it is the oldest male householder, or the husband/male partner of the oldest female householder. Else, the oldest female householder is the household head.

Household dependency ratio The ratio between those who are not economically active (and therefore dependent), and those who are economically active.

Household reference person The householder, in whose name the home is owned, being bought, or rented. If there are joint householders, the one with the highest income is the household reference person. If their income is the same, then the eldest one is the household reference person.

Total fertility rate This is the average number of children that would be born alive to a woman during her lifetime if she were to pass through her childbearing years conforming to the age-specific fertility rates of a given year. The replacement rate, a TFR of 2.1, is the rate at which a population would remain stable, excluding migration.

Households and Families as Socioeconomic Institutions

Families and households are both fundamental socioeconomic institutions. Defined in terms of shared residence, they are basic units of social reproduction, consumption, and, in certain times and places, economic production. Private households are distinct from public households such as residential homes; only private households are considered here. There has been much criticism of functionalist approaches which present the standard nuclear family as a universal social institution necessary for producing or rearing children, or meeting the instrumental and expressive tasks of breadwinning and caregiving. Nevertheless, families remain key social and cultural units that are consequential for human behaviour and well-being. Changes in families and households can have profound social and economic consequences at both the individual and societal levels.

The ways in which people conduct their intimate relationships and organise their living arrangements are both causes and consequences of social and societal change. Households are key drivers of sociospatial processes. The size and composition of households impact on housing consumption and demand. Consumption practices and mobility patterns of households shape urban development and the built environment. Contemporary changes mean functions such as caregiving are increasingly provided beyond the household. The significant transformations undergone by families have policy implications for resource planning, care provision, and housing, and effective policies require understanding the changing shape and needs of families and households.

Conceptualising Households and Families

The terms household and families refer to distinct concepts, relating to either residential arrangements or kinship/relatedness. Nevertheless, the household may be simultaneously a spatial and social unit – the space within which intimate relationships are maintained. These concepts are often conflated in academic scholarship as well as popular everyday understandings: notions of 'home' for example are often associated with the familial realm.

Since the first modern census, demographers have aimed at identifying and defining households as primary sampling units for collecting data about individuals. Household-based understandings of the family unit draw on notions of the conventional life course to conceptualise the family as forming when a man and woman marry and have children, creating a nuclear household unit. Traditional household models assume functions such as shared residence and income pooling. Historical and cross-cultural research demonstrates that such models fail to adequately capture the diverse nature and meanings of families or households. Preindustrial households included extended kin, such as grandparents or adult siblings, as well as nonkin, such as servants or lodgers. Anthropology illustrates the limitations of the household concept to adequately account for diversity in patterns of residence, kinship, and economic organisation in developing countries. Feminist analyses of the political economy of the family draw attention to intra-household inequities in resources such as time and income. Sociological theorising emphasises that kinship can be expressed in many ways, and argue that the concept of family has come to signify the subjective meanings of intimate connections, rather than biological or conjugal ties. This scholarship highlights the need to consider diverse 'family practices', shaped by differences such as ethnicity and sexuality. Disciplinary approaches reflect the differing purposes that concepts such as the family serve. Nevertheless, these concepts remain useful tools for describing and understanding human behaviour.

How households and families are conceptualised influences their classification in official surveys. Evidence from various disciplines suggests that the social units that people live in may not correspond fully to the household as defined by survey practitioners. Households and families are dynamic: increasing transitions in and out of these at the individual level contribute to difficulties in classification. Recent changes in family formation raise issues as to whether the current formal definitions can capture contemporary complexities of living arrangements and familial relationships. Changes in household structures, for example the rise in one-person households, indicate 'family practices' may increasingly be taking place beyond the household. However, population surveys rarely collect information about kin relationships beyond the household, thus the social and economic interactions with such individuals may be overlooked. It is also unclear as to what extent same-sex couples are counted in surveys or censuses.

In some countries, household registration is required by law, for example, China (*Hukou*) or Japan (*Jyuminhyou*). In addition to formal arrangements for residency registration, registration of family-related information may also be required. Government-administered family registers recording events such as births, deaths, marriages, and divorces have been common in many European nations and in countries which use continental-style civil law; however, several have recently been abolished. For example, the *Hoju* system in South Korea, seen as innately patriarchal, ended 1 January 2008. Since 1 January 2009 German *Familienbücher* are no longer issued.

Definitions and Measurement

The household is almost universally used as a unit of enumeration. There are ongoing attempts to standardise classification of households, and of relationships within households, for purposes of comparability across place and time, and in relation to the requirements of government departments. Networks of relationships pose formidable problems to those with an interest in identifying and quantifying these relationships. New measurement tools such as relationship matrices are emerging to improve enumeration of increasingly complex households.

Common elements of household identification are that they comprise a single person, or a group of people living at the same address who share certain aspects of domestic life, for example, eating together. Not all private households contain families. Nonfamily households consist of people who live alone or who share their residence with unrelated individuals, for example, shared student households. Standard classifications distinguish private households according to the family units they contain. Family is conventionally defined in terms of consanguinity (blood ties) and conjugality (marriage). 'Family' in official statistics almost always refers to a single nuclear family unit living together.

The diversity of both households and family types is recognised in various classification schemas that have emerged to measure complexity, that is, the extent to which nonnuclear members are present. Thus, a simple family household consists of a partnered couple (married or cohabiting) with or without children, or a sole parent with one or more children. More complex or extended family households include members of more than two generations or siblings, or through the addition of other more distant relatives or nonrelatives. There are many ways of grouping or classifying households into household types, including the age, sex, and number of household members, as well as according to the family units they contain. Official definitions of the family unit, or family nucleus, may preclude some relatives being classified as living in family households, for example, adult siblings living together would be classified as a nonfamily household. Similarly, same-sex cohabiting couples would not be classified as a family unit.

The identification of a household reference person in household censuses and surveys enables the enumeration of relationships between members within households. The household reference person is the householder, the person responsible for the accommodation. This concept, defined in relation to householder status, income, and age, replaces the notion of a head of household, defined in relation to sex and age, although this may still be used. In Great Britain, where the concept of household reference person was adopted on all government-sponsored surveys from 2001–02, the household reference person and head of household are the same person in about 90% of households.

Contemporary Change in Families

A society's population structure, that has in developed societies been increasingly shaped by demographic trends such as increased longevity and declining fertility, is consequential for household size and composition. Ageing populations have meant more and smaller households. Across industrialised societies, there is an increasing gap between population rates (declining) and household rates (increasing), with declining fertility rates as a crucial determinant of this divergence. **Table 1** shows the total fertility rate (TFR) for selected countries between 1980 and 2000; with the exception of the United States, all have a TFR below the replacement rate of 2.1. Household projections indicate that overall population trends will continue to have a major influence in the years to come, with the average household size likely to continue to decline.

The transformation of the household structure in industrialised countries is a long-standing trend going back well over a century. It is associated with what has been termed the First Demographic Transition, starting in the latter part of the nineteenth century, as both fertility and mortality fell and household size decreased. Dramatic changes in recent decades in the timing and extent to which individuals partner and bear children have led to the destandardisation of family and household forms across industrialised countries. Several scholars identify contemporary demographic and associated changes as the Second Demographic Transition.

The Second Demographic Transition

Trends in family formation since the 1960s include the delay and decline in marriage and childbearing, alongside an increase in cohabitation, divorce, separation, and remarriage, and extra-marital births. **Table 1** shows the increasing average age at first birth, and in lifetime childlessness, for women. Alongside this are changes such as increasing tendency and ability of the elderly to live alone, and the legal recognition of same-sex couples. Families have become less stable, smaller, and more diverse. These trends have led to the transformation of household structures, a pluralisation of household arrangements, for example, dual-career households or

Table 1 Mean age of women at first birth, total fertility rate, and definitive childlessness for women, by selected countries and years

Country	Mean age of women at first birth[a] 1980	2000	Total fertility rate[b] 1980	2000	Definitive childlessness[c] Women (%) born in 1940	1965
Austria	–	26.4	1.6	1.4	11.9	21.1
Belgium	24.7	–	1.7	1.6	13.1	–
Canada	26.5	29.9	1.7	1.5	–	–
Denmark	24.6	27.3	1.6	1.8	–	12.7
Finland	25.5	27.4	1.6	1.7	–	19.9
France	–	27.8	2	1.9	8.3	–
Germany	25.2	29	–	1.4	10.6	–
Hungary	22.9	25	1.9	1.3	9.1	9.6
Ireland	25	27.4	–	1.9	19.8	15.6
Israel	–	–	3.1	3	–	–
Italy	–	–	1.6	1.3	14.6	15.3
Netherlands	–	–	1.6	1.7	11.2	18.3
Norway	–	27.3	1.7	1.8	9.5	12.1
Poland	23.4	24.5	–	1.4	–	10.8
Portugal	23.6	26.5	2.2	1.6	–	4
Spain	25	29.1	2.2	1.2	–	13.1
Sweden	25.3	27.9	1.7	1.5	13.2	12.9
Switzerland	26.3	28.7	1.6	1.5	16	–
United Kingdom	–	29.1	1.9	1.6	10.7	18.9
United States	22.7	24.9	1.8	2.1	7.4	14.4

[a, b]Source: UNECE Statistical Division Database, compiled from national and international (Eurostat, UN Statistics Division Demographic Yearbook, WHO European Health for All database and UNICEF TransMONEE) official sources.
[c]Source: OECD Family database, brings together information from different OECD databases, and databases maintained by other (international) organisations.

step-families, and a rise in the frequency of transitions between different household types. There is some debate as to the extent to which changing sociocultural attitudes, such as increasing individualisation and greater emphasis on personal autonomy, secularisation, or changing expectations of the roles of men and women, underpin these trends. A substantial body of evidence links demographic changes to broader economic and social processes. These impact differentially on various socioeconomic groups. There are also important regional differences in the rate and extent of demographic changes. Nevertheless, the pattern of trends is similar across industrialised countries.

Changing Household Structures

The role that demographic factors play in shaping the size and composition of households varies across societies. The partnership and parenthood behaviours of men and women are related to wider social and economic changes. The interaction of factors such as education and labour market circumstances, housing, and employment conditions with localised norms and values underpins the considerable heterogeneity in household structures across and within countries. Nevertheless, there are common patterns across industrialised countries. The average household size has been decreasing – an outcome of the decline in family households and concomitant increasing numbers of one-person and lone-parent households. There has also been a decline in extended or multihouseholds containing more than one family unit, although such households constitute more than 10% of all households in the United States, Mexico, Korea, Japan, as well as some former Eastern European countries (see **Table 2**). These broad trends in living arrangements are mediated by factors at the individual level, such as age and stage in the life course, gender, and routes into solo living.

One-Person Households

One of the more remarkable changes has been the increase in people living alone, or solo living. This trend has been interpreted by some commentators as signifying a decline in family. The increase in nonresident parenthood as an outcome of partnership dissolution as well as 'living-apart-together' relationships, however, illustrate the 'family practices' that may be conducted across household boundaries.

Living alone, or solo living, has been a steadily increasing trend across a wide range of industrialised countries in recent decades, with a significant proportion of people now living alone in countries of Northern Europe (see **Figure 1**). People who live alone however are not a homogeneous group, and routes into solo living vary by socioeconomic circumstance. Men of working age are more

Table 2 Type of household, selected countries, latest year

Country	Couple family households	One-person households	Lone-parent households	Other private households
Australia	58.7	26.5	5.8	9
Austria	52.9	33.5	9.7	3.9
Canada	57.4	26.8	15.7	0.1
Czech Republic	53.6	30.3	12.9	3.2
Denmark	50.9	36.8	5.1	7.2
Finland	49.8	37.3	7.6	5.3
France	58.3	31	8	2.7
Germany	55.4	35.8	5.9	2.9
Hungary	57	26.2	10.7	6.1
Ireland	59.2	21.6	11.7	7.6
Italy	62.3	24.9	8.9	3.9
Japan	49.5	29.5	8.4	12.1[a]
Korea	72.6	–	9.4	18.6
Netherlands	59.9	33.6	5.8	0.7
Norway	52.2	37.7	8.6	1.5
Poland	56.4	24.8	12.6	6.2
Portugal	69.1	17.3	8.6	5
Spain	62.9	20.3	9.9	6.9
United Kingdom	53.5	30.2	9.8	6.6
United States	51.7	27.3	9.2	11.8

[a]This proportion includes potentially lone-person households which cannot be identified separately from the data.
Data concern 1999 for France; 2000: Finland, Korea, and the United States; 2001: Austria, Czech Republic, Denmark, Hungary, Italy, the Netherlands, Norway, Portugal, Spain, and the United Kingdom; 2002: Ireland, Poland; 2005: Japan; 2006: Australia and Canada.
Source: OECD Family database, brings together information from different OECD databases, and databases maintained by other (international) organisations.

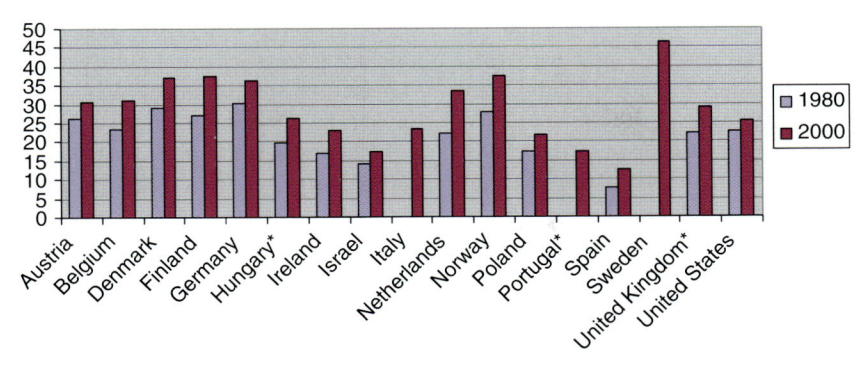

Figure 1 One-person households as a percentage of all households, by selected countries, 1980 and 2000. *Figures for 2001. Source: United Nations Economic Commission for Europe (UNECE) Statistical Division Database, compiled from national official sources.

likely to be living alone than their female counterparts. This is in part related to increasing rates of partnership dissolution and the tendency of women to retain custody of any children, thereby forming a lone-parent household (the overwhelming majority of lone-parent households are headed by women). At retirement age, women are more likely to live alone. This is in part related to their greater life expectancy, but also reflects a shift from previous patterns of elderly people living with their adult children.

The increase in living alone is also evident amongst young adults, in part related to the later age at which people are entering partnerships, whether marital or cohabiting. Whereas previously young adults would typically leave the parental home and set up their own household on marriage, a period of living independently, either living alone or sharing with peers, has become more common. Living alone or in shared households may be transitional for some, however for others it may become a more settled living arrangement. Individuals may experience several transitions, for example, moving from living alone to cohabiting, and recommencing solo living following partnership dissolution.

The rise in one-person households has been accompanied by other trends, such as an increase in young adults returning to or remaining in the parental home. These trends are situated in broader economic and social, as well as demographic, changes. Alongside shifts in the timing of partnership and parenthood, the availability and affordability of housing, as well as education and employment markets, interact with specific cultural attitudes regarding practices such as remaining in the parental home or living alone, with consequent regional differences in household structures. The proportion of one-person households in Nordic countries such as Sweden and Finland, for example, is around twice those of Mediterranean countries such as Spain or Portugal.

Relationships beyond the Household

Censuses and surveys have traditionally used the household as the unit of analysis, and the household is, in most cases, composed of a single nuclear family living together. Nevertheless, it is important to be aware that intimate relationships are not simply limited to those people that one lives with at a particular point in time, resulting in increasing obligations beyond the household.

Living alone is not the same as being single, and people in one-person households may have a sexual partner or be in an established nonresidential partnership. The phenomenon of couples 'living apart together' (LAT) has been increasingly documented. LAT is generally accepted as monogamous, and more than a temporary, fleeting, or casual relationship. Defining and measuring its prevalence is very difficult. Individuals in LAT relationships may be of the same sex as well as opposite sexes, and either partner may be living in a household containing other people.

Another striking trend in household structures is the increase in lone-parent households, and thereby an increase in nonresidential parents. Although not all nonresident parents will be involved parents, and only the function of child maintenance is regulated by legislation, increasingly children may be living across households, with nonresident parents providing support to children. Parenting across households is common in some ethnic minority communities. Nonresident parents however may be treated similarly to single people by housing authorities, and thus not be allocated accommodation sufficient for their children to stay overnight. There is also increasing attention given to the role of grandparents in postseparation agreements. Family structure is often used in research on children's well-being; however, studies looking beyond the household suggest that differences in indicators of disadvantage across one- and two-parent households may have diminished.

As average life expectancy increases, alongside the decreasing likelihood of older people living with their children (who are major providers of informal care), their needs will be met increasingly from outside the household. The household, having given up its economic and educational roles in the past, is now increasingly sharing its caring responsibilities with both formal and informal sectors. Other practices such as increased migration and mobility may also result in family members residing elsewhere providing remittances. While the decrease in average household size means a trend towards smaller, less complex households, more and more people will have commitments and networks beyond its confines. Analyses conducted at the household level, for example household dependency ratios, do not take into account economic contribution or other support from those outside the household.

Implications for Family Formation

There are complex interrelationships between demographic trends such as the postponement of partnership and parenting. Factors such as education and employment markets, alongside the availability, quality, and type of housing, are also influential. Changes in family formation are consequential for household structures, and for future housing demand. At the same time, both housing availability and type of household influence demographic trends. Changing housing markets, the rise of owner-occupation, and assessment of housing as a financial asset constrain partnership formation. Housing inaffordability, alongside the perceived undesirability of private rental housing, in certain contexts undermines fertility rates.

There is a long-standing relationship between forms of households and the availability of housing. Another central factor is the availability of familial support. In the past, at times of housing shortage, many young couples commenced married life in the parental household, a custom that has declined in practice and cultural acceptability in many industrialised countries. In the United Kingdom, the expansion of lone-parent households has been in part attributed to an increase in the provision of first public, and then private, housing in the 1970s and 1980s: lone-parent families, who have historically been more likely than others to live in multifamily households, increasingly set up independent households throughout this period. As the recent dramatic increase in first-time buyers receiving financial support from parents for deposits and repayments illustrates, declining housing affordability may also reinforce familial connections.

Changes in the affordability and demand for private rented housing from those living outside a family have been identified with the increase in one-person households, particularly amongst certain groups such as young professionals, concentrated in urban centres. This residential sorting of household types has particular sociospatial implications, including specific consumption patterns and social networks. Qualitative studies on solo living suggest that duration of living alone, alongside a sense of stake in their current home, whether owner-occupied or a tenancy, impacts on the sense of risk associated with future partnership.

Future Convergence?

Demographic transition theory assumes convergence, that is, the size and complexity of households decreasing as societies industrialise. This view assumes current heterogeneity in household structures merely reflects different rates of transition. Debates over the extent of convergence relate to different interpretations of cultural or ideational factors on demographic trends, rather than solely economic determinants. Trends in household size and composition in Europe and North America since the mid-nineteenth century are consistent with convergence theory. Nevertheless, differences between broad categories of countries, for example, the Nordic countries compared with Southern Mediterranean countries, are indicative of the impact of distinct political cultures and policy contexts across industrialised nations. There is limited support for convergence in developing countries, and some indication of trends to smaller and predominantly nuclear households.

See also: Children and Parenting; Demographic Perspectives in Economic Housing Research; Experiencing Home; Gender Divisions in the Home; Gender and Urban Housing in the Global South; Life Course; Residential Segregation: Experiences of African Americans; Risk in Housing Markets.

Further Reading

Alders MPC and Manting D (2003) Household scenarios for the European Union, 1995–2025. *Genus* LVII(2): 17–47.

Bongaarts J (2001) Household size and complexity in the developing world in the 1990s. *Population Studies* 55: 263–279.

Brandon PD and Hogan DP (2008) New approaches to household diversity and change. *Journal of Population Research* 25(3): 247–250.

Ford J, Rugg J, and Burrows R (2002) Conceptualising the contemporary role of housing in the transition to adult life in England. *Urban Studies* 39(13): 2455–2467.

Hareven TK (1991) The home and the family in historical perspective. *Social Research* 58(1): 253–285.

Heath S and Cleaver E (2003) *Young, Free and Single: Twenty-Somethings and Household Change*. Basingstoke, UK: Palgrave Macmillan.

Hofferth SL and Casper LM (eds.) (2007) *Handbook of Measurement Issues in Family Research*. Mahwah, NJ: Lawrence Erlbaum Associates.

Laslett P and Wall R (eds.) (1972) *Household and Family in Past Time*. Cambridge, UK: Cambridge University Press.

Madigan R, Munro M, and Smith SJ (1990) Gender and the meaning of the home. *International Journal of Urban and Regional Research* 14(4): 625–647.

Myers D (ed.) (1995) *Housing Demography: Linking Demographic Structure and Housing Markets*. Madison, WI; London: University of Wisconsin Press

Stillwell J (ed.) (2009–2010) *Understanding Population Trends and Processes* (3 Volumes). Dordrecht, The Netherlands: Springer.

Stillwell J, Coast E, and Kneale D (eds.) (2009) *Understanding Population Trends and Processes: Fertility, Living Arrangements, Care and Mobility*. Dordrecht, the Netherlands: Springer.

van Imhoff E, Kuijsten A, Hooimeijer P, and van Wissen L (eds.) (1995) *Household Demography and Household Modelling*. New York; London: Plenum Press.

Relevant Websites

www.oecd.org – OECD Family database, information on family size and household composition.

http://epp.eurostat.ec.europa.eu – New family relationships and living arrangements – demands for change in social statistics. 35th CEIES Seminar 24–25 January 2008, Warsaw, Poland.

Household Waste Recycling

M Watson, University of Sheffield, Sheffield, UK

© 2012 Elsevier Ltd. All rights reserved.

Glossary

3Rs In relation to waste, standing for reduction, reuse, and recycling, the three most preferable options of the waste hierarchy which together reduce the total quantity of materials entering the final waste stream.
Landfill Method of solid waste disposal by filling low-lying land areas. Where regulated, waste is covered with layers of soil and the site is subject to pollution control measures.
Recycling Using materials from waste products to make new products.
Reuse Using a product again after its first use in its original form, whether for the same or a different purpose.
Waste Substances or objects disposed of, or intended for disposal.
Waste hierarchy Hierarchical ranking of waste management options based on environmental impact, typically ranking reduction over reuse, over recycling, over recovery, with disposal the last resort.
Zero waste An ideal future scenario in which all materials discarded are resources for reuse.

Introduction

Household waste recycling is profoundly mundane. At the scale of the household, it is a matter of sorting paper and cardboard, and cleaning bottles and cans. However, the rapid rise of household waste recycling over recent decades in developed countries is a fascinating phenomenon. It represents specific convergences of global environmental concern and international political agendas with routine practices and mundane infrastructures of the home. Exploring the dynamics of recycling also brings us face to face with how we relate to the materials which pass through our houses, and how the ways in which we process and classify those materials helps in establishing the space of home.

Defining Household Waste Recycling

To begin to approach this topic, we need to give basic definitions of the key terms of the article. To begin with, what is waste? According to the 1989 Basel Convention, a landmark treaty in the modern history of waste management, "[w]astes are substances or objects which are disposed or are intended to be disposed." This chimes with our common sense understanding of waste as matter to be rid of. However, as will shortly be explored, once we go beyond abstract definitions working out what makes something waste is a complex and culturally contingent process of classification. Partly due to the difficulties of classifying what material counts as waste, it is difficult to quantify how much is produced, but a rough indication is that the Organization for Economic Co-operation and Development (OECD) estimated that, in 2001, its 25 member countries produced approximately 4 billion tons of waste.

A relatively small proportion of the billions of tons of waste produced globally each year is considered to be household waste. For example, in the United Kingdom, household waste accounted for 11% of the 288 million tons produced in 2008. However, the ranking of household waste on public and policy agendas is disproportionate relative to its volume. This is partly a consequence of its high visibility in everyday life, making it relatively present in the public consciousness. It also results from its profoundly complex nature: compared to larger-scale waste streams from extractive industries, manufacturing or construction, household waste is messy and heterogeneous, with small quantities of diverse materials mixed up in the bin. This makes it difficult to work with to recover value, given that different materials must enter different processing and market streams.

Recycling is the use of materials from waste products to make new products. In popular discourse, recycling can also refer to what is more formally referred to as reuse. In reuse, a product is used again in its original form, whether or not for its original purpose. In recycling, products are reduced to raw materials, to reenter manufacturing processes.

Conceptualising Waste and Home

While the definition presented above of waste as matter to be disposed seems straightforward, it can in fact indicate that for something to become waste it must pass a profoundly contingent line, over which the value of keeping it is understood to be less than the costs of keeping it. For example, a householder might recognise the potential value of a plastic food-packaging container to be reused for keeping food leftovers in the future, but the costs of time and space entailed in cleaning and storing it, weighed against the likelihood of that future use value being realised, mean that it goes straight in the bin. The massive volumes of waste travelling from households to be buried in landfill sites or burned in incinerators are the material accumulation of millions of moments of tacit calculation through which something passes over the line of tacit valuation to become waste. Mostly, these moments of calculation are not conscious, but are instead enactments of routine, established patterns of action whereby handling particular materials ends up with putting them in the bin. Household waste, then, can be understood as the fallout of the ways in which we organise the accomplishment of our daily existence, amidst the flows to things and materials that we coordinate into our home lives.

While the classification of matter as waste can be framed as pragmatic actions informed by questions of value and costs, it cannot be reduced to economics. The value of objects, and the costs of keeping them, can clearly be symbolic and emotional rather than only economistic and pragmatic. While waste is an inevitable result practically of the processes of social reproduction, it can be argued from anthropological approaches that the symbolic processes of delineating possessions from rubbish, or resource from waste, are bound up with the reproduction of fundamental cultural categories. Not least among these can be the construct of home itself. The processes of consigning matter to the category of waste are constituted spatially, as that matter is put on a journey beyond the boundaries of the home, often via the bins which provide spatial containment for troublesome matter on its way. The spatial and symbolic processes of consigning matter as waste so contribute to the reproduction of the home itself, both as space and as category.

Household Waste and Recycling Across Time

Waste is inevitable, a universal characteristic of human societies. However, through most of human history, waste management was largely local and informal. In advance of industrialisation, material economies typically operated on a relatively local scale, with overall flows of material which are infinitesimal in scale in comparison to industrial societies. Additionally, the range of materials circulating was considerable smaller than it is today. Finally, the balance of value between materials and human labour was substantially different than it is in affluent countries now. Consequently, a far higher proportion of materials were kept in productive circulation than is the case in contemporary industrialised societies.

Industrialisation and urbanisation have been the drivers of waste, becoming a significant concern of policy and public administration, with calls for the formalisation of waste collection in London emerging from the mid-eighteenth century. Industrialisation not only increases the throughput of materials in an economy, but also increases the scale and spatial concentration of production. As the circuits of material flows run to greater scales, the opportunities for keeping materials within the productive economy once they have passed through consumption become less attractive. The growing diversity of materials flowing through the economy, especially from the early twentieth century also brought difficulties as waste streams became more heterogeneous and with a greater range of risks of toxicity. Meanwhile urbanisation concentrates settlement and so the sources of household waste, at the same time as making space for dealing with it scarce. Finally, increasing typical affluence both reduces the relative value of materials and increases the effective costs of the time it takes to do the work involved in realising the residual value in products and materials.

While processes of urbanisation and industrialisation have been running for centuries, economically self-sustaining activities of reuse and recycling from household waste kept running on a significant scale to the mid-twentieth century even in countries like Britain. Ironically, it was just as environmental consciousness began to emerge in the 1960s and 1970s that activities like scrap metal or textile collections in residential areas went in to serious decline. It was this period which saw the fullest embedding of what has been termed the disposal paradigm of waste management in industrialised countries. This paradigm is characterised by a linear flow of materials, from primary extraction through processing, manufacturing, exchange, use, and ending in final disposal. Waste is understood as worthless matter to be got rid of at least cost without falling foul of prevailing environmental regulation. Waste management is so conceptualised under this paradigm as a technical, end-of-pipe service operation, collecting and disposing of whatever enters the waste stream, typically through either landfill or incineration.

The Rise of Modern Household Waste Recycling

Within this paradigm, the householder has perhaps the most convenient relation to waste materials in human history: everything to be rid of goes into one bin which, in return for a small proportion of local taxation, the local government will remove from your property once a week.

This system of household waste management, and the particular character of household waste practice that is part of it, are therefore relatively historically recent. Nevertheless, their normality was thoroughly embedded in most industrialised countries by the late twentieth century. In short, the norm of chucking everything in to one bin was a relatively short-lived and culturally specific moment.

However, by the late twentieth century, pressure that had been building against the disposal paradigm since the late 1960s became increasingly irresistible. Through the later decades of the twentieth century, waste and its dominant modes of management under the disposal paradigm became increasingly problematised within policy. Growing concerns around local pollution from landfill leachates and incineration emissions provided the initial impetus, and the regulation of waste disposal infrastructures have become steadily more stringent. The 1970s saw the codification of basic principles of more sustainable waste management. For example, the 1975 European Economic Community (EEC) Waste Framework Directive formalised the concept of the waste hierarchy, which prioritises approaches to waste. At the top of the hierarchy, as the most preferable option, is reduction through targeting waste at source, for example, through increasing production efficiency or extending product life spans. Reducing overall material consumption levels would be the clearest realisation of this imperative, but one which is not easily consistent with hegemonic ideals of societal progress through particular models of economic development. The second most preferable option where waste cannot be prevented is to reuse end-of-life products. The third option is to recycle. Recycling comes below reuse because recycling typically involves more input of energy and other resources to return the material to productive use. Together, these options, the '3Rs' or reduce, reuse, and recycle, should minimise the quantities of material entering the final waste stream for disposal. The hierarchy carries on down to prioritising options for final disposal, with recovery of energy from incineration preferable to incineration without energy recovery, with landfill as the least preferable option.

While this foundation for a shift to a more sustainable paradigm of waste management was formalised in international policy in the 1970s, through to the end of the century it was visible more as a declaration of principle than as recognisable features of waste management practices. Despite both the OECD and the EEC adopting the waste hierarchy as principle in the mid-1970s, by 2005 49% of municipal waste in the European Union (EU) was still going to landfill. Household waste volumes continued to grow with or ahead of growth in gross domestic product (GDP). For example, between 1995 and 2003, the GDP of the nations that became the EU25 increased by 19%, and the generation of municipal solid waste (substantially composed of household waste), increased by the same percentage. While the disposal paradigm might have relatively shallow historical roots, it had become thoroughly embedded throughout society. Institutions, from divisions of responsibility within national government down to the local authorities tasked with service delivery developed around a particular framing of waste. Expensive infrastructures and long-term contractual obligations evolved around formulations of waste collection and disposal services. Finally, the everyday practices of people working in waste collection, and of the householders dealing with the matter that goes in to the waste stream, are shaped within the infrastructures and services that are part of that disposal paradigm. There is a complex social, cultural, institutional, and technical system which comprises a particular way of doing waste management.

Given this, it is unsurprising that declarations of principle in international and national governments have limited immediate impact. However, from the end of the twentieth century, indications of a nascent shift in the management of household waste became visible. This reflected the growing recognition of waste management's contribution to climate change, especially through methane emitted from the decomposition of organic waste in landfills, adding a new scalar dimension of environmental concern to established concerns about local pollution. Pushed along by international legislation that was binding rather than declarative, such as the EU 1999 Landfill Directive, national legislatures increasingly took meaningful action to change household waste practices, as part of broader strategies to drive waste management towards increased sustainability. Increasing recycling has been a major component of these strategies. For long in many countries, promotion of recycling was limited to publicity and education campaigns and the provision of recycling 'bring sites' – where householders have to deliver recyclables to centralised facilities. Around the turn of the century, the provision of kerb side collection of a growing range of recyclables became increasingly common.

Meaningful interventions like the provision of convenient infrastructures for householders brought a step change in the progress of household recycling. For example, in the United Kingdom, recycling grew from 11% of household waste by mass in 2000–01 to 58% in 2008–09. With the provision of bins and collection services, household practices became reshaped on a significant scale, with a significant proportion of households enrolled to the small but inconvenient practices of recycling. Things that were previously thrown into one bin now have to be rinsed, sorted, stored, and put out for collection on the right day. Yet surveys suggest that taking on this additional burden in the already crowded patterns of daily household activity is not dependent on active commitment to environmental sustainability. Whereas surveys of recyclers in the United Kingdom up until the mid-1990s found a strong correlation between stated environmental commitment and doing recycling, surveys in recent years find the relationship much less evident. Through the provision of specific bins, the development of specialist collection services, together with continued information and advertising campaigns, recycling has become increasingly both normal and normative. The likelihood of a household putting out their recycling bins can correlate more with whether or not their neighbours do, than with their commitment to environmental responsibility. This in part results from spatial variations in residence, with middle-class areas generally more likely to recycle than working class, for example. Related to this, variations in housing stock make a big difference to the practicalities of doorstep recycling. Systems based on multiple household bins can work well in a leafy suburb of houses with gardens, but clearly face problems in high-density multiple occupancy dwellings.

While active recycling is not dependent on environmental commitment, for householders recycling can nevertheless stand as emblematic of their fulfilment of responsibilities to the environment, in some sense legitimating the continued pursuit of normal but environmentally damaging practices such as car dependency or international air travel. This reflects the emphasis put upon recycling as an environmental obligation in public discourse, but active recycling of waste makes a tiny difference to the environmental impact of a typical household.

Recycling has become part of the routine practices of many households in industrialised countries, a variation on the ways in which we perform and reproduce home through the categorisation and handling of wastes to take them beyond the boundaries of our domestic spaces. The normative role of recycling both demands and enables a distinctive moral configuration of these practices, through the possibility of realising residual value in at least some of the materials that flow through and out of our homes. This is not a return to preindustrial local material stewardship. Rather, it represents a mode of maintaining materials within the productive economy that develops from the industrial system of waste management that evolved under the disposal paradigm, with the materials collected from households passing into markets on a global scale.

The Limits of Household Waste Recycling

The progress seen in household recycling in recent years represents a quite remarkable success. Interventions into routinised practices to enhance sustainability are profoundly difficult. Here, it is possible to trace a narrative from global concerns about climate change through international and national legislation to local policy and service changes, translated ultimately into the transformation of mundane household practices. Through an optimistic lens, the successes of interventions to promote household waste recycling might give hope for the broader-scale radical transitions in household practices which are required as part of moving towards environmental sustainability.

However, there is reason to be more cautious. As indicated above, recycling ranks only third in the waste hierarchy, beneath reduction and reuse. Yet, not least in relation to households, among these options recycling has been the principal focus of political attention. In comparison, there has been limited progress in reuse or in reduction other than that which can be accounted for through economic decline. This relative prioritisation of recycling has been explained by the relative ease of pursing it over the higher-ranking options in the 3Rs. Progress on household recycling has demanded major changes. Collecting diverse materials and getting each into a suitable market stream for recycling is clearly more complicated than collecting a single bin full of mixed waste and delivering to the nearest landfill site or incinerator. Providing a number of bins to households and developing the network of vehicles to collect the materials is a major undertaking. Enrolling householders to undertake practices which are demonstrably less convenient than what went before without either legislation or financial incentives is in many ways an astonishing feat. However, all of these changes are modest when compared with what it would take to effectively pursue either reuse or reduction. Recycling involves intervention into a relatively small proportion of the overall cycle of materials flow through the economy. Getting materials from its point of collection at the kerbside to its point of next use remains a largely technical set of activities that fits relatively well within the existing infrastructures and competences of waste management. In comparison, pursuing the options higher up the waste hierarchy demands much broader, reaching interventions. Enabling reuse demands that specific goods find their way to situations where they are worth acquiring, keeping, and using. This is more exacting than feeding generic raw materials from recycling back into manufacturing. Pursued fully, promotion of reuse would require intervention into product design and production, to enable reuse and into the different conduits through which things travel from one situation of use to another, which range from informal social networks through second-hand retail networks to Internet-enabled second-hand exchange across national boundaries. Reduction of waste directly is more potentially demanding again, intervening in processes, practices, and situations throughout the economy to reduce overall material throughput.

Conclusion

The rapid rise of contemporary household waste recycling provides a lens into the ways in which global environmental concern becomes translated to interventions in mundane household practices. It also serves to highlight the shifting role of disposal and wasting of materials in the reproduction of the home as dwelling space and as locus of cultural meaning.

The success of concerted promotion of household recycling over recent years could give hope to policy-makers and activists concerned with engendering shifts in everyday life towards more sustainable patterns. However, attention to recycling in comparison to other demands entailed by moving towards sustainability reveals that it has been a relatively easy win in terms of the changes demanded from national government to the household. Transition to a sustainable materials economy will require far more radical interventions throughout systems of production, exchange, consumption, and disposal, to shift norms and practices in households and elsewhere.

See also: Environmental Consciousness; Home Objects; Material Cultures of Home; Neighbourhood Effects; Sustainability; Sustainable Lifestyles.

Further Reading

Darier E (1996) The politics and power effects of garbage recycling in Halifax, Canada. *Local Environment* 1(1): 63–86.

Davies AR (2003) Waste wars – public attitudes and the politics of place in waste management strategies. *Irish Geography* 36(1): 77–92.

Gandy M (1994) *Recycling and the Politics of Urban Waste*. London: Earthscan.

Gregson N, Metcalfe A, and Crewe L (2007) Moving things along: The conduits and practices of divestment in consumption. *Transactions of the Institute of British Geographers* 32(2): 187–200.

Hawkins G (2006) *The Ethics of Waste*. Maryland: Rowman and Littlefield Publishers.

Murray R (2002) *Zero Waste*. London: Greenpeace Environmental Trust.

O'Brien M (2007) *A Crisis of Waste? Understanding the Rubbish Society*. London: Routledge.

Pellow DN (2002) *Garbage Wars: The Struggle for Environmental Justice in Chicago*. Cambridge, MA: Massachusetts Institute of Technology.

Petts J (1995) Waste management strategy/development: A case study of community involvement and consensus-building in Hampshire. *Journal of Environmental Planning & Management* 38: 519–536.

Scanlan J (2004) *On Garbage*. London: Reaktion Books.

Strasser S (2000) *Waste and Want: A Social History of Trash*. New York: Owl Books.

Watson M, Bulkeley H, and Hudson R (2008) Unpicking environmental policy integration with tales from waste management. *Environment and Planning C: Government and Policy* 26: 481–498.

House Price Expectations

R Martin, Federal Reserve Board of Governors, Washington, DC, USA

Published by Elsevier Ltd.

Introduction

Over the past 15 years the level of real house prices in the United States has taken off. Between 1996 and 2006, real house prices increased almost 60% (**Figure 1**). To put this number in perspective, total real house price appreciation was a meagre 6%. That is, the average annual gain in house prices in the latter period was comparable to the total house price gain in the first part of the sample. Other house price indexes, such as the Case–Shiller home price index, show an even larger increase. Not as exceptional but still shocking, real house prices have declined nearly 8% since reaching their peak in 2006.

The rapid rise and subsequent collapse of the housing market has led many to ask whether or not the housing market was a bubble. There is no single accepted definition of the word bubble. The most common use of the word seems to be associated with any rapid rise in prices, particularly if the rise is followed by a sharp decline.

For our purposes, we define a housing bubble to refer to any situation in which households or investors purchase property because they expect future prices to rise. These expectations of future prices then feed back into current prices as households bid for the limited supply of houses currently on the market.

These heightened expectations work through two channels. The one most people think of is the household (or investor) that purchases a home that would under normal circumstances be too expensive for them. They expect to benefit from future price increases either by selling their house at the higher price or by withdrawing equity from their home in the form of a mortgage equity withdrawal. The other channel comes through households who know they want to buy a larger (or a first) home in the future. Given their expectations of future house price increases, they may fear that not buying today will price them permanently out of the market. This fear brings their purchase forward and puts pressure on today's prices.

If these expectations of future price increases are not well-founded, then the rise in home prices resulting from these false expectations is likely to reverse. That is, at first the expectations themselves provide a self-fulfilling prophecy: households expect extraordinary returns and they get them as more agents reinforce this belief. However, at some point, reality takes hold and all return-driven investment is removed from the market. At this point, households correctly perceive a high probability of a negative return and house prices return to their fundamental level often with a detour below on the way down.

Identifying a market whose behaviour is driven by exuberant expectations is important to policymakers. Irrespective of the direction of causality, bad macroeconomic outcomes are generally associated with bubble-like episodes. The rapid rise in house prices may have masked an underlying deterioration in credit quality that led to the wave of recent foreclosures and is among the foremost of explanations for the severity of the 2007 US recession. House prices may directly affect households through balance sheet effects. The fall in prices has led to a record fall in household net worth. According to standard permanent income models, this fall in wealth should lead to lower household consumption. However, the direction of causality is not firmly established. House prices and consumption may well be driven jointly by a third factor, for example, future expected income growth. In this case, the fall in house prices is not itself a macroeconomic problem. Nonetheless, timely data from the housing market may help policymakers identify future problems, even if their source is unclear.

This article studies household beliefs and their relationship to real house prices in the United States between 1975 and 2009. The first part examines direct evidence on house price beliefs from the Michigan Survey of Consumers. In the second part, we write down a model of real house prices. We compare the model to the data in two ways. First, we examine the aggregate household Euler equation, using quantities of housing and consumption from the National Income Accounts. Second, we replace components of the Euler equation using market data. We find that survey data are a poor predictor of future house price performance. However, the pricing equations from the model indicate that household expectations for future house prices are unbiased, on average, and are reasonably accurate predictors of future house prices.

The views and opinions expressed herein are solely those of the author and do not reflect the views and opinions of the Board of Governors, the Federal Reserve System, or their respective staffs.

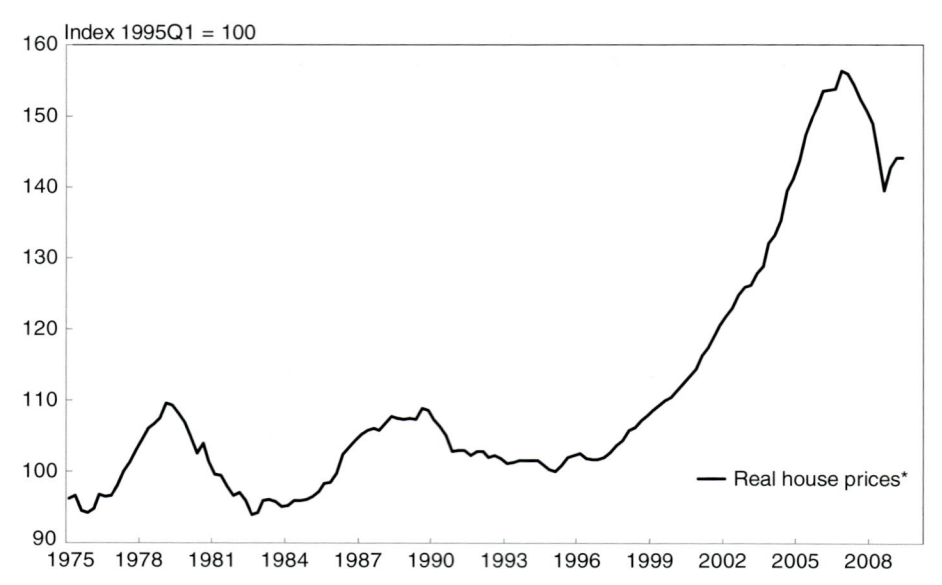

Figure 1 Real house prices in the United States between 1975 and 2008. *Real house prices are the FHFA quarterly house price index divided by the index of headline consumer prices.

Household Expectations from Survey Data

In this section, we study household beliefs about future house prices. The Michigan Survey of Consumers asks households whether or not it is a good time to purchase a house and why. Among the possible reasons for it being a good time to buy is that prices will increase in the future. We take the percent of respondents expecting future price increases as a proxy for aggregate expectations of future price growth. In other words, periods when this measure is high forecast greater than average expectations of future house price growth.

Figure 2 plots the percent of households expecting price increases against the eight-quarter ahead change in nominal house prices (we use nominal rather than real house prices because all of the price questions in the Michigan survey focus on nominal prices and we believe it likely that households are answering with respect to their nominal beliefs). That is, the house price and survey data are aligned such that at each date the survey response corresponds to house price appreciation that occurs over the next 2 years.

While we take the survey data as accurately reflecting household expectations, those expectations are a poor

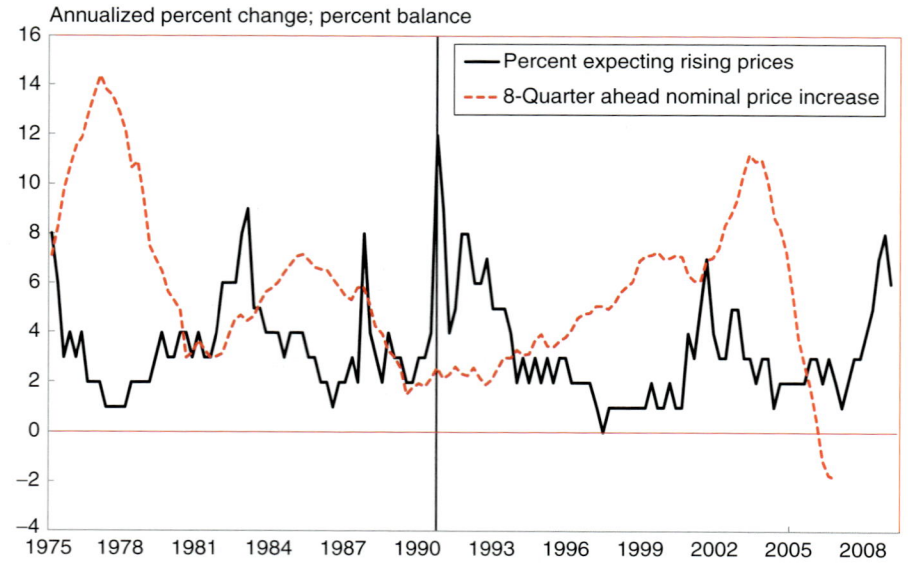

Figure 2 Percent of households expecting price increases against the eight-quarter ahead change in nominal house prices.

forecast of 2-year ahead price changes. Starting in 1975, households became systematically more pessimistic over future house price growth at a time when nominal house price appreciation was entering a series high. The same pattern occurred in the early 1980s. Households were optimistic in the very early portions of the boom but became discouraged over future prospects well before house prices hit their peak appreciation. In the early 1990s, households kept high appreciation expectations until house prices actually began to increase at which point they became pessimistic once again. In the early 2000s, households almost got it right, missing the peak by only a year or so. Despite the nominal fall at the end of the sample, households were no more pessimistic in 2006 than they were in the early 1990s and actually optimistic relative to their expectations in the late 1990s.

An Asset Pricing Model

In this section, we build a stylised real model of housing with the intention of deriving data-based equations containing household price expectations. The model is based on the iconic endowment asset pricing model of Lucas. The economy is populated by a single, infinitely lived, representative consumer who derives positive utility from the consumption of two goods: market consumption and housing services.

Because we are only interested in obtaining pricing equations for housing, we abstract from the production sector and focus only on the household problem. We also make the heroic assumption that housing investment costs less. Agents conduct all of their savings through a series of risk-free bonds. The households receive income y each period. Solving the model more fully does not change the asset pricing implications of the model; such additions only have an impact on quantities. We will follow the finance tradition of replacing equilibrium quantities with those observed in the data.

Individual Agent Optimisation

Households seek to maximise lifetime utility by choosing sequences of consumption and housing capital subject to a period-by-period budget constraint as follows:

$$\max_{c_t, b_t, B_{t,t+s}} E \left\{ \sum_{t=0}^{x} \beta^t U(c_t, H_{t+1}) \right\}$$

s.t.

$$c_t + \sum_{s=1}^{\infty} \rho_{t,t+s} B_{t,t+s} + p_t H_{t+1} \leq y_t + \sum_{s=1}^{\infty} B_{t-s,t} + p_t H_t$$

where c is consumption and H is units of housing. For simplicity, we assume that the quantity of housing purchased today, H_{t+1}, enters the current period utility function. That is, housing is available for consumption in the period purchased. The bond terms are written for ease of notation. In each period the agent chooses a portfolio of bonds. Each bond pays off one unit of consumption in a single future period and has price ρ. For example, a bond paying one unit of consumption s periods in the future is denoted as $B_{t,t+s}$. This bond trades at price $\rho_{t,t+s}$ and represents the discount factor between t and $t+s$. Without loss of generality, the bond is not traded in the intermediate periods. These bonds are assumed to be in zero net supply.

We have the following first-order conditions for the model:

$$c_t : U_c(c_t, H_t) = \lambda_t$$
$$H_{t+1} : \lambda_t p_t = \beta^t U_b(c_t, H_{t+1}) + E\{p_{t+1} \lambda_{t+1}\}$$
$$B_{t,t+s} : E\lambda_{t+s} = \delta_{t,t+s} \lambda_t$$

These conditions are standard.

House Price Expectations

An expression for house prices including households' expectations of future prices can be derived by combining the first-order equations for market consumption and housing as follows:

$$p_t = \frac{U_b(c_t, H_{t+1})}{U_c(c_t, H_{t+1})} + \beta \ E \left\{ \frac{U_c(c_{t+1}, H_{t+2})}{U_c(c_t, H_{t+1})} p_{t+1} \right\}$$

The first term $(U_b(c_t, H_{t+1}))/(U_c(c_t, H_{t+1}))$ is the utility value of holding h units of housing today. This term is commonly called the rental value of housing and can also be viewed as the real dividend for holding housing. The second term is the value of selling the house in period $t+1$. This pricing equation is entirely standard. The price of housing is ex dividend and the rental value is the period-by-period dividend.

Household price expectations are captured in the last term, $\beta \ E\{(U_c(c_{t+1}, H_{t+2}))/(U_c(c_t, H_{t+1})) p_{t+1}\}$. Future price expectations influence today's prices. All else equal, a household will pay more for a house today if the return is expected to be higher. This is the sense in which housing is an asset. However, as with any pricing equation, tomorrow's prices are not merely pulled from the air. Those prices themselves are a function of the utility value of housing and market goods.

Following standard practice we can substitute for next period's price, deriving an expression for today's house prices solely in utility terms.

$$p_t = E \sum_{s=0}^{\infty} \beta^s \frac{U_b(c_{t+s}, H_{t+s+1})}{U_c(c_t, H_{t+1})}$$
$$= E \sum_{s=0}^{\infty} \beta^s \frac{U_c(c_{t+s}, H_{t+s+1})}{U_c(c_t, H_{t+1})} \frac{U_b(c_{t+s}, H_{t+s+1})}{U_c(c_{t+s}, H_{t+1+s})}$$

Hence, the price of housing at time t is equal to the discounted value of future rents. The term $\beta^s(U_c(c_{t+s},H_{t+s+1}))/(U_c(c_t,H_{t+1}))$ is the stochastic discount factor. This specification uses the future path of consumption and the housing stock to price housing. Nothing else is needed. We will use a version of this equation in the next section.

Because future quantities are hard to measure, we can transform the equation to take advantage of available market prices. We can use the first-order condition for bonds to substitute market prices for this discount factor.

$$p_t = E\sum_{s=0}^{\infty} \delta_{t,t+s} \frac{U_b(c_{t+s},H_{t+s+1})}{U_c(c_{t+s},H_{t+s+1})} = E\sum_{s=0}^{\infty} \delta_{t,t+s} \text{Rent}_{t+s}$$

This is the standard equation used to evaluate house prices. The current price of housing is directly related to the real interest rate and the flow of future housing rents. All else equal, higher rents or lower interest rates yield higher house prices. This formulation is convenient because future interest rates (and to a lesser extent future rents) can be inferred from market data. However, there is substantial comovement between the interest rate and the value of future rents: both elements incorporate the marginal utility of future market consumption. We will use the one-period ahead version of this equation below, using data on interest rates and rents.

The Euler Equation Using Quantities

In this section, we take the asset pricing equation to the data in an attempt to infer household expectations of future prices. We use the one-period ahead equation derived earlier:

$$p_t = \frac{U_b(c_t,H_{t+1})}{U_c(c_t,H_{t+1})} + \beta E\left\{\frac{U_c(c_{t+1},H_{t+2})}{U_c(c_t,H_{t+1})} p_{t+1}\right\}$$

To proceed, we need a functional form for utility and quantity data on sequences of c and H. We follow standard practice and assume utility takes a CES form:

$$U(c_t,H_{t+1}) = \frac{\left(\alpha c_t^{\varepsilon} + (1-\alpha)H_{t+1}^{\varepsilon}\right)^{1-\sigma/\varepsilon}}{1-\sigma}$$

the parameter ε lives on the interval $-\infty$ to 1. When $\varepsilon = 1$, the two types of consumption are perfect substitutes. When $\varepsilon = 0$, utility is assumed to be Cobb–Douglas. If $\varepsilon = 1 - \sigma$, then utility is separable. We will use the Euler equation itself to calibrate the utility parameters.

For house prices, we use the FHFA (Federal Housing Finance Agency) National House Price Index, which is available from 1975Q1 through 2009Q2. Consumption data are real personal income taken from the National Income Accounts. In general, consumption data should be cleaned of its housing components; but, since this exercise is illustrative on house price expectations, total consumption suffices.

We construct a series of housing stock from the National Income Accounts. We use data on residential investment between 1947 and 2009. To arrive at the stock estimate, we assume a depreciation rate on residential structures of 1%. We also assume that in 1947 the housing stock was in equilibrium and the housing investment in that year was set to maintain that stock. Therefore, the stock in 1947 is obtained from the following steady-state equation: $H=\text{Res Inv}_{1947}/1-0.01$. This equation yields a housing stock of about 10 trillion 2005 dollars in 1947. The time series for the level of both consumption and the housing stock is shown in **Figure 3**.

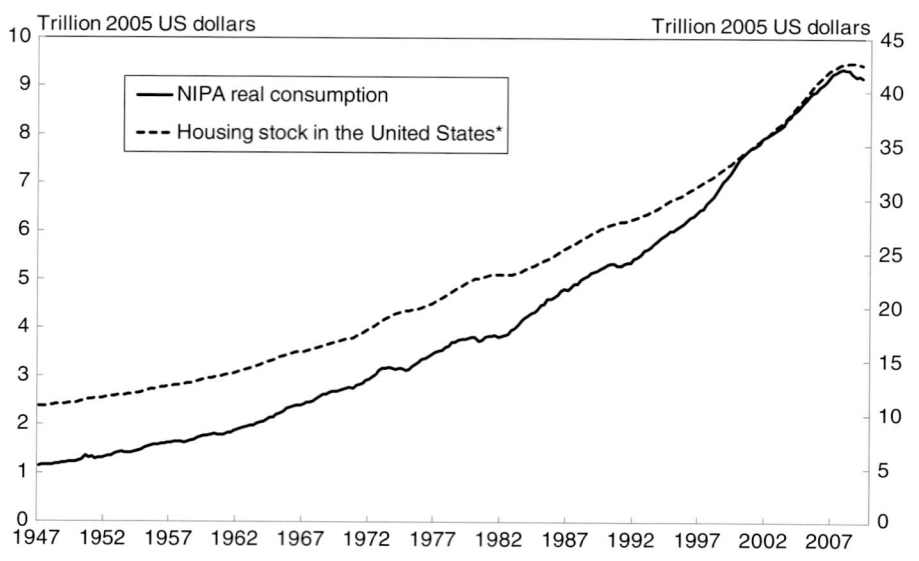

Figure 3 Time series for the level of both consumption and the housing stock. *Housing stock calculated using real residential investment flow and a 1% depreciation rate.

If these calculations are roughly correct, the rise in house prices over the past 20 years is not entirely surprising. Over the time shown, consumption has increased at about twice the pace of the housing stock. Most of the growth differential has occurred since the late 1980s. The resultant relative scarcity of housing should be expected to have a price effect on housing.

It turns out that the level of the housing stock at the beginning of the period is not important. A greater problem arises because we know neither the level of prices (we have only an index) nor the true mapping of the housing stock into period utility. Surely the entire stock of housing does not enter in each period; but rather, its flow value enters. We resolve both problems by adding a scaling factor to the housing stock in the Euler equation. The scaling factor is constant over time.

We calibrate the utility parameters (and the scaling parameter) to set the sample average of the above Euler equation to zero. We find that the minimum average error is achieved when the within-period utility function is Cobb–Douglas, σ is set to 3, and $\beta = 0.995$. The parameter α is of course not identified because of the scaling parameter.

We show the results of the exercise in **Figure 4**. The solid black line centred around 1 translates the Euler equation errors into one-period ahead pricing errors. The value of the black line gives the multiplier on the next period's prices that would make the Euler equation hold with exact equality. That is, we replace p_{t+1} in the equation with mult* p_{t+1} and the value of the black line is mult. The two dashed lines in the background give the series of real house prices and the series of real house prices that incorporates the one-step ahead error.

These pricing errors are very small for empirical Euler equations. Ninety percent of the errors are smaller than 2%.

It seems that the Euler equation gives a good picture of household pricing expectations on average over time.

What do the pricing equations have to tell us about household price expectations during the recent housing boom? Look at the circled section in **Figure 4**. The multiplier on the next period's prices is consistently below one. A number below one implies that households received a positive surprise to house prices: the realised price in the next period was above the price needed for the Euler equation to hold.

This is strong evidence, given the fit of the equations elsewhere, that the house price appreciation during this period was not driven by exuberant expectations on the part of households. During the height of the boom, households' expectations seem to have placed downward pressure on prices. They were underexuberant.

Although the equation is only designed to yield one-step ahead forecast errors, we can accumulate the errors to achieve a sample path of implied house prices. We take the implied growth rate of house prices, (mult* $p_{t+1})/p_t$, to create an alternative house price index, assuming the aggregate correction is zero in 1975 (**Figure 5**).

The dotted line is the actual series of real house prices. The dashed line is the one created by the above exercise. Focusing entirely on the period between 1996 and 2006, we can see that the house price boom can be cleanly separated into two periods: 1996–2000 (enclosed in the rectangle) and 2001–06 (enclosed in the circle). During the early period, the expected return on housing was clearly greater than the realised return. Viewed on this scale, this period may be an example of expectations leading prices.

But, in the latter period at the peak of the episode, the expectations for house price appreciation were clearly lower than the realised outcomes. Expectations did not

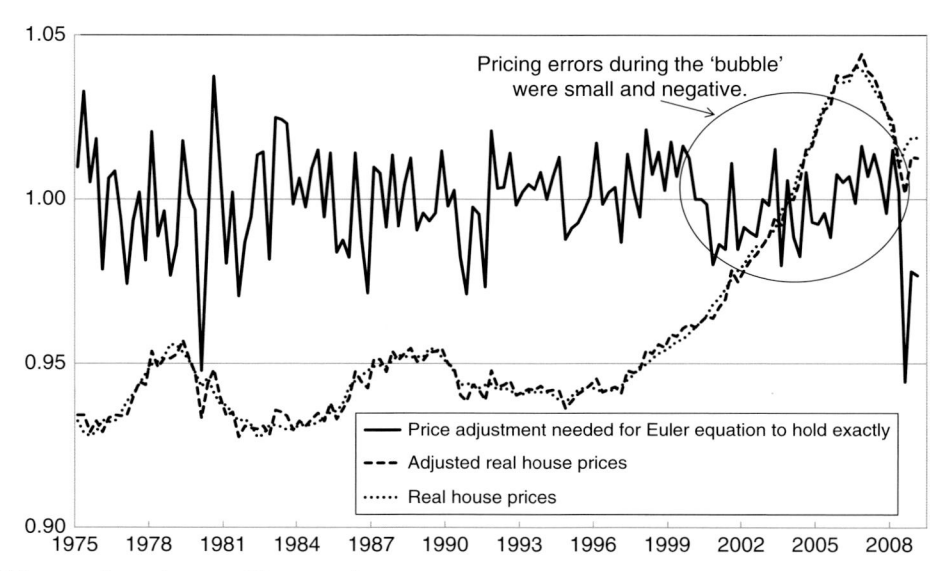

Figure 4 The Euler equation using quantities – result.

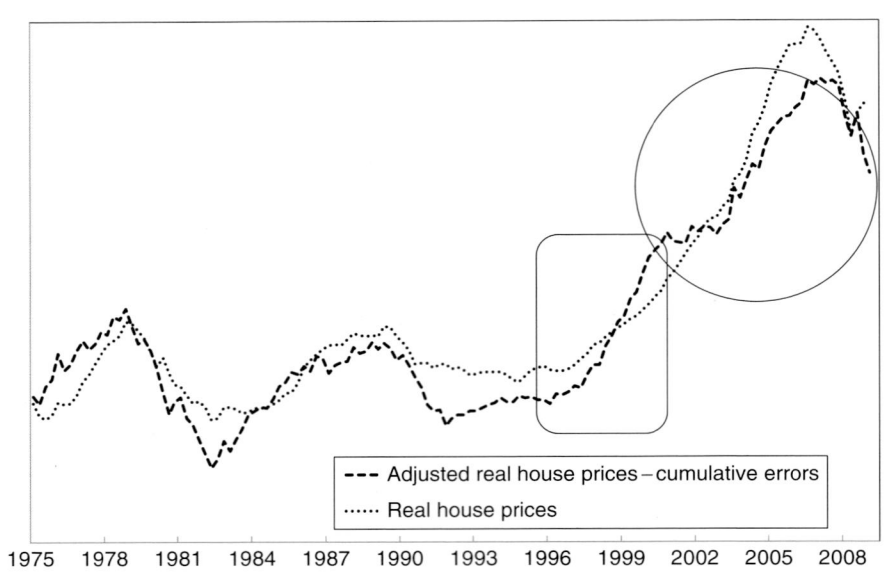

Figure 5 Implied growth rate of house prices to create an alternative house price index.

lead the latter part of the cycle. Rising home prices in the early part of the cycle spurred additional supply of credit. The relaxed borrowing constraints pushed up the price of housing in the current period as more households entered the market, competing for the fixed supply of homes. Households did not anticipate the change in credit and hence were surprised by the price increase. Throughout the boom, households (and indeed policymakers and economists) were continually surprised by the further expansion of credit, leading to consistent errors in the pricing equations.

The Euler Equation Using Market Prices

Of course, data on the levels of consumption or the housing stock may be faulty (especially the latter). Therefore, it is a useful exercise to use the same pricing equation substituting market observations where possible. We can use the same pricing equation as in the last section.

$$p_t = \frac{U_h(c_t, H_{t+1})}{U_c(c_t, H_{t+1})} + \beta\, E\left\{\frac{U_c(c_{t+1}, H_{t+2})}{U_c(c_t, H_{t+1})} p_{t+1}\right\}$$

and replace the discount factor, $\beta(U_c(c_{t+1}, H_{t+2}))/(U_c(c_t, H_{t+1}))$, with a one-period real interest rate and the rental rate, $(U_h(c_t, H_{t+1}))/(U_c(c_t, H_{t+1}))$, with market rents:

$$p_t = \text{Rent}_t + E\{\delta_{t,t+1}\, p_{t+1}\}$$

Prices, rents, and the interest rate are all, in principle, observable in the current period. In this version of the Euler equation, there are no utility parameters to calibrate but we must still find market prices that are reasonable series.

For this exercise, we will use the Bureau of Labor Statistics (BLS) series on actual rents. This rent series is available from 1981 onwards. For the interest rate, we choose the 10-year treasury rate deflated by headline inflation. We deflate each series using the overall consumer price index (CPI). There are many ways to deflate nominal series but, because of the stability of inflation in recent years, the methods tend to yield very similar series.

The two series are shown in **Figure 6**. Real interest rates fell on average from the early 1980s through 2006, falling from almost 9% to <2%. Real rents rose sharply in the late 1980s but then were unchanged or negative on average for the next 10 years. Rents began to rise again in the late 1990s, increasing substantially between 1996 and 2007 coinciding with the increase in house prices. Both rents and interest rates seem to have contributed to the rise in house prices during the recent housing market boom.

We show the results of the exercise in **Figure 7**. The solid black line centred around 1 translates the Euler equation errors into one-period ahead pricing errors. The value of the black line gives the multiplier on the next period's prices that would make the Euler equation hold with exact equality. That is, we replace p_{t+1} in the equation with $\text{mult}^* p_{t+1}$ and the value of the black line is mult. The two dashed lines in the background give the series of real house prices and the series of real house prices that incorporates the one-step ahead error.

By this metric, house price expectations do not seem to be driving the recent run-up in house prices. The pricing errors are consistently negative, indicating that households were surprised by the acceleration in house price growth. Indeed, these errors are large enough to reverse the trend in house prices. That is, households expected

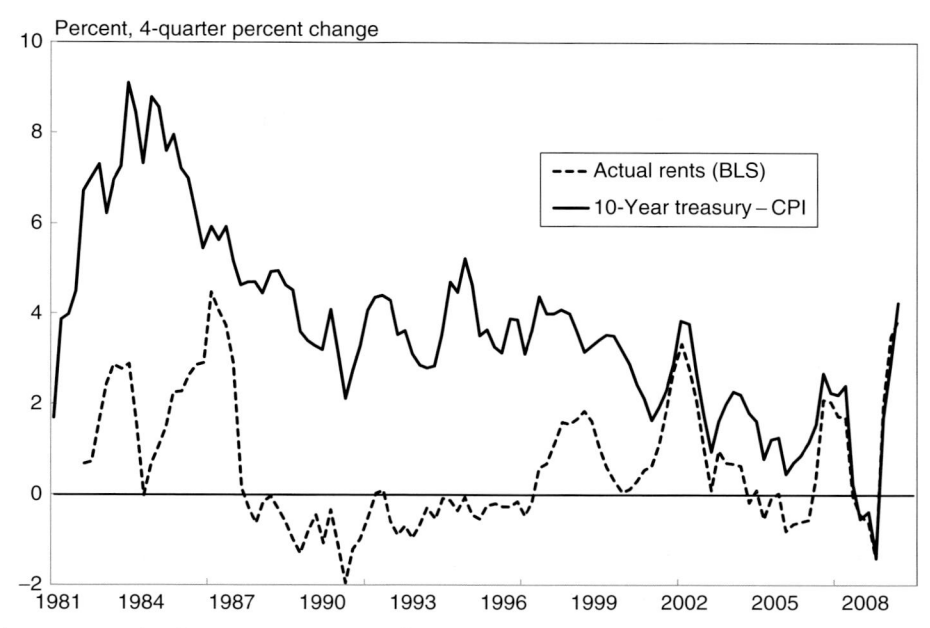

Figure 6 Actual rents versus the 10-year treasury rate deflated by headline inflation.

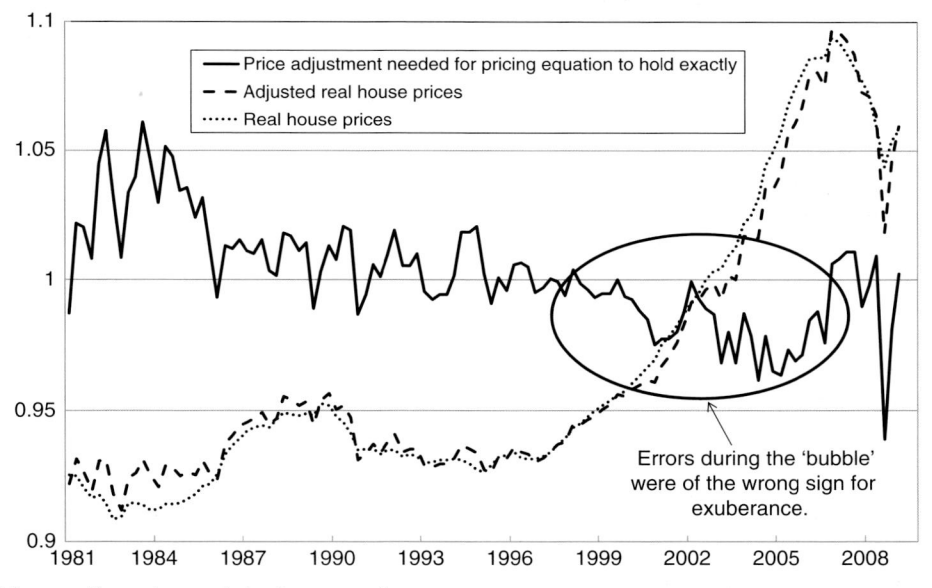

Figure 7 The Euler equation using market prices – results.

prices to fall during this period. Perhaps, the households believed house prices would return to their long-run average.

But Regional House Price Expectations Could Still Be Exuberant

The above results provide fairly convincing evidence that, at the national level, house price expectations were formed rationally. However, these aggregate results may offer wildly inaccurate views of regional markets. Exuberant expectations in Boston may be offset by housing market pessimism in Cleveland – Boston prices surged while house prices in Ohio remained largely stagnant over the period.

Robert Shiller has long believed, and provided extensive evidence in support of his views, that house prices were driven by irrationally high expectations of future price gains and that the housing bubble was driven by irrational consumer demand. The evidence he presents is more regional in nature. For example, Case and Shiller sent questionnaires to both 'hot' and 'cool' housing markets. Their main finding was that households seem to form future house price expectations based almost entirely on past house price movements. In contrast to the national Michigan survey, Case and Shiller find a strong correlation between expectations of high house price growth and future house price growth. As well, Shiller points out that the Michigan survey is not designed per se to measure house price expectations but rather is designed to study overall consumer sentiment. This lack of design in the survey may lead to misleading interpretations of the results.

Although data do not exist to replicate the Euler equation method at the local level, we can use those results to judge what the results might look like for hot markets. Florida serves well as an illustrative example.

At the national level, the long-term correlation between GDP growth and consumption growth is about 0.8. Assuming this relationship holds at the state level, we can use state GDP growth to proxy for consumption growth in the Euler equations above. Focusing just on the years 2005 and 2006, Florida's peak GDP growth, we can see that Florida grew quite strongly compared with the country as a whole, with a 6.1% expansion in 2005 and a 3.9% expansion in 2006, a differential of 2–3 percentage points. This greater income growth should be associated with high house price growth.

The question is how much extra house price growth. Given our model calibration used above with the same future expected house price gains, this higher growth should have led to an increase of 2–6%, depending on assumptions of how fast the housing stock rises. In reality, house prices rose >25% in 2005, following 4 years of double-digit increases. According to our model, Florida households would have to expect roughly 6–8% income growth per perpetuity to justify these increases. This is a very different picture than was painted at the national level.

Although still not proof of a bubble, the regional markets, like Florida, provide strong evidence that something was amiss at the local level. Are there other explanations which might explain the behaviour of regional price movements? Possibly. But given the size of the errors and the pure magnitude of the house price increases, the explanations need to be large. One would think that these types of explanations should be readily apparent, but they are not.

Conclusion

Economists will never know how households form house price expectations. Nonetheless, house price expectations can be, to some extent, measured from the household Euler equation. The raw data plugged into a simply calibrated Euler equation do a good job of matching the data. The pricing errors implied by the Euler equation are small even during the height of the boom.

This article provides evidence on the rationality of house price expectations (small errors in the Euler equation) at the national level and the informational efficiency of residential housing markets. It also provides evidence that the recent boom and ensuing bust in the housing market was not driven by exuberant expectations on the part of households. For their part, households consistently underestimated the extent of house price appreciation. We believe that evidence points away from the household sector and, perhaps, towards the lending sector as an explanation of the extremes in the most recent housing cycle. For regional movements, the possibility of house price bubbles and irrationally formed beliefs remains.

See also: House Price Indexes; Housing Wealth as Precautionary Savings; Price Determination in Housing Markets; Price Dynamics in Housing Markets.

Further Reading

Attanasio O, Blow L, Hamilton R, and Leicester A (2009) Booms and busts: Consumption, house prices and expectations. *Economica* 76: 20–50.

Case K and Shiller R (1989) The efficiency of the market for single-family homes. *American Economic Review* 79(1): 125–137.

Case K and Shiller R (2003) Is there a bubble in the housing market? *Cowles Foundation Paper No. 1089.*

Davis M and Heathcote J (2007) The price and quantity of residential land in the United States. *Journal of Monetary Economics* 54(8): 2595–2620.

Davis M and Martin RF (2009) Housing, home production, and the equity and value premium puzzles. *Journal of Housing Economics* 18(2): 18–91.

Giradi K, Lehnert A, Sherland S, and Willen P (2008) Making sense of the subprime crisis. *Brookings Papers on Economic Activity, Fall, Conference Draft.*

Mayer C, Pence K, and Sherlund SM (2008) The rise in mortgage defaults. *Finance and Economics Discussion Series No. 2008-59.*

Meese R and Wallace N (1994) Testing the present value relation for housing prices: Should I leave my house in San Francisco? *Journal of Urban Economics* 35(3): 245–266.

Verbrugge R (2008) The puzzling divergence of rents and user costs, 1980–2004. *Review of Income and Wealth* 54(4): 671–699.

House Price Indexes

SC Bourassa, University of Louisville, Louisville, KY, USA

© 2012 Elsevier Ltd. All rights reserved.

Glossary

Constant-quality index An index that controls for changes in housing characteristics so that index changes are due to price differences rather than to changes in the composition of properties sold.

Hedonic index An index based on models that regress prices for houses – that transact during one or more periods – on measures of the characteristics of the houses. If a single model is estimated for multiple periods, then time variables are included as independent variables along with the house characteristics.

Hybrid index An index based on a model that combines the hedonic and repeat sales methods.

Median index An index constructed from the medians of the prices of houses sold during each period.

Repeat sales index An index that is based on price changes for the houses that sell more than once during the period of study.

Sale price appraisal ratio index An index that is based on the ratio of transaction prices to earlier appraised values.

Purposes of House Price Indexes

Like other price indexes, such as the consumer price index, house price indexes are intended to allow for the comparison of price levels over time. Indexes may be constructed for entire nations, for regions within countries, and for metropolitan areas and cities. Indexes serve a variety of useful purposes. One of these relates to the measurement of the affordability of homeownership. As house prices increase or decrease over time, it may become more or less difficult for households to purchase homes. The level of this difficulty depends on household incomes, wealth, interest rates, and other factors that affect the affordability of homeownership. House prices affect the access of new households or renting households to homeownership; they also affect the ability of existing homeowners to relocate. A homeowner living in a community with low house prices may find it difficult to move to one with high prices. Steep declines in house prices may also inhibit mobility by making it impossible for households to satisfy mortgage debt with sales proceeds: in such cases, homeowners are considered to have negative equity.

Given the importance of housing in households' wealth in many countries, house price indexes help households to estimate the values of their homes without the need to obtain regular appraisals. This information is useful in making decisions about home improvements, home equity loans, relocation, and other investments such as for retirement purposes. House price indexes are also used by institutional investors, such as holders of mortgage loans or mortgage-backed securities, who need to keep track of the values of their assets.

House price indexes are needed for various research purposes, including efforts to understand how housing markets function. This broad area of research includes efforts to understand the determinants of house price levels and changes in prices, the measurement of the efficiency of housing markets, and the analysis of price bubbles. Information about house price movements also helps to inform housing and related policies, such as the design of tax incentives or other subsidies intended to encourage homeownership.

Finally, reliable house price indexes are essential for the operation of housing derivatives designed to hedge against housing market risk. Although not in wide use, these instruments can be used to create insurance products that allow homeowners to protect themselves against potential losses in home equity due to changes in the local housing market. They do not protect against the idiosyncratic risk associated with individual properties, just the marketwide risk over which the homeowner has no control.

Several methods have been used to measure house price changes over time. The most simple method is to construct a series of median sale prices, although in some cases the sales data are stratified and weighted to make them more representative of the housing stock. Most of the other methods for constructing indexes use multiple regression techniques. The hedonic method regresses sale prices on property characteristics and, in some cases, uses dummy variables for time periods. The repeat sales method regresses changes in the prices for the same properties on a series of dummy variables for time periods. Hybrid methods combine the hedonic and repeat sales methods. Finally, appraisal-based methods typically compare sale prices with appraised values to measure price changes.

Issues in the Design of Indexes

Quality Changes

As houses are quite heterogeneous with respect to a large number of structural and locational characteristics, it is relatively difficult to measure price movements over time. This difficulty occurs because the characteristics of houses change over time and this is reflected in the characteristics of houses that transact during any given period. Moreover, changes in market conditions cause the composition of houses that transact to shift over time. Consequently, simple measures of mean or median house prices may be reflecting differences in the characteristics of the houses sold rather than actual price movements. Therefore, all the preferred methods for constructing price indexes aim to limit quality changes, so that the index is measuring only or mainly price changes. These types of indexes are referred to as constant-quality indexes. The repeat sales and hedonic methods are examples of techniques designed to produce constant-quality indexes.

Sample Selection Bias

Only a small fraction of houses transacts during any given time period. These houses may not be a representative sample of all the houses in the relevant housing market. Consequently, movements in their prices may not reflect what is happening in the market as a whole. There is some evidence, for example, that smaller homes trade more frequently in the United States. This suggests that price indexes may be influenced to a disproportionate effect by what is happening at the lower end of the market. Moreover, as already noted, the composition of the sample of properties sold may shift over time suggesting that the nature of the bias changes. Econometric techniques designed to control for sample selection bias may be used to correct for the impacts of unrepresentative transactions data. Another approach is to apply weights to the data to make the sample look more like the entire housing stock. This may involve stratifying the data.

Revision

A third problem with house price indexes is that addition of new data may cause revisions in index numbers that have already been calculated, published, and relied upon for various purposes. This is particularly a problem, for example, for an index used to hedge house price risk. Some research has explored the impacts of late addition of data for time periods for which indexes have already been calculated. This issue is more a matter of the administration of index production, particularly the timing of data collection and index calculation, than of index methodology per se. The more important issue arises when the addition of data for new time periods causes the revision of index numbers for historical periods. This is typically a problem with methods for constructing indexes that involve regression models with time dummies, such as repeat sales or longitudinal hedonic indexes. In some cases these revisions can be substantial.

Administrative Complexity

Government agencies and other organisations that regularly produce house price indexes face a trade-off between complexity and accuracy. Some organisations persist in using simple methods that do not adequately control for quality changes. In other cases, the choice of index methods is driven more by the availability of data than by any technical considerations about methods. For example, repeat sales methods are used to construct the main indexes in the United States, owing in part to the lack of standardised data on hedonic characteristics. In contrast, the small owner-occupied sector in Switzerland implies that repeat sales data there are particularly thin. However, the concentration of the Swiss banking sector means that hedonic characteristics for properties that transact can be collected from mortgage lenders. Consequently, the best indexes in that country make use of hedonic techniques.

Types of Indexes

Median

Indexes based on median house prices are quite easy to calculate. Indexes based on means would be equally easy to produce, but these are generally avoided owing to the excessive influence of outliers. Examples of median indexes include those produced by the National Association of Realtors (NAR) in the United States, by similar organisations in Canada, Australia, and New Zealand, or by Wüest and Partner (W&P) in Switzerland. The US indexes are based on sale prices for existing houses sold by real estate agents who are members of the NAR, while the Swiss indexes are based on advertised list prices. The latter method raises questions about whether relative list prices are an adequate indicator of relative sale prices. This seems unlikely to be the case, given that the relationship between sale and list prices varies over the course of a property cycle. Sale prices are more likely to be above asking prices in a hot market and below asking prices in a weak market.

Consequently, most median price indexes are based on actual transaction prices rather than list prices.

The primary problem with indexes based on medians is that they are affected by the changes in the composition of the houses sold as well as by changes in prices. If a large number of relatively small (and inexpensive) houses are sold during a period, then price levels will appear to be lower than if a large number of high-end houses are sold. One way to deal with this problem is to stratify the sales data and apply weights to the strata to make the sample of properties that transact more like the entire stock of properties. The W&P index method involves stratification of the properties listed by characteristics such as the location, size, and quality of the property. Separate indexes are produced for single-family houses and condominiums. Research by the Reserve Bank of Australia on that country's median-based indexes has shown that they can be improved significantly if the property transactions are stratified geographically, with the geographical areas defined in terms of average price levels. This approach may be appealing to some governments or other organisations because the method is relatively simple to apply. It needs limited data and technical requirements; yet it can apparently yield a constant-quality price series.

Hedonic

The hedonic method is used widely to control for the heterogeneous nature of properties when constructing price indexes. Hedonic models involve regression of sale prices on a set of attributes of the properties. The estimated coefficients on the attributes are considered to be the implicit prices of those characteristics. The attributes are related to (i) the physical characteristics of the property itself, including both the structure and lot, if any, and (ii) the property's location, including characteristics of the surrounding neighbourhood and proximity to various places, such as central business districts.

There are two basic ways to construct hedonic price indexes. The cross-sectional method involves estimating a separate hedonic regression for each time period. In this case, the index is constructed by multiplying the vector of implicit prices by a vector of standardised attributes. One attractive feature of this method is that there is no revision of previously calculated index numbers. The other, longitudinal, approach involves estimation of a single regression equation that includes time dummy variables. The estimated coefficients on the time dummies yield the price index. The longitudinal method assumes that implicit prices remain constant over the period of time covered by the index. In the longitudinal case, historical index numbers will change each time data for a new period are added to the model.

The hedonic method is the most data-intensive of the primary index construction techniques. Lack of data about property attributes may preclude the use of this method. For example, the main price indexes in the United States are repeat sales rather than hedonic indexes because there is no consistent set of hedonic characteristics available nationwide. Some countries, such as Sweden or New Zealand, which have nationwide appraisal systems for property taxation purposes, are in a better position to implement hedonic indexes. In other countries, such as the United Kingdom or Switzerland, lenders or property valuers collect property characteristics at the time of mortgage origination, and these data are then used to construct hedonic indexes. The US situation is changing, however, as more property data are being collected in electronic form. The online residential property data company Zillow, for example, is attempting to collect hedonic characteristics for a large fraction of the US housing market.

Repeat Sales

The repeat sales method was first proposed in the 1960s by Martin Bailey, Richard Muth, and Hugh Nourse. When sufficient data on hedonic characteristics are not available, the index can instead be based on differences in transaction prices of the same dwellings at different times. With the assumptions that the characteristics of the houses remain the same from one transaction to the next and that the implicit prices of those characteristics are unchanged, the repeat sales model regresses the differences in the logarithms of prices on a set of time dummy variables, which are equal to −1 for the time of the first in each pair of transactions, 1 for the time of the second transaction, and 0 otherwise.

One obvious problem with this method is that the characteristics and their implicit prices may have changed between transactions. By definition, the house is older and it may have depreciated owing to lack of maintenance or obsolescence. On the other hand, it may have been improved. One way to address this problem is to include some hedonic variables in the model to capture the impacts of changes in certain characteristics, such as the condition of the property. However, the need for hedonic characteristics removes some of the appeal of the repeat sales method relative to the hedonic method.

A less obvious problem with the basic repeat sales model was identified by Karl Case and Robert Shiller in the late 1980s. They observed that the variance in repeat sales models tends to increase over time. One way to address this would be to weight the observations using a measure that takes into account the length of time between transactions. This weighted repeat sales approach is used to produce both of the two main sets of house price indexes in the United States: those of the Federal Housing Finance Agency (FHFA) and those of Standard & Poor's Case–Shiller Home Price Index.

The sample selection bias that affects all indexes is aggravated when the transactions data are limited to repeat sales because repeats make up only a fraction of all transactions. This obviously depends on the rate of turnover in the market and the amount of time covered by the index. In a study of house prices in Stockholm over a 19-year period, Eric Clapham and his colleagues found that less than a third of the dwellings that transacted during the period sold more than once; moreover, the dwellings that transacted represented less than half of the total stock. To the extent that properties that transact more frequently appreciate at different rates than other properties, a repeat sales index will diverge from the true market index. The same study of Stockholm found that repeat sales indexes are more subject to revision than hedonic techniques. Consequently, they do not provide a stable basis for derivatives intended to provide a hedge against house price risk.

Hybrid

Hybrid price indexes combine hedonic and repeat sales, making use of transactions for all properties rather than only those that sell more than once during the period of analysis. Hybrid models therefore take advantage of the information that is contained in both hedonic and repeat sales data. The hybrid method is both data-intensive and computationally complicated and therefore has seen little practical application.

Sale Price Appraisal Ratio

Methods that take advantage of the information available in official property appraisals are used in several countries to construct price indexes. The popular variant of this method, the sale price appraisal ratio (SPAR) index, is used in at least four countries: Denmark, The Netherlands, New Zealand, and Sweden. The SPAR index is a type of repeat index, in which the first of each pair of values is the official government appraisal of the property, while the second is the transaction price. One advantage of using the official appraisal as the first in each pair of values is that all appraisals for a geographical area are typically as of a particular date. This eliminates the need to use a regression technique to calculate the index. When properties are reappraised, the new appraisals become the base for the calculation of the index. In the case of New Zealand, for example, the appraisals are adjusted for subsequent improvements that require building permits, thereby controlling for major quality changes.

One advantage of the technique is that it makes use of sales data for almost all properties that transact, unlike the repeat sales method. However, the method does require accurate information about properties' hedonic characteristics for appraisal purposes. A comparative study of New Zealand's SPAR index found that it was most closely correlated with a repeat sales index, which is perhaps not surprising, given that both rely on analyses of paired values for properties that are appraised or transact at different times.

Comparison of Alternative Index Types

There is no ideal index method, but some methods are clearly better than others. The least satisfactory method of those in current use is the median index because it fails to satisfy the constant-quality criterion. In fact, some would claim that the simple median index is not a price index because it is not designed to measure price changes. Nevertheless, such measures are widely referred to and used as if they were price indexes. The problem with median price indexes can be addressed, however, by stratifying and weighting the transactions data to make them more representative of the housing stock.

All of the constant-quality indexes are subject to sample selection bias to a greater or lesser extent, because they all depend on the set of properties that transact, which may not be representative of the entire market. Repeat sales indexes are more prone to sample selection issues because they are based on only the properties that transact more than once during the period of analysis. This is typically only a fraction of all properties that transact and, of course, an even smaller fraction of the entire housing stock. Repeat sales and longitudinal hedonic indexes are also subject to revision of index number estimates for previous periods, as data for new time periods are added. These methods also rely on the assumption that implicit prices of housing characteristics remain constant during the period of analysis, which seems unlikely. Cross-sectional hedonic indexes avoid the revision problem and the assumption of constant implicit prices. However, they require sufficient transactions data to support the estimation of a separate regression model for each time period. The hedonic methods generally require more data than the repeat sales method. The best way to apply the latter method involves the use of at least some information about housing characteristics, to control for changes in the quality of dwellings between transactions.

An alternative constant-quality index technique involves the use of appraisals. As the SPAR index uses ratios of transaction prices to appraised values, it is able to take into account almost all transactions, unlike the repeat sales index. However, the SPAR method does require some information about housing characteristics in order to control for quality changes between appraisals and sales. The appraisals themselves are presumably based on hedonic regressions or other types of analysis of comparative sales, which require detailed information about housing characteristics.

The choice of index method depends to a significant extent on the availability of data. Consequently, the primary indexes in the United States use the repeat sales methods owing to the lack of consistent hedonic data. In other contexts, such as Switzerland, the repeat sales data are relatively thin; yet good housing characteristics data are available; and the best indexes use hedonic methods. The choice of method may also reflect the technical expertise within an organisation. In some instances, an organisation may be more comfortable with a familiar simple method than one that may be more accurate, but technically complex.

See also: House Price Expectations; House Price Indexes: Methodologies; Price Determination in Housing Markets; Price Dynamics in Housing Markets; Residential Property Derivatives.

Further Reading

Bailey MJ, Muth RF, and Nourse HO (1963) A regression method for real estate price index construction. *Journal of the American Statistical Association* 58: 933–942.

Bourassa SC, Hoesli M, and Sun J (2006) A simple alternative house price index method. *Journal of Housing Economics* 15: 80–97.

Case KE and Shiller RJ (1987) Prices of single-family homes since 1970: New indexes for four cities. *New England Economic Review* (September/October): 45–56.

Case B, Pollakowski HO, and Wachter SM (1991) On choosing among house price index methodologies. *Journal of the American Real Estate and Urban Economics Association* 19: 286–307.

Clapham E, Englund P, Quigley JM, and Redfearn CL (2006) Revisiting the past and settling the score: Index revision for house price derivatives. *Real Estate Economics* 34: 275–302.

Englund P, Quigley JM, and Redfearn CL (1998) Improved price indexes for real estate: Measuring the course of Swedish housing prices. *Journal of Urban Economics* 44: 171–196.

Englund P, Hwang M, and Quigley JM (2002) Hedging housing risk. *Journal of Real Estate Finance and Economics* 24: 167–200.

Gatzlaff DH and Haurin DR (1997) Sample selection bias and repeat-sales index estimates. *Journal of Real Estate Finance and Economics* 14: 33–50.

Gatzlaff DH and Ling DC (1994) Measuring changes in local house prices: An empirical investigation of alternative methodologies. *Journal of Urban Economics* 35: 221–244.

Green RK and Malpezzi S (2003). *A Primer on U.S. Housing Markets and Housing Policy. AREUEA Monograph Series No. 3*. Washington, DC: Urban Institute Press.

Kain JF and Quigley JM (1970) Measuring the value of housing quality. *Journal of the American Statistical Association* 65: 532–548.

Prasad N and Richards A (2008) Improving median housing price indexes through stratification. *Journal of Real Estate Research* 30: 45–71.

Quigley JM (1995) A simple hybrid model for estimating real estate price indexes. *Journal of Housing Economics* 4: 1–12.

Shiller RJ (2003) *The New Financial Order: Risk in the 21st Century*. Princeton, NJ: Princeton University Press.

Wang FT and Zorn PM (1997) Estimating house price growth with repeat sales data: What's the aim of the game? *Journal of Housing Economics* 6: 93–118.

House Price Indexes: Methodologies

NE Coulson, Penn State University, University Park, PA, USA

© 2012 Elsevier Ltd. All rights reserved.

Price Indexes

In 2005, both forbes.com (see Relevant Websites) and cnnmoney.com (see Relevant Websites) published online articles on the topic of the most expensive housing markets in the United States. Each of the two articles constructed rankings of housing markets based on the price of a 'typical' house, but the method of defining typical was quite different in the two surveys. The ranking by forbes.com used the US zip code as the area of analysis; that is, each zip code was defined as a distinct housing market. For each zip code, the survey constructed a *median sales price*, the price which is at the halfway point in a list of most expensive to least expensive units in that zip code. As forbes.com itself noted, the unit that has the median price can differ substantially from place to place, and comparing prices across these locations will be like comparing apples to oranges. Atherton, California, a community located in the bay area of Northern California, had the highest median sales price (of $2.4 million), but one of the reasons for this was because the median house in Atherton is a large house, on a large plot of land with many expensive amenities. According to the 2000 census, the median number of rooms in Atherton's zip code (94 027) is 8.2, which is certainly larger than the national median of 6.2. And so the comparison is of apples to oranges.

The comparison at cnn.com took a different approach. They asked a leading real estate brokerage service to find, for each housing market, the price of "a 2200-square-foot house with 4 bedrooms, 2 ½ bathrooms, a family room and a two-car garage" located in a neighbourhood "typical for corporate middle-management transferees". They were trying to compare apples to apples. The cnn.com survey seems to use market areas larger than zip codes, so it is a little bit difficult to compare its findings to that of the forbes.com report. Nevertheless it is quite instructive to note that the top place on the cnn.com list was La Jolla, California, a beach area in San Diego County. On the forbes.com list, the zip code corresponding to La Jolla ranked only 73rd. It is tempting to infer that homes in La Jolla are smaller than the mansion communities seen at the top of the Forbes list, but that on a size- and quality-adjusted basis, La Jolla is the pricier location. Indeed, the median number of rooms for owner-occupied units in its 92037 zip code was at the national median of 6.2.

The heterogeneous nature of housing precludes our ability to make price comparisons over space and time simply by taking averages in different locations or in different years. We must compare like to like using price indexes. In the case of 'ordinary' price indexes like the Consumer Price Index, a basket of n commodities of quantities $x = x_1 \ldots x_n$ is posited. The prices of those commodities in market 1 are given as $p_1 = p_{11} \ldots p_{1n}$ and the resultant expenditure is $\Sigma p_{1i} q_i$, where summations throughout are over the index $i = 1 \ldots n$. Prices from a spatially or temporally distinct market 2 are also gathered and the expenditure *on the same basket* is also computed. Comparison is usually taken in the form of a ratio, where market 1 (the numeraire market) expenditure is in the denominator and the comparison is in the numerator and for clarity the result is multiplied by 100:

$$P = \frac{\Sigma p_{2i} q_i}{\Sigma p_{1i} q_i} \times 100$$

Regression Methods and the Hedonic Price Index Status

In the case of comparing housing prices, the situation is somewhat more intricate. The quantities, X_i, are not items on the grocer's shelves but attributes of a 'typical' house. In the case of the cnn.com survey these were quantities of square feet, bedrooms, baths, garage spaces, family rooms, and neighbourhood quality. But what 'prices' were assigned to these 'commodities'? The usual answer lies within regression estimation, in this context sometimes called mass appraisal. A sample of sales within a particular market i, including the sale price and characteristics 1 through k of the associated property, are gathered, and a regression of the form

$$P_i = \beta_{0i} + \beta_{1i} X_1 + \ldots + \beta_{ki} X_k + e \quad (1)$$

is run. The β's, that is, the regression weights, or parameters, for each characteristic, are estimated for each city, and interpretable in this linear case as the *implicit prices* of the associated characteristics are estimated. For any given house, the set of attributes, X_1 through X_k can be fed into the equation and a valuation, an *appraisal*, of that house can be calculated. As the weights are specific to each market, a price index similar to (1) can be calculated. One market is chosen as the numeraire market and cross-sectional price indexes can be calculated. The existence of the intercept term, β_0, absent from the calculation of traditional price indexes, should be noted. Informally speaking, the value of this term will derive from all of the characteristics of the housing market that are constant across the units in that market. Representing, as it does, things like sunshine and proximity to ocean, it can be a major contributor to housing price differentials across cities. Omitted price factors are gathered in e, the error term.

The study by Palmquist (1984) is convenient for exemplary purposes. Palmquist, using Federal Housing Administration (FHA) mortgage insurance filings, estimated appraisal equations for the Atlanta, Denver, Houston, Louisville, Oklahoma City, and Seattle metropolitan areas. **Table 1** provides a list of characteristics used in the regression and the β-weights for each city. A zero entry means that that particular attribute was not included in the regression for that city, a circumstance which arose because the FHA did not collect all the information for all the cities, possibly because of a dearth of houses with the said attribute (as perhaps is the case for swimming pools in Seattle). In any case, we set the values of the quantities of characteristics to the values in the column labelled $X*$. These are zero for any attribute that is missing from any of the cities' hedonic regressions. The row labelled 'Constant quality price' provides the appraisal of a house with $X*$ in each metropolitan area – that is, $\beta_0 + \Sigma\beta_i X_i$ for each city.

There are differences. Seattle's price is the highest, at over $60 000 (recall this is 1984), followed by Denver, at just over $50 000. Atlanta and Houston are the lowest-priced markets at just over $35 000. In order to transform these numbers into a price index of the form above, we need to choose one city as a *base city* (against which all the other cities are compared). Any of them can be chosen; in this case Atlanta serves that role. We can then construct the price index as

$$P = \frac{\beta_{i0} + \beta_{ij}X_j}{\beta_{A0} + \beta_{Ai}X_j} \times 100 \quad (2)$$

where the A subscripts identify parameters from Atlanta. The last row of **Table 1** shows the results of this calculation. Obviously, Atlanta's index is 100; Houston's value of 98.1 indicates that a comparable house in that area costs about 2% less, while Seattle's value of 170 indicates that it costs 70% more there than it does at Atlanta.

We noted above that comparing indexes depends rather importantly on the quantities. So it is with the hedonic price indexes here. It can be the case that the ranking of 'most expensive cities' using one set of attributes can be reversed when using another set of attributes. An example of this phenomenon is also on display in **Table 1**. In the last column (labelled $X**$), a second set of attribute values is displayed. This set of attributes is meant to suggest a home of somewhat lower overall quality. In particular, both the size of the home and the size of the lot have been reduced. The last line of the table provides the index number for each city, where it can be seen that changes in the ordering from most expensive to least expensive have taken place. In particular Denver is now the most expensive city, taking over from Seattle, whose price has taken a substantial drop in this new index. Thus, care must be taken to ensure that the attribute sizes chosen are truly 'representative' dwellings, although what constitutes representative will depend on the purpose of constructing the index.

There are three important issues that the previous simple example has ignored:

1. Omitted variables: The vector of variables will not necessarily contain all of the important determinants of housing prices. This is understood in regression analysis, and the role of the error term is to encompass all of the unobservable influences on housing prices within the database. The problem arises when there are, roughly speaking, systematic differences in those unobservables across markets as this can cause bias in the estimated prices and therefore in the price indexes.

2. Nonlinearity: Because housing attributes are tied bundles of attributes, there is no particular reason why the relation between housing attributes and building price should be linear. Many alternatives to the linear model have been hypothesised, and one popular alternative used below is the semilog function:

$$\ln P_i = \beta_{0i} + \beta_{1i}X_1 + \ldots + \beta_{6i}X_6 + e \quad (3)$$

in which case the parameters are not prices, per se, but semielasticities. The Laspeyres price index [2] is replaced by:

$$P_i = \frac{\exp(\beta_{0i} + \beta_{ij}X_j + 0.5s_i^2)}{\exp(\beta_{01} + \beta_{1j}X_j + 0.5s_1^2)} \times 100 \quad (4)$$

where s^2 is the estimate of the variance term of the error in [3], and is included to provide an estimate of the mean value of price rather than the median (Malpezzi et al., 1998). Other nonlinear forms are of course possible.

3. Parsimony: Estimating eqn [2] or [3] separately for each city market may be too much to ask of the available data. It can be plausible to assume that the intercept term is the major difference in the index parameters, as the difference in capital prices (i.e., the price of structural characteristics) may be arbitraged across locations. Thus, the following regression can be employed, using data from all markets and assuming semilog form:

$$\log P = \beta_0 + \beta_1 X_1 + \ldots + \beta_k X_k + \gamma_1 M_1 \\ + \gamma_2 M_2 + \ldots + \gamma_h M_h + e \quad (5)$$

where the γ parameters are coefficients of the h indicator variables M_j representing h of the $h+1$ cities in the database. Note that the semilog specification implies that these are estimates of the percentage difference between the constant quality

Table 1 Palmquist (1984) estimates of hedonic price indexes for six US cities

Attribute	Atlanta	Denver	Houston	Louisville	Ok. City	Seattle	Value of X_*	Value of X_{**}
Intercept	−9337.32	4398.511	−12156.8	1116.21	2901.192	−9526.05	1	1
Lot area (square feet)	0.0813	0.1474	0.0998	0.0745	0.1423	0.6542	40000	25000
Improved area (square feet)	15.0576	12.7203	12.7237	8.4252	8.6116	17.921	1400	1000
Improved area^2	−0.0002 2	−0.0019	−0.00002	−0.00023	0.0007	−0.00032	1960000	1000000
Number of baths	1821.32	1881.861	477.7357	3611.45	1169.399	2527.32	2	2
Year built	134.4473	79.34	111.402	71.27	106.004	101.9034	70	70
Number of stalls in garage	1451.094	21989.28	1838.58	1602.43	1694.6060	1319.142	2	2
Number of stalls in carport	1198.081	601.4742	682.5717	999.5843	1097.116	483.6459	0	0
=1 if garage is detached	−1006.91	−820.9986	−739.4174	−409.3972	−1277.08	−479.62	0	0
=1 if wiring is underground	710.0944	510.15	1239.945	2156.105	449.7995	672.2081	1	1
=1 if dishwasher	1710.118	984.5379	1153.738	2027.138	1028.8940	1006.522	1	1
=1 if garbage disposal	292.5529	473.8454	783.4335	1214.163	866.3541	696.6563	1	1
=1 if central air conditioning	1937.391	0	1998.0340	2113.566	1606.441	0	1	1
=1 if wall air conditioning	604.6657	0	984.1632	642.5249	285.40880	0	0	0
=1 if ceiling fan	344.714	570.0075	−165.0138	977.5475	560.0915	300.8057	0	0
=1 if sold in 1976	−1114.5	−2432.459	−1758.73	−1179.69	−1616.08	−2207.6	0	0
=1 if 'excellent condition'	1007.502	1434.456	759.2975	384.2958	1084.787	1243.15	1	1
=1 if 'fair condition'	−2227.37	−2095.13	−1352.85	−2538.34	−1042.07	−1626.36	0	0
=1 if 'poor condition'	0	−4316.13	0	−3390.74	−8880.12	153.1606		
=1 if brick or stone exterior	622.333	979.6494	1568.272	2390.842	1241.053	3981.132	0	0
=1 if full basement	1852.194	2229.443	0	3219.733	0	3712.41	1	1
=1 if partial basement	1108.292	2218.805	0	2201.489	0	2748.483	0	0
=1 if fireplace	1114.569	2118.643	2418.986	1604.151	2416.365	1334.085	1	1
=1 if swimming pool	3274.725	0	0	0	3426.925	0	1	1
Level of air pollution	−45.47	−26.0403	−11.8616	−1.5987	−0.2232	−8.865	0	0
Median age in census tract	−58.1812	49.0941	119.2348	47.7201	2.8702	−108.976	36	36
Median family income in census tract	0.0788	0.1655	−0.0044	0.0249	−0.0976	0.3854	25000	25000
% of workers in tract with blue-collar jobs	−52.1812	−15.0316	27.0144	−44.1273	−51.5020	−76.8352	45	45
% of houses in tract with new occupants (<5 years)	−32.4515	−61.5007	−30.7873	5.9894	−2.7746	−30.8822	14	14
% of tract population that is nonwhite	−1516.5	−4465.67	−2455.11	−5561.16	−3412.13	−6155.91	0	0
% of tract population over 24 that is HS graduate	1.2341	0.3271	0.4575	0.9166	0.2563	−0.3471	68	68
% of structures with >1 person per room	35.9097	64.3941	80.8062	−16.2552	−39.3587	199.9203	0	0
Number of work destinations per square mile in tract	16.6915	13.9396	26.8967	3.7791	−7.0332	8.7971	0	0
Constant quality price ($)	35695.53	50235.08	35038.77	40020.18	41373.61	60748.87		
Index (X_*) (Atlanta = 100)	100.0	140.32	98.1	112.1	115.9	170.2		
Index (X_{**}) Atlanta = 100	100.00	145.86	93.27	123.86	114.02	144.31		

price in the indicated city and the base city represented by β_0, and so it itself an index number. That is to say, the price index [4] reduces to:

$$P_i = \frac{\exp(\beta_0 + \beta_j X_j + \gamma_i + 0.5s^2)}{\exp(\beta_0 + \beta_j X_j + 0.5s^2)} \times 100 = \exp(\gamma_i) \times 100 \quad (6)$$

For small γ, we can use the approximation $\exp(\gamma) = 1 + \gamma$ and interpret it directly as the percentage difference between the base market price and the ith market price.

We then turn to the problem of estimating housing price indexes for a given location/housing market over time. At its heart this presents no new issues. In the first instance one can gather data where the sales or appraisals occur at different points in time, and treat those points in time as if they were different markets. The (say) Atlanta market in 1990 is a distinct market from Atlanta in 2000 or any other year, and one can estimate separate hedonic regressions for each of the two markets, and proceed as above. Or in the spirit of comment (3) above, one can simply estimate a single regression with indicator variables for the different time periods in the data. These can be over any level of time aggregation that the data will support: years, quarters, and even months. The regression would then take the form:

$$\log P = a_0 + a_1 X_1 + a_2 X_2 + \ldots + a_k X_k + b_1 T_1 + b_2 T_2 + \ldots + b_h T_h \quad (7)$$

where T_j is a binary variable indicating that the sale, or the observation of the housing price, took place in time period j. There are $h + 1$ distinct time periods, and β_0 is the intercept term representing the normalised period. This is exactly analogous to eqn [5] and the construction of the index is as in [6].

In research applications this latter method seems to be preferred over the use of separate hedonic regressions for each time period. Researchers seem to be more willing to assume constant hedonic coefficients for the same location over time than for different locations at the same time. This makes some intuitive sense. Spatially distinct markets will have large differences in supply and/or demand that would contribute to creating statistically significant differences in the regression parameters. This is less likely to be an issue when the same market is examined at different points in time, although there are no guarantees that this would be the case.

A parsimonious version of [7] would replace the time variables with a time trend:

$$\log P = a_0 + a_1 X_1 + a_2 X_2 + \ldots + a_k X_k + cW$$

The variable W takes on the value 1 for the chronologically first time period in the database, 2 for the second, and so on. It thus assumes that the time index increases at a constant percentage (if the model is logarithmic) or amount (if it is in levels) during each period. This model is a specialised case of the previous approach where the coefficients in [7] behave according to the pattern $c*j = \gamma_j$. Thus, the time trend can be tested using usual hypothesis testing procedures. Note also that c can be negative, if the data indicate falling housing prices.

There are obvious problems using time trends, since the restriction on the b_j's may not be true, and certainly will not if housing prices exhibit both increases and decreases over the sample period. One then has to balance the flexibility of the form to allow increases and decreases over time, with the desirability of 'smoothness'. One might alleviate this problem with the use of higher exponents of W in the regression. Including W^2 in the model would allow either a fall and subsequent rise, or the opposite. Additional cubic or even higher terms would capture any possible pattern in prices. Even more flexible functional forms may be used.

The Repeat Sales Method

A temporal price index can alternatively be constructed using the increasingly popular method of repeat sales. Suppose you had a database of actual sales, and moreover that it included the same house twice: a repeat sale. For convenience, label these observations 1 and 2 and equally conveniently assume that the sales took place in time periods 1 and 2. The individual appraisals for these two observations are:

$$\log P_1 = \beta_0 + \beta_1 X_{11} + \ldots + \beta_k X_{k1} + \gamma_1 T_1 + e_1 \quad (8)$$

and

$$\log P_2 = \beta_0 + \beta_1 X_{11} + \ldots + \beta_k X_{k1} + \gamma_2 T_2 + e_2 \quad (9)$$

because of course the values of all other time indicators are equal to zero. Now subtract [8] from [9]. If none of the attribute sizes changed between the two sales (i.e., the X values are constant), the price difference would be:

$$\log P_2 - \log P_1 = \gamma_2 T_2 - \gamma_1 T_1 + e_2 - e_1 \quad (10)$$

Now, the difference between two error terms is just another error term (although perhaps one with different properties; Case and Shiller (1989)). Therefore we can write the above down in the following way:

$$\Delta \log P = b_2 T_2 - b_1 T_1 + v \quad (11)$$

so that the percentage change in price is just the difference in index values b_2 and b_1 plus an error term specific to that observation.

Now imagine an entire database that has such pairs of observations of home sales. That is, each house has two observations, a first sale, and a second sale. Combine each pair into a single repeat-sales observation, and write down a regression model of the form:

$$\Delta \log P = \gamma_1 T_1 + \gamma_2 T_2 + \ldots \gamma_b T_b + v \quad (12)$$

where the T_j's are no longer indicator variables in the strictest sense. Instead, they take on the value of -1 for those observations which had 'first sales' in that time period and $+1$ for those observations which had their second sale during the time period (and zero otherwise). For any given observation, the 'fitted value' will be something like eqn [11] with 1 and 2 being replaced by the appropriate first and second sale time periods.

Running the above regression provides estimates of the b_j's and, with one further modification, the sequence of γ_j's form a 'multiplicative repeat sales index' as presented originally by Bailey et al. (1963). The modification is the usual one, that an index needs a normalisation. The usual procedure, following these authors, is to let the first time period be the normalisation. In the logarithmic model above, this amounts to setting the initial price equal to zero. The γ-terms are then values relative to the first time period and the index proceeds accordingly. This model basically underlies the well-known price indexes provided by the US Federal Housing Finance Agency (see Relevant Websites).

Examination of the repeat sales regression reveals the obvious advantage of this method, which is that the actual attributes of the property are not among the regressors, and so it is unnecessary to estimate attribute prices. This is especially significant as both observed and unobserved attributes are eliminated and thus comment (1) above no longer has as much force. The differencing operation which takes place in the repeat sales model removes all attribute levels and so source of bias is eliminated from the parameter estimates. If the goal of the investigator is not to estimate attribute prices but merely to derive constant quality time indexes of property, then the repeat sales model has considerable appeal. The research of Case and Shiller (1989) and the increased availability of databases with repeat sales in them have caused an explosion in the use of this model.

The repeat sales model is not, however, without its own faults (Meese and Wallace, 1997). One, the database is restricted to properties with multiple sales, which may be a small portion of the overall database, and, moreover, such properties may be a nonrandom sample. Properties that sell multiple times within a given time frame may be systematically different. Also, the premise of the model is that the attributes do not change between sales, and that the coefficients of those attributes do not change either. This pair of assumptions is what allows the cancellation to take place. But if these assumptions are not true, then some modifications of the model are required.

As an example, there is one attribute that is clearly not constant over the inter-sales period, and that is the age of the dwelling. Allowing this X variable to change over time causes the difference between [8] and [9] to become:

$$\Delta \log P = a_1 \Delta \text{Age} + b_1 T_1 + b_2 T_2 + \ldots b_b T_b + v \quad (13)$$

although in some such specifications collinearity can become problematic (Coulson and McMillen, 2008). What is always true of age might sometimes be true of almost any other structural or neighbourhood characteristic, but with any such change, as long as it is observable (i.e., involves the X characteristics), similar modifications can be made. The repeat sales price index can still be characterised by the sequence of γ's assuming that all of the ΔX terms are set to zero.

Potential changes in the β coefficients themselves are somewhat more difficult to handle. The most general case is when each β coefficient has a different value in each time period. Case and Quigley (1991) discuss the possibility that each β has a distinct deterministic trend, but also the more general model:

$$\log P_t = \beta_0 + \beta_{1t} x_{1t} + \ldots + \beta_{kt} x_{kt} + e_t$$

(also see Clapp and Giaccotto (1998)). Subtracting the repeat sale at time period $t - r$ we get the individual change in appraisal:

$$\log P_t - \log P_{t-r} = (\beta_{1t} - \beta_{1r}) x_{1t} + \ldots + (\beta_{kt} - \beta_{kr}) x_{kt} + e_t - e_r \quad (14)$$

and for the sample as a whole, the regression model becomes:

$$\log P_t - \log P_s = \sum_{i=1}^{T} \sum_{j=1}^{k} T_{ij}(\beta_{ij}) x_j \quad (15)$$

where, as before, i indexes the time period, j indexes the attribute, and, in a fashion similar to the original Bailey, Muth, and Nourse models:

$$T_{ij} = 1 \text{ if } i = t$$
$$= -1 \text{ if } i = s$$

Several things can be noted. First, each sequence of β parameters may be interpreted as a repeat sales index not for the unit, but for the X characteristic itself. Second, a consequence of this is that one of the advantages of the repeat sales index is lost; a set of benchmark values $X*$ must be selected, in the manner of **Table 1**, in order to construct the price index sequence for housing itself, but this is a straightforward modification of the above methods. Third, if temporal parameter variation is suppressed, then this model reverts to what was described in text following eqn [13]. Finally, as Case and Quigley (1991) and Clapp and Giaccotto (1998) note, it is straightforward to combine this repeat sales model with data on one-time sales, as the β parameters from a one-time sale at time t ought to be equal to the corresponding β's in [15], although doubts about the comparability of such samples expressed above may prevent this.

References

Bailey MJ, Muth RF, and Nourse HO (1963) A regression method for real estate price index construction. *Journal of the American Statistical Association* 58: 933–942.

Case B and Quigley J (1991) The dynamics of real estate prices. *The Review of Economics and Statistics* 73: 50–58.

Case K and Shiller R (1989) The efficiency of the market for single family homes. *American Economic Review* 79: 125–137.

Clapp J and Giacotto C (1998) Price indices based on the hedonic repeat-sales method: Application to the housing market. *Journal of Real Estate Finance and Economics* 16: 5–26.

Coulson E and McMillen D (2008) Estimating time, age and vintage effects in housing prices. *Journal of Housing Economics* 17: 138–151.

Malpezzi S, Chun GH, and Green RK (1998) New place-to-place housing price indexes for U.S. metropolitan areas, and their determinants. *Real Estate Economics* 26: 235–274.

Meese R and Wallace N (1997) The construction of residential housing price indices: A comparison of repeat-sales, hedonic-regression and hybrid approaches. *The Journal of Real Estate Finance and Economics* 14: 51–73.

Palmquist R (1984) Estimating the demand for the characteristics of housing. *The Review of Economics and Statistics* 66: 394–404.

Further Reading

Thibodeau T (ed.) (1997) Special Issues on House Price Indices. *Journal of Real Estate Finance and Economics* 14: 1–255.

Relevant Websites

www.fhfa.gov – Federal Housing Finance Agency.
www.freddiemac.com – Freddie Mac Housing Price Indexes.
www.forbes.com – Forbes (Clemence, Sarah, 'Most Expensive Zip Codes, 2005', Forbes.com).
www.money.cnn.com – Money ('Most Expensive Housing Markets', cnn.com).
www.standardandpoors.com – Standard & Poor's (S&P/Case–Shiller Home Price Indices).

House Prices and Quality of Life: An Economic Analysis

JF McDonald[1], Roosevelt University, Chicago, IL, USA

© 2012 Elsevier Ltd. All rights reserved.

Glossary

Amenity Feature external to housing unit that enhances well-being (e.g., nearby park).
Bubble Situation in which price of something is rising simply because its price is rising.
Cost–benefit analysis Technique of evaluating public programme or project which compares monetary values of costs and benefits.
Disamenity Feature external to housing unit that reduces well-being (e.g., crime in the neighbourhood).
Discrimination In economics, willingness to pay to avoid association with certain types of people.
Foreclosure Process in which homeowner defaults on the home loan and loses title to the property.
Hedonic analysis Economic model that relates the value of a good such as a house to its physical features and the features of its location.
Microeconomics Field of economics that studies the decisions of individual households and firms and the markets in which they participate.
Public good Good that is jointly consumed by a large number of people and is costly to exclude people from consuming (e.g., national defence).
Tax price Cost in taxes paid by an individual household for an additional unit of a public good or service.
Tiebout model Model of resource allocation decisions made by the local public sector in which households choose jurisdictions based on the quality of public services and local taxes.
Urban economics Field of economics that studies urban areas, including housing markets and spatial patterns within urban areas.

Introduction

The topic of home prices and quality of life calls forth many aspects of applied microeconomic theory. Housing is a consumer good, as well as an economic asset, so basic economic analysis of consumer behaviour is relevant. Beyond that, housing is a big part of people's lives and the largest user of land in an urban area. Housing is unique among consumer goods in other respects as well. When one selects a particular housing unit, a choice of residential location has been made. The neighbourhood surrounding the house contains neighbours, schools, and many other things that people care about. The location choice is made with reference to employment location, access to transportation, shopping, and other factors. Houses and apartments are very complicated commodities that contain numerous features that have value for the consumer. In short, the housing market is a market that is characterised by complicated, highly durable units, each of which is located in a neighbourhood with many attributes. To a certain extent all housing units are unique, and there is considerable truth in that thought. However, it is also true that the housing market functions. Each day houses and apartment buildings are bought and sold and housing units are rented. The operation of the housing market determines housing prices, and those prices both reflect and have major impacts on quality of life. This raises the question of how we define quality of life.

The report commission established by President Sarkozy of France (Stiglitz et al., 2010) states that:

> Quality of life is a broader concept than economic production and living standards. It includes the full range of factors that influence what we value in living, reaching beyond its material side.

The report recommends that the following dimensions should be included:

- Material living standards,
- Health,
- Education,
- Personal activities including work,
- Political voice and governance,
- Social connections and relationships,
- Environment,
- Insecurity, of an economic as well as a physical nature.

It can be said that the household's housing unit and the neighbourhood in which the unit is located influence all

---

[1] The author is the Gerald W. Fogelson Distinguished Chair in Real Estate at Roosevelt University in Chicago.

of these dimensions. Housing and quality of life are connected intimately. The purpose of this article is to explore the relationships between home prices and these dimensions of quality of life. I will consider each of these dimensions briefly in turn.

Material living standards obviously include housing – one component in the three basics of food, clothing, and shelter. Expenditures on housing are the largest share of the household budget. A person's health depends in part on the quality of the housing unit, which includes sanitation, bathroom facilities, food preparation facilities, proper heating and cooling, ventilation, and so on. Educational attainment of children depends upon having a place to study at home – and perhaps more importantly depends upon the location of the home, because the choice of location often determines the quality of the school that the child attends. A person spends more time at home than anywhere else, so the quality of many personal activities depends upon the housing unit and its location. Political voice can also depend upon the choice of the housing location, as can the quality of social connections and relationships. Indeed, the neighbourhood in which the home is located supplies the social environment in which children live – in school and otherwise. That social environment is known to have powerful influences on children and their chances for success in life. The environment (air quality, water quality, noise, and so on) are part of one's quality of life and depend upon housing location as well. Lastly, personal security (especially crime rates) depends upon housing location and upon the security of the housing unit itself.

Basic Microeconomics of Housing

Microeconomics theory begins with the proposition that consumers allocate income to consumer goods to maximise utility – the economist's proxy for well-being. Suppose that utility (U) is a function of the amount of housing services consumed (H) and expenditures on everything else (Z). A household has an income amount (Y) and faces a price of a unit of housing services (R). So the problem is to maximise

$$U(H, Z) \text{ subject to } Y = RH + Z$$

where H is a general index for the quality of the housing unit, and R is the price of a unit of quality. The solution to the problem is to allocate income to H and Z so that the last dollar spent on each of the two goods produces the same addition to utility.

This basic model has important implications. First, an increase in the price of a unit of housing quality will reduce the household's level of utility. A price increase lowers the household's level of 'real' income, so the household is less well off. Second, an increase in the price of housing raises the price of housing relative to other consumer goods, which causes the household to reduce the consumption of housing and increase the consumption of other goods. These are the income and substitution effects of basic consumer theory, and both effects work to reduce the consumption of housing when the price of housing rises.

What can cause the price of a unit of housing quality (H) to rise? There are many causes that will be considered in this article. One set of causes stems simply from the cost of producing housing services. Those costs include construction costs (materials and labour), financing costs, and the costs of operating housing units (heating, cooling, water supply, maintenance and repairs, and so on). These factors are similar to the costs of buying and operating any consumer durable good. In addition, housing is subject to many public policy laws and regulations that can affect its price. Local governments have building codes, housing codes, and zoning ordinances that influence building costs and operating costs or operate to restrict supply directly. Indeed, government regulations are implicated in high housing prices in many urban areas. The price of housing is also determined in part by the price of land. Housing requires the use of land, and the price of land depends upon its location. The values of features external to the housing unit itself – the value of the location – are built into the value of land.

As noted above, a household simultaneously chooses a housing unit and a residential location. The typical household consumes the services of one housing unit and resides in one location. This fact is the founding principle of the field of urban economics. (Some households have two housing units – including a 'vacation' home, and a very small number of households have more than two units. This complication is ignored here.) The most basic urban economics model supposes that a member of the household must travel to work at a central workplace location and must spend part of household income on commuting costs. This model implies that the price of housing must decline with distance to the central workplace. If the price of housing were the same at all locations, a household that resides at a great distance from the central workplace would bid more to live nearer to work – in order to save on commuting costs. If all households are the same and the housing market works perfectly, the decline in the (annual) price of housing with respect to distance to the central workplace will equal the increase in (annual) commuting costs as the distance increases. Households pay different prices for housing, but are all equally well off because the higher price 'pays for' reduced commuting costs. In equation form:

Change in commuting cost $= -$ Change in housing price

This basic result shows that the price of housing depends upon an important feature of its location and has been applied to many other location or neighbourhood features of housing units. The model originates with Alonso (1964) and Muth (1961). See McDonald (2007) for a brief discussion on the history of the development of this important result. The particular analysis of commuting costs is contingent on the validity of the assumption that distance to work and travel costs are most important. If other factors are taken into account, the relationship between house price and location changes.

The fundamental point is that a higher home price is related to a better location. In effect, households pay for the better location. Do households located at the better location experience a better quality of life? In the basic Alonso–Muth model, they do not because the higher price of housing exactly offsets the advantages of the better location for all households. However, households vary in their willingness to pay for an economic good. The market price for a good (including a better location) is established by the willingness of the 'marginal' household to pay. Households who choose to locate at the better location are willing to pay an amount that is equal to or greater than the price of that location. The excess of this willingness to pay above the actual price is called consumers' surplus, and it means that the quality of life is enhanced for all households at that location (except the marginal household). For example, suppose that public transit service is improved (using funds from the national government) and housing prices near the stations increase – which they do in fact as shown by McMillen and McDonald (2004) and others. The households that choose to live near the stations are willing to pay an amount equal to or more than the increase in the price of housing to have access to the improved transit service. These households as a group benefit by an amount that is greater than the increase in housing prices.

Components of Housing Unit Quality

Literally, hundreds of empirical studies show that many features of the housing unit contribute to housing quality. Those studies are known as hedonic analyses and involve multiple regressions with the selling price (or rent) as the dependent variable and numerous physical features of the housing unit as independent variables. In terms of the analysis in the previous section, the dependent variable is house value $V = PH$ (where P is the price of a unit of housing quality) or annual rent RH (recalling that R is the rent for a unit of housing quality). A partial list of the physical features of the housing unit that have been found to add to value (or rent) is:

- floor area of the unit,
- lot area,
- age of unit,
- architectural type (colonial or contemporary versus other types),
- assessment of interior quality,
- remodelling,
- number and sizes of bedrooms,
- family rooms,
- number of full bathrooms,
- number of half bathrooms,
- fireplaces,
- type of exterior construction (stone, brick, stucco versus others),
- assessment of exterior quality,
- partial basement,
- full basement (unfinished or finished),
- attic (unfinished or finished),
- central heating,
- central air conditioning,
- appliances,
- garage (one-car, two-car),
- exterior deck/terrace,
- underground yard/garden sprinkler system,
- swimming pool, and
- single storey (compared to over one storey).

The two most important variables in many of the studies are the amount of interior space and the age of the unit. Some typical results are that the selling price of a house declines by 0.5–1.0% per year as the house ages. Additions to the floor area of a housing unit are found to have a declining marginal value; it is not correct just to multiply the square footage of the house by an average value per square foot to estimate house value. Ignoring other factors, suppose that the market value (V) for a housing unit can be specified as a function of square footage (F):

$$V = aF^b.$$

If $b = 1$, then the market value for the unit is strictly proportional to the square footage, but if $b < 1$, the market value is less than proportional to the square footage. In particular, $\Delta V/\Delta F = ba/F^{1-b}$. (Here, Δ stands for 'change in.') For example, McMillen and McDonald (2004) found that $b = 0.25$. This result means that the effect of additional square footage declines as the quantity of space increases.

A fundamental issue with hedonic studies is the set of independent variables that should be included in order to obtain accurate results. The technical term from econometrics is omitted variables bias. If an important variable is left out of a study, then the coefficients that are estimated for the included variables will be biased. For example, suppose that the presence of central air conditioning and a yard sprinkler system are positively correlated. If central air conditioning is omitted, then the estimated effect of a yard sprinkler will be biased upward. Part of the value attributed to the yard sprinkler is really the value of central air conditioning. At this point, there is no standardised set of independent variables that all researchers agree should be included. Rather, the variables that are used are determined by the cost of collecting the data. A typical study includes a set of 'control' variables, and then adds another variable to determine whether that additional feature adds to (or subtracts from) the value of the house. But we really do not know whether the study has included an adequate set of control variables. The number of control variables that researchers include appears to have been growing over time, so perhaps the confidence one can place in the empirical studies is increasing.

Amenities and Disamenities External to the Housing Unit

Those same hedonic studies of housing prices (or rents) have found that there are numerous features of the locale of the housing unit that affect its market value. Recall that, in principle, these features affect the value of the land upon which the physical housing unit rests. The values of vacant lots reflect these features (assuming that houses can be built on those lots). Those neighbourhood features affect market value because they add to (or detract from) the well-being of the household. This section of the article considers only those features for which the household does not make direct payment in the form of taxes or fees. Analysis of public goods and services is provided in the next section. A partial list of the neighbourhood features that have been found to affect market values in at least one study is as follows:

- Neighbourhood income (positive effect),
- Property in gated community (positive effect),
- Percentage of neighbours with college education (positive effect),
- Percentage of neighbourhood population under age 18 (negative effect),
- Percentage of vacant parcels (negative effect),
- Number of foreclosures in the neighbourhood (negative effect),
- Value of houses in the neighbourhood (positive effect),
- Air pollution (negative effect),
- Airport noise (negative effect),
- Proximity to contaminated areas (negative effect),
- Proximity to nuclear power plant (negative effect),
- Proximity to park (positive effect),
- Industrial noise (negative effect),
- Heavy traffic on street (negative effect),
- Location on main road (negative effect),
- Location proximate to fast food restaurant (negative effect),
- Location proximate to night club (negative effect),
- Location in a floodplain (negative effect),
- Distance to employment (negative effect),
- Distance to shopping (negative effect),
- Distance to airport (negative effect),
- Rating of quality of houses on the block (positive effect),
- Within walking distance of public transit or commuter rail station (positive effect),
- Adjacent to rail line, highway, or transit line (negative effect),
- Proximity to highway interchange (positive effect),
- Proximity to a church (negative effect),
- Existence of zoning or restrictive covenants versus their absence (positive effect),
- Previous price increases in the neighbourhood to capture expectation of future price increases (positive effect),
- Crime in the neighbourhood (negative effect),
- Proximity to hog farm (negative effect).

This is a long list, and each variable clearly has some connection to one or more of the dimensions in the quality of life listed above. But how can anyone possibly take all of these factors into account when choosing a housing unit and its location? Indeed, it is amazing that variations in housing prices (sometimes, at least) capture variations in all of these variables. A reasonable behavioural model of the search for a housing unit might posit that the household specifies a desired set of characteristics in the housing unit itself and a price range, and the real estate agent identifies units that meet these criteria. If a subject house meets the basic criteria, then the household will take a look at the neighbourhood characteristics that are regarded as most important – near transit stop, not proximate to hog farm, and so on. That said, these neighbourhood effects (both positive and negative) mean that there is a positive relationship between home prices and the quality of life.

There is one more characteristic that is important (at least to a sizable number of people) – the racial composition of the neighbourhood. Gary Becker, in his classic book (1971: 14), defines discrimination in economic terms as follows.

> If an individual has a 'taste for discrimination,' he must act *as if* he were willing to pay something either directly or in the form of reduced income, to be associated with some persons instead of others. When actual discrimination occurs, he must, in fact, either pay or forfeit income for this privilege.

In particular, numerous empirical studies are consistent with the hypothesis that white households are willing to pay and in fact do pay something to avoid residing among or near African-American households. This willingness to pay a premium not to live near African-Americans means that such households feel that their quality of life is influenced by this factor. The *US Fair Housing Act of 1968* makes it illegal to discriminate actively in the sale or rental of housing units on the basis of race, colour, religion, or ethnic origin. No exemptions are made for racial discrimination. However, no law can legislate away the willingness to pay to avoid certain groups of people. With that said, government policy does not need to recognise the 'legitimacy' of this particular preference in cost–benefit analyses of proposed or actual programmes. As a general rule the benefits of public programmes are based on estimates of the willingness of people to pay for them. (For example, transportation projects reduce commuting time, so the main benefit is the value of that time saved.)

This preference for discrimination, along with the willingness to act on it, leads to racial segregation. Segregation often involves a process known as neighbourhood tipping. Consider an all-white neighbourhood that is adjacent to a black neighbourhood. Houses are put up for sale on a regular basis as people change jobs, retire, and so on. The process begins when a black household buys a house in the adjacent white neighbourhood. The purchase may have been made because of demand growth in the black portion of the housing market. White households continue to buy houses in the neighbourhood because they are not influenced by the presence of one black household. However, soon more black households buy houses in the neighbourhood. Now some potential white buyers 'avoid' the area, and more and more of the houses that are put on the market are sold to black households. Put another way, potential buyers make lower bids than do potential black buyers because of the presence of black households in the area. The tipping point is defined as the percentage of houses in the neighbourhood occupied by black households at which white buyers begin to avoid the area for racial reasons (i.e., make lower bids than potential black buyers). Although some white households may remain, and some white buyers may continue to move in, racial transition occurs. See Schelling (1971) for a theoretical study of neighbourhood tipping and segregation, and Massey and Denton (1993) for a detailed discussion of the causes and effects of racial segregation in the United States.

Local Public Goods and Services and Taxes

The primary function of local government is to supply public goods and services, including education, hospitals and health care, transportation (streets, transit), public safety (police, fire protection), parks, community development and planning, waste management, and other infrastructure. Revenue sources to pay for these public goods include local property taxes (and other taxes), user fees, and revenues from higher levels of government (school aid funds from state governments, and so on). All of these items influence the quality of life and home prices.

The prevailing economic theory of local government originates with a classic article by Charles Tiebout (1956), and is known as the 'vote with the feet' model (or Tiebout model). The model is based on the idea that people in an urban area can change residential locations easily, and therefore can express their demands for local public services by voting with their feet. They set up local governments to satisfy these demands, and people join the 'club' that most closely matches their preferences. In the pure Tiebout model, local public services are financed entirely by taxes on the residents, and each household pays the same amount in local taxes. For example, suppose that a local government is set up with 1000 home sites and supplies a public good that costs Π per unit. Each household sees the price of the public good as $\Pi/1000$. Households that demand exactly Q^* units of the public good at that price will reside in this jurisdiction, and each will pay exactly $\Pi Q^*/1000$ in taxes. Any household that does not demand Q^* units of the public good at price $\Pi/1000$ will not choose to reside there. In short, the households in effect purchase the public good in exactly the same manner as a crowd at a sporting event buys a ticket to see the game. In this simplified world, the price of the home (in this case, the home site) is unaffected by local government activities.

The real world is far more complex, of course. The Tiebout model relies on the assumption of a sufficiently large number of local governments in an urban area to permit households to sort themselves in an optimal manner. Large urban areas in the United States have many suburban jurisdictions – probably for Tiebout-type reasons. But the large central city contains many types of households with very different demands for public services and willingness to pay for them. In addition, as noted above, local government services are supported by revenue from the state and national governments. Another complication is that local taxes are levied on commercial and industrial property as well as on residential property, and these properties generally require far less in public services than do residents. The taxes contributed by commercial and industrial property exceed the cost of providing the services that they require, so local jurisdictions compete to attract these tax-paying assets. Yet another complexity is the fact that the property tax is not a uniform tax on households in the jurisdiction. The tax base is the assessed value of the home, and this can vary considerably even in suburban jurisdictions. Households in fact do not see the same 'tax price' for public services.

These real-world complications mean that local public services and taxes do affect home prices. Households do not get exactly the public services for which they pay in local taxes and user fees. The central city will tend to cater to the 'median' household. Households that demand more public services (e.g., better schools) who live in the central city insist on paying less for their homes than otherwise (so they can pay for private schools, for example). A jurisdiction with a great deal of commercial and industrial property is able to supply more public services to residents at a given tax rate (or charge a lower tax for a given amount of public services). This net advantage will be reflected in higher home prices. Better public services (holding local taxes constant) and higher local taxes (holding public services constant) are capitalised into home prices. The operation of the housing market tends to equalise net advantage. A low home price (given all other factors) means that public services are of low quality or local taxes are high (or a combination of the two), but the low home price is a compensation. Again, the outcome is a positive relationship between home prices and the quality of life.

Housing Price Bubbles and Quality of Life

The decade of the 2000s produced an unprecedented bubble in housing prices in the United States and in several other countries. See Shiller (2008) for a detailed explanation of this phenomenon. A price bubble can be defined as a situation in which prices increase because prices are increasing. People somehow become convinced that prices will continue to rise, so they want to buy now and take advantage of the trend – which tends to drive up prices even more. Price bubbles always 'pop' eventually, of course. The end of the housing price bubble in the United States started in 2006 after the supply of housing had increased dramatically. How is the quality of life related to this unusual event?

The impact on the household's quality of life depended critically on the timing of the household's participation in this market. Outcomes for households that purchased homes before the bubble had generated outlandish price increases varied considerably. Some households sold houses for inflated prices and walked away with large gains – and realised those gains if they moved to rental units or to places with lower housing prices. Other households took out additional loans based on the increased equity to pay for consumption, college tuition, and so on, but later found that the house turned out to be worth less than the outstanding loan balances ('under water'). These households face the choice of continuing to make the loan payments or to default and reduce housing expenses by moving to a rental unit. Most households that purchased the home before the bubble simply remained in the home and rode out the storm with no material impact on their quality of life, unless they live in an area with a high density of foreclosures sufficient to put their homes under water. In this latter case, if and when the household needs to move, the selling price will be insufficient to pay off the loan.

Households that purchased the home during, at, or near the peak of the bubble are the big losers. Many of these households were persuaded to take out loans that they could not afford – unless housing prices continued to rise. For example, many 'subprime' loans were made with interest rates that were relatively low for the first 2 or 3 years, and then would reset to higher rates after this initial period. If the value of the house declined, these households had little choice but to default after the initial 'teaser rate' period and suffer the consequences of a poor credit rating. While many of these borrowers had little or no equity in the home, any downpayment that was made has been lost. Those households that bought at the peak of the bubble for whom the house payments were affordable have lost their equity and face the choice of whether to default. In short, the lives of the people who made the home purchase during the bubble have experienced serious disruptions and they may have suffered substantial financial losses.

Conclusions

This article has discussed the relationships between home prices and the quality of life. Higher home prices have a number of causes:

- Higher costs of building and operating housing units, which mean that high home prices are associated with a lower quality of life.
- Higher quality of the housing unit itself, which means that the household has purchased a higher quality of life by having a bigger and/or better house.
- Better neighbourhood features (proximity to employment, lower crime rate, better neighbourhoods), which mean that the household has paid more for land at a better location.
- Combination of better public goods and services and/ or lower local taxes, which means that the household has paid more to live in a better municipal jurisdiction.
- A housing price bubble, which means that housing prices went up simply because prices were rising. This is a dangerous situation because the household that makes a home purchase at or near the peak of the bubble will suffer personal disruptions and substantial financial losses when the bubble deflates.

See also: Economics of Housing Choice; Mortgage Default: Well-Being in the United States; Neighbourhood

Effects: Approaches; New Urban Economics and Residential Location; Residential Segregation.

References

Alonso W (1964) *Location and Land Use*. Cambridge, MA: Harvard University Press.
Becker G (1971) *The Economics of Discrimination*, 2nd edn. Chicago, IL: University of Chicago Press.
Massey D and Denton N (1993) *American Apartheid*. Cambridge, MA: Harvard University Press.
McDonald J (2007) William Alonso, Richard Muth, Resources for the future, and the founding of urban economics. *Journal of the History of Economic Thought* 29: 67–84.
McMillen D and McDonald J (2004) Reaction of house prices to a new rapid transit line: Chicago's Midway Line, 1983–1999. *Real Estate Economics* 32: 463–486.
Muth R (1961) Economic change and rural-urban land conversion. *Econometrica* 29: 1–29.
Schelling T (1971) Dynamic models of segregation. *Journal of Mathematical Sociology* 1: 143–186.
Shiller R (2008) *The Subprime Solution*. Princeton, NJ: Princeton University Press.
Stiglitz J, Sen A, and Fitoussi J-P (2010) *Mis-Measuring Our Lives: The Report of the Commission on the Measurement of Economic Performance and Social Progress*. New York: The New Press.
Tiebout C (1956) A pure theory of local expenditures. *Journal of Political Economy* 64: 416–424.

Further Reading

McDonald J and McMillen D (2011) *Urban Economics and Real Estate*, 2nd edn. Hoboken, NJ: John Wiley & Sons.

Housing Agents and Housing Submarkets

C Donner, Formerly Lecturer at Technical University Vienna, Vienna, Austria

© 2012 Elsevier Ltd. All rights reserved.

Housing Agents

The Emergence of Housing Agents

In early history, migrant mankind relied on self-provision for housing. Individuals or human groups found and adapted natural shapes and materials into makeshift and transitory shelters. The development of civilisations based on agriculture, which necessitated fixed settlement, led to the evolution of more permanent homes, still produced by the later occupants themselves. At that point, and as a basis for any structure, entitlement to a specific plot of land had to be ensured.

Later, with specialisation of trades, various craftsmen, such as masons, carpenters, and others, began to offer their services in exchange for goods or cash. These services were later bundled by professional builders and eventually consolidated into contemporary construction companies. With this, provision of new housing required two partners: the individual client and investor, who owned a plot and needed a home for his household, and the builder, who supplied materials, labour, and expertise.

Today, in many countries, housing production based on individual contracts – with or without appointment of an architect – has become a minority undertaking or has almost vanished. In highly developed countries, professional developers commission construction enterprises of varying size to build the great majority of new housing, both in single-family homes and in multistorey buildings. The developer has thus become the third essential partner in providing new housing. Finally, many households in need of a dwelling cannot (or do not want to) pay the price of a dwelling. Thus, they assume the role of tenant, representing the fourth partner in housing provision, with the original developer (investor) becoming a landlord. Essentially, operation of housing markets only requires actions of the two to four agents mentioned above. However, additional agents often contribute their services in upstream markets, such as the land property market, the construction service market, and the financing service market. In highly developed societies, these roles may become further differentiated or combined into multiple functions of many housing agents.

Land Property Owners

In Europe, in premodern times, property rights implicitly included the right to build. With increasing urban population density and competing land uses, specific authorisation had to be obtained for any construction project. Therefore, in developed countries, any contemporary residential construction project requires appropriate zoning, a building permit, and compliance with the building code. Utilisation of land for construction may be based on ownership or on lease agreements, which are usually long term, but essentially temporary. In British history, a structure with several layers of (partial) leaseholds developed, greatly adding to the complexity of real estate acquisition and use.

Private property owners may sell land to the developer of a housing project or arrange a lease, or also they may keep it for later personal use or for speculative reasons. Landowners hoarding land restrict access to building sites for potential developers and hence drive up land prices. On the other hand, this prevents land from being built up too quickly. The pressure on land prices mainly depends on demand and on holding cost. Apart from selling land, for specific fiscal reasons, private land owners may prefer to provide a plot to a builder of a residential building and later receive a preestablished part of the joint project profit, a practice previously common in Mediterranean countries. In socialist countries (e.g., in Eastern Europe until 1989), land was owned by the state and citizens only received permanent usage rights for their dwellings. However, in capitalist countries, too, the state – or municipal bodies – often holds large land reserves for future infrastructure, commercial, and/or housing projects.

Ample land reserves are also essential for large construction companies specialised in residential developments in order to maintain a steady output. By thus restricting the readily available land on offer, they also contribute to general land price inflation and hence increase their gains.

Developers

The developer of a housing project is the organiser who initiates the process of housing provision involving some or many of the agents presented here. In the simplest case, the developer plays the role of landowner and investor at the same time, procuring a single-family home for himself by contracting a professional builder. When they aim at anonymous clients, housing developers act as housing market agents that guide real estate investment projects, all through their planning, financing, and building stages. During this process, they assume the complex and risky role of coordinator of many other agents. This task requires multifaceted skills related to housing market analysis, project organisation, financial bargaining, and product marketing.

Developers have to study housing supply and demand in the local housing market, present preliminary planning schemes and architectural designs, determine construction schedules and foreseeable costs, ensure adequate financing, evaluate various risks, and present a comprehensive feasibility study to investors, who must then approve the entire scheme.

In order to determine economic feasibility, that is, profitability, developers estimate the maximum price (or discounted rental income) obtainable on the local market for the maximum usable floor area allowed on a specific site. Building cost, on the other hand, is relatively well known for any chosen housing standard. Therefore, subtracting building cost (including planning and financing) from anticipated revenue indicates the maximum price that a nonprofit developer would be willing to pay for the respective site. Profit might then result from negotiating a lower price with the current landowner. Developers, who already own a particular site and discover that the price they paid for it would result in too low profit or even loss, will have to wait until market demand for housing increases, or they may try to convince the authorities to rezone their property allowing additional profit-generating use.

After approval of the investment, the developers then apply for a building permit, contract a building company, secure a construction supervisor, and, finally, market the completed dwellings. If they act as (main) investors, they can sell the completed dwellings to future owner-occupiers, professional large-scale lessors, or individual small-scale landlords. On the other hand, they may also act as (long-term) landlords themselves. Depending on the housing sector in question, a great variety of developers act on local housing markets, often competing with each other, but sometimes enjoying a unique selling proposition, mainly when provision of state subsidies is exclusively linked to specific types of developers.

Developers of market-oriented owner-occupied housing

Developers of owner-occupied housing may be legal persons, that is, enterprises that own a number of building sites already equipped with technical infrastructure, or raw land that still awaits zoning and development. For example, around 1900, the German 'Terraingesellschaften' (land development companies), acquired large expanses of agricultural land on the perimeter of major cities and then sold large shares to wealthy families or to commercial builders, as well as individual plots to families wanting to build their own homes. Over time, these companies also became involved in extensive home building. In Great Britain, large-scale development of future owner-occupied housing by a few companies holding considerable land reserves is standard practice. While extended residential developments with quite uniform row houses are generally accepted in some countries, in other countries large-scale developers try to mitigate the monotony by more attractive urban layout and by varying the design of individual dwellings.

Physical persons acting as individual housing developers usually intend to build a single-family home for personal use. This type of housing may be relatively low cost, with developers sometimes contributing their own labour and protracting the building period over several years in order to stretch construction expenditure. This procedure, of course, has been widely practised in developing countries. Also in Europe, this form of individual housing development has traditionally been quite popular, for example, in Austria, Belgium, Greece, Italy, and Slovenia. At the other extreme, individually developed housing may also be of a high standard, based on a made-to-measure individual architectural design. On the other hand, developing of subsidised owner-occupied housing may be restricted to limited-profit developers (often for multifamily housing) or be open to commercial developers with size and price limitations.

Developers of market-oriented rental housing

Production of rental housing is technically quite similar to that of owner-occupied housing, but financing differs, as rental housing requires long-term investors acting as landlords. Market-oriented developers of rental housing are mostly legal persons, either with available capital (e.g., insurance companies and pension funds) or backed by capital providers, such as real estate funds. Other investors already own a building site and want to obtain rental income while keeping their property.

Developers of rental housing have to maintain a particularly careful and conservative approach when undertaking a feasibility study, since the risk of negative future economic development always looms large over long-term investments such as rental housing. However, when eventually leaving the rental market, private landlords may, depending on land market development and on applicable tax law, profit from (considerable) capital gains, enhancing overall yield on their investment.

Developers of subsidised rental housing

Developers of subsidised rental housing supplied at below-market rent make up a more varied group. In order to ensure that supply-side subsidies actually reach tenants who occupy these dwellings, some form of rent regulation usually applies. Also, in principle, these developers are not profit-oriented, thereby potentially reducing production cost.

State/regions/local authorities

The first subgroup of this kind of developer is part of the public sector at state, regional, or, above all, municipal level. In some countries, such as Austria and Great Britain, local authorities have been very active as rental housing developers and providers. Sweden has opted for a system of municipal housing companies operating at arm's length from local city councils. As part of special efforts to provide affordable dwellings, particularly France and Great Britain, have developed a number of large New Towns, where public authorities provide dwellings on similar terms.

Limited-profit housing associations/housing cooperatives

The second subgroup of subsidised housing developers are legally private enterprises, operating under limited-profit legislation. They may originate from state, church, or trade union initiatives for below-market-rent housing provision, sometimes addressing specific groups of households. These developers generally enjoy preferential access to subsidies for rental housing. While limited-profit housing associations are usually free to generate profits and to accumulate reserves, they are not allowed to distribute dividends over and above a low ceiling. In case of sale or dissolution of a limited-profit housing association, distribution of windfall profits may be problematic. Housing cooperatives operate along similar guidelines but originate from 'bottom-up' initiatives, when groups of households needing a home combine efforts for a joint solution of their housing problem. However, beyond a certain size, housing cooperatives become quite similar to housing associations.

Legal and physical private persons

Last but not least, in some countries (e.g., Germany), profit-oriented legal and physical private persons may also act as developers of subsidised rental dwellings, if they adhere to rent regulation applying to limited-profit developers. In this case, rent regulation normally applies for a certain period of time only, for example, until full repayment of preferential loans.

Investors

Housing investors are owners of capital who want to transform their cash or similar liquid assets into real estate in order to obtain short-term gains via sale of housing to owner-occupiers, or to receive long-term income via letting to tenants. In the latter case, possible capital gains at termination of the investment may add to profitability. However, as such expected gains occur in the distant future, they are hard to quantify. Via feasibility studies, potential housing investors compare expected net yields with other investments of similar risk and liquidity structures. In particular, investors in rental housing carry long-term risks regarding prolonged vacancies, substantial rent arrears, or profit-limiting changes in housing and tax law.

In some cases and for physical persons, the importance of net rent income compared to capital gains may fade, particularly if the former is taxed and the latter is not.

Planners

Planning services may be provided by large-scale developers themselves or outsourced to specialists. Urban planners, architects, and engineers for structural design and technical equipment all contribute their designs and calculations, coordinated by the developer. Contracts with outside planners are usually based on official or negotiated fees, sometimes following a design competition.

Builders

Professional builders offer more comprehensive expertise than layman self-builders can usually muster. Therefore, they are able to offer a guarantee covering state-of-the-art procedures and high-quality craftsmanship. Influenced by regional traditions, competing interests, and potential state incentives, and in cooperation with architects and other planners, construction enterprises have developed new and more efficient building and energy conservation technologies. Already from the 1950s, prefabrication of residential buildings became available. Structural and complementary elements were produced in permanent or temporary plants and later assembled on the site. With increasing efficiency, a good deal of manual labour is being economised.

As a rule, contracts with construction companies are based on a general or restricted bidding process. Builders are usually not involved in financing a construction project, except when specifically agreed upon. This is a solution sometimes chosen for infrastructure work. However, large construction enterprises aiming at stable output volumes may also act as housing developers.

Financing Institutions

Buyers of single-family homes are rarely able to pay cash for their home. Even less can investors in multifamily housing comprising dozens of dwellings pay cash immediately. Therefore, in market-based housing production, developers must secure substantial capital-market finance to complement their equity. Housing loans are mostly based on mortgages with land and buildings serving as collateral. Depending on market conditions, the lifetime of loans, interest rates, and annuity design vary. Due to a widespread lack of stable long-term refinancing, more often than not, these terms must be renegotiated in the course of the repayment period.

Parting from traditional practice, in recent years, banks have often sold most of their outstanding mortgage loans to third parties via securitisation. Since 2007, imprudent rating and excessive speculation have caused the collapse of many major banks and a worldwide crisis of the finance system.

In addition to mortgage loans from banks, various other financing sources have emerged, such as real estate companies or funds, private equity funds, and real estate investment trusts, which split the entire financial engagement among a number of individual investors and sometimes enjoy preferential taxation.

Pension funds and insurance companies collecting employee contributions for future pension payments, or insurance premiums for risk coverage, are special cases. They sometimes directly develop housing projects and fund the required investment without recurring to the capital market.

Finally, grants and preferential loans provided by the public sector or by state-controlled institutions have become a typical component in the finance mix required for provision of new housing. These housing policy instruments may cover the major part of total cost, particularly for new rental housing. (From 2001, the Hungarian government even offered grants of up to 70–80% of total cost for new municipal rental housing.) As a rule, subsidies for owner-occupied housing have been considerably less generous.

Landlords

In the rental housing sector, in addition to the owner/investor and the builder, another essential agent appears: the landlord. Landlords acquire one or several dwellings, not for personal use but for letting them to other households, thereby generating a stream of rental income for themselves.

Some landlords mostly operate in the private (market) rental sector, while others provide subsidised and/or regulated rental housing.

Real Estate Agents

The complexity of real estate markets and the variety of transactions required to procure a home often overwhelm the prospective buyer or tenant, who quite rarely has to deal with such matters. Therefore, real estate agents act as consultants, intermediaries, or sales agents. Depending on their customer, they cater to different needs and interests. Most balanced information may be expected from independent surveyors.

Real estate agents provide information on available dwellings with specific characteristics such as location, size, type, and price, or they assist a potential buyer or tenant to find a certain kind of dwelling. Collecting and interpreting this information requires constant market observation and updating of accumulated material. Clients pay a fee for this service, sometimes only if a contract actually comes through.

Typically, real estate agents do not participate in housing markets with their own capital.

Legal Advisers

Real estate transactions have far-reaching consequences. Therefore, formal aspects are of great importance. Property law and tenancy law are often complex and their correct application is difficult to interpret for a layperson. While a lease contract may still be based on clauses jointly agreed upon between the contracting parties, or on standard clauses formulated by interest group specialists, the sale of a dwelling or of a residential building regularly requires assistance by a lawyer or public notary. The cost of their services has to be taken into account when computing total yield of an investment.

Of course, legal counsellors also intervene when upstream contracts are concluded, for example, contracts related to acquisition of a site, to bidding or to procurement of construction services and to financing arrangements.

Housing Stock Managers

After completion, new dwellings cannot be left to themselves. In order to ensure a continuous stream of 'housing service', every building requires continuous management and upkeep. While owners of single-family homes may take care of this matter personally, things become more complicated in condominiums, where several co-owners must coordinate their joint responsibility for administration, maintenance, and repair. Co-owners sometimes take turns attending to these tasks, but condo management is normally outsourced to specialised companies and remunerated. Outsourcing is generally the case in rental housing, even where the owner is a physical person, as soon as the number of tenancies exceeds a few dwellings.

Households

Households are on the receiving end of housing supply. Housing developers try to meet the needs and preferences of households regarding location, size, amenities, and so on. Households secure user rights by various tenures: owner occupation, housing cooperatives, or rental tenancies. In addition, employers may provide housing for their employees.

While during periods of scarcity (e.g., following mass destruction in war) many households had to double up with others, in developed societies and on balanced housing markets almost all households live in their individual dwellings. Exceptions may refer to flat sharing by students, to joint living of unrelated elderly persons in apartments with private and common rooms, to single persons living in institutions, and so on. Mirroring positive economic development, there is a long-term trend for average household size to decrease and for floor area per person to increase.

Housing Politicians

In spite of a wide gamut of ideas ranging from faith in the self-balancing forces of free markets to the ambitious conviction that society must support the weak, contemporary European social policies pledge to prevent, or at least combat, open poverty resulting from insufficient primary market income.

Therefore, in most countries, housing markets are not entirely left to the free interaction of private interests. Against a prevailing background of redistributive income policies, housing politicians aim at preventing inadequate housing or even homelessness among low-income households and at ensuring acceptable housing expenditure ratios for lower-income and middle-income households. Striving for adequate housing provision, governments and housing politicians apply a great variety of instruments, such as subsidies and transfers, tax benefits, provision of nonmarket housing, and allocation rights.

Of course, housing subsidies and benefits all cost money. During periods of acute housing scarcity, most governments are willing to tolerate high housing policy expenditure, even if this means increasing state debt. However, when the general level of housing consumption seems to be acceptable but state indebtedness keeps increasing, governments tend to press for more parsimonious forms of housing policy and for more efficient and effective housing policy instruments.

Housing Researchers

Although most citizens have at least vague notions how housing markets function, even housing politicians often lack reliable information on actual housing conditions in local housing markets and on the effectiveness and efficiency of specific housing policy instruments. While detailed statistics may provide part of the answers, housing researchers try to gain a deeper understanding of the workings of housing markets, of the outcome of interdependent housing policy instruments, of data reliability, and of probable future housing market developments.

Depending on their location in universities, independent research institutions, or private industry, housing researchers may provide theoretical analyses, useful practical conclusions, or merely supportive lobbying for private interest groups.

Government Branches and Agencies

Whatever the decisions taken by governments regarding their housing policy, implementation of agreed-upon instruments requires effective agents, either within the government structure itself or as dependent, state-controlled institutions.

Nongovernmental Organisations

Numerous nongovernmental organisations (NGOs) representing the interests of specific groups, such as tenants, landlords, or property owners, are active in the field of housing. Some NGOs represent initiatives regarding specific forms of housing and living, or pursue ecologically motivated research into future-oriented urban design and housing technology, or carry out societal experiments through housing cooperatives, self-building, and similar activities.

Housing Submarkets

The Constitution of Housing Markets

Transactions between suppliers and consumers of housing services basically involve two agents: a seller or landlord on the one side and a buyer or tenant on the other side. In principle, purchase and a tenancy agreement are individual legal acts. However, a large number of such contracts in a given area collectively generate local housing markets, where large numbers of residential buildings and individual dwellings change hands in a steady flow of transactions. In theory, the number of all potential interactions is almost unlimited. However, differentiation by tenure, location, and physical characteristics such as age, amenities, and state of repair result in subdivision into local submarkets by sector and segment. Based on their personal preferences and financial possibilities, households in demand of a dwelling must decide which submarket to focus on and then critically compare available objects, in order to make an informed choice.

The main sectors of housing markets refer to owner-occupied housing (with or without subsidies), to (private) market-oriented rental housing, and to nonmarket (subsidised) rental housing, with housing cooperatives occupying an intermediate position. In all housing submarkets, supply predominantly consists of second-hand dwellings, while new housing, being added to the existing stock, represents a distinct but smaller share.

Owner-Occupied Housing

Owner occupation is typically the largest sector in national housing stocks, although in urban areas it may still represent a minority tenure. In Europe, there are but few exceptions to this, such as Germany and Switzerland, where the owner occupation ratio remains well below 50%. This tenure represents large shares of total housing stock in Southern Europe and Ireland, as well as in former socialist countries in Central and Eastern Europe due to their large-scale privatisation schemes. Therefore, owner-occupiers are prominent agents on housing markets. As a rule, acquisition of an owner-occupied home requires considerable effort. Therefore, a household able to attain this tenure usually enjoys higher social standing. Also, identification of occupants with their homes is usually stronger than in other tenures and hence they are more interested in maintenance. Due to relatively high transaction costs, owner-occupiers tend to remain in their homes longer than tenants.

Owner-occupied housing is generally considered the top rung of the 'housing ladder' and offers the most comprehensive property rights, such as the right to use or to permit use, to profit from, to exclude others, to bequeath, to mortgage, to sell, and to destroy. In addition to these property rights, owner-occupiers over time generally profit from an increase in the value of their home. However, while this is common practice, their gain cannot be considered an entitlement. Both for original construction and for subsequent major alterations, owners have to apply to local authorities for a building permit. As a rule, property owners have to pay real estate tax both on land and on buildings – regardless of actual occupation. Also, owner-occupiers must abstain from any use that severely affects the property and usage rights of other parties.

Owner-occupied housing does not exclusively consist of single-family homes on individual plots. In order to save on plot size and cost, developers of owner-occupied housing often group units in pairs ('semidetached housing'), rows ('terraced houses' in the United Kingdom or 'townhouses' elsewhere), or clusters. The pressure of rapidly increasing urban populations often led to the construction of sometimes quite narrow rows of houses with three or four storeys (e.g., in France, the Netherlands, and Great Britain). Apartment buildings were originally identified with rental housing only, but with the advent of condominium legislation in the twentieth century, flats became an individually tradable commodity too.

Rental Housing

Rental housing differs fundamentally from owner-occupied housing by separating the functions of owner and user. Basically, the landlord lets a specific dwelling to the tenant for a predetermined or undetermined period of time. The tenant periodically pays the rent specified in the tenancy contract and enjoys the right to occupy the dwelling together with other members of his or her household.

Through the tenancy contract, some of the property rights are transferred from owner to tenant, particularly user rights. Whether upkeep of the dwelling remains the owner's responsibility or (partly) shifts to the tenant depends on national tenancy law. Essentially, any arrangement could be considered valid as long as the distribution of risks is properly reflected in the agreed-upon rent.

The inherent instability of private tenancies may benefit employees with a frequently changing workplace. On the other hand, private rental housing generally conveys lower social prestige than owner-occupied housing.

Within rental housing in general, topics of particular legal interest are payment of rent, use of the dwelling by third parties, payment of maintenance and other running costs, and, last but not least, the conditions for termination of contract by tenant or landlord. However, entitlements and obligations in rental housing vary according to the subsector of rental housing in question. Some parts of national tenancy law may refer to market rental housing only, while others may exclusively regulate nonmarket rental housing. As in owner-occupied housing, owners of rental housing usually benefit from a progressive increase in value of their property, which adds to total yield.

Tenancies in this subsector are often quite short, that is, a few years or even less (e.g., in Great Britain). In part, this reflects frequent changes of residence during the early years of professional careers. However, a short period of notice to quit may cause considerable hardship for affected households. Low-income households in private rental housing may or may not be entitled to housing benefit payments.

Rental housing is not linked to a specific form of dwelling. While in some countries most rental housing takes the form of apartments in multistorey buildings with only a small share of single-family homes being let to tenants, in other countries (e.g., the Netherlands and Great Britain) many homes in row houses are occupied on the basis of a tenancy contract.

'Non-market-oriented rental housing' is made up by municipal rental housing, nonprofit rental housing, charity housing, and other forms. Tenants in this subsector usually enjoy unlimited tenancy rights and rent is determined by some form of rent regulation and hence it is usually considerably lower than corresponding market rents. Low-income households occupying a nonmarket (i.e., subsidised) rental dwelling are, in principle, entitled to complementary housing benefit payments. Special forms of low-rent or rent-free housing refer to employer housing and to dwellings let to relatives of the owner.

Cooperative Housing

Cooperative housing is based on collective property of land and buildings by all co-op members. Each member has one share and one vote and may participate actively in managing the cooperative, which, in turn, lets the dwellings to individual households.

This double-headed tenure thus offers a blurred picture, with some characteristics typical for owner occupation and others typical for rental housing. Essentially, housing cooperatives represent a joint enterprise of a group of people in need of a home, regardless of household income. However, in practice, housing cooperatives are important mainly because of their ability to procure subsidies from public or private sources.

Historically, housing cooperatives not only provided housing but also fostered a new communitarian way of life, with interactive participation by members and various complementary services, such as meeting places and play and recreation areas.

Co-op membership is transferable to spouses and children, but withdrawal from the cooperative did not entitle members to participate in any capital gain. Therefore, capital gains were accumulated by cooperatives. Over time, more individualistic co-op members tried to remedy this imbalance, which sometimes led to a redefinition of property rights, allowing members to transfer their homes at near-to-market prices.

Informal Housing

In addition to formal housing of various tenures, low-income households sometimes cover their basic housing needs by occupying the property of others. This might take the form of squatting on public or private land and building makeshift shelters that later grow into more stable homes. In other instances, squatters occupy vacant buildings, often derelict and slated for demolition, sometimes only in need of renovation but temporarily not in use.

Spontaneous occupation of property may occur on an individual basis or by squatters organised in groups that stand a better chance to resist later efforts by authorities to evict them. While informal and illegal housing has been occurring in European countries, particularly during periods of economic hardship and in less developed regions, it is a common and widespread approach to housing provision in developing countries.

Informal housing seemingly avoids the cost of land acquisition or even that of building, but entails a loss of confidence in state structures and policies, which represents a cost to society. Also, arbitrary and ambiguous application of the law often reflects inadequate social policy.

Tenure Changes and Transitions

Tenures are not always as clear-cut as they may seem. Owner occupation and cooperative housing are typical examples of different meanings for given terms. Also, the concept of a particular tenure may shift over time.

Economic ownership of mortgaged property

For instance, buyers of homes are often referred to as owners, although most of them are still repaying a mortgage loan. Legally, those buyers are registered as owners in public land registers together with the mortgage that serves as collateral for the loan. However, no reference is usually made to the proportion of the outstanding balance to the purchasing price or to net equity. Only in periods of widely diminishing property values, lenders keep a close eye on the ratio of that balance and the current market value of the home, particularly when net equity becomes negative and repossession is in the offing.

France shows a more transparent approach, as housing specialists distinguish between *accédants* – who are still paying annuities – and *propriétaires non accédants* – who have repaid their loan and thereby have become full economic owners of their home.

Shift between owner-occupied and rental housing

A more important aspect of tenure interrelation is a shift from owner occupation to rental housing or vice versa. Owner-occupiers may decide to move to another dwelling and let their previous dwelling, whereby it switches to the rental housing sector, or landlords may terminate their current tenancy contract and opt for using the dwelling themselves. Also, current tenants may desire to purchase their dwelling by any of various transition schemes. Evidently, in this case, the current owner and landlord must be willing to sell on these terms, unless obliged to do so by law.

Shared ownership

A shared ownership scheme offers the tenant the possibility of purchasing his or her dwelling by progressively paying parts of a – usually – preestablished price and thereby acquiring (additional) equity. To facilitate this operation, each share normally has to represent, for example, 20% or 25% of the total. Every time an additional share changes hands, the balance that remains as rental housing decreases. Such schemes have been operated by city councils in Great Britain and Ireland.

Rental housing with purchasing option

A similar scheme provides the tenant with an option to buy his or her home at a certain point in time. However, the sales price may not have been established beforehand, so that tenants willing to buy have to approach a court and have it decide on the price (e.g., in Austria). Neither shared ownership agreements nor purchasing options consider part or all of paid rent as part of the acquisition price.

Rent-purchase

Contrary to the above, in a scheme of rent-purchasing, paid rent is taken into account as step-by-step (instalment) payment towards an initially agreed-upon total purchasing price.

Legalisation of illegal housing

Over time, and based on lobbying action by participants in squatter movements, informal settlements may gain initial tacit acceptance and later legal recognition from authorities, sometimes via some compensation payment to the owner – and often in exchange for support for local politicians and bribery of officials.

However, legalisation cannot always be achieved. Authorities have razed many illegal settlements and dispersed or even prosecuted their inhabitants.

Relative Advantages for Users of Owner-Occupied, Rental, and Co-Op Housing

All housing tenures have specific advantages and drawbacks. While owner occupation offers the most comprehensive property rights, residential mobility is usually limited. Also, in some countries, certain forms of housing, for example, single-family homes, may only become available through purchase.

One of the most important differences between owner occupation and rental housing is the distribution of housing expenditure over time and its total amount. Also, owner-occupiers may profit from future capital gains of their property, which tenants do not. Finally, owner-occupiers need not contribute to any landlord's profit nor incur risks of extended vacancy. On the other hand, moving within the rental housing sector is less expensive.

Cooperative housing is a tenure quite similar to renting but with the advantage of more direct tenant participation and – possibly – with a chance to profit from capital gains.

Cost

When financing the purchase of an owner-occupied home fully with mortgage loans, buyers face high annuities during the early years of repayment. High interest rates – often a consequence of inflation – cause front-loading, that is, a steep increase in initial capital cost, excluding many households interested in acquiring a home. Previous savings may mitigate this effect by contributing a substantial down payment, which reduces the need for capital market financing. On the other hand, progressive devaluation of annuities over time gradually reduces the annuity load, especially during periods of high inflation.

This tenure is particularly attractive for persons who plan to repay their mortgage loan while they are economically active and who expect to enjoy their home free of capital cost on retirement.

Compared to this picture, rental-housing expenditure remains more stable in real terms. Initial rent will generally be lower than the annuity for a 100% loan-to-value (LTV) loan. On the other hand, by indexing, nominal rent continues to increase, eventually outpacing the equivalent expenditure for owner occupation. As rent payment continues after all loans are repaid, the investor/landlord receives net rent income, contributing to the anticipated yield.

For all tenures, running cost for physically identical homes is fairly similar, although the legal framework may differ. However, owner-occupiers of single-family homes may save on maintenance expenditure by contributing their own labour.

Risk distribution

Owner occupation provides maximum security of tenure. Rental housing, on the other hand, offers much greater flexibility but less tenure security.

During periods of varying interest rates for mortgage loans and hence annuities, rents fluctuate considerably less. While annuities for buyers may be similar to annual rent for tenants during low-interest periods, they remain exposed to rapid increase, as soon as variable interest rates rise.

Prestige/political preference

Apart from purely economic factors, owner-occupiers generally enjoy higher social prestige than tenants. Many housing politicians also believe that owner-occupiers tend towards political stability, while tenants might be more inclined to opt for political change.

See also: Housing Developers: Developed World; Housing Market Institutions; Housing Policy: Agents and Regulators; Institutions for Housing Supply; Intermediate Housing Tenures; Real Estate Agents; Rights to Housing Tenure; Submarkets.

Further Reading

Balchin P (1995) *Housing Policy – An Introduction*. London: Routledge.
Donner C (2000) *Housing Policies in the European Union*. Vienna: Donner.
Donner C (2006) *Housing Policies in Central Eastern Europe*. Vienna: Donner.
Donner C (2011) *Rental Housing Policy in Europe*. Vienna: Donner.
Jenkis WH (ed.) (1996) *Kompendium der Wohnungswirtschaft*. Munich, Germany: Oldenbourg.
Kofner S (2004) *Wohnungsmarkt und Wohnungswirtschaft*. Munich, Germany: Oldenbourg.

Housing and Labour Markets

P Flatau, University of Western Australia, Perth, WA, Australia

© 2012 Elsevier Ltd. All rights reserved.

Glossary

Housing assistance The provision of housing and financial support to households by government to meet housing needs.

Labour supply The decision of individuals and households as to whether or not they will participate in the labour market and, if so, their preferred hours of work.

Marginal effective tax rate The combined rate at which tax is levied and government income and housing support payments are withdrawn for each extra dollar of private income.

Neighbourhood effects The independent effect of neighbourhoods on labour market and other outcomes for residents.

Oswald hypothesis The thesis that a rise in the rate of homeownership leads to higher unemployment.

Regional mobility The movement of households across regions.

Spatial mismatch hypothesis The thesis that there is a mismatch between where people who face poor labour market prospects live and where jobs are located; discrimination by employers and in housing markets limits opportunities for relocation.

Introduction

Housing affects the labour market in a number of different ways. One important channel, which has received significant attention in recent years, links housing tenure to the regional mobility of labour and hence the efficiency of the labour market. Relocation costs are not neutral with respect to housing tenure. They are higher for homeowners than for renters. The high cost of selling in one location and buying in another, impedes the free movement of homeowners in reaction to spatially differentiated labour market shocks. Consequently, the labour market is less flexible than it would otherwise be and unemployment is higher. This hypothesis is commonly referred to as the Oswald thesis following the author's discussion of the idea in the 1997 volume of the *Journal of Economic Perspectives*.

A housing tenure–residential mobility–unemployment nexus is also advanced with respect to public housing. In the case of public housing, it is not so much high transaction costs that impede the movement of households from one region to another, but the location-specific nature of public housing allocations. Such allocations make it very difficult for tenants to transfer from one public housing authority to another in a different region, local government area or jurisdiction. Greater portability in public housing tenancies across regions and jurisdictions would assist in increasing the mobility of public housing tenants.

The literature that has developed around the Oswald thesis has provided rich insights into the channels through which housing tenure affects unemployment. The evidence generally supports the view that homeowners are less mobile between regions than private renters. However, homeowners also stay longer in their jobs and accrue higher returns to firm-specific human capital. Moreover, they may overcome the adverse impacts of regional immobility on unemployment outcomes by commuting longer distances to work, and being able to access jobs in their local areas more successfully than private renters. Furthermore, it would appear that the stresses of meeting high mortgage repayments results in mortgagors experiencing lower probabilities of unemployment, shorter unemployment durations, and higher rates of reemployment than outright owners. The same may also be true for renters seeking to become homeowners as they also face pressures to save for a down payment.

A related literature considers the impact that trends in the housing market, particularly those relating to house prices, may have on regional migration and commuting. Regional migration and commuting patterns respond to a range of housing market signals including actual house price levels, expected house price appreciation and housing scarcity. A two-way relationship exists between the labour market and the housing market: Strong labour market conditions and earnings draw migrants into regions, but strong housing market conditions prevent movement since expensive housing can deter entry into a region.

Another link between housing and labour markets, which has received considerable attention in both the research literature and among policy-makers, is that of the impact of housing assistance on labour supply decisions (see article Housing Subsidies and Work Incentives). The value of a rental subsidy together with eligibility and entitlement criteria may reduce the incentive of housing assistance recipients and those on housing assistance waiting lists to either participate in the labour force or increase their hours of work beyond very low levels. At the same time, however, the stability and security of tenure of public housing (relative to homelessness and short stays in marginalised housing) improves the educational and health outcomes of children, all other things being equal, leading to improved labour market prospects down the track.

Following Kain's (1986) seminal paper, there has been a sustained interest in mismatch between the location of low-income households and the location of employment opportunities. Under the spatial mismatch hypothesis (see article Policies to Address Spatial Mismatch), a loss of employment opportunities in a particular area may maroon households who are constrained by their limited housing opportunities in high-unemployment, low-income locations.

More recently, the spatial dimension of housing and labour markets has received attention in terms of neighbourhood effects: those living in very low-income low-employment neighbourhoods with deep social and health problems may have access to fewer educational, health and community resources, reduced access to transportation, and be stigmatised when applying for jobs (see article Housing and Neighbourhood Quality: Urban Regeneration).

This article considers only the direct link between housing and the labour market. However, housing impacts on a range of nonlabour market social outcomes and these outcomes may have important downstream effects in the labour market. For example, there is the argument that homeownership produces positive neighbourhood social capital effects as well as a range of positive impacts on family well-being and children's educational outcomes. Another claim is that policies favouring housing may drive up land and property prices displacing commercial and industrial sites so reducing employment-generating opportunities. On the other hand, house price inflation can be the source of wealth effects that prop up aggregate demand in the economy (see articles Housing Markets and Macroeconomic Policy; Monetary Policy, Wealth Effects and Housing).

In examining evidence on the labour market impacts of housing, it is important to recognise that isolating the independent effect of housing on labour market outcomes is a difficult matter, and much of the existing literature has not always been able to successfully deal with the statistical issues involved. There are four particularly important difficulties associated with measurement of the impact of housing on the labour market.

First, housing is only one of many factors influencing labour market outcomes and the omission of nonhousing influences will result in biased estimates of housing's impact. Second, while housing impacts on the labour market, the labour market influences housing. For example, accessing the owner-occupied market relies on some measure of success in the labour market, while the opposite is often true in terms of public housing. We expect, therefore, a strong association between housing tenure and labour market outcomes, but such an association is not proof of a causal relationship running from housing to the labour market. Third, housing may affect labour markets indirectly via its impact on some intermediate channel, and isolating this mechanism is tricky. Finally, both positive (and negative) housing and labour market outcomes could be the product of a range of other determinants, but these determinants are not easily measured, and their link to housing and labour markets not well understood.

This article is divided into four topic areas. The first concerns the nexus between housing tenure and unemployment. The second considers the broader link between housing and labour market dynamics. The relevant literature in both areas places considerable emphasis on the role of residential mobility. The third issue addressed in the article involves the impact housing assistance has on the supply of labour. A final section examines the spatial mismatch hypothesis and the role of neighbourhood effects.

Housing Tenure and Unemployment

A long-standing concern in the literature has been on whether public housing impedes interregional labour mobility and so increases unemployment over and above what it might otherwise be. Public housing tenants may be less mobile than private renters because of their security of tenure, and the nonportable nature of indirect subsidies.

A more recent point of interest is Oswald's hypothesis that the rise of homeownership and the decline in private renting in Organisation for Economic Co-operation and Development (OECD) countries has resulted in an increase in unemployment. Oswald's hypothesis is based largely around a residential mobility argument; namely, that relocation costs are higher for homeowners than for renters, a differential that some governments contribute to (and could alleviate) when transaction taxes are applied on property conveyance (see article Taxation Policy and Housing).

Public Housing and Regional Mobility

In a series of papers through the 1980s, Gordon Hughes and Barry McCormick examined the nexus between public housing, regional and local mobility, and unemployment in the United Kingdom. Hughes and

McCormick (1981, 1985) present evidence that public housing tenants exhibit different patterns of actual and planned migration and moving activity than households in other tenure categories, principally homeowners. The authors define a 'migrating' household as one in which the current address is in a different region to that a year previously and a 'moving' household as one that moves in the past year to any destination. Migration therefore typically represents long-distance moves between local government jurisdictions.

These papers report findings that public housing tenants were less likely to migrate between regions than owner-occupiers do, even though public housing tenants did not differ from homeowners in respect to their intentions to migrate. Nor did public housing tenants differ from homeowners in terms of the probability of making local moves. In a subsequent paper, Hughes and McCormick (1987) suggest that public housing policies – rental subsidies, policies in regard to transferring between regions, security of tenure, and waiting lists – act as an impediment to labour mobility while rent controls in the private rental market limit the availability of private rental accommodation. They further suggest that lower migration rates in the United Kingdom than in the United States reflect in part lower levels of public housing in the United States.

One difficulty with these early studies is that they do not account for the fact that unobservable characteristics may be correlated with both entry to public housing and a tendency to be less mobile across regions. This means that part of the observed regional mobility differentials found between housing tenures may be due to unobserved heterogeneity effects as compared to housing tenure effects per se. Nevertheless, the findings from this and other residential mobility studies have been used to support the case of those advocating privatisation of public housing (see article Privatisation of Social Housing), and measures to deregulate and revitalise private rental housing (see article Access and Affordability: Rent Regulation).

The Oswald Hypothesis

In a series of unpublished papers, Andrew Oswald argued that an important explanation for the secular rise in unemployment in OECD countries over the last 30 years was the increase in the rates of homeownership (Oswald, 1997). Based on a series of descriptive and simple time series analyses, Oswald concluded that for every 5% point increase in the rate of homeownership, the unemployment rate rose by 1% point.

Oswald's key explanation for the posited relationship between homeownership and unemployment is that homeowners are less willing, than private renters, to move when they become unemployed because they face higher transaction costs of relocation than private renters. He suggests that a decline in labour mobility feeds into higher rates of 'equilibrium unemployment'. Government policy actions, designed to increase homeownership rates, Oswald argues, have worsened the efficiency of the labour market. For example, because of higher rates of regional immobility, homeowners accept jobs for which they are not fully suited, and located in distant parts of a city or region. Homeowners then commute more than renters do, which results in transport congestion leading to higher costs of production and distribution in the economy, as well as external costs from carbon emissions and other air pollutants. Because of these additional costs, the efficiency of the economy declines and jobs are destroyed. The strong policy implication of this conjecture is that subsidies provided to households to enter homeownership have detrimental impacts on the labour market.

Despite the weak econometric foundations to Oswald's thesis, it has generated considerable interest in the literature. The evidence from a range of international studies supports the proposition that high transaction costs (including, importantly, taxes on property conveyance) inhibit regional moves by homeowners. Nevertheless, there is little support for the more general hypothesis that homeownership increases unemployment; countervailing positive impacts from homeownership having not been accounted for in the Oswald thesis.

In a contemporaneous US study, undertaken independently of Oswald but addressing the same issues, Goss and Phillips (1997) examined the impact of housing equity on the duration of unemployment using the 1986 US Panel Study of Income Dynamics (PSID). The authors found that homeownership reduces the duration of unemployment by between 11 and 17 weeks. The impact of homeownership on unemployment was stronger for mortgagors as compared to outright owners suggesting that mortgage repayments have a significant effect on labour market behaviour. Such a result is common across those studies, surprisingly few in number, which distinguish outright owners from mortgagors. In a subsequent US study, Coulson and Fisher (2002) find that homeowners have significantly lower probabilities of being unemployed and typically earn significantly higher wages than renters. They also find that homeownership exerts a significant negative influence upon the duration of unemployment.

Flatau et al. (2003) use Australian microdata to consider the role of different states of ownership (degrees of leverage) and types of tenancy (private, public, and rent-free) on unemployment. They find that higher homeownership causes lower unemployment and owners have significantly quicker exits from unemployment than do private renters. More importantly, however, they show that the key to these results is owners with mortgages who have a lower probability of being unemployed and exit a spell of unemployment faster. Both public housing tenants and those living rent-free are more likely than private renters to become unemployed. Public renters who become unemployed have longer durations of unemployment than do private or rent-free renters. On the basis of a Netherlands micropanel data set for the period 1989–98, Van Leuvensteijn and Koning (2004) find that homeowners who lose their jobs are more geographically mobile than renters who lose their jobs; a finding which contradicts Oswald's theory. Employed homeowners, in contrast, are found to be less mobile than renters are and less likely to switch jobs.

In their analysis of housing and unemployment linkages, Munch et al. (2006) distinguish between the case of an exit from unemployment to a local job and an exit to employment in a geographically distant labour market. They hypothesise that homeownership will have a positive effect on exits to local labour markets but not to distant labour markets (i.e., homeowners are immobile across regions relative to renters). Using Dutch data, they find that homeownership reduces the propensity to move regionally for job reasons (as suggested by Oswald) but improves the chances of finding local jobs. In net terms, and in contrast to the Oswald hypothesis, their study finds that homeownership reduces the duration of unemployment.

Battu et al. (2008) also examine the relationship between housing tenure and the duration of unemployment. They allow for different types of exit from unemployment and find that unemployed homeowners are more likely to gain a job locally (relative to private renting) and less likely to obtain a job nonlocally (with a move), but these effects are not large when all relevant statistical issues are accounted for. They also find that, relative to private renters, homeowners are less likely to leave their current job for nonlocal jobs. This then results in lower unemployment outcomes for homeowners.

Munch et al. (2008) switch attention to the duration of jobs (rather than the duration of unemployment) and argue that because of transaction costs, employed homeowners are less likely to move to nonlocal jobs than renters and will, therefore, stay longer in their jobs. This makes them more attractive to employers seeking to fill job vacancies, which require long-term investments in firm-specific human capital. The consequence is that homeowners will be offered higher wages, and will be less likely to leave their current job for other local jobs. Munch et al. (2008) find that homeowners have lower transitions to new local jobs, new nonlocal jobs, and into unemployment than private renters. They also receive higher pay. In other words, homeowners are more likely to stay put and reap the wage dividends of long tenures with the same employer.

Housing Market Dynamics and the Labour Market

Closely related to the studies surveyed above is a relatively large literature examining broader interactions between housing and labour markets, again with an emphasis on the role of regional migration.

Henley (1998) utilises longitudinal data from the British Household Panel Survey for the period 1991–94, to investigate the extent to which low or negative housing equity impedes individual household mobility, and whether a stagnant housing market impairs labour market flexibility. In the early 1990s, a collapse of the housing market in the United Kingdom was associated with a decline in turnover in the owner-occupied residential property market. The argument is that a household that cannot sell its home (or cannot sell at a sufficiently high price to meet a required deposit on the next home purchase) may find itself 'locked' into a home that provides an inappropriate level of housing services given current needs. Immobile households may seriously impair the ability of the labour market to match vacancies with potential employees. Their results suggest that households who bought their home as former local authority tenants are less likely to move, confirming the hypothesis that such households may be less mobile due to 'lock in' clauses in their contracts of sale that prevent instant arbitrage gains. Outright owners are also significantly less likely to move.

Other studies find that mortgagors had lower levels of residential mobility (particularly intra-regional moves) than those in other housing tenures, which may reflect the incidence of low and negative housing equity in the United Kingdom over the 1990s. The same finding is evident in US studies examining the impact of the recession of the early 1990s.

Bover et al. (1989) examine the dynamics of the housing and labour markets using time series data. Their model of the UK economy includes a number of housing and labour market interactions. One of these is the lower homeowner regional mobility channel examined above, but they also consider the role of house and land prices, and expectations of future house and land price movements on mobility. Their results suggest that house price differentials between regions increase unemployment at the aggregate level. The presumed channel is that of high house prices in South-East England depressing in-migration to a prosperous region, which results in higher than otherwise unemployment elsewhere (and higher earnings in the South East).

In subsequent work, Cameron and Muellbauer (1998) provide evidence on the role of both commuting and net migration between British regions. Their argument is that commuting can act as a substitute for migration when high house prices impede migration to prosperous areas. Using

UK census sources for 1981 and 1991, the authors suggest that, despite strong relative labour market pressures, there was a sharp decline over the 1987–89 period in net migration to the South East. High relative house prices during the 1980s house price boom discouraged in-migration to the South-East region, but rising relative earnings and falling relative unemployment encouraged 'in-commuting'. The evidence presented supports the hypothesis that migration responds strongly to relative earnings and relative employment prospects, as measured by the unemployment rate. However, high relative house prices discourage net migration to a region, though expected house price rises can act to partly offset this impact. Investment in transport and other infrastructure that facilitate in-commuting might help ease house price pressures, though whether there are efficiency gains is an open question.

Housing Assistance and Labour Supply

Housing assistance (subsidy) to consumers of housing involves the provision of rental subsidies to tenants in public housing; portable rental subsidies to low-income households in the private rental market (vouchers); and various forms of assistance to facilitate the accessibility and affordability of homeownership (see article Housing Markets and Macroeconomic Policy). There has been considerable interest in the literature on the impact that housing assistance may have on labour supply decisions and in the policy implications of the existing evidence.

The labour supply effects of housing assistance are generally modelled within a neoclassical economic framework in which individuals and households make rational utility maximising decisions on the hours of labour they wish to supply subject to the (after-tax and after-subsidy) wage rates they face, and their receipt of nonlabour income.

Within the neoclassical economic model, the provision of housing assistance may either increase or decrease the supply of labour, though there is a general presumption that housing assistance reduces the supply of labour. The provision of a housing subsidy leads to an improvement in the (non-labour-related) income position of a household, though that increase is tied to the consumption of housing. Economists generally assume that gains in non-labour-related income are associated with increases in the 'consumption' of 'leisure' (or a reduction in work hours), and losses with decreased consumption of leisure (an increase in work hours).

Housing subsidies are means tested in most jurisdictions. In other words, the value of housing assistance benefit is withdrawn at some fixed rate as the private market income (e.g., wage income) of the eligible recipient increases. With each extra dollar of wage income resulting in a loss of housing assistance, recipients face a marginal effective tax rate on their earnings that is higher than the statutory marginal income tax rate. Indeed the marginal effective tax rate on earnings may be very high at very low earnings. Highly effective marginal tax rates generate an incentive to substitute away from the now less rewarding work and into nonlabour activities (i.e., 'leisure'). This is known as the substitution effect. On the other hand housing assistance increases the income of recipients, and this could result in either more or less work. Typically, it is assumed that people prefer to devote more time to nonwork activities as their income increases, and if so, this 'income effect' reinforces the 'substitution effect' and hours of work fall.

In a targeted income support system, allowances and benefits are also means tested. Those receiving housing assistance will generally receive other forms of assistance. If the design of the housing allowance is such that it is withdrawn at the same time as other income support benefits, then this will further blunt work incentives. This 'multiple stacking' problem may be alleviated by ensuring that housing allowances are not withdrawn until other income support is exhausted. In-work incentives can be sharpened if social housing rents that are income related are not immediately adjusted on getting a job. The provision of rent holidays and the payment of other bonuses for obtaining employment are other policy options that some governments have introduced.

The standard neoclassical treatment of the impact of housing assistance on the supply of labour needs to be extended to take into account the nonfungibility of housing assistance (it cannot be cashed out and transferred to other goods). Recipients of the housing assistance may therefore consume higher levels of the subsidised good than would otherwise be the case if the transfer were in a cash form. If housing and leisure are substitutes (in the sense that they, at least partly, satisfy the same needs of people so that one can be used in replacement of the other) then the increase in the consumption of housing will be associated with a decrease in the consumption of leisure, or alternatively, an increase in the supply of labour. The opposite is true if housing and leisure are complements (consumption of one is valued more if accompanied by consumption of the other).

Many housing assistance programmes are rationed and require those seeking assistance to apply and join waiting lists; once they reach the top of the queue their application is considered. Examples of such approaches include housing vouchers in the United States, public housing in the United Kingdom, Australia and much of Western Europe. To remain eligible for support and move up the waiting list, households must maintain their low incomes in order to remain eligible for housing assistance. This can deter search for and acceptance of job offers. The waiting list (welfare lock) effect further adds to the negative labour supply consequences of housing assistance.

Any analysis of the impact of housing assistance on labour supply must take into account a number of indirect effects of housing assistance on the supply of labour over the longer term. As discussed above, the nontransferability of public housing subsidies means that such subsidies may lock in recipients to areas that have poor labour market prospects. Furthermore, if housing assistance provides greater security of tenure than would otherwise be the case, it may improve human capital accumulation, which in turn will result in improved labour market outcomes down the track. There is some evidence to suggest that living in public housing during childhood increased employment and raised earnings in young adulthood.

Shroder (2002) provided a comprehensive review of the US evidence on the labour supply impacts of housing assistance and concludes that the evidence is not conclusive with respect to employment effects. In part, this reflects the difficulties involved in deriving robust estimates of the independent impact of housing assistance on the supply of labour. However, Shroder's (2002) conclusion also echoes the conflicting findings of the studies themselves; some concluding that housing assistance reduces labour supply, others increasing labour supply, but the majority finding no significant effect of housing assistance on labour force participation and hours of work. In reviewing more recent US evidence on the labour supply impacts of housing assistance, Shroder (see article Housing Subsidies and Work Incentives) suggests that housing assistance in the United States has a net negative impact on labour supply but the "impact appears to vary among subgroups, may change over time, and seems rather small relative to the amounts paid out in subsidy."

In a recent study of the long-run employment participation of Australian public housing tenants, Wood et al. (2009) use a series of cross-sectional data sets to find that between 1982 and 2002, the proportion of male public renters in employment effectively halved. Almost all of this reduction in employment rates, however, was due to the changing composition of those in public rental housing rather than changes in-work incentives. In 2002, as compared to 1982, more male public housing tenants were less 'employable', relative to males in other tenures, because of their lower levels of human capital and past employment histories. This was not the case for female public housing renters where both compositional and economic incentive effects seem to have played a role in the decline in employment rates.

The Spatial Mismatch Hypothesis and Neighbourhood Effects

The spatial mismatch hypothesis asserts that in many cities and regions poor people reside in areas distant from where jobs are located and may face barriers in trying to overcome this spatial disadvantage thereby perpetuating patterns of poverty and inequality (see article Policies to Address Spatial Mismatch). In the United States, the spatial mismatch hypothesis was advanced in response to a specific concern, namely, the poor labour market outcomes of African American inner-city residents who are disconnected from suburban job opportunities; racial discrimination in the suburban housing market and among employers being viewed as critical impediments to improved outcomes. In Australia and Europe, the opposite spatial mismatch concerns motivated policy discussion – cheap housing at the periphery attracting unskilled workers, but many unskilled jobs remained in inner-city areas.

Gobillon et al. (2007) posit a number of channels through which spatial mismatch may occur. On the supply side, unemployed people may decide not to take up jobs because commuting costs are too high relative to the wage offered, their job search efficiency decreases with distance to jobs (individuals get less information on distant job opportunities), and workers may incur high search costs in more distant neighbourhoods. On the demand side, employers may discriminate against those from poorer neighbourhoods because of the stigma or prejudice associated with their residential location, or because they are satisfying the prejudice of their local customers. Finally, and most importantly, those seeking to move from low-employment areas to areas where jobs are more abundant may face high housing costs and discrimination in those housing markets where jobs are more plentiful. Of the above channels, some such as commuting costs are market driven. Those channels linked to discrimination in housing and labour markets motivated Kain's (1968) seminal statement of the spatial mismatch hypothesis.

Gobillon et al. (2007) report that the trend towards suburbanisation in the United States began in the postwar period, continued throughout the twentieth century and was accompanied by a movement of jobs to the periphery of cities. They suggest that the key link to the spatial mismatch hypothesis is that "entry level jobs grew in the suburbs and declined in city centres where low-skilled minorities remain located" (p. 2404). Two arguments are presented for this proposition. First, that service industries using low-skilled workers grew in the better-off outlying residential suburban areas to meet growing consumer demand. Second, firms that hire low-skilled workers wanted to avoid central locations where land was scarcer and becoming more expensive.

The evidence is limited with respect to the importance of major channels through which spatial mismatch can arise. However, there is clear evidence from existing studies that commuting costs and discrimination may play a significant role in sustaining higher than otherwise unemployment among inner-city residents (the US case). Weaker evidence exists for the other supply-side determinants; namely, the increase in search costs and the decrease in search efficiency with distance.

Closely connected to the spatial mismatch hypothesis is the neighbourhood effects model. This suggests that neighbourhoods may have independent positive and negative effects on their residents (see article Policies to Address Social Mix in Communities). For example, those in low-income low-employment neighbourhoods typically have poorer access to educational, health and community resources, and experience higher crime and drug-related problems. These problems then may exacerbate any underlying individual- and housing-level adverse labour market impacts.

There is a large US literature attempting to estimate the size of independent labour market-related neighbourhood effects. In particular, this literature has focused on the role of housing assistance programmes designed to offer relocation opportunities to residents from distressed neighbourhoods. This evidence includes findings from a randomised control trial of the US Department of Housing and Urban Development's Moving to Opportunity (MTO) programme (see article Social Housing and Employment). Housing-assisted tenants living in neighbourhoods with high concentrations of poverty were invited to volunteer for the MTO programme and then randomly assigned to one of three groups: Group 1 was offered rent assistance vouchers that could only be used in areas with less than 10% poverty rates; Group 2 was offered rent assistance vouchers that could be used in any location, and Group 3 was an in-place control group who continued to receive their current project-based assistance in poverty-concentrated locations. MTO and other similar programmes aim to move people to jobs to address spatial mismatch. There is also a case for moving jobs to people, using financial incentives and spatial programmes such as neighbourhood renewal (see article Housing and Neighbourhood Quality: Urban Regeneration). A related US programme is HOPE VI which seeks to improve social and economic outcomes for public housing tenants through individual incentives designed to improve self-sufficiency, planning mechanisms designed to reduce the concentration of public housing by placing public housing in nonpoverty neighbourhoods and improving partnerships with government agencies, local governments, nonprofit organizations, and private businesses (see article HOPE VI).

Conclusion

Housing impacts on labour market outcomes through a number of channels. One that has received significant attention is that of housing tenure, residential mobility, and unemployment. High relocation expenses inhibit the movement of homeowners from one location to another in reaction to spatially differentiated labour market shocks. Public housing tenants may also find themselves locked into areas because of difficulties in accessing affordable housing options in areas of higher employment. However, while there is good evidence that the hypothesised housing tenure and residential mobility channel operates, it is also clear that there are a number of offsetting effects. Homeowners stay longer in their jobs, commute longer distances to work (so partially offsetting their regional immobility) and access jobs in their local areas more successfully than private renters; all of which acts to lower unemployment. As there is significant evidence to suggest that mortgagors experience lower probabilities and shorter spells of unemployment, it is clear that additional factors are at work in influencing labour market outcomes. The relatively high housing costs experienced by mortgagors as compared to outright owners may represent an important driver of outcomes. The fact that high transaction costs and public housing allocation mechanisms may impair labour market flexibility through reducing residential mobility provides an important avenue for policy intervention.

Neoclassical labour supply theory does not provide a clear-cut answer to the question of whether housing assistance reduces or increases labour supply. However, there is a greater presumption in favour of the proposition that housing assistance reduces labour supply, particularly in light of the fact that traditional forms of means testing of housing assistance lead to high marginal effective tax rates at low levels of wage income; reforms to rent setting in social housing may act to negate such negative impacts especially when combined with programmes which provide positive incentives for individual self-sufficiency.

A long-standing interest in the literature on housing and labour markets is the mismatch between the location of low-income households and the location of employment opportunities. In the United States, the spatial mismatch hypothesis was developed to explain the poor labour market outcomes of African American inner-city residents who became disconnected from growing suburban job opportunities. Racial discrimination in the suburban housing market and among employers is advanced as a critical impediment to improved outcomes and provides an obvious avenue for policy action. One area where there has been significant policy intervention in the United States is in respect of support to residents of distressed neighbourhoods who move in search of new opportunities. Neighbourhood renewal programmes and location-specific financial targets have also been implemented in enhancing opportunities for residents of disadvantaged and distressed neighbourhoods.

In examining the evidence on the impact of housing and neighbourhoods on the labour market, a cautionary approach should be adopted. Isolating the independent effect on labour market outcomes is a difficult matter and much of the existing literature has not always been able to successfully deal with the statistical issues involved. Moreover, housing and neighbourhoods may impact on a range of variables such as educational opportunities which will feed through to the labour market only after a period of time.

See also: Access and Affordability: Rent Regulation; HOPE VI; Housing and Neighbourhood Quality: Urban Regeneration; Housing Markets and Macroeconomic Policy; Housing Subsidies and Work Incentives; Monetary Policy, Wealth Effects and Housing; Policies to Address Social Mix in Communities; Policies to Address Spatial Mismatch; Privatisation of Social Housing; Social Housing and Employment; Taxation Policy and Housing.

References

Battu H, Ma A, and Phimister E (2008) Housing tenure, job mobility and unemployment in the UK. *The Economic Journal* 118: 311–328.
Bover O, Muellbauer J, and Murphy A (1989) Housing, wages and UK labour markets. *Oxford Bulletin of Economics and Statistics* 51: 97–136.
Cameron G and Muellbauer J (1998) The housing market and regional commuting and migration choices. *Scottish Journal of Political Economy* 45: 420–446.
Coulson NE and Fisher NM (2002) Tenure choice and labor market outcomes. *Housing Studies* 17: 35–49.
Flatau P, Forbes M, Hendershott P, and Wood G (2003) *Unemployment and Homeownership: The Roles of Leverage and Public Housing*. NBER Working Paper 10021.
Gobillon L, Selod H, and Zenou Y (2007) The mechanisms of spatial mismatch. *Urban Studies* 44: 2401–2427.
Goss EP and Phillips JM (1997) The impact of home ownership on the duration of unemployment. *Review of Regional Studies* 27: 9–27.
Henley A (1998) Residential mobility, housing equity and the labour market. *The Economic Journal* 108: 414–427.
Hughes GA and McCormick B (1981) Do council housing policies reduce migration between regions? *Economic Journal* 91: 919–937.
Hughes GA and McCormick B (1985) Migration intentions in the UK: which households want to migrate and which succeed? *Economic Journal* 95(Conference Supplement): 76–95.
Hughes GA and McCormick B (1987) Housing markets, unemployment and labour market flexibility in the UK. *European Economic Review* 31: 615–641.
Kain J (1968) Housing segregation, negro employment, and metropolitan decentralization. *Quarterly Journal of Economics* 82: 175–197.
Munch JR, Rosholm M, and Svarer M (2006) Are home owners really more unemployed? *The Economic Journal* 116: 911–1013.
Munch JR, Rosholm M, and Svarer M (2008) Home ownership, job duration, and wages. *Journal of Urban Economics* 63: 130–145.
Oswald AJ (1997) Thoughts on NAIRU. *Journal of Economic Perspectives* 11: 227–228.
Shroder M (2002) Does housing assistance perversely affect self-sufficiency? A review essay. *Journal of Housing Economics* 11: 381–417.
Van Leuvensteijn M and Koning P (2004) The effect of home-ownership on labor mobility in the Netherlands. *Journal of Urban Economics* 55: 580–596.
Wood GA, Ong R, and Dockery AM (2009) The long-run decline in employment participation for Australian public housing tenants: an investigation. *Housing Studies* 24: 103–126.

Further Reading

Murphy A, Muellbauer J, and Cameron G (2006) *Housing Market Dynamics and Regional Migration in Britain*, University of Oxford, Department of Economics Discussion Paper Series, No. 275. Oxford, UK: University of Oxford Press.

Housing and Neighbourhood Quality: Home Improvement Grants

P Leather, University of Manchester, Manchester, UK

© 2012 Elsevier Ltd. All rights reserved.

Glossary

Amenities Features of the dwelling such as water supply, WC, washing and bathing facilities, kitchen facilities, and facilities for the disposal of sewage and waste.

Enveloping (sometimes Group Repair, Block Repair) Repairs and improvements to a number of adjacent dwellings carried out simultaneously to secure greater effectiveness and economy, usually focussing on repairs to external areas/features such as roof, walls, and windows.

Home improvement agencies Organisations specialising in assisting owners (especially older or disabled people) to organise and carry out repairs and improvements to their homes.

Home improvement (or repair) grant Financial assistance, normally nonrepayable, provided by the state to assist an owner with repairs or improvements to the home.

Improvements Works to a dwelling designed to add features not previously present or to upgrade existing features to a higher standard.

Repairs Works to a dwelling designed to remedy defects or deterioration.

Reverse mortgages Financial mechanisms to assist owners to borrow money secured against the value of their homes, usually distinguished from normal mortgages by arrangements for the deferral or rolling up of interest and capital repayments.

Introduction

It is inevitable that the physical condition of dwellings deteriorates and that investment is required to maintain them, or in extreme cases to remove them from the housing stock. This is partly a function of time and of climatic conditions, but initial construction standards, ongoing usage, and levels of investment also play a part in determining dwelling condition. Expectations over what are reasonable standards of accommodation, and the facilities and features which are required to make houses habitable, also evolve over time.

Housing standards of course vary enormously, both between and within developed and developing countries, in part as a function of national and individual economic circumstances. This article cannot consider housing standards and approaches to maintaining or improving them across the many different international contexts. It focuses in particular on state interventions to address perceived poor housing conditions and housing improvements in the United Kingdom, and specifically in England and Wales, since the middle of the twentieth century. The United Kingdom experienced the Industrial Revolution and large-scale urbanisation at a relatively early stage, leaving it with a large stock of ageing dwellings built to meet the needs of industry at a time when building standards were often poor and relatively few amenities were provided. Dealing with this legacy has proved a challenging process because of the inability or unwillingness of many owners to invest and the constraints posed by the nature of the stock requiring investment.

This experience is of wider interest, perhaps mostly to other European countries with similar forms of housing, but beyond this to other developed countries, as an example of the difficulties associated with sustaining the housing stock in good condition, and increasingly, minimising the impact of housing on carbon emissions and climate change.

The article first looks at the factors which created a need for state intervention to improve poor housing conditions in England and Wales. It goes on to describe the introduction of state-funded grants to homeowners, initially for the installation of basic amenities which were not provided when dwellings were constructed but subsequently, as awareness of the causes of under-investment grew, to provide assistance with essential repairs and maintenance. The article goes on to look at the emergence of other policy issues on which housing condition can impact, notably the link between housing conditions and poor health, the disproportionate effect of poor conditions on older people, and the impact of housing usage on carbon emissions.

Poor Housing Conditions

The Industrial Revolution in Great Britain led to the creation in the nineteenth century of a large volume of housing to accommodate workers in cities, towns, and industrial areas. Most of the housing created was of poor quality, constructed to extremely high densities using poor materials and techniques and lacking modern amenities. Throughout the nineteenth century and well into the twentieth, most industrial workers rented their accommodation from private landlords, whose main aim was to extract the maximum return from rents. As a result, there was a chronic level of investment in repairs or improvements. From 1919, state controls on rent levels further depressed investment in the housing stock (see article Access and Affordability: Rent Regulation).

Increasing awareness of poor housing conditions and a growing understanding of the potential links between poor housing and health were the early drivers of intervention by the state in the housing market in Britain in the late nineteenth century, and such policies have remained an important strand of intervention (see article Health and Housing). The first form of intervention was the demolition and replacement of substandard housing, which the state acquired compulsorily from private landlords at very low cost. But as the very worst stock was removed and compensation levels rose, this policy was abandoned and clearance activity has shrunk to almost negligible levels in the privately owned stock. In the latter part of the twentieth century, the refurbishment of poor-condition dwellings has become the main means of intervention, either through the acquisition and renovation of dwellings by housing associations or through the provision of capital grants to owners.

Scale of Grant Provision

Since 1949, more than five million grants have been provided in England and Wales (**Table 1**). The programme peaked in the 1980s, and has subsequently declined in scale, but it remains significant with average annual expenditure of £460 million in England over the past 10 years. As **Table 1** shows, the type of grant provided has changed over time, as explained below.

Grants as an Expedient

Renovation grants were first introduced on a significant scale in 1949. At this stage, grant aid was seen as a short-term expedient to tide over the older dwelling stock until it could be demolished. With the majority of poor condition private housing owned by private landlords, local authorities made some use of compulsion to require landlords to undertake works, but this proved difficult and grant aid (covering 50% of improvement costs) was made available to encourage landlords to invest. The scale of activity was small and there was political opposition in many areas to the provision of grants to landlords for arrears of repairs. Assistance was focussed on the provision of basic amenities such as an indoor cold water supply or indoor WC (water closet; toilet) which had never been present in the affected dwellings. Grants were seen as an incentive to owners to invest and as compensation for the lack of return on investment, arising from regulation of rent increases. Maximum value limits were set to restrict grants to smaller dwellings.

Although grants were targeted at landlords, owner-occupiers responded most actively to the initiative. Since 1949, private landlords had begun to sell off their holdings of older dwellings and increasing prosperity allowed many tenants to purchase the dwellings they lived in. In his book *Housing Policy in Britain*, Holmans (1987) estimates that 1.25 million dwellings in England and Wales were transferred from the private rented sector into owner-occupation between 1953 and 1961, with a further 850 000 in the following decade. The average number of grants approved for private owners increased from around 40 000 per annum in the late 1950s to 90 000 in the early 1960s.

Renovation rather than Demolition

By the mid-1960s, the view of renovation as a temporary expedient before clearance was revised. Owner-occupation levels in the older housing stock continued to rise, and the costs of acquisition for demolition and compensation mushroomed. There was growing opposition among owners to clearance, and housing in the very worst condition had by then been dealt with. The issue was one of neglect or disrepair rather than inherently substandard construction or layout. Commentators have also stressed the importance of the mid-1960s fiscal crises, which led the government to look for cheaper alternatives to clearance policies.

After a period of review, the 1969 Housing Act changed the framework of grant aid to meet the new objective of giving poor-condition dwellings a longer life. Grant levels were substantially increased, and importantly repair work (as distinct from the addition of absent amenities or facilities) became eligible for grant assistance. It was recognised that poor-condition dwellings tended to be concentrated together and that such concentrations were a disincentive to individual owners to invest, so local authorities were given powers to designate General Improvement Areas (GIAs), neighbourhoods of around 250–500 dwellings, where rates of grant were more generous. This led to a rapid growth in take-up (see article Housing and Neighbourhood Quality: Urban Regeneration).

No account was taken of the ability of applicants to finance investment from their own resources. It soon

Table 1 Grants to homeowners, England and Wales, 1969–2008

Year	Improvement	Intermediate	Repair	Renovation and disabled facilities	Renovation only	Disabled facilities only	Total
1969	23 298	50 311					73 609
1970	29 795	47 375					77 170
1971	48 937	48 724					97 661
1972	88 624	48 484					137 108
73	144 209	39 989					184 198
1974	186 888	30 188					217 076
1975	79 660	13 000	89				92 749
1976	63 738	11 377	160				75 275
1977	54 303	9 425	244				63 972
1978	54 869	8 354	362				63 585
1979	62 791	8 191	493				71 475
1980	72 598	8 555	660				81 813
1981	54 656	15 523	5 862				76 041
1982	59 782	21 836	33 399				115 017
1983	86 762	28 925	131 468				247 155
1984	92 295	31 643	135 147				259 085
1985	57 798	32 524	63 242				153 564
1986	50 978	28 213	52 708				131 899
1987	53 860	23 146	50 999				128 005
1988	53 357	20 207	51 926				125 490
1989	54 433	16 803	47 187				118 423
1990	57 526	15 073	41 590	954			115 143
1991	18 536	5 247	12 515	33 894			70 192
1992	2 880	958	1 260	61 481			66 579
1993	464	141	164	65 441			66 210
1994	236	56	58	70 367			70 717
1995		14		73 098			73 112
1996					73 940	20 060	94 000
1997					108 923	24 552	133 475
1998					119 969	26 230	146 199
1999					130 976	26 910	157 886
2000					109 814	29 500	139 314
2001					91 854	29 758	121 612
2002					77 604	35 017	112 621
2003					64 400	41 598	105 998
2004					68 080	43 143	111 223
2005					66 100	40 208	106 308
2006					97 080	43 169	140 249
2007					100 910	43 960	144 870
2008					118 360	41 790	160 150

Sources: Leather P and Morrison T (1997) *The State of UK Housing*. Bristol: The Policy Press. Department of Communities and Local Government Live table 313, Welsh Assembly Government Welsh Housing Statistics 2003, table 3.2.

emerged, particularly in London, that landlords were using grant aid to renovate housing previously occupied by low-income tenants and selling these units to more affluent owner-occupiers. Accordingly, there were revisions to grant provision in 1974 to target assistance on low-income owner-occupiers. The underlying problem was that such owners could not in many cases raise their share of the costs of work. One response was a new 75% grant rate, but in addition an entirely new grant, the Repair Grant, was introduced to assist solely with repairs rather than improvements. This was a radical shift from the initial objective of grant aid. Most importantly, it was an implicit recognition that wider state policies to encourage more households to own their homes were not practical, or sustainable, without the provision of further assistance to low-income owners of poor-condition dwellings. Older people, those who had become unemployed, and single-parent households were highlighted in circular advice from government.

The Rise of Repair Grants

The new repair grants were only available to residents of GIAs, and those living in a new type of area, the Housing Action Area (HAA), intended to assist local authorities address the problems of neighbourhoods with social and economic deprivation as well as poor physical conditions.

But activity levels during the later 1970s failed to regain the impetus of the early years of the decade, and in 1980, the government extended the provision of repair grants to areas of pre-1919 housing outside HAAs and GIAs. In 1982, during a period of recession in the economy, the government announced a temporary 1 year increase in repairs grants to over 90% of costs for all pre-1919 dwellings. Local authorities were deluged with applications which peaked at 135 000 in 1984.

This boost to investment was less significant in improving housing conditions than it seemed. Under the sudden pressure of demand, the supply of builders was overwhelmed and many 'cowboy' operators entered the market. Most applications came from people living in dwellings which were not in the worst condition. There was still no test of the applicant's resources and many would have been able to afford to carry out work anyway. Older homeowners, who were particularly likely to live in poor conditions, were seriously underrepresented.

One impact of the growth in repair grant aid was its impact on the attitudes and expectations of homeowners in older housing areas. The availability of 90% grants supported the view that the state, rather than individual owners, would take responsibility for major repair work in older homes. Grant aid was thus, arguably, a disincentive to further work rather than the incentive originally intended.

Enveloping

This approach reached its zenith in the mid-1980s when some local authorities developed an approach known as enveloping. This involved the simultaneous repair of the external elements of blocks or terraces of older privately owned housing through large contracts organised by a local authority. Enveloping had the advantage over piecemeal grant provision of allowing for professional design and contract management to ensure that work was carried out to a high standard. As contracts were large, they attracted larger builders and obtained economies of scale and professional project management techniques. In most cases, occupants or owners were not required to contribute at all to the costs of schemes. In effect, therefore, the grant represented 100% of the costs of works. It was hoped that owners would be encouraged to invest resources in internal works, although these could also be grant aided. Block Repair and Group Repair were similar concepts that sometimes required contributions from owners.

Means Testing

Grant provision had been transformed from its original focus as a temporary source of funding to private landlords to tide poor-condition dwellings over until demolition, to a major mechanism for assisting low-income owners to undertake repairs and improvements which they otherwise could not afford. The change in the ownership pattern of pre-1919 housing from private renting to home-ownership was the driver of this shift. Remarkably, the expansion of grant provision in the 1980s took place against a background of severe reductions in many other areas of housing public expenditure. In Leather and Murie's study published in 1986, the authors argue that grants should be seen as part of a package of measures to support and enhance owner-occupation including increased spending on mortgage interest tax relief.

By the mid-1980s, however, the government had decided to draw back from this commitment. The key development was the introduction in 1990 of a means test for grant aid to target assistance on low-income owners and the replacement of Repair and Improvement Grants by a new all-embracing Renovation Grant. Surprisingly, grant was initially made available as of right (subject to the means test) for all works necessary to meet a minimum standard of fitness for human habitation, but this was soon amended in 1996 when the provision of grant aid became discretionary to limit spending. In 2002, local authorities were given a wider power to offer their own tailor-made forms of assistance through grant aid, repayable loans, or assistance in kind. **Table 1** shows the continuance of grant aid since then, but there are no readily available data on the scale of other activity. The policy has featured little in policy debate, as considered further below.

Area-Based Renewal and Urban Regeneration

The debates which resulted in the introduction of Renovation Grants in 1990 covered a range of other emerging issues. As already indicated, area-based renewal mechanisms such as GIAs and HAAs had long been part of private sector housing renewal policy. Despite the introduction of means-testing, area renewal measures were reinvigorated through a new mechanism, the Renewal Area. These covered much larger areas than GIAs or HAAs. Parallel developments in urban regeneration policy at the time concluded that successful regeneration would require housing renovation to be accompanied by broader measures such as the provision of training and creation of employment opportunities, the provision of social and community facilities, improved educational facilities, environmental improvements to eliminate pollution, and measures to combat crime and antisocial behaviour (see article Housing and Neighbourhood Quality: Urban Regeneration). Renewal areas were seen as a focus for these initiatives.

Community Care

Older people living in private rented or owner-occupied housing had long been identified as one of the groups most likely to experience poor housing conditions, but they are also among those most unlikely to make use of grant aid. There were several reasons for this. Low incomes prevented many older people from meeting their matching contribution to the grant aid. Inflexibility in regulations about the work required to be eligible for grant assistance often made work too disruptive for older people to cope with. The practical difficulties of organising repairs and improvements were also argued to be too great for more vulnerable older people. During the 1980s, pressure groups such as Shelter and sheltered housing providers such as Anchor Trust lobbied for measures to make grant assistance more accessible to older people, and pioneered the establishment of home improvement agencies to provide older people with practical help in carrying out work. These issues became increasingly prominent in the 1990s as a result of the steady ageing of the population, and as more people entered old age as homeowners with responsibility for the repair and maintenance of their homes.

There were two responses. The first was the introduction in 1990 of a new small grant, Minor Works Assistance, that was restricted initially to older people. This was replaced in 1996 by Home Repair Assistance, a grant with a maximum value of £2000, also available to younger households on means-tested state benefits. The purpose of this grant was to assist people to live independently rather than to secure the repair or improvement of their dwelling – a significant distinction.

The second major link with community care policy was provided by the introduction of grant aid to cover adaptations to dwellings for disabled people. Grants had been used in the past for this purpose but mainly as a by-product of repair work. The new Disabled Facilities Grant (DFG) was, like the Renovation Grant, means-tested, but significantly the grant was made mandatory (available as of right) for most types of adaptation work. After a slow start, demand for these grants increased rapidly. By 1996, DFGs had come to account for almost 20% of spending on private sector renovation and by 2008 they represented 53%. This growth in spending at the expense of funding for renovation has been a cause of debate, but an equally strong debate is concerned with the extent to which actual spending on DFGs falls short of what is required to meet the rising need for assistance.

Climate Change and Sustainability

Other issues have also impacted on private sector renovation policies. As the need to reduce CO_2 emissions has gained prominence, measures to achieve higher standards of insulation and improvements to the efficiency of heating systems in private housing have become more prominent (see articles Climate Change and Building Regulations for Energy Conservation). These are established uses for grant funding in association with repair and improvement works, and at various times other dedicated pots of funding have been made available.

Housing and Health

Growing awareness of the specific impacts of poor housing on health has also become increasingly important. During the 2000s, and after long debate, the minimum standard for housing in Britain was changed to take more specific account of risks to health. Initiatives have also been developed to combat environmental pollutants such as radon, carbon monoxide, and lead in water pipes.

There are arguments that other agencies (such as the National Health Service or local authority Social Services Departments) should contribute to the funding of this kind of assistance, because of the preventative benefits which would be achieved, but these have achieved only limited success.

Housing Market Renewal

In the late 1990s, evidence emerged of increasing vacancy rates in some parts of the older private housing stock, generally in the inner areas of the conurbations or in smaller industrial areas which had experienced serious decline. Often the housing in these areas had previously enjoyed large-scale public investment through grant aid, but the benefit appeared to be short-lived. Research identified this problem as being caused by low or weak demand for housing, arising from population loss and low levels of new household formation, both in turn being caused by economic decline.

This led to a major programme of investment from 2004 onwards through the designation of nine Housing Market Renewal Pathfinders, which served as the channel for larger-scale public funding aiming to regenerate housing markets in the worst-affected areas. However, the programme has been a major channel for public funding directed to private sector housing renovation since 2004, mostly through Group Repair schemes, accounting for an equivalent sum to that made available through dedicated private sector renewal funding channels. Some 32 local authorities in England have benefited from this source. Further discussion of this important initiative can be found in the study conducted by Leather et al. (2007) on behalf of the Department of Communities and Local Government in Britain.

Equity Release

The introduction of means-tested grants from 1990 onwards focussed attention on other potential sources which homeowners might access to fund renovation work. The equity which some owners had accumulated in their homes was identified as a major potential source, although policy-makers in many other areas also eyed its potential. The significance of equity was highlighted by the steep increase in property values nationally in the late 1990s and early 2000s which affected even low-value areas. In some cases (especially younger people who had recently purchased a home with a mortgage), the amount of equity available was limited, but for outright owners, or those with a small mortgage relative to the value of their home, the potential of this source was greater. Unfortunately, many of these equity-rich owners (many of whom were older people) often lacked sufficient income to meet the repayment costs of a loan, or were otherwise ineligible. Many older people were also reluctant to borrow because they had no experience of debt, or wished to retain the equity in their homes to bequeath to heirs. More generally, there was also the paradox that dwellings requiring greater expenditure on repairs or improvements tended to have lower values, irrespective of the circumstances of the owner. In the late 1990s and early 2000s, some financial institutions developed equity-release products permitting the deferral of loan and interest repayments (mainly aimed at older people), but these were unpopular because accumulated interest charges could quickly mount up, and the resulting outstanding debt could even exceed the resale value of the home.

Despite these limitations, a few local authorities and other agencies sought to develop specialist equity release or loan products. These sought to tap into private sector finance (e.g., by using capital from banks or building societies), but mainstream lenders were cautious about involvement in this market. Most schemes sought public sector funding to meet start-up costs and initial lending, even if they aimed to sell their loans on to the private sector. Funding for this was in short supply. None of these schemes took off on a substantial scale, ultimately because of a lack of demand rather than the supply of finance. Since 2007, the schemes have been marginalised as a result of the more general restrictions on lending resulting from the credit crunch, and latterly from cuts in public funding.

Individual investors, of course, have always been responsible for the majority of investment in the private housing stock. Much investment is undertaken by more affluent households, often on the improvement of newer housing, or on the gentrification of some parts of the older housing stock (see article Gentrification and Neighbourhood Change). The problem is that levels of private investment in older housing occupied by those on lower incomes are more limited and often fall short of what is required to keep up with normal deterioration.

The Revival of the Private Rented Sector

One of the key developments in the British housing market since the late 1990s has been the growth of the private rented sector after almost a century of decline (see article Private Rental Landlords: Europe). Some of the growth in private renting has occurred in the new build market, but there has also been a large volume of investment in lower-value older dwellings, attracted by the potential for high rates of return, especially during periods of rapid growth in values. Although a range of measures have sought to attract institutional capital into housing investment, most investors have been individuals with small portfolios, often less than five dwellings. Many are reluctant to reduce returns by investing in high-quality repairs or in improvements which may not recoup their costs in terms of increased rental yield or capital growth. Others simply lack the resources to invest. Surveys of housing condition such as the Department of Communities and Local Government's English Housing Survey consistently show that privately rented dwellings are more likely to be in poor condition than those in the owner-occupied or social rented sector. They are also least likely to be energy-efficient. This suggests that a decline in housing conditions can be expected in some parts of the private rented sector and, more importantly, in neighbourhoods where there are concentrations of housing in this tenure.

Conclusion

Grants for the improvement and repair of private sector housing were conceived initially as a mechanism for the short-term amelioration of poor housing conditions in older housing pending demolition and replacement, in a context where most dwellings were of very low value and in the ownership of private landlords. With the subsequent transfer of much of the pre-1919 housing stock into owner-occupation, the function of grant aid shifted to fund the provision of basic amenities and improved facilities which many low-income owners could not afford to carry out. The policy became one-directed as much at sustaining homeownership among those on low incomes as at securing improvements to physical conditions. Over time, grants shifted from being an equal partnership between the owner and the state to a situation where the state bore most or even all of the costs. For a long time, grant aid was shielded from the impact of the 1980s cuts in public spending because of the importance of homeownership in government policy, but eventually in the 1990s means testing was introduced to restrict aid to those on low incomes.

From the 1990s onwards, the objectives of grant provision also became increasingly diverse, playing a part in wider area regeneration, community care, and environmental sustainability. Efforts were made to develop other mechanisms including better access to loan finance to bring more private sector investment into the improvement of older houses, with limited success.

With the prospect of major retrenchment in public expenditure more generally, it is difficult to see the survival of a major programme of public investment in housing renovation. Equally unlikely is any extension of powers to compel owners to undertake investment for their own or their tenants' benefit. The abolition of a simple and low-cost measure (the Home Information Pack) to compel people selling homes to make buyers aware of potential repair costs and energy efficiency was one of the first actions of the 2010 Coalition Government, suggesting that such issues are a very low priority. Yet a potentially serious hazard as measured under the Housing Health and Safety Rating System was present in around 4.8 million homes in 2008, representing 22% of the housing stock. Some 7.4 million homes (33% of the total in England) fell below the Decency Standard in 2008 and 1.2 million vulnerable households were living in homes that failed to meet the decency standard. Houses are one of the major sources of greenhouse gas emissions. The number of older people in private sector housing needing adaptations and other amenities continues to rise. All this suggests that poor housing conditions will quickly return to the top of housing policy agendas.

See also: Access and Affordability: Rent Regulation; Building Regulations for Energy Conservation; Climate Change; Gentrification and Neighbourhood Change; Health and Housing; Housing and Neighbourhood Quality: Urban Regeneration; Private Rental Landlords: Europe.

References

Holmans A (1987) *Housing Policy in Britain*. London: Croom Helm.
Leather P and Morrison T (1997) *The State of UK Housing*. Bristol, UK: The Policy Press.
Leather P and Murie A (1986) The decline in public expenditure. In: Malpass P (ed.) *The Housing Crisis*, pp. 25–56. London: Routledge.
Leather P, Cole I, Ferrari E, et al. (2007) *National Evaluation of the HMR Pathfinder Programme: Baseline Report*. London: Department for Communities and Local Government.

Further Reading

Communities and Local Government (2010) English Housing Survey, Headline Report 2008–09. http://www.communities.gov.uk (accessed 19 April 2011)
Department of the Environment (1975) *Circular 13/75: Housing Act 1974: Renewal Strategies*. London: HMSO.
Department of the Environment (1979) *English House Condition Survey 1976, Part 2: Report of the Social Survey*. London: HMSO.
Department of the Environment (1983) *English House Condition Survey 1981, Part 2: Report of the Interview and Local Authority Survey*. London: HMSO.
Department of the Environment (1993) *English House Condition Survey 1991*. London: HMSO.
Gibson MS and Langstaff M (1982) *An Introduction to Urban Renewal*. London: Hutchinson.
Hamnett C (1973) Improvement grants as an indicator of gentrification in Inner London. *Area* 5(4): 252–261.
Leather P (2000) Grants to home-owners: A policy in search of objectives. *Housing Studies* 15(2): 149–168.
Leather P and Mackintosh S (1992) *Maintaining Home Ownership: The Agency Approach*. London: Longman; Institute of Housing.
Nevin B, Lee P, Goodson L, Murie A, and Phillimore J (2002) *Changing Housing Markets and Urban Regeneration in the M62 Corridor*. Birmingham, UK: University of Birmingham Centre for Urban and Regional Studies.
Smith SJ, Easterlow D, and Munro M (2004) Housing for health: Does the market work? *Environment and Planning A* 36(4): 579–600.

Housing and Neighbourhood Quality: Urban Regeneration

R Paddison, University of Glasgow, Glasgow, UK

© 2012 Elsevier Ltd. All rights reserved.

Glossary

Housing quality The provision of housing so that it meets basic needs and expectations. Initially, quality is defined in absolute terms, in particular, basic needs. With a rising standard of living housing quality becomes defined in more relative and subjective terms. Its definition extends beyond the physical qualities of provision to include attributes more related to the neighbourhood in which it is located.

Neighbourhood disparities The differences that exist between neighbourhoods (in a city) in their quality, real and imagined.

Neighbourhood effect The contribution 'good' or 'bad' neighbourhoods have on influencing the life-chances of individual residents living within it.

Neighbourhood quality The characteristics – including its amenities, social composition, image, and others – that help define neighbourhoods as 'good', 'bad', 'desirable', and 'undesirable'.

Scale and multilevel analysis The contribution processes operating at different scales (or levels) – global, national, through to the individual – have in influencing life-chances. Identification of the relative importance of scalar-defined processes is possible through multilevel statistical modelling.

Introduction

The questions of housing and neighbourhood quality have profound implications for the quality of life enjoyed – or endured – by residents of the city. Housing bears on questions of security as well as meeting the needs of the household in terms of its space requirements and the basic services it provides. The quality of the neighbourhood not only has a bearing on the life experiences of its residents but it has also become linked with their opportunities and life-chances in which relatively deprived neighbourhoods are associated with the socially excluded. Urban regeneration policies represent an attempt to redress the inequalities of housing and neighbourhood quality, and in particular those experienced by the more disadvantaged. Before looking at these neighbourhood policies, it is necessary to tease out how residential satisfaction differs within the city and explore the definitions of quality (of housing and the neighbourhood) and its implications.

As a measure of residential satisfaction, housing and neighbourhood quality are two sides of the same coin. How satisfied residents tend to be with their current housing position reflects not only the attributes of their house or flat, including the conditions of their tenure, but also the attitudes they hold towards the neighbourhood in which they live. As a recent report offering guidance on the improvement of housing in England suggests "When asked what makes a good place to live, people give just as much importance to the wider neighbourhood as to their own house or flat" (Department for Communities and Local Government, 2006: 7). Such a finding is recurrent in other national housing surveys confirming intuition that while the standards of housing provision, both in the private and, particularly, in western European experience, in the social sector, improved in the latter half of the twentieth century, the quality of the neighbourhood in which residents live and their perceptions of it, especially in the more deprived areas of cities, contributed to the dissatisfaction felt by a significant minority towards their housing.

Differences in residential satisfaction between households broadly reflect their market position. For the relatively affluent, the development of gated, privatised communities demonstrates the ability of wealthy and influential households to opt out of the perceived disadvantages of city living, yet maintain their accessibility to its benefits. Gated communities have become a globalised phenomenon within the last two decades, developing rapidly in North America but also emerging rapidly in cities as different as Guangzhou, Sofia, and Sao Paulo (see articles Gated Communities: Developed Countries and Gated Communities: Global South). In certain respects, they represent the ultimate expression of the importance of neighbourhood quality as a contributory factor to residential satisfaction and city living in which an ability to afford a privatised local environment is a key motivation explaining household relocation.

While the gated community arguably represents an extreme case, it is a variant of an endemic feature of cities, the inequalities surrounding housing and neighbourhood quality. In the global South, these inequalities can be highly visible. In Sao Paulo, for instance, the manicured and fully serviced gated compounds in some cases exist adjacent to the *favelas* defined not just by their overcrowding and slum housing but also by their neighbourhoods that lack basic amenities, including the provision of a proper water supply and of sewerage and drainage networks. It may be true that in northern cities the inequalities between households living in privileged and disadvantaged neighbourhoods do not compare with their southern counterparts, but in 'relative' terms, the contrasts between rich and poor areas of the cities of Europe and North America are striking reminders of the inequalities defining the quality of urban living in late capitalism. These inequalities have become more palpable under urban neoliberal practices, and the spread of gentrification has regenerated areas of the city previously occupied by lower-income groups producing landscapes of privileged consumption whose housing and environmental amenity contrast with those of old adjacent neighbourhoods, whose future development may also become embroiled in the spread of further gentrification.

Issues of housing and neighbourhood quality have become subsumed within the wider policy objective of urban regeneration. Just as at an earlier stage in the twentieth century, and particularly in those states where welfarism became adopted as a key instrument of state policy, the provision of state housing had sought to reduce the inequalities in the housing conditions experienced between social groups, so too in recent decades the state has sought to influence neighbourhood quality, again so that the lifestyles of the less privileged are not blighted by poor neighbourhood environments. This has been the case in Britain, which since 1997 has been particularly active in promoting how residential neighbourhoods can be improved and through a programme of partnership initiatives has actively sought to bring about such improvements in the more deprived neighbourhoods. While it is against these developments that the issues arising from housing and neighbourhood quality need to be understood, it is important to point out that in different ways the experience is repeated elsewhere in western Europe as well as beyond, in Australian cities (such as Newcastle and Wollongong) as well as in North American cities. Before beginning to look at how such programmes have been defined and their implications, it is important to define how quality is expressed both as a measure of housing as well as of the neighbourhood. What becomes clear is that if housing quality is not uncontentious in its definition, these difficulties become magnified in the case of neighbourhood quality. In particular, there is the thorny problem of separating out the role of the neighbourhood in influencing life-chances as opposed to processes operating at different scales, including macroeconomic and household-specific factors. Little wonder, then, that these problems in measuring quality become mirrored in the mixed outcomes arising from the methods by which improving neighbourhood quality have been sought through policy practice.

Conceptualising and Measuring Quality: Some Problems

Whether applied to housing or to other consumer goods, quality is a slippery concept to define largely because of its subjective interpretation. More frequently considered in relation to retail purchases what constitute quality becomes subjectively appreciated, reflecting preferences, taste, and other criteria, which will in turn clearly reflect personal dispositions. To the extent that housing quality can be defined objectively – as meeting minimum standards of provision, for example – these too may incorporate value judgements as to what should define these standards. New postwar housing in Britain, for example, was expected to be built to minimum standards of provision, as was made explicit in *Homes for Today and Tomorrow* (the 'Parker Morris Report') (Ministry of Housing and Local Government, 1961) and later in *Homes for the Future* (RIBA/IoH, 1983). These attempts to define minimum standards of provision were to continue a debate that had begun much earlier in the century, the unfolding of which reflected how such standards would need to be responsive to the changing demographic, social, and technological contexts in which they were played out. In other words, the problem of defining what objective standards new housing provision should meet could not assume that quality was reducible to a fixed set of stable criteria.

Notwithstanding the complexities of defining appropriate standards of provision (minimal criteria defining the quality of provision), certain basic attributes of housing provision should be agreeable consensually. In southern cities, this has become forcefully expressed through a rights-based approach; that is, where a substantial proportion, often a majority, live in squatter settlements, their upgrading should meet minimum standards of quality provision so that households have access to basic services as well as enjoying security of tenure, measures that are more taken for granted amongst householders in northern cities.

Beyond the provision of basic needs, there is considerable divergence as to how housing quality should be defined. One attempt by the UK Government in 2000 to define housing quality indicators listed 10 factors including location, site considerations such as visual impact, layout, and landscaping, accessibility, noise, and other forms of pollution, environmental, and sustainability criteria, as well as measures that provide an indication of how housing units meet needs and perform in use. Whether such factors are to be given equal weighting and, if so, how their relative importance is to be decided raises additional complications. Further, such a listing reflects the professional norms of architects, urban designers, as well as urban planners, those closely involved in housing provision. More fundamentally, it assumes that householders, in choosing where to live, are able to articulate preferences with respect to housing unit attributes independently of the neighbourhood it is located in.

Neighbourhood quality is monitored in some countries – such as the Netherlands, England, and Scotland – reflecting concern about disparities within cities and the wider problems of social deprivation. In the United Kingdom, surveys monitor measures of environmental problems such as vandalism and other incivilities (e.g., litter), together with assessment of air quality and the presence of indicative problems such as boarded-up dwellings. In recognition of the importance of perceptions, the English House Condition Survey and its Scottish counterpart, the Scottish Household Survey, monitor how satisfied residents are with their neighbourhood.

The factors linked to inter-neighbourhood disparities within a city are more complex than these surveys suggest. Typically, residents of a city will have a mental map of its neighbourhoods to which they are able to add affective terms such as 'good', 'bad', 'desirable', and 'undesirable'. Though as stereotypes such images may counter the 'lived reality' of particular neighbourhoods, they are based on an understanding of the factors that distinguish high- and low-quality neighbourhoods. Environmental problems and neighbourhood incivility may be a component of the stereotype, but also important, for example, will be the quality of the neighbourhood schools and of the general environment for rearing children, alongside more intangible, but nonetheless important, characteristics relating to social and behavioural norms defining the values of the local area. In what analysts term the 'neighbourhood effect' there is a claim that such characteristics can have a bearing on the life-chances of the residents in an area, and hence on their quality of life.

Appreciation of the significance neighbourhood disparities have for quality of life has been recognised by urban policy for several decades, and in western countries, particularly those in Europe, have been the subject of considerable political attention. This is particularly so where statistical analysis is able to identify them as being multiply deprived. Multiple deprivation is defined in terms of the cumulative effects there may be for individuals living in areas characterised by high levels of relative poverty and unemployment, of crime together with other social problems such as high levels of drug dependency and alcohol consumption, high rates of morbidity, and relative disengagement from (local) political processes. Successive analyses in cities undertaken in different countries in Europe and elsewhere identify the existence of the disadvantaged neighbourhood in which the exclusion of its residents, economic, social, and political, is its hallmark. The processes underpinning such exclusion will be contingent reflecting differences, for example, of welfarist policies decided by national-level governments – that is beyond the city. Even so, the overriding conclusion to be drawn from the reality of intra-urban neighbourhood disparities is that neighbourhood quality, and particularly in areas that are relatively disadvantaged, can have profound consequences for its residents.

While the reality of relatively disadvantaged neighbourhoods – what are variously termed 'areas of multiple deprivation', 'sink estates', or 'urban sores' – is a hallmark feature of cities in the advanced capitalist economies, the reasons for their existence, together with the formulation of urban policy aimed at amelioration, are the source of significant contention and difference. As in diagnoses of the problems of cities in the global South, the persistence of poverty and of low incomes is frequently cited as a core factor underpinning the poor quality of life experienced by residents of the disadvantaged neighbourhoods of northern cities. Similarly, the causes of such poverty have drawn on widely different types of explanation, ranging from those relatively close to the 'culture of poverty thesis' – in which the poor become blamed themselves for the disadvantaged position which they occupy – to those explanations which emphasise the structural factors that under capitalism spell out the seeming inevitability of socioeconomic inequalities that, in turn, become mapped out in neighbourhood disparities. Between these extremes – and occupying the ground on which much welfarist urban policy is located – are explanations which are defined around reformist aspirations; that through state intervention allied to building neighbourhood capacity, a process that draws on the participation of residents, neighbourhood regeneration can be achieved and the cycle of multiple deprivation reversed. Given such differences in the diagnosis of the disadvantaged neighbourhood, it is not surprising to find that how urban policy addresses the problem is variable, not only across countries but also within them over time, where the emphases of intervention will reflect the ideological positions of ruling (national and local) political parties.

Notwithstanding the reality of relatively disadvantaged (poor) neighbourhoods, unequivocal demonstration that the neighbourhood effect is significant is far from established. As intuitively plausible as the neighbourhood effect may be – that living in a relatively deprived area is likely to have negative consequences for the individual household (and presumably vice versa) – establishing that this is the case has been proved contentious among social scientists. A different but also plausible explanation is that poor neighbourhood amenity might accelerate depreciation of the housing stock with negative efficiency and distributional consequences. Both arguments tend to assume that the individual resident is passive, rather than able to have constructive effects on their life course and that the factors influencing the latter are largely endogenous (contained within) to the local area itself. Statistically, there are methods, such as multilevel modelling, that are available to separate out the effects of neighbourhood from other factors on inter-neighbourhood variations in performance. For example, the degree to which variations in school performance indicators (as in examination performance) are attributable to neighbourhood characteristics is identifiable using these methods. Where there may be growing acceptance from such analyses that the neighbourhood effect has consequences for residents, statistically, this is likely to be relatively small, particularly by comparison with characteristics defining the individual such as whether they are in employment. In other words, neighbourhood quality, or rather its absence, may matter but there are far more significant factors originating from other scales of analysis – the individual as well as nationally through, for example, changes in taxation or social policy – that impact on neighbourhood disparities and which have material, if variable, consequences for the residents of different neighbourhoods.

These caveats to the neighbourhood effect emphasise an important distinction that also impacts on neighbourhood quality – that its determination is the outcome of exogenous as well as endogenous factors. That is, the wider position of the neighbourhood within the metropolitan area of which it is a part may also affect quality; in turn this positioning may be the outcome of structural factors affecting the city as a whole and are processes over which individual neighbourhoods lack the capacity to control. Thus, in the United States and also in some European cities there has been much debate about the so-called spatial mismatch hypothesis, the lack of access certain neighbourhoods may have to job opportunities whose residents may have the skills (see article Policies to Address Spatial Mismatch). Frequently this becomes evident through the mismatch between the residents of relatively deprived inner-city neighbourhoods, defined by race and high levels of unemployment, and their accessibility to employment opportunities on the edge of the metropolitan area. What the problem underlines is how neighbourhood quality becomes defined in part by processes operating at scales beyond that of the neighbourhood itself.

It may be useful at this juncture to summarise some major points of the discussion. First, however hard to define, access to quality housing that meets not only the needs of security but is also able to meet household needs and also lifestyle preferences, together with access to good neighbourhoods, represents an ideal. Its realisation in market societies is limited to those who are defined by their relatively powerful market position – hence their access to high-quality housing and neighbourhoods. Second, the introduction of social housing has had positive outcomes for the quality of provision, but because quality in the more affluent economies becomes measured in relative terms, problems of housing quality tend to be persistent. Thus, while the problems defining housing quality in cities in the global South – security of tenure and the provision of basic needs – are largely resolved for residents of cities in more affluent economies, problems of quality are not eliminated. Problems of physical condition remain for some housing in northern cities, while recent political policies (as in the UK) emphasising the consumer-voter has sought to link choice with quality in the (social) housing market. Third, housing and neighbourhood quality have profound consequences for the quality of life (and life-chances) of householders. Whether for reasons of social control or cohesion, the inequalities associated with these variations in quality become difficult to ignore politically; in European countries (in particular), they have become the object of concerted policy attention.

Urban Regeneration

Urban regeneration, particularly as it has evolved in recent decades in the United Kingdom and in several other European countries, is a holistic strategy that specifically targets these questions of quality. Its goal is transformational, at redressing the inequalities experienced by those living in the disadvantaged neighbourhoods. Its holistic nature – simultaneously targeting economic, social, political, and environmental objectives along with physical reconstruction – distinguishes it from programmes of urban reconstruction or renewal that were more circumscribed in their objectives, focusing frequently on physical reconstruction alone.

The term urban regeneration has wider currency than this argument suggests. In what have become hallmark redevelopments in many cities, urban regeneration is linked to the recapitalisation of city spaces – city centres and waterfront development, for example – the rationale for which in turn relates to a broader goal of enhancing the competitive position of cities. Such regeneration can be linked with the processes of gentrification, the result of which tends to exacerbate inequalities in the quality of housing and of neighbourhoods. Yet, in such regeneration it has become increasingly common practice (as in the United Kingdom) to insist that a proportion of the housing stock is affordable, thereby catering for lower-income households (see article Inclusionary Zoning to Support Affordable Housing). Further, in other regeneration schemes – notably the development of Thamesmead on the eastern edge of London – the development of new housing estates has deliberately sought to create high-quality design and sustainable forms of housing development at affordable prices that counter the problems experienced by many essential (sometimes professional) workers otherwise unable to access the London housing market (see article Inclusionary Zoning to Support Affordable Housing). Such developments directly address some of the key issues of housing and neighbourhood quality.

In the United Kingdom and following the election of the Labour Government in 1997, neighbourhood renewal strategies became the hallmark of social justice policy, seeking to address the multiple disadvantages of deprived communities, many of which stemmed from their problems of housing and neighbourhood quality. The details of the policies differed between England, Scotland, and Wales (as a result of devolution to the minority nations in 1999) though they shared a holistic appreciation of the problems and sought to 'close the gap' between poor neighbourhoods and the rest. Thus in England, the New Deal for Communities programme tackled five key indicators linked to social deprivation – unemployment, crime, poor health, and problems associated with housing quality and the environment. In Scotland, the newly created (in 2001) Communities Scotland, focusing its attention on identified areas of multiple deprivation, had as its remit

- to improve the quality of existing housing and ensure a high quality of new build,
- to improve the quality of housing and homelessness services,
- to increase the supply of affordable housing where it is needed most,
- to improve the opportunities for people living in disadvantaged communities,
- to support the social economy to deliver key services and provide job opportunities.

Not dissimilar initiatives aimed at neighbourhood renewal were introduced in other European countries including the Netherlands, Denmark, and Germany.

Such programmes were transformational not only in their intention but also in the processes through which their objectives were sought. This was apparent in their holistic interpretation of neighbourhood quality and also in the place given to partnership working, and in the attempt to bring community residents into the regeneration process. In practice, considerable problems arose in these governance processes and, at best, outcomes had mixed success in addressing fundamental inequalities. Critically, such programmes may underscore the structural (exogenous) factors linked to poor housing and neighbourhood quality. Further, some of the assumptions around which they were constructed attracted extensive criticism. This has been particularly the case in the assumptions surrounding the advocacy of social mixing, that by bringing together relatively advantaged households with those less so, poorer households would become less excluded (see article Policies to Address Social Mix in Communities). Perhaps even more so than in the case of the neighbourhood effect, the reality of mixing has not achieved what was expected of it.

Such a conclusion, if tentative, reflects the experience where social mixing has resulted from the movement of higher-income (middle-class) households into areas undergoing renewal in inner city areas otherwise associated with social deprivation and concentrations of low-income households. The location of such neighbourhoods together with the provision of new-build housing, especially flats suitable for single-person or small-sized households, meets the lifestyle preferences of particular types of household emergent in the 'new' city. Such mixing results, then, from the movement of higher-income households into areas otherwise characterised by relatively high levels of poverty and social exclusion.

For political reasons (witness, the intentions underpinning exclusionary zoning in metropolitan suburbs in the United States), as well as, more obviously, economic factors, achieving a greater degree of social mixing through the opposite process – the movement of poor households from disadvantaged neighbourhoods to low-poverty areas – is only likely to result from direct policy intervention. A recent programme of the federal Housing and Urban Development Department (HUD) – Moving to Opportunity (MTO) – sought to assess the impacts on low-income households that had been enabled to take such a move. In fact, there was a precedent. In an earlier programme in Chicago – which followed from a housing segregation lawsuit initiated by a tenant activist, Dorothy Gautreaux – some 7000 black families had been moved in the 1970s to predominantly white or racially mixed neighbourhoods. Apparently, the move had positive outcomes for the moving households, educationally, in employment terms, and in satisfaction with the new housing and neighbourhood conditions. MTO, first implemented in 1992, was structured more carefully to meet the conditions of statistical testing, overcoming the possible problems of the Gautreaux programme, namely that the moving households were self-selecting and the absence of any control group. MTO was structured as a randomised experimental model in which very low-income households were enabled to move to low-poverty neighbourhoods in five participating cities: Baltimore, Boston, Chicago, Los Angeles, and New York. The results were mixed: while satisfaction with the new neighbourhood and a greater feeling of safety was a common response by moving households and while the mental health of adults and young females improved, the interim results were more neutral educationally and in employment terms. In fact, the impacts of such a programme are likely to unfold fully over the longer term, though even so our ability to be assured of the extent to which positive (or other) impacts are attributable to policy is undermined by the effects of the changing exogenous (e.g., macro-economic) environment on neighbourhoods and households (see article Mobility Programmes for Disadvantaged Populations: The Moving to Opportunity Programme).

Policies such as MTO, together with those of neighbourhood regeneration, raise the fundamental question of scale, which has been recurrent in this article. Are the problems of low-income households living in public housing developments the result of high concentrations of such households living in poor neighbourhoods or is it more the result of attributes of the household itself? Most probably, it may often be the result of both, though the mix will differ contextually – realities that pose formidable challenges to effective policy intervention.

See also: Gated Communities: Developed Countries; Gated Communities: Global South; Housing Policy and Regeneration; Inclusionary Zoning to Support Affordable Housing; Key Worker Housing Policies; Mobility Programmes for Disadvantaged Populations: The Moving to Opportunity Programme; Policies to Address Social Mix in Communities; Policies to Address Spatial Mismatch.

References

Department for Communities and Local Government (DCLG) (2006) *English House Condition Survey 2004: Annual Report, Decent Homes and Decent Places*. London: DCLG.
Ministry of Housing and Local Government (MHLG) (1961) *Homes for Today and Tomorrow*. The Parker Morris Report. London: HMSO.

Further Reading

Andersson R, Musterd S, Gaslter G, and Kaupipinen TM (2007) What mix matters? Exploring the relationships between individuals' incomes and different measures of their neighbourhood context. *Housing Studies* 22(5): 637–660.
Atkinson R and Kintrea K (2001) Disentangling area effects: Evidence from deprived and non-deprived households. *Urban Studies* 38: 2277–2298.
Caldeira T (2000) *City of Walls: Crime, Segregation and Citizenship in Sao Paulo*. Berkeley, CA: University of California Press.
Department of the Environment, Transport and Regions (DETR) (1999) *Towards an Urban Renaissance: The Report of the Urban Task Force Chaired by Lord Rogers of Riverside*. London: Routledge.
Goodchild B (2008) *Homes, Cities and Neighbourhoods: Planning and the Residential Landscapes of Modern Britain*. Aldershot, UK: Ashgate.
Jones P and Evans J (2008) *Urban Regeneration in the UK*. London: Sage.
Office of the Deputy Prime Minister (ODPM) (2003) *Sustainable Communities: Building for the Future*. London: HMSO.
Office of the Deputy Prime Minister (ODPM) (2005) *Sustainable Communities: People, Places and Prosperity*. London: HMSO.
Royal Institute of British Architects/Institute of Housing (RIBA/IoH) (1983) *Homes for the Future: Standards for New Housing Developments*. London: Institute of Housing.

Relevant Websites

www.cabe.org.uk – Commission for Architecture and the Built Environment has material on the role of design in creating attractive neighbourhoods.
www.communities.gov.uk – Department for Communities and Local Government in England, useful site to trace regeneration policies.
www.hud.gov – US Department of Housing and Urban Development holds evaluative material on Moving to Opportunity besides other material on housing and neighbourhood quality.

Housing and Sustainable Transport

E Holden, Sogn and Fjordane University College, Sogndal, Norway

K Linnerud, Cicero Centre for International Climate and Environmental Research, Oslo, Norway

© 2012 Elsevier Ltd. All rights reserved.

Glossary

Centralists Supporters of the compact city theory as sustainable urban form.

Compact city A theory that encourages high-density development close to or within the city core with a mixture of housing, workplaces, and shops. Development of residential housing areas, in particular single-family housing, on the urban fringe is banned.

Decentralised concentration An urban form that combines compactness at a city level and decentralisation at a national/regional level. The energy efficiency gained from a compact urban form with the broader quality-of-life aspects gained from the dispersed city.

Decentralists Supporters of the dispersed city theory as the sustainable urban form.

Dispersed city A theory that encourages the green city, that is, a more open type of urban structure where buildings, fields and other green areas form a mosaic-like pattern.

Land use planning Branch of physical and socioeconomic planning that includes how we design (i.e., housing type) and locate (i.e., distance to city centre) houses. Land use planning involves studies and mapping, analysis of environmental and hazard data, and formulation of alternative land use decisions and design.

Sustainable development Development that meets the needs of the present generation without compromising the ability of future generations to meet their needs. It contains two key concepts: the concept of 'needs', in particular the essential needs of the world's poor, to which overriding priority should be given; and the idea of limitations imposed by the state of technology and social organisation on the environment's ability to meet present and the future needs.

Introduction

Passenger transport, environmental problems relating to transport, and housing are interrelated through land use planning. Unfortunately, most Western countries have for several decades practised a form of land use planning which favours – and in many cases requires – the use of cars, which in turn has contributed to a substantial increase in environmental problems caused by transport. But land use planning is not just a cause of increased transport and environmental problems; it is also a possible solution. By reversing the planning practices of recent decades, it is fully possible to reduce the environmental problems caused by transport. In other words, this has to do with a sustainable form of land use planning, also referred to as a sustainable urban form

Transport

For more than a million years, travel has been important to man: he has escaped poverty or fled from aggressive invaders; he has travelled to explore the world; and he has travelled to hunt for food or to trade. Put briefly, he has travelled in order to improve his life. Whatever the reason, travelling then was uncomfortable, hazardous, and time-consuming. Today some would claim that little has changed; travelling is still uncomfortable, hazardous, and time-consuming. There are, however, two major differences between travelling then and travelling today: in modern society, we have experienced an explosive growth in the use of motorised transport for our journeys and an equally explosive growth in the environmental problems caused by them.

In order to put this growth in travel (or transport as we refer to it here) in perspective, we can compare it with population growth. In the course of the previous century the world's population quadrupled, while the world's total volume of transport of passengers and goods increased by a factor of 100. The growth in transport has in turn contributed to the fact that we use increasingly more energy for transport. On a worldwide basis, transport accounts for 20% of the total energy consumption – and is likely to increase. By 2030 it is estimated that the increase in the world's annual energy consumption for transport will be 2.1% – a growth rate that is higher than for any other sector.

Transport and Sustainable Development

Along with energy consumption come the environmental problems. With around 25% of man-made emissions of carbon dioxide (CO_2) to its credit, transport is a major contributor to climate changes. Emissions of sulphur and nitrogen contribute to regional environmental problems such as acid rain. Emissions of nitrogen oxide and particles contribute to local environmental problems in the form of poorer air quality in towns and cities. All this is before we even mention accidents, congestion, consumption of building materials for infrastructure, splitting up of natural habitats for animal and plant life, and discharges into water and soil. It is therefore no exaggeration to say that no other sector in society contributes to – and will continue to do so for many decades to come – such a broad spectrum of serious global, regional, and local environmental problems as transport.

Since the UN-commissioned report from the World Commission on Environment and Development, *Our Common Future*, set the agenda more than 30 years ago, it has become usual to include environmental problems in the broader concept of sustainable development. When studying environmental problems caused by transport in particular, it is usual practice to use the term 'sustainable transport'. The large-scale environmental problems mentioned above have led researchers and environmental bureaucrats all over the world to reach the rather one-sided conclusion that we now have a nonsustainable transport system. Furthermore, the same researchers and environmental bureaucrats conclude that things will only get worse unless we take some dramatic action, and soon.

Transport, Sustainable Development, and Land Use Planning

There are many reasons for these discouraging conclusions. One of them is many decades of ineffective land use planning. Housing, workplaces, and public and private services are spread across large areas, a situation which has gradually made it practically impossible to get from one place to another without having to use a car or other means of motorised transport. There is little doubt that such land use planning has contributed to the explosive increase in transport.

The overall technical framework for the relationships between transport, sustainable development, and land use planning is planning research. We refer here to the branch of planning research that deals with the study of the effects of physical planning. This branch is often referred to as research on planning products as opposed to research on planning processes. In the latter case, the focus is placed on how planning work is conducted. Although the planning process is important, it will not be discussed here. Within this framework, the debate on sustainable urban forms appears to be fundamental.

Sustainable Urban Form

Until the 1960s, planning was an important instrument for realising visionary ideas. Based on a long history, planning provided credible answers about how we should form our built environment and, subsequently, our society. However, in the beginning of the 1960s, the public lost confidence in the planners, and, subsequently, the planners lost confidence in themselves. But this did not last for long. Following the publication of *Our Common Future*, a new optimism about planning emerged, and a debate about the role of planning in promoting sustainable development has been going on ever since. The crucial question is: Which urban forms will most effectively deliver sustainable development?

Regarding sustainable urban form, two important questions arise. First, and most fundamentally: Does planning matter? Second for those who answer 'yes' to the first question: What is sustainable urban form?

Does Planning Matter?

Even though planning seems to have regained much of its legitimacy, there has been a lot of scepticism about and even rejection of the very idea that planning has an important role in promoting sustainable development. The fundamental dispute has been about energy consumption and urban form: Does changing urban form tend to reduce the frequency and length of journeys, and hence energy consumption?

To this day, disagreement persists and the critiques against planning have many different forms, including:

- Claims that engine technology, taxes on gasoline, and road pricing are more effective measures for reducing energy consumption than urban planning.
- The assertion that socioeconomic and attitudinal characteristics of people are far more important determinants of travel behaviour than urban form. Critics taking this position assert that the importance of form is highly overestimated in empirical studies.
- Casting doubt on the assumption that proximity to everyday services and workplaces will contribute to reduced travel in a highly mobile society.

- That the relationship between nonwork travel, especially long leisure-time travel, and urban form has been neglected.
- The assertion that travel preferences rather than urban form influence travel behaviour; people live in city centres because they prefer to travel less, and not that they travel less because they live in city centres (the 'self-selection bias').

Even though these aspects should not be taken lightly, there seems to be overwhelming support in the literature for the idea that planning does matter in determining the level of energy consumption in urban areas. This view is based on both theory and empirical studies. Thus, planning is an important instrument for promoting sustainable development in general and sustainable transport in particular.

What Is Sustainable Urban Form?

Even among the supporters of planning, there is a lively debate about which urban form and land use characteristics actually promote a more sustainable society. There are two dominant and contradictory theories about sustainable urban form: the compact city and the dispersed city.

The main principle in the compact city theory is high-density development close to or within the city core with a mixture of housing, workplaces, and shops. This implies dense and concentrated housing development, which favours semidetached and multifamily housing. Under this theory, the development of residential housing areas on (or beyond) the urban fringe, particular single-family housing, is banned. Furthermore, central, high-density development supports a number of other attributes that are favourable to sustainable energy use: low energy use for housing and everyday travel, efficient remote heating systems, proximity to a variety of workplaces and public and private services, as well as a highly developed public transport system.

The supporters of the compact city theory believe that the compact city has environmental and energy advantages as well as social benefits. The list of advantages is remarkably long and includes a better environment, affordable public transport, the potential for improving the social mix, and a higher quality of life. However, the main justification for the compact city is that it results in the least energy-intensive activity pattern, thereby helping us cope with the issue of global warming.

The supporters of the dispersed city suggest the green city, that is, a more open type of urban structure where buildings, fields, and other green areas form a mosaic-like pattern. The list of arguments against the compact city theory is even longer than the list in support of it, such as: it rejects suburban and semirural living, neglects rural communities, affords less green and open space, increases congestion and segregation, reduces environmental quality, and lessens the power for making local decisions.

Until fairly recently an international consensus in favour of the compact city as a sustainable development approach dominated the debate. Thus, the move towards the compact city is now entrenched in policy throughout Europe.

The Compact or the Dispersed City?

Which of these camps, the centralists supporting the compact city or the decentralists supporting the dispersed city, can claim the sustainable urban form? Ultimately, that depends on the sustainability issue in question. Five major issues are discussed here: energy consumption, the global environmental problem, accessibility to transport, urban environment, and quality of life. The first three issues are discussed jointly.

Energy Consumption, Global Environmental Problems, and Accessibility

Regarding these three sustainability issues, compact cities are more sustainable for five reasons: first, compact cities give shorter distances between different activities. This means shorter trips and increases the likelihood of cycling or walking instead of driving a car, all of which result in lower energy consumption and fewer emissions of greenhouse gases.

Second, compact cities contribute to higher population densities. Increased population densities offer possibilities for more public and private services where people live, something which also means shorter trips and, hopefully, more trips by bicycle and on foot. Moreover, increased population densities provide a practical and economic basis for a good public transport system. A good public transport system increases the likelihood that people will choose not to use their cars, something which contributes to lower energy consumption and emission levels. Moreover, a good public transport system is necessary for ensuring that those who do not own a car have their transport needs met.

Third, compact cities offer better possibilities for good public transport solutions *between* cities. When there are more people living at each end of a train line than people living along the stretch in between, more people will probably make use of the train – something which again provides a basis for an even better public transport system.

Fourth, compact cities increase the possibilities for using energy-efficient and environmentally friendly vehicles. For example, the success of the electric car is dependent on the distances between the places to which people need to travel not being *too long*. The electric car, which is far more energy-efficient than petrol and diesel vehicles and also has lower life cycle emissions of greenhouse gases, is more at home in compact cities. It would also be easier to facilitate more charging stations.

Finally, compact cities entail less overall land use change, thereby leaving a lot of natural landscapes untouched. That is good news for animals and plants, or for what is often referred to as biological diversity, which must continuously make way for humans on the eternal hunt for new land to develop.

Overall, there is much to suggest that high-density and concentrated development of our cities and towns is favourable in terms of reducing energy consumption, protecting the global environment, and achieving better accessibility to transport for low-mobility groups. As already mentioned, this conclusion is strongly supported by national and international research communities.

Urban Environments

The need for a safe urban environment in terms of health was strongly emphasised in *Our Common Future*. Even though the situation is most precarious in developing countries, pollution, traffic accidents, and other health hazards represent serious problems in many cities in developing countries, too.

This is the result of the fact that very large numbers of people live and travel within a fairly limited area. In other words, it is the result of densification. Further densification, as the centralists envisage it, could easily make conditions even worse. The compact city would therefore unavoidably struggle with a poor urban environment. On the other hand, the decentralists want to enjoy the benefits of having pollution spread over larger areas and thereby having urban air that was less hazardous to health. Moreover, the decentralists claim that densification would unavoidably lead to a gradual reduction in the number of green areas in the cities and would thereby reduce the cleansing effect that these areas have on pollutant emissions. Regardless of the fact that decentralised development could lead to more emissions overall, the individual inhabitant will at least be spared from too much of it wherever he or she happens to live.

However, the fact remains that increasingly more people already live in cities and towns. According to the UN's population programme, 2008 was the year when – for the first time in history – more than half of the world's population of 6.7 billion people lived in cities. In 2030 the figure will rise to 60%. All future population growth will take place in the cities, predominantly in the developing countries, where the cities' populations will double in the course of one generation. Large sections of these cities will become even more densely populated and more compact than they already are. Large and compact cities are therefore not something one can just cast aside in favour of the decentralists' ideal of smaller cities with low densities.

It then becomes even more important to combine increasing density with measures to improve urban environments, or 'high-quality densification'. So the picture need not necessarily look so bleak. The reason for this is that, in the first place and as already discussed, densification leads to shorter journeys and provides the basis for a better public transport service and nonmotorised transport. These are conditions that will improve the urban environment. Secondly, adherents of densification also place an emphasis on preserving green lungs in the cities. If so-called brown areas in cities were taken into use (disused factories and industrial plants), then the green areas could be spared. Furthermore, much of the land that is used for roads and parking areas could be used for housing and workplaces. This would be possible if the public transport service was good. Third, a densification strategy must in any case be combined with other ways of improving the urban environment, such as physical restrictions on traffic; economic instruments that make it cheaper to travel on public transport and more expensive to drive a car; and increased use of zero-emission vehicles. Nonetheless, there is no reason to hesitate in proclaiming the smaller and low-density cities as the winners if you look at the connection between urban form and urban environment in isolation.

Quality of Life

Quality of life is a concept which is used increasingly more in psychology and other branches of the social sciences. It is a concept which invites contemplation about what a good life entails and what the premises are for experiencing a certain quality in life. A question which arises in discussions on quality of life is who should assess what a good quality of life is for someone. If researchers were to assess the quality of life of others, their own values would easily become the basis for their assumptions. As a psychological concept, quality of life is therefore defined on the basis of the individual's experience of his/her own life and life situation. One often talks of a *subjective* quality of life as opposed to an *objective* quality of life, which embraces much of what has already been said about health under the section 'Urban Environments'. The way in which we use the term 'quality of life' here has to do with the individual's perception of his/her own life as good or bad.

Strictly speaking, the issue of quality of life is one which we do not consider to have anything to do with sustainable development. If you set aside obvious situations such as protecting yourself against harmful air and noise pollution and hoping that the bus comes along when it should, then quality of life is something which individuals decide for themselves. Whether it is better to live in a high-density city, as the centralists claim, or a low-density city, as the decentralists claim, should be up to you to decide (we acknowledge, however, that not all have to the resources to *make* such a decision). All the same, quality of life very often emerges as a distinct dimension in sustainable urban development and it is often the case that it is one's own personal and often ideological preferences about the 'right' quality of life that lie behind it. In this debate, we often find that both camps make attempts at developing an ownership relationship with whatever gives quality of life.

The Troublesome Leisure-Time Travel

An important question that arises from looking at the wider issue of energy use and greenhouse gas emissions is whether reduced local everyday travel will be compensated for by increased long-distance leisure travel at other times. Is it the case that the sum of 'environmental vices' is constant and that households managing on a small everyday amount of transport create even heavier environmental strain through, for instance, weekend trips to a cottage or long-distance holiday trips by aeroplane?

In the professional debate, some have claimed that people living in high-density, inner-city areas will, to a larger extent than their counterparts living in low-density areas, travel out of town on weekends to, for instance, a cottage in order to compensate for the lack of access to a private garden. In addition to this 'hypothesis of compensation', others have launched a 'hypothesis of opportunity' which asserts that the time and money people save due to shorter distances in their daily travel will probably be used for long-distance leisure-time travel. Such compensatory travel might counteract the advantages of the compact city.

Studies have found such compensatory travel by car and plane among households in Norway, Denmark, Sweden, and Switzerland (**Box 1**). The reasons for compensatory travel behaviour are numerous and will not be presented here. There is, however, little to indicate that the volume of compensatory journeys by car is greater than the

---

Box 1 Compensatory Travel Housing Density, Everyday Travel, and Long-Distance Leisure-Time Travel by Plane

The figure shows relations between housing density, everyday travel, and long-distance leisure-time travel by plane from a household study in the Greater Oslo area (Norway). The figure illustrates that, compared to the residents in low-density areas, the residents in high-density areas consume far less energy for everyday transport and far more energy for leisure-time travel by plane.

Moreover, multivariate regression analysis shows that the negative relation between housing density and energy consumption for everyday travel and the positive relation between housing density and energy consumption for leisure-time travel by plane are significant even when relevant socioeconomic and attitudinal factors are controlled for. Thus, the multivariate regression analysis resoundingly confirms that increased housing density affects people's everyday travel and leisure-time travel by plane in opposite ways. The identified pattern in the figure lends some support for the 'hypothesis of compensation' and 'hypothesis of opportunity' discussed in the text.

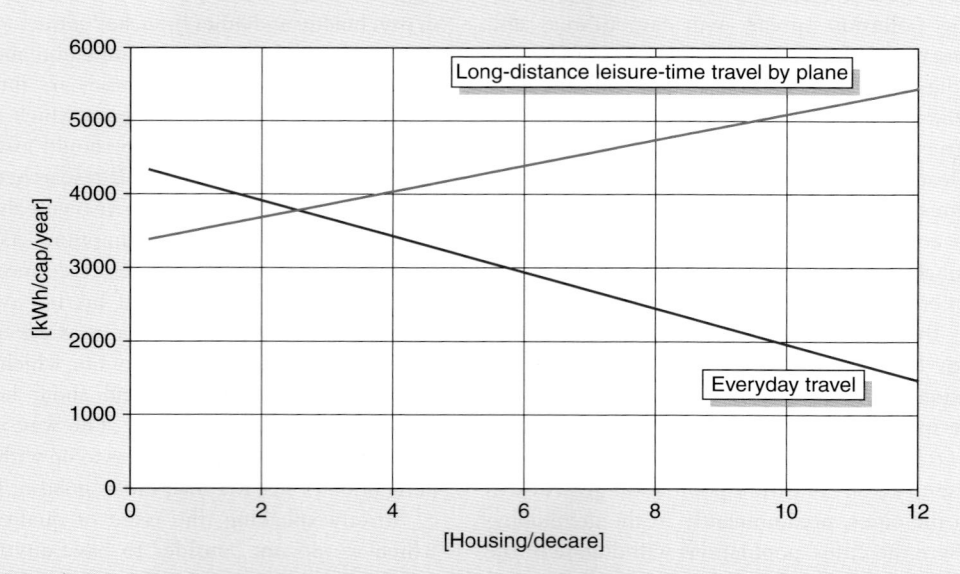

Relation between housing density in residential areas, everyday travel and long-distance leisure-time travel by plane ($N = 703/840$).
Source: Holden E (2007) *Achieving Sustainable Mobility: Everyday and Leisure-Time Travel in the EU*. Aldershot: Ashgate.

journeys that are being compensated for. The significance of urban form and urban plan factors is therefore important, though a little less important than what they were before researchers began to take a closer look at leisure-time travel. Density and concentration are still preferable if we are to reduce our energy consumption on transport.

It is a different case for the long air journeys. If we include these, the difference between those who live in high-density areas and close to the city centre and those who live in less densely populated areas in the outskirts of cities and in small towns is almost evened out. There is, however, good reason to ask whether long aeroplane journeys during leisure time do in fact have anything to do with urban form. On the one hand, it is maintained that such air travel is a result of an urban lifestyle: young, sociable people wanting to live close to the city centre and explore the world in their leisure time. On the other hand, there is evidence to support that those who live in the most densely populated areas fly the most in their leisure time, controlled for age, education, and income. We can therefore not disregard the fact that increasing densification and centralisation towards the cities has had the undesirable side effect of an increase in the desire to travel.

Consequently, the conclusion to be reached about this troublesome leisure-time travel and different forms of compensatory travel behaviour is that the proponents of centralisation are right. owever, there is good reason to ask whether there are any limits to how densely populated and large the cities should be. Cities that are too densely populated and too large could be the reason for direct and indirect compensatory travel behaviour, particularly by air.

Decentralised Concentration

Centralisation, then, results in low energy consumption for everyday travel and decentralisation seems to result in lower energy consumption for leisure-time travel. How can we achieve the best from both camps? The answer is decentralised concentration, which combines the energy efficiency gained from the compact urban form with the broader quality-of-life aspects gained from the dispersed city (there are other 'middle positions' such as the urban village, new urbanism, the sustainable urban matrix, transit-oriented development, and smart growth).

To achieve decentralised concentration it could be useful to take a closer look at the concepts of 'centralisation' and 'densification'. These two concepts are often regarded as being two sides of the same coin, but this does not have to be the case at all. On the contrary, it is two other conceptual pairs which are often confused: 'centralisation–decentralisation' and 'concentration–dispersal'. By combining these two pairs, we get four models of urban form (**Figure 1**).

Susan Owens, the respected English planning theorist from Cambridge University, asserts that in theory 'decentralised concentration' often emerges as relatively efficient in terms of travel and energy requirements. This is not simply a theory; empirical studies also confirm this view. It is a view which is supported by a large number of prominent transport and planning researchers around the world (Breheny, 1992; Holden, 2007; Jenks et al., 1996; Williams and Jenks, 2000).

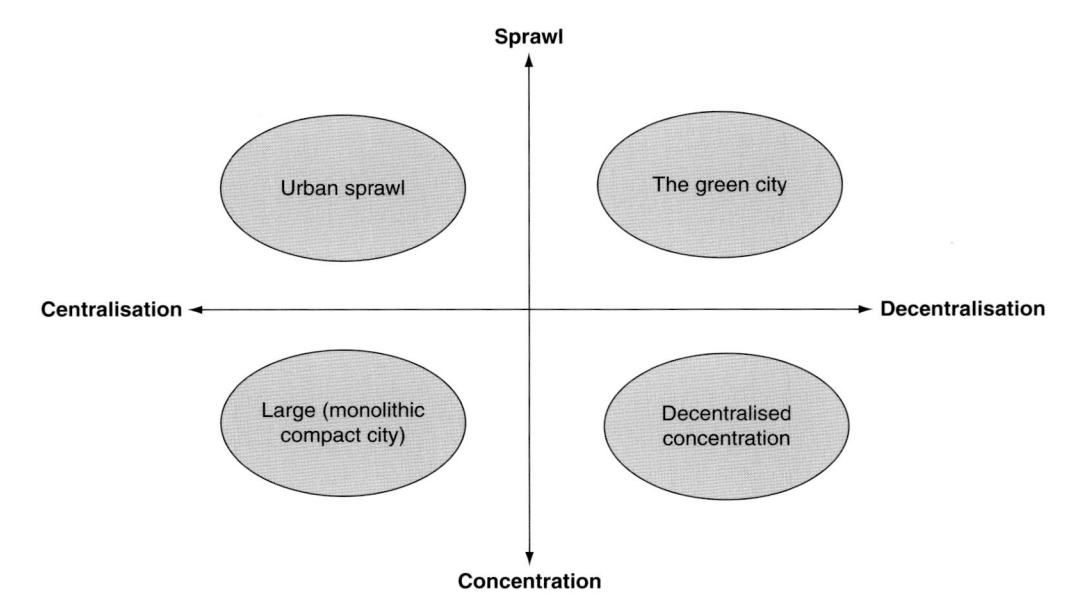

Figure 1 Four models of sustainable urban form.
Reproduced from Holden E (2004) Ecological Footprints and Sustainable Urban Form. *Journal of Housing and the Built Environment* 19(1): 91–109.

See also: Residential Urban Form and Transport; Sustainable Urban Development.

References

Breheny MJ (ed.) (1992) *Sustainable Development and Urban Form*. London: Pion Limited.

Holden E (2004) Ecological Footprints and Sustainable Urban Form. *Journal of Housing and the Built Environment* 19(1): 91–109.

Holden E (2007) *Achieving Sustainable Mobility: Everyday and Leisure-Time Travel in the EU*. Aldershot: Ashgate.

Jenks M, Burton E, and Williams K (eds.) (1996) *The Compact City: A Sustainable Urban Form?* London: E & FN Spon.

Williams K and Jenks M (eds.) (2000) *Achieving Sustainable Urban Form*. London: E & FN Spon.

Further Reading

Boarnet MG and Crane R (2001) *Travel by Design. The Influence of Urban Form on Travel*. New York: Oxford University Press.

Elkin T, McLaren D, and Hillman M (1991) *Reviving the City: Towards Sustainable Urban Development*. London: Friends of the Earth.

Frey H (1999) *Designing the City: Towards a More Sustainable Urban Form*. London: Spon Press.

Holden E and Norland IT (2005) Three challenges for the compact city as a sustainable urban form: Household consumption of energy and transport in eight residential areas in the greater Oslo region. *Urban Studies* 42(12): 2145–2166.

Jacobs J (1961) *The Death and Life of Great American Cities: The Failure of Town Planning*. New York: Random House.

Næss P (2006) *Urban Structure Matters*. Abingdon: Routledge.

Organisation for Economic Co-operation and Development (OECD) (2000) Environmentally sustainable transport, futures, strategies and best practices. *Synthesis Report of the OECD Project on Environmentally Sustainable Transport EST*. Vienna: OECD.

Owens S (1992) Energy, environmental sustainability and land use planning. In: Breheny MJ (ed.) *Sustainable Development and Urban Form*, pp. 79–105. London: Pion Limited.

Sperling D and Gordon D (2009) *Two Billion Cars. Driving Toward Sustainability*. New York: Oxford University Press.

Housing and the Macroeconomy

J Muellbauer, University of Oxford, Oxford, UK

© 2012 Elsevier Ltd. All rights reserved.

Glossary

Dynamic stochastic general equilibrium models Dynamic stochastic general equilibrium (DSGE) models aim to describe the behaviour of the economy as a whole by analysing the interaction of many microeconomic decisions. The decisions considered in most DSGE models correspond to some of the main quantities studied in macroeconomics, such as consumption, saving, investment, and labour supply and labour demand. The decision-makers in the model, often called 'agents', may include households, business firms, and possibly others, such as governments or central banks. These agents are typically assumed to be rational utility or profit maximisers facing linear budget constraints and efficient financial markets. They typically assume rational, 'model consistent' expectations: in other words, they assume that agents have the same understanding of the structure of the economy as is embodied in the rest of the model. DSGE models are dynamic, studying how the economy evolves over time. They are also stochastic, taking into account the fact that the economy is affected by random shocks such as technological change, changes in preferences, or errors in macroeconomic policy-making. Before the 1999 paper by Bernanke, Gertler, and Gilchrist, DSGE models assumed away financial frictions, agency costs, and the information asymmetries central to the operation of credit markets. That paper introduced a simple static friction applying to firms, but entirely ignored any credit channel effects operating via households. The 2005 paper by Iacoviello is generally considered the first fully worked out DSGE model with housing and a financial friction for households. DSGE models were particularly ill-equipped as tools for understanding interactions between the financial system and the economy. The technical difficulties of incorporating heterogeneous asymmetric information in DSGE models with credit markets remain ferocious.

Housing equity withdrawal It (sometimes termed mortgage equity withdrawal) is the difference between the change in the stock of mortgages for residential property and the amount of residential property acquired by the household sector. Before the liberalisation of mortgage markets, housing equity withdrawal was usually negative in that first-time and other buyers of housing injected equity (cash) in the form of the deposit required by mortgage lenders. Later, as loan-to-value ratios fell and home equity loans became easily available, new borrowings by existing households taking advantage of the increases in collateral caused by higher house prices often caused the increase in borrowing to exceed the amount of housing acquired.

Mortgage defaults A mortgage payment delinquency occurs when a borrower falls behind with mortgage payments. If the arrears mount, the lender may choose, through legal processes, to take possession of the home pledged as collateral for satisfactory servicing and repayment of the mortgage debt. Borrowers may short-circuit this process and voluntarily hand over access and ownership of the home to the mortgage lender. US terminology for either outcome is 'foreclosure'; UK terminology is 'mortgage possession' or 'repossession'. The consequences of mortgage default can differ greatly across countries and indeed between US states. At one extreme, in California, the lender's rights are restricted to the value of the collateral, at least for some types of mortgage. In the United Kingdom, mortgage defaulters can be pursued also for any losses the lender makes upon resale of the home for a period up to 7 years. UK lenders may also be able to obtain court orders giving them recourse to the borrower's regular income or other assets, if any.

Negative housing equity Negative housing equity arises when a borrower's mortgage debt exceeds the value of the home on which that debt is secured. It is often a precursor to mortgage default. When the borrower is still able and willing to service the mortgage debt, negative equity often constrains geographic mobility as sale of the home would require repayment of the mortgage. With negative housing equity, this would typically require unsecured debt or other assets.

The banking channel The banking channel is the most important part of the credit channel by which shocks are transmitted through the economy. The key idea is that quantities of credit offered to potential borrowers are subject to shocks and have a direct effect on the spending decisions of potential borrowers. In other words, it is not just the price of credit that influences such spending decisions, though changes in central bank policy rates can be among the shocks that trigger shifts in credit availability. A build-up in bad loans, a fall in the share price of banks or shifts in liquidity, or capital requirements set by regulators can be other triggers that alter the credit supply and credit terms offered by the banking system.

> **User cost of housing** The user cost is defined as the price of housing multiplied by a factor made up of the deterioration rate plus a tax rate, if any, plus the interest rate (the opportunity cost of tying up cash or the cost of borrowing funds to purchase the durable) minus the expected rate of capital gains. For example, with a deterioration rate of 2%, a property tax rate of 1%, an interest rate of 6%, and an expected rate of appreciation of 5%, the user cost would be 4% of the price of the durable.

Introduction

Housing has three main interactions with macroeconomic activity: these operate through the investment, consumption, and banking channels. First, residential construction is a substantial share of gross domestic product (GDP). In the 2007–09 crisis, the collapse of residential construction had large effects on GDP and on unemployment in the United States, Spain, and Ireland. Second, though there has been great controversy over whether there is a 'housing wealth effect' on consumption, theory and evidence suggest that in economies with liberal financial systems, housing has an important collateral role for raising relative cheap debt and so funding consumption spending, as well as other activities, see article Monetary Policy, Wealth Effects and Housing for further details. Higher house prices then increase access to credit and enhance the potential 'buffer stock' role of housing wealth where consumers face individual income risk. Finally, when housing loans go bad, this can have major effects on bank balance sheets and hence on the ability of banks to extend credit to households and businesses. Conversely, in economic upswings in which house prices rise, the reverse occurs as existing loans look more secure and profits rise. Through all three channels, house price fluctuations tend to amplify the business cycle in certain types of economies. This led Leamer to argue dramatically in 2007 that in the United States, 'housing is the business cycle'. These channels are illustrated in **Figure 1**, taken from Duca et al. (2010).

The institutional dependence and so heterogeneity of these mechanisms across countries is a key feature of the following discussion. The article begins with a discussion of what drives house prices, followed by an examination of each of the three channels discussed above. The potential for amplification and transmission of initial shocks in each of the three channels will be discussed.

However, interactions between housing and the macroeconomy do not end there. Housing costs account for around 30% of the US consumer price index, measured by rents, imputed rents of owner-occupiers, and maintenance costs. What happens in housing markets is therefore important for understanding inflation. Housing affects labour mobility and so labour markets. Potentially, economies with more constrained housing supply or high transaction costs may operate at lower levels of efficiency, with greater mismatch in labour supply and demand and so less favourable inflation–unemployment trade-offs. Finally, because housing accounts for half or more of household assets in many advanced countries, fluctuations in house prices have important effects on the distribution of wealth between individuals and across generations, with long-term macro-consequences.

What Drives House Prices?

In many countries, house prices appear to be subject to boom/bust cycles. In the decade 1997–2007, the rise in real house prices was unprecedented in many countries, though absent in a few, notably Japan and Germany. The three panels of **Figure 2** illustrate with real house price data from the OECD. The first panel is for four Anglo-Saxon economies: the United States, the United Kingdom, Canada, and Australia. These are all economies with liberal credit markets and independent monetary policies. The United Kingdom shows the highest appreciation in

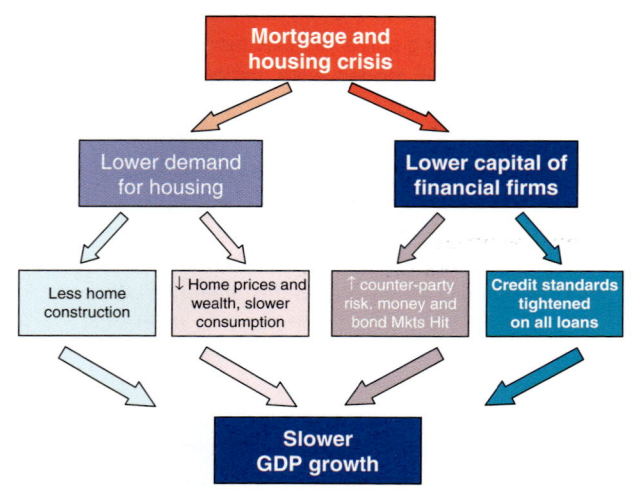

Figure 1 The channels of transmission of the mortgage and housing crisis.

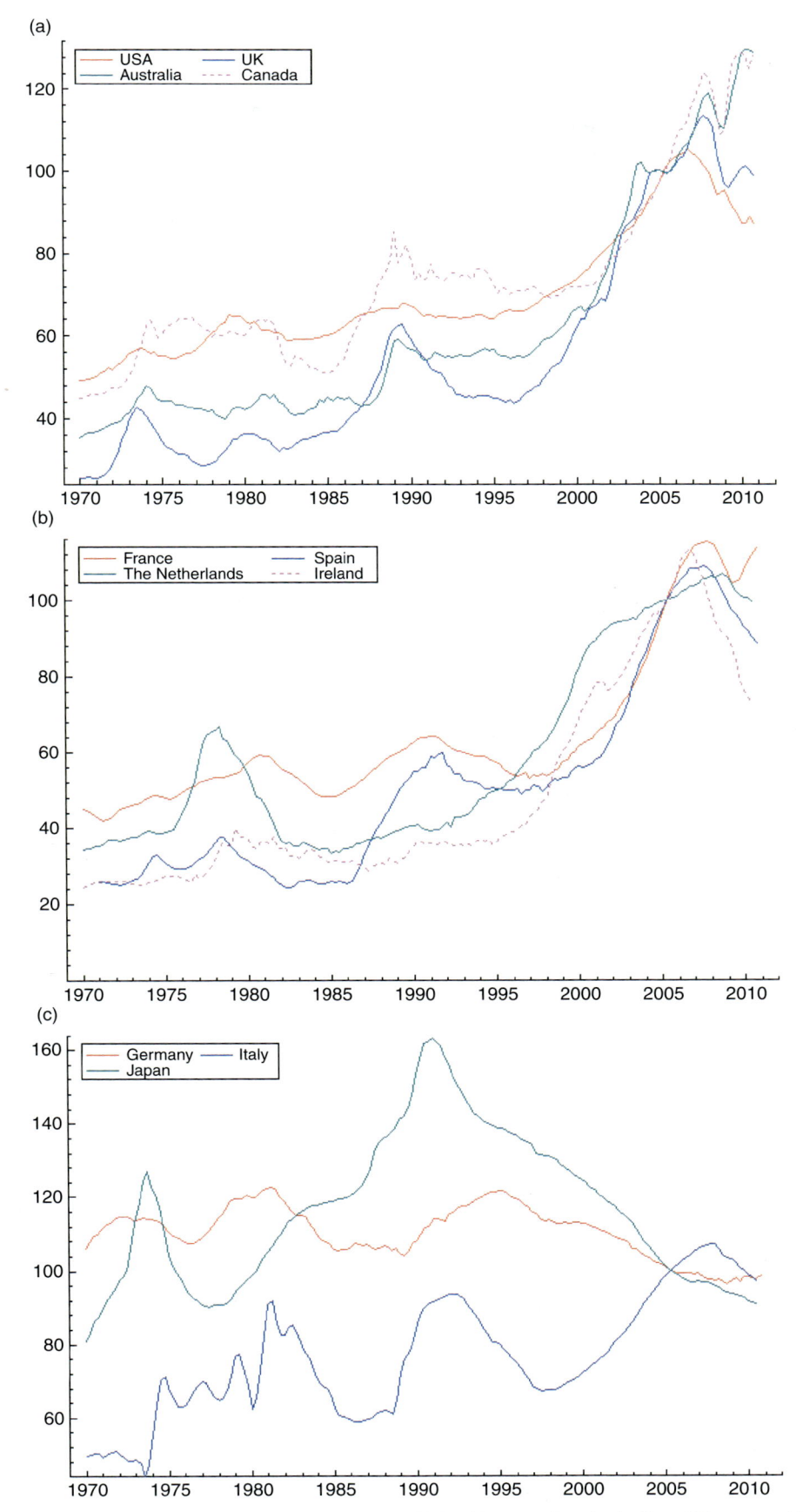

Figure 2 (a) Real house prices in the Anglo-Saxon economies. (b) Real house prices in the liberal Eurozone. (c) House prices in Germany, Italy, and Japan.

real house prices since 1970, followed by Australia, Canada, and the United States, though from 1970 to 2005, appreciation was similar in the United States and in Canada. The United States pattern is smoother than that of the other economies, reflecting averaging over heterogeneous regional markets. The United States has experienced the greatest fall in real house prices since 2006 while house prices in Australia and Canada rose to new highs after the global financial crisis.

The second panel is for a group of Eurozone economies, France, Spain, the Netherlands, and Ireland, where mortgage credit availability in the past decade also appears to have been strong. Spain and Ireland experienced a similar rise in real prices from 1970 to 2007, and all four economies went through large appreciations from the late 1990s to 2007, with the largest later falls in Ireland followed by Spain.

The third panel is for Germany, Italy, and Japan where mortgage credit availability has long been restricted and where there is little evidence of major shifts in the past decade. Japan experienced a great rise in real house prices (actually housing land prices).

As the major differences in outcomes illustrated in **Figure 2** hint, careful econometric work can make an important contribution to understanding what has happened to house prices and contribute to an early warning system of overvaluation and subsequent destabilising crashes, the ramifications of which were seen in the recent international financial crisis. Such research can uncover the most relevant fundamentals. Large recent deviations of house prices from levels predicted by models estimated on historical data are one symptom of overvaluation. But overvaluations are perfectly possible without such deviations. For example, there are likely to be inherent regularities in house price dynamics consistent with systematic overvaluation, since a large psychological element appears to drive the behaviour of many housing market participants, as Shiller has argued, for example, in his book on 'Irrational Exuberance'. It is also possible for credit availability, interest rates, and income to deviate from sustainable levels.

Indeed, almost the entire empirical literature on house price determination agrees that the housing market is not efficient: systematic mispricing can persist. In their literature review, Muellbauer and Murphy (2008) point to much evidence that house price changes are positively correlated and past information on fundamentals can forecast future excess returns. A number of authors find evidence against the hypothesis of rational home price expectations. Many empirical models find important effects on current house prices of lagged appreciation, termed the 'bubble-builder' by Abraham and Hendershott (1996), consistent with an important extrapolative element in expectations. The deviation of prices from long-run fundamentals is then the 'bubble-burster'.

For example, a series of positive shocks to fundamentals can lead to rising prices and the expectation of further appreciation leading to greater and greater overvaluation. In due course, the increasing negative pull from fundamentals reduces the rate of appreciation. When prices eventually fall, the falls can then be exaggerated by expectations of further falls.

In the United States, from the late 1990s, financial innovations in securitisation and changes in procedures by rating agencies resulted in the subprime revolution, extending loans to borrowers whose credit histories would previously have denied them such access. The growth of credit derivatives (see article Credit Derivatives and the Housing Market, C King and A Pavlov) played a vital role in expanding the investor base backing mortgages. Behind this increase in household leverage lay an increase in leverage at banks and financial institutions, (see Geanakoplos (2010) and Duca, Muellbauer, and Murphy (2010) for further discussion). Many nonprime mortgages were at adjustable rates, which particularly benefited from the lowest interest rates for decades in 2001–03. The house price increases these credit supply and interest rate changes set in train fooled many participants, as seen in surveys of house price expectations, into thinking that such rises would be sustained. In 2003, the fundamentals began to change as interest rates belatedly and only slowly began to return to more 'normal' levels, as argued by John Taylor in his book Getting Off Track. High rates of building expanded the housing stock, so that house prices became increasingly overvalued, and began to fall from 2006, with more and more borrowers with negative equity (i.e., homes worth less than their mortgages). As the extent of bad loans gradually became clear, the fundamentals changed again, as the supply of credit not only for subprime but also for mortgages more generally contracted as illustrated in Figure 1. The global financial crisis triggered by a mix of liquidity and solvency problems at banks and other financial institutions, well explained by Brunnermeier (2009), caused a massive rise in unemployment in the United States, exacerbating the mortgage foreclosure crisis (see further discussion below).

The Theory of House Price Determination

There are two basic theories of house price determination. The first is based on supply and demand functions, and a price adjustment process which brings supply and demand into balance. The second is based on finance and assumes arbitrage brings house prices and rents into an equilibrium relationship, again after a price adjustment process towards equilibrium. In both approaches, interest rates as well as shifts in access by households to credit provide an important link between the macroeconomy and house prices.

The supply and demand approach

In this approach, the supply – the stock of houses – is given in the short run. This is a simplification of the more general approach set out by G. Meen (see article Price Determination in Housing Markets). Then, prices are given by the inverted demand curve (i.e., by the stock of housing and the factors driving demand). Let log housing demand be given by

$$\ln h = -\alpha \ln hp + \beta \ln y + z \quad [1]$$

where hp = real house price, y = real income, and z = other demand shifters. The own-price elasticity of demand is $-\alpha$ and the income elasticity is β. Solving yields:

$$\ln hp = \frac{(\beta \ln y - \ln h + z)}{\alpha} \quad [2]$$

An advantage of the inverted demand function approach (i.e., expressing price as a function of quantity and the other factors shifting demand) is that it is well grounded theoretically, unlike many 'ad hoc' approaches. In addition, we have strong priors regarding the values of the key long-run elasticities, corresponding to the 'central estimates' set out in Meen's 2001 book on modelling spatial housing markets. For example, many estimates of the income elasticity of demand suggest that β is in the region of 1, in which case the income and housing stock terms in the above equation simplify to log income per house, that is, $\ln y - \ln h$.

The demand shifters included in z cover a range of other drivers. Since housing is a durable good, intertemporal considerations imply that expected or 'permanent' income and 'user cost' should be important drivers. The user cost takes into account that durable goods deteriorate, but may appreciate in price and incur an interest cost of financing as well as tax. The usual approximation is that the real user cost is:

$$uc = hp(r + \delta + t - \Delta hp^e/hp) = hp(uch) \quad [3]$$

where r is the real after-tax interest rate of borrowing, possibly adjusted for risk, δ is the deterioration rate, t is the property tax rate, and $\Delta hp^e/hp$ is the expected real rate of capital appreciation (see article Price Determination in Housing Markets), eqn [9].

The ex-post user cost, neglecting the risk premium, can take on negative values as rates of capital appreciation in house price booms have sometimes exceeded interest and other costs of owning a home. An important practical issue for the modeller is how to measure expected house price appreciation, since only in recent years have surveys begun to ask households about this. A reduced form approach in which expected appreciation is assumed to be a function of lagged appreciation, interest rates, and of log income, log housing stock, and other components of z is most often taken. Real house prices are explained by this same set of variables (see article Price Determination in Housing Markets, eqn [16] for a general formulation of an equilibrium correction model for house prices).

Other factors are also likely to be relevant, given that many mortgage borrowers face limits on their borrowing and may be risk averse. These include nominal as well as real interest rates, credit supply conditions, expected income growth, demography (such as the proportion of people aged 25–44 who tend to be the most active in the housing market in economies where down payment requirements are low), and proxies for downside risk, particularly of mortgage default. Credit supply conditions are particularly important given the international evidence on their influence on house price appreciation. Meen (see article Price Determination in Housing Markets) notes that in the theoretical derivation of the link between user cost and demand for housing which allows for mortgage rationing constraints, the shadow price on the rationing constraint enters the demand relationship. This provides a formal rationale for the inclusion of a credit conditions index, measuring household access to credit, in house price equations.

The rent–arbitrage approach

House prices have also been modelled using the house price-to-rent approach, particularly in the United States where rental markets are well-developed, and rents are generally market-determined, in contrast to the more heavily regulated rental markets of some European countries. This approach is grounded in finance and assumes that in the absence of substantial frictions and credit restrictions, arbitrage between owner-occupied and rental housing markets implies the house rent-to-price ratio is a function of the real user cost of capital term uch defined as, in eqn [3], by the nominal user cost of mortgage finance minus expected appreciation:

$$\text{rent}/hp = uch \quad [4]$$

A similar result is also obtained when agency costs make renting housing services more expensive than owning a home. Inverting and taking logs of eqn [4] implies:

$$\ln(hp/\text{rent}) = -\ln(uch) \quad [5]$$

where the elasticity of the price-to-rent ratio equals -1.

However, in a 2007 paper, Kim showed in an equilibrium model that when rental agency costs are accompanied by binding, maximum LTV ratios on marginal home-buyers, the equilibrium log price-to-rent ratio is more complicated:

$$\ln(hp/\text{rent}) = f(\ln(uch), \text{ maximum LTV}) \quad [6]$$

where the size of the negative real user cost elasticity can be smaller than 1, in line with empirical results, see Duca, Muellbauer and Murphy (2011) for evidence and discussion. Kim's result is close in spirit to Meen's eqn [11] (see article Price Determination in Housing Markets), which shows that when there is a binding credit constraint, the user cost term in the optimal house price-to-rent ratio includes the shadow price of the credit constraint (such as a maximum LTV bound), which will be related to the pervasiveness of such constraints.

Empirical evidence

One widely cited study is in IMF Economic Outlook, April 2008, 'Assessing Overvaluation in House Prices', a development of its 2004 Economic Outlook article. For each country, house price growth is modelled as a function of the lagged ratio of house prices to personal disposable income (PDI), growth in PDI per capita, short-term interest rates, long-term interest rates, credit growth, and changes in equity prices and working-age population. The unexplained increase in house prices from 1997 to 2007 defines the 'house price gap', a measure of overvaluation (see **Figure 3**). The IMF study does not have a clear theoretical foundation. The omission of the supply side and the imposition of a long-run income elasticity of 1 for house prices, when the true figure is likely to be in the 1.5–2.5 range are serious shortcomings in the approach. Also, permanent shifts in credit conditions and shifts in the age–structure of the population play no role in the analysis. This makes the conclusions from its house price gap figures unreliable.

The relationship between these estimated gaps and subsequent falls in real house prices is poor, apart from Ireland. The United States, ranked thirteenth, has experienced a sharper fall in real house prices than all countries ranked as higher risks, except for Ireland and Spain. Australia, France, Norway, Belgium, Sweden, and Finland had all experienced rises in real house prices by the third or fourth quarter of 2010 relative to the first quarter of 2008 despite their supposed overvaluations.

Research by Duca, Muellbauer, and Murphy confirms the role of credit market liberalisation in accounting for the rise in US house prices from 1996 to 2006, while the credit crunch then explains much of the subsequent fall. Data on loan-to-value ratios of first-time buyers, extracted from the American Housing Survey, are shown to be important for obtaining a cointegrated solution for the log house price both for the house price/rent–arbitrage model and the inverted demand approach. The important role of extrapolative expectations in the user cost confirms that US house prices temporarily overshot relative to 'fundamentals' as given either by credit conditions, interest rates, and rents or in place of rents, income, population, and the housing stock. However, some of the 'fundamentals' also proved unsustainable, most obviously the expansion of access to mortgages since 2000, based on excess leverage and other aspects of the subprime revolution.

In many other countries, little reliable time-series information is available on loan-to-values for first-time home-buyers or other indicators of credit market liberalisation. However, an alternative is to combine information from several credit sensitive indicators and extract a credit conditions index as a common latent variable. Research by Blake and Muellbauer for the European Commission on early warning indicators of imbalances and risks in European housing markets used information from a mortgage stock and house price equation jointly estimated for each country. This suggested that Ireland, Spain, France, and the United Kingdom all had a substantial rise in access to mortgage credit since 2000, with Ireland experiencing the largest subsequent credit crunch. In Germany, there was little evidence of change in access, while in Italy slight liberalisation since 2002 accounted for under 10% of the rise in real house prices. In all countries, the movements of the housing stock relative to real income and population make important contributions to explaining fluctuations in real house prices, for example, largely explaining the stagnation of real house prices in Germany compared to strong rises in the United Kingdom. One potential problem with the latent variable approach, even when supported by qualitative institutional information, is that other unobserved factors

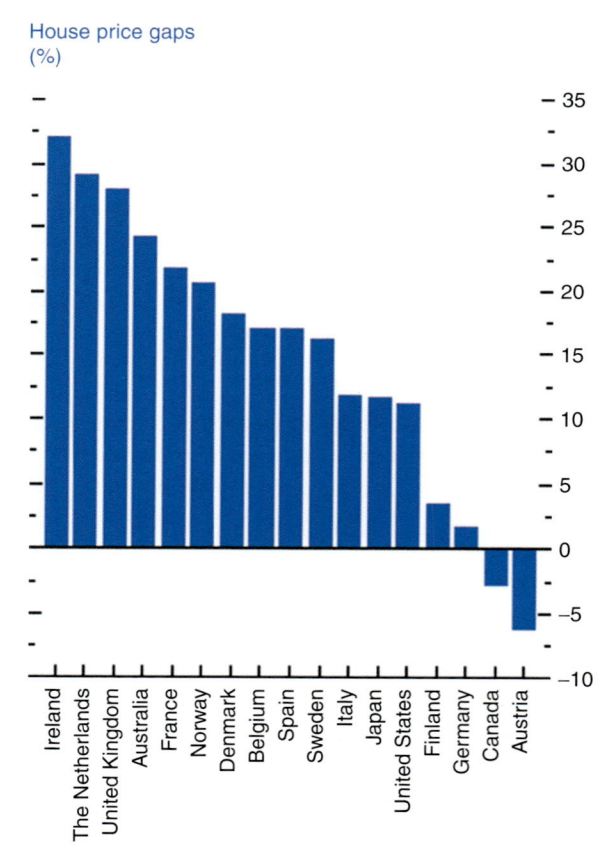

Figure 3 IMF house price gaps estimated in early 2008. Source: World Economic Outlook 2008:1 http://www.imf.org/external/pubs/ft/weo/2008/01/c3/Box3_1_1.pdf

might also be accounting for the rise in house prices and the mortgage stock which the standard controls such as income, interest rates, population, the housing stock, and demography cannot explain. Of these, perhaps the most plausible is a change in the subjective risk premium in the minds of housing investors. Adding more equations and other proxies for the risk premium should reduce the possibility of confusing credit conditions with a risk premium, but this remains a topic for future research.

Further evidence of the importance of credit market liberalisation and on an increased role for real interest rates for house prices comes from Muellbauer and Williams (2011). They estimate a four-equation system for Australian house prices, mortgage stock, consumption, and housing equity withdrawal (HEW) in which a common latent variable is a household credit conditions index. This index is estimated from a flexible spline function whose shape is consistent with institutional information about credit liberalisation in Australia. The rise in the credit conditions index (CCI) accounts for about half of the rise in real house prices between 1987 and 2008 and also from 1996 to 2008. Under-building relative to rising real income and population only begins to drive up house prices after 2002. In contrast, in the United Kingdom, the latter is the biggest single factor driving up real house prices from 1996 to 2007, though the rise in the UK CCI runs a close second.

Residential Construction

The determinants of the supply of housing are extraordinarily complex, as demonstrated by Vandell (see article Housing Supply). The literature on the econometrics of new house building is correspondingly diverse and contradictory. In a 1999 article in the Journal of Real Estate Finance and Economics, Pasquale explains some of the reasons why we appear to know so little about housing supply. Housing supply comes from new build as well as conversions and rehabilitation of the existing stock. Data on expenditure on improvements suggest that it has become a substantial fraction of total gross investment in housing. But the behaviour of builders and owners is likely to be different, while among owners, owner-occupiers may behave differently from landlords. New construction can be for owner-occupation, the private rental sector, or for the social rental sector, each with different drivers. Housing is heterogeneous and the available data on numbers of units usually ignore this heterogeneity by type and location.

Finally, government intervention in some countries is or has been on a massive scale. For example, as a matter of policy, the construction of social housing in the United Kingdom (and, for that matter, in many other countries, such as the Netherlands) has declined sharply since the 1970s. The incidence of rent controls has varied greatly.

Where the literature on private residential construction has found some convergence in recent years is in agreeing on the importance of land supply and, hence, zoning and planning restrictions and other interventions, such as taxation of developers (see Muellbauer and Murphy (2008) for further references, and Quigley (2007) for a review of the US literature).

Wide disagreements on details remain. Many of the estimates for housing-supply elasticities differ greatly, even when they are meant to refer to the same country and time period, sometimes even within the same study. In their 2000 article in the Journal of Urban Economics, Mayer and Somerville argue that residential construction responds not to the level of real house prices but to the rate of appreciation, and that this could be part of the reason for the great instability of estimates of the supply elasticity. Stripped to the essentials, they advance two main arguments. The first is that residential construction is a stationary series while real house prices are nonstationary, so that a cointegrated relationship cannot exist explaining the former by the latter. The second is that house values are basically land values plus the value of the bricks, mortar, and so on, erected by builders on the land. The structures are reproducible and their supply price is given by costs little affected by demand in the long run. Land, however, is nonreproducible. Builders effectively sell on the same land they acquired earlier so that their profit consists of the normal markup on construction costs plus the capital gain on land. Capital gains in land are approximately capital gains in housing adjusted for the rise in other construction costs. Hence, expected capital gains in land (or housing) will be important drivers of residential construction volumes. To be more precise, because builders also need to take the cost of capital into account, a user cost concept analogous to that which influences household demand for housing should help explain variations in residential investment. The relevant interest rate will be the rate at which builders can borrow, which will be correlated with but not identical to mortgage interest rates. Furthermore, access to borrowing by large and small construction companies may sometimes move differently from access to mortgages by households. It is also possible that builders may have better informed capital gains expectations than households. Nevertheless, it is likely that an extrapolative element governs these expectations. Hence, it is likely that quite similar factors, namely, extrapolative expectations of capital gains, low interest rates, and easier access to borrowing, explain both the overshooting of residential construction volumes in housing booms and the overshooting of house prices in, for example, Ireland, Spain, and the United States.

Most housing economists when asked, say in 2003, would have argued that economies where the supply responsiveness of housing is relatively high, as in

Ireland, Spain, and the United States, should experience lower house price volatility than economies where housing supply is unresponsive as in the United Kingdom. The smaller fall in house prices in the United Kingdom relative to the other three economies seems to contradict this. Part of the explanation lies in the common drivers of overshooting noted above – clearly if supply overshoots, then the subsequent fall in home prices to restore equilibrium will be greater; part lies in the greater relaxation of credit conditions and poorer lending quality, and hence greater reversal after 2007, in at least Ireland and the United States; and part lies in the macroeconomic feedback on unemployment and incomes which occurs when residential construction volumes collapse.

Interestingly enough, though there was hardly any increase in the volume of residential investment in the United Kingdom during the 1997–2007 house price boom, construction volumes in 2009–10 still fell from low levels to even lower levels, so that the United Kingdom built fewer homes in 2010 than in any year since 1923. The impact on GDP was just over 1% compared with 3% or more in Ireland, Spain, and the United States. It seems likely that the new supply market in the United Kingdom was in disequilibrium in 2010 in that home completions were governed more by demand than by what builders would have liked to sell at prevailing prices, or by the supply of building land.

In his 1988 book on the UK construction industry, Ball argued that the UK's volatile house price environment, in contrast to Germany's stable one, has had consequences for relative productivity and industry structure: the acquisition and management of land banks has been the main source of profits for UK house-builders. In a volatile house price environment, he argues, it has dominated the business agenda of house-builders to the neglect of concern for technological advance in building methods, design quality, or workforce training, which count for more in more stable house price environments.

Consumption and Housing Wealth

There is much disagreement among economists on whether variations in housing wealth matter for consumption. For example, Attanasio et al. (2009) take the view that house price fluctuations reflect shifts in income expectations and play no causal role for consumption. The Bank of England long argued similarly that there is no housing wealth effect on consumption. Muellbauer (see article Monetary Policy, Wealth Effects and Housing) explains that classical theory, in which credit constraints and buffer stock saving play no role, suggests that there could be a small housing wealth effect on nonhousing consumption but that on the standard national accounts concept of consumption, including imputed rent from housing, the housing wealth effect was likely to be negative.

Moving beyond classical theory to take credit constraints into account, the conclusions are quite different: a liberal credit market tends to result in a positive effect of house prices on consumption as collateral constraints on owners are relaxed and because the need to save for a housing deposit by the young is then limited even at higher prices. However, in the long run, the accumulation of higher debt will eventually reduce consumption. With an illiberal credit market, the collateral effect is weak, while the need of the young to save for a housing deposit is greater with higher house prices. In the latter case, higher house prices reduce consumer spending, as seems to have been the case in Italy and Japan. Institutional differences between countries therefore matter greatly, and so does the proper control for changing credit conditions in econometric work.

With proper controls for shifting access to credit, for income growth expectations, interest rates and the change in the unemployment rate, empirical estimates of the shifting marginal propensity to consume out of housing wealth tend to be lower but more accurately determined than estimates widely found in the literature, see the discussion in Muellbauer (see article Monetary Policy, Wealth Effects and Housing).

Depending on the structure of credit markets and other institutions, the housing collateral channel is an important part of the transmission of monetary policy and credit shocks to consumer spending and hence economic activity. In countries such as the United States, the United Kingdom, Spain, and Ireland, the housing collateral channel was a major factor in the strong growth since the early 2000s in consumer spending and its subsequent decline, as it was in the United Kingdom and the Scandinavian countries in the 1980s.

The Banking Channel

The banking channel is the third of the major macrochannels involving the housing market. This can be illustrated by the differing experiences of the United States, Spain, Ireland, the United Kingdom, and Germany in the financial crisis beginning in 2007. To summarise, the subprime crisis in the United States triggered major falls in US house prices, a surge in mortgage defaults, and a wider banking and credit market crisis spreading contagion among overleveraged banks and financial institutions globally.

Banks in Ireland were caught both by contagion from the United States and by a double domestic lending problem: reliance on short-term money markets, which seized up in August 2007, and overextension and poor quality of lending both to property developers and households (see Kelly, 2009). By mid-2011, it was estimated that over half of Irish mortgages were in negative equity The overwhelming bad loan problem led to a massive bank bailout by the government, and a credit crunch with sharply tighter loan conditions. The hastily given 2-year guarantee of the Irish banks by the Irish government and the collapse of tax revenue contributed to a more than doubling in 2 years of the ratio to GDP of government debt and to a sovereign debt crisis in 2010–11. International bond investors no longer believed in the capacity of the Irish government to service its bonds and hence spreads against safe Eurozone government bonds rose to levels requiring external support. The severity of the Irish economic crisis, accompanied by a massive rise in unemployment, falls in income and prospects by households of having to service a vast government debt in decades to come, led to substantial net outmigration. With one of the most mobile labour forces in Europe, some households could, in effect, walk away from the country's sovereign debt.

UK banks were far less extended to UK mortgage markets and UK property developers but faced a similar funding problem to that of the Irish banks and were also hit by contagion. Indeed, by 2010, bad domestic mortgage loans accounted for only a small part of the bad loan book of UK banks. Highly leveraged take overs, poor commercial lending decisions, and bad loans on unsecured lending did more to impair the balance sheets of domestic UK banks far more. However, without unprecedented monetary policy actions, including dramatic reductions in the policy rate and 'quantitative easing', there would have been severe problems in the UK mortgage market also. In the United Kingdom, mortgage loans are full recourse loans and defaulting borrowers can be pursued for up to 7 years for the shortfall between the loan and what the lender receives from the sale of the foreclosed property. This makes it more likely that foreclosure (mortgage possession or repossession) involves both a weak debt/equity position and a cash flow problem with debt service. Moreover, with most mortgages at adjustable interest rates, shocks to the debt–service ratio from variations in interest rates can be an important cause of both foreclosure and payment delinquencies (mortgage arrears), together with negative net equity and with income loss, for example, due to unemployment. In the analysis of UK arrears and possessions by Aron and Muellbauer, these factors are analysed together with estimates of the effects of lower loan quality in the late 1980s and the 2005–07 period and the subsequent tightening of access to refinancing possibilities, and of the impact of government policies. Policy involved urging increased forbearance on lenders through the enforcement of a code of practice and increasing the generosity of income support for those with payment difficulties. The UK government also brought in other policy measures to support those at risk of defaulting.

Figure 4 below shows the estimated long-run contributions to explaining the log possessions or foreclosure rate in the United Kingdom from the debt–service ratio (defined as the mortgage interest rate multiplied by average mortgage debt and divided by income), the proportion of mortgages in negative equity and the unemployment rate.

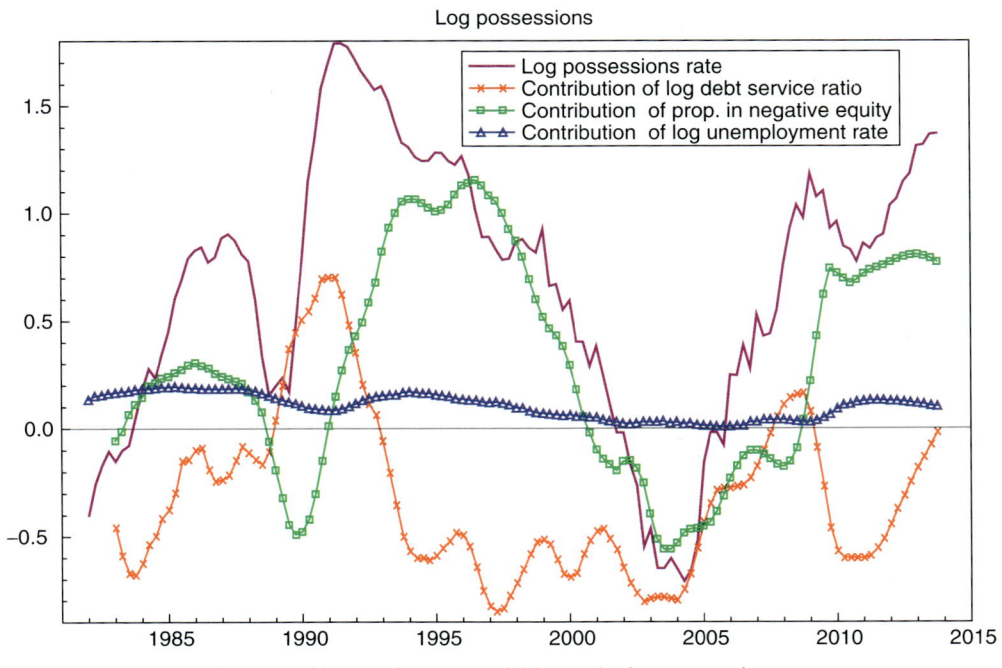

Figure 4 Estimated long-run contributions of key explanatory variables to the log possessions rate.

The outcomes from 2010 onwards are based on an assumed economic scenario in which interest rates start a return to more normal levels in the latter half of 2011. The figure shows the contribution of higher interest rates in 1989–92 in driving up foreclosures, the contribution of dramatically lower rates in 2008–10 to preventing a larger rise in foreclosures and the effects of simulated interest rate normalisation from 2011. The rise in the proportion in negative equity explains why foreclosures did not fall more rapidly in the mid-1990s and a major part of the rise in the foreclosure rate from 2004 to 2010.

Figure 5 suggests that increased forbearance policy reduced the foreclosure rate by about 12% below where it would otherwise have been both from 1992 and from the end of 2008. The figure also shows the estimated effect of the combination of loan quality, access to refinancing opportunities, and income support policies. It suggests that more generous income support from 2009 roughly cancelled the impact of the earlier deterioration in loan quality and of reduced access to refinancing opportunities. As an order of magnitude, it suggests that more generous income support probably reduced foreclosures by around 10–12% below the rate that would otherwise have occurred.

Models for mortgage arrears driven by the same determinants can be linked to the bad loan books of mortgage lenders used for stress testing the stability of the financial sector of the economy under different economic scenarios. The models should contain an important nonlinearity or amplification in the transmission of shocks via the housing market to the financial sector and so the economy. This arises because of the nonlinear link between house prices and the incidence of negative equity illustrated in **Figure 6**. This shows the distribution of log debt/equity with the area under the right tail showing the fraction of mortgages with negative equity (with home equity less than debt). If average house prices fall by 10% say, the distribution shifts to the right and the area under the tail increases by much more than 10%. Thus, beginning in 'normal' times, even a large rise in house prices has little effect in reducing further the already low level of foreclosures. But a fall in house prices raises the level of foreclosures while a large fall will sharply raise foreclosures. This is an important asymmetry which helps account for the fact that business cycle contradictions are often far sharper than business cycle expansions.

To date, the most complete quantitative model which captures the right-hand side of the flow chart shown in **Figure 1** is the Bank of England's Risk Assessment Model for Systemic Institutions (RAMSI) (see **Figure 7**). The following flow chart explains how this model works.

At the start of the period, some macro or financial shocks arrive. These affect yields and probabilities of default (PDs). The credit risk module models UK probabilities of default for mortgages, unsecured household lending, corporate defaults in the United Kingdom and abroad, and scales by loss given default. These losses are distributed across banks given each banks' exposure to each sector, using detailed balance sheet information for each bank. The profit and loss accounts of each bank are then

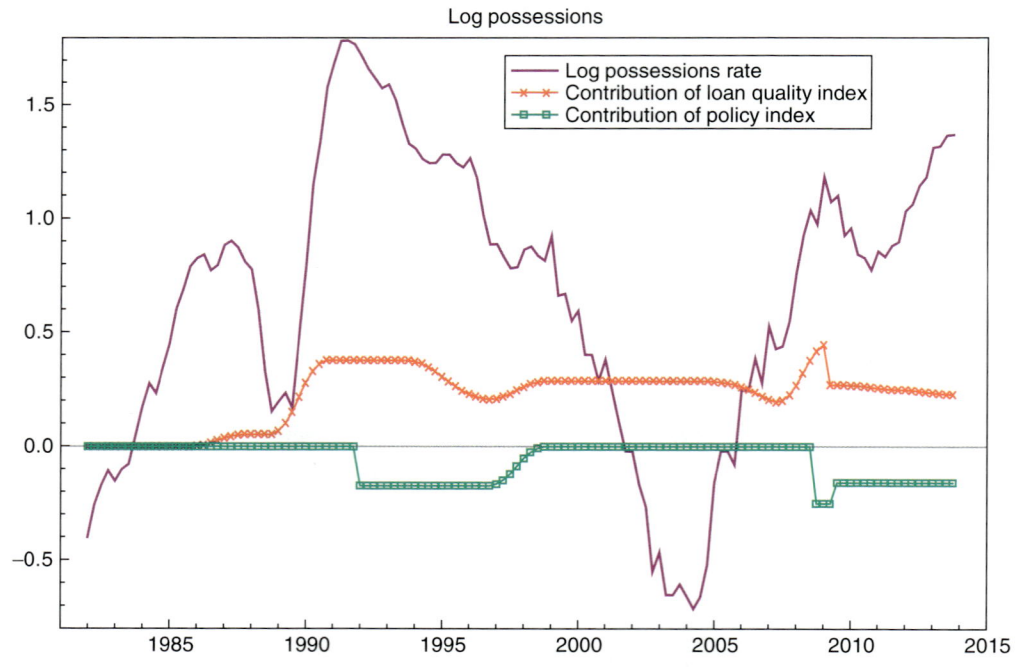

Figure 5 Estimated long-run contribution of lending standards and forbearance policy to the log possessions rate.

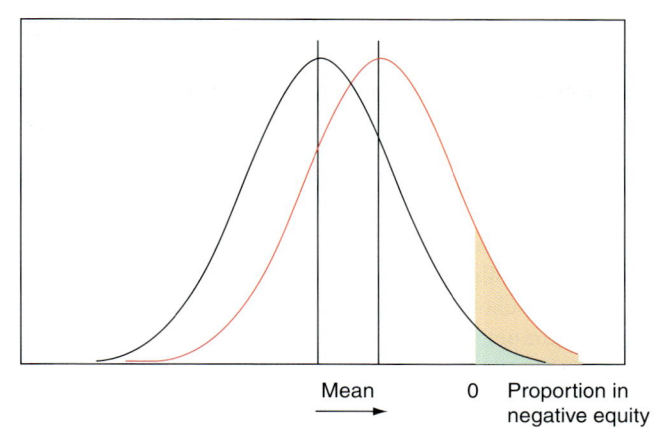

Figure 6 The impact of an increase in the average debt equity ratio on the proportion of mortgages in negative equity.

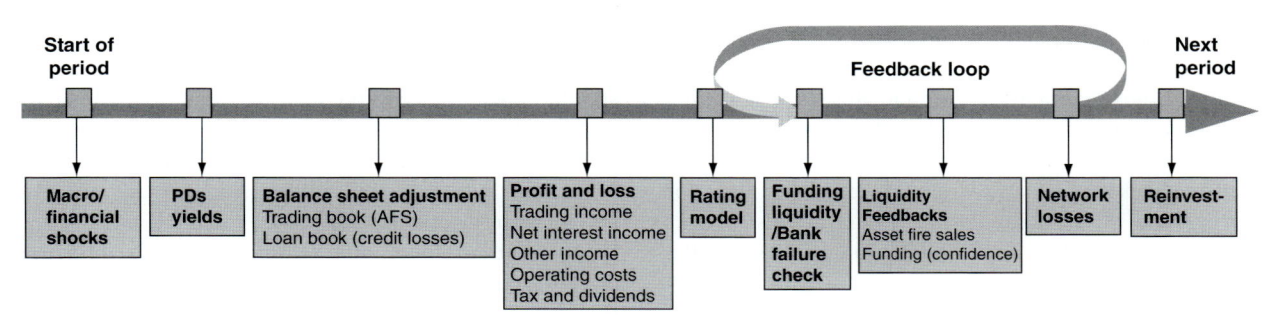

Figure 7 Model dynamics for Bank of England risk assessment model. Figure 2, p. 9 in David Aikman, Piergiorgio Alessandri, Bruno Eklund, Prasanna Gai, Sujit Kapadia, Elizabeth Martin, Nada Mora, Gabriel Sterne and Matthew Willison, 2009, Bank of England Working Paper No. 372 'Funding liquidity risk in a quantitative model of systemic stability'.

determined, given the models for trading income and expenses. A net interest model implies that the pricing structure of each bank's balance sheets, especially the mismatch between assets and liabilities, influences each bank's vulnerability to shocks to interest rates, spreads, and default probabilities. This influences the ratings banks receive from ratings agencies, which can affect funding costs and liquidity and possibly even bank failure. Banks may engage in fire sales to boost liquidity. A model of interactions between banks with network externalities, where counterparty risk constrains behaviour, generates the possibility of further losses, and this feeds back on funding liquidity and the possibility of bank failure. Survivors bear credit losses which impair their balance sheets and assumptions need to be made on the portfolio/risk strategies pursued by the survivors. At the end of the period, balance sheets, loan, and trading books are set for the beginning of the next period. Bank lending determined in the period also feeds into the macroeconomic picture for the beginning of the next period, when new macro or financial shocks arrive and the model continues.

The Banking Channel gives a good flavour of the kinds of realistic feedbacks and shock amplification which arose in the global financial crisis and which potentially could arise again. Simulations of the model highlight risk to funding liquidity and contagion and allow stress tests to be carried out under different scenarios. The model can also calculate how bank recapitalisation reduces systemic risk. The model highlights the risks associated with higher interest rates in the aftermath of the financial crisis and the role played by housing and mortgage markets in transmitting these risks.

DSGE Models with a Housing Sector

In recent years, the new Keynesian dynamic stochastic general equilibrium (DSGE) model has been the dominant paradigm for macroeconomists and central banks. As noted in the Glossary, DSGE models until recently excluded financial frictions and had no active role for asset prices and money. Drawing on a paper by Iacoviello in the American Economic Review, a 2010 paper in the American Economic Journal by Iacoviello and Neri presents the first fully calibrated DSGE model with a housing market and a financial friction. Because of the influence of this approach, it is worth a more detailed examination.

There are two sectors, one producing goods from capital and labour and one producing new homes from capital, labour, land, and intermediate goods. There are two types of households. Patient households differ from impatient ones by saving and lending to the impatient households who always want to borrow as much as they can using the value of their homes as collateral. The financial friction is that the patient households are not willing to lend more than some maximum fraction of value, 85% in the calibrated model. The wage share of the impatient households is fixed (21% in the calibrated model). There is a different trend in technological progress across sectors. Prices in the nonhousing sector and wages are sticky but house prices adjust instantaneously to clear the housing market. The central bank runs monetary policy by setting interest rates. There are several real rigidities including habits in consumption, lags in labour mobility, adjustment costs in capital, and variable capital utilisation. Apart from sectoral technology shocks, six other shocks drive the economy. Three household preference shocks affect the discount rate, the taste for housing, and the taste for leisure. There are also shocks in the interest rate function, the inflation process, and the central bank inflation target.

The model is calibrated to quarterly US data from 1965 to 2006. Simulating the model over this period makes it possible to explain variations in house prices, housing construction, consumption, business investment, inflation, and other variables in terms of the original shocks. It is also possible to compare the properties of simulated economies with and without the financial friction. For example, running a regression of the growth rate of consumption on the growth rate of house prices gives a coefficient of 0.1 without the financial friction. This makes the point that there may be little 'causal' relationship between house prices and consumption: it is just that the shocks driving both happen to be positively correlated. Adding the financial friction, which introduces a causal link, via the role of housing collateral, between house prices and consumption raises the above regression coefficient by 0.024.

However, the model fails major reality tests. The model implies that aggregate housing equity withdrawal (HEW) defined as the increase in household mortgage debt minus the accumulation by households of residential property is always negative. The ratio of HEW to non-property income in the United States, often positive and subject to swings from +7% to −8%, is a hugely important part of financial flows in the national accounts. Their closed economy model without a banking system could never generate such swings. The model therefore fails this simple first reality test, despite being calibrated on US data.

A second problem is that there are no defaults on loans and therefore there is no default risk. Thus, mortgage foreclosures discussed above, now at record levels in the United States, are outside the scope of such models. A third problem is that unexplained housing preference shocks play an implausibly large role in explaining real house prices and housing investment. Generally, apart from habit formation or gradual evolution, economists prefer preferences to be stable, and not subject to cyclical shocks. Fourth, there is no role for extrapolative expectations of house price appreciation or other housing market inefficiencies which ignores the large literature on housing market inefficiency. Extrapolative expectations are one major amplification channel for the financial accelerator discussed in the section 'What Drives House Prices?'. A fifth problem is that the model also ignores an important part of life-cycle saving: young households need to borrow, but their need to save first for their initial housing deposit is omitted from the model. Their saving should depend on both the loan-to-value ratio constraint and level of real house prices (see the discussion in 'Consumption and Housing Wealth' section above). Next, precautionary and buffer stock saving are also absent, as in most DSGE models.

A seventh problem is the assumption of a fixed fraction of credit constrained households, omitting the impact on the desire to borrow of time-varying expectations of income, capital appreciation, and uncertainty, and also giving no role for financial innovation and credit market liberalisation. A micro-theorist could argue that credit rationing, driven by consumers' exogenous taste differences and an unexplained loan-to-value ratio limit, lacks microfoundations in asymmetric information. Finally, a generic problem in such DSGE models is the assumption that consumers and firms have 'rational' or model consistent expectations, in a world where central banks even with their large and sophisticated research staffs and superior access to data, are hugely uncertain about the future and often make systematic forecasting errors arising from changes in the structure of the economy.

This suggests that a more evidence-based approach, based on less restrictive assumptions about the economy, but with appropriate controls to reduce the risk of causal confusion, is a better way of acquiring an understanding of the issues, relevant for policy-makers.

Extensions

Housing and the Consumer Price Index

Housing costs account for around 30% of the US consumer price index, measured by rents, imputed rents of owner-occupiers, and maintenance costs. Imputed rents are based on data from rental markets so the latter are important for understanding US inflation. Rents tend to follow the general price level, borrowing costs and house prices with a substantial lag. This means that, for example, US rents are likely to continue falling or rise less strongly relative to other prices even after US house prices stabilise and then begin to recover. Interest rate policy pursued by the Federal Reserve can therefore continue to be more accommodative than in previous recoveries from recession.

Not all countries use imputed rents to measure owner-occupied housing costs. At first sight, the obvious alternative is to use a user cost measure based on eqn [3]. But the difficulty is that expectations of capital gains and the risk premium are unobservable and no generally agreed proxies exist. In the Euro currency area, because of institutional differences and disagreements over concepts, the harmonised consumer price index excludes owner-occupied housing altogether. Housing costs are therefore underrepresented in the official inflation measure, most of all in countries with high rates of owner-occupation such as Spain, and in the monetary policy response. It is likely that high rates of increase of house prices in Spain and labour market demands from the expansion of the building industry contributed to higher rates of wage inflation in Spain. These damaged the economy's competitiveness in the Euro area and therefore contributed to the deep economic crisis in which Spain found itself by 2009.

Housing and Labour Mobility

Potentially, economies with more constrained housing supply or high transactions costs may operate at lower levels of efficiency, with greater mismatch in labour supply and demand and so less favourable inflation-unemployment trade-offs and so somewhat higher average rates of unemployment. High rates of owner-occupation combined with high transactions costs, due to Stamp Duty or other turnover taxes, are likely to reduce average labour mobility (see article Housing and Labour Markets). Perhaps even more serious are the constraints on labour mobility associated with low or negative housing equity. At the end of 2010, estimates by CoreLogic suggested that 22.5% of US homes with mortgages had mortgages exceeding the value of their homes. Given transactions costs of perhaps 5 or 6% in realtors fees and a substantial deposit on a new purchase, many more households would have found a move to another owner-occupied home difficult or impossible. With a large private rental sector in the United States and a walk away option in some but not all states for mortgage borrowers, the United States had a mobility safety valve. Nevertheless, it seems likely that these restraints on labour mobility were part of the reason why US unemployment rates were slow to fall in 2010 and 2011.

Housing and Intergenerational Inequality

Finally, because housing accounts for half or more of household assets in many advanced countries, fluctuations in house prices have important effects on the distribution of wealth between individuals and across generations, with long-term macro-consequences. In their 2010 paper, Barrell and Weale show, in an overlapping generation model, that higher land prices raise the consumption of the current generation of owners at the expense of future generations. There is thus a formal similarity between higher land prices and a fiscal deficit resulting in future generations having to reduce consumption to finance the extra consumption enjoyed by their parents' or grandparents' generation. They argue that in countries with strongly rising real land prices, fiscal policy should be tightened to compensate for the resulting intergenerational redistribution. This redoubles criticism of excessively loose fiscal policy in the United Kingdom and in the United States in the years before the financial crisis.

Conclusions

Nothing could illustrate more strikingly the relevance of housing and mortgage markets for the macroeconomy than the global financial crisis which began in 2007. In countries such as the United States, Ireland, and Spain, where house building had been very responsive to the house price boom before the financial crisis began, and where mortgage credit had been liberally available, the collapse in housing contributed to a dramatic reduction in GDP. This was the result of the fall in residential construction, the fall in consumer spending and the impact on other economic activity of the credit crunch triggered by mortgage defaults and worries about the liquidity, and solvency of major financial institutions. In the United Kingdom, where land supply constraints had prevented house building from responding to rising prices, the fall in GDP from the fall in residential construction was far smaller, while dramatic falls in interest rates helped to stabilise house prices and consumption, and employment was supported by currency depreciation. In Germany, the absence of credit market liberalisation and the absence of a preceding house price boom and an associated building boom, left house prices, consumer spending, and house building little affected by events in domestic housing and mortgage markets. Germany's banks still suffered some impairment from foreign loans and foreign, mainly

United States, real estate asset-backed securities. Output fell as a result of the shock to demand for exports but subsequently recovered more firmly than in the United Kingdom with the recovery of world trade.

As explained in the penultimate section, there are three further issues raised by the structure of housing and mortgage markets for the macroeconomy. The first concerns the measurement of owner-occupiers' housing costs in the consumer price index used to set monetary policy. This could have important implications for whether monetary policy 'leans against the wind' of rising house prices. The second concerns housing market impediments for labour mobility, which affect the inflation–unemployment trade-off. The third concerns the intergenerational redistribution caused by a house price boom, with major implications for saving behaviour, pensions, and tax policy.

Acknowledgements

The author acknowledges the financial support from the ESRC via the UK Spatial Economics Research Centre. This research was supported in part by grants from the Open Society Institute and the Oxford Martin School. This article draws on joint research over many years with Anthony Murphy and Janine Aron and more recently with John Duca.

See also: Credit Derivatives and the Housing Market; Housing and Labour Markets; Housing Supply; Monetary Policy, Wealth Effects and Housing; Price Determination in Housing Markets.

References

Abraham JM and Hendershott PH (1996) Bubbles in metropolitan housing markets. *Journal of Housing Research* 7: 191–207.

Aron J and Muellbauer J (2010) Modelling and forecasting UK mortgage arrears and possessions. CEPR discussion paper 7986.

Attanasio O, Blow J, Hamilton R, and Leicester A (2009) Booms and Busts: Consumption, House Prices and Expectations. *Economica* 76(301): 20–50.

Barrell R and Weale M (2010) Fiscal policy, fairness between generations, and national saving. *Oxford Review of Economic Policy* 26(1): 87–116.

Brunnermeier MK (2009) Deciphering the liquidity and credit crunch 2007–2008. *Journal of Economic Perspectives* 23(1): 77–100.

Duca J, Muellbauer J, and Murphy A (2010) Housing markets and the financial crisis of 2007–2009: Lessons for the future. *Journal of Financial Stability* 6(4): 203–217.

Duca J, Muellbauer J, and Murphy A (2011) House prices and credit constraints: Making sense of the US experience. *Economic Journal* 121(552): 445–461.

Geanakoplos J (2010) Solving the present crisis and managing the leverage cycle. *Federal Reserve Bank of New York Economic Policy Review* 16: 101–131.

Iacoviello M and Neri S (2010) Housing market spillovers: Evidence from an estimated DSGE model. *American Economic Journal: Macroeconomics* 2(2): 125–164.

Kelly M (2009) The Irish credit bubble. University College Dublin Centre for Economic Research, WP09/32.

Muellbauer J and Murphy A (2008) The assessment: Housing markets and the economy, Special Issue on *Housing Markets and the Economy, Oxford Review of Economic Policy* 24(1): 1–33.

Muellbauer J and Williams D (2011) Credit conditions and the real economy: The elephant in the room. CEPR discussion paper 8399.

Quigley JM (2007) Regulation and property values in the United States: The high cost of monopoly. In: Ingram GK and Yu-Hung H (eds.) *Land Policies and their Outcomes*, pp. 46–66. Cambridge, MA: Lincoln Institute.

Further Reading

Leamer E (2007) Housing is the business cycle. *Housing, Housing Finance, and Monetary Policy Symposium*, sponsored by the Federal Reserve Bank of Kansas City, Kansas City, USA, 149–233.

Housing and the State in Australasia

B Badcock, Housing New Zealand Corporation, New Zealand

© 2012 Elsevier Ltd. All rights reserved.

Glossary

Accommodation Supplement The Accommodation Supplement (AS) is a nontaxable income and asset-tested supplement that provides assistance towards private accommodation costs in New Zealand, including rent, board, and the short-term costs of owner-occupied homes (where owners can demonstrate good cause). The amount takes account of family size, tenure, and income, varies according to market rents in four composite regions, and is adjusted periodically in line with living costs.

Commonwealth Rent Assistance Rent assistance in Australia is provided to tenants renting in the private rental market through two programmes: Commonwealth Rent Assistance (CRA) and (formerly) CSHA private rent assistance (PRA). In 2005–06, the federally funded CRA programme allocated $2.1 billion of assistance to low-income private renters. CRA is a uniform payment regardless of variations in regional housing costs. By contrast, PRA, which is provided by the states and territories, was a comparatively modest $78.4 million in 2005–06.

Commonwealth State Housing Agreement The first Commonwealth State Housing Agreement (CSHA) setting out the responsibilities and funding arrangements for a government housing programme in Australia was signed in 1945. It fell somewhat short of a 'comprehensive' housing policy. This first agreement advanced funds to the states primarily for rental stock. The agreement was renegotiated and priorities adjusted every 4 years or so until it was replaced by the National Affordable Housing Agreement at the beginning of 2009.

Economic rationalism Economic rationalism is a term that was adopted in Australia to apply to the market-oriented economic policies favoured during the 1980s and 1990s. Economic rationalists supported deregulation, privatisation of state-owned industries, lower direct taxation and higher indirect taxation, and a reduction in the size of the welfare state.

First Home Owner Scheme The First Home Owner Grant Scheme (FHOGS) is a joint Australian and State Government venture that provides a $7000 grant to eligible applicants. Between October 2008 and June 2009, the First Home Owners Boost (FHOB) doubled and trebled the existing grant on established and new home, respectively.

National Affordable Housing Agreement The National Affordable Housing Agreement (NAHA) is one of a series of Intergovernmental Agreements ratified by the Council of Australian Governments in November 2008. The Commonwealth and the States agreed to a new NAHA which commenced on 1 January 2009. It consolidates previous Special Purpose Payments that support government programmes in social housing, assistance to people in the private rental market, support and accommodation for people who are homeless, and home purchase assistance.

National Rental Affordability Scheme National Rental Affordability Scheme (NRAS) is a 2007 Australian federal government commitment to: increasing the supply of affordable rental dwellings; reducing rental costs for low-to-moderate income households; and encouraging large scale investment and innovative delivery of affordable housing. Annual tax offsets will be available for 10 years on the condition that throughout the period the dwelling is rented to eligible low and moderate income households. The rent will be charged at 20% below the market rate. The scheme will fund 50 000 rental dwellings by 2012, and possibly a further 50 000 units after July 2012, subject to demand.

New Zealand Housing Strategy The New Zealand Housing Strategy, which was launched in 2005, set out the Government's programme of action for housing over the ensuing decade. Primary and supporting initiatives were designated to: stimulate a sufficient supply of new housing to meet future demand, and help stabilise market conditions; improve housing assistance and affordability; improve access to home ownership; develop the private rental sector; improve housing quality; strengthen housing sector capability; and meet diverse needs.

Supported Accommodation Assistance Program Supported Accommodation Assistance Program (SAAP) is one of the two most important Australian programmes providing assistance to people experiencing homelessness. SAAP was established in 1985 and is jointly funded by the Australian Government and states and territories. The programme delivers accommodation and short-term income support to meet crisis needs and to help transition people into independent living. SAAP was reviewed in 2008–09 and now has two headline goals: to halve overall homelessness by 2020; and, to offer supported accommodation to all rough sleepers who need it by 2020. The other programme is the Crisis Accommodation Program (CAP), which provides the capital funding for about 7300 units of emergency accommodation in the NGO sector.

Introduction

This article outlines the evolution of government intervention and housing policy settings in Australia and New Zealand-Aotearoa (hereafter NZ) with an eye to the implications for welfare and well-being. The scene is set by describing essential defining features of Australia and NZ as separate nation states. This is followed by a brief history of housing provision which, despite the common threads, inevitably faces the twin liabilities of overgeneralisation and omission. Coverage of current arrangements for housing assistance and housing outcomes dominates the remainder of the discussion. While the main purpose is to describe the housing outcomes resulting from state intervention in Australasian housing markets, this contribution concludes by noting some of the wider implications for debates about the direction of housing theory and policy.

Australia and NZ as Nation States

Australia and NZ are New World colonies settled during the nineteenth century by Anglo-Celtic stock. Both have parliamentary systems modelled on Westminster, except that the Australian colonies opted for a federal system in 1901, while NZ developed a unitary system.

During the nineteenth century, successive waves of immigrants subjugated the Aboriginal and Māori inhabitants as the rural frontier was pushed further into 'the bush'. British land tenure and property systems were enshrined in legislation and superimposed on the landscape. The seeds of collective organisation sprung out of dissatisfaction with conditions on pastoral stations in Australia (in the case of the union movement) and overcoming barriers in the pioneering dairy industry in NZ (in the case of farmer's coops). These developments helped to frame the expectations of citizens with respect to minimum wages, women's suffrage, public health, and housing, and provided a future platform for the creation of the welfare state in both countries.

The growth of the two economies depended upon agricultural exports and until the mid-1970s, tariff protection for domestic producers. From the early days NZ and Australia's eastern seaboard have been tied together by trade and trans-migration. Bilateral trade and investment have grown significantly since the Australia–New Zealand Closer Economic Relations Free Trade Agreement (CER) was signed in 1983. Port cities like Sydney, Melbourne, Brisbane, Adelaide, Perth, and Auckland continue to dominate the settlement systems of two of the most highly urbanised countries in the OECD. By 2005, the populations of Australia and NZ had passed 21 million and four million, respectively. While indigenous people constitute less than 2% of the Australian population, Māori and Pacific peoples in NZ account for 15 and 7% of the population and are projected to grow faster than Pakeha people of European origin. Immigration continues to increase the multicultural diversity of Australian society, while the dominance of immigrants from Pacific neighbours and Asia, together with Māori, is steadily 'browning' NZ society. The indigenous populations of both countries, especially Aborigines, score less well on many indicators of human well-being, including housing.

All these factors have influenced the evolution of distinctive and remarkably similar housing systems which are often type-cast, along with Britain, Canada, and the United States, as 'property-owning democracies'. In both countries, by 2010: owner-occupiers accounted for about 68% of privately occupied dwellings (though, in the case of NZ, the rate had fallen sharply from 74% in 1991); private renters accounted for 26–28%; and social renters for just 5–6%.

This dominance of home ownership reflects the strength of state support for the tenure in the recent past. During the middle of the twentieth century, housing policy in Australasia was tailored to suit the prosperous economic conditions underpinning occupational mobility and entry into home ownership; and with the private rental sector offering choice and flexibility to households not ready to own, there was little cause in either country to develop 'not-for-profit' community-based housing as an alternative to state housing. For this reason, with under 2% of the total stock, the community housing sector is still in an embryonic state. And while the third sector now has government backing, growth will be painstaking rather than spectacular.

A Brief History of State Housing Intervention

Early Experiments in 'Nest Building'

State intervention has been central to shaping the early development of Australia and NZ. In NZ, direct intervention in the housing market dates back to the beginning of the twentieth century (Ferguson, 1994: 59–69). In NZ, a Liberal Government passed the Workers' Dwellings Act (1905) and advanced finance to 'respectable' households on moderate incomes wanting to move out of overcrowded terrace housing to build in the suburbs (Advances to Workers Act 1906). In the event, up until 1935, about three times the number of loans to city dwellers were issued to farmers for rural housing and improvements.

In Australia, where the New South Wales government granted its Savings Bank permission to advance home finance in 1912, this quickly caught on in other states. Immediately after the Great War, the Commonwealth financed 12 000 War Service Homes for owner-occupation. Suburban house building then went through a boom in the 1920s, but virtually ceased during the depression of the early 1930s. At the same time, housing surveys conducted in NZ under the Housing Survey Act (1935), and a growing clamour for slum clearance in Australia's largest cities, heightened public awareness of the unfit state of much of the older housing stock.

Housing Becomes a Pillar of the Welfare State

The first Labour Government in NZ came to power at the end of the Depression (1929–34) and laid the foundations for the 'wage earner's welfare state'. With markets unable to adequately meet basic needs in health, education, housing, and retirement, the state stepped in. This presaged later developments in Australia, when a referendum held in 1946 granted powers to the Commonwealth so it could institute a national social security scheme. In effect, a social contract was struck around guarantees to provide citizens with a reasonable standard of living, including work opportunities, adequate schooling and health care, a pension in retirement, and decent housing within their means (Thorns, 1988: 6).

Increasingly, governments in Australasia approached housing expenditure as one of the Keynesian tools to be used countercyclically to support the building industry and stimulate economic activity. For example, in NZ under Labour (1936–49), about 32 000 state rental units were built, in the process helping to prime the housing industry and create jobs. This relieved some of the pressure on the private rental market by replacing the worst housing, while rent controls and a minimum wage policy made accommodation more affordable. In South Australia, it was a conservative Liberal Government in 1936 that created an 'arms length' authority with the powers to manage rental housing built under contract by private builders. The South Australian Housing Trust deliberately set rents below market rates as a wage subsidy to industry. This gave the state a competitive advantage in attracting new jobs and over time helped to stabilise rents in the private sector (Badcock, 1989).

While governments gave priority to building state housing through the 1940s, some set up agencies – such as the State Advances Corporation in NZ – to provide subsidised loans to households with low to moderate earnings and savings. Despite this, by the end of the Second World War, even though 52–54% of households in Australia and New Zealand owned or were buying their own homes, both countries faced mounting housing shortages. At a time when the Commonwealth Housing Commission estimated a shortfall of 300 000 dwellings, the 1947 Census counted over 10% of households 'sharing' and over 80 000 people 'sleeping out' (Greig, 1995: 31–37).

Nation-Building and Achieving the 'Dream'

For 25 years after the Second World War, major public investment in infrastructure, full employment, real wage gains, and government housing programmes ensured that home ownership levels expanded in line with a fairer distribution of earnings for Australasian workers (Badcock and Beer, 2000). Indeed, during the 'long boom', when living standards exceeded those in most other OECD countries, Australia and NZ were constructing more housing per capita for owner-occupation than any other industrialised country and dispensing subsidised home loans to significantly bolster otherwise rationed bank finance. As a consequence, 'the dream' of home ownership came to be embedded in the national psyche and undoubtedly played its part in attracting migrants from all over Europe where home ownership was unattainable for many groups.

The single measure that did the most to make home ownership affordable in NZ throughout the 1960s was the option to capitalise an allowance paid to mothers of each child under 16 years (i.e., the 'family benefit'). This helped bridge the deposit gap towards a subsidised mortgage underwritten by the State Advances Corporation which, at the peak in the 1960s, financed more than half the homes built in NZ. Similarly, in Australia, amendments to the 1956 Commonwealth State Housing Agreement (CSHA) diverted funds to a Home Builders Account to assist low-income home buyers, and paved the way for the sale of public rental stock. By 1968–69 almost 90 000 of these dwellings had been sold Australia-wide, with New South Wales and Victoria accounting for nearly two-thirds of the total (Jones, 1972). Home ownership in Australia peaked at 71.4% in 1966, and at 74% in NZ by 1986.

For a time in South Australia (1950–66), with the blessing of the state's Premier, the Housing Trust made the most of its statutory independence to extend business well beyond the supply of rental housing for workers, to the acquisition of land in the right locations, and to the provision of fixed capital and labour. It actively sought out and contributed to the establishment costs of major employers such as General Motors-Holden, BHP, Phillips, Chrysler, and Vacuum Oil, and indirectly subsidised their production costs. There are parallels here, therefore, to the role played in nation-building by the Singapore Housing and Development Board. Also, by restricting access to tenants in steady employment, the Housing Trust largely avoided the complications of defaulting and arrears, and was able to operate profitably between 1938 and 1962. According to Stretton, "Central economic planning ran half a century ahead of a central lack of compassion – saving on that was where the winning margins in cheap land, water, power and housing came from" (quoted in Badcock, 1989: 441). Thus, in its heyday, although lacking a priority system, the Housing Trust housed over 11% of South Australian households – almost double the share of most other states.

'Downsizing' the State and Establishing a 'Safety Net'

The last quarter of the twentieth century found structural imbalances and fiscal pressures bearing down upon the welfare systems of most OECD countries – 'the fiscal crisis of the state'. This forced governments, and none more so than New Zealand's, to thoroughly reexamine all forms of public expenditure and social protection (including housing assistance). In Australasia, the political consensus and policies that had underpinned the 'dream' of home ownership since the late 1940s finally gave way to the politics of economic rationalism (Pusey, 1991).

By the 1980s, criticism of the welfare state and its public sector offspring, including the public housing agencies, was mounting in Australasia as elsewhere. A blend of neoliberalism, institutional economics, and public choice theory inspired a fundamental questioning of the respective roles of markets and the state. Trade barriers were lowered, markets were opened up and exposed to greater competition and flexibility, services were overhauled at the same time that economic restructuring was eliminating jobs, deinstitutionalisation was in full swing, and social security was being cut back. The relative impact upon living standards in both countries by the end of the twentieth century is apparent in the growing income gap: between the mid-1980s and 2000, income inequality in NZ jumped by 3 times the increase recorded in Australia, and was the largest of the group of 20 nations included in an OECD study.

In 1991–92, a 'pro-market' government in NZ introduced sweeping reforms in the housing sector: state housing should serve as a safety net, operate as a commercial enterprise, and return a dividend each year to the Crown (Thorns, 2000). The aims of shifting to an income supplement for housing were as follows: to establish a *de facto* voucher system so all renters could access their tenure of choice (tenure neutrality); to equalise the level of subsidy received by social and private tenants (horizontal equity); and to reduce dependency on the more generously subsidised state housing. Statistics NZ calculates that the National Government's 'market referencing' of rents for state house tenants increased their housing costs by 106% between 1992 and 1999. Private rents rose by 23% over the same period (DTZ, 2004: 51–52). Hence, by the late 1990s, some 60% of state tenants were paying more than 30% of their income in rent. Lots of state tenants were driven out of their homes and began sharing in the private market in an attempt to contain their housing costs. Turnover rates climbed from 14% in 1991 to peak at 35% in August 2000 before the reinstatement of income-related rents for state tenants, as did the increase in crowding-related illness.

Australia's National Housing Strategy, developed in the early 1990s, recommended reducing CSHA funding for public housing and diverting more of it into community housing, as well as extending rent assistance to more private tenants. This shift in the flow of housing expenditure from the supply-side to the demand-side, which paralleled the switch to the Accommodation Supplement (AS) in NZ, was a watershed event in state housing intervention in Australasia. Whereas expenditure on the CSHA in 1990–91 was 44% higher than on Commonwealth Rent Assistance (CRA), from 1995 to 1996 onwards annual outlays on the CRA exceeded the CSHA (Australian Institute of Health and Welfare, 2008: 7).

Between 1990–91 and 2000–01, capital funding for public housing in Australia declined by 25% in real terms (Hall and Berry, 2004: iv). Meanwhile, as allocation criteria tightened, revenue from rents began a descent due to the growing concentration within public housing of the 'nonworking' poor and households with high and complex needs receiving statutory income. With the Australian states facing mounting operating deficits (**Figure 1**), total state stock numbers fell from 380 000 to 375 000 dwelling units between 1996–97 and 2000–01 (and have since dropped to 340 000). In NZ, a transformed housing department was required to pay an annual dividend to the Crown, so began selling off large tranches of state houses: stock numbers fell from about 70 000 to 58 000 between the mid-1990s and 2000–01.

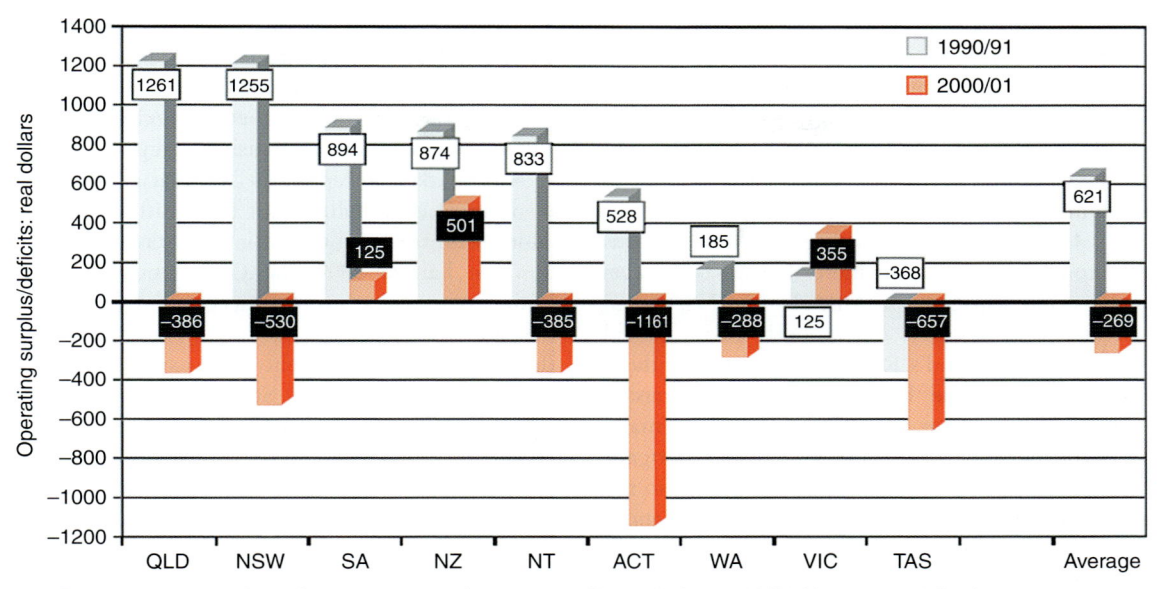

Figure 1 Real operating surpluses/deficits per state housing dwelling 1990/91–2000/01 (June 2001 dollars). Reproduced with permission from Hall J and Berry M (2004) *Operating Deficits and Public Housing: Policy Options for Reversing the Trend*. Australian Housing and Urban Research Institute. www.ahuri.edu.au.

Therefore, funding for state housing in Australia and NZ, which in earlier decades had been available to a much broader cross section of wage earners, began to decline in real terms. This eventually forced public housing agencies into the position of residual providers of welfare housing (Hall and Berry, 2004); and although this found favour philosophically with proponents of a 'safety net' approach to social security, state housing in Australasia gained the reputation of 'tenure of last resort' (Thorns, 2000).

The Supported Accommodation Assistance Program (SAAP) in Australia and Community Group Housing in NZ formed other strands in the welfare housing 'safety net'. SAAP which was introduced in 1985 under the Hawke Government created a national system of homelessness services. While these programmes were phased in at a time when people were leaving institutional care, SAAP and Community Group houses and hostels also extend to women's refuges, halfway housing for ex-prisoners, foyer housing, and the like. In 2005–06 over 160 000 people, including 54 000 children, accessed SAAP.

Home ownership assistance also changed in a major way. Following the liberalisation of the financial sector in both countries, governments progressively withdrew the direct subsidies that had formerly supported bank lending to home buyers on modest incomes. In addition, the NZ Government sold off the Housing Corporation (HCNZ) (formerly State Advances) mortgage portfolio. Between 1992 and 1999, $2.4 billion of HCNZ prime-rate mortgages, which had been progressively adjusted upwards to prevailing market rates, were on-sold to private investment houses. Otherwise, in Australia the Commonwealth established a First Home Owner Scheme (FHOS), while NZ governments focussed assistance more narrowly on a few small-scale home loan products aimed at poorly serviced segments of the market. These include low deposit home loans for buyers in rural areas, loans for houses on Māori land in multiple ownership, and loans for people wanting to build a home as part of a Group Self-Build venture.

However, it remains the case that the tax concessions available to residential property investors, including home buyers and owners, far outweigh the direct housing assistance available to public and private tenants in both countries. For example, NZ estimates suggest that under tax regulations operating in 2007 implicit assistance to existing home owners and investors in rental property was equivalent to NZ$5.3 billion, as opposed to NZ$1.3 billion for tenant subsidies – $877 million for the AS paid to private tenants and $436 million for income-related rents set for state tenants (Department of the Prime Minister and Cabinet, 2008: 19–20).

Current Arrangements for Housing Assistance

A Return to Greater Intervention in Markets

In the face of state housing deficits, shrinking home ownership rates, and an emerging 'intermediate' market segment, questions were being asked once more in the early 2000s about the adequacy of prevailing policy settings (Housing New Zealand Corporation, 2005; National

Affordable Housing Forum, 2006). The difference from the past, however, was that the unaffordable house prices and rents emerged in a time of near-to-full employment and plentiful home finance. The New Zealand Housing Strategy and Australia's National Affordable Housing Agreement formed the core government responses to the new dimensions of housing stress.

With global savings multiplying, excess liquidity was pumped into residential and commercial property markets around the world, especially in Australia and NZ due to the high yields on offer. As the property boom gained momentum, New Zealand's Reserve Bank tried without much success to subdue housing inflation by raising interest rates. House prices in Australia and NZ actually peaked before the collapse of the US subprime mortgage market towards the end of 2007 which, in turn, led to the collapse of credit and the onset of global recession. Central governments were forced to step in to salvage the wreckage left by market failure. But in the main Australasia's better regulated banking system averted the market collapse experienced in the United States and Britain. Over a 3-year period (2009–12) the social housing sectors in both countries stand to benefit from the additional spending undertaken by central governments as part of larger stimulatory packages.

Housing Affordability

Overheated markets distorted supply and exacerbated housing affordability issues. An 'intermediate' market segment has emerged in Australia and NZ comprising working households who are earning too much to qualify for social housing, but not enough to buy their own home without some assistance. The difficulties facing 'would-be' home buyers prompted enquiries in both countries. Significantly, experience diverged in the respective private rental markets. Rents in NZ tracked the Consumer Price Index during the boom due to the comparatively healthy supply response and liberal bank lending to residential property investors (Department of the Prime Minister and Cabinet, 2008: 22). In Australia, on the other hand, housing supply stalled, and by the time the market peaked in 2003–04 vacancy rates were at historically low levels. At this stage, an estimated 750 000 lower-income households had housing costs above the affordability benchmark of 30% of income (Yates, 2007).

At the beginning of 2009, the CSHA was replaced by a National Affordable Housing Agreement (NAHA) to respond to affordability issues and stimulate supply. It consolidates a variety of housing programmes into one of the five Special Purpose Payments agreed by the Council of Australian Governments (COAG) in November 2008. This $10 billion jointly funded package addresses housing affordability, homelessness, and indigenous housing disadvantage. A National Rental Affordability Scheme (NRAS) (2008–12 and beyond) is using tax credits to stimulate the supply of 100 000 new affordable rental dwellings. The scheme provides incentives to financial backers and developers willing to partner with community housing groups.

Any market correction in NZ that adversely impacts on rents is eventually offset by adjustments to the AS. Along with tax liability and interest rates falling through the first half of 2009, the Government expects other initiatives to also improve access and affordability for first home buyers. They include the following: amending the Resource Management Act to speed up consenting; issuing a National Policy Statement to ensure that local councils adequately plan for a forward supply of new house sites; and a Gateway Housing scheme whereby land in public ownership is developed and made available at a discount to first home buyers or community housing organisations to build new houses.

Public and Community Housing Programmes

In Australia, the Commonwealth never got directly involved in owning or supplying public housing. That role was delegated to the States which also hold the head leases on most of the community housing stock. In addition to existing allocations, the 2008 NAHA increased the social housing budget by $400 million over 2 years. Then, early in 2009, with the Australian economy facing recession, the Rudd Government announced a $6.6 billion package to build 20 000 additional social housing units. Not only does this represent the single largest investment in social housing ever, but the federal Minister is using the funding to reform Australia's social housing system. Growing a number of sophisticated not-for-profit housing organisations to operate alongside existing state-run housing authorities is to be the "centre-piece of the government's reform agenda".

In NZ, immediately after Labour's return to power in 1999, income-related rents were reinstated and state house sales were halted. Over the next decade stock numbers were rebuilt to the level preceding the sales programme. However, housing provision in NZ is still dominated by a single centrally owned and operated public housing agency; and despite the reinvestment in state and community housing, the portfolio continues to fall as a proportion of the total stock as this is growing at a faster rate. For the foreseeable future, both the main political parties appear committed to income-related rents for state tenants, to the AS for private tenants, and to holding state housing numbers at current levels (86 700). Also, in order to stimulate growth and jobs during the recession, a further $124.5 million was added to the budget allocation in 2009–10 for modernising dilapidated state rental stock.

Indigenous Housing Needs

As well as the burden of excessive housing costs, long-standing and seemingly intractable housing issues beset many indigenous communities. They have their basis in land tenure, economic marginalisation, poverty, and poor health. These problems are compound in remote rural communities. Compared with their share of the population at the 2006 Census (see above), indigenous people, along with the Pacific population in NZ, are overrepresented in the public and community housing sectors, and are more prone to inferior housing and overcrowding in the private rental market, and to homelessness. Tenure disparities are evident in home ownership rates that are much lower than for other Australasians and declining: 48% for Māori; 34% for Pacific peoples; and, 34% for Aboriginal and Torres Strait Islanders.

In 2007–08, with government programmes failing indigenous Australians, the Commonwealth embarked on a wide-ranging review of prevailing policies and funding arrangements (including housing assistance). COAG's Working Group on Indigenous Reform proposed closing the gap on Indigenous disadvantage. Almost $2 billion over 10 years was set aside for remote Indigenous housing. It bears some of the hallmarks of the Clarke Government's short-lived programme in the early 2000s to close the social and economic gaps between Māori and non-Māori in NZ.

Homelessness

The extent of homelessness appears to be one of the few points of difference between the housing systems in Australia and NZ. While about 100 000 people are homeless on any given night in Australia, surveys have yet to detect an equivalent rate in NZ. Firstly, it appears that a boarder's allowance paid to about 50 000 individuals as part of the Accommodation Supplement lowers vulnerability. Secondly, it is still commonplace for Māori and Pacific peoples to live as extended families and take in relatives at times of need. But this does give rise to localised overcrowding and associated health issues, especially in the southern and western suburbs of Auckland.

The Australian Government's Green and White papers on homelessness, which were prepared during 2008, resolved to intervene early to prevent homelessness, to end rough sleeping and halve overall homelessness by 2020, and offer supported accommodation to all rough sleepers who need it. COAG (in the financial year 2009–10) has agreed to raise programme funding by an additional $800 million over 4 years.

Implications for Housing Debates

The housing booms in the early 2000s exposed the limitations of demand-side assistance in dealing with an insufficient supply of affordable housing. Hence, after a period of overreliance on income support to address housing stress in Australia and New Zealand, housing policy is now returning to a more efficacious mix of demand- and supply-side interventions.

Even so, although the policies developed to respond to unaffordable first homes will pay dividends in the years ahead, it is less certain that these supply-side initiatives will be sufficient to stabilise home ownership at current levels in Australia and NZ. Yet such is the traditional dominance of home ownership in private wealth – 62 and 76% of gross household assets in Australia and NZ, respectively – that asymmetries in market power will continue to feed the concentration of housing wealth which, under present public policy settings, holds the key to material well-being and security in later life. Extending the benefits of home ownership to people facing the prospect of renting throughout their working lives and on into retirement is one of the greatest challenges in housing policy confronting governments in Australia and NZ.

Finally, a major implication of the uncertainty surrounding the future of home ownership in Australasia goes to the heart of the social bargain struck between governments and workers during the era of the 'wage earner's welfare state'. Central governments subsidised mortgage finance and left ownership largely untaxed in return for lower rates of personal taxation and reduced spending on social security and pensions. This has been called the 'really big trade-off' to distinguish the traditional encouragement of home ownership by governments in Australia and NZ from the alternative social housing models pursued by social democratic states in Europe (Kemeny, 2005). However, policy reversals in Australia and NZ are progressively eroding the social bargain in anticipation of the growing dependency of ageing societies upon the state.

See also: Access and Affordability: Developed Countries; Access and Affordability: Housing Allowances; Demand Subsidies for Low-Income Households; First Home Owner Grants; Foreclosure Prevention Measures; Health, Well-Being and Housing; Housing Need in the United Kingdom.

References

Australian Institute of Health and Welfare (2008) *Housing Assistance in Australia*. Cat. No. HOU 173. Canberra: Australian Government. www.aihw.gov.au

Badcock B (1989) The role of housing expenditure in state development: South Australia, 1936–88. *International Journal of Urban and Regional Research* 13: 438–461.

Badcock B and Beer A (2000) *Home Truths. Property Ownership and Housing Wealth in Australia*. Carlton, VIC: Melbourne University Press.

Department of the Prime Minister and Cabinet (2008) *Final Report of the House Prices Unit: House Price Increases and Housing in New Zealand*. www.dpmc.govt.nz/dpmc/publications/hpr-report/index.html

DTZ (2004) *Changes in the Structure of the NZ Housing Market*. Wellington: Centre for Housing Research Aotearoa New Zealand. www.chranz.co.nz

Ferguson G (1994) *Building the New Zealand Dream*. Palmerston North: Dunmore.

Greig A (1995) *The Stuff Dreams are Made of. Housing Provision in Australia 1945–1960*. Carlton, VIC: Melbourne University Press.

Hall J and Berry M (2004) *Operating Deficits and Public Housing: Policy Options for Reversing the Trend*. Australian Housing and Urban Research Institute. www.ahuri.edu.au

Housing New Zealand Corporation (2005) *Building the Future: The New Zealand Housing Strategy*. Wellington: HNZC. www.hnzc.co.nz

Jones MA (1972) *Housing and Poverty in Australia*. Carlton, VIC: Melbourne University Press.

Kemeny J (2005) 'The really big trade-off' between home ownership and welfare: Castles' evaluation of the 1980 thesis, and a reformulation 25 years on. *Housing, Theory and Society* 22: 59–75.

National Affordable Housing Forum (2006) *Achieving a New National Affordable Housing Agreement*. www.housingsummit.org.au

Pusey M (1991) *Economic Rationalism in Canberra: A Nation-Building State Changes Its Mind*. Cambridge: Cambridge University Press.

Thorns DC (1988) Housing issues. In: *Report of the Royal Commission on Social Policy (Te Kōmihana A Te Karauna Mō Ngā Āhuatanga-Ā-Iwi), Vol. III, Part Two: Future Directions Associated Papers*, pp. 5–23. Wellington: The Royal Commission on Social Policy.

Thorns DC (2000) Housing policy in the 1990s – New Zealand a decade of change. *Housing Studies* 15: 129–138.

Yates J (2007) *Housing Affordability and Financial Stress*. AHURI Research Paper. Melbourne: Australian Housing and Urban Research Institute. www.ahuri.edu.au

Relevant Websites

www.workandincome.govt.nz – Accommodation Supplement

http://fahcsia.gov.au/sa/housing/payments/Pages/Rentassistance.aspx – Commonwealth Rent Assistance

www.coag.gov.au – National Affordable Housing Agreement

http://fahcsia.gov.au/about/publicationsarticles/corp/BudgetPAES/budget2008-09/FactSheets/Pages/NationalRentalSchemeFS13.aspx – National Rental Affordability Scheme

www.hnzc.co.nz – New Zealand Housing Strategy

Housing and the State in China

F Wu, Cardiff University, Cardiff, UK

© 2012 Elsevier Ltd. All rights reserved.

Glossary

Commodity housing This refers to privately developed housing on the leased land. Proper commodity housing has a deed. It is commonly used to refer to new housing developed by development companies, although initially the purchase of commodity housing was subsidised. It differs from 'affordable housing', which refers to a specific type of government-subsidised owner-occupied housing. In theory there is sale restriction, which is based on income qualification.

State work-units These include state-owned enterprises and institutes controlled by the state. The state work-units are the basic units for organising social lives. The workplace, hence, is dominant in housing consumption. This is a unique phenomenon in China (but it is perhaps also present in other socialist countries).

Transformation of Housing Provision

The Chinese housing system in the period of the planned economy (from 1949 to 1998) was characterised by the dominance of public housing. However, a large proportion of so-called public housing was actually built, owned, and managed by state work-units (*danwei*). This sector – work-unit housing – is similar to 'enterprise housing' in the former Soviet Russia. Work-unit housing accounted for about 60–75% of the total housing stock. Its quality is usually better than the public housing that is directly managed by the municipality. This is because municipal public housing was created mainly by converting previous private housing built before 1949.

As the state provided work-unit housing, Chinese cities saw a relatively high level of social mix. Households with different socioeconomic statuses usually lived within the same residential compound built by their workplace. The role of the workplace in housing provision meant housing inequalities unfolded along the dimensions of the *danwei* (such as the nature, rank, and size of the *danwei*).

In rural areas, however, housing was self-built and privately owned. The role of the state in housing provision was insignificant. In recent years, some rural collectives in the more developed coastal regions have begun to tap the profitability of township and village enterprises (TVEs) to build planned residences for farmers, while making a profit by selling to urban households.

Housing reform in China began in the early 1980s. However, despite various experiments in raising rents and in selling public housing in selected cities, the overall reform of housing was slow and piecemeal until 1998. In contrast to the swift privatisation in Central and Eastern Europe, China adopted a gradualist approach. Instead of privatising existing public housing, housing reform started from 'commodification' or 'marketisation'. In other words, newly built housing was required to be developed either for selling or for renting in the housing market.

The Chinese housing system came to a turning point in 1998 when the state launched a 'big bang' approach to ending 'in-kind' allocation of housing. China adopted a more radical approach than that proposed by the World Bank economists. The real motivation for ending the welfare state was not a neoliberal political ideology but rather a very practical imperative in the aftermath of the Asian financial crisis, which threatened the export-oriented development strategy that had hitherto been applied successfully in China. The strong Chinese currency – in comparison with other Asian currencies – halted China's exports. The Chinese economy was in peril. The state launched investment programmes to boost domestic demand. Housing was regarded as one of the key investment areas. To facilitate house purchase, housing finance was introduced. In fact, mortgage lending became 'low-risk' to banks in comparison with nonperforming loans granted to state-owned enterprises. The development of a mortgage market helped banks find an outlet for surplus capital.

The 1998 policy proposed to transform the housing system into three segments: about 70–80% of housing would be 'affordable housing'; about 10–15% would be high-standard 'commodity housing' developed through the market to serve higher-income households; and about 10–15% would be subsidised 'rental housing' supported by employers or municipal governments.

In reality, however, the 'big bang' approach pushed middle-income families into commodity housing markets; whereas affordable housing has never been fully developed as expected. With the abolition of in-kind housing allocation and the establishment of mortgages, the housing market entered a period of boom after 2000. Ownership became a preferred tenure. State-owned enterprises, managers, and state cadres benefited as they obtained discount housing and gained ownership. Seniority in the workplace proved to be an advantage for getting better housing, according to the studies on the Chinese public housing system (see Further Reading).

Housing Affordability

Chinese cities witnessed a housing market boom from 2001 to 2005. According to the China Real Estate Index, house prices in Shanghai increased from 600 points in 2001 to about 1900 points, an increase of 3.3 times. In other words, in just 7 years, house prices in Shanghai more than tripled. The above figure is just an average. For properties in premium locations, the price inflation is more dramatic. New commodity housing prices nationwide have increased 1.5 times since 2001. However, the figure is a very conservative estimate. The actual increase might have been far more significant.

With escalating house prices, the issue of affordability has become acute. The ratio of house price to family disposable income ranges as high as 8:1–10:1. Even the capacity of the middle-class buyers has been overstretched. Homebuying is increasingly motivated by investment and asset appreciation. The issue of housing affordability has become one of the key public discourses, which is constantly raised in the Peoples' Congress. The rapid increase in house prices is seen as a threat to social cohesion, especially to the newly proposed 'harmonious society'. A term has even been invented to describe the heavy mortgage burden on risk-taking homepurchasers, who are called the 'slaves of housing' (*fang nu*). Stabilising house prices became an objective of the new housing policy.

Although the issue of affordability is often raised to suggest the high pressure faced by 'ordinary people', in the discourse on affordability, the focus of this issue is specifically on middle-class buyers of market-price housing. The real challenge of affordability is, however, the provision of housing to low-income households and rural migrants.

Housing Mortgages

Housing mortgages started in the early 1990s, as part of the government's overall effort to encourage reforms of the public housing system. However, the development of housing mortgages has been very slow. A Housing Provident Fund was developed in some cities such as Shanghai as a form of subsidised financial support to former state employees. However, commercial housing mortgages had not fully developed in the 1990s, as – in case of mortgage default – banks were not vested with the right of housing foreclosure. However, the Asian financial crisis led to a very proactive economic policy to boost domestic demand. With the deterioration of state-owned enterprises' profitability, the banks realised that the risk of housing mortgages to individual households was actually low; and mortgages thus became a profitable sector of financial services. In the 2000s, along with the housing boom, the mortgage market has also developed. Some households, comprising mostly middle-income groups, managed to use mortgages to buy subsidised affordable housing and other commercially developed housing, and managed to get a handsome economic return. There are some instances of people aggressively taking out mortgages to buy multiple houses for speculation. However, it is not entirely clear how widespread this kind of behaviour is.

As mortgages are mainly issued by the banks without going into the secondary market (i.e., mortgages are not securitised), the Chinese housing finance system is still stable, and the default rate is still low. It is most likely that the middle-income class has benefited from the development of residential mortgages. However, as discussed in the section about housing affordability, some of the middle-class homebuyers, especially the younger generation, have undertaken a heavy burden of mortgage repayments, which is becoming a hotly debated topic.

Housing Tenure

Housing tenures in China are more complicated than their Western counterparts in their market economies; this fact reflects the nature of China's market transition. In a market economy, the classical tenure categories include housing that is owner-occupied, privately rented, and rented from the local authority or from social-housing sectors. In China, the owner-occupied sector includes market housing with full property rights, 'reform housing' with partial property rights, private housing inherited from the presocialist period, and self-built rural housing restricted from the urban housing market (i.e., it cannot be sold to urban households; only a 'use right' can be transacted among rural households).

Commodity housing, or *shang ping fang*, refers to the housing privately developed in the market, on leased land. Commodity housing has a proper certificate of property rights, issued by the local housing and land-administration bureau. Within this category is resettlement housing, which is sold to relocated households at a discount price or as 'in-kind' compensation. Private housing (*si fang*) also has full property rights but the term usually refers specifically to housing that has been privately inherited or reinstituted.

'Reform housing' (*fang gai fang*) is a transitional form of housing that refers to privatised public housing. Because of the gradual process of reform, some owners only have partial property rights with sales restriction (e.g., not for sale within 5 years) and the workplace has the priority to buy it back. However, many sales restrictions have been lifted since the early 2000s because the government hoped to promote the secondary market and, in turn, to stimulate the primary housing market. Consequently, the category will eventually diminish.

Affordable housing (*jingji shiyong fang*) – literally 'economic and suitable housing' or 'economic and comfortable housing', depending on the translation – is a specific type of government-subsidised owner-occupied housing. It is better developed in Beijing than in Shanghai because Shanghai has only recently – in 2008 – announced some schemes.

As land price constitutes a major component of the house price, the government exempts affordable housing from the process of competitive bidding for land. In other words, affordable housing receives the land without paying the premium for land. The government regulated the profit rate of affordable-housing production to a maximum of 3%. Although affordable housing is targeted towards middle-income and low-income families, in reality it has been difficult to check buyers' qualifications. Although the buyers are required to file an application form, because of 'grey' incomes and an underdeveloped system of personal income tax, it is impossible to identify the exact incomes of the applicants. Another reason is that after the Asian financial crisis, the government has shifted its emphasis from providing affordable housing to using housing development for boosting economic growth. As a result, income-qualification checks were not implemented rigorously.

Affordable housing has been sold to better-off households, which has caused criticism and debates. Because of the land-premium exemption, it is cheaper than ordinary market housing. However, market-housing developers felt that they were disadvantaged by paying a land premium to the government; whereas affordable housing could get free land that was actually sold to the same group of consumers. Because better-off households were the buyers of affordable housing, the size of the units became larger, much bigger than can be considered affordable. Although affordable housing is cheaper than market housing, it is still too expensive for low-income families. The unit price is much higher because these properties are oversized. However, large affordable housing schemes are located in the periphery of the city. They are planned in new towns or residential areas such as Huilongguan and Tiantongyuan in Beijing, creating difficulties of long-distance commuting. Now the procedure of applying for affordable housing has been tightened. In Beijing, the applicants must have Beijing residential permits (*hukou*). There is now a very detailed qualification check based on per capita income, which varies with the sizes of the households. The application needs to go through a two-round public notice.

Social rental housing (*lian zhu fang*) is a new type of public rental housing, specifically supplied to low-income families. There are stringent criteria of income and housing conditions. For example, in Guangzhou, tenants must earn an income lower than the minimum living standard support (MLSS) – the Chinese poverty line; per capita living space must be below $5\,m^2$; and the applicant household should not enjoy any housing subsidy under preferential housing policies. The social rental-housing sector is underdeveloped. In 2006, the Ministry of Construction (MoC; now Ministry of Housing and Urban and Rural Development) found that more than 70 cities had not developed any social rental housing. The new housing policy in 2007 requires local governments above the county level to cover all MLSS families by 2008.

In China because of the urban and rural duality, rural housing is not allowed to be circulated in the formal urban-housing market, even though the expansion of the city may have transformed former rural villages into de facto urban areas. These villages are called 'urban villages' (*chengzhongcun*). However, farmers try to capitalise on their right to self-built housing on the land reserved for their own housing or on the land of the rural collectives. They build extra units to sell in the market. This type of housing is not recognised by the state; thus it does not possess a deed. Consequently, compared with housing that enjoys full property rights, this type of quasi-commodity housing is called 'small property-right housing' (*xiao chanquan fang*) or also 'township property-right housing'. The root cause lies in the different urban and rural land systems. The land used by 'small property-right housing' does not go through the formal procedure of land acquisition and leasing.

The change in housing tenures has transformed China's social space from a mixed one to one that is based on tenure divisions. Residential segregation between the households owning commodity housing and households entitled to public rental is significant. Social groups with different housing tenures see a remarkable concentration in different areas. For example, in periurban villages, private rental is mainly developed for migrant workers. To sum up, since the late 1990s, market housing has now become the dominant form of new housing supply, with limited availability of affordable housing and an underdeveloped social rental sector.

The State's Retreat from Direct Housing Provision

Through 30 years of economic reform, the state has retreated from direct housing provision. The course of reform has been gradual, but the cumulative effect is significant. Since the abolition of in-kind housing provision in 1998, China's housing policy has been geared to prioritising market provision. The public housing sector is declining and becoming residual. The shift in housing tenures has been radical. China is now a nation of homeowners. The population census in 2000 shows that the rate of homeownership had reached 72% in the cities and 78% in the towns. In 2007, the rate of homeownership in both cities and towns reached 87%. Housing, which used to be an important item of collective consumption, is now becoming an asset of capital appreciation. Those who bought discounted housing in the sale of public housing or purchased new market housing gained windfall wealth, because house prices have appreciated annually in double digits since 2000. People have begun to buy second or even third properties and to collect handsome rents while enjoying asset appreciation.

However, the state's retreat is not a straightforward process. The state is actually behind housing commodification, which was initiated to tackle the chronic housing shortage left by the socialist era. Before the late 1990s, China saw a very interesting situation: the commodification of housing production with a lingering role for work-units in housing consumption. This 'muddling-through' approach reflects the gradual nature of housing reform. This gradual approach was politically successful because it smoothed the resistance towards housing privatisation and allowed the establishment of the housing market under conditions of very low affordability. Various ad hoc policies helped to overcome the bottleneck of affordability. Affordable housing – with the waiving of the land-leasing premium by the government – helped better-off households to become homeowners. The mortgage market had been established to enhance purchase capacities, although it again favoured high-income households. The sale of public housing was also muddled through with heavy discounts; however, its resale was restricted by 'partial property rights'. These partial rights became fully recognised and were later converted to tradable rights in the post-1998 reform, which again benefited those who had housing advantages under work-unit socialism. Through state promotion, a large proportion of housing stock was produced through quasi-market approaches after the economic reform.

The Resurgent Role of the State

To counter real-estate speculation, the state has attempted to regulate the land supply since 2002. The central state, in particular the Ministry of Land and Resources (MLR), tightened the land-leasing regulations. In 2002, the MLR issued No. 11 Decree (*Regulation of Granting State-Owned Land Use Right by Tender, Auction and Quotation*), which was intended to make the land market more transparent. It requires all land used for business purposes (commerce, tourism, entertainment, and commodity housing) to be transferred publicly, either through tender, auction, or quotation. This bans land dealings through under-the-table negotiations.

However, the decree was not effectively implemented. The local governments were more passive in tightening land regulations because they had vested interests in land development. Land revenue constituted major local revenue, and land leasing was used to boost the local economy. To tighten land regulations further, the central state issued No. 71 Decree, which set the deadline of 31 August 2004 for all the cities to ban negotiated conveyances for commercial development. The decree had a major impact on land hoarding and speculation. Land-supply control thus became a new mechanism of macro-economic intervention when the mechanism of project approval of the planned economy was abandoned. The role of the state in land and housing regulation is thus increasing once again.

The task for the Chinese state before the global economic downturn was to regulate a booming housing market. Since 2005, the central government and its agencies have been issuing a series of policies to tighten the control over housing development. Before the global financial crisis in 2008, China had a problem of hyperliquidity, meaning that too much 'hot money' was released into circulation. Real-estate development, together with the stock market, became the outlet for capital-seeking asset appreciation. To curtail the potential financial risks, the policies were to tighten credit provision, stabilise house prices, control the supply of housing, adjust the structure of housing provision, enhance low-income housing provision, and constrain the pace of demolition.

The policy to tighten credit provision includes the decree made by the Bank Monitoring Commission in 2007 to raise the deposit amounts for second properties. In 2005, the State Council announced the *Notice for Thoroughly Stabilizing House Price* (known as the 'old eight points' because the notice contains eight orders) and *Eight Measures to Strengthen the Regulation and Adjustment of the Real Estate Market* (known as the 'new eight points'). The new eight points include a sale tax on the resale of housing within 2 years of purchase, to reduce speculation.

Later in the same year, the State Council approved a joint order made by seven central ministries, *The Position Document for Stabilizing House Prices*, known as Document No. 25. In 2006, nine ministries of the central government jointly promulgated *The Position Document for Adjusting the Structure of Housing Supply and Stabilizing Housing Prices* (known as Document No. 37). This decree requires local governments to prepare their construction plans for ordinary commodity housing, affordable housing, and social rental housing. The decree also specifies that housing projects should meet the requirements of tenure structure. That is, more than 70% of total floor space should be developed into smaller units of under 90 m^2. This decree is also known as the 90/70 policy.

Subsequently, the central government began to emphasise the need to achieve social objectives in housing policies. In 2007, the State Council promulgated *The Position Document for Solving Housing Difficulties of Urban Low Income Families*, known as Document No. 24. The policy requires the development of social housing provision. To constrain the pace of urban demolition, the central government tightened land leasing. In 2007, the MLR announced the Order 39, which requires that all land premiums must be fully paid up before land deeds can be released. This increased the capital requirements for development projects. In the same year the *Property Law* became effective. Urban demolition must follow the legal procedure and should respect property rights. The enforcement of the property-rights procedure slows down the pace of demolition. The demand for new housing by relocated households is thus reduced.

It is surprising that so many orders, decrees, and policies have been promulgated in such a short period. Although the state has retreated from direct housing provision, it still heavily regulates housing production and consumption. After a period of deregulation, the state is apparently attempting to reregulate housing and to perhaps realise the social costs of unconstrained clearance and redevelopment.

The promulgation of Document No. 24 (on urban low-income housing) marks a significant turn in housing policy. The document specifies that social rental is the major approach to low-income housing provision. The MLSS recipients should be completely included in the social rental system. The document also sets a timetable to include other low-income families into social rental. It requires local governments to prepare a plan for affordable housing. The unit size should be below 60 m^2, and 10% of net land revenue should be used for social rental construction. The policy also requires income-qualification checks for affordable housing. Overall, it seems that housing policies since 2006 have included social objectives. The scope of housing policies has been greatly expanded.

To sum up, in the process of transformation of China's housing system, we see that the role of the state has experienced a series of changes. Initially, it acted to promote commodification for the sake of opening up funding sources to alleviate the housing shortage and to reduce the financial burden on the state. Later, faced by the Asian financial crisis, a radical approach to privatisation was launched, to use housing development to boost local economies. With increasing speculation, stretched affordability, and rising social problems, the state has had to intervene in the housing market. The state's role in direct housing provision has shrunk; nevertheless, its regulatory role has persisted and has grown stronger. With the deepening of the global financial crisis and a decline in the export-production sector, a new package of economic stimuli has been proposed. There are early signs that the government has eased off the controls on the housing market: for example, in Beijing, foreign buyers have once again been allowed to purchase properties, after the ban in 2006.

Housing Redevelopment, Displacement, and the State

The Chinese cities have seen large-scale urban redevelopment and residential displacement since the 1990s. Unprecedented demolition of old housing estates has significantly changed inner urban communities where traditionally strong social bonds existed. According to a survey by Si-ming Li in Shanghai, about one-third of the total households randomly surveyed experienced residential displacement – 'displaced residents' are defined as those whose original residences have been demolished. The majority of displacement activities occurred after 1992.

Housing redevelopment has experienced a shift towards a market-oriented approach, which can be characterised as 'neoliberalisation'. However, China's redevelopment demonstrates more than a simple retreat of the state from housing development. Instead, the state, through a series of institutional reforms, helps to facilitate and legitimise the operation of the market in housing development. For example, the standard of compensation for demolished housing was modified in 2001: the practice of on-site and in-kind housing allocation was changed to off-site allocation and monetary compensation. This reduced compensation requirement greatly facilitated housing redevelopment. Rampant housing redevelopment, added to an inflationary housing market, created new housing problems for relocated households.

Housing demolition has led to resistance by displaced households, which, as seen by the state, jeopardised social stability. The state then began to intervene and constrain the speed of residential demolitions. Since 2003, new ordinances have been published to prohibit enforced demolition. In the meantime, households have found various ways to negotiate with developers and even delay projects, escalating compensation costs in the process. The result is that housing redevelopment has slowed down. Consequently, the role of the state in housing redevelopment is a complex one. On the one hand, it helps to create the conditions for market-oriented development. On the other, the state is crucial for softening the problems generated by market operations.

Despite the many problems reported in the media, residential surveys show that the relocated households as a whole are generally satisfied with their new housing. This is because the inner-city housing was undermaintained and lacked necessary facilities. The new housing is comparatively much better in terms of physical conditions and facilities. The process of residential relocation changed residents into 'active consumers', raising their awareness of their interests and rights.

Migrant Housing

The migrant housing issue results from the rural–urban duality in China. The economic system, including the ownership and management of land and housing, is profoundly different between the rural and urban areas. In the cities, land is state-owned but its property rights are leased in the land market; housing in rural areas is mostly privately owned, whereas in the cities it is predominantly public rental. Rural and urban populations are separated by the system of household registration (*hukou*). When labourers are formally recruited from the rural areas, or absorbed through formal channels such as the entrance to universities and the army, they gain the urban *hukou* and subsequently qualify for state housing allocation. However, migrant workers, when they move to the cities by themselves for employment, are excluded from the formal housing provision in the cities. They find difficulties settling in public housing areas because the supply of private rentals is limited there. They mostly cluster in the peripheries of cities, where the farmers in urban villages develop housing on their plots for migrants.

Besides living in the dormitories provided by their employers, rural migrants mainly rely on private rental housing provided by local farmers. Local governments such as street offices (a subdistrict agency of the district government) and township government may develop migrant housing complexes but the practice is not widespread. Informal squatting is impossible in China because of the relatively stringent management of urban land. Therefore, Chinese cities do not see the phenomenon of squatter settlements, despite the 'informal' and underregulated migrant housing market. Clustered migrant housing areas have formed in the suburbs, for migrants originating from the same place. These migrant villages are nicknamed after the place of origin of their inhabitants, such as Zhejiang village, Henan village, Anhui village, and Xinjiang village. Increasingly there are signs that migrants have also begun to settle in central areas, as original local residents have moved into better housing in the suburbs leaving their properties to be let out as private rentals. Now the courtyards (*hutongs*) in central Beijing are shared by many migrant families and other low-income locals.

The condition of migrant housing is generally poorer than that of locals. However, this housing disadvantage is more complicated than just being a simple issue of discrimination. Migrants may prefer living together in migrant villages because they provide a sense of community to newcomers, similar to the ethnic enclaves occupied by immigrants in the developed world. Migrants consciously adopt a cost-saving strategy to minimise housing costs. Without a local *hukou*, they are not able to buy housing in the second market (i.e., privatised municipal or enterprise housing, or 'reform housing'). With house-price inflation, even the second-market housing is too expensive for migrant workers. Although *hukou* can be blamed for its discriminatory effects, the root cause of the discrepancy is the unstable nature of the labour market for migrant workers. Faced with uncertainty, renting in a substandard market is perhaps the best survival strategy that can be adopted by migrants. It appears as if granting a *hukou* to migrants will not automatically solve the migrant housing problem. In the open market of commodity housing, migrants are allowed to buy properties and by doing so even gain a so-called blue-seal *hukou*. However, the commodity housing market is not a solution for all migrant workers. Although migrant villages are crowded and lack public services – and are thus regarded by the officials as eyesores and backward areas – demolishing low-quality private rentals in urban villages may not achieve the purpose of the upgrading of migrant housing. Low labour-market wages seem to be the cause for poor housing conditions in urban villages.

See also: Homeless People in China/East Asia; Mortgage Market, Character and Trends: China; Rights to Housing Tenure; Social Housing Landlords: China; Welfare States and Housing.

Further Reading

He S and Wu F (2008) China's emerging neoliberal urbanism: Perspectives from urban redevelopment. *Antipode* 14(2): 282–304.

Huang Y and Clark WAV (2002) Housing tenure choice in transitional urban China: A multilevel analysis. *Urban Studies* 32(1): 7–32.

Li SM (2000) Housing consumption in urban China: A comparative study of Beijing and Guangzhou. *Environment and Planning A* 32(6): 1115–1134.

Li SM and Song Y-L (2009) Redevelopment, displacement, housing conditions, and residential satisfaction: A study of Shanghai. *Environment and Planning A* 41(5): 1090–1108.

Li Z and Wu F (2008) Tenure-based residential segregation in post-reform Chinese cities: A case study of Shanghai. *Transactions of the Institute of British Geographers* 33(3): 404–419.

Logan JR, Bian YJ, and Bian FQ (1999) Housing inequality in urban China in the 1990s. *International Journal of Urban and Regional Research* 23(1): 7–25.

Wang YP (2001) Urban housing reform and finance in China: A case study of Beijing. *Urban Affairs Review* 36(5): 620–645.

Wang YP and Murie A (2000) Social and spatial implications of housing reform in China. *International Journal of Urban and Regional Research* 24(2): 397–417.

Wu F (1996) Changes in the structure of public housing provision in urban China. *Urban Studies* 33(9): 1601–1627.

Wu WP (2002) Migrant housing in urban China: Choices and constraints. *Urban Affairs Review* 38(1): 90–119.

Wu F, Xu J, and Yeh AG-O (2007) *Urban Development in Post-Reform China: State, Market and Space*. London: Routledge.

Housing and the State in Latin America

C Zanetta, University of Tennessee, Knoxville, TN, USA

© 2012 Elsevier Ltd. All rights reserved.

Glossary

Agro-export growth model The economic model that fuelled the growth of most Latin American countries during the late nineteenth and early twentieth centuries, based on the exports of primary goods, such as wool, grain, beef, coffee, rubber, and minerals, mainly to European markets.

Import-substitution industrialisation The economic model that replaced the agro-export model in Latin America after the Great Depression and the Second World War closed the region's export markets. It sought to reduce dependency on foreign exports and investments by protecting the local production of industrialised products.

Laissez-faire policies Economic system that supports a free-enterprise system with minimal state intervention. This doctrine has infused the liberal economic policies implemented during the beginning and the end of the twentieth century.

Washington Consensus It refers to the set of free-market reforms that were implemented in most Latin American countries during the 1980s and 1990s. These reforms were aimed at reducing the role of the state in the economy, enhancing fiscal discipline, and promoting financial and trade liberalisation.

Introduction

During the twentieth century, the production of housing in Latin America became increasingly intertwined with the state. Some of the roles undertaken by the state, such as defining the housing standards through building codes and land-use regulations, have become widely accepted. Other roles are more controversial, as their legitimacy was grounded on the specific economic model prevailing in the region at the time. Thus, as these economic models were successively replaced by others, the role of the state with respect to housing also evolved. In this way, the state was intermittently directly involved in the production of the housing stock as well as its destruction. At times it facilitated the production of housing by the private sector while, at others, it added obstacles to the workings of the market. During some periods, it firmly eradicated illegal settlements, while during others it supported self-help upgrading programmes. Thus, to understand the evolving relationship between housing and the state in Latin America, it is important to first understand the successive economic models that prevailed in the region during the last century as well as the roles assigned to the state in the framework of each of these models. For purposes of simplification, the relationship between housing and the state is summarised over three periods: (1) the liberal export-led growth model of the early twentieth century; (2) the import-substitution industrialisation model of the post-Second World War period; and (3) the neo-liberal policies of the late twentieth century. The experiences of Argentina, Mexico, and Chile are used to illustrate how local socioeconomic, demographic, and political conditions shaped the way each economic model was adopted by individual countries and the housing policies that were pursued during each period.

The Early Twentieth Century: Housing under the Liberal Agro-Export Growth Model

The late nineteenth and early twentieth centuries were an expansionary phase for Latin America as a whole, during which most countries in the region achieved remarkable economic growth under a liberal agro-export-based model. During this period, there was little state intervention in the economy, with most governments pursuing laissez-faire policies that were fully supportive of free markets and private ownership. Fuelled by the growth of the world economy, the export of primary commodities (wool, grain, beef, coffee, rubber, and minerals) led to the fast economic growth of Latin American economies, including Argentina, Mexico, and Chile. During this period, Latin America's largest economies were highly integrated into the international economy – Great Britain, Germany, and France in particular – not only as importers of manufactured commodities but also as avid recipients of foreign investments. By 1913, 20% of all British capital overseas was in Latin America. Foreign investments, in turn, served to build the infrastructure needed to support export activities, such as railroads, ports, and other basic infrastructure. Expansion of the railroads gained momentum after 1870, reaching a network of almost 3500 km in Argentina and Brazil alone by 1913 (Thorp, 1998).

During this period, politics were dominated by groups tied to the export economies. However, although income was concentrated in the hands of the ruling class – particularly the landed oligarchy – the rapid expansion in public infrastructure and services helped spread some of the benefits among the broader segments of society. Efforts aimed at improving the living conditions of the poor were limited and ad hoc, often under the mantel of charity organisations sponsored by the wealthy. This lack of concern towards poverty remained unchanged until low-income workers began to organise into labour movements and had a more active political participation.

Labour and social movements were introduced by the large inflows of immigrants who had arrived in the Americas during the late nineteenth and early twentieth centuries. Some countries had pursued active immigration policies, seeking the influx of European immigrants to populate the large extensions of unpopulated lands. More that 10 million people immigrated to Argentina and Brazil alone, mostly between 1860 and 1914 (Thorp, 1998). These newcomers were absorbed into these countries with remarkable ease, becoming an intrinsic part of their ethnic make-up and national identity.

The relationship between the state and the production of housing during this period was consistent with the overall liberal economic model, with laissez-faire policies towards land development and self-help housing. The experience of Argentina, which achieved its golden age under the agro-export model during this period, serves to illustrate the liberal housing policies and their impact on the production of housing at the turn of the century.

As in the economy as a whole, market forces were the determinant factor shaping the production of housing under Argentina's liberal regime. The private sector was the main actor in the housing sector and the state intervened only to facilitate the workings of the market, such as with the creation of the National Mortgage Bank (*Banco Hipotecario Nacional – BHN*) in 1860. The BHN was conceived as a source of financing for lower-middle-income households that had the savings capacity necessary to afford the full cost of housing with the help of long-term credit and low interest rates. It served as a financial intermediary, relying on publicly traded savings certificates to attract private investors, mainly from overseas. However, despite the sound reputation of the BHN savings certificates during that initial period, the loans were not widely affordable and resulted in the financing of few housing units (Yujnovsky, 1984).

Low-income households, including many of the newcomers arriving at Argentina's cities as part of the successive migratory waves, were not able to afford formal housing and had to resort to informal housing arrangements, particularly in Buenos Aires and other large metropolitan areas. The particular responses to unmet housing needs evolved over time, starting with the overcrowded *conventillos* in which poor European migrants took refuge towards the end of the nineteenth century and the beginning of the twentieth century. Tenement housing similar to Argentina's *conventillos* was also a common phenomenon in other Latin American cities, including La Habana, Montevideo, Lima, Santiago, and Mexico City. These *conventillos* were first located in the large houses that the wealthy had abandoned in the south of the city to escape the outbreaks of yellow fever and typhus that plagued the city in 1870. Later, buildings with numerous small rooms, precarious quality, and inadequate sanitary services were built in large numbers for that specific purpose. Tenement landlords frequently owned numerous *conventillos*, and were among the richest and most respected men of Buenos Aires (Scobie, 1974). However dismal, these *conventillos* offered newcomers affordable accommodations in the proximity of employment opportunities (Cravino, 2003).

As the migrants moved up the social ladder and began to integrate into the larger society, they started to abandon the *conventillos*, moving towards the urban periphery, in which the same laissez-faire approach helped provide formal housing for the rapidly growing urban population. Urban development legislation, including subdivision and land-use regulations, was not enacted until the mid-1940s. Even then, regulations were not very strict, and, combined with readily available credit, resulted in an abundant supply of inexpensive land on the periphery of the Buenos Aires metropolitan area – the so-called *loteos económicos*. In this way, many working-class households were able to purchase a plot of land in monthly instalments and progressively build their houses (Clichevsky, 1997). Despite the typical deficiencies of this type of housing, such as overcrowding and lack of services, self-help developments were integrated into the urban fabric, both physically and socially. As a result, self-help housing in Argentina has not been traditionally associated with extreme poverty, illegality, and spatial segregation as in other Latin American cities. In fact, self-help has been an important component of Argentine cities, giving access to formal housing to popular sectors of the population during periods of fast urban growth (Clichevsky, 1990).

As the liberal elites' grip on power began to loosen, housing policies gradually increased their focus on expanding access to housing among the less wealthy. The Economical Housing National Commission (*Comisión Nacional de Casas Baratas – CNCB*) was created in 1915 to provide affordable housing with transfers from the national government and proceeds from horse racing.

Likewise, from 1916 onwards, the BHN established a new line of credit (*préstamos de fomento*) to target lower-income sectors of the population. However, the impact of these programmes was insignificant, and access to these programmes remained restricted to high-paid employees (Yujnovsky, 1984).

As part of the reforms introduced in favour of popular sectors of the population, rent control legislation was enacted in 1921. This highly interventionist approach towards rental housing was in stark contrast to the laissez-faire policies towards land development and self-help housing characteristic of the period. It responded to mounting social pressures and the worsening living conditions, particularly in central areas of the capital city. Despite the dismal living conditions in the *conventillos* and other substandard rental housing, prices had continued to increase and, not surprisingly, tenants began to organise and social pressures kept mounting (Torres, 1975). After decades of indifference, the claims of the tenants were finally addressed in 1921, when, for the first time in Argentina's history, rents were frozen and evictions were suspended in the capital city and territories under the jurisdiction of the federal government. These controls were extended in 1923, 1924, and 1925 (Yujnovsky, 1984). Although rent control legislation may have helped release social pressures in the short run, they provided a negative precedent. Rent control legislation was enacted once again in 1943, marking the beginning of a period lasting over three decades during which time the rental markets were virtually dismantled (Zanetta, 2004).

The Post-War Era: Housing under the Import-Substitution Industrialisation Model

A shift in the development paradigm occurred in response to drastic changes in the international environment triggered by the economic crisis of 1930 and the Second World War. These two events resulted not only in the loss of traditional export markets but also supplies, forcing many Latin American countries to produce many products that had been previously imported. As a result, Latin American countries emerged from the Second World War aware of their vulnerability to external shocks and with a deep pessimism about exports (Sikkink, 1991). Disillusioned by the fragility exhibited by the export-model during the Great Depression and the Second World War, Latin American leaders turned towards import-substitution industrialisation (ISI) strategies in the post-War period.

Under the ISI model, the state played a central role in economic development, fostering production for the domestic market through an elaborate system of incentives to both consumers and producers (Cornelius, 1996). Domestic producers benefited from protection from foreign competition while workers, at least unionised ones, benefited from relatively high real wages and generous benefits. Often the largest single employer, investor, and source of financing, the state was the main force guiding Latin America's development process in the post-Second World War era. It regulated foreign investment, provided subsidies for key domestic industries, and stepped in when necessary to help avoid bottlenecks in the industrialisation process (Bruhn, 1996). It channelled massive public investment into infrastructure, including roads, energy, dams, and telecommunications. It also facilitated private capital accumulation by providing the private sector with abundant, cheap credit through state-owned development banks, making possible higher rates of accumulation that, in turn, stimulated higher levels of investment by domestic and foreign investors (Cornelius, 1996).

The economic performance of Latin American economies under the ISI model was remarkable, exhibiting an average growth rate of 5.3% between 1945 and 1973 (GDP growth for continental Latin America – i.e., excluding the Caribbean countries). Growth of the manufacturing sector, which served as the engine of growth for the economy as a whole, fuelled the flow of rural migrants to cities. As a result, all countries in the region faced rapid urbanisation rates: urban population grew at an average annual rate of 4.1% between 1950 and 1980. Rapid urbanisation put great pressure on urban centres' ability to provide housing, infrastructure, and basic services to the large number of migrants arriving every year. Not all of the newcomers found formal employment in the expanding private and public sectors, resulting in the emergence of important urban informal sectors. While the salaries and benefits of formal workers improved under the ISI model, the informal sector lagged behind. Thus, the ISI model ultimately reinforced the existing patterns of income and social inequality, despite the bold efforts at land reforms that were undertaken in many countries (Thorpe, 1998).

Mexico's housing policies between 1925 and the early 1980s serve to illustrate the increasingly important role played by the state in the provision of housing, particularly low-income housing, under the ISI model. The Mexican government first became involved in public housing in 1925, when several agencies were established with the purpose of building housing for government workers. However, the rapid expansion in coverage failed to translate into the actual provision of housing for those who were eligible. Due to the limited capacity of the various agencies, only a few privileged government workers benefited from these early public housing programmes (Zanetta, 2004).

A second phase in Mexican housing policy occurred during the 1960s, when the production of low- and middle-income housing was revitalised with the injection of substantial sources of financing. Funds from the United States' Alliance for Progress programme were coupled with compulsory lending requirements for private banks to fund the Housing Finance Programme (PFV), with a focus on low-income housing (Ward, 1990). Private banks were required to deposit 30% of their total savings in two funds established within the Bank of Mexico, which, in turn, were used to issue state-guaranteed loans for the purchase and construction of low-income housing (Ward, 1990). These funds effectively channelled substantial financial resources into housing construction, resulting in the private sector producing most of the formal low-income housing that was constructed between 1965 and 1970 (Gilbert, 1993). These efforts, however, were dismal relative to the magnitude of the existing illegal housing stock and the continuously growing housing needs that resulted from the relentless rural–urban population flow.

While the expanded housing stock effectively attended to the needs of middle-income and working segments of the population, housing accommodations were too expensive for families on the lower rung of the income ladder (Gilbert, 1993; Ward, 1990). By the late 1960s, it became evident that government efforts were insufficient to address the housing needs of a rapidly growing urban population. Mounting social unrest and increasing pressure from labour unions set the stage for the next phase in Mexico's housing policy (Ward, 1990). In 1970, a period of intense production and financing of housing for salaried workers began when national pension funds were channelled into the production of housing (Gilbert, 1993; Ward, 1994). Three major housing institutions – INFONAVIT, FOVISSSTE, and FOVIMI – were established to attend to the housing needs of private-sector workers, federal employees, and the military, respectively. Modelled after Brazil's National Housing Bank, INFONAVIT was financed by a 5% payroll tax paid by workers and matched by the employer and the government (Ward, 1990). The huge expansion that resulted from the use of pension funds boosted annual formal low-income housing production without imposing a major burden on fiscal finances. The three new housing institutions became the major players in the production of low-income housing, being responsible for more than half of all formal low-income housing units built during the 1971–82 period (Zanetta, 2004).

Despite these improvements, housing interventions were still far from perfect. While between 1973 and 1976 the housing produced by INFONAVIT was randomly allocated among blue-collar workers, the institution became controlled by the labour unions from 1977 onward, which used the institution mainly as a tool for patronage (Ward, 1990). Also, despite the marked increase in housing production as a result of the newly created funds, the public sector was able to satisfy only a small proportion of the estimated total demand for low-income housing (Ward, 1990). In view of their inability to access housing through formal channels, the poor had taken it upon themselves to build their own housing in irregular or illegal settlements generally located on the periphery of large urban agglomerations. As a result, self-help or progressive housing has played a major role in the production of Mexico's low-income housing stock. In Mexico City, for example, the proportion of the population living in self-help housing increased from only 2% in 1947 to almost half of the overall population by 1970 (Gilbert, 1993).

Before the 1970s, official policies towards informal settlements had been erratic. Urban renewal programmes rooted in a philosophy of public health improvement contributed towards the destruction of much of the rental and low-income housing located in the urban core, as slum areas and decaying tenements (the so-called *vecindades* in Mexico) were cleared and replaced with new developments (Coloumb, 1989). At the periphery, government officials and politicians intermittently promoted land invasions, turned a blind eye to illegal subdivisions, or manipulated regulations to legalise settlements formed on communal land (Gilbert, 1993).

The policies implemented from 1970 onwards constituted a significant shift from the past, not only in terms of the increase in housing production, but also in qualitative terms. For the first time, housing policies were aimed at low-income segments of the population, resulting in a marked improvement in housing conditions and accessibility to urban services for the genuinely poor (Ward, 1994). The National Institute for Community Development and Housing (INDECO) was established to provide housing solutions for the lower-income groups that were not served by the principal funds (Ward, 1990). Similarly, public policy took a more pragmatic approach, which included the revalorisation of informal settlements and housing construction. The pattern of government policy towards land development for low-income housing started to shift from inconsequential, ad hoc actions built around clientelism to a more systematic type of government intervention characterised by less partisanship and more rationality in the management of resources (Jones et al., 1993). *Vecindades* improvement programmes were introduced by INDECO and INFONAVIT. Slum improvement programmes also became an important goal of local housing agencies, such as the Federal District's Directorate for Popular Housing (DDF) (Gilbert, 1993).

Policies aimed at providing affordable housing solutions continued to evolve throughout the 1970s. Influenced by the UN Habitat Conference held in Vancouver in 1976, major housing institutions resorted to nontraditional low-income housing solutions on a significant scale. In 1981, FONHAPO became an independent agency and was charged with the responsibility of providing housing to low-income, self-employed workers and those in the informal sector living mainly in Mexico's secondary cities (Gilbert, 1993; Ward, 1990). To meet the challenge of producing affordable housing, FONHAPO focussed mainly on nontraditional housing alternatives, such as sites-and-services, core units, self-help and upgrading programmes, and the acquisition of apartments by renters (Ward, 1990). Similarly, the regularisation of land titles in existing settlements intensified after 1977, as the agencies charged with regularisation became more efficient and the processes were simplified. While land regularisation brought obvious benefits to illegal settlers, it also allowed local governments to increase their tax base, increase collection of service fees, and improve the effectiveness of planning and building regulations (Ward, 1990).

In summary, Mexico's housing policies in the three decades after the Second World War were characterised by the important role played by the government in the country's housing financial market and the production of low-income housing. The evolution of housing policies during this period was incremental, with new housing agencies and programmes being added to the ones already in place, resulting in a patchwork of multiple institutions that dominated the housing market. These public-sector institutions provided direct and indirect assistance to both households and developers through a complex and rather segmented array of programmes. From 1970 onwards, there was a shift towards more pro-poor housing policies and programmes that more effectively responded to the needs of the poor. Despite these efforts, the Mexican housing system still offered few options for the poor. Moreover, it became increasingly apparent that, even though the patchwork of government programmes offered much room for improvement, the ability of the state to boost housing financial markets and produce low-income housing was clearly insufficient to meet the housing needs of the rapidly increasing urban population (Zanetta, 2004).

The Late Twentieth Century: Housing under the Washington Consensus

The ISI model was not without its internal weaknesses, including the serious inefficiency of the industrial sector that resulted from the heavy protectionism. Sheltered from external competition and with a secured domestic market, firms tended to maximise profits and minimise investments. Minimal capital investments in technology and almost no research and development resulted in a strong reliance on foreign technology, which, in turn, tended to increase production costs (Cornelius et al., 1989). Over time, Latin America's industrial sector became increasingly obsolete and inefficient, unable to compete in international markets. Another weakness was the structural reliance on the importation of capital goods, which, together with a long-term shortage of capital, forced Latin American countries to borrow from international credit markets, ultimately accumulating unsustainable levels of debt. By the early 1980s, as most Latin American countries were struggling with mounting inflation, large public-sector deficits, and considerable debt-servicing obligations, there was increasing disillusionment with the protectionist policies. In this way, the conceptual model for development predominant in Latin America started to shift from one of heavy state interventionism to one of economic liberalisation reforms that emphasised a reduced role of the state, fiscal discipline, and financial and trade liberalisation. The forged agreement among Latin American leaders of the need to widely adopt neoliberal policies came to be known as 'the Washington Consensus' (Krugman, 1997; Williamson, 1997).

The economic crises of the 1980s and 1990s forced many Latin American countries to undertake economic reforms along the lines defined by the International Monetary Fund and the World Bank, implementing structural adjustment that emphasised macroeconomic reforms reflecting the thinking embedded in the so-called 'Washington Consensus' (Pugh, 1994, 1995). Against the backdrop of the free-market reforms that were being successfully implemented in most Latin American countries, the formulation and implementation of housing and urban policies became significantly internationalised, favouring the approaches formulated by the Washington-based development institutions, such as the World Bank and the Inter-American Development Bank. In this context, Latin America's housing and urban agenda of the 1990s was conceived within the broader objectives of economic development and macroeconomic performance, seeking to maximise the positive 'macroeconomic linkages', or the potential of urban economies to contribute to a country's macroeconomic performance through financial, fiscal, and economic links (Cohen and Leitmann, 1994; Jones and Ward, 1994; Lee, 1994; Pugh, 1995). With a central focus on the revalorisation of market mechanisms, sound housing and urban policies were defined as those aimed at eliminating barriers that restricted the productivity of urban economic agents, both formal and informal, so as to maximise their contribution to the national economy (Jones and Ward, 1994; Pugh, 1995). The role of the public sector was defined in terms of 'enabling' markets to work by providing the legislative, institutional, and financial frameworks in which firms and households could prosper (Pugh, 1995). Urban services, including water and sewer, electricity, roads, transport, and social services were now conceptualised as factors promoting urban productivity

(World Bank, 1993). Even the potential productivity of the urban poor through the informal sector came to be recognised as an asset, which could contribute to the urban and national economies (World Bank, 1993).

The housing policies implemented in Chile from the early 1970s onwards anticipated the 'enabling approach' that was to be widely adopted in the region during the 1990s. These policies were adopted by the military government that took control in 1973 through a military coup and remained in power for 17 years. These policies were maintained after Chile returned to democratic rule in 1990, as the centre-left coalition that ruled the country between 1990 and 2010 sought to enhance poverty alleviation within the capitalistic free-market economic model adopted in the early 1970s. Thus, the housing policies implemented in Chile over the past three decades provide a good illustration of enabling housing policies as well as the weaknesses and challenges of the overall approach.

Chile's preoccupation with housing dates back to 1906, when the progressive housing legislation – the Workers' Housing Councils – was first enacted. However, despite the good intentions, the housing policies implemented in Chile until 1970 were deficient in ways similar to those of the other Latin American countries. Specifically, while the private sector succeeded in supplying housing to higher-income groups, a myriad of government programmes tried, unsuccessfully, to address the housing needs of lower-income sectors of the population. As a result, the housing deficit continued to increase. The democratically elected socialist government of Salvador Allende (1970–73) attempted to use housing construction as an engine of economic growth and employment. It sought to speed up public housing programmes through advanced technology and direct state construction. These initiatives, together with the decision to put an end to the indexation of mortgage repayments, brought fierce opposition from the construction and banking sectors. The socialist housing policies were abruptly disrupted when the military coup took place in 1973 (Gilbert, 2002).

From 1977 onwards, the military government undertook a thorough reform of the housing sector according to the neoliberal principles that had been applied to the economy as a whole. Under the new paradigm, which has been maintained until today, the private sector was to be the main actor in the production and financing of housing, with the state playing a subsidiary role, boosting the purchasing power of low-income households with up-front subsidies financed by the central government. In addition, the new policies supported the development of capital markets as a whole, including the securitisation of mortgages, as a way to increase access to private long-term housing financing among higher-, medium-, as well as lower-income households. Additionally, urban land markets were deregulated in 1978, when many growth restrictions and land-use regulations were lifted, freeing massive amounts of new land for development (Rojas, 2001). Finally, the focus shifted away from the production of fully finished low-income dwellings and a stronger emphasis was laid instead on progressive self-help models aimed at providing minimal housing solutions that could be later incrementally improved by the beneficiaries themselves (Greene and de Dios Ortúzar, 2002).

While housing production has increased steadily and the private sector has played an increasingly important role in the financing and construction of housing, the strong role played by the state has been a critical factor in ensuring the ultimate success of Chile's housing policies. The need for government intervention proved to be particularly urgent in the low-income segment of the market, as Chilean developers and banks showed no interest in building and financing houses for households earning less than US$200 per month. As a result, the government had to assume a more active role than originally envisioned and, to this day, it directly contracts the construction of low-income housing with private companies and assigns the houses to beneficiaries registered in a national list of applicants. Likewise, the government has been providing the supplementary loans required by low-income beneficiaries to pay for the homes because banks have not been interested in financing these loans (Rojas, 2001).

The Chilean experience is widely regarded as a success: the production of new housing since the 1980s has been above the rates of new household formation and replacement of the old housing stock, opening the possibility that Chile's housing deficit will be soon eliminated (Rojas, 2001). Illegal land occupation has also been brought to an end. This is not a minor achievement, taking into consideration that, by the early 1970s, illegal land occupation had become common practice not only on the urban fringes but also on more valuable land located in the urban centres (Ducci, 2000). Moreover, the private sector now plays a leading role in the production and financing of housing for the middle- and higher-income households, which constitutes a significant achievement considering that in the 1970s most housing was built and financed by the state. Further, government assistance is reaching the poor in an effective manner and most public resources are benefiting low-income households (Rojas, 2001). There are, however, significant challenges still pending, such as the low quality of the housing and the concentration of poverty in low-income housing projects, which, in turn, are located at the urban periphery without sufficient access to jobs, services, and urban amenities. Moreover, chronically high levels of delinquent debt in government-provided low-income housing loans are still to be addressed systematically, as they are threatening the entire low-income housing system in Chile (Ducci, 2000).

Chile's approach towards housing during the past two decades seems to have found a point of equilibrium between the minimalist and expansionary roles that were alternatively assigned to the state in the housing sector in Latin America during the twentieth century. At this equilibrium point, both the state and the private sector play an important and complementary role. While the Chilean experience has demonstrated that private markets can deliver efficient housing solutions and financial mechanisms for those segments of the population that can afford them, it has also shown that the vision of a housing sector mostly driven by the private sector is unattainable. Alternatively, Chile's housing policies have underscored the need for the state's continuous engagement to ensure the development of sound housing markets and to effectively respond to the housing needs of low-income households, as well as the persistent challenges that this task presents.

See also: House Building Industries: Latin America; Housing Finance Institutions: Africa; Housing Markets and Macroeconomic Policy; Informal Housing: Latin America; Self-Build: Latin America; Social Housing Landlords: Latin America; Squatter Settlement Clearance; Welfare States and Housing.

References

Bruhn K (1996) Social spending and political support: The 'lessons' of the national solidarity in Mexico. *Comparative Politics* 28(2): 151–177.
Clichevsky N (1990) *Construcción y administración de la ciudad latinoamericana*. Buenos Aires: Grupo Editor Latinoamericano.
Clichevsky N (1997) Regularización dominial: ¿Solución para el hábitat 'popular' en un contexto de desarrollo sustentable? In: Cuenya B and Falú A (eds.) *Reestructuración del Estado y Política de Vivienda en Argentina*. Buenos Aires: Centro de Estudios Avanzados, Universidad de Buenos Aires.
Cohen M and Leitmann J (1994) Will the World Bank's real new urban policy please stand up? *Habitat International* 18(4): 117–126.
Coloumb R (1989) Rental housing and the dynamics of urban growth in Mexico City. In: Gilbert A (ed.) *Housing and Land in Urban Mexico*, Monograph Series, No. 31, San Diego, CA: Center for US–Mexican Studies.
Cornelius W (1996) *Mexican Politics in Transition: The Breakdown of One-Party Dominant Regime*, Monograph Series, No. 41. San Diego, CA: Center for US–Mexican Studies, University of California.
Cornelius W, Gentleman J, and Smith P (1989) The dynamics of political change in Mexico. In: Cornelius W, Gentleman J, and Smith P (eds.) *Mexico's Alternative Political Futures*, Monograph Series, No. 30, San Diego, CA: Center for US–Mexican Studies, University of California.
Cravino M (2003) Las transformaciones en la identidad villera. La conflictiva construcción de los sentidos. *Cuadernos de Antropología Social*, No. 15. Facultad de Filosofía y Letras, Universidad de Buenos Aires, Buenos Aires.
Ducci ME (2000) Chile, the dark side of a successful housing policy. In: Tulchin J and Garland A (eds.) *Social Development in Latin America: The Politics of Reform*. Colorado: Lynne Rienner Publishers.
Gilbert A (1993) *In Search of a Home: Rental and Shared Housing in Latin America*. London: UCL Limited Press.
Gilbert A (2002) Power, ideology and the Washington Consensus: The development and spread of Chilean housing policy. *Housing Studies* 17(2): 305–324.
Greene M and de Dios Ortúzar J (2002) Willingness to pay for social housing attributes: A case study from Chile. *International Planning Studies* 7(1): 55–87.
Jones G and Ward P (1994) The World Bank's new urban management programme: Paradigm shift or policy continuity? *Habitat International* 18(3): 33–51.
Jones G, Jimhez E, and Ward P (1993) The land market in Mexico under Salinas: A real-estate boom revisited? *Environment and Planning A* 25: 627–651.
Krugman P (1997) 1995 and beyond: The era of deflated expectations. In: Costin H and Vanolli H (eds.) *Economic Reform in Latin America*. Fort Worth, TX: Dryden Press.
Lee B (1994) A comment on the World Bank's new urban management programme: Paradigm shift or policy continuity? *Habitat International* 18(4): 139–144.
Pugh C (1994) Housing policy development in developing countries: The World Bank and internationalization, 1972–93. *Cities* 11(3): 159–180.
Pugh C (1995) Urbanization in developing countries: An overview of the economic and policy issues in the 1990s. *Cities* 12(6): 381–398.
Rojas E (2001) The long road to housing sector reform: Lessons from the Chilean housing experience. *Housing Studies* 16(4): 461–483.
Scobie J (1974) *Argentina: A City and a Nation*. New York: Oxford University Press.
Sikkink K (1991) *Ideas and Institutions: Developmentalism in Brazil and Argentina*. Ithaca, NY: Cornell University Press.
Thorp R (1998) *Progress, Poverty and Exclusion: An Economic History of Latin America in the 20th Century*. Baltimore, MD: The Johns Hopkins University Press.
Torres H (1975) Evolución de los procesos de estructuración espacial urbana: El caso de Buenos Aires. *Desarrollo Económico – Revista de Ciencias Sociales* 15(58): 281–306.
Ward P (1990) Mexico. In: van Vliet W (ed.) *International Handout of Housing Policies*. New York: Greenwood Press.
Ward P (1994) Social welfare policy and political opening in Mexico. In: Cornelius W, Craig A, and Fox J (eds.) *Transforming State–Society Relationships in Mexico: The National Solidarity Strategy*. San Diego, CA: Center for US–Mexican Studies.
Williamson J (1997) Latin American reform: A view from Washington. In: Costin H and Vanolli H (eds.) *Economic Reform in Latin America*. Fort Worth, TX: Dryden Press.
World Bank (1993) *Housing: Enabling Markets to Work*, Policy Paper. Washington, DC: World Bank.
Yujnovsky O (1984) *Claves Políticas del Problema Habitacional Argentino: 1955–1981*. Buenos Aires: Grupo Editorial Latinoamericano.
Zanetta C (2004) *The Influence of the World Bank on National Urban Policies: A Comparison of Mexico and Argentina during the 1990s*. Aldershot, UK; Burlington, VT: Ashgate.

Further Reading

Ward P (1986) *Welfare Politics in Mexico: Papering Over the Cracks*. London: Allen & Unwin.

Housing and the State in South Africa

C Lemanski, University College London, London, UK

© 2012 Elsevier Ltd. All rights reserved.

Glossary

ANC The African National Congress. The ruling political party in South Africa since 1994.

Apartheid Political, economic, and spatial system of racial segregation and discrimination enforced in South Africa from 1948 to 1994.

Informal housing Housing that is informal in structure (e.g., wood, corrugated iron lacking foundations) and/or situated on land without legal right of ownership or occupation.

Postapartheid The political era in South Africa since the demise of apartheid, signalled by the 1994 democratic elections. Characterised by legacies of the apartheid system.

The Role of History in South Africa's Housing Landscape

Housing in South Africa is highly politicised with a long history of state interference, exemplified by the contemporary postapartheid drive towards private ownership via public provision. South Africa's housing landscape is heavily influenced by the legacies of apartheid, and thus the present cannot be fully understood without comprehending the past. The prohibition of home-ownership for Africans (with restrictions for Coloureds and Indians) during apartheid, coupled with insufficient housing construction and poor service provision in areas designated African, resulted in significant overcrowding and severe housing shortages by the 1970s, not to mention lack of access to services, as well as the absence of formal assets and tenure insecurity amongst South Africa's poorest social groups. (The apartheid labels of African/Bantu (updated to Black African), Coloured, Indian/Asian, and European (updated to White) are used as they continue to dominate discourses, policies, and statistics in South Africa.) It is thus onto a canvas of massive housing inequality, projected both racially and spatially, as well as untenable housing shortages and a consequent reliance on informal forms of housing for many households, that contemporary state interventions are painted.

Parts of this article are republished from Lemanski C (2010) Moving up the ladder or stuck at the bottom? Homeownership as a solution to poverty in South Africa. *Journal of Urban and Regional Research* 34.4 In press; and Lemanski C (2009) Augmented informality: South Africa's dwellings as a by-product of formal housing policies. *Habitat International* 33: 472–484, with permission.

The State's Changing Conceptualisation of Housing

Since the establishment of democracy and inauguration of the ANC-led government, the provision of housing for the poor has been a major priority in South Africa. In 1994, the government pledged to build 1 million houses for low-income households over the following 5 years. The meaning of this housing provision has shifted over time: the initial 1994 Reconstruction and Development Programme (RDP) conceptualised housing as a basic human right, enshrined in the constitution, but since the 1996 introduction of the more macroeconomic Growth Employment and Redistribution (GEAR) strategy, government perceptions of housing have become increasingly neoliberal, conceptualising housing as primarily a capital-accumulating asset for the poor. This contemporary focus is encapsulated by the following quotation from the Minister of Housing Lindiwe Sisulu during a 2005 interview:

> We are moving towards the concept of a house as an asset. You have to give people title deeds to give them complete ownership of the house. Then they can re-bond a house and have access to more money ... or they can improve the house and sell it a few years down the line and make a profit. (quoted in *Delivery*, 2005, 'Talking to Lindiwe Sisulu...', May/July)

South Africa's National Housing Subsidy System

One outcome of the contemporary state focus on private property ownership as a form of capital accumulation for the poor has been state withdrawal from housing markets;

for example, ownership of municipal housing is gradually being transferred to private occupiers, and the state is increasingly reluctant to act as landlord. In practice, the emphasis on private homeownership operates primarily through the National Housing Subsidy Scheme which provides low-income households with a one-off housing subsidy from the state that effectively results in ownership of a newly built fully serviced (usually one-bedroom) house or apartment. Although early houses were as small as 25 m^2, subsidy houses approved post 1998 are now a minimum of 30 m^2. To be eligible for the housing subsidy, households must earn below 3500 ZAR per month (1 US$ = 7.14 ZAR, 1 GBP = 11.15 ZAR at current exchange rates), be headed by a South African citizen, have a married member or a dependant, and have never owned property or previously received a housing subsidy. Under the project-linked subsidy system (through which most subsidised houses are constructed) a pool of subsidies are paid to a contractor to build houses and install services on a plot. A group of beneficiaries are then relocated to this land by provincial or local government and awarded title deeds. Houses built under the subsidy system are colloquially known as 'RDP houses' (from the 1994 Reconstruction and Development Programme).

The Limits of South Africa's National Housing Subsidy System

The scale of construction is significant: between 1994 and 2007 approximately 2.4 million RDP subsidies have been offered, costing more than 44.1 billion ZAR. Albeit an impressive record, the backlog of 2.4 million houses continues to grow faster than delivery, primarily due to household fragmentation and migration. Thus informal housing remains important, with 15 million people continuing to live in informal shacks throughout South Africa's cities, as eligible households wait more than a decade for RDP houses (while those ineligible are restricted to informal housing). Indeed, according to South Africa's 2006 General Household Survey, 14.5% of households in South Africa live in an informal dwelling, and more recent data indicate that the scale of informality is growing.

In addition to the inability of the housing subsidy to meet housing demand, this form of state-provided private homeownership itself is not without problem. Specifically, critics have argued that the location of most RDP homes on the urban periphery results in the creation of isolated and poverty-ridden slums that do not produce valuable assets. Furthermore, anecdotal evidence indicates large numbers of RDP property transactions (despite a 2002 amendment to the Housing Act preventing RDP house sales), typically selling for amounts that are drastically below value and operating via informal unregistered processes. As vendors typically return to informal housing, this process undermines the very ethos of the state's emphasis on homeownership and the eradication of informality, whilst also revealing the limits of homeownership as an antipoverty strategy.

A New Approach to Housing

Recognising the failure of the National Housing Subsidy Scheme to resolve South Africa's housing shortage with sufficient speed or quality, the 2004 Breaking New Ground (BNG) Housing Strategy was introduced. BNG promotes integrated and sustainable human settlements, mixing housing and income types in nonperipheral locations, close to economic opportunities, social and infrastructural services, as well as promoting alternative tenure options. Unlike the previous RDP focus on mass delivery of an end product (i.e., a house), BNG promotes property ownership as a poverty-alleviating asset for wealth creation and empowerment by seeking to create settlements that are sustainable, incorporating social amenities and infrastructure, rather than a collection of houses situated in isolated dysfunctional ghettos. BNG also addresses and seeks to promote tenure alternatives such as rental stock, gap housing (for those in the affordability/eligibility 'gap': ineligible for subsidy housing but unable to afford private housing), and informal settlement upgrading. This represents a major change of emphasis. Rental options were not part of the initial postapartheid housing package, and in fact local authorities decreased their existing rental stock in the late 1990s, while informal housing was viewed as temporary, a trend that would disappear as low-income households moved into subsidised houses. However, evidence that approximately 20% of South African households live in rented accommodation and that new tenants are predominantly accommodated in backyard dwellings and informal settlements has forced the government to acknowledge the necessity and dominance of rental (and, to a lesser extent, informal) housing for low-income households. Although translating this 'recognition' into policy has been slow, for example, the 2005 Draft Social Housing Policy remains unimplemented 4 years later, the 2007 Rental Housing Amendment Bill has substantially increased tenants' rights, and programmes providing affordable rental housing for low-income households are slowly emerging. For example, the Community Residential Units (CRU) programme launched in 2008 provides rental options for low-income households by upgrading and maintaining existing public housing stock. However, many rental programmes are yet to have an impact on the ground, and homeownership remains the primary product, albeit a product that is failing to meet demand, leaving many low-income households reliant on rental and/or informal accommodation.

Is the South African State Effective in Meeting Its Housing Goals?

In analysing South Africa's housing policy, the basic premise is that poverty alleviation at an individual or household level is intrinsically linked to homeownership. In the words of South Africa's Housing Director General, Itumeleng Kotsoane, "We need to educate people about title deeds ... that having a house is a great asset as property appreciates over time" (*Mail & Guardian*, 2007, SA reels under housing backlog, 29 March). In other words, the state provides beneficiaries with their first step on the property ladder and then hands them over to the existing capitalist housing market in which they now have a stake, with the implicit assumption of market integration, upward mobility, and collateral security. Thus, in South Africa's neoliberal economic climate RDP housing represents the final major form of state provision for the poor (although in reality state provision continues, for example, through the indigent policy), with beneficiaries expected to use this provision as their primary means for individual and household advancement. Although South Africans have a constitutional 'right' to housing (broadly upheld in the 2000 Grootboom case), this neoliberal policy emphasis promotes housing primarily as a financial asset, demonstrating the state's desire to eradicate informality and promote a nation of homeowners; or, in the words of social anthropologist Steven Robins, an idealistic state vision of 'suburban bliss'. (The Grootboom case, heard by the South African Constitutional Court, was brought by a group of informal dwellers (represented by Irene Grootboom) who were evicted by the City of Cape Town from land they had invaded. With legal assistance they successfully brought legal action against the government under the South African Constitution's provision for the right to adequate shelter and children's right to basic shelter. The High Court (and later in appeal at the Constitutional Court) ruled that the housing programme needed to cater for vulnerable people living in intolerable conditions (i.e., the destitute, especially women and children).) These policy goals clearly resonate with the ideas of Peruvian economist Hernando de Soto, as summarised in his book *The Mystery of Capital* (2000). De Soto insists that poor people's homes are significant assets, but that without formal title deeds guaranteed by a unified legal system these assets are 'dead capital'. At a simplistic level, he argues that by giving poor people legal title to something they already informally 'own', they will consequently grow in social and economic empowerment, engaging with the capitalist property dream by building an asset and securing collateral. Although South Africa has not strictly followed the de Soto path, favouring primarily the provision of new housing for the poor rather than titling existing informal property, his ideas have certainly influenced contemporary housing policy. However, alongside this neoliberal focus, it is important to stress that South Africa's housing policy also incorporates a pro-poor redistributive element, providing opportunities for poor blacks to become homeowners after prohibition under apartheid. This indicates the tensions and complexities of South Africa's dual policy focus on economic neoliberalisation alongside a pro-poor agenda within the housing context.

See also: House Building Industries: Africa; Housing Finance Institutions: Africa; Housing Policy Trends; Housing Subsidies in the Developing World; Mortgage Market, Character and Trends: Africa; Private Rental Landlords: Developing Countries; Securing Land Rights and Housing Delivery; Self-Build: Global South; Shanty Towns; Slums; Urbanisation and Housing the Poor: Overview.

Reference

De Soto H (2000) *The Mystery of Capital*. New York: Basic Books.

Further Reading

Department of Housing (DoH) (2004) *Breaking New Ground: A Comprehensive Plan for the Development of Sustainable Human Settlements*. Pretoria, South Africa: DoH.

Gilbert AG (2004) Helping the poor through housing subsidies: Lessons from Chile, Colombia and South Africa. *Habitat International* 28: 13–40.

Huchzermeyer M (2001) Housing for the poor? Negotiated housing policy in South Africa. *Habitat International* 25: 303–331.

Huchzermeyer M (2003) Housing rights in South Africa: Invasions, evictions, the media, and the courts in the cases of Grootboom, Alexandra and Bredell. *Urban Forum* 14: 80–107.

Huchzermeyer M (2003) Low income housing and commodified urban segregation in South Africa. In: Haferburg C and Oßenbrügge J (eds.) *Ambiguous Restructurings of Post-Apartheid Cape Town*, pp. 115–136. Hamburg, Germany: Lit Verlag.

Lemanski C (2009) Augmented informality: South Africa's backyard dwellings as a by-product of formal housing policies. *Habitat International* 33: 472–484.

Lemanski C (2011) Moving up the ladder or stuck at the bottom? Homeownership as a solution to poverty in South Africa *International Journal of Urban and Regional Research* 35(1): 57–77.

Robins S (2002) Planning for 'suburban bliss' in Joe Slovo Park, Cape Town. *Africa* 72: 511–548.

Royston L (2006) Barking dogs and building bridges: A contribution to making sense of Hernando de Soto's ideas in the South African context. In: Huchzermeyer M and Karam A (eds.) *Informal Settlements: A Perpetual Challenge?*, pp 165–179. Cape Town: UCT Press.

Tomlinson MR (1999) South Africa's housing policy: Lessons from four years of the new housing subsidy scheme. *Third World Planning Review* 21: 283–296.

Relevant Website

www.dhs.gov.za – South African Department of Housing (recently renamed Department of Human Settlements).

Housing and the State in South Asia

S Kumar, London School of Economics and Political Science, London, UK

© 2012 Elsevier Ltd. All rights reserved.

Glossary

Chawls These are four- to five-storied tenement buildings, mainly constructed by textile mill owners in Mumbai in the 1950s to accommodate their workers on a rental basis. A chawl typically consists of one room and a kitchen with a number of households sharing a bathroom and a toilet.

Housing policy In many developing countries housing policy is not necessarily set out in the form of a policy document – it often consists of the design and implementation of a series of housing programmes and projects that are subject to change over time. Policies in the plural sense of the term is perhaps more appropriate.

Housing tenure This is the relationship between a resident and the land or a dwelling they occupy. A household renting the land or dwelling is a tenant, whereas the person (or institution) involved in letting is the landlord; the former pays rent to the latter. The letting relationship is separate from the legal status of the land or dwelling. Sharers are those individuals or households who reside in a dwelling but do not pay rent.

Slums These are legal dwellings displaying conditions such as over-crowding, poor water and sanitation, damp, and a deteriorating physical fabric. Slums are not squatter settlements. The latter is defined primarily as the illegal occupation of land (including pavements) or buildings. Squatter settlements, however, display the same poor environmental conditions present in slums.

South Asia: The Development Context

In 2010, South Asia (Afghanistan, Bangladesh, Bhutan, India, Maldives, Nepal, Pakistan, and Sri Lanka) was home to 25% of the world's population (1.73 billion) and 14% of its urban population (0.5 billion). The urban population (29% in 2007) is projected to rise to 37% by 2025 and exceed 50% by 2050. **Table 1** highlights three key points. First, that growth rates are uniformly higher in urban areas across the region. Second, although urbanisation levels in South Asia are lower compared to other regions of the world, the contribution of agriculture to gross domestic product (GDP) varies from a low of 12% in Sri Lanka and a high of 35% in Nepal (1992–2001). Urban India, for example, is forecast to contribute as much as 70% of GDP, making urban policy ever more important.

Third, the spatial patterns of urbanisation are highly variable. It would therefore seem reasonable to expect urban housing policy for Male (with almost 100% of the urban population of the Maldives) to be different from that for Bhutan or Kabul (with 50% of urban population concentrated in the main city) and from that of India, Pakistan, and Sri Lanka. This is not the case: quick reviews of the national housing policies of Bhutan (2002), Maldives (2007), Nepal (1996), or India (1988) show little recognition of these differences – the policy language and emphasis contained within them can hardly be differentiated.

Historically, poverty has been a predominantly rural phenomenon. Recent trends, however, indicate that rural poverty has declined faster than urban poverty. Based on the World Bank's $1.08 per day poverty line (1993 purchasing power parity), the poverty headcount ratio for South Asia as a whole declined by 4.28% between 1993 and 2002 – the figures for rural and urban areas being 3.28 and 0.87%, respectively. India, which currently accounts for almost three-fourths of the region's population, witnessed a much steeper decline in rural poverty: 5.01% compared to 1.09% for urban areas. However, these percentages mask the challenge in absolute numbers: a decline in the rural poor by 8.31 million was accompanied by an increase in the urban poor by 4.23 million in the same period. Inequality remains high in urban South Asia, varying from 0.34 (Pakistan, 2004) to 0.43 (Nepal, 1996, and Sri Lanka, 2006–07).

Labour market opportunities for the urban poor are, by and large, confined to either wage work or self-employment in the 'informal economy'. In the absence of comparable figures for South Asia as a whole, selected countries are used as an illustration. In 2000, Indian non-agricultural employment in the informal economy accounted for 86% of total employment; the figures for total urban and rural informal employment were 66 and 92%, respectively. In Bangladesh, Pakistan, and Sri Lanka, the proportion of those in the informal economy was 88% (2005–06), 86% (2001–02), and 66% (2006), respectively.

Table 1 South Asia: Basic populations and urban indicators

Country	Population (2008)	Growth rate (%) (2005–10) Urban	Rural	Urban (%) (2007)	Largest urban agglomeration (2007) Agglomeration	Population	Share (%)
Afghanistan	27 208 000	5.4	3.4	23.6	Kabul	3 277 000	51.03
Bangladesh	160 000 000	3.5	1.0	26.6	Dhaka	13 485 000	31.68
Bhutan	687 000	4.9	−0.3	33.3	Phuntsholing	106 000	46.33
Maldives	305 000	5.3	−0.3	36.6	Male	111 000	99.44
Nepal	28 818 000	4.9	1.4	16.7	Kathmandu	895 000	18.60
India	1 181 412 000	2.4	1.1	29.9	Mumbai	18 978 000	5.37
Pakistan	176 952 000	3.0	1.2	35.7	Karachi	12 130 000	19.20
Sri Lanka	20 061 000	0.5	0.5	15.1	Colombo	656 000	21.66

Source: UN data – Country profile.

The informal economy remunerates wage workers poorly, is highly segmented and is characterised by disproportionate levels of insecurity in terms of work, wages, and social protection. These labour market features have generally received short shrift in the formulation of urban housing policies. With the region accounting for about 37% of the developing world's poor in 2002 (32% urban and 37% rural), there is an urgent need to revisit the linkages between labour markets and housing as a basis for determining affordability and tenure options.

Housing conditions are a reflection of poverty levels and labour market constraints, and vice-versa. A majority of the urban poor in South Asia lack access to affordable land, water, and sanitation, and low-cost credit. Significant numbers are forced to find housing solutions outside formal frameworks of provision (public as well as private) despite the constant threat of eviction. South Asia and India account for 27 and 17% of the World's 'slum' dwellers, respectively, with 63% of the region's slum dwellers residing in India. Slum dwellers, as a proportion of their respective national urban populations in 2001 were Sri Lanka (25%), India (60%), Bhutan (70%), Pakistan (79%), Bangladesh (87%), Nepal (97%), and Afghanistan (99%), compared to 59% for South Asia as a whole. Although the proportion of slum dwellers in the region declined from 57% in 1990 to 35% in 2010, their population increased by 10 million over the same period, indicating the sluggishness of housing policy. UN-Habitat notes that 66% of slum dwellers in the region suffered from one of five shelter deprivations and 29% from two deprivations in 2005. Although the fifth deprivation of insecure tenure is difficult to quantify, it is important to note that it is not an indicator of 'housing tenure' but of how secure slum households feel from the threat of eviction.

The State and Housing

A perennial question for housing policy is what role, if any, should the state play? Should it continue to naively assume that economic development and poverty reduction are the most prudent ways of resolving housing problems? Should it be less risk-averse politically and adopt more socially just housing policies? Should it acknowledge that there are no quick-fix solutions to housing problems and that a more fragmented approach is the only realistic option? Despite the diversity of development challenges, these questions are pertinent for all countries in South Asia provided certain overarching themes are taken to form realistic starting points. These are that urbanisation is a positive force that needs to be managed, the links between housing and labour markets are vital for the livelihoods of the poor, the poor will benefit more from the universal provision of basic services and that they have the ability to pay for them, and that although ownership may be the preferred end-goal of housing policy, adopting options commensurate with the lived-lives of the urban poor in the interim is more realistic. This article now turns to an overview of housing and the state using a set of episodes which can be characterised thus: (1) benign neglect; (2) premature aspirations; (3) reluctant acceptance; (4) asymmetrical partnerships; and (5) full circles. These episodes are not distinct from one another in either time or space – they merge, diverge, disappear, and re-emerge with different sets of actors attempting to influence policy at a given point in time.

Benign Neglect: Housing as Consumption Good

Post-independence nation-building aspirations in South Asia sought to foster economic growth and reduce unemployment by modernising the so-called productive sectors of agriculture and industry. Housing was seen to be a consumption good with occasional references in policy statements being confined to identifying investments required for housing some public and private sector employees as tenants. In India, for example, remnants of such a focus are evident in the public-sector steel township of Bhilai in the state of Chhattisgarh and 'chawls' (privately constructed low-rise rental units housing employees within easy reach of the factory gate) in the city of Mumbai. Only on rare occasions, such as in Pakistan in the late 1950s, can one find expressions of intent to provide the poor with serviced plots of land. Unfortunately, these attempts were prone to gentrification by better-off groups as their housing demands were not met by either the state or the market.

As a consumption good, the benign neglect of housing was justified by the need to use scarce resources more prudently. Modernisation, the dominant development paradigm of the time, provided the conceptual underpinning for development: industrial development would absorb surplus rural labour, generate income gains, and create housing demand which would then incentivise supply. Demographic data were used to forecast housing demand and any mismatch with supply expressed as 'housing shortages'. For example, the fifth 5-year plan (1997–2002) for Bangladesh notes that the housing shortage in 1991 was 3.1 million (2.15 million rural units) and estimated to rise to 5 million by the year 2000. In 1998, Pakistan estimated its housing shortage at 8.25 million units (5.3 and 3 million rural and urban units, respectively).

The notion of a 'housing shortage', used as a planning expression as well as a political slogan, should not detract from a questioning of its relevance for housing policy formulation in South Asia. It may be relevant in the industrial world where it is used as a benchmark against 'formal' norms in order to galvanise a range of actors into action. Reconciling demand and supply is predicated on well-established institutional structures and procedures. In South Asia, shortages expressed in millions of units have little meaning in the context of widespread poverty, low levels of affordability, precarious labour markets, restricted access to affordable institutional finance, exclusionary land markets, weak property rights, a low tax base, and weak institutional capacity. More importantly, the use of the notion of a 'housing shortage' as a planning tool not only discounts the actions that the poor pursue to address their housing needs but also considerably narrows down the range of politically 'acceptable' housing outcomes. For example, evidence of the benefits that the poor gain from accessing a range of housing submarkets (such as renting and sharing) has not only been ignored but also actively discouraged: housing policy myopically pursues 'ownership' as the preferred tenure choice instead.

Premature Aspirations: Visions of Modernisation

Economic modernisation was also accompanied by overseas aid regimes which included, among others, technical assistance and overseas training in the fields of planning and housing. Armed with concepts such as 'new towns' and 'slum redevelopment', government planners were encouraged to design and implement 'modern' low-income housing projects. In doing so, the state appropriated the centre ground of policy.

However, with rural to urban migration showing little signs of abating, settlements of the poor continued to develop around, for example, the newly commissioned national capitals of Islamabad (Pakistan) and New Delhi (India), and the regional one of Chandigarh (Punjab state, India). Existing postcolonial cities also witnessed the growth of squatter housing, located predominantly on pockets of public land in between residential areas of the better-off. The resultant juxtapositioning of poverty and wealth is a very visible feature of housing outcomes in South Asia.

As this was antithetical to the development project, Slum Clearance Boards were established with the purpose of evicting squatter residents and relocating those deemed eligible in low-rise walk-up tenements. Eligibility for resettlement was based on the ability of identified evictees being able to prove that they had been resident before an arbitrary cut-off date set by the political party in power. Those unable to do so were often physically transported to the periphery in the hope that they would not return. In addition, present and future land values were used to filter out those who could not be resettled in situ. This majority found themselves relocated a considerable distance away: this only served to increase their vulnerability as ties with labour markets and social networks were either punctured or severed.

Two observations are worth making at this point. First, the relevance of housing policies involving eviction and resettlement must be located in the context of government fiscal capacity, institutional arrangements, and industrial labour market opportunities prevalent in the West at that time. They are unsuitable for South Asia. Second, as will be seen later, although this policy went into partial hibernation for a couple of decades, it reemerged with a vengeance in the 1990s. National development concerns driven by modernisation have been replaced with an urge to become part of an elite global circuit. The mantra of modernisation has been replaced with that of globalisation, while interest in nation building has been replaced with that of conspicuous consumption.

Reluctant Acceptance: Housing as a Productive Good

Academic research, the first housing policy paper by the World Bank in 1975 and the first United Nations Conference on Human Settlements in 1976, coalesced to demonstrate the limited impact of the 'prescriptive' top-down eviction and resettlement approach. It was argued that it would be more beneficial if governments concentrated their efforts on the provision of water and sanitation, access to affordable land and institutional finance (as these were seen to be beyond the reach of the individual households), leaving the poor to organise the construction of housing in line with their individual household lifecycles and affordability. In sum, an 'enabling' bottom-up set of housing policies with two main strands emerged: 'settlement upgrading' (initially, in situ environmental improvements with the view to preserving existing social networks; title to land was added later) and 'sites-and-services' (the development of new partially serviced housing lots for self-help housing construction). The 'Hundred Thousand', 'One Million', and 'One and Half Million' houses programmes (1978–94) in Sri Lanka, and the World Bank-assisted 'bustee' (slum) improvement programme in Calcutta (1977–84) are examples of the former. 'Khuda-ki-Basti' (an incremental development scheme) instigated by the city authority of Hyderabad, Pakistan is an example of the latter. The World-Bank-financed Madras Urban Development Programmes I and II (1978–86) and the Tamil Nadu Urban Development Programmes I, II, and III (1988–97, 1999–2004, and 2005 to date) exemplify a combination of upgrading, sites-and-services, and urban basic service provision.

By the early 1990s, however, site-and-service projects were gradually phased out, the purported reason being that vacant land was harder to find and more expensive to service. Just after the turn of the century, governments at different levels used natural disasters (such as the Asian Tsunami of 2004) as a justification for preventing the poor returning to coastal locations; the resettlement of fisher folk, for example, significantly impacted on their livelihoods as well as on the livelihoods of those providing ancillary services. Globalisation sceptics would argue that this had little to do with the well-being of the relocated households and more to do with the influence of powerful vested commercial interests.

Asymmetrical Partnerships: Non-State Actors and Housing

South Asian non-state actors have used three main pathways to engage with the state and the housing question. One is to adopt an antagonistic stance with the view to hold the state to account for not meeting the housing needs of the poor. As this is highly dependent on the politics of governance, its occurrence is fragmented and is evident mainly in parts of India (such as the activities of YUVA, an NGO in Mumbai) and preconflict Sri Lanka. The second is by changing tactics from confrontation to cooperation. For example, in Mumbai, the National Slum Dwellers Federation (NSDF) with a history of antagonistic relations now partners with SPARC (an NGO) and Mahila Milan (a women's organisation) – under the banner of the 'Alliance' – to negotiate access to land, housing, and services. This has involved, for instance, the proactive identification of alternative sites for those households threatened by eviction – arguably turning 'forced' evictions into 'voluntary' ones. Such cooperative relations with the state have also enabled the Alliance to bid for and successfully win projects involving the construction of toilets for slum dwellers as part of the World-Bank-assisted Mumbai Slum Sanitation Programme (1996–2005). A third approach is one based on organising the poor and self-provisioning. Two well-known examples are the Orangi Pilot Project (OPP) in Karachi, Pakistan, and the Self-Employed Women's Association (SEWA) in Gujarat, India. The motivation behind OPP was the lack of sanitation in the 'Katchi Abadi's' (informal settlements) of Karachi and the absence of any corrective state action. Adopting the principles of participation, OPP organised residents on a lane-by-lane basis to invest their labour and savings in laying sanitation pipes. This community commitment was successfully used to convince local government of the benefit of connecting these neighbourhoods to the city's mains. In contrast, SEWA adopted the principles of trade unionism to organise self-employed women so as to negotiate better wages (for labourers) and prices (for producers). SEWA has now widened its portfolio of services to include, among others, housing, infrastructure, health, and legal services.

Private sector partnerships in housing have also been attempted, albeit mainly in India. 'Parivartan' (meaning change) used multiactor partnerships (involving poor communities, nongovernmental organisations, the city government, and the private sector) to improve access to water, sanitation, education, health, and livelihood opportunities in a number of squatter settlements in the city of Ahmedabad, Gujarat state. The city of Chennai, Tamil Nadu, experimented with 'guided urban development' which encouraged private developers to build housing for sale on subsidised government land in return for 25% of the housing units produced being handed over to them for allocation to poor households. CLIFF (Community-Led Infrastructure Financing Facility) is a multiactor partnership piloted in India. It involved the 'Alliance' in Mumbai (local facilitator and savings groups), a private sector bank (lender), Homeless International (a UK-based charity and northern facilitator), and the World Bank (the collateral provider). The thinking behind this was that the poor could demonstrate their capacity to save but did not have the necessary collateral for leveraging private sector loans which the multiactor partnership would help overcome.

Although such innovative examples are to be welcomed, their ability to influence wider policy outcomes is patchy for several reasons. First, nongovernmental organisations that have been able to make some inroads into policy (such as SEWA) have done so due to charismatic leadership which remains in short supply and constrains scaling-up. In addition, the constitutional makeup of membership-based organisations (such as the Alliance) results in benefits mainly accruing to their members. This is in contrast to, for example, the minimum wage or the right to information which having become institutionalised are accessible to all citizens. Second, despite the inspiration for 'Khuda-ki-Basti' (winning the Aga Khan award for Architecture in 1995) emanating from progressive city leadership, wider policy change did not follow for similar reasons. Third, even multiactor partnerships such as 'Parivartan' have not produced institutionalised policy outcomes; sustaining private sector participation has proved to be more difficult than assumed. In sum, innovative practices in housing remain localised and fragmented. This is not to suggest that they should be jettisoned; it only serves as a reminder that innovation should not lose sight of the aim of policy transformation.

A Full Circle: The Re-Domination of the State

Housing policies and programmes, in the years leading into the twenty-first century, have seen a re-domination of the state, albeit with different agendas. In India, bids for resources to fulfill national development aims have been overshadowed by intra-country rivalries between regions and cities seeking to attract foreign direct investment in a race for global prominence; Mumbai aims to be like Shanghai and Bangalore is seeking to emulate Singapore. Squatter settlements, once outside the circuit of propertied capital, now find themselves on prime real estate and thus a target for new market-driven forms of eviction. For instance, Dharavi in Mumbai, with a population of around 1 million (purportedly the largest squatter settlement in Asia), is at the centre of a disputed private development initiative which proposes to resettle households in high-rise tenements free of cost; paid from the massive real estate profits that the vacated land is forecast to generate. This also suggests a revisioning of the 'right to the city' (see article Rights to the City). Evidence of a shift in the position of contemporary judicial rulings, in New Delhi, for instance, is emerging. Previous judgements, unequivocally placing the onus of responsibility for unserviced squatter settlements on local government have now given way to squatters themselves having to justify their rights to the areas they occupy. A recent newspaper article reports that the Government of India is (with the view to make urban areas 'slum free') in the process of finalising a model law that will make it mandatory of state governments to frame laws on legal ownership. It proposes that every homeless urban household will be guaranteed a minimum of 24 sq m in walk-up tenements constructed by the private sector, located wherever possible in situ. Beneficiaries will have to pay only 10–15% of the cost (the rest being borne by the central and state governments) with assistance from an interest subsidy scheme from the Ministry of Housing and Poverty Alleviation. To prevent encroachments in the future, the law also proposes a maximum 3-year prison term or a minimum fine of Rupees 100 000 (approximately GB£1400 or US$2200) or both. This is not redistribution; it only serves to maintain the status quo.

Forced evictions have shown no signs of abating. They continue to be explicitly justified in terms of city beautification or infrastructure and implicitly in relation to real estate gains. In Karachi, Pakistan, the Lyari Expressway project is estimated to have displaced 230 000 inhabitants since 2002 – in the 5 months to May 2006, some 23 000 people are said to have been evicted in several parts of the city. Approximately, 30 000 families are estimated to have been evicted in Dhaka, Bangladesh, in a 2-year period between 2007 and 2009 on grounds of legality and it is alleged that Sri Lanka's Colombo Plan (designated as an 'economic war' to rebuild the nation) would involve the eviction of thousands of families.

In sum, housing policy in large parts of South Asia has come full circle. The tenement as the dominant housing form disappeared for several decades but has now resurfaced. Advances in poverty reduction may have been made in aggregate terms but the livelihoods of the majority poor are still dependent on the informal economy making the tenement as inappropriate a housing form as ever. Moreover, the extreme peripheral location of these tenements places the greatest burden on the poor – the cost and time involved in commuting has a domino effect on a number of other aspects of well-being such as the increased burden on the reproductive role of women. It would seem that housing policy aims not so much to alleviate poverty as to 'visibly' banish it. The state has vacated the driving seat of policy formulation and become the navigator of policies propelled by a range of private vested interests instead.

Housing and the State: Potential Pathways

There are several housing pathways worth pursuing. First, one needs to acknowledge that incumbent governments in South Asia are likely to continue to pursue policies in those areas they deem to be most pressing – for Afghanistan, Nepal, Pakistan, and Sri Lanka these are understandably likely to be political stability and physical security within a wider economic reform agenda. Bangladesh is likely to prioritise rural poverty alleviation and economic growth in the medium term. However, such macrolevel concerns should not ignore the potential contribution that housing can make at the local, provincial, and regional levels. A recent report by UNHCR found that a majority of returnees in Afghanistan cited employment, housing, and water as top priorities. Housing can act as a catalyst in bringing about inclusionary objectives: thoughtful reconstruction could help reconcile perceived injustices, stimulate investment, and develop human and institutional capacity. Pakistan, with a history of innovation in housing and basic services has the potential to reconcile potential tensions between displaced populations and local communities at low-end labour market entry points, housing, and basic services. Nepal could explore housing tenure issues given that more than a quarter of its urban residents are tenants.

Second, rural to urban population movements are yet to peak in South Asia (apart from Afghanistan where conflict may have temporarily skewed population distribution). A key challenge facing Bangladesh, Nepal, Pakistan, and Sri Lanka is the primacy of certain cities as destinations for economic and political migrants. This spatial concentration of urbanisation should inform policy-making.

Third, although idiosyncratic urban land markets have been identified as a major housing bottleneck, the jury is still out on how best to reconcile this with the insatiable appetite of vested property interests whose profit margins from its development surpass older forms of rent seeking.

Fourth, access to housing finance seemed less problematic until the recent emergence of doubts surrounding the role of microcredit as a poverty reduction strategy. In addition to the venerable objective of creating more opportunities for secure and stable income flows, private financial institutions should be encouraged to explore ways to create new savings and insurance-related packages for the poor.

Fifth, housing tenure has received short thrift from policy-makers. Homeownership as a policy goal needs to be placed on the back burner for the time being as there is sufficient evidence of the more immediate benefits that both tenants and landlords stand to gain from a wider range of tenure options. These are creating and enhancing livelihood opportunities; building and expanding social networks; advancing forms of social inclusion in class, ethnicity, religion and gender; and promoting a sense of psychosocial security. The 'housing ladder' remains a pertinent analogy: the move from renting to ownership to landlordism does take place, albeit gradually.

Finally, there is little evidence of the sharing of good practice and lessons within South Asia. The plethora of NGOs active in rural Bangladesh, for example, is in stark contrast to their absence in urban areas. Exchange programmes between Indian civil society organisations and their counterparts as far afield as Colombia and South Africa are almost nonexistent within the South Asian region. There is also little by way of intercountry government dialogue and learning; a recent hallmark of many government policy transfers in Latin America. Intra- as well as intercountry dialogue must be fostered between the wide gamut of actors involved in housing policy and practice.

See also: Rights to the City.

Further Reading

Afghanistan Independent Human Rights Commission (2007). *Economic and Social Rights in Afghanistan II*. Geneva: UNHCR.

Aldrich BC and Sandhu RS (eds.) (1995) *Housing the Urban Poor: Policy and Practice in Developing Countries*. London: Zed Books.

Aliani AH and Yap KS (1990) The incremental development scheme in Hyderabad: An innovative approach to low income housing. *Cities* 7(2): 133–148.

Anwara B (2007) Urban housing as an issue of redistribution through planning? The case of Dhaka city. *Social Policy and Administration* 41: 410–418.

Badshah AA (1996) *Our Urban Future: New Paradigms for Equity and Sustainability*. London: Zed Books.

Brun C and Lund R (2009) 'Unpacking' the narrative of a national housing policy in Sri Lanka. *Norsk Geografisk Tidsskrift-Norwegian Journal of Geography* 63(1): 10–22.

Joshi S and Sohail Khan M (2010) Aided self-help: The million houses programme – Revisiting the issues. *Habitat International* 34(3): 306–314.

Kumar S (2001). *Social Relations, Rental Housing Markets and the Poor in Urban India*. London: Department of Social Policy, London School of Economics. http://www.dfid.gov.uk/r4d/pdf/outputs/R6856.pdf. (accessed 1 September 2011).

Rahman MM (2001) Bastee eviction and housing rights: A case of Dhaka, Bangladesh. *Habitat International* 25: 49–67.

Ravallion M, Chen S et al. (2007). New evidence on the urbanization of global poverty. *Policy Research Working Paper No. 4199*. Washington, DC: World Bank, Page 40.

Russell S and Vidler E (2000) The rise and fall of government – Community partnerships for urban development: Grassroots testimony from Colombo. *Environment and Urbanization* 12: 73–86.

Shakur T (1988) Implications for policy formulation towards sheltering the homeless: A case study of squatters in Dhaka, Bangladesh. *Habitat International* 12: 53–66.

UN-Habitat (2011) *The State of Asian Cities 2010/11*. Fukuoka: UN-Habitat.

Wagle UR (2008) How have the poor in South Asia fared between 1980 and 2004? An assessment of living conditions. *South Asia Economic Journal* 9(2): 261–292.

Weerapana D (1986) Evolution of a support policy of shelter – The experience of Sri Lanka. *Habitat International* 10: 79–89.

Relevant Websites

http://go.worldbank.org/GBUHVXX420
http://m.timesofindia.com/PDATOI/articleshow/8521581.cms

Housing and the State in the Middle East

AM Soliman, University of Alexandria, Alexandria, Egypt

© 2012 Elsevier Ltd. All rights reserved.

Glossary

NGOs Non government organisations.
CBOs Community-based organisations.
ILO's International labour organisations.
Madinet Al Awqaf Madent in Arabic means a city, Al awqaf is the traditional religious form of trust tenure in Islamic countries. Waqaf land means that this land is held in trust for many years for a certain purpose, and it could be released after the period of Waqaf ends.

Introduction

The emergence of urban informality in most Third World cities was the main outcome of the rapid urbanisation and the tremendous conversion, either formally or informally, of socioeconomic, political, military, and spatial spaces. As reported throughout this encyclopaedia, for the first time in history, more than half the world's population lives in urban areas. Over 90% of urbanisation is taking place in the developing world. Rapid urbanisation, if not well managed, will increase poverty and slums. An estimated one billion people currently live in urban slums in developing countries. Cities need to be prepared to absorb the demographic growth and to minimise the expansion of slums.

In almost all countries in the Third World, especially in the Middle Eastern countries, the influx into the cities of migrants from rural zones markedly accentuates the cultural diversity and, in ethnically divided countries such as Lebanon, Israel, and Palestine, reflects the ethnic diversity. (Among the many definitions for this area, the Middle East is perhaps most easily defined in terms of the peoples who speak Arabic, Persian, and Turkish, the main Semitic historic languages of Islam. The geopolitical term Middle East, first coined in 1902 by a US naval officer Alfred Thayer Mahan, originally referred to the Asian region south of the Black Sea between the Mediterranean Sea to the West and India to the East. In modern scholarship, the term refers collectively to the Asian countries of Bahrain, Cyprus, Iran, Iraq, Israel (and the Palestine-occupied Gaza Strip and West Bank), Jordan, Kuwait, Lebanon, Oman, Qatar, Saudi Arabia, Syria, Turkey, the United Arab Emirates, and Yemen, and the African country of Egypt. A broader and more cultural definition might include the Muslim countries of Morocco, Algeria, Tunisia, Libya, Sudan, Afghanistan, and Pakistan. The Middle East and North Africa Region covers a wide array of countries from Morocco in the West to Iran in the East. Each country has a long and rich history and strong individual characteristics such that no region-wide strategy can do justice to the specific situation of a particular country. Nevertheless, a number of similarities exist that constitute a good basis for general principles and overall guidance, which then needs to be adapted in what must remain country-specific strategies. It is important to keep this caveat in mind while reading the strategy. The Economic and Social Commission for Western Asia (ESCWA) region contains 13 countries, the six Gulf Cooperation Council, namely, Bahrain, Kuwait, Oman, Qatar, Saudi Arabia, and the United Arab Emirates, together with the more diversified economies, namely, Egypt, Iraq, Jordan, Lebanon, Palestine, Syria, and Yemen. Thus, wherever Middle Eastern countries are mentioned, it will include the ESCWA region, Iran, Turkey, and Arab countries in Africa. For further discussion of different definitions and arguments, see Rashid Khalidi (1998). On the other hand, the Middle Eastern countries also witnessed extensive regional migratory movements of refugees caused by hunger and war. (In Lebanon during the civil war, in Egypt during the Suez Canal crisis of 1956, and in Egypt and Syria during the defeat of the 1967 war, in Iraq during and after American invasion in Sudan in Darfur and the subdivision of the country, and in the current conflict between Israelis and Palestinians in Palestine, there has been increasing support for the growing numbers of refugees.) All these conflicts have caused some sort of burden on national governments, especially for allocating houses for hundreds and thousands of refugees. During the last five decades, international and local agencies, concerned with developing urban policies within cities in the Third World, have influenced the natural and urban landscape and this has led to a host of new proposals of governance and municipal management at the local level. After 11 September 2001, in order to tackle terrorism, innovations in institutional form and practice were introduced, along with new reforms and readjustment of laws and regulations of governments in the Middle Eastern countries.

The year 2011 has brought the Middle Eastern countries into a new era for social movements, where on 14 January the departure of the Tunisian president Zine El Abidine Ben Ali after massive popular protest in Tunisia, was followed by the resignation of the Egyptian president Hosni Mubarak on 11 February after the white revolution of Egyptian youth on 25 January. The great revolt of people in Tunisia and Egypt was to protest against poverty, low wages, rampant unemployment, government corruption, and the autocratic governance of the regimes. Other countries such as Yemen, Libya, Oman, Syria, and Bahrain are following the Egyptian and Tunisia models for social, economic, and political freedom and justice. The common demands of these popular revolts are the eradication of poverty, social justice, democracy, freedom of expression in the opinion, a decent life for every person in the society, and injustice of the housing delivery systems as a prime concern for human rights.

This article illustrates the role of the state in formulating housing policies in the Middle East and demonstrates how changes in these policies affected the local society. (The vast majority of the population in the Middle East is Muslim (primarily Sunni), but there are numerous other religious groups, including Christians, Alawis (concentrated in Turkey and Syria), Jews (almost all in Israel), and Druze (present in Syria, Lebanon, Israel, and Jordan). The most prominent ethnic group in the Middle East is the Arabs, representing about half of the total population of the region (including Iran and Turkey, but not North Africa). Among the remainder, 25% are Turks, 12% Persians, 7% Kurds, 2% Jews, and 4% an amalgam of smaller ethnic groups, such as Armenians and Baluch (Omran and Roudi, 1993; Weeks, 1988).) The article endeavours to develop an understanding of the recent transformations in selected Middle Eastern countries under different political regimes and diversified economies and their influence on varied forms of urban conflicts. The discussion focuses on the shifting liaison between the states and civil societies. The transformation of socioeconomic, spatial spaces, political and urban housing is examined in the light of social exclusion and its relationship to urban informality. The study concludes with an analysis of policy options designed to ameliorate housing informality.

The Shifting Liaison between the State and Civil Society

With the beginning of new millennium, the political arena of the Middle Eastern countries has changed and a new state of socioeconomic and political order has emerged. (For example, the invasion of Iraq, the changing presidency of Syria, the assassination of Rafiq El Hariri in Lebanon, the assassination of Sadat and the resignation of Mubarak in Egypt, the death of King Hassan of Jordan, the death of Yasser Arafat, and the growing conflict between Israel and Palestine. At the global level, the attack on the World Trade Center on 11 September has been, and continues to be, a perpetual challenge for the Middle Eastern countries. Increased globalisation has added to the stress on world trade.) At the regional level, political changes driven by the popular revolutions in Egypt and Tunisia will be accompanied by significant economic, social, and cultural changes, in order to make a real and comprehensive transformation towards a modern civil state based on principles of fair opportunities, transparency, and effective accountability. Therefore, the roles of the states in the Middle Eastern countries and their relationship with civil societies are being recast in their attitude both towards the rest of the world and to their civil societies. Thus, one observes shifting roles of the states in housing policies and towards civil society.

Informal residential areas are often argued to be an important source of cheap labour, making possible the lowering of the social wage assumed by the capital or the state in the economies of developing countries (AlSayyad and Roy, 2004). Housing is a tool of economic development (Arku and Harris, 2005) and governments may use it to reduce unemployment or improve health and productivity. Moreover, they may turn existing informal settlements and insecure wealth into productive capital by regularising the ownership claims of squatters (De Soto, 2000). As experience and insight grew, it became evident that local people, who had previously been viewed as passive 'subjects', 'clients', or 'beneficiaries', had much to contribute to the development process (Miltin and Thompson, 1995). Soliman (2008) argues that the rise of this informal urban proletariat is an original development that was unforeseen by both classical Marxism and neoliberal theory and that it contributes informally and formally to economic and political development. After the popular movements in the Middle East countries, it became apparent that this strata of the society has a major effect and strong articulate on the development process, and on the right of being secure in the place that the reconciliation are today's realities to ensure better practices for the future depending upon a good integration between the society and a responsible performance by the state.

It is argued that power is flowing away from the nation state upwards to the global level, while power is also flowing downwards to subnational organisations (local and regional authorities, communities, nongovernment organisations (NGOs), community-based organisations, etc.) (Castells, 1997). Globalisation processes have unleashed the pursuit of a new basis for community and group identity, presenting welcome opportunities for more powers of self-determination and the expansion of democracy, participation, and personal as well as group freedom. Regulations and the question of spatial scale in the prospect of increasing globalisation have become important, although the current attempts to address these pressures within the formula 'think global, act local', or through 'glocalising' activities are unlikely to be sufficient by themselves.

Some progressive social movements have also appealed to themes of security and antiterrorism to bolster their legitimacy and forward their agenda after the 11 September attacks (Marcuse, 2006). Therefore, worldwide, and especially in the Middle East, the role of governments is being reconsidered and reconfirmed to strengthen the essential functions of facilitating markets and correcting market failures, endorse democratic systems, promote socioeconomic stability, and ensure distributional equity.

In the Middle East, it appears that petty commodity production is an ever-present feature of the capitalist economy and that the informal economy constitutes a high proportion of the Middle Eastern countries' national economy. According to the 1996 Egyptian government survey data, some 1.4 million entrepreneurs – 82% of all entrepreneurs in Egypt – worked in the informal sector, which employed 8.2 million workers – more than the number employed in the formal private sector (6.8 million) or in the government (5.9 million) (Galal, 2004). In Amman, with a population of 2.17 million (out of 5.47 million of Jordan as a whole, 35% of whom are Palestinians), two-thirds of the workers were in the informal sector (Potter et al., 2009). One million Palestinians live in Lebanon, 50% of whom work in the informal sector. In Syria, in 2006, informal employment reached more than 35% of total employment (Kattaa and Al Cheikh Hussein, 2009). Since the blockade began in 2007, Gaza's private sector has collapsed and 42% of the workforce is currently unemployed. The United Nations Relief and Works Agency (UNRWA) recognises that the current blockade has increased the problem of housing in the Gaza strip, which is considered the largest squatter settlement in the world (Yiftachel and Yacobi, 2004). It seems that the proportion of the informal sector will increase as the added population growth in the Middle East would be within the figure of 100 million within the next decade (see **Table 1**), an almost 30% increase over the current population.

Since the 2003 Gulf War, the Syrian Arab Republic has hosted some 1 000 000 Iraqi refugees, half of whom are children. Jordan has an equal number of Iraqi refugees; Lebanon and Egypt are also hosts to Iraqi refugees. This external emigration, along with internal national migration, have put further pressure on the Middle Eastern states to provide sound housing to accommodate the rapid increase in population in urban areas, and it is projected that the proportion of the populations living in urban areas in the Middle East will approach 73.7% by the year 2020 (see **Table 2**).

Due to the presence of the informal economy, the accumulation of capital resulting from production from this sector has become large scale and forms an important

Table 1 Projected population of the Middle Eastern countries between 2002 and 2020

Country	Capital city	Area (km^2)	Population growth rate 1990–95	Population estimate 2002	2010	Projection 2015	2020
Algeria	Algiers	2 381 740	2.3	32.278	38.718	43.38	48.603
Bahrain	Manama	665	2.1	0.656	0.775	0.86	0.954
Egypt	Cairo	1 001 450	1.9	70.712	82.203	90.315	99.227
Iran	Tehran	1 648 000	1.7	66.623	76.241	82.946	90.24
Iraq	Baghdad	437 072	2.8	24.002	29.936	34.368	39.457
Israel	Jerusalem	20 770	2.2	6.03	7.176	8.001	8.921
Jordan	Amman	92 300	3.1	5.307	6.776	7.893	9.195
Kuwait	Kuwait	17 820	3.1	2.112	2.696	3.14	3.658
Lebanon	Beirut	10 400	1.8	3.678	4.242	4.638	5.07
Libya	Tripoli	1 759 540	2.4	5.369	6.49	7.307	8.227
Morocco	Rabat	446 550	1.8	31.168	35.949	39.303	42.97
Oman	Muscat	212 460	3.4	2.713	3.546	4.191	4.953
Qatar	Doha	11 437	1.8	0.793	0.915	1	1.094
Saudi Arabia	Riyadh	1 960 582	3.4	23.513	30.724	36.315	42.922
Syria	Damascus	185 180	2.6	17.156	21.066	23.951	27.231
Tunisia	Tunis	163 610	1.4	9.816	10.97	11.76	12.607
Turkey	Ankara	780 580	1.7	67.309	77.027	83.8	91.17
United Arab Emirates	Abu Dhabi	82 880	2	2.446	2.866	3.164	3.493
Yemen	Sanaa	527 970	2.2	18.701	18.701	18.701	18.701
Total		11 741 006		390.382	457.017	505.033	558.693

Source: http://www.mongabay.com/igapo/population_projections.htm

Table 2 Changes in the urbanisation rates of selected Middle Eastern countries (1950–2030)

	1950	1960	1970	1980	1990	2000	2010	2020	2030
Algeria	22.3	30.4	39.5	43.5	51.4	57.1	62.2	67.5	71.7
Morocco	26.2	29.2	34.6	41.3	48.4	55.5	61.7	66.7	71
Tunisia	31.2	36	44.5	51.5	57.9	65.5	71.3	75.2	78.4
Libya	18.6	22.7	45.3	69.3	81.8	87.6	89.7	90.9	92
Egypt	31.9	37.9	42.2	43.8	43.6	42.7	44	48.2	54.4
Jordan	35.9	50.9	56	60.2	72.2	78.7	80.1	82.2	84.4
Israel	64.6	77	84.2	88.6	90.3	91.6	93.3	93.9	94.6
Palestine	37.3	44	54.3	61.1	64	66.8	70	73.5	76.9
Lebanon	22.7	39.6	59.4	73.7	84.2	89.7	92.1	93.1	93.9
Syria	30.6	36.8	43.3	46.7	48.9	51.4	55.4	60.6	65.6
Turkey	21.3	29.7	38.4	43.8	61.2	65.8	69.9	73.7	77
Average	31.15	39.47	49.25	56.68	63.99	68.40	71.79	75.05	78.17

Source: UN-HABITAT (2006). *The State of the World's Cities Report 2006/2007*. London: Earthscan.

contribution to the national economy. Thus, Middle Eastern states have come to rely on the working classes and upon the informal economy. A major component of social consumption provided by the states pertains to public housing, land provision, and so on, which are increasingly important for securing the supply of labour power and social relations in capitalist cities. Petty commodity production represented in building housing units for the workers actually interacts with and depends upon capitalist production; neither of the two can be separated from the country's national economy. In fact, recent economic investment in Egypt, Syria, Jordan, and Lebanon has brought about increasing land and property investments, generating a 'construction boom' in 2007 and 2008, especially with new groups of executives demanding high-end housing. According to the preliminary estimates of the International Labour Organisation for the year 2007, unemployment currently stands at 11.8% in the Middle East (World Bank, 2010).

The inability of private capital and the weakness of the states in providing collective means of consumption (housing, services, and infrastructure), especially housing for low-income groups, have led to the emergence of new forms of informal development within the Middle Eastern cities that are often characterised by complex and bizarre intersections of urban and rural restructuring. The popular revolt on such a large scale in Egypt, and maybe all over the world, was for social equity and poverty reduction, where at least 17 million Egyptians reside in informal areas around cities (Egypt Human Development Report 2010, 2010). Informality is no longer the domain of the poor in the cities of the Middle East, but has also become a primary avenue to homeownership for the lower-middle and middle classes (Soliman, 2004). Urban informality has thus become noticeable and fits the realities of the contemporary urban landscape of the Middle Eastern cities (AlSayyad and Roy, 2004).

The State, Housing, and Emerging Political Strains

The Middle Eastern governments responded to community participation, in socioeconomic development and in increasing housing production, in five principal ways: (1) demobilisation mode, (2) the participatory mode, (3) the manipulative mode, (4) the cost-recovery mode, and (5) the 'transitional socioeconomic and political mode'. Of course, these are idealized type of responses that do not fit every situation and sometimes exist in combinations or variations.

First, in the 'demobilisation mode', the government actively sought to promote community mobilisation, from rural to urban areas, and its contribution as a mechanism for sustaining the political system, and the low-income groups were used by politicians for strengthening their own political power and continuance. During the Nasserism era in Egypt, from 1954 to 1970, most of the states of the Middle East followed the paradigm of Nasserism, which reflected socialist ideology and trend, both at the regional and national levels, in attracting the lowest strata of the society towards the new political transformation. Thus, Nasser's ideology was spread throughout the Middle East, such as in Syria, Libya, Lebanon, Iraq, Algeria, Yemen, and Palestine, attracting the lowest strata of the society against the external international powers. It was aimed at satisfying the urgent needs for goods and services, for the bottom strata of the societies, in order that they would be a buffer against the external 'imperialism'. It was to be the basis to establish a 'Socialist society' and to mobilise the working classes from rural to urban areas in order to accelerate the development processes.

In the late 1950s, most of the Middle Eastern countries witnessed the introduction of the development of social housing programmes for constructing low-cost housing to accommodate middle- and low-income groups. In Egypt, the first public housing programme was introduced in 1954. The construction of workers' housing, sometimes called dormitory towns, was mainly for workers and employees who were attached to major industrial centres established at that time. In Syria, after the establishment of the union with Egypt in 1958, similar policies were applied after 1960 when President Nasser (then President of the United Arab Republic) initiated public housing programmes that were assigned the roles of securing land to set up housing projects, provide utilities, and sell and distribute plots. Other Middle Eastern countries followed suit, countries such as Libya, Iraq, and Algeria, supplied social housing for low-income groups. The socialist movement was in full swing as governments endeavoured to become solely responsible for providing housing for middle- and low-income groups, while the involvement of the private sector was reduced (Hopkins, 1969).

In the mid-1960s, housing policy shifted into condominiums in new large-scale land subdivisions such as *Madinet Al Awqaf*, in *Maadi*, and *Heliopolis* districts near Cairo, Egypt, and in the periphery of Damascus and Aleppo in Syria, taking advantage of the liberal credit terms available under the government-subsidised cooperative housing programmes. Libya and the Sudan followed the Egyptian model following the announcement of the new union between the three countries in 1968. In Syria, after 1968, the law was changed so that Palestinians were allowed to own one house per person, but they were still not allowed to own farm land (United Nations, 2005), and the Syrian government had allocated land plots for housing development to low-income groups. Similarly, Jordan, Yemen, and Lebanon witnessed a transformation in housing policy with the elimination of the role of the private sector in housing supply, causing a sharp decline in the housing market.

However, the 1967 war with Israel, the subsequent war of attrition, and the run up to the 1973 war froze formal housing programmes in the Middle Eastern countries, as public funds were reserved for the war effort. Large urban centres had to accommodate a significant number of internal and external migrants, especially in Egypt, Syria, and Jordan. Shifting demobilisation – from one urban to another urban area – had taken place, with the landscape of the cities in confrontation with Israel changing radically, resettlement of many residents from war-front cities, and a huge increase in housing production in other cities, but much of it was informal, such as in Cairo, Alexandria, Damascus, Aleppo, Amman, and Beirut. The informal housing development accounted for between 25 and 35% of the total housing production.

Secondly, the 'participatory mode' was characterised by an elastic housing programme through encouraging involvement of the private sector in decision making and in housing production for accelerating the development process. During the era from 1973 to 1981, the Middle Eastern countries witnessed a period of active but ad hoc intervention. After the 1973 war, the socio-economic and political milieu in the Middle East changed dramatically, and the oil prices increased exponentially. The next phase of alteration, from 1978 to 1983 (often referred to as the 'boom years'), was based on the large contingent of emigrants coming from Jordan (Kadhim and Rajjal, 1988), Syria, and Egypt (Soliman, 2004), who worked in the oil-rich states of the region, many of whom sent back substantial remittances, and this accelerated the boom in housing productions.

Consequently, Middle Eastern governments intervened more positively in the housing market and recognised that the private sectors offered an important means to tackle the housing shortage. Housing policies involved the private developers and embraced three sets of actors, the formal and informal private sectors, and the public sector, where the private housing developers were considered an important actor in the housing development in new and old towns. Thus, the private sector had gained the privilege of becoming the main supplier for housing production. At the same time, for low-income groups, the states adopted self-help that was advocated by the first congress of UN-HABITAT in 1976. This was achieved by facilitating the flow of subsidised building materials, forming cooperative housing societies, and allowing a free market within the formal private housing sector. In the late 1970s, the role played by the informal sector as an indispensable part of housing production was recognised in the Middle Eastern countries with at least 75, 55, and 60% of housing construction being undertaken by the uncontrolled private sector in Egypt, Syria, and Jordan, respectively (Kattaa and Al Cheikh Hussein, 2009; Potter et al., 2009; Soliman, 2004).

Adequate shelter for all was the declared objective to be achieved through private and public sectors. The idea was a shift of focus from providing completely subsidised housing to providing other means of housing in terms of goods, services, or both. As a consequence, site and services and upgrading programmes, core housing, and wet core units were developed to house this bottom stratum of the society. Many projects were introduced in different Middle Eastern cities, for example, in Egypt – Alexandria, Ismailia, Helwan, Aswan, Cairo; in Syria – Damascus and Aleppo; in Jordan –Amman; in Lebanon –Saidon, and in Sudan – Khartoum. This was based upon two main principles: first, to allocate large land plots in various locations within the cities to cover various social classes of the required population, and second, to leave housing production in the hands of private developers who catered only to a small minority of the privileged who could afford to build their own homes.

Thirdly, the 'manipulative mode' constituted a vaguely formulated or poorly implemented policy whereby at the beginning of the 1980s, the governments played an arbitrary role within the housing market and had begun to impose new restrictions on private developers in terms of building procedures and regulations. Yet by 1986, the new-found orientation of international agencies induced new economic reforms, and the states once again recognised the private sector as the principal housing sector to develop housing construction for middle- and low-income groups (Soliman, 2004). This era witnessed a great fluctuation in housing policies and the real estate market, where new private developers in the form of money-lending companies became a major supply of housing units, not for the poor, but for the middle and the upper-middle classes. The urban poor continued to rely on informal methods to shelter themselves. Due to the arbitrary housing policies in this era, many laws were passed and later on amended and replaced by new ones (e.g., Egypt, Syria, Lebanon, and Jordan) where many informal areas had been created on the periphery of the major urban centres in the Middle East.

Therefore, the states had accepted a status quo for the arbitrary urban growth in seeking to recover from the financial burden that it had inherited from the 1973 war, housing shortages in the 1970s, and the increasing price of oil, and began to speed up the process of implementing new economic policies, making the best use they could of the substantial remittances from people who worked abroad.

Fourthly, the 'cost-recovery mode' was an attempt to involve community participation programmes and the private sector on a cost-recovery basis for increasing the level of housing production and for the states' own ends. Lack of resources, in cash, in kind, or both, forced the states to follow the cost-recovery mode in order to increase housing production for the urban poor. One of the main issues to be tackled was taking account of the invisible resources of middle- and low-income groups and guiding their efforts to participate in housing construction. As De Soto (2000) identified, 'the potential value of an asset, to effectively "unlock" $9.3 trillion of what he calls "dead capital", and so allows us to control it'. Therefore, with the beginning of the New Millennium, and after 11 September, the roles of governments were recast to strengthen their essential functions of facilitating real estate markets and correcting market failures, promoting socioeconomic stability, and ensuring distributional equity. The governments, especially in Egypt, Syria, and Jordan, initiated a new economic policy through privatisation programmes that paid attention to the urban poor. This process included efforts to expand opportunities for citizen participation; to increase innovation, openness, and cost-effectiveness; and to promote public–private partnership. All these efforts were challenges for local governments for ensuring an environment conducive to good business, a strong civic society, and for alleviating the heavy financial burden to be paid on housing projects. Egypt, Syria, Jordan, Algeria, Libya, and Yemen were committed to poverty alleviation and had acquired clear momentum through the explicit adoption of the goal of reducing poverty to 15% by 2015 (United Nations, 2005). The governments of Egypt, Syria, and Jordan explicitly articulated a package of actions and programmes designed to empower the poor on cost-recovery basis.

The cost-recovery programmes, policies, and strategies were rapidly developed with the participation and consensus of all stakeholders under different national and international housing projects. However, the important point was the stability of the implementation of the housing policies and its contribution to the development process within the Middle Eastern countries. In the meantime, after 10 years of relative deprivation in real estate market investment (between the years 1994 and 2004), a boom in the private housing development occurred in the Middle Eastern countries, especially in Egypt, Syria, Lebanon, and other Gulf countries. International, regional, and national real estate companies entered the Middle Eastern market; prices rapidly rose, forcing the urban poor to acquire their goods and services in their own way. Urban informality was perceived as potentially dangerous, and states introduced new approaches to attack the poverty belts on the periphery of urban areas, and to prevent the growing of illegal housing development (Potter et al., 2009; Soliman, 2007).

Fifthly, the 'transitional socioeconomic and political mode' was an attempt to cope with the transitional state of affairs that occurred after the peaceful revolution in Egypt and other Middle Eastern countries in responding to the increasing demand for housing units to absorb the massive anger of the societies. The role of the state shrunk, while the housing mechanisms controlled by the private sector in informal housing development being flourishing. As an immediate response of the interim governments in Egypt and Tunisia to modify the current housing delivery system for low-income groups and to meet the rapid demand for housing units, these governments intervened in several ways.

First, an inventory all public housing units located in different Egyptian and Tunisian cities, either completed or non-finished housing units to distribute them to applicants who most in need for shelter. It is estimated that about one million and 150 000 applications were handled to the responsible authorities in Egypt and Tunisia, respectively, in a short period of less than 15 days after the fall of the Mubarak and Ben Ali regimes.

Second, speeding up the housing production in a short time by distributing of serviced land plots (with an average area ranging between 350-450 square meters) on the outskirts of cities or in the new urban communities in Egypt to private real estate developers at prices to suit low-income groups to build residential blocks up to ten floors in height. This technique is dependent on self-assistance through the formulation of owners' associations between a private developer and those seeking access to housing on a cost recovery basis. The idea is to formulate cooperation between the public and private sectors, where the former will provide goods in the form of serviced land that the private sector is incapable of doing, while the latter will be enabled to carry out the construction process on an incremental basis at its own expense.

Third, inventory of the actual number of closed and vacant housing units in the cities, in order to exploit them as rental units in the real estate market. Some privilege will be allocated to the property owners of vacant units by exempting them from paying properties tax, and providing financial support to the property owners ranges between 25 000–30 000 Egyptian Pounds (LE) without interest. This financial support is to be paid off in monthly installments of 120 LE for the state out of the actual rental value of a free contract between property owners and tenants. The differences between the actual rent agreed upon with the owner of the property and the imbursement of loan to be covered by the tenant over a period between 10–15 years. It is estimated that the total closed and vacant housing units in Egypt is about 4.58 million housing units of which 1.18 million were closed and 3.40 million were vacant.

Fourth, governments try to temporarily control the unregulated construction on agricultural land and existing buildings, where some individuals took advantage of the transitional circumstances that the countries are passed through for personal interest, building on agricultural land and the exploitation of what can be exploited in the absence of a security presence in Egypt. It is estimated that the illegal conversion of agricultural land into informal residential development was about 25–30 000 Faddan (one Faddan equals 4200 square metres) within a period of 20 days after the outbreak of the youth revolution in January 2011. This is unlike the many roles of the establishment in violation of the conditions to build on the existing buildings in cities of Egypt, estimated at around 15–20 000 residential units in the same period. The interim government is reluctant to implement laws for fear of the negative perception at street level to the responsible authorities in the country.

It could be said that during this critical transitional period, the housing mechanisms are fully controlled by the masses of the people without adhering to the laws governing the construction process, and the shrinking role of government in controlling the real estate market. In other words, the role of the state shifted from an enabler to an observer, in which it lost control over the built environment. It is expected that Egypt and other Middle Eastern countries will face many urban problems because of the indiscriminate construction and the rapid erosion of agricultural lands in over time.

Social Exclusion

A significant theoretical analysis of the interrelations between the social and the spatial aspects of the urban phenomenon refers to the urban as an arena of power relations, shaping cities' meaning and space (Castells, 2000). This school views urbanisation as a process that produces spatial structures and forms, supporting the recreation of social relations for the reproduction of capital which may represent the conflict between the state and society. But it hardly affects the urban poor. (The recent world financial crisis, rise in food prices, and increase in oil prices, revolutionary movements have added to the burden on most governments in the Third World; this sharply affects the urban poor in obtaining goods and services for their survival. This has created a new section of Middle Eastern societies that are prepared to do things that would threaten national security. The states do not realise that the greater the social exclusion, the greater the danger to national security. Revolts, riots, disturbance, and conflicts between the poor and the Middle Eastern governments have occurred, for example, the recent revolts in Egypt, Tunisia, and Libya, the one in West and East Beirut, and the confrontation of *Nahar El Bared* in Tripoli in Lebanon.)

A conjunction of conditions linked with urban poverty, violence, ethnic, and migrant concentration is spatially expressed in 'invisible' urban enclaves (Sibley, 1995), especially in Lebanon, Syria, Palestine, Israel, and Jordan (Fernandes, 2009; Potter et al., 2009; Soliman, 2008; Yiftachel and Yacobi, 2004). Very often, these places – in spite of their often large scale – are not marked on city maps, and are categorised by the majority as 'illegal'. These places become the signifiers of the socially constructed and demonised image of the 'other'. These communities are all the result of labour exploitation, poverty, ethno-national antagonism and socioeconomic exclusion that have pushed people – occasionally residents of the city in question – to act 'illegally' and claim their right to the city, and even more excluded a whole region such as the Gaza strip in Palestine from being integrated within the national, regional, and international regions.

On the other hand, various economic regimes in the Middle East are adopting social policies and institutional arrangements that have a differential impact on the quality of life. Middle Eastern cities increasingly separate people: this is visible in the spaces they occupy and inhabit such as the social divides of *Imbabha* and *El Zamalek* areas in Cairo, the segregation in West and East Beirut (Soliman, 2008), and the differentiation between the Eastern and Western sectors of Amman where the former is a district for the poor, while the latter occupied by the elite (Potter et al., 2009). Traditional physical planning decisively reinforces processes of social exclusion. Disadvantaged groups are considered to be come apart from the informal economy society.

The spatial organisation of the Middle Eastern cities is not an organic or natural process reflecting solely socio-economic differences. Rather, it is integrated into unequal urban niches that spatially express power relations that are currently stemming from the rapid increase in information technology. The political arenas in Egypt and other countries in the north of Africa have changed. Many of these organisations' grassroots activists in Egypt, furthermore, were directly involved in the January 28 'day of rage' that kicked off the series of protests, both through social media like Youtube, Twitter, and Facebook, and also through hands-on planning on the ground by which President Hosni Mubarak was deposed on 11 February, 2011. In Middle Eastern cities, social exclusion is currently taking two forms. One is the problematic nature of disadvantaged groups on the periphery or in the most dilapidated quarters of large urban centres. Residential segregation and consolidation is not only a product of enforcement by others; it can also be self-determined by the residents themselves. Specific groups may prefer to isolate themselves in order to protect their common political entity and collective consciousness – for example, the Palestinian camps in Damascus, Beirut, and Amman. The segregated group is able to establish communal functions and a sense of security, as well as political organisation when necessary, such as the Moslem Brothers movements and groups in Egypt, Syria, and Hamas in the Gaza strip in Palestine. This is also true in the case of Israel/Palestine, where the informal land rights of settlers have been so intensely ethnicised that they are now a major hurdle to the prospects of peace. The Israeli state, having prevented the Palestinians from building legally, has left them with no alternative but to expand informally, by which the state created ethnocratic urban informality (Yiftachel and Yacobi, 2004). These segregated battlefields are the locations, or the worst locations, in which struggles for the right to the city take place, such as the *Ezbet El Haghana* and *Dewiqa* areas in Cairo, the *Dahiya Janubiyya* and *Ouzai* areas in Beirut, the Eastern sector in Amman, and the Gaza strip in Palestine. Hence, understanding the patterns of segregation in housing, economic activities, and everyday life is tightly linked with the analysis of minority–majority power relations in terms of network urbanisation and in terms of socioeconomic and political conflict.

Social exclusion within different classes of the society also occurs from their respective abilities and capacities to take advantage of information technology. Social media played a huge role in connecting many of the people who would eventually join the protests which boasted half a million members on January 25, 2011 in Tahrir Square and adjacent parts of the city center of Cairo, and were instrumental, so much so that a new expression has entered the Egyptian lexicon. The politicised, Internet-savvy generation that organised the initial events is known as the 'Facebook kids'. Some people have the capital and knowledge to benefit from information technology, while others are as yet incapable of being integrated. For example, new residential compounds on the periphery of Cairo, Damascus, Amman, Beirut, and so on, reflect and assist differentiations between the haves and have nots. This has led to a paradox: an acute housing crisis in urban areas in the Middle East, while at the same time a very large number of housing units remaining vacant and unused. There are several reasons for such a large housing stock remaining unused or vacant (World Bank, 2007): most of the vacant houses are within the category of high-income, and above middle-income, housing.

Epilogue: A Credible Future

During the last four decades, cities in the Middle East have witnessed a remarkable and, in many ways, unprecedented increase in levels of urban informality. Urban informality is often construed as a land-use problem. Yet it arises and persists due to socioeconomic and culture necessities and material deprivation, physical and social insecurity, and ethnic and class prejudices. As a result failing housing policies, poor development of social services, and changing demographic trends, contemporary urban informal areas remain the growth points in society and are also the potential lightning rods for political and social unrest as happened in Egypt, Libya, Yemen, and Tunisia.

In a context characterised by disengagement of the state and meagre local finances, Middle Eastern countries face the contradictory goals of meeting the aspirations for integration in a globalising economy with the growing difficulties of meeting the needs of the local population and effective management of the urban environment. This is particularly pronounced in the largest cities. With the rapid growth of population, governments will continue to face an increasing demand for housing and will need to facilitate land delivery systems paying special attention to the needs of the poor and to the need to increase access to employment and income-earning opportunities.

Four main challenges are facing the Middle Eastern governments in tackling housing informality in urban areas. The first is that new changes that are taking place within civil society, where NGOs and international agencies have come to play a major role in the relationship between the state and the society. The second is the change in the nature of the state and the influence of globalisation requiring good governance in which the state becomes the principal enabler of housing production for the bottom strata of society. The third is that public sector management reform and private sector development cannot proceed effectively unless and until they are adapted to the requirements of good urban governance that can be implemented at the municipal level. The fourth is that a new era for democracy has emerged in various Middle Eastern countries (the revolt in Egypt and Tunisia) in which civil society, CBOs and NGOs will play a major role in conducting the development process, especially in housing delivery system.

Perhaps the perpetual challenge that faces the current transitional circumstances in the Middle Eastern countries is the absence of deep understanding of the seriousness of loss of stability, security, retreat of priorities, and the collapse of the economy. The accomplishment of all targets, enhancing housing delivery system and poverty reduction would require a creation of an environment capable of implementing incrementally the priorities of a comprehensive development and to speed the return to a life of natural conditions for the welfare of the societies.

A more appropriate balance between rural and urban economic and noneconomic opportunities also appears to be necessary for the amelioration of urban and rural unemployment problems and to slow down the pace of rural–urban migration and regional migration. The challenges facing the Middle Eastern governments are the following: to rectify the imbalances between housing demand and supply, to redistribute demographic concentration from the old urban centres, and to close the gap between what the low-income groups can afford to pay and the minimum cost of a legal plot with basic services. Middle Eastern governments need also to integrate development activities and link housing to larger urban systems of employment and production. They must also decentralise resources to support local enterprise and home building at the local and national levels, providing transparency, accountability, responsibility, and trust in their vision for the future. Closer collaboration or partnership between various stakeholders is required in order to create the required capital for the development process. Urbanisation is not exclusively a challenge for cities alone, rather it is a challenge to face chaos in cities as a result of transitional circumstances in the Middle Eastern cities.

References

AlSayyad N and Roy A (2004) Prologue/dialogue. In: Roy A and AlSayyad N (eds.) *Urban Informality: Transnational Perspectives from the Middle East, Latin America, and South Asia*, pp. 1–6. Lanham, MD: Lexington Books.
Arku G and Harris R (2005) Housing as a tool of economic development since 1929. *International Journal of Urban and Regional Research* 29(4): 895–915.
Castells M (1997) *The Power of Identity*. Malden, MA: Blackwell Publishers Inc.
Castells M (2000) *The Rise of Network Society, Vol. 1: The Information Age: Economy, Society and Culture*, New edition. Malden, MA: Blackwell Publishers Inc.
De Soto H (2000) *The Mystery of Capital: Why Capitalism Triumphs in the West and Fails Everywhere Else*. New York: Basic Books.
Egypt Human Development Report 2010 (2010) United Nations Development Programme, and the Institute of National Planning, Egypt.
Fernandes E (2009) Informal settlements in Syria: A general framework for understanding and confronting the phenomenon. *Municipal Administration*. Syria: Damascus.
Galal A (2004) *Potential Winners and Losers from Business Formalization*. Working Paper Series 95. Cairo: The Egyptian Center for Economic Studies.
Hopkins H (1969) *Egypt, the Crucible: The Unfinished Revolution of the Arab World*. London: Martin Secker and Warburg Limited.
Kadhim AM and Rajjal Y (1988) City profile: Amman. *Cities* 5(4): 318–325.
Kattaa M and Al Cheikh Hussein S (2009) Women entrepreneurs facing the informality in rural and remote areas in Syria. *European Journal of Social Sciences* 11(4): 624–642.
Khalidi R (1998) The 'Middle East' as a framework of analysis: Re-mapping a region in the era of globalization. *Comparative Studies of South Asia, Africa and the Middle East* 18(1): 74–80.
Marcuse P (2006) Security or safety in cities? The threat of terrorism after 9/11. *International Journal of Urban and Regional Research* 30(4): 919–929.
Miltin D and Thompson J (1995) Participatory approaches in urban areas: Strengthening civil society or reinforcing the status quo? *Environment and Urbanization* 7: 231–250.
Omran AR and Roudi F (1993) The Middle East population puzzle. *Population Bulletin* 48(1): 1–38.
Potter R, Darmame K, Barham N, and Nortclif S (2009) 'Ever-growing Amman', Jordan: Urban expansion, social polarisation and contemporary urban planning issues. *Habitat International Journal* 33(1): 81–92.
Sibley D (1995) *Geographies of Exclusion: Society and Difference in the West*. London: Routledge.
Soliman A (2004) *A Possible Way Out: Formalizing Housing Informality in Egyptian Cities*. Lanham, MD: University Press of America.
Soliman A (2007) Urban informality in Egyptian cities: Coping with diversity. *Fourth Urban Research Symposium*. Washington, DC: World Bank.
Soliman A (2008) Diversity of ethnicity and state involvement on urban informality in Beirut. *Theoretical and Empirical Researches on Urban Management* 9: 15–32.
United Nation (2005) *Second National Report on the MDGs in the Syrian Arab Republic*. Syrian Arab Republic.
UN-HABITAT (2006) *The State of the World's Cities Report 2006/2007*. London: Earthscan for UN-HABITAT.
World Bank (2007) *Arab Republic of Egypt: Analysis of Housing Mechanisms*. Report Number 41180. Washington, DC: World Bank.
World Bank (2010) *Middle East and North Africa Region – A Regional Economic Update, April 2010: Recovering from the Crisis*. Washington, DC: World Bank.
Yiftachel O and Yacobi H (2004) Control, resistance, and informality: Urban ethnocracy in Beer-Sheva, Israel. In: Roy A and AlSayyad N (eds.) *Urban Informality: Transnational Perspectives from the Middle East, Latin America, and South Asia*, pp. 209–239. Lanham, MD: Lexington Books.

Relevant Website

http://www.mongabay.com/igapo/population_projections.htm (accessed 20 November 2011).

Housing and the State in the Soviet Union and Eastern Europe

I Tosics, Metropolitan Research Institute, Budapest, Hungary

© 2012 Elsevier Ltd. All rights reserved.

The Socialist Ideology about Housing

According to Demko and Regulska (quoted by Smith, 1996: 72), socialist ideology aims for the equality of the people. Within this wider aim, ensuring nondiscriminatory and nonspatially differentiated housing was considered an important goal. "No social or occupational group would have better or more favourably located residential sites so that one would find a randomly distributed housing pattern."

In the fight to achieve equality, the abolition of private property was one of the very first aims and actions of the 1917 revolution in Russia. Except for the peasant households' landownership, all other land was taken away by the state, resulting in the total nationalisation of urban land. Later, in the 1936 Constitution, the concept of personal ownership was introduced, limited for a household to one house "without the right to derive 'non-labour income' from its ownership" (Marcuse, 1996: 129). These radical regulations resulted in a very one-sided tenure structure: in 1990, by the end of socialism, 79% of Soviet urban housing was state owned, 5% was owned by public and construction cooperatives, and 15% was in personal ownership (Berezin, 1992, quoted in Marcuse, 1996: 130).

In the other socialist countries – where socialism ruled for a shorter period – similar principles were applied but to varying extents. The nationalisation of property was an important part of the development of the socialist state; nevertheless, in all these countries, a significant share of land and housing remained in private ownership. In Hungary, for example, buildings with fewer than six rooms were exempt from nationalisation: as a result of this the share of state ownership of housing always remained below one-third (in Budapest below two-thirds) of the total stock.

The state ownership of land and housing was not the sole factor controlling the housing system in socialist countries. To understand the logic of state control in housing, first the basic features of socialism have to be mentioned: state monopoly of the means of production, the system of one-party rule, and the single-rank hierarchical social order with the cadre elite at the top (Szelényi, 1996: 308). Second, it is important to understand the main aspects of the socialist economic system (Hegedüs and Tosics, 1996: 16): a central planning system (centralising economic decisions to a narrow political elite), and strict income regulation, paying low wages without adding the costs of housing, education, health care, and infrastructure (i.e., centralising these elements into the state budget). On that basis the following additional political-institutional factors were introduced, which became specific determinants of East European socialist urban and housing policies (Tosics, 2005):

- strong and direct state control over land use, leading to very specific land-use patterns expressing the preferences of the socialist state (Bertaud and Renaud, 1997);
- administrative limitation of housing consumption (one dwelling per family);
- state control over the most important housing-policy factors (state-financed housing construction, social housing policy, subsidised private housebuilding, loan origination, and construction industry and materials);
- control over the private housing market (private rents) and indirect regulation of the self-financed form of housing construction;
- administrative limitation of the size and development (inflow of population, industrial growth) of major cities; and
- direct control over the financial resources of the cities, and control over the political decision-making process.

All these factors made it possible for the East-Central European countries to exert strong control over the functioning of the land market and housing system, even if they did not own all – or even the majority of – the land and the housing stock. Owing to the basic similarity of the framework conditions, the notion of the East European (Socialist) Housing Model has been introduced (Hegedüs and Tosics, 1996: 16).

The Real Functioning of the Socialist Housing Model

The label 'Socialist Housing Model' indicates that this housing system was qualitatively different from other Western housing models. Western models were based on market relationships regarding the land and the housing, which were also considered market commodities (although state interventions were always present to correct market failures). The distinctiveness of the socialist housing system coincides with the view of Iván Szelényi who states that "urban development in the socialist epoch in Eastern Europe was quite different from urban development in Western countries at a similar stage of economic growth" (Szelényi, 1996: 286).

How did this socialist housing model function in reality, and to what extent has the socialist state fulfilled its promises to supply housing to everyone in an equitable way?

The detailed analysis of the logic and real functioning of the socialist housing system (Hegedüs and Tosics, 1996) shows how different the reality was compared with the ideology. First, the control of the state over housing construction and private transactions was never total – in practice the private sphere, with some limited market relationships, was always present. It is possible to prepare a rough periodisation according to the strengths of state control over the private or market sphere. Periods of strong control were followed by periods of less control (1947–56: introduction of strict control with redefinition of property rights; 1957–68: concessions to the private sector; 1969–80: a new wave of centralisation; 1980–90: decentralisation due to economic crisis; Hegedüs and Tosics, 1996: 22). Second, even when the state control was at its strongest, the system did not function according to the original principles regarding the supply and allocation of new housing.

These two basic aspects of the malfunctioning of the socialist housing systems are connected with each other. In the first decades of socialism, the quantity of new housing production was very low. Infrastructure investments in general and housing construction in particular were subordinated to the need for 'productive' investments (i.e., development of industry). Most of the state's resources were allocated to industry. Political leaders used the slogan, 'cutting the chicken before the eggs are coming out', to describe the use of resources for the production of housing, as it would take away money from industrial development.

The low level of new housing construction led to a shortage in housing similar to the shortages in the other sectors of the socialist economy (see the famous book of János Kornai on the shortage economy; Kornai, 1980).

The general and equal accessibility of social services was one of the important political goals of socialism. However, in housing this was never achieved – education and health care came closer to the principle, although the standards were still low. Szelényi and Konrád (1969) carried out an empirical sociological analysis about the residents of four new housing estates in Hungary. They were thus the first to prove that the politically determined processes of the planned economy did not function according to egalitarian principles. Moreover, these processes increased social inequalities, achieving just the opposite of the ideological statements. In the allocation of the freely or very cheaply distributed (but scarce) new state and cooperative flats the more deserving' members of the society have got systematic advantages, at the expense of the blue-collar workers who were substantially underrepresented. "... from 1950 to 1968 class inequalities in housing did not diminish, they increased.... But the people themselves were not generally conscious of increasing housing inequalities, or depressed by them, chiefly because the housing situation of all classes had visibly improved through the years" (Szelényi, 1983: 73).

According to Szelényi and Konrád this allocation mechanism was neither a failure nor a result of corruption, but followed from the very functioning of the system. As housing became one of the scarcest goods – for which long queues developed – the state used the allocation of new housing to reward 'deserving' people. For the political and economic ruling classes, the cheaply allocated flat was a compensation for their low incomes (the income distribution was very much flattened out in the socialist system). These are the main reasons for the 'merit-based allocation' of housing, in which party and state functionaries were the main beneficiaries.

The logic of the socialist housing model did not apply just to state rental housing. There were many other tenure forms, such as cooperative housing or even state-built owner-occupied housing, where the state had direct control over the land, permissions, construction processes, costs, and allocations of flats. Individual efforts and market relationships played a role only in the single-family housing form (and from the late 1970s, small condominiums). However, these housing forms were not allowed to attain a significant share of the housing in socialist cities.

Interestingly enough, in the Hungarian reform period (1968–72) the real functioning of the socialist housing system could openly be surveyed and discussed. Nevertheless, not much later in 1975, Szelényi was expelled from Hungary, while Konrád had to accept a publication embargo. They had further developed their theory about the real functioning of the socialist system: their book describing the path of the intelligentsia to class power (Konrád and Szelényi, 1978) was far too radical, questioning the whole ideology of socialism.

As emphasised, the socialist housing model was an integral part of the socialist model of economic and political development. The dominance of state ownership in land and in the means of new housing production also resulted in significant changes in the spatial structures of the cities. After the nationalisation of the housing stock (late 1940s to early 1950s), housing authorities "were under tremendous pressure to keep rents low in order to match low wages, and to build as much new housing as possible" (Szelényi, 1996: 304). Consequently, there was no spending at all on existing public housing, whereas new constructions took place in larger developments. These developments were located on sufficiently large, unoccupied territories in the outskirts of the cities and were suitable for new housebuilding technologies using prefabricated elements.

Figure 1 Large prefabricated housing estate from the socialist period (aerial view, Kőbánya Újhegy housing estate in Budapest built in late 1970s).

The consequences of the lack of market relationships in land and housing were large new housing estates in peripheral areas and neglected old housing stock in the inner areas of the cities. Flats on large estates of over 2500 units constituted 20–40% of the total housing stock compared with 3–7% in West European countries. It is hard to imagine that people in East European countries liked such estates more than their Western counterparts did – this, of course, was not the case. In the state-controlled system, the real preferences of the population did not count at all. These preferences were substantially modified anyway by the artificially low rents and the huge subsidies granted not only for the construction of prefabricated housing (see **Figure 1**) but also for the renting and buying of such flats (Tosics, 2004: 80).

The social structure of the cities changed accordingly: the beneficiaries of state housing allocation moved to the new housing estates, while the rest remained in the deteriorating inner-city areas, which became increasingly dominated by older and poorer tenants (see **Figure 2**). This sociospatial development was the complete antithesis of the patterns of housing in the presocialist period, when higher-status social groups congregated in the prestigious inner-city areas. In some other parts of the city, the changes were less visible from the outside but were very important in the structural aspects. The elitist character of the best-located green areas with villa-type buildings was preserved: the presocialist elite was swept out and the new cadre-elite occupied the villas. The agglomerations around the cities remained low-status areas with little or no infrastructure services. These areas grew in density because of people moving to the large cities without being able to acquire housing within them.

The Transition from Socialism to Capitalism

Soon after the collapse of socialism it became clear that these countries had inherited large, very inefficiently managed and run state rental sectors. A careful analysis of all the aspects of housing has shown that the main housing problem in these transition countries was not the nonavailability (shortage) of housing but the low quality, bad location, and misallocation of the stock (Hegedüs et al., 1996). In addition to this 'internal' factor, external factors for radical change were at work in the economy. This change necessitated the restructuring of the existing housing systems and policies in the 1990s, and not new construction.

At the beginning of the transition, the hypothesis was raised that housing could become the 'agency of change'. One sector – in which market mechanisms (e.g., bank financing, market rents, and targeted housing benefits) were quickly introduced – could induce market-oriented changes in the other sectors of the economy as well. Instead of this progression, however, in all the postsocialist transition countries "housing was designated to be a 'shock absorber' while other reforms went forward – implying rents remained frozen and few other changes occurred besides cuts in subsidies in new construction and handing over of some units to tenants ('privatization')" (Struyk, 1996: 3).

Figure 2 Deteriorated inner-city area, no improvements in the socialist period (Budapest, District VIII, Józsefváros).

Two steps were relatively quickly performed in most of the transition countries: first, the transference of the ownership of public housing from the central state to local governments; second, the denationalisation of the public housing stock.

Regarding the denationalisation of the public housing stock, three options were available, as the nationalisation of the stock could be reversed in different ways. The least-applied method was the privatisation of the management companies: this happened in Germany only. The second method was the 'restitution' of the stock, involving handing back the buildings to the heirs of the former owners, who had been stripped of their landlord statuses as part of nationalisation. The process of restitution raised a lot of legal questions (e.g., confirming the identity of the owner of the house exactly 40–45 years earlier; protecting the present tenants from sudden rent increases). This method was applied in many of the countries, but not all – Hungary was among the exceptions where this method was not followed for the housing stock. The third method was the 'privatisation to the sitting tenants', in effect, selling the flats to the actual renter families.

Most of the Western advisers arriving in the early 1990s to the transition countries came from Anglo-Saxon countries and argued for quick privatisation. There were two main arguments: if the housing stock was sold at market price, it could provide the state with substantial funds to manage the transition. Second, privatisation would decrease inflationary pressures as the excess demand of the households is soaked up by buying their flats and they become interested in saving more. There were, however, counterarguments as well: if units are sold below their market values, the allocation of gained subsidies becomes important. Moreover, it is important to keep a substantial rental stock for many reasons – geographical mobility, starter families, lowest-income families, and so on. If privatisation is successful, the rental sector can easily shrink below the minimally required level, that is, below the proportion of poor families.

A compromise between these various factors could have been reached by balancing the scale of privatisation with the level of discount offered on the market value of the flats. With relatively low discounts, privatisation could have helped the state in overcoming the economic difficulties while the rental sector preserved a sizeable share within the housing stock (see **Figure 3**).

Rational considerations, however, could not play a large role in the transformation of the housing sector. In most transition countries there was a strong political push for large-scale privatisation, on the parts of both the households (who were uncertain about future rent levels and wanted to become owners) and the politicians (who wanted to gain popularity by offering large discounts to the population).

Consequently, in the process of housing privatisation, larger discounts were offered in most transition countries than in the United Kingdom in the 1980s by Margaret Thatcher. This was despite the fact that the sale of the UK council housing was very sharply criticised by housing analysts owing to the many negative externalities. Using the 'give-away' principle in most postsocialist countries caused the public rental sector to decrease dramatically. The quickest and most dramatic changes were to be found in the South-East European countries (e.g., Albania and Romania), while Poland, the Czech Republic, and Russia were slower to follow, as can be seen from **Table 1**.

Figure 3 Consequences of privatisation: Tirana, rain-pipe on the house is broken, but the owners, who invested a lot into their dwellings (see the new satellite dishes and shutters) do not pay any attention to that, as it does not belong to their own flats.

Table 1 Housing privatisation between 1990 and the early 2000s

	Public rental in 1990	Public rental after 2000	% Privatised
Albania	35.5	1.0	97.2
Lithuania	60.8	2.4	96.1
Romania	32.7	2.7	91.7
Croatia	24.0	2.9	87.9
Bulgaria	6.6	3.0	54.5
Slovenia	31.0	3.0	90.3
Hungary	23.0	4.0	82.6
Estonia	61.0	5.2	91.5
Slovakia	27.7	6.5	76.5
Latvia	59.0	16.0	72.9
Poland	31.6	16.1	49.1
Czech Republic	39.1	17.0	56.5
Ukraine	47.3	20.0	57.7
Russian Federation	67.0	29.0	56.7

Source: From Hegedüs J and Struyk R (2005) Divergencies and convergencies in restructuring housing finance in transition countries. In: Hegedüs J and Struyk R (eds.) *Housing Finance. New and Old Models in Central Europe, Russia and Kazakhstan* OSI/LGI, pp. 3–39.
Table is based on data from the *UN-ECE Bulletin of Housing Statistics for Europe and North America*, 2002.

Housing in the Postsocialist Countries

As the process of privatisation was dictated by the 'give-away' principle, the manner of the allocation of the large discounts to the population became important. The discount usually increased with the value of the flat; thus the social effects largely depended on the ways in which public rental housing had been allocated in the earlier (socialist) times.

In the course of the give-away housing privatisation, the unequal distribution of advantages that accompanied the socialist period became marketised (Tosics, forthcoming). In 1992 the Metropolitan Research Institute, Budapest, and the Urban Institute, Washington, carried out empirical research on a sample of public tenants in Budapest. The results showed that privatisation continued the unequal distribution pattern of the rent subsidy, transferring – and even worsening – the unequal situation from the rental stock into the private sector. In this manner, give-away privatisation was a large gift to sitting tenants in general, the additional effect being the further increase in inequalities in favour of the higher-income tenants (Hegedüs and Tosics, 1994).

Little empirical data are available about the spatial allocations of advantages and disadvantages. According to popular belief housing privatisation strengthens sociospatial segregation, as the marketisation of the value of the housing unit enables the ex-tenant (new owners) to become mobile on the housing market. The larger the subsidy value is, the larger will be the chances of mobility. In the privatised buildings qualified majority decision (in the Hungarian condominiums at least 80%) is needed for the renovation of the common parts of the building. In the lower-status parts of Budapest it is more difficult to achieve the qualifying majority, as the share of low-income and elderly families is substantial. Thus there is a chance that the better-off families will sell off their units in these buildings. They can then move to higher-status areas where residents belong to the same financial strata and where larger-scale improvements to the buildings are possible.

As a consequence of this give-away privatisation, by the end of the 1990s, housing in most of the transition countries changed formally into systems dominated by property-ownership. This had far-reaching consequences both on the privatised housing stock and on the remaining public rental housing.

The privatised housing sector developed gradually into a real market sector. In the first years of transition the privatisation of housing did not entail the development of real housing markets. The new owners did not yet consider their flats as commodities; there was little cooperation between owners within the same building; mobility remained low; and the banks did not accept the privatised units as collateral for bank loans (Hegedüs and Tosics, 1998: 161). In the more advanced postsocialist countries, however, the newly privatised multifamily buildings quickly adapted to the usual characteristics of multifamily owner-occupied housing listed below.

- The process of homogenisation of the household structure within the houses started, partly in connection with the 'renewal effect' described above.
- The chances of renovations of the buildings started to be differentiated according to geographical position (land and property value).
- This newly emerged sector offered flexible opportunities for nonresidential activities, as flats could be easily converted to office use.

By the end of the 1990s, banks started to issue mortgage loans. In the more advanced postsocialist countries this signalled the development of all the important aspects of owner-occupied housing: the transition to the owner-occupied sector was complete.

The public rental sector became residualised in most postsocialist countries as the direct consequence of the give-away privatisation: only the 'leftovers of privatisation' stayed in the public rental sector. This implies the presence of all the usual deficiencies of marginalised social housing – the concentration of poor families and the slender hope for renovation. As the better-off families 'ran away' with the better-quality housing stock, the remaining stock was not self-sustaining anymore (rents could not cover costs). Maintenance and renovation thus became even more dependent on the decisions of the already financially overburdened local authorities (see **Figures 4** and **5**).

The process of residualisation of public rental stock is characteristic of most postsocialist countries – only the Czech Republic, Poland, and Estonia kept more than 5% of stock as public rental housing. With this the postsocialist countries – together with the South European countries – form a special type of social housing provision within the typology of the EU countries (**Table 2**). They all belong to the targeted approach, which is based on the assumption that the objectives of housing policy will be met predominantly by the market. Only those households for whom the market is unable to deliver housing of decent quality at an affordable price will benefit from social housing. Moreover, most of the postsocialist countries (with the exception of the Czech Republic and Poland, where social housing is allocated to households falling under a certain income ceiling) subscribe to the most restricted version of social housing provision, focusing exclusively on the most vulnerable sections of society.

The development of a dominant owner-occupied sector – with a very small, residualised public rental sector – indicates radical changes in the housing systems of the East-Central European countries. "... current mortgage arrangements, income levels and house prices make housing unaffordable to a large number of households. The previous shortage of housing has been replaced by a shortage of affordable housing" (Tsenkova, 2000: 132).

Summary

It is not the task of this article to give a full overview of the housing policies of postsocialist countries after the end of the transition. However, by focussing on the

Figure 4 Gentrification of inner-city areas (Budapest, District V, Belváros-Újlipótváros).

Figure 5 Ghettoisation of the poorest strata (Budapest, District VIII, Józsefváros).

transition and its effects on the development of the new capitalist system, it is possible to conceptualise the direction of change.

Table 2 Typology of approaches to social housing provision in EU countries

Size of the sector	Allocation criteria		
	Universalistic	Targeted Generalist	Residual
20% and more	The Netherlands Denmark Sweden	Austria	United Kingdom
11–19%		Czech Republic France Finland Poland	France
5–10%		Belgium Germany Italy	Ireland Belgium Estonia Germany Malta
0–4%		Slovenia Luxembourg Greece	Hungary Cyprus Portugal Bulgaria Lithuania Latvia Spain

Source: From Cecodhas (2007: 16) *Housing Europe 2007. Review of Social, Cooperative and Public Housing in the 27 EU Member States*. Brussels: Cecodhas European Social Housing Observatory.

The East-Central European countries were forced in the 40–45-year-long socialist period to introduce a specific housing policy (called the socialist housing model) with strong state control over all aspects of housing policy. After the collapse of the socialist politicoeconomic system, in the course of the transition to the capitalist system, the housing sector was not a forerunner for free market forces. Even so, in most of these countries the state quickly declined any responsibility for housing. This resulted in a development path that headed towards the South-European housing systems, where market regulations dominate without any state-sponsored overarching welfare protection system. In this sense the housing in postsocialist countries remained as different from the mainstream European housing systems as they had been earlier during the socialist period.

See also: Housing and the State in China.

References

Bertaud A and Renaud B (1997) Socialist cities without land markets. *Journal of Urban Economics* 41(1): 137–151.
Cecodhas (2007) *Housing Europe 2007. Review of social, cooperative and public housing in the 27 EU member states*. Brussels: Cecodhas European Social Housing Observatory.
Hegedüs J Struyk R (2005) Divergencies and convergencies in restructuring housing finance in transition countries. In: Hegedüs J and Struyk R (eds.) *Housing Finance. New and Old Models in Central Europe, Russia and Kazakhstan* OSI/LGI, pp. 3–39.
Hegedüs J and Tosics I (1994) Privatization and rehabilitation in the Budapest inner districts. *Housing Studies* 9(1): 41–55.
Hegedüs J and Tosics I (1996) with Kay H *Housing Privatization in Eastern Europe*. In: Clapham D, Hegedüs J, Kintrea K and Tosics I

(eds.) *Disintegration of the East European Housing Model*, pp. 15–40. Westport, CT: Greenwood Press.

Hegedüs J and Tosics I (1998) Social change and urban restructuring in Central Europe. In: Enyedi G (ed.) *Towards new models of the housing system*, pp. 137–168. Budapest: Akadémiai.

Hegedüs J, Mayo S, and Tosics I (1996) Transition of the housing sector in the East Central European countries. *Rewiew of Urban and Regional Development Studies* 8: 101–136.

Konrád Gy and Szelényi I (1978) *Az értelmiség útja az osztályhatalomhoz (The Road of the Intelligentsia to Class Power)*. Európai Protestáns Magyar Szabadegyetem (Bern), later published by Gondolat, Budapest, in 1989.

Kornai J (1980) *Economics of Shortage*. Amsterdam; New York: North-Holland Publishing Company Vol. I and II, pp. XVII, 650.

Marcuse P (1996) Cities after socialism. Urban and regional change and conflict in post-socialist societies. In: Andrusz G, Harloe M, and Szelényi I (eds.) *Privatization and its Discontents: Property Rights in Land and Housing in the Transition in Eastern Europe*, pp. 119–191. Oxford, UK: Blackwell.

Smith DM (1996) Cities after socialism. Urban and regional change and conflict in post-socialist societies. In: Andrusz G, Harloe M, and Szelényi I (eds.) *The Socialist City*, pp. 70–99. Oxford, UK: Blackwell.

Struyk R (1996) Economic restructuring of the former Soviet Bloc. The case of housing. In: Struyk R (ed.) *The long road to the market*, pp. 1–68. Washington, DC: The Urban Institute Press.

Szelényi I (1983) *Urban Inequalities under State Socialism*. New York: Oxford University Press.

Szelényi I (1996) Cities after socialism. Urban and regional change and conflict in post-socialist societies. In: Andrusz G, Harloe M, and Szelényi I (eds.) *Cities under Socialism – And After*, pp. 286–317. Oxford, UK: Blackwell.

Szelényi I and Konrád Gy (1969) *Az új lakótelepek szociológiai problémái* (Sociological problems of the new housing estates). Kiadó: Akadémiai.

Tosics I (2004) European urban development: Sustainability and the role of housing. *Journal of Housing and the Built Environment* 19: 67–90.

Tosics I (2005) Transformation of cities in Central and Eastern Europe: Towards globalization. In: Hamilton I, Dimitrovska FE, Andrews K, and Pichler-Milanovic N (eds.) *City Development in Central and Eastern Europe since 1990: The Impact of Internal Forces*, pp. 44–78. Tokyo; New York: The United Nations University Press.

Tosics I (forthcoming) From socialism into capitalism: The restructuring of cities and the social outcomes. In: Carmon N and Fainstein S (eds.) *Planning and People: Looking Back for the Future*. Penn Press.

Tsenkova S (2000) *Housing in Transition and Transition in Housing*. Sofia: K Reklama.

Housing and the State in Western Europe

P Boelhouwer and J Hoekstra, Delft University of Technology, Delft, The Netherlands

© 2012 Elsevier Ltd. All rights reserved.

Introduction

The reason why governments intervene in the housing market can be explained on the basis of two important motives. The first motive is based on the poor results of a housing market which is completely steered by the free market. Almost all developed countries have established the right to decent housing in their constitution. Also, most countries have established minimum quality standards for housing in their legislation, which could in most cases not be realised in the free market. The second motive for government intervention in the housing market is the relation between housing and other policy areas. For instance, the battle against diseases and epidemics was the most important reason for many West European governments to start interventions in the housing markets in the nineteenth century. Also today, housing policy operates as a vehicle to reach policy goals across a broad spectrum of policy areas including social integration, environmental policy, spatial policy, and labour market policy.

Despite the close relation between housing and government policy, housing policy forms quite a specific element of the welfare state. As Torgersen put it: "Housing is the wobbly pillar under the welfare state" (Torgersen, 1987: 116). In contrast to social security, education, and health care, for example, identical and clear standard criteria which could be politically tested are lacking for housing. Politically it is not common that on the basis of certain objective criteria specific housing situations will be altered when the household situation changes. This is quite obvious, however, for health, education, and social security. The unclear way governments pay attention to the definition of housing need and the way this definition changes in time, changes in the housing situation of those who got certain benefits (like the increase in property prices and inheritances), or more broader policy goals like the creation of mixed neighbourhoods are the main reasons for the existing complex relation between the welfare state and housing. Also, Harloe states that housing is "the least decommodified and most market determined of the conventionally accepted constituents of welfare states" (1994: 2). Not only is the provision of housing mainly market determined, but it also differs in that, the costs of decommodified housing, and in particular social rented housing, are to a large extent charged to consumers. Finally, Bengtsson (2006) argued that housing policies, in contrast to other policies, are best understood as state correctives to the market.

This complex relationship was for Esping-Andersen the justification for leaving out housing in his study, *The Three Worlds of Welfare Capitalism* (Esping-Andersen, 1990). Moreover, the position of housing within the welfare state is far from obvious and has provoked a good deal of discussion. Some authors (e.g., Kemeny, 1992, 2001) focus on the relationships between the housing system and the welfare state, while others predominantly lay stress on the private market characteristics of housing (Harloe, 1995). The second part of this article pays attention to the way housing could be incorporated in the welfare state theory of Esping-Andersen and how this could be related to the development of the social rented sector in Europe. On the basis of the results of this elaboration, we also present a proposal for a modification of the welfare state typology of Esping-Andersen. Kemeny's visualisation of corporatism plays a key role in this attempt.

The problematic relationship between housing and government policy does not mean that governments do not have an important role to play in the housing market. On the contrary, despite the fact that exact definitions are difficult to formulate, almost all governments in the Western world have formulated general policy goals to establish enough affordable housing of good quality in the right place. Governments can hardly accept a full introduction of the iron law of the housing market which states that those with the lowest incomes have to live in the least attractive houses (Doling, 1997; Priemus, 1978). After establishing the more general policy goals for housing by the government, the question arises as to what extent the government itself has to intervene actively in the housing market. The government has a choice of the following six policy options: doing nothing, exhortation, regulation, taxation, subsidisation, and self-realisation (Doling, 1997: 42). Only when using the last three instruments does the government actively step in and become, together with households and housing suppliers, a direct player on the housing market.

In this article, we first elaborate on the development of theories about housing and the welfare state. Since the 1970s, different theoretical frameworks have been developed to explain and describe this complicated relationship. In the second part of the article, we next focus on Esping-Andersen's welfare state theory. His theory and typology have attracted considerable attention in international comparative housing research. Various researchers have discussed the position of housing within the welfare state in general and within Esping-Andersen's framework in particular (see Boelhouwer and Van der Heijden, 1992; Brandsen, 2001; Doling, 1999; Harloe, 1995; Kemeny, 1992, 1995, 2001, 2006; Kemeny and Lowe, 1998; Kleinman, 1996; Matznetter, 2002). Most of the debate, however, has been at a conceptual or theoretical level. Esping-Andersen's work has rarely been tested, or directly related to housing practices. One exception is the study by Barlow and Duncan (1994), who relate the Esping-Andersen typology to housing production in the United Kingdom, France, and Sweden. Another exception is the research of Domburg-De Rooij and Musterd (2002) investigating the relationship between welfare state regimes (The typology of welfare states used by Domburg-De Rooij and Musterd differs from that of Esping-Andersen.) and segregation. And finally, Hoekstra tested the connection between welfare state regimes and dwelling type (Hoekstra, 2005). On the basis of an analysis of the conceptual framework of Esping-Andersen, the last section will present a modification of his welfare state typology.

Theories of the Development of Welfare States and Housing

The way the government chooses to play a role in the housing market has a central position in research on the development of housing systems and their relations to the development of welfare systems. This research discipline commenced towards the end of the 1970s and was dominated by convergence theories. Wilensky et al. (1987) showed that social and economic convergence theories had dominated decades of research into the development and functioning of the welfare state. This enduring paradigm presumes a relationship between the level of economic development and the level of public expenditure on welfare, such as social security, housing, and education. Notwithstanding the differences in cultural and social characteristics of different countries or societies, economic progress undermines the traditional structure of care, including assistance offered by families, the private sector, and charitable institutions. This process is also explained by the development of a complex post-industrial society. Much of this comparative research on housing can be traced back to the work of Donnison, and in particular his 1967 book, *The Government of Housing*. His central idea is that housing policy also converges because of an increasing correspondence between economic and demographic developments in countries despite party-political, ideological, and/or institutional differences between countries. In 1982, Donnison and Ungerson published a modified version of this important book. In this book, they distinguish between a marginal and an institutionalised housing policy. The former seeks to ensure a basic level of housing quality and concentrates on helping the weakest in society. The authors argue that this form of housing policy is principally followed by moderately developed industrial societies. As industrial growth continues, housing policy also takes on a more institutional form. The government then develops a complex policy directed not only to the construction of housing but also to the distribution and the management of the dwelling stock. In order to achieve this, an extensive set of policy instruments is developed. These are designed to ensure a degree of equity, an increase in the quality of housing, and a reasonable distribution of expenditure on housing. Despite clear differences in the political backgrounds of the respective governments, the increase in the scope of government activity has been both quantitative (involvements in more fields of policy) and qualitative (more far-reaching policy aims). This increase is related to the rising expectations of a postindustrial society.

During the last few decades, several critical remarks have been made on the convergence theory. First, there is little empirical support for the principles on which the theory is based. The theory itself has led to hypotheses and a number of descriptive studies. Another problem with the convergence theory is the scale at which it can be applied (see also Doling, 1990). The theory was originally formulated to describe the development of a society in broad terms. In order to test such theories, it often suffices to refer to aggregate data on government expenditures for core activities and other general macroeconomic and demographic trends. However, expenditure levels and policy goals may fluctuate widely by sector and through time. A third point of criticism concerns the supposed outcome of the housing systems. In contrast to Donnison's position, government may be said to retreat rather than expand as the level of affluence rises. When housing-market shortages ease up, government supposedly retreats from housing, giving market forces more leeway.

An alternative approach to research in the tradition of convergence theory, which has proved its value in comparative housing research since the mid-1970s, is the 'structure of housing provision' (SHP). This approach distinguishes social groups that can influence the way in which the provision of housing and housing services comes about. The relationships between these groups must be defined in order to investigate many issues associated with housing. This approach explicitly recognizes that processes of change take place. As a result, the investigation of institutional changes forms a key empirical question for housing-related research (Ball and Harloe, 1990: 1). The context in which housing-market processes operate is subject to continual change. To understand the changes in the provision of housing and housing services, it is precisely these institutional changes that have to be recognised.

The SHP approach analyses the relations of consumption and production, as well as those of exchange. The SHP approach is explicitly not presented as a theory of housing. It provides a context within which many housing-related issues can be examined. It certainly does not specify what theoretical approach should be adopted in explaining the differences observed. For this, one has to rely on existing explanatory models, such as those based on neoclassical, Weberian, or neo-Marxist theories.

Harloe and Martens (1987) also subscribe to the proposition that housing-market processes in every country are a product of the specific interaction between political, economic, and ideological factors. For instance, the size of the owner-occupied sector cannot be explained by the mere fact that a country supports a policy of privatisation. In practice, the owner-occupied sector in the underdeveloped regions of France fulfils a completely different function than it does in, say, the southeast of England. Furthermore, countries organise their nonprofit rented housing sector very differently. As a result, public-sector rented housing in, for example, Great Britain is much more vulnerable to policies of privatisation than in the Netherlands or Denmark.

As noted above, those subscribing to the SHP approach argue that it is important to describe and account for institutional structures in order to provide a satisfactory explanation of housing-market processes. Among these structures, they include the different financial mechanisms, the development of the construction industry, and the government's land-use policy. Of course, these structures have their origins in past ideological, political, and economic developments.

As a reaction to these quite mechanistic convergence theories in which 'politics doesn't matter' forms a key element, a new group of divergence theories became popular in the 1990s. These theories pay more attention to country- and region-specific cultural processes and actors. The view that institutionalised relationships and structures within the housing system themselves become formative of new structures over time has led to the proposition that housing and welfare systems more generally may be expected to diverge to an increasing extent (Milligan, 2003: 37). These theories are sometimes addressed as middle-range theories (Kemeny and Lowe, 1998). These authors stress the specific political, ideological, and cultural differences to explain the differentiation between housing systems (see also Mandic and Clapham, 1996; Merton, 1957). To help explain the perpetuation of different national characteristics in housing systems, a number of researchers have introduced the concept of 'path dependency' (Boelhouwer and van der Heijden, 1992; Kleinman, 1996: 15). This concept refers to the tendency for solutions to problems or policy decisions, whether accidental or deliberately chosen, to become locked in through institutional and ideological processes and, subsequently, difficult to change (Kleinman, 1996: 15).

One of the most influential scholars of the divergence approach is Jim Kemeny. Kemeny distinguishes a direct relation between the development of housing systems and the social structure of a society which in his terms is strongly influenced by the dominant ideologies. For Kemeny, it is the wider social arrangement and ideological dispositions in different countries, not the economic logic of capital or particular configurations of political power, which better explain how the choices of policy strategies come about and are maintained. Essentially, in his view, societies are either more collectivised in their social consciousness or more privatised. The continuum between privatisation and collectivism is presented in two different models: home-owning societies against cost-rental societies (Kemeny, 1995). Anglo-Saxon countries are defined as home-owning societies and are characterised by a dual rental market. Against a large owner-occupied sector, a small social rented sector is placed which is only accessible for low-income groups and which is highly segmented. Rent setting is organised by the private rented sector. The State stimulates by management of speech and direct and indirect subsidies the growth of homeownership. In the continent of Europe, more cost rental societies can be seen. The rental sector is well developed and the rents are based on the cost price and not on the market value. The division between the private and social rented sector is small and both are subject to the same legislation.

Kemeny's approach provides a theoretical basis (the maturation process) for explaining the potential for differences in housing outcomes to arise from long-term differences in housing policy strategies. With maturation, Kemeny is referring to the growing difference between the debt per house for the existing stock and for newly built houses. The way the maturation process is developed determines the position of the social rented sector on the housing market. If the government allows the introduction of the principle of rent pooling, a high maturation will also be reflected in the rent level of the social rented sector. The impact of the social sector increases, and gives the organisations the possibility to become an important player at different policy arenas. In those systems, it is also the social rented sector which is in charge of rent setting and not the private rented sector (Kemeny, 1995). According to Kemeny, because of the central position of housing in the welfare state, the choice for a unitary or dual rented system also has consequences for other policy areas. A dual rental system often corresponds with a social security system that is based on a safety net for the most vulnerable households in society. In such a model, the housing allowances often have residual characteristics.

A society which is based on a safety net for the most vulnerable households has also some correspondence with another type of welfare system: the 'asset-based' or 'property-based' welfare system (Doling and Ronald, 2010; Elsinga et al., 2007; Horsewood and Neuteboom, 2006; Ronald, 2008). The principle underlying an asset-based approach to welfare is that, rather than relying on State-managed social transfers to counter the risks of poverty, individuals accept greater responsibility for their own welfare needs by investing in financial products and property assets which augment in value over time (Doling and Ronald, 2010). These can, at least in theory, later be tapped to supplement consumption and welfare needs when income is reduced. The potential wealth tied up in owner-occupied housing has been considered, more or less explicitly, to be a solution to the fiscal difficulties involved in the maintenance of welfare commitments, and through that, the asset in asset-based welfare has frequently become property or housing assets (Doling and Ford, 2007).

The above sections have summarised several methods and approaches employed in international comparative housing research. Given the vehement polemics that occasionally erupt among exponents of these approaches, both in the literature and at conferences, it would seem that the differences between these approaches are unbridgeable. In practice, though, this is not the case. In several publications, these authors acknowledge that each of the methods contains valuable features that sometimes complement each other (see Lundqvist, 1991; Oxley, 1990). In addition, these approaches do not purport to employ a universal explanatory model. Rather, they suggest methods and techniques which seem to provide insight into housing-market processes. For an explanation of these developments, it is often necessary to revert to more general theories, such as neoclassical, Weberian, and neo-Marxist explanatory models. Exponents of the various approaches tend to agree on the subjects and aspects that comparative research should treat. All these different approaches recognise the importance of factors outside the sphere of housing. It is only in terms of actual interpretation that they differ from one another. According to convergence theory, these factors explain the differences between housing systems. Other approaches regard these factors more as the context within which housing processes take place. But all of these approaches devote attention to how adaptation to changing circumstances takes place. This can occur as the result of government policies (policy-oriented approach) or through activities of various social groups that influence the provision of housing and housing services (provision-oriented and institutional approaches).

As mentioned in the introduction, in the next part of this article, we will again discuss in general the complex relationship between the development of welfare states and housing. Esping-Andersen argues that welfare states can be reduced to three ideal typical welfare state regimes, which differ fundamentally from each other. This has resulted in his well-known and widely used typology of welfare state regimes.

In his theory of welfare state regimes, Esping-Andersen explains how the differences between the three welfare regime types came about. Three factors were of particular importance: the way in which the mobilisation of the working class took place; the coalitions between the political parties; popular support for the conservation and expansion of the welfare state (Esping-Andersen, 1990). It is important to recognise that the Esping-Andersen typology is of ideal typical nature. Most countries will only to some extent correspond to the welfare regime they are classified in (see, e.g., Kvist, 1999). Therefore, the typology should not be seen as an exhaustive classification system. Rather, it is an analytical device that can be used to interpret differences in welfare systems between countries. The section 'The Theory and Typology of Esping-Andersen' gives a brief explanation of Esping-Andersen's welfare state theory. An application of his theory for housing is presented in the section 'The Welfare State Typology Applied to Housing'. The resulting scheme of analysis shows how the three welfare state regimes differ on some important aspects of the housing system. As a result of this analysis, the section 'The Relation between the Modified Theoretical Framework and the Development of Social Housing in Europe' gives a short elaboration of how this theory could be connected to the development of social housing in Europe.

The Theory and Typology of Esping-Andersen

Three Welfare State Regimes

The typology of Esping-Andersen makes a distinction between the three welfare state regimes. The most important characteristics of these three regime types are briefly discussed below. We identify some countries belonging to each of the regime types.

In social-democratic welfare state regimes, the provision of welfare services is dominated by the State. There are universal welfare services of a high level, to which a large proportion of the population has access. As a result of the redistributive effects of the welfare state, income differences are relatively low. Sweden is the classic example of a social-democratic welfare state, although other Scandinavian countries also belong to this regime type.

In corporatist welfare state regimes, the State is fairly active in the provision of welfare services. However, this does not lead to income redistribution, since preservation of the existing hierarchy in society is the starting-point for welfare polices at State level. Consequently, the welfare provision is segmented; different groups are entitled to different welfare services; and the traditional family is often explicitly favoured. Furthermore, the State is definitely not the only provider of welfare services. In this respect, the family and private nonprofit organisations (churches, trade unions, and so forth) also play an important part. Austria, Germany, Italy, and Belgium are representative corporatist welfare state regimes. In this article, like Esping-Andersen (1999: 4), we also treat the Mediterranean welfare state regime as part of the corporatist welfare state.

The liberal welfare state regime is characterised by little State interference and a strong market orientation. Private companies are responsible for the majority of the welfare services. The State only provides help for a limited group of people with really low incomes (safety net). As a result, the society is characterised by dualism. There is equality (but also poverty) among the recipients of state welfare, while there is differentiation in income in the rest of the society. The United States, Australia and, to a lesser extent, the United Kingdom and Ireland represent liberal welfare state regimes, although the United Kingdom is sometimes seen as a mixed regime with both social democratic and liberal elements, though perhaps moving more towards the latter.

The Welfare State Typology Applied to Housing

Esping-Andersen discriminates between the three welfare state regimes on the basis of three (strongly interrelated) criteria: decommodification; stratification; the arrangements between the State, market, and family. These three criteria are applied to housing and translated into four specific housing aspects, which are expected to cover an important part of the housing system. **Figure 1** shows the relationship between Esping-Andersen's three criteria and the four aspects of the housing system to which they have been converted.

Decommodification

When applied to housing, decommodification can be defined as the extent to which households can provide their own housing, independent of the income they acquire on the labour market. Thus, governmental interference (It should be noted that the State is not the only actor responsible for decommodification, since the family can also have decommodifying effects. However, following Esping-Andersen, we focus on the decommodification caused by the State.) is involved with the price of housing and with household incomes. The welfare state can decommodify housing not only via price regulation and production subsidies (affecting the price of housing), but also via subject or to the household directed subsidisation, which influences the household income (Lundqvist, 1991). The latter can involve both general income support (pensions, unemployment benefits) and subject subsidies that are specific to the field of housing. In this article, we have restricted ourselves to the last category. Thus, the decommodification is translated into the following two housing aspects: housing subsidisation (both object and subject subsidies), and price regulation.

Stratification

The welfare state is a system of stratification; the way in which the welfare state distributes welfare services has

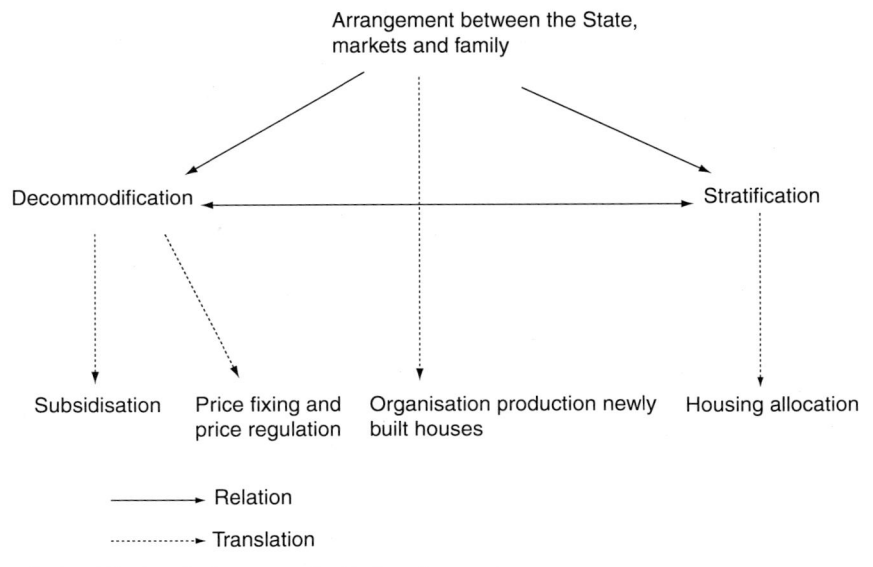

Figure 1 The three criteria of Esping-Andersen applied to housing.
Adapted from Hoekstra J (2003) Housing and the welfare state in the Netherlands. An application of Esping-Andersen's typology. *Housing Theory and Society* 20(2): 58–71.

consequences for the hierarchy in society. In this respect, a distinction can be drawn between economic stratification and social stratification. Economic stratification refers to income distribution within a society, whereas social stratification is related to differences in social status. Social stratification can be related to economic factors (income), as also to noneconomic factors such as ancestry, or occupation. In the field of housing, stratification is reflected in the process of housing allocation. Without State interference, housing allocation could be expected to be a direct reflection of the economic stratification in a society; households with the most resources would obtain the best and most expensive houses. However, the State is able to regulate the housing allocation process. Certain groups can be favoured by applying allocation rules. These State interventions can have different objectives. They can aim not only at increasing the choice for low-income groups, but also at the preservation of status differentials.

The State, Market, and Family Mix

Welfare services can be provided by the State (or public sector), as also by the market or the family (or household sector). The differences between the State, market, and family are connected with the so-called 'decision units' and the way the decisions are coordinated (Priemus, 1983). For the State, the decision units are public bodies; for the market, suppliers and buyers; and for the household sector, small groups (households, families, friends, and associations). Every sector is characterised by a specific kind of coordination of decisions. Public bodies are responsible for the decisions that are taken in the public sector (supported by laws or regulations), while the coordination of decisions in the market sector takes place on the basis of the 'market-mechanism' (with the price as an important point of orientation). In the household sector, the coordination of decisions occurs without financial transactions and prices, often on the basis of reciprocity.

It has to be noted, however, that the above-mentioned trichotomy between the State, market, and family refers to an ideal typical situation. In reality, there are many graduations and mixes, both with regard to the decision units and the coordination of decisions. First of all, it is obvious that the decision units in the State and the household sector frequently enter the market (mostly as buyers, but sometimes also as suppliers). On the other hand, nowhere in the world is a market totally free; every market is subject to government regulations and has some informal aspects. Eventually, it is important to realise that there are decision units that do not properly fit within one of the three sectors. In virtually every country, there are institutions that combine private (household sector and market) and public (state) interests and tasks. The housing associations in the different European countries are a good example of such institutions.

The relationships between the State, market, and family determine which welfare services are provided, how they are distributed, and for which groups they are destined. In other words, the mix between the State, market, and family is decisive for the decommodification and stratification in a country. Although Esping-Andersen is not explicit on this matter, we assume that the mix between the State, market, and family is superior to decommodification and the stratification. The specific configuration between the State, market, and family in a certain society then represents the essence of the welfare state. The implication is that the criteria discussed earlier in this section are in fact all influenced by this configuration. The most direct influence can be seen in the organisation of the production of newly built dwellings and the way in which actors from the public, market, and household sectors participate in this process.

Towards a Scheme of Analysis

We hypothesised that the four housing aspects in **Figure 1** differentiate between the three welfare state regimes. The hypothesis led to the scheme of analysis (see **Table 1**), which could be applied to the housing system of a specific country. The scheme of analysis was deductively constructed on the basis of the welfare state typology of Esping-Andersen. A more detailed underpinning of this deductive process can be found in Hoekstra and Reitsma (2002). This implies that the scheme is of an ideal typical nature; when constructing the scheme, developments that are specific for a particular country were not taken into account. Accordingly, the scheme should be considered as a mere analytical device that can be used to make sense of empirical country data on housing. The scheme solely applies to the national level. It does not take into account territorial differences within countries.

Kemeny's View of Corporatism

According to Kemeny (1995), Esping-Andersen uses an unusual definition of corporatism, since he clearly relates this concept to conservative elements, like the preservation of status differentials in society and the preferential treatment of the traditional family. In the political sciences, the definition of corporatism is more neutral: there, corporatism is a system of cooperation and compromise between capital and labour, coordinated by the State. Following this line of thought, Kemeny comes to the following working definition of corporatism: A system of institutionalised political representation of different interest groups that is essentially founded on compromise, and accommodation between

Table 1 Differences between the housing systems of the three welfare state regimes

Criterion	Social-democratic	Corporatist	Liberal
Decommodification	• Large	• Quite large	• Low
Stratification	• Relatively low	• High, mainly based on social status	• High, mainly based on income
Mix of the State, market, and family	• Dominant position of the State	• Important position for the family • Considerable influence for private nonprofit organisations	• Dominant position of market parties
State regulation	• Strong central government influence	• Functional decentralisation, incremental, problem-solving policies	• Relatively little State regulation (at both central and local levels)
General housing policy objectives	• Guaranteed universal high level of housing quality	• Preservation of the social stratification in society • Preferential treatment of the traditional family • Stimulation of households and other private actors to take initiatives on the housing market	• Dominant position for the market • State only supports marginal groups
Subsidisation	• Large-scale production subsidies • Subject subsidies for large target groups	• Segmented subsidies; specific arrangements for specific groups	• Means-tested subject subsidies • Few production subsidies
Price setting and price regulation	• Strong State influence on price setting and price regulation	• Moderate State influence • State regulation of prices to correct negative effects of the market	• Market determination of house prices
Housing allocation	• Allocation on the basis of need	• State intervention to correct the market • Certain groups may be favoured in the allocation process	• Market determination of housing allocation in a large part of the housing stock • Regulated allocation in a small part of the housing stock (reserved for low-income groups)

Adapted from Hoekstra J (2003) Housing and the welfare state in the Netherlands. An application of Esping-Andersen's typology. *Housing Theory and Society* 20(2): 58–71.

conflicting power groupings – whether these be based on class, religion, or ethnicity (Kemeny, 1995: 65–66). Kemeny asserts that, when so defined, corporatism applies to corporatist as well as social-democratic welfare state regimes. He argues that both the continental European countries (corporatist welfare state regimes) and the Scandinavian countries (social-democratic welfare state regimes) are characterised by a political structure that is based on corporatism (in the political science definition). In the Anglo-Saxon countries on the other hand, there is little political corporatism and often a dual political system (two main parties).

According to Kemeny, the Scandinavian and continental European countries differ from each other in one important aspect: the influence of the labour movement in a historical perspective. In Scandinavia, the strong position of the labour movement has resulted in a welfare state in which the central government has a dominant position and social equality is of great importance. Kemeny refers to this as labour-led corporatism, where the workers have a relatively strong position (Kemeny, 2006: 8). In continental Europe, however, the labour movement was less strong. As a result, private nonprofit organisations played an important part in the provision of welfare services in continental Europe, and the ability to cope on one's own was strongly stimulated. Kemeny refers to welfare states of this kind by the term 'capital-led corporatism' (Kemeny, 2001: 62).

A Proposed Modification of the Theoretical Framework

Kemeny's ideas suggest that the political structure criterion should have an important position in the theoretical framework. Kemeny's distinction drawn between liberal and corporatist (labour-led and capital-led corporatism) welfare states is made principally on the basis of this criterion. On the basis of the changing role of the central government in many Western European countries in the 1990s, we subdivide Kemeny's capital-led corporatism into two types: conservative corporatism and modern corporatism. Conservative corporatism corresponds with corporatism as defined by Esping-Andersen, whereas modern corporatism refers to a style of governance whereby the central government switches to a more indirect mode of governance, by defining the policy frameworks within which the local authorities and the private actors operate (see Hoekstra, 2003, for an elaboration for the Dutch housing market). Thus, next to liberalism, we distinguish three different kinds of corporatism: labour-led, conservative, and modern. In short, we have arrived at a modified theoretical framework that differs from the original framework (see section 'The Theory and Typology of Esping-Andersen', **Table 1**) on the following three points:

- The political structure criterion has been added to the criteria listed in **Table 1**.
- The social-democratic welfare state regime is considered to be a specific form of the corporatist welfare state regime: labour-led corporatism.
- The corporatist welfare state regime of Esping-Andersen is subdivided into two types: a conservative corporatist welfare state regime (coinciding with Esping-Andersen's original corporatist welfare state regime) and a modern corporatist welfare state regime.

Table 2 shows how the various welfare state regimes of the modified theoretical framework differ with respect to these characteristics. **Figure 2** shows the same information in the form of a diagram, based on Evers' State–market–family triangle (1988).

The Relation between the Modified Theoretical Framework and the Development of Social Housing in Europe

The modification of the theoretical framework in the previous section was constructed inductively. Adaptations were partly derived from concepts defined by Kemeny. The modified theoretical framework could be used as a basis for the interpretation of the developments within country-specific housing systems. In this article, we will connect in short, the new theoretical framework to the development of social rented housing in Europe.

The development of the social rented sector in Europe has been described by several authors in the past (Boelhouwer and van der Heijden, 1992; Danermark and Elander, 1994; Harloe, 1992, 1994; Murie, 1992). As noted by many of these authors before (see Danermark and Elander, 1992: 2 for an overview), the concept of social housing, although used as if its meaning was self-evidently clear, takes on different meanings in various national contexts. Sometimes it is connected to council housing (like in the United Kingdom), sometimes as publicly subsidised housing, irrespective of ownership (like in Germany), sometimes as intermediate housing (like in the Netherlands), or as an umbrella concept, covering various types of housing in terms of ownership and tenure. Nevertheless, despite these and other differences, historically, the term social housing has been ascribed some dimensions that are quite similar from country to country, thus making comparative discussions meaningful (Danermark and Elander, 1992: 2). As summarised by Harloe (1992), social rented housing can be very broadly characterised as having three major characteristics: First, it is provided by landlords at a price which is not primarily determined by considerations of profit. Second, it is administratively allocated according to some conception of 'need'. Thirdly, government control over social rented housing is extensive and has become more over time. With regard to this last characteristic, things have changed in the last decade. Social landlords, for instance, in the Netherlands are much more independent of the government than they were before.

Table 2 Main characteristics of the four welfare state regimes according to the modified theoretical framework

	Labour-led corporatist	*Conservative-corporatist*	*Modern corporatist*	*Liberal*
Decommodification	High	Relatively high	Relatively high	Low
Influence of central government	High and direct	Quite high and often indirect	Quite high and often indirect	Low
Degree of political corporatism	Many corporatist structures and processes	Many corporatist structures and processes	Many corporatist structures and processes	Few corporatist structures and processes
Fragmentation in the provision of welfare services	Fragmentation on the basis of measurable criteria	Fragmentation on the basis of occupation and/or social status	Fragmentation on the basis of measurable criteria	Fragmentation on the basis of measurable criteria
Treatment of the traditional family in welfare policies	No preferential treatment for the traditional family	Preferential treatment for the traditional family	No preferential treatment for the traditional family	No preferential treatment for the traditional family
Role of the State, market, and family in the provision of welfare services	Dominant position of the State	Important (if not dominant) position of the family	Welfare services are provided by both market and the State	Dominant position of the market

Adapted from Hoekstra J (2003) Housing and the welfare state in the Netherlands. An application of Esping-Andersen's typology. *Housing Theory and Society* 20(2): 58–71.

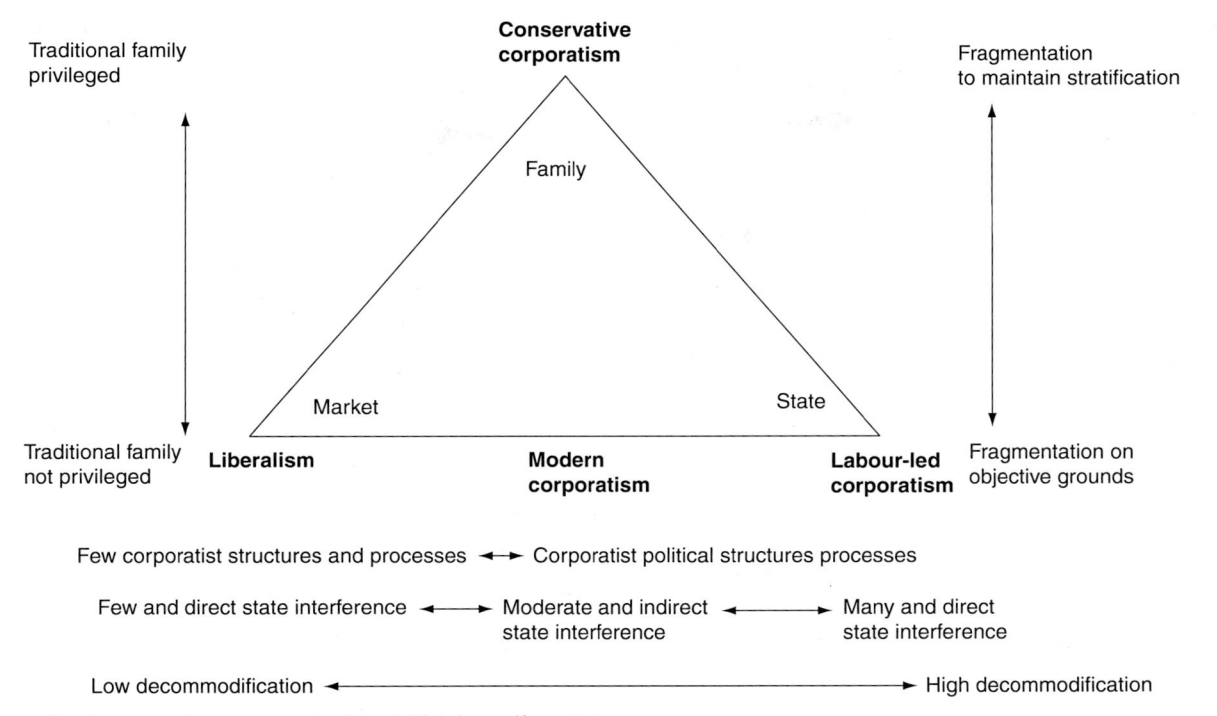

Figure 2 A proposed new conceptual model for the welfare state.
Adapted from Hoekstra J (2003) Housing and the welfare state in the Netherlands. An application of Esping-Andersen's typology. *Housing Theory and Society* 20(2): 58–71.

With our adjusted welfare state typology, it is possible to structure the position of the social rented sector more precisely. As explained in the section 'Theories of the Development of Welfare States and Housing', Kemeny's elaboration between home-owning and cost-rental societies could be the starting point. In his article 'Corporatism and Housing Regimes', Kemeny (2006) argues on the basis of a division between capital-led and labour-led corporatism that there is a connection between the specific corporatistic welfare state and the existence of an integrated rental market with a strong social rented sector. Kemeny argues that the corporatist power system indicates the need to achieve compromises. Corporatist compromise solutions entail a political solution that takes into consideration several different interests. The fragmentation of political parties resulting in coalitions and minority governments being the norm may be part of the explanation for the rise of an integrated market and a strong social rented sector. The latter can take many shapes and forms such as municipality-owned companies, voluntary or charitable societies, trusts, rental cooperatives, and even privately owned nonprofit enterprises (Kemeny, 2006: 12). For right-wing hegemonic coalitions who could be classified as liberal welfare states, it is quite clear that there will be a choice for a dualist rental system where nonprofit activities are restricted and nationalised. Social rented housing is incorporated into a publicly controlled planned economy and shaped into a low-income housing sector (command economy means-tested public renting). Examples are the United States, Canada, Australia, New Zealand, and, to a lesser degree, the United Kingdom. The corporatist welfare states are more related to an integrated rental market with a specific leading role for the social rented sector (Kemeny, 2006: 13). In conservative corporatist countries, we could still observe a strong influence of right-wing parties and a social rented sector which is limited and has a limited impact on the rental market. We also could expect a variety of ownership forms of social rental housing. Examples of these countries are Germany and Switzerland. In the labour-led corporatist countries, we would expect a bigger and more uniform social rented sector and a very small profit rented sector. The social rented sector is then big enough to have a leading position on the rental market. Also, the influence of the tenant and/or the State could be more explicit. Clear examples of these types of corporatist states are Sweden and Denmark. In the modern corporatistic welfare state, the role of the State is smaller and the role of the market, also for the social rented sector, is bigger than in the labour-led corporatistic state. A clear example of that is the social rented sector in the Netherlands. With 33% of the housing stock, the social rented sector in the Netherlands still has a dominant position not only in the Dutch rental market, but also in the overall housing market. The State largely confines itself to creating the conditions and to formulate the policy frameworks within which local government authorities and private actors operate. This new policy framework brought the housing associations in the Netherlands into a very powerful position. They are financially very strong and are in the bigger cities dominating the local rental market with regard to their housing stock and have a crucial role in urban renewal developments. A relevant question for the future is if more corporatist welfare states will develop in the direction of a modern corporatist welfare state and if the right-wing/conservative parties and the liberal-oriented neoclassical economies will approve such a development. More specifically, the role of the European Commission and the way the policy of free competition is implemented in the near future by specific laws from Brussels will probably provide an answer to the question of whether corporatist welfare states in general will have a bright future.

See also: Asset-Based Welfare; Economics of Social Housing; Gender and Urban Housing in the Global South; Housing Subsidies and Welfare; Social Housing and Social Problems; Social Theory and Housing.

References

Ball M and Harloe M (1990) Rhetorical barriers to understanding housing provision, what the 'provision thesis' is not. Paper presented at the *International Housing Research Conference 'Housing Debates – Urban Challenges'*. Paris, France, 3–6 July.

Barlow J and Duncan S (1994) *Success and Failure in Housing Provision, European Systems Compared*. Oxford, UK; New York; Tokyo: Elsevier Science Ltd.

Bengtsson B (2006) Swedish housing corporatism, a case of path dependency? Paper presented at the *ENHR 2004 Conference 'Housing: Growth and Regeneration'*. Cambridge, UK, 2–6 July 2004.

Boelhouwer PJ and van der Heijden HMH (1992) *Housing Systems in Europe, Part I: A Comparative Study of Housing Policy*. Housing and Urban Policy Studies 1. Delft, The Netherlands: Delft University Press.

Brandsen T (2001) Bringing actors back in: Towards an institutional perspective. *Housing, Theory and Society* 18: 2–14.

Danermark B and Elander I (1992) *Social Rented Housing in Europe: Policy, Tenure and Design*. Housing and Urban Policy Studies 9. Delft, The Netherlands: Delft University Press.

Danermark B and Elander I (1994) *Social Rented Housing in Europe: Policy Tenure and Design*. Housing and Urban Policy Studies 9. Delft, The Netherlands: Delft University Press.

Doling J (1990) Housing policy and convergence theory: Some comments on Schmidt, Research note. *Scandinavian Housing and Planning Research* 7: 117–120.

Doling J (1997) *Comparative Housing Policy. Government and Housing in Advanced Industrialized Countries*. London: Macmillan Press Ltd.

Doling J (1999) De-commodification and welfare: Evaluating housing systems. *Housing, Theory and Society* 16: 156–164.

Doling J and Ford J (2007) A union of home owners, editorial. *European Journal of Housing and Planning* 7(2): 113–127.

Doling J and Ronald R (2010) Home ownership and asset-based welfare. *Journal of Housing and the Built Environment* 24: 1.

Domburg-De Rooij T and Musterd S (2002) Ethnic segregation and the welfare state. In: Schnell I and Ostendorf W (eds.) *Studies in Segregation and Desegregation*, pp. 107–131. Aldershot, UK: Ashgate.

Donnison D (1967) *The Government of Housing*. Harmondsworth, UK: Penguin.

Donnison D and Ungerson C (1982) *Housing Policy*. Harmondsworth, UK: Penguin.

Elsinga M, De Decker P, Teller N, and Toussaint J (2007) *Home Ownership Beyond Asset and Security*. Housing and Urban Policy Studies 32. Amsterdam: IOS Press.

Esping-Andersen G (1990) *The Three Worlds of Welfare Capitalism*. Cambridge, UK: Polity Press.

Esping-Andersen G (1999) *Social Foundations of Postindustrial Economies*. Oxford, UK: Oxford University Press.

Evers A (1988) Shifts in the welfare mix – introducing a new approach for the study of transformations in welfare and social policy. In: Evers A and Wintersberger H (eds.) *Shifts in Welfare Mix*. Vienna: European Centre for Social Welfare Training and Research.

Harloe M (1992) The social construction of social housing. In: Danermark B and Elander I (eds.) *Social Rented Housing in Europe: Policy, Tenure and Design*, pp. 37–52. Housing and Urban Policy Studies 9. Delft, The Netherlands: Delft University Press.

Harloe M (1994) *The People's Home? Social Rented Housing in Europe and America*. Oxford, UK; Cambridge, MA: Blackwell.

Harloe M and Martens M (1987) Innovation in housing markets and policies. In: Turner B, Kemeny J, and Ludqvist L (eds.) *Between State and Market: Housing in the Post-Industrial Era*, pp. 190–214. Gävle, Sweden: Almqvist & Wiksell International.

Hoekstra J (2003) Housing and the welfare state in the Netherlands. An application of Esping-Andersen's typology. *Housing Theory and Society* 20(2): 58–71.

Hoekstra J (2005) Is there a connection between welfare state regime and dwelling type? An exploratory statistical analysis, *Housing Studies* 20(3): 475–495.

Hoekstra J and Reitsma A (2002) *De zorg voor het wonen. Volkshuisvesting en verzorgingsstaat in Nederland en België [The Care for Housing. Housing and the Welfare State in the Netherlands and Belgium]*. Volkshuisvestingsbeleid en Woningmarkt 33. Delft, The Netherlands: DUP Science.

Horsewood N and Neuteboom P (2006) *The Social Limits to Growth*. Housing and Urban Policy Studies 31. Amsterdam: IOS Press.

Kemeny J (1992) *Housing and Social Theory*, pp. 64–81. London; New York: Routledge.

Kemeny J (1995) *From Public Housing to the Social Market. Rental Policy Strategies in Comparative Perspective*. New York: Routledge.

Kemeny J (2001) Comparative housing and welfare: Theorising the relationship. *Journal of Housing and the Built Environment* 16(1): 53–70.

Kemeny J (2006) Corporatism and housing regimes. *Housing, Theory and Society* 23(1): 1–18.

Kemeny J and Lowe S (1998) Schools of comparative housing research: From convergence to divergence. *Housing Studies* 13(2): 161–176.

Kleinman M (1996) *Housing, Welfare and the State of Europe*. Cheltenham, UK; Brookfield, WI: Edward Elgar Publishing Limited.

Kvist J (1999) Welfare reform in the Nordic countries in the 1990s: Using fuzzy-set theory to assess comformity to ideal types. *Journal of European Social Policy* 9(3): 231–252.

Lundqvist LJ (1991) Rolling stones for the resurrection of policy as the focus of comparative housing research. *Scandinavian Housing and Planning Research* 8: 79–90.

Mandic S and Clapham D (1996) The meaning of home ownership in the transition from socialism: The example of Slovenia. *Urban Studies* 33(1): 83–97.

Matznetter W (2002) Social housing policy in a conservative welfare state: Austria as an example. *Urban Studies* 39(2): 265–282.

Merton RK (1957) *Social Theory and Social Structure*. Glencoe, IL: The Free Press.

Milligan V (2003) *How Different? Comparing Housing Policies and Housing Affordabilty Consequences for Low Income Households in Australia and the Netherlands*. Netherlands Geographical Studies 318. Utrecht, The Netherlands: University of Utrecht.

Murie A (1992) Public rented housing in Britain. In: Danermark B and Elander I (eds) *Social Rented Housing in Europe: Policy, Tenure and Design*, pp. 77–94. Housing and Urban Policy Studies 9. Delft, The Netherlands: Delft University Press.

Oxley M (1990) The aims and methods of comparative housing research. Paper presented at the *International Housing Research Conference 'Housing debates – Urban Challenges'*, Paris, France, 3–6 July.

Priemus H (1978) *Volkshuisvesting; begrippen problemen en beleid*. Alphen aan den Rijn, The Netherlands: Samson Uitgeverij.

Priemus H (1983) *Volkshuisvesting en woningmarkt [Housing System and Housing Market]*. Volkshuisvesting in theorie en praktijk nummer 1. Delft, The Netherlands: Delft University Press.

Ronald R (2008) *The Ideology of Home Ownership*. Basingstoke, UK; New York: Palgrave Macmillan.

Torgersen U (1987) Housing: The wobbly pillar under the welfare state. In: Turner B, Kemeny J, and Ludqvist L (eds.) *Between State and Market: Housing in the Post-Industrial Era*, pp. 116–127. Gavle, Sweden: Almqvist & Wiksell International.

Wilensky HL, Luebbert HL, Hahn GM, et al. (1987) *Comparative Policy Research*. Berlin: Gower.

Further Reading

Boelhouwer PJ (2002) Trends in Dutch housing policy and the shifting position of the social rented sector. *Urban Studies* 39(2): 219–235.

Bourne LS (1981) *The Geography of Housing*. London: Arnold.

Leibfried S (1992) Towards a European welfare state: On integrating poverty regimes into the European Community. In: Ferge Z and Kolberg J (eds.) *Social Policy in a Changing Europe*, pp. 245–279. Frankfurt, Germany: Campus Verlag.

Housing and Wealth Portfolios

M Flavin, University of California, San Diego, CA, USA

© 2012 Elsevier Ltd. All rights reserved.

Introduction

The household's decision to invest in a home is complicated by the fact that owner-occupied housing plays a dual role as both a physical good generating housing services and as a component of the wealth portfolio. For many homeowners, housing represents both the largest single element of the monthly expenditure and the most important asset in the wealth portfolio. Given the availability of rental markets for houses, a family could, in principle, independently choose its desired level of consumption of housing services and its desired holdings of residential real estate as an asset; for example, renting a 2500 square foot single family house for its own use and at the same time owning and renting out a 1000 square foot condo. However, using rental markets in order to separate the consumption decision (the quantity of housing services consumed) from the investment decision (the quantity of residential real estate held as an asset) would require the household to engage in the landlord–tenant relationship (once as a landlord and once as a tenant) on both houses. Understandably, the vast majority of homeowners avoid the double landlord/tenant roles by choosing a single residential property, which then simultaneously determines the family's level of consumption of housing services and the quantity of real estate in the portfolio. We consider the role of owner-occupied housing in the asset portfolio, assuming that the household owner-occupies a particular house, and thus the quantity of housing held as an asset coincides with the household's consumption of housing services.

Determining the Price of Housing

Both the expected return and the risk associated with investment in residential real estate depend on the behaviour of house prices over time. To understand the determination of real estate prices and identify the main factors that drive house prices, consider the interaction of supply and demand in two markets: the market for existing, or resale, houses, and the market for new construction. As drawn in **Figure 1**, a distinctive feature of the market for existing houses is the vertical, or completely inelastic, supply curve. That is, the stock of existing houses is fixed in the short run in the sense that driving up the price of existing houses will not increase the stock of available houses immediately. Of the pool of existing houses, it may be the case that in response to an increase in house prices, a greater fraction of houses are formally listed as 'for sale'. However, by the 'supply of existing houses' we are referring to the entire stock of houses currently habitable, whether or not the house is listed as 'for sale'. An owner-occupied house that is not formally listed for sale can be thought of as both one unit of the supply of existing housing and is currently satisfying the demand (on the part of the owner) for one unit of housing.

While different houses have different individual values, depending on their location, size, and physical attributes, consider a house price index, P, which reflects the average level of house prices at a point in time. If the demand for houses is relatively low, as indicated by the demand curve to the southwest in the left-hand graph, the average level of house prices, P, will be the price at which the demand for houses is equated with the current, fixed supply of existing houses. Since the price of resale homes determines the price at which builders can sell their newly constructed homes, the market price of new construction homes will also be P_0. (More realistically, a newly constructed home probably sells for a premium over an otherwise comparable resale home. However, if the premium paid for a newly constructed house is reasonably constant, the market price of existing homes will move one-for-one with the market price of resale homes. While a positive premium for new construction could be incorporated, it would not affect the basic mechanism which determines the market price of new construction.)

While the supply of existing homes is fixed at any moment, and changes only slowly over time as new houses are built, the demand for houses can shift rapidly due to changes in (1) mortgage interest rates, (2) the strictness of mortgage underwriting standards, (3) the level of per capita income, (4) population size and demographics, and (5) expectations concerning the path of future house prices. The effect of the first four factors on the demand for housing is straightforward. For a given house purchase price, a lower mortgage interest rate reduces the monthly mortgage payment required to buy the house, increasing the pool of buyers who are able to afford the house, and shifting the demand curve to the right. Similarly, relaxation of mortgage underwriting standards in the form of lower required down payments, no-documentation loans, and 'interest-only' or negative amortisation loans will increase the pool of buyers at a given price level. An increase in population, an increase in household

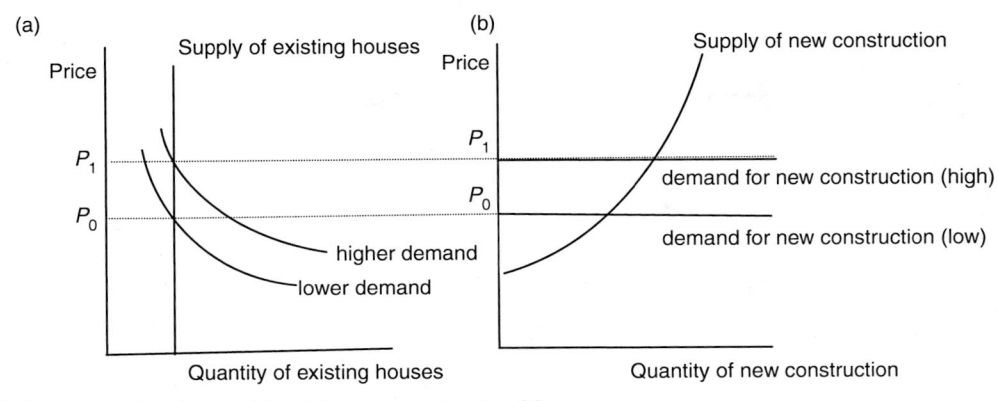

Figure 1 Markets for existing homes (a) and for new construction (b).

formation, or an increase in per capita income will also increase the pool of potential buyers who can afford to buy at a given price level, and therefore shift the demand curve to the right. Since, in the short run, the supply of existing houses is fixed, any factor that shifts the demand curve to the right – for example, a reduction in the mortgage interest rate, relaxation of underwriting standards, or an increase in population – will require a higher price in order to maintain equilibrium in the real estate market.

If the price of a unit of the existing housing stock rises from P_0 to P_1, the price of newly constructed homes also rises, inducing builders to increase the rate of construction of new homes. Over time, as these newly built houses are added to the housing stock, the supply of existing houses will increase (shift to the right).

The final factor that affects the demand for houses is the expected path of future home prices. In contrast to most of the goods it purchases, the household plans to resell the house at some point in the future. Consider a household deciding between renting a home or owning a comparable home, and assume that the monthly expenses on both homes are equal in the sense that the rental rate on the rental is approximately the same as the monthly expenses (mortgage payments, property taxes, and insurance) on the purchased home. If real estate values are expected to rise over time, the household will prefer to own rather than rent (even if the houses and the monthly expenses are comparable) because by owning the household expects to benefit from the capital gain on the house. Therefore, an increase in the expected growth rate of real estate values (from 4 to 8% annually, for example) shifts the demand curve to the right. Note that an increase in the expected rate of appreciation of houses increases the demand for the asset, and increases the current price. Likewise, a decline in the expected rate of appreciation or an expected decline in house prices will shift the demand curve to the left, and cause the current price to fall.

Housing Risk and Return

Because an owner-occupied house is an investment, or asset, its risk and return can be defined analogously to the risk and return to financial assets such as stocks and bonds. The holding period return to a stock or share of equity has two components, the capital gain and the dividend payment. Expressed as a rate of return, or the return as a percentage of the value of the stock at the beginning of the period, the holding period return, R_S, to a stock is as follows:

$$R_s = \frac{P_{t+1}^S - P_t^S + D_t}{P_t^S}$$

where P_t^S is the value of the house at the beginning of the period, P_{t+1}^S is the value of the stock at the end of the period, and D_t is the total dividend payments during the period. Analogously, the holding period return to an owner-occupied home, R_H, can be thought of as follows:

$$R_H = \frac{P_{t+1} - P_t + \text{NRV}_t}{P_t}$$

Here the prices refer to the value of the stock at the beginning and the end of the period and NRV_t refers to the net rental value of the house over the time interval. The asset income generated by an owner-occupied house is received in the form of the flow of housing services provided by the house during the holding period. To the extent that the homeowner incurs maintenance costs, the net rental value would be the market rents the house would command on the rental market (i.e., imputed rent), net of the homeowner's maintenance costs.

With this notion of the holding period return to an owner-occupied home, the expected return and variability of returns on housing can be compared with the risk and return characteristics of financial assets. **Table 1** reports the average return and the standard deviation of return on short-term government debt (T-bills), long-term

Table 1 Average return and standard deviation of return on T-bills, bonds, stocks, mortgage, and houses

	T-bills	Bonds	Stocks	Mortgage	House
Average return	−0.0038	0.0060	0.0824	0.0000	0.0659
Standard deviation	0.0435	0.0840	0.2415	0.0336	0.1424

Source: Flavin M and Yamashita T (2002) Owner-occupied housing and the composition of the household portfolio. *American Economic Review* 1: 345–362.

government debt (bonds), the S&P 500 stock market index (stocks), 30-year fixed-rate mortgages (mortgage), and owner-occupied homes (house), for the United States over the period from 1968 to 1992. All returns are annual, after-tax returns, and have been adjusted for inflation.

Stocks provide the highest after-tax inflation-adjusted return at 8.24%. The after-tax, inflation-adjusted return to government debt was close to zero in the case of long-term bonds, and slightly negative in the case of short-term Treasury bills. Because mortgage interest payments are tax-deductible in the United States, and because the 1968–92 period was characterized by high, unexpected inflation, holders of long-term fixed-rate mortgages ended up paying, on average, an after-tax, inflation-adjusted mortgage interest rate of zero. At 6.6%, the inflation-adjusted return to housing is comparable to, although somewhat smaller than, the return to stocks. With a standard deviation of 14.24%, the variability of the return to houses is substantially smaller than the variability of stock returns.

When constructing a portfolio of assets, the household cares about the expected, or average, return to the portfolio as a whole. Similarly, the 'riskiness' of an individual investment depends on how the riskiness, or variability of return, to the portfolio as a whole is affected by the addition of the asset. Because the household ultimately cares about the average return and riskiness of return to the portfolio as a whole, the optimal holding of a particular risky asset – such as a house – depends on the asset's contribution to the diversification of the portfolio as a whole. For example, if we consider two risky assets, A and B, which are identical in terms of their individual average return and a standard deviation of return, the two assets will nevertheless make very different contributions to the effective diversification of the overall portfolio if the return to asset A is strongly positively correlated with the return to the portfolio (i.e., asset A tends to have higher than average returns when the return to the rest of the portfolio is higher than average) while the return to asset B is negatively correlated with the return to the portfolio (i.e., asset B tends to have higher than average returns when the return to the rest of the portfolio is lower than average, and vice versa). Thus, even if the return to risky asset B has the same average return and variability of return as risky asset A, by having a return which is negatively correlated with the rest of the portfolio, the addition of asset B provides more effective diversification than asset A. By creating greater diversification of the portfolio, asset B will allow the household to achieve a lower level of portfolio risk than asset A.

Thus, in assessing the contribution of owner-occupied housing to the risk and return of the overall portfolio, it is important to determine whether the return to housing is positively correlated (like asset A) or negatively correlated (like asset B) with returns to the financial assets that make up the rest of the portfolio. Using the same data series as **Table 1**, **Table 2** reports the correlation coefficients for each pair of assets.

T-bills, bonds, and mortgages are each debt contracts, and differ primarily in the maturity of the contract and the nature of the issuer. Not surprisingly, the returns to any pair of these three assets are strongly positively correlated, with correlation coefficients ranging from 0.68 to 0.84. Stock returns are positively correlated with the returns to T-bills, bonds, or mortgages, but the degree of correlation is smaller, ranging from a correlation of 0.47 between stocks and mortgages, to a correlation of 0.02 between stocks and T-bills. The correlation between the return to owner-occupied housing and any of the financial assets is either slightly negative, in the case of T-bills or bonds, or zero, for stocks and mortgages. Since the correlation coefficients are

Table 2 Correlation between returns to pairs of assets

	T-bills	Bonds	Stocks	Mortgage	House
T-bills	1				
Bonds	0.69	1			
Stocks	0.02	0.20	1		
Mortgage	0.84	0.68	0.47	1	
House	−0.03	−0.01	0.00	0.00	1

Source: Flavin M and Yamashita T (2002) Owner-occupied housing and the composition of the household portfolio. *American Economic Review* 1: 345–362.

either zero, or if negative, close to zero, the bottom row of **Table 2** indicates that the return to owner-occupied housing is essentially uncorrelated with the returns to any of the financial assets, and therefore provides substantial diversification to the portfolio as a whole. Owning a home rather than renting is a good investment for several reasons: First, the average annual return to housing, after taxes and adjusting for inflation, is 6.6%, almost as large as the average return to stocks. Second, adding owner-occupied housing to a portfolio of financial assets is an effective way of achieving diversification and thus lowering the risk of the overall portfolio.

Optimal Portfolio Allocation

Owner-occupied housing as an asset has several disadvantages compared to financial assets. Financial assets are extremely liquid in the sense that they can be bought or sold quickly, and in the sense that the transactions costs incurred in a purchase or sale are very small relative to the value of the asset that changes hands. In contrast, the seller of a house incurs significant monetary costs in order to liquidate his investment in real estate, in addition to the time and effort required to physically move from one house to another. Less obvious, but probably more important, is the fact that housing investment is not divisible in a similar way to that of financial investments. While an investor has complete control over the scale of his investment in shares of equity, given the ability to buy one share or a thousand shares at essentially the same price per share, an investment in owner-occupied housing is 'lumpy' in the sense that the choice is between not owning at all (i.e., an investment of zero) or owning an entire housing unit. For homeowners with mortgages, their equity in the house may be small compared to the value of the house. However, since a homeowner with a mortgage still bears all of the risk associated with changes in real estate prices, the magnitude of the investment is determined by the value of the house, rather than value of the equity.

Once the household determines its desired level of consumption of housing services – that is, once the household determines the quantity of housing it prefers for consumption purposes – it then faces the decision of whether to own the house or to rent. In contrast to most financial assets, for which the optimal strategy is to own small amounts of a large number of assets, the fact that housing serves a dual role as both a consumption good and as an asset implies that the household must choose between being a renter (and investing in no real estate at all), or being a homeowner (and therefore making a large investment in real estate). The idea that, for homeowners, the quantity of housing held as an asset must coincide with the quantity of housing chosen for consumption purposes is referred to as the 'housing constraint' on the wealth portfolio.

In order to purchase a house, most households borrow funds in the form of a mortgage. After acquiring both the mortgage and the house, the net wealth or equity of the household may be fairly modest. However, instead of considering the household's net position (the home equity), both the gross investment in the house and the borrowing in the form of a mortgage as separate asset positions. The household can also invest in T-bills, bonds, and stocks. Since the typical household does not buy stocks on margin or sell stocks short, the portfolio analysis assumes that the household can hold T-bills, bonds, and stocks only in nonnegative amounts. Further, it is assumed that the household can borrow only in the form of a mortgage, and that the size of the mortgage is no greater than 100% of the value of the house when initially purchased.

Table 3 reports the average holdings of cash (defined as bank deposits and short-term debt such as T-bills), bonds, stocks, owner-occupied housing, and mortgages for a sample of US families in 1989. All amounts are expressed as a fraction of the household's net wealth. Since a mortgage is a liability rather than an asset, the fraction of net wealth held in the form of a mortgage is expressed as a negative number. Since each of the assets in **Table 3** is a component of net wealth (and because the mortgage is represented as a negative asset), the five numbers in any row of **Table 3** add up to unity by construction.

Table 3 Ratio of particular assets to net worth, average for US households in 1989

Age of head	Cash	Bonds	Stocks	House	Mortgage
18–30	0.193	0.072	0.056	3.511	−2.833
31–40	0.169	0.067	0.068	2.366	−1.671
41–50	0.148	0.060	0.085	1.588	−0.882
51–60	0.200	0.058	0.092	0.969	−0.319
61–70	0.254	0.048	0.113	0.757	−0.171
71+	0.264	0.029	0.098	0.648	−0.038

Source: Flavin M and Yamashita T (2002) Owner-occupied housing and the composition of the household portfolio. *American Economic Review* 1: 345–362.

In **Table 3**, the data are broken into subsamples according to the age of the head of household, and the allocation of net wealth across different assets is reported separately for each age-group. For the youngest cohort of homeowners, with household heads age 18–30, the value of the house is about 350% of net wealth. On average, this cohort of homeowners are encumbered with a mortgage with a principal value about 280% of net wealth. About 19% of their wealth is held in the form of bank deposits (checking accounts, savings account, CDs) and short-term government debt, 7% in bonds, and 6% in equities. On average, the household's net wealth increases with age. Since the consumption of housing services is relatively stable over the lifecycle, the fact that net household wealth increases with age implies that the ratio of the value of the house to net wealth falls with age. For the cohort aged 51–60, average net wealth is approximately equal to the value of the house. While the typical household in this age-group could (almost) pay off their mortgage, doing so would involve holding no financial assets, including cash. Instead, the typical household in the 51–60 age-group carries a mortgage with remaining principal equal to about 30% of the value of their home, and owns substantial amounts of cash, equities, and bonds.

The value of the house as a fraction of net wealth and the remaining principal on the mortgage continue to fall as the household passes age 61 and 71.

Even in the absence of housing as an asset, the optimal portfolio will depend on the household's degree of risk aversion. A simple way of characterising risk aversion in this context is to think of the household as evaluating different possible portfolios by computing the following function of the average, or expected return, $E(r_p)$, and the variability, or variance of return, σ_p^2.

$$E(r_p) - \frac{A}{2}\sigma_p^2$$

All households are assumed to be risk averse, in the sense that for a given average return they would like to minimise the riskiness of the portfolio, as measured by the variability of its return. However, households differ in the degree of their risk aversion, as reflected by the value of the parameter A. A household with a relatively high degree of risk aversion (e.g., $A=10$) is more sensitive to portfolio risk than a household with a low degree of risk aversion (e.g., $A=1$). Depending on their degree of risk aversion, households will choose different portfolios on the risk and return trade-off: relatively risk-averse

Table 4 Optimal portfolios

Ratio of house value to net wealth	Assets in portfolio	Degree of risk aversion Low	Moderate	High
0 (Renters)	T-bills	0	0.47	.83
	Bonds	0	0.15	0
	Stocks	1	0.38	.17
3.51	T-bills	0	0	0
	Bonds	0	0.60	.81
	Stocks	1	0.40	.19
	Mortgage	−1	−1	−1
2.37	T-bills	0	0	0
	Bonds	0	0.61	0.79
	Stocks	1	0.39	0.21
	Mortgage	−1	−1	−0.93
1.59	T-bills	0	0	0
	Bonds	0	0.61	0.70
	Stocks	1	0.39	0.30
	Mortgage	−1	−1	−0.72
0.97	T-bills	0	0	0
	Bonds	0	0.52	0.51
	Stocks	1	0.48	0.49
	Mortgage	−1	−0.76	−0.28
0.76	T-bills	0	0	0
	Bonds	0	0.47	0.38
	Stocks	1	0.53	0.62
	Mortgage	−1	−0.61	0
0.65	T-bills	0	0	0.38
	Bonds	0	0.44	0.20
	Stocks	1	0.56	0.42
	Mortgage	−1	−0.47	0

households will choose portfolios with modest expected returns and low variability of return, and relatively risk-tolerant households will choose portfolios with higher expected returns and higher variability (risk).

With the addition of owner-occupied housing to the list of assets, and assuming that the quantity of housing held is determined by the household's consumption demand for housing services, an additional constraint is imposed on the household's portfolio allocation problem. At any given moment, both the value of housing owned and the total net wealth of the household are fixed, and therefore the ratio of house value to net wealth is a fixed value. The household's optimal holdings of financial assets will depend on both the value of the housing constraint (i.e., the ratio of house value to net wealth) and on their degree of risk aversion.

Table 4 reports the optimal portfolio for different levels of the housing constraint, and for low, moderate, and high degrees of risk aversion. The first row reports the optimal portfolios when the ratio of house value to net wealth is zero; that is, for nonhomeowners. In this table, the holdings of T-bills, bonds, and stocks are stated as a percentage of the sum of those three assets, and the size of the mortgage is stated as a percentage of the value of the house (i.e., −1 for the mortgage indicates that the mortgage is 100% of the value of the house).

Households with a very low degree of risk aversion will hold a portfolio with high expected return (and high risk) by continuing to borrow against their home in the form of a 100% mortgage, and investing all of their net wealth in stocks. By maintaining the 100% mortgage, these risk-tolerant households leverage their portfolio and hold only the two highest average return assets, houses and stocks. For households of moderate to high risk aversion, young families with a high value of the ratio of house value to net wealth will achieve their optimal portfolio by creating leverage with a 100% mortgage and dividing their net wealth among bonds and stocks. As the household ages, and the ratio of house value to net wealth falls, the optimal portfolio involves less leverage in the sense that the mortgage principal, as a percentage of house value, falls. Highly risk-averse households pay off their mortgages sooner in the lifecycle than households of moderate risk aversion, since paying off the mortgage reduces the degree of leverage and reduces portfolio risk. For a given level of the ratio of house value to net wealth, more risk-averse households also reduce risk by holding relatively smaller amounts of stocks and relatively greater amounts of bonds and T-bills.

Reference

Flavin M and Yamashita T (2002) Owner-occupied housing and the composition of the household portfolio. *American Economic Review* 1: 345–362.

Further Reading

Sinai T and Souleles N (2009). Can owning a home hedge the risk of moving? *NBER Working Paper No. 15462*, October 2009.

Housing Auctions

D Brounen, Rotterdam School of Management, Rotterdam, The Netherlands

© 2012 Elsevier Ltd. All rights reserved.

Glossary

Default The financial status at which households can no longer meet their financial obligations to their mortgage lender.

Fair market value The most likely sale value a house would generate on the open market under standard sale conditions.

Foreclosure The legal process by which a creditor obtains title to property offered as security following default by the borrower.

Information asymmetry The circumstance at which not all relevant information is known to both parties involved in a transaction.

OTC fire sale The sale of a house organised by a local broker in order to salvage the outstanding loan balance of the mortgage lender. In this type of sale, the house is sold in the open market after repossession by the mortgage lender.

Price discount The percentage difference in the sale price generated at a foreclosure sale and the fair market value of the dwelling.

Auctions

An auction is a process of buying and selling goods by offering them up for bid, taking bids, and then selling the item to the highest bidder. The origins of auctioning date as far back as the Roman Empire, when auctions were used to liquidate the assets of debtors whose properties had been confiscated. But, compared to the alternatives of haggling and sale by set-price, auctions have always been a relatively unpopular way of negotiating the exchange of goods. For a long time, auctioning was not very common, and it is only since the eighteenth century that auctions have become fashionable, especially in the arts world where auction houses like Sotheby's and Christie's have been auctioning fine art on a regular basis since 1744.

From the perspective of economic theory, the auction platform ought to be an appealing method of selling assets. The seminal work by Milgron and Weber (1982) demonstrates that the competitive element at auction sales ought to result in sale prices that exceed the outcomes generated at other sale platforms. Competition among bidders is a crucial condition for this claim. This means that one needs to organise auctions such that large audiences will consist of multiple bidders independent of each other. This independence is needed, since bidders need to compete in order to arrive at the highest price.

Auction Methods

In the literature, four principal methods of auctioning are defined.

English Ascending Auction

The English ascending method is the most popular method of auctioning. The auctioneer starts with a low price, and calls successively higher prices until there is only one bidder remaining. This type of auctioning is publicly held and all the participants know who the successive bidder is. An advantage for the seller of property is the 'winner's curse', when the buyer due to strong competition gets carried away in the heat of the moment.

Dutch Auction Method

This method starts with a high starting price determined by the auctioneer, and calls gradually a lower price until one bidder accepts the bid price. This method is famously used during the Dutch flower auction in Aalsmeer.

The First Price Sealed-Bid Auction

In this type of auctioning, bidders submit a concealed bid in which the buyer with the highest bid wins the item. This type of bidding should theoretically give the same results as the Dutch auction method, in relation to the game theory, where the result depends on the choices of others.

The Second Price Sealed-Bid Auction

In this method, the buyer with the highest bid wins just like the first price sealed-bid auction; however the winner pays only the amount of the second bid. This method was designed by Vickrey (1961). The main advantage of this type of auctioning is the incentive for bidders to target the true value.

Research by Lucking-Reiley (1994) compared the price outcomes of these different auction formats and documented that Dutch auctions result in the highest price results, almost 30% higher than in the price auction setting.

Auction Mispricing

Although auctions are set out to be a very competitive sale platform, which facilitates competitive bidding to achieve the highest possible bids, auctions are also notorious for yielding prices that are less than optimal for the seller involved.

The main driver of potential mispricing at auctions is information asymmetry. In order to arrive at a price that is fair to both seller and bidder, both parties need to agree on the quality of the good. This implies that all relevant information concerning the good is known to both parties at the same time. This, however, is typically not the case. In most cases, sellers have more experience with the good involved, which offers them an informational advantage. They know exact specifications and the current technical conditions of the product, which allows them to set the price at a level that favours them. Buyers/bidders, who cannot assess all quality elements, need to make an educated guess when placing their bid. This puts the bidder at a disadvantage and creates the so-called 'lemons problem' as set out first by Akerlof (1970). In this situation, bidders will bid conservatively for goods of which not all information is readily available to them. The chance of buying a product of lower than average quality is significant, and therefore they will demand, on average, a price discount.

At auctions, the organiser of the sale ideally needs to work hard on disseminating all the relevant information before the bidding process. This will reduce the information asymmetry, will comfort the bidders, and thereby increase the price result at the end of the day.

For housing, the issue of informational asymmetry is very relevant. Dwellings tend to be very heterogeneous in their specifications. Hence, disclosing full information on the quality of the house for sale is vital for the sale process. Compared to buying an authentic seventeenth century statue, buying a house requires more due diligence. Given the size of the product and the technical complexity of the quality aspects, obtaining all relevant information during the limited time span before the bidding process is a challenge.

Typically, the extent to which the price formation at auctions succeeds is measured by benchmarking the sale prices at auctions to that of sales in the open market.

Housing Auctions

The auction system is applied in the housing market in different ways. Like in other markets, such as the market for fine arts, auctions are used as a sale mechanism in open-market sales. In some contexts, for instance, in the United Kingdom and Australia, a significant share of regular home sales are organised at home auctions. Here, the seller voluntarily puts the house up for sale, and hopes that the competition among prospective buyers will yield the highest possible proceeds. The fact that an auction also speeds up the sale is another important advantage. While other sale mechanisms may involve lengthy negotiation processes, visits to the dwellings, and expensive advertisement periods, auctions deliver results on the spot. As long as there are reasonable bids, the sale is a fact at the end of the auction day.

This relative speed of sale is also one of the key drivers of the second type of home auction platforms – foreclosure auction sales. In this case, the house is put up for sale by the mortgage lender once the original buyer fails to meet his or her financial obligations. Selling a home at a foreclosure auction guarantees a swift result. The proceeds are first used to pay off the outstanding loan balance (to the lender) before any money is paid out to the financial delinquent.

Worldwide, mortgage foreclosures have been on the rise. In the United States, the credit quality of residential mortgages fell substantially in 2008 (Bovenzi, 2009), and it is expected that the number of mortgage foreclosures will only rise over the next few years (Bair, 2008; White, 2009). This means that apart from home retention measures, banks must try to ensure that foreclosure sales indeed help to recover the outstanding debt. Under Basel II financial guidelines, banks are required to have a good understanding of the recovery rates of their outstanding loans, particularly during economic downturns.

Open-Market Housing Auctions

Previous studies of auction sales versus private sales have used various methodologies to determine the outcome of real estate auctions. In Australia and New Zealand, for example, auctioning of real estate is seen as a viable alternative for selling by private treaty. Using various variables for comparison and quality control, Lusht (1996) found that, in Australia, higher-quality properties sold by auction have an average premium of 8%. The study by Dotzour et al. (1998) of auctions in New Zealand suggested that auctions are most successful when houses are more desirable and in a higher price range. Dotzour et al. (1998) used a hedonic model to compare auctions with private negotiations and observed that highly priced and unique properties are sold at a premium ranging from 5.9 to 9.5%. In line with this result, Ashenfelter and Genesove (1992) also found that auction prices for New Jersey condominiums were higher than private listings.

In contrast with these results, auctioned properties are sold at a discount, which increased in down-market areas for the regions of Dallas and Los Angeles. In line with this result and using a hedonic model, it has been identified that properties sold at an auction fetch significantly lower prices than comparable properties sold in the private market. The above studies, however, only look at nondistressed sale auctions. The conditions surrounding a distressed sale by auction are not comparable with a nondistressed sale. Often, properties that are sold during a distressed auction have a higher discount to fair market value than nondistressed properties. The following section discusses issues concerning properties in distress in further detail.

Foreclosure Housing Auctions

Buying a home at foreclosure auctions is costly. The sale is managed by a notary on behalf of the bank. In these events, notaries charge a higher fee than the standard, given the additional work that is involved in filing the distressed background of the mortgagee. The auction itself will also induce additional costs, for instance, renting the auction house and hiring an auctioneer. On average, these fees amount to around 4% of the sale proceeds, whereas a regular sale only requires a notary fee of around 1%. This cost difference, of course, will depress sale proceeds at auctions. Moreover, buyers at foreclosure auctions are typically professional real estate traders and (re)developers, whereas in an over-the-counter (OTC) fire sale, the buyer is more likely to be a private household that is less calculating or profit-driven when bidding for a home. At auctions, it is typical that buyers are only allowed to participate in the bidding process when they are able to deposit a bank guarantee that vouches for the line of credit. Private individuals may be naive concerning such practices and auctions may thus be biased in favour of professional traders.

In the Dutch market, foreclosure auctions are associated with various elements that create informational asymmetry. For instance, buyers at foreclosure auctions rarely have the opportunity to inspect the properties that are for sale, which greatly limits their information-gathering process. Furthermore, during the auction, little information concerning the characteristics of the house is communicated beyond the location and legal status. Buyers need to make speculative guesses and often bid on the basis of scant information such as the address and a single photograph of the front of the house.

Mortgage Foreclosure

A borrower may enter into technical default in a case of a mortgage loan delinquency of at least 30 days. Where the borrower may be expected to be able to meet loan (re)payments in the long run, but currently faces a temporary income dip, the bank and borrower may voluntarily agree to add past due principal and interest payments to the balance of the loan and renegotiate the monthly payments. In spite of these efforts, however, some homeowners enter into default, which is often a first step into a process that ultimately leads to foreclosure (see Ambrose et al., 1997; Lambrecht et al., 2003). In a US study, Ambrose et al. (1997) illustrate that, depending on state law, the time span between initial action and foreclosure may vary between 6 weeks to 18 months. Some alternatives still exist to prevent foreclosure: short sales and deed-in-lieu of foreclosure. In both cases, the borrower and lender agree that the borrower sell the home for a price that may be less than the face value of the mortgage. Eventually, the lender collects the proceeds of the short sale and may sometimes absorb a loss. The borrower is penalised by having their personal credit score reduced, and the creditor may still try to collect the loss through a deficiency judgement. The main difference between these sales methods is the speed of the process, which is generally quicker for the latter. Both the short sale and the deed-in-lieu of foreclosure tend to be cheaper for the lender than a regular foreclosure and are thus preferred. Yet, when mortgages have been securitised (i.e., the loan is not retained by the lender but broken up and resold on the securities market), the securitisation system may not allow the terms of the underlying mortgages to be modified at all (see White, 2009). This failure to renegotiate securitised mortgages seems to have substantially contributed to the recent surge in foreclosures. Since, in many countries, most mortgage debt has been securitised (in the United States some 60%), the outcome for the foreclosure process is a significant concern.

In a foreclosure, the lender is entitled to seize the collateral. Lenders are, usually, not legally allowed to begin foreclosure proceedings until two payments are missed and the third is due. Although conditions vary from country to country, typically, once a borrower is behind on his or her mortgage payments, the lender may send a 'notice of default' (NOD). Lanzerotti (2006) noticed only a small percentage of homeowners who receive an NOD actually lose their homes to foreclosure. If the due payment cannot be resolved, the lender files a 'notice of sale'. In the United States, the property is then sold at a public auction, and if the minimum bid set by the lender is not met, then the property becomes a 'real estate owned' (REO) by the lender and is sold through regular channels. The foreclosure auction and REO sales through mainstream channels are the two extreme sales mechanisms often considered in prior research (e.g., Ashenfelter and Genesove, 1992). For a discussion on the realised auction bids and the reserve price, due to unobservable attributes of the house, quality signals, and bidder estimates of the house, we refer to McAfee et al. (2002).

In the Dutch mortgage market, residential mortgage contracts clearly state the process of foreclosure. In the event that the mortgagee fails to meet his or her monthly mortgage duties, the bank automatically obtains the right to repossess the home. After notifying the mortgagee, the bank can evict the client from the home within 2 months and organise a public sale of the property to redeem the loan balance. The fastest sales method is the foreclosure auction where the home will be sold on the spot, assuming that a predetermined minimum sales' proceed is met. Alternatively, the house can also be sold at an OTC fire sale. In this case, a local real estate broker is hired by the bank to facilitate the sale in the open market. Here, the home will be advertised in the traditional manner, without signalling the distressed state of the mortgagee. Prospective buyers are offered the opportunity to visit the property and the home is sold after bilateral negotiations between the brokers of the buyers and the sellers. Also, during this sale process, the bank is in charge of the sale and collects the proceeds up to the amount of the outstanding loan balance. Given that the average sales period of these OTC fire sales typically exceeds 120 days, banks often opt for the foreclosure auction to swiftly salvage their loan. Though auctions yield faster sales, they are also more expensive. The main costs include the notary managing the sale, the fees of the auction house, and the auctioneer.

Foreclosure Auction Pricing

The conditions surrounding distressed auction sales are more constrained than normal real estate auctions. In the case of foreclosure, the seller does not have a broker to represent him or her and often becomes passive in the process, diminishing his or her ability to negotiate. Shilling et al. (1990) found that the net realised values of properties that are in distress are usually understated. Lenders expect a short time interval between bankruptcy and sale of a property. Therefore, lenders will offer a discount in order to sell the property quickly. Investigations, with a hedonic analysis, have revealed the impact of physical location, time, and neighbourhood variables on auction sale outcomes for distressed properties. Their results demonstrated significant effects of location and neighbourhood factors. It has been found that impatient sellers, who want to sell their properties quickly, tend to sell their property with significantly higher discounts than patient sellers. Studies by Forgey et al. (1994) and Hardin and Wolverton (1995) also report that foreclosed properties sell at a 23% discount in comparison with nonforeclosed properties. They therefore suggest that financial institutions should be more patient when disposing of real estate assets.

A main reason why foreclosed properties sell for less is that borrowers who have a low income and a greater risk of default spend much less on maintaining a property, which results in lower house prices. From the perspective of financial institutions, another reason why foreclosed properties sell for less is that acquiring properties through foreclosures can have an impact on institutional credit ratings. If a financial institution keeps a nonperforming property on the books, it affects their credit rating, thus providing financial institutions an incentive to accept below-market prices in order to sell the property quickly. An additional aspect for foreclosed properties is the fact that, often, potential buyers cannot view the property from the inside or do a proper appraisal because of time constraints. Therefore, the possibility that the property has some hidden defects influences the sale value.

In an empirical analysis of 279 foreclosed home auction sales in the Netherlands, an average price discount of 36%, which equals an amount of €52 000, was documented. In another sample of 403 OTC fire sales, the price oscillation proved to be milder. Here, a negative price difference of less than €28 000, which equals around 15% of the free market value, was evident. All in all, these results are in line with previous studies on US foreclosure sales that documented price discounts of 22–25%.

Given that the average forced sale in the Netherlands occurs around 4 years after the house is acquired and typically financed at a loan to value of 115%, the bank needs a price appreciation of more than 8% a year to compensate for the loss that is realised in the foreclosure auction. In the study of 403 OTC fire sales, the bank still recovered its outstanding mortgage as long as the house price had risen at least 3.5% a year during the 4 years preceding the default. Since 1970, the average nominal price appreciation in the Dutch housing market has equalled 6% per annum. However, over the 10 most recent years, this average price appreciation fell to less than 4% a year, and during 2008, house prices in the Netherlands fell by 2%.

When focusing on the cross-sectional variation of these price discounts at auction sales, we find that the price discounts among forced sales are predominantly a function of the type of sale and the neighbourhood in which the home is located. It appears that structural characteristics like the age and the size of the house do not matter when explaining the price discount, especially among the auction sales. This may be explained by the poor information supply at these auctions. In the Dutch sample of OTC fire sales, where information on the dwelling was shared with all bidders during the site inspection, a more prominent role for these specific factors was documented. In this case, bids better reflected the quality of the home and not just the status of the neighbourhood.

In the Dutch auction sample, the only factors that appeared to be significant drivers of the price discount were related to the neighbourhood of the dwelling. Homes located in weak neighbourhoods, where the sale time is relatively long and average house values are low, will earn only a low price at auction. Bidders at auction, who will need to base their bid on very little information other than the address, appear to discount the quality of the neighbourhood into their pricing strategy.

This result is not surprising, but is, at the same time, alarming. The results show that as long as foreclosure auctions are poorly organised with respect to information for bidders, auction sales will not succeed in collecting a fair price for the seller. In fact, the same neighbourhood factors that seem to inspire banks to select the auction platform to swiftly recover the outstanding loan balance inspire buyers at the auction to bid low and thereby hamper the recovery of the loan. As long as information on the dwelling is absent, location is the sole factor that will drive bids away from the fair market value.

See also: Foreclosure Vulnerability.

References

Akerlof GA (1970) The market for 'lemons': Quality uncertainty and the market mechanism. *Quarterly Journal of Economics* 84: 488–500.

Ambrose BW, Buttimer RJ, Jr, and Capone CA (1997) Pricing mortgage default and foreclosure delay. *Journal of Money, Credit and Banking* 29(3): 314–325.

Ashenfelter O and Genesove D (1992) Testing for price anomalies in real-estate auctions. *American Economic Review* 82(2): 501–505.

Bair SC (2008) *Statement of Sheila C. Bair to Committee on Financial Services*; US House of Representatives. www.fdic.gov/news/news/speeches/archives/2008/index.html (accessed 19 May 2011).

Bovenzi JF (2009) *Statement of John F. Bovenzi to Committee on Financial Services*; US House of Representatives. Speech of 3 February 2009. www.fdic.gov/news/news/speeches/archives/2009/spfeb0309.html (accessed 19 May 2011).

Dotzour M, Moorhead E, and Winkler D (1998) The impact of the auctions on residential sales prices in New Zealand. *Journal of Real Estate Research* 16(1): 57–72.

Forgey F, Rutherford R, and Van Buskirk M (1994) The effect of foreclosure status on residential selling price. *Journal of Real Estate Research* 9(3): 313–318.

Hardin WG and Wolverton ML (1995) The relationship between foreclosure status and apartment price. *Journal of Real Estate Research* 12(1): 101–109.

Lambrecht BM, Perraudin WRM, and Satchell S (2003) Mortgage default and possession under recourse: A competing hazards approach. *Journal of Money, Credit and Banking* 35(3): 425–442.

Lanzerotti L (2006) Homeownership at high cost: Foreclosure risk and high cost loans in California. *Study Conducted for the Federal Reserve Bank of San Francisco*.

Lucking-Reiley D (1994) Using field experiments to test equivalence between auction formats: More magic on the internet.

Lusht KM (1996) A comparison of prices brought by English auctions and private negotiations. *Real Estate Economics* 24: 517–530.

McAfee RP, Quan DC, and Vincent DR (2002) How to set minimum acceptable bids, with an application to real estate auctions. *Journal of Industrial Economics* 50(4): 391–416.

Milgron PR and Weber RJ (1982) A theory of auctions and competitive bidding. *Econometrica* 50(5): 1089–1122.

Shilling JD, Benjamin JD, and Sirmans CF (1990) Estimating net realizable value for distressed real estate. *Journal of Real Estate Research* 5(1): 129–140.

Vickrey W (1961) Counterspeculation, auctions, and competitive sealed tenders. *Journal of Finance* 16(1): 8–37.

White MJ (2009) Bankruptcy: Past puzzles, recent reforms, and the mortgage crisis. *American Law and Economics Review* 11: 1–23.

Further Reading

Danis MA and Pennington-Cross A (2008) The delinquency of subprime mortgages. *Journal of Economics and Business* 60(1–2): 67–90.

Gardner MJ and Mills DL (1989) Evaluating the likelihood of default on delinquent loans. *Financial Management* 18(4): 55–63.

Piskorski T, Seru A, and Vig V (2008) Securitization and distressed loan renegotiation: Evidence from the subprime mortgage crisis. *Chicago Booth School of Business Research Paper No. 09-02*.

Posner EA and Zingales L (2009) The housing crisis and bankruptcy reform: The prepackaged Chapter 13 approach. *Chicago Booth School of Business Research Paper No. 09-11*.

Housing Careers

M Abramsson, University of Linköping, Linköping, Sweden

© 2012 Elsevier Ltd. All rights reserved.

Glossary

Housing career Series of dwellings occupied by a household during the life course.
Housing pathways Patterns of interaction concerning house and home, over time and space.
Housing trajectories Long-term housing patterns of individuals or households.
Life course Sequence of socially defined events and roles that the individual passes through over time.
Life cycle Series of predetermined stages that households pass through during life.

Introduction

Housing career is a frequently used term and can objectively be defined as the series of dwellings a household occupies during the course of life. Other terms used to describe a similar sequence are *housing trajectories* or *housing pathways*.

The term *housing career* is well established in housing research and depicts the moves conducted by an individual over time. The concept has been criticised for being insufficient and mainly focused on changes in tenure and location. However, it does imply more than only moves from one place to another or from one tenure to another. Nothing inherent in the concept excludes the use of it in a way that combines objective as well as subjective criteria. Thus, it could be argued that the fault is not in the concept but in its insufficient use.

The housing careers of individuals and households are dependent on housing policies in different countries. To a large extent, these influence the choices and constraints of individuals acting on the housing market. Different welfare state regimes explain the political constraints (and choices) encountered. A housing career cannot be seen as isolated from other careers in an individual's life course. This article discusses the importance of choices and constraints surrounding the housing career and parallel careers. These vary for different groups depending on factors such as experiences, education, or socioeconomic status. Resources, preferences, and possibilities are other terms used as tools to describe the way households act on the housing market.

Individuals often face the task of having to make major decisions related to the housing situation – to move or to stay in a current dwelling. This leads to a number of theoretical considerations regarding the possibilities individuals and households have in improving their housing conditions. This concept, housing career, is somewhat problematic, as in the word *career* as such is a connotation of progression. Also, it is related to the possibilities individuals have or the restrictions they face to move. Thus, the concept implies a matter of resources, which is related to a discussion on politics, division of resources, and institutional structures. Housing careers are also related to other life course events, changes to household size and composition, change of jobs, and so on.

Although many housing careers involve a progress in standard, quality, and desirability of housing, this is often also a normative public goal. Considering the changes to the welfare state as well as preferences of households the concept of housing career can be viewed in a broader sense. Housing careers can be classified as upwards, downwards, and sideways moves in housing careers. The concept includes voluntary and forced decisions to stay or to move that differ between different age and socioeconomic cohorts.

Housing conditions improved considerably in all Western countries, in the prosperous years after 1945. In this period of economic growth, the means were available for the governments to improve housing conditions and the housing stock was enlarged and renewed. Subsidies were introduced in most Western countries to reduce the cost of housing for the households. This was part of the welfare policies introduced to various degrees. However, as the constant economic growth was cut off in the 1970s and despite subsequent recovery, the governments' willingness to spend money on housing was reduced, affecting the housing situation.

The balance between choice and constraints changes according to resources and restrictions. An individual's possibility to choose is determined by the stage in the life cycle, resources, and individual and institutional constraints encountered in the housing market. The terms *choice* and *constraint* reflect the change in housing consumption over time for various groups of households.

The aforementioned constitutes the background to housing careers and households with progressing, descending, and stagnating housing careers. During the life course, an individual progresses through various careers, the housing career being one. Others may be education, occupation, and family careers. To which extent an individual is successful in these careers depends on institutional and structural as well as local and individual conditions. Life course analysis and time geography are theoretical approaches that provide helpful tools in the study of housing careers. The approach in time geography is to allow the individual to interact with the environment. A housing career is not only the result of an individual choice but also the result of the interaction within and between different households as they cooperate or compete and the interaction between households and institutions and the structural factors at work.

Decisions, Choices, and Constraints as Explanators for Residential Mobility

An individual's decision to move and change place of residence depends on a variety of factors. One is the importance of an individual's goals, from low-order (physical) needs to higher-order (nonmaterial) intellectual needs and the relationship between behaviour and preferences. To the individual, some goals or preferences in life are more important than others are. When current conditions do not allow fulfilment of these goals, the individual tends to improve these conditions, the housing situation providing one example. The decision to move is thus rationally taken considering the preferences of the individual, perceived possibilities, resources, and constraints. Residential mobility can be seen from a life course perspective. The behaviour of an individual is determined by previous actions in that these provide the means and the capabilities for future actions.

For arriving at a decision to move, there needs to be a trigger. Several factors influence the decisions or possibilities for a household to move. These can be defined as preferences, opportunities, resources, and constraints. Lifestyle preferences are noneconomic motivations for migration and vary between different individuals. Opportunities are the options available to individuals, such as housing vacancies. Once the decision to move has been taken, different opportunities are searched for and they are in turn accepted or rejected. What is considered an opportunity depends on individual preferences, resources, and constraints. There is a distinction between perceived and real opportunities. Perceived opportunities are those taken into consideration by the individual. Real opportunities are all opportunities, although the individual may not recognise some because of social background and lack of experience or information. In the course of time, intervening opportunities can arise, as new opportunities, which may alter or delay the original plan, that is, alter the housing career. Resources are individual possibilities as determined by financial means and freedom to move. The latter is often restricted by other parallel careers, such as family formation. Constraints or restrictions are the counterparts of the opportunities and the resources. Restrictions limit access to some parts of the housing market for various households and in some cases make residential mobility impossible. They also help in forming attitudes and preferences. They can be exogenous as well as endogenous – the latter, for example, being a shortage of housing or an unfavourable economic development. Endogenous restrictions are a lack of individual resources, attachment to place, or an individual dislike for change.

Moves (in this case, a move from one dwelling to another) or nonmoves of individuals can be studied using a time geographic approach as the actions of each individual can be followed over time and in space. Time and space determine our activities such as workplace or recreation, and as such limit our possibilities to choose where to live. In a time geographic model, the possibilities of individuals to realise their projects (or goals) in a certain time space are described and analysed.

Hägerstrand describes three types of constraints governing our actions: capability, coupling, and authority constraints, which in some parts are similar to those mentioned earlier. Capability constraints are biological and physical restrictions that limit our possibilities to move in time and space. How far we can get in a daily time space path depends on our means of transport. Coupling constraints are the meetings required for certain activities to take place, as individuals need to join time space paths. Authority constraints limit accessibility, as some places are accessible only at certain times. Rules and legislation also limit the freedom of movement. These restrictions are derived from the more basic type of restrictions characterised by the term *indivisibility*. The most important in a study on housing careers perhaps is the indivisibility of the human being (and many other entities); the fact that movements between points in space consumes time and the fact that every situation is inevitably rooted in past situations, previous experiences determine our current and future actions.

The life cycle model showed how residential mobility occurs as families move as their needs change. Later research has emphasised a relationship between the various stages of the life cycle and moves. However, residential mobility cannot be limited only to events in the life cycle. In the life-course concept, the way individuals move through different stages and positions in various careers during the course of life is taken into account. It can be used not only to describe but also to analyse housing careers, thus including experiences such as education, work, family, housing, and social skills. It allows for structural changes in society, that is, changes in the supply of housing as well as social and economic conditions affecting the housing market and the mobility of households and individuals on this market. Trajectories and parts of these, transitions, such as marriage, divorce, and change of work are important themes in life course studies.

There are *subjective* views of the optimal housing conditions for individuals. Factors of importance vary for each individual or household. In addition to these subjective views, there are guidelines for how we shall be housed. This *institutional* aspect on housing is provided as national guidelines on living space per person and standard that can be considered acceptable in a modern society. The housing stock and thus the type of housing available on the housing market is mainly an effect of current and previous housing policies. Our choice of housing is restricted, to a large extent, by the type of housing available in each tenure.

Housing Career

The term housing career is somewhat controversial as it is not an analytical concept but has an inherent meaning of what a housing career involves – a progression, or a change to something better. A progressing, or upward, housing career has typically been described as stepping up a ladder. The first step is usually the move from home to an inexpensive dwelling of one's own or shared with others. This is followed by further steps: as the standard gets higher, the living area becomes larger, and tenancy changes from rent to ownership. This usually goes hand in hand with a rising income and a larger family. In this case, the housing career follows the housing changes across the life cycle as described by Rossi. Moreover, its connection to life course changes is clear: towards the top of the ladder, the final goal is reached – owner-occupation and the detached single-family house. This type of dwelling – owner-occupation – is considered the most favourable for the individual as well as for society. A number of studies on housing preferences have clearly shown that the most preferred type of housing is the single-family, owner-occupied dwelling. As a result, this has been the focus of much of the research in this area. However, the concept of housing career describes all types of moves upwards, downwards, or sideways along a housing ladder.

Gober describes housing career as the way people change their housing as they progress through the life course. As a definition, housing career involves all changes to an individual's housing. As such, a housing career can be defined as a change to a larger and more modern dwelling as well as a move to a dwelling of one's preference, even if it is smaller and of a lower standard. Renovating a current dwelling would also involve making a housing career. If a housing area changes its status from a socially deprived area to a popular and upmarket area, would it mean that original inhabitants have made a housing career? In this case, the change of housing conditions is not related to life course changes.

To move from ownership to rent is an important change for the individual. Such moves take place following a separation, loss of a partner, financial problems, or in conjunction with long-distance moves. Older people can move from the maintenance of house and garden. If a migration decision is rational, a decision to move and change housing would always be a change for the better, that is, a downward housing career is not necessarily a change to poorer housing conditions. Rather, it is a change to conditions more suitable to the specific household. Another example are older households changing housing type as the children have left the parental home and their housing needs have altered.

With a change in household composition follows an increase in nonstandard housing careers. The number of one-person households has increased, as has the number of single parents. These groups of households might not be attracted by a single-family detached house. Many immigrants after a certain period of finding their way in a new country end up in the same categories of housing as the rest of the population: some groups seem to remain outside the owner-occupied sector in particular, despite the same income levels. In this case, the housing situation can be said to be a consequence of a choice made by the households. However, it is important to note that the housing situation may as well be an effect of discrimination or a lack of social contacts, in that some households are denied access to certain parts of the housing market.

Measuring Housing Career

In many countries, housing policy was more or less part of the general welfare policy. The material standard was pointed out first. The environment only later became important when the quality of the dwelling and the neighbourhood were discussed. Housing began to involve more than only the physical dwelling. Individuals born at different times have different housing experiences, a reflection of the changing values in society. Older individuals may view a dwelling in terms of standard and modernity, whereas younger individuals may view their dwelling as part of a lifestyle. This change of view reflects the difficulties in measuring housing career. There are quantitative and qualitative dimensions to the concept, and different methods are needed to tackle these dimensions.

All criteria on which the selection is based have to be important as well as representative of the housing market.

One criterion is the standard measured as modernity, number of rooms, and area of living. Crowdedness and the norms designed for measuring crowdedness are examples of standard issues that relate to housing policy. Following this characteristic, the area of living as well as the technical standard of a dwelling is of importance.

Tenure is another variable in measuring housing careers but the meaning of different tenures vary between countries. In some countries, housing policy has aimed at supporting and encouraging public housing as an alternative to the private rental market as well as private ownership. In others, ownership and private rental housing dominate, and public (or social) housing is aimed only at specific groups. To that extent, tenure can be used as a measurement, but may have different meanings in different countries.

A variable that has come to play a more important role in the choice of housing is the characteristics of a housing area. This field includes a number of components: the type of households living in the area (such as demographic, socioeconomic, and ethnic characteristics), the reputation of the area, service level, the layout of the area, and the way different tenures are mixed.

Housing Careers: A Framework

The attributes explaining variations in the housing careers of different households on the basis of the

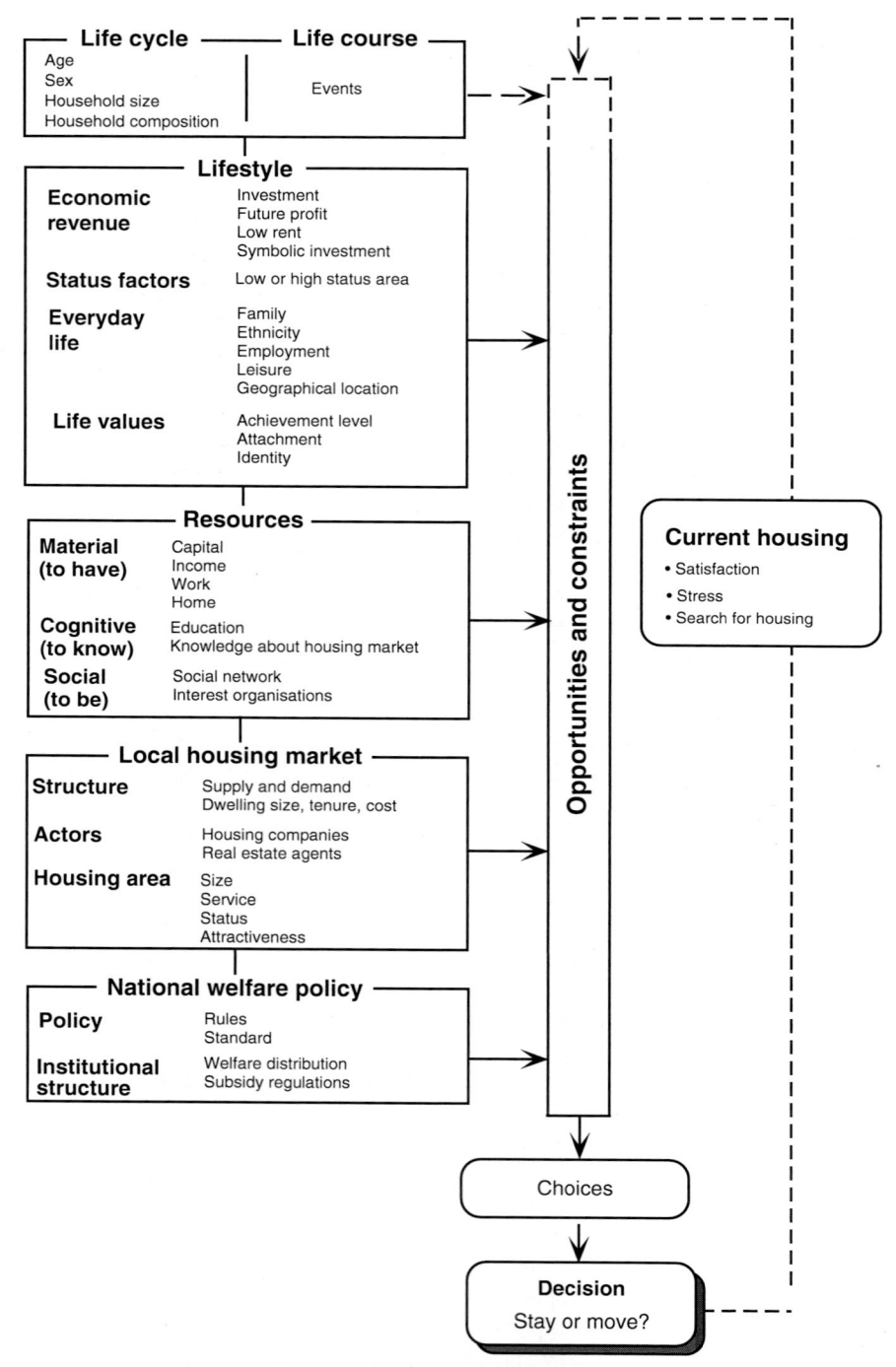

Figure 1 Housing careers. A figure explaining variables that interact depending on the relationship between choices and constraints.

aforementioned factors are presented in **Figure 1**. The explaining attributes are divided into five interactive groups. The importance of each depends on where in the course of life the individuals or households find themselves and their lifestyle preferences or resources. The local housing market and national welfare policies then provide different possibilities or inhibits certain actions.

The households are able to act on the housing market according to their degree of material (to have), cognitive (to know), or social (to be) resources. How they choose to act depends on their lifestyle preferences. Preferred housing can be seen not only as a suitable place to live but also as a good investment, perhaps while waiting for more suitable housing; as a symbolic investment as in second homes or that it provides housing at low cost. The preferred housing can be considered the correct place to live according to the status of the area, as a way to make a residential career. Family, ethnicity, employment, and leisure are important attributes as they influence our choice of housing to a large extent.

Without financial resources, a change of housing according to the household's preferences may prove impossible. Besides the individual preferences and resources, the institutional and structural factors as presented in **Figure 1**, has to be taken into consideration, as has the structure of the housing market, the relationship between supply and demand, housing policies, rules, standards, acting institutions, organisations, and agents. Other factors of importance are the neighbourhood as well as the attractiveness of a housing area.

The actual housing career, to stay or to move, then is a result of the relationship between choices and constraints, that is, to what extent the attributes limit or make different actions possible.

See also: Choice and Government Intervention in Housing Markets; Gentrification and Neighbourhood Change; House Biographies; Housing Market Search; Housing Preferences; Life Course; Place Attachment; Welfare States and Housing.

Further Reading

Bourne LS (1981) *The Geography of Housing*. New York: Winston.
Cadwallader M (1992) *Migration and Residential Mobility. Macro and Micro Approaches*. Wisconsin: The University of Wisconsin Press.
Clapham D (2002) Housing pathways: A post modern analytical framework. *Housing, Theory and Society* 19: 57–68.
Clark WAV and Dieleman FM (1996) *Households and Housing. Choice and Outcomes in the Housing Market*. New Brunswick, NJ: Center for Urban Policy Research, Rutgers University.
Desbarats J (1983) Spatial choice and constraints on behavior. *Annals of the Association of American Geographers* 73(3): 340–357.
Elder GHJ (1985) Perspectives on the life course. In: Elder GHJ (ed.) *Life course dynamics.* Trajectories and transitions, 1968–1980, pp. 23–49. Ithaca, NY: Cornell University Press.
Faulkner D (2007) The older population and changing housing careers: Implications for housing provision. Review article. *Australasian Journal of Ageing* 26(4): 152–156.
Gober P (1992) Urban housing demography. *Progress in Human Geography* 16(2): 171–189.
Hägerstrand T (1975) Space, time and human conditions. In: Karlqvist I, Lundqvist L, and Snickars F (eds.) *Dynamic Allocation of Urban Space*, pp. 3–14. Farnborough: Saxon House.
Kendig HL (1984) Housing careers, life cycle and residential mobility: Implications for the housing market. *Urban Studies* 21: 271–283.
Kreibich V and Petri A (1982) Locational behaviour of households in a constrained housing market. *Environment and Planning A* 14: 1195–1210.
Michelson W (1977) *Environmental Choice, Human Behavior, and Residential Satisfaction*. New York: Oxford University Press.
Pickles AR and Davies RB (1991) The empirical analysis of housing careers: A review and a general statistical modelling framework. *Environment and Planning A* 23: 465–484.
Rossi PH (1955) Why families move. A study in the social psychology of urban residential mobility. Glencoe, IL: The Free Press.
Saunders P (1990) *A Nation of Homeowners*. London: Unwin Hyman Ltd.
Wolpert J (1965) Behavioral aspects of the decision to migrate. *Papers of the Regional Science Association* 15: 159–169.

Housing Classes and Consumption Cleavages

SG Lowe, University of York, York, UK

© 2012 Elsevier Ltd. All rights reserved.

Glossary

Consumption sector The division between the public or the private form of the delivery of a service.
Collective consumption Services such as social housing, public transport, and education that are provided by the state. These services, however, can lose their nonmarket anchorage and become increasingly accessed commercially.
Urban system The arena in which collective consumption services are delivered and can match and even override the industrial workplace as a source of anticapitalist conflict.
Urban social movements The political mobilisation of social bases that are rooted in the politics of urban systems and stand outside formal party politics. They tend to be unhierarchical and incorporate cultural issues and stress the collective push towards change of some kind.
Housing class Groups of households that share a common form of occupancy of housing in local housing markets such as tenants of rooms in lodging houses, council house tenants, and outright owners of a property.

Introduction

The intellectual roots of the idea of consumption sectors, from which consumption cleavages and housing classes are derived, are to be found in the work of the great German sociologist Max Weber. Weber argued, against Marx, that social class was an important but not necessarily determining form of social stratification. Instead other crosscutting statuses and consumption opportunities could equally shape people's life chance and expectations. He suggested that status groups are 'stratified according to the principles of their consumption of goods'. This theme is taken up in a very diverse sociological literature and has become prominent in recent years in the work of scholars looking at modern mass consumption opportunities and also surfaces in the literature on postglobalisation welfare states in which 'social consumption' (social policy) is more closely integrated into supporting economic performance. Traditional sociological concepts such as alienation, social class, and the division of labour have been challenged in these literatures. In other words it is not one's position as a factory/office worker, manager, or owner that wholly determines social position but equally, and perhaps more so, it is the ability to engage in consumption, and the consumption process itself, that shapes social relations, social meaning, and according to one variant of this school impacts on voting behaviour.

The literature emphasises the division of a household's consumption of services into two forms of delivery: those accessed principally through the private sector and, on the other hand, households that are mostly state dependent (Dunleavy, 1980). Where households stand in relation to this essentially *vertical* public/private division of society, as opposed to the horizontal stratification of the traditional social classes, shapes political attitudes, life chances, and cultural identities, all the key social indicators of postmodern society. An influential strand of this debate, which connects to the idea of housing classes, is found in the work of the Spanish sociologist Manuel Castells and a number of other writers who were concerned particularly with the *urban* domain as the source of social conflict and what they initially referred to as 'secondary contradictions' created in modern urban life (as opposed to the primary contradiction created by the means of production) but which they eventually came to see as principal sources of social tension and by how modern society is stratified by new forms of social division.

The next section focuses on the debate about 'the urban' and how this links to consumption cleavages. The idea of housing classes needs to be read within this context. This concept, which is discussed in the final section, may be thought of as an illustration of microlevel consumption sectors. In this case they arise from households' socioeconomic position in local housing markets (Rex and Moore, 1967).

The Urban System

The main source of the idea that there are autonomous material interests outside the social class system and that there is a distinctive 'urban system' which is the 'location' of these crosscutting social bases is found in the work of

Castells. His ideas have evolved through a number of distinct phases including his current work on 'networked capitalism'. For this purpose it is necessary to trace out two of his earlier positions because these are the source of the idea of consumption cleavages (for more detail on this, see Lowe, 1986).

Castells' earliest perspective on urban systems derives from a debate in the 1960s among neo-Marxist intellectuals about the later writings of Marx, dealing with the question of whether the clash between capital and labour was sufficient on its own to create a social revolution. Althusser, for example, argued that although the economy is the primary determinant of the social system there is a matrix of 'secondary contradictions' caused by the interaction of economic, ideological, and political elements. These three factors he argued needed "...to fuse into a ruptural disunity" for a social revolution to be successful (Althusser, 1969: 116).

In *The Urban Question* Castells argued that it is within the urban system that new sources of contradiction arise mainly due to the necessity for the state to intervene to stabilise the economic and social system of modern capitalist nations (Castells, 1977). His thinking gradually abandoned the idea of the determining influence of economic structure in favour of defining 'the urban' as the key arena for the politicisation of society. Here is the place and context for the so-called reproduction of labour power – meaning, according to classical Marxism, replenishing the workforce and making it functional at the point of production, and incorporating consumption process. Schools, hospitals, transport services, leisure amenities, and housing are all part of the means of ensuring an available and compliant workforce. As capital became increasingly global in character, the urban system and the organisation of space became the locus of the consumption process and the reproduction of labour power. This definition is not necessarily congruent with the idea of the urban (as opposed to rural) in everyday parlance or which is found in the classic urbanism thesis of the Chicago School sociologists (Park et al., 1925; Wirth, 1928). The point of Castells' idea of 'the urban' is that it is the setting within which consumption processes are located, the provision of which is highly politicised.

Consumption Sectors

In a second layer of argument Castells observed that increasingly these consumption services were provided or planned by the state, so-called collective consumption, creating a new source of potential conflict.

> The contradiction it [monopoly capitalism] developed in the sector of collective goods and services leads to an intervention by the state which, far from regulating the process exacerbated contradictions and politicized issues. (Castells, 1978: 174)

The political repercussions of state intervention in the provision of public services stem largely from the fiscal crisis that large-scale spending programmes can potentially create. Disengagement from everyday consumption services is difficult without either increasing taxation or causing social unrest as consumers and public service workers protest against cuts. This is why Castells argued that the urban system is a highly politicised domain. Indeed new forms of political campaigning and direct action, so-called urban social movements, develop within this arena. One reason for this is that these issues create the potential for interclass alliances. In his book *City, Class and Power* Castells called for a popular unity front between 'the new petite bourgeoisie' and the workers' movement, giving a particularly prominent role to professional and salaried workers, creating what he called Citizens' Movement (Castells, 1978). From here Castells began his work to investigate the historical basis of 'urban contradictions', prefiguring his massive collection of case studies published in *The City and the Grassroots* (1983).

Castells' break with his earlier structuralist neo-Marxism therefore opened up the idea that there can be autonomous material interests unconnected in principle to social class. These crosscutting interests are based on public or private access to consumption provision. One of the main proponents of this idea in British social science was Patrick Dunleavy. Dunleavy argued that sectoral consumption cleavages were a consequence of the rapid post-Second World War expansion of consumption services and that, taken together, these services constituted a new 'urban system' very much in line with Castells' position. Dunleavy outlined a list of key urban services based on two fundamentals: first, whether the service was collectively or individually consumed ('mode') and, second, whether its provision was principally in the public or private sectors with access granted by market or nonmarket criteria. In this logic utility services such as gas supply or telephones were excluded from the urban system because they are marketed to individuals and are commercially funded. But a facility such as public housing was included because of its allocation to those in need on a nonmarket test of eligibility. In Britain the education system is also predominantly a state-provided service with a small private sector. Similarly in the health services there is a large state-funded national health system with a small – albeit growing – but influential private sector. Dunleavy argued that private education and private health provision, although both small, have a disproportionate impact in terms of their ideological and political influence on the overall service.

Dunleavy followed Castells in identifying housing and transport as the source of two major and powerful consumption cleavages in contrast to the largely state-dominated services, because they are principally provided in the private sector with smaller, residual public sectors. At the time Dunleavy was pursuing this argument, in the 1980s, home ownership had risen to over two-thirds of households. He pointed out that the large and expanding private sector in housing did not correspond to the social class system because more than 50% of manual workers were home owners, producing a consumption sector that cuts vertically through the manual worker social strata. In a later version of this work Dunleavy echoed the neo-Marxist roots of this argument by suggesting that new types of 'urban' intervention and the general increase in welfare state spending in market economies were a response to the crisis of overproduction/underconsumption (Baran and Sweezy, 1968). The switch towards socialised consumption during the twentieth century was one of the key methods of coping with underlying economic problems of modern capitalism, "...a widely available strategy for combating underconsumption tendencies". Dunleavy argued that many of these social/collective consumption services are compulsory such as the education of children between the age of 5 and 16, social services regulation over family life, and many aspects of the town planning system. Compulsory consumption provides a unique nonmarket link between state and society.

A second feature of this interpretation of socialised consumption in combating underconsumption results from the 'coerced exchange' character of many of these involvements (Mishan, 1967). In other words once people become dependent on a service or facility they may have to switch from an initial reliance on public provision to a marketed solution in order to avoid a deteriorating standard. For example, in order to retain flexibility in transport and to sustain mobility, car ownership, once an option available only to the very wealthy, gradually spreads down the income hierarchy.

> Large scale 'exiting' from one mode of consuming a product or from one sector to another may be a market choice as far as initial (high income) movers are concerned; but it becomes progressively a coerced exchange as the residual mode or sector shrinks to an uneconomic size... or becomes a low status, under-financed refuge of the disadvantaged, or simply becomes progressively more costly and less efficient. (Dunleavy, 1983: 25)

Dunleavy suggested that the social structure of societies is shifting in the wake of social consumption processes while economies become increasingly dependent on the compulsory production of new demands and the extension of unmet wants. Cuts in public spending can be thought of as shifts in exchange relationships. For example, the sale of council houses in the United Kingdom since the 1980 Housing Act should not be seen as a 'recommodification' (returning public assets to the private sector) but as a switch of resources from one subtype of socialised consumption to another; that is to say, according to his classification of consumption processes, from a purely 'collective consumption' category (where access is based on measured 'need') to a 'quasi-individualised consumption' (where services are privately supplied but marketed with a subsidy).

Dunleavy's development of Castells' ideas on collective consumption and the urban system prefigures a later debate about the nature of modern capitalism which points to significant shifts in the ways in which the state guarantees the economic and social conditions required for capital accumulation (see Burrows and Loader, 1994). Jessop, for example, argued that there have been fundamental changes in the way in which the world economy operates that have forced governments to reform their economic and social policies in order to maintain national economic competitiveness. "Opening of national economies makes it harder to pursue social policy in isolation from economic policy" (Jessop, 2000: 182). A variant of this thesis can be found in recent work on the idea of the 'competition state' by Cerny and Evans (2004). This line of argument leads us beyond the remit of this article but it is important not to lose sight of the bigger picture of debate in the wider social sciences about the impact of consumption processes on contemporary society.

In the narrower debate about consumption cleavages Saunders argued that it was relatively easy for most households to transition from public to private means of access to services as state subsidies were withdrawn. He particularly highlighted the growth of home ownership, which he argued provided an autonomous source of financial resources through growth in the value of housing equity (Saunders, 1981). The capital accumulation potential of owner-occupied housing created a major consumption sector cleavage based around housing. The ability of home owners to withdraw equity by remortgaging or trading down in the market gave housing a particularly resonant place in debates that developed in the 1980s and 1990s about life chances, living standards, and, crucially, the development of the wider welfare state. Following ideas outlined by Kemeny (1981), Lowe argued that home-owning societies tended to have residual welfare states and that one reason for this was the ability of home owners to utilise housing assets to provide for welfare and care needs. He cited the rapid expansion in the 1980s of private sector sheltered housing and residential care of the elderly in the United Kingdom as cases of this (Lowe, 1990). In a later argument Lowe suggested that welfare at all stages in the life course could be underpinned by these resources especially via the thousands of mortgage equity release products that became available following the deregulation of the banking system in the 1980s (Lowe, 2004). Although many of these have been withdrawn following the 'credit crunch' of 2008/09, the logic that housing equity can sponsor access to privately supplied services remains intact. The cyclical nature of the housing market and the potential for house prices to decline in real terms are a salutary warning against the withdrawal of public services in favour of privately sponsored welfare. Nevertheless, the consumption cleavage around public and private access to housing remains a key part of this wider debate echoing Castells' claim that the urban domain would be a major source of social and political conflict.

Housing Classes

One earlier classic statement of consumption-based political and social processes is found in the work of Rex and Moore who, writing in the mid-1960s, found evidence of housing classes in the inner city of Birmingham. This microlevel research revealed that distinct consumption interests could be identified through the operation of local housing markets. The urban social system, so they argued, is predicated by the socioeconomic forces that shape these markets.

> ...that the basic process underlying urban social interaction is competition for scarce and desired types of housing. In this process people are distinguished from one another by their strength in the housing market, or more generally in the system of housing allocation. (Rex and Moore, 1967: 274)

In other words these different groups comprised low-level consumption cleavages that divided the local community both socially and spatially, based on their occupancy of different types of housing tenure. In Sparkbrook, an inner-city neighbourhood of Birmingham, they distinguished seven main housing class affiliations:

1. Outright owners of large houses in desirable areas
2. Mortgagors who occupy whole houses in desirable areas
3. Council house tenants
4. Council house tenants in slum dwellings awaiting demolition
5. Tenants of whole houses owned by private landlords
6. Owners of houses bought on expensive short loans who let rooms
7. Tenants of rooms in lodging houses

Rex and Moore's famous study was subject to various criticisms; for example, that what they had discovered were not classes but status groups and that they depended to a large extent on the role of local authorities and building societies, both acting as gatekeepers in managing the allocation process (Haddon, 1970; Saunders, 1979). Lowe argued that one overlooked part of the debate on this research was the key question of whether members of these different 'classes' would subjectively recognise their connections and be able and willing to mobilise to defend or advance this interest (Lowe, 1986). According to Castells a test of the salience of a consumption process was precisely the extent to which it became politicised. Two factors seemed to be at work here. First, one of Rex and Moore's key findings was that there was a system of status grading in which people would aspire to move up the housing class ladder. Second, because Sparkbrook was a neighbourhood with a large immigrant population, that housing classes were overlaid by other associational interests which migrants formed as a means "...to partial, temporary, pluralistic integration" (Rex and Moore, 1967: 172). The incipient housing class structure of the area is thus dissipated and mediated by local churches, mosques, political parties, tenants' associations, drinking clubs, ethnic cultural associations, and local residents' groupings, all of which provide alternative means of expression of political sentiment and in which the values of immigrant communities were externalised. In later work Rex extended this argument by suggesting that it was within these groups that housing classes could be seen to become 'classes-in-themselves'. In addition the social functions provided by these voluntary associations created the framework for 'colony structures' (Rex, 1973).

The extension of this argument is that these 'classes' are subject to a variety of alternative sources of consciousness that overlie implicit housing market interests and, as a result, there may be no clear-cut awareness of belonging to a particular housing class. Not only is there an absence of collective consciousness but there appears to be no readily available organisational structure through which such an objective interest can become fulfilled, an active 'class-for-itself'. Thus although it is possible to identify microlevel consumption cleavages such as housing classes and a variety of other possible consumption interests, their mobilisation is suppressed by a range of crosscutting associational groups. This finding echoes the many community studies (of working-class neighbourhoods) conducted by sociologists in the 1950s and 1960s, in which some organisations came to have an expressed political base, such as council house tenants' associations, but whose activity was sporadic and poorly organised in conventional terms. Although tenants' associations were a conscious expression of a consumption interest – public housing – their associational role (providing social activities, pastoral care, and bargaining with landlords) mitigated their impact as a politically conscious force, just as Rex argued in the case of his housing classes in Sparkbrook. For these reasons the most common outcome of the activity of these nascent social movements was their co-option or dissipation into wider social and cultural settings (Lowe, 1986).

Conclusion

The debate over consumption cleavages has a very long-standing provenance that is sourced in the work of the great German thinker and scholar Max Weber. In the modern period a major debate opened up in the 1960s and 1970s concerning the thoughts expressed in the later writings of Marx on the conditions in which a social revolution might occur. Leading European philosophers and sociologists such as Althusser, Poulantzas, and Castells all contributed to this discussion. Castells in particular explored a number of ideas in his work on the 'urban system'. It is here that notions of consumption, especially 'collective consumption', are discussed, leading to later work that debated and defined in more detail consumption cleavages. Dunleavy and Saunders were particularly prominent in the United Kingdom. British scholars were receptive to this sort of thinking because at the time the country was maturing as a home-owning society (having historically been dominated by landlords) and a major consumption sector had opened up between owner occupiers and council house tenants. In recent years a considerable research effort has shown the extent to which home owners have been able to access and use housing equity as a result of the deregulation of the banking system (Smith, 2008). The existence of financial resources of huge magnitude has impacted on how people think about their housing (as an asset) and their ability to convert this resource into other goods and services (e.g., to sponsor children into private education). Although beyond the scope of this article it is clear that the consumption cleavages around housing, health, and education continue to be controversial and much debated in the literature.

Although a somewhat ageing contribution, the idea of 'housing classes' is still resonant in the housing studies literature and the wider social sciences. Rex and Moore's classic research showed then as now that local housing markets generate their own subdivisions and social interests. In the wider debate about consumption processes their work showed the existence of microlevel cleavages generated by housing market processes. It is an area of scholarship and practical policy that is ripe for reinvestigation because the forces that shape and determine housing markets continue to be rather poorly understood.

See also: Asset-Based Welfare; Gentrification and Neighbourhood Change; Housing Equity Withdrawal in the United Kingdom; Housing Wealth and Consumption; Housing Wealth Over the Life Course; Resident and Neighbourhood Movements; Residential Segregation: Experiences of African Americans; Residential Segregation: Race and Ethnicity; Social Class and Housing; Social Movements and Housing.

References

Haddon R (1970) A Minority in a Welfare State Society. *New Atlantis 2*.
Jessop B (2000) From the KWNS to the SWPR. In: Lewis G, Gerwirtz S, and Clarke J (eds.) *Rethinking Social Policy*. London: Sage Publications.
Rex J and Moore R (1967) *Race, Community and Conflict*. London: Oxford University Press.
Saunders P (1979) *Urban Politics: A Sociological Approach*. London: Hutchinson.
Saunders P (1981) *Social Theory and the Urban Question*. London: Hutchinson.

Further Reading

City, Class and Power (1978) is Castells' shortest and most accessible book. During this phase of his output he explains in some detail his idea on 'the urban' and the role of urban social movements. *Urban Political Analysis* (1980) is a classic work by Dunleavy, a leading British political scientist, which discusses the theme of urban politics including a detailed analysis of the role of consumption cleavages. In *Housing Policy Analysis* (2004), Lowe explored the consequences of the United Kingdom becoming a home-owning society and the crosscutting division of the country by housing tenure. He suggested a powerful case for the impact on living standards and on access to welfare provision of the division between more or less state-dependent tenants and home owners who in general have a much wider range of choices, an argument redolent of the original ideas on 'the urban domain' outlined by Castells.

Althusser L (1969) *For Marx*. London: Allen Lane.
Baran P and Sweezy P (1968) *Monopoly Capital*. Harmondsworth: Penguin.
Burrows R and Loader B (1994) *Towards a Post-Fordist Welfare State?* London: Routledge.
Castells M (1977) *The Urban Question*. London: Edward Arnold.
Castells (1978) *City, Class and Power*. Houndmills: Macmillan.
Cerny P and Evans M (2004) Globalisation and public policy under New Labour. *Policy Studies* 25: 51–65.
Dunleavy P (1980) *Urban Political Analysis*. Houndmils: Macmillan.
Dunleavy P (1983) *Socialized Consumption and Economic Development*. Anglo-Dutch seminar on Local State Research: University of Copenhagen.
Kemeny J (1981) *The Myth of Home Ownership*. London: Routledge and Kegan Paul.
Lowe S (1986) *Urban Social Movements: The City after Castells*. Houndmills: Macmillan.
Lowe S (1990) Capital accumulation in home ownership and family welfare. In: Manning N and Ungerson C (eds.) *Social Policy Review. 1989–90*. Harlow: Longman.
Lowe S (2004) *Housing Policy Analysis: British Housing in Cultural and Comparative Context*. Basingstoke: Palgrave/Macmillan.
Mishan EJ (1967) *The Cost of Economic Growth*. Harmondsworth: Penguin.
Park RE, Burgess EW, and McKenzie RD (1925) *The City*. Chicago: Chicago University Press.
Rex J (1973) *Race, Colonialism and the City*. London: Routledge and Kegan Paul.
Smith S (2008) *Banking on Housing: Spending the Home: Full Research Report*. ESRC End of Award Report, RES-154-25-0012. Swindon: ESRC.
Wirth L (1928) Urbanism as a way of life. *American Journal of Sociology* 44: 1–24.

Housing Construction Industry, Competition and Regulation

D Hayward, RMIT University, Melbourne, VIC, Australia

© 2012 Elsevier Ltd. All rights reserved.

Glossary

Innovation It involves the development and adoption of new techniques or activities that represent an improvement on what went before. Innovation may involve individual tasks undertaken by one or more people (the use of inputs). Alternatively, it may involve the product or service that is produced (the output). Innovation may be a one-off event or it might involve continuous improvement.

Productivity It is measured by the quantity of outputs from any given level of inputs, assuming a constant level of quality. Increasing productivity leads to higher rates of production or to improved quality. We can measure productivity by considering units produced per unit of labour (labour productivity) or units produced relative to all factors of production (multi-factor and total factor productivity). Broadly speaking, productivity change can occur through improvements in the organisation of production, the adoption of new techniques or tools in production, or as a result of more efficient use of existing plant and equipment such as increased use of existing capacity. High levels of research and development typically characterise industries with high rates of productivity improvement.

Regulation They are formal and informal rules that specify the standards (measured by certificates of competency or effectiveness) required of a particular activity or product. Formal rules are codified in laws that can be enforced by government. Informal rules are those developed by industry and professional associations. While regulatory frameworks vary in their complexity, they are essential to all modern forms of housing construction.

Introduction

Housing construction plays an important role in national economies, accounting for between 3 and 7% of gross national product. It is a sector of the economy that has long been criticised for its lack of ongoing innovation and productivity improvement, in turn acting as a drag on the overall economic growth. These criticisms are not restricted to one or two countries, but are widespread across the developed world. There are two broad explanations for these problems. One focuses on excessive or ill-considered government regulation or intervention, which can prevent competitive markets from being a spur for innovation, heightened productivity, and high levels of consumer satisfaction. An alternative explanation is that the problems stem from the way housing construction, distribution, and use are organised rather than the regulatory framework within which they take place.

These two explanations are not necessarily competing positions. Housing construction consists of a broad set of relationships within it (e.g., between house builders and between builders and building workers) as well as outside of it (e.g., between house builders, financiers, land developers, and the ultimate consumers). It is in the context of these broader sets of relationships that government regulations must be understood, for they not only help shape these relationships but also influence the strategies and tactics of the agents as they try to secure their goals.

This article explores how and to what extent regulation affects innovation and productivity in housing construction. The focus is on Australia and Britain and to a lesser extent on the United States. Although high-density residential construction and apartment building dominate residential construction in some countries and cities (e.g., Hong Kong and Singapore, this article concentrates on low-density housing and multi-unit (condominium)) construction. The article is divided into five sections. 'Innovation and Productivity in Housing Construction: The Evidence' discusses the evidence relating to housing construction productivity and innovation. 'How Regulations Can Affect Competition in and Outcomes from Housing Construction' identifies the key points of actual or potential government regulation that can affect housing construction. 'Competition, Regulation, Productivity, and Innovation in Housing Construction' examines the nature and type of regulations that affect housing construction and explains how they can affect productivity and innovation, while 'An Alternative Explanation' looks to nonregulatory explanations for relatively low productivity and innovation.

Innovation and Productivity in Housing Construction: The Evidence

Official data on productivity and innovation within housing construction are limited in their availability. There are no commonly agreed international data, and there is significant variation in the quality of the data that are gathered. The focus of most of the data is productivity rather than innovation, with the latter being notoriously difficult to measure.

Moreover, cross-country comparisons are made difficult by the adoption of widely different production methods, techniques, and use of building materials. These are affected by wage rates, availability of building materials, and weather conditions. The demands of building in European countries that experience harsh winters are vastly different to those of a country such as Australia where winters are typically mild. These differences are not just limited to days lost due to poor weather; they also extend to the robustness of materials and construction methods that are used.

With these limitations in mind, the productivity data that are available paint a similar picture for a broad range of countries including Canada, Australia, the United Kingdom, Denmark, France, and the United States. As **Figure 1** shows, over the past 30 years, the annual output has shown two distinctive patterns. Over the longer term, there is a longer-term boom–bust pattern of output, with a severe fall occurring in the early to mid-1990s following the boom of the previous decade. This is then followed by a 15-year trend of rising output, followed by the severe recession of the late 2000s, which saw a collapse in housing output in all countries except for recession-free Australia. Within this longer-term pattern are shorter periods of annual variation, which is especially noticeable in Australia. This can involve substantial increases and decreases of up to 30% per annum. The most recent downturn saw housing output in Denmark and the United Kingdom more than halve in the 3 years to 2009. It should be borne in mind that these data do not show output relative to inputs, and therefore should not be interpreted as necessarily being a measure of productivity gain and decline. The volatility of housing construction appears to be an entrenched feature of most developed economies, a point to which we shall return presently.

One way of measuring productivity is to compare specific tasks undertaken in housing construction with a similar task undertaken in other construction sectors. There is evidence that productivity rates in housing construction for specific tasks are higher than similar tasks undertaken for the commercial building sector. For example, research in Australia has found that the costs of completing the same tasks such as installation of windows and construction of plasterboard and carpentry walls were up to 25% lower in residential construction. The Australian Royal Commission into the Construction Industry suggested that much of the explanation for this productivity gap could be due to high levels of unionisation on commercial construction relative to domestic house building, which is relatively union-free, and dominated by independent subcontractors.

This static measure of productivity is considered by economists to be less important than productivity trends over time. These longer-term measures of productivity improvements in residential construction – particularly in low-rise accommodation – have been relatively slow, and those that have occurred have tended to stem from developments outside of the industry rather than within it.

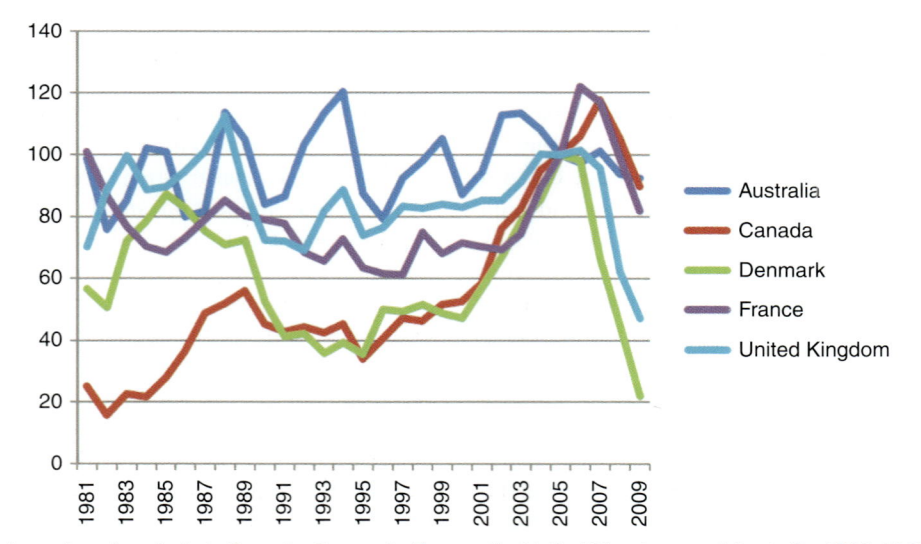

Figure 1 Index of new housing starts in Canada, Denmark, France, the United Kingdom, and Australia, 1981–2009 (2005 = 100). Source: Data from OECD statistics database (oecd.org), accessed on 8 December 2010.

Examples here include the invention and widespread adoption during the mid to late twentieth century of increasingly portable power tools including saws, nail guns, digging machinery, and so on. There has been little overall, long-term take-up of off-site prefabrication, and despite the volume of dwellings built each year, mass production techniques have yet to be widely adopted. Similarly, innovation within housing construction has been slow, with most of the change coming from appliances, environmentally sustainable materials, and designs rather than the construction process itself.

In the 1960s, 1970s, and 1980s, a number of Scandinavian countries attempted to redress this situation through large-scale social housing projects, with government subsidies being used to encourage firms to experiment with large-scale industrialised production techniques. These experiments proved costly and were abandoned in the 1990s.

How Regulations Can Affect Competition in and Outcomes from Housing Construction

Market-based economies are premised on the idea that the best resource allocation decisions are made when the provision of goods and services is determined by actors competing with one another to supply commodities to consumers. Markets are said to exist whenever one or more provider supplies one or more consumers with a given good or service at an agreed price. Over the past 30 years, the goal of public policy has been to develop markets in places where they previously were not present, and to increase competition within markets in places where they already exist. Advocates claim that competition leads to innovation and productivity improvement, because suppliers compete with one another to lower unit costs, increase market share, develop new products that will give them a competitive edge, and increase consumer choice (see article Choice and Government Intervention in Housing Markets).

Housing is a difficult area for policy makers who are keen to move toward a low level of regulation (see article Regulation Theory). It is a complex area that has developed in response to forms of market failure that require government intervention. Most consumers do not have the technical skills to be able to tell how well a dwelling has been constructed, or whether over time it remains in good order. Also, it is difficult for consumers to secure information about the standard of work by a builder or one or more of their workers. The United States is one of the few countries to have a national Internet-based system enabling consumers to rate the quality of building work. There is, nevertheless, an all too often asymmetry of information between purchasers and sellers, and this cannot easily be resolved through relying on industry codes of conduct or self-regulation. There is a moral hazard in doing so, with financial incentives encouraging privatised entities to behave in ways that would be contrary to the interests of consumers. This has been demonstrated by various attempts to privatise aspects of the housing regulatory regime, including insurance schemes on new housing where industry representatives have been reluctant to find in favour of the consumer and building inspections where builders have an incentive to hire 'light-touch' inspectors.

Government regulations can affect levels of competition, innovation, and productivity in housing construction in a number of direct and indirect ways. Direct regulations include those affecting building standards, including site location, construction techniques, materials, and employee entitlements, qualifications, and working conditions, while indirect regulations are those that affect related industries such as regulations relating to mortgage products. A flowchart illustrating the Australian Federal and State Government regulatory framework from a consumer's perspective is shown in **Figure 2**. Broadly speaking, a similar framework exists in all Anglo-American countries, with the main variation being the level of government that is responsible for the regulations, the organisation that is responsible for implementing and enforcing the regulations (in some countries some parts are privatised whereas in others they are not), and the degree to which the regulatory regime is light touch in its design.

Indirect regulations can often have significant effect on housing construction as the direct ones. For example, regulations governing housing finance can have a major effect on the ability of consumers to secure funding for house purchases. It was the liberalisation of regulations governing housing finance in the United States and Britain (especially during the 1990s and 2000s) that is said to have been responsible not only for a prolonged building boom in those countries, shown in **Figure 1**, but also the subsequent dramatic slump that ensued when the financial bubble burst (with the notable exception of Australia).

Each set of regulations must be considered in their broader regulatory context, for changes in one set of regulations may produce the opposite effect to what was intended. For example, during the 1990s, South Eastern Europe introduced a range of regulatory reforms designed to improve the availability of housing finance, which were not accompanied by measures designed to increase the supply of housing. The result was a bout of house price inflation and little new building.

Relatedly, regulatory frameworks are rarely integrated and complete. Important gaps may exist and these in turn can put pressure on other parts of the regulatory system. For example, imperfect, absent, or incomplete home building warranty insurance can lead to significant

398 Housing Construction Industry, Competition and Regulation

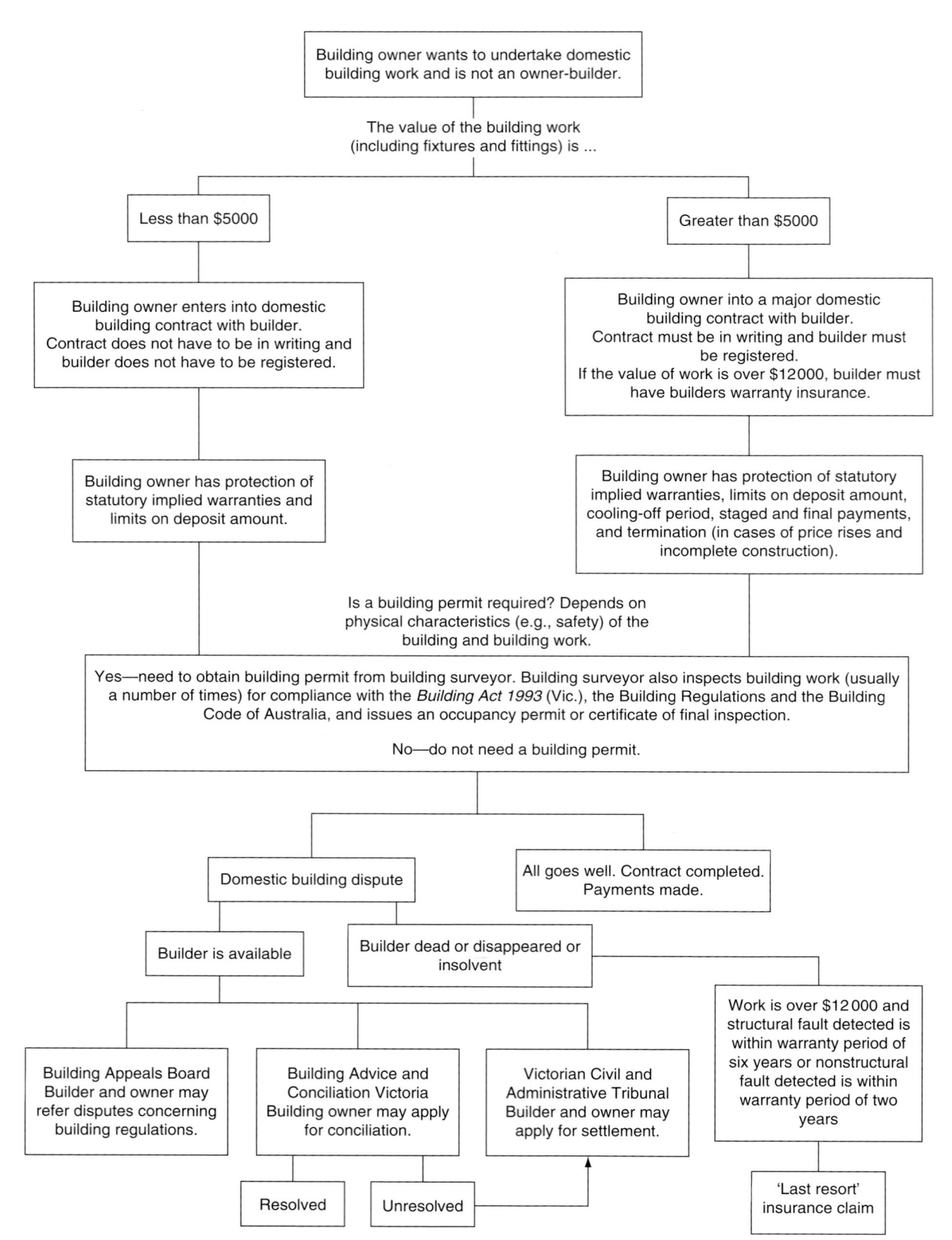

```
                 Building owner wants to undertake domestic
                      building work and is not an owner-builder.

                         The value of the building work
                      (including fixtures and fittings) is ...

         ┌───────────────────────────────────────────────────┐
  Less than $5000                                      Greater than $5000

  Building owner enters into domestic           Building owner into a major domestic
  building contract with builder.               building contract with builder.
  Contract does not have to be in writing and   Contract must be in writing and builder must
  builder does not have to be registered.       be registered.
                                                If the value of work is over $12000, builder must
                                                have builders warranty insurance.

  Building owner has protection of              Building owner has protection of statutory
  statutory implied warranties and              implied warranties, limits on deposit amount,
  limits on deposit amount.                     cooling-off period, staged and final payments,
                                                and termination (in cases of price rises and
                                                incomplete construction).

                  Is a building permit required? Depends on
                  physical characteristics (e.g., safety) of the
                               building and building work.

  Yes—need to obtain building permit from building surveyor. Building surveyor also inspects building work (usually
  a number of times) for compliance with the Building Act 1993 (Vic.), the Building Regulations and the Building
  Code of Australia, and issues an occupancy permit or certificate of final inspection.

                       No—do not need a building permit.

      Domestic building dispute            All goes well. Contract completed.
                                                    Payments made.

   Builder is available        Builder dead or disappeared or
                                          insolvent

                                                              Work is over $12 000 and
                                                              structural fault detected is
  Building Appeals Board    Building Advice and   Victorian Civil and   within warranty period of
  Builder and owner may     Conciliation Victoria Administrative Tribunal six years or nonstructural
  refer disputes concerning Building owner may apply Builder and owner may   fault detected is within
  building regulations.     for conciliation.    apply for settlement.   warranty period of two
                                                                                  years

                     Resolved      Unresolved                        'Last resort'
                                                                   insurance claim
```

Figure 2 Regulations and housing construction in Australia from a consumer's perspective.
Source: Victorian Competition and Efficiency Commission (2005) *Housing Regulation in Victoria. Building Better Outcomes*. Melbourne, VIC: VCEC.

consumer dissatisfaction, incomplete dwellings, or dwellings that are unfit for habitation. In Australia in the 1990s, for example, the privatised house building warranty insurance schemes collapsed, when the largest and rapidly growing private insurer went broke after underquoting on premiums to gain market share. This in turn led to home purchasers being unable to secure a mortgage because housing financiers required warranty insurance prior to authorising a loan on a new dwelling. Many builders went bankrupt as work dried up during this time, perhaps leading to the higher levels of building industry concentration referred to below. To this day, warranty insurance is still unavailable for multi-storey dwellings.

While it is often assumed that regulations can impede innovation and productivity growth, this is not always the case. Indeed, sometimes regulations drive innovation by, for example, requiring new standards in building design that adopt the latest environmental standards. Such standards may not become an industry norm without government regulations. Some of the most important innovations or attempts at innovations in recent decades have come from work undertaken for the social housing and public sector, who were early to embrace a sustainability agenda.

Furthermore, the costs of such regulatory involvement must be balanced against the potential benefits. Government regulations do not arise without reason, and most typically they are put in place to address important market failures. Occupational health and safety regulations, for example, may stifle innovation in building techniques, but they stem from the need to maintain acceptable standards of workplace safety. Their intent is to ensure that the time that might otherwise be lost as a result of workplace injuries is reduced, not to mention the social costs to individual workers, families, and friends that inevitably accompany serious injury, sometimes for a lifetime.

Similarly, regulations surrounding building standards and materials are often said to be a drag on innovation, for developers and builders (including owner builders) often say they are loath to try new designs or materials that may not secure planning approval or a building permit. The threat of substantial delays in completing the dwelling is said to be enough to discourage innovation. However, these regulations are in place to protect the interests of neighbouring households whose amenity and property value may be affected by the nature and quality of the building work next door. Also, strict building standards and home warranty insurance are intended to protect the interests of the immediate and importantly future consumers from substandard building work, including the possibility of death or injury in the case of seriously flawed work. As one recent detailed Australian study put it, "homebuyers have little understanding of the building process and its pitfalls, even though buying a home is the most important financial transaction most people make in their lives" (Percy Allen and Associates, 2002).

Table 1 Percentage of customers who are very satisfied or fairly satisfied with their house builder, United Kingdom, 2003

	2000	2001	2003
Overall satisfaction with quality of home	87	87	83
Overall satisfaction with quality of service	69	70	65
Would you recommend your house builder	52	49	46

Source: Housing Forum National Satisfaction Survey, 2003.

The other main reason for government regulation is that the different participants in the residential construction industry often have conflicting interests and would be unable to reach agreement on industry codes of practice and conduct. The Australian and British housebuilding industries, for example, have been tardy in promoting consumer interests, and both have tended to have relatively low levels of consumer satisfaction, particularly the United Kingdom (see **Table 1**).

In recent decades, there have been some high-profile cases where governments facing significant demographic and industry pressure have watered down, removed, or failed to improve important regulations governing builders and building codes, only to subsequently create a major policy problem. While the reforms led to important short-term 'innovations' in construction, they also produced serious longer-term social costs that were deemed to be unacceptably high. During the early 1990s in New Zealand and British Columbia (in Canada), governments modified building standards associated with multi-unit developments, and builders responded by using inappropriate and ultimately dangerous building techniques, prompting major government inquiries (in the case of Canada, a Royal Commission) and extensive remedial action. Both cases left in their wake a repair bill worth up to NZ$1.8 billion in New Zealand and up to C$3 billion in British Columbia. It is estimated that the cost of fixing the problem significantly exceeded the cost of doing the job properly in the first place, by as much as 280%.

The regulatory framework may be the responsibility of one tier of government. But often it is split between different tiers. In unitary systems of government such as that which exists in the United Kingdom, the regulatory regime is shared between national and local governments. In federal systems such as that which exists in the United States and Australia, state and local governments play the key roles. The more important is the role of subnational tiers of government in developing and enforcing regulatory standards, the more likely it is that significant variations will occur within nations, which adds to the complexity of the regulatory systems. This can unnecessarily inflate the compliance costs of builders undertaking work on anything other than a local basis. In Australia, the degree of variation can be significant, embracing everything from home warranty insurance, the wording of building contracts, qualifications needed to be registered as a builder, planning schemes, the issuance and enforcement of building permits, and planning schemes. It is partly in response to this that the Federal government has taken on an increasingly prominent role in setting national building standards, and to state governments becoming increasingly important players in setting and enforcing planning standards with the full support of peak industry bodies. The complexity of Australia's regulatory regime is illustrated in **Figure 3**, which shows the type of regulation in place by state and territory.

It is also the case that even the best regulatory regime needs to be enforced and monitored to be fully effective. Again using the case of Australia, during the 1990s, most states applied competition policy to the issuance of building permits, enabling private certifiers to compete with local government for work from builders. The private surveyors were paid by the builder to issue a certificate and then also undertook compliance checks, again on a fee-for-service basis. A number of these private certifiers were found to have strong links with major firms, raising questions about the veracity of their work. The privatised system effectively created a 'moral hazard' in which private certifiers could receive more income by guaranteeing to certify work no matter how poor the quality was, because their payment was made by the builder. The moral hazard can be compounded by 'loose' standards governing information vendors are

	NSW	Vic	Qld	SA	WA	Tas	ACT	NT
Builders must warrant their work	Yes	Yes	Yes	Yes	Yes	Yes	Yes	No
Builders must enter into formal building contracts in addition to warranting their work	Yes	Yes	Yes	Yes	Yes	No	No	No
Building contracts must be worded in 'Plain English'	No	No	Yes	Yes	No	No	Not applicable	Not applicable
Builders warranty insurance covered by legislation	Yes, Home Building Act 1989	Yes, Building Act 1993 and Domestic Contracts Act 1995	Yes, Building Services Authority Act 1991	Yes, Building Contracts Act 1995	Yes, Home Building Contracts Act 1991	Yes, Housing Indemnity Act 1992 Building Act 2000 still to be proclaimed	Yes, Building Act 1972	Yes, Building Act 1993
Private insurers permitted	Yes	Yes	No	Yes	Yes	Yes	Yes	Yes
Private insurers must be approved by government in addition to APRA	Yes	No	Not applicable, only BSA permitted	No	Yes	No	Yes	No
Government fully or partly guarantees or underwrites insurance	Yes, but only for BSC and HIH claims, claims in excess of $10 million for a single builder and insurance for high-rise units	Yes, but only for HGF and HIH claims, and claims in excess of $10 million for a single builder	No, Formal guarantees or re-insurance by Government	Yes, but only for HIH claims and claims in excess of $10 million for a single builder	Yes, but only for HIH claims and claims in excess of $10 million for a single builder	Yes, but only for HIH claims	Yes, but only for HIH claims	Yes, in respect to TIO
Current insurance providers ranked by share of market	Dexta, HIAIS, and Reward	Dexta, HIAIS and Reward	BSA	HIAIS	HIAIS and Reward	HIAIS and Reward	HIAIS	TIO
Insurers must submit regular statistical reports to government	Yes, but not provided in a standard format	No	Yes, but only through annual report of BSA	No	No	No	Yes, but do not comply	No
Professional builders must have insurance before commencing building work	Yes, (Checked by local council)	Yes, except for spec homes	Yes	Yes	Yes, (checked by local council)	Yes	Yes, Except for spec homes	Yes
Agency for administering insurance legislation	Fair Trading	Infrastructure	Housing	Consumer and Business Affairs	Builders' Registration Board	Consumer Affairs and Fair Trading	Planning and Land Mgt	Infrastructure, Planning and Environment
Private certifiers permitted to approve buildings	Yes	Yes	Yes	Yes	No, Certification done by local councils	Yes	Yes	Yes
Government audits private certifiers	No	Yes	Yes	No	Not applicable	No	Yes	Yes

Figure 3 Housing regulations by State, Australia. Spec, speculative.

required to disclose to prospective buyers. In some countries, such as the United Kingdom, information packs disclosing details on warranty insurance claims, condition report, and so on must be provided to those seeking to buy (see article Education Programmes for Home Buyers and Tenants).

Competition, Regulation, Productivity, and Innovation in Housing Construction

Regulations can have a significant impact on the nature and extent of competition, which in turn can affect levels of innovation and productivity. This is one reason why there has been a trend in developed economies toward deregulation and the embrace of competition policies over the past two decades. In this spirit, most developed countries have reviewed or tried to simplify the regulatory framework covering housing construction, whether this be through a shift to outcome-based building and planning codes, or moves to simplify approval processes.

However, it is not clear that this policy thrust has had the desired effect. Some countries that have been pursuing active competition policies (Australia and Britain) subsequently experienced worsening or at best stable house building concentration ratios, while in others there remains considerable regional variation. The British and Australian housing construction industries, for example, have become increasingly concentrated in recent decades. Within Australia, there is marked regional variation in concentration ratios. Western Australia's housing industry is highly concentrated as is the industry in South Australia. The larger states of New South Wales and Victoria, on the other hand, are much less concentrated (**Tables 2–4**).

Importantly, while there is evidence of increased industry concentration in countries like the United Kingdom and Australia, it is also true that by comparison with other industry sectors, the housing construction industry is, nevertheless, competitive. Barriers to entry into the industry are relatively low, with labour laws enabling high rates of labour subcontracting. This allows new building firms to form with very low overheads. Australia is a good, if not extreme example. Most industries – from airlines, banking, retailing, and communications – are dominated by two to three companies, whereas in housing construction, the number of firms/companies in most states is much higher than this.

Table 3 Market shares in US house building

% of total housing units produced

Firm Rank	2002	2005	2006
Largest	2	2	3
Top 10	11	14	15
10–25	5	5	5
26–45	4	4	4
46–100	5	5	5
Top 100	24	28	29
101–400	8	7	7
Top 400	32	35	36

Source: Ball M (2008) *Firm Size and Competition: A Comparison of the House Building Industries in Australia, the United Kingdom and the USA.* London: RICS Research.

Table 4 Market shares in UK house building

% of total housing units produced

Firm Rank	2001	2002	2003	2004	2005
Largest	9	9	8	8	8
Top 4	29	29	29	28	27
Top 10	46	47	46	45	44
11–20	13	13	11	12	11
21–30	6	6	6	5	6
31–50	6	10	8	9	9
51–100	2	4	4	4	4
Top 100[a]	73	76	71	71	70

[a]2001 top 75, 2002 top 97, and 2003 top 95 only.
Source: Ball M (2008) *Firm Size and Competition: A Comparison of the House Building Industries in Australia, the United Kingdom and the USA.* London: RICS Research.

Table 2 Market shares in Australian house building, 1994/95–2005/06

% of total housing units produced

Firm Rank	1994–95	1995–96	1996–97	1997–98	1998–99	1999–2000	2000–01	2001–02	2002–03	2003–04	2004–05	2005–06
1–10	10	12	14	15	16	15	17	16	16	14	13	14
11–20	5	6	6	6	8	6	8	9	9	8	6	7
21–30	3	3	4	4	5	4	5	5	5	5	5	5
31–50	5	5	5	5	5	5	7	5	5	7	7	7
51–100	5	6	6	6	6	5	7	6	6	6	7	7
Top 100	28	31	35	36	40	35	44	41	41	40	38	40

Source: Ball M (2008) *Firm Size and Competition: A Comparison of the House Building Industries in Australia, the United Kingdom and the USA.* London: RICS Research.

This in turn raises one of the paradoxes of the housing construction industry: It has relatively high rates of competition by comparison with other industry sectors, yet as was shown earlier productivity, innovation, and also consumer satisfaction remain relatively low. If the regulatory framework is not the sole or even main cause of low longer-term productivity growth and innovation, what might be an alternative explanation?

An Alternative Explanation

Five factors have been identified as playing a major role.

The first factor is the degree to which house builders are able to generate profits from other aspects of the housing development process. Foremost here is land development, which in countries like Britain generates the largest return (although it brings with it higher risks). There house builders focus on the broader development gains to be had from converting raw land into finished allotments with dwellings on them, rather than productivity and innovation improvements in construction. The key factor here is the timing and location of land acquisitions rather than improved profitability derived from the construction of a dwelling.

A second factor is that relatively high rates of competition may paradoxically inhibit innovation, especially in the context of a volatile market. Builders may be inclined toward building designs and materials that appeal to a mass market, and will be reluctant to drive change and innovation for fear of striking financial difficulty, for example, during a market contraction. In Australia, new dwelling construction is undertaken on a contract basis, with builders constructing display homes on allotments assembled by a land developer. Consumers typically see what is on display and then order one of the predesigned dwellings to be built on their plot of land. House builders have a strong incentive to remain relatively conservative in their design, especially smaller firms that have capital tied up in the display homes that must eventually be sold, but are also crucial for the number of dwellings that are sold.

A third factor is that housing construction industries are not homogeneous, but instead vary across countries and over time. It is an unusual industry in that at its edge is an informal sector that includes owner builders and a self-build market that expands and contracts relatively quickly, and which operates often through informal agreements and methods of payment. At the other end of the spectrum are listed companies that operate nationally and which engage in reasonably sophisticated marketing campaigns. Much building work can be done on a cash-in-hand basis, using production techniques that professional builders would not employ but which can be financially feasible because of the informal nature of the work done. This is not possible in commercial construction or, for example, in manufacturing. Finally, multinational housing companies are rare as are examples of national companies successfully moving offshore. The technology transfers that often accompany such multinational corporate activity do not therefore occur via direct foreign investment in the way that they do in many other industries, especially manufacturing but also certain services.

A fourth factor is the nature of housing production, especially in countries where detached dwellings are the dominant form of accommodation. Production takes place at individual sites that may be spread over a considerable geographical scale, punctuated by significant spatial gaps and involving timing driven by individual patterns of demand. This is a very difficult context within which to further mechanise or modernise the production process.

This in turn raises a final and probably the most important single factor affecting innovation and productivity. This is the degree of industry volatility discussed in earlier sections. Faced with a volatile market, individual builders are understandably reluctant to invest in high levels of research and development, or to experiment with and undertake large-scale investment in new techniques and methods of production, for fear that an unexpected market decline may render them unprofitable. The risks are great and the returns potentially low. It makes far more sense to structure their businesses in ways that keep overheads low and off-loads risks to other players. Extensive subcontracting of building labour is one way of doing this, with subcontracting rates of pay, conditions of work, and quality of building labour effectively becoming the balancing mechanism to adjust output to market conditions.

Conclusion

This article has considered productivity and innovation in the housing construction industry. While there is some evidence of the industry being able to lift productivity rates rapidly, and while there is also evidence that higher rates of productivity may be evident in certain tasks relative to the construction industry as a whole, over the longer-term productivity growth and innovation have both been tardy.

Government regulations may have contributed to both of these sets of outcomes. However, they do not seem to be the major cause, and even if this were to be true, it is difficult to see how the major regulations could be watered down without seriously compromising health and safety standards or harming the interests of current and future consumers. While industry representatives frequently portray government regulations as the cause of most of the industry's problems, hard evidence to support this is difficult to come by. For example, a recent very detailed study in the state of Victoria, Australia, concluded that the costs of regulations added only 4% to the price of a dwelling.

The single most important paradox is that although there are significant variations in the degree of industry concentration within and between nations, housing construction, nevertheless, appears to be a relatively competitive industry by comparison with industries renowned for their productivity growth. A far more likely explanation is that the broader institutional context of housing construction acts as an impediment to these developments, with the single most important one being the relatively high degree of industry volatility and the capacity of builders to adjust their costs and output through the use of subcontracting.

See also: Building Regulations for Energy Conservation; Choice and Government Intervention in Housing Markets; Education Programmes for Home Buyers and Tenants; Housing Standards: Regulation; Housing Supply; Policy Instruments that Support Housing Supply: Supply-Side Subsidies; Regulation Theory.

Reference

Percy Allen and Associates (2002) *National Review of Home Builders Warranty Insurance and Consumer Protection*, p. 27. Sydney, NSW: Ministerial Council for Consumer Affairs.

Further Reading

Allen J, Barlow J, Leal J, Maloutas T, and Padovani L (2004) *Housing and Welfare in Southern Europe*. Oxford, UK: Blackwell.

Ball M (2003) Markets and the structure of the housebuilding industry: An international perspective. *Urban Studies* 40(5): 897–916.

Ball M (2006) *Market and Institutions in Real Estate and Construction*. Oxford, UK: Blackwell.

Barker K (2004) *Delivering stability: Securing our future housing needs. Final Report*. London: HM Treasury.

Barlow J and Duncan S (1994) *Success and Failure in Housing Provision: European Systems Compared*. Oxford, UK: Pergamon Press.

Barlow J and Ozaki R (2005) Building mass customised housing through innovation in the production system: Lessons from Japan. *Environment and Planning A* 37: 9–20.

Bosch G and Philips L (eds.) (2003) *Building Chaos: An International Comparison of Deregulation in the Construction Industry*. London: Routledge.

Buzzelli M (2001) Firm size structure in North American housebuilding: Persistent deconcentration, 1945–98. *Environment and Planning A* 33: 533–550.

Buzzelli M and Harris R (2006) Cities as the industrial districts of housebuilding. *International Journal of Urban and Regional Research* 30: 894–917.

Dowling R (2005) Residential building in Australia, 1993–2003. *Urban Policy and Research* 23(4): 447–464.

Overview Group on the Watertightness of Buildings (2002) *Report of the Overview Group on the Weathertightness of Buildings to the Building Industry Authority*. New Zealand: Building Industry Authority.

Parliamentary Library of New Zealand (2002) *Leaky Buildings, Background Note*. New Zealand: Parliamentary Library.

van der Heijden J (2009) International comparative analysis of building regulations: An analytical tool. *International Journal of Law in the Built Environment* 1(1): 9–25.

Wellings F (2006) *British Housebuilders: History and Analysis*. Oxford, UK: Blackwell.

Housing Demand

S Malpezzi, University of Wisconsin-Madison, Madison, WI, USA
SM Wachter, University of Pennsylvania, Philadelphia, PA, USA

Published by Elsevier Ltd.

Glossary

Consumption demand Demand for housing as living quarters, whether an owner or a renter.
Demand for housing The amount (space, quality, location) of housing that consumers desire. In market equilibrium, consumers reveal these preferences through their rental or purchase of a dwelling.
Elasticity Responsiveness of supply or demand to market conditions and budget constraints. Demand elasticities, considered here, summarise how consumers' demands change in response to changes in prices, incomes, household size, and so on.
Investment demand For a homeowner, additional demand for housing as an asset, above and beyond what is demanded for consumption.

Housing Demand

Understanding the demand for housing is central to solving many academic and practical problems. Housing is roughly half the national and global capital stock, and typically on the order of 20% of consumption and 30% of investment (Malpezzi and Mayo, 1987). Private market participants naturally want to understand demand patterns in order to better understand market conditions, pricing points on mortgages, and so on; the demand for housing undergirds no small part of the financial markets (and the recent financial crisis and 'Great Recession'). Housing demand undergirds the proper design of government interventions in housing and related markets (e.g., the design of housing subsidies). Assumptions about housing demand are often embedded in a wide range of economic models, for example, in several recent macroeconomic models that incorporate housing explicitly (Leung, 2004, and see article Housing and the Macroeconomy).

Economists define the income elasticity of demand for housing as the ratio between the percentage change in housing demanded and the percentage change in income:

$$\varepsilon_Y^D = \frac{dQ^D/Q^D}{dY/Y}$$

where ε represents elasticity, Q the quantity of housing services, and Y is income. The formulation is quite general, so we can refer to price elasticities of demand, elasticities of supply, and so on, by straightforward substitution of prices, quantities supplied, or for that matter other arguments such as demand elasticities with respect to population growth, interest rates, and so on.

An oft-used and natural empirical structure that yields constant elasticities is based on a regression of the logarithm of housing consumption against the logarithms of determinants (incomes, prices, demographic variables). The form was long in use before Hausman (1981) worked out an explicit utility function that yielded logarithmic demand functions. The other approach is to start with a plausible utility function, for example, Cobb–Douglas or Stone–Geary (displaced Cobb–Douglas) and then work out demand functions. These approaches are discussed in general in Deaton and Muellbauer (1980) and applications to housing are discussed in Mayo (1981) and Olsen (1987). One difficulty is that the quantity and price of housing are not usually directly observable, at least in microanalyses (household level). Housing economists use hedonic index techniques to decompose housing expenditures into prices and quantities using regression techniques (Green and Malpezzi, 2003).

Literally, hundreds of studies have been carried out examining the demand for housing. Early studies, such as those by Reid (1962) and Muth (1960), examined housing demand using aggregate data on how housing expenditures and incomes changed over time. These studies generally found income elasticities around 1.0. If the income elasticity is 1, then the fraction of income devoted to housing stays constant as income rises and falls.

In the 1970s, a large number of papers appeared based on household survey data, such as that from the Experimental Housing Allowance Programme, and later the American Housing Survey. Generally, these studies found lower income elasticities, and (to the extent that comparisons are possible) lower price elasticities, than the aggregate studies. **Figure 1** (from Green and Malpezzi (2003)) is a representative result; while in a simple

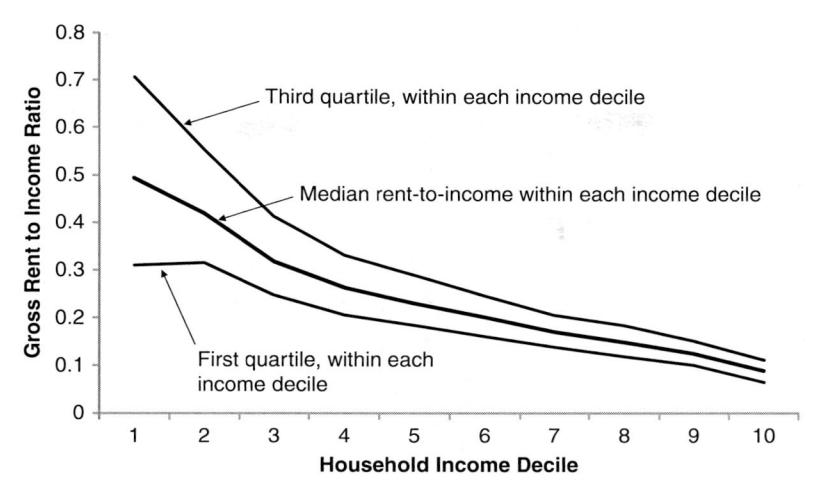

Figure 1 Housing expenditure: Rent-to-income ratio, by income decile, 1993 American housing survey.

tabulation, many multivariate econometric estimates turn out to be remarkably similar (Mayo, 1981). Of course, these cross-section regression-based studies are not without their own problems. From Muth onward, analysts have wrestled with the proper specification of income. Milton Friedman's permanent income hypothesis posits that current income can be decomposed into so-called permanent and transitory components. Further, households 'smooth' their consumption by making consumption decisions mainly on the permanent (or long-run) component. Positive transitory income is saved, and if current income is below permanent income, households borrow against or use savings.

Since permanent income is never directly observed, different papers adopted different proxies for it. Some studies rely on an instrumental variables approach; that is, using a regression model to predict or estimate permanent income based on age, job status, and other life-cycle variables. Other studies use total consumption for a proxy. Papers such as Ihlanfeldt (1981) Goodman (1995), and Goodman and Kawai (1985) analyse demand based on those who have recently moved, who would be presumed to be closer to equilibrium, with corrections for selectivity bias borrowed from the labour economics literature. Generally, when these corrections are made, the income and price elasticities of demand get larger in absolute value, often approaching 1.

Which elasticity is relevant depends upon the purpose. For example, demand estimates based on proxies for permanent income, and limited to recent movers closest by their true demand curve, may best reveal the true underlying elasticity. Often estimates from such models suggest unitary or greater elasticity. But such estimates may be of little direct use in explaining observed patterns of housing expenditure within the market, which clearly exhibit inelastic behaviour. The latter estimates may be more relevant when, for example, predicting housing budget shares for programmes where eligibility is, indeed, based on current (not permanent) income. And only a few papers, such as Follain (1979) and Rothenberg et al. (1991), examine the proposition that 'the' elasticity actually varies systematically in different segments of the market.

Housing demand can also vary across tenure types (owners and renters), notably because while renters' demand is presumably based solely on the desire to consume housing services (space, quality and facilities, neighbourhood and location), homeowners may also have a separable investment motive. Ioannides and Rosenthal (1994) provide a good representative of this strand of literature. Using data that include both owners and renters, some of whom own other properties, they are able to tease out separate estimates of consumption and investment demand by assuming that renters' principal residences reveal only consumption demand; homeowners' principal residences always reveal some consumption demand, and sometimes investment demand; and some of both tenures hold additional properties, which are assumed held largely for investment. Ionnides and Rosenthal find that generally investment demand elasticities with respect to income and wealth are higher than the corresponding income and wealth consumption elasticities. They find that consumption demand elasticities with respect to demographic variables like age, education, and household size are larger than the elasticities of these variables with respect to investment demand.

The studies discussed in the previous paragraphs mainly examine demand within a market. However, there is evidence that housing expenditures across markets increase at least as fast as income. Davis and Ortalo-Magné (2010) find the median rent-to-income ratio is surprisingly constant across US metropolitan areas, implying a cross-market elasticity of about 1; and we have already noted that many studies using time series data

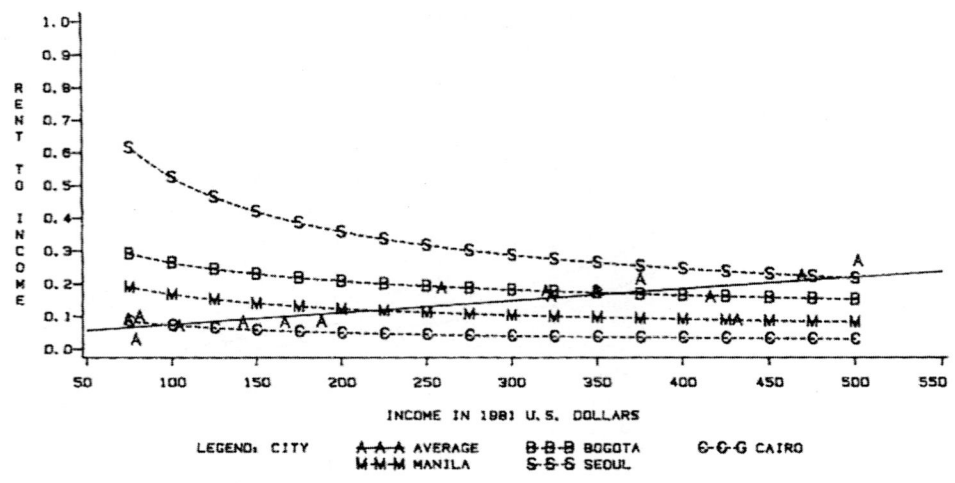

Figure 2 Rent-to-income ratios by income for renters.
Note: Average is for each LDC city at its average income.

also have higher elasticities. Malpezzi and Mayo (1987) argue that cross-market comparisons reveal a longer time frame; following the well-known Le Chatelier principle such elasticities tend to be higher as markets have greater latitude to respond.

These patterns of owner and renter housing consumption are surprisingly similar across countries; Whitehead (1999) provides a review. For example, in the Malpezzi and Mayo (1987) study of 14 cities in developing countries, for both tenure groups the cross-section elasticity is less than 1, and the long-run time series elasticity is about 1, although the level of owner consumption is higher.

Income and price elasticities of demand within cross sections were remarkably similar to those found in developed countries. Cross-market elasticities were generally in the range of 0.5–0.8 for owners and renters. Tackling issues like price specification and permanent income as well as the simultaneity between demand and tenure choice tended to push elasticities up to the higher end of this range but they generally remained less than 1 in absolute value; Lee and Trost (1978) is the classic reference on this question.

While within-market elasticities were broadly similar across markets, Malpezzi and Mayo (1987) noticed that the intercept terms were quite different. Estimating cross-country models using, for example, the median rent-to-income ratio within markets, Malpezzi and Mayo found elasticities of 1 or a little higher; **Figure 2** illustrates this. The dotted lines represent four of the 14 cities studied, namely Bogota, Cairo, Manila and Seoul; the other 10 are not drawn but are qualitatively similar. Specifically, all 14 city curves show declining rent-to-income ratios as incomes rise within the city. But the level of each city's curve tends to rise with the average income of the city (Cairo's average household income is low, among the sample cities; Seoul's average income is the highest). The rising solid line in **Figure 2** is the regression line through 14 points that represent each of the 14 cities' rent-to-income ratio at each city's average income. Over the very long run, as cities develop, elasticities will tend to be higher than within cross section. That is to say that housing markets take significant time to adjust, and single cross sections do not reveal truly long-run behaviour. Studies along the lines of Ortalo-Magné and Rady (2006) are modelling the dynamics of this adjustment more explicitly, and define a significant portion of the current research agenda on housing demand.

See also: Housing and the Macroeconomy; Neoclassical Models of the Housing Market; Supply Elasticity of Housing.

References

Davis MA and Ortalo-Magné F (2010) Household expenditures, wages, rents. *Review of Economic Dynamics* 14(2): 248–261.
Deaton A and Muellbauer J (1980) *Economics and Consumer Behavior*. New York: Cambridge University Press.
Follain JR (1979) A study of the demand for housing by low and high income households. *Journal of Financial and Quantitative Analysis* 14: 769–782.
Goodman AC (1995) A dynamic equilibrium model of housing demand and mobility with transaction costs. *Journal of Housing Economics* 4(4): 307–327.
Goodman AC and Kawai M (1985) Length of residence discounts and rental housing demand: Theory and evidence. *Land Economics* 61(2): 93–105.
Green RK and Malpezzi S (2003) *A Primer on US Housing Markets and Policy*. Washington, DC: Urban Institute Press for the American Real Estate and Urban Economics Association.
Hausman JA (1981) Exact consumer's surplus and deadweight loss. *American Economic Review* 71(4): 662–676.
Ihlanfeldt KR (1981) An empirical investigation of alternative approaches to estimating the equilibrium demand for housing. *Journal of Urban Economics* 9(1): 97–105.

Ioannides YM and Rosenthal SM (1994) Estimating the consumption and investment demands for housing and their effect on housing tenure status. *Review of Economics and Statistics* 76(1): 127–141.

Lee L-F and Trost RP (1978) Estimation of some limited dependent variable models with application to housing demand. *Journal of Econometrics* 8: 357–382.

Leung C (2004) Macroeconomics and housing: A review of the literature. *Journal of Housing Economics* 13(4): 249–267.

Malpezzi S and Mayo SK (July 1987) The demand for housing in developing countries. *Economic Development and Cultural Change* 35(4): 687–721.

Mayo SK (January 1981) Theory and estimation in the economics of housing demand. *Journal of Urban Economics* 10: 95–116.

Muth RF (1960) The demand for non-farm housing. In: Harberger A (ed.) *The Demand for Durable Goods*. Chicago, IL: University of Chicago Press.

Olsen EO (1987) The demand and supply of housing services: A critical review of the empirical literature. In: *Handbook of Regional and Urban Economics* (Mills ES (ed.) *Handbook of Regional and Urban Economics*, Vol. 2. Amsterdam: Elsevier.

Ortalo-Magné F and Rady S (2006) Housing market dynamics: On the contribution of income shocks and credit constraints. *Review of Economic Studies* 73: 459–485.

Reid MG (1962) *Housing and Income*. Chicago, IL: University of Chicago Press.

Rothenberg J, Galster GC, Butler RV, and Pitkin JR (1991) *The Maze of Urban Housing Markets: Theory, Evidence, and Policy*. Chicago, IL and London: University of Chicago Press.

Whitehead CME (1999) Urban housing markets: Theory and policy. In: *Handbook of Regional and Urban Economics* (Chesire P and Mills ES (eds.) *Handbook of Regional and Urban Economics*, Vol. 3. Amsterdam: Elsevier.

Housing Developers and Sustainability

A Congreve, University of Hertfordshire, Hatfield, UK

© 2012 Elsevier Ltd. All rights reserved.

Glossary

ALMO These are not-for-profit companies which have been set up by local authorities to manage all or part of their housing stock. The stock that ALMOs manage used to be managed directly by the local authority. Some ALMOs are increasing their stock of housing by developing new projects. ALMOs were first set up in 2002 and now manage housing in over 60 local authority areas.

Housing associations Build and manage housing at below market rents for people who would otherwise have difficulty entering the commercial housing market. They are established as not-for-profit companies which means any developments they carry out which make a profit must be put back into building new affordable housing or improving their existing neighbourhoods. They vary considerably in size with very small associations that manage less than 100 homes to over 50 000.

Introduction

Increasing attention on the environmental impacts of climate change is forcing a number of sectors of the economy, including house building, to give more weight to environmental issues. Concern about climate change has been heightened in the United Kingdom following the publication of the Stern Review that highlights the damage to the UK economy by failing to take action. Domestic energy use contributes almost a quarter of greenhouse gas emissions from the United Kingdom (DEFRA, 2008). Choice of building materials, their extraction and processing, transport, and as the building process all have environmental implications. These include the landscape impacts, not just of greenfield building but the extraction industries that support them, pollution, impact on water resources, and energy costs. The environmental standards to which a house is built will have long-term implications for sustainability issues such as energy efficiency. The way in which we build houses is therefore an issue of global environmental importance. This section examines the environmental implications of the residential construction industry during various stages of the building process.

Funding the Development Process

House building is a unique industry in that its product is not only expensive for the individual consumer, many times their annual salary, but also expensive initially for the builder. Before a sale can be made the builder must set capital aside to purchase land, buy materials, fund the building process including associated infrastructure, and meet any other requirements in regulations. The structure of the industry varies considerably between countries. The United States has a tradition of the private sector meeting most housing needs. The United Kingdom has a more mixed housing market although the trend is towards private provision. In the past, local authorities used to be the major developers of new housing. House building reached a peak in England in 1968 with over 352 000 new houses built – of these, 41% were by local authorities. There are some important differences between local authority housing and the way in which private sector housing is developed. Local authorities would supply the land and usually detailed design guidelines. There would be a contract with a house builder to supply the housing at a fixed price (Wellings, 2006). In England today, most house building is carried out by private sector developers. A private house builder acts as a developer – buying the land and carrying out most or all of the building work before a contract is signed with the purchaser. In 2007/08, 167 000 new houses were completed; of these, 86% were for the private sector. Only 23 000 were completed as affordable houses, available for rent at below market rates. Until the late 1970s, housing associations made a relatively modest contribution to the new housing stock, typically completing between 1000 and 5000 units per year, far less than local authorities. Now, almost all new affordable housing is completed by housing associations, with local authorities having almost entirely withdrawn from new housing construction (DCLG, 2008).

Private capital needs to be raised to enable the development process making the private house building industry vulnerable to economic cycles of growth and recession. The industry has reduced its risk exposure by being able to alter levels of production significantly from year to year. Purchasing option agreements to develop land many years in advance can reduce the risk of land price inflation and employing subcontractors rather than having a large, permanent staff allows quick adaptation to housing booms or recessions. Over time, housing developers have focused on land assembly, securing planning permission and sales, often leaving the physical construction work to subcontractors (Wellings, 2006). Development by private sector house builders in the United Kingdom is increasingly dominated by the 10 largest companies. This is in marked contrast to the United States where the domestic market is dominated by a large number of small businesses. Recent figures from the US economic census show that the share of new houses built by larger companies is declining (Melman, 2010). In the UK, in the 1930s, house building was mainly a local activity confined to individual towns. There was some competition for sites between neighbouring towns and larger builders including Costain and Wimpey would build on large greenfield sites. The market share of the top 10 house builders was only 6%. This began to change in the 1960s with the emergence of regional companies. This trend from local to regional to national companies continued, so by 2004 the top 10 companies had a market share of 44% (Wellings, 2006). This is in marked contrast to the United States where large companies in 2009 constructed 23% (Melman, 2010). The speculative housing market in Britain is particularly volatile, and this volatility has been exposed by the recent economic downturn. It is reflected in the number of new starts for properties and in the number of staff employed. Applications to start building new homes (registered with the National Housebuilding Council) were 75% lower in August 2008 than in August 2007. Between June and October 2008, the six largest house builders made 4000 staff redundant (Merrick, 2008). In the United States, the larger house builders have been particularly badly affected by the recession. They focused their activities on the fastest-growing markets in Las Vegas, Phoenix, Miami, and larger urban areas in California. These areas have been the worst hit by the recession. These larger developers are now attempting to reposition themselves, focusing on quality lots but are still experiencing difficulty, while large numbers of unsold homes remain in these areas (Melman, 2010). This volatility is significant because as we shall see later it acts as an important factor inhibiting innovation.

Location and Land Assembly

The first phase of new development will be the selection of the location in which to build and the acquisition of suitable land. In an industry now dominated by private builders this places the initiative in the hands of the building industry. Developers' decisions about where to build are taken in the context of planning or zoning requirements. Agricultural land prices varies, ranging from £4000 to £25 000 per acre. Land with planning permission is typically valued at 8–10 times the value of land without planning permission. Ideally for the industry the purchase of land at agricultural rates and its subsequent transfer to development status for housing represents a high financial return and the industry will devote much of its resources to achieve this. This diverts manpower and expertise from other elements of the industry such as research and development, site and project management, attention to particular physical characteristics on development sites, and so on.

In the case of the United Kingdom, it is interesting to note that many of the best practice examples in sustainability take place when this speculation element is removed through the land being subsidised by local or national government. Such subsidies are used to encourage development on problematic sites such as contaminated land or to encourage regional growth where market forces are not providing sufficient housing. Such subsidies, however, allow the authorities to have more input into the quality and form of the development including sustainability issues such as energy conservation. The site may also have environmental features or concerns such as wildlife interest or the risk of flooding which force some environmental issues to be taken onboard. Articles in the housing and regeneration trade press, environment press, and mainstream media regularly feature examples of environmentally sound housing projects. These projects typically show development on land acquired cheaply by the developer, often on previously developed land by a public sector or voluntary body with an interest in environmental issues. The site may also be part of a national government programme and receive special funding – and additional scrutiny as a result. Finally, the site may be in an area with a high level of green activism and a history of promoting green projects. The best know of all the green housing projects in the United Kingdom is BEDZED (Beddington Zero Energy Development) in south London. The project was developed in partnership between Sutton Council, an NGO called Bioregional, an architectural practice ZED factory, and the housing association Peabody. While the figures for low energy use and low water use on the site are impressive, the innovation came at a cost. Some of the green measures – including sourcing local and recycled building materials and the combined heat and power (CHP) energy system – proved particularly challenging. The large number of environmental and social innovations on the site also created project management difficulties which led to the project being substantially over budget. Flagship projects will always have difficulties when they are the first in the field and the technology is unfamiliar. Costs reduce as technologies become mainstream and expertise in specifying and installing technology increases.

The location of housing raises various sustainability issues. Its distance from amenities in the context of creating mixed neighbourhoods will have a high impact on transport and energy use. There are some areas of consensus between builders' locational preferences and planning constraints. In the United Kingdom, there has been a consistent planning policy framework to encourage new development within key settlements or along transport corridors. Builders' attitudes reflect a similar preference for 'building where the chimney pots are'. Local amenities such as nearby schools and shops encourage house sales and these locations also minimise infrastructure costs for the developer. In other areas, however, there is potential conflict between the building industry and planners. Builders show a preference for greenfield sites on the periphery of urban centres. There is the potential for an attraction such as riverside location to bring development at risk of flooding or an attractive landscape with potential damage to wildlife sites. If the site is prime agricultural land there are also obvious losses in farm production. Loss of local high-quality farmland could lead to more food being transported at greater distances and has implications for long-term food security. UK planning has promoted brownfield rather than greenfield developments to minimise these impacts and aid in urban regeneration.

Planning Regulations

Following land acquisition and drawing up initial designs, the next phase of development would be gaining formal approval from the planning process and building regulations. Again the planning context will vary from country to country. At a minimum some form of zoning is likely to be in place to separate residential from other land uses. In the United Kingdom, the Building Regulations relate to the construction of the individual house and the land-use planning system addresses broader issues. Although local government has almost entirely withdrawn from building new housing, it still maintains an active role in enforcing the Building Regulations and in developing policy and then enforcing planning conditions. Building Regulations were first developed to address public health concerns and to prevent buildings causing injury through fire or collapse. There has been a broadening of their scope increasingly in aspects of sustainability such as energy efficiency. Britain's Building Regulations that improve the energy efficiency of new housing have been in place since the 1970s. They were developed in response to the rising fuel costs as a result of the oil crisis. Throughout the 1980s, the Building Regulations were criticised as being the weakest in Northern Europe (Webb and Gossop, 1993). A major problem with the regulations was that they allowed developers to offset improvements in one area against another; for example, by increasing loft insulation and decreasing thermal efficiency in walls. This is a particular problem where improvements are expensive and technically difficult to retrofit, such as windows and walls. It is quite easy for a householder to put in an extra layer of roof insulation, compared to the costly and difficult process of adding thermal insulation to walls. Since the late 1990s the Building Regulations have been successively tightened and are now more closely aligned with other northern European countries. In Germany, Austria, and Scandinavia, the Passivhaus standard has become widely adopted which focuses on a high-quality building fabric that minimises the need for heating systems combined with planned ventilation. From 2005, the UK government began moving towards more ambitious carbon-neutral building standards. One of the criticisms of the Building Regulations was the very short time builders and those supplying materials to the house building industry had to adapt to changes. In response, the government developed the Code for Sustainable Homes that sets out the future Building Regulations up until 2016 including phasing in the increased environmental targets proposed in 2005.

There has been an increasing trend for industry to become actively involved in its own regulation (Rehbinder, 1997). House builders can choose to use a building inspector provided by the local authority to show they have conformed to the Building Regulations. This is a common practice with many small house builders. It is much more common for larger house builders to appoint their own approved inspector to show they have conformed to the regulations. With any system of regulation there are issues of compliance. There is no point in legislating to require higher environmental standards if those standards are widely flouted. The Energy Saving Trust in the United Kingdom looked at compliance in one area: the rate at which cold air leaks into buildings. It found that 43% of the new houses checked should have been failed by building inspectors but were instead passed (Grigg, 2004). Since the introduction of the Building Regulations in the 1970s, there has not been one prosecution brought for failure to meet insulation standards in buildings (Warren, 2006). The key problem here is the culture of inspection which does not regard compliance with energy efficiency requirements as a priority issue. This was found in work carried out by Future Energy Solutions (2006), who interviewed 59 building control inspectors. It found that energy efficiency issues were viewed as 'not life threatening'. Future Energy Solutions found that while the levels of compliance with the Building Regulations are generally high, energy efficiency in buildings has one of the poorest levels of compliance.

The Building Regulations are prescribed by central government and local authorities are left purely with an implementation role. The land-use planning system works differently, and local authorities have a stronger role in developing as well as implementing policy. Any development of new housing will require house builders to seek planning permission from the local authority. If planning permission is approved, then this will be subject to a number of conditions such as the location, number and size of units on a plot. It is also common practice for housing developers to have to meet environmental conditions. These often relate directly to the specific site and may include preserving existing landscape and wildlife features, such as trees or hedges, within the development. There may also be requirements to enhance landscape and biodiversity through planting new trees and adding other landscape features. This is often the environmental issue that house builders are most enthusiastic to follow. Retaining and improving the landscape can create a more attractive setting for houses, increasing the speed of sale and perhaps the sale price (Congreve, 2012). There is increasing pressure for other site issues to be given more consideration. Building new housing will usually increase the amount of hard surfaces – roofs, roads, and pavements – which in turn increases the speed of runoff following rainfall. This increased runoff can lead to flooding in the new development or lead to flooding downstream. The planning process can be used to require housing developers to include sustainable urban drainage systems (SUDSs). The Environment Agency thinks that all new housing developments should incorporate SUDS into the development (Environment Agency, 2007). In practice, take-up has been limited outside a small number of demonstration projects. Other aspects of estate design which may be considered by planners include CHP, transport issues, amenities, and infrastructure. District-level CHP is more energy-efficient than heating each individual home separately and is widely used in many northern European countries including Germany and Finland. Estate layout and housing density affect the viability of public transport and alongside the local provision of amenities will affect the number of trips taken by private car.

The Construction Process

After planning approval has been gained, the construction process can begin. For house building to be more environmentally sound, materials should come from sustainable sources and minimise the environmental impact in their processing, transportation, and disposal at the end of their life. Embodied energy provides a useful measure to compare the environmental impacts of different building materials; it measures the energy needed to change raw building materials into finished building products. Within this energy used in the construction phase, it is estimated that about half is used in the extraction and processing of materials, the rest is consumed by transport, both transport of the products to the construction site and the transport of products for processing (Sustainable Homes, 1999). There is scope for improvement in energy savings in the manufacture of building products. Cement, for example, currently contributes 5% to total global greenhouse gas emissions, the equivalent of the aviation industry. Cement makes such a significant contribution because it requires high temperatures as part of its production process and also releases carbon dioxide from the limestone as heat is applied. Choice of what building materials to use, how they are processed, how locally they can be sourced, and how they are assembled on site all have sustainability impacts. Wood, for example, is widely promoted as a renewable and sustainable building material. Unlike cement, bricks, and PVC, it requires little energy to turn it from a raw material into a useable product in construction. However, if the wood is sourced internationally, its bulk means that energy used in transport is high giving it an unexpectedly high embodied energy. It is also important how much of a particular material is used. Steel, for example, has a very high embodied energy because of its production process but is only used in small amounts in some domestic construction methods. Once materials are assembled on-site, the construction method can impact on the environmental quality of the finished house and raise other issues such as the amount of waste. In the United Kingdom, most housing is built on-site using a brick and block method on cement platforms. The only prefabricated units tend to be doors and windows usually of PVC construction. Lovell (2007) points out that domestic residential construction is essentially unchanged in the past 100 years. The masonry construction materials and methods have changed very little over this time. Industry lobby groups including the Traditional Housing Bureau have been established since the 1980s to help maintain the dominance of masonry construction. 'Traditional' is compared to other 'nontraditional' building techniques that are presented as unreliable (Lovell, 2007). Here, UK house-building techniques diverge from many other developed countries including the United States and Germany where other methods, particularly timber frame, dominate and can be built more easily to high environmental standards. Why do house builders wish to keep using traditional masonry methods? A major reason is the volatility in the housing market described earlier. It is relatively easy to hire and sack staff or subcontractors as the housing market changes. Building a factory to make timber frame panels or moving towards fuller factory-based preconstruction (MMC) is a significant investment and there is less flexibility to increase or decrease the output from a factory in response to market variability. Traditional on-site construction leads to more waste of unused and damaged building materials, increasing the environmental impact of the construction process. There are also sustainability issues with the long-term disposal or recycling of building materials. Wood can biodegrade but other products like PVC do not and cannot be recycled into new PVC products. Plastic materials can only be turned into lower-grade products such as plastic bags, a process called down-cycling.

A general picture emerges of a conservative industry with limited interest in new products or building methods. Within the construction sector as a whole, research and development is a paltry 0.9% of sales. This compares poorly with other sectors that have a major impact on people's lives like pharmaceuticals (15%) and information technology (18%) (Bonfield, 2008). The response of the housing sector, represented by the Home Builders Federation (Slaughter in Scott, 2008), is that companies that do innovate by using new materials and systems should be given tax breaks to support their research and development. If the industry itself is not focused on research and innovative changes, this raises the question of where the drivers for change will come from. Government has a role particularly in raising environmental standards of the building process and finished product, flagship projects can provide an opportunity for developers to learn about new materials and techniques, and consumer pressure for greener products which has appeared in other sectors could influence developer's behaviour.

In what aspects of house building is further innovation needed? Bonfield (2008) argues that there are key areas where greater innovation could take place: microgeneration; modern methods of construction; and improved installation methods. Solar water panels and photovoltaics are well-established technologies, although the uptake varies internationally. Best results occur in countries such as Germany where a feed-in-tariff rewards the householder not just with cheap energy but also for any excess energy they supply back to the grid. Further product development could take place in a number of renewable technologies including: CHP, ground source heat pumps, and micro-wind. Similarly, some countries minimise on-site construction by building prefabricated panels or pods that can simply be assembled on-site. Despite the innovation that has taken place in these modern methods of construction since the 1990s – in producing light-gauge steel frames, closed panel timber frames, prefabricated brick walls, and structurally insulated panels (SIPS) – all of these systems could be further developed (Bonfield, 2008). Plaskett, the sustainability director of Crest Nicholson, argues that there is little experience among British house builders of CHP and other renewable technologies (in Scott, 2008). She cites instances where the benefits of these systems have been compromised by poor installation. Innovation is not just about developing new technologies, but gaining greater experience with which technology best suits a particular site and the best ways of installing a particular technology. Another factor that inhibits innovation is the lack of permanent staff in the main house building companies. The use of subcontracts gives flexibility in a recession but also acts to inhibit investment in staff training in the use of new materials and technologies. The volatility in the housing market also acts as a barrier to developing factories for modern methods of construction. There is a large capital investment in a factory and to make a profit there must be a regular demand.

The BEDZED projects – and other green demonstration projects like Hockerton Housing Project (completed 1998) and the Milton Keynes Energy Village (built in 1986) – have not impacted significantly on the behaviour of mainstream house builders. Is innovation and change more likely to succeed when development is carried out by other agents? How will the structure of the industry change in the future? It is very unlikely there will be any return to the mass local authority housing projects of the 1950s and 1960s. However, other new bodies could take an increasingly significant role. Some arms-length management organisations (ALMOs) are beginning to develop new housing as well as managing the existing housing stock (Thorpe, 2007). Another important trend is the increased importance of self-build housing. During 2008, the self-build market accounted for about 14 000 units or 8% of total completions. The main problem limiting the expansion of this sector is the difficulty in securing plots. If this sector is to expand, this problem needs to be addressed. One solution could be to assist the formation of co-operatives, so self-builders can develop larger sites (AMA research, 2009). Another solution is to make every new development site provide space for self-build plots. As traditional planning obligations face problems regarding their financial viability, this could appeal to both larger developers and local authorities (Morrison, 2009). Although by definition each self-build project will be individual, many self-builders are more concerned about the environmental performance of their house than mainstream developers. This approach has been particularly successful in Freiburg in Germany. Here in the new development at Rieselfeld, a proportion of plots were allocated for community self-build groups. These groups could take out an option to purchase land at a reduced rate and had a year to assemble a group and the funding required. These resulted in developments that were built to high environmental standards and were more architecturally imaginative than developer-led projects. The success in Freiburg has led to of community self-building being promoted in other German cities.

Selling and Occupancy

A key factor in driving up environmental standards in other sectors, as described below, has been consumer pressure. Some consumers have been willing to pay a premium for 'green' white goods such as washing machines and fridges. Models with very poor environmental standards are no longer produced – it is no longer possible to buy a new G-rated refrigerator or washing machine. Cost savings from reduced energy and water bills can compensate the consumer for the higher initial price of the green product. Consumers have also been willing to express their identity through buying green products (Moisander and Pesonen, 2002). Are similar forces working to encourage house builders to develop houses with higher environmental standards? Although some consumers will be looking to buy a new house, most new houses are also competing with existing houses for buyers' attention (Office of Fair Trading, 2008). This makes houses fundamentally different from other products like white goods or organic food. The market for second-hand washing machines and refrigerators is very small compared to the market in 'second-hand' houses. Also, consumers view housing as an investment and, while they may be willing to experiment more with other consumer products, they tend to be conservative when buying houses. Edge and associates found that homebuyers still have negative views of innovative housing, based on the failure of postwar 'prefab' construction. This makes them resistant to any innovation that changes what a traditional house looks like (Edge et al., 2002). The high importance of housing as an investment vehicle across a range of different income groups is explored by Smith and associates (2009). The evidence is also patchy that having a green home or installing green features will add value to a property – in the same way as improving the kitchen or bathroom. Research by Roy and Caird (2008) found that a fifth of households, who considered microgeneration but did not go ahead, thought it would not add any value to their property – and may even reduce property values. Increasing energy costs and improved finance mechanisms are beginning to focus buyer's attention on the energy costs of running a home. For such issues to be influential at the point of purchase, a clear and prominent green labelling scheme for housing is required.

Greener building is further developed in the commercial property sector rather than private housing. This includes office buildings (including those commissioned by the public and third sector organisations), educational buildings, and recreational facilities such as visitors' centres. The economic case for greener commercial property development is addressed in the Royal Institution of Chartered Surveyors report Green Value (RICS, 2005). This puts an economic case for green building. The report argues that green buildings can:

- be quicker to secure tenants,
- command higher rents or prices,
- enjoy lower tenant turnover,
- cost less to operate and maintain in most cases, and
- improve business productivity for the occupant.

Some factors from the commercial building sector translate more readily into the residential sector than others. The first, securing tenants (or in this case buyers), could apply to the residential sector. Builders, particularly smaller developers, benefit from quick sales and avoiding having capital tied up in unsold properties. If greener housing did attract a higher price, this would also be an incentive for developers to produce greener housing. The point about tenant turnover is not really applicable, as the developer has no interest in the property once sold. The number of apartment-type developments where this applies is very small in the United Kingdom. The fourth point about costing less to operate and maintain does not apply in the same way as the commercial sector. When the property is sold, this is a benefit for the owner and is of no interest to the developer. It could only become of interest to the developer if the buyer was willing to pay more for a building that costs less to operate and maintain. Similarly, a more productive building in which to work (or in the case of a house, a healthier and more pleasant building in which to live) will be of interest to the developer but only as a selling point. While issues such as energy costs are of importance to commercial property users who will have the expertise to measure these costs for similar consumer pressure to appear in the housing sector, buyers will need to understand and calculate their own personal costs.

Post-Occupancy

Changes are occurring within the sector which aim to secure the longer-term management of developments. A range of green features including public open space, sustainable urban drainage systems, microgeneration, and green transport measures will require ongoing management and maintenance. One option is to hand over these responsibilities to local authorities but their track record in some areas, for example, running energy systems such as district heating, has been poor. The culture within the industry is of developers leaving as soon as the houses are up and having no long-term interest in the sites' impacts on environmental performance. As we have seen, it is one of the reasons why the commercial sector is more concerned about environmental performance than the residential sector. Despite this, a number of different models of the 'build and stay' approach are already being developed. At Great Notley near Braintree, Countryside Properties have set up a trust which is responsible for the long-term management of the properties. According to the Countryside Properties Director, these sold for a 20% premium compared to neighbouring similar properties (Cherry in Blackman, 2008). Residents' concerns about a safe and secure environment are addressed through good management rather than security measures on individual properties. A different model has been developed at the Greyfriars site in central Gloucester. Here, English Partnerships forced the developer to enter into a 10-year agreement covering the ongoing management of the site. This covers traditional topics including public open space, but the developers also have responsibility for a range of other issues from community cohesion to recycling (Blackman, 2008). One of the longest-established schemes is the Greenwich Millennium village development – also developed by Countryside Properties. Here, residents pay a service charge of approximately £1400 for services. Part of this new interest among housing developers may also be attributed to the lack of interest from mainstream energy companies. The Galion's Park development in East London, a 260-home zero-carbon energy project, has had difficulties in attracting an energy company partner. The development partners have had to take on the role of green energy supply themselves, something that is outside the core business for the companies involved (Arup, BioRegional Qunitain, Crest Nicholson, and Southern Housing Group).

Conclusions

Internationally there is considerable variation in the structure of the development industry and the way in which it interacts with other stakeholders including government and consumers. However, compared with other consumer products, the housing sector shows a marked conservatism and this impacts on its ability to address environmental issues. Economic factors and the lack of research within the industry mean that the drivers for change are often external. Government at international, national, and local level can use both regulatory powers and incentives to influence the location, design, and layout of new housing. Some of the main areas of innovation have been in specific components on the house rather than in overall redesign. Microgeneration of energy at the individual house level has benefits both for the householder, and by reducing energy loss during transmission, reduces the overall energy needs. New building materials such as improved insulation and better installation methods can also improve energy efficiency. Modern methods of construction have the potential to bring about significant improvements in environmental performance as well as reducing waste and could be the major change in the building industry as governments put more pressure on developers to achieve environmental targets, particularly reduced carbon emissions.

See also: Building Regulations for Energy Conservation; Community Energy Systems; Eco-Communities; House Building Industries: Western Europe and North America; Housing Construction Industry, Competition and Regulation; Housing Developers: Developed World; Modern Methods of Construction.

References

AMA Research (2009) *Self Build Housing Market*. AMA Research, Cheltenham, UK: AMA.

Blackman D (2008) Is this the end of build and bugger off. *Regenerate.* 16–24 January/February.

Bonfield P (2008) How innovative is construction? *Sustain* 9(1): 24–25.

Congreve A (2012) *Sustainability and New Housing Development.* London: Routledge.

DCLG (2008) *Housing Statistics 2008*. London: DCLG.

DEFRA (2008) *The UK Climate Change Programme Annual Report to Parliament*. London: DEFRA.

Edge M, Craig A, Laing R, et al. (2002) *Overcoming Client and Market Resistance to Prefabrication and Standardisation in Housing*. Research Report of RTI/EPSRC Link Programme, Meeting Client's Needs Through Standardisation. Aberdeen, UK: Robert Gordon University.

Environment Agency (2007) *Sustainable Drainage Systems (SUDS): An Introduction*. Bristol, UK: Environment Agency.

Future Energy Solutions (2006) *Compliance with Part L1 of the 2002 Building Regulations Energy Efficiency Partnership for Homes*. Southampton, UK: Future Energy Solutions.

Grigg P (2004) *Assessment of Energy Efficiency Impact of Building Regulations Compliance*. Building Research Establishment. Report for the Energy Savings Trust and Energy Efficiency Partnership for Homes. Watford, UK: BRE.

Lovell H (2007) Exploring the role of materials in policy change: Innovation in low energy housing in the UK. *Environment and Planning A* 39: 2500–2517.

Melman S (2010) Structure of the Home Building Industry. Available at URL: http://www.homebuyertaxcreditusa.net. (accessed 10 November 2011).

Merrick N (2008) Crisis management. *Inside Housing,* 31 October, 30–34.

Moisander J and Pesonen S (2002) Narratives of sustainable ways of living: Constructing the self and others as a green consumer. *Management Decision* 40(2): 329–342.

Morrison D (2009) Voyage of self discovery. *Property Week.* 13 February, 38–39.

Office of Fair Trading (2008) *Homebuilding in the UK*. London: Office of Fair Trading.

Rehbinder E (1997) Environmental agreements – A new instrument of environmental policy. *Environmental Policy and Law* 27(4): 258–269.

RICS (2005) *Green Value: Green Buildings, Growing Assets*. London: RICS.

Roy R and Caird S (2008) Low and zero carbon pioneers: Expanding the UK household market for microgeneration heat. *Green Building.* Autumn.

Scott M (2008) Ready steady build. *Sustainable Business* 130: 30–32.

Smith SJ, Searle BA, and Cook N (2009) Rethinking the risks of home ownership. *Journal of Social Policy* 38: 83–102.

Sustainable Homes (1999) *Embodied Energy in Residential Property Development*. Kingston-Upon-Thames, UK: Sustainable Homes.

Thorpe C (2007) New breed (new house building). *Inside Housing.* 14 September, 26–29.

Warren A (2006) Time to put a stop to the disdain for regulations. *Energy in Buildings and Industry Magazine.* March.

Webb A and Gossop C (1993) Towards a sustainable energy policy. In: Blowers A (ed.) *Planning for a Sustainable Environment* (Report by the Town and Country Planning Association). London: Earthscan.

Wellings F (2006) *British Housebuilders: History and Analysis*. Oxford, UK: Blackwell Publishing.

Housing Developers: Developed World

W Amann and A Mundt, Institute for Real Estate, Construction and Housing, Vienna, Austria

© 2012 Elsevier Ltd. All rights reserved.

Glossary

Public–private partnership (PPP) In housing this describes an approach in which private companies fulfil public service obligations, such as housing provision for defined households with need. For this purpose they have access to public funds (state aid). Successful PPP models are in place in several Western European and Asian countries, but their presence is insignificant in transition economies.

Social rental sector Part of housing provision set up with the goal of satisfying the needs of those income classes that are excluded from homeownership or the open market rental sector.

Welfare regimes Country groups that arrange their social policy frameworks according to different guidelines and principles. Esping-Andersen conceived the social democratic, the conservative, and the liberal welfare regimes. Often a Southern European welfare regime is added.

Introduction

Housing provision in developed countries is increasingly being formalised and institutionalised. This is because the supply of building land is regulated, and individuals, firms, public bodies, and limited-profit entities that engage in the production of living space are usually embedded in a tight legal framework. Yet, there are considerable differences in the way housing developers operate and which sphere they belong to on a continuum from private to public ownership.

Housing developers usually define their product, buy the necessary building land, coordinate and supervise the planning and building process, arrange for adequate financing, and place the dwellings on the market. Sometimes they also ensure the long-term management of the buildings they produced. There is a whole bundle of literature on the adequate classification and analysis of housing developers in relation to national housing systems (Barlow and Duncan, 1994; Golland and Oxley, 2004; Healey and Barret, 1990).

One such very interesting study, by Barlow and Duncan in 1994 analyses the process of housing development in European states in the context of Esping-Andersen's (1990) classification of different welfare regimes. Not surprisingly, there are great differences in housing development across welfare states as regards the average size of production firms, the profit regimes under which they operate (building profits, development gains), the type of land supply (public ownership versus speculative), and the promotional form of housing (nonprofit and self-promotion versus private sector). For example, countries belonging to the liberal welfare regime (United Kingdom, Ireland) tend to have large builders and developers that rely more on speculative development gains than on building profits and largely belong to the private sector. Social democratic regimes, on the other hand, have large builders that rely on building profits exclusively, since land supply is under tight public control. The operation of builders is supervised by nonprofit developers. Barlow and Duncan's very preliminary study unfortunately has not found many successors since 1994 (exceptions: Arbaci, 2007; Keivani and Werna, 2001: 70).

For the sake of this very short introduction, it is useful to differentiate the following formal (i.e., through official channels of recognised institutions) forms of housing development in developed countries:

- Direct government housing providers, usually municipalities or the federal level.
- Limited-profit housing providers, such as cooperatives and social housing associations.
- Commercial housing providers, often focusing on large rental housing estates and condominiums or on single-family houses.
- Self-built housing provision.

Up until the interwar period, housing provision was usually done by commercial housing providers and individuals. To some extent company and cooperative housing played a minor role in some countries even earlier, but building activity only started to soar once government provided adequate backing for these initiatives. In the 1920s and 1930s direct state provision of housing in the form of municipal apartments started to gain a foothold in Germany and many surrounding countries. In the United Kingdom too, municipal housing started to become the cornerstone of housing provision.

In the current millennium, traditional public housing developers, so prominent in the aftermath of the Second World War, have phased out their building activity in favour of limited-profit housing developers such as housing associations and other forms of housing organisations (United Kingdom, Belgium, Denmark, France, the Netherlands, and Austria). This form of housing production is unique to some fully developed countries and will therefore be the focus of attention in the following sections.

Housing Development between the State and the Market

The functioning of housing developers of the 'Third Sector' varies considerably across countries (Czischke, 2009) and the stock resulting from this development does not exclusively belong to the social rental stock aimed at low-income households, but may be accessible to middle-income households as well. There is a large variety of legal forms (associations, foundations, cooperatives, limited companies, publicly or privately owned or under mixed ownership). Usually there is some form of government control or approval of social housing developers that operate under special rules overriding ordinary law. Often their field of operation is confined to the local or regional level. In some countries, housing developers of the 'Third Sector' depend heavily on public funding, whilst in others, private financing is increasingly channelled towards them (**Figure 1**).

Country Examples

Limited-Profit Housing Associations in Austria

By providing discounted building land, grants, public loans, or tax-favoured investment, the federal government of Austria, together with its regional (Länder) and municipal governments, has strategically promoted the development of limited-profit, cost-capped housing with estate-based cost rents. Limited-profit housing is procured and managed mainly by limited-profit housing associations (LPHA) but also by municipal housing companies. LPHA in Austria comprise altogether 190 housing cooperatives and private-limited and public-limited companies with a total housing stock (rental dwellings and owner-occupied apartments) of some 865 000 units (approximately 22% of the total housing stock in Austria). The LPHA are responsible for a third of new residential construction. That is more than half of all multistorey housing construction. With this very high market share, LPHA have not only outperformed municipal housing, but also private multiapartment housing construction. The housing associations are cooperatives or are owned by public authorities, charity organisations, parties, unions, companies, banks, or private persons. To avoid moral hazard, it is prohibited for construction firms to be owners of LPHA (Amann and Mundt, 2009).

LPHA are undertakings organised according to private law and a strict federal law. They are exempt from corporate tax, are not classified as state or 'charitable' undertakings, and are limited in the extraction and distribution of profit and in their field of operation. They aim at creating a housing sector that is characterised by a legally defined long-term binding of the built-up capital within the housing sector and the constraint to therefore reinvest in housing matters. The aim of LPHA is the provision of affordable housing for large parts of the population.

In short, the limited-profit housing system is characterised by four principles (Amann et al., 2009):

- Cost coverage principle: the obligatory calculation of rents based on construction costs in combination with rent limitation defined by the subsidy schemes guarantee a low and continuous level of rents (€3–5 per m^2 net).
- Limited field of action: the housing associations have to focus on housing construction, refurbishment, and housing management. In fact, it is an important requirement for long-term success of the system that housing associations in general manage the houses they have produced before.
- Binding of property – limited-profit: Housing associations ought to make profits. But these profits have to be reinvested: in purchase of land, refurbishment, or new construction. A limited part of the profit (maximum 3.5% of registered capital) may be divided among the owners or shareholders.
- Control: Self-control through an umbrella organisation; supervision through provincial governments.

The present system of social housing finance in Austria provides guarantee-like effects, even without using explicit guarantees. This derives from the combination

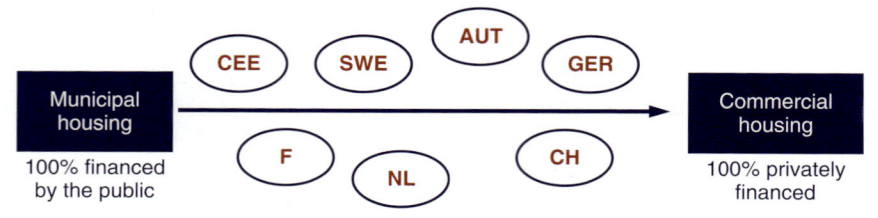

Figure 1 Public–private partnerships in housing. Adapted from IIBW.

of public subsidies (low interest loans, annuity grants), the prior role of LPHA in new construction, and the effectiveness of housing banks ('Wohnbaubanken'). Therefore, LPHA are regarded as low-risk borrowers. The guarantee-like functioning of the housing subsidy scheme in all its complexity – financial support as well as control and supervision – is responsible for the very good conditions LPHA face on the capital market.

HLM in France

The social rental sector in France is centred around the concept of subsidised rent projects, called 'low-cost housing' (Habitations à Loyer Modéré: HLM). The associations providing HLM vary in legal form, ownership, and management. Yet, some general features of HLM providers can be distinguished (Levy-Vroulant and Tutin, 2009).

- They receive supply-side subsidies for building new dwellings or buying and refurbishing existing ones, but no subsidies to cover operating costs.
- The social rental housing supply is financed mainly through off-market long-term loans, with the aid of state subsidies and local authorities. There are three broad types of social housing, corresponding to the three types of loans used to fund them. The three types vary in the maximum income level controlling access and the level of social rents charged.
- The loans are obtained from a public bank funded by deposits in the housing savings scheme. Guarantees are provided for these loans by local authorities or by a mutual fund. In addition, off-market loans are provided from an employers' fund financed by a housing tax on wages. HLM often benefit from state and local land subsidies.
- HLM organisations can take various legal forms: HLM Public Offices, HLM Public Planning and Construction Offices, and privately run HLM (capital companies, subject to commercial law). Some HLM also take the form of semipublic companies, foundations, and cooperatives, some of which focus on homeownership.
- HLM are designed in a way that a sound financial balance is maintained. They are managed according to public accountancy standards, with (in the case of privately run HLM) profits limited to a certain share of capital invested. HLM organisations are financially and legally controlled by the Ministries of Housing and of Finance, and they are monitored so that their activities conform to their social objectives.
- The allocation of HLM dwellings is subject to family circumstances, housing conditions, and income. Local authorities are allocating a percentage of the housing stock according to their access criteria.

From these general concepts it is quite clear that the system of HLM in France has many similarities with the Austrian Limited-Profit Housing Associations, as described in the previous section. Yet, one important difference remains in the funding, which in Austria relies on capital market sources to a much greater extent. The HLM scheme was used as a model when introducing the TBS system in Poland (see below).

'Woningcorporaties' in the Netherlands

Nowhere in Europe is limited-profit housing more dominant than in the Netherlands. It is owned and managed by housing associations ('woningcorporaties'), which in many cases are foundations without real owners. These have to act on a commercial basis, but any profits they make must be reinvested in housing. They participate in one of seven performance areas, such as providing target groups with suitable housing, maintaining the standards of homes, ensuring financial security, and contributing to the quality of life in neighbourhoods (Boelhouwer, 2007). Housing associations are very flexible and may buy and sell their dwellings on the market.

After a process of deregulation in 1995, housing associations became financially independent through the so-called grossing and balancing operation ('brutering'). Over the last decade, the stock of limited-profit housing remained stable (around 2.4 million), because the number of sold and demolished dwellings more or less equalled the number of new-built and purchased dwellings. At present, there are around 500 housing associations that are increasingly going for mergers due to reasons of efficiency.

Despite its independence from the government, the limited-profit housing sector is subject to two 'safety bodies': the Guarantee Fund for Social Housing (WSW) and the Central Housing Fund (CFV). Both are financially independent from the government and act as guarantors to housing association loans, which results in loans that are cheaper than those available on the capital market. Associations must register with the WSW and undergo a credit check. The fund is now financed by contributions from housing associations, which are required to set aside a certain amount, in case the assets of the WSW fall below a minimum level. If, for any reason, a housing association is not able to meet the financial demands of the WSW and is unable to obtain funds, it may be eligible for financial support from the CFV. The CFV maintains financial supervision on behalf of the Minister of Housing and may restructure financially weak associations. In return, associations must consent to undertake reorganisation in order to establish financial stability. Once CFV support is accorded, the association can once again apply for membership and, in turn, WSW loan guarantees.

An internal supervisory body advises management, monitors the work of associations, and takes action where necessary. Although the central government withdrew from the field, the Minister of Housing still retains some powers of intervention. The Minister of Housing also has the power to block plans adopted by the associations without his prior permission. The associations endeavour to show that they act responsibly towards society by promoting transparency in their policies and by encouraging collaboration with others. A very recent decision of the EU Commission (15 December 2009) demanded a clearer separation of commercial and social activities of housing associations, and ensured that the allocation of dwellings is conducted in a transparent and objective manner, focusing more on a predefined target group of socially less advantaged persons. Other than that, the Commission confirmed that the operation of Dutch housing associations was in line with EU competition law.

Municipal Housing Companies in Sweden

In Sweden, providing adequate housing is the responsibility of the municipalities. Most municipalities have their own independent nonprofit housing company. SABO is the federation for the municipal housing companies (see Relevant Website) and now includes approximately 300 member organisations. These member organisations own and manage around 780 000 dwellings all over the country (18% of the total stock, 2005). Since the early 1950s, municipal housing companies are run as independently as possible from wider municipal budgets and are usually organised as limited companies. Municipalities have the primary responsibility for planning and supplying good housing for the local population and for those who wish to move to the area, while the federal government is responsible for providing the necessary legal and financial instruments.

Municipal housing companies combine commercial aims with social responsibilities, and may only engage in a business activity if it is conducted without the prospect of profit and is essentially concerned with providing municipal amenities or services for the residents of the municipality. The social responsibility of the municipal housing companies today primarily means that they focus on offering good-quality, safe housing at a reasonable cost. The dwellings are allocated by the housing organisation itself or by a housing association run by the municipality.

New construction by the municipal sector roughly corresponds to its share in the total housing stock (around one-fifth). It is funded on the open credit market, with loans sometimes backed by municipal guarantees. Up to 90% of building costs of a typical project might be financed by long-term loans; the rest is covered by the housing company's own capital (Turner, 2007).

The solidity of municipal housing companies has improved over time as their net worth, i.e., their assets minus liabilities, averaged 20% in 2005. The recent increase in property values contributed considerably to the rising solidity of municipal housing companies. The return on capital invested is around 6–7%. It is usually reinvested in building activities. Municipal housing associations' rents are set by negotiation with local tenants' associations and function also as a benchmark for the rent levels in the private rental market, which has in the past caused problems with EU law with respect to competition and level playing fields.

In addition, there is a very particular system of housing cooperatives in Sweden. HSB and Riksbyggen are the main actors in this sector, both of which are umbrella associations for many small cooperatives. Housing dependent on these cooperatives is equivalent to 700 000 apartments or 17% of the total housing sector. HSB currently represents close to half of this market.

Transition Countries

In a study commissioned by the EIB, the Hungarian research institute Ecorys Research and Consulting (2005) described housing policy development in CEE (Central and Eastern Europe) and SEE (Southeast Europe) countries by referring to a general model (**Figure 2**):

1. In the first period of transition, housing construction is reduced to owner-built, particularly single-family houses. The traditionally rather strong state involvement in financing, building, allocation, and management decreases sharply. Housing production drops drastically and privatisation and restitution take place.
2. In the following years legal reforms are undertaken and the banking sector establishes and develops mortgage instruments. The private sector recovers with the development of owner-occupied apartments. The authors include the present situation in Romania and Bulgaria in this stage.
3. Subsequently, the states develop subsidy policies. This is the case in CEE countries and Croatia today.
4. The final stage is described as having reestablished social housing schemes and urban renewal policies. As a complementary sector, the nonprofit sector with housing cooperatives, housing associations, and housing corporations may operate under some kind of government supervision, enjoying government subsidies.

Figure 3 summarises the dynamics of housing delivery systems throughout the stages of transformation. The lack of housing development because of reduced public sector

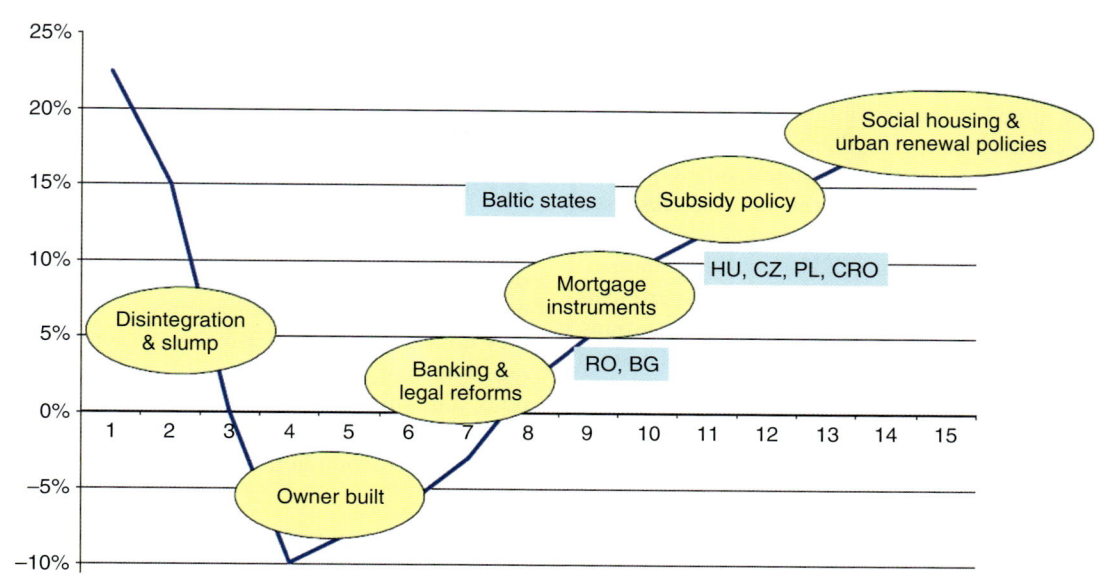

Figure 2 Policy development in transition countries, housing output and time.
Adapted from Ecorys Research and Consulting (2005) Housing sector study in Central Eastern and South Eastern Europe. *Study Prepared for the European Investment Bank. Final Draft Report, 25/07/2005*. Budapest: Ecorys.

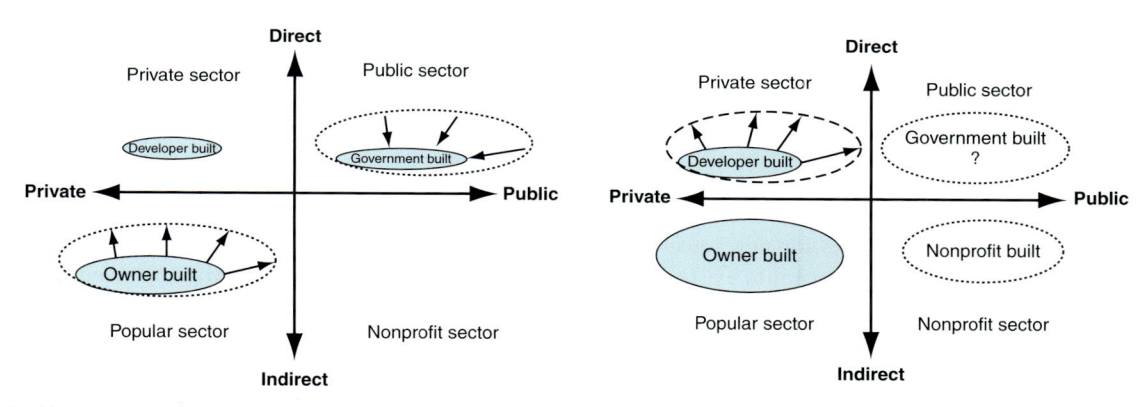

Figure 3 Housing delivery dynamics during transition.
Adapted from Ecorys Research and Consulting (2005) Housing sector study in Central Eastern and South Eastern Europe. *Study Prepared for the European Investment Bank. Final Draft Report, 25/07/2005*, pp. 15–18. Budapest: Ecorys.

development is being balanced by private developer-built housing construction and, in some countries, by the emergence of nonprofit or limited-profit housing production only around a decade after the transformation process was initiated.

Although construction of owner-occupied apartments has recovered, this is not the case for rental and especially limited-profit affordable housing (Tsenkova, 2005). Public housing experienced a sharp decline in the 1990s and has not staged a recovery. Municipalities are active in housing construction in only a few countries (e.g., Poland). Generally, the public sector has done away with owners' obligations by privatising big parts of rental stock (Hegedüs, 2007).

The profession of rental housing developers is not established in the majority of CEE and SEE countries. Currently, housing developers are often subsidiaries of construction companies. Their primary motive is to employ their own construction division and to get returns on investment as soon as possible. Long-term investments are neither their core business nor in their interest. Affordable rental housing developers in contrast must have a long-term perspective. So far, only some attempts at a nonprofit or limited-profit housing sector can be observed.

The Polish TBS Model

In 1997, Poland introduced a rental housing construction programme aimed at municipalities. Some 100 000 units have been constructed so far. The administration of this programme is carried out by the state-held BGK Bank and finance consists of long-term interest-subsidised loans (3.5% double-indexed). Construction is realised by nonprofit housing associations (TBS) owned by municipalities and by a few cooperatives. The rental apartments are targeted more at middle- than at low-income groups. Co-funding by private equity has to reach 30% of costs in order for the remaining 70% of costs to qualify for subsidies by the National Housing Fund (KFM), which is financed predominantly out of the state budget. Since 2002, the funding has to a large extent been provided by state-guaranteed loans from the EIB and the CEB (Le Blanc, 2009). The significant requirement for outstanding public loans is also a considerable problem. Also, within the political debate, insufficient targeting of the subsidies has been criticised, because objective criteria for allocating these very cheap dwellings are lacking. There is an urgent need for narrowing the gap with market conditions. Therefore cofinancing and refinancing through commercial banks and the issue of domestic bonds should be considered to relieve the pressure of budgetary funding. Meanwhile, production output of the TBS sector has decreased strongly.

Cooperatives in the Czech Republic

In the Czech Republic, neither social housing nor nonprofit housing associations are legally defined. Yet, in 1995, special subsidy programmes for new 'quasi-rental' municipal housing construction came into existence, with total subsidies amounting to approximately one-fourth to one-third of average dwelling construction costs. The programme allowed for the creation of cooperatives (public–private partnership: PPP) between municipalities and participants (future tenants): a municipality, with the help of a commercial developer, secured the state subsidies. The remaining costs of development were covered by downpayments from future tenants and by commercial mortgage loans. Though a right to buy was allowed only after 20 years from the year of completion, the share in a housing cooperative could, under valid legislation, be liquidated immediately, resulting in a quasi-ownership structure. Even though this programme helped to increase new construction considerably, it was highly criticised for several reasons. Amongst these were the emergence of a black market in rent-regulated municipal dwellings and the illegal 'sale' of rental contracts on rent-regulated municipal apartments, carried out via fictitious dwelling exchanges. Also, there were no limitations concerning the maximum cost per square metre or the maximum area of the dwelling, and no means-testing was applied in the allocation. Owing to this body of criticism, the system was largely amended in 2003. The cooperative form was forbidden, cost and income ceilings were introduced, and the participation of private capital was further encouraged. Apartments constructed with this state subsidy now have to remain in the ownership of the municipality and have to be used for the purpose of housing based on a lease right. Only some income groups (lower-income groups) may become tenants in such apartments, on condition that they do not own any other real estate intended for housing. The rent level corresponds approximately to cost rents. The subsidy programme for 'quasi-rental' municipal housing has contributed considerably to the high rate of new construction in the Czech Republic.

The Slovak Nonprofit Housing Scheme

Only 4% of the Slovakian housing stock consists of municipal dwellings and 14% of cooperative dwellings. Due to the scarcity of social housing, rental contracts with the municipalities are generally limited to 3 years. As a result, the existing law on nonprofit organisations was extended to the area of housing. The tax reductions that were introduced benefit associations and cooperatives, but they do not apply to capital companies. Owners may be municipalities or private individuals. Nevertheless, only housing associations that are predominantly owned by municipalities may receive state subsidies. They also have to respect specific building cost caps. After a setup period of several years, in 2004 and 2005, the first two housing associations following this model were founded. One of them is owned by the city of Bratislava (90%) and the bank Istrobanka (10%). The other one, based in the northern Bohemian city of Martin, received important help from the Dutch housing fund DIGH (Dutch International Guarantees for Housing). These two associations have just begun building activity. The foundation of these associations met with considerable difficulties. Approval had to be obtained from the local authorities. The authorities are concerned about a capital outflow and have therefore established strict control mechanisms.

Conclusion

In economically advanced European countries, housing development is often carried out by specific housing developers of a so-called Third Sector, which is situated between the state and the market. Limited-profit housing providers may take various legal forms. Yet, they have to act in accordance with public interest and therefore get assigned subsidies of various forms or building land. Rent levels and access to their dwellings are legally restricted.

An analysis indicates that there are two important prerequisites for establishing affordable limited-profit housing in CEE countries: First, the operation of limited-profit housing developers must be defined by law, as building of assets is promoted by public funding. Second, a sound financing model is required.

Limited-profit housing development is designed as an alternative to both private and public housing. Developers are managed on a private market basis, but have to accept thorough public supervision and auditing. Over the years, business operations may generate substantial assets. This results in economically strong companies with a sound and secure position in financing markets and markets for construction services. This also requires strict regulations regarding the treatment of profits and assets. Therefore an adequate legal framework has to define that profits should be made, but must be reinvested in housing.

The IIBW (Institute for Real Estate, Construction and Housing Ltd., Vienna) and DIGH have designed a financing model, following the principles of a Housing Finance Agency for Countries in Transition (H!FACT) towards the implementation of an affordable rental housing market in several CEE countries. The fundamental aim is to provide inputs from housing systems in 'old' Europe for an efficient framework for the operation of limited-profit developers.

See also: Cooperative Housing/Ownership; Economics of Social Housing; Housing Finance Institutions: Transition Societies.

References

Amann W, Lawson J, and Mundt A (2009) Structured financing allows for affordable rental housing in Austria. *Housing Finance International* S14–S18.
Amann W and Mundt A (2009) Indicators of a unitary rental market in Austria. *Paper Presented at the ENHR Conference*. Prague, Czech Republic, 28 June–1 July.
Arbaci S (2007) Ethnic segregation, housing systems and welfare regimes in Europe. *European Journal of Housing Policy* 7(4): 401–433.
Barlow J and Duncan S (1994) *Success and Failure in Housing Provision, European Systems Compared*. Oxford, UK; New York; Tokyo: Elsevier Science Ltd.
Boelhouwer PJ (2007) The future of Dutch housing association. *Journal of Housing and the Built Environment* 22: 383–391.
Czischke D (2009) Managing social rental housing in the EU: A comparative study. *European Journal of Housing Policy* 7(2): 121–151.
Ecorys Research Consulting (2005) Housing sector study in Central Eastern and South Eastern Europe. *Study Prepared for the European Investment Bank. Final Draft Report, 25/07/2005*. Budapest: Ecorys.
Esping-Andersen G (1990) *The Three Worlds of Welfare Capitalism*. Princeton, NJ: Princeton University Press.
Golland A and Oxley M (2004) Housing development in Europe. In: Golland A and Blake R (eds.) *Housing Development. Theory, Process and Practice*, ch. 12, pp. 295–320. London; New York: Routledge.
Healey P and Barret SM (1990) Structure and agency in land and property development processes: Some ideas for research. *Urban Studies* 27(1): 89–104.
Hegedüs J (2007) Social housing in transition countries. In: Whitehead C and Scanlon K (eds.) *Social Housing in Europe*, pp. 165–177. London: LSE.
Keivani R and Werna E (2001) Modes of housing provision in developing countries. *Progress in Planning* 55: 65–118.
Le Blanc D (2009) Residential rental housing finance. In: Chiquier L and Lea M (eds.) *Housing Finance Policy in Emerging Markets*, pp. 363–394. Washington, DC: The World Bank.
Levy-Vroelant C and Tutin C (2007) Social housing in France. In: Whitehead C and Scanlon K (eds.) *Social Housing in Europe*, pp. 90–104. London: LSE.
Tsenkova S (2005) *Trends and Progress in Housing Reforms in South Eastern Europe*. Paris: Council of Europe Development Bank (CEB).
Turner B (2007) Social housing in Sweden. In: Whitehead C and Scanlon K (eds.) *Social Housing in Europe*, pp. 148–164. London: LSE.

Relevant Website

www.sabo.se – SABO website.

Housing Developers: Developing World

C Acioly Jr. and M French, United Nations Human Settlement Programme (UN-HABITAT), Nairobi, Kenya

© 2012 Elsevier Ltd. All rights reserved.

Introduction: Urban Informality and Housing Development

The majority of the housing stock in cities of the developing world is built by informal self-built housing processes. Rapid urbanisation and population growth, lack of formal employment, and insufficient supply of affordable housing force a significant proportion of urban dwellers to become housing developers who plan, finance, and construct their house outside the domain of official planning and development control. The production of such housing comes about in a much less well-defined manner than housing development in the developed world. Yet, this method shares similar basic underpinnings of what it means to be a housing developer: in essence the use and modification of the physical environment in an effort to add value for economic gain.

There are many housing development modalities in the developing world, with informal self-built housing, as described above, being only one. This article will first explain how the range of modalities is best conceptualised on a continuum from informal to formal, rather than be seen as formal–informal binary modalities. The concept of 'housing developer' is useful to undertake this analysis because through looking at the field through the housing developer lens one can look at the housing system in terms of adding value, rather than just the initial provision of houses for immediate commercial gain. Accordingly, development approaches such as incremental housing processes and slum upgrading are also considered housing developer modalities, even though they typically do not include the direct provision of housing units.

After presenting the 11 developer modalities on the formality continuum, this article will describe the three housing development modalities of the developing world at the informal end of the continuum: unauthorised owner-occupier self-build, unauthorised subdivision, and rental property. Overall, then, this article gives an overview of all development modalities and a focused description of the three informal modalities. It demonstrates that informal housing developers that operate outside formal controls are largely building the cities of today in the developing world.

Housing Developers in the Developing World

In the developed world context, a 'housing developer' is traditionally considered to be an actor or entity whose central activity is the modification of the physical environment for the purpose of their own economic gain. Developers can be one person, a group of people, or a partnership or corporation. Housing development is a commercial enterprise that is profit driven and highly speculative and the primary activity is investing in land and/or buildings and subsequently improving them, typically through the construction of new buildings or the provision of infrastructure and services. Therefore, a property developer seeks to add value to the physical environment and capitalise on this added value through selling the improved property, to extract the added value.

Using this conceptualisation of a housing developer as an actor who seeks to add value and create wealth by modification of the physical environment, there are many actors in the developing world that can be considered as housing developers. There are those who follow a similar model to developers in the developed world: private companies who work within the formal real estate sector to produce housing with the aim of making a profit. Likewise, governments of developing countries act as housing developers, either directly or indirectly for low-income housing.

There are also a variety of informal housing developers operating in the developing world. By far, the most significant is the unauthorised owner-occupier self-build developers who occupy slums and squatter settlements that currently account for a significant proportion of the world's construction activity. They are not 'commercial housing developers' whose primary activity is conventional housing development as noted above, but rather can be considered as 'everyday developers' whose development activities are tied up with daily living activities, a motivation to attain shelter and improve their economic situation. There is also a unique type of housing developer widely active in Asia and Latin America that illegally subdivides land, sells plots to individuals who will ultimately build their homes on it with or without support from the land developer. Cities like Bogotá, São Paulo, and Karachi have large parts of their territory developed through this informal land subdivision modality.

There are, therefore, key differences between housing developers in the developed and developing worlds, even though they are both engaged in the same process of producing housing and adding value. Housing developers in the developed world are risk-averse, driven almost exclusively by economic gain, and work at large scales in a fast manner. In contrast, informal developers in the developing world often take high risks, are motivated primarily by their shelter needs, and predominantly work at small scales, often the unit of the household, at a much slower pace dictated by their financial capabilities.

The Formality Continuum of Housing Development in the Developing World

Housing developer modes in developing countries have typically been referred to as either formal or informal. In practice, the conceptual binary is between informal, illegal squatter settlements and formal private sector and government housing development. The level of formality typically concerns the degree to which an entity acts within the government regulatory framework. This includes aspects such as housing finance, real estate, and infrastructure; and relates to if the entity acts within the official structure (for instance, obtains building consents, pays property taxes, and for the use of municipal services, etc.). Drakakis-Smith (1981) provides an overall conceptualisation of the housing sector, and divides housing production into conventional and unconventional (formal and informal). Keivani and Werna (2001) develop Drakakis-Smith's framework and retain the conventional–unconventional binary. The conventional modes are public, cooperative, and private development and unconventional modes are squatters, informal subdivision, and rental development.

Rather than seeing housing production as pertaining to either a purely formal or informal system, as an informal/formal binary, housing development in developing countries is best seen on a continuum from informal to formal modes. A continuum recognises that even in formal modes there are certain practices, activities, and processes that are informal. Likewise, in informal methods, there are often links with, for example, formal government structures, private finance entities, or material suppliers. Therefore, a continuum better reflects the intricacies of different housing development methods, especially those 'hybrid' approaches such as self-help or cooperative housing which explicitly include both formal and informal components and processes. Eleven prevailing housing developer modalities in the developing world are identified and outlined in **Table 1**.

Informal Housing Development Modalities

Throughout the developing world, informal housing production accounts for the majority of housing activity. According to UN-HABITAT, in Africa and in some subregions of Asia, urban growth is largely synonymous with slum formation, meaning that cities are growing on the basis of informal land and housing developments and not as a result of planned processes within the formal housing market. For example, in sub-Saharan Africa urban growth and slum growth are almost identical: 4.58 and 4.53%, respectively (UN-HABITAT, 2005). Informal modes of housing are those that are undertaken outside of the official planning framework, often contravening building codes and norms, and out of the control of the state, city, or local authorities. Informal modes are not regulated by state building and planning codes, are financially independent (they do not pay taxes or receive any subsidies), and, at least initially, are not formally recognised by any state agencies (for instance, listed on land and building registries).

A key feature of informal development is the reversal of formal development stages. Baross (1987) highlights how the failure of formal housing provision in the developing world has been due to the inadequacy of conventional housing and development models. The formal approach of planning, servicing, building, and subsequent occupation (PSBO) model is an inadequate method to provide housing in a context of rapid urbanisation and increasing demand for housing, land, and infrastructure such as those found in the developing world. This PSBO model is the opposite of informal housing approaches, which can be explained as the OBSP model: occupation, building, servicing, and planning model (**Figure 1**). It is this reversal of formal development stages that characterises informal development modalities (Acioly, 2010).

The prevalence and scale of informal development depend on several factors. Along with rapid population growth, high levels of sustained urbanisation have significantly increased urban housing demand. Vast numbers of poor rural migrants, who relocate to the city in search of employment and greater opportunities, seek housing that is affordable and centrally located for employment purposes. Informal housing such as squatter settlements and slums suits the needs of recent migrants (Turner, 1976) and are much cheaper than formal housing. Combined with this demand, there is insufficient supply of affordable housing, especially centrally located housing, and formal housing is prohibitively expensive in terms of the initial purchase price and operating cost.

Resulting from this drastically mismatched supply and demand, informal housing developers construct a significant proportion of the housing stock in the developing world. Generally, informal housing development depends on land availability, with cities that have large tracts of public land having higher rates of informal settlements than those with higher levels of private land (UNCHS, 1996), as well as the level of tolerance and lenience afforded by the national and city governments to informal development. Across the developing world, there are three main informal developer modalities: unauthorised owner-occupier self-builders which is by far the most widespread; unauthorised land subdividers which is becoming increasingly dominant as available

Table 1 Housing developer modalities in the developing world

	Modality	Characteristics	Key actor(s) leading development	Geographic location and examples
Informal	1. Unauthorised owner-occupied self-build	Incremental construction of housing units over many years and decades led by households on land that is (at least initially) occupied illegally	Low-income households and self-formed informal neighbourhood organisations	Throughout the developing world, especially in countries that have tolerant governments towards such processes
	2. Unauthorised subdivision	Land is subdivided into individual plots and either sold on the informal market or upon which housing units are developed and then sold	Private developers acting outside formal system. In some cases, 'land grabbers'	Pirate land subdividers of Colombia; clandestine land subdividers of Brazil; 'land grabbers' in Pakistan
	3. Rental property	Construction of units or rooms that are rented to low-income households and recent migrants, outside of formal controls	Middle- and upper-income citizens, dedicated rental property developers, landowners	Africa, with very low-quality construction, very common in West African cities; The *Bustees* of Calcutta
			Unauthorised self-builders who have incorporated rental rooms/units into their houses	Very common in Latin America: rooms/units in self-built unauthorised houses (modality 1)
Informal–formal hybrid	4. Community slum upgrading and resettlement	The community organises themselves, agrees on their needs and priorities, works with the government to secure funding, and implements the urban upgrading or resettlement project	Community organisations, often with support from NGOs; local government; local and international funding providers	For example, resettlement partnership in Manila, Philippines (UN-HABITAT and UNESCAP, 2008). For example, Baan Mankong Programme, Bangkok, Thailand (UN-HABITAT and UNESCAP, 2008)
	5. 'Self-help' housing	Government provision of serviced plots of land on which residents incrementally construct their house, often known as 'Sites & Services'. Sometimes incremental land development schemes with unserviced land	Government leads land and service provision, after which low-income households lead the house building process	For example, Villa El Salvador, Lima, Peru (Ivo and Rustler, 2003). For example, Samambaia, Brasilia, Brazil
	6. Cooperative housing partnerships	Cooperatives organise themselves, save, obtain land from government, and construct houses either communally or individually	Cooperatives lead the process, often with support from NGOs, with government support through land provision	For example, Barrio Hardoy, Buenos Aires, Argentina Almansi and Tammarazio (2008). For example, Prek Toel, Phnom Penh, Cambodia (UN-HABITAT and UNESCAP, 2008)
	7. Owner-occupier transformations of social housing	Occupants who have received a government 'social' house incrementally modify/enlarge it	Once occupied the owner-occupier leads the process. Government regulations and building type restrict opportunities	In Egypt, even mid-rise multifamily blocks have been subject to informal expansion
Formal	8. Government-led slum upgrading	Informal slum settlements are upgraded through infrastructure and service provision and regularisation of tenure, which can add considerable value through encouraging further investment in housing	National governments, local authorities, NGOs, professionals (architects, engineers, etc.)	For example, Favela-Bairro project in Rio de Janeiro, Brazil (Machado, 2003). For example, Kampung Improvement Programme (KIP) in Indonesia

(Continued)

Table 1 (Continued)

Modality	Characteristics	Key actor(s) leading development	Geographic location and examples
9. Legally established community groups	Organised community groups, recognised by law, apply for public funding, and develop housing on self-management, mutual aid, and assisted self-help building processes supported by technical assistance from NGOs	Community-based organisations, supported by NGOs	São Paulo's FUNACOM programme, later brought to scale for the State of São Paulo and now a national model recognised by the Brazilian National Social Housing Fund (Denaldi, 1994)
10. Private	Typically either speculative or individual owner-occupier. Profit-seeking developers often partner with governments for low-income housing ('public–private partnership')	Commercial housing developers. Built environment professionals. Middle- and high-income citizens	Throughout the developing world but especially in countries with well-functioning construction industries and supportive regulatory frameworks: El Salvador, India, Brazil, Malaysia, and Zambia
11. Direct government 'social housing'	Land and housing is developed by the government (sometimes via the private sector) and is sold or rented to low-income households	The government leads and finances the process with support from the private sector	For example, Ethiopian Condominium Housing Programme (UN-HABITAT, 2011); South Africa national housing programme

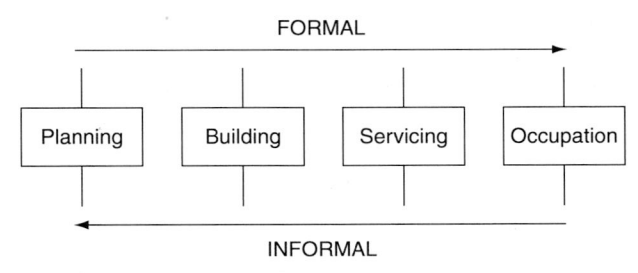

Figure 1 Formal and informal housing development approaches.
Source: Adapted from Baross P (1987) Land supply for low-income housing: Issues and approaches. *Regional Development Dialogue* 8(4): 29–45; and Acioly C Jr. (2010) The informal city and the phenomenon of slums: The challenges of slum upgrading and slum prevention. In: International New Town Institute (ed.) *New Towns for the 21st Century: The Planned vs. the Unplanned City*, pp. 222–231. Amsterdam: SUN architecture.

land for individual household squatting is becoming increasingly difficult; and rental property developers, both small-scale petty (household) landlords and dedicated landlord developers who often have large rental property portfolios.

Unauthorised Owner-Occupied Self-Build

The unauthorised owner-occupied self-build mode of housing provision includes squatter settlements, informal settlements, and self-built slums. Throughout the last four decades, it has been the dominant method of housing provision. The unauthorised owner-occupier developer secures a plot of land (either squatting illegally, through organised mass invasion or gradually by families or small groups, or informally through de facto tenure agreements with landowners) and then constructs a housing unit, almost always without official permission, registration, or building code compliance.

Although there is regional variation, the housing development process follows a similar general trend. Initially, the shelter quality is rudimentary, constructed from inexpensive and impermanent materials. Seldom is there infrastructure and service provision. If eviction is resisted and de facto tenure secured, owner-occupiers consolidate the rudimentary shacks into more permanent, often multistoried houses. Concurrent with individual house development, the neighbourhood secures services such as electricity, water, and sanitation and installs infrastructure such as roads, street lighting, and public spaces. The consolidation process typically takes many decades after which time these informal settlements are often indistinguishable from neighbouring formally developed areas. The consolidation process, however, is not a given and it does not always take place; often the rudimentary settlements remain so, depending on the level of community cohesion, investment capacity in housing, tenure security, and owner-occupation (Gilbert, 1990).

While the unauthorised self-build housing developer is largely independent, acting according to their own interests and financial capacity, they often have connections to local neighbourhood organisations, working with them to improve communal neighbourhood aspects and lobby the government or municipality for land title registration and service provision. While the owner-occupier largely constructs the initial house, specialised tasks – or in some cases all of the construction tasks – for the consolidated house are outsourced to informal building contractors (Drakakis-Smith, 1981). Housing finance is largely dependent on the individual developer's resources and capacity. In many parts of the developing world, this mode is increasingly difficult for the low-income sector due to increased pressure on limited land supply that forces land prices up and reduces the number of invasions (Ward and Macoloo, 1992).

Unauthorised Subdivision

Unauthorised subdivisions are developed by small- and medium-sized private developers who secure an area of land, undertake a detailed site survey, and divide the land into plots that are then sold to owner-occupier self-builders. The whole process is by and large undertaken outside government control. This mode contrasts with the unauthorised owner-occupied self-build mode in terms of the initial land acquisition and development process; however, the house building and infrastructure provision process is largely the same. As inner-city land for squatting becomes increasingly unavailable, this mode is gradually becoming the dominant informal settlement approach in developing countries (Baross and Van de Linden, 1990; Keivani and Werna, 2001; UNCHS, 1996). These developments are often located on the periphery of cities where there is a greater availability of land, often agricultural land, and a greater chance that the land capture and resale will be unchallenged by authorities.

The approach is very similar to formal land speculators, but these developers operate outside the formal system, thus no formal planning approval is sought and the settlement may not meet official urban planning and land use regulations (for instance, minimum plot size, rights of way, density limitations, floor area ratio, etc.). Service provision is not usually given at the time of individual plot sale due to the high costs incurred by the developer. Rather, unserviced plots are sold under contract between the developer and the purchaser. Then, as with unauthorised owner-occupier self-build, houses are incrementally constructed, often with a greater reliance on subcontraction of construction tasks and a greater focus on speculation than in the typical squatter approach of modality 1. Over time, infrastructure and service provision follow and it is rather common to find small-scale informal building contractors operating on the basis of commissioned tasks of the housing construction process. In some cases, such as in Bangkok, these developers also build low-income housing on the plots, yet this remains an uncommon approach and the main business of the developer in this modality is to expedite the development and sale of land plots (Keivani and Werna, 2001).

The land can be either privately or publicly owned. In both cases, the developer is the central actor negotiating the development proposal and financial incentive for the existing landholder. Because of the nature of land subdivision schemes, there is an intrinsic illicit practice of securing land to make it available for housing. Conversion of use is often not authorised by government planning agencies, for example, from agricultural to residential land use, and the initial land sellers may not necessarily be the same entity as the legal landowners meaning that land has been grabbed and used without knowledge or permission by the one who has the freehold rights.

For private land, the developer negotiates the extent of the proposed development and the financial compensation arrangement for the private landholder. For public land, the developer may find ways to unofficially negotiate with government officials to ensure that the proposed land development will go unchallenged, with officials receiving financial benefit either through personal allocation of plots or a proportion of overall development profit (Keivani and Werna, 2001).

This form of development is common where customary landownership exists, such as in many West African countries, where tribal chiefs, rather than the government or municipalities, have strong control over land and are therefore relatively capable of facilitating this process unhindered by state regulations. It is also evidenced in Latin America, for example, the *Ejidal* in Mexico that are developed outside state control (Gilbert and Ward, 1985; Moser, 1982). This modality best illustrates the fact that in the developing world housing is produced under different modalities which are bound to the local political context and the degree of government tolerance towards certain modes of production, even if they contravene the law.

Rental Units

A significant proportion of low-income urban dwellers in the developing world rent rather than own the housing they occupy. This is especially the case with the 'poorest of the poor' and recent urban migrants, who are financially excluded from formal housing systems, cannot afford to purchase land through unauthorised subdivisions, or secure owner-occupied housing in existing slums and informal settlements. Rental housing has both benefits and disadvantages: it is cheap, centrally located, and offers flexibility, yet it can place renters in situations of exploitation by landlords, it is typically of a very low environmental quality, and tenants have less security of tenure (UN-HABITAT, 2003b).

There are two main types of informal rental housing developers in the developing world. The first type is the dedicated rental property developer who specifically develops rental accommodation on a large scale outside formal controls. They take a variety of guises: property owners who develop their property independently, middlemen who operate on behalf of property owners, and dedicated informal private enterprises that develop property in opportune locations specifically for rental. They either build new units or adapt existing buildings to accommodate many housing units for rent. In general, the dwelling quality is low, which keeps rental costs low (desirable for the low-income tenants). The *Bustees* of Calcutta provide a clear example of the large-scale development of rental housing by large-scale property owners and middlemen.

The second type is small-scale rental property developers who modify their informal owner-occupied house to include rental accommodation. As they incrementally consolidate, their house owner-occupiers add extra rooms or independent housing units to accommodate other households or extended family. Such development is financially advantageous as it generates an income that can be used to further improve the house, construct additional units, and increase the overall financial security of the landlord. Such small-scale rental property development is common throughout the developing world, especially in countries with high housing demand (due to high urbanisation and population growth rates) and already dense inner-city informal settlements where land is scarce.

Both types are informal in that they are developed outside official planning and city development plans, their developments do not conform to building and planning regulations, and they do not pay taxes. Therefore, rental properties and arrangements are usually kept quiet and as a result, the scale and intricacies of this mode of housing provision are the least documented and understood of all housing modalities (UN-HABITAT, 2003b).

Conclusion: The Dominant Role of Informal Developers

There are significant differences between housing developers in the developed and developing worlds, yet there are also many similarities: they mobilise resources and modify the physical environment in an effort to add value. In outlining a typology continuum and identifying the 11 main housing developer modalities, this article has demonstrated the wide spectrum of housing approaches in the developing world. The majority of cities in the developing world are being built by informal housing developers who act outside official control in a variety of ways. Unauthorised owner-occupied self-build is the most well-known classic modality that represents the largest share of informal development. Increasing in scale, however, is unauthorised land subdivision on the periphery of cities where land is divided into plots and sold with or without services. Likewise, as urban land becomes increasingly scarce and expensive, large- and small-scale rental housing developments are becoming common.

Having looked at the field through the conceptual lens of 'housing developer', this article has highlighted that low-income citizens are not only striving for adequate shelter but to use housing as a form of investment and security, and, importantly, for economic gain. Many see housing as a guarantee of a type of pension and social security in their old age, as well as an important asset to pass on to their family.

The continuum highlights that in reality modes of housing production do not fit neatly into the formal–informal dichotomy. Rather, within each mode, there is either more or less influence of informal and formal elements. Local and international policy must acknowledge that the informal sector is a major force of housing production in the developing world. With such a range of modalities, the challenge for the public and private sectors is how to encourage and facilitate the growth of all modes of housing provision in order to 'go to scale' and meet the high demand. While the growth of informal housing modes is not desirable per se, attention must be given to the hybrid approaches (e.g., housing cooperatives) as well as government-supported self-management models and autonomous housing building process to ascertain how they can be supported. This is essential because it is highly unlikely that formal approaches alone will meet the massive housing demand – both existing and future – in developing countries. The challenge, then, is how governments and the private sector in the developing world can capitalise on the creativity and entrepreneurship of informal housing developers to expand access to adequate and affordable housing.

See also: Housing Developers: Developed World; Housing Institutions in Developing Countries; Housing Policies in Developing Countries; Housing Policies in Developing Countries: Sites-and-Services and Aided Self-Help; Informal Housing: Latin America; Private Rental Landlords: Developing Countries; Self-Build: Global South.

References

Acioly C Jr. (2010) The informal city and the phenomenon of slums: The challenges of slum upgrading and slum prevention. In: International New Town Institute (ed.) *New Towns for the 21st Century: The Planned vs. the Unplanned City*, pp. 222–231. Amsterdam: SUN Architecture.

Baross P (1987) Land supply for low-income housing: Issues and approaches. *Regional Development Dialogue* 8(4): 29–45.

Baross P and Van de Linden (1990) *The Transformation of Land Supply Systems in Third World Cities*. Aldershot, UK: Avebury.

Denaldi R (1994) *Viable Self-Management: The FUNACOM Housing Programme of the São Paulo Municipality*. IHS Working Paper Series No. 9. Rotterdam, The Netherlands: IHS.

Drakakis-Smith D (1981) *Housing and the Urban Development Process*. London: Croom Helm.

Gilbert A and Ward P (1987) *Housing, the State and the Poor: Policy and Practice in Three Latin American Cities*. Cambridge, UK: Cambridge University Press.

Gilbert A (1990) The costs and benefits of illegality and irregularity in the supply of land. In: Baross P and Van der Linden J. (eds.) *The Transformation of Land Supply in Third World Cities*, pp. 17–36. Aldershot, UK: Avebury.

Ivo I and Rustler J (2003) *Slum Upgrading and Participation: Lessons from Latin America*. Washington, DC: The World Bank.

Keivani R and Werna E (2001) Refocusing the housing debate in developing countries from a pluralist perspective. *Habitat International* 25: 191–208.

Machado R (ed.) (2003) *The Favela-Bairro Project*. Harvard, MA: Harvard University Graduate School of Design.

Moser C (1982) A home of one's own: Squatter housing strategies in Guayaquil, Ecuador. In: Gilbert A, Hardoy J, and Ramirez R (eds.) *Urbanization in Contemporary Latin America*. Chichester, UK: Wiley.

Turner JFC (1976) *Housing by People: Towards Autonomy in Building Environments*. London: Marion Boyars.

UNCHS (1996) *An Urbanizing World: Global Report of Human Settlements*. Oxford, UK: Oxford University Press.

UN-HABITAT (2003b) *Rental Housing: An Essential Option for the Urban Poor in Developing Countries*. Nairobi: UN-HABITAT.

UN-HABITAT (2005) *Global Urban Observatory, Urban Indicators Programme, Phase III*. Nairobi: UN-HABITAT.

UN-HABITAT (2011) *Condominium Housing in Ethiopia: The Integrated Housing Development Plan*. Nairobi: UN-HABITAT.

UN-HABITAT and UNESCAP (2008) *Housing for the Poor in Asian cities: 6: Community-Based Organizations: The Poor as Agents of Development*. Nairobi: UNON.

Ward P and Macoloo CG (1992) Articulation theory and self-help housing in the 1990s. *International Journal of Urban and Regional Research* 16:1, 60–80.

Further Reading

Almansi F and Tammarazio A (2008) Mobilizing projects in community organisations with a long-term perspective: Neighbourhood credit funds in Buenos Aires. *Environment and Urbanization* 20.1, 121–147.

Davis M (2006) *Planet of Slums*. New York: Verso.

Tipple G (2000) *Extending Themselves: User Initiated Transformations of Government-built Housing in Developing Countries*. Liverpool, UK: Liverpool University Press.

UN-HABITAT (2003a) *The Challenge of Slums: Global Report on Human Settlements*. London: Earthscan.

UN-HABITAT and International Co-Operative Alliance (ICA) (2001) *Shelter Co-operatives in Eastern and Southern Africa: Contributions of the Co-operative Sector to Shelter Development*. Nairobi: United Nations Centre for Human Settlements.

Housing Dynamics: Environmental Aspects

G Powells, Durham University, Durham, UK

© 2012 Elsevier Ltd. All rights reserved.

Glossary

Building code A building code is a set of rules that specify the minimum acceptable level of safety for constructed objects such as buildings and nonbuilding structures. Building codes are set by national, federal, or state-level institutions.

Embodied emissions Embodied emissions are those CO_2 or GHG emissions produced across a product or service's entire life cycle. This includes raw material extraction, transport, manufacture, assembly, installation, disassembly, deconstruction, and/or decomposition.

Introduction

The demand for housing is a constant feature of any society, one which drives economies, supply chains, labour markets, and governments more powerfully than almost any other sector, as evidenced by the extremes of wealth and worry caused by the recent economic booms and subsequent financial crisis, both inextricably linked to housing economics. This powerful economic driver, however, is also very profoundly linked to the wider environment in which it is located – our planet. The impacts of adequately providing housing and the associated domestic services (such as heating, lighting, water, and waste collection) on the environment are many, significant, and growing.

The amplification of environmental impacts comes at a time when sustainability is a mainstream concern of every government institution, every firm, and, increasingly, every community. Whether for reputational advantage, operating efficiency, or ethical reasons, minimising the impacts of housing on the environment has in the twenty-first century moved from being a concern of a vocal minority to a major feature of housing strategy, construction, and governance.

However, while awareness of the challenges associated with sustainable housing is more widely acknowledged, major challenges persist in delivering homes which minimise a wide range of environmental impacts while creating the best possible homes for people. This tension between discourses of sustainability and practices structured by legacies of house building, construction skills and techniques, economic realities, and unrelenting consumer demand for more space, luxury, and convenience animates the interaction between housing and the environment.

There are several registers in which the environmental impacts of housing markets can be observed. The article attempts to provide an outline of these impacts on various supply- and demand-side housing issues.

Supply Side: Regulating Construction

Increasingly, the sustainable building agenda is widening in scope to include low-carbon energy technologies, affordability, and waste minimisation as well as the associated environmental impacts of transport and utilities connectivity. Across Western economies, increasing recognition of the need for sustainable housing has led to the creation of sustainable building codes to which constructors must adhere.

In the United Kingdom, the Building Research Establishment's Code for Sustainable Homes sets out targets for cooking appliances, space heating, lighting, cooling ventilation, and hot water with the aim of introducing practices and design components previously found in niche ecobuilds to mainstream house building. Similar schemes and building codes exist in other nations, including the Building Code of Australia, Spain's Building Technical Code (CTE – Código Técnico de la Edificación), and the Model Energy Code in the United States. Several state- and local-level building codes exist in North America, the North Carolina State Energy Code, the Arizona State Energy Code, and the Massachusetts Energy Conservation Code.

While building codes have emerged as a core element of governmental responses to the challenge of sustainability in the built environment, their deployment differs geographically. Research has found considerable differences between North American, UK, and Australian building codes as well as between codes within the United States. Governmental efforts to tackle climate change take place at various scales, from the international to the local, and it is certainly the case that in large federally governed states, subnational governmental institutions have acted with powerful effects to control the energy performance of new house building in their territories driven by a motivation to reduce greenhouse gas emissions.

At the other end of the spatial scale, intergovernmental action on sustainable homes can be found in the EU, where since 2008 Energy Performance Certificates (EPCs) have been required whenever a dwelling is built, sold, or rented out. This not only creates an industry in energy certification and inspection, and develops associated skills, but also creates marketplace advantages for low-energy homes – whether due to the reduced running costs or through appeals to environmental values of buyers and renters. The effectiveness and design of EPCs, however, has been called into question.

A relatively new debate in this area is around the GHG emissions embodied in new build homes. While it is generally the case that new homes built to contemporary building codes have better energy performance and result in lower operational emissions (from occupants' activities), the construction activities and materials used bring with them significant, under-acknowledged carbon emissions. These embodied emissions are those generated by the mining of raw materials and the processes such as making concrete, firing bricks, and transporting building materials to the construction site gate. Minimising the embodied carbon built into construction materials and processes remains an area of environmental accountability in the shadows and largely out of sight on mainstream efforts to create sustainable homes, but as more scrutiny is applied to the area, the environmental impacts of what happens before the site gate begin to enter into the discussion.

The Existing Housing Stock

Regardless of the impacts of new low-impact building codes, creating sustainable housing in the twenty-first century is a project which cannot start with a clean slate. The brute indifference of the existing housing stock and its resolute durability means that the biggest and most difficult challenge is dealing with the homes that we inherit from previous generations. Studies of the UK housing stock, for example, have led to an alarming consensus. In particular, two points demand attention: first that the current housing stock is made up in large part by dwellings more than 25 years old which have poor energy performance and second, they are here to stay. Consequently, refitting and demolition become matters for serious consideration:

> Results from the UKDCM show that the (2050) 60% reduction target can only be met if there is a step change in the quality of the fabric of the housing stock. Demolition and construction rates both need to rise; the average energy consumption of the existing stock needs to be brought up to a SAP (Standard Assessment Procedure) rating of 80, and all new homes need to achieve close to zero space heating demand from 2020 at the latest. (Boardman et al., 2005: 38)

They rightly highlight the problems associated with making the existing housing stock more sustainable, acknowledging the fact that the housing discourses of previous generations are in many ways still exerting influence over contemporary experiences of housing and home. In 2004, they argued for a fourfold increase in demolition in the United Kingdom to accompany a rigorous refit of all homes able to be sufficiently improved. Ravetz agrees:

> The highly topical issue of new housing, and the national target of 3 million new dwellings by 2020, is actually at the margins of a much bigger but less focused question, of the continuation of the existing building stock. Moreover, such existing buildings are not only physical structures and financial commodities. They are often central to the fabric of everyday lifestyles, communities, cultures and livelihoods. They are also embedded in the spatial form and structures of existing settlements, at various scales, and these too may need to be adapted or re-engineered for future requirements. (Ravetz, 2008)

However, there is an alternative perspective to the challenge presented by the poorest-performing homes, which reframes the worst-performing housing stock as a 'strategic opportunity' rather than a problem. Progress is being made in the United Kingdom, albeit slowly, to address this issue, through a combination of policy initiatives such as grants, subsidies, and building improvements, and as a result the average energy efficiency rating has improved over the last 20 years.

The focus of sustainable retrofit activities has been on minimising energy use in order to reduce greenhouse gas emissions, as energy consumption by occupants plays a large role in the impact of housing on the environment. In the United Kingdom, for example, over 27% of greenhouse gas emissions originate in domestic energy use, while in the United States, homes account for 18% of CO_2 emissions. While the energy intensity of everyday life grows, however, 5 million UK households are thought to have needed to spend more than 10% of their income on energy bills in the winter of 2008–09, a rise of 2 million from 2004 when fuel prices were at their lowest for decades, pushing more households than ever deeper into energy poverty. These entangled issues of domestic emissions of greenhouse gases and the affordability of energy push domestic energy use to the forefront of efforts to avoid the worst effects of climate change and to make everyday life financially as well as environmentally sustainable. In the UK context, however, the policy emphasis on fuel poverty has not been matched by wider-reaching reform of the housing market.

Changing Energy Demand

There are several factors which through their interaction and combined effects have inflated energy demand from homes in the postwar period. The primary drivers for increased demand are dealt with below: They are demographic change, increased appliance ownership, expectations of comfort, and cleanliness and heating needs of older people.

First, as is widely acknowledged, many Western societies are facing significant demographic changes. One of the most significant of these in the context of energy use in homes is the division of larger households, often families, into smaller, more numerous households. In the UK context, official figures predict 5.5–6 million new households by 2031, an increase of 25% from 2006; 70% of these new households will be single-person households meaning that the energy required for heat on a per-person basis will rise dramatically, in turn leading to a rise in emissions. By 2026, 38% of all households are expected to be single-person households, meaning that energy savings made possible by sharing heated spaces and the energy used in bathing, refrigeration, and cleaning will be realised in far fewer homes. Boardman et al. (2005) estimate that per-person energy use is 60% higher in single-person households than in two-person households, while Shorrock and Utley add concern over this issue in their observation that there has been a strong correlation between the number of households and domestic energy consumption between 1970 and 2001 in which period the number of homes grew by 36% and energy use in homes rose by 32%.

This trend also suggests that per-household consumption has changed little between 1970 and 2001 as the modest improvements achieved in average thermal performance in the period have been offset by increased demand for electricity:

> Since 1970, gains in the thermal efficiency of dwellings and their heating systems have reduced per household heating demand, even as homes have increased in size per person and people have achieved higher internal temperatures. But this improvement in thermal performance (averaging approximately a 1% reduction in SAP rating per annum) has been offset by an increase in demand of over 70% for electricity use in appliances and lighting. (Roberts, 2008: 630)

A related research focus is the dramatic rise in recent years in demand for electricity for domestic appliances and more recently information and leisure technologies such as digital radios, ever-larger TV screens, personal computers, and games consoles. Furthermore, the trend is widely predicted to continue as older generations of technology are replaced and as technology becomes more and more affordable as a result of global supply chain.

The other major demographic change is the increasing average age of Western populations, and crucially the increase in the number of those eligible to retire from employment will have serious long-term consequences for societies and economies. For the environment, however, one impact is the increased need for heating and cooling by older people. Risks associated with cold indoor climates include increased vulnerability to respiratory, circulatory, and infectious disease as well as impaired mobility and well-being. In warm climates, problems associated with overheating can be equally detrimental to health. Minimising these problems requires older people to maintain comfortable, dry homes. When coupled with the reality that retired people spend considerably more time in the home, the demand for heating and cooling results in considerably more energy use, and thus more emissions.

Water

While much attention has been placed on energy demand associated with house building and domestic life, these activities have wider environmental impacts. As well as carbon footprints, the water footprints and resource footprints of homes have entered into policy and academic debates around sustainable housing.

Water scarcity is becoming an increasing risk to both ecosystems and human health. Accessible fresh water resources are, in many places, unable to provide adequate clean water to human populations. At the same time, modern agriculture and population growth mean that water, which would otherwise reach unpopulated areas, is diverted to provide water for increasingly unsustainable farming practices and urban developments.

As expectations of comfort and, in particular, cleanliness have increased dramatically in the postwar era, a clean, unlimited water supply has become taken for granted in the West. Furthermore, hot water on demand and homes with several WCs have become similarly normalised. Shove's (2003) influential study claims that processes such as bathing, laundry, cooking, and cleaning have changed considerably.

Several approaches are being experimented with as governments across the world become aware of the environmental impacts of water demand from the growing number of households, and The University of Twente's internationally supported Water Footprint Network provides a comprehensive set of resources and literature as well as a wealth of water consumption data for a wide range of nations, broken down to domestic water demand, highlighting the huge differences between nations. Research has for some time critically assessed demand-side management, price sensitivity of demand, and the time sensitivity of demand, but more recently the focus of research has shifted from demand- to supply-side issues. Featuring heavily in this is research into the potential offered by water trading, which after being pioneered in Australia at a regional level has been reformulated at a variety of scales. Problems remain unresolved in such schemes, often surrounding the lack of governance structures such as the current water use auditing and technical issues such as the requirement for metering on all participating supplies.

Another side of the water debate is the impact of house design and urban planning on water absorption and, as a result, flooding. As more and more land is developed and covered with impervious materials such as concrete, asphalt, and buildings, water is prevented from sinking into soil where it would be retained and possibly utilized in local ecosystems. Instead, water runs over the tops of such surfaces into urban drains where it can create flooding, particularly in rain storm conditions where drains are deluged and can flood, often damaging property. Furthermore, urban run-off has the effect of drying out the land, lowering the water table, and making droughts more likely as moisture is kept within closed drainage systems rather than being allowed to enter the groundwater. Efforts to reduce urban run-off have most recently focused on urban green spaces such as parks and gardens and green roofs.

Waste

Research into domestic waste issues is another feature of academic interest in the environmental impacts of housing. The huge volume of waste generated by UK households has risen dramatically in the last 50 years.

In terms of waste arising from domestic practices, emphasis is most often placed on recycling and composting rather then waste reduction. This emphasis on redirecting rather than reducing the waste stream flowing from homes is also linked to using waste to generate energy. There is a growing interest in waste-to-energy projects and exploring the possibilities, potentials, and challenges associated with turning household waste into useful energy in the form of heat and power. Several technical approaches are available in this regard, including micro generation options shown in **Table 1**, community-scale energy projects, and grid supply projects.

Community-scale projects use combustible waste to provide heat for use in so-called district heating schemes which provide heat to neighbourhoods via shared hot water circulation systems and in some cases use combined heat and power plants to create electricity as well as hot water. Alternative configurations use waste to create energy for export to national grids by injecting grid-compliant cleaned biogas from anaerobic digestion of organic waste or by generating electricity

Table 1 Major technology options for dwelling-scale energy generation

Technology	Type of energy produced	Applications
Solar thermal	Hot water	Roof and wall-mounted piping absorb heat. The heated water can be stored or distributed around the dwelling
Solar photovoltaic panels	Electricity	Solar PV panels turn sunlight into electricity which can be used in the property and/or exported to the electricity grid
Wind	Electricity	Small vertical or horizontal blades turn when wind speed is between cut-in and cut-out speeds, creating electricity which can be used in the dwelling and/or exported to the electricity grid
Air source heat pump	Hot water	Ambient heat in the air is drawn into the unit by a fan and is passed through an electrically powered compressor to create hot water which can be used to heat the property or for hot water. Operates all year round but is more efficient in summer than winter
Ground source heat pump	Hot water	Ambient heat in the ground, which is a relatively stable temperature all year round, is absorbed and condensed by pipes laid underground in horizontal or vertical arrangements. This is passed through an electrically powered compressor to create hot water which can be used to heat the property or for hot water. Operates all year round but is more efficient in summer than winter
Micro-hydro	Electricity	Where available, a water wheel is turned by flowing water to create electricity, which is used in the dwelling or is sold to the grid
Biomass	Heat, transport	Materials such as wood, oils, and other organic waste products are used to fire engines or boilers which produce heat. The heat produced can be used in combustion engines for transport or can be used to heat water or to power a combined heat and power unit

for the national electricity grid through Combined Heat and Power (CHP) installations.

Whether for local or for national energy production, a principal concern is the nature of the waste stream. Turning domestic waste into useable energy depends heavily on the quality of the waste and often the separation of waste at the source – which often means in the kitchen. As well as providing infrastructure to promote separation of organic from inorganic waste for biopower energy projects, and indeed for recycling of other wastes, research has shown that behavioural drivers such as attitudes, time availability, and householder's preexisting norms and values play important parts in determining readiness to participate in such schemes.

Without source segregation, domestic waste is considerably more difficult to turn into energy, as even the most sophisticated mechanical separation devices run up against technical barriers in isolating materials such as paint and items like batteries from otherwise organic waste streams. Furthermore, environmental protection measures which regulate waste processing create obstacles to using household waste for energy production. While such measures are designed to protect the environment from harm, they have also been found to have a stifling effect on innovative practice in reducing the environmental impacts of waste arising from households. Such regulatory challenges require coordinated efforts from highly engaged networks which include private and public sector entrepreneurs if they are to function effectively in protecting the environment from poor-quality recovered waste products rather than prevent the recovery of waste by slowing or stalling waste-to-energy projects, many of which rely on regulatory approval as a condition of project finance.

Homes Not Islands

While it is tempting to look at housing as a science of many dwellings, it is in many powerful ways also the study of communities. Homes are located in places which have particular economic, infrastructural, and social characteristics, which both impact upon housing and also affect housing policy and home building. Indeed, the environmental impacts of housing activities are multiscalar, ranging from global effects of greenhouse gas emissions to local impacts of visual amenity, waste, and the considerable impacts of home construction and demolition. This is reflected in a global interest in sustainable communities reflected in a large, growing, and empirically diverse research. In particular, the sustainable communities agenda has focused on urban rather than rural settlements, overlapping with urban regeneration and sustainable cities research themes.

In the UK context, sustainable communities agenda was crystallised in the publication of a government white paper that sets out the priorities for a new, multi-dimensional approach to sustainable housing, which encompasses land use and urban economic viability and prioritises the 'liveability' of urban spaces. This fusion of environmental and economic sustainability in urban design, architecture, planning, and house building has been a theme in critical studies of urban development for several decades, but it is only relatively recently that efforts to modernise and remake urban housing across the globe in the post-Bruntland era have so directly attempted to fuse economic, social, and environmental outcome in a single concept and policy discourse.

Micro Generation

As well as maximising energy efficiency of homes, a major part of reducing energy demand is micro generation. By generating energy from renewable sources, households can minimise their consumption of grid-sourced energy, thus minimising their emissions of greenhouse gases. A number of renewable energy options exist at the domestic scale. These micro-generation technologies are very often long-established technologies which are being applied in new ways, in new combinations, and in new contexts. **Table 1** provides an introduction to the major technology options for dwelling-scale energy generation.

The potential offered by each technology varies considerably in different places. Factors such as latitude, longitude, and prevailing meteorological conditions significantly alter an area's natural energy resources, but local technical and economic factors can be just as, if not more, powerful in determining the popularity and deployment of domestic micro-generation technology. International comparisons are particularly enlightening in micro-generation deployment, as factors such as feed-in-tariffs and government subsidies and market manipulations at work in different countries create very different outcomes.

In Europe, there have been considerable differences between micro-generation deployment schemes, which have interacted with national politics and economies to create diverse outcomes. However, due to the policy learning and policy transfer activities of EU member states and the general exchange of best practice through international networking, there has been a convergence in recent years and a reduction in the differences between renewable energy supplies in European nations, suggesting a maturation of practice in countries with previously low share of European renewable capacity including Estonia, Hungary, Belgium, Luxembourg, the United Kingdom, and the Netherlands. Considerable differences in installed capacity persist however, with nation-specific barriers of regulation and market conditions identified as targets for governmental reform if more capacity is to be achieved.

Adaptation to Climate Change

As well as adapting homes to minimise emissions of greenhouse gases, and thus the extent of climate change, there is also considerable work underway to adapt to the reality of a warming planet. Roberts argues that homes built for climatic conditions which prevailed in the past, at the time of their construction, are now challenged by rapidly evolving weather conditions.

Moser and Satterthwaite (2008) provide a review of how the issue of climate change adaptation affects the urban populations in low- and middle-income countries, arguing that there are a variety of risk profiles and particularly vulnerable groups and that there are key roles to be played by governments and international donors as well as urban communities. They argue that supporting communities as they interface with local institutions is key to successful adaptation. Furthermore, while emissions reduction policies have in various ways attempted to address the problems associated with the affordability of low-carbon energy, adaptation to a warming climate presents a similar problem of equity of outcomes.

Challenges likely to face housing in a warmer world can be grouped into three categories: avoidance of overheating, minimisation of flood risk, and water scarcity.

First, overheating problems are expected to arise from waste heat escaping from light fittings, cooking, and the increased use of electrical equipment; solar radiation through windows; thermal gain through external surfaces; and higher external air temperatures which will warm indoor temperatures if windows and doors are not air tight or if they are used for ventilation. Solutions being developed to avoid overheating include passive heating through choice of wall colours and materials for greater absorbency or reflection as desired; green roofs which absorb water and provide thermal insulation, increasing the thermal mass of homes and choosing materials which allow walls and floors to operate as effective heat sinks and emitters (such as removing carpets and other furnishings acting as internal insulation in winter months); waterproofing and water ingress management.

Second, the flooding risk to homes is associated with increased precipitation, sea level rise, and increased frequency and strength of storms. Measures required to prepare homes for this increased flood risk include resistance measures aimed at minimising the ingress of water into homes and resilience measures aimed at minimising the damage done to flooded homes and reducing recovery times.

Third, the water scarcity risk posed by climate change stems from rising demand for water (as discussed above) which can not be satisfied by supplies drawn from precipitation and groundwater in areas likely to face warmer, dryer climates, such as Southern Europe, Southern England, Australia, and large areas of many nations in the Global North and South. As well as posing problems for homeowners, the increased demand for water created by contemporary domestic lifestyles also poses environmental risks associated with overextraction of water. Policy responses to water scarcity have ranged from hose pipe bans during summer droughts to water metering, tariff manipulation, and technology redesign. Research into the deployment of such initiatives questions their effectiveness and suggests that manipulating market conditions is more effective than technological fixes or behavioural change campaigns.

> in the trade-offs between prices, people, devices, and rules, prices and rules are the most certain and, because they can be applied generally to all households, their cumulative effects can be great ... simply giving households engineered devices is not effective (as) offsetting behaviour is so strong that effectiveness is swamped.
> (Campbell et al., 2004)

See also: Building Regulations for Energy Conservation; Climate Change; Domestic Technologies and the Modern Home; Fuel Poverty; Housing and the Macroeconomy; Sustainable Regeneration.

References

Boardman B, Darby S, Killip G, et al. (2005) 40% House. *Environmental Change Institute Research Report Number 31*. Oxford, UK: University of Oxford.

Campbell HE, with Johnson RM and Hunt Larson E (2004) Prices, devices, people, or rules: The relative effectiveness of policy instruments in water conservation. *Review of Policy Research* 21(5): 637–662.

Moser C and Satterthwaite D (2008) *Towards pro-poor adaptation to climate change in the urban centres of low- and middle-income countries, Human Settlements Discussion Paper Series*. http://www.iied.org/pubs/display.php?o=10564IIED.

Ravetz J (2008) Resource flow analysis for sustainable construction: Metrics for an integrated supply chain approach. *Proceedings of the Institute of Civil Engineering, Waste and Resource Management* 161(WR2): 51–66.

Roberts S (2008) Demographics, energy and our home. *Energy Policy* 36: 4630–4632.

Further Reading

Noorman KJ and Uiterkamp TS (1998) *Green Households: Domestic Consumers, the Environment and Sustainability*. London: Earthscan.

ONS (2007) *Social Trends no 37. Office for National Statistics*. Basingstoke, UK: Palgrave Macmillan.

Parker DS (2009) Very low energy homes in the United States: Perspectives on performance from measured data. *Energy and Buildings* 41(5): 512–520.

Pérez-Lombarda L, Ortizb J, Gonzáleza R, and Maestrec IR (2008) A review of benchmarking, rating and labelling concepts within the framework of building energy certification schemes. *Energy and Buildings* 41(3): 272–278.

Raco M (2005) Sustainable development, rolled-out neo-liberalism and sustainable communities. *Antipode* 34: 324–346.

Roberts S (2008) Altering existing buildings in the UK. *Energy Policy* 36(12): 4482–4486.

Shorrock L and Utley J (2003) *Domestic Energy Fact File 2003*. Watford, UK: BRE.

Shove E (2003) *Comfort, Cleanliness and Convenience*. Oxford, UK: Berg.

Housing Equity Withdrawal in the United Kingdom

A Holmans, University of Cambridge, Cambridge, UK

© 2012 Elsevier Ltd. All rights reserved.

Glossary

Flexible mortgages A mortgage which allows the borrower to vary the total amount borrowed at his/her discretion subject to limits. A home equity line of credit in the United States is similar.

Housing equity withdrawal The process by which households can convert some or all of the equity in their dwelling into cash.

Mortgage equity withdrawal Withdrawing housing equity by increasing the mortgage debt secured on the dwelling.

Mortgage equity withdrawal in situ Mortgage equity withdrawal that does not depend on a move, that is, remortgaging, further advances, and flexible mortgages.

Over-mortgaging Taking a larger mortgage on a house being bought than would be needed if all the proceeds of the previous sale (selling price minus the outstanding mortgage) were put towards financing the purchase of the house being bought.

Reverse mortgage A mortgage on which interest accumulates (or rolls up) until the house is sold. The sum borrowed is usually but not necessarily used to generate an income.

Scope and Definitions

This article is concerned with housing equity withdrawal (HEW) in the United Kingdom. The process by which housing equity can be withdrawn depends on financial systems and institutions, which vary from country to country, and structure of house purchase transactions and their financing. In the interest of clarity the data in this article are for the United Kingdom only. A broader picture is presented in Munro's article (see article Mortgage Equity Withdrawal).

The channels through which housing equity may be withdrawn may be summarised as:

	Mortgage related (mortgage equity withdrawal)	Nonmortgage related
Involving trade or move	Over-mortgaging	Trading down by outright owner Move from owner-occupation to renting
No trade or move involved	Remortgaging Further advances Flexible mortgages Equity release schemes	Bequest and inheritance

These channels are described and discussed by Munro.

Two categories of information about HEW are used: aggregate amounts derived from national income and financial accounts and interviews with households about amounts of equity withdrawn and how it was used.

Aggregate Measures of Housing Equity and Withdrawal in the United Kingdom

To set the scene for measures of HEW, it is useful to show estimates of the total of personal housing wealth and loans secured on dwellings over a long run of years. The figures in **Table 1** are mainly of owner-occupiers' house value and debts but include as well dwellings owned by households and rented out to tenants. In 2009, loans on rented dwellings were about 12% of the total.

The effect of deregulation of financial markets in the 1980s is shown by the increase in loans secured on dwellings relative to personal housing wealth between 1980 and 1990, notwithstanding the effect of the house price boom of the 1980s on house values. The amount of housing equity owned by households is sensitive to the state of the housing market. House prices fell between 1990 and 1995 and again after 2007 and housing equity diminished as a result.

The distribution of mortgage debt and hence of housing equity is strongly related to age. **Table 2** shows estimates of the value of owner-occupied dwellings and mortgage debts in England in 2003–05 analysed by households' age and divided into owners with mortgages and outright owners.

Of the total value of housing equity, some 62% belonged to outright owners and 38% to owner-occupiers with mortgages. Mortgage debt was equal to about 50% of the total value of mortgaged dwellings. In terms of age, **Table 2** shows that 20% of housing equity belong to 'younger' (under 45) households, 45% to 'middle-aged' households (45–64), and 35% to 'older' households (65 and over).

Table 1 Value of households' dwellings and loans secured on dwellings in the United Kingdom: Selected years (£billion)

	Personal housing wealth	Loans secured on dwellings	Personal housing equity	Loans as percent of housing wealth
1980	311	53	258	17
1985	550	127	423	23
1990	1 145	295	850	26
1995	1 089	391	698	36
2000	1 968	536	1 432	27
2005	3 361	967	2 394	29
2007	4 077	1 187	2 890	29
2008	3 689	1 226	2 463	33
2009	3 827	1 236	2 591	32

Source: Savills Housing Investment Consultancy (2011) *UK Housing Review 2010/11*. London: Chartered Institute of Housing.

The distribution of housing equity between age groups is affected by changes in house values. **Table 3** shows an updated version of **Table 2**. It shows the situation in 2009, after the fall in house values from their 2007 peak.

Comparison with **Table 2** shows that mortgage debts were higher in relation to house values for all age ranges, but especially for younger age ranges. For owner-occupiers under age 45 with mortgages, their equity in 2009 was equal to only 23% of the gross value of their dwellings, as compared with 39% in 2003–05. The explanation lies in the course of house prices, especially the fall after 2007.

Ownership of housing equity by older people can allow income to be supplemented by withdrawal of equity through equity release schemes. Older people do not all have low incomes, but there is often thought to be scope for such schemes to assist people who are 'house-rich but income-poor'. Some evidence is in **Table 4**, which cross-analyses the distribution of house values of outright owners by the distribution of their incomes. The quintiles are of all households: the table shows, for example, 12% of outright owners aged 70 and over having incomes in the top 20% of the distribution, and 23% having house values in the top 20% of all house values.

Table 4 shows that for outright owners aged 70 and over, house values and incomes are related. There are

Table 2 Aggregate house values and mortgage debts in England 2003–05: Age analysis (£billion)

	Age 16–34	35–44	45–54	55–64	65–74	75 and over	Total
Outright owners							
Total house values = equity	18	59	142	301	317	284	1 121
Owners with mortgages							
Total house values	260	490	398	197	30	7	1 382
Mortgage debt	178	282	166	58	7	1	693
Equity	82	208	232	139	23	6	690
Ratio of debt to house values (%)	68	58	42	29	23	14	50
All owner-occupiers							
Total equity	100	267	374	440	340	290	1 810
Distribution of housing equity (%)	5.5	14.8	20.7	24.3	18.8	16.0	100.0

Source: Holmans AE (2008) *Prospects for Housing Wealth and Inheritance*. London: Council of Mortgage Lenders.

Table 3 Updated analysis of age of house values and mortgage debts in England in 2009 (£billion)

	Age 16–34	35–44	45–54	55–64	65 and over	Total
Outright owners						
Total house values = equity	20	64	155	329	656	1 224
Owners with mortgages						
Total house values	284	534	435	215	41	1 509
Mortgage debt	251	377	187	65	9	889
Equity	33	157	248	150	32	620
Ratio of debt to house values (%)	88	71	43	30	22	59
All owner-occupiers						
Total equity	53	221	403	479	688	1 844
Distribution of housing equity (%)	2.9	12.0	21.9	26.0	37.3	100.0

Source: Author's estimate (not thus far published) made by working forward from the sources for Table 2.

Table 4 House values by range of incomes: Outright owners aged 70 or over in England in 2005–07 (thousands)

House value quintiles	Income quintiles					
	First (lowest)	Second	Third	Fourth	Fifth (highest)	Total
First (lowest)	128	63	62	24	9	288
Second	196	126	71	46	19	456
Third	201	148	105	56	34	544
Fourth	167	156	119	140	79	660
Fifth (highest)	82	108	108	135	158	592
Total	773	601	467	403	298	2 542

Source: Analysis by the author of data from the English House Condition Survey made available by the Department of Communities and Local Government.

comparatively few with incomes in the top two quintiles (the top 40% of incomes) with house values in the bottom two quintiles (the bottom 40% of house values). Twenty-nine percent of all outright owners had house values in the two bottom quintiles (of house values in all tenures), but only 14% of those in the top two income quintile ranges. 'House-rich and income-poor' is open to argument. A more stringent definition would take the bottom income quintile and the top two house value quintiles, which would give a figure of about 250 000. With the bottom two income quintiles and the top two quintiles of house values, there would be 500 000 outright owners aged 70 and over who would count as house-rich and income-poor. These are substantial numbers; but even on the broader definition of 'income poor', only one-fifth of owner-occupiers aged 70 or over are 'house-rich and income-poor'. With the narrower definition of 'income-poor', an income in the bottom quintile, the number of owner-occupiers that are house-poor and income-poor way exceeds the number that are house-rich and income-poor.

Thus far, use of home income plans has been on a comparatively small scale in Britain, but even so they have been less developed elsewhere in the European Union. Suggestions have been discussed but so far not acted on, that the reverse mortgage mechanism might be used to enable costs of personal care for older people in their own homes to be paid for by drawing on the value of their dwellings. This would be a highly contentious form of HEW.

The amount of housing equity belonging to the owner-occupier is the starting point for a consideration of HEW. It can be looked at in the net terms or gross. Equity can be injected into housing, for example, by first-time purchasers' deposits and by repayment of mortgage loans. Net HEW is the difference between gross amounts withdrawn and amounts injected. To estimate gross equity withdrawn, estimates are required by flows of funds through house purchases and sales and mortgage loans advanced and repaid. How complex are these flows can be seen from Holmans (2001).

Gross flow estimates of HEW and mortgage equity withdrawal in the United Kingdom are taken from the research by Holmans (2001). These are now somewhat dated, but have to be used because the work done to produce them has not been repeated. It requires estimates of a very complex set of financial flows which must be internally consistent. Each flow must come from somewhere specific and go somewhere. Owing to the complexity it is not possible to describe in an article of this length the sources and methods used. **Table 5** shows estimated gross flows in 1998, 1999, and 2000 and the number of households withdrawing equity by each method. The numbers withdrawing equity are important for the economic effects of equity withdrawal that might be looked for.

Table 5 shows that at the time to which it refers, gross equity withdrawal financed by mortgage lending was about one-half of the total. The other half consisted mainly of last-time sales, of which sales resulting from bequest and inheritance of house property is the largest category. Mortgage finance for equity withdrawal from housing amounted to about £28 billion a year, which was about 1.5% of total owner-occupied housing wealth (see **Table 1**) and slightly more than 4% of households' disposable income.

In a gross flows analysis, the counterpart to gross equity withdrawal is gross equity 'injection', that is, flows that work to reduce the total of mortgage debt relative to the value of owner-occupied dwellings. These 'injections' can be financial, which reduce the total of mortgage debts, or they can be investment in owner-occupied dwellings, which increases the value of the owner-occupied housing stock relative to debts secured on it. The total of mortgage debts can be reduced in a variety of ways, including entire mortgage loans repaid when mortgaged dwellings are sold, entire mortgage loans repaid in the course of remortgaging, and partial repayments of loans. In the 3 years included in **Table 5**, the total of equity 'injected' is estimated at an average of £50 930 million (see Table 8 in Holmans

Table 5 Gross flows of housing and mortgage equity withdrawn: Amounts withdrawn and numbers of households making equity withdrawals (£million)

	1998	1999	2000	Average
Amounts withdrawn				
(1) Over-mortgaging	11 977	15 711	14 629	14 106
(2) Remortgages	4 539	6 145	5 845	5 510
(3) Further advances	5 280	8 891	10 436	8 202
Subtotal: withdrawals that depend on mortgage lending	21 796	30 747	30 910	27 818
(4) Outright purchasers trading down	1 947	2 171	2 048	2 055
(5) Last-time sales	19 073	23 500	27 346	23 306
(6) Sales by households to other sectors of the economy	2 358	2 747	3 132	2 746
Subtotal: withdrawals not depending on mortgage lending	23 378	28 418	32 526	28 107
Total, all housing and mortgage equity withdrawal	45 174	59 165	63 436	55 925
Estimate of number of owner-occupiers withdrawing equity				
(7) Over-mortgaging	290	347	313	303
(8) Remortgaging	398	499	529	475
(9) Further advances	424	666	687	592
(10) Outright purchasers trading down	56	68	63	62
(11) Last-time sellers	369	403	403	392
Total	1 537	1 943	1 995	1 825

Source: Holmans AE (2001) *Housing and Mortgage Equity Withdrawal and Their Component Flows: A Technical Report.* London: Council of Mortgage Lenders.

(2001)), and hence net withdrawal of equity £4 995 million.

Much less demanding of data than gross flows of equity into and out of privately owned housing are net measures of housing and mortgage equity withdrawal. Whereas constructing estimates of gross housing and mortgage equity withdrawal is a major research exercise, a net measure can be produced from series in regularly produced financial and national accounts statistics. A substantial part of the saving of data requirements is in the financial flows. Net lending secured on dwellings rolls together a large number of different ways in which mortgage debts are repaid, and the forms of new lending. For some forms of lending through 'flexible' mortgages, gross lending cannot be clearly defined. Furthermore, lenders require totals of outstanding loans for their own purposes; amounts lent and repaid, particularly amounts repaid in different ways, tend to be of less operational interest and so less often collected.

The problems with net measures of HEW are comparability of coverage of net lending secured on dwellings and investment of households in dwellings as measured in the national income accounts. As noted above, in the UK National Accounts the 'household' sector includes 'non-profit institutions serving households' among which are housing associations. Since the mid-1990s these associations have been the main providers of new social housing for letting at rents below market levels, which are financed partly by loans from banks and building societies and partly from government grants. The component series used by the Bank of England to calculate mortgage equity withdrawal in the 3 years included in **Table 5** are shown in **Table 6**. These are among the selected years for which the table shows the components of net equity withdrawal, to illustrate their different magnitudes and how they have changed with economic conditions in the short term, and in the longer term also. In the table, HEW column (G) equals (A) plus (B) plus (C) minus (D) minus (E) minus (F) 'Housing Equity Withdrawal' is the term used by the Bank of England, though Mortgage Equity Withdrawal could equally well be used.

Comparison of the HEW column with the other columns shows clearly that HEW is driven predominantly by net lending secured on dwellings. There have been extreme fluctuations in the period covered by **Table 5**, with very large increases in the boom years to 2007 and then large falls with the credit crisis and housing market slump. There have been fluctuations as well in households' investment in dwellings, and on a smaller scale in transfer costs of nonproduced assets (mostly houses brought and sold second hand). These costs are mainly estate agents' commission, legal fees, and to an increasing extent Stamp Duty on purchase of houses. The amount varies with the volume of housing market transactions.

Mortgage equity withdrawal makes its impact through the gross flows discussed earlier in this article, so the relationships between the gross flows of mortgage equity withdrawal and net HEW and net lending secured on dwellings are important. **Table 7** shows these comparisons, for 1998, 1999, and 2000, the years included both in **Tables 5** and **6**.

Table 7 shows how the year-to-year changes in net HEW are closely related to net lending secured on dwellings. The link between gross mortgage equity withdrawal and net HEW is not as close, though the increases between 1998 and 1999 were similar. A longer run of

Table 6 Components of housing equity withdrawals, Bank of England's measure (£million)

	(A) Net lending secured on dwellings	(B) Capital grants to personal sector	(C) Capital grants to HAs	(D) Household investment in dwellings	(E) Household costs of transfers	(F) Household net purchases of land	(G) Housing equity withdrawal (net)
1994	19 216	1 226	1 563	17 996	3 617	185	207
1998	24 285	1 267	798	23 046	3 793	17	−506
1999	37 444	1 142	1 042	23 642	6 279	−138	9 845
2000	40 713	965	935	25 301	5 284	−67	12 095
2003	100 886	1 130	1 743	34 390	12 449	−210	57 130
2006	110 111	1 348	1 848	48 650	15 090	−358	49 925
2007	108 941	1 781	1 772	50 648	19 296	−340	42 890
2008	43 975	1 442	2 745	45 082	9 781	−340	−6 361
2009	11 141	3 048	3 625	34 648	5 853	−348	−22 339

Note: HAs, means housing associations. The column heading (E) in full reads: 'Household cost associated with the transfer of ownership of nonproduced assets'. The figures in this table are subject to revision.
Source: Bank of England.

Table 7 Gross mortgage equity withdrawal, net housing equity withdrawal, and net lending secured on dwellings in 1998, 1999, and 2000 (£million)

	1998	1999	2000
Gross mortgage equity withdrawal (**Table 5**)	21 796	30 747	30 910
Net housing equity withdrawal (**Table 6**)	−506	9 845	12 095
Net lending secured on dwellings (**Table 6**)	24 285	37 444	40 713

years would be required for the relationship of gross to net to be studied more closely.

Information about Mortgage Equity Withdrawal by Households, Who Withdraws Equity, How Much Is Withdrawn, and How Is It Used

Tables 2 and 3 showed which age groups owned housing equity and which had mortgage debt. In 2009, two-thirds of the total equity in owner-occupied dwellings belonged to outright owners. For them to withdraw equity, new loans secured on hitherto unmortgaged dwellings would be required. One-third of the equity belonged to owner-occupiers with mortgages, who could potentially withdraw equity through further advances or remortgaging. Equity could be withdrawn in these ways without moving house, which sometimes is referred to as in situ mortgage equity withdrawal. There were 10.2 million owner-occupiers with mortgages in the United Kingdom in 2009, of which 5.9 million were aged under 45 and 4.3 million were aged 45 and over; those under age 45 owned just over 40% of the equity that belonged to owner-occupiers with mortgages. Households aged 45 and over had on average nearly twice as much equity available for in situ mortgage equity withdrawal as did young households.

Household information about mortgage equity withdrawal is of two kinds. One is from a specialist survey of households that have made mortgage equity withdrawals. The other is from questions in multipurpose surveys about mortgage amounts and activities. Specialist surveys depend on a 'sift' survey to find a sample of households that have made withdrawals of mortgage equity, who can then be resurveyed to collect more detailed information.

An example of a specialist survey of households that had withdrawn mortgage equity is that undertaken for the Bank of England and the Council of Mortgage Lenders and reported in Chapter 6 of Davey and Earley (2001). The sample was found from a survey on financial subjects run by a commercial survey research firm. Samples were found by households that had withdrawn equity in the course of moving (over-mortgaging), remortgaging, and taking further advances. Not all the sample of movers and households who remortgaged withdrew equity; all those who took further advances did so, by definition.

Information was collected about the amount of equity withdrawn. For moving households who sold one house to buy another, questions were asked about the price received from the house being sold and the mortgage outstanding on it, and about the price paid for the house

Table 8 Equity withdrawn by over-mortgaging and remortgaging (%)

Amount	Movers over-mortgaging[a]	Remortgage with different lender	Remortgage with same lender or further advance
Under £5000	19	15	10
£5000 but less than £10 000	37	12	20
£10 000 but less than £15 000	16	24	18
£15 000 but less than £20 000	5	8	10
£20 000 but less than £40 000	13	24	26
£40 000 or more	10	16	17
Total	100	100	100

[a]Excludes movers 'trading down'.
Source: Davey M and Earley F (2001) *Mortgage Equity Withdrawal*. London: Council of Mortgage Lenders.

being bought, and the mortgage. Questions were not asked about transaction costs (e.g., stamp duty, estate agent's commission, and legal fees) which are sometimes taken into account in estimating amounts withdrawn by over-mortgaging. **Table 8** shows the survey information, in summary form, about amounts of equity withdrawn.

The size distributions of amounts withdrawn through the different forms of in situ mortgage equity withdrawal were similar, but the amounts withdrawn by over-mortgaging were smaller. Fifty-six percent of withdrawals by over-mortgaging were below £10 000 as opposed to 27% by remortgaging with a different lender and 30% by remortgaging with the same lender or through further advances. At the other end of distribution, 40% of withdrawals by remortgaging with a different lender and 43% by remortgaging with the same lender or further advances were of £20 000 or more, but only 23% of withdrawals was by over-mortgaging. On the evidence of the survey, the amounts withdrawn by in situ mortgage equity withdrawal were substantial: averages of £25 500 by remortgaging with a different lender, £28 400 by remortgaging with the same lender (equivalent to a further advance and treated as such in statistics of lending secured on dwellings), and £22 000 for further advances. These are much higher figures for average amounts withdrawn in situ than those that can be derived from the aggregate amount withdrawn and the numbers of loans shown in **Table 5** (£11 600 for remortgaging and £13 900 for further advances). The survey figures were derived from small samples and there is some uncertainty about the number of households withdrawing equity through remortgaging and the number receiving further advances. There is a discrepancy here.

Next to consider is what the survey reported about how in situ mortgage equity withdrawal was used. This is in two parts: an analysis in which 'spent some' is one category, 'paid off debts' is another, and 'saved some' is another; and an analysis of what the 'spent some' money

Table 9 Uses of in situ mortgage equity withdrawal (percent)

	Remortgages	Further advances
What was done with the money withdrawn		
Spent some	59	74
Paid off debts	22	22
Saved some	11	8
Other or don't know	21	14
Total	100[a]	100[a]
What the money was spent on		
Improvements to the home	75	80
New goods for the home	25	13
Car/vehicle	6	6
General expenditure	12	7
Other	14	11
Total	100[a]	100[a]

[a]Multiple responses were permitted.
Source: Davey M and Earley F (2001) *Mortgage Equity Withdrawal*. London: Council of Mortgage Lenders.

was spent on. **Table 9** shows these data in summary form first, what proportion of households withdrawing equity 'spent some', and then the proportions reporting the different categories of expenditure, within the first 6 months after withdrawing the equity.

Of interest is what proportion of households withdrawing equity in situ used at least some of it for improvements to the home. Before the early 1980s when building societies were the dominant lenders for housing and rationed their lending, paying for home improvements was effectively the only purpose for which further advances were made. Remortgaging was then nonexistent. At the end of the 1990s, though, the survey for the Bank of England and Council of Mortgage Lenders indicates that about 60% of households withdrawing equity through further advances and 45% of those withdrawing equity through remortgaging used at least some of the equity

Table 10 In situ mortgage equity withdrawal: Life stages

	United Kingdom		Australia	
	Total	Proportion withdrawing equity (%)	Total	Proportion withdrawing equity (%)
Age				
15–24	94	33.8	74	36.3
25–34	1 219	35.4	946	38.9
35–44	1 712	31.4	1 717	33.6
45–54	1 081	23.2	1 204	25.5
55–64	381	8.3	440	11.6
65 and over	118	1.8	125	2.4
Total	4 605	18.5	4 506	21.0
Family type				
Couple family without children	1 180	12.1	1 023	12.9
Couple family with children	2 397	32.9	2 692	34.2
Couple family with only independent children	377	16.2	203	15.3
Lone parent with children	276	26.8	235	27.6
Single person	340	8.4	334	10.1
Other	35	12.3	19	20.9
Total	4 605	18.5	4 506	21.0

Source: Parkinson S, Searle BA, Smith SJ, Stoakes A, and Wood G (2009) Mortgage equity withdrawal in Australia and Britain: Towards a wealth-fare state? *International Journal of Housing Policy* 9(4): 365–389.

withdrawn to pay for home improvements. Paying for home improvements was the largest individual use of mortgage equity withdrawn in situ; but it was also a source of finance for a wide variety of other expenditures.

More common than specialist surveys about mortgage equity withdrawal are questions placed in surveys that collect a wide range of other information. In Britain, these surveys include those primarily concerned to collect information for official policy purposes; and also an important social science research survey. The former are the Family Resources Survey (FRS) and Survey of English Housing (SEH, now English Housing Survey). The latter is the British Household Panel Survey (BHPS). FRS is run by the department responsible for state pensions, unemployment, and sickness and disability benefits and basic income support, currently the Department for Work and Pensions. This government department requires information about incomes, assets, and debts to analyse the effects of its policies on the incomes of different sections of the community, and for appraising and costing possible policy changes and innovations. The English Housing Survey is run by the department responsible (in England) for housing policy, currently the Department for Communities and Local Government. The information collected is summarised in Smith and Searle (2008).

The British Household Panel Survey is a resource for research in the social sciences and is funded by the Economic and Social Research Council (ESRC). It is a longitudinal survey in which the sample is reinterviewed annually. This feature makes it possible to relate episodes of mortgage equity withdrawal to life course events, to investigate whether and how far it is used to protect against adverse financial effects of life events (Parkinson et al., 2009). Some information about the proportions of households withdrawing equity in different life stages and ages is shown in **Table 10**. It comes from a comparative study from data for Australia and the United Kingdom, so results for both countries are included. The table reports the proportion of household-years in 2002 in which mortgage equity was withdrawn.

The age analysis and the analysis by type of household are different aspects of the same finding, that in situ equity withdrawal is used primarily by couple households with children. The analysis by age should be seen alongside the data in **Tables 2** and **3** about how ownership of houses with mortgages, and the amount of equity that mortgaged homeowners have, is related to age. The 35–44 age group has the most owner-occupiers with mortgages, with an average equity in their homes equal to above 30% of the total value, or between £40 000 and £45 000 per households.

Table 3 shows that owner-occupiers with mortgages in the 55–64 age range are far from numerous, and at age 65 and over very few. **Table 10** shows that such mortgaged owner-occupiers as there are in these age groups are not inclined to use in situ mortgage equity withdrawal.

See also: Monetary Policy, Wealth Effects and Housing; Mortgage Contracts: Flexible; Mortgage Equity Withdrawal.

References

Davey M and Earley F (2001) *Mortgage Equity Withdrawal*. London: Council of Mortgage Lenders.

Holmans AE (2001) *Housing and Mortgage Equity Withdrawal and Their Component Flows: A Technical Report*. London: Council of Mortgage Lenders.

Holmans AE (2008) *Prospects for Housing Wealth and Inheritance*. London: Council of Mortgage Lenders.

Parkinson S, Searle BA, Smith SJ, Stoakes A, and Wood G (2009) Mortgage equity withdrawal in Australia and Britain: Towards a wealth-fare state? *International Journal of Housing Policy* 9(4): 365–389.

Savills Housing Investment Consultancy (2011) *UK Housing Review 2010/11*. London: Chartered Institute of Housing.

Smith SJ and Searle BA (2008) Dematerialising money? Observations on the flow of wealth from housing to other things. *Housing Studies* 23(1): 21–43.

Housing Estates

F Wassenberg, Delft University of Technology, Delft, The Netherlands; Nicis Institute, The Hague, The Netherlands

© 2012 Elsevier Ltd. All rights reserved.

What are Housing Estates?

No Overall Definition

A universal definition for housing estates does not exist. According to the popular free encyclopaedia Wikipedia, a housing estate is a group of buildings built together as a single development. The British urbanist Anne Power defines estates as groups of housing built in defined geographical areas that are recognised as distinct and discrete entities. Patrick Dunleavy, referring to mass housing estates, talks about estates of uniform housing quite distinct in form from the kinds of housing provided by market mechanisms. Van Kempen et al. mention that housing estates are artificial areas in that they are self-contained, planned developments rather than organically developed neighbourhoods. Common in these definitions are the grouping of buildings (with dwellings), the uniform and distinct character, the similar and planned construction, and the geographical concentration. Combining the definitions, we define a housing estate as a group of housing quite distinct in form built together as a single development.

The British phrase 'housing estate' is not easily and equally translated into other languages, providing different connotations. In Germany and Austria we can find many 'Siedlungen' or 'Wohnsiedlungen', but these have a connotation of socialist advocates of the 1920s. The French cité's or ensembles associate with remote postwar constructions in the notorious banlieue. The Dutch 'complex' associates with the administration unit of the owning housing associations. In Spanish, the term 'housing estate' as such does not exist; 'polígonos de vivienda' is the closest, which is clearly associated with Franco's dictatorship strategy to build large housing estates for blue-collar workers in major cities such as Madrid, Barcelona, or Bilbao.

Housing estate is more British English, as in the United States and Australia, 'housing developments' and 'tract housing' are more widely used. Moreover, housing estates differ not only between countries, but also within countries, depending on local circumstances.

Features of Housing Estates

Housing estates are most common in Britain, in the continent of Europe, and in developed and populated countries such as Hong Kong and Singapore. Keeping in mind the working definition of housing estate mentioned earlier in this article, we distinguish eight features of housing estates:

- *Planned development*: A housing estate is the result of urban planning, not of the organic growth of cities. Estates contain thousands of dwellings, depending on the local context; so an average housing estate in Moscow or London will be larger than one in the provinces. However, a housing estate has a quite large scale in the local context. We will deal with large housing estates later in this article.
- *Urbanity*: Housing estates can be found in urban or suburban areas, including new towns in developed countries, where houses have been built in relative or absolute large quantities.
- *Appearance*: Housing estates are usually built by a single contractor in a limited period of time and according to one prevailing design, resulting in a uniform and distinct appearance.
- *Building periods*: Although the history of housing estates starts in the nineteenth century, most housing estates were built in the post-Second World War decades.
- *Housing types*: Housing estates vary from single-family developments to large-scale housing constructions, like high-rise blocks. However, modern constructions with detached or semi-detached housing in new suburbs are considered housing estates as well.
- *Tenure*: Housing estates can be owner-occupied, public (or social) housing, and private rented housing. A mix is possible. The focus often is on monotenure estates, usually social housing.
- *Function*: Housing estates usually contain houses, dwellings. Only in large developments are supporting functions like neighbourhood centres, community services, and schools included. Often, the function of housing is clearly separated from other functions.
- *Location*: Most housing estates are developed outside the then existing city limits, where sufficient territory was available and affordable. Some of these once peripheral spots become central within cities, while others remain in isolated locations.

Ideas, Expectations, and Historical Notions Behind Housing Estates

There are many kinds of housing estates, but most of the focus nowadays is on the post-Second World War housing estates in trouble: large-scale estates, monotenure social housing, low-rise or high-rise flat blocks, inhabited by the least well off and built mainly during the postwar decades. This has not always been the case. On the contrary, when those currently abused housing estates were built, the populations aimed at were the higher-working classes and the lower-middle classes, the 'class workers', not the poor and the underprivileged who live there so often at present.

Every Time Provides its Own Housing Estates

During the nineteenth century, industrialisation attracted masses of job-seeking people to the urban areas, where new industries were concentrated. The cities were not equipped for these large flows of migrants, resulting in poverty, overcrowding, poor hygiene, diseases, and other miseries. Cities like Berlin, Paris, or Vienna tripled or quadrupled within half a century (see Lévy-Vroelant et al., 2008, for an essay on the backgrounds of housing estates). The first housing estates were built on a small scale in the late 1800s by philanthropic aristocrats and utopian industrialists. The idea behind such dwellings was ensuring social justice, providing healthy workforces, controlling urban diseases, and preventing uprisings.

At the turn of the century, Housing Acts were passed in all European countries, with Belgium being the first in the world in 1889, incorporating government involvement for housing. Government support emerged in the early 1900s with municipal support for idealistic housing estates, but actual implementation took some time, hitting a peak after the First World War. This second generation of housing estates was initiated by local governments and had not only a housing function, but also a symbolic and moral function to uplift the working classes. Social housing became a key element of the emerging welfare system.

The great depression of the 1930s stopped government intervention in housing, and the private sector took the lead in the construction of housing estates. Most housing estates in this third period were market-oriented constructions, originally private rented, and often being sold now. Housing estates of these years have their own characteristics and distinction.

Housing for the Millions

The three decades following the Second World War are often considered to be the golden age for social housing. In all European cities millions of houses were built, the majority in housing estates with the features mentioned earlier. Social housing was aimed not only at the working classes as before, but also at the middle classes, key workers, and otherwise, the lowest classes. Social housing policy allowed the majority of the population to share the wealth of the economic boom and was a key factor in establishing national welfare states, following the Scandinavian examples. Most housing from these days was built in distinctive housing estates. Unlike the case with previously built housing estates, in this fourth period national governments took the lead with the supply of large brick and mortar subsidies for the construction of housing estates.

A Housing Estate as a Neighbourhood Unit

The development of housing estates is related to the development of neighbourhoods. Housing estates are planned constructions, while neighbourhoods refer to a geographical part of a town.

Architects and urban planners had not only thought about better housing, but also about better living environments instead of the overcrowded, unhygienic, and gloomy slums.

Urban planning reformers thought about solutions, resulting in the garden city movement from Ebenezer Howard, the functionalist high-rise areas according to Le Corbusier and his CIAM-friends, and the neighbourhood unit planning ideas from the American planner Perry, elaborating on the enlightened ideas of the human ecologists of the Chicago school. Neighbourhood planning to support ideal living was being developed before the Second World War, but was implemented on a wide scale after the war. The urban planning of the postwar housing estates heavily leaned on these important neighbourhood planning ideas. Good neighbourhoods should provide a solid basis for people as a protection against the anonymous urban society, and as a defence against totalitarian regimes – Communism or Nazism.

Many postwar housing estates were built according to the ideas of the neighbourhood unit, a neighbourhood that would flourish by itself, where houses and all services needed were within the same unit or area. The postwar large housing estates were well-planned units, contrary to the chaotic urban planning that characterised the prewar years. The carefully developed neighbourhood planning ideas took shape before the Second World War, but gained momentum after the war.

High-Rise Housing Estates

By the 1960s, a series of influences and pressures had coincided to build housing estates in larger sizes and with higher levels. High-rise became the expression of a new world, being the most uniform, the most dominating, the most direct, and the most visible result of postwar urban planning, as Turkington et al. call these estates. Postwar urban planning was very much influenced by the ideas of the CIAM-movement, the organisation of modern architects led by the famous Swiss architect Le Corbusier. High-rise estates in Western countries were built in a concentrated period, starting somewhere in the 1950s, and the building activity stopped rather suddenly some 10 years later – in England after a horrifying gas explosion, in the United States after a major debacle at St. Louis, in the Netherlands and Sweden after it became clear that the market demanded something else. However, in Eastern Europe the construction of high-rise housing estates continued until the fall of the Wall, and in Southern Europe but also in South America and South East Asia there has been a continuous construction of high-rise estates during the last sixty years. In all of these countries there hasn't been the aversion to high-rise, that flew over the Western countries throughout the 1970s. This is why more high-rise estates can be found in countries such as Spain, Italy, Ukraine, and Hong Kong compared with the Scandinavian countries, Germany, Britain, or the United States.

After a standstill from the mid-1970s to the 1990s, new high-rise housing is being constructed in Western countries, following Asian initiatives. At present, Asian high-rise, including the housing function, serves as an example for the rest of the world, including African, Australian, Latin American cities, and a revival of high-rise in Europe. The new high-rise housing in Western cities, however, is not built in large housing estates like the 1960s, but in tower blocks, promoted as residential parks or communities. Moreover, these are aimed at another population group, young wealthy or elderly urban-oriented citizens, not the working-class or the middle-class families as in the 1960s.

Booming Housing Estates During the Golden Years

After a period of relative standstill in the field of housing after the great depression, the Second World War and the decades following it turned out to be the golden years for the construction of housing estates. The French speak of *les trentes glorieuses*, the 30 golden years following 1945. Most urban housing was planned in these estates: large-scale, uniform, monotenure, monofunctional housing constructions at the outskirts of most cities. This large-scale planning boosted housing, 'mass housing', needed to solve the massive housing shortages. Building in concrete, employing large prefabricated components, establishing housing factories on site, and rationalising the building process stimulated building in high-rise. In both Sweden and Hungary famous 'million programmes' were launched to successfully develop one million new dwellings in mass-produced housing estates dominated by high-rise blocks. All high-rises in the nowadays problematic *grands ensembles*, the French large housing estates, belong to this programme.

Besides being based on technological progress and quantitative needs, housing estates were heavily ideological. Many housing estates were developed according to egalitarian ideas, in which a modernist urban planning could deliver a more equal and fair society, opposite to the bourgeois narrow lifestyles of the 1930s. There was a strong belief that urban planning could control social development. The egalitarian ideas focused on the common use of facilities within the building (e.g., entrees, galleries, washing machines, and libraries) and in the surroundings (e.g., greens and playing facilities).

The Outcomes: Many Large Housing Estates

The outcomes of these golden years are evident. Housing production reached a peak in the late 1960s and early 1970s, not coincidentally the same years that high-rise housing peaked. Housing estates were built as mass housing, in large quantities and at high speed. In France, for example, the average time taken to produce a dwelling dropped from nearly 2 man-years in 1950 to 7 months in 1960. In France more dwellings were built between 1960 and 1980 every 4 years than in the whole of the 1920s and 1930s. Dwellings in housing estates were produced to uniform standards, with the use of prefabricated constructions in housing factories on the spot. In Germany and Eastern Europe the postwar estates are often referred to as *Plattenbau*, because of the concrete panels used. Influenced by the 1950s and 1960s planning model of 'towers in the park', in Toronto approximately 1000 high-rise apartment towers were built, making it second on the continent, after New York. In Brazilian cities like Sao Paulo, Rio de Janeiro, and the newly built Brasilia, tempting condos in newly constructed high-rise blocks became the norm for modern urban living.

Many postwar large housing estates were built in easy and inexpensive locations, so at the then outskirts. The present location depends on the local urban development since then; some housing estates are still far out of town, while others are swallowed up by further urban expansions.

The postwar housing estates, culminating in the high-rise estates of the 1960s and early 1970s, represented the ideal housing of that era, egalitarian and modern dwellings which were spacious, comfortable, well designed, and often suitably located. However, these qualities would be questioned in the next era.

Developments Once Built

The postwar housing estates were by the 1970s a multiple of the ones built before the Second World War. Built in times of tremendous housing shortages, people were happy to get a dwelling in the new housing estates. The focus was on enlarging production numbers, developing speedy building techniques, and rationalising the building process to solve urgent needs. Once the housing market became more relaxed – after the peak productions of the early 1970s – people got more choice. Growing prosperity, greater mobility, and more household differentiation stimulated diversified housing demands. People made demands and did not take for granted the top–down supplied large housing estates as they did before.

After the housing estate boom, from the 1970s onwards developments started to be more diverse. We can divide developments worldwide into two groups: those where housing estates meant a normal way of urban housing, and those where housing estates became synonymous with problems.

In Southern European countries, but also in Brazil, Argentina, and other South American countries, living in large housing estates was accepted as the normal urban style of living. In Asian countries like Japan, China, and Malaysia living in a city means living in a flat in a housing estate. Housing estates do not have the negative image they often possess in Western countries.

The countries in the former Soviet bloc represent a different situation: There was no choice in housing there until the 1990s. Until the fall of the Wall, millions of dwellings were built within cities, the vast majority built in similar housing estates.

Problems in Housing Estates

Many Western countries soon revealed construction problems and low housing demand concentrated in the newly built housing estates. Problems were aggravated when new attractive housing estates that better suited consumers' needs were built, that is, single-family houses. In the Netherlands half of all housing consists of single-family houses in rows with a garden at the back and in the front. Moreover, the hitherto neglected slums started to be refurbished or renewed from the 1970s onwards, soon providing more appreciated housing than the early postwar housing estates. Gradually, it became clear that the supplied housing stock of the large housing estates could not match the individual preferences of people.

Problems in housing estates are plenty and manifold. One classification of problems includes:

- Structural problems: poor-quality materials, poor insulation, asbestos pollution, deterioration, and so on
- Internal design problems: small rooms, outdated floor plans, and no room for modern equipment
- Spatial problems: high building densities, poor locations, and poor services
- Liveability: safety, crime, and antisocial behaviour
- Segregation of low-income households and immigrants, social exclusion, social and racial tensions, and decreasing social cohesion
- Concentration of deprived people, high unemployment, low education, poor schooling, many dropouts, homeless, and limited self-empowerment
- Low demand and vacancies in the estate, caused by a low ranking in the local housing market
- A negative image
- Management and organisational problems
- Legislative problems, especially in some Central and Eastern European countries, where the responsibility for public spaces in large housing estates is unclear
- Financial problems: housing costs for inhabitants, large operating costs for landlords.

This classification covers most problems in the large housing estates owned by social landlords and built during the 1950s–70s. These housing estates, and the dwellings within them, were once appreciated as modern, spacious, luxurious, and egalitarian, but now the same estates are often considered as monotonous, uniform, dull, and small. The middle-class families are grown old and have been replaced by low-class families, often from other cultures, with other habits, and speaking other languages.

However, some estates, especially large post–Second World War housing estates, suffer from a range of problems like the ones just classified. Moreover, problems tend to influence each other. In fact, spirals of technical, social, and economic decline influence each other. In most problematic estates more problems occur, which interfere. Some merely blame the physical layout; most famous among those are Oscar Newman (1972) and Alice Coleman (1985), who accused the designers of horrible postwar 'modernistic' architecture. Indeed, sometimes estates were miserably designed with clumsy and unsafe entrances, corridors, and walkways, creating semi-public spaces nobody felt responsible for. Sometimes new techniques were tested, bad materials were used. Thus, the physical deterioration is evident. However, often other factors are more important than only physical.

Some of these other factors are outside the housing estate itself, or even outside the regional situation. Economic relocations in old industrial cities, large immigration or emigration flows may cause oversupply in weak parts of the housing markets, not unusually the large housing estates. The development of attractive new housing nearby may cause deprivation in older housing estates. Sale of popular housing estates at low prices, like in England in the 1980s, or in some East European countries in the 1990s, may lead to a concentration of problematic households in the remaining stock, often large housing estates. However, in Spain, Italy, and Brazil, housing estates have been sold to inhabitants on a large scale, resulting in many cases in more social cohesion and less problematic neighbourhoods. Obviously, there is no single reason causing problems, nor is there a single solution to address (or prevent) the problems.

Redevelopment of Housing Estates: A Policy Perspective

Problems differ locally, depending on the local context, building and development histories, the local or regional housing market, and local and national policies. Renewal of housing estates will vary across local contexts as well. Redevelopment, renewal, regeneration, reconstruction, or other terms may differ slightly. In this text no difference is made between them.

It is important to state that many housing estates of all ages are doing satisfactorily to very well, and do not need any major redevelopment at all. This is true for the old pre-Second World War estates, brand new estates, as well as many postwar estates. Ordinary maintenance will do there. With the passage of time, every building needs refurbishing, such as fresh painting, a new kitchen, or a new roof – routine responsibilities for any homeowner.

Rising problems, however, lead to rising needs for redevelopment schemes. Most developed countries have policies to redevelop housing estates. Redevelopment of housing estates is dependent on a range of variables such as the seriousness of the problems, the housing market situation, available finances, and investing capacity and willingness among actors. In short, urgency and priority are key factors. Most vulnerable estates belong to the postwar era; among those are many flats belonging to the period from the 1950s to the mid-1970s, including the large high-rise housing estates. In other cases, the derelict prewar tenement buildings need redevelopment. The larger an estate, the more vulnerable it is when people's preferences change. Large postwar housing estates therefore appear to be more vulnerable, and are more prominent in contemporary urban renewal schemes.

Area-Based Approaches

In most countries a shift in urban renewal can be seen towards area-based approaches, which means a focus on the estate. The area or estate is a natural scale to create a good framework for concerted actions of the actors in the process. One of the strongest advantages of an area-based approach is visibility: It is clear for everyone when a former gloomy area has changed over time into an attractive area. Such an approach to redevelop a deprived estate may be a good platform to coordinate cross-sectional efforts, but issues like poverty, jobs, or bad schooling do not keep to the area limits. Solutions to those issues should be found at a higher-scale level. Another side effect of an area-based approach is that some problems cannot be solved on the spot, but will be transferred to adjacent areas, the so-called waterbed effects.

There are several physical options for redevelopment, varying from improving maintenance to upgrading or extreme makeover to a total demolition. With drastic measures, inhabitants have to be rehoused, which could be temporarily when they are going to move back, somewhere else in the estate (when dwellings are successively being renewed), or elsewhere in the city. The choice for the types of measures has to do with the seriousness of the problems, with the needs of the residents (if they are asked anything), with future market prospects, and with the overall housing market situation.

In areas with a loose housing market, oversupply, vacancies and decreasing housing prices, demolition is a quantitative way to lose dwellings. Major examples are the east of Germany and the Detroit area in the United States; northern England, southern Italy, and northern France have also experienced the results of major economic and demographic changes. In tight housing markets – which can be found in other areas within the same countries – there will be demand for even problematic housing estates.

Integrative Approach

Redevelopment of large housing estates is not only a matter of restructuring of the housing stock, as housing problems go along with serious economic, employment, social, ethnic, and environmental problems. This means any redevelopment approach has to deal with these issues as well, resulting in an integrative approach. Only providing better housing while neglecting other problems leads to better-housed people who remain deprived and socially excluded. We can state this sharper: Improving the housing situation without improving social and economic problems, is a lost chance; physical improvements open ways to contact people and to pull them into personal improvement.

At the start of any redevelopment scheme it is worthwhile to analyse the qualities of estates, which could be the open structure, the greens, or the logical layout of the neighbourhood. An existing estate is not a 'tabula rasa', an empty piece of land, characteristic of the planning habits of half a century ago. It is a challenge to redevelop an estate while maintaining its original qualities.

Sustainability plays a role as well. Most problematic housing estates do not know a history of successes. The redeveloped estates should better serve future demands and should be more sustainable. Energy spending is a major problem in many postwar housing estates, causing high expenses for inhabitants and adding to the worldwide climate change issues. Rising energy prices are causing major problems in all estates in Eastern and Central European countries, where costs for energy exceed the costs for housing.

The Process of Renewal

Measures and strategies cover the 'what' of an approach, while the 'how' is related to the way the several actors implement the process. Times when governments could decide about society are a long way behind: 'Government' has become 'governance'. Most housing estates that are subject to redevelopment at present were constructed in times when the government had a firm idea about what society in general, and living in particular, should be like. Many housing estates were developed not only to provide shelter, but to provide in a future way of living.

However, times have changed, and redevelopment is an issue for many actors: local, national, or regional governments, land and property owners, social and commercial investors, present and future residents, tenants and owner-occupiers, policemen, shopkeepers, and social workers. Partnerships between relevant actors are necessary; cooperation is more important than steering from the top. Citizens have a far more important role than their parents or grandparents, during whose time the original estates were planned; in those days planners and politicians were thought to know what was best for people, but today people want to be involved in their future.

Involving all vital actors; combining various measures and sectors; working at the levels of the dwellings, the housing estate, and the city; and combining future-oriented policies with today's urban reality can make for successful redevelopment of housing estates.

See also: High Rise; High-Rise Homes; HOPE VI; Housing and Neighbourhood Quality: Urban Regeneration; Housing and the State in Western Europe; Neighbourhood Effects; Neighbourhood Planning; Peripheral Neighbourhoods; Post-Disaster Housing and Reconstruction.

References

Coleman A (1985) *Utopia on Trial*. London: Hilary Shipman.
Lévy-Vroelant C, Reinprecht C, and Wassenberg F (2008) Learning from history, changes and path dependency in the social housing sector in Austria, France and the Netherlands (1889–2008). In: Whitehead C and Scanlon K (eds.) *Housing Strategies in Europe*. London: LSE.
Newman O (1972) *Defensible Space: Crime Prevention through Urban Design*. New York: Macmillan.

Further Reading

Droste C, Lelevrier C, and Wassenberg F (2008) Urban regeneration in European social housing areas. In: Whitehead C and Scanlon K (eds.) *Housing Strategies in Europe*. London: LSE.
Dunleavy P (1981) *The Politics of Mass Housing in Britain, 1945–1975*. Oxford, UK: Clarendon Press.
Esping Andersen G (1990) *The Three Worlds of Welfare Capitalism*. Cambridge, UK: Polity Press.
Hall P (1988) *Cities of Tomorrow*. Oxford, UK: Basil Blackwell.
Hall P (2002) *Urban & Regional Planning*, 4th edn. London: Routledge.
Hall S and Rowlands R (2005) Place making and large estates: Theory and practice. In: Van Kempen R, Dekker K, Hall S and Tosics I (eds.) *Restructuring Large Housing Estates in Europe*, pp. 47–62. Bristol, UK: The Policy Press; University of Bristol.
Howard E (1898) *Tomorrow: A Peaceful Path to Real Reform*. London: Swan Sonnenschein.
Nystrom L (2006) Neighbourhood Centers in Europe. *Built Environment* 32(1): 12–31.
Perry CA (1929) *Neighborhood and Community Planning*. New York: Regional Plan of New York.
Power A (1997) *Estates on the Edge: The Social Consequences Of Mass Housing In Northern Europe*. London: Macmillan.
Prak NL and Priemus H (1986) A model for the analysis of the decline of post-war housing. *International Journal of Urban and Regional Research* 10(1): 1–17.
Slob A, Bolt G, and van Kempen R (2008) *Na de sloop, waterbedeffecten van gebiedsgericht stedelijk beleid [waterbed effects of area based approaches]*. The Hague: Nicis Institute.
Temkin K and Rohe WM (1996) Neighbourhood change and urban policy. *Journal of Planning Education and Research* 15: 159–170.
Turkington R, van Kempen R, and Wassenberg F (eds.) (2004) *High-rise housing in Europe: Current trends and future prospects*. Delft, the Netherlands: Delft University Press.
Van Kempen R, Dekker K, Hall S, and Tosics I (eds.) (2005). *Restructuring Large Housing Estates in Europe*. Bristol, UK: The Policy Press.
Wassenberg F (2006) The Netherlands: Adaption of the carefully planned structure. In: Nystrom L (ed.) *Neighbourhood Centers in Europe. Built Environment* 32(1): 12–31.
Wassenberg F, van Meer A, and van Kempen R (2007) *Strategies for Upgrading the Physical Environment in Deprived Urban Areas: Examples of Good Practice in Europe*. Den Haag: European Urban Knowledge Network EUKN/NICIS Institute.
Whitehead C and Scanlon K (eds.) (2007, 2008) *Social Housing in Europe*, vols. I, II, London: LSE.
Yuen B, Yeh A, Appold SJ, Earl G, Ting J, and Kurnianingrum Kwee L (2006) High-rise living in Singapore public housing. *Urban Studies* 43(3): 583–600.

Housing Finance: Deposit Guarantees

JR Barth and H Hollans, Auburn University, Auburn, AL, USA

© 2012 Elsevier Ltd. All rights reserved.

Glossary

Deposit guarantee A system where financial institutions guarantee the safety and security of customer deposits. This system is often supported by direct sanction from a sovereign government or quasi-private institution backed by government sanction.

Deposit insurance A specific form of depository guarantee backed by an insurance fund.

Explicit guarantee A form of guarantee backed by the full faith and credit of a sovereign government having jurisdiction over the institution, often offered in cooperation with a private financial organisation such as a bank or savings institution.

Fractional reserve banking A system of banking in which institutions are required only to keep a (oftentimes small) percentage of bank deposits in reserves to cover deposit withdrawals. The larger portion of those deposits are then used for extending credit, including commercial and consumer loans, as well as mortgages, secured against both commercial and residential housing.

Implicit guarantee A form of guarantee backed only by the assumption that a guarantor, such as a sovereign government, will stand ready to support the security of deposits in the event of an institutional failure.

Introduction

In the world of modern financial institutions and markets, guaranteeing the safety of deposits has become a widely accepted principle in promoting the stability of financial institutions. Deposit guarantees may take many forms, such as a direct or explicit guarantee that is fully supported by a particular guarantor. In order for a guarantee to be successful in providing stability to a financial system, the performance and acceptability of that guarantee are critical for its market acceptance. The emphasis on the financial soundness of the guarantor has led to the creation of deposit guarantee institutions which are usually established by sovereign governments and then backed by the government's overall financial strength. An alternative to this form of guarantee is the creation of a quasi-governmental institution to which support is extended through government intervention if necessary.

The need for a deposit guarantee arises due to fractional reserve banking. When a banking system is built on this basis and banking institutions do not hold 100% in reserves, there is a potential problem. If depositors lose confidence in the ability of a financial institution to return those deposits at full value, the potential for panic behaviour exists. The term bank panic or bank run is an apt description of what potentially could happen when depositors converge on an institution to withdraw their deposits. In order to support the viability of fractional-reserve-banking systems, deposit guarantees have been put in place in many countries throughout the world.

A common form of a deposit guarantee system that is most frequently found in countries is the creation of deposit insurance institutions. These types of institutions have a long history dating back to the early American experiments of the 1800s. Today, many countries around the globe protect depository accounts from loss with some form of deposit insurance. These deposit insurance institutions are usually backed by government guarantees. The typical way in which a deposit insurance scheme works is that depository institutions pay a premium based on their deposits or assets in an insurance fund, which guarantees up to a certain limit the safety of deposits.

Deposit Guarantees

The US Experience

In terms of the history of deposit insurance schemes, one of the oldest and most recognised institutions for this purpose is the Federal Deposit Insurance Corporation (FDIC). The history of insuring bank deposits in the United States, however, dates even earlier to the period of the early 1800s when many insurance schemes were established and then funded and guaranteed at the level of the state government as opposed to the federal government. A primary motivation for these schemes emerged between 1836 and 1863, which is often referred to as the wildcat banking era. This was a period marked by unsound banking practices and numerous bank panics and failures. During this period, just prior to the Civil

War, state-chartered banks issued their own currency and state authorities were primarily responsible for overseeing the safety and soundness of the banking institutions within the different states. In order to provide for greater stability of their banking systems, states like New York created deposit guarantee systems.

During the 1860s, the United States experienced a significant change in its monetary system as federally chartered banks and the federal government became the primary issuers of currency that served as legal tender. Two acts, in particular, the National Currency Act of 1863 and the National Banking Act of 1864, facilitated this transition. At this time, the Office of the Comptroller of the Currency was created. This agency was established to charter federal banks. The National Banking Act that superseded the Currency Act prohibited federal banks from engaging in lending for residential housing. Not until 1913, the year in which the US Congress passed the Federal Reserve Act, could commercial banks issue home loans. Prior to this, residential mortgages were dominantly provided through savings and loan associations or through private placement by mortgage brokers with insurance companies being a significant source of funds.

The next most significant events in the history of US housing finance and commercial banking came during the period of the Great Depression. The stock market crash of 1929 heralded the beginning of a catastrophic failure in the US financial system. During this period, the banking system experienced a widespread panic that triggered significant institutional failures as depositors lost confidence in the safety and soundness of the entire system. Under President Roosevelt's New Deal legislative initiatives, numerous changes occurred in the regulatory environment. Two important innovations at this time were the creation of the Federal Home Loan Banking system and the creation of the FDIC. Federal Home Loan Banks were a set of 12 regional wholesale banking institutions created for the purpose of extending credit to the savings and loan industry to support housing. As a way to promote greater stability in the savings and loan industry, the Federal Savings and Loan Insurance Corporation (FSLIC) was created in 1934 to guarantee deposits at these institutions.

Both the FDIC and the FSLIC served as a foundation for deposit guarantees at banks and savings and loan associations for much of the following half-century. These two organisations were established as insurance funds which required all member institutions offering insured deposits to pay a small premium based on their deposits to the fund. The history of these two organisations illustrates the positive and negative aspects of deposit guarantees. During the 1980s, the savings and loan industry was engulfed in a financial crisis which led to the bankruptcy of the FSLIC. The crisis was a period when hundreds of institutions became insolvent. In order to deal with the fallout of numerous costly failures, Congress passed the Financial Institutions Reform, Recovery, and Enforcement Act (FIRREA). This Act dissolved the FSLIC because it could no longer meet its obligation to insure depositor funds. In its place, the FDIC was given the task of administering a second insurance fund for the deposits of the remaining and viable savings and loan institutions. As a result, the FDIC was responsible for administering two parallel insurance funds, the Savings Association Insurance Fund (SAIF) and the Bank Insurance Fund (BIF). In the wake of this crisis, it was necessary to expend tremendous amounts of taxpayer money to restore the financial system to solvency. The two funds were subsequently merged.

In 1991, the FDIC was granted greater power to take corrective action against deteriorating banks before they become insolvent. Nevertheless, the financial crisis of 2007 engulfed the US banking system, and led to the FDIC playing a lead role in supporting the safety and soundness of the depository financial system. One action taken in this regard was to increase the level of deposit insurance for depositors. When FDIC deposit coverage went into effect in 1934, the level of coverage was $2500 per depositor. At the start of the most recent financial crisis, the FDIC insured deposits at the level of $100 000 per depositor per institution. The FDIC during the most recent crisis increased this limit to $250 000 per depositor per institution. This increase sought to instil greater confidence in depository institutions.

An International Perspective

When considering the nature of deposit guarantees in the context of world financial markets, it is helpful to assess the extent to which there has been a general acceptance of this type of innovation across multiple sovereign economies. **Table 1** illustrates the coverage of explicit deposit guarantees across 19 of the G20 nations. The existence of these schemes varies across financial systems, with countries such as Australia, China, Indonesia, and South Africa yet to establish an explicit deposit guarantee system as of 2007. The reasons for this undoubtedly vary by country. For example, the size of the nation's economy and the overall role and importance of depository institutions may dictate the perceived importance of establishing such deposit guarantees. One might think that the level of financial assets relative to GDP might have been a factor in a country's decision to implement a deposit insurance scheme. However, **Table 1** illustrates that even among countries with high levels of financial assets relative to GDP some still have not implemented deposit guarantee systems. In contrast, countries with relatively small financial asset to GDP ratios such as Mexico, Turkey, and Argentina have set up deposit guarantee systems.

Table 1 Selected financial and bank allowable activity information by country

Country	Financial assets to GDP ratio (%)	Homeownership rate (%)	Residential mortgage debt to GDP ratio (%)	Residential mortgage debt per capita (thousand)	Explicit deposit system	Allowable real estate activities for banks - Investment	Allowable real estate activities for banks - Development	Allowable real estate activities for banks - Management
Argentina	79.2	77.0	3.8	0.29	Yes	No	No	No
Australia	301.2	70.0	51.0	23.9	No	Yes	No	No
Brazil	188.2	74.4	7.4	0.3	Yes	Yes	No	No
Canada	322.7	68.4	42.6	28.5	Yes	Yes	Yes	Yes
China	280.4	81.0	10.0	0.15	No	No	No	No
France	376.2	57.4	35.9	11.0	Yes	Yes	No	Yes
Germany	351.8	43.2	46.1	14.0	Yes	Yes	Yes	Yes
India	161.9	86.8	2.2	77.0	Yes	No	No	No
Indonesia	77.5	n.a.	1.8	n.a.	No	No	No	No
Italy	347.6	80.0	19.8	5.2	Yes	No	No	No
Japan	579.1	60.0	37.0	14.2	Yes	No	No	No
Mexico	95.0	84.0	9.0	0.5	Yes	Yes	Yes	Yes
Russia	142.4	63.8	2.4	0.2	No	Yes	No	Yes
Saudi Arabia	124.2	n.a.	n.a.	n.a.	No	No	No	No
South Africa	334.3	56.0	24.8	4.5	No	Yes	No	No
South Korea	270.5	62.9	13.4	1.4	Yes	Yes	No	No
Turkey	107.6	68.2	0.22	0.1	Yes	Yes	Yes	Yes
United Kingdom	597.7	70.0	80.5	23.8	Yes	Yes	Yes	Yes
United States	413.9	67.8	83.6	26.7	Yes	No	No	No

Source: The Milken Institute, 2010 data.
n.a., not available.

Another important issue is the extent to which depository institutions are allowed to engage in various real estate activities. Some countries such as the United States are very restrictive in regard to the types of real-estate-related assets that banks may hold on their balance sheets. It is generally believed that participation in relatively risky real estate ventures might pose problems that can undermine public perceptions regarding the safety of deposits. Three of the important areas of real estate activity involve investment in, development of, and management of property. Frequently, the bank regulatory regime within an economy might permit investment in real estate, but would not permit the development and management of property. Some notable economies such as Canada, Germany, Mexico, and the United Kingdom permit depository institutions to participate in all three primary activities. With the exception of China, the countries that permit a broader range of real estate activities generally have an explicit deposit guarantee system.

Recent innovations in risk mitigation strategies, such as risk-based capital requirements and various provisions of Basel I, II, and III, have significantly affected how deposit insurance might be structured to enhance the performance of a specific country's depository institutions. Regarding guidance on this issue, a report published in 2009 jointly by the Basel Committee on Banking Supervision and the International Association of Deposit Insurers sets forth a framework for implementation of a deposit insurance scheme. The agreed-upon set of guiding principles includes the following discussion:

> In order to be credible, and to avoid distortions that may result in moral hazard, a deposit insurance system needs to be part of a well-constructed financial system safety net, properly designed and well implemented. A financial safety net usually includes prudential regulation and supervision, a lender of last resort and deposit insurance. (Basel Committee on Banking Supervision (BCBS) and International Association of Deposit Insurers (IADI) (2009))

It is clear from this discussion that deposit insurance is likely to play a major role going forward in promoting the safety, soundness, and stability of world financial markets, especially in regard to depository institutions. Further discussions within this set of guiding principles clearly note that deposit insurance is not sufficient by itself to ensure a well-functioning financial system and adequately guarantee against a 'systemic crisis'.

Linking Deposit Guarantees and Mortgage Lending

When considering the importance of deposit insurance to housing finance, it is important to understand the structure of the housing finance system within each country.

Consider, as a point of comparison, the United States which has a two-tiered system of housing finance. The first tier of housing finance is found in the role that depository institutions play in underwriting or originating mortgage loans. US banking organisations play a significant part in the operation of the housing finance system by creating mortgages which may be retained in their asset portfolio or sold in the second tier of the system. This second tier represents the secondary mortgage market where market participants trade previously written securities, that is, mortgages. The principal players in this second tier of the mortgage market include organisations such as Fannie Mae and Freddie Mac, as well as numerous private label investment groups. Large commercial banks in the United States such as Wells Fargo and Bank of America also play a major role in this two-tiered market. These two institutions along with numerous others work extensively to help create a highly liquid mortgage market.

Originate-to-Hold Model versus Securitisation

Depending upon the position that a depository institution takes in regard to mortgage-related assets, the role that deposit insurance plays can be significantly different. Depository institutions may take one of two approaches to mortgage-related activity. Institutions can primarily be in the business of underwriting mortgage loans, which are then converted into portfolio assets and become a part of that banking institution's overall asset portfolio. An alternative to this would be a depository institution serving primarily as a mortgage broker; after underwriting mortgages, they are sold to secondary market investors. The structure of the US housing finance system followed this path over the past several decades, as has that in many other countries.

When comparing the US housing finance system of the 1980s to that in 2008, it is clear that the Originate-to-Hold model that was common before the 1980s has been replaced to a significant degree by the Originate-to-Distribute model. During the period of the early 1980s, savings and loan institutions dominated the home mortgage market, holding a 49% share of the source of funding for residential mortgages. By contrast, commercial banks accounted for only 17% of the market with various mortgage pools and private label investment groups accounting for nearly another 20% market share. By 2008, this paradigm had radically shifted. Commercial banks' share had slightly increased to a 19% share, but saving institutions' share declined to only 8% with credit unions' contributing an additional 3% of total funding. However, the largest single source of funding had shifted toward the securitisation market. Government-Sponsored Enterprise mortgage pools, led by Fannie Mae and

Freddie Mac, accounted for 41% of funding, with private mortgage pools contributing an additional 18%.

The monumental shift away from depository institutions holding the lion's share of residential loans to large-scale securitisation significantly impacted the capital structure of these institutions. Historically, institutions that pursued an originate-to-hold strategy gained a steady and acceptable rate of return on capital from mortgage investment. The period of the mid-to-late 1980s fuelled significant changes in this strategy as savings and loan institutions gave way to commercial banks in terms of market share. This transition also impacts the public's perceived risk of deposits in depository institutions that rely heavily upon investment in housing finance as a primary source of revenue. These institutions are somewhat insulated from market downturns in regard to mortgage portfolio value losses, given that a significant portion of the mortgages they create are sold in the secondary market. This behaviour by deposit institutions serves to weaken the rationale for linking housing finance activity with deposit insurance requirements, as the risk of holding mortgage assets is shifted to investors in securities backed by pools of mortgages.

Conclusions and Policy Implications

It is clear that during times of financial crisis a focus on enhancing public perception as to the safety, soundness, and stability of the financial system is a primary consideration for financial regulators. One of the principal methods of achieving this goal is through the proper use of deposit guarantees, possibly in the form of establishing a formal deposit insurance scheme. Quite often during periods of tranquillity in the banking industry, deposit insurance schemes go unnoticed in terms of their importance to the financial system as a whole. In order to maintain a healthy posture on an ongoing basis, it is necessary for deposit insurance institutions to be granted appropriate regulatory authority to deal with both institutional-level deficiencies and provide some level of oversight to minimise risk to the financial system as a whole.

An illustration of the importance of insuring deposits can be seen in **Figure 1(a)** and **1(b)**. These charts show the composition of the liabilities of US depository institutions in two different time periods. **Figure 1(a)** illustrates the composition of the industry in the early stages of the financial crisis of 2007. During this period of time, insured deposits were 33% of total liabilities. By June 2010, insured deposits had grown to 39% of total liabilities, as shown in **Figure 1(b)**. The transitioning of bank balance sheets towards heavier reliance upon insured deposits clearly indicates the importance of deposit insurance as a way to better entice the larger public to retain their confidence in banks as well as their deposits. This was particularly important during the mortgage market meltdown that was occurring at the time.

With regard to the financial crisis of 2007, the FDIC took a lead role in helping promote the recovery of confidence in the entire financial system. In conjunction with the Federal Reserve, the FDIC is front and centre in the effort to help restore public confidence. The FDIC has served as a major broker in the process of disposing billions of dollars in troubled assets at failed depository institutions. The FDIC has accomplished this through assisting in the placement of performing assets and core deposits of failed institutions with depository institutions considered on a solid footing. For troubled assets which are more difficult to market, the FDIC has played a lead role in providing these assets to auction markets.

For any policy-maker, it is important to understand the argument that deposit guarantee systems create a

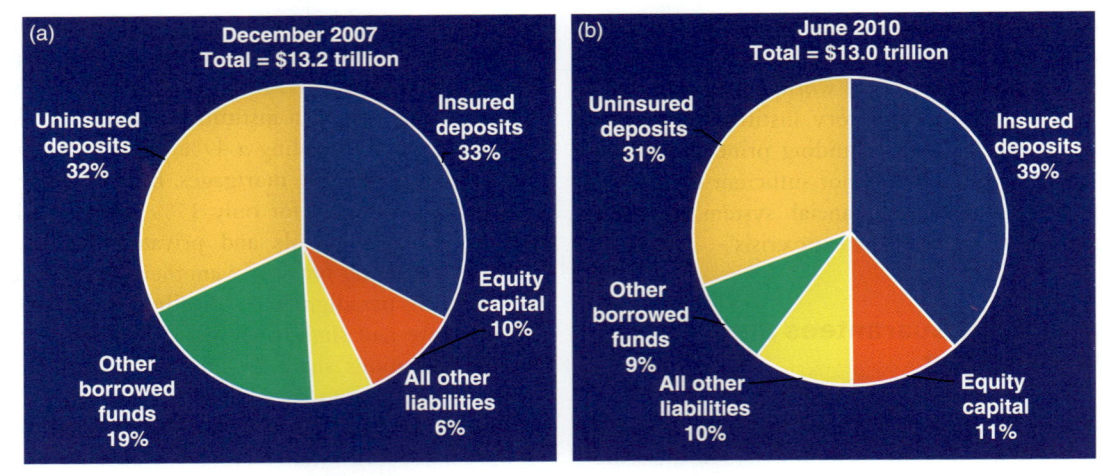

Figure 1 Sources of funding for all FDIC Insured Depository Institutions.

'moral hazard' in regard to promoting excessively risky behaviour by lending institutions. In order to deter institutions engaging in risk-taking behaviour which might threaten the safety of depositor accounts, a system of regulatory oversight must also be provided. The regulatory structure must not only be effective in identifying problem institutions in advance of catastrophic failures, but also be empowered to intervene so as to prevent those failures from causing a significant public burden, as is often the outcome when financial systems experience widespread institutional failures. This is an ongoing and difficult task.

See also: Access and Affordability: Mortgage Guarantees; Contract Saving Schemes; Credit Derivatives; Housing Policy: Agents and Regulators; Mortgage Insurance; Industrial Organisation of the US Residential Mortgage Market; Mortgage Lenders and Loans; Mortgage Market Regulation: Europe; Mortgage Market Regulation: North America; Mortgage Markets and Macro-Instability; Mortgage Markets: Regulation and Intervention; Mortgage Payment Protection Insurance.

Further Reading

Barth JR (1991) *The Great Savings and Loan Debacle*. Washington, DC: The AEI Press.

Barth JR and Dan Brumbaugh R, Jr. (1992) *The Reform of Federal Deposit Insurance: Disciplining the Government and Protecting Taxpayers*. New York: HarperCollins Publishers.

Barth JR, Nolle DE, and Rice TN (1997) Commercial banking structure, regulation, and performance: An international comparison. *Economics Working Paper*. Washington, DC: Office of the Comptroller of the Currency.

Barth JR, Nolle DE, Phumiwasana T, and Yago G (2003) A cross-country analysis of the bank supervisory framework and bank performance. *Working Paper Series*, New York University Salomon Center. Malden, MA: Blackwell Publishing Inc.

Barth JR, Caprio G, Jr., and Nolle DE (2004) *Comparative International Characteristics of Banking* Washington, DC: Office of the Comptroller of the Currency.

Barth JR, Caprio G, Jr., and Levine R (2006) *Rethinking Bank Regulation*. New York: Cambridge University Press.

Barth JR, Li T, Lu W, Phumiwasana T, and Yago G (2009) *The Rise and Fall of the U.S. Mortgage and Credit Markets: A Comprehensive Analysis of the Market Meltdown*. Hoboken, NJ: John Wiley & Sons.

Basel Committee on Banking Supervision (BCBS) and International Association of Deposit Insurers (IADI) (2009) *Core Principles for Effective Deposit Insurance Systems*. Basel, Switzerland: Bank for International Settlements.

Division of Research and Statistics (1998) *A Brief History of Deposit Insurance in the United States*. Federal Deposit Insurance Corporation. Washington, DC: International Conference on Deposit Insurance.

Housing Finance: Global South

K Datta, Queen Mary University of London, London, UK

© 2012 Elsevier Ltd. All rights reserved.

Glossary

Global South A term first coined in the 1980s to distinguish between the richer industrialised countries of the North and the poorer countries in the South.

Housing finance Housing finance is the organised mobilisation of loans/credit, savings, and subsidies.

Housing microfinance Housing microfinance is small-scale lending typically aimed at housing consolidation and improvement.

Progressive housing/incremental housing This refers to housing which is built gradually and incrementally as and when households have the resources to improve or consolidate their housing.

Introduction

The human settlement dimension of poverty is inadequate housing which – despite numerous interventions across the global South – looks set to increase. Recent reports estimate that one in three urban dwellers in the developing world lives in slums, with the total slum population poised to rise from 998 million in 2006 to 1.4 billion people in 2020. This increase can be partly explained by the twin processes of high rates of urbanisation and the urbanisation of poverty. In turn, there is increased consensus that this deficit in adequate housing has to be urgently addressed due to the critical links between housing and household productivity: income, health, and sustainable livelihoods. Furthermore, the role that housing can play in local, regional, and national economic and financial development is also increasingly recognised.

Informed by wider economic reform and broader changes in urban management approaches in the 1990s, housing finance has emerged as a key initiative in addressing this housing deficit. Embedded within economic, financial, legal, and institutional reforms, housing finance is credited with having the potential to both improve housing conditions and facilitate housing markets. Over a period of time, housing finance programmes have matured, with researchers noting the substantial experience and innovation evident in the range of financial products on offer; the diversity of organisations and agencies involved in the extension of housing finance programmes; as well as the partnerships being forged between governments, private sector organisations, nongovernmental organisations, and microfinance organisations, which span the formal and informal divide.

This article aims to provide an overview of housing finance in the global South. It begins with a definition of housing finance and an examination of the types and sources of housing finance available. It then moves on to identify the key institutions involved in the delivery of finance. The article concludes with a discussion of the challenges faced by housing finance programmes. Divided into three sections, the article draws upon relevant examples throughout. The article concludes with a discussion of the challenges faced by housing finance programmes particularly within the context of the recent economic downturn.

Defining and Identifying Key Types and Sources of Housing Finance

Housing finance, or shelter finance as it is also referred to, can be broadly defined as the organised mobilisation of loans/credit, savings, and subsidies. Three further points are important here. First, despite the distinctions between credit, savings, and subsidies, it is important to recognise that these are vitally interconnected as reflected by the financial behaviour of households which utilise a complex combination of all three to satisfy their housing needs. Second, the supply of credit, subsidies, and savings instruments span the formal, semiformal, and informal sectors. Third, the types of housing finance available do not always meet the financial needs or preferences of those on lower incomes.

It is clearly evident from research that credit is a predominant source of housing finance. This said, while it is typically provided in the form of mortgage finance in the global North, it has taken much more diverse forms in the global South including not only conventional mortgage finance but also housing microfinance. Further, it can be accessed individually or via group membership in Rotating Savings and Credit Clubs (ROSCAs) as well as Accumulated Savings and Credit Associations (ASCrRs). In contrast to credit finance, the role of savings as a source of housing finance has not always been recognised although it is highly significant in housing improvement and consolidation. In part, this invisibility is attributable to a long-held assumption that people on lower incomes do not save because they do not want to or are unable to do so. Yet, research notes that even while many poorer households lack safe and convenient ways of saving (particularly in the formal sector due to criteria such as the maintenance of minimum balances or lack of positive rates of interest), they do engage in a range of income-maximisation and consumption-minimisation strategies in order to accumulate savings. In turn, the recognition of the role of savings in housing finance signals a consensus that the extension of credit is not always the best way of helping poor people as loans turn into debts. Indeed, despite the importance of credit finance, research illustrates that low-income households generally express an aversion to debt and that repaying loans can in fact harm the financial viability of households. Recent studies of the Kuyasa Fund in South Africa as well as the Shack Dwellers Federation in Namibia, for example, report that a significant proportion of poor households prefer to use savings rather than loans to finance a range of housing improvements.

Subsidies are a third source of housing finance, although some would argue that their relative importance is diminishing. It is of course important to recognise that subsidies have played a role in financing housing for a considerable period of time and were particularly utilised in both mass public housing and site and service schemes which were implemented with high levels of subsidisation in order to address the problem of affordability. Identified as 'supply side' subsidies, these programmes were largely unsuccessful, unsustainable, and failed to keep abreast of housing demand. Debates continue as to the role of housing subsidies in housing finance programmes, with critics arguing that they undermine financial sustainability and private sector involvement as well as inculcate cultures of dependency and nonpayment, while proponents point out that the shelter needs of particularly poor households cannot be addressed without recourse to subsidies.

The synergies between credit, savings, and subsidies are variously captured by different housing finance instruments, of which three are further detailed here: namely conventional mortgage finance, direct demand subsidies, and housing microfinance. Conventional mortgage finance is usually directed at the purchase of completed housing units. It consists of a large loan extended for a term of 10–30 years with a minimum and regular income requirement, and the provision of immovable tangible assets and registered title deed as collateral. Typically, borrowers are also required to demonstrate savings ranging from 10 to 30% of a housing unit's value. There have been attempts to expand and strengthen mortgage instruments in a number of developing and transitional societies – such as in the Ukraine, for example, where the number of formal sector organisations offering mortgage finance has risen from 6 commercial banks in 2002 to nearly 100 banks in 2007, as well as the development of more innovative mortgage programmes such as the Dual Index Mortgages in Mexico.

However, notwithstanding these initiatives, an enduring feature of mortgage finance is that it is primarily targeted at middle- to high-income households, with a number of studies reporting that mortgage finance has played a relatively minor role in providing finance to those on lower incomes in the global South. For example, a study by the UNHCS (2005) put the proportion of households unable to afford a conventional mortgage at 40% in Latin America, rising to 70% of households in sub-Saharan Africa. At a national scale, it is estimated that nearly 80% of all urban housing in Indonesia is constructed without recourse to mortgage finance. In turn, the unavailability of mortgage finance in Mexico through the 1980s was reflected by the fact that while 84% of the total housing stock was owner-occupied, less than 10% of it was financed through mortgage loans.

The inability of mortgage finance instruments to go 'down-market' as it were can be partly explained by a disjuncture between the financial needs of lower income groups and the product on offer as well as the perceived risk of engaging in a financial relationship with poorer households. Taking these in turn, the fact that mortgage finance often translates into a large loan taken over a long period of time means that it is unsuited to the needs of lower-income households. Research from across the global South reflects that poor households prefer to minimise their exposure to debt through acquiring small loans for short periods of time. Perceptions of the risk associated with lending to lower-income groups also structure relations between financial institutions and these households. Financial institutions are often wary of extending loans due to difficulties in verifying incomes (which may be particularly difficult to do if households are employed in the informal economy) as well as a lack of willingness to innovate or learn from the financial practices of low-income groups. Lower-income households may themselves lack faith in formal financial institutions based in part on very limited interactions.

As such, the inappropriateness of conventional mortgage finance persists, which in turn has necessitated finding alternative ways of financing housing for lower-income groups including subsidy programmes. Learning from (some of) the mistakes of the past, subsidy programmes have been transformed from being 'supply side' (evident in the 1960s and 1970s, see above) to 'demand side' products with the latter credited for being better targeted and operating in a more accountable manner. Pioneered in Chile in 1977, direct demand subsidies as they have come to be known have since been introduced in a number of countries including Colombia, Costa Rica, Ecuador, Panama, and South Africa, with some variation evident across different programmes. Thus, for example, while housing subsidies have been linked to a savings record in Chile on the premise that this reflects the willingness of poorer households to help themselves, in South Africa, subsidies have been linked to the provision of credit on the basis that savings take far too long to accumulate. Notwithstanding some innovation, limitations remain in the design and implementation of direct demand subsidy programmes. In particular, they are prone to suffer from a 'financial gap', which is attributable to the difference in the level of the subsidy and the actual cost of construction. In turn, this effectively means that poorer households have to operationalise a range of other financial mechanisms including savings; and income raised through micro-enterprises and/or personal networks in order to raise sufficient shelter finance to improve or consolidate their housing. Furthermore, government funding for subsidy programmes may not be sufficient relative to the housing demand.

Within this context, housing microfinance is seen by many as the key innovation in the provision of housing finance to lower-income households. Defined as small-scale lending usually aimed at housing consolidation and improvement, housing microfinance loans are typically used to construct more durable roofs, walls, floors; connect essential services to plots (including water, sewage, and/or electricity); and construct additional rooms. There is broad consensus that housing microfinance can play a critical role in slum upgrading programmes which often disregard housing, concentrating instead on the improvement or extension of basic urban infrastructure, land tenure, and other services. Households who may be left to their own devices regarding finance for housing can be offered a home improvement loan, an option being explored in slum upgrading programmes in Vietnam and India.

It is important here to distinguish between two broad approaches to housing finance for the poor: namely, Shelter Advocacy to Housing Finance and Micro-Credit to Housing Finance. A key distinction between the two approaches is their respective origins, with the former growing out of slum upgrading programmes with a focus on extending land rights as well as shelter advocacy with a secondary focus on the provision of credit. In contrast, Micro-Credit to Housing Finance has evolved out of the microfinance industry and it is important to trace its roots in the 'microfinance revolution' in order to understand how it works. Microfinance is a product of a third wave of financial experimentation following on from the failure of state-mediated and subsidised credit and deregulated financial markets in the 1980s. Consisting of small working capital loans often extended on the basis of group lending, and spearheaded by innovative microfinance institutions in countries as diverse as Bangladesh (and most famously the Grameen Bank), Bolivia, and Indonesia, microfinance has been critical in meeting the needs of financially excluded people, a significant proportion of whom are on low incomes. Evidence of its ability to do so, and the growing euphoria surrounding microfinance, is reflected, among other things, by the fact that 2005 was declared 'the UN Year of Microfinance'.

Even while the focus of microfinance has been, and indeed continues to be, on the provision of loans for income generation projects, a number of large microfinance institutions have since expanded their portfolios to include lending for housing. In turn, housing microfinance loans appear to be particularly suited to the financial needs and preferences of lower-income households and rest somewhere in between conventional mortgage finance and microfinance loans. In relation to mortgage finance, housing microfinance loans are typically smaller and borrowed for shorter periods of time and, perhaps even more importantly, are not usually tied to conventional collateral and/or secure land titles. In comparison to microfinance loans, housing microfinance loans typically have longer terms; are for larger amounts; have lower interest rates; and come with adapted loan appraisal techniques. As an example, the Indian Self-Employed Women's Association (SEWA) Bank's (which is essentially a cooperative bank which belongs to the SEWA, a trade union representing the interests of informally employed women) housing products are longer in term (60 months compared to 35 months) and cheaper (interest rate of 14.5% per year compared with 18%) than microfinance working capital loans.

There is some variation across institutions in terms of housing microfinance loan products, size, and terms. For example, home improvement loans in Latin America and the Caribbean are short- to mid-term and range from 3 to 36 months, although some institutions offer terms of up to 60 months. This is in contrast to the experience in Asia where the typical duration of loans is from 12 to 36 months, with some of the larger microfinance organisations such as the Grameen Bank in Bangladesh and the SEWA Bank in India offering terms of up to 10 years. Loan sizes also vary, and within the Latin American region, they average at US$2800 but range from US$900 to US$3500. Further, while interest rates are generally fixed, they may vary during the lifetime of the loan as evident in the case of housing microfinance loans extended by Banco Sol in Bolivia, which has developed a variable rate product. Interest rates may also be below those for working capital loans but again can vary, with a typical range of 24 to 36% per annum.

Perhaps, the key to the success of housing microfinance programmes is that they are particularly suited to the ways in which poorer households construct their homes – essentially housing microfinance is incremental finance directed at incremental or progressive housing. Further, the flexibility which lending organisations are able to deploy in relation to adjusting loan amounts and terms often means that housing microfinance repayments are affordable with relatively low rates of default. The provision of construction/technical assistance and establishment of multi-stakeholder partnerships also enables poorer households to access housing microfinance programmes. A number of housing microfinance programmes have also recognised the synergies between credit and savings such that the majority of schemes enable households to build up both a savings and credit history, which in turn reduces the risks incurred by lenders leading to lower interest rates in the long term. As such, housing microfinance loans are typically the third or fourth loan issued to any individual allowing for the establishment of a savings history.

While the potential growth of housing microfinance varies across regions, it appears to be highest in those countries which share the following common characteristics: high levels of financial exclusion from traditional forms of mortgage lending; lack of collateral which may be attributable to problems in determining land tenure; a preponderance of low to moderate, as well as irregular, income; and high levels of urbanisation as well as the existence of a strong microfinance industry. By the early 2000s, researchers estimated that there were 40 housing microfinance programmes in operation, which stretched across the globe from Africa, Asia, and the Middle East to Latin America and the Caribbean.

Organisations Involved in the Provision of Housing Finance

Having outlined the main sources and instruments of housing finance, this section identifies the key organisations involved in the provision of housing finance. As noted by researchers, the number and types of organisations involved in the provision of housing finance has been facilitated by financial deregulation. In turn, these organisations operate across the formal, semiformal, and informal spectrum and consist on the one extreme of formal sector organisations including banks, credit unions, and cooperatives through to informal mechanisms including registered or unregistered moneylenders. As indicated above, microfinance institutions are also critical in the provision of housing finance. These may in turn be registered as NGOs, cooperatives (e.g., the SEWA Bank in India), private commercial banks or banks with a special charter (of which the most well known is the Grameen Bank in Bangladesh), credit unions, and nonbanking financial intermediaries. Two points are important here. First, there is general consensus that while formal financial institutions tend to be supply driven, informal financial institutions are more demand driven. Second, a key innovation is the collaborations between these different types of organisations, particularly between governments and NGOs, in order to deliver a range of financial instruments to lower-income households.

Before looking at some of these organisations in more detail, the state deserves special and separate attention. There is broad consensus that the advent of neoliberal economics and politics in the late 1980s has had a fundamental impact upon the role and function of the state. Within the realm of shelter, the state has been transformed from being a key provider of housing to an enabler responsible for getting the conditions right to facilitate the smooth and efficient running of housing markets. Urged to undertake regulatory reform and forge partnerships with the private sector by influential organisations such as the World Bank, this has entailed a fundamental shift in housing policy formation and implementation across the global South.

Yet, as researchers note, while the state may no longer play a pivotal role in the production of housing, it still does – and critically, for some, should – exert considerable influence. The continuing influence/intervention of the state in housing markets can be partly understood as arising out of the politicisation of shelter, whereby housing is recognised as being crucial to individual and household well-being and as such an important potential vote-bank. Even in its role as an 'enabler', the state has important roles to fulfil. For example, where housing programmes are linked to broader shelter issues including service provision and land regularisation, some level of state intervention is necessary. State intervention is also a necessary prerequisite for getting the policy framework right in order to facilitate the flow of housing finance. Research in a number of developing countries documents that building codes and standards as well as financial laws are premised on the assumption that people acquire their homes through the purchase of fully constructed units. Yet this does not reflect the reality on the ground – studies report that anywhere between 75 and 90% of all housing in developing world countries is incremental or progressive housing. Ironically, however, financial institutions may be restricted from lending for incremental housing, a good example of which is the Kenyan Banking and Building Societies Act. Reform of such laws is crucial given that they potentially disrupt both the supply and the demand for shelter finance as well as slow down the process of housing consolidation and improvement. Further, the importance of the state in championing housing microfinance can also not be underestimated with a number of national governments playing an instrumental role in its promotion. For example, the Mexican and Colombian governments have been working to integrate housing microfinance as a crucial ingredient of their housing and urban development strategy. The governments of Indonesia and South Africa have also developed policies which support commercially based housing microfinance programmes. The state can also play a key role in forging new partnerships as evident in the case of South Africa where the links between the national and local government and the NGO sector have been strengthened and are crucial both for the provision of technical assistance and subsidies in shelter programmes.

Moving on to consider the role of NGOs in the provision of housing (micro) finance programmes, the first NGO-led programmes have been traced back to the 1970s although NGO involvement accelerated through the 1980s and 1990s. Housing finance programmes promoted by NGOs often share a range of characteristics including the tying of credit facilities with a savings history; community-based approaches with the adoption of group lending mechanisms; as well as the extension of technical assistance in construction and planning. Largely supported by donor funding, NGO housing finance projects have often operated in collaboration with governments as evident in Mexico, the Philippines, Thailand, and South Africa, which has enabled more widespread coverage. This in itself is an important step in the right direction, given the often fractious relationship between state and civil society prior to the 1990s when broader changes related to the urban governance democratisation and decentralisation agenda had an important impact upon this relationship. This said, it is equally important to acknowledge that the demand for what are effectively financial services often places a high burden on NGOs who may lack such expertise while also recasting the 'special' relationship between NGOs and the communities which they serve.

In practice, it is the microfinance institutions that have spearheaded the provision of housing microfinance, which is not surprising perhaps given their track record in engaging with lower-income households. Over a period of time, both the number of microfinance institutions offering home improvement loans and the relative importance of their respective housing finance portfolios have expanded. Thus, for example, not only have leading agencies such as Banco Solidario in Ecuador, Calpia in Honduras, Banco Ademi in the Dominican Republic, Mibanco in Peru, and Banco Sol in Bolivia established a housing finance programme, the latter two have experienced a particularly significant growth in their housing portfolio as a proportion of their total portfolio (35 and 15%, respectively). Other examples are the URI in Uganda which launched its housing product in 2004, which in turn accounted for over 10% of its total portfolio just a year later and the SEWA Bank of India whose home improvement and infrastructure loans account for 40% of its total portfolio. Another impressive example of the success of microfinance institutions in providing housing microfinance loans is Mibanco in Peru. Mibanco is Latin America's second-largest microfinance institution with over 70 000 clients. A private commercial bank, Mibanco was established in 1972 and launched its home improvement loan programme, Micasa, in 2000. The growth of the Micasa programme has been impressive – within 12 months, it was reported that it had 3000 active clients and was generating almost $16 000 a month in incremental net income. Further, it is anticipated that home improvement loans will increase to 50% of its overall portfolio by the late 2000s.

The involvement of microfinance institutions in the provision of housing microfinance has largely come in response to two factors: first, there were clear indications that a significant proportion of microfinance loans (20% in some cases) were, in fact, being used for housing consolidation, improvement, or construction. For example, research from Mexico estimates that the demand for housing microfinance (US$ 122 million) is more than 6 times greater than the demand for microfinance ($20 million). Second, a significant proportion of enterprises started through microfinance loans are in fact home-based enterprises which clearly benefit from housing improvements. In practice then, it has been difficult to distinguish between housing microfinance and microfinance loans, as the latter may be invested in housing improvements where businesses are based. In turn, the fact that housing consolidation and improvement can lead to significant increases in the productivity of home-based enterprises also has the added advantage of enabling clients to service their loans. For example, a survey of the SEWA Bank's slum upgrading programme reported a 35% average increase in weekly earnings from home-based enterprises following the disbursal of loans for home improvements and water and electricity connections.

A key advantage of adding housing loans to the facilities that microfinance institutions already offer is that it enables them to extend their market in terms of both loan size and attracting new customers. This in turn strengthens their performance and enhances their financial sustainability. Further, the addition of housing microfinance loan facilities to the existing portfolios of microfinance institutions enables these organisations to sell other financial products such as savings schemes, remittance services, and other types of credit. There is emerging evidence that so-called multiproduct financial relationships can also foster higher customer loyalty. For example, the Grameen Bank in Bangladesh offers housing loans as a reward to existing clients who have performed well in the repayment of past loans.

Challenges and Opportunities

As noted at the start of this article, it is increasingly recognised that housing finance can play a vital role in local, regional, and national economic and financial development. This was graphically illustrated – albeit in a perverse manner – in the 2007–10 economic downturn which was precipitated by the subprime mortgage market in the United States. Researchers note that while there is a significant demand for housing finance among low-income households, particular challenges remain in the supply of such finance. This is attributable to a number of factors. Poorer countries in the global South suffer from a lack of financial resources, more generally, but also specifically in terms of the financial resources available to devote to housing. This is reflected in one of the key assessments of a UNCHS (2005) report on housing finance which concluded that it was unlikely that "many developing countries will have the required finances to fund urban infrastructure and housing needed in the next 20 years." In particular, poor countries have limited access to longer-term capital flows which financial institutions engaged in the provision of housing finance require. While this presents a particular problem for formal financial organisations providing mortgage finance, funding for 'housing' microfinance programmes may also be particularly difficult to source, given that it falls between the gaps of microfinance loans directed at income generation and conventional mortgages, both of which have received relatively more attention and funding.

Arguably, this financial gap has been exacerbated by the 2007–10 global economic downturn which has resulted in a significant decline in financial flows to the global South and a particular slowdown in housing markets. Taking microfinance as an example, even while this sector emerged relatively unscathed from previous recessions (including the 1990s currency crisis in East Asia as well as the financial crisis in Latin America in the same decade), the greater integration of microfinance in both domestic and international capital markets from 2000 onwards, as well as the geographic scale and intensity of the global recession has rendered microfinance institutions vulnerable. Following a period of significant growth, the sector as a whole has been at best stagnant or at worst shrinking, depending upon the economic and regulatory environments adopted in specific countries and regions; the institutional liabilities, financial state and funding structure of individual organisations as well as the economic health of their clients. Broadly, smaller and medium-sized microfinance institutions have faced a more acute liquidity crisis particularly in sub-Saharan Africa and South Asia, while deposit-based institutions have proven to be more resilient then either debt- or equity-based organisations due to funding diversification and access to savings portfolios. The quality of microfinance loan portfolios has also been noted as being in decline due to the higher incidence of loan delinquency as microfinance clients struggle to cope with higher food prices, job losses, and economic contraction.

It is also important to recognise that the types of housing finance which are available may be inappropriate for lower-income groups. While programmes which seek to extend formal mortgage finance to such households have foundered in a number of countries, showing that these programmes have limited applicability to poorer households, housing microfinance should not be seen as a panacea itself. For a start, the underwriting of housing microfinance loans presents challenges. Unlike microfinance loans which are judged against an evaluation of the income stream that they generate, it is not the case that all housing microfinance borrowers are entrepreneurs. Furthermore, improvements in housing do not necessarily result in improved income and more sustainable livelihoods as opposed to the perceived and real impacts of microfinance loans. Indeed, the main strengths of housing microfinance may be the indirect savings which accrue due to the use of better-quality building materials and savings in the time spent in executing housing improvements. Perhaps most importantly, it is clearly evident that housing microfinance programmes continue to suffer from problems of scale, with commentators observing that despite the increases noted above, the majority of microfinance institutions remain solely focused upon the disbursal of small working capital loans for income generation such that housing microfinance remains a small (albeit increasingly significant) proportion of total microfinance lending. Given that these challenges of integrating breadth and depth in housing finance programmes remain, housing microfinance programmes should not be seen as a solution to either addressing a large and in some cases growing housing deficit or alleviating poverty. It is also vitally important to recognise that housing finance programmes by themselves cannot resolve the problem of inadequate housing in the global South which requires an integrated approach which incorporates tenure security, service provision, and housing consolidation.

Despite these diverse challenges, there are some grounds for cautious optimism. For a start, the microfinance sector is expected to make a strong recovery in the post-recession period, although this is dependent upon its ability to innovate and diversify. Research also suggests that problems of scale are not insurmountable. The involvement of large microfinance institutions, such as Banco Sol in Peru, have played a vital role in illustrating the viability of housing finance programmes as well as demonstrating that those on lower incomes are both creditworthy and potentially profitable. In so doing, such organisations have aroused the interest of both high street retail banks as well as credit unions partly due to the fact that they are more comfortable with the terms and conditions of housing microfinance – as opposed to microfinance – loans. Importantly, then (some) microfinance institutions have illustrated that they can provide financial services to the poor at scale and on commercial terms. It is also evident that households are unwilling to invest in the consolidation or improvement of their dwellings unless issues of tenure have been addressed with a growing consensus that the provision of secure (as distinct from full legal) tenure is key to the success of home improvement programmes. One innovation is for the state to provide intermediate tenure security as evident in the case of the Ahmadabad Municipal Corporation in India, which granted slum dwellers in the city 10 years security of tenure which has been sufficient to generate investment in housing. Some research also suggests that lower-income households are primarily interested in accessing good-quality efficient financial services with the costs involved being a secondary concern. In such a context, it would appear that initiatives such as interest rate ceilings, subsidies, or debt-forgiveness policies may inhibit financial sector involvement which may be counter-productive.

See also: Housing Subsidies in the Developing World; Industrial Organisation of the US Residential Mortgage Market; Microfinance for Housing; Mortgage Market, Character and Trends: Africa; Mortgage Market, Character and Trends: Brazil; Mortgage Market, Character and Trends: China; Mortgage Market, Character and Trends: India; Mortgage Market, Character and Trends: Korea; Mortgage Market, Character and Trends: Mexico.

References

United Nations Human Settlement Programme (UNHCS) (2005) *Financing Urban Shelter: Global Report on Human Settlements*. London: Earthscan.

Watson Y (2009) From crisis to catharsis: How microfinance can make it through the global recession. *Microfinance Insights* 11 (1).

Further Reading

Biswas S (2003) Housing as a productive asset – housing finance for self-employed women in India. *Small Enterprise Development* 14(1): 49–55.

Buckley RM (1996) *Housing Finance in Developing Countries*. Basingstoke, UK: Macmillan.

Daphnis F and Ferguson B (2004) *Housing Microfinance: A Guide to Practice*. Bloomfield, CT: Kumarian Press.

Datta K and Jones GA (eds.) (1999) *Housing and Finance in Developing Countries*. London: Routledge.

Datta K and Jones GA (2001) Housing and finance in developing countries: Invisible issues on research and policy agendas. *Habitat International* 25: 333–357.

Ferguson B (2004) Scaling up housing microfinance: A guide to practice. *Housing Finance International* September: 3–13.

Gilbert A (2004) Learning from others: The spread of capital housing subsidies. *International Planning Studies* 9(2–3): 197–216.

Mitlin D (2007) Editorial: Finance for low income housing and community development. Special issue on Finance for low income housing and community development. *Environment and Urbanization* 19(2): 331–336.

Mitlin D (2008) Editorial: Finance and shelter improvements. Special issue on Finance for low income housing and community development. *Environment and Urbanization* 20(1): 3–12.

Rogaly B and Johnson S (1997) *Microfinance and Poverty Reduction*. Oxford, UK: Oxfam/Action Aid.

Stein A and Vance I (2008) The role of housing finance in addressing the needs of the urban poor: Lessons from central America. *Environment and Urbanization* 20(1): 13–30.

Tibaijuka A (2009) *Building Prosperity: The Centrality of Housing in Economic Development*. London: Earthscan.

Yunus M (2003) *Banker to the Poor: Micro-Credit Lending and the Battle against World Poverty*. New York: Public Affairs Books.

Housing Finance: Mexico

M Lea, San Diego State University, San Diego, CA, USA

© 2012 Elsevier Ltd. All rights reserved.

Glossary

Dual index mortgage (DIM) Mortgage instruments in which the payments are linked to the minimum wage index and the accrual rate is based on a variable market interest rate. The loans have a flexible term and can create negative amortisation.

INFONAVIT A housing pension fund for private sector formal workers. Infonavit obtains funds through payroll deduction and provides mortgages to its members. Infonavit also provides retirement income to its members. FOVISSSTE is the public sector equivalent.

Price level-adjusted mortgage (PLAM) A fixed rate mortgage with the balance and thus payments periodically indexed to inflation.

Sociedad Hipotecaria Federal (SHF) A development bank focused on housing.

Sofol A nondepository finance company specialising in mortgage lending (both construction and permanent finance).

Introduction

Mexico has a large and well-known housing deficit. It is estimated that the magnitude of the deficit was 8.9 million households at the end of 2010 – mainly due to poor quality of the existing housing stock (SHF, 2011). In addition, household formation is expected to top 600 000 in 2011 of which only 51% are able to afford a loan. Mexico has a high proportion of informal workers – nearly 29% in 2010 – who have difficulty obtaining mortgage finance.

Historically, private lenders have been unable to meet much of the housing finance needs in Mexico. This reflects several macro and structural reasons, including the informality of the lowest income segments, financial crises that have kept interest rates high and volatile, high costs and taxes in real estate transactions, weaknesses of judicial enforcement of real estate collateral, and poor state of local property registries. The Tequila crisis caused the banks to withdraw from mortgage lending in the mid-1990s, and they have returned only slowly to this sector after nearly a decade of macro-stabilisation.

Faced with a pressing socioeconomic need for housing, the government has participated actively in providing housing finance, especially for low-income borrowers. The government established Instituto del Fondo Nacional de la Vivienda para los Trabajadores (INFONAVIT) and Fondo de la Vivienda del Instituto de Seguridad y Servicios Sociales de los Trabajadores del Estado (FOVISSSTE) in 1972 and 1973, respectively, to channel mandatory pension contributions into home mortgages for private and public sector formal workers, respectively (the 'Institutes'). It set up Fondo de Operación y Financiamiento Bancario a la Vivienda (FOVI) in 1963 and the Sociedad Hipotecaria Federal (SHF) in 2002 to promote housing finance, while creating the Sociedades Financieras de Objeto Limitado (Sofoles), an entirely new class of nondepository mortgage lenders, in 1995. It introduced home mortgage interest rate deductibility, and direct subsidies for home acquisition, improvement, and rental for low-income individuals.

A new law in 2004 provided for a discontinuation of SHF's direct lending to the Sofoles by 2009, and the government's direct backing of SHF liabilities a few years thereafter. However, SHF's role was expanded to provide mortgage insurance (MI), support issuance of mortgage-backed securities (RMBS) by Sofoles, and give liquidity and credit enhancement for RMBS. The financial crisis and problems with several Sofoles led the government to continue lending and providing security guarantees through SHF. Starting in 2000, significant governance, managerial, and operational improvements have been implemented at both INFONAVIT and FOVISSSTE to improve their functioning and return on pensioners' savings. As a result, both Institutes have become more effective in serving their members and their market share has increased.

The public sector currently dominates the housing finance in Mexico. As of the end of 2010, the mortgages provided by INFONAVIT and FOVISSSTE represented nearly 70% of the outstanding stock of mortgage loans. The public sector also has a considerable involvement in housing finance through SHF's provision of MI, purchases of RMBS, and market maker of RMBS.

A Brief History

The dominant role of the government dates back to the late 1960s and 1970s when directed lending and interest rate caps were used to allocate credit to housing (Renaud, 1989). Six percent of total bank credit had to be directed to housing finance at fixed or capped nominal interest rates. Rising inflation in the late 1970s led to negative real interest rates and large portfolio losses for banks ultimately leading to nationalisation of the banking sector in 1982. During this period of high inflation, banks were authorised to issue 'dual indexed mortgages' (DIM) to create mortgage affordable instruments. Payment on DIMs was linked to the minimum wage index with the accrual rate based on a variable market interest rate (Lea and Bernstein, 1996). The DIM construct can result in negative amortisation if the payment rate is less than that required to amortise the loan at the accrual rate. As a result, the DIM is a flexible term mortgage – with the term extending when there is a balance outstanding at the end. During the 1980s and 1990s, the government absorbed the risk of indefinite term extension by capping the maximum term at 20 years and agreeing to pay off any outstanding balance at the end of the term.

Mexico privatised the banking system in the early 1990s. The banks significantly increased their lending to housing with the ratio of mortgage debt to GDP increasing from 1.3% to 2.4% between 1989 and 1994 (Zanforlin and Espinosa, 2008). They began offering a new inflation-indexed instrument – a price level-adjusted mortgage or PLAM. This instrument is a fixed rate mortgage with the balance and thus payments periodically indexed to inflation. The sharp inflation and interest rate spike in the aftermath of the Tequila crisis triggered a wave of bank mortgage defaults, as borrowers could not cope with the payment increases (bank mortgage default rates peaked at 34% in 1997 (Pickering, 2000)). The government was forced to restructure most mortgages and bail out the banks. As a result, the banks left the sector and did not return until the mid-2000s.

With the banks departing the market, the government through the Institutes and loans made by FOVI to the newly created Sofoles provided housing finance. The Sofoles are nonbank financial intermediaries specialised in housing finance focusing mainly on low- to moderate-income households (6–20 minimum wages (MW)) (as of March 2011 Mexico's minimum wage is 59.82 pesos per day, equivalent to US$4.7). The Institutes use funds from mandatory payroll deductions from formal sector workers to provide mortgage finance also focused on low- to moderate-income households (2–11 MW). Through the 1990s the Institutes had a reputation for corruption and inefficiency thus limiting their contribution to housing finance.

Beginning in the early 2000s, the government embarked on an ambitious reform effort designed to stimulate greater provision of housing finance. The creation of SHF, a development bank with a sovereign guarantee, was a catalyst to revive private sector lending, initially through the Sofoles and subsequently through the banks. SHF provided MI, partial guarantees on construction loans, and partial guarantees on mortgage-backed securities. They developed standards for appraisal and mortgage security (Borhis) design. As part of their mandate to stimulate the private sector development, they brought US-based private mortgage insurers and bond insurers to the Mexican market to credit enhance loans and securities. Reform efforts at Infonavit and more recently Fovissste led to significant increases in their volume of lending.

Housing finance began to grow rapidly in Mexico starting in 2003 (**Figure 1**). Most of the growth came

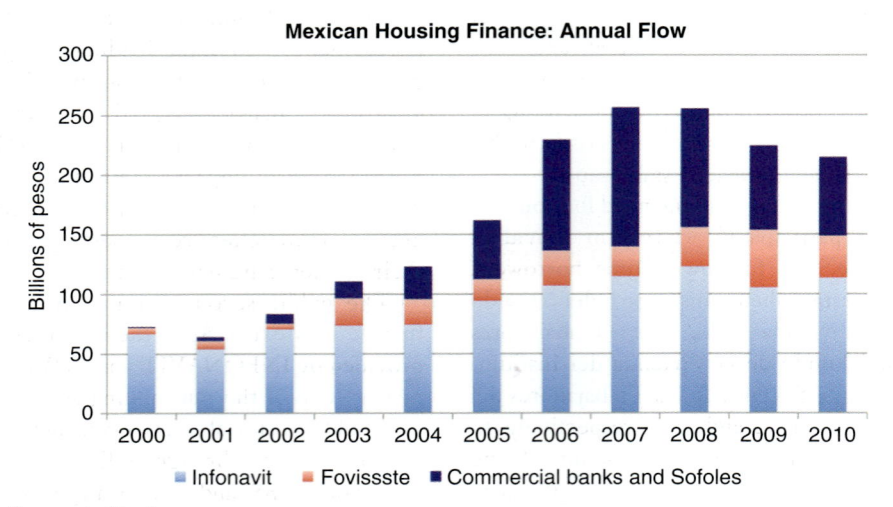

Figure 1 Housing finance in Mexico.
Source: BBVA (2010).

from the private sector, the market share of which climbed from 1.4% in 2000 to a peak of 45.6% in 2007. The private sector share has fallen by 44% since its peak in 2007, while the public sector funding has remained relatively constant. In 2010, the public sector through the Institutes accounted for nearly 70% of mortgage originations. Factoring in SHF lending the public sector share of funding was even greater.

The Sofoles initially drove the increase in private sector housing finance. They were responsible for a majority of the private sector share through 2005. In that year the Spanish bank BBVA purchased the largest Sofol, Hipotecaria Nacional, and the bank market share began to surpass that of the Sofoles. Both banks and Sofoles continued to expand through 2007. The recession resulted in a sharp decrease in Sofol lending with their portfolios down 64% through mid-2010 (BBVA, 2011). Bank lending was curtailed but has since restarted.

Despite a decade of growth, the outstanding residential mortgage debt (peso 1.264 trillion) represents only 10.6% of the GDP by the end of 2009. This situation is favourable compared to most other LAC countries (including Colombia, Brazil, and Argentina), but still reflects an underdeveloped stage of market penetration, compared to the growing housing demand in Mexico.

There has been significant progress in expanding the financing options available to borrowers. In 2000, the only instruments available were the DIMs and PLAMs developed for an inflationary environment. Loans were short term with high down payment requirements. By 2008, there were fixed peso as well as variable rate loans, for uses other than new home purchase, with significantly lower down payment requirements (**Table 1**). Deductibility of mortgage interest was introduced in 2008.

In 2009, the recession led to a deep contraction in demand, due to a loss of jobs, real income, and deterioration of consumer confidence. The crisis impacted the housing finance sector restricting liquidity and contributing to the failure of several Sofoles. Financing problems of the Sofoles impacted both builders and housing buyers in the low- and medium-income segments. A decline in Sofol construction lending (known as bridge lending in Mexico) created problems for smaller builders. As shown in **Figure 2**, bridge lending declined by over 50% in real terms between the second quarter of 2008 and the first quarter of 2009. The large public builders were not affected, as they were able to access the capital markets. More recently, banks have stepped in to replace Sofol bridge lending with the result that such lending has increased every quarter since the third quarter of 2009. Bridge lending is a critical component of Mexican housing finance as more than 80% of credit goes to new construction.

The Mexican housing finance market substantially recovered in 2010. Outstanding mortgage balances rose slightly during the year. Mortgage defaults fell – to less than 6% for permanent mortgages and 10% for

Table 1 Loan Characteristics

	2000	*2008*	*2009*	*2010*
Interest rate	Variable	Fixed	Fixed with incentives for timely payments	Fixed with incentives for timely payments
Up front fees	6%	3%–0%	3%–0%	0%
Term	10–15 yrs	Up to 30 yrs	Up to 30 yrs	Up to 30 yrs
Products	Acquisition	Multiple uses	Multiple uses	Multiple uses
Payment pesos per thousand	$22.0	$9.5–$11.0	$10.5–$12.0	$10.5–$12.0
Down payment	+35%	10%–20%	10%–20%	10%–20%
Mortgage insurance	No	For high LTV's	For risk mitigation	For risk mitigation
Unemployment insurance	No	Yes	Yes	Yes
Interests *tax* deductible /	No	Yes	Yes	Yes

Multiple uses →
- Acquisition
- Substitution
- Construction
- Remodelling
- Co-financing INFONAVIT FOVISSSTE
- 2nd Home
- Home Equity
- Saving Account[a]

[a]income disponibility for mortgage monthly payment.
Source: ABM.

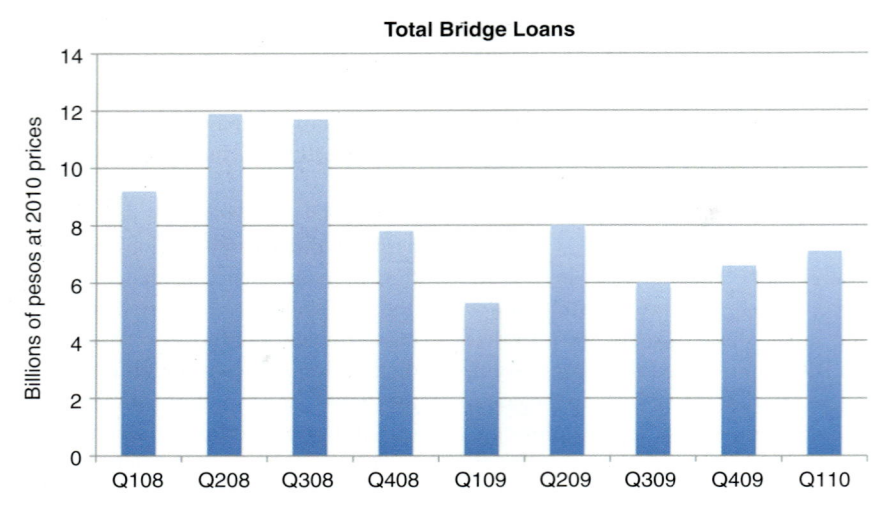

Figure 2 Bridge lending.
Source: BBVA (2010).

construction loans. Bank lending has picked up with double-digit annual growth in the second half of 2010. Both Infonavit and Fovissste exceeded their lending targets during the year, making up for the reduction in Sofol lending. The bridge loan market also recovered as banks replaced Sofoles as the major source of debt capital for mid-size developers.

Despite turning the corner housing finance in Mexico faces significant challenges going forward. Affordability is a big challenge. **Table 2** shows the distribution of households by income and house price. Twenty-six percent of households earn less than US$9000 annually (5 MW). It is difficult to build or buy a decent housing unit for less than US$24 000, an investment out of reach of households earning less than 5 MW. The minimum required by most bank lenders is a household income above 8–10 MW. Infonavit targets households in the 4–8 MW and has recently expanded its lending down to 2 MW (for used or incremental housing).

Mortgage interest rates remain high (**Figure 3**) reflecting the risks of mortgage lending and a weak infrastructure. The spread between the 15-year mortgage rate and 10-year government bond rate (fixed, nominal peso for both) was 6.9 percentage points at the end of 2010 – equal to the average spread over the past 6 years. (The mortgage rates are the average of those offered by private lenders – banks and Sofoles. The rates offered by the institutes are significantly less but are indexed and adjustable.) Infrastructure deficiencies include long and uncertain foreclosure processes in most state, a costly and antiquated property registration system and appraisal weaknesses – particularly for used housing.

The Role of Infonavit and Fovissste

INFONAVIT and FOVISSSTE were created as government-sponsored construction and housing development funding agencies. Infonavit serves formal private sector workers and Fovissste serves formal public sector workers. They have a unique tripartite governance structure between unions, employers, and the government. They have been funded by a mandatory contribution of 5% of gross wages. In 2010, Infonavit made over 475 000 loans to its members and co-financed over 93 000 loans with private lenders totalling over US$9 billion (Infonavit, 2011). Fovissste made over 91 000 loans for more than US$4

Table 2 Mexico housing and income segmentation

Type	House price range	Income segment minimum wage	Income segment $annual	% of familes
Minimum	<$9 000	<2 MW	<$3 400	9
Social	$9 001–$24 000	2–5 MW	$3 400–$9 000	17
Economic	$24 001–$45 000	5–11 MW	$9 000–$20 000	45
Middle	$45 001–$111 000	11–25 MW	$20 000–$45 000	21
Residential	$111 001–$250 000	25–65 MW	$45 000–$100 000	5
Residential Plus	>$250 000	>65 MW	$100000+	3

Minimum wage in 2009 approximately $150 per month.
Source: Softec 2009.

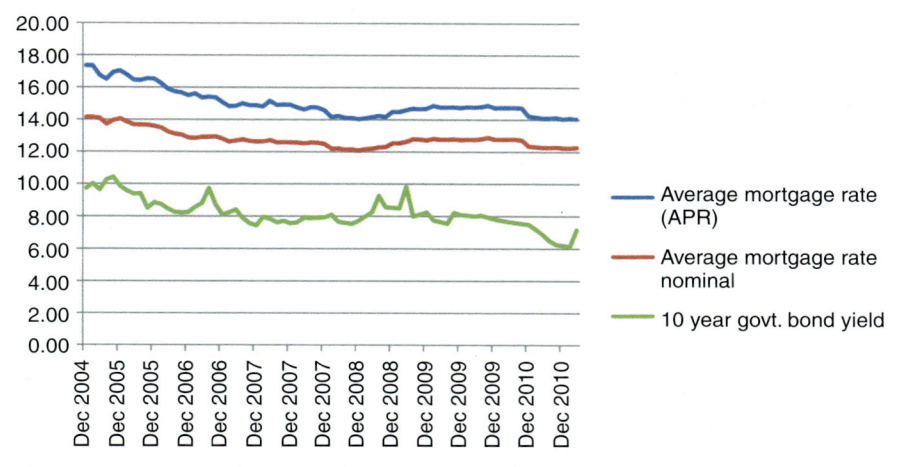

Figure 3 Mexican interest rates.
Source: Branco de Mexico.

billion (Fovissste, 2011). Their joint loan portfolios total over US$65 billion.

The institutes have several important advantages over other lenders. They have a dedicated source of funds through the payroll deduction. They also receive loan payments through payroll deduction – a privilege only they enjoy – which contributes to a lower default rate and servicing costs on their loans. Although they do not have an explicit government guarantee, market participants view them as too big to fail with an implicit guarantee similar to that enjoyed by Fannie Mae and Freddie Mac in the United States. They are exempt from taxation.

By law the institutes must use a mortgage instrument in which the payments and balances are indexed to the minimum wage. Infonavit cross-subsidises its members charging a sliding scale of $MW + 4$ to $MW + 8$ based on income. Fovissste charges $MW + 4$ to all borrowers.

The institutes have a dual mission as housing lenders and pension funds. This duality creates an inherent conflict. On the one hand, their mission is to provide affordable housing loans to their members. On the other hand, they are supposed to provide adequate retirement income to the same members. Infonavit targets a remuneration of $MW + 3$ but their ability to provide it depends on the performance of the mortgage portfolio. The ability of the institutes to provide a market rate of return on mandated savings is also affected by securitisation, which is a higher cost of funds than savings. A final point is the lack of diversification of the retirement fund assets – almost all of which are real estate loans.

The institutes operate with numerical goals for delivery of housing loans. Their dedicated funding source, augmented with securitisation, has allowed them to regularly achieve these goals. In particular, they played an important stabilising role through the crisis as both banks and Sofoles sharply cut back on new lending. Adherence to quantitative targets has led to quality problems in some new housing developments. According to Infonavit, nearly 26% of housing financed between 2006 and 2009 with its loans are uninhabited, for the most part due to problems of location and the urban environment associated with the housing development (Infonavit, 2011). The institutes allocate blocks of funding for large developments that produce standardised housing often on the periphery of the cities.

As in the United States there are questions about the large role played by government institutions in the mortgage market. Infonavit's successful transformation has resulted in a substantial decline in the backlog of members demanding loans. It has forecast an excess of funds in the near future and is looking at new lending markets – for example, informal lending, co-financing of loans to nonmembers. In turn, this has led to concern about potential crowding out of private sector lenders. In 2010 there was a proposed amendment to the Infonavit Law that would gradually reduce the pension contribution to housing funds from 5% to 1% with the difference deposited into a separate and regulated pension fund. The amendment would also allow Infonavit to make nominal peso loans. As of March 2011, it has not yet passed the Congress.

Securitisation

The capital markets are an increasingly important source of funding for Mexican housing finance. Projections by SHF showed that the resources of the banking system would be inadequate to meet the future housing finance funding needs.

Mortgage-backed securities were first issued in 2003 in Mexico (**Figure 4**). The initial issues (2003–06) were guaranteed by SHF (BORHI) or issued Infonavit

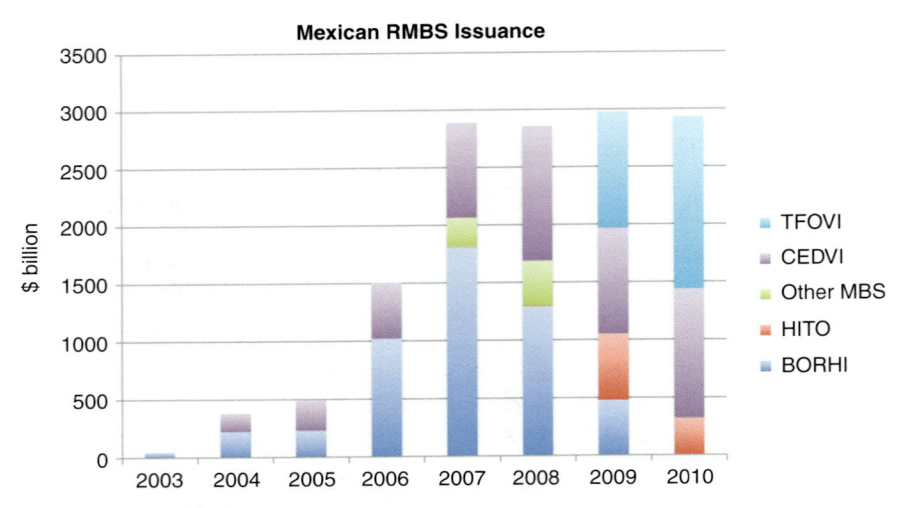

Figure 4 Mortgage securitisation in Mexico.
Source: SHF.

(CEDVI) (BORHI issues have a first loss position by the originator. CEDVIs are a form of structured finance with a waterfall of loss positions. In both cases, the guarantor/issuer is a public or quasi-public entity.). The private sector entered the market in 2007 with structured finance issues by banks and Sofoles. Fovissste, another public sector entity, entered the market in 2009 (TFOVI) and was the largest issuer in 2010. Both Infonavit and Fovissste have used a private sector issuance platform, HITO, as well. Hito (Hipotecaria Total) was created as a multilender issuer of Danish-style covered bonds. SHF is a minority investor. The covered bond market has yet to take off, due in part to the lack of a covered bond law.

SHF has been a pioneer in creating the RMBS market in Mexico. It provides partial mortgage default loss insurance and partial guarantees on mortgage securities. It has created a performance database for mortgage securities.

The private and Borhis RMBS markets shut down in the crisis due to the failure of two large Sofol issuers and the resulting lack of confidence in issuers (the main investors in Mexican RMBS have been Afores, which are the private pension plans). As a result, all recent issuance has been by public-sector-backed entities, with issuance remaining close to precrisis levels. SHF has stepped in to support the market by purchasing a significant volume of outstanding Borhis. This step has stabilised the market but has strained SHF's resources.

Going forward there is a need for more standardisation and transparency in MBS issues. There were several variants of the Borhis issued by different lenders with significantly different characteristics and a lack of good information about performance and servicer capabilities. SHF and CNBV (the banking and capital markets regulator) have been advancing proposals for a standardised issue structure, better information to facilitate trading and a back up liquidity source (e.g., CNBV is requiring more timely and complete performance information and SHF has created a pricing calculator to aid in investor analysis). One possibility is to have the central bank (Banco de Mexico) act in this capacity as is the case in the United States and other developed markets.

Low-Income Housing Finance

One of the main challenges of Mexican housing finance is affordability and qualification ability of informal households. The housing deficit, which affects about 9 million households, is largely concentrated in the lower-income segments categories that are not served by the financial sector: income below 6 MW (6.8 million), informal/independent labour sector households (1.6 million), rural and peri-urban population (5.2 million). Infonavit has stated a goal of 60% of its 2010 lending for borrowers at or below 4 MW in an attempt to address this shortage. One of the main challenges is the high level of informality. The banks and institutes only lend to the formal sector though Infonavit has announced an initiative aimed at the informal sector. The Sofoles had started to do some down market lending but the problems of funding these institutions has largely cut off this form of lending.

The Mexican government has two types of subsidy programmes (BBVA, 2011). The first, administered by Sedesol, focuses on the very low income with grants (between 6000 and 15 000 pesos) for home improvement and infrastructure. The second, administered by Conavi, focuses on the urban population, both formal and informal, with incomes up to 5 MW and access to housing finance. Their Ésta es tu casa (this is your home) programme provides up-front grants up to 30 000 pesos mainly for down payments. It is available to both institute and private sector borrowers.

Conclusions

The Mexican housing finance system had marked improvement in the past decade. There is greater variety of instruments, funding sources, and lenders in the system today relative to 2000. The system was able to finance a significant expansion of housing investment helping the government achieve historically high production goals. The system was able to withstand the shock of the financial crisis – in part because lenders avoided many of the excesses that plagued the United States.

The Mexican housing finance system faces significant challenges going forward. Currently the government provides (or backs) most of the finance for the housing market. A sustainable housing finance system must depend more on the private sector for the mobilisation and allocation of resources. Attention needs to focus on improving the lending infrastructure to bring down the cost of credit. Separation of the lending and pension obligations of the institutes will help rationalise both the mortgage and pension sectors of the financial markets. And programmes to provide finance to lower-income and informal households are essential for the continued progress of the sector.

See also: Industrial Organisation of the US Residential Mortgage Market; Mortgage Market, Character and Trends: Mexico.

References

BBVA Research (2010) *Mexico Real Estate Outlook,* July.
BBVA Research (2011) *Mexico Real Estate Outlook,* January.
Fovissste (2011) *President Calderon's Fovissste 2007–2011 Presentation,* February. www.mexicanhousingday.com (accessed 20 November 2011).
Infonavit (2011) *2010 Results and outlook: Mexican housing day.* www.mexicanhousingday.com (accessed 20 November 2011).
Lea M and Bernstein S (1996) Housing finance in an inflationary economy: The experience of Mexico. *Journal of Housing Economics* 5(1): 87–104.
Pickering N (2000) *The Mexico Mortgage Market Boom, Bust and Bail Out: Determinants of Borrower Default and Loan Restructure After the 1995 Currency Crisis.* Harvard University Joint Center for Housing Studies, Working Paper 003, April.
Renaud B (1989) *The role of housing finance in development: Issues and policies.* The World Bank.
Sociedad Hipotecaria Federal (SHF) (2011) *Outlook for Mexican housing industry and SHF role and perspectives Presentation,* February. www.mexicanhousingday.com (accessed 20 November 2011).
Softec (2009) *The Mexican Housing Market,* May.
Stauffer C and Rucker P (2010) *Mexico's economy swells through recovery.* Reuters. August.
Zanforlin L and Espinosa M (2008) Housing finance and mortgage backed securities in Mexico. *IMF Working Paper 08/105,* April.

Further Reading

Deschamps I (2011) *Mortgage lending in Mexico.* Presentation of Mexican Banking Assn February. www.mexicanhousingday.com (accessed 20 November 2011).

Housing Finance Institutions: Africa

F Roy, World Bank, Washington, DC, USA

Published by Elsevier Ltd.

Glossary

Enabling environment It encompasses laws, regulations, and market infrastructure and should allow for conditions conducive to housing finance.

Financial Sector Charter (FSC) It is the charter signed in 2003 by members of the financial sector in South Africa in which they collectively committed themselves to providing more than ZAR 70 billion of development finance over the next 5 years (by the end of 2008), including ZAR 42 billion for housing finance to low-income earners with a monthly income of between ZAR 1500 and ZAR 7500.

Housing Provident Fund (HPF) It is a specialised financial institution that collects mandatory savings from employees (public and/or private) expressed as a defined percentage of their salary. Contributors typically have access to a housing loan or are entitled to withdraw their contributions for housing purposes.

***Organisation pour l'Harmonisation du Droit des Affaires en Afrique* or 'Organisation for the harmonisation of business law in Africa' (OHADA)** It is an international organisation established in 1993. Its members are 17 African States (Benin, Burkina Faso, Cameroon, Central African Republic, Comoros, Congo, Democratic Republic of Congo, Ivory Coast, Gabon, Guinea-Bissau, Guinea, Equatorial Guinea, Mali, Niger, Senegal, Chad, and Togo). The organisation pursues two main objectives: (1) to harmonise business law, promote arbitration, and to consolidate economic environment and (2) to support the development of an African Economic Community. The OHADA Code has already made a major impact on legislation in member countries.

Reconstruction and Development Programme (RDP) It is the programme that provides subsidised small standard houses to low-income South Africans (about 30–40 m^2 on a plot of 80–100 m^2). Since 1994, about 1.8 million RDP houses have been built (data per 2005).

The East African Community (EAC) It is the regional intergovernmental organisation of the Republics of Kenya, Uganda, the United Republic of Tanzania, Republic of Rwanda, and Republic of Burundi with its headquarters in Arusha, Tanzania.

The West African CFA franc (*Communauté financière d'Afrique*, Financial Community of Africa) It is the currency of eight West African states (Benin, Burkina Faso, Côte d'Ivoire, Guinea-Bissau, Mali, Niger, Senegal, and Togo). The currency is issued by the BCEAO (*Banque Centrale des États de l'Afrique de l'Ouest*, Central Bank of the West African States), located in Dakar, Senegal, for the members of the UEMOA (*Union Économique et Monétaire Ouest Africaine*, West African Economic and Monetary Union).

Introduction

Limited access to housing finance is common in all sub-Saharan African (SSA) countries due to a number of factors, such as the poor framework for identification and registration of titles and mortgages, the restricted access to long-term finance in local currency, and so on. This article provides an overview of housing finance institutions in SSA countries and the environment in which these institutions operate. A description of the general market conditions and country characteristics is followed by an overview of housing finance institutions with South Africa and Nigeria as examples.

The SSA comprises 48 African countries with a total population of around 740 million people. It does not include the five Maghreb countries (i.e., Morocco, Tunisia, Algeria, Libya, and Mauritania) and Egypt. Before the outbreak of the global financial crisis in 2008, SSA countries experienced nearly a decade of economic growth. Growth rates averaged between 5 and 6% over the previous 5 years. Inflation rates fell to single-digit levels. These positive developments were fostered by strong economic policies; a favourable external environment, especially rising commodity prices; debt relief; and aid from the international community. **Table 1** shows key macroeconomic indicators of the region.

The findings, interpretations, statements, and conclusions expressed herein are those of the author alone and do not necessarily reflect the views of the International Bank for Reconstruction and Development/The World Bank and its affiliated organisations, or those of the Executive Directors of The World Bank.

Table 1 Key economic indicators of SSA (2006–10)

	2005	2006	2007	2008	2009[a]	2010[a]
GDP growth (% change)	6.2	6.4	6.9	5.5	1.1	4.1
Consumer prices (annual average, % change)	8.9	7.3	7.1	11.6	10.5	7.2

[a]IMF estimates.
Source: IMF African Department database.

The global financial crisis has had an impact on the continent since the last quarter of 2008. The positive trend in growth has been reversed. According to the IMF, growth is projected to fall from 5.5% in 2008 to 1.1% in 2009 and to recover slowly in 2010 to 4.1%. Inflation is expected to fall below double-digit levels in 2010 again. Due to their stronger linkages to international capital markets, South Africa, Nigeria, Ghana, and Kenya have been affected more severely than other SSA countries. Box 1 provides an overview of the impact of the global financial crisis on SSA countries.

Characteristics of SSA Countries

SSA is a highly fragmented region. The median GDP is about US$3 billion. A third of its population lives in landlocked and resource-poor countries. This prevents many countries from exploiting economies of scale and raising production efficiencies. Access to international financial markets is often restricted.

The South African economy has a dominant position in SSA. South Africa and Nigeria make up nearly half of SSA's GDP and have about one-fourth of the population. A 1 percentage point decline in the South African economy is associated with a half to a three-quarter percentage point decrease in the rest of Africa (IMF, 2009). Its banking sector dwarfs the other countries' financial sectors. In terms of bank assets, South African banks account for about 70% of all bank assets in the region (South African banks in comparison with the largest 200 banks in SSA) (2007 data from *Jeune Afrique*).

The region faces considerable demographic pressures. African countries' populations grew more rapidly than those of other developing countries. At the same time, HIV/AIDS has had a major impact on life expectancy since the 1980s. Approximately 2 million people die of AIDS every year. There are 2.7 million new infections each year. Short and uncertain life expectancies among mortgagors have generated significant credit risk for lenders.

In comparison with other regions, financial sectors in SSA have not contributed significantly to economic growth. Typically, they are shallow (relative to the size of the economies) with a narrow range of institutions and limited access to basic financial services (in particular for low- and middle-income groups). Banking systems are reasonably sound. The capital adequacy ratio averages 16% of risk-weighted assets. Banks are profitable even though they are less efficient than those in other countries.

Remittances play a major role in supporting the SSA economies. The volume of international remittances into

---

Box 1 Impacts of the 2008 global financial crisis on SSA countries

The financial crisis affected SSA through the real estate sector as well as a decline of capital flows that impacted the financial sector. Traditional export markets deteriorated, commodity prices declined, and the volume of remittances decreased. According to estimates of Deutsche Bank Research, the value of capital flows has halved since 2007 (about US$32 billion).

It seems, however, that the region has, in general, avoided the major macroeconomic instabilities that followed previous contractions in the region. Foreign exchange reserves are still close to their historic highs which should leave room for economic stimulus packages. Typically, lenders in most countries were not allowed to invest in toxic assets. Thus, the need to mark down has not impacted on their performance. However, nonperforming loans after a period of rapid credit growth and a contraction of business activities could lead to rising credit risk for lenders.

With the exception of South Africa, national mortgage markets have not come under severe strain. Mortgage/housing loan portfolios of lenders are still quite small. The volume of mortgage lending to GDP accounts for 1–2% in most SSA countries (South Africa: 34%). Additionally, loan-to-value ratios (LTVs) are quite low (typically around 50%) and banks have granted mortgages mainly to upper-middle- and higher-income groups. In terms of asset–liability management, lending has been done mainly in domestic currency. Although short-term deposits have been the main funding instrument, liquidity risk has been manageable due to the small mortgage portfolios. Specialised lenders (mainly state-owned housing banks) have been marginally affected due to their reliance on governmental budget allocations.

Source: IMF (2009) *Regional Economic Outlook: Sub-Saharan Africa*. Washington, DC: IMF; Deutsche Bank Research (2009) *African Frontier Capital Markets: More than a Flash in the Pan*. Germany: Frankfurt am Main.

Africa in 2005 reached an estimated US$8 billion. In some countries, they have reached 5% of GDP (Senegal, 5.4%; Uganda, 5.8%). A considerable amount of remittances are used for housing purposes (e.g., modernisation and incremental house-building process).

Market Conditions for Housing Finance Institutions in SSA

Despite governments' concerted efforts to improve regulatory and institutional frameworks, the enabling environment for housing finance is considered weak: most countries lack efficient property registries, functioning credit bureaus, or clear foreclosure rights. Often, lenders cannot trace ownership rights since changes of ownership are often not registered. In Nigeria, for example, banks require a title search to assess the legal situation of property offered as collateral. This procedure is regularly followed by updating the title to facilitate the registration of a mortgage. The cost of these measures can amount to up to 20% of the loan amount.

Different forms of law (often within one country) are a further reason for underdeveloped formal land systems and have resulted in the coexistence of overlapping systems. A mixture of traditional or tribal with state and private laws is very common. Where land is held on a tribal basis, decisions on the use of land are made according to the customs of the tribe. Such decisions are rarely recorded in writing, creating no evidential basis for the use of rights. The different legal systems impede regional cooperation. Kenya, Malawi, Tanzania, Uganda, and Zambia are ruled by Common Law, whereas countries in West Africa and Rwanda are governed by Napoleonic Law. Portuguese Law roots are embedded into the law of Angola and Mozambique.

Poorly functioning property markets have led to a lack of affordable housing supply: on the one hand, most markets do not have appropriate land zoning policies, building, and property valuation standards, as well as the required infrastructure (pipes, electricity, sewage systems, etc.), when new sites are developed. Typically, developers are responsible for the development of the necessary infrastructure. The cost of construction material is another reason. Land-locked countries like Rwanda or Burkina Faso suffer from high construction material costs due to the lack of adequate transport infrastructure. On the other hand, most developers do not possess the required skills to manage the property construction, sales, and financing process or they are too small to work on larger developments. Coupled with this is the general aversion of lenders to financing housing construction since most lenders do not have the skills to assess the implied risks.

Rising urbanisation has put further pressure on urban property markets, limiting the supply of affordable housing. According to UN-HABITAT, the region will have an urban majority by 2030, with more people in towns and cities than the total population of Europe (about 492 million). Rapid urbanisation creates a considerable growth in informal housing. According to a Financial Times Special Report on Urban Infrastructure (21 November 2006) by 2030, about 72% of urban residents will live in informal settlements. Not only the urban poor live in these areas, but also low- and middle-income groups that are unable to access affordable housing. As a consequence, the majority of the urban population (in particular, new migrants from rural areas) end up in informal settlements. The lack of title often prevents them from obtaining formal housing finance.

To date, land and housing policy responses have been limited and/or weak. Despite considerable efforts to implement subsidised housing programmes (e.g., the South African Reconstruction and Development Programme or the 10 000 Social Housing Programme in Burkina Faso, 'programme 10 000 logements sociaux et économiques'), the execution has been hampered by non-transparent allocation mechanisms, poor administration, and so on. In addition, municipalities or local governments do not have the capacities to zone new land, administer it well, or improve infrastructure networks as required.

Mortgage Markets in SSA

Low market penetration and limited access to financial services is a predominant feature of SSA financial sectors. The ratio of private sector credit to GDP amounts to 18%. The M2-to-GDP ratio is 42% in SSA (2004). The M2 indicator measures the broad money supply (cash in the hands of the public, the deposits, and the quasi-cash) in relation to GDP.

Thus, cash is still the most dominant financial instrument. The assets of the largest 200 SSA banks amount to US$481.5 million (as per 2007) which is not sufficient to place the whole continent's banks within the 30 largest banks worldwide.

Only a small fraction of the population across the region are served by a formal financial institution. The number of branches per 100 000 people is about 2.8. Approximately 20% of African adults have an account at a formal or semiformal financial institution. Often, the costs of banking services work as a deterrent to people banking with a formal financial institution.

Figure 1 shows the mortgage lending to GDP ratios of major SSA countries. The low ratios in housing finance reflect the small scale of the national banking sectors.

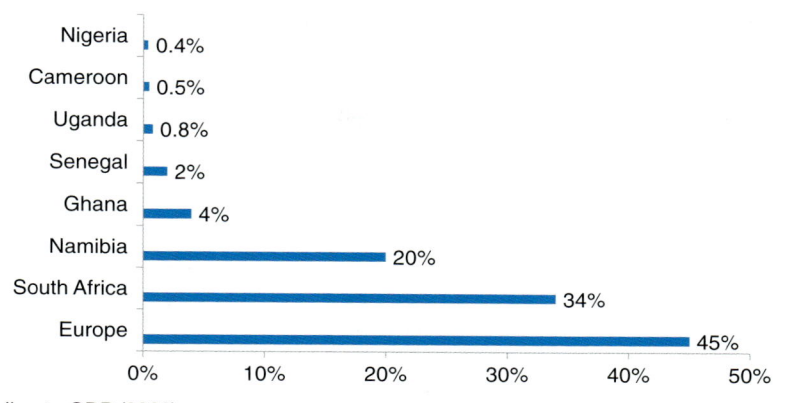

Figure 1 Mortgage lending to GDP (2009).
Source: World Bank, various national statistical databases, and authorities.

- Nigeria: 0.4%
- Cameroon: 0.5%
- Uganda: 0.8%
- Senegal: 2%
- Ghana: 4%
- Namibia: 20%
- South Africa: 34%
- Europe: 45%

Notable exceptions are the markets in South Africa (34%) and Namibia (20%).

The lack of long-term local currency funding has been a major impediment to the financing of long-term mortgages. The financial systems are still greatly dominated by banks. Short-term deposits are the main funding instruments for housing finance which exposes lenders to significant interest and liquidity risks. Capital markets do not play a significant role. Among the 19 existing stock markets, none reaches the 100% of GDP capitalisation level of South Africa. Though growing rapidly, the domestic debt market accounted for about 20% of GDP at the end of 2008 (emerging markets, 39%; developed countries, 139%). Sovereign debt is the most important debt instrument. Except in South Africa, there have been no issuances of mortgage debt securities. The most important institutional investors are banks and the national pension funds. The insurance industry is not yet developed so as to become an important institutional investor.

Due to the small size, low liquidity, and general lack of long-term maturities, as well as a limited investor base, there are no reliable yield curves, pricing benchmarks, and financial products to hedge risk. Secondary trading is very limited.

The offer of housing loans is limited and mainly concentrates on upper-middle- and high-income groups. According to FinMark Trust, only 15% of local populations are eligible for mortgage finance. Products which take into consideration the needs of low-income groups are rarely offered by banks. These products are usually offered by microfinance institutions, cooperatives, or NGOs.

Most banks do not possess appropriate risk management systems and staff usually lack the necessary skills in housing finance. To date, most banks have been active in corporate finance but have only moved slowly into retail banking. The high share of informal incomes, inadequate legal systems for collateralisation, as well as the lack of credit bureaus, have prompted bank managers to consider housing finance a high-risk business.

Table 2 provides an overview of housing finance product features in selected markets in SSA. Typically, loans are offered in local currency and are secured by a mortgage and/or personal guarantees.

The LTV ratios in South Africa may be as high as 100%. In Nigeria and Ghana, the loan amount depends on salary. The typical payment-to-income ratio is about 35%. The interest rate shown in **Table 2** in Ghana is for loans denominated in US dollars. For loans denominated in Ghanaian New Cedi, the interest rate ranges from 28 to 30%. In Ethiopia, the interest rate on mortgages with a term longer than 10 years rises to 10.75%.

In most countries, housing microfinance products are offered by microfinance institutions, cooperatives, or NGOs. Loan amounts vary from US$400 to US$5000 and tenors from 1 to 5 years. Interest rates are usually in the range of 20% and higher. The loans often serve to finance home improvement or the incremental house-building process.

Operating Housing Finance Institutions in SSA

The diversity of housing finance institutions in SSA is broad, as in many other regions. It is thus useful to adopt a broad conceptualisation of the term 'housing finance institution' to encompass financial institutions that offer other products, such as commercial banks and microfinance institutions, cooperatives as well as NGOs. They are often the most important providers of housing finance and housing microfinance products (including incremental house financing).

The type of institution ranges from specialised lenders, building societies, cooperatives, mortgage insurance providers to commercial banks, or microfinance institutions. In many countries, governments have intervened through

Table 2 Housing product features in selected countries in SSA

	South Africa	Nigeria	Ghana	Senegal	Mali	Burkina Faso	Ethiopia	Uganda	Kenya	Rwanda	Zambia	Malawi	Mozambique
Average size of loan (in US$)	Minimum 10 000			50 000	30 000	10 000	15 000–20 000	35 000–60 000	Up to 100 000	30 000	10 000–12 000	Up to 35 500	
Term (years)	20–30	Up to 20	15	15–20	4–15	8–10	Up to 10	Up to 20	7–20	5–10	Up to 10	Up to 20	12–25
Interest rate (%)	11 (prime rate)	16–20	13.50	9.5–11	10–14	10.5–12	9.75	16–18	12.5–15.5	15–16	25–28	19–24	16–22.5
LTV ratio (%)	80		Up to 75	50 to 80	50–70	Up to 75	Up to 80	Up to 70				80	Up to 70

Source: FinMark Trust, World Bank, AfD, Roland Igbinoba Real Foundation for Housing and Urban Development.

the establishment of state-owned housing banks and state-owned developers. Sometimes, these banks have both functions. In Rwanda, for example, the *Banque de l'Habitat du Rwanda* is both a bank and a developer.

For activities of foreign-owned financial institutions in housing finance, three groups can be differentiated:

1. Financial institutions from SSA countries: South African (e.g., Standard Bank) and Nigerian banks (e.g., Access Bank, Guaranty Trust Bank) have been the most active banks expanding into other SSA countries. Other important African banking groups with housing finance activities are Ecobank (Togo) and Bank of Africa (established in Mali in 1982). Bank of Africa is also an active lender to low-income groups.
2. Financial institutions from other countries: In particular, British banks (e.g., Barclays) and French banks (e.g., BNP Paribas, Société Générale) are active in the region, although their expansion strategies have followed former colonial ties. They mainly concentrate on corporate finance, but in selected countries, they have started to enter into retail banking and housing finance (e.g., Madagascar, South Africa, Uganda, and others). However, they have remained small players in this segment with a major concentration on upper-middle- and high-income groups.
3. Activities of international NGOs (e.g., Habitat for Humanity) and foreign-owned microfinance lenders (such as ProCredit Group): In many SSA countries, these institutions operate in areas where commercial lenders are not active, that is, the informal sector (e.g., rural areas, urban peripheries, and informal settlements).

Table 3 shows examples of housing finance institutions in selected markets in SSA.

The following describes two SSA markets in detail since they demonstrate the greatest variety of institutions in SSA. The first one is South Africa and the second one is Nigeria.

South Africa

The South African housing finance market is the most complex and diversified in SSA. The state-owned institutions established are mainly the result of the National Housing Accord (1994) created to address the massive housing backlog of about 3 million dwellings and low levels of housing affordability. At that time, only about 13.9% of the population earned more than ZAR 3500 annually. Today, housing finance is offered by commercial banks, credit unions, retailers, and nonbank microlenders. On the one hand, state-owned institutions have support functions, for example, provision of liquidity to the market (e.g., NHFC or RHLF). On the other hand, they offer financing (e.g., NURCHA), guarantees (e.g., Home Loan Guarantee Company), or knowledge dissemination (e.g., Social Housing Foundation). **Figure 2** provides a more detailed overview on the structure of the housing finance market in South Africa.

The four major banks (ABSA, Standard Bank, Nedbank, and First National Bank) are the most important providers of housing finance. They have a market share of about 85% (2008) which accounts for about ZAR 167.1 billion (US$22.6 billion). Although the target group of the commercial banks typically starts from the middle-income groups, they have committed themselves to the Financial Sector Charter to provide ZAR 42 billion to low-income households for housing finance purposes within 10 years (income from ZAR 1500 to 7500). The initiative came into effect on 1 January 2004. Between January 2004 and 31 December 2007, lenders have made ZAR 37.99 billion worth of mortgages, fully guaranteed (pension-backed), unsecured, developer, and wholesale loans.

SA Home Loans was established by Standard Bank and JP Morgan to use securitisation as a funding instrument for mortgage loans. SA Home Loans originates loans and sells the loans to a Special Purpose Vehicle (called Thekwini Fund), but continues to service them. To date, it has issued residential mortgage-backed securities (RMBS) worth ZAR 27 billion. It is the second largest issuer of RMBS in South Africa behind Standard Bank. With the global financial crisis, its business model has been put under serious strain.

To support the supply of housing finance, the government established the National Housing Finance Corporation (NHFC) and the Rural Housing Loan Fund (RHLF). Both institutions are wholesale financiers providing funding to eligible small credit lenders and microfinance institutions. NHFC predominantly works with small lenders in urban areas, whereas RHLF focuses on rural areas. NHFC disbursed ZAR 652 million and RHLF ZAR 252 million (2005) to its lending partners.

The Home Loan Guarantee Company was established in 1989 to provide insurance to banks and other lenders to cover losses incurred by lenders in cases of default on housing loans. It can provide a mortgage default guarantee of up to 50% of the loan amount. The guarantees also cover default as a result of HIV-/AIDS-related illnesses. The company has provided guarantees for home loans exceeding ZAR 3 billion in the lower-income segment.

NURCHA and Thubelisha Homes are two state-owned companies, the operations of which concentrate on supporting the supply of affordable housing. NURCHA, for example, offers bridging finance to small and medium-sized and large contractors and developers. The volume of loans outstanding amounts to ZAR 132 million.

The microlending industry in 2004 provided some ZAR 17.6 billion of consumer loans. The most important lenders are African Bank and Capitec Bank. The rest are nonbank

Table 3 Housing finance institutions in selected markets in sub-Saharan Africa

	South Africa	Nigeria	Senegal	Mali	Ethiopia	Kenya	Zambia	Mozambique
State-owned or state-sponsored institution	1. National Housing Finance Corporation (NHFC) 2. Rural Housing Loan Fund (RHLF)	1. Federal Mortgage Bank of Nigeria 2. National Housing Fund (NHF)	Banque de l'Habitat du Sénégal (BHS)	1. Banque de l'Habitat du Mali (BHM) 2. Fonds de Garantie Hypothécaire du Mali (FGHM)	Construction and Business Bank (CBB)	Housing Finance	1. Public Sector Pension Fund (PSPF) 2. Local Authorities Super Annuation Fund (LASF)	Fundo de o Fomento da Habitacao (Housing Promotion Fund, FFH)
Function and products offered	NHFC and RHLF are wholesale financiers	1. Administration of provident fund scheme, refinancing of PMIs 2. Provident Fund	Offer of housing loans is one of major business activities	1. Housing loans to private households and developer loans 2. Mortgage insurance	CBB was a traditional housing bank, but now universal bank	Housing loans to private individuals and developer loans	PSPF and LASF are pension funds which are legally allowed to offer housing loans. As per 2007, no lending activities	Promote social housing for low-income families, qualified technicians, and young families
Form of shareholder structure	Both institutions are state-owned	State-owned	State is minority shareholder	1. State-owned 2. Majority in private ownership	State-owned	Majority in private ownership	State-owned	State-owned
Other specialised lenders	1. SA Home Loans 2. Home Loan Guarantee Company	Primary mortgage institutions				1. Savings and loans 2. East African Building Society Bank	1. Zambia National Building Society (ZNBS) 2. Finance Bank	
Function	see **Figure 2**	Collect deposits and offer loans, distribution channels for NHF loans				Operate in the form of building societies	Both institutions are building societies	

Form of shareholder structure	Private			Private ownership	Private ownership
Products offered	1. Private ownership 2. Government ownership				
	1. Mortgage loans and refinancing through securitisation 2. Mortgage insurance				1. Building material loan 2. Loans for housing purposes. For loan eligibility, membership required
Microfinance institutions/ NGOs	Microlenders, credit unions (SACCOs), nonbank microlenders	Crédit Mutuel du Sénégal (CMS)	Nièsigyso	National Cooperative Housing Union, Kenya Affordable Shelter Project (NGO), K-REP Development Agency, Jamii Bora	ProCredit, SOCREMO, Banco Oportunidade
Form of shareholder structure	Private or cooperative	Cooperative	Cooperative	Private ownership, cooperative	Private
Products offered	Loans for housing purposes	Loans for housing purposes	Loans for housing purposes	Loans for housing purposes	Loans are used for housing purposes

Source: FinMark Trust, World Bank, AfD, Roland Igbinoba Real Foundation for Housing and Urban Development.

Figure 2 Housing finance institutions in South Africa.
Source: FinMark Trust, UN-HABITAT, KfW.

Portfolio lenders and non-bank financial institutions	Whole sale lenders	Institutions supporting supply of housing	Other institutions
• Commercial banks • Credit unions • Retailers • Non-Bank Microlenders • SA Home Loans	• NHFC • RLHF	• Thubelisha Homes • National Urban Reconstruction and Housing Agency (NURCHA)	• National Housing Finance Corporation • Social Housing Foundation • Servcon Housing Solutions • Home Loan Guarantee Company

lenders ranging from single-branch owner-operated cash lenders to multi-outlet franchises and nonprofit organisations providing microenterprise credit.

Credit unions in South Africa operate under a self-regulatory statute of Savings and Credit Co-operatives (SACCOs). They take savings deposits from, and make loans to, members rather than to the public at large. Their operations are on a quite modest scale. Annual loan volume of the total SACCO movement is estimated at just over ZAR 300 million.

Nigeria

The size of the Nigerian Housing Finance market is very small in comparison with the size of the population. The housing deficit is estimated at about 12–16 million dwellings (according to the World Bank). Private commercial banks have slowly entered into housing finance which reflects rising incomes and the emergence of a middle class. The government's housing policy is based on the following institutional structure in housing finance (Nigeria: Housing Finance by M. Boléat and S. Walley, First Initiative, March 2008):

- The Federal Mortgage Bank of Nigeria (FMBN) has two roles: (1) administration of the housing provident fund (National Housing Fund (NHF)) and (2) supporting access to capital market funding by mortgage institutions.
- The NHF is a compulsory provident fund. Every employee has to pay 2.5% of his or her salary into the fund. Proceeds of the fund can be used for the purchase of a home. After saving for 6 months with the NHF, a saver is entitled to a mortgage loan of up to NGN 15 million (about US$100 000) at an interest rate of 6%.
- Primary mortgage institutions (PMIs) are specialised mortgage lenders. They collect deposits and provide housing loans. In addition, they are the distribution channels for the loans from the NHF.

Since its existence, the NHF has disbursed NGN 5 billion (US$33 million) in 13 years, and at the end of 2005, there were only 5250 beneficiaries out of 2.8 million contributors.

Conclusion

To date, the state has assumed a dominant role in providing housing finance in most SSA countries, through state-owned institutions. Most of these institutions are exposed to a considerable number of nonperforming loans, poor corporate governance regulations, poorly working risk management systems, nontransparent procedures as well as political influence in their decision-making procedures.

The positive economic conditions during the past years and the emergence of a stronger financial sector have, however, increased competition on state-owned lenders and have put pressure on these institutions to restructure to respond to these changes. In Ghana, Ghana Home Loans, a private specialised mortgage lender, has become the second largest mortgage lender behind the traditional mortgage loan provider, HFC Bank. With more lenders entering the market and a growing middle class, competition is expected to rise in the market (despite recent setbacks resulting from the global financial crisis). The World Bank estimates the SSA middle class will be 43 million strong by 2030, up from 12.8 million in 2000. Another example is Kenya where the Housing Finance Company of Kenya (now Housing Finance) was privatised through an initial public offering (IPO) in July 2007 and an additional rights issue in June 2008. The government reduced its stake to 3.7%. Private shareholders hold 93.2% of the lender's capital.

The pressure for reform and new lenders entering housing finance is likely to continue despite the effects of the global financial crisis, albeit at a slower pace. The enormous backlog in the supply of housing is a factor supporting this trend. In this context, the advancement of regional cooperations and economic areas (such as the East African Community), including harmonisation of legal systems (e.g., OHADA legislation), could facilitate the supply of housing finance since long-term capital could be raised through one regional entity. With one currency (West African CFA Franc) in a number of West African States, tapping regional capital markets could be a promising alternative for financing the housing markets of these countries.

See also: House Building Industries: Africa; Housing Market Institutions; Industrial Organisation of the US Residential Mortgage Market; Mortgage Lenders and Loans.

References

Deutsche Bank Research (2009) *African Frontier Capital Markets: More than a Flash in the Pan*. Germany: Frankfurt am Main.
IMF (2009) *Regional Economic Outlook: Sub-Saharan Africa*. Washington, DC: IMF.

Further Reading

Centre for Affordable Housing Finance (2009) *Scoping the Demand for Housing Microfinance in Africa: Status, Opportunities and Challenges*. Johannesburg: FinMarkTrust.
Dowden R (2008) *Africa: Altered States, Ordinary Miracles*. London: Portobello.
IMF Working Paper (2009) *Understanding the Growth of African Financial Markets*. Washington, DC: IMF.
IMF Working Paper (2009) *What Determines Bond Market Development in Sub-Saharan Africa*. Washington, DC: IMF.
Roland Igbinoba Real Foundation for Housing and Urban Development (2009) *The State of Lagos Housing Market*. Lagos: Roland Igbinoba Real Foundation for Housing and Urban Development.
Rust K (2008) *Housing Finance in Sub-Saharan Africa: Reflections from South Africa*. Abuja.
UN-HABITAT (2008) *Housing Finance Systems in South Africa*. Nairobi.

Relevant Websites

www.mhu.gof.bf – Burkina Faso social housing programme.
www.finmark.org.za – FinMark Trust under the theme area for housing finance; there are various housing finance countries studies. Currently, the following countries are analysed: Ethiopia, Kenya, Malawi, Mozambique, Namibia, Rwanda, and Zambia.

Housing Finance Institutions: Asia

H Zhu, Bank for International Settlements, Hong Kong, China

© 2012 Elsevier Ltd. All rights reserved.

Glossary

Adjustable-rate mortgage (or floating-rate mortgage, or variable-rate mortgage). A mortgage loan in which the interest rate is periodically adjusted on the basis of a prespecified benchmark (a base rate or index).

Central provident fund A compulsory social security savings plan that was first introduced in Singapore in 1955, which aims to benefit workers in their retirement. Under the scheme, a part of workers' monthly income is set aside and accumulated until retirement, when the savings can be withdrawn. As an exception, the savings can be withdrawn for the purpose of home purchase.

Chonsei An informal housing finance system that used to be very popular in Korea. Chonsei is a rental contract in which the tenant pays an upfront payment (deposit) at the beginning of the contract period. There is no monthly rental payment, and the deposit is fully refundable at the end of the contract period. The landlord's rental income comes from revenues generated by the deposit during the contract period.

Fixed-rate mortgage A mortgage loan in which the interest rate remains the same through the term of the loan.

Loan-to-value ratio The size of a mortgage loan as a percentage of the total appraised value of the property.

Primary mortgage market The market where borrowers and mortgage originators meet to negotiate terms and arrange mortgage contracts.

Secondary mortgage market The market for the sale of mortgage loans, typically via securitisation.

Background

In most Asian economies, housing finance markets have grown rapidly over the past decade. Nevertheless, the levels of development remain widely different. Growth has been particularly remarkable in China and Korea and has led to a fundamental change in the mortgage market landscape. In China, housing mortgages were launched as late as 1998, but the market quickly expanded to RMB 3 trillion at the end of 2007 (~12% of GDP). In Korea, total mortgage debt outstanding almost tripled in less than 5 years from $67 billion at the end of 2001 to over $200 billion in 2006. In terms of relative size, the two front-runners are Singapore and Hong Kong, with mortgage loans accounting for 61 and 44% of GDP, respectively. At the other end of the spectrum are Indonesia and India, where the mortgage market accounts for only 2% of GDP (**Figure 1**).

The development of mortgage markets in Asia can be attributed to demand and supply factors. On the demand side, the strong economic growth in the region in the past decade has boosted household income. Moreover, the rapid development in the urbanisation process has also generated strong demand for housing. According to the United Nations, the urban population in Asia increased from 594 million in 1980 to 1565 million in 2005. Or, equivalently, the percentage of urban population increased from 26.3 to 39.7%. In Hong Kong and Singapore, almost the entire population live in urban areas. Even in China – the most populous country in the world, with the majority of the population still living in rural areas – the change has been dramatic. Urban population totalled 531 million (or 40.4% of the total population) in 2005 compared with 196 million (19.6%) in 1980. On the supply side, mortgage markets in Asia have generally become more market oriented. Intensified competition, lower cost of housing finance, and a wider range of mortgage products have improved the availability and affordability of mortgage loans to households in the region.

Characteristics of Housing Finance Systems in Asia

The housing finance systems in Asia share certain commonalities, but there exist substantial differences across countries as well. The subsequent sections discuss them in three major aspects: primary mortgage markets, secondary mortgage markets, and the role of government support.

Primary Mortgage Markets

Primary mortgage markets in Asia typically remain national in nature, with distinct legal and regulatory regimes. Domestic commercial banks are often the

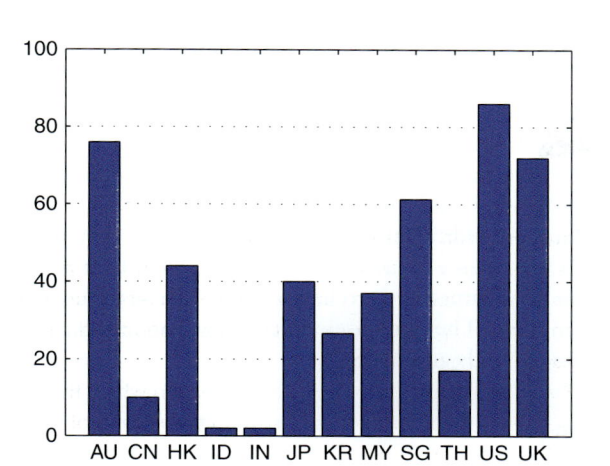

Figure 1 Mortgage debt, as a percentage of GDP (2005). Note that definitions may differ across countries.
Data Sources: BIS; National data. Abbreviations: AU = Australia; CN = China; HK = Hong Kong SAR; ID = Indonesia; IN = India; JP = Japan; KR = Korea; MY = Malaysia; SG = Singapore; TH = Thailand; US = United States; UK = United Kingdom.

dominant lender (with the important exception of Singapore), and there is a general trend that their market shares have increased over time. Government housing finance agencies play an important role in loan origination in some countries such as Korea, Singapore, and Thailand. Foreign banks, however, typically are confined to a rather limited role on the origination side, and their market share is quite small in most Asian economies. The degree of competition among mortgage lenders varies across countries and is sometimes affected by government policies such as interest rate controls that existed in some Asian economies at a certain period.

Lending practices share certain commonalities in Asia. In terms of the payment of mortgage interest, most Asian economies (except Japan) have relied primarily on adjustable-rate mortgages. Fixed-rate mortgages exist but lack popularity. In terms of the length of mortgage contracts, average mortgage terms typically range between 10 and 20 years, with maximum terms between 20 and 30 years. A noticeable exception is Korea, where 3-year bullet-type mortgages are most popular. In terms of lending criteria, the typical maximum loan-to-value (LTV) ratio ranges from 70 to 80% and is normally based on an appraisal evaluation. This constitutes relatively conservative practice compared to market norms in industrialised economies.

Secondary Mortgage Markets

The secondary mortgage market has grown rapidly in Asia in recent years. Malaysia, the front-runner in this area, issued its first mortgage-backed security (MBS) in 1987. The market has exploded since 2001. Hong Kong, Singapore, Japan, and Korea have established relatively advanced MBS markets, and China issued its first MBS in 2005.

Nevertheless, MBS markets in Asia are far from full-fledged. In some countries, there are legal, tax, and accounting impediments to the development of secondary mortgage markets. Even in more developed markets, trading of MBS instruments has not been very active. The market illiquidity may be attributable to various reasons, including insufficient information, lack of expertise in risk management, and banks' unwillingness to remove mortgage loans from their balance sheets as the loan quality is usually high.

Overall, the growth in MBS markets has helped mitigate the maturity mismatch risk in the banking system, improve liquidity in the primary mortgage market, and deepen the local debt market. By contrast, another function of MBS instruments, credit risk transformation via risk enhancement techniques, has so far been limited in Asia.

The Role of Government Support

At present many Asian economies, including Bangladesh, Hong Kong, India, Japan, Korea, Malaysia, Pakistan, Singapore, Sri Lanka, and Thailand, have active government-supported housing finance agencies. The business objectives of these government agencies are different across countries.

A conventional role of government housing finance institutions is to cater to mortgage financing needs of households, particularly low-income households, and to promote homeownership. In some countries, such as the Philippines and Thailand, government housing finance institutions provide concessional residential loans to low- to moderate-income households. In Singapore, the very comprehensive government housing finance benefits the majority of households.

Another major function of government housing finance institutions is to facilitate securitisation. For instance, the National Mortgage Corporation of Malaysia (called Cagamas) and the Hong Kong Mortgage Corporation undertake the function of securitisation and do not engage in direct lending to households. In Korea, the Korean Housing Finance Corporation (KHFC) performs dual functions of lending to households and MBS issuance. By contrast, government housing finance agencies in China, the Philippines, and Singapore do not perform the mortgage securitisation function.

National Housing Finance Systems

China

Traditionally, urban residents in China lived under a welfare housing system in which state sector employers owned properties and provided essentially free housing for their workers. In 1998, the government put an end to the welfare housing system and began to encourage workers to buy their own homes. Because the land is owned by the state, homeowners purchase the right to occupy the building for a specific period (typically 70 years) and could transfer the title to another party. Since then, the privatisation of residential housing has developed quickly. Currently, the majority of residential units were traded at market prices.

The mortgage market in China was underdeveloped before the 1990s. In 1998, along with the abolishment of the welfare housing system, the People's Bank of China issued guidelines to banks on granting housing loans. The primary mortgage market has grown exponentially since then. At the end of 2007, the mortgage loan outstanding reached RMB 3 trillion. However, China's residential mortgage loans were still quite small in that they accounted for only about 12% of GDP.

Commercial banks are currently the dominant lender in the primary mortgage market, supplemented by the Housing Provident Fund (HPF) scheme established in 1990. The HPF scheme, which follows the Singapore model (see section 'Singapore'), requires compulsory saving by employees (plus contributions from employers) for entitlement to a housing loan in the future. The practice of the HPF scheme was pioneered in the city of Shanghai and was implemented nationwide in 1994. Currently, HPF loans represent ~12% of total mortgage balances outstanding and the number of participants represents about 60% of total employed staff and workers in the urban area.

Hong Kong SAR

The mortgage market in Hong Kong is one of the most developed in Asia. Housing is an important component of household assets and mortgage loans account for ~25–30% of bank loans. Traditionally, the government has played an important role in the housing market. On the supply side, it runs a large public housing programme (including low-cost housing and public rental units) that provides accommodation for about half of Hong Kong's population. In addition, landownership and land restrictions by the government often restrict the adjustment of housing supply to changing demand. On the demand side, the government affects the availability of housing finance via various measures, including limits on banks' exposure to mortgage loans and maximum LTV ratio (which stands at 70%).

Commercial banks are the predominant source of housing finance, and there is no government-run housing loan bank in Hong Kong. Mortgage loans are typically at variable, market-determined rates.

In 1997, the Hong Kong Mortgage Corporation (HKMC) was established to promote wider homeownership in Hong Kong. The HKMC is wholly owned by the government and hence is viewed by market participants as having a strong implicit government guarantee. A main function of the HKMC is to offer a large mortgage insurance programme, which allows banks to offer loans with a maximum LTV ratio of 95% without taking on additional credit risk. In addition, the HKMC also provides a reliable source of liquidity to mortgage loan originators by purchasing pools of mortgage loans from them. The purchases are typically funded by issuing agency bonds and MBSs.

India

The Indian mortgage market has experienced fundamental changes in the past several decades. Traditionally the government played an important role. In 1970, the central government established the Housing and Urban Development Corporation to finance housing and urban infrastructure activities. In 1988, the Indian National Housing Bank (NHB) was established to promote a sound and cost-effective housing finance. The NHB is wholly owned by the Reserve Bank of India (RBI) and has an explicit government guarantee. The NHB provides funding to banks and housing finance companies and exercises regulatory and supervisory authority over housing finance companies. On the funding side, the NHB raises resources by issuing bonds or by borrowing from the RBI and financial institutions. Currently, the NHB is playing a leading role in facilitating mortgage-backed securitisation and in launching a Mortgage Credit Guarantee Scheme for protecting the lenders against default.

Housing finance in India is mainly provided by housing finance companies and commercial banks. The first private housing finance company, Housing Development Finance Corporation (HDFC), was established in 1977. Traditionally, the mortgage market was dominated by housing finance companies as commercial banks were rather reluctant to lend for housing. Towards the end of the 1990s, against the backdrop of lower interest, industrial slowdown, and ample liquidity, banks started to plunge into the business of housing finance to maintain their profit margins. Since the early 2000s, commercial banks have overtaken housing finance companies as the main mortgage lenders in India. Nevertheless, HDFC remains the single largest lender in the market.

Indonesia

Since the 1970s, the housing development policy of the Indonesian government has focused on providing low-cost housing for low-income households, by imposing a compulsory '1:3:6' rule for developers and providing subsidised loans for low-cost housing through state-owned mortgage banks. The '1:3:6' rule requires that, for every high-cost house, developers must build a minimum of three middle-class houses and six simple or very simple houses. Despite this, medium- and high-cost houses, which represent only 10% of housing units, have dominated the market in terms of sales value. Given that private sector lenders (including a number of domestic banks and one large foreign bank) have been actively involved in housing finance for high-end houses, they have played an important role in the primary mortgage market alongside two state-owned mortgage banks.

Japan

Mortgage loan funding in Japan used to be characterised by heavy dependence on government treasury investment, which was based on subsidies. After the bubble era, commercial banks were forced to restructure their business models from lending to industrial enterprises to financing home purchases. Currently, the Japanese government is restructuring its housing finance institutions by redefining their role in the market.

In 1950, the Government Housing Loan Corporation (GHLC) was established to provide a stable supply of housing finance. The GHLC was wholly owned by the government. Although it was without a formal government guarantee, the market generally perceived it as having strong implicit government support. Traditionally, the GHLC focused on providing long-term, fixed-rate housing loans directly to households and purchasing mortgages from banks. It retained these loans on its balance sheet, funding them using a combination of agency bonds and Fiscal Investment and Loan Programme (FILP) – a government loan issued for public purposes. As a result, the GHLC carried the market risk arising from the duration gap of its housing loan assets and funding liabilities. In April 2007, the GHLC was reformed into Japan Housing Finance Agency (JHF). In contrast to the GHLC, JHF abolished direct housing loans to the general public and changed its business model to focus on enhancing securitisation and enabling private financial institutions to create a steady supply of housing finance. By securitisation, the majority of the market risk was shifted to the capital market. In addition, JHF also succeeded loan guarantor responsibilities previously held by the Housing Loan Guarantee Corporation, a GHLC-related public corporation.

Korea

Korea's housing and housing finance system used to be heavily regulated. The primary mortgage market used to be dominated by the National Housing Fund (NHF) that provided below-market loans to low- and moderate-income households and the Korea Housing Bank (KHB) that catered to higher-income customers. Mortgage loans were mostly extended on a short-term basis.

Since 1991, this sector has experienced major changes due to interest rate liberalisation and financial deregulation. Price controls on new apartments were abolished, and market-based housing finance emerged. In 1996, commercial banks were allowed to provide long-term mortgages. The following year, the KHB was privatised. After a decade of rapid growth, housing banks and commercial banks have become the major source of mortgage loans for medium- and high-cost houses. However, for low-income homebuyers, policy loans of the NHF remain the primary funding source.

In Korea, an informal housing finance system known as the chonsei also exists. Chonsei is a unique rental contract arrangement between tenants and landlords. It used to represent a large chunk of housing finance in Korea but has become less important in recent years.

Traditionally, housing finance in Korea was dominated by short-term loans with floating rates. In 2004, the KHFC was established to provide more liquidity and allow for the lengthening of the maturity of mortgage loans. The KHFC is wholly owned by the Korean government with a formal government guarantee. It offers 30-year fixed-rate mortgages to households and also enables purchasing mortgage loans from banks, which is funded by issuing KHFC-guaranteed MBSs.

Malaysia

Banking institutions, including commercial banks, finance companies, Islamic banks, and merchant banks, are the biggest lenders in the primary mortgage market in Malaysia. Among them, foreign banks play a significant role, originating nearly one quarter of mortgage loans. Apart from banking institutions, development finance institutions, and a number of insurance companies also provide financing for the purchase of residential properties. The Treasury Housing Loan Division (THLD) of the Ministry of Finance is also involved in the housing loan market by providing financing to public sector employees.

Typically, banking institutions in Malaysia would offer two types of mortgage loans: conventional housing loans and Islamic house financing. Islamic house financing products generally share the same characteristics as do normal housing loan products except that they are based on Syariah principles. Under the Syariah principles, the payment and receiving of interest is not allowed. Instead, it encourages profit sharing when conducting banking-related business. The financing of home mortgages are usually based on Bai Bithaman Ajil (deferred payment sale). This refers to the sale of goods on a deferred payment basis at a price that includes a profit margin agreed upon by both the buyer and the seller. Islamic house financing is mostly fixed-rate financing, but as of 2003, banking institutions have begun to offer variable-rate Islamic house financing products.

Secondary mortgage markets started early in Malaysia, when Cagamas was established in 1986. Cagamas does not receive any government support. The central bank (Bank Negara Malaysia) owns one-fifth of Cagamas, with the remaining majority shares held by domestic and foreign banks. The main function of Cagamas is to turn mortgage loans into debt securities through a securitisation process. Cagamas is the largest issuer of debt securities in Malaysia, and its business expansion has helped improve market liquidity and mitigate the maturity mismatch problem for primary lenders.

The Philippines

In the Philippines, the government housing finance system consists of various government agencies with finance-linked subsidies such as those by the Home Development Mutual Fund, Government Service Insurance System, and the Social Security System. The main function of these agencies is to provide housing finance assistance to low- and middle-income households.

Singapore

Homeownership in Singapore is segmented into private and public housing markets. It is worth noting that public housing in Singapore can be purchased by upper- or middle-income groups and therefore is not equivalent to low-cost housing as in other Asian countries. The public housing sector is dominant and accommodates over 80% of all households. It is strictly under the authority of the Housing Development Board (HDB), which was set up in 1960 to oversee the entire gamut of housing-related programmes, from planning and development to housing management and housing finance. The HDB is wholly owned by the government and has a formal government guarantee. The majority of citizens are eligible for the public housing provided by the HDB, and the public houses can be traded at market prices after fulfiling a 5-year minimum occupancy requirement. In addition, the HDB also provides housing finance at concessionary interest rates to first-time buyers or to second-time homebuyers who upgrade to another HDB flat. Before 2003, it also provided housing finance at market rates to high-income households.

Since the 1990s, the government has taken measures to encourage the development of private housing and the share of private housing has increased rapidly. In 2005, the value of contracts awarded for new private sector construction work was almost twice as great as the value of contracts for public housing. For the purchase of private housing units, commercial banks provide mortgages at market rates, typically up to seven times the household annual income.

In addition, private property buyers can use their savings in the Central Provident Fund (CPF) – a mandatory social security savings plan – to make downpayments and monthly mortgage repayments. A majority of the homeowners fund their home purchases through the CPF.

Thailand

Domestic commercial banks, the Government Housing Bank (GHB), and the Government Savings Bank (GSB) are the biggest lenders in the primary mortgage market, with market shares of 51.4, 39.4, and 9%, respectively. Commercial banks usually compete for middle- and high-income segments. By contrast, the GHB, which was established in 1953 and is wholly owned by the Ministry of Finance (with a formal government guarantee), has rather focused on serving moderate-income households. After the 1997 crisis, the GHB experienced higher housing loan growth than domestic commercial banks. The market share of the GHB was even higher for the newly originated credits in 2006, around 47%. The combined market shares of both the GHB and the GSB represented 48% of the outstanding mortgage debt and 56% of the new mortgage loans.

Conclusion

Overall, housing finance systems in Asia have developed rapidly in the past several decades, although still lagging behind those in the industrialised economies in terms of the size, the range of mortgage products, and secondary market activity. Asia is now an important engine for global economic growth. Because the economy is growing strongly and the urbanisation process continues, private housing and housing finance will continue to develop in the coming decades in the region.

See also: Government/Public Lending Institutions: Asia-Pacific; Housing Institutions in Developing Countries; Housing Policy: Agents and Regulators; Industrial Organisation of the US Residential Mortgage Market; Islamic Housing Finance; Mortgage Market, Character and Trends: China; Mortgage Market, Character and Trends: Japan; Mortgage Market, Character and Trends: Korea; Private Sector Housing Management: Asia Pacific; Social Housing Landlords: Asia Pacific.

Further Reading

Arner D, Booth C, Hsu B, Lejot P, Liu Q, and Pretorius F (2006) Property rights, collateral, and creditor rights in East Asia. In: Dalla I (ed.) *East*

Asia Finance: Selected Issues, pp. 383–428. Washington, DC: World Bank.

Chan E, Davies M, and Gyntelberg J (2006) MBS markets in Asia: The role of government-supported housing agencies. *BIS Quarterly Review* December: 71–83.

Ghosh (2006) *East Asian Finance – The Road to Robust Markets*. Washington, DC: World Bank.

Committee on the Global Financial System (2006) Housing finance in the global financial market. *CGFS Papers No. 26*. Bank for International Settlements.

Glindro E, Subhanij T, Szeto J, and Zhu H (2008) Determinants of house prices in nine Asia-Pacific Economies. *BIS Working Papers No 263*.

Gyntelberg J and Remolona E (2006) Securitisation in Asia and the Pacific: Implications for liquidity and credit risks. *BIS Quarterly Review* June: 65–75.

OECD (2005) *Housing Finance Market in Transition Economies: Trends and Challenges*. OECD publication. ISBN-92-64-010165.

Remolona E and Shim I (2008) Credit derivatives and structured credit: The nascent market of Asia and the Pacific. *BIS Quarterly Review* June: 57–65.

Sing TF and Ong SE (2004) Residential mortgage-backed securitization in Asia: The Singapore experience. *Journal of Real Estate Literature* 12(2): 159–179.

Tsatsaronis K and Zhu H (2004) What drives housing price dynamics: Cross-country evidence. *BIS Quarterly Review* March: 65–78.

Warnock V and Warnock F (2008) Markets and Housing Finance. *Journal of Housing Economics* 17: 239–251.

Zhu H (2006) The structure of housing finance markets and house prices in Asia. *BIS Quarterly Review* December: 55–69.

Housing Finance Institutions: Latin America

WB Gwinner, International Finance Corporation, Washington, DC, USA

© 2012 Elsevier Ltd. All rights reserved.

Glossary

Covered mortgage bond A bond issued by a mortgage lender that is secured by a pool of mortgages that is maintained on the asset side of the issuer's balance sheet.

Currency peg A currency policy whereby a country seeks to maintain the value of its own currency in terms of that of another economy.

Financial crisis A period marked by a sharp drop in confidence in and the value of financial institutions, resulting in a rapid contraction in lending and economic activity.

Mortgage lien A legal agreement that encumbers an asset as collateral until a related loan is repaid.

Nonbank financial institutions (NBFIs) NBFIs are lenders that lack some of the functions of depository banks, generally the privilege to raise demand deposits.

Price-level adjusting mortgages (PLAMs) PLAMs are structured to maintain the real value of the principal lent in an inflationary environment.

Residential mortgage-backed security (RMBS) A bond or series of bonds that are secured with the cash flows from a pool of mortgages that are maintained in a separate legal vehicle that in turn is bankruptcy remote from the institution that issues the RMBS.

Sovereign debt crisis A period in which investors lose confidence in the ability of a sovereign to service its debt. Generally follows an extended period of economic expansion and increased public and private debt issuance in one or more countries.

Introduction

Latin American housing finance markets are small in comparison to the size and level of development of their national economies. Single-family mortgage debt generally ranges from 2% to 5% of GDP. Only Chile, Panama, and Mexico exceed 10%, dramatically lower than the 60–100% levels prevalent in North America and Western Europe. Constraints to long-term housing finance include limited penetration of financial markets, periodic economic crises, high inflation in the 1980s and 1990s, the prevalence of informal incomes, and the rapid and widespread growth of squatter settlements in the latter part of the twentieth century.

Economic and political instability has restricted the development of Latin American mortgage markets. High inflation in the 1970s through the 1990s in many countries in Latin America was accompanied by several sovereign debt crises and by financial crises in Mexico and Colombia in the late 1990s. Argentina and Uruguay experienced a crisis in 2001 related to the collapse of Argentina's currency peg. Mexico suffered more than any other country in the region since the 2008 international financial crisis, with GDP shrinking by 6% in 2009.

In most of Latin America, access to financial markets is limited to the highest-earning third of the population. Moderate- and low-income households generally conduct transactions in cash, lacking any kind of savings or checking account, or access to credit. As a result, mortgage lending is something of a luxury good in the region.

Half or more of the economic activity of most Latin American countries occurs in the informal sector. Informal wage earners by definition have more difficulty documenting their income for a mortgage application, and their incomes are generally more volatile than formally employed workers, making it difficult to support a long-term debt obligation.

Latin America's urban population grew from 49.3% of total in 1960 to 79.6% in 2005. Urban planning and land markets in most of the region failed to adequately adjust to the rapid growth of cities. A great deal of this urbanisation took the form of illegal invasions of land on the periphery of cities, such as Villa El Salvador in Lima, or the 'favelas' of Rio de Janeiro and other Brazilian cities. Residents of squatter settlements generally lack formal title for their properties, and their self-built structures generally are inadequately constructed to qualify as registered dwellings, and so are not adequate to serve as mortgage collateral. About one-third of the housing supply in Latin America is overcrowded, of deficient construction, or missing an important amenity such as electricity, running water, or connection to a sewage system.

It would take many pages to do justice to the variety of approaches that Latin American countries have taken to stimulate the supply of housing and mortgage finance. This article introduces some of the key themes with references to individual market developments. The article also provides a brief introduction to four of the larger and more advanced economies in this diverse region.

Characteristics of Housing Finance Systems in Latin America

Each Latin American government has intervened at some point to increase the supply of housing, mortgage finance, or both. In recent years, several have sought to encourage more private sector lending, notably Chile, but also including Mexico, Colombia, Peru, and Panama. The region's private financial systems are driven predominantly by depository bank lenders, but a few countries have developed nonbank lenders and capital market funding for mortgages, notably Colombia and Mexico. Public lenders remain important in many markets, and they dominate lending in Mexico (*Infonavit* and *Fovissste*), Brazil (*Caixa Economica Federal*), and Jamaica (National Housing Trust).

Primary Mortgage Markets

Institutional Structure

In Latin America, most mortgages are originated by banks and held on their balance sheets, funded with short-term deposits. Several countries, notably Mexico, Colombia, Brazil, and Panama, have permitted the creation of nonbank financial institutions (NBFIs) to compete with banks. However, NBFIs have had trouble competing to provide mortgages since commercial banks and government-owned retail lenders benefit from lower cost of funds. Mexican NBFIs have suffered particularly after losing access to capital markets in the wake of the 2008 international financial crisis.

Provident funds were created as a form of forced retirement savings in several countries. These are public mortgage lenders that are funded with payroll taxes and that make mortgage loans as investments. Formally employed individuals generally have individual accounts with provident funds. Leading examples have been in Mexico (*Infonavit* for private sector employees and *Fovissste* for state employees), Brazil, Colombia, Jamaica, and Ecuador. When efficiently run and well targeted, provident funds provide a steady supply of mortgages. Well-run provident funds in Latin America have included *Infonavit* since it was reformed in the late 1990s. However, even in the best of circumstances, provident funds tend to offer sub-market rate mortgages, thereby distorting primary market pricing and arguably provide a sub-optimal investment choice for fund members, who would normally want access to a well-diversified range of investment vehicles that provide a market rate of return. In the worst of cases, political influences have overwhelmed financial decisions, and provident funds have failed to provide a positive real return to contributors.

Mortgage loan maturities run between 15 and 30 years in most countries in the region. Fixed-rate lending has become more prevalent in the 2000s as inflation has fallen to low levels in many countries. In Panama, Guatemala, Peru, and the Dominican Republic, lenders retain the right to adjust rates as their funding costs change, a form of administrative floating rate.

Inflation-Linked Lending

Between the 1980s and the early part of the 2000s, inflation-indexed loans were prevalent in many countries. Price-level adjusting mortgages (PLAMs) with 20- and 30-year maturities were the norm until recently in Mexico, Colombia, Brazil, Chile, Peru, Argentina, and Uruguay. PLAMs come in several varieties. A common design is to carry an interest rate that is fixed in real terms, expressed as a spread over an inflation index, for instance, Colombia's *Unidad de Valor Real* (UVR). Loan principal and payments on such loans rise with inflation. PLAMs work well for lenders and borrowers so long as (1) inflation remains close to a rate in the single digits; (2) the product design permits complete amortisation of principal within the original maturity; and (3) salaries rise at least at the same rate as the index, enabling borrowers to afford the increasing nominal monthly payments.

In countries where inflation has remained low, lending is increasingly denominated in fixed or variable rates in nominal local currencies, often with shorter maturities of 10 and 15 years. In Chile, inflation of 3% or less since the early 1990s made indexation largely irrelevant to consumers. Since the early part of the 2000s, Chilean mortgages have increasingly been made in nominal pesos and funded by banks with a blend of short-term deposits and medium-term corporate bond issues. Similarly, most new lending in Mexico and Colombia has been in nominal fixed-rate pesos.

Foreign Currency Lending

A more risky way to manage inflation is to lend in a more stable foreign currency. Lending in US dollars was prevalent throughout the 1990s in Peru, Argentina, and Uruguay. In inflationary economies, a more stable foreign currency often appears attractive to borrowers in the short term because the nominal rate of interest is lower than that of the local currency. For example, US dollar lending was popular in Argentina from 1991 until 2001, during which the exchange rate of the Argentine currency was fixed to the US dollar. However, US dollar mortgage payments jumped by 400% in local currency terms by the end of 2002 when deteriorating macroeconomic fundamentals forced Argentina to abandon the currency peg.

When borrowers are paid in local currency, it is important to also denominate their long-term debts in local currency. Otherwise, a sudden and sharp devaluation like that of Argentina in 2001 can make foreign currency denominated loans unaffordable and lead to widespread mortgage defaults.

One means to eliminate inflation is to adopt a more stable foreign currency as the national currency. Panama, Ecuador, and El Salvador have each adopted the US dollar as their official national currency, and in each case have effectively ceded monetary policy to the US Federal Reserve. As a result, salaries are paid in US dollars and mortgages are made in dollars, at fixed and variable rates. Variable rates tend to be subject to adjustments at the discretion of the lender rather than to a mechanical link to a market rate of interest or a rate index.

Housing Microfinance

Given the importance of the informal housing market in Latin America, nonmortgage lending for housing renovation and progressive construction has come into being. In squatter settlements, individuals typically accumulate savings in the form of building materials, and then add a room or a feature such as a concrete floor. A series of small loans without mortgage liens can permit these households to speed up the construction process and improve their quality of life. Microfinance lenders in Bolivia, Peru, Guatemala, and Mexico make such microfinance housing loans, often less than US$ 1000 for maturities of less than a year.

Secondary Mortgage Markets

The picture for capital markets funding for Latin American mortgages is a mixed one and has been particularly constrained in the wake of the 2008 international financial crisis. In many countries, the development of private pension funds, mutual funds, and the growth of life insurers has created demand for bonds. Since the 1990s, markets for residential mortgage-backed securities (RMBSs) have come into being in Colombia, Chile, Mexico, Brazil, Argentina, Ecuador, Panama, and Peru. Covered bonds in the form of *cedulas hipotecarias* or *letras hipotecarias* that match a single mortgage to a single bond are feasible in law in most countries in the region, but are actively issued only in Chile and Guatemala. Covered mortgage bonds that are backed by portfolios of mortgages held on the books of the bond issuer are not actively issued in the region.

Actual issuance of both RMBS and covered bonds is quite limited in most countries. In general, corporate bond markets suffer from inadequate issuance compared to demand, and thin and illiquid trading. Argentine RMBS issues flourished for a short time in the late 1990s until the 2001 currency crisis. Brazilian RMBS issuance has been limited by technical issues with the indexes used to price the majority of mortgages. Chilean RMBS issuance grew in the late 1990s, and then fell off when investors were surprised by a refinancing wave in 2000. Still, about 12% of Chilean mortgages have been securitised. Mexican RMBS issuance grew from 2000 to 2008, reaching 9% of stock, and then almost completely stopped as a result of the 2008 international financial crisis. The only RMBS market in Latin America that grew through 2008 and 2009 was Colombia, with an average of roughly US dollar equivalent 141 million in issuances each quarter, reaching 37.5% of stock in 2010. Colombian RMBS are issued by a securitisation company that is owned by the country's largest banks, and demand for its issues comes from pension funds, insurers, and its bank shareholders.

National Housing Finance Systems

Brazil

Mortgages make up 2.1% of GDP, a small portfolio relative to the size and sophistication of the financial system and relative to GDP. The market is segmented by income level, with private lenders serving upper-income households. The largest primary mortgage lender is the state-owned bank Caixa Economica Federal, which serves predominately moderate- and lower-income formal sector households. Caixa Economica is the most significant channel for funding from national savings plans. Caixa lends these funds, which are raised through either payroll taxes or tax-advantaged savings accounts, at a rate of interest that is generally less than or equal to the inflation rate.

Private securitisation companies have had a certain amount of success creating RMBS. Demand by private pension funds and insurers is strong for long-term bonds; however, the supply of collateral for RMBS is limited to mortgages offered by private banks or the few nonbank lenders at market rates of interest.

Mexico

Mortgages make up about 11% of Mexico's GDP. Predominant lenders are the provident funds *Infonavit* and *Fovissste*, private banks, and NBFIs. Since 2000, the government has encouraged private sector lending through a series of reforms and institutional changes. The strategy included reforms to the legal and regulatory environment for mortgage lending, including faster enforcement of mortgage liens in case of default, improved property appraisals, and reforms of state property registration systems. The government created *Sociedad Hipotecaria Federal* (SHF) in 2002 as a provider of liquidity lines of credit to NBFIs and to support securitisation by providing portfolio guarantees. Between 2000 and 2008, total lending grew from about 150 000 units financed per year to just over 600 000 units, matching the household formation rate, and holding out the possibility of reducing the housing deficit. NBFIs grew to be significant lenders and regular issuers of RMBS and construction loan securitisations.

In the wake of the 2008 financial crisis, mortgage lending has fallen. Mexico was the Latin American economy worse hit by the crisis. Two Mexican NBFIs failed, *Metrofinanciera* and *Credito y Casa*; with each failure, the result of causes was specific to the institution. Nevertheless, investors lost confidence in the entire NBFI sector and demand for commercial paper and RMBS issued by NBFIs evaporated.

Since 2008, investors have been willing to buy only RMBS issued by *Infonavit*, by *Fovissste*, or by large international banks. Without wholesale funding, NBFIs can fund lending only with loans from the state-owned development bank SHF, which is not adequate to grow at the rate that they had been growing. NBFI lending has dramatically declined. In the vacuum left by the NBFIs, *Infonavit* and *Fovissste* have returned to their role as the prominent lenders to moderate- and low-income households. Until they can again convince investors to buy their RMBS, the future of mortgage NBFIs in Mexico is in doubt.

Colombia

Banks dominate primary lending in Colombia, but since the securitisation company *Titularizadora Colombiana* began business in 2002, the banks have sold increasing amounts of loans as collateral for RMBS. Private Colombian mortgage lenders have been active since the 1970s. The overall portfolio grew to 12% of GDP in 1998, and then shrank by one-third in the wake of the financial crisis that year. In the years immediately prior to the crisis, real estate prices had risen at unsustainable rates. In a bid to match lending and funding costs for specialised mortgage lenders, the inflation index for mortgages had been based on short-term interest rates. When short-term rates jumped during the crisis, mortgage payments also rose rapidly. But salaries did not rise as quickly, and as a result, roughly one-third of mortgage borrowers defaulted in the wake of the 1998 crisis. In response, the courts forced a rewrite of the terms of inflation indexing. Originations slowly recovered, particularly in the latter part of the 2000s, but only in 2009 did they equal the volumes reached in 1998. By 2010, more than 90% of new originations were fixed-rate peso-denominated loans, with inflation-linked lending falling out of favour with increased macroeconomic stability.

Chile

Since the 1980s, Chile has consistently pursued a model that complements private lending with capital market funding and capital subsidies for low-income households. The result has been a steady growth in the mortgage portfolio, to just over 20% of GDP at the end of 2010. Capital market instruments include *letras hipotecarias*, which link an individual bond to each mortgage, and securitisation. Demand for *letras* has been consistent from insurers and from private pension funds, also created in the 1980s. In recent years, banks have developed the market position to issue medium-term bonds at funding rates that are lower than *letras* or securitisation. The predominant issuers of *letras* in recent years have been NBFIs that are wholly owned by life insurers, and which exist to provide *letras* to their corporate parents for long-maturity duration matching. Chilean mortgage originations from the 1980s through the early 2000s were predominately inflation linked. But inflation has been below 4% annually since the early 1990s, and in recent years, the vast majority of mortgages have been fixed rate, denominated in nominal pesos, for terms up to 30 years.

The Way Forward

The 2008 crisis interrupted the supply of finance for housing in some countries, but the demand for quality housing in the region persists. Chile and Panama have each reduced their housing deficits dramatically by providing a range of legal and financial instruments that permit lenders to manage the risks of mortgage lending, while each has provided a wide-ranging subsidy programme that permits lenders to serve households earning less than the median income.

The prevalence of low inflation and steady economic growth in most Latin American economies over the past 10 years creates new opportunities for mortgage finance. The economic prospect for the near term is positive in many countries in the region, with high commodity prices driving further growth. Some of this growth has resulted in reduced poverty rates. To the degree that the middle class grows, and inflation remains under control, then mortgage markets can be expected to expand.

Acknowledgement

WB Gwinner is a Housing Finance specialist in the International Finance Corporation. The views in this article represent his personal perspective, and do not necessarily represent IFC's official position.

Further Reading

Chiquier L and Lea M (eds.) (2009) *Housing Finance Policy in Emerging Markets*. Washington, DC: The World Bank.
Cuéllar MM (2006) *A la vivienda quién la ronda? Situación y perspectivas de la política de vivienda en Colombia*, lst edn., Vols: 1 and 2, Bogotá: Universidad Externado de Colombia.

Relevant Websites

www.ahm.org.mx – Association of Mexican mortgage lenders
www.caixa.gov.br – Brazil's Caixa Economica Federal
www.titularizadora.com – Colombia's securitisation company
www.hofinet.org – Housing Finance Information Network
www.housingfinance.org – International Union for Housing Finance
www.uniapravi.org – The Latin American Union for Housing Finance

Housing Finance Institutions: Transition Societies

W Amann, Institute for Real Estate Construction and Housing, Vienna, Austria
E Springler, Vienna University of Economics and Business Administration, Vienna, Austria

© 2012 Elsevier Ltd. All rights reserved.

Glossary

Housing funds Designed as public or semipublic entities to help finance the construction of a social rental sector.

Mortgage-backed securities Debt obligations, which represent claims on cash flows from pooled mortgage loans. These obligations are bought from financial institutions (mostly banks) by governmental, private, or semiprivate entities, which in turn issue securities based on the claims of payments of the basket of pooled loans.

Public–private partnership In housing this describes an integrated approach wherein private companies fulfil public service obligations, such as housing provision for defined households with need. For this purpose they have access to public funds (state aid). Successful PPP models are in place in several Western European and Asian countries, but hardly in any transition economies.

Social rental sector Part of housing provision set up with the goal to satisfy the needs of those income classes that are excluded from homeownership or the open market rental sector.

Structural Funds From the EU Structural and Cohesion Funds the European Regional Development Fund (ERDF) is most important in terms of housing. Today it is possible to spend a small portion of it on housing refurbishment issues.

Structured housing finance products These were developed to mitigate risks and reduce costs of capital. They can be defined by three key characteristics: pooling of financial assets, delinking of the credit risk of the asset pool from the credit risk of the originator, and tranching of liabilities that are backed by the collateral assets.

Introduction and Background

After the shaky economic developments in the 1990s most transition economies entered a phase of stability in the past decade until recently. In line with overall economic development the financial structure also faced massive changes, which were accompanied by numerous banking crises and credit crunches. While these widely underdeveloped banking structures were reconciled, the structure of housing finance did not seem to modernise (see among others OECD, 2005; UNECE, 2005). In the current crisis all transition countries are affected by an economic downturn although the effects differ in intensity. For most housing markets the current slump is even more harmful than for the average of Western European countries, although economic actors are affected differently. Compared to some Western economies, households have fewer negative effects when they became homeowners after transition. Conversely, housing supply is under even more severe pressure than in many Western European economies. The reasons for this can be found in the housing supply structure and development of housing finance products.

In the first years of transition numerous economies privatised their formerly public or cooperative housing stock and enabled renters to become homeowners. In some countries more than 30% of the housing stock was privatised (PRC, 2005). Homeownership rates rose and are well above EU15 average, while retail financing products appeared only in the early 2000s. They were responsible for a boom in new construction of housing in all metropolitan areas. But the excessively high ownership rates derive primarily from high rates even before transition and privatisation.

For many years new construction of multistorey dwellings in Central and Eastern European (CEE) countries was largely orientated towards the upscale condominium market. There was neither hardly any social housing construction nor rental housing construction. International investors, (domestic) construction companies, and the banking sector with its newly developed retail mortgage products were the major players in housing development.

For a discussion on development in residential debt to GDP ratios and rationale for homeownership in CEE economies see among others Amann (2005). As shown in **Figure 1**, the residential debt to GDP ratio in CEE and Southeastern European (SEE) countries remains well below the level of advanced European countries and the United States. Despite the small size, the lending market for housing in the region has grown sharply, with an average growth of well above 50% per year. In the

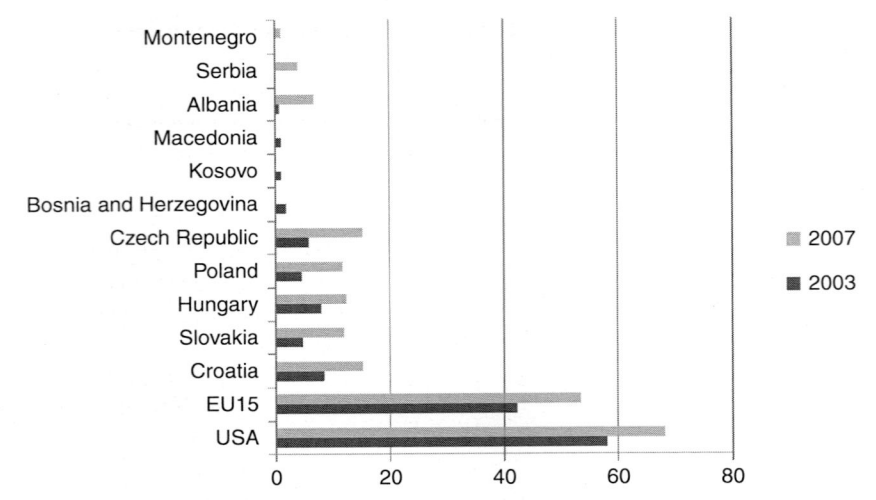

Figure 1 Residential debt to GDP ratio in percentage in Central and Eastern Europe in comparison to the United States and EU15 for 2003 and 2007.
ECORYS (2005), EMF (various issues), IMF (2008), and own calculations.

EU15 countries, the growth rates were mostly less than 10% in the same period, but starting from a much higher level (OECD, 2005).

Therefore this article first gives a short overview of the main developments in the banking sector, which are classified as a traditional view of housing finance institutions. But they can only partly comply with the financing needs of social housing in CEE economies. Hence, focus is laid on alternative views of housing finance and the role of different housing finance institutions. In this respect national and international finance institutions are distinguished.

Traditional View on Housing Finance Institutions

The necessity for developments in housing finance was not primarily driven by an increased demand for financial means, but was fostered by international commercial banks to enlarge their business share in CEE economies. In this respect especially international financial institutions such as the European Bank for Reconstruction and Development (EBRD) have been of high importance for the promotion of liberalised housing finance markets.

Banking Institutions

While the efficiency of the banking sector was improved in all CEE economies in major consolidation phases in the late 1990s that led to a sharp increase in the market share of foreign banks, the efficiency of the legal background followed an individual national basis. Both aspects, the deepening and restructuring of the banking sector itself and the accomplishments regarding the efficiency of mortgage lending, vary substantially across CEE and SEE countries. In a cross-country analysis that measured the legal efficiency of national mortgage markets at the multidimensional level, countries like Croatia, the Slovak Republic, and Slovenia reached the best score (EBRD, 2007). This means that in these countries the mortgage system developed more efficiently compared to Poland and Serbia, but also compared to Hungary and the Czech Republic. Despite these differences between transition countries the overall increase in efficiency is acknowledged. Mortgage lending in CEE/SEE economies by financial institutions was further improved among others by the introduction of contract saving schemes, following to a large extent the system of Bausparkassen, which was implemented with different success in the Czech Republic, Slovakia, Hungary, Romania, and Croatia in the 1990s, or by the set up of specialised mortgage banks.

Development of Structured Products

Similar to indirect finance systems the institutional structures of housing finance too have to fulfil the basic function of providing liquidity. As mortgage finance systems deepen, different forms of structured finance products emerge, despite changes in the underwriting criteria of mortgage lenders like maximum loan to value ratios. Lenders in CEE and SEE countries show great interest in the securitisation of mortgage loan portfolios. In Romania, for example, several laws were passed or adapted in order to facilitate mortgage-backed security (MBS) issues. Still in other countries like Serbia, Bosnia and Herzegovina, Montenegro, Kosovo, and Albania, capital markets are in a very early stage of development and, thus, cannot yet serve as a resource for long-term finance. However, it is likely that, in the next few years, these countries will reinforce their efforts to develop these markets by enacting the necessary legislation and establishing the relevant institutional framework (e.g., supervisory bodies).

Impact of International Financial Integration

The impact of increasing international financial integration for CEE economies mainly covers two aspects: to diminish interest rate spreads in combination with an increase in efficiency in local mortgage markets and to increase mortgage lending in foreign currency (until currently). Competition among banks together with an increase in the respective banking sector's depth and financial support of the EBRD in terms of loans, equity, and guarantees decreased interest rates on mortgages and increased the flexibility of existing mortgage products. This counts especially for the new EU member states and to an even larger extent for the new member states of the Euro zone. Another aspect of international financial integration that pushed mortgage supply was the increase in mortgage lending in foreign currency. Especially Romania, Poland, Hungary, and Croatia took advantage of this possibility of lending in the past years. Following the current financial and economic crisis, foreign currency loans turned to be very problematic. In some cases, at the time devaluation of the local currency increased mortgage payments, real estate market slump reduced the value of the dwelling and jobs became insecure. Today, foreign currency loans are mostly prohibited or discouraged. Existing loans had to be converted.

Housing Finance Institutions at the National Level

The possibilities of public authorities changing the market results of demand and supply on the housing market are multidimensional. The role of the state can be manifested by direct and indirect housing subsidy schemes as well as tax incentives. For the question of housing finance especially, state guarantees, tax reliefs on income tax, and legal action are important. Furthermore, the respective national institutional setting accounts for specific financial funding possibilities.

Figure 2 shows different forms of organisational structure of housing finance at the national level. Moving from structures of mortgage providers, which might be pure market actors as well as state administrated entities, to state guarantees, national housing

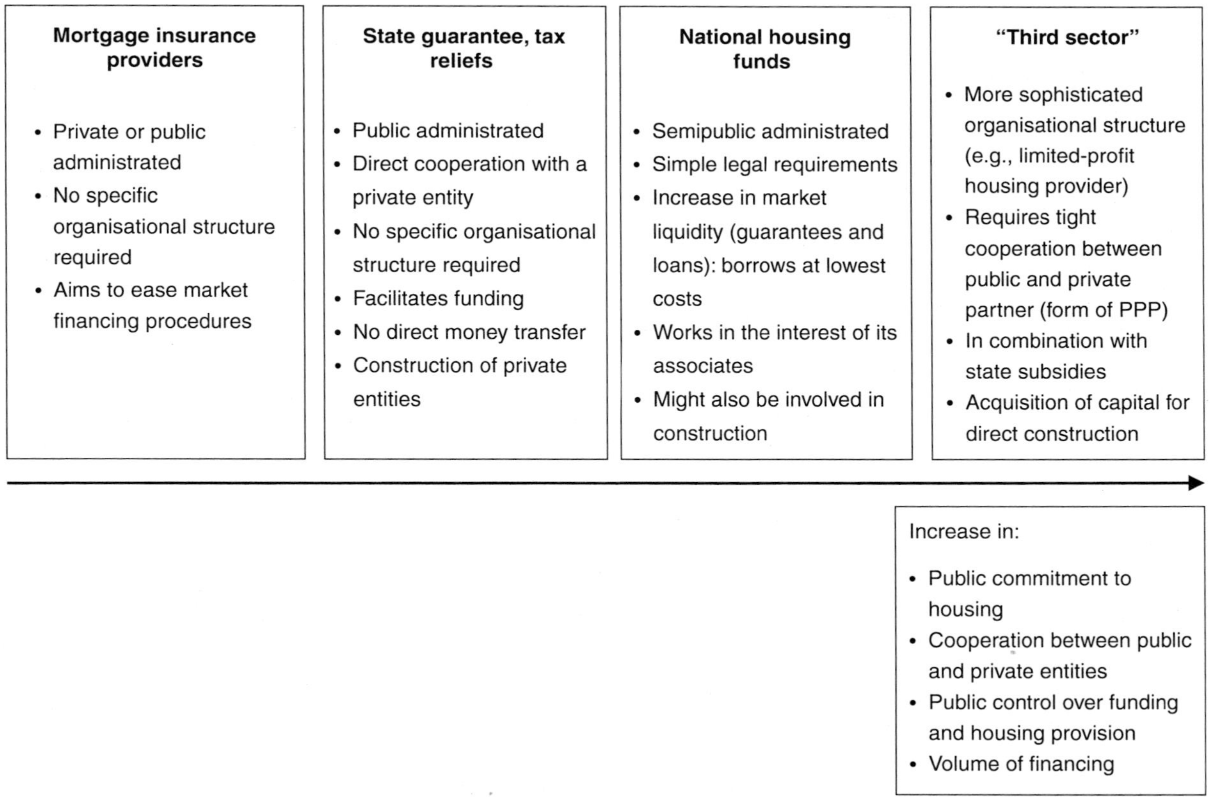

Mortgage insurance providers	State guarantee, tax reliefs	National housing funds	"Third sector"
• Private or public administrated • No specific organisational structure required • Aims to ease market financing procedures	• Public administrated • Direct cooperation with a private entity • No specific organisational structure required • Facilitates funding • No direct money transfer • Construction of private entities	• Semipublic administrated • Simple legal requirements • Increase in market liquidity (guarantees and loans): borrows at lowest costs • Works in the interest of its associates • Might also be involved in construction	• More sophisticated organisational structure (e.g., limited-profit housing provider) • Requires tight cooperation between public and private partner (form of PPP) • In combination with state subsidies • Acquisition of capital for direct construction

Increase in:
- Public commitment to housing
- Cooperation between public and private entities
- Public control over funding and housing provision
- Volume of financing

Figure 2 Housing finance: Organisational structures at the state level.

funds, and to a so-called 'third sector' in housing finance, housing provision requires a stronger cooperation between public and private entities. In the following section the use and structure of these different organisational forms at the state level in selected CEE and SEE countries are discussed.

State Guarantees and Tax Reliefs

While public funding is constrained by national and international fiscal requirements, public guarantees are less affected by these constraints and can serve as important factors for cheap housing finance, as investors benefit from the creditworthiness of the public sector and financing security is increased. As all transition economies have tight limits in providing guarantees, which they might also allocate preferable to other investments but housing, the effectiveness of state guarantees is limited. A precondition for the success of state guarantees is the supervision of provision, which includes the fact that only institutional finance should be provided via this channel, as negative effects on payment behaviour may be caused when private persons are the immediate beneficiaries. Alternatively, structures of tax reliefs can be chosen to obtain similar well-guided financing effects for private households. Unlike direct monetary subsidies by the state, which are designed as unconditional grants, tax reliefs promote the financial capacity of the individual household. In this case the financial sector is not enlarged; however, it can be shown that homeownership financing for households becomes more attractive (Springler and Wagner, 2009).

CEE countries like the Czech Republic, Hungary, and Slovakia introduced such schemes already in the 1990s and used it throughout the past years to a different extent. In Hungary, for example, the mortgage payment allowance on personal income tax had no major influences when introduced in 1994, but with the discussions and structural changes in 2000 and 2002, which led to a substantial increase in tax deductibles and widened the base for deductions, its impacts for loan demand increased (Hegedü, 2009).

National Housing Funds

Some Western European and a growing number of CEE/SEE countries use the instrument of housing funds. A particularly successful example is the Dutch Waarborgfonds Sociale Woningbouw (Social Housing Guarantee Funds), which was set up already in the 1980s and provides a triple loan guarantee (through the structure of the association, the capital assets of the fund, and the state and local authorities) (Boelhouwer, 2003).

A housing fund may issue loans, grants, or guarantees for the rental sector as well as offer a finance possibility for homeownership. It may work more efficiently than public administration, presuming that its mandate and control are properly regulated. For such a fund, public guarantees may be an appropriate and cheap form of public commitment, but, at the outset, direct public funding seems to be indispensable, at least in the initial phase. The effectiveness of such a fund is dependent on its size. The national housing funds in place rely partly on revenues from housing privatisation, partly on loans of international financing institutions, and partly on budget grants as sources of their capital. Especially Poland, the Czech Republic, Slovakia, Slovenia, Romania, and Albania take advantage of national housing funds as funding source. The Housing Fund of the Republic of Slovenia emerged as an important provider of finance for the social housing sector after transition, when mortgage finance was developing slowly and housing policy was inadequate. The Polish National Housing Fund (KFM) has financed since the mid-1990s, when it was established, more than 60 000 new rental units. The administration of the fund is done by the state-owned Bank Gospodarstwa Krajowego (BGK) (Chiquier and Lea, 2009). By 2006 around 60% of the fund's volume had been funded by government budget grants (World Bank, 2006). Despite the current crises, discussions to promote the fund's stability were ongoing in the last years; possible strategies include the aim to narrow the gap between KFM loans with market conditions and the search for new alternative forms of public–private partnerships (PPPs). Such measures reshape the tasks of national housing funds from the provision of a social rental sector for lower-income classes to a broader provision for middle-income tenants.

A 'Third Sector' in Housing

Some CEE economies started in the last years with the establishment of 'third sectors'. As the developments of nonprofit and cooperative housing schemes for example in Slovakia and the Czech Republic show, which are rather restricted in their operations due to considerable political commitment or heavily criticised for their structure and forbidden after a few years in place, the establishment of a 'third sector' as a special form of the PPP requires a strong political commitment, a well-organised legal background, as well as provision of financial means. In Poland, a concentrated semiprivate nonprofit sector Towarzystw Budownictwa Spolecznego (TBS) (Society for Social Housing) is responsible for rental housing construction and receives financial support from BGK bank, the National Housing Fund, and in the last years from European Investment Bank (EIB) and Council of Europe Development Bank (CEB), which are presented in the following section, in the form of state guaranteed loans. A new approach to establish PPP for affordable housing is taken by the Austria-based IIBW – Institute for Real Estate, Construction and Housing.

Current projects in Romania, Montenegro, and Albania follow a dual strategy to establish a legal framework for this new business type with a PPP Housing Law and to develop a funding scheme including sources from international financing institutions.

International Financing Institutions

In addition to financial structures and institutions at the state level, the international financing institutions International Finance Corporation (IFC), a member of the World Bank, EIB, CEB, and others promote housing finance in transition economies. Furthermore, the European Union has an impact on housing developments in those transition economies that are already member states of the European Union within the setting of the Joint European Support for Sustainable Investment in City Areas (JESSICA) programme (see below).

World Bank/International Finance Corporation

The World Bank has followed closely the changes in housing policy in transition economies since 1990. It has carried out substantial analytical work (sector reports) and has worked closely with researchers and policy analysts across Central and Eastern Europe on all relevant aspects of housing policy reform. Financial support was granted to housing projects in Poland, Russia, Albania, and Latvia in the form of loans or guarantees (Tsenkova, 2005). In the last years (2004–08) especially land administration and management projects were financed in Montenegro, Serbia, and Bosnia and Herzegovina through the World Bank.

European Investment Bank

The EIB is the financing institution of the European Union and, as such, aims at providing long-term finance for specific capital projects. Housing projects, especially housing renovation, have traditionally found support in the context of the urban renewal objective, but recently a wider opening to social housing finance, in support of the social cohesion objective, has taken place. The EIB is involved in implementing EU development aid and cooperation policies through provision of long-term loans. These loans are derived from the bank's own resources, subordinated loans, and risk capital from EU or member states' budgetary funds. In 2002 for example, the EIB decided to lend a total of EUR 200 million to Poland for urban renewal and energy-efficient social housing. The 25-year loan to state-owned BGK is aimed at renovating housing stock that shows evidence of severe deferred maintenance. Investments are mainly concentrated in the urban areas with the largest housing deficits.

In addition to these direct financing methods of projects by the EIB, the bank has an important role in the JESSICA programme, which is described below.

Council of Europe Development Bank

The CEB especially aims to support housing policy measures for vulnerable groups and persons. In Bosnia and Herzegovina, Bulgaria, Croatia, Macedonia, Serbia, Montenegro, Albania, and Romania, funds were invested in projects for the housing of refugees, the reconstruction of war-damaged dwellings, and the social integration of the Roma community. The bank is also contributing to large-scale public programmes for the construction of social dwellings and housing projects for young people and low-income families (Tsenkova, 2005: 99).

European Union: Structural Funds and the JESSICA Programme

In 2006, after several years of discussion, an agreement was reached that allowed European Regional Development Fund (ERDF) spending on housing under certain conditions. With this agreement direct financial support of social housing measures through the ERDF was made possible and replaced the only indirect assistance via the general engagement to support economic and social conversion in urban areas. In order to avoid the split-up of ERDF funds for housing issues among different programmes, overall housing-related expenditure should be limited to 4% (until 2009 only 2%) of total ERDF funds (Cecodhas, 2009). With the opening of the structural funds for housing measures, it has become clear that a need for action in CEE and SEE countries has been declared at the highest political level.

Unlike the traditional grant funding, JESSICA focuses on the support and development of financial engineering instruments in the field of sustainable urban development with the use of equity, guarantees, and subordinated loans. National Structural Funds managing authorities should establish urban development funds (EIB, 2007: 3–8) with grants from the structural funds and loans from the development banks – EIB and CEB. These urban development funds should in turn attract further national contributions, aim to find private capital investors, and invest in selected PPPs or other eligible projects for urban renewal. In addition to a national intermediary between urban development funds and the managing authority, a holding fund may be established. These requirements prove to be difficult to be implemented, worsened by the request to design integrated urban development plans, without being defined clearly.

So far, the implementation of the programme in the EU member states is in progress. But until June 2009 only two JESSICA agreements have been signed for CEE regions, namely the region Wielkopolska in Poland and Lithuania (Regio, 2009). The problems with the implementation of the JESSICA programme are pointed out clearly in the evaluation studies of the two projects: the unclear legal structure of the urban development funds, the weakly defined relationship of the involved institutions, and a lack of well-developed equity markets in CEE regions. Furthermore, the necessity to promote social housing in addition to urban renewal is clearly expressed.

Conclusions

In the light of the current financial crisis, which tightens the possibilities of conventional market financing in the housing sector, the impact of adequate national and international housing finance institutions is even higher. The experience of the last years in CEE and SEE economies shows that all economies try to overcome the gap in the social rental sector by implementing different forms of alternative finance. Housing finance structure has to be improved to be a stable market player in an integrated European housing finance environment. The European Union manifested in the last years its willingness to promote urban regeneration with the set-up of the JESSICA programme. Its real impact cannot be forecast as implementation is still on shaky legal grounds and financial funding has not reached the necessary level. An extension of the programme to social housing construction is urgently recommended. Furthermore, additional housing finance sources from PPPs ('third sector' of social housing finance, as represented here) seem a necessary alternative to the common sources of traditional housing finance.

See also: Cooperative Housing/Ownership; Covered Bonds; Economics of Social Housing; Housing and the State in the Soviet Union and Eastern Europe; Industrial Organisation of the US Residential Mortgage Market; Public-Private Housing Partnerships.

References

Amann W (2005) How to boost the rental housing construction in CEE/SEE countries. *Housing Finance International* 20(2): 24–31.

Boelhouwer P (2003) Social housing finance in the Netherlands: The road to independence. *Housing Finance International* 17(4): 14–21.

Cecodhas (2009) *Housing and the EU Structural Funds in Action.* Bruxelles: Cecodhas – European Social Housing Liaison Committee.

Chiquier L and Lea M (2009) *Housing Finance Policy in Emerging Markets.* Washington, DC: World Bank.

EBRD (2007) *Mortgages in Transition Economies. The Legal Framework for Mortgages and Mortgage Securities.* European Bank for Reconstruction and Development.

EIB (2007) *JESSICA, Preliminary Evaluation Study.* http://www.eib.org/attachments/jessica_preliminary_evaluation_study.pdf

EMF (various issues). *Hypostat.* A Review of Europe's Mortgage and Housing Market, Annual Publication European Mortgage Federation. http://www.hypo.org

Hegedüs J (2009) Towards a new housing system in transitional countries – the case of Hungary. In: Arestis Ph, Mooslechner P, and Wagner K (eds.) *Housing Market Challenges in Europe and the United States – Any Solutions Available?* pp. 178–202. Houndmills: Palgrave MacMillan.

OECD (2005) *Housing Finance Markets in Transition Economies, Trends and Challenges.* Paris: OECD Publishing.

PRC Bouwcentrum International (2005) Sustainable refurbishment of high-rise residential buildings and restructuring of surrounding areas in Europe. *Report for European Housing Ministers' Conference held in Prague.* The Netherlands: PRC, 14–15 March.

Regio DG (2009) *Jessica in Progress.* Brussels, Belgium, 17 June. http://ec.europa.eu/regional_policy/funds/2007/jjj/doc/pdf/jessica/20090617_1_progress.pdf

Springler E and Wagner K (2009) Determinants of homeownership rates: Housing finance and the role of the state. In: Arestis, Mooslechner, and Wagner (eds.) *Housing Market Challenges in Europe and the United States – Any Solutions Available?* pp. 60–84. Palgrave MacMillan.

Tsenkova S (2005) *Trends and Progress in Housing Reforms in South Eastern Europe.* Paris: Council of Europe Development Bank (CEB).

UNECE (2005) *Housing Finance Systems for Countries in Transition, Principles and Examples.* New York, Geneva.

World Bank (2006) *Poland Housing Finance Policy Note.* Washington: World Bank.

Housing Governance

A Beer, University of Adelaide, Adelaide, SA, Australia

© 2012 Elsevier Ltd. All rights reserved.

Glossary

Governance A set of arrangements for the achievement of public sector objectives that explicitly include a range of nongovernment actors.

Governmentality The set of institutions, cultural devices, and mores established and maintained by society to encourage individuals to adhere to social norms.

Residualisation The outcome of increasing the proportion of disadvantaged persons in a system of welfare provision.

Introduction

Governance is a signal feature of contemporary life and the delivery of programmes and services in developed economies, but it is a dimension of housing that has received relatively little explicit attention among housing researchers and policy-makers. The concept of 'governance' stands in contrast to established notions of government, in that it incorporates a broader range of actors in the delivery of social and economic well-being, and generates a diffuse set of relationships and decision-making structures. Governance arrangements, in some respects, reduce the capacity of governments or the state to directly determine outcomes. On the other hand, they open up the potential for a wider range of outcomes that may be more effective in their reach because of the engagement of diverse stakeholders. This article begins by considering the definition of governance before moving on to examine its evolution and expression in developed economies over recent decades. It notes that governance arrangements may differ between nations and systems of government, and considers the ways in which governance has been applied in a number of settings, including urban regeneration projects and the provision of social housing. The article then examines a number of examples of governance arrangements in the housing sphere, before concluding with a discussion of the implications for the future.

Understanding Governance

Over the past two decades, one of the most important shifts in the philosophy of public assistance evident in developed nations has been a shift away from hierarchical forms of government to more porous forms of governance. This transformation has reshaped lifetime experiences of housing in many locations and under a range of policy regimes. The concept of governance lies at the heart of much contemporary theory concerned with the role of the state and the implementation of major housing, urban, and regional programmes. Governance is a challenging concept because while it has been the subject of a great deal of scholarship and research, there is ongoing debate about its definition and even the broad scope of phenomena encompassed by this term. However, while the detail may be open to dispute, research and writing on governance recognises a number of common elements that are taken to be typical of governance arrangements, and these include the shift away from a reliance on the formal structures of government to the incorporation of a wider range of interests in public decision-making and the achievement of public-sector programme objectives. Frequently governance is associated with the rise of partnership arrangements for the delivery of programmes and a reduced ability for governments to directly determine outcomes. Governance, then, is more broadly constituted than conventional public-sector administration and commonly involves a range of government and nongovernment entities working to achieve a mutually agreed set of goals or outcomes.

The rise of governance can be linked to wider shifts in the relationship between the public sector and society. A number of authors have argued that governance structures emerged as part of the broader response to stalling economic conditions in many developed economies in the late 1970s and early 1980s. The reform of national economic management away from Keynesian economics to monetarist approaches resulted in a retreat from direct government intervention in the economy and society, lower rates of personal and business taxation, deregulation of labour and financial markets, and, in some nations, the privatisation of industries and enterprises previously owned by governments. Importantly, public-sector fiscal restraint has resulted in an emphasis on using state funding to 'leverage' private investment and expertise. In return, nongovernment and private sector partners have become integrated into the decision-making and implementation activities of the state. Governance has served both fiscal and ideological objectives: private sector participation in some types of initiatives has reduced direct costs to governments, while in other arenas it has allowed governments to claim efficiencies as a consequence of the involvement of private sector or contracted entities in the delivery of programmes.

Governance takes different forms in different nations. Much of the literature on governance has its origins in nations with unitary systems of government, that is, countries such as New Zealand, the United Kingdom, or France where the national government serves as the focus of state power and may be the sole tier of constitutionally based government authority. Under these circumstances, governance arrangements may be relatively unambiguous as the national government retains a determinant influence and in large measure can shape how and when power is shared, and to what effect. Governance arrangements are commonly more complex in nations with federal systems of government, such as the United States, Canada, Germany, and Australia. Within federal systems, governance is marked by both horizontal links between agents and institutions and vertically defined interactions that may be hierarchical, competitive, or co-operative. Under these circumstances, governance can lead to complex forms of interaction with both positive and negative relationships characterising governance arrangements. Importantly, within both unitary and federal systems of government policy, approaches and initiatives that are ostensibly decentralised often reveal very little true sharing of power and resources. That is, governments continue to exert a dominant controlling influence, even if they are no longer directly involved in the provision of services or supports. Their role as the financier and regulator of service provision maintains their central position in determining the distribution of welfare.

Urban regeneration projects – which may or may not include specific housing objectives – are an example of the types of partnership arrangements that typify governance in the contemporary era (see articles Housing Policy and Regeneration and Housing and Neighbourhood Quality: Urban Regeneration). Commonly urban regeneration projects will take place within a governance framework where responsibility – and risk – is shared across a number of actors. The private sector, for example, may be responsible for the development and marketing of housing and commercial real estate, while one or more tiers of governments furnish land or other facilities in exchange for a commercial return. Local governments may provide additional services in the expectation of achieving social objectives and raising tax revenues, while the not-for-profit sector may be engaged by the project partners to co-ordinate and manage the supply of affordable housing.

The 'roll-out' of governance structures has not been limited to urban regeneration or equivalent programmes. Governments in many nations, including Australia and the United Kingdom, have sought to expand nonstate forms of assisted housing provision and involve private and other nongovernment sources of finance and expertise in the development of subsidised rental housing. For example, the introduction of Housing Benefit in the United Kingdom marked a substantial shift away from the direct subsidy of housing supply to subsidising the consumption of rental housing, with the payment of benefit decoupled from the provision of housing by specific forms of landlords (see article Access and Affordability: Housing Allowances). Housing Benefit became payable to tenants of nonstate landlords, especially housing associations, and also private landlords. Housing associations in the United Kingdom, moreover, increasingly made use of private sector finance for capital development projects, while the availability of private finance was underpinned by a system of public sector subsidies, which was relatively generous and guaranteed the repayment of such loans. In the 30 years post-1945 financial and other assistance with housing was likely to be provided by government agencies but in the contemporary era governance arrangements have, in large measure, replaced those arrangements and created new support arrangements. In all likelihood, that new form of assistance will come with altered terms, conditions, and management practices.

Housing Governance: The Management of Housing and Tenants

As noted previously, the boundaries of the term governance remain open to debate and discussion among both the academic community and practitioners. The term housing governance is frequently employed in two separate, but related, dimensions of housing. In the first, the term governance is often linked to the formal structures and processes of management found among social housing providers. In the second instance, researchers have used governance as a heuristic tool for examining the ways in which the behaviours of tenants or other housing consumers have been managed. Both uses of the term draw implicit and explicit links to the broader literature on the changing role of the state and the rise of new forms of government intervention within the economy and society.

The term housing governance has been used to describe the management structures found within many systems of social housing provision and in particular to draw attention to the shift from direct state provision – council housing in the United Kingdom, public housing in New Zealand and Australia, and municipality housing in Canada – to the use of a broader set of social landlords with legal and fiscal structures that include the public, private, and nongovernment sectors (see article Policy Instruments that Support Housing Supply: Social Housing). It is worth noting that 'governance' structures in this sense arrived relatively late to the housing field. Policy arenas such as urban regeneration and regional development saw the widespread introduction of governance structures some decades before their implementation in the housing sphere. This reflects the intuitively tighter fit between economic development and land use policy and the private sector, and the fact that the development of housing governance was of necessity dependent upon system-wide transformation rather than piecemeal innovation. Pivotal markers of the transformation from the government of housing to housing governance in this sense include the shift in the United Kingdom in the 1980s and 1990s away from council-provided housing, to a reliance on registered social landlords with access to public subsidies. Over a similar period, public housing provision in New Zealand was reduced and corporatised, while central governments in Australia and Canada have reduced, or walked away from, their commitment to state provision of housing. Nations such as China, Singapore, the Czech Republic, and Hungary have also witnessed a comparable transition to housing governance, as the private sector has become a more important feature of their economy and as previous systems for the direct provision of housing have been wound down. In Australia, recent policy development at both the level of the Australian Federal Government and among the six State and two Territory governments has sought to encourage the development of a more broadly constituted social housing sector, akin to Britain's housing associations.

In some respects, the term 'governance' is used by public policy researchers as shorthand to summarise substantial shifts in the way services and public goods are provided. In the housing sphere, this type of governance gives rise to internal governance issues as social housing providers seek to manage their affairs within an environment made more complex by the need to balance competing sectoral interests, a reliance on accountability models borrowed from the private sector, and a potentially complex funding system. The term governance, in this instance, is employed in a more conventional manner to reflect upon systems of management and representation. Several authors have noted that in many nations there are a large number of organisations operating as social housing providers, with some commanding considerable assets and revenues. Critically, some commentators have questioned the accountability of such agencies and suggested that there is a 'governance gap' in that their operations and use of public sector monies are not fully transparent. Work undertaken in the United Kingdom has suggested that there are at least five fundamental concerns in this vein: there is a need to question the honesty and competence of administrations across the sector; such organisations are nominally independent but may be unduly influenced by governments; agencies may develop agendas and objectives that run counter to their original purpose; formal regulatory mechanisms are unduly cumbersome; and there will be a loss of consumer and taxpayer influence over the delivery of services. In Australia, there has been a long-running debate on the governance of Indigenous housing organisations, fuelled in part by the small size and very remote locations of many of these entities. This issue has been brought into focus because some organisations have become bankrupt, while others have not been able to meet demand with respect to both the quality and quantity of accommodation provided.

A key challenge to arise out of the new model of housing governance is the need to reconcile conflicting agendas. Recent investigations have documented the tensions within social housing providers where boards of management represent a range of interests, including tenants, the private sector, management, the representatives of central governments, and independent members. In the United Kingdom, the structure of housing associations may result in the internalisation of tensions that were previously resolved at a policy or programmatic level. Issues such as rent levels, policy on eviction or redevelopment, and growth opportunities must now be decided by independent boards with greater or lesser degrees of expertise and management. There is evidence that in some instances failures of governance at the board level have contributed to the rationalisation of the social housing sector, with organisations either lacking confidence in their capacity to manage their future or recognising gaps in their administrative competence.

One of the ways housing governance has been explored by the research community draws upon the work of the French philosopher and sociologist Michel Foucault. It establishes an explicit link between his writings on 'governmentality' and the regulation of tenant behaviour in social housing. This body of work focuses upon the ways in which the management of social housing is used to enforce social norms on tenants, who may under other circumstances exhibit preferences beyond socially sanctioned expectations. Housing governance in this sense has a long history with Octavia Hill, the social reformer and a leading figure in the development of the social housing sector in the United Kingdom, establishing a system focused on managing both the tenant and the rental property. A central feature of Octavia Hill's approach to housing governance was a weekly visit to the tenant to collect rent, and a number of social landlords across the globe – but not all – maintain the tradition of housing officers visiting tenants on a more or less frequent basis. In the past, housing governance was largely focused on matters directly related to the tenancy: the management of rent arrears, the appropriate maintenance of the dwelling, the need to repair or upgrade the dwelling, and changes in circumstance, including shifts in household composition and employment status.

More recently, commentators and researchers have noted a shift in emphasis to a broader housing governance agenda, with a growing focus on the social control functions of landlords. Measures to address crime and antisocial behaviour have emerged as a major feature of housing governance employed by some social landlords. It is argued that the instruments of housing regulation – tenancy agreements, housing allocation procedures, incentive programmes, tenancy support, and access to enhanced services – are used to ensure conformity in behaviour. As a number of commentators have noted, this shift has taken place within the context of a broader rethinking of the philosophy of government and society. Current social and political discourse places a greater emphasis on personal responsibility rather than the rights of the individual to equitable outcomes. Public debate is focused on social inclusion rather than achieving equivalent outcomes across society. Policies emphasise strengthening education and engagement with the formal labour market, the use of public–private sector partnerships to social and economic objectives, and a commitment to limiting public sector expenditures. Measures that reflect this approach include the termination or suspension of a tenancy because of the complaints of neighbours, the use of leases that are provisional – subject to some period of demonstrated good behaviour, the exclusion of some types of tenants from the more desirable housing stock, and the explicit targeting of antisocial behaviour in social housing estates.

The new paradigm of housing governance encompasses measures to censure unacceptable behaviour as well as provide incentives that reward actions seen to be beneficial to society and the housing provider. For example, the tenant incentive schemes popularised through innovation at the Irwell Valley Housing Association in the United Kingdom enhanced the day-to-day management of the housing stock by encouraging the prompt payment of rent and the upkeep of dwellings while also addressing broader social concerns, including the development of a sense of community. Such schemes have been promoted widely and adopted in various localities around the globe. In other instances, governments have chosen the 'stick' over the 'carrot', looking to implement a range of sanctions that provide social landlords with the capacity to exert greater control over the behaviour of their tenants. In part, this reflects the 'residualisation' of social housing provision: the supply of social housing has not kept pace with need in many nations, and so a growing percentage of tenants are drawn from the most marginalised groups within society, including the homeless, those who were previously incarcerated, persons with a psychological disability, and persons who have lived precarious lives. Overall, the objective has been to create a framework that encourages, supports, and, to a certain degree, requires individuals to act as rational beings with respect to their tenancy while also reducing their reliance on state support.

Conclusions

Housing governance emerged in many nations in association with broader changes in the ways governments seek to assist low-income and vulnerable households with their housing. These new models of support have created new challenges for the effective delivery of housing assistance, but to date there has been relatively little attention directed to this set of issues. It is clear that the evolution of new structures of governance – public sector–private sector partnerships, nongovernment agencies for the delivery of services, and so on – has been paralleled by a new agenda of governance actions, especially the regulation of tenant behaviour. Issues of housing governance warrant more explicit attention in order to advance our knowledge of the sector and manage the housing stock more equitably and efficiently.

See also: Access and Affordability: Housing Allowances; Foucauldian Analysis; Housing and Neighbourhood Quality: Urban Regeneration; Housing and the State in Australasia; Housing and the State in China; Housing and the State in the Soviet Union and Eastern Europe; Housing and the State in Western Europe; Housing Policy and Regeneration; Policy Instruments that Support Housing Supply: Social Housing; Social Housing Landlords: Asia Pacific; Social Housing Landlords: Europe; Social Housing Landlords: North America.

Further Reading

Bradley Q (2008) Capturing the castle: Tenant governance in social housing companies. *Housing Studies* 23(6): 879–897.

Clapham D and Kintrea K (2000) Community based housing organisations and the local governance debate. *Housing Studies* 15(4): 533–559.

Flint J (2002) Social housing agencies and the governance of anti social behaviour. *Housing Studies* 17(4): 619–637.

Flint J (2003) Housing and ethopolitics: Constructing identities of active consumption and responsible community. *Economy and Society* 32(3): 611–629.

Flint J (2004) Reconfiguring agency and responsibility in the governance of social housing in Scotland. *Urban Studies* 41(1): 151–172.

Relevant Websites

www.ahuri.edu.au – Australian Housing and Urban Research Institute.

www.irwellvalleyha.co.uk – Irwell Valley Housing Association.

www.octaviahill.org – Octavia Hill.

Housing Indicators

J Flood, AHURI-RMIT, Melbourne, VIC, Australia

© 2012 Elsevier Ltd. All rights reserved.

Glossary

Benchmarking A methodology for improving organisational performance in which performance indicators are developed, similar organisations are found that perform better on these indicators, and the good practices which result in outstanding performance are copied.

Holistic approach Taking a comprehensive view of some area of social policy, rather than focusing on one or two key issues that are currently in the public eye.

Indicator A single item of data which is tied to a policy goal and points the way to 'improvement' according to some norm.

Monitoring Reporting to stakeholders on progress towards meeting organisational objectives; often using indicators.

Norm A judgement by one or more groups of stakeholders as to what constitutes better outcomes or a better situation in some area of social policy. Different stakeholders may have opposing norms.

Performance indicators Indicators adopted by organisations for reporting.

Stakeholder Anyone with a vested interest in the performance of an organisation.

What Are Indicators?

Indicators are small 'models' simplifying a complex subject to a few numbers which can be easily grasped and understood by policy-makers and the general public. They are generally highly aggregated and consist of ratios so that they are normalised in some fashion. They should be policy- and stakeholder-driven so that each indicator has one or more associated objectives and is valuable to some significant group of stakeholders.

Some of the characteristics of good indicators are that they should be (1) important, (2) measurable, (3) responsive, (4) simple and robust, (5) timely, (6) stakeholder-driven, (7) action-oriented, and (8) informative. The characteristics of a good indicator 'system' are that it should (1) cover the most important issues, (2) represent the interests of all stakeholders, and (3) be structured in a modular, logical manner. A well-structured system will also show linkages – different indicators may reinforce each other to give a picture of the overall effectiveness of a tightly linked system such as a housing market.

The major groups of stakeholders who may benefit from the use of indicators are as follows:

Governments: Governments most commonly use indicators as part of prescriptive reporting structures, or integrated within strategy documents or national sectoral reports. Most housing strategy documents are structured around examples of indicators as measures of conditions or of past successes and failures, and improvements resulting from such strategies are generally anticipated in terms of indicators. Spatial indicators of need may also be used to distribute funding for infrastructure or social housing.

Private sector: The private sector (builders, developers, and real estate agents) needs timely information for investment and sales purposes, concerning economic conditions in cities, government performance, supply/demand imbalances, and the consumption requirements of residents. Consequently, organisations representing private sector interests are often involved in presenting national housing data series, particularly those relating to prices and market conditions. These are also used in the role of advocacy on behalf of their constituents.

In some cases, private organisations have become important suppliers of housing data, particularly relating to prices. For example, Fiserv Pty Ltd owns and maintains the S&P/Case-Shiller US National Home Price Index, and Standard and Poor's disseminates the results. Data analysis firms in most countries provide advice and reports on real estate and investment conditions in national and local markets.

'Nongovernment and community organisations' are the major users of indicators in their advocacy and lobbying role, in submitting funding proposals, and, particularly, because through indicators they can monitor the performance of governments. In the sustainability area, not-for-profit organisations have taken on the major role in publishing indicators of community well-being including housing indicators (see Relevant Websites).

The 'public, media, and tenants of housing organisations' may be informed by indicators of the efficient and equitable performance of markets and satisfactory management of housing policy and administration.

History of Housing Indicators

From the time of Biderman (1966) and Sheldon and Moore (1968), indicators have been nominated as a means by which progress towards a whole system of social goals could be measured. The importance of indicators to housing policy has also been recognised for a long time, and fairly extensive bibliographies of early contributions in the field have been produced (Horowitz, 1980, 1986). Generally, these contributions were related to particular parts of housing policy, such as housing needs or housing and neighbourhood quality (Goedert and Goodman, 1977; Ingels, 1980; US Bureau of the Census, 1976) rather than to the housing sector as a whole.

The United Nations took an interest in shelter and its adequacy from the early 1960s (UNSD, 1993; UNSO, 1962), and in the 1970s, the UN Ad Hoc Group of Experts on Social Indicators for Housing and Urban Development (UN, 1973) sustained this concern.

From the late 1970s, there was a massive surge in urbanisation in the developing world, resulting in burgeoning slum or shanty populations surrounding most cities. In the late 1980s, there was a resurgence of interest in monitoring and indicators as it became apparent that sectoral, government-based approaches to solving urban and housing problems had not worked in the developing world and that a multisector, enabling strategy was the preferred approach to achieving improvements (World Bank, 1993). This was underlined by a rapidly emerging interest in sustainability issues, which stressed the interrelatedness of all aspects of human activity with the natural environment.

The Housing and Urban Indicators Programme

Following the International Year of Shelter for the Homeless, in 1988, the Global Shelter Strategy to the Year 2000 was adopted. This strategy was influenced by market liberal economies, and called for a fundamental shift in government policy away from the direct provision of housing towards an enabling legislative and regulatory environment which 'facilitates, energises, and supports the activities of the private sector'. In 1989, the United Nations Centre for Human Settlements (now UN-HABITAT) was requested to provide cost-effective national monitoring of progress towards realising the goals of the Strategy.

In October 1990, the World Bank and UNCHS (now UN-HABITAT) jointly initiated the Housing Indicators Programme (HIP), which was funded and supported by USAID. The methodology and the indicators were largely the brainchild of Dr Steven Mayo, a principal economist with the World Bank, and Dr Schlomo Angel, an Israeli expert on slums and urban development. The indicators had a macroeconomic emphasis and some of the indicators were novel and original. The pilot programme resulted in a detailed comparison of the housing sectors in major cities in 52 countries, through the collection of about 40 key indicators on a comparable basis (World Bank/UNCHS, 1991). The final results of the original HIP were not published until after the untimely death of Mayo (Angel, 2004) (see Relevant Websites and the 1996 and 2001 values are available from the author).

Subsequently, 10 of these housing indicators were collected globally as part of a much more comprehensive urban indicators system in the run up to the Habitat II conference in Istanbul in 1996, and again in 2001, along with tenure data. In this case, data for 237 cities were collected which were sufficient for a global sample and analysis (Flood, 1997; UNCHS, 1997; UN-HABITAT, 2002).

The long-term aim of the Programme was ambitious: to engage countries in a lasting process which would place housing issues on the national policy agenda. The major original contribution of the Programme was not just an innovative indicators set but a whole new philosophy about the way data should be used in organisations. Indicators were to be developed and prioritised through participative stakeholder consultations (Flood, 1993), they were to be a holistic collection measuring the health of a whole sector, and every indicator should have an objective and strategy associated with it. They were to be maintained within operational departments or special-purpose monitoring groups and should not reside or be under the control of central statistical agencies. The statistics were also to be collected at the city level – which had not previously been attempted.

One of the main purposes of the housing indicators was to establish a set of diagnostics for a 'well-functioning housing market' and the indicators were chosen with this in mind. For example, various indicators might show a market in which land was being inadequately supplied, resulting in housing shortages and high prices. Deviations from standard benchmarks might show the presence of market-distorting policies like rent control.

It cannot be overstated the effect that the Housing Indicators movement had on thinking about housing policy in the developing world, although its 'soft' market-oriented philosophy was rarely adopted. Some of the indicators, most notably the median house price-to-income ratio (see Relevant Websites), have been accepted globally and by many agencies and are still at the centre of considerable controversy. Separate HIPs were conducted in the early 1990s in a number of countries in the Caribbean, Southern Africa, and Eastern Europe (see Hegedus and Tosics, 1993; Ministry of Public

Construction and National Housing, Zimbabwe, 1990), generally funded by USAID, as part of an attempt to vitalise or revive the housing sectors of those countries.

Aftermath

In general, the housing indicators were well received. The main criticisms were in keeping with the origins of the system – that they referred largely to the economic part of the economic–social environmental nexus, and had little distributional or environmental content. Data issues and the costs of data verification remained a major obstacle. Flood (1997) concluded that "The housing indicators have been less well understood than the other (urban) indicators, partly because they represent data that are not commonly collected, and partly because they represent complex concepts or have difficult collection methods".

To change institutions is a harder task than collecting indicators, and the funds or political will to do this were never really there. Ultimately, the 'enabling approach' appealed neither to the growing sustainability movement nor to the economic right. After 15 years of promotion through the Global Urban Observatory movement, the strategic emphasis on a holistic, sectoral approach and on participative development of indicators through stakeholder meetings has not been widely adopted, although particular indicators retain a considerable following.

The main follow-up to the Habitat Agenda in 1996 was to construct a network of National and Local Urban Observatories who were tasked with collecting key urban and housing indicators and making sure they were applied to policy. This was to be coordinated by the Global Urban Observatory located in Nairobi. This still exists with limited support, and a few local observatories are active (Vancouver, Barcelona, Jeddah, Medina, and Tehran), though none have a housing focus. Within UN-HABITAT after 2003, most effort has gone towards collecting the Millennium Indicators, http://mdgs.un.org/unsd/mdg, through national statistical bodies rather than collecting key indicators through operational departments.

Several of the original supporters of the HIP, most notably the National Association of Realtors and the Canada Mortgage and Housing Corporation, have continued to be independently active in the indicators area.

The most lasting legacy of the HIP has probably been Indicator H1, the Median House Price to Income Ratio, which has become the primary indicator of the general health and efficiency of housing and land markets (HJCHS, 2009; Wilcox, 2003, and many other sources).

Mainstreaming Housing Indicators

The emphasis after 1995 was less about maintaining whole systems of housing indicators to measure the health of the sector – which in practice rarely had a champion agency within national governments – and was more directed towards including indicators of performance within policy documents and as part of government reporting. By the mid-1990s, most annual reports of government agencies were required to include indicators of performance.

However, the laissez-faire 1990s were anti-planning even within a market liberal framework: the role of government was to be as a regulator rather than a guiding hand. Even monitoring was discontinued in many housing markets, as specialist departments of housing tended to disappear, retaining only a narrow residual role within much larger social security ministries. Much of the effort in collecting and maintaining housing market indicators devolved to the private sector and to sustainability organisations.

The world paid the price for this lack of attention to housing markets and for leaving monitoring largely to partisan delivery agencies or lobbying groups in October 2007, when the subprime mortgage crisis precipitated the largest economic downturn since the Great Depression. Closer monitoring of the health of overstressed housing markets using indicators might have prompted policy action to take the pressure off prices in the worst-affected areas, and to improve accountability and obtain better compliance with prudential norms.

Housing Indicators

Housing and Urban Indicators Programme

The 10 housing indicators that were collected for Habitat II in 1996 and Istanbul+5 in 2001, for approximately 235 cities around the world on each occasion, were:

H1: House price to income ratio – Median house price/median household income; a primary indicator of the health of housing markets.

H2: House rent to income ratio – Median rent/median income of renters. Less than 20% usually means that rent control is in place.

H3: Floor area per person – Consumption indicator, highly correlated with GDP or city product.

H4: Permanent structures – Per cent structures of permanent materials; measures the very poorest communities.

H5: Unauthorised housing – Per cent stock 'not in compliance' with current regulations; establishes the strength of the informal sector.

H6: Land development multiplier – Ratio of median land price of a developed plot at the urban fringe and the median price of raw, undeveloped land; potentially useful, but hard to measure consistently.

H7: Infrastructure expenditure – Total annual expenditures on infrastructure services per person; a community wealth measure.

Table 1 Mean value of the 10 key housing indicators, by development quintile, Habitat II collection, 1996

	Very low	Low	Medium	Higher	Developed
H1. Price to income	6.6	8.1	8.8	8.3	4.7
H2. Rent to income (%)	29.1	28.2	15.4	11.7	18.0
H3. Floor area per person (sq m)	7.3	8.0	13.2	17.3	31.4
H4. Permanent dwellings (%)	46.9	77.9	78.8	91.7	95.6
H5. Dwellings in compliance (%)	42.5	52.5	72.9	85.5	96.2
H6. Land development multiplier	5.1	4.9	3.9	4.6	5.3
H7. Infrastructure expenditure per capita ($)	16	15	48	136	421
H8. Mortgage to credit ratio (%)	5.9	7.1	12.0	20.3	27.1
H9. Dwelling production per 1000 population	4.7	6.0	8.5	5.6	4.8
H10. Housing investment ratio (%)	7.7	12.2	6.2	5.1	3.2

The development level of cities was defined using the City Development Index, which is described in Flood (1997).
Source: Flood J (1997) Urban and housing indicators. *Urban Studies* 34(10): 1665–1667; Tables 13 and 14.

H8: Mortgage to credit ratio – Ratio of mortgage loans to all loans; can only be measured at the national level. Over 25% in developed countries, almost negligible elsewhere.

H9: Housing production – Net number of housing units produced per 1000 population. A major measure of boom/bust or vigour of the sector; usually unknown when informal sector is large.

H10: Housing investment – Investment in housing/gross city product; measures importance of housing in the local economy and is difficult to calculate.

Table 1 shows the 1996 averages for these indicators over cities of different levels of development. Indicators H3, H4, H5, H7, and H8 increase with the level of development, as they represent increased consumption, improved dwelling quality, and more developed mortgage systems. House prices are highest with respect to income at middle levels of development – probably because formal sector construction standards are enforced before incomes have risen sufficiently to justify them. Rents H2 fall with development until the final quintile. The construction indicators H9 and H10 are correlated with rates of urban household formation.

Other Indicators

Several other indicators from the extended housing indicator system are widely used in OECD countries.

HA1. Mortgage affordability – Proportion of households who are eligible for and can afford the maximum loan on a median-priced formal sector house.

HA2. Excessive housing expenditure – Proportion of households in the bottom 40% of incomes who are spending more than 30% of their incomes on housing; known as 'core housing need' in Canada and 'housing stress' in Australia.

HA6. Overcrowding – Households with too few bedrooms.

HA8. Inadequate housing – Requiring substantial repairs to bring them to accepted standards.

HA11. Homelessness – Number of people per thousand who sleep outside dwelling units or in temporary shelter.

Other housing indicators and statistics that are frequently cited include:

Supply: Prices, stock turnover, second homes, building approvals and completions, and supply of unsold homes.

Affordability: Proportion able to afford median home.

Housing gap: Shortfall in supply of affordable housing. Usually rhetorical rather than numeric.

Mortgage finance: Mortgage applications, mortgage approvals, interest rates, foreclosures, and equity withdrawal.

Rental: Yields and returns, vacancy rates, and rental distributions.

Public housing: Length of waiting lists, subsidies, occupancy, match with client needs, and special needs.

Consumer: Report cards, indexes of satisfaction, and security for the public and for public tenants.

Other Systems

There are a number of standard systems or frameworks for classifying and organising indicators, which can be useful in reducing the amorphousness of metrics established through stakeholder consultations. For environmental indicators, these include the Extended Urban Metabolism system for urban sustainability (Newton et al., 1998), and for organisational performance indicators, outcome-based management (Hatry, 2007). By and large, these classifications do not work very well for housing indicators, since many of these are prices and macroeconomic measures which can adopt different roles depending on the context.

Statistical Publications

A number of statistical investigations of the condition of housing and housing markets in various countries have been undertaken (Canada HRSD, 2009; CSO Ireland, 2008). These frequently use indicators as part of the exposition, and in some cases have led to indicator systems being developed (DETR, 1997, 1998).

Performance Indicators

In Britain, the Netherlands, Scandinavia, and other parts of Europe, the move away from public and council housing towards housing associations has strongly encouraged the development of performance indicators. There is now a very substantial literature in the area (Clapham and Satsangi, 1992; Smith and Walker, 1994). The British literature demonstrates the move away from prescriptive central programme indicators to a more community-based approach with no central monitoring.

In 1993, the Australian government laid down a common framework for performance indicator reporting across all departments. It took some years before the public housing indicators selected to fit this external framework settled into the system currently used (AIHW 2009; see Burke and Hayward, 2000; Urban Resources and SGS, 1999, for critiques).

Benchmarking

In benchmarking, workers in organisations examine their internal processes to try to improve effectiveness, establish benchmark indicators for performance, find other organisations that perform better or have good practice, and adopt their methods and internal organisation. This seems to have been very rarely done for housing delivery organisations, and it is an area where considerable improvements could be achieved in construction, service delivery, asset management, financial monitoring, and other aspects of organisational processes (Flood, 1999).

Use and Abuse – Indicator Controversies

Indicators form one important input to the policy process, but only one input of many that will lead to the usual negotiated process of policy setting. Even if there is a good connection between a specific policy instrument and an indicator, there are normally other policy actions that will influence significantly a particular outcome measured by one indicator. The multidimensional nature of most policies is significant, and it is unlikely in most cases that a single indicator will express every desired outcome of a particular policy.

Some people may assume that because an indicator is established and shows a positive result or improvement, then no more needs to be done. Others may disguise bad outcomes by quoting indicators which are not really relevant, while other important indicators which do not show a positive result are conveniently forgotten.

In a few cases, different indicators can be associated with very different policy approaches or can be associated with contradictions in political thinking. Once an indicator gains a life of its own, it may be subject to attack or denigrated by stakeholders who have a vested interest in ensuring no action is taken.

These general principles can be demonstrated through several topical examples.

Affordability Indicators

Housing markets are particularly vulnerable to 'bubble behaviour' and policy confusion, since correcting a bulge in one part of the market tends to create pressure or undesirable outcomes in others. All governments would like house prices to be both low and rising, which cannot continue. Everyone agrees that affordable housing is a good thing, but governments will frequently take action to support high house prices.

Three different groups of stakeholders have conflicting interests in housing affordability – developers who want controls and levies removed and house prices lowered, real estate agents who want rapid turnover and rising prices, and environmentalists who want cities to stop expanding. Preventing the expansion of cities has environmental and cost advantages in limiting 'sprawl', but in a growing market, it will invariably cause a substantial upward revision in price and greater congestion costs.

These different objectives are generally expressed through different indicators which will suggest different policy responses. For example, H1, the median house price-to-income ratio is regarded as a primary measure of affordability which should be kept below the value of 3. However, following financial deregulation in the early 1980s, the indicator began to run substantially higher than this, and again in the period after 1996, it ran to extremely high levels, over 6 in a number of countries, particularly in Ireland, Spain, and Australia which were exposed to boom conditions (Performance Urban Planning, 2009).

However, if alternative measures of affordability such as HA1 or HA2 above are used, the problem appears to go away. HA2 appears to show that interest rates should be kept low, while HA1 encourages the removal of prudential constraints on lending. Frequent citation of HA2 has prevented governments from increasing interest rates to keep a lid on house prices.

Even the very widely used indicator HA2 has been subject to an extensive measurement controversy. The indicator as stated always shows higher levels of housing stress in small households (who naturally devote a higher proportion of their income to housing), and as well it is not comparable between income groups. It is generally agreed that 'residual income' after housing is a better and more comparable measure of the stress caused by high housing expenditure.

In the end, there is no escaping the reality that high house prices are bad for the economy and for intergenerational equity, and that in the very long term they are caused by limiting urban expansion (Angel, 2004).

The Slum Indicator

The only housing indicator included in the United Nations Millennium Development Goals was "7.10. Proportion of people living in slums". While this referred to the extremely important concept of delineating areas of social deprivation and poor housing, the term 'slum' had not been included in official housing documents since the 1920s, except in India, mostly because it was regarded as impossible to define or measure. However, the notion of slums had substantial political and emotive power for advocacy, and these political advantages ultimately led to the reintroduction of the term (UN-HABITAT, 2003, 2005).

It was clear that the concept was multidimensional and very difficult to measure objectively. After several unsuccessful attempts at a definition, UN-HABITAT took a dwelling to be a slum if it had any one of the following: (1) lack of access to improved water supply; (2) lack of access to improved sanitation; (3) overcrowding (three or more persons per room); and (4) dwellings made of nondurable materials. In practice, the only information widely available at the household level was water and sanitation, and the slum indicator ended up as a proxy for either of these – which somewhat defeated the original intention.

Conclusions

The original aim of the World Bank/UN-HABITAT housing indicators – to provide an overall diagnostic tool for looking at the effectiveness of the whole housing system – has rarely been emulated except perhaps in medical diagnosis, which was frequently used as an analogy.

The Indicators Programme succeeded in its aims of espousing an enabling market-oriented approach to housing through much of the developing world. Like many indicators activities, it was not so successful in maintaining a sustained collection within policy departments, or in gaining a widespread appreciation of the use of the indicators for diagnostic purposes. It was not until the Global Financial Crisis that some of the key indicators began to be used for this purpose on a global scale – and mostly in the developed countries.

A number of community-based indicators projects have made wide use of other housing indicators covering issues of equity and sustainability. There has been insufficient use of indicators for benchmarking the performance of housing organisations and using these in adopting best practice.

There is room for an expanded system of National and Local Observatories that can maintain housing and urban indicators and push forward with educating policymakers in their use.

See also: Housing Statistics.

References

Angel S (2004) *Housing Policy Matter: A Global Analysis*. Oxford, UK: Oxford University Press.
Australian Institute of Health Welfare (AIHW) (2009) *Public Rental Housing 2007–08*. Canberra: AIHW.
Biderman AD (1966) Social indicators and goals. In: Bauer RA (ed.) *Social Indicators*, pp. 68–153. Cambridge, MA: MIT Press.
Burke T and Hayward D (2000) Performance Indicators and Social Housing in Australia. http://researchbank.swinburne.edu.au (accessed 18 June 2011)
Canada Human Resources and Skills Development (Canada HRSD) (2009) *Indicators of Well Being in Canada: Housing*. http://www4.hrsdc.gc.ca/d.4m.1.3n@-eng.jsp?did=7
Central Statistical Office Ireland (2008. Construction and Housing in Ireland 2008 Edition. Dublin: Stationery Office.
Clapham D and Satsangi M (1992) Performance measurement and accountability in British housing management. *Policy and Politics* 20(10): 63–74.
Department of the Environment, Transport the Regions (DETR) (1997) *Housing in England 1995/6*. London: DETR.
Department of the Environment, Transport the Regions (DETR) (1998) *Developing a System of Housing Quality Indicators*. DEGW Consulting. London: DETR.
Flood J (1993) Housing indicators in Australia: A consultative method. *Netherlands Journal of Housing and the Built Environment* 8(1): 95–124.
Flood J (1997) Urban and housing indicators. *Urban Studies* 34(10): 1665–1667.
Flood J and Spiller Gibbins Swan (SGS) (1999) Methodology for developing benchmarking for housing outcomes. *AHRF 208, Final Report*. Nairobi: UNCHS-HABITAT.
Goedert JE and Goodman JL, Jr. (1977) *Indicators of the Quality of US Housing*. Washington, DC: Urban Institute.
Harvard Joint Centre for Housing Studies (HJCHS) (2009) *The State of the Nation's Housing 2009*. Cambridge, MA: Harvard University.
Hatry H (2007) *Performance Measurement, Getting Results*, 2nd edn. Washington, DC: Urban Institute.
Hegedus J and Tosics I (1993) Housing indicators in transitional economies: A new tool for policy making: The Hungarian housing indicators program intensive survey. *Netherlands Journal of Housing and the Built Environment* 8(1): 85–94.
Horowitz CF (1980) *Housing Indicators and Housing Policy*. Monticello, IL: Vance Bibliographies.
Horowitz CF (1986) *Housing Indicators and Public Policy*, 2nd ed. Monticello, IL: Vance Bibliographies.

Ingels M (1980) *Housing Data Resources: Indicators and Sources of Data for Analyzing Housing and Neighborhood Conditions.* Washington, DC: Bureau of the Census.

Ministry of Public Construction and National Housing, Zimbabwe (1990) *Monitoring of the Shelter Sector Performance Using the Shelter Indicator Methodology.* Zimbabwe: MPCNH.

Newton P, Flood J, Berry M, et al. (1998) *Environmental Indicators for National State of the Environment Reporting. Human Settlements.* Canberra, ACT: Department of the Environment.

Performance Urban Planning (2009) *5th Annual Demographia International Housing Affordability Survey.* http://www.demographia.com/dhi.pdf (accessed 18 June 2011)

Sheldon EB and Moore WE (1968) *Indicators of Social Change: Concepts and Measurement.* New York: Russell Sage Foundation.

Smith R and Walker R (1994) The role of performance indicators in housing management: a critique. *Environment and Planning A* 26(4): 609–621.

United Nations. Ad Hoc Group of Experts on Social Indicators for Housing and Urban Development (1973) Social Indicators for Housing and Urban Development. Dublin: UN.

United Nations Centre for Human Settlements (UNCHS) (1997) Indicators Programme 1994–96. Programme activities. Analysis of the data collection. *Report to Commission for Human Settlements.* Canberra: AHRF.

UN-HABITAT (2002) *State of the World's Cities Report 2002.* Nairobi: UN-HABITAT.

UN-HABITAT (2003) *The Challenge of Slums: Global Report on Human Settlements 2003.* London: Earthscan.

UN-HABITAT (2005) *State of the World's Cities Report 2004/5.* London: Earthscan.

United States, Bureau of the Census (1976) *Financial characteristics by indicators of housing and neighborhood quality.* Washington, DC: US Bureau of the Census.

United Nations. Statistical Division (1993) *Housing in the World: Graphical Presentation of Statistical Data.* New York: UN.

United Nations Statistical Office (1962) *Statistical Indicators of Housing Conditions.* New York: United Nations.

Urban Resources and Spiller Gibbins Swan (1999) Methodology for Developing Benchmarking for Housing Outcomes. AHRF 208, Final Report, April 1999.

Wilcox S (2003) *Can Work Can't Buy.* York, UK: Joseph Rowntree Foundation.

World Bank (1993) *Housing: Enabling Markets to Work.* Washington, DC: World Bank.

World Bank/UNCHS (1991–1993) *The Housing Indicators Program, Vol. 1: Report of the Executive Director, Vol. II: Indicator Tables, Vol. III: Preliminary Findings, Vol. IV: The Extensive Survey Instrument.* Washington, DC: World Bank/UNCHS.

Further Reading

Demographia (2010) *6th Annual Demographia Internationl Housing Affordability Survey.* http://www.demographia.com

United Nations Centre for Human Settlements (UNCHS-HABITAT) (1995) *Monitoring Human Settlements: Abridged Survey.* Indicators Programme. Nairobi: UNCHS.

Relevant Websites

www2.standardandpoors.com – Benchmarks, research, data, and analytics.

www.manhattan-institute.org – Manhattan Institute.

www.mortgageguideuk.co.uk – Mortgage guide UK.

www.realtor.org/research/research/ecoindicator – National Association of Realtors.

http://soer.justice.tas.gov.au/2003/indicator – State of the Environment Tasmania.

www.sustainablemeasures.com/Database/Housing.html – Sustainable Measures. Links to a number of community-based housing indicators.

www.un.org/esa/dsd/index.shtml – UN Commission on Sustainable Development.

ww2.unhabitat.org/programmes/guo/ – United Nations Human Settlements.

http://mdgs.un.org/unsd/mdg – United Nations Statistical Division. Millennium Development Goals Indicators.

www.bus.wisc.edu/realestate/documents/inthsg2.xls – Wisconsin Real Estate Programme. The values of the original housing indicators collected for the 1993 pilot.

Housing Institutions in Developing Countries

A Pal, Erasmus University, Rotterdam, The Netherlands
W Van Vliet, University of Colorado, Boulder, CO, USA

© 2012 Elsevier Ltd. All rights reserved.

Glossary

Developing countries Countries characterised by a comparatively low GNP per capita and with large proportions of the population living in poverty, generally located in the southern hemisphere.

Freehold title A form of ownership right that gives the holder full ownership of the land and buildings on it for an indefinite time period.

Microfinance The provision of financial services in the form of loans of very small amounts to low-income clients, including consumers and the self-employed, who traditionally lack access to banking and related services.

Mortgage The transfer of an interest in property to a lender as a security for a debt – usually a loan of money.

Participatory budgeting A process of democratic deliberation and decision-making, in which ordinary residents decide how to allocate part of a municipal or public budget.

Property rights A bundle of rights accompanying a given property (e.g., use rights, transfer rights, rights to subdivide), owned by multiple parties.

Property tax The tax imposed usually by municipalities on the owners of property within their jurisdiction based on the value of such property.

Security of tenure A constitutional or legal guarantee that a resident cannot be removed from his or her housing except in exceptional and specified circumstances.

Zoning A device of land-use regulation used by local governments that designates permitted uses of land based on mapped zones, which separate one set of land uses from another.

Introduction

What do we understand by housing institutions? A more conventional understanding is that of a social organisation supporting the specific housing and housing-related needs of society. Such a conception excludes those who emphasise the need to see institutions more broadly as the norms, rules, and regulations, that is, the entire body of mechanisms and structures of social order and cooperation that govern the behaviour of a set of individuals. In such a view, housing institutions can be seen as the set of norms and rules that govern the process of fulfilling a society's need for adequate housing. For the purpose of this article, we have defined housing institutions according to the conception that housing supply and housing needs, not just market demand, are viewed as a result of the complex interactions of these various factors.

This article is about how people access housing in developing countries (either for their own use or as investments with an eye on future returns). Here, access refers not just to acquiring the physical asset, but it also includes its maintenance, services (water, sanitation, access roads), regulations (to prevent externalities), tenure security (for preventing eviction), and finance for the actual creation of the asset and also for purchasing or renting it. Housing provision therefore runs from finance through land development, design and construction, and maintenance to management. All these activities can occur through a combination of more or less formal processes. (It is important to emphasise that informal is not necessarily illegal.) Since all this happens not in isolation but within a social, economic, political, cultural, and legal context, some of the dimensions of access to housing have been institutionalised over time into more permanent norms and rules implemented with varying degrees of formality by agencies or organisations of the state, market, or civil society. This article describes those institutions through which people in developing countries come to access housing.

How Are Housing Institutions in Developing Countries Different?

Housing institutions that cater to the needs of the middle- and higher-income groups in the developing countries are not very different from those in more developed countries. Private developers, banks offering mortgages, and planning and regulatory institutions, for instance, do not differ much from their counterparts in western and northern countries. Differences arise mainly in the forms of housing institutions that serve the poor in these countries.

1. Most cities in the developing countries have a large population living in high-poverty areas, often called slums. This is an indication of the failure of many of the formal institutions to make housing available to the people. Formal institutions may meet market demand, as expressed by those households able to generate financial gain for profit-oriented suppliers through their ability to pay. However, those who cannot translate their housing needs into an effective market demand fall by the wayside. Although homelessness and inadequate or unaffordable housing are not unique to cities in developing countries, the nature and extent of the problem makes the tasks of the housing institutions for the poor significantly more challenging in the developing countries.

2. There is a general lack of technical and financial capacities among state housing actors in developing countries. Unlike, for example, Western Europe, North America, or Australia, availability of state subsidies for housing the urban poor is limited in developing countries. The private and civil society sectors seek to address this gap in state capacity. In most developing countries, the formal markets for land, housing, or housing finance cater to a relatively affluent minority of its urban households. The urban poor often access housing through an informal market, using a variety of strategies that include, for example, squatting on someone else's land and constructing housing in violation of zoning or building regulations. In addition, civil society organisations, such as nongovernmental organisations (NGOs), religious, youth, or women's groups, or other community-based organisations (CBOs) play an important role in providing access to housing for the poor.

3. Informality and the lack of clarity make housing difficult to access for the urban poor. Informal institutions for housing provision are more common in cities of the developing countries. Often, a significant number of households in these cities access housing and its components, such as access to water and sanitation, from the informal market. Much of their housing stock does not conform to formal regulations, which are either remnants of old colonial regulations or overly ambitious, often set to unrealistically high construction standards and insensitive to real community needs.

Diversity in Housing Institutions in the Developing World

The institutions vary in their form on the basis of their historic paths and their political, social, economic, and cultural contexts. For instance, institutions that govern urban land rights in China are based on socialist principles of state ownership, but recent efforts towards market reforms have put pressure on them to evolve. In the current property rights regime in urban China, use rights for specified periods (40–70 years) can be obtained from the state through the upfront payment of land-use fees. These fees are determined by the location, type, and density of the proposed development. This separation of landownership and use rights allows the trading of land-use rights while maintaining state ownership of land. For the Chinese government, this separation offers three advantages: first, market mechanisms can help guide the allocation of land resources; second, land-use fees provide local government with a new source of revenues; and, third, by retaining state ownership, social and political conflict is minimised (Ding and Knaap, 2003). Such a system has very little in common with the institutions that govern property rights in postcolonial Kenya, where traditional forms of collective ownership coexist with the private freehold system inherited from British colonial rule.

Housing institutions also vary between cities within the same country or even within the same city, according to income, religious, ethnic, linguistic, or other categories. For instance, institutions through which Mumbai's slum dwellers (Appadurai, 2001) access housing finance (in the form of loans from a community credit and savings scheme, as part of an international fund, described later) are very different from the mortgage products available through formal commercial banks to middle- and higher-income residents of the same city.

Two dimensions categorise the wide variety of housing institutions in developing countries. One is based on the categories of actors (state, market, or civil society) that help shape access to housing. The other dimension relates to the components that together make up the process of housing provision. **Table 1** shows the variety of housing institutions on the basis of this categorisation.

What follows below is a broad overview of each of the three main housing actors as related to their roles in each of the four components of the process of housing provision.

Public Sector Institutions

Housing is not just a market commodity but also part of a basket of basic needs for all. The provision of housing is often an enormous economic activity for any nation, with significant effects on the wider economy. These characteristics have made a strong case for a significant role of state actors at the national, regional, and local levels in shaping demand and supply of housing.

The role of state institutions cuts across all four components of the housing process. The state plays important

Table 1 Housing actors and their roles in different components of the housing process

Housing process components	Housing actors			
	State	*Market*	*Civil society*	
Land	Land administration, agencies maintaining cadastres, and development authorities responsible for land acquisitions	Land developers, and formal and informal land markets	Land-related NGOs and CBOs	
Finance	Subsidies, property tax office, central bank, grants, budgeting, and budgetary institutions	Financial institutions such as mortgage companies, MFIs, and banks	Community-managed savings and credit schemes, charity, microfinance NGOs, and community budgeting	
Construction/ maintenance/ management	Municipal housing associations, state developer, and development authorities	Developers, promoters, construction companies, and condominium management companies	Nonprofit housing associations, housing cooperatives, condominium associations, and homeowners' associations	
Policy and regulatory framework	Planning agencies, planning laws, zoning building by-laws, courts, constitution, and financial regulations	Condominium contracts, private contracts, and agreements between parties	Rights and responsibilities relating to housing	

roles in land administration, for example, maintaining cadastral information, capturing land-value appreciation through property taxation, regulating land and housing markets through zoning and land-use restrictions, and managing institutions that increase supply of land, such as land banks. Institutions for land-use planning, zoning, and taxation all play important roles in shaping housing delivery and maintenance of housing stock. The laws and regulations that relate to human settlements also have significant effects on housing in developing countries. These laws and regulations can have positive and negative consequences for urban residents (Fernandes and Varley, 1998). The public sector is predominant in some parts of the housing provision process, for example, land administration. In many developing countries, it has been very difficult to reconcile the informal and formal processes through which the urban residents access land for housing.

States have, at times, acted against the interests of the urban poor by forcibly evicting households. Forced evictions have occurred in various circumstances. They may have complex, interconnected causes, including tenure insecurity or absence of formal rights, development and infrastructure projects, large international events, such as the Olympic Games, urban redevelopment, and beautification initiatives, property market forces and gentrification, absence of state support for the poor, political conflict, ethnic cleansing, and war (Coalition of Housing Rights and Evictions (COHRE, 2009)).

Despite continuing cases of forced eviction, more progressive local and national authorities in a number of developing countries have evolved innovations such as land readjustment, land pooling, and land sharing to increase urban land supply and regularise squatter settlements (e.g., in Bangkok). State land banks set up in Colombia and other Latin American countries have also made land more affordable for social housing.

State actors at different levels play a role in improving people's access to housing finance. Traditionally, states used to subsidise supply of low-cost housing by direct housing production. But in low-income countries, where the middle-income populations too experience housing deficits, subsidised housing often benefits the middle- and lower-middle-income households, while leaving out the very poor. Direct demand-side subsidies have been suggested as a solution, as these can be better targeted to the very poor. State institutions have been used for administering direct subsidies in the form of low-interest housing loans and one-time cash handouts for housing in some Latin American countries such as Chile, Costa Rica, and Venezuela. State-owned housing mortgage banks may administer interest rate subsidies or grant family housing certificates to those below a certain threshold income. But such demand-side subsidies can have side effects. They may increase land values and the cost of construction materials, thus resulting in the subsidy finally benefiting landowners, speculators, and the construction industry more than the poor.

At the national level, institutions such as central banks that determine monetary policy play a significant role in controlling the supply and cost of capital. Lax monetary policies in the form of long periods of low interest rates without adequate savings rates have led to boom and bust cycles in housing markets in developing countries, much like in the US housing market.

Most states both in the developed and developing countries have reduced the extent to which they are engaged in actual construction, maintenance, and management of housing. The states in most developing countries lack the resources to construct and manage housing estates large enough to meet the housing shortfall. Unlike many Western housing institutions that own many housing units, which they rent below market rates, most of the new housing being constructed by state agencies and development authorities in the developing countries are owner-occupied units. South Africa, after apartheid, started large-scale public housing projects to address its housing shortage. It has constructed over 1.4 million housing units since 1994. But its housing programme has evolved towards a kind of public–private partnership. In India, state governments set up metropolitan development authorities in many cities, which have constructed and sold many housing units, mostly in the form of apartments. They have also made available large amounts of serviced land for housing construction by private developers. But these efforts have not targeted the urban poor most in need.

State actors play their most important role by providing regulatory frameworks for the provision of housing. Planning, zoning, and building regulations directly affect the supply and nature of housing. These regulations allow public authorities to control land use, density, construction type, design and aesthetics, and costs of residential development. In most countries, local authorities set and enforce these rules and regulations. In many developing countries, implementation of these regulations is weak. The reasons for lax enforcement are not just insufficient capacity among the local authorities or corruption, but also unrealistic and inappropriate standards. While some regulations help improve housing conditions for middle- and upper-income households, they also burden the urban poor by making housing less affordable, thereby pushing them towards informal housing outside the purview of regulations.

In addition to these local regulations, there are also national and local laws with indirect effects on housing supply. For instance, financial regulations (such as those that regulate the extent to which foreign direct investments or pension funds can invest in real estate) set by independent regulatory authorities and the central bank in a country determine, among others, the demand and therefore the cost of land for residential development.

Market Institutions

Since the late 1980s, many countries in Asia, Africa, and Latin America adopted neoliberal policies to encourage the market to play a greater role in housing provision, spurred by the IMF's structural adjustment programmes that forced countries to cut their fiscal deficits by reducing spending on social programmes. Public investments for developing housing were one of the first to be cut. Governments adopted policies to encourage the private sector to invest in all aspects of housing, from land to housing finance to management and regulation of housing estates.

Land is an important component of housing provision. Most countries allow land to be traded within a land market with varying degrees of regulations. Even in countries like Mozambique, Ethiopia, China, and Cuba, where the state holds most urban land, a land market operates. In these countries, the state issues use rights in the form of leases. However, over the years, a market for land-use rights has evolved, where these use rights can be bought and sold – informally if not formally. Land markets allocate limited urban land to different users based on their willingness and ability to pay for land. Among the residential users, the higher- and middle-income households can pay a much higher price, thereby using up most of the convenient locations and leaving distant or dangerous locations for those with limited means.

Land markets, like markets for other commodities, work best when their information on demand and supply is transparent. But land has other important characteristics that make it unique. When demand for a commodity such as a television set increases, its price also increases, thus encouraging the manufacturers of television sets to increase supply to maximise profits, but then eventually bringing down the price to match the new demand. In the case of land, it is not easy to increase supply of land within an urban system without significant investments in extending city infrastructure. This unique attribute of land encourages speculators to invest in land without developing housing with the hope of selling the land later at a higher price. Therefore, land markets are often accompanied by a regulatory framework that includes a penalty for speculative investments (e.g., higher property taxes for landowners, who keep their land idle or underutilised).

Not all rules to regulate land markets in developing countries have the intended effect. For instance, India passed an Urban Land Ceiling Act in 1976 to prevent the concentration of urban land in the hands of a few persons who might profit from speculation and to bring about an equitable distribution of land. The Maharashtra state government purchased large tracts of land in Mumbai under provisions of this Act for low-cost housing. However, this land continues to lie vacant, thus reducing the amount of land available in the market and thereby increasing land prices.

Land markets are not the only institutions where the private sector plays an important role in providing housing. Private land developers and construction companies play an important role in putting services and other infrastructure on site and building new housing. But these developers typically do not consider investing in housing for low-income households as profitable. Developing countries sometimes provide incentives to private developers, or mandate them to cater to the housing needs of low-income residents. One such incentive is allowing higher floor–area ratios (FAR) than normally permissible if developers include some low-income housing in the project site. Some cities require developers to set aside a certain percentage of low-income units of new developments as a condition of approval.

Many cities have a large informal land market that is more vibrant than the formal one. This market mostly involves trading in use rights of public or private land, which may be illegally occupied or land that is not zoned for residential use (such as forest or agricultural land). It may also include trading of rights to use land in hazardous locations – flood plains, landslide-prone areas, or dump sites. These locations are sometimes the only option for those who cannot afford the high land rents within the formal land market.

Like land, capital for housing provision is also shaped by market competition. Formal financial institutions that supply capital for housing in developing countries are mostly in the private sector, with few exceptions. Some Latin American countries have created large state-supported financial institutions that offer subsidised credit for new home construction or home improvements targeting low-income households. Also, some countries nationalised large parts of their banking sector in the 1950s and 1960s, with very limited roles for private banks in home loans and the mortgage market. Despite these exceptions, for-profit financial institutions such as banks, mortgage companies, and microfinance institutions (MFIs) play an important role in financing housing in many developing countries.

Formal (meaning state-regulated) housing finance institutions offer credit only to those who build housing on authorised land and meet local planning standards and building regulations. In developing countries, many households cannot afford to acquire land in the formal land market or to meet the high (and sometimes locally irrelevant) standards and therefore they cannot access housing credit from formal sources. In some cases, formal financing options are inaccessible because income is irregular. Consequently, such households often fall victim to informal lenders and pawn shops that offer credit to those who cannot access formal housing loan and mortgage products. Some traders who sell building materials for home improvements in slums and squatter settlements also offer credit to their customers. Most often such informal access to credit comes with very high interest rates (sometimes as high as 100% per year).

The emergence and rapid spread of MFIs in many parts of the world is a noteworthy development in housing finance for the urban poor. MFIs offer microcredit in amounts that are too small for regular banks to lend in a cost-effective way. These institutions also place fewer conditions about meeting planning and building regulations and often do not ask for collateral in the form of land title. MFIs in the Asia-Pacific region charge rates ranging from 30 to 70% a year. These rates are still much higher than those charged by commercial banks. Larger loan amounts offered by commercial banks mean lower transaction costs, which results in lower interest rates.

In many developing countries, the proportion of owner-occupied housing units relative to the total housing stock is rising, and the proportion of public rental housing is falling. Owner occupancy increased in Bangkok during the 1970s, although less rapidly in the 1980s. Ownership increased rapidly in most of South Asia in the 1960s and 1970s. In urban Pakistan, the proportion of owners increased from 48 to 68% between 1961 and 1980 and in India the proportion of urban households living in their own home increased from 46 to 54% 20 years later. During this period, owner occupancy increased in 112 out of the country's 140 largest cities. In some cities, the shift was startling: in Mumbai from 30% in 1961 to 61% in 1981; in Ahmedabad from 18 to 42%; in Delhi from 34 to 53%. By 2001, the rate of owner occupancy in urban areas of India had increased to 67%. Housing market deregulation and policies that grant tax incentives for homeownership are contributing to this trend. Similar trends can be seen in South Africa since 1994 (Gilbert and UN-Habitat, 2003).

Civil Society Institutions

Civil society institutions are important actors in housing provision in most developing countries. They play particularly significant roles in housing the poor and marginalised groups in cities. With the growing prominence of the neoliberal paradigm, the state has increasingly withdrawn from providing housing for the poor and is encouraging market actors to address the housing needs of its people. Since the needs of the very poor often cannot be translated into an effective market demand, their needs do not get addressed by market mechanisms alone. Therefore, civil society institutions, such as NGOs, CBOs, religious and other philanthropic organisations, try to fill in the gap.

Some CBOs take a leading role in land-use planning processes in the developing countries. For example, Dar-es-Salaam and Mwanza, Tanzania, have set standards for informal settlement upgrading. The process comprises preparation for project execution, including preparation of base maps, reconnaissance and mapping of infrastructure facilities and utilities, conducting general assembly or meetings, elaborating tasks, developing community consensus in determining planning standards and allocating infrastructure facility and utilities, identifying major access roads and areas for public services, and negotiating plot demarcation for public land and private facilities (Magigi and Majani, 2005). Civil society organisations in developing countries have also developed innovative housing finance for those excluded from formal financial markets. The International Urban Poor Fund (IUPF) is one such example. It supports improvements in secure tenure and basic services developed through grassroots initiatives. Each initiative is designed to show national and local governments and international agencies what grassroots organisations can achieve. For instance, the construction of houses that are larger, of better quality, and much cheaper than those built by contractors; or community-designed and -managed toilet blocks that work much better than conventional public toilets; or detailed enumeration and maps of informal settlements that provide the information base for slum upgrading and tenure regularisation. The Fund is a joint venture of the International Institute for Environment and Development (IIED) and Shack/Slum Dwellers International (SDI), a transnational network of federations of slum/shack dwellers and homeless groups and their support NGOs in 15 countries. The IUPF provides small grants to support savings groups formed by low-income urban dwellers to secure land for housing. The Fund obtains tenure for land urban dwellers already occupy or for alternative sites, and assists them in building or improving their homes and accessing basic services. The Fund supports the initiatives designed and implemented by local savings groups that form the base organisations for the slum/shack dwellers' federations. The local savings groups also offer very low interest rate housing loans to its members. For example, the Urban Community Development Office (UCDO, which is the SDI affiliate in Thailand) makes home loans available to its members at rates as low as 3%.

Community-managed savings and credit schemes, run mostly by women, federate at the city and national level to create institutions that can share assets and resources (mainly knowledge and finance), thereby, strengthening and extending the capacity of local savings groups (Mitlin and Satterthwaite, 2007). SDI and its affiliates have used such saving schemes to form robust federations, which allow other forms of collective action, such as bargaining for secure tenure or better government services.

The role of civil society institutions in financing housing or related services is not restricted to raising capital, but also managing it. Neighbourhood, regional, and city-wide assemblies in several Latin American countries now decide on how to spend public money for community improvements and building infrastructure and services through participatory budgeting. The first full participatory budgeting process was developed in the city of Porto Alegre, Brazil. Participatory budgeting was part of innovative reform programmes, started in 1989, to overcome severe inequality in living standards among city residents. One-third of the city's residents lived in isolated slums in the city outskirts, lacking access to public amenities (water, sanitation, health care facilities, and schools). Participatory budgeting in Porto Alegre takes place annually, starting with a series of neighbourhood, regional, and city-wide assemblies, where residents and elected budget delegates identify spending priorities, and vote on which priorities to implement. Around 50 000 residents of Porto Alegre now take part in the participatory budgeting process (compared to 1.5 million city inhabitants), with the number of participants growing every year. Participants are from diverse economic and political backgrounds. A World Bank paper suggests that participatory budgeting has led to improvements in facilities in Porto Alegre. For example, sewer and water connections increased from 75% of households in 1988 to 98% in 1997. The number of schools quadrupled since 1986. Based on the success in Porto Alegre, more than 140 municipalities in Brazil, and several other Latin American cities, have adopted participatory budgeting.

Non-profit, non-government housing associations providing subsidised rental housing to lower-income households, such as those in the Netherlands or the United Kingdom, are not common in developing countries. Where they do exist, they only cater to a very small proportion of households. However, housing cooperatives are common in many developing countries. For example, Egypt created its General Authority of Housing and Building Cooperatives (GAHBC), in 1954, to assist cooperatives to provide housing for teachers, engineers, and police officers. GAHBC has no capital, does not take deposits, and its annual overhead is paid out of the national budget. It advises cooperatives and reviews building sites and construction plans for members. It also supervises construction, acquires and develops sites, and designs, plans, and builds projects. Of primary importance to the cooperatives are the loans made to the members of the cooperative, with each loan given on the basis of the cost of the dwelling unit. Loan payments are generally on an annual basis, and the cooperatives are required to see that their buildings are properly cared for and maintained.

As an initiative for the civil society in the social housing sector in Egypt, the Future Housing Foundation was established, in 1998, as a non-profit organisation with a mission to provide affordable and decent housing for the needy sectors of society. The foundation is committed to providing homes for people in need through government land grants, private donations, and the proceeds of fund-raising events. The Future Foundation channels private funds and technical resources into the design and construction of attractive low-income apartment housing. The government contributes the land and the infrastructure, while the foundation covers half the cost of the apartments. More importantly, the foundation provides financing arrangements under which new homeowners are able to pay off the balance over an extended period. This initiative is the key to the foundation's effort to promote low-income households as responsible, 'bankable clients' for both banks and non-bank lenders. However, the number of provided dwellings is still limited, and the foundation is not supervised by any authority (Aref, 2005).

There are individuals and households with special needs whose shelter needs are not met by the market or the government. There are nonprofit institutions, mostly religious or philanthropic organisations, that house people who cannot help themselves such as orphans or very old people without care-giving relatives or communities rehabilitated after natural or man-made disasters. Varying degrees of government support are available for civil society organisations offering shelter to vulnerable groups. This is evident from the widespread homelessness in many of these countries.

Public–private and public–community partnerships: In recent years, partnership between the public, private, and the community sectors have emerged. There are also examples of communities partnering with the local government to extend sanitation and water-supply services to informal settlements. In the case of the Orangi Pilot Project in Karachi, community participation is complemented by the use of microfinance, low- or moderate-income land development, and direct demand subsidy. The delivery of housing is done by the private sector, but the financing is subsidised by the taxpayer. Another example of partnership is between the private sector and cooperatives, such as the one in Porto Alegre (see Fruet, 2005).

International Institutions

Several international institutions work to provide housing in developing countries. UN-Habitat (United Nations Human Settlements Programme) is the primary UN agency with a mandate to implement the Habitat Agenda and Target 11 of the Millennium Development Goals to significantly improve the living condition of 100 million slum dwellers in the world by 2020. Although the mandate includes slums from North America, Europe, and Australia, its work focuses on the developing countries. Most of its activities relate to advocacy around the need for adequate and affordable housing for all. It relies on several modalities, ranging from publishing periodic reports on housing and human settlements, awarding and publicising international best practices in related fields, and two campaigns, that is, the campaign for secure tenure and the campaign for good governance.

The World Bank and the regional development banks (Asian Development Bank (ADB), African Development Bank (AfDB), and Inter-American Development Bank (IADB)) also have a number of housing-related projects in developing countries, mostly in the form of loans to national, regional, or local governments for developing new housing or for upgrading existing slum settlements. The World Bank is also a key player in developing knowledge of urban housing. It funds applied research on housing finance, security of tenure, and slum upgrading through the World Bank Institute. Research supported by the World Bank has tended to have a neoliberal bias, with an emphasis on individual property rights and relying on enabling markets to provide housing.

In addition, international NGOs based in the developed world work to improve access to housing in developing countries. Some of them conduct advocacy campaigns to make governments recognise housing as a basic right. COHRE is an international human rights organisation campaigning for the protection of housing rights and the prevention of forced evictions. It offers access to legal resources to communities under threat of forced evictions, in addition to naming and shaming the worst-offending countries by publishing reports on evictions. Other international NGOs, such as Habitat for Humanity International (HFHI), seek to eliminate housing poverty and homelessness and to make decent shelter a matter of conscience and action worldwide. Habitat volunteers in more than 100 countries are building houses for families in need of shelter.

Recent Trends

Two important trends have greatly affected the nature of housing institutions in the developing countries. First is the move from the state-as-provider paradigm to state-as-supporter paradigm in the 1980s. After the end of colonial rule in many developing countries, the state began participating in large-scale provision of housing. Because of its inability to meet the demand for new housing, its role in providing its citizens with adequate housing gradually shifted from that of being a housing provider to that of an enabler to support the housing market to match the demand for housing with adequate supply. This shift has been accompanied by a similar adoption of neoliberal thinking in relation to the provision of other services, such as water supply or solid waste management, that had traditionally been seen as public goods.

The second trend has been more gradual but equally profound in shaping contemporary housing institutions in developing countries. The process of decentralisation of state responsibilities to local and regional levels has meant that the local government is increasingly seen as a significant housing actor. Institutions for land-use planning, zoning, taxation have all had varying degrees of devolution from the national to local levels.

The two trends mentioned above are interlinked in a way that reinforces each other. Decentralisation or devolution is inevitably linked to the move towards markets and privatisation because lower levels of government just do not have the resources – financial and human – needed to carry out their new responsibilities. So they partner with the private sector to deliver housing or related services. But this does not automatically address the needs of those living in poverty whose needs cannot easily be translated into a market demand. So, a more recent trend is the emergence of trisector partnerships that include the public and private sector, as well as civil society (NGOs, CBOs, etc.) (van Vliet, 2008).

In terms of access to land for housing, for instance, informal occupation of land is of growing importance in cities of the developing world. The widespread presence of so-called 'illegal' housing has led to a questioning of whether this housing should be termed 'illegal'. The legal status of housing is particularly complex, where there are different entities bestowing legality. It is increasingly recognised that informal land development is a solution for land access by the urban poor, where formal supply is inadequate and inflexible and where both the state and the market are weak. New forms of associations and partnerships reconciling formal and informal processes of land management have therefore been suggested. These new forms of partnership are based on structures within civil society and draw from resources of both the state and private sector actors (Jenkins, 2001).

A recent study of such public–private–civil society partnerships suggests that most partnerships with a housing programme aim at upgrading existing housing in slums and squatter settlements (in situ upgrading) rather than building new projects to replace derelict housing. Upgrading programmes reach a much larger number of households, have a longer average duration, and cost less per household than new construction. Perhaps due to their complexity, cost, and diversity of partner types, programmes of housing-focused partnerships are less frequently replicated than partnership programmes in other programme domains.

Also, housing partnerships experience more challenges in scaling up than do partnerships that are focused differently. The reasons may be the difficulties in forming more complex partnerships and acquiring the larger resource base that is often required for housing projects.

See also: Housing Standards: Regulation; Microfinance for Housing; Slums; Squatter Settlement Clearance.

References

Appadurai A (2001) Deep democracy: Urban governmentality and the horizon of politics. *Environment and Urban* 13(2): 23–43.

Aref HM (2005) Social housing sectors: Lessons learned by others. *Paper presented at the XXXIII IAHS World Congress on Housing: Transforming Housing Environments through Design.* http://www.up.ac.za.

COHRE (2009) Causes of forced evictions. http://www.cohre.org/view_page.php?page_id=100 (accessed 16 July 2009).

Ding C and Knaap G (2003) Urban land policy, 2009 reform in China. *Land Lines* 15(2): 1–3.

Fernandes E and Varley A (1998) Law, the city and citizenship in developing countries: An introduction. In: Fernandes E and Varley A (eds.) *Illegal Cities: Law and Urban Change in Developing Countries*, pp. 3–17. London; New York: Zed Books Ltd.

Fruet GM (2005) The low-income housing cooperatives in Porto Alegre, Brazil: A state/community partnership. *Habitat International* 29(2): 303–324.

Gilbert A and UN-Habitat (2003) *Rental Housing: An Essential Option for the Urban Poor in Developing Countries*. Nairobi: United Nations Human Settlements Programme.

Jenkins P (2001) Strengthening access to land for housing for the poor in Maputo, Mozambique. *International Journal of Urban and Regional Research* 25(3): 629–648.

Magigi W and Majani BBK (2005) Planning standards for urban land use planning for effective land management in Tanzania: An analytical framework for its adoptability in infrastructure provisioning in informal settlements. *Paper Presented at the From Pharaohs to Geoinformatics: FIG Working Week 2005.* www.fig.net/pub/cairo/papers/ts_19/ts19_03_magigi_majani.pdf

Mitlin D and Satterthwaite D (2007) Strategies for grassroots control of international aid. *Environment and Urbanization* 19(2): 483–500.

van Vliet W (2008) *Broad-Based Partnerships as a Strategy for Urban Liveability: An Evaluation of Best Practices*. Nairobi: United Nations Human Settlements Programme (UN-Habitat).

Further Reading

Aldrich BC and Sandhu RS (1995) *Housing the Urban Poor: Policy and Practice in Developing Countries*. London; Atlantic Highlands, NJ: Zed Books.

Buckley RM (1996) *Housing Finance in Developing Countries*. New York: St. Martin's Press.

Datta K and Jones GA (2001) Housing and finance in developing countries: Invisible issues on research and policy agendas. *Habitat International* 25(3): 333–357.

Keivani R and Werna E (2001) Modes of housing provision in developing countries. *Progress in Planning* 55: 65–118.

Kigochie PW (2002) Extending themselves: User-initiated transformations of government-built housing in developing countries. *Cities* 19(1): 81–82.

Mathur GC, Centre for Science and Technology of the Non-Aligned, and Other Developing Countries (1993) *Low-cost Housing in Developing Countries*. New Delhi: Centre for Science & Technology of the Non-Aligned and Other Developing Countries; Oxford, UK: IBH Publishing Co.

Mukhija V (2001) Upgrading housing settlements in developing countries – the impact of existing physical conditions. *Cities* 18(4): 213–222.

Pugh C (2001) The theory and practice of housing sector development for developing countries, 1950–99. *Housing Studies* 16(4): 399–423.

Tipple AG (2000) *Extending Themselves: User-Initiated Transformations of Government-Built Housing in Developing Countries*. Liverpool, UK: Liverpool University Press.

Van Vliet W (1990) *International Handbook of Housing Policies and Practices*. New York: Greenwood Press.

Housing Market Search

WAV Clark, University of California, Los Angeles, CA, USA

© 2012 Elsevier Ltd. All rights reserved.

Glossary

Anchor point search Households select vacancies for search which are at some selected distance and direction from an 'anchor point', a current residence or a job, for example.

Area-based search Households select areas (neighbourhoods) and examine vacancies in those areas.

Risk A state of uncertainty where some outcomes may be undesirable or involve a loss.

Stopping rules Models which include rules that specify how long a household will search and when a household will end the search process.

Uncertainty The existence of more than one possibility. In search, uncertainty is related to the inability to be certain about the number of available vacancies for purchase. In addition, the uncertain information about those vacancies, even though they may be listed in a real-estate catalog, further increases uncertainty in decision making.

Search and Choice in the Housing Market

Our choices of where to live are necessarily influenced by where we search. Our neighbourhood and community search behaviours in the end determine, at least for that relocation, where we will buy or rent housing. Our searches are of course conditioned by budget constraints, and our preferences for particular neighbourhood characteristics and population compositions. A family with small children may well search only in neighbourhoods and communities where there are likely to be other small children and good schools. The neighbourhoods they will select to search in will be constrained by the housing stock characteristics and the costs of housing. Young singles beginning their careers may well search only in inner-city locations where there are other young singles. Because they are in the early stages of their housing career, and are likely to be renters, the housing costs may be a lesser constraint on their choices. In either of these cases, the search process is the precursor to the selection of a particular dwelling or apartment.

Knowing something about the search process, how individuals and families go about choosing housing is a central part of the operation of the housing market. But it is not only a matter of where people look – which neighbourhoods they choose to examine – it is also about the availability of information and the length of their searches. Now the search process is undergoing significant changes as households move to internet access, processing, and evaluation. The internet is making more information available and may be increasing the range over which households search and evaluate housing opportunities.

A Conceptual Setting for Search Behaviour

Most research on residential choice suggests that we think of the residential mobility as a two-stage process, in which the decision to move and the decision to search precede the neighbourhood and housing choice itself. In this formulation, households (families or individuals) evaluate their current living conditions and if they are not in equilibrium (or in some formulations, if they are 'under housing stress') they consider moving. This decision sets in motion the search and evaluation process to examine whether some set of vacancy opportunities can better fulfil their housing needs than the current house does. It is this two-stage process which informs much of our thinking about residential mobility and residential choice.

The choice process itself is an evaluation process which involves examining and considering a set of alternatives to the current residence. The process is necessarily both spatial and temporal. Search is across one or more neighbourhoods and commonly occurs over days, weeks, or even months. Search is information-dependent but has both visual and numerical dimensions. Few households select a house without 'seeing' the house, and the availability of size, room shapes, and architectural details are essential parts of the evaluation process. Renters and more especially buyers face a distribution of housing units with given characteristics, and it is that set of opportunities within which the household makes a residential choice. Often search involves comparing quite different housing units. Some may have the required number of rooms but be architecturally unappealing, while others may be appealing but the room configuration would not suit the household.

Conceptually, housing search, like all search behaviour, is (a) goal directed (b) information dependent (c) budget constrained, and (d) uncertain. Each of these concepts which are general to search behaviour has specific dimensions in housing search. Search is goal directed because we know that households do not select from a random set of offers, but rather the search process involves filtering a set of alternatives from a larger set of opportunities. That filtering process is dependent on the supply of information about the housing units. It is not simply an issue of locating alternatives; it is the detailed information about those alternatives which is central to the choice process and the decision making that occurs. Some models suggest a hierarchical approach to information gathering, in which data on neighbourhoods are assembled before specific houses are evaluated for their suitability. Of course, the search process takes place under a budget constraint and not all neighbourhoods and houses are available to all searchers. The constraints can be financial, time, and limited access to information. Information channels can limit search, perhaps more so in the past when real-estate agents carefully guarded their listings and the information in those listings. Now the internet provides greater information but not necessarily the information which is the most useful to housing market searches and the ultimate selection decision.

Perhaps the most critical issue in housing market search relates to uncertainty. It is not possible to know the complete set of opportunities; housing is necessarily complex and apart from easily resolved differences among units (number of bedrooms, for example), how does the searcher evaluate a three bedroom and office against a three bedroom and family room. Clearly the information being presented has implications for the choice. Uncertainties can be resolved to some extent with additional search and at additional cost, but in some instances the uncertainty is only resolved after the decision is made.

The large literature on decision making under risk and uncertainty is as critical in housing market search as in other search behaviours. Uncertainty, the lack of complete certainty, is created by the existence of more than one possibility, certainly a truism in the real-estate market. Risk, on the other hand, is used to describe the situation where some outcomes may be undesirable or involve an actual loss. A particular uncertainty in the housing search decision is that even after an alternative is selected, what is the appropriate offering price, and how to negotiate the most advantageous mortgage rates for the house that has been selected.

Characteristics of Search

The choice of a residence is perhaps the most significant consumption decision that a household makes. Certainly, housing expenditures are probably the largest component of most household's expenses, and the house and its neighbourhood defines the living environment for the household. But as the commentary above suggested, it is also a decision which is surrounded by uncertainty. Housing is a multidimensional good and it is far more complex than the choice of any other consumer durable and much more complex than buying a car for example. Even renting will have near-term, if not long-term effects on a household. The household cannot be sure of the way in which the housing unit will meet the needs of the household over the coming years. Not only is the 'good' being purchased complex, there are significant transaction costs in the selection and purchase of a dwelling. Even renters do not change residences that often and buyers enter the market even more infrequently. The search strategy then is a way of reducing uncertainty; narrowing the number of possibilities that will best meet the needs of the household. It is also a way of reducing the uncertainty about the costs and benefits of particular dwellings. These strategies revolve around search effort which in turn can be broken down into the length of the search, the number of units that the household considers (of course not independent of the length of the search), and the number and type of information that a household uses in the search process.

Studies in the United States suggest that owners, not unexpectedly given the potential investment decision, search longer than renters do and examine many more alternatives before selecting a new residence. The median time for a rental search was between a week and 2 weeks but owners searched between 5 and 6 weeks. Still, while 40% of renters searched for less than a week, even 20% of buyers made their decision within a week or less. Clearly there is considerable diversity within both renter and owner searches. Another significant difference between renters and potential buyers is the use of different information sources. While friends and newspaper advertisements played an important role for both groups, real-estate agents were much more important to buyers. This difference is changing quite rapidly as special-purpose rental sites now dominate the basic information for rental searches while real-estate agents are still an important part of the functioning of the purchasing market.

For buyers, several independent variables are associated with search behaviour. The number of houses examined in the search process is a function of the number of real-estate agents used, and the number of areas considered in the search process is negatively related to education (the more educated search fewer areas which can be either a function of the greater ability to process information or alternatively the limited number of areas available to more educated (and possibly more affluent) buyers). The length of search is most closely predicted by age of the head of household, for example, older heads search for shorter times (based on their experience and knowledge). Finally, distance of the search area is characterised by age, household size, the size of the dwelling, and the price and number of realtors used in the process. Older and larger households searched in more confined areas but over greater distances if the dwelling was large. Interestingly, searches for higher-priced units took place over more confined areas. This is a topic of some interest and is reexamined in the discussion of specific models of spatial search.

Models of Search

Disequilibrium Models

Models of housing search while derived from models of job search and selection have developed an individuality that is specific to the housing market. Three basic approaches have been developed to understand residential search and mobility. First, disequilibrium models of search are based on the broader notions of disequilibrium models of mobility (Clark, 1982). In these models, the probability that a household will search is a function of the benefits and costs of moving. These approaches to search have tended to use an 'income equivalent variation' approach – that is, the additional income necessary to make the household as well off with its current consumption of housing as it would be with its equilibrium consumption. In the search models using a disequilibrium approach, the models estimate the gains and/or losses from a move from actual to equilibrium consumption, with specific assumptions about the form of the household's utility function. These disequilibrium models have been used to examine the household's rate of search and moving. Logit functions are used to estimate the probability of search on the basis of a set of socioeconomic characteristics of the household controlling for race, previous mobility, and reported housing satisfaction. In these models, dissatisfaction with housing and neighbourhood are the most important predictors of the likelihood of search. And, as expected, age of household head is important, and younger heads are more likely to search, which is consistent with what we know about mobility in general.

Stopping Rule Models of Search

Studies of job search were the basis for models of when to stop searching for a house (McCall, 1970). In job search models, the decision is about whether to accept a job offer and stop searching or to continue evaluating further jobs as they come on line. The models examine the trade-off in the costs of continuing search and possibly securing a 'better' (higher-paying) job or accepting the job that is currently being offered. Some of the more sophisticated job search models utilise a strategy, in which the job searcher can revise his or her expectations about the wage levels which may be offered. The extension to search in the housing market employs the same conceptual structure – whether to accept a house which the searcher has seen or to incur the costs of further search.

Early research on stopping rule models for housing search used the terminology of house hunting which of course it is – a process of 'hunting for a house' rather than hunting for a job. In this conceptualisation, each house can be assigned a value and the net payoff to the searcher is maximising a criterion value, and the strategy of the searcher is to accept the first alternative whose value exceeds the criterion value. Some researchers who have used this strategy suggest that the criterion for stopping search and the cost of search are both functions of time (Smith et al., 1979). These normative models have been modified to incorporate criterion values which cannot be determined a priori, but rather evolve as part of the evaluation process.

Nested Hierarchical Models of Search

Models which invoke hierarchical search in the main depend on versions of the discrete choice modelling strategy developed by MacFadden (1974). In these models, the issue is a selection process which proceeds through a set of discrete choices nested within one another. In these models, it is assumed that a household views the mobility and choice process as a selection from a set of ordered choices. In the selection process a household decides to move or not, or in alternative formations to search or not and then given that decision proceeds through a set of choices – neighbourhood, dwelling type, and dwelling unit. At each of these levels, the household is making a selection from a choice set. Of course, the choice set assumes that the choices within a branch of the preference tree are more similar, or substitutable, than the choices at other levels of the preference tree.

The ordering of the choices from high to low reflects the relative degree of similarity. Thus, dwelling units in a given neighbourhood are more alike by definition and are dissimilar to dwelling units in another neighbourhood. This does not mean that units in a neighbourhood cannot be similar to dwelling units in another neighbourhood, but by definition being in a different neighbourhood will mean that they have different associated characteristics. A preference tree suggests the nature of hierarchical models of search and choice. A household can decide to search or not and then follow a decision to search the hierarchical approach suggests a sequence of choices of first, a selection of a neighbourhood to search, then which dwelling unit types to search, and finally which actual dwellings to search. Thus, we can imagine a household examining four hierarchical choices each of which is more similar within the choices at each level than between the levels. The relative degree of similarity increases as the choice structures are constrained.

Limited applications of the hierarchical choice model provide some evidence that indeed households do search for their new locations in a hierarchical fashion. However, what does emerge is that to the extent that neighbourhoods possess different supplies of dwelling units of a specific type, there will be powerful effects on the likely choices of households. Overall, the models exhibit weak relationships with the observed data. The research literature on neighbourhood characteristics is growing but we are still some way from identifying the critical variables that determine neighbourhood choice.

Obviously, a link between hierarchical models of search and stopping rule models of search is a natural extension of hierarchical models alone. In this conceptualisation, a household is faced with a standard stopping rule decision — whether to accept the offer (a house) or continue searching. The difference from the standard stopping rule model is the introduction of the decision of which neighbourhood to search if search is to continue. To this extent, the hierarchical model is a model of search strategy in contrast to the standard disequilibrium model which is a model of housing demand. The models differ substantially, in the household's knowledge of the housing market, the search and moving costs, and the relationship between housing price and characteristics. This latter variation is important because it is the hierarchical model which assumes a joint distribution of price and characteristics, while the standard disequilibrium model assumes that housing price and characteristics are correlated.

Information Decision-Making Models of Search

Some models of housing search specifically privilege the nature and role of information in the decision making and strategy related to search behaviour (Smith and Clark, 1980). This work has attempted to model the way in which search is conditioned by the acquisition and use of information. These models have shown that variations in cost are critical determinants in both the temporal and spatial sequences of search behaviour. In one analysis, it was possible to show that the nature and success of the spatial search was especially dependent on the quality of the real-estate agent input and the way in which search occurred with that agent. In other words, the external input of the agent was a central part of the way in which search occurred.

These information models assume that the decision-maker has subjective beliefs about the spatial structure of the market, the chances of finding an acceptable vacancy, and of the characteristics of four specific channels of information flow. The first precondition built into the model is that the searcher believes that the housing market is partitioned into a set of distinctive subareas and that these subareas are relatively homogeneous, akin to neighbourhoods with similar housing types. The second precondition is that the decision maker has a set of beliefs about the likelihood of finding an acceptable vacancy in any of these areas in a given period of search. In a simple form of the model, areas have two probabilities of success, high or low. Real-estate agents can improve the chance of success and are viewed either as successful (good agents) or not successful (poor agents). Two other conditions are used in the model — that the searcher does not have certain knowledge about whether an area has a higher or low probability of success, and the decision maker has four channels of information available to them, but each channel of information has a cost of acquisition. With these conditions, the decision maker then contacts and searches with an agent he has information about or an agent for whom there is no prior information.

Simulations of this model provide new insights into the search process. In particular, costs of search become an important constraint on successful search. When information is inexpensive (or alternatively when it is readily available), individuals search the areas of greatest likely success and seldom search in other areas. All individuals buy in the best area. As costs of information increase, the number of searches in the best area declines. Consequently, there are lower likelihoods of finding acceptable vacancies in those areas. In this model, the role of real-estate agents was important. The changing availability of information is a critical element in the search process. The good real-estate agent is a substitute for other kinds of information when the cost of that information is high.

Spatial Search

Although spatial search was a component of the previous model, specific spatial search models have been devised to examine how a household selects from areas under certain locational constraints (Huff, 1986). Area-based search models use a probability function of visiting a particular vacancy based on the conditional probability that an area contains a vacancy. Areas with larger numbers of vacancies are more likely to be included in the search space. The likelihood of search is also conditioned by prior search experience in particular areas. Area selection is then followed by intensive search in that area with higher probabilities of visiting vacancies near to the last vacancy visited. In one formalisation of the area-based search model it can be shown that under some simplifying assumptions the search process can be described as a Markov chain, in which the probability of searching in a given area is a function of the last vacancy seen and the indirect cost of identifying a member of the possibility set in the area of search and the direct cost of actually visiting the vacancy.

An alternative spatial search model, the anchor point search model, also assumes that the search pattern will reflect the underlying distribution of vacancies. The difference between the two models, however, is that search in the anchor point model is concentrated around a focal point, such as the existing residence, job location, or other focal point which is relevant to the choice outcome. Search declines in intensity around the focal point. Clearly, search is geographically biased and households do not search a set of randomly arriving vacancies as is sometimes suggested in economic approaches to search behaviour. In general, the economic approaches to search have not incorporated the geographic dimensions of search.

In tests of the model, the anchor point model was able to predict the observed search distribution over half of the time, but both the area and the anchor point models emphasise that the search process has strong spatial regularities.

The Role of Information in Housing Search

There is little doubt that more and more accurate information will enable more successful search outcomes. The availability, amount, and quality of information have a direct influence on the timing and success of the search. Detailed information on relative prices and the prices of alternative units will enable a more realistic assessment of the 'real price' of units. We still, however, do not have good models of the access and use of information in housing choice.

Recent work has suggested a three-stage information acquisition process (Menzio, 2007). In the orientation phase an individual or a household attempts to pre-structure a later more detailed search by identifying areas which seem to provide housing types and neighbourhood characteristics which are consistent with initial housing aspirations. The orientation phase is followed by a phase in which specific vacancies are identified, followed by an evaluation phase in which direct visits are used to accept or reject specific vacancies. At this stage, actual likes and dislikes of specific properties, maintenance issues (quality of the dwelling), and prices were the determinants in whether to pursue a bid.

While these observations on search are still generally relevant, the way in which housing information is now being transmitted is changing rapidly. Websites, both general and specific, provide details and photo montages of almost all properties on the market. Certainly this is true for much of the North American real-estate market. Large search engines such as Zillow, Truilla, Redfin, and the venerable MLS (Multiple Listing Service) in the United States now provide details on what is for sale, pictures of the properties, and important details of the property. It is true that a real-estate agent can provide processing and document arrangement, but they are much less central to the search process than they were two decades ago. Yet, they are still the final arbiters who negotiate the actual sale and to that extent they fulfil an important role in the search process. However, the search process itself is changing as the web and the internet change. How this will affect the outcomes of the search process in the future is an ongoing question.

See also: Economics of Housing Choice; Migration and Population Mobility.

References

Clark WAV (ed.) (1982) *Modelling Housing Market Search*. London: Croom-Helm.

Huff J (1986) Geographic regularities in residential search behavior. *Annals Association of American Geographers* 76: 208–227.

MacFadden D (1974) Conditional logit model analysis of qualitative choice behavior. In: Zarembka P (ed.) *Frontiers in Econometrics*, pp. 105–142. New York: Academic Press.

McCall J (1970) Economics of information and job search. *Quarterly Journal of Economics* 84: 113–126.

Menzio G (2007) A theory of partially directed search. *Journal of Political Economy* 115: 748–769.

Smith T and Clark WAV (1980) Housing market search: Information constraints and efficiency. In: Clark WAV and Moore E (eds.) *Residential Mobility and Public Policy*, pp. 100–125. Beverly Hills, CA: Sage Publications.

Smith T, Clark WAV, Huff J, and Shapiro P (1979) A decision making and search model for intraurban migration. *Geographical Analysis* 11: 1–22.

Further Reading

Albrecht J, Anderson A, Smith E, and Vroman S (2007) Opportunistic matching in the housing market. *International Economic Review* 48: 641–664.

Albrecht J, Gautier P, and Vroman S (2009) *Directed Search in the Housing Market*. Bonn, Germany: Institute for the Study of Labor.

Huff JO (1984) Distance decay models of residential search behavior. In: Gaile GL and Willmott CW (eds.) *Spatial Statistics and Models*, pp. 345–366. New York: Reidel Publishers.

MacLennan D (1979) Information networks in a local housing market. *Scottish Journal of Political Economy* 26: 73–88.

MacLennan D (1982) *Housing Economics: An Applied Approach*. New York: Addison Wesley Longman.

Weinberg D, Atkinson R, Vidal A, Wallace J, and Weisbrod G (1977) *Locational Choice, Part 1: Search and Mobility in the Housing Allowance Demand Experiment*. Cambridge, UK: Abt Associates.

Housing Markets and Macroeconomic Policy

S Whelan, University of Sydney, Sydney, NSW, Australia

© 2012 Elsevier Ltd. All rights reserved.

Glossary

Aggregate demand The total sum of expenditure in an economy, often characterised as consumption expenditure plus investment expenditure plus government spending.

Business cycle The tendency of the real level of output to fluctuate over time. During booms output levels are high relative to trend levels and during recessions output is relatively low.

Consumer Price Index (CPI) A measure of the general level of prices in an economy. The CPI or some related measure is often targeted by monetary authorities when determining monetary policy settings.

Fiscal policy The use of government spending and taxation to achieve desirable economic outcomes such as full employment.

Global financial crisis A term commonly applied to the period beginning in 2007 when financial markets in the world's advanced economies were characterised by major instability and those economies fell into recession.

Gross Domestic Product A measure of the total output of the economy measured over some period of time, usually one year.

Keynesian pump priming The use of an active fiscal policy to increase aggregate demand and the level of total output in the economy during periods of recession.

Monetary policy The setting of interest rates or some other monetary variable such as the money supply to influence the level of economic activity and the general level of prices in the economy.

Stagflation The occurrence of high inflation and high unemployment simultaneously.

Housing in the Macroeconomy

An understanding of housing and its relationship to macroeconomic policy in developed economies is best appreciated by first considering the place of housing in the macroeconomy. In modern capitalist economies, the housing sector remains a significant component of aggregate demand. **Table 1** indicates the relative importance of the housing sector in the economy by considering expenditure on housing construction as a proportion of total output or Gross Domestic Product (GDP). For those economies listed, housing construction alone accounts for between 3.2 and 6.5% of GDP per annum. Perhaps more significantly, the figures in **Table 1** indicate that investment in the construction of residential dwellings represents a large component, approximately 20–30%, of total annual investment expenditure.

The importance of housing construction in total investment revealed in **Table 1** draws attention to the key role of the housing sector in macroeconomic policy settings over time. Fluctuations in economic activity that are usually associated with changes in the level of unemployment generally coincide with large swings in the level of investment expenditures in the economy. Other components of aggregate demand, such as household consumption expenditures, are far more stable over the business cycle. It is variation in investment expenditure, especially the construction of residential dwellings, which represents a disproportionately large share of the swings in output that are characteristic of the business cycle. Evidence from the United States indicates that – in the majority of the recessions experienced after the Second World War – the decline in investment in residential dwellings has been the largest single contributor to the weakening GDP in the year preceding the recession. This role of investment in residential dwellings as a leading indicator of economic activity is considered in more detail below.

Investment in residential dwellings has a direct effect on aggregate levels of economic activity. In addition, it has important spillover effects on the other components of aggregate demand. Construction of new dwellings generally necessitates the purchase of consumer durables such as furnishings. Evidence from the United States indicates that, like the expenditures on residential construction, decreasing expenditures on consumer durables also signal the onset of an economic downturn. Moreover, this spillover effect of expenditure on residential dwelling construction has made housing attractive to policymakers. In the past, it has often been argued that activity in the housing sector has a multiplier effect on overall economic activity.

The focus of this discussion is the current contribution of activity in the housing sector to the macroeconomy. The characteristic of housing as a durable good consumed over time is increasingly important to contemporary

Table 1 Housing in the macroeconomy, 2005

Country	Expenditure on housing constructions as a percentage of GDP	Expenditure on housing constructions as a percentage of investment
Australia	6.5	22.0
Canada	5.9	25.3
France	4.2	20.7
Germany	5.4	30.3
United Kingdom	3.2	17.7
United States	5.4	27.5

GDP – Gross Domestic Product
Reproduced with permission from Organisation of Economic Co-operation and Development (OECD) (2009) *National Accounts of OECD Countries*, Vol. 1, Main Aggregates 1996–2007. Paris: OECD.

macroeconomic policy-makers. For homeowners, the residential dwelling usually represents an important means of saving and is the largest single asset in their wealth portfolio. From a countrywide perspective, the accumulated stock of housing represents a large stock of wealth with potentially important implications for the functioning and settings of macroeconomic policy. The role of housing as a stock of wealth and its significance for macroeconomic policy is highlighted by noting the increase in the value of the US housing stock between 2000 and 2007. During this period, the value of housing is estimated to have increased from 1.1 to 1.4 times personal income. Concurrently with this change, the role of housing, as a store of considerable wealth and its relative magnitude have become increasingly important in debates surrounding the nexus between macroeconomic policy and the housing sector.

Macroeconomic Policy-Making and the Housing Sector

Macroeconomic policy objectives have traditionally been couched in terms of a desire to achieve high and growing levels of employment (or output), coupled with low rates of inflation. The tools generally available to macroeconomic policy-makers are fiscal policy and monetary policy. Fiscal policy focuses on the taxing and spending decisions of governments. For the housing sector, this has involved direct intervention in the housing market through the construction of public or social housing. More often, fiscal policy measures emphasise the role of the private sector and encourage the construction of dwellings by means of targeted subsidies or tax expenditures, which reduce the cost of constructing residential dwellings for private agents (see article Access and Affordability: House Purchase Certificates). Contemporary debates about macroeconomic policy and the housing sector focus more on monetary policy measures. That is, interest rates or some other monetary aggregates are targeted, to achieve the desired policy objectives.

It is important to emphasise the change that has occurred in the role of housing for macroeconomic policy over time. At times, the housing sector has been used as a means to achieve the desired policy objectives. At other times, the housing sector has been seen to be an important determinant of macroeconomic settings. At all times, the unique nature of housing has meant that understanding policy settings requires acknowledgement that policy-makers generally have a variety of objectives that they wish to achieve. Social objectives such as the redistribution of income and wealth, the provision of adequate shelter, or the promotion of homeownership have often dominated the debates about housing, masking the important underlying macroeconomic objectives.

The Keynesian Paradigm and Demand-Management Policies

After the Great Depression, with its ensuing misery and high rates of unemployment, governments around the world sought policies that would prevent or alleviate such downturns in economic activity. Before and for a time after the Second World War, it was widely accepted that governments could fill the gap created by decreases in private-sector activity. These Keynesian demand-management policies – named after the British economist John Maynard Keynes, who popularised them – emphasised the use of fiscal measures to smoothen out the fluctuations in aggregate demand. Downturns in private-sector activity could be offset either by higher government spending or lower taxes. Conversely, excessive private-sector activity that potentially exacerbates inflationary pressures in an economy can be mitigated by an increase in taxes or a reduction in government expenditure.

From the perspective of housing, activist demand-management policies could conceivably take a number of forms: all these were evident in different countries over time. Direct policy measures, such as expenditure on the construction of public housing, represent perhaps the most obvious way in which governments acted to increase the overall levels of economic activity and to manage aggregate demand. These measures were an important consideration in the creation of public or social housing in Australia and Canada in the decades following the war. The construction of dwellings by the government or by quasi-governmental agencies was designed to moderate seasonal and cyclical fluctuations in economic activity, especially in the construction sector. This intervention would also ensure that an adequate housing stock would be available for the continued expansion of the economy over time.

In an economic sense, however, governments sought to encourage economic activity in the housing sector by more indirect measures, in the face of weak aggregate demand. These policies have included direct subsidies to households purchasing their own dwellings or tax incentives (expenditures) designed to reduce the effective cost of purchasing a residential dwelling. Although the rhetoric that accompanied such policy announcements often alluded to other objectives, such as the encouragement of homeownership, the underlying rationale of the policy remained the Keynesian 'pump priming' or the stimulation of aggregate demand. This characteristic of public policy for the housing sector is best exemplified by the experience of the United States. A succession of policies was implemented, which had ostensibly been put in place to encourage homeownership. The timing and the temporary nature of the measures – such as tax credits for the purchase of new homes in 1975 and concessional tax arrangements on savings instruments during the 1981 recession – underscore their roles as demand-management measures.

Stagflation and the Rise of Monetarism

The prevailing orthodoxy that had provided the bedrock for macroeconomic policy settings during the postwar period was undermined by the oil-price shocks of the 1970s and the resulting stagflation. Keynesian demand-management policies seemed incapable of responding to the simultaneous presence of stubbornly high inflation and high unemployment. The period coincided with a number of developments in the policy arena, typified by the popular adherence to the monetarist views of the economy. There were a number of components to the monetarist's view of the macroeconomy, exemplified by the belief that inflation was at its core a monetary phenomenon and that reducing inflation required strict adherence to a rule targeting the growth of the money supply.

The monetarist view of the economy explicitly rejected the Keynesian tenet of demand management through activist policy settings. The ideological shift that accompanied the embracing of monetarist ideals coincided with a belief on the parts of numerous governments that the market remained the most efficient means by which to allocate resources. This belief was prevalent especially among those in the Anglo-American tradition, such as the United States, the United Kingdom, and Australia. Activist government policy was seen as being either ineffective or counterproductive. For example, if governments reduced taxes and increased borrowing to stimulate economic activity, private agents would respond by decreasing expenditure on the understanding that future governments would need to increase taxes to repay the accumulated debt. Similarly, government investment would crowd out equivalent amounts of private-sector investment, so that total investment – and therefore the level of output – remained unchanged. Governments were no longer seen as the solution to the problem, rather they were the source of the problem.

To be clear, the embracing of monetarism did not result in the abandonment of Keynesian ideals completely. In the United States, temporary tax measures have been used to kick-start the economy under the guise of some overriding aim, such as the promotion of homeownership. Similarly, in Australia, direct subsidies were made to first home buyers, ostensibly to assist in attaining the aspiration of homeownership; they were used to provide a fillip to the construction industry. This ideological shift did, however, have important implications for the role of housing and the housing sector. In the United Kingdom, the decade following 1978 was marked by a reduction of around 70% in the number of new housing start-ups by the government. Moreover, concern at the size of government spending and the associated level of public-sector debt led to large-scale sell-offs of publicly owned dwellings to private individuals. During the 1980s alone, over 1.3 million publicly owned dwellings were sold to tenants as part of a large-scale policy of privatisation (see article Privatisation of Social Housing).

The Place of Housing in the New Macroeconomic Policy

The reassessment of the role of macroeconomic policy had important implications for the relationship between the housing sector and macroeconomic policy settings. As noted above, a central tenet of monetarism was that inflation remained a monetary phenomenon and that governments could best contribute to economic growth over the long term by maintaining low and stable rates of inflation. After the 1980s, the primary role of central banks, most notably in Australia, North America, and Western Europe was redefined as maintaining low rates of measured inflation. Changes in the general level of prices are measured with reference to the spending behaviour of an 'average household' and are reflected by the changes in the consumer price index (CPI). Typically, housing represents the largest single component of most household budgets; so the manner in which the cost of housing is included in the measured level of price changes potentially affects the measured level of inflation.

To date, there remains a lack of consensus among academics and statistical agencies about the appropriate technique to use when incorporating the cost of housing – especially of owner-occupied housing – into the CPI. In the United States, the Bureau of Labor Statistics uses the observed market rent of similar types of dwellings to estimate the cost of housing for owner-occupiers. It has been suggested that using a different approach – incorporating information on the selling prices of homes sold after 2000 – would have yielded a measured rate of inflation of approximately 3.8% per annum, around 1.5 percentage points higher than the reported figure. If so, it is unlikely that interest rates in the United States would have remained as low as they did over such a protracted time period.

How to correctly incorporate measures of housing costs into the broad measure of the general price level is a somewhat mundane characterisation of a far more fundamental question faced by central banks during the 1990s and 2000s. Following the periods of expansionary monetary policy in the 1990s and 2000s, many expressed concern that asset-price bubbles could potentially destabilise the economy. A key question that occupied the minds of policy-makers during this time was whether monetary policy should 'lean against the wind' and attempt to proactively limit these asset-price bubbles before they burst and had detrimental effects on the real economy (see article Monetary Policy, Wealth Effects and Housing). The steep increases in housing prices at various times during this period in the United States, Europe, and Australia brought the issue into sharp focus, although the debate remains unresolved.

The 2000s – a Keynesian Revival?

The period following the early 1980s had been described as the 'great moderation' by macroeconomists. The variations in overall levels of economic activity that characterise the business cycle continued, but these fluctuations were significantly smaller during the post-1980 period relative to the period following the Second World War. Admittedly, economic growth since 1980 has been punctuated by periods of recession, most notably in the early 1980s and the 1990s, but output growth during this period exhibited a relatively steady trend. This feature of the overall economy was mirrored in the behaviour of the housing sector. In the United States the standard deviation in residential investment relative to the trend rate was around 13% before the 1980s. After the 1980s, it was around 5%. For many, the faith in macroeconomic policy that had characterised this period – especially the role of monetary policy – had been vindicated.

The 'global financial crisis' (GFC) that first manifested itself in 2007 has again focussed attention on macroeconomic policy settings. The exact cause or causes of the GFC remain a matter for ongoing debate among policy-makers and academics. Undermining of confidence in the financial markets climaxed in the second quarter of 2008. There was broad agreement that developments in the financial sector dealing with the residential mortgage market had a large role to play in this. These developments in the financial markets quickly spread to the real economy: during 2007 and 2008, all major Western economies entered a period of acute recession. Ironically, the responses of the governments took on a decidedly Keynesian flavour. The stance of monetary policy became markedly more expansionary; nominal interest rates were driven to historical lows; and central banks in Europe and North America embarked on a policy of quantitative easing or printing of money.

Fiscal policy also took on a familiar flavour at this time as governments sought to cushion their national economies from the downturn. Governments around the world announced large fiscal packages designed to stimulate the real economy. Support to the housing sector – either directly through the construction of additional housing stock or indirectly through subsidies and tax expenditures – was a part of the fiscal stimulus package announced by all European and North American governments.

It is premature to argue that Keynesian demand-management policies have again found favour and that the monetarist approach that had dominated macroeconomic policy-making since the 1980s has been abandoned. The GFC has presented a set of challenges to policy-makers not experienced since the depression of the 1930s and the long-term effects of the GFC are yet to emerge. Notwithstanding this uncertainty, it is clear that events that had their genesis in the housing sector of the economy have highlighted the continuing role of housing in macroeconomic policy-making.

Macroeconomic Policy and Housing – Where to Now?

The debates about macroeconomic policy since the depression of the 1930s have been profound and remain active today. Housing and the housing sector occupy a central position in these debates because of the importance of housing to the business cycle. Nonetheless, housing policy has at times been couched in terms of broader policy objectives, which reflect the role played by housing as a merit good and in achieving other objectives.

Contemporary debates about housing and its relationship to the macroeconomy and macroeconomic policy settings have focused on new issues such as the long-run growth performance of the economy rather than short-run fluctuations in economic activity. For example, there is concern that policies explicitly or implicitly favouring the housing sector might have long-run repercussions on the economy and constrain its capacity to grow. The favourable tax benefits for housing and the continued housing-price inflation have encouraged overinvestment in housing at the expense of investment in other more productive sectors of the economy. In the long run, such an outcome is likely to diminish the growth of output. Others have questioned whether the housing sector should be used as a leading indicator when determining policy settings. While evidence suggests that declines in investment in residential dwellings precede a more widespread decline in economic activity, it is not clear that this justifies 'targeting' the sector when setting monetary policy. Key proponents of the monetary regime that coincided with the great moderation since the 1980s noted that fluctuations in the housing sector during this period have also been moderated without explicitly targeting it.

Arguably, the linkages between housing and macroeconomic policy settings have become more important over time, as the role of housing in the real economy has become more sophisticated. The housing sector is no longer seen simply as a component, although an important one, of aggregate demand. Rather, those responsible for monetary policy settings acknowledge the multitude of ways, direct and indirect, in which the housing sector and monetary policy are linked. Monetary policy influences the user cost of capital directly through interest rates. Therefore the demand for housing can be manipulated through interest-rate changes. Monetary policy also has implications for expected appreciations of future house prices, and, therefore, for housing demand. Similarly, by influencing the value of housing, monetary policy has the potential to impact the net worth of households and consumption expenditures (see article Housing Wealth and Consumption). This latter transmission mechanism has gained increasing importance in the eyes of policy-makers, in the light of the significant fluctuations in house prices experienced in recent years.

The complexities of the relationship between macroeconomic policy settings and the housing market are underscored by the macroeconomic models used by central banks such as the Federal Reserve in the United States. The main macroeconomic model of the economy used by the Federal Reserve, namely the FRB/US model, incorporates some but not all of the hypothesised linkages between housing and the other components of the economy. Moreover, even for the transmission mechanisms included in the model, considerable uncertainty remains about the magnitude of the relationships posited.

The relationship of housing to the macroeconomy and macroeconomic policy settings is likely to become more, not less, vigorously debated in the aftermath of the GFC. It is unclear where this discussion will lead in terms of the exact role played by housing in macroeconomic policy debates. Ideally, it will lead to a deeper understanding of the role of housing and the housing sector in the macroeconomy.

See also: Access and Affordability: House Purchase Certificates; First Home Owner Grants; Housing Wealth and Consumption; Monetary Policy, Wealth Effects and Housing; Privatisation of Social Housing.

Further Reading

Bernanke B and Gertler M (2001) Should central banks respond to movements in asset prices? *American Economic Review Papers and Proceedings* 91: 253–257.

Carliner MJ (1998) Development of federal homeownership 'policy'. *Housing Policy Debate* 9: 299–321.

Dalton T (2009) Housing policy retrenchment: Australia and Canada compared. *Urban Studies* 9: 63–91.

Diewert WE and Nakamura AO (2009) Accounting for housing in a CPI. *Federal Reserve Bank of Philadelphia, Working Paper No. 09–4*.

Goodhart C (2001) What weight should be given to asset prices in the measurement of inflation? *The Economic Journal* 111: F335–F356.

Leamer EE (2007) Housing is the business cycle. *Proceedings of a Symposium Sponsored by the Federal Reserve Bank of Kansas City on Housing, Housing Finance and Monetary Policy*, Jackson Hole, WY, USA, 30 August–1 September.

Leung C (2003) Macroeconomics and housing: A review of the literature. *Journal of Housing Economics* 13: 249–267.

Maclennan D and Gibb K (1999) Housing finance and subsidies in Britain after a decade of 'Thatcherism'. *Urban Studies* 27: 905–918.

Mishkin FS (2007) Housing and the monetary transmission mechanism. *Proceedings of a Symposium Sponsored by the Federal Reserve Bank of Kansas City on Housing, Housing Finance and Monetary Policy*, Jackson Hole, Wyoming, USA. 30 August–1 September.

Organisation of Economic Co-operation and Development (OECD) (2009) *National Accounts of OECD Countries, Volume 1, Main Aggregates 1996–2007*. Paris: OECD.

Prince MJ (1995) The Canadian housing policy context. *Housing Policy Debate* 6: 721–758.

Taylor JB (2007) Housing and monetary policy. *National Bureau of Economic Research, Working Paper 13682*.

Taylor JB (2009) The financial crisis and policy responses: An empirical analysis of what went wrong. *National Bureau of Economic Research, Working Paper 14631*.

Housing Market Institutions

K Hawtrey, Hope College, Holland, MI, USA

© 2012 Elsevier Ltd. All rights reserved.

Glossary

Cooperative A nonprofit, autonomous, voluntary association of members, constituted for the purpose of achieving a common community goal of an economic, social, or cultural nature; and often a democratically controlled and jointly owned enterprise.

Government-sponsored enterprise A commercial agency created by the government to assist groups of the housing-needy, by facilitating access to dwellings, loans, and other resources, usually self-funding by the revenue gained from its activities.

Hedonic pricing This model of pricing is one that decomposes the price of an item into separate determinants of the price; for example, the price of a house may depend on factors such as both its size and location.

Institutional economics The study of the role and evolution of institutions in the economy, and their relation to firms, governments, market norms, households, and organisations.

Nonprofit entity An incorporated enterprise set up for a charitable or civic purpose, by capital holders who do not receive and direct personal monetary gain.

Principal–agent problem An economic transaction where one person (the agent) acts as a representative of the other (the principal), and where the agent has imperfect information about the principal or vice versa.

Transactions costs Costs incurred when buying or selling a house, which may include agent's commission, search costs, advertising costs, and so on.

Introduction

To fully understand housing systems and outcomes, it is essential to gain an appreciation of the institutional nature of housing markets. Different historical pathways mean that housing systems display diverse institutional characteristics, and the interplay between institutions has a significant effect on housing futures. The diversity of institutional tone that exists both within and between different markets invites a comparative approach. Private sector, community-based, and public sector organisations each contribute to a rich and dynamic mix that makes the housing industry unique. In addition to formal organisations, informal and organic institutional forms need to be considered, such as player perceptions and market customs.

This article provides an introduction and overview of the institutions of housing markets. It begins with a consideration of conceptual issues of interpretation and methodology, using institutional economics as a starting point, and develops the idea of institutional forms in housing markets. The discussion then moves to identifying the main private, community, and public groups in housing markets. Finally, the article then explores issues surrounding the interaction of different housing market institutions, noting certain key directions that research is currently taking.

Institutions and Markets: Conceptual Issues

While individual rational choice theory has been the predominant view of human decision-making among economists, institutional economics has played a significant supporting role in explaining economic performance (North, 1990). Institutional economics tells us that agents may make choices as social groups, based on social calculation and groupthink. It emphasises the governance structure of markets, and the role that is played by collective action in the pursuit of common goods.

The institutional quality of markets has a number of important consequences for economic outcomes. Institutional patterns can give rise to path dependence of the economy through time, where the sequence of market changes depends in part on past events and external forces. Institutional factors will also have significant impact on the costs of market exchange: transactions costs will rise because fees are likely to be higher for utilising and enforcing property rights or territorial claims; information costs will rise because of searching and market negotiation; social costs, defined as the sum of private costs incurred by an agent and public costs borne by others, will be affected because of altered externalities.

An important theoretical question concerns the definition of market institutions. In the scholarly literature, the collective action envisaged by an institutional view of markets can mean a range of things: natural human rights, formal organisations, a matrix of laws, how agents commonly behave en masse, a set of forces for dynamic change, and so on. A seminal paper in Commons (1931) defined an institution as "collective action in control, liberation and expansion of individual action" and suggested that "collective action ranges all the way from unorganised custom to the many organised going concerns, such as the family, the corporation, the trade association, the trade union, the reserve system, and the state". In other words, while the scope of an institutional view of markets includes visible organisations, it extends well beyond that to encompass all the invisible ingredients that make up the 'governance' of a market. Market institutions can be seen as the 'rules', written or unwritten, coerced or persuasive, that structure human economic interaction, both explicitly (such as constitutions and legislation) and implicitly (such as market conventions or codes of conduct). Together, these human networks and market conventions are the contexts in which contracts and trades are nested.

Recently, the field of new institutional economics has developed, seeking to capture even richer views of market institutions (Coase, 1988). It is a socioeconomic theory that moves beyond a pure atomistic conception of markets, to include an interdisciplinary ingredient. New institutionalism is an interdisciplinary enterprise that combines economics with other disciplines including political science, sociology, psychology, anthropology, law, organisation theory, and so on. By rethinking competition, and exploring alternative choice theories, it seeks to analyse markets as an economic, social, and political unity. It provides a way of viewing how institutions shape the behaviour of individual members and market outcomes.

An Institutional Perspective on Housing Markets

Applied to housing markets, the term 'institution' can accordingly carry a broader meaning than organisations per se, although these remain core to institutional economics. The term refers to the full set of norms of a given marketplace, stated and unstated, including organisations but extending to embrace the cultural fabric in which the housing market is nested, because all of this goes to make up the structural framework that supports human interaction. The institutions of the housing sector can accordingly encompass not merely commercial practices but also such aspects as ethics, the social expectations of the local population, demographics, tastes and preferences of the market, tenant mindset, ethnic customs, and so on. Indeed, if housing demand is understood not just as the dwelling structure but as a "continuous quantity that represents the flow of housing services" (Zabel, 2004) then a host of habits and behaviours comprise the infrastructure of a housing market. Factors such as the propensity for homeownership among the population, housing tenure, location, size, quality, tenant or landlord characteristics, willingness of the population to move location, modes of transportation, available mortgage instruments, neighbourhood segmentation, racial discrimination, degree of speculation in the market, pension systems, monetary policy transmission mechanism, capital markets, institutional investors' perceptions of housing investment, ageing of the population, the emphasis placed on environmental considerations, generational changes, and national traditions represent the dimensions of a given housing market's fabric. All these have roots in the economic histories of each city or locality (Ruonavaara, 2005). They contribute to the so-called implicit economy.

Immediately it becomes clear that each housing jurisdiction is institutionally unique. Diversity in housing institutional arrangements across countries is significant, and these discrepancies in turn lead to diverse market outcomes. For instance, Italy has its own legal process governing the use of housing as collateral; the mortgage market in Germany is relatively closed to outside entrants, while France has rental subsidies and introduced an upfront subsidy to homeownership. In Switzerland, nonprofit renting has a low profile in the market, whereas in the Netherlands community-based housing is a mainstay. Japan's housing system has its own distinctive polices, such as an income tax deduction system for capital losses of owner-occupied households, and the Rental Act that provides renters protection from eviction. Chinloy and Megbolugbe (1994) identify key differences about the UK housing markets compared with the United States', including the mortgage instrument and long-term price declines. Hawtrey (2009) discusses multiple institutional differences in housing systems between the United States, the United Kingdom, and Australia.

Others observe distinct differences in the homeownership between cultures. Ronald (2007) argues that a contrast between homeowner societies can be identified that fits an 'East–West model', where all the institutional factors we have discussed blend to create distinguishable patterns of mass homeownership between English-speaking, Anglo-Saxon societies on the one hand, and East Asian societies on the other. These are derived from divergences in systems, regimes, and socio-ideological relationships. Even the meaning of a commercial 'contract' can vary between jurisdictions in the degree to which it is a legally enforceable agreement, depending on the diversity of institutional landscapes, say between western and eastern Europe, or North and South America (e.g., see Méndez, 2006). In other words, each housing market is distinctive. Indeed, the differences between jurisdictions have led to calls for institutional reforms to reduce the tensions within and between markets.

Equally it is true, notwithstanding the above, that housing jurisdictions in the industrialised world generally share certain institutional characteristics in common. Many of these shared structural experiences, interestingly, seemingly contain internal contradictions. The social housing sector is often underserved, at the same time that housing supply firms are looking for more work. Neighbourhood and resident groups form cooperatives – even gated communities – while urban planners are looking for ways to better integrate the city. The proverbial 'location, location, location' mantra exerts its effect on prices, while at the same time international integration of housing markets means that property values are increasingly part of a global cycle. Mortgage lenders urge borrowers to take on greater risk; yet housing finance institutions struggle to manage their own risk properly. Developers seek to build new residential stock on the outskirts of the urban fringe, while parts of the older inner city precincts are vacant and decaying, such as the older inner suburbs in metropolitan America (Hanlon, 2008). Government-sponsored enterprises proliferate with a myriad of market support programmes, yet certain social subgroups – ethnic, women, elderly – continue to experience housing difficulty. Estate agents' language extols the marketing attributes of a sale property, while green groups seek to emphasise the environmental attributes of dwellings. This is not an exhaustive list, but it gives the flavour that in housing markets today, paradoxically, institutional diversity and common institutional patterns happen to be juxtaposed.

It is instructive to ask whether the textbook market mechanism is one of the universal institutional characteristics of housing markets. Does the perennial challenge of supply responding to demand side at the right price get resolved by the classic price mechanism, in the world of housing? Some of the time 'yes', but a lot of the time 'no'. Because of its institutional forms, housing is not like other markets: there are long lead times in bringing product to market, each dwelling is unique, and the commodity of housing is immobile by its very nature. The durability, fixity, and heterogeneity of dwellings mean that transactions costs are significant in the housing market (Jaffe, 1996). Moreover, many institutional factors can bear upon the supply of housing in the economy including construction standards, zoning regulations, development levies, environmental priorities, skill shortages, workplace culture, land supply, infrastructure provision, tax laws, and so on. This can impart a 'kinked' supply curve (Goodman, 2005). Demand for housing can be impacted by demographic shifts, worker attitudes, banking practices, and government incentives. The net result can be shortages in some locations at the same time as gluts in others, exaggerated swings in the housing cycle between boom and bust, and unfair disparities across different segments of the population. Institutional differences are an important explanation for why house price cycles move differently in different regions (Gros, 2007) and time periods.

In short, housing markets typically exhibit idiosyncrasies – personalities almost – that make housing a unique case study in institutional economics. Arguably, institutional economics has not received the attention it deserves in housing studies (Lowndes, 2001), yet there are signs that this state of affairs is gradually beginning to change (Lambooy and Moulaert, 2009). Developing a richer institutional perspective on housing markets may help us move closer to explaining some of the puzzles in housing markets catalogued above.

Housing Market Institutional Groups

One institutional pattern that is almost universal across advanced housing markets is the presence of a mix of private sector, community-based, and public sector players. This provides a useful taxonomic system for classifying the range of housing market institutions.

Private Sector

Private sector participants generally operate on a commercial, for-profit basis. The leading examples are developers, master builders, landlords, real estate agents, and architects who each perform a key role in providing housing. These players are the traditional backbone of the industry, have a considerable influence over urban outcomes and housing policy, and are represented by various professional bodies.

Developers and builders

Builders and developers act as the physical providers of housing. How well they do their job of delivering tangible built product has a huge bearing on the technical efficiency of the economy, in terms of making the most effective use of factors of production, and on housing affordability (see, e.g., Cho, 2003). Cost effectiveness is very important to builders and developers, and is a major driver for forming industry associations. In the United Kingdom, the Federation of Master Builders was founded 60 years ago and today it is the largest trade association in the UK building industry, with 12 000 members. An independent and not-for-profit body, its members are primarily builders and specialist tradesmen. Since 1942 in the United States, the National Association of Home Builders (NAHB) has sought to enhance national appreciation for the importance of housing and promote policies that support the residential building industry. Its annual convention, the International Builders Show, is the largest expo of the light construction industry, and the association seeks to be a premier resource for housing education and technical expertise. The NAHB is a federation of more than 800 local affiliates and has more than 175 000 members, and the organisation's members build some 80% of the new homes constructed each year in the United States.

Landlords

Landlords serve consumers who rent instead of buy. Investors are partly represented by landlord bodies such as Britain's National Landlords Association (NLA). This is a confluence of private residential landlords ranging from small-time owners of single-bedroom apartments, through to full-time landlords with large property portfolios. The NLA promotes a high code of management practice in the private-rented sector, and offers a range of member services with a view to encouraging private landlords to join the sector. Also in the United Kingdom, other institutional groups operate along these lines, such as the Residential Landlords Association (RLA) in England and Wales. The RLA was historically the first NLA in the United Kingdom and represents over 7800 landlords with a combined portfolio in excess of 150 000 properties. In the United States, the Landlord Association.org is an online company developed by landlords and other property investors and who want to support those involved in real estate investing. The association's prime directive is to provide members with information: news, resources, and 'tricks of the trade' to help improve investor's earnings. The Landlord Association provides answers to common questions posted on its website, and looks at issues such as landlord insurance, tenant laws, lease termination notices, rent collection, and so on.

Estate agents

Real estate agents play the role of 'market makers' in the housing industry. By bringing together buyers and sellers to facilitate two-way trading, they act as market makers. This 'middleman' function helps improve the allocative efficiency of the economy. Bagnoli and Khanna (1991) provide an economic analysis of buyers' and sellers' agents in the housing market, arguing that agents reduce principals' search costs. This is consistent with the theory of pricing behaviour under demand uncertainty, and with search theory. Changing reservation prices during the marketing of a heterogeneous asset is also consistent with such theory, and research shows that sellers who have better information about the value of their home are less likely to change price, while sellers who have relatively high costs of continuing a search for a buyer are willing to change price more often. This provides further rationale for employing an agent. The advent of the internet as a search tool has altered the home buying process and affected the role of estate agents.

Researchers have found that the web reduces search costs and encourages buyers to search more intensively, by allowing buyers to visit more properties in a shorter time (Zumpano et al., 2003).

Like developers, real estate agents have their own associations. In the United States, many estate agents are represented by the National Association of Realtors (NAR). Membership of the NAR comprises those engaged in various aspects of the residential and commercial property industry where a state license to practise is required, including real estate brokers, property managers, and appraisers. On the other side of the Atlantic, the National Association of Estate Agents (NAEA) and The Independent Network of Estate Agents are leading examples of real estate agent associations in the United Kingdom. The NAEA, founded in 1962, has around 10 000 members, while the INEA has over 2000 members. Why do estate agents form associations? Bishop (2004) evaluates the reputation of estate agents within the context of principal–agent problem. The poor reputation of estate agents often arises from product characteristics, where the buyer lacks full information about the dwellings (which are heterogeneous) and from the nature of the market (in which trading takes place infrequently). Bishop canvasses various solutions such as certification, and this explains a major rationale for estate agents to form associations: reputation building. In most countries, a legal requirement exists for estate agents to belong to a registered professional organisation in order to trade as an estate agent, and actors can be penalised if they are operating without a licence. Such associations serve as a scheme of governance to discipline improper practices and to guide practitioners. Members are bound by a code of ethics, by standards of practice that include responsibilities to clients, the community, and fellow estate agents.

Other private sector groups

The other groups in this business include mortgage lenders, mortgage insurers, mortgage guarantee companies, property valuers, retirement homes, building material suppliers, home security firms, urban planning professionals, engineers, and architects.

Community-Based

Community housing organisations are (usually) private, not-for-profit cooperatives that supply and manage housing, particularly affordable housing, through a semi-commercial (or even noncommercial) business model. Or they are advocacy bodies for particular subgroups such as tenants or single-parent families.

Community housing providers

Known officially as housing associations in the United Kingdom and community housing development organisations in the United States, such enterprises generally do not earn profits: any financial surplus is reinvested in homes and community services. Although these organisations normally employ paid staff, they are often controlled by voluntary committees or boards, and work closely with local authorities. They are frequently a tax-exempt charity, and are recognised as providing a social service by increasing the supply of affordable rented accommodation. These cooperatives vary in the way they allocate homes: some deal directly with applicants, while others accept nominations from local authority housing lists or make use of welfare referral agencies. Their objectives are more social than financial in nature, and commonly include expanding affordable housing and homeownership, stimulating local economic development and enhancing housing services among target groups. Typically they are dedicated to seeing that people on the lowest incomes have access to affordable housing, and addressing the gap between housing costs and the earnings of those on low incomes.

An important contrast can be observed between the British and American models of community-based housing. Britain's housing system is very much the product of history: as an old-world country, much of the built housing dates back centuries, which still shapes the urban form today. As well, the Second World War saw the destruction of thousands of homes, and the postwar reconstruction that followed was led by council housing. Consequently, a relatively large proportion of dwellings in the United Kingdom have traditionally been quasi-social housing. In the 1980s, the Thatcher government initiated a new path with the Right to Buy scheme, beginning a trajectory towards private ownership that continues to this day. Yet there remains in British housing a deep connection to community housing, evidenced by the widespread role of housing associations (HAs). These associations are independent, not-for-profit social businesses set up to provide affordable homes for people in housing need. The HAs vary in size from just a handful of dwellings, to more than 50 000 homes under management. Together, housing associations provide about two-and-a-half million homes across England, and most are rented at affordable rates. Some properties are even sold through low-cost homeownership schemes. HAs are also often engaged in building new houses, supplying specialist housing, or regenerating neighbourhoods (e.g., in programmes such as the Market Renewal Pathfinders). Most of the income of HAs comes from rents, though many also receive government funding. Although they are not part of the public sector, all housing associations are required to be registered with the Tenant Services Authority (TSA). Houses for social rent are under the long-term management of Registered Social Landlords (RSLs), independent housing organisations registered with the TSA under the Housing Act 1996. RSLs may be provident societies, registered charities, or companies.

The community housing system in the United States has quite a different feel. As a new-world country, its geographic form and built inventory is less permanent. It is indicative of the differing cultures that British homes are built using lasting brick, while American homes are made of aluminium siding, a lighter material. There is not the same postwar legacy of council or social housing. Rather, community housing in the United States is more entrepreneurial and supported by private charitable donors, or by tax incentives or subsidies from the government. Rather than the national uniformity of Britain, American community housing is more customised to local circumstances. The CDFI (community development financial institution) Coalition is the national voice of CDFIs in the United States. With the aid of a paid secretariat, the CDFI Coalition and similar peak bodies help resource local community housing associations and provide vital technical support on a range of national matters such as accreditation and legislation. Another peak body is the National Low Income Housing Coalition (NLIHC). Established in 1974, with hundreds of members nationally, the Coalition's singular focus is on the needs of extremely low-income people, including particular segments of the population such as women, Hispanics, and farm workers. The NLIHC conducts research and policy analysis and has a voice in Washington that helps to shape housing policy. Landmark examples of policy-making where the NLIHC has played a significant role include the earmarking of 30% of Section 8 units for low-income households in 1974, the creation of the Low Income Housing Tax Credit in 1986, and the launch of the Federal Home Loan Banks' Affordable Housing Program in 1989. More recently, the NLIHC played a part in the establishment of the national Housing Trust Fund in 2008. The NLIHC aims to preserve existing levels of federal assistance for housing, to expand the supply of low-income housing through the federal government increasing its own production, and to enhance neighbourhood stability which is conducive to better health, employment, and education.

One example of a US community group is Wilmington Housing Partnership (WHP). Established in 1989, the Partnership is a 501(c)(3) organisation in California chartered to increase the City of Wilmington's housing stock, lift homeownership, raise the quality of dwellings, and stabilise neighbourhoods in the city. WHP partners with investors, acts sometimes as a developer, at other times works with nonprofit community entities, or functions as a facilitator for housing developments by raising the funding available for qualifying projects. It purchases and renovates vacant properties, or facilitates construction of new homes. WHP is a nonprofit corporation and obtains its funding from the programme income generated from its activities, and through applications to local governments, banks, and foundations.

Melendez and Servon (2007) study a sample of urban community development corporations (CDC) and note that the typical urban CDC has a diversified portfolio of economic development activities and is likely to have a housing development programme on some scale. However, relatively few (18%) are large-scale housing producers, defined as having produced at least 500 units during the previous 10 years. Supplying housing on a big scale is correlated with a large organisational capacity, affiliation with national bodies, the length of executive directors' tenure, and the share of funding devoted to housing programmes. While this accords with the goals of many community housing cooperatives, it is not the reality for many of them, in turn raising the question of what barriers currently exist to their advancement. One hypothesis is that other institutional groups in the system (private, public) are inhibiting the performance of community-based players.

Other community-based groups

Neighbourhood cooperatives, resident associations, tenant groups, self-builders, sustainable/green movements, ethnic communities, women's housing cooperatives, seniors, and special-needs housing are some of the other groups in this sector.

Public Sector

In addition to legislating policy norms for housing in its role as social umpire, governments are major players at an operational level, directly supplying or facilitating housing. Compared with some other sectors in the economy, government agencies are often heavily involved in the housing market itself, as active suppliers. Public sector housing delivery agencies' mission may involve supporting renters, managing housing estates, helping borrowers refinance or modify their existing mortgage to avoid foreclosure, helping consumers avoid predatory lending, underwriting loan risk, encouraging new financial instruments for housing, advising on the home buying process, improving housing affordability, and so on.

Housing ministries

Housing departments typically have a wide brief. In the United States, the Department of Housing and Urban Development is a pivotal institution. In the United Kingdom, the Homes and Communities Agency is the national housing and regeneration delivery agency for England. Such departments may build and manage public housing estates themselves. And they frequently forge partnerships with community (including faith-based) organisations to leverage resources that will help make an impact at the community level, to increase homeownership, and increase access to affordable housing. To make home-buying more affordable, housing departments get involved in assisting homeowners to refinance to take advantage of lower mortgage rates, or modify their monthly mortgage payments, perhaps because their income has dropped or their interest rate has been reset higher due to earlier contractual agreements. This line of activity has quickened especially in the wake of the global financial crisis of 2008. The departments also address diverse policy questions such as low-income housing tax credits, disaster recovery accommodation, and greener housing in the form of savings on energy. In conjunction with local partners such as housing associations and private sector developers, these agencies encourage the delivery of affordable homes in high-quality, sustainable neighbourhoods.

When they get involved in the provision of affordable housing, national housing bureaus seek to target areas of greatest need. They may do this by providing funding for low-income housing, increasing land supply, rehabilitating declining urban areas, developing investor tools, leveraging housing estates in inner-city/rural/mining localities, and promoting quality and design standards (including environmental impacts and room sizes). For example, England's HCA does this through its Decent Homes Standard. It has also published a Model Shared Ownership Lease, for use by all lenders and housing providers, using plain English and clarifying the rights and obligations of banks, housing cooperatives, and consumers. Dwellings for affordable sale are made available by such agencies, and in conjunction with community-based not-for-profit cooperatives, the departments provide affordable homes for people in housing need.

Government-sponsored enterprises

Government-sponsored enterprises (GSEs) operate on a quasi-commercial basis, to build housing estates or provide mortgage funding. The latter may be buyers of home mortgages rather than originating mortgages themselves, instead operating in the secondary mortgage market and working with a national network of mortgage lending clients. The stated aim is to keep money flowing to mortgage lenders in support of homeownership and rental housing. GSEs often support a portfolio of mortgage-backed securities that is used to foster a stable supply of funds for banks to make new loans to home-buyers, and to facilitate financing for low-income housing. They act like a mortgage insurer: if a borrower stops making monthly payments, the agency steps in and makes those payments on behalf of the homeowner, in return for collecting a credit guarantee fee from the lender. Managing this 'credit risk' is how the GSE generates revenue.

Fannie Mae provides a case study of a government-sponsored enterprise. Operating in US housing and capital markets, and established in 1938, Fannie's broad mission is to operate in securitisation markets so that banks can increase the volume of funds available in order to make homeownership and rental housing more affordable and available. The organisation deals in mortgage securitisation, a process which sees the purchase of home loans originated by banks, the packaging of these loans into mortgage-backed bonds, and the selling of these bond instruments to investment houses. The vast bulk of loans involved are long-term, fixed-rate mortgages. By packaging mortgages into MBS (mortgage-backed securities) and guaranteeing the timely payment of principal and interest on the underlying mortgages, Fannie (and its counterpart, Freddie Mac) expand the pool of funds available for strategic housing by attracting to the secondary mortgage market investors who might not otherwise put their money into housing. That makes the secondary mortgage market more liquid and helps lower the interest rates paid by homeowners and other mortgage borrowers.

Are GSEs like Fannie effective? Fannie Mae seeks to enhance liquidity and affordability of the US mortgage market. It does this not by making mortgage loans available directly to home buyers, but by working with bankers in the secondary mortgage market. The aim is to ensure that primary mortgage market partners have funds to lend to consumers at reasonable rates, but Fannie Mae funds its mortgage investments primarily by issuing debt securities in the domestic and international capital markets. This led to problems during the Wall Street meltdown. Although Fannie Mae was chartered in 1968 as a private shareholder-owned company, in September 2008 at the height of the global financial crisis, the Federal Housing Finance Agency was appointed as conservator of Fannie Mae and the federal Department of Treasury effectively had to bail out Fannie, agreeing to provide the capital needed to correct any 'net worth deficiencies'. Like Fannie, Freddie also needed a Federal Government bail out in 2008. This institutional form has had a huge impact on the rest of the housing market, often for good, though not always positive.

International government agencies
Sustainable urbanisation is recognised by international agencies such as the United Nations and others as one of the greatest ongoing challenges facing the world community in the twenty-first century.

The United Nations Center for Human Settlements operates the UN's human settlements programme, UN-HABITAT, and is mandated by the UN General Assembly to facilitate adequate, sustainable shelter for all people. Disease, crime, poverty, and social unrest are threats when human populations seeking resettlement are inadequately housed, and slums can deprive the population of access to shelter, water, sanitation, or medicine. UN-HABITAT's aim is to broker workable solutions to the challenges posed by human settlements, to attain the goal of cities and towns without slums. It does this through research and policy development, and by capacity building and financial programmes. The United Nations Millennium Declaration outlines a goal for member states to improve the lives of at least 100 million slum dwellers by the year 2020, and reduce by half the number of people without sustainable access to safe drinking water.

The World Health Organization is interested in housing conditions because they influence people's health. For instance, poor design or construction of dwellings causes many accidents in the home, and damp indoor conditions can cause respiratory diseases. The WHO looks at a range of relevant issues, including thermal energy in the home, residential environments as they affect physical activity, effects of housing on mental health, and the challenge of ageing populations. It then works towards the implementation of action plans for better housing, and promotes better health through the technical aspects of housing.

Other public sector groups
Urban planning authorities, elected officials, local councils, lawmakers, and welfare professionals are the several other public sector groups in the housing activity.

Interaction between Private, Community, and Public Institutions

How the three broad interest groups – private, community, and public sector – interact is important, because they jockey for influence over the market. Sometimes they work together, and other times at cross-purposes. Each forms its own interest group, an identifiable collective of actors who have common interests. The three groups see value in cooperating with others in their own respective grouping, towards shared objectives. As outlined in the previous section, they often form organisations and participate in external policy processes, launch new industry initiatives, or provide flagship member services. They seek to create the conditions for their affiliates to thrive, and to influence the housing policy agenda nationally. At stake is the housing market 'food chain', their daily give-and-take in the market. And their success or otherwise will be evident in numerous ways, ranging from transaction costs to spatial hierarchy, through to public choice.

How does the interplay between the three major institutional groups of the housing industry affect housing market outcomes? This question is increasingly at the frontier of research into housing markets, and takes many forms. Typically, it involves exploring bilateral relationships between, say, government and developer, or consumer and housing cooperative.

Consider, for instance, the interaction between private developers and community-based providers. Kemeny et al. (2005) draw a distinction between dual rental systems and integrated rental markets, in which nonprofit providers are able to compete with private developers on an equal footing. They explore the scenario of markets in which nonprofit providers influence, lead, and dominate the market. Bratt (2008) presents a discussion of the effectiveness and attributes of not-for-profit housing providers and compares them with for-profit organisations in developing and owning subsidised rental housing. In some ways, community-based suppliers are found to have the advantage, while for-profit developers have an edge in other areas. The author suggests that nonprofit and for-profit organisations pool their strengths by joining together more in partnership arrangements. Clearly, the degree to which this happens is one of the institutional challenges that will shape the future of many housing jurisdictions.

Next, consider the nexus between government and private developers. Sometimes, government housing providers are themselves operating in direct competition with the private sector, and there is a robust debate in the literature about whether government as provider crowds out provision of housing stock by the private sector. At other times, the government's role is more akin to that of an urban planner. Developers often face a potential 'holdout' problem, where some landowners wish to sell but others refuse at the offer price, effectively raising the cost of development. To minimise this extra cost, developers prefer land whose ownership is less dispersed, but Miceli and Sirmans (2007) argue that this creates a bias towards development at the fringes of metropolitan areas, resulting in urban sprawl.

Yet an institutional approach to housing markets holds out the promise of finding more market-oriented solutions to problems of this nature. For example, Winfree and McCluskey (2007) use a game-theoretic model to analyse the interaction between the landowner and the government, and show that efficiency can be reached when compensation is tied to the private value of developed land, provided the landowner is compensated by the full amount of any positive externality. Mohamed (2010) discovers in the US context that profits decrease as time to complete the subdivision increases, because of delays due to regulations which make it more difficult for outside developers to enter the market, thus limiting competition among developers. This suggests that streamlining red tape may make a tangible difference. Considerations such as these have led some commentators to call for an institutional approach to strategic planning (Salet et al., 2000). Research shows that restrictions on residential development near major cities correlate with the regional distribution of economic activity, and demonstrate that zoning by metropolitan local governments can have adverse effects on housing production and affordability.

As we noted in the conceptual framework developed earlier, housing attitudes and values of the population form part of the institutional makeup of the market. Researchers are increasingly exploring the ways in which demographic and related factors influence housing market outcomes. Andrew et al. (2006), for example, look at the institutional differences in the transition of young adults from renting to first-time homeownership in Britain and the United States (Britain has relatively higher ownership rates among young adults), and hypothesise this is because young adults in Britain are more responsive to income and wealth, and face differences in relative risk. Others find evidence that values relating to the quality of housing are transmitted between generations: the value of the parents' home is an important predictor of housing value of their adult children, even after controlling for parental income, age, and social status.

The relationship between resident neighbourhood groups and local authorities is another fascinating aspect of institutional housing economics. Consumers of housing, despite being the largest and arguably the most important group of stakeholders in the housing sector, probably experience the least degree of formal organisation as a collective interest group. In particular, ordinary residential home-buyers are typically not part of any association, because the actual experience of purchasing a home tends to be an infrequent one, and the interests of buyers are so diverse. Indirectly, certain groups and think tanks provide thought leadership for consumers, and their common interests are often reflected implicitly through watchdogs. Yet one emerging way that homeowners' interests are increasingly being reflected in an explicit manner is through gated communities.

Why are walled neighbourhoods proliferating? The goal of these exclusive suburban enclaves is a transformation of homeownership experience and a shift more towards resident-controlled governance. Researchers have observed that private walled residential neighbourhoods are the predominant form of new housing development across much of the United States. McKenzie (2005) argues that their proliferation is driven by structural forces such as rising land costs, local government fiscal constraints, and consumer preferences for security and control over space. Indeed in some places, for example Las Vegas, gated neighbourhoods are being actively promoted by the authorities: new housing developments must be governed by private homeowner associations, and even existing neighbourhoods are under pressure to become private communities. Le Goix (2005) looks at gated communities in California and notes that one key driver is that local governments consider them a valuable source of revenue because suburbanisation costs are paid by the private developers and the home-buyer, rather than the local authority. The author's empirical study in the Los Angeles region evaluates the nexus between walled suburbs, socioeconomic segments, and ethnic patterns, and concludes that gated communities increase social segregation. Gated neighbourhoods are a phenomenon that is spreading globally. In Canada, gating is not yet as common as in the United States, but Grant (2005) observes that the number of gated subdivisions in that country is increasing. Even so, for the most part, Canadian planning authorities have been slow to include explicit policies related to gating. Homeowners' associations – or 'contractual democratic neighbourhoods' – are seen as illustrating consumers' demand for private governance capacity; and the authors suggest that governments need to reduce the costs of such collective action by providing enabling legislation. Gated communities effectively represent a partial privatisation of the housing sector by the government, through the handing over of civic services supply and management to property companies.

Besides quantitative research, we can also analyse the relationship between institutional groups by way of qualitative case study. For instance, consider the question: is the partnership between the government and community housing cooperatives working? The US Government, through its Department of Housing and Urban Development, recognises community housing associations under its Community Development Entity (CDE) programme. Examples include the Community Reinvestment Committee in Los Angeles, Coconut Grove Collaborative Inc. in Florida, Shorebank Corporation in Chicago, and the Michigan Housing Trust Fund. A CDE, as defined under IRC 45D(c)(1), must be a legally established entity whose primary mission is serving, or providing investment capital for, low-income communities and which is accountable to local residents through representation on a governing board. Of particular interest for our purposes is the category known as Community Housing Development Organization, which is a CDE-type body endorsed by the Department of Housing and Urban Development, the US housing administration. Under the New Markets Tax Credit programme, taxpayers may claim a credit against Federal income taxes for Qualified Equity Investments made to acquire stock in designated CDEs. The funds must, in turn, be applied to a Qualified Low-Income Community Investment, as defined under IRC 45D(d)(1). A defined CDFI is a community-based financial institution dedicated to community development. Grants, loans, equity instruments, deposits, credit union shares, and tax credits are variously available to help promote CDFI access to capital and thereby assist local underserved markets to grow economically. We can see the impact of this programme by observing that over 1000 CDFIs operate across the United States, providing financial services that are often not obtainable from mainstream banks.

Conclusion

In the literature, it is recognised that housing is different because it exhibits hedonic pricing: prices that are determined by more than one factor. In this article, we have seen how housing markets reflect both universal forces (demand and supply) and unique forces (location and culture). This article has outlined a conceptual framework emphasising that housing market outcomes are the product of both traditional economics and institutional forms, to a significant degree. The institutional economics of housing involves the interaction between the rules of the game (institutions) and the players (organisations). Here, the 'rules' include formal laws, and also unwritten codes of behaviour, along with the recognition that control is not the same as influence, and that both are important in shaping market outcomes.

By way of application of the framework, this article has canvassed the diversity of institutional landscapes between countries and even within cities, in the knowledge that different housing systems affect different market outcomes.

The relationship between different public, private, and community-based institutional forms has been explored, and illustrations provided using both quantitative research and qualitative case studies, which is consistent with the empirical style of institutional economics.

By providing an overview of an institutional perspective on housing markets, this article lays the groundwork for later articles exploring particular facets of this essential strand of thought.

See also: Central Government Institutions; Housing Estates; Housing Governance; Housing Supply; Institutional Economics: New; Institutional Economics: Traditional; Institutions and Governance Networks in Housing and Urban Regeneration; Institutions for Housing Supply; Institutions that Represent Housing Professionals; Stakeholder Analysis for Housing; Submarkets; Time and the Economic Analysis of Housing Systems.

References

Andrew M, Haurin D, and Munasib A (2006) Explaining the route to owner-occupation: A transatlantic comparison. *Journal of Housing Economics* 15(3): 189–216.

Bagnoli M and Khanna N (1991) Buyers' and sellers' agents in the housing market. *Journal of Real Estate Finance and Economics* 4: 147–156.

Bishop P (2004) Despised, slippery and untrustworthy? An analysis of reputation in estate agency. *Housing Studies* 19(1): 21–36.

Bratt R (2008) Nonprofit and for-profit developers of subsidized rental housing: Comparative attributes and collaborative opportunities. *Housing Policy Debate* 19(2): 323–365.

Chinloy P and Megbolugbe I (1994) Real estate market institutions in the United Kingdom: Implications for the United States. *Housing Policy Debate* 5(3): 381–399.

Cho Y (2003) Economic efficiency of multi-product structure: The evidence from Korean housebuilding firms. *Journal of Housing Economics* 12(4): 337–355.

Coase R (1988) *The Firm, the Market, and the Law*. Chicago, IL: University of Chicago Press.

Commons J (1931) Institutional economics. *American Economic Review* 648–657.

Goodman A (2005) Central cities and housing supply: Growth and decline in US cities. *Journal of Housing Economics* 14(4): 315–335.

Grant J (2005) Planning responses to gated communities in Canada. *Housing Studies* 20(2): 273–285.

Gros D (2007) Bubbles in real estate? A longer-term comparative analysis of housing prices in Europe and the US. *Economic Policy CEPS Working Documents*. October. Brussels: Centre for European Policy Studies. October.

Hanlon B (2008) The decline of older, inner suburbs in metropolitan America. *Housing Policy Debate* 19(3): 423–456.

Hawtrey K (2009) *Affordable Housing Finance*. Macmillan Series in Banking and Finance Institutions. New York; Basingstoke, UK: Palgrave Macmillan.

Jaffe A (1996) On the role of transaction costs and property rights in housing markets. *Housing Studies* 11(3): 425–435.

Kemeny J, Kersloot J, and Thalmann P (2005) Non-profit housing influencing, leading and dominating the unitary rental market. *Housing Studies* 20(6): 855–872.

Lambooy J and Moulaert F (2009) The economic organization of cities: An institutional perspective. *International Journal of Urban and Regional Research* 20(2): 217–237.

Le Goix R (2005) Gated communities: Sprawl and social segregation in Southern California. *Housing Studies* 20(2): 323–343.

Lowndes V (2001) Rescuing Aunt Sally: Taking institutional theory seriously in urban politics. *Urban Studies* 38(11): 1953–1971.

McKenzie E (2005) Constructing the *Pomerium* in Las Vegas: A case study of emerging trends in American gated communities. *Housing Studies* 20(2): 187–203.

Melendez E and Servon L (2007) Reassessing the role of housing in community-based urban development. *Housing Policy Debate* 18(4): 751–783.

Méndez F (2006) The value of legal housing titles: An empirical study. *Journal of Housing Economics* 15(2): 143–155.

Miceli T and Sirmans CF (2007) The holdout problem, urban sprawl, and eminent domain. *Journal of Housing Economics* 16: 309–319.

Mohamed R (2010) Are profits from subdivision development higher in areas with more regulations? A case study of South Kingstown, Rhode Island and some implications for land use planning. *Housing Policy Debate* 20(3): 429–456.

North D (1990) *Institutions, Institutional Change and Economic Performance*. Cambridge, UK: Cambridge University Press.

Ronald R (2007) Comparing homeowner societies: Can we construct an East–West model? *Housing Studies* 22(4): 473–493.

Ruonavaara H (2005) How divergent housing institutions evolve: A comparison of Swedish tenant co-operatives and Finnish shareholders' housing companies. *Housing, Theory and Society* 22(4): 213–236.

Salet W, Salet W, and Faludi A (2000) The institutional approach to strategic planning. In: Salet W, Salet W, and Faludi A (eds.) *The Revival of Strategic Spatial Planning*, pp. 13–24. Amsterdam: KNAW.

Winfree J and McCluskey J (2007) Takings of development rights with asymmetric information and an endogenous probability of an externality. *Journal of Housing Economics* 16(3–4): 320–333.

Zabel J (2004) The demand for housing services. *Journal of Housing Economics* 13(1): 16–35.

Zumpano L, Johnson K, and Anderson R (2003) Internet use and real estate brokerage market intermediation. *Journal of Housing Economics* 12(2): 134–150.

Further Reading

Cochrane A (2007) *Understanding Urban Policy*. Oxford, UK: Blackwell.

DiPasquale D and Wheaton W (1996) *Urban Economics and Real Estate Markets*. Englewood Cliffs, NJ: Prentice Hall.

Furubotn E and Richter R (1997) *Institutions and Economic Theory: The Contribution of the New Institutional Economics*. Ann Arbor, MI: University of Michigan Press.

Harsman B and Quigley J (eds.) (1991) *Housing Markets and Housing Institutions: An International Comparison*. Boston/Dordrecht/London: Kluwer Academic.

Le Gals P (2002a) *European Cities; Social Conflicts and Governance*. Oxford, UK: Oxford University Press.

Malpass P and Murie A (1999) *Housing Policy and Practice*, 5th edn. London: Macmillan.

Murie A, Niner P, and Watson C (1976) *Housing Policy and the Housing System*. London: George Allen & Unwin.

Olson M (1965) *The Logic of Collective Action: Public Goods and the Theory of Groups*. Cambridge, MA: Harvard University Press.

Housing Need in the United Kingdom

A Clarke, Cambridge University, Cambridge, UK

© 2012 Elsevier Ltd. All rights reserved.

What is Housing Need?

Housing is a basic human need. People need shelter to keep them warm, dry, and safe, to care for children, cook, and store possessions. There is therefore some extent to which it is a universal need. People in all societies must find some way of meeting these needs, and in most societies they do so by means of permanent built structures to live in. The term housing need, however, is also a culturally defined term. It refers not just to those who are in absolute need of housing, being completely without it (though homelessness of course is one form of housing need), but also to those whose housing is in some way unsuitable and fails to meet their needs. These needs are culturally defined, and based on the norms of the society. This article explores housing need in relation to the UK context. It first discusses the way in which housing need is defined and the role of housing need in the UK housing system. It then proceeds to look at the issues that arise when efforts are made to measure it, and then discusses the ways in which it can be measured.

Housing need is something quite distinct from housing demand. Housing demand includes the amount, type, quality, and location of housing that a household chooses and can afford to buy or rent on the market. In developed countries, most households have sufficient income that they can afford to purchase or rent housing of an adequate standard at market rates, and most that can, will choose to do so.

However, a significant minority of households lack the resources to provide themselves with housing which meets either their basic human needs, or the socially accepted norms of the society in which they live. There are particular concerns that children growing up in poor-quality housing may suffer in terms of health or educationally, and also that leaving people to live only in the housing that they can afford, which may be badly overcrowded, may pose risks to the whole of society from the resultant ill-health or poor fire safety (Harker, 2006; Marsh et al., 1999; Wilkinson, 1999). The outcome of leaving it to the market to determine how much housing everyone can consume is therefore considered unacceptable and definitions of acceptable housing standards have therefore been developed. Households living in housing need are those whose accommodation fails to provide this accepted standard.

Regulations tend to govern issues such as fire safety and public health concerns. However, the UK 1996 Housing Act attempted to go beyond this to define the major forms of what was regarded as housing need at the time. It listed categories of people to whom local authorities should give 'reasonable preference' in allocating social housing. The housing needs of refugees are considered under this system. The housing needs of asylum seekers, in contrast, are dealt with by a separate system, outside of the local authority housing department's control.

Homeless People

People who are homeless and sleeping rough are clearly in housing need, as are those sleeping involuntarily in cars, tents, or other unsuitable accommodation. In addition, people living in hostels, refuges, bed and breakfast accommodation, or other accommodation intended for homeless people are generally regarded as being in housing need, on the grounds that this accommodation is not intended to be a permanent home for them. People living informally on friends' floors temporarily with no rights to remain are also regarded as being in housing need, as are those under immediate threat of homelessness. People who are under the threat of violence if they remain where they are and others who cannot 'reasonably be expected' to remain safely in their homes are regarded as being homeless and hence in housing need.

Overcrowded Households

There are two differing standards of overcrowding in use in the United Kingdom. Both compare the composition and size of the household to the number of bedrooms in the dwelling. 'Statutory overcrowding' happens when a household is unable to allow each couple, pair of children of the same sex, pair of children of either sex aged under 10, or other member of the household to sleep in a separate room. Rooms suitable for use as sleeping accommodation, however, can include living rooms as well as bedrooms. There are also rules about the size that bedrooms must be to allow one or two people to use them.

The other way in which overcrowding is assessed in the United Kingdom is the more generous 'bedroom standard'. This also works out the number of rooms required in the same way as statutory overcrowding rules, but assumes that only bedrooms (rather than living rooms) are suitable for sleeping in. A household of six consisting of two parents, two daughters, and two sons living in a two-bedroom flat would therefore be overcrowded according to the bedroom standard but not statutorily overcrowded, so long as they had two bedrooms and a living room which were each large enough to accommodate two people.

People Whose Housing is Insanitary or Otherwise Unsatisfactory

Most local authorities regard people as being in housing need on these grounds if their accommodation lacks facilities such as an indoor toilet, a bath or shower, cooking facilities, or a hot water supply. Some local authorities also include households who have to share facilities with other households to be in some degree of housing need. Housing in a very poor state of repair such that it poses a serious ongoing risk to health would also be considered unsatisfactory, as would that which is uninhabitable, for instance because of flooding or collapse of the roof.

People Who Need to Move for Medical or Welfare Reasons, including Grounds Relating to a Disability

Some people are considered to be in housing need because the accommodation they live in creates or exacerbates an existing medical condition. For instance, people who cannot safely climb the stairs of their property and lack a downstairs bathroom would be considered to be in housing need.

People Who Need to Move to a Particular Location

This may include people who need to move to be nearer training opportunities, special medical facilities, or to give or receive care from family members. It is an interesting example of 'housing need' as it relates not to the actual accommodation, but to its location, in recognition of wider needs, which in some cases can only really be met by living in a specific location.

We can therefore see that the term 'housing need', as it is used in the United Kingdom, covers a wide variety of people whose accommodation fails to provide them with a basic standard that the society they live in expects. In other societies, standards may be quite different as a result of different climates, levels of affluence, and norms around the way in which space within the home is used. Even within the United Kingdom, research has found that views on acceptable forms of housing vary between locations (Platt et al., 2004) and ethnic groups (Markkanen et al., 2008).

What Role Does It Play in the United Kingdom?

The main role that housing need plays in the UK housing system is in determining access to social (pubic sector) housing. It also plays a part, along with other factors, in influencing levels of new social housebuilding that local authorities aim to ensure is provided. Social housing is housing that is allocated by some mechanism other than the market. It was traditionally provided in the United Kingdom by local authorities but much of it today is instead managed by registered social landlords, who are responsible for almost all new construction. It takes the form mainly of social rented housing. The rents are regulated and maintained at submarket levels, meaning that it is a major source of subsidy available to households who are unable to afford adequate market housing. (The other main form of subsidy is Housing Benefit, which is paid directly to low-income households in order for them to afford private sector rents. Whether the housing needs of those unable to afford market rates should be met by the private sector (using Housing Benefit) or in the form of a bricks and mortar subsidy remains a subject of debate but is beyond the scope of this article.) It is allocated primarily on the basis of housing need, though there are other factors that may also determine who is given priority, including length of time waiting, length of local residence, employment status, and past behaviour (CLG, 2002; CLG, 2009).

In contrast, private rented housing is rented to whoever the landlord chooses, and rents are established generally by whatever the market is prepared to pay. Many households, if they are in housing need, will have the resources to find better housing for themselves, and owner-occupation is the tenure of 68% of households in England and Wales with an additional 14% renting privately (see Relevant Websites). Households with sufficient resources would therefore usually be in housing need for only a short period until they buy or rent adequate housing.

The concern around housing need in the United Kingdom has therefore focused on those who are unable to solve their own housing needs because they lack the financial resources. The cost of market housing in the United Kingdom is high, relative to incomes, and despite the recent downturn it remains difficult for many households to afford to buy properties (Pannell, 2010). The rental market is easier to access, though still hard for many households on low incomes, who are in receipt of state benefits or unable to raise the deposit required. Social rented housing has traditionally been seen as the tenure of housing that should be looking to ensure that households unable to provide adequately for themselves in the private market are nevertheless able to live in adequate housing.

The needs-based allocation of social housing was established in the 1977 Housing Act. This legislation (together with later amendments and good practice guidelines) clarifies for local authorities the groups of people to which they owed the most duties to provide housing. It also gives clear guidelines that housing should be allocated on the basis of need and not allocated to sons and daughters of existing tenants in priority above others, allocated solely on the basis of time waiting, or any other factors which run contrary to the principle of housing need. The legislation was broadly welcomed by housing rights campaign organisations and has been defended since as a crucial piece of legislation to ensure that housing need is addressed. The 1996 Housing Act, as discussed above, offered further clarification on the groups who should be afforded the greatest priority, but maintained the emphasis on housing need as the primary consideration.

The system is, however, controversial, as there are perceived to be perverse incentives for households to ensure that their housing is as poor as possible, or do little to improve it, in order to achieve priority for social housing (Dwelly and Cowans, 2006; Turner, 2009). In high-pressured areas, such as London, the difference between social rents and private rents is stark. It has been estimated that a social tenancy has a financial worth of between £35 000 and £75 000 over its lifetime, if the household were otherwise to buy or rent at market levels (Leunig, 2009). It is therefore unsurprising that demand for social rented housing is high, particularly in areas such as London. There are many households unable to access it, but also unable to buy housing, who remain in private rented housing, or are forced to commute long distances to work and often resent the people who enjoy the low rents and very central location of much of the social housing. The tension of the situation is further exacerbated by political parties on the far right who exploit concerns that too much social housing is allocated to immigrants, rather than to long-term local residents (Rutter and Latorre, 2009; Turner, 2009).

It has been suggested that allocating social housing on the basis of housing need has contributed to the declining rates of economically active households in the sector as seen over the past 30 years (Hills, 2007; Martin and Watkinson, 2003; Page, 1993). Solutions are therefore sometimes put forward for adjusting allocations methods, or to diversify tenure so as to produce "a mix of housing types and tenures that are attractive to a wider range of households" (ODPM, 2005a). Social landlords have been responding to this pressure by adjusting allocations systems with a view to increasing social mix (Cole et al., 2001).

Housing is a difficult public good to distribute fairly. Many other forms of welfare are either freely available to all (such as health care or schooling in the United Kingdom) or else allocated on the basis of need, but with a taper, withdrawing support from better-off households at a rate which preserves some incentive to better themselves (such as the UK tax credit system). Social housing does neither of these in a situation of excess demand and therefore creates a harsh divide between those who can and cannot access it. This has led to a political drive to allocate it more fairly to "help and encourage people towards greater economic independence and social mobility; matching responsibility with opportunity...we will deliver greater fairness and make best use of our resources" (Caroline Flint MP, Housing Minister, 17 June 2008 (see Relevant Websites)).

The implication here is that allocating social housing on the basis of housing need is in some sense unfair and fails to encourage people towards economic independence. However, it has been argued that the increasing proportions of economically inactive households in the social rented sector is more related to the inability of these households to access any other sector, than it is a function of the allocation system.

The Government's recent statutory guidance issued to local authorities on allocating social housing (CLG, 2009) was responding to concerns that 'local people' should be given greater priority for accommodation, and encouraged local authorities to make the most of their freedoms and flexibilities already enjoyed in order to achieve this. However, it retained housing need as the overriding priority that must govern allocation:

> We believe it is right that social housing – which brings with it the dual benefits of security of tenure and sub-market rents – should continue to provide a stable base for those who are likely to have more difficulty fending for themselves in the private market. For this reason, we remain of the view that, overall, priority for social housing should go to those in greatest housing need. (CLG, 2009: 10)

It remains to be seen to what extent this new guidance will change the emphasis of allocation systems and move away from allocation based on housing need. It is already the case that some allocation systems give greater priority for length of residence than all but the most severe forms of housing need (see, for instance, www.anglesey.gov.uk, where applicants are awarded a maximum of 50 points for living and working in the parish they wish to live in, but only 30 points if they are sleeping rough). There is also a growing emphasis in the United Kingdom on the use of the private rented sector to alleviate housing need (CLG, 2010; Rugg and Rhodes, 2008). Local authorities have been encouraged to take a wider strategic overview in helping people to access housing in the private rented sector. If people in housing need are able to access private rented housing, and pay for it with housing benefit, this may negate the need for housing need to be the overriding factor in social housing allocation. However, accommodating benefit-dependent households in the private rented sector creates a potentially large housing benefit bill (see Hamnett, 2009), which could only be curtailed by rent regulation (unlikely in the United Kingdom) or further caps to the amount of rent that will be paid, causing difficulties for tenants.

Measuring Housing Need

There are two main reasons why we would want to measure levels of housing need. One relates to the needs of local authorities who are charged with allocating social housing according to a fair and transparent allocation policy which takes account of the identified categories of people in priority housing need. The concern here is not so much to count overall numbers of households in housing need, but to measure it on an individual (i.e., household) basis in order to prioritise between applicants in order to allocate housing to those who are in the greatest need. Differing systems have therefore evolved in different market conditions that also reflect local priorities. The other reason for measuring (or rather, estimating) housing need relates to measuring overall levels of need in order to establish whether more social housing ought to be built. This is the main focus of the remainder of this article.

There are parts of the United Kingdom with weaker housing markets where the cost of social housing, relative to its quality, means that it effectively competes with the private rented sector. In these areas, there have been concerns over the past 30 years that there could be an excess supply of social housing (Bramley and Pawson, 2002; Power and Mumford, 1999; Scottish Executive, 2003). These concerns have been less apparent in the last 5–10 years as the housing market has boomed, and (social) housing construction has failed to keep pace with demand (Ferrari, 2007). Instead, there have been growing problems with excess demand for social housing and growing numbers of households on waiting lists (Shelter, 2008).

Leaving aside questions about whether overall levels of housebuilding impact upon price (Barker, 2004) – and therefore reduce levels of housing need – it is generally recognised that more social housing is required in order to cater for the large and growing numbers of households on housing waiting lists (Barker, 2004; CLG, 2006). The regulated rents mean that social housing construction requires money from the public purse. It is therefore deemed necessary to establish levels of housing need to justify levels of new construction.

There are a variety of approaches used nationally to estimate the amount of new social housing that is required. Some focus more on affordability measures (Bramley and Karley, 2005; Stone, 2007) and others on demographic estimates (CCHPR, 2008). Local authorities in the UK are required to have an up-to-date assessment of the need for affordable housing in order for planners to enforce that new housing developments above a certain size contain a proportion of affordable housing. Affordable housing in this context refers to both social housing and other nonmarket housing, which is more affordable than market housing. Housing assessments are an important aspect of the evidence base that supports the planning system in England and Wales. Their aim is to "provide local authorities with a robust evidence base which will inform the development of policies in local development frameworks....to help ensure that the information underpinning local housing strategies is robust and comprehensive" (ODPM, 2005b: 5).

Local housing need assessments have for many years been used in the United Kingdom to assess levels of housing need, predict future levels of need, and therefore provide an estimate of the amount of new social housing that is required to meet predicted levels of need. In the last few years, many local authorities have taken a broader approach to understanding the whole housing system, carrying out Local Housing Market Assessments (CLG, 2007). Within these assessments, there is generally an element which seeks to establish levels of housing need and hence the need for additional social housing construction. There is also an increased emphasis upon subregional working, in recognition of the fact that in most parts of the country housing markets operate across local authority boundaries, and that a group of neighbouring districts is usually a better approximation of a housing market area than a single district (DTZ Pieda Consulting, 2004; ODPM, 2005b).

Housing need/market assessments are usually commissioned jointly by the housing and planning departments of local authorities. They generally follow the model set out in the guidance issued to local authorities (CLG, 2007), which estimates the number of households falling into and out of need annually, as well as estimating the current number of households in housing need (the backlog). A time period is then chosen over which the local authority can aim to address the backlog (typically 5 years), so the annual requirement for new social housing will be:

- annual number falling into need
- (minus) annual number falling out of need
- (plus) the backlog divided by number of years over which it is to be met.

In order to calculate the numbers who fall into need, whose need is met each year, who could afford to meet their needs on the market, and who are already in housing need, a range of data are required, some of which involve making subjective judgements regarding what should count as a household, or which households should be considered to be able to solve their own housing needs via market housing. Households' own views as to what they can afford to pay by way of mortgage or rent vary, as do mortgage lending criteria, making it difficult to assess accurately who can and cannot afford to purchase or rent in the open market. It is also difficult to establish how many households who are currently living within another household (such as an adult child, or young couple living with parents) intend, or could be said need, to leave home.

Some use can be made of secondary data sources, though national survey data tend not to be robust at the local authority level (Whitehead et al., 2008). Many housing need assessments therefore make use of local household surveys. These involve either interviews or postal questionnaires carried out with a sample of households across the local authority or housing market area (usually several neighbouring local authorities who are working together). Local authorities do not generally have the resources to carry out this kind of work themselves, so they usually commission a consultant to carry it out for them.

Carrying out housing need surveys in a consistent manner and producing clear and uncontroversial findings is however a challenge. Different consultants can carry out a study on the same district and produce very different levels of need. This has meant that studies are frequently challenged at Local Plan Enquiry by developers seeking to reduce the proportion of social housing that has been required of them. Developers are sometimes able to show that the housing needs assessment that the council has commissioned is flawed. In some cases they have commissioned an alternative consultant to carry out a new study that has found very different levels of need for affordable housing.

Planning inspectors find it hard to establish which study should be believed, but would often need to have a detailed understanding of statistical research methods in order to do this. For instance, at one planning enquiry in West Devon, the planning inspector was presented with two alternative assessments which had been carried out, one commissioned by the council and the other by a local developer, finding very different levels of housing need. The inspector examined the two in detail and concluded that in many areas it was not possible to conclude whether the output can be affected by differing judgements at each stage and that there were ambiguities in guidance issued to local authorities at the time, which were capable of interpretation depending on one's point of view (West Devon Borough Council, 2003, Ch. 4: 84). The guidance issued has since been updated (CLG, 2008) and some more recent assessments have started to make use of new resources such as Internet-based property websites which list house prices and rents with coverage of much of the available local stock. However, there do remain difficulties in depending on household surveys funded by limited budgets, with response rates typically below 30% to produce accurate levels of housing need.

An alternative to local housing surveys to measure levels of housing need is to draw on housing registers. However housing registers are produced as administrative systems and are not primarily intended for research purposes. As discussed above, their purpose is to record applicants' need and preferences and to prioritise households for the available lettings, rather than to produce accurate estimates of the total number of households who are 'in housing need' or 'not in housing need'. There have been concerns expressed that in some areas, where the length of time on the housing register is a deciding factor, people may register for social housing at times when they are not in housing need, as 'insurance' for the future (Bramley et al., 2000). Conversely, in areas of high demand where only those in the most severe housing need will have any chance of being offered a social housing tenancy, there is evidence that a great many households do not register for social housing, even though they are in housing need and would like to live in it.

Nevertheless, there is one strong advantage to using housing registers, particularly in areas with relatively low demand: they measure demand for social housing as well as simply need. People are not compelled to live in social housing. It is often a stigmatised tenure, being associated in some areas with large and rough council estates and poor conditions. Some households may choose to remain in private accommodation or share with another household rather than apply for social housing. Indeed, surveys have shown that large numbers of people who would appear to be unable to afford private housing state that they have no desire for social housing (Clarke et al., 2008), meaning that demand for social housing has a role to play, as well as need.

Conclusions

The concept of housing need therefore recognises that housing has a role to play above and beyond meeting the basic human needs of providing shelter. It acknowledges that people suffer from housing that fails to let them live according to the norms of their society. Social housing, once seen in the United Kingdom as the tenure for large sections of the working classes, is today seen as a means by which society can alleviate housing need. Whilst levels of unfit dwellings have fallen hugely over recent years, it has proved harder to tackle overcrowding and other mismatches between households and their accommodation in a housing system that continues to suffer from overall pressure from growing numbers of households, affordability pressures, and excess demand for social rented housing. This excess demand is likely to mean that allocating social housing will remain controversial, and pressure to move away from needs-based allocation will remain.

Linking the construction of new social rented housing to estimated levels of housing need, whilst providing for it through developer contributions in the planning system, also looks likely to ensure that levels of housing need too will remain contested, given the methodological challenges of assessing it.

The growing UK policy interest in the role of the private rented sector in alleviating housing need presents a challenge to the assumed role of social housing as the means by which housing need should be met. If social housing is no longer seen as the only, or even the preferred, way to alleviate housing need, the reason for allocating it on the basis of housing need will surely be further questioned in the future. Determining levels of new social housing that should be built also becomes more a policy decision, rather than hinging solely on levels of housing need in an environment where social housing is no longer seen as the only way to meet housing needs.

See also: Access and Affordability: Developed Countries; Homeless People: Care Leavers in the United Kingdom; Housing and the State in Western Europe; Policies to Support Access and Affordability of Housing; Social Housing: Allocation; Urbanisation and Housing the Poor: Overview.

References

Barker K (2004) *Review of Housing Supply: Delivering Stability: Securing Our Future Housing Needs*. London: HMSO.
Bramley G and Karli K (2005) How much extra affordable housing is needed in England? *Housing Studies* 20(5): 685–715.
Bramley G and Pawson H (2002) Low demand for housing: Incidence, causes and UK national policy implications. *Urban Studies* 39(3): 393–424.
Bramley G, Pawson H, and Parker J (2000) *Local Housing Needs Assessment: A Guide to Good Practice*. London: DETR.
CCHPR (2008) *Homes for the Future: A New Analysis of Housing Need and Demand in England*. London: Shelter.
Clarke A, Fenton A, Markkanen S, Monk S, and Whitehead C (2008) *Understanding the Demographic, Spatial and Economic Impacts on Future Affordable Housing Demand: Paper Four – Moving into Social Housing*. London: Housing Corporation.
CLG (2002) *Allocation of Accommodation: Code of Guidance for Local Housing Authorities. November 2002 Revision*. London: Communities and Local Government.
CLG (2006) *Delivering Affordable Housing*. London: Communities and Local Government.
CLG (2007) *Strategic Housing Market Assessments Practice Guidance Version 2*. London: Communities and Local Government.
CLG (2009) *Fair and Flexible: Statutory Guidance on Social Housing Allocations for Local Authorities in England*. London: Communities and Local Government.
CLG (2010) *The Private Rented Sector: Professionalism and Quality – Consultation. Summary of Responses and Next Steps*. London: Communities and Local Government.
Cole I, Iqbal B, Slocombe L, and Trott T (2001) *Social Engineering or Consumer Choice? Rethinking Housing Allocations*. Coventry, UK; York, UK: Chartered Institute of Housing; Joseph Rowntree Foundation.
DTZ Pieda Consulting (2004) *Housing Market Assessment Manual*. London: ODPM.
Dwelly T and Cowans J (2006) *Rethinking Social Housing*. London: The Smith Institute.
Ferrari E (2007) Housing market renewal in an era of new housing supply. *People, Policy and Place On-Line* 1(3): 124–135.
Hamnett C (2009) Spatial divisions of welfare: The geography of welfare benefit expenditure and of housing benefit in Britain. *Regional Studies* 43(8): 1015–1033.
Harker L (2006) *Chance of a Lifetime: The Impact of Bad Housing on Children's Lives*. London: Shelter.
Hills J (2007) *Ends and Means: The Future Roles of Social Housing in England*. London: London School of Economics.
Leunig T (2009) *The Right to Move*. London: Policy Exchange.
Markkanen S, Clarke A, Fenton A, Monk S, and Whitehead C (2008) *Understanding the Demographic, Spatial and Economic Impacts on Future Affordable Housing Demand: Paper Seven – BME Housing Needs and Aspirations*. London: Housing Corporation.
Marsh A, Gordon G, Pantazis C, and Heslop P (1999) *Home Sweet Home? The Impact of Poor Housing on Health*. Bristol, UK: Policy Press.
Martin G and Watkinson J (2003) *Rebalancing Communities: Introducing Mixed Incomes into Existing Rented Housing Estates*. York, UK: Joseph Rowntree Foundation.
ODPM (2005a) *Planning for Mixed Communities, PPG3 Draft*. London: ODPM.
ODPM (2005b) *Housing Market Assessments, Draft Practice Guidance*. London: ODPM.
Page D (1993) *Building for Communities: A Study of New Housing Association Estates*. York, UK: Joseph Rowntree Foundation.
Platt S, Fawcett W, and de Carteret R (2004) *Housing Futures: Informed Public Opinion*. York, UK: Joseph Rowntree Foundation.
Power A and Mumford K (1999) *The Slow Death of Great Cities?* York, UK: Joseph Rowntree Foundation.
Rugg J and Rhodes D (2008) *The Private Rented Sector: Its Contribution and Potential*. York, UK: Centre for Housing Policy.
Rutter J and Latorre M (2009) *Social Housing Allocation and Immigrant Communities*. Manchester, UK: Equality and Human Rights Commission.
Scottish Executive (2003) *Low Demand Housing in Scotland*. Edinburgh, UK: Chartered Institute of Housing in Scotland.
Shelter (2008) *Research Report: Homes for the Future: A New Analysis of Housing Need and Demand in England*. London: Shelter.
Stone M (2007) A housing affordability standard for the UK. *Housing Studies* 21(4): 453–476.
Turner E (2009) *Reforming the Social Housing Waiting Game*. London: Public Policy Research.
West Devon Borough Council (2003) *Inspector's Report on the WDBC Local Plan*. http://www.westdevon.gov.uk/doc.asp?doc=8922&cat=2397 (accessed 9 August 2010).
Whitehead C, Monk S, Clarke A, Holman A, and Markkanen S (2008) *Measuring Housing Affordability: A Review of Data Sources*. Cambridge, UK: National Housing and Planning Advice Unit.
Wilkinson D (1999) *Poor Housing and Health: A Summary of the Research Evidence*. Edinburgh, UK: The Scottish Office.

Relevant Websites

www.communities.gov.uk – Communities and Local Government.
www.anglesey.gov.uk – Serving Anglesey.

Housing Paradigms

T Iglesias, University of San Francisco, San Francisco, CA, USA

© 2012 Elsevier Ltd. All rights reserved.

Glossary

Paradigm Thomas Kuhn defined the term paradigm as an integrated cluster of substantive concepts, variables, and problems attached with corresponding methodological approaches and tools.

Theories of middle range A "theory of the middle range" as defined by Robert K. Merton is a theory with limited scope intended to explain a specific set of phenomena, rather than a 'grand theory' that purports to explain phenomena comprehensively at a societal level.

Social constructionism Explains how social phenomena develop in social contexts through human interaction and communication.

Jim Crow laws Laws enacted after the Civil War in the United States employing explicitly racial categories intended to maintain segregation.

Mount Laurel cases A series of exclusionary zoning cases decided by the New Jersey Supreme Court which found that cities had a duty under the state constitution to set zoning and other land use policies to create a reasonable opportunity for the production of housing affordable to all economic classes.

Common interest/planned community A housing development in which owners own their own dwelling in fee simple, share certain common areas as tenants, and by virtue of ownership are members of a self-governing body which has certain duties and rights regarding the common areas and the entire planned community.

Habitat I and II Conferences United Nations-sponsored conferences in which participants further defined the 'right to housing' and began work to implement it globally.

Framing devices Framing devices are value-laden images, metaphors, or turns of phrase that structure and direct a reader's attention regarding an issue or problem.

Social norms Social norms are informal rules which identify expected conduct within particular social groups.

Discourse analysis Discourse analysis uses dialogue, conversation, and other communication among actors as the primary data from which to interpret and to understand the social meanings of those actors' intentions and decisions in their interactions.

Introduction

Housing paradigms are historically contingent, value-laden organising principles that shape the whole range of housing issues (viz. financing, production, location, and the use of housing) at all levels of government through an ongoing social dialogue. More specifically, a housing paradigm is an organising principle that affects housing law and policy by directing attention to certain kinds of facts and issues as more or less relevant to policy and decision-making. Beyond just categorising the world, each housing paradigm incorporates a normative dimension; it is poised towards decision and action in a value-laden way, operating as a lens that privileges certain goals by shaping perceptions of the social reality. Each housing paradigm problematises housing in a different way and enables a particular discourse with its own concepts and vocabulary. Housing paradigms may be consciously employed (e.g., for advocacy purposes) or prereflective. In the absence of an agreed-upon grand housing theory, housing paradigms are theories of the middle range. They are consistent with many theoretical frameworks, especially with social constructionism, discourse analysis, and narrative theory. However, the identification and elaboration of housing paradigms implicitly challenges the claim that any one housing paradigm is true or accurately encompasses the entire field. Housing paradigms are useful concepts for housing researchers and scholars because by identifying a society's housing paradigms researchers can reveal and understand the deeper structures of a society's housing law and policy. When a society's housing paradigms have been identified, researchers can use them to explore topics (e.g., affordability and tenure) to determine the effect of a housing paradigm on a law or policy concerning that topic. This understanding in turn provides a basis for critique of, and enables effective improvements in, housing law and policy.

An Example of Housing Paradigms: The United States of America

There are five distinct and stable housing paradigms deeply embedded in the USA's housing policy and law that in turn influence contemporary housing law and policy through an ongoing social dialogue. They are: (1) housing as an economic good, (2) housing as home, (3) housing as a human right, (4) housing as providing social order, and (5) housing as one competing land use in a functional system. Each housing paradigm is now briefly explained. In addition, there is one emerging housing paradigm: housing as a focal point for self-governance. (The USA's housing paradigms are neither normative nor exceptional, but do provide specific examples.)

Paradigm 1: Housing as an Economic Good

The housing as an economic good paradigm directs attention to the fact that most housing is financed, produced, and distributed by the private market. For many Americans, their house is their largest single investment and housing costs are one of their largest monthly expenditures. Substantial capital gains are regularly made and lost in the housing market. Therefore, this paradigm focuses attention on economic principles as critical to the formation of good housing law and policy. This familiar paradigm is evidenced in real estate transactions law and a wide range of policies at all levels of government. From the perspective of this paradigm, any proposed legal rule or policy affecting housing should be scrutinised on the basis of how this proposal will affect investment in housing development, applications for housing development permits, residential property values, and related economic consequences.

Paradigm 2: Housing as Home

The housing as home paradigm concentrates on the fact that homes are *special* places for the people who live in them. There they create their lives, their families, and their very selves. Therefore, this special space must be protected and expectations deriving from it should receive legal recognition. This paradigm is expressed in a wide range of laws and policies generally benefiting current residents of housing. By and large, these laws and policies concern noneconomic rights and privileges affecting safety, freedom, and privacy. This paradigm inquires of any proposed rule or policy: How will this proposal affect domestic privacy, security, household composition, and related values?

Paradigm 3: Housing as a Human Right

The housing as a human right paradigm contends that adequate, safe, and affordable housing is critical to proper human development. Such housing enables individuals to be healthy, to take advantage of educational opportunities, to be productive members of the workforce, and to form nurturing families. Because housing is fundamental to proper human flourishing, this paradigm urges that all people should have rights to housing protected by law. This paradigm is expressed in the widespread adoption of the implied warranty of habitability as well as by more selective adoption of rent control policies and requirements for just cause when evicting tenants and enforcing rent control policies; it was addressed (although not embraced) in the important case *Lindsey v. Normet*. 405 US 56 (1972) (refusing to recognise an individual's right to housing under the Due Process and Equal Protection Clauses of the US Constitution). The question it asks of any new proposal is: How will this proposal affect access to and tenure in safe, decent housing for all people? (It is important to distinguish the use of law in a housing as human right paradigm from law as a typical means to implement a policy adopted because of any housing paradigm.)

Paradigm 4: Housing as Providing Social Order

The housing as providing social order paradigm notes that housing settlement patterns – the relative location of housing, types of housing, and who lives in them – create a particular social order. Where and among whom one lives structures important parts of individuals' lives. Therefore, housing law and policy should respect and promote what are deemed good communities, by respecting who people want to associate with in their neighbourhoods. One critical dimension of this paradigm is relative inclusivity versus exclusivity. Evidence of this paradigm's effects on the USA's housing law and policy include Jim Crow laws, racial and classist restrictive covenants, exclusionary zoning cases (e.g., the famous *Mount Laurel* cases), and the enactment of fair housing law. This paradigm continually asks: How will this proposal affect who will live in my community?

Paradigm 5: Housing as One Competing Land Use in a Functional System

The housing as one competing land use in a functional system paradigm draws attention to the fact that housing is only one of many land uses that are necessary for a healthy, well-functioning city or town. And, housing, like any land use, may have both positive and negative externalities. Therefore, housing law and policy (including financing, producing, designing, and siting) should be conscious and deliberate about the relationships between housing and other land uses in the relevant geographical unit. The marks of this paradigm on USA's law and policy include comprehensive planning law, subdivision law, and environmental law. The primary concern of this paradigm is: How will any housing law or policy affect nearby land uses, infrastructure and schools, the jobs-housing balance, and the environment?

Emerging Paradigm: Housing as a Focal Point for Self-governance

Housing as a focal point for self-governance paradigm may be an additional emerging housing paradigm in the United States. This paradigm is grounded in the relatively recent flourishing of common interest/planned communities. Currently, approximately 50 million Americans live in some form of common interest/planned communities in which housing ownership is linked to membership and voting rights in a self-governing body. This paradigm focuses attention on the relationship between housing and civic engagement in one's housing community. Some argue these developments enable community formation, social capital building, and citizenship skill building. Others argue that common interest/planned communities are the latest form of exclusion and represent privatisation of government. To any proposed new housing law or policy, this paradigm would ask: How will the law or policy affect residents' involvement and democratic participation with their housing community?

Pluralism in Housing Paradigms

A multiplicity (or pluralism) among housing paradigms exists because human housing is such a complex and multifaceted reality. Human housing (the subject of governmental policy and law) is always more complicated than mere 'shelter' because of the social relationships implicated in its financing, production, location, and use. These intricate social relationships create the potential for distinct interests, values, and meanings associated with housing. These, in turn, create the potential for distinct laws and policies that will serve various interests, values, and meanings.

The relationships among housing paradigms can be complex. For example, in the United States each paradigm is not monolithic; there are several versions or strands of each paradigm. For example, versions of the housing as an economic good paradigm vary depending upon each one's interpretations of housing markets and the appropriate role for government policy in establishing and regulating them. Historically this paradigm grounds much of the scholarly debate regarding housing policies. And, each paradigm can support more than one social value, for example, the housing as one land use in a functional system paradigm can be concerned with efficiency, environmental quality, and affordability. In addition, the housing paradigms are not consistently aligned with any particular interest group. One or more of the five identified housing paradigms often combine with each other in support of a particular legal rule or policy. For example, housing antidiscrimination law can be supported by the housing as a human right paradigm and by an inclusionary version of the housing as social order paradigm. A policy or law is most stable when supported by several housing paradigms. For example, the enduring priority for homeownership can be explained in part by the fact that a version of each of the five housing paradigms supports homeownership. The paradigms also function as reciprocal constraints on each other. For example, effects on the cost of housing (housing as an economic good paradigm) are raised as a criticism to policies that would ensure habitability (housing as a human right paradigm).

Coexistence among the housing paradigms has been the norm historically in the United States, and is likely to persist. However, there is a potential for temporary or limited hegemony by one or more paradigms. In the last few decades, a deregulatory (or neo-liberal) version of housing as an economic good paradigm has been rising and become, arguably, dominant. The deregulatory version of housing as an economic good paradigm is founded on the view that the housing affordability problem is caused by the cumulative effect of government regulations raising the production costs of housing. Deregulation is offered as the proposed solution. On this view, government subsidies for housing become unnecessary if government lets the markets work. This particular version of the housing as an economic good paradigm is in profound conflict with the stability and flourishing of the affordable housing movement. In response, the affordable housing movement has articulated a different version of this paradigm, analysing the USA's chronic affordable housing crisis as an effect of various market failures justifying governmental regulation.

Housing Paradigm Perspective as a Tool for Comparative Housing Studies

The housing paradigm perspective can be a useful tool for comparative housing studies. The potential variety (or heterogeneity) of possible housing paradigms is vast because of the multidimensionality of interests, values, and meanings in human housing. However, the meanings and roles of housing in different locations tend to converge around a relatively small number of common practices. In practice, therefore, there may be only a limited number of actual housing paradigms worldwide.

There are two types of housing paradigm pluralism: global variety and local variety. Global variety expresses the overall multiplicity of distinct housing paradigms in different cultures worldwide. For example, Zimbabwe may generate a housing paradigm that never emerges in Canada. Local variety pluralism recognises that due to the sociological richness of the human experience of housing probably each culture will have more than one operative housing paradigm at any time in its history. As described above, the United States currently has at least five operative housing paradigms.

There are two forms of commonality among housing paradigms: static shared housing paradigms and dynamic commonality. Because housing fulfils similar functions in many societies it is likely that some societies will share some common housing paradigms. For example, the housing as home paradigm operates in both the United States and the United Kingdom. Comparative housing scholars can investigate and measure the extent and degree of shared housing paradigms globally. Due to the influence of local factors and conditions, researchers may expect different versions and/or combinations of these paradigms in different societies, a form of latent pluralism.

In addition, comparative housing scholars can investigate and measure the direction of change in housing paradigms globally or within a society. It is possible that a version of some common housing paradigms, for example housing as an economic good, may be converging and possibly even nearly universal globally or within a region or society. This does not mean that it would be the dominant housing paradigm within these societies, only that it is nearly always present as one of the housing paradigms in a certain set of societies. However, over time researchers may find patterns of dominance or trends towards hegemony of certain housing paradigms. Alternatively, housing paradigms in different societies might further diverge. These changes could occur because of external/exogenous factors (e.g., pressure from the World Bank or International Monetary Fund), internal/common experiences, or (more radically) because of some universal aspect of the human condition. For example, a version of the housing as an economic good paradigm may be common and may be becoming dominant because of the expansion of market-based economies or neo-liberal ideology in the last 25 years. Alternatively, the United Nations' work resulting from the Habitat I and II Conferences in 1987 and 1996 may be promoting a version of the 'housing as human right' paradigm as a dominant paradigm worldwide. For example, countries as diverse as France and Ecuador have recently legally recognised housing as a human right. The housing as one land use in a functional system paradigm may be coming into the forefront because of a broader recognition of important causal relationships between land use patterns (including housing settlement patterns) and climate change, and the resulting focus on environmental sustainability. Yet, given the multifaceted nature of human housing and the variety of factors shaping housing paradigms, it is likely that housing paradigm pluralism will be persistent both within particular societies and globally.

Three key factors are likely to shape housing paradigms in any particular country and suggest when and how they might change: its economic system and stage of economic development; its political and civil society (including religious traditions); and, the relative dominance of its urban, suburban, or rural settlement patterns. Housing paradigms are most clearly expressed and are most likely to change in times of significant social, political, or economic transition. For example, the dominance of the housing as an economic good paradigm in postsocialist transition economies has led to widespread privatisation of housing, and the right to housing enshrined in the new constitution of postapartheid South Africa is molding its housing law and policy.

Consequences of Housing Paradigm Pluralism

Housing paradigm pluralism may help explain the difficulty housing scholars have encountered in identifying a single grand housing theory. For example, the housing as an economic good paradigm cannot explain certain common phenomena, for example, inefficient remodelling expenses by homeowners. If there is persistent housing paradigm pluralism, then it is likely that national housing policies will never be as coherent as some scholars, policymakers, and advocates hope or expect. For example, the USA's housing paradigm pluralism supports numerous, diverse goals and interests but not in a consistent or coherent way. Thus the USA's housing paradigm pluralism helps account for the past and current muddle of its housing law and policy. And to the extent that housing paradigm pluralism persists, the United States is not likely to ever have a completely coherent, efficient, and equitable housing policy. Still, further research might offer a different notion of coherence that is more appropriate, for example, substantial fit with the society's core values and aspirations. And, housing paradigm pluralism may illuminate ongoing housing policy conflicts, such as: what housing production and financing systems (i.e., market, private, nonprofit, or government) should be promoted and subsidised; the appropriate balance between homeownership and rental housing; which forms of housing ownership should be promoted; and to what degree local units of government should decide the types, amounts, and location of housing build in its jurisdiction.

Understanding the operative housing paradigms in a given society presents housing scholars and advocates with the challenges and opportunities that a specific housing paradigm pluralism presents to the achievement of particular policy goals, for example, advancing affordability or homeownership. Employing a housing paradigm perspective, housing researchers can consider local instances of housing paradigms or particular mixes of housing paradigms in specific societies or regions as local laboratories of housing law and policy. And such studies will enable societies to learn from each other.

Outstanding Research Questions

Housing studies is often criticised as under-theorised, in part because housing studies are often conducted employing a positivist empirical method framed by neoclassical economic theory. The housing paradigm perspective can shed new light on traditional topics in housing studies as well as opening up a wide range of new questions.

To date, many scholars have explicated one or more housing paradigms in their own societies. The housing as an economic good paradigm has been investigated in detail by economists and provides the context for traditional debates about the relative roles of the market and the society in housing policy. The critical debates about housing affordability are usually carried out within this paradigm. The housing as home paradigm has been explored under the rubric of the meaning of home, frequently within the context of the tenure of homeownership. The housing as a human right paradigm is commonly the focus of human rights advocates and lawyers, particularly those inspired by the United Nations Habitat work. The housing as social order paradigm has been considered by numerous scholars under the categories of discrimination, social exclusion, and segregation. The housing as one land use in a functional system paradigm is primarily discussed in the context of planning and environmentalist literature. As such, the housing paradigm framework offers a middle range theory to put all these literatures under one conceptual roof.

As an emerging field, there are numerous important methodological and conceptual questions for the housing paradigm perspective. Housing paradigms may function as rhetorical devices, metaphors, narratives, framing devices, ideologies, separate rationalities, or some combination of these. Therefore, the primary conceptual issue is clarifying the conceptual status of housing paradigms within other housing theories and in relation to other theories of the middle range, for example social norms. A related issue is clarifying the mechanisms by which housing paradigms operate to influence law and policy formation and development. Identifying housing paradigms is an interpretative exercise, and, as such, is inherently contestable. The primary methodological issue is agreeing upon methods to identify housing paradigms and the processes by which they are generated and changed. The answers to the preceding conceptual and methodological questions would inform the necessary empirical work. This work includes identifying operative (and emerging) housing paradigms in each society; cataloguing the panoply of extant variations; and identifying trends towards commonality, convergence, dominance, or divergence in societies and globally along with the causes of such changes.

See also: Comparative Housing Research; Complexity; Construction of Housing Knowledge; Critical Realism; Cultural Analysis of Housing and Space; Discourse Analysis; Discrimination in Housing Markets; Economic Approaches to Housing Research; Human Rights and Housing; Policies to Promote the Environmental Efficiency of Housing; Political Ideologies; Regulation Theory; Social Class and Housing; Social Construction; Social Policy Approaches; Social Theory and Housing; Socio-Legal Perspectives.

Further Reading

Barros DB (2006) Home as a legal concept. *Santa Clara Law Review*. 46, 255–290.
Bengtsson B (2001) Housing as a social right: Implications for welfare state theory. *Scandinavian Political Studies* 24(4), 255–275.
Benjamin D (ed.) (1995) *The Home: Words, Interpretations, Meanings, Environments*, Aldershot: Ashgate.
Bratt RG, Stone ME, and Hartman CW (2006) *A Right To Housing: Foundation for a New Social Agenda*, Philadelphia: Temple University Press.
De-Vos P (2001) Grootboom: The right of access to housing and substantive equality as contextual fairness. *South African Journal on Human Rights* S48(17): 258–276.
Fox L (2007) *Conceptualising Home: Theories, Laws and Policies*, Hart Publishing Ltd: Oxford.
Goodchild B (2003) Implementing the right to housing in France: Strengthening or fragmenting the welfare state? *Housing, Theory & Society* 20(2): 86–98.
Haworth A, Manzi T, and Kemeny J (2004) Social construction and international comparative housing research. In: Jacobs K, Kemeny J, and Manzi T (eds.) *Social Construction and International Comparative Housing Research*, pp. 159–185. Aldershot: Ashgate.

Iglesias T (2007) Our pluralist housing ethics and the struggle for affordability. *Wake Forest Law Review*, 42(2): 511–593.

King P (2000) Can we use rights to justify housing provision? *Housing, Theory and Society* 17: 27–34.

Mandic S and Clapham D (1996) The meaning of homeownership in the transition from socialism: the example of Slovenia. *Urban Studies* 33(1): 83–97.

Massey D, and Denton N (1993) *American Apartheid: Segregation and the Making of the Underclass,* Harvard University Press: Harvard.

Misra PC (1998) Right to shelter: A human right perspective. *Journal of the Indian Law Institute* J65(40): 230–242.

Reinders L and Van Der Land M (2008) Mental geographies of home and place: Introduction to the special issue (see articles within). *Housing, Theory & Society* 25(1): 1–13.

Youngs R (2004) Human rights in the housing sphere: German comparisons. *The King's College Law Journal* K7(15): 145–158.

Relevant Website

http://www.unhabitat.org – United Nations Habitat Project.

Housing Pathology

A Thomsen, Delft University of Technology, Delft, The Netherlands

© 2012 Elsevier Ltd. All rights reserved.

Glossary

Building pathology Study of building deficiencies, concerning identification, investigation, and diagnosis of defects in existing buildings, prognosis of defects, recommendations for the most appropriate course of action, and appropriate programmes of remedial works.
Demolition Intentional physical deconstruction of buildings.
Housing pathology Holistic approach to identify, investigate, and diagnose housing deficiencies, specify preventive measures and remedial interventions, and evaluate their effects.
Housing quality The ability of residential buildings to fulfil adequate shelter for specified groups of residents.
Life cycle (of buildings) The cycle from initiation, conception, realisation, exploitation, and adaptation through demolition.
Lifespan The length of time during which buildings physically exist.
Pathology Study of diseases with the aim of understanding their causes, symptoms, and treatment.
Real service life The period a dwelling actually is used and/or meets demand.
Social pathology Study of social problems as the result of human behaviour within specific social, cultural, economical, and physical circumstances.
Urban pathology Study of urban problems. Individual events negatively valued by society in general and aggregated into neighbourhood grades.

Introduction and Definition

Housing pathology can be defined as a holistic approach to understand the nature and life cycle of residential buildings and their environment, in order to identify, investigate, and diagnose deficiencies, specify preventive measures and remedial interventions, and evaluate their effects. In common parlance, the term housing pathology is sometimes used to point at all kinds of major social problems with a housing or urban background. In the more broad scientific definition in this article, housing pathology refers to pathological knowledge and skills about residential buildings in their social and physical environment, making use of building pathology (Harris, 2001; Watt, 2007) as well as social pathology (Gerhard, 1997; Lemert, 1951) and urban pathology (Choldin, 1978).

The term pathology has its origin in the medical science and is generally defined as the systematic study of diseases with the aim of understanding their causes, symptoms, and treatment. The term has since been applied in many different disciplines, in the context of the built environment being, in particular, building pathology and social and urban pathology. In analogy with health as the core condition for the quality of human life, the health of housing accommodations stands for housing quality, being the ability of residential buildings to fulfil adequate shelter for specified groups of residents. On the other hand, this analogy falls short on one essential difference: Unlike living things, houses and other building are not god given but immobile man-made artefacts intended to serve specific needs, and their health and the lifespan are the result of men's decisions. Consequently, the appreciation of the housing quality mirrors the concerns of the partaker involved.

Though buildings can physically exist long after being abandoned, the relevant lifespan of dwellings is the real service life: the period a dwelling actually meets demand (Awano, 2005). Housing pathology concerns this phase. Pathological studies are directed at the physical as well as the functional and economical performance of dwellings and to what extent they satisfy their stakeholders – residents as well as proprietors – demands.

Existing Stock and Paradigm Shift

The twentieth century saw an enormous worldwide growth of the housing stock. In particular, the building boom after the Second World War, during which the housing stock in most countries was multifolded, focused the attention of the housing sector primarily on the planning and realisation of new construction; the consciousness of the enormous maintenance and management task to come was still a far cry away.

The beginning of the twenty-first century shows a completely different situation that urges for a paradigm shift. As **Figure 1** shows, new construction in most Western countries has faded down below an annual production of 1% of the existing stock, and often well below.

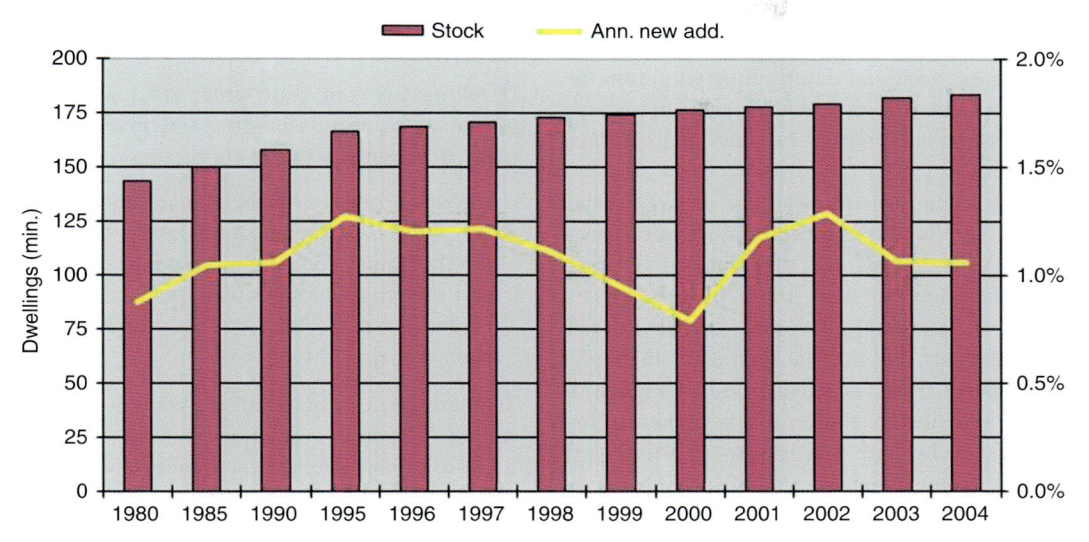

Figure 1 European housing stock, annual addition (8/15 Western European countries + CH).

Parallel to this, the ageing existing stock draws growing attention. As **Figure 2** shows, two-thirds of the Western European housing stock is built after the Second World War. In most Western European countries, over 60% of the stock – in some countries like the Netherlands and Finland even over 75% – is younger than 50 years and over half is younger than 30 years.

Though still relatively young, the existing stock is ageing fast. In particular, the older part of the stock is increasingly facing deficiencies and shortcomings, large parts do not satisfy residents' needs and preferences and are far from energy-efficient, and numerous postwar neighbourhoods are in trouble. The necessary investments in major repairs, renovation, adaptation, and redevelopment count at present for a total turnover well beyond that of new construction. Improving the energy efficiency to the required standards of tomorrow will give these investments a strong extra boost. Though the change from large-scale new construction to maintenance and improvement of the existing stock is well under way, the knowledge about how and when to successfully maintain a healthy housing stock has still a long way to go. This otherwise also refers to the fast-growing urban areas in developing countries. At the same time, the awareness grows that housing problems are only partly related to the physical supply side and solving them requires more than bricks and mortar. This shows the relevance of housing pathology as a relatively new knowledge field, combining expertise, skills, and instruments for a healthy housing stock.

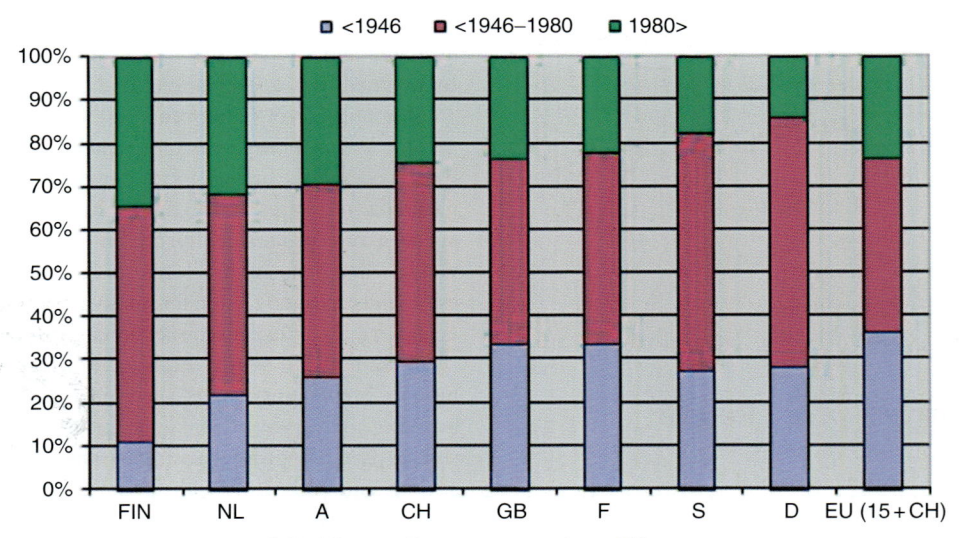

Figure 2 European housing stock by age (8/15 Western European countries + CH).

Holistic and Sustainable Approach

As housing is a basic need and determining condition for the quality of human life, the quality and supply are subject to governmental control by laws, regulations, and public bodies.

Housing, be it single private dwellings or large social housing estates, implies complicated interrelated processes with multiple actors. On the scale of existing dwellings and their environment, these processes basically consist of the supply = the dwelling, the demand = the residents, and the management = the landlord and/or property trade, as schematised in **Figure 3**. To understand the nature of these processes, their influence on the life cycle, and deficiencies of residential buildings and their environment, a holistic approach is essential.

The results of these processes have far-reaching and long-lasting social, economic, ecologic, demographic, and geographic effects on different levels of scale, making a sustainable approach indispensable (see **Figure 4**).

Figure 3 Holistic approach.

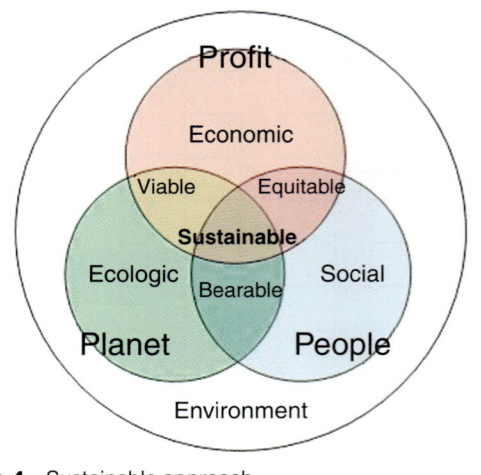

Figure 4 Sustainable approach.

Nature and Life Cycle of Dwellings

Dwellings are composite structures, consisting of a multiplicity of building elements and materials and serving many different and partly conflicting functions as follows:

- shelter: protection from climate and external threats; the physical or technical quality;
- family home: cocooning, cooking, dining, recreating, and sleeping; the functional quality; and
- capital good: a source of actual or future income; the economical quality.

These three main functions are conditional for the quality and the lifespan of residential buildings and housing stocks.

As a human artefact, the quality and the lifespan of a dwelling is not limited by given physical conditions, but can in principle be endlessly prolonged, as long as it keeps being useful by the application of maintenance, adaptations, improvements, transformations, and possibly reuse of building parts and functions.

The life cycle of buildings consists of three main phases: the initial phase or building phase, consisting of the initiative, the design, and the construction phase; the use phase or real service life; and the final end-of-life phase. In the initial phase, the initial quality, determining for the future quality development, is established. Afterward, change of the initial quality will require capital-intensive modifications and adjustments.

Housing Quality

What is housing quality, and what is a decent – healthy – housing quality?

As shown above, the quality of residential buildings is determined by the physical or technical quality, the functional quality, and the economical quality. Clear standards for what these qualities are – or should be – are hardly available and strongly depend on the country and culture. In practice, the appreciation of the housing quality will considerably diverge between residents and other parties involved: landlords, residing tenants, applying tenants, owner-occupiers, or real estate developers, all having their particular measures. In the rented sector, landlord attitudes are as a rule professionally driven by property value and yield – though social landlords also by more societal interests – and tenants by value for money and emotions. Owner-occupiers, by nature nonprofessionals, face both sides.

Since housing quality highly determines the quality of human life, governments interfere in the housing and building market by means of legislation, inspection, and subvention. To protect residents and citizens from dangerous and unhealthy substandard building conditions, building regulations for the existing stock set a bottom line for the minimal acceptable dwelling quality, and to enforce a minimum quality of new construction, building regulations set a wide range of minimal conditional quality standards. Both quality levels though do not answer the question what decent housing quality is: the bottom line for existing stock is too low and the standard for new construction too high to serve as a feasible and acceptable standard for the maintenance and management of the existing housing stock.

Traditionally, housing quality is assessed by the presence and acceptability of defects and shortcomings. Actual housing management approaches aim at the more positive question of what quality level is needed for maintaining a healthy lifespan of residential stock. The answer is attempted by, as an example, successively distinguishing the market potency, using product–market combinations (PMCs); the corresponding physical and functional conditions for optimal performance, using critical success factors (CSFs); and the underlying physical, functional, and economical performance requirements. This approach will further be discussed below.

Lifespan

What is, and what should be, the average lifespan of a building?

To assess what quality is needed to maintain a healthy housing stock, this question is vital. There are several approaches to answer this question. The most common approach is based on the precalculated amortisation of the capital investment, generally 50 years for buildings and 75 years for the land. In practice, however, most buildings last much longer – according to a recent expert enquiry 125 years – while many of the composing materials have a much shorter lifespan. **Figure 1** shows that the housing stock is so young that reliable ex-postevaluation data to measure the lifespan are not available. The question can also ex ante be approached by computing the minimal needed service life of the existing stock using the actual available replacing capacity. This results in a minimal time to replace the existing stock – using all the available building capacity – in the Netherlands and in the United Kingdom of roughly 100–125 years. As the actual replacement is much lower – in the Netherlands 0.25% annually of the stock and in the United Kingdom substantially lower – this results in a minimal necessary net lifespan of 350 and 1000 years, respectively.

Life Cycle Models and Approaches

Most lifespan theories and life cycle models of buildings originate from the broader research field of consumer goods manufacture, covering all phases from initiative, production, and retail through use and disposal or recycling. As decisions in the design phase are decisive for the performance, knowledge about the use phase is essential for the design. In particular, aircraft and automotive manufacturers have a strong interest in safe, reliable, and long-lasting products, and as a consequence, most research in the field of technical maintenance of buildings is derived from that source. On the other side, marketing surveys make up essential input about consumer needs and preferences. In the housing field, marketing has still a long way to go.

Life cycle models of buildings can be divided into three basic types: cyclic models, linear models, and process models.

Cyclic models cover all phases: the initial phase consisting of research, programme, design, production, and distribution; the use phase; and the end of life phase. Specific for buildings as complex composite and long-lasting structures is the recurring repetition of the cycle during the use phase as major repairs, renovation, transformation, and so on follow the same cycle. Cyclic models are mainly descriptive, ordering the process without explaining or predicting possible outcomes.

Linear models describe the life cycle of a building as the development of a value over time. **Figure 5** depicts

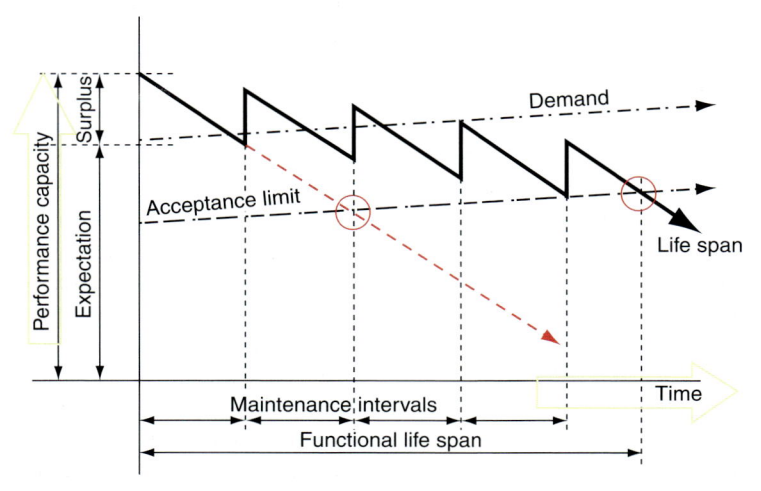

Figure 5 Dwelling decay process.

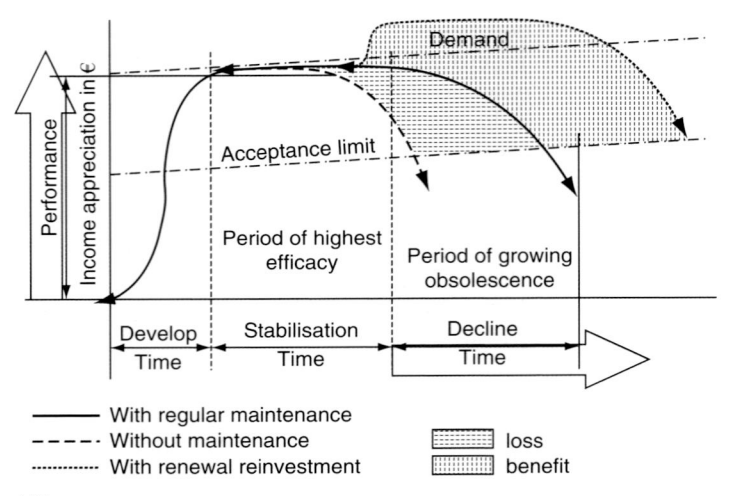

Figure 6 Real estate project life.

the development of the building performance as linear declining due to ageing, and the required performance to satisfy the user's demand as increasing due to economic growth and prosperity. Problems arise where the actual performance falls through the limit of acceptance, causing tenant complaints and loss of market position. This model shows the main intervention strategies to prevent this: maintaining by carrying out maintenance and major repairs, upgrading by improvements to increase the performance capacity, or downgrading by changing the target group to less demanding residents.

Depicted as the income appreciation over time, **Figure 6** shows the development of the economic performance. In the same way as the physical performance, this model shows the strategic and managerial intervention potentials. During the development phase, a revision of the planned appreciation, that is, the design, and/or of the objectives is required and possible, whereas during the stabilisation phase and the decline phase, the variables lie in changing the performance by additional earning potential or accepting a lower profit and/or shorter profitable lifespan.

Comprehensive process models are intended to relate the life cycle of buildings to determining factors, usually being technical/physical, social/functional, and economical aspects.

Figure 7 shows a recent version of this kind, a diagnosis and decision support model shaped as a decision tree with tangible suggestions for interventions following survey outcomes. Based on the results of an international comparative survey of aged housing stock (Van Kempen et al., 2006), this model can serve as a backbone for housing pathology analyses.

What Determines the Lifespan?

Empirical knowledge about the lifespan of buildings is limited. This may have to do with the relatively young age of the existing stock and the prevailing attention to new construction as stated above.

The main sources of knowledge about the lifespan of buildings are quantitative statistical data on withdrawal from the national stock, generally consisting of the total of, respectively, demolition, end of use, merge to other buildings, and loss by calamities. Most countries only maintain statistics on withdrawal of residential stock. Some countries like Finland do not (yet) collect statistical data on withdrawal at all.

In recent decades, some surveys have been executed on the qualitative side of the lifespan, more in particular on demolition and demolition motives of dwellings.

Theoretically, the main determining factors of fatal building decay can be divided into technical, functional, and (micro)economical decay, generally related to underperformance by, on the one hand, declining quality and/or, on the other hand, rising needs.

Unlike what most people think, technical causes are generally not decisive for the end of life of buildings. Based on Dutch sources, the determining factors for demolition of residential stock were found to be tenure, age, building type, location, and proprietor motives.

According to these findings, there is a strong correlation between tenure and demolition rate. Though technically the best part of the Dutch housing stock with no share of substandard dwellings, the demolition rate of social rented dwellings is 3–4 times higher than that of the owner-occupied stock; on the other hand, the demolition rate of the worst part, the commercial rented stock with a substantial substandard share, is almost zero. Regarding tenure, demolition often occurs after property transfer to developers and municipalities with the intention to realise new urban plans and developments. This also applies to the owner-occupied stock where demolitions almost always occur after purchase by new owners often in search of land for a new home.

Within the social rented stock, there is some correlation between age and demolition rate. Though the age of

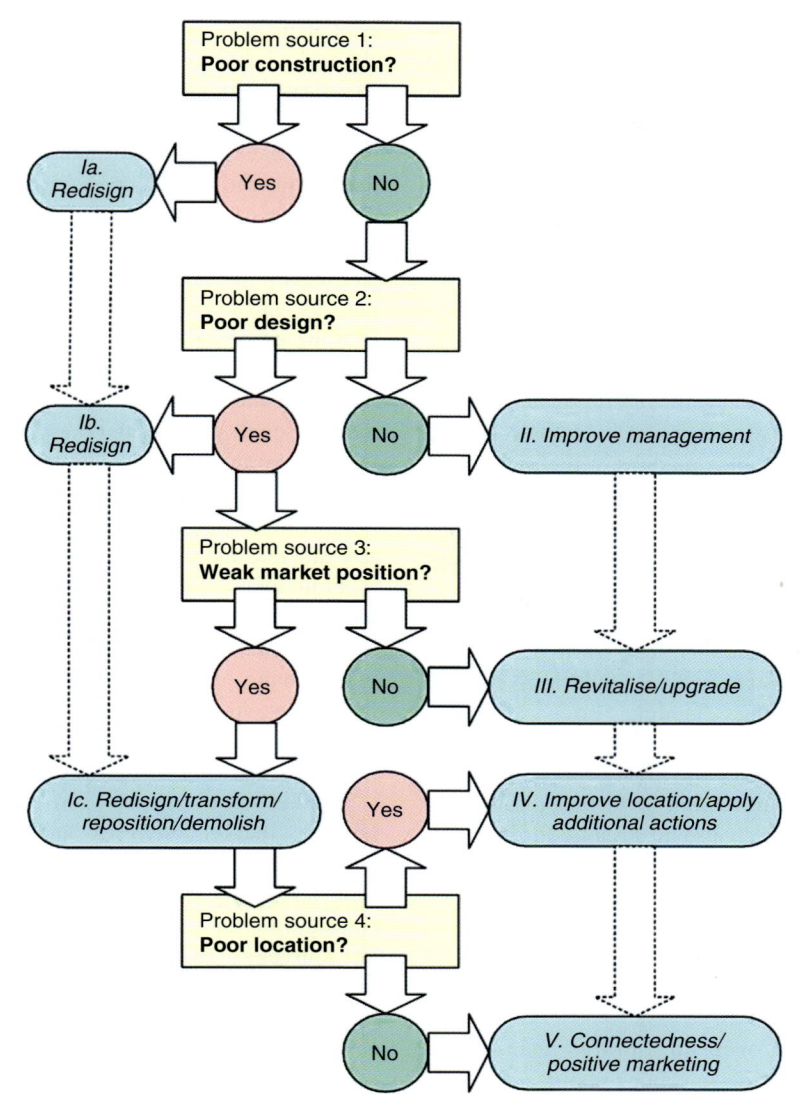

Figure 7 Diagnostical model.

buildings generally determines the technical and functional quality, this correlation is not generally valid in the owner-occupied and the commercial rented stock, where it only occurs within the same building type (detached, semi-detached).

Also within the social rented stock, there is some correlation between building type and demolition rate. The demolition rate of social rented apartment buildings is significantly higher than that of single-family dwellings. The opposite occurs in the owner-occupied stock, where demolition is concentrated in the detached dwelling type; demolition of owner-occupied row houses and apartments is rare.

In contrast to previous analytical assumptions, no general correlation between location and demolition rate or between the type of housing management and demolition rate was found. On the other hand, there are indications that motives and ambitions of the management play a significant role in the demolition policy of housing associations.

Based again on Dutch sources, demolition motives should be divided into two different underlying grounds: the quality of the existing property and the value of land and location.

Quality-related motives can be linked with insufficient technical quality, functional quality, or economical quality and oversupply. In line with the correlation between age and quality, technical motives increase with the age and as such dominate in the prewar stock; in the same way, functional motives dominate in the early postwar stock and economic/oversupply motives dominate in the younger stock and fade with age. Profit-related motives can be linked with a high potential land development value after and/or low value/yield before demolition.

Not a motive but an important reason for demolition is urban planning, also with either a qualitative or a profit background.

Demolition motives are often mixed, unclear, and – in the case of profit-related motives – hidden.

Housing Pathology in Practice

Derived from its origin in the medical science, the practice of housing pathology basically consists of six steps: anamnesis, diagnosis, remedy, care, evaluation, and prevention.

The way these steps are employed in practice largely depends on the tenure, professionalism of the proprietor, and the actual circumstances. In the case of professionally managed property, most of the six steps are part of common strategic housing property and asset management cycles.

Next to this, generally unplanned reasons to start these steps are sudden serious quality loss, be it by internal (deformation, leakage, stench, fire, explosion, etc.) or external (storm, lightning, flooding, etc.) calamities, often in addition to assessment of liability and loss. This kind of assessment belongs to the highly specialised field of building pathology and will not be further discussed.

Property transactions can also be a reason for in-depth examination of the health of the property involved. In any case, fulfilment of the next steps requires proficient professional knowledge, skills, and experience.

Anamnesis

Like medical anamnesis, or medical history, gained by a physician by asking specific questions about a patient's troubles and possible causes, referred to as symptoms, completed with direct clinical examination, the anamnesis phase of housing pathology can be described as a systematic data collection of historical and actual data about the health of houses, in case of emergent problems, completed with additional specific on-site inspection.

The anamnesis is a vital part of professional strategic housing management. It usually consists of a collection of data about the construction, renovation, adaptation, and maintenance history, and the technical, functional, and economic/market performance, preceded by formal and legal information, like land register records, building permits, and so on.

Sources are all necessary legal documents for each building, including land and ownership registration, building, land and use permits, (revision-)drawings, (periodical) quality and safety assessments, EPBD energy labels, guarantee documents, user manuals, and so on; rental administrations, including contracts, inspections, modification permits, and so on; periodical condition assessments; and long-term maintenance plans.

Functional performance is in practice largely intertwined with economical performance. Sources are internal data, that is, portfolio management plans, including strategic planning of supply and target groups and PMCs, re- and disinvestments, and comparative assessment, that is, rent valuation or property valuation scores and long-term market and profit assessments.

Market performance sources are, for example, housing market analyses and performance analyses based on exit interviews, denied lettings, resident satisfaction, tenant preferences, client panels, complaints, and consultation of tenant organisations. In particular, the last sources are of vital importance for timely observation of, and anticipation on, possible failures and underperformance, be it that the outcomes should always be combined with regular inspection of the physical condition.

Table 1 shows an overview of the respective normative and relative criteria and related project data sources. The interval and urgency of these reviews mainly depend

Table 1 Housing quality assessment, standards, and criteria

	Normative standards	Relative criteria	Project data source
General	Property regulations Housing regulations	General rating systems	Property portfolio
Technical/physical	Building code Technical standards EPBD	Condition rating criteria (EN-NEN 2767) EPBD criteria	Condition inspection Maintenance register Resident complaints EPBD label
Functional	Building code Functional standards	Functional assessment criteria (WWS) Quality certificate requirements	Functional assessment score Letting register Resident satisfaction Exit interviews
Economical	Rental housing regulations	Property value criteria Performance rating systems Property index	Property value Performance/index score Balance sheet Yield

on the risk and gravity of possible consequential damage and loss and partly covered by formal governmental and/or institutional regulations. The latter concerns, in particular, the growing importance of quality certification.

Accidental anamnesis in case of calamities and so on is generally directed at specific characteristics and symptoms of the disorder concerned and the underlying causes. It will generally require specialised expertise.

Diagnosis

Like the medical diagnosis, which refers to as well the determination process as to the resulting opinion about the nature and possible causes of a disease or disorder, the diagnosis phase of housing pathology can be described as the systematic search for the nature and possible causes of housing problems, starting with careful analysis of the symptoms found in the anamnesis. Thorough knowledge of the symptoms and underlying possible disorders and their causes is an essential prerequisite.

In professional practice, the diagnosis follows, as part of the strategic housing management cycle, the analyses of the anamnesis. Diagnostic procedures can be carried out using a variety of techniques and approaches: deductive, deterministic, and/or probabilistic. The analytical model of **Figure 7** offers a useful tool for this purpose. Results are most often obtained by elimination of other reasonable possibilities and, in case of physical/structural disorders (leakage, noise, etc.), diagnostic tests.

The diagnosis phase of housing pathology is of vital importance; poor diagnoses can have severe and sometimes fatal consequences.

As for housing pathology in general, the only criterion for a sound diagnosis is the health or residential quality: the ability of residential buildings to fulfil adequate shelter for specified groups of residents. As long as clear standards to assess and measure residential quality are practically not available (see above), each diagnosis requires a separate quality analysis, with the minimal level of the national and local building regulations as a bottom line. Specific interests of the parties involved can only be of secondary influence and should be explicitly referred to. This regards not only direct material interests but also attitudes and habits. In the construction and property trade, it is not uncommon to automatically combine a rough indication of apparently clear disorders with simple technical remedies, that is, leaking roofs should be replaced, damp walls are caused by ill-occupancy, and aged obsolete housing blocks should be demolished. These 'diagnoses' are often more the result of prejudices and biased opportunism than clear analyses. In particular, the latter examples entail the risk of planners blight: self-fulfilling authoritative disqualifications, because the accused residents will not bother anymore and few will invest in turned-down property.

As argued above, housing deficiencies are seldom single-sided. To serve as a reliable input for possible remedies, the diagnosis phase should therefore cover all relevant causes of and influences on the central problem, including starting points for alternative strategies and excluding hidden biases.

Remedies and Treatment Plan

Searching for adequate remedies for housing problems may well be the most difficult step in professional housing management. It implies weighing a range of considerations between often conflicting interests and goals, short- or long-term solutions and consequences, investments and returns, and risks and feasibilities. As mentioned above, some problem–solution combinations may be – or look – simple, but often are not.

Following the diagnosis, remedies should in the first place solve quality problems, that is, the ability to fulfil adequate shelter for specified groups of residents. This means that the criteria for decent solutions may vary between students, family with children, and the elderly. Property ownership is of course an essential input in the whole process: it is determining for the professionalism of the housing management and pathological approach, from the anamnesis through the conceptualisation of and the decision-making about a treatment plan. But a well-developed treatment plan should consider all interests concerned and, in the case of ill-combinable concerns and contradictory outcomes, provide alternative solutions.

Major structural solutions will require long-term investments and accordingly additional burdens. To assess these and compare alternative approaches and options, the use of advanced financial assessment methods based on net constant value is essential.

In particular, in the case of combined problems in older stock, a differentiated larger-scale approach including the environment and infrastructure should be taken into account. In the past decades, a growing number of specialised architects and research and development offices have focused their expertise on this subject. But, as experience shows that a preceding adequate and thorough diagnosis is essential for successful results, remedies should follow and never precede clear analyses. In particular, architects and housing managers should bear this well in mind.

Evaluation and Prevention

Though often neglected, evaluation is of vital importance, as well to check if and to what extent the treatment was successful, as to gain knowledge to be applied in similar cases. The analytical model of **Figure 7** is an example of the fruitful results of case evaluations and secondary analyses. Similar extensive case evaluations are aimed at developing preventive 'thermometers' for the health of residential stock and CSFs as described above. While large-scale comparative surveys are of great importance for the development of pathological knowledge, in practice every single dwelling, row, or block has its own characteristics, values, and weaknesses.

For the health of the housing stock, the knowledge and experience of the directly responsible housing manager, proprietor, and/or consultant are essential. As the ability of the building trade to learn from experience is not strong, a growing number of intermediary knowledge and support organisations, often associated with branch organisations of housing associations, owner-occupiers, or tenants, are trying to fill the gap.

On the other hand, some promising recent developments show the emerging awareness of the paradigm shift within the building trade. In the Netherlands, a group of maintenance contractors launched a model for performance-based long-term maintenance contracts for residential property. This initiative not only acknowledges the physical and economical importance of long-term quality care but also implies a shift in tasks and responsibilities between property managers and contractors. As a more international development, more and more building material manufacturers show long-term concern with their products by offering guarantees in combination with operating and maintenance instructions, service, and support, provisions that as a matter of fact are regular in most other markets. A few property developers and contractors follow with long-term guarantees in combination with operating, maintenance, and service concepts, but as far as comparison also with capital-intensive products like aircrafts, trains, automotive, and so on goes, there is still a long way to go.

See also: Housing Paradigms; Health and Housing.

References

Awano H (2005) *Towards the Sustainable Use of Building Stock*. Paris: OECD.
Choldin HM (1978) Urban density and pathology. *Annual Review of Sociology* 4: 91–113.
Gerhard U (1997) The dilemma of social pathology. In: Porter D (ed.) *Social Medicine and Medical Sociology in the Twentieth Century*. Amsterdam-Atlanta, GA: Editions Rodopi.
Harris SY (2001) *Building Pathology*. New York: Wiley.
Lemert EM (1951) *Social Pathology: A Systematic Approach to the Theory of Sociopathic Behavior*. New York: McGraw-Hill.
Van Kempen R, Murie A, Knorr-Siedow T, and Tosics I (2006) *Regenerating Large Housing Estates in Europe*. Utrecht, the Netherlands: Restate/Urban and Regional Research Centre Utrecht, Utrecht University.
Watt DS (2007) *Building Pathology*. Oxford, UK: Blackwell.

Further Reading

AEEBC (1994) *Academic Guidelines; Policy Regarding Degree Validation*. London/Brussels: Association d'Experts Européens du Bâtiment et de la Construction.
Kohler N and Hassler U (2002) The building stock as a research object. *Building Research & Information* 30(4): 226–236.
Miles ME, Berens GL, and Weiss MA (2007) *Real Estate Development: Principles and Process*, 3rd edn. Washington, DC: Urban Land Institute.
Thomsen AF and Van der Flier K (2009) Replacement or renovation of dwellings: The relevance of a more sustainable approach. *Building Research & Information* 37(5–6): 649–659.
Van der Flier K and Thomsen A (2006) The life cycle of dwellings and demolition by Dutch housing associations. In: Gruis V, Visscher H, and Kleinhans R (eds.) *Sustainable Neighbourhood Transformation*, pp. 23–41. DUP, Amsterdam: IOS Press.

Housing Policies in Developing Countries

PM Ward, University of Texas at Austin, Austin, TX, USA

© 2012 Elsevier Ltd. All rights reserved.

Introduction

Housing policies towards low-income settlements and neighbourhoods in less developed countries are a relatively recent phenomenon, dating in most countries to the post-1970s and -1980s. Before that time, with the exception of apartheid South Africa and some colonial land and housing policies directed to schedule Black populations and other low-income ethnic groups to certain areas of town, policies were often 'nonpolicies' of laissez faire, in which the government did little leaving housing provision to the private sector, much of which was unregulated and developed informally by private landlords and by individual self-builders. As urbanisation rates began to quicken (from the 1950s onwards in Latin America and Southeast Asia, and later in the case of Africa, and elsewhere), land captures through squatting or low-cost purchase led to the creation and expansion of irregular self-help settlements which began to comprise significant portions of the built-up area. Only then did irregular settlement for housing provision and production come onto the policy-making agenda initially in the form of large-scale eviction programmes (Perlman, 1976) and subsequently in the form of ex-post interventions to improve conditions in these largely unserviced settlements. Even here, however, the nature and development of those policies was slow in coming, and have evolved as government and governance practices have changed alongside democratisation, decentralisation, and economic development – as outlined below.

Prior to the 1950s, most low-income households rented usually in the city centre areas. Renting was commonplace in older housing that had been converted into rooming houses – as was the case in the old colonial palaces of downtown Mexico City which became high-density *vecindades* (tenements) made famous by Oscar Lewis's anthropological and popular writings such as *The Children of Sanchez*. Elsewhere, rooming houses and tenements were built to accommodate migrants and recent arrivals to the cities. Sometimes, too, homes were also the workplace, such as the classic Chinese 'shop houses' in Southeast Asia, in which the family lived above the ground floor store. Similarly in Hong Kong and elsewhere, rows of houseboats in the harbour were both home and place of work. 'Company towns' constructed for workers were relatively rare, although some neighbourhoods in São Paulo, Brazil, were built by factory owners in the late nineteenth and early twentieth centuries to accommodate workers and provide schools for their children. Other company towns were associated with interior mining settlements, although these were also private developments. If the government intervened at all, it was to attend to unrest among renters (rent strikes), and to defuse 1920s renter social movements, and occasionally to impose rent control ceilings upon landlords although this was often to maintain low wage levels and reduce inflation rather than out of concern for living conditions and costs.

Changing Paradigms of Housing Policies

The emergence of planning ideas and housing policies vary in time and space. Different countries have different political systems and ideologies, levels of development and urbanisation, rates of urban growth, and different challenges in providing or sponsoring housing for their populations. Understanding this is essential to any interpretation of housing processes and practices in any individual country or region, and, as one would expect, patterns vary greatly between Asia, Africa and North Africa, South and Central America and the Caribbean, and Eastern European and former Soviet Bloc nations – to the extent that the latter might be considered to be 'developing' countries. In Socialist (or former socialist/communist) countries state intervention in housing policy is likely to be overarching; while in capitalist developing countries it will vary markedly and often be quite muted – as this article will show.

Broad political philosophy aside, housing ideas, broad policy approaches, and the specific policies adopted emerge from within the wellspring of thinking at the time. The various ways in which housing development and public policy has been intellectually understood or 'constructed' during the past 50 years are summarised briefly below, and highlight the several paradigms and paradigm shifts that have framed thinking at different periods. These shifts do not apply equally nor have the same period of expansion in all regions, of course, but it is interesting to observe how conventional wisdoms about housing policy 'travel', and how they break out of a particular development model and intellectual critiques of their day.

Housing Policies Associated with Modernisation Theory and Functionalism in the 1950s and 1960s

After the Second World War, the dominant economic model that informed economic development was that of 'Import Substituting Industrialisation' developed and promoted by UN ECLA/CEPAL which sought to promote a manufacturing industrial base in developing countries that would obviate the need for extensive imports of basic and intermediate consumer goods, taking advantage of national primary produced materials and a supply of low-waged labour. In the 1950s and 1960s, ISI (import substituting industrialisation) strategies were adopted with considerable success especially in Latin America where they were formulated. However, they also fostered rapid urbanisation and rural to urban migration to 'man' the factories (most industrial formal sector labour was male at that time, with female migrants working informally in services – as domestics for example). Enter stage left the beginnings of perceptions that a housing 'problem' existed.

The economic philosophy underpinning ISI was one of 'Modernisation theory' which viewed development as a predominantly linear process of economic and social change, as societies moved from being rural, traditional, small scale, and familial to more complex, corporate and international levels of economic activity and labour organisation, with quickening rates of urbanisation, and changing value systems oriented towards consumerism, and based upon broader associational criteria and networks (rather than familial ones or those based upon ascription). Functionalism grew out of classical late nineteenth- and early twentieth-century sociology of Durkheim and Tonnies which characterised traditional and modern dualities (*gemeinschaft* vs *gesellschaft*), namely rural (community) versus urban (association) patterns of social organisation. It emphasised cultural rather than class-based values, while social change involved a fundamental recasting of those values from traditional ones to more modern ways of thinking and more modern (urban) patterns of behaviour.

At this time, urbanisation was often viewed as 'parasitic' and dysfunctional for the process of economic development as rural peasants flocked to cities and reconstructed their rural lifestyles, in what was a throwback to functionalist thinking of the late 1930s in which ideas about urbanisation, 'breakdown', and social anomie flourished. It was posited that migrants to cities were undergoing a similar 'breakdown' as their rural traditional values systems were thrown into disarray by the modern patterns of behaviour and social codes of the city. These were largely stereotypes, of course, and were only later debunked by younger scholars researching these settlements (e.g., Perlman, 1976), and by others working in these barrios as peace corps volunteers or as 'barefoot architects' and socially committed practitioners.

In terms of housing policy, modernisation theory lauded the new social engineering and architectural norms of large-scale project housing, while the early nomenclature of many spontaneous (self-help) worker settlements that began to develop at the margins of many cities reflected the social constructions of the day which saw them as dysfunctional throwbacks to rural technologies and to marginal areas of intense poverty. This led to a range of housing policies being adopted to cater for this expanding poor worker population. At first the philosophy was one of state promotion of housing projects – small apartments in what were usually 5–7 storey walk ups. In Latin America, these broke out of the post-1961 'Alliance for Progress' international initiative for rural land reform and social development projects aimed at fostering stability against the backcloth of rapid urbanisation and population growth, as well as what was increasingly perceived in the United States as a communist threat being exported from Cuba after the Castro-led revolution in 1959. Many national housing agencies and ministries were created or expanded at this time as a direct result (ICT in Colombia, INVI in Mexico, and worker housing agencies such as BNH in Brazil and INFONAVIT in Mexico). These agencies were charged with resolving the emerging housing crisis by building or financing good amenity workers' housing, targeting often relocated populations from the unserviced slums and shanty towns (Perlman, 1976, 2010). But they were invariably overwhelmed by the pace of urbanisation and even well-resourced housing agencies could barely touch the demand of workers' needs, let alone accommodate evictions from irregular settlements, which continued to grow pretty much unrestricted, subject only to occasional evictions of selected (high visibility) settlements – as in the case of the favelas on the south side of Rio de Janeiro in Brazil, or the Tondo foreshore of Manila (Philippines). And because wage levels were so low, the private sector was not interested in providing mortgages and other financing for formal housing production to meet this demand: thus it was left to the state to take the lead (Turner, 1976). This was the norm in Latin America and Southeast Asia during the 1960s and 1970s.

City states such as Singapore and Hong Kong did rather better at this time and demonstrated considerable success in developing housing for their middle classes and worker population through high-rise apartments of varying types and specifications. The fact that they did much better was a result of their very small and constrained national territories which required much tighter planning controls (often nonexistent or ignored elsewhere), higher level of economic development, better wage levels, lower population and urbanisation growth rates, and, in the case of Singapore, an authoritarian iron-hand of nondemocratic government. Similarly, economic growth and strong government in South Korea and Taiwan lay the basis for more successful large-scale housing programmes for workers, in contrast to Indonesia, Thailand, the Philippines, and South Asia where poor irregular settlements and shanty towns were the usual paths to housing the poor.

With these two city–state exceptions, as well as contemporary China, developing countries have not seen public housing policies akin to those found in the United Kingdom and Europe, or in communist East Europe and the USSR. Thus, the private sector was and continues to be the primary provider in a number of ways, much of which is 'informal' (unregulated and outside of formal financing institutions). Some private sector formal housing for rental was always important, but it invariably targeted middle- and upper-income households. Similarly, better-off groups using private resources and/or bank loans could afford custom-built housing developed in (often) 'fancy' residential neighbourhoods in high amenity areas of the city away, or walled off from, poorer neighbourhoods. This new upper-class housing expansion was the leitmotif of housing dynamics, while middle-income groups often 'filtered' into the vacated residential areas of the wealthy. Some city-centre and longtime deteriorated middle end elite residences were turned into tenements for poor migrant workers, while other landlords built tenements for incoming migrants who worked in and around the central city, although this was rarely a large-scale or profitable enterprise (UNCHS, 2003), especially after some governments sought to impose rent controls, and so on. In short, most of this low-end rental development was unregulated and informal.

From the late 1950s and early 1960s onwards, the private sector in many countries was also responsible for much of the low-income informal sector housing, whether this was squatter settlements and low-income subdivisions at the periphery of cities or shantytowns in and around the centre. The nature of land acquisition, housing production, and dwelling structure varied between, and within, countries, but commonalities were illegal forms of land acquisition; absent or limited basic services such as water, drainage, and often electricity; high levels of community mobilisation and activism; and self-help housing construction by the people themselves. Home building was largely through self-help, and dwelling expansion took place gradually over 15–20 years (**Figure 1**), with local authorities providing basic infrastructure. The essence of this process was an inversion of what one would usually associate with the planning process as a sequence of stages: Planning – Servicing – Building – Occupancy (PSBO), such that self-help started with occupancy and building and only involved planning and formal intervention latterly (OBSP – Baross, 1990).

Thus, informal private sector actors (developers, leaders, or communities themselves) took responsibility for creating shelter, and 'irregular' settlement quickly began to emerge as the primary mode of housing production in cities in developing countries, making up anything between 20 and 60% of the built-up area of cities. Although the majority of these pioneer self-builders were migrants, many of whom came originally from rural areas, they were quickly incorporated into city live life – as home builders, consumers of cheap manufactured goods and food products and building materials, as voters. Far from being a marginalised mass steeped in their own traditional mores, they now formed part of the mainstream of modern city life – albeit poor (Perlman, 1976).

Was public policy entirely absent at this time therefore? Invariably yes, and apart from some periodic eviction programmes mentioned above we may appropriately view this as the period of extreme *laissez faire* in so far as governments and policy-makers quietly ignored the growth of irregular settlements, knowing that they did not have the wherewithal (resources principally) to provide alternative shelter, and recognising the advantages that self-build and other informal housing arrangements offered to capital accumulation and labour needs of ISI (through low wages levels). Often, too, there were political gains to be had through clientelism, vote catching, and co-optation of potentially unstable and radical populations. In short, given the ISI economic model in place, and the often authoritarian and undemocratic nature of many governments of the time, *laissez faire* was a rational response, even if the resulting physical fabric of shanty towns and poorly serviced settlements did not conform to 'modern' constructs.

Structuralist Paradigms of the 1970s to Mid-1980s

The so-called 'dependency theory' rather unceremoniously shoved aside modernisation theory in the late 1960s and early 1970s. Most closely associated with writers such as Andre Gunder Frank, Samir Amir, and Paul Baran, and Marxist at its theoretical core, the main thrusts of the structuralist thesis was that the asymmetric relationships between richer and poorer countries characterised by colonialism were in effect continuing after independence due to the highly dependent relationships that continued to exist between developed and less developed countries. The core, or 'metropole' as it was sometimes called, was able to exploit peripheral-dependent countries by controlling the terms of trade and by taking advantage of lower costs of production and exports of primary products in the less developed countries. Later, once ISI industrialisation had taken root in the less developed world, national and transnational companies were able to exploit lower labour costs in the rapidly

Figure 1 Lot plans showing sequence of self-building in informal settlements, from 1960s to present, Lima case. Courtesy of Susana M. Rojas Williams.

industrialising and urbanising cities – and informal settlements and self-help housing were an integral part of that process.

Although dependency theory was at first widely embraced, by the mid- and late 1970s it was widely criticised for being a-historical and overarching in its thesis, such that adherents tended to bifurcate; some scholars went back to Marxism for their inspiration seeking to examine how urbanisation was tied to capital accumulation, class, and relations to the means of production and means of collective consumption, while others – either from a Marxist or non-Marxist perspective – adopted a more loose 'political economy' framework that was holistic in nature and sought to understand first and foremost how economic development and political structures and processes shape the behaviour of the state on the one hand, and social and political relations on the other hand (for elaboration, see Gilbert and Ward, 1985; Ward, 1982). For these latter authors, development also centered on economic structures, but focused upon the way in which these impacted upon development, social, and political organisation, and upon the ways in which housing was an important form of mediation by the state.

Indeed, this was a period of state bureaucratic expansion in many developing countries, and although these governments were often authoritarian and undemocratic in nature, social policy (of which housing was an important element) became the basis of statecraft including patronage, clientelism, and manipulation of popular groups (Gilbert and Ward, 1985). The take home point here is to recognise that there was a close intersection between housing policy formulation and the dominant economic paradigm of the day. Even though ISI remained in place during the 1970s and the 1980s, its effectiveness was slowing as internal market limits became saturated, and as the majority remained poor with low internal purchasing power. 'Structuralism', therefore, constructed poverty as structurally derived, class-based in which poverty was ongoing and reproduced by those relations; rather than being culturally determined by inappropriate or backward value systems that had characterised the modernisation school, and which assumed some sort of lineal development trajectory over time. This was a sea change since it required us to focus upon and analyse how economic (and state) relations were shaping employment structures, well-being, state intervention, and public policy formulation.

In the housing field this change may be characterised as a shift from state-centered paternalism in which previously 'marginal' populations learned how to live in modern housing projects and changed their lifestyles as they moved into the 'mainstream' of modern society to a growing understanding that poverty was structurally determined by the nature of an industrialisation process that was predicated upon maintaining relatively low wages in the production of goods and services. Tied to rapid urbanisation to fuel that industrialisation process, a new set of housing policy approaches were required that could be large in scale, affordable, and inclusive of low-income populations, yet without incurring impossible demands upon the state's fiscal resources. Enter stage right self-help housing policies, and advocacy.

The emergence of more active support for self-help policies now made a lot of sense in the developing world given the rising economic pressures associated with rising urbanisation and the incapacity (or unwillingness) of governments to follow more orthodox housing policy approaches. Also, as in Europe and the United States, by the late 1970s there was a growing critique of modernist housing solutions and projects, many of which were being torn down as 'great planning disasters'. In less developed countries, however, the stakes were much higher given the very rapid growth rates of cities (often 3–5% per annum), the widespread illegal capture of unserviced land, and the burgeoning of spontaneous settlements. Inspired often by international agencies such as the World Bank, self-help policies of upgrading and home improvement by the people themselves was like manna-from-heaven, and made good sense for governments (Gilbert and Ward, 1985). State-assisted self-help policies helped to spread scarce resources much more widely, while embracing a large (majority) populace. It also brought much needed services to poor areas while offering important dimensions of political mediation and negotiation tied to the process of housing provision and land titling, thereby creating new arenas of capturing political capital (support and votes). Self-help also kept wages low, since a key component of wage inflation is the cost of housing (rent or purchase). Thus, self-help offered a relatively low-cost solution to housing demand in so far as people basically housed themselves. The downside was that governments had to turn a blind eye to illegal land development which it generally did unless the land was very valuable or owned by those influential enough to secure an eviction. A further downside was that governments had to ensure that they responded at least partially by assigning sizeable resources to low-income infrastructural needs albeit in ways that could be achieved gradually and pacify demand making. The middle classes and elites were catered for through the private market, and they accepted laissez faire so long as their neighbourhoods were protected from, and not threatened by, nearby poor residential districts.

However, the structural nature of poverty and the often undemocratic and inequitable nature of these new-found housing policies evoked considerable criticism from Marxist and non-Marxists alike (Burgess, 1982; Mathey, 1992). It was no longer as easy to ignore large swathes of low-income spontaneous settlements, but even as self-help housing advocacy was beginning to take off as a policy 'solution' and was beginning to be widely adopted, some authors began to question the appropriateness of viewing self-help as a solution at all (Ward, 1982). These authors pointed to the high social costs associated with life in unserviced self-help settlements, and suggested that informal private sector housing of this nature fostered exploitation, political clientelism: it was an abrogation of both the public and private sector's duty to provide adequate housing for citizens and worker populations, respectively.

The merits of the debate aside, the slowing down of economic development in the 1980s, and the lack of any appreciable trickle down in wealth to the poorer sectors meant that self-help and self-reliance took on even greater urgency, and for pragmatic reasons it became a more central plank in national housing policies. In the late 1960s and early 1970s, architects and planners began to advocate for state assistance towards existing irregular settlements in the form of ex-post housing interventions to provide basic service infrastructure, improve road access, and sometimes to provide formal titles. This was generally known as 'upgrading policies' since they sought to accelerate the process of home consolidation and settlement physical integration to the city. 'Regularisation' policies usually refer to servicing or to the provision of clean legal property titles. The aim was for state intervention to provide those 'elements' that could not easily be provided by the populations themselves (such as water, drainage, power, street paving, and access), while leaving house building and home consolidation to the residents themselves (Gilbert and Ward, 1985 [2008 reprint]; Turner, 1976): 'housing that works' as Turner described it. Laissez faire was now replaced by pragmatism and active intervention. These ideas emerged from research from the late 1960s onwards, but only began to gain traction when promoted by the World Bank from the early 1970s onwards, and especially after the first UN Habitat conference held in Vancouver in 1976 and the creation of a UN Habitat Center in Nairobi that same year.

In addition to the upgrading of existing settlements housing policies sought to adapt to self-help by creating planned sites-and-services programmes which provided land to poor households who then built their homes themselves. An extension of this pragmatic planned self-help approach was to offer sites with basic 'wet cores' already installed – a WC/bathroom or kitchen – around which households could self-build a home with at least a basic level of services in place from the outset (**Figure 2**). However, such planned formal settlements, albeit low cost, were often too expensive and many sites were unoccupied. Whatever their merits – and they are still occasionally promoted today as in the case of the UNDP project in Neuquen Argentina (**Figures 2** and **3**) – these policies had only limited implementation since they

Figure 2 'Wet Core' slab, electricity, and water provision to sites with services, Neuquen, Argentina.

Figure 3 Wet core with self-built additions, Nuequen, Argentina. The original core is left-centre with the black water tank above.

proved difficulty to replicate on a scale. Also the mood of international orthodoxy was already beginning to change as the world international economic order began to shift.

From the structuralist point of view one of the key critiques was the need to fully appreciate the important linkages between macro- and microeconomic performance and the relative success of self-help housing policies. To be sure, at the macro-level ISI (import substituting industrialisation) had generated large-scale formal employment largely for a male labour force who were paid the minimum wage. This was an important feature of growth in many Latin American and Southeast Asian economies during the 1960s and 1970s. However, by the early 1980s growth had stalled in many parts of Latin America, and in what came to be called the 'lost decade' (of development), many formal jobs disappeared, while the informal sector expanded dramatically. As real incomes declined or flat-lined, and as the costs of building materials increased, so the rates and capacity of successful self-building consolidation slowed (Ward, 1982). In summary, these insights demonstrated quite clearly that self-help, by itself, was unable to overcome structural constraints, especially macro- and microeconomic ones.

Middle-income households were also often hard hit, especially if devaluation eroded the value of their savings and where their lines of credit were tied to the US dollar and their indebtedness burgeoned. Others, faced with declining supply of affordable housing, sometimes 'raided' downwards buying out or taking over housing projects that were designed ostensibly for lower-income and lower-middle income workers, and as in India sometimes occupied sites and services – a bizarre form of gentrification that was born of an insufficient supply of affordable public or private sector housing for the middle classes.

Neoliberal and Globalisation Paradigms from the Mid-1980s

Economic development did not stall everywhere, however. By the 1980s, several Southeast Asian countries were fast developing around a model of export-oriented growth targeting the world market and a decade later Latin American countries followed suit and began to throw off the shackles of ISI and restructure their economies (and polities) to accommodate to globalisation pressures. Since the 1980s there have been three major and largely sequential currents that have shaped thinking about urban development planning in general, and about the nature and direction of housing policies in particular. To summarise these briefly: first was the emerging 1980s IMF/World Bank-led philosophy to downsize the state, reduce direct state intervention, and make markets 'work' more efficiently. This was itself closely shaped by the IMF requirements to downsize public investment and was often tied to what were called structural adjustment loans (SALs) which under the specific terms of the support package required a series of macro-level economic adjustments designed to reduce inflation and debt, the creation of greater consistency and uniformity in national accounting systems, and the improvement of government performance through the cutting of inefficient spending programmes. This restructuring was part-and-parcel of a paradigm shift away from closed markets and protection, towards open markets, free trade, and competition in the global market place.

Second, from the late 1980s through the 1990s, the development paradigm began to predicated upon improving the quality and efficiency of urban management and public administration (especially in land, infrastructure provision, and environmental control), in order to enhance levels of cost recovery and to ensure greater fiscal sustainability of cities. Third, and following on from the urban management programme, was the goal of moving decision-making and responsibility down the urban hierarchy by embracing a genuine commitment to decentralisation and devolution of policy-making to subnational governments (state and city), and by ensuring good governance (Ward, 2005).

In the housing and public policy fields, these macro-level economic changes informed a number of important shifts in state behaviour and policy-making. First, there was less room for manoeuvre in terms of the scope and range of urban projects such as sites-and-services. The cut backs in public expenditure, and the downsizing in the state apparatus, forced central governments to reduce their direct intervention through state-sponsored housing schemes, which were no longer likely to be well-disposed to subsidisation of direct housing production and intervention. At the same time, declining or static real wages was eroding housing affordability. Second, was the demand for greater efficacy of public policy and better value for public expenditure and investment which it was anticipated could be achieved by organisational streamlining (reducing overlaps and waste), improving the content of policies by bringing them closer to what people wanted or needed most, and by more targeted approaches especially focusing upon the most vulnerable populations. Although this more routine and systematic mode of policy implementation reduced political clientelism, it also sometimes led to greater segmentation and stratification among low-income constituencies, and to the reproduction of stratification patterns between those housing sectors or classes who were excluded and those who were included, and the terms of that inclusion. A third feature was the decline in the margins for (political) error. The shift from authoritarian rule in many countries from the 1980s towards more representative and participatory democracies brought with it a sharper and more articulated potential unrest, and instead of being able to fall back on co-optation or authoritarian control, political parties now needed to win friends and influence people at the ballot box. Finally, there was an overarching need for more sustainable policies that no longer depended upon a strong central state and centralised resources, but looked increasingly towards priming the marketplace, generating more resources locally, and to encouraging the participation of the private sector.

As one might expect, these changes in the wider political and policy-making environment fostered a new generation of housing policies. In the arena of self-help housing policies beginning in the early 1980s, one sees the World Bank's withdrawal from self-help project interventions and a corresponding move to make the private housing market system work more smoothly (Gilbert and Ward, 1985). In part this entailed removing the perceived impediments to the housing and land supply system that generated scarcity, and which, it was argued, made for higher prices. The policy instruments advocated here were actions to reduce monopolies, open up competition, regularise 'clouded' land titles in order to encourage de jure (full) ownership, and to provide infrastructure in order to reduce the scarcity of serviced land – again in order to reduce land prices. In addition, investment in housing development was to be predicated upon cost recovery, minimal subsidies (or at least full transparency of any subsidy), and greater effective cost recovery in real terms of service and consumer charges for water, electricity, gas, and other utilities. Moreover, it was proposed that from now on special encouragement should be given to the private sector to promote housing production through guarantees and new financing schemes. The message was clear: wherever possible, governments and multilateral agencies should stay out of direct production of housing and urban projects such as self-build, and instead encourage the private sector and the market to open up new housing opportunities. In effect the era of sponsored self-help had been relatively short lived – less than a decade. Thus, rather than urban projects-based approaches and support spearheaded by the World Bank, policy focused instead upon "urban operations on city-wide policy reform, institutional development, and high priority investments – and to put the development assistance in the urban sector in the context of broader objectives of economic development and macroeconomic performance" (World Bank, 1991: 4).

By the 1990s, this neoliberal philosophy was being firmly translated into urban policy embodied in what was now to be called 'The New Urban Management Programme'. In essence this argued for urban 'management' over urban 'administration', to free housing and land markets from constraints, and to formalise their operations (Jones and Ward, 1994), and these ideas presaged what were to become the buzz words of the twenty-first century and the directions of future policy: namely, 'decentralisation' and (good) 'governance'.

The effects of these changes were dramatic. Many countries developed a serious housing mortgage market for the first time. In the housing sphere the effect was also to speed up and improve public policy responsiveness, especially in servicing provision. Moreover, in the two decades since the mid-1980s these measures have primed the private sector production of housing for the lower middle classes and better-off working-class end of the market – often on an enormous scale and in which there is no scope for self-help activity. By insisting upon transparency, cost recovery, and the ratcheting up the real-cost of consumption charges, this shift in policy and approach is undermining many of the informal practices such as self-help, household extension, multiple family sharing on lots, reciprocity, multiple earning strategies, and so on, that have protected low-income populations in the past. Indeed, in many countries a 'new poverty' has emerged leading to harder lines of social segmentation and social exclusion (LARR, 2004).

More stable and less volatile macroeconomic management appears to have benefited the middle-income groups who can access formal financing through the emerging mortgage markets, banks, and state-guaranteed funding by the private sector. From the 1980s the larger-scale formal sector housing institutions such as Brazil's (now defunct) BNH or Mexico's INFONAVIT increasingly became 'second line' housing providers, offering credits to worker groups and organisations to build housing apartments blocks and duplex homes for their workers. In parallel, sometimes government promoted housing funds for informal sector workers, although these were often poorly financed and rarely had a significant effect upon housing demand or needs. Since the 1990s, as neoliberal macro-level economic strategies have been advanced, governments have sought to strengthen the emerging mortgage market, particularly where these target lower-income and lower middle-income groups. Working with for-profit developers, national and regional governments, they have offered financial guarantees, access to low interest loans, tax holidays, and other incentives in order to dramatically ratchet up housing production at the lower end of the formal market.

The Contemporary Development Paradigm: Decentralisation, Institutional Strengthening, and Good Governance

Decentralisation has been on the development policy agenda issue for many years, but until the last two decades it was almost always rhetorical and largely ineffectual. Democratisation also changed all that, and 1990s decentralisation has been described as the 'The Quiet Revolution' (Campbell, 2003). This is particularly true if one views decentralisation as both a vertical process, devolving decision-making power down the hierarchy to subnational levels of government; and as a horizontal process, namely the opening up of the political spaces between the branches government (Wilson et al., 2008). Equally important in this process is the opening up of opportunities for participation in governance and planning. But as noted above, the promotion of decentralisation now has as its handmaiden the notion of good governance, as well as the goal of strengthening the administrative and governmental capacity – especially at the subnational and local level – in order to provide for greater urban sustainability. Achieving this requires a number of strategies: inter alia, the streamlining of government itself and public sector programmes, their modernisation, maximising transparency, regularising informal practices, embracing new techniques, and sharing best practices and innovations.

So how might self-help fit into this brave new world? In some respects hardly at all if recent housing developments in Mexico are anything to go by. In Mexico, the past 10 years have witnessed dramatic (and impressive) state and local government promotion of low-income (social) housing production through the private sector, allowing private developers to profitably construct massive housing estates in peripheral and peri-urban locations, at costs that are affordable to lower middle-income groups and better-off working classes (**Figure 4**). Clearly there is a demand for such housing, and many who would probably have been self-build consolidators in the past are now opting for these housing projects. The cookie-cutter designs offer minimal variation and scope for self-help adaptation, or for individualising the home. In some ways we appear to be returning to the Latin American social interest housing projects of the 1960s, to the Levittown suburbs in the United States, and to the large municipal and local government housing of Western Europe. Future research will need to ascertain the relative success and viability of such large-scale developments, but it seems likely that self-help activities will be extremely limited in such physical environments.

Elsewhere, however, it is anticipated that self-help process will extend and intensify many of the housing policies that emerged under neoliberalism, namely to ensure that housing production is fiscally sustainable through tax-and-spend programmes for infrastructure, incorporation of irregular settlements into the (property) tax register, paying service and other consumption charges, and so on. Of course, this requires much greater regulation and less informality, such that regularly updated property registers and cadasters have become a *sine qua non* for effective land use controls, for the activation of planning and construction permissions, as well as forming the basis of property tax assessments. Tied to all this is a process of social (re)construction that promotes a sense of citizenship, and the privileges and responsibilities that go with being citizens rather than squatters or supplicants.

Sociologically, we are also facing a different socioeconomic scenario borne of globalisation. Mention was made earlier of the 'new' poverty and the possible emergence of a new marginality and 'culture of poverty', and it appears that today's poor are indeed segmented on the basis of a number of dimensions: age, ethnicity, migration status, types of job and benefits, education type and levels, and inclusion in government and nongovernment programmes. Internally, too, settlement populations are sometimes taking action to protect themselves from drug peddlers, local delinquents, and gangs, by informally 'gating' their streets in order to reduce access and to protect their properties (**Figure 5**). Gated communities are not just the preserve of rich neighbourhoods, but are also a feature of self-help, and one observes a retreat to the super-local – the block, or the street, or subsection of large barrios which are perceived to be 'safer' comprising of 'good' folks compared with those beyond.

Segmentation can lead to social exclusion, and even to the creation and acceleration of poverty cycles. In particular, certain populations are becoming more vulnerable: immigrants and ethnic minorities as the 2008 backlash against immigrant populations in many tropical African

Figure 4 Large-scale private sector developed social interest housing estate, peri-urban area of Guadalajara, Mexico.

Figure 5 Informal 'gating' of a side street in a low-income self-help settlement, Santiago, Chile.

squatter settlements demonstrated (most notoriously in South Africa). More generalised segmentation and vulnerability occurs among the elderly, not least because until recently many less developed societies were overwhelmingly youthful, and it is only now that longer life expectancy and a middle-ageing demographic structure has begun to highlight housing needs for the elderly (Varley and Blasco, 2003).

These sociological changes highlight the need for creative thinking when it comes to identifying the contemporary issues and housing policy directions. A recent thrust in the literature that has emerged to provide some resistance to the outcomes of neoliberal and globalisation processes is a refinement of understandings about what is meant by citizenship – its rights and responsibilities – as well as promotion of a 'rights to the city' movement (Fernandes, 2007; Harvey, 2008). The central idea here is that as a part of urban citizenship people have rights to make full use of the city and to live a rich urban life. In particular, among more marginalised groups, ensuring adequate access to public spaces is emphasised as a counterweight to the trends towards the privatisation of such spaces. Faced with a lack of state-sponsored affordable housing, and the fact that access to adequate shelter is now considered a basic human right by the United Nations, rights-to-the-city arguments will have increasing weight in the coming years for citizenship demands, politics, and participation.

Within this framework a number of self-help policies are being promoted. Regularisation and infrastructure provision continues to be a priority in order to bring services to unserviced populations and to encourage upgrading, but now it is parsed within a context of (fiscal) sustainability and citizenship responsibilities to pay for the installation and consumption charges. Some major schemes such as the *Favela Bairro* programme are heavily underwritten by international agencies, but the expectancy is that, once established, they will be self-sustaining and charge the real costs of consumer charges. Regularisation of land title – the provision of full legal title – has become something of a mantra in many policy-making circles.

Tied to the need to ensure registration as a basis for inclusion in the property tax base, and to bring informal settlements into systems of planning and land use controls (see above), full legal property is also argued to be essential for the market to work more smoothly (de Soto, 2000). In fact, many researchers have long since demonstrated that title per se is not a prerequisite for successful consolidation: more significant factors are other indicators: of security, service and infrastructure provision by local government, settlement size, and age. Alternative (customary law) systems of land holding have been argued to offer equal (and better understood) security of tenure, without recourse to full legal title under conventional law. However, the de Soto argument is that full property title enhances and makes more effective one's participation in the market – using home equity as a collateral for credit, buying and selling a home, providing for testamentary succession, and so on. In fact, such propositions are hotly debated, and few low-income self-builders appear to be interested in using their homes as collateral in order to access credit. Nor is there much interest in making a will (although not for title reasons), and formal title per se appears to make little difference in facilitating market place and the ability to sell one's home. But even though de Soto's assertions about title may be overstated and poorly conceived, the issue of land market performance of self-help settlements remains important, and it merits further study and analysis. Although the primary function of self-help has been the use value to which the dwelling is put (i.e., a place to live, raise one's family, enjoy relative security, benefit from social support and protection from economic predation, etc.), self-help housing also has significant exchange value – as an asset – if the dwelling is sold. Titled or untitled, 'For Sale' notices are common for homes and lots in self-help settlements, but they only remain more or less affordable to other low-income residents at the earlier phases of their development when land and home prices are still quite low. Sales are far less common after the settlement is consolidated, once families have invested large amounts of time and money into upgrading and extending their home. This low effective demand further depresses land and house prices in established self-help segments of the market place.

Thus, while the poor can benefit in terms of both use and exchange value, their gains tend to be considerably lower than those of the formal sector, thereby intensifying existing patterns of social segmentation. The implications for policy call for financing mechanisms and mortgage-type support instruments that will assist interested lower-income households to buy out self-builders who, for one reason or another, need to move. Currently there is minimal mobility (Gilbert, 1999; Ward, 2012), and future policy needs to consider how people can liberate the exchange value of their sweat equity and investment. While not a significant issue in the past, it is likely to be increasingly important in the future.

For many, too, the home doubles up as workplace and this is especially true for self-help housing. During the so-called lost decade of the 1980s, many household members became petty entrepreneurs working out of their home places, producing goods for sale, taking in goods for repair, or offering services (hairdressing, manicures, etc.). Sometimes, too, a section of the dwelling or lot is turned over into rooms to rent, or the creation a workshop, thereby providing the basis for a family business. Yet, despite widespread recognition of the urban productivity in self-help settlements, housing policies rarely encourage home-based enterprises. The intersection of family-based enterprises, household organisation, and the home merits further greater study, not least since an increasing proportion of the low-income city dwellers work in the informal sector.

Future Policy Arenas for Low-Income Settlements

The globalisation paradigm of today seems likely to continue well into the next decade or two. Global summit meetings of political leaders at the turn of the millennium regularly confronted major protests in developed countries by coalitions and movements concerned about the adverse impacts of globalisation upon job creation, incomes, and the life chances of low-income groups worldwide. Those protests have abated somewhat, and it is probably fair to suggest that there has been some softening of social development policies under globalisation as national governments realise that they have to develop housing policies within a free trade context. Also the emerging experiences of housing policy development among the rising economic powerhouses of China, India, and Brazil illustrate, in very different ways, the alternative housing strategies targeting their very large urban populations. How these three countries, in particular, tackle the challenges of slum upgrading and of promoting new housing production opportunities will be illustrative for the developing world at large, not least since the housing strategies adopted by the big three are quite different.

The backdrop of globalisation and housing policies is also being shaped and nuanced by new and important considerations which have increasing saliency: specifically these are the need for urban sustainability and the need to arrest climate change; citizenship and 'rights to the city', especially among lower-income populations; and improved financing systems, whether in the form of widening mortgage markets or through microcredit schemes (Datta and Jones, 1999). Mortgage markets and 'subprime' lending were dealt a serious setback by the 2008 housing crisis in the United States, but they have become increasingly important features of the housing production landscape since 2000 in Mexico (**Figure 4**), Brazil, and China, occasionally embracing modest 'green' initiatives such as lower energy homes, solar panel water heaters, and more economical systems of water use. However, their location at the periphery and urban hinterland beyond contradicts the basics of green and sustainable solutions, especially given the inadequate public transportation systems for workers, and the heavy reliance that these suburban commuters have upon private car ownership. As a counterpoint, in the developed world suburbanisation has slowed, and there is an important swing 'back-to-the city' that focuses upon housing processes of densification, housing rehab, redevelopment and infill using energy efficient applications, community participation and strengthening, and public transportation and pedestrianisation – all of which are designed to provide more local community systems of living that will also help to reduce a neighbourhood's carbon footprint.

Self-Help Housing Challenges

There are several arenas of self-help housing policy that are likely to become important policy arenas in the next decade but are, as yet, often largely unformulated. First are policies that provide for asset management targeting elderly householders who have created the self-built housing stock (Varley and Blasco, 2003). Many of the successful self-helpers of the past, especially those who started out in the 1960s and 1970s and were in their twenties and thirties at the time, are now dying or approaching old age, and their consolidated home represents a substantial asset of US$25 000–$50 000 or more. These elderly pioneer self-builders invariably remain living in their homes, as do some of their adult children and their families (the grandchildren), for whom it will continue to be the family home once the parents pass away. As well as having 'exchange (sale) value' as an asset if the property is sold, the dwelling has ongoing 'use value' as a place of residence for children and grandchildren. How these self-built properties are transferred upon death is important and potentially conflictive given the different stakeholder interests of those who inherit. Countries have different inheritance and succession practices of willed inheritance or 'forced heirship', but given that so few low-income people make wills, property transfers often follow implicit understandings and informal practices of housing transfer. Disputes often occur, and in the case of controversy or conflict it will hinge upon the local laws that provide for inheritance and intestacy. Future policies will need to address title changes relating to informal agreements, as well as provide for low-cost probate processes, adequate dispute resolution mechanisms, and for (sibling) share buy-outs from those adult children wishing to remain in the family home and retain it as their own (Ward et al., 2011).

Second, new policies will be required for self-build rehab and retrofitting. Many of these same earlier self-help settlements that began over 30 years ago are now located in the intermediate rings of city – they are the 'first suburbs' or the 'innerburbs' as I describe them elsewhere (see article Urban Regeneration in Latin America). Built gradually over time, and intensively used, they are now often dilapidated and in urgent need to repair and renovation. Recent research has begun to systematically analyse the housing conditions and needs of such 'consolidated' settlements (www.lahn.utexas.org), and has begun to provide a blueprint for the next generation of housing policies towards irregular settlements that will focus upon renovation and retrofits, rather than upgrading and self-build. Housing rehab and urban regeneration in working-class communities are widely recognised policy arenas in the developed world, but there is an urgent need to think creatively about their counterparts in developing countries.

Third, just as housing policies and practices in developed countries are becoming more 'green', so too do policy-makers in the developing world need to think about sustainable housing applications for self-help that target the poor as well as the better-off income groups. Much of the thinking to date focuses upon renewable energy applications (solar panels and the like), most of which remain unaffordable to the poor. However, insulation, weatherization, prefabricated energy saving windows and doors, all present DIY (do it yourself) opportunities for self-builders. Also, many other sustainable housing applications and improvements are not costly: rain water harvesting for 'spot' watering; low energy light bulbs; minor modifications to save water in the home and improve air quality; microenvironmental (garden and yard) management; composting and recycling are all applications that can be usefully (and cheaply) incorporated into future self-help housing practices in developing countries. Given the extent of informal settlements and building practices worldwide, these modest behavioural and dwelling adaptions would make a dramatic difference to future sustainability (Sullivan and Ward, 2012). The important point to recognise is that, as a proportion of household income, energy reduction, and other sustainable applications invariably offer greater value relative to low-income householder budgets than to those of middle- and upper-income groups.

Renting and the Need for New Rental Housing Policies

As noted at the outset, informally produced private-sector renting was commonplace before the rapid rise of spontaneous settlement and opportunities for ownership afforded through self-help. And while a broad range of housing policies have been developed to promote housing ownership and to intervene and support self-help, there has been an almost total neglect of policies for those who rent – and they are many. Gilbert in his contribution to this encyclopaedia estimates that perhaps as many as one billion people still rent accommodation, and renting is especially high in Africa where many squatter (self-help) settlement lots are developed by landlords who sublet rooms in tenements (Huchzermeyer, 2007). Elsewhere – in Latin America especially – renting opportunities are created by owners who sub-let to one or two tenants (as in Bogotá), or on lots where several unrelated families share

facilities in new tenement arrangements (Gilbert, 1993). Other households, which contain second generation or extended relations to the owner, often share the lots and dwelling, and while they may not pay rent or be thought of as renters, they add significantly to rising population densities. Located in the past periphery, as cities continued to grow, communications improved, and land-uses changed, many of these former irregular settlements now in the inner city or intermediate ring and some may even find themselves in prime locations, where they are subject to buy outs by middle-income 'gentrifiers' and even by developers for multistorey apartment blocks (see **Figure 6**).

Thus in many cities low-income renting is on the rise, and is expected to increase in the coming decades. And yet, as Gilbert comments in his contribution, the past 30 years have seen remarkably little policy development towards low-income renting: it has become the new arena of laissez faire (UNCHS, 2003). In the past, rent controls have been the one area of government policy to control inflation (and pressures on wages), and to help low-income households, but such policies have often backfired: distorting the land market; favoring longer term tenants over more recent ones; reducing the profitability for landlords, and discouraging further investment and growth of the rental housing stock. A number of policy opportunities to improve accessibility for renters exist, including the encouragement of landlords to create

Figure 6 Middle-income gentrification of a consolidated former squatter settlement, in Mexico City. Apartments in construction.

more space, offering modest incentives and microcredit to landlords, as well as legal protection to ensure that they are not penalised. Similarly, self-help upgrading schemes rarely address the notion of promoting renting, either in newly developed peripheral areas or in the older often dilapidated 'innerburbs'. Of course, some safeguards of tenants' rights are always necessary, and here, too, arbitration panels, informal dispute resolution offices, and well-targeted subsidies can help to mitigate the tension between profit and rent-seeking, and between environmental quality and affordability.

Conclusions

The broad-brush overview offered in this article has sought to emphasise that housing policies are formulated in a particular paradigm of development thinking that is in vogue at different time periods, and we have observed how such thinking has shifted from modernisation theory in the 1950s and 1960s to structuralism and dependency theory in the 1970s, governmental downsizing and withdrawal of the state in the 1980s, to more neoliberal and market-driven policies of the 1990s which continue today. Regrettably, perhaps, each paradigm of housing policy is only marginally informed by the state of the art of quality housing research, and the shape of housing policy appears to be more a product of national income and poverty level profiles, political ideologies, level of democratic practices and types of governance, international agency advocacy, and so on. In short, housing policy research and ideas often do not sit comfortable with national governments (especially authoritarian ones), nor do they travel well unless they also dovetail with the prevailing political economy and ideology in any one country or region (Harris, 1998; Jones and Ward, 1994). This is one main reason why housing policies in developing countries vary so much. Occasionally, too, housing actions undertaken appear to be stuck in time warp, as in Zimbabwe where Robert Mugabe's savage eradication schemes (informed in his case by attempts at ethnic cleansing), hark back to many of the policy missteps of the 1960s.

As pointed out earlier, it will be especially interesting to observe how Brazil, China, and India adapt their housing policies in their very different development contexts. In particular for us to gauge how they attempt to 'square the circle' and develop housing policies against the backdrop of democratisation, decentralisation, urban sustainability, climate change, and lower dependence upon nonrenewable energy resources – all of which are considerations that appear to have emerging saliency in our time and paradigm.

There is little doubt that since the beginning of the twenty-first century, policy-making has become much more aligned with people's actual needs and is informed by better research, but production continues to be left to the private sector, much of which is produced informally. With one or two notable exceptions (e.g., China), the private sector appears likely to remain at the centre of most housing production in developing countries, and the state's role will be to provide guarantees, incentives, and to ensure regulation of those efforts. Recent efforts to prime formal housing production for working-class populations in middle-income developing countries such as Brazil, Mexico, South Korea, China, Singapore, and Taiwan suggest that significant inroads are being made in ratcheting up the housing stock, whether through high-rise apartment blocks or through massive low-rise peripheral and peri-urban estates (see **Figure 4**). However, there is also the danger that these may become the slums and tenements of the future, not least since their peripheral and distant locations appear to be running in the opposite direction to recent thinking about city densification and improving the opportunities and livability in the inner city. There is also likelihood of intensifying segmentation and exclusion between different groups of the poor: owners and renters, new migrants and city born; couples and singletons, different ethnicities; formal and informal sector workers, and so on. Finally, no matter how far housing policies appear to have progressed across these various paradigms in the past half century, we should recognise that in absolute terms more people live in poor housing conditions today than ever before. The challenge of yesteryear remains: how to formulate policies that will provide access to a decent standard of housing for everyone.

See also: Gentrification; Rental Market and Rental Policies in Less Developed Countries; Residential Segregation: Apartheid; Rights to the City; Urban Regeneration in Latin America.

References

Baross P (1990) Sequencing land development: The price implication of legal and illegal settlement growth. In: Baross P and van der Linden J (eds.) *The Transformation of Land Supply Systems in Third World Cities*, pp. 57–82. Aldershot, UK: Avebury.

Burgess R (1982) Self-help housing advocacy: A curious form of radicalism. A critique of the work of John F.C. Turner. In: Ward P (ed.) *Self-Help Housing: A Critique*, pp. 55–97. London: Mansell.

Campbell T (2003) *The Quiet Revolution: Decentralization and the Rise of Political Participation in Latin American Cities*. Pittsburgh: University of Pittsburgh Press.

Datta K and Jones G (eds.) (1999) *Housing and Financing in Developing Countries*. London: Routledge.

De Soto H (2000) *The Mystery of Capital: Why Capitalism Triumphs in the West and Fails Everywhere Else*. New York: Basic Books.

Fernandes E (2007) Constructing the 'Right to the City' in Brazil. *Social and Legal Studies* 16(2): 201–219.

Gilbert A (1999) A home is forever? Residential mobility and homeownership in self help settlements. *Environment and Planning* 31: 1073–1091.

Gilbert AG (1993) *In Search of a Home*. London: UCL Press.

Gilbert A and Ward P (1985) (2008 reprint). *Housing the State and the Poor, Policy and Practice in Latin American Cities*. Cambridge, UK: Cambridge University Press.

Harris R (1998) The silence of the experts: 'Aided Self-help Housing', 1939–54. *Habitat International* 22(2): 165–189.

Harvey D (2008) The right to the city. *New Left Review* 53: 23–40.

Huchzermeyer M (2007) Tenement city: The emergence of multi-storey districts through large-scale private landlordism in Nairobi. *International Journal of Urban and Regional Research* 31: 714–732.

Jones G and Ward P (1994) Tilting at windmills: Paradigm shifts in World Bank orthodoxy. In: Jones G and Ward P (eds.) *Methodology for Land Housing Market Analysis*, pp. 8–23. London: University College London Press.

Latin American Research Review (LARR) (2004). From marginality of the 1960s to the new poverty of today (Mercedes González de la Rocha, Elizabeth Jelín, Helen Safa, Janice Perlman, Bryan Roberts and Peter Ward). *Latin American Research Review* 39(1): 183–203.

Mathey K (ed.) (1992) *Beyond Self-Help Housing*. London; New York: Mansell.

Perlman JE (1976) *The Myth of Marginality: Urban Poverty and Politics in Rio de Janeiro*. Berkeley, CA: University of California Press.

Perlman JE (2010) *Favela: Four Decades of Living on the Edge of Rio de Janeiro*. New York: Oxford University Press.

Sullivan ME and Ward P (2011) Sustainable housing design and technology applications and policies for low-income self-help settlements (in press).

Turner JFC (1976) *Housing by People: Towards Autonomy in Building Environments*. London: Marion Boyars.

UNCHS (2003) *Rental Housing: An Essential Option for the Urban Poor in Developing countries*. Nairobi: UNCHS.

Varley A and Blasco M (2003) Older women's living arrangements and family relationships in urban Mexico. *Women's Studies International Forum* 26(6): 525–539.

Ward PM (ed.) (1982) *Self-Help Housing: A Critique*. London: Mansell.

Ward PM (ed.) (2005) The lack of 'Cursive Thinking' with social theory and public policy: Four decades of marginality and rationality in the so-called 'Slum'. In: Roberts B and Wood, C (eds.) *Rethinking Development in Latin America,*, pp. 271–296. Pennsylvania, PA: Pennsylvania State University Press.

Ward P (2012) "A Patrimony for the Children": Low income homeownership and housing immobility in Latin American cities. *Annals of the Association of American Geographers (AAAG)* (in press).

Ward P and Jiménez E, in collaboration withErika Grajeda and Claudia Ubaldo Velázquez (2011) 'The house that mum and dad built': Self-help housing policies for second generation inheritance and succession. *Habitat International* 35: 467–485.

Wilson R, Ward P, Rodriguez V, and Spink P (2008) *Governance in the Americas: Decentralization Democracy and Subnational Government in the USA, Mexico, and Brazil*, p. 337. Notre Dame, IN: University of Notre Dame Press.

World Bank (1991) *Urban Policy and Economic Development: An Agenda for the 1990s*. Washington, DC: World Bank.

Further Reading

Puentes R and Warren D (2006) *One-Fifth of America: A Comprehensive Guide to America's First Suburbs*. Washington, DC: The Brookings Institution Press.

Rojas Williams SM (2005) "Young Town" growing up – Four decades later: self-help housing and upgrading lessons from a squatter neighborhood in Lima. MCP and SMArchS Thesis, Massachusetts Institute of Technology.

UN-HABITAT (2005) *Global Report on Human Settlements: Financing Urban Shelter,* Earthscan.

Relevant Website

http://www.lahn.utexas.org – Latin American Housing Network.

Housing Policies in Developing Countries: Microfinance

P Smets, VU University, Amsterdam, The Netherlands

© 2012 Elsevier Ltd. All rights reserved.

Glossary

Incremental building A stepwise building process.
Incremental financing A method of financing accompanying an incremental building process or home improvement.
Informal finance Financial arrangements taken place not under jurisdiction of a central bank.
Microfinance Savings as well as credit in small amounts.
Mortgage financing Housing finance secured by land, house, or property.
Social collateral Loan security obtained through a network the client belongs to and based on notions of trust and social control.

The Microfinance Revolution

The UN World Urban Forums in Vancouver (2006), Beijing (2008), and Rio de Janeiro (2010) have collectively drawn attention to the housing crisis affecting the urban poor. It is increasingly recognised that these individuals and households have to rely on self-help housing which is financed through their savings or credit, derived from the informal financial sector. Attempts to provide formal mortgage finance to poorer sections of society have proven to be relatively unsuccessful. Within this context, housing microfinance presents a viable alternative for poor households.

The United Nations proclaimed 2005 as the 'International Year of Microfinance'. Microfinance has been afforded special attention because it is believed to help people out of poverty. In addition to clear financial goals, the UN declaration states that microfinance has been found to increase the empowerment of women and contribute to social and human development processes in general. Microfinance is expected to be more than just a financial service used in the fight against poverty and can therefore be described as a means to empowerment and the creation of a social environment that is essential to people's well-being. The microfinance revolution started in the 1990s and focused mainly on the provision of income-generation loans and less on consumption credit. A relatively new development is housing microfinance, which represents a new loan portfolio for the microfinance industry offering possibilities for building in an incremental way.

Microenterprise finance and housing microfinance differ. Microenterprise finance is intended for working capital or fixed assets, for microenterprises. Eligibiity for microenterprise finance is premised upon applicants' ability (dependent on income and cash flow), and willingness to repay. Furthermore, these loans can be secured against collateral ranging from business equipment, assets, and/or property. Housing microfinance is designed for housing development or improvement. Once a microentrepreneur with a good repayment record applies for a small housing loan, he/she is more eligible for housing microfinance, but not all applicants are (micro-)entrepreneurs. Risks are reduced by asking for compulsory savings, participation in a savings group and/or cosigners. Some microfinance institutions rely on payroll deductions from those being employed in the formal sector. Collateral may encompass property and land which is part of the microenterprise. In practice, both types of finance are not always distinguishable as evidenced in cases where entrepreneurs use part of their house for his/her business such that microenterprise loans are effectively used for housing.

Housing microfinance has drawn a lot of attention due to its relationship with the microfinance industry. Small home improvement loans offer a useful product that microfinance institutions can add to their core business of microenterprise lending. Microfinance institutions can successfully apply their existing loan methods and installations for microenterprise loans to small home improvement loans with little or no modification. Furthermore, evidence suggests that roughly 20% of funds nominally borrowed for microenterprise are invested in housing improvement in the absence of an explicit housing product. This article is built up as follows. Firstly, an overview will be given of housing microfinance and how it may fit or compete with other financial products; informal finance, community-based finance and consumer credit for building materials. After this overview, microfinance institutions will be discussed including bottlenecks for expansion: financial sector and capital market barriers, land, and infrastructure. Finally, the focus will be on housing microfinance and beyond.

Housing Microfinance

Housing finance, however, is not always an easy endeavour for microfinance institutions. Although there are geographical differences, the prototypical housing microfinance loan consists of a small, short-term credit (US$500–2000) with a term of 2–5 years (depending upon context), to a homeowner for expansion or remodelling of their informally built house. Sometimes, microfinance institutions offer somewhat larger loans (US$3000–7000) over a longer period of time (5–15 years), for a family to construct a new home (often on land that they already own), occasionally secured by a mortgage although the majority are secured by social collateral. Small home improvement credit, however, is the main market for which microfinance institutions have developed a housing microfinance product. This said, small loans could also finance a wide range of other housing investments useful for low- and moderate-income households. These include plot purchase, title regularisation, (prescribed) construction of floor/joist/roof extensions that a homeowner may build to add rental units onto the property through horizontal or vertical expansion, individual and communal infrastructure, and vertical or horizontal build out of a developer-built core unit or humid core (a bathroom/kitchen area containing plumbing and electricity). Investments could also be made into the completion of an unfinished condominium shell in a high-rise building, for example, the addition of fixtures, cabinets, electrical equipment, extra plumbing, and painting.

Despite stumbling blocks in the expansion of the housing microfinance portfolio (see below), housing microfinance has the potential to serve many low- and moderate-income households. These families neither want nor can afford a large long-term traditional mortgage to purchase a complete unit built by a developer. Instead, these households build progressively, by acquiring and upgrading land title, building a makeshift shelter, replacing this makeshift shelter with permanent materials, expanding it, and lobbying for public services. A series of small short-term loans can fund this progressive housing process with payments affordable to households. Small serial loans can increase the speed and lower the high cost of the incremental housing process.

Despite evidence of progressive building practices, a number of microfinance institutions continue to prioritise the construction or purchase of a complete housing unit. Consequently, large loans extended for a longer period are undertaken even while these harm the building and financing strategies of the poor, which are an essential part of their survival strategy. Several organisations in the housing microfinance sector face difficulties in thinking small. Thinking small refers to housing finance loans which fit the building and financing strategies of poorer sections of society, also called incremental building and financing strategies. This has to do with affordability, determined by the borrower's ability and willingness to take and repay a loan at that moment. Here affordability is not just a matter of determining a specific percentage of their income which could be spent on a housing loan. Moreover, some clients may also have their daily lives adversely affected by being required to repay these small loans over a short period of time.

Progressive building practices should also be linked with some insights in the growing market of housing microfinance. In many developing countries, social support programs joined with growth of gross domestic product have stimulated a rapid increase in the household income of families in the bottom half of the income pyramid. The potential market for small home improvement loans remains huge and is often relatively uncontested; 50–80% of the population in most developing countries build their homes progressively. Market studies typically show that about 25% of these families want, and can afford a small home improvement loan at any one time. The demand for somewhat larger loans (US$2500–10 000) for the rapidly growing lower middle class in developing countries also remains largely unserviced. Although each individual project is small to modest in size, the huge numbers result in an impressive total market potentially financed by such credit: US$331.8 billion worldwide. Affordable housing finance markets will grow exponentially as 90% of the net increase in world population of 4 billion people is projected to reside in the urban areas of developing countries by the year 2050. The focus of studies of housing finance markets generally is on formal financial institutions. However, lessons could be learned from the operations of the informal financial sector.

Informal Finance

Informal housing finance is often not taken seriously by microfinance institutions. Microfinance institutions often assume that low-income clients have no access to finance at all and need financial services. This assumption neglects the fact that many poor people are served by the informal financial sector, where a kaleidoscope of pure commercial and social relationships can be traced. Roughly, a distinction can be made between personal lenders (friends, neighbours, relatives, colleagues, and employers), commercial lenders (moneylenders and pawnbrokers), and financial self-help groups.

Housing microfinance can compete with informal sector finance and in doing so enlarge the opportunities for the clientele, allowing lenders to make a choice for the product that fits them best. However, when microfinance institutions make use of social guarantees to secure loans, it is of crucial importance that trust relations among the dwellers will not be harmed. Negative experiences with social collateral can have a negative impact on participation in 'informal' financial self-help groups. Once mutual trust is harmed people are not willing to join forces any longer. It can take a long period of time before mutual trust relations are restored: a period of 7 years is not exceptional.

Community-Based Housing Finance

Traditional mortgage–finance institutions have typically lacked the low-cost community-based systems which offer the alternative of social collateral for securing loans.

Typically, individual loans to families best finance house construction. Community-based housing finance groups offer an alternative solution. These groups form not only to fund individual house construction but also to purchase land parcels and acquire communal infrastructure (roads, drainage, water distribution and connection, etc.). Acquiring these communal components of residential development typically involves negotiations with the other stakeholders involved, such as the original landowners of the parcel and government.

Community-based housing finance groups typically organise households to save and/or borrow sums necessary for the development, construction, and maintenance of the resulting housing. Such community funds encourage community empowerment, land acquisition or security of tenure, infrastructure development along with obtaining, or improving shelter.

Governments often support community-based housing finance in some form. In the Philippines, the Community Mortgage Programme offers groups of 'informal' settlers a mortgage for an undivided track of land. Such land can be obtained initially by occupation with or without permission from the owner; however, the private or public owner must agree to sell their land as part of the program. Once land is acquired, this program provides loans for site development and housing. For projects without a defined site, it is hard to organise heterogeneous groups. Even projects with a defined site sometimes face problems with group size, cohesion, and mutual cooperation. A weak monitoring system in combination with corruption and poor enforcement of internal rules results in low repayment rates and high arrears, complicating the operation of this program. One of the lessons derived from the experiences with the Community Mortgage Programme is that group-based loans with a short term (e.g., 90 days) are administered and repaid more easily than larger, longer-term group credit. The experiences of microfinance institutions in the Philippines show that excessively large group loans encourage members to withdraw from the effort and drop their financial commitment.

The Village Savings and Loan Associations (VS&LA) that started in 1991 in Niger has now spread to over 16 African, 2 Latin American, and 2 Asian countries offering quite a different approach. Originally, this organisation focused only on rural areas, but now urban areas are also included. VS&LA are independent financial self-help groups in which members pool savings from which credit can be distributed. The participants determine the purpose for which loans are eligible. These financial self-help groups encompass Accumulating Savings and Credit Associations (ASCAs) and rotating savings and credit association (ROSCAs). In an ASCA, participants pool money in a fund from which loans can be provided. These loans, often including interest, have to be paid back to the common fund. After a specific period the fund will be terminated and all money will be divided among all participants. These self-help groups can be more flexible with regard to the purpose for which credit is taken out. In India, ASCAs have even formed federations. Such federations offer the possibility of transferring surplus finance from one group to another financial self-help group in need of finance.

In India, many auction 'chit funds' are nonbanking financial institutions under jurisdiction of the central bank. These chit funds are a type of ROSCA, they pool savings and then allocate the funds at a highly reduced rate to the participant, accepting the highest discount. All participants obtain the pooled savings once during a cycle. Any remaining amount gets distributed among all members.

In Brazil, a system of housing cooperatives and associations (*consorcios*) pools savings of groups of households in order to find and purchase land parcels, subdivide, and build housing projects. A housing *consorcio* is typically a group of 100–144 families that agree to make monthly payments for a specified number of months. They take the pool of funds gathered each month and allocate them to one or more members enabling them to buy a house. This system is currently highly controlled by the Central Bank.

Consumer Credit for Purchase of Building Materials

Studies of consumer credit for the purchase of building materials conclude that households select the place where they buy construction materials from, based mainly on price, method of payment, store brand, and the distance of the store from their houses. Many pay for their building materials by cash, but serial consumer credit for building materials is on the rise. Moreover, consumer credit for building materials already covers 20% of housing investments in Sao Paulo and has a huge potential for growth. More favourable interest rates, terms, products, and services can facilitate a sustainable expansion. Otherwise, a consumer credit explosion may occur, with mass defaults.

Here microfinance expertise can be brought in through business alliances with building material retailers.

Microfinance Institutions

Housing microfinance is growing fairly rapidly. The number of institutions providing housing microfinance is growing worldwide. At this point of time, roughly 200 microfinance institutions worldwide have become commercially viable. Housing microfinance is more established in Latin America and is expanding in Asia and Africa. Moreover, housing microfinance is only a small part of the total portfolios of microfinance institutions. Increasing competition had slowed growth opportunities available to microfinance institutions in some markets, such as Bolivia and Bangladesh.

Housing microfinance also fits well with the transformation of many microfinance institutions from NGOs into financial institutions, this is required because they take deposits from the public. The ability to take deposits can vastly reduce the costs of microfinance institution funding, which otherwise comes typically from other financial institutions or donors. The aspiration to own or build a house has historically proven to be the main motivation for families to save money; normally saved in banks, in both developed and developing countries where savings groups and housing cooperatives serve the same purpose. Hence, adding a home improvement credit as well as savings products makes sense for microfinance institutions seeking to take deposits (the least expensive type of funding), and therefore becoming regulated financial institutions.

Three interrelated factors which seriously limit the expansion of housing microfinance within microfinance institutions can be identified.

First, an explicit housing product typically has a slightly lower interest rate and longer tenure, and can cannibalise their existing microenterprise loan business. That is, the microfinance institution's microentrepreneur clients could nominally borrow for housing to fund their business and get better terms than they would under a microenterprise credit. Thus, the development of an explicit housing product might mainly lower profits, unless marketed to a new clientele or unless the microfinance institution monitors the use of the funds for housing.

Second, microfinance institutions often consider housing an adjunct secondary product. From the perspective of most microfinance institutions, housing credit deserves little attention and is unrelated to their core mission of 'promoting economic development'. Many studies, as well as common experience, show that most households build wealth mainly through homeownership and that housing investment plays a crucial role in national economies. Nevertheless, microfinance institutions continue to relegate housing to a trivial role in their business strategy, aimed supposedly at 'economic development'. With a few notable exceptions, microfinance institutions lack the interest to make housing a major focus.

Third, microfinance organisations offer far too small an institutional base in many countries to allow for the expansion of housing microfinance to a scale relevant to demand, even if microfinance institutions were interested in this role. Even after 25 years of development, the microfinance institution industry consists of less than 300 commercially viable institutions and serves only a fraction of the market for microenterprise loans in most countries, therefore offering housing microcredit in minuscule volumes relative to demand.

Bottlenecks to Housing Microfinance Expansion: Financial Sector and Capital Market Barriers

There is a rapid growth of housing microloan volume within microfinance institutions, although from a small base. Microfinance institutions have discovered that housing microfinance is profitable and has immense potential for expansion. Thus, housing microfinance, in particular, small home improvement loans, is now well established as a recognised niche product for microfinance institutions. From the perspective of many microfinance institutions, their housing product is on track to fulfil its institutional missions: to diversify risk, to support development of savings products and the transition to a regulated deposit-taking financial institution, and to offer an additional product popular with their core microentrepreneur clients.

The 'lack of funding', cited as the main stumbling block by microfinance institutions, hindering the expansion of housing microfinance, is on its way to a solution. For example, Mexico's second-tier housing development bank, the *Sociedad Hipotecaria Federal*, which previously offered liquidity only for mortgage loans, mainly for middle-income home purchase, has (since 2005) a housing microfinance window and now offers a subsidy that can be joined with a small housing loan. Many Latin American countries join market-rate credit with subsidies (in the form of vouchers) and down payments of households in affordable housing programs. Such 'direct-demand subsidy programs' started with Chile (which has served as a model for other countries) and have spread widely to Costa Rica, Mexico, Ecuador, Jamaica, Brazil, El Salvador, Columbia, and elsewhere. These ABC programs (named after the Spanish terms for their financial components: *ahorro* – household savings, *bono* – direct-demand subsidy, *credito* – credit) typically work well for the middle class and, sometimes, moderate-income households, but have had difficulties reaching low-income households. The government of Colombia has tried to start a secondary market for housing microfinance. Investment groups and capital market institutions are establishing financial vehicles to fund home credit for microfinance institutions. There is considerable progress in issuing securities on public markets for on-lending to microfinance institutions to finance low- and moderate-income housing in developing countries.

Apart from incomplete liquidity of banks and capital markets, there are limited linkages between banks, microfinance institutions, and the capital market, but also with private sector enterprises. These linkages could enable capital streams between financial institutions. Under such circumstances, private sector entrepreneurs, such as building materials suppliers, work together with microfinance institutions. Moreover, building materials could be financed through microfinance institutions.

Land and Infrastructure

In the shelter sector, there are problems with the lack of tenure security, land titles, and infrastructure. In many sub-Saharan African countries such as Rwanda and Kenya, few urban low- and moderate-income households individually own the land on which their houses stand, this land is often communal tribal property or owned by others. In such contexts, some microfinance institutions have begun to accept evidence of security of individual tenure (rather than ownership rights), such as 'land leases' for underwriting small housing credits. Housing microfinance can play an important role in financing low-income urban land development, the largest stumbling block to housing the poor as the example of Saiban in Pakistan shows.

In Karachi, a citizen sector organisation Saiban has acquired land parcels, organised, financed, and provided the internal infrastructure for over 60 000 people. The process to apply for and buy a lot is handled onsite and involves minimal paperwork. Saiban offers a flexible payment schedule consisting of a down payment of 20–40% (about US$175) of the total price. Households pay the remaining amount of US$525 in monthly instalments over a period of 100 months. These monthly payments of US$5.25 are affordable even to the lowest-income households and virtually none drop out of the process. Saiban keeps ownership of the lot until the last payment, after which it delivers full legal title to the families. Saiban has also worked with commercial banks to offer mortgage finance to those earning at least US$3 per day.

In this project, the initial infrastructure is minimal, partly to discourage speculation. It consists of a communal water supply, a soak pit for sanitation, and public transport from private suppliers. Underground sewerage, piped water, electricity, and paved roads are extended incrementally once instalment payments are made. Saiban develops the service infrastructure internal to the subdivision funded by the monthly instalments from purchasing households. The relevant government agencies develop external infrastructure including trunk sewer lines, sewage treatment plants, bulk water, electricity supply, and access roads. In order to discourage speculation, Saiban requires that a poor family stay at a reception site for up to 2 weeks to demonstrate need. On making the down payment at the end of the 2-week waiting period, the family gains possession but not title to the plot. Saiban also arranges for a wide variety of other services. Perhaps most important, Saiban transfers clear title to the lot when households make the final payment on their land and ensures public safety in its settlements through agreements with local police (usually, not to intervene) and others.

Various types of public-private partnerships and alliances between different stakeholders - public and private sector organisations and civil society - have potential for providing basic communal infrastructure and services to the poor, which can be financed by housing microfinance loans.

Housing Microfinance and Beyond

In addition to the many new uses for micro credit, a huge unmet demand exists for somewhat larger loans (US$2500–10 000) for the housing solutions preferred by the rapidly growing lower middle class of dynamic developing countries, especially in Asia and Latin America. Meeting this demand requires longer loan duration (e.g., 10 years) and lower interest rates, new methods for funding, underwriting, processing, servicing and collecting loans, risk management, and institutional innovation. The development of distinct products and institutions for this market has largely yet to occur. Thus, housing microfinance is only one step in the creation of a wide spectrum of innovative credit products necessary to meet the massive demand for affordable housing in developing countries.

See also: Housing Finance: Global South; Housing Finance Institutions: Africa; Housing Finance Institutions: Asia; Housing Finance Institutions: Transition Societies; Housing Policies in Developing Countries; Housing Subsidies and Welfare; Microfinance for Housing; Self-Build: Latin America; Urbanisation and Housing the Poor: Overview.

Further Reading

Daphnis F and Ferguson B (eds.) (2004) *Housing Microfinance: A Guide to Practice*. Bloomfield, CT: Kumarian.
Ferguson B (2003) Housing microfinance: A key to improving habitat and the sustainability of microfinance institutions. *Small Enterprise Development* 14(1): 21–31.

Ferguson B and Smets P (2010) Finance for incremental housing: Current status and prospects for expansion. *Habitat International* 34(3): 288–298.

Merrill S (2009) Microfinance for housing: Assisting to the 'Bottom Billion' and the 'Missing Middle' *IDG Working Paper No.* 2009. Washington, DC: Urban Institute Center on International Development and Governance.

Merrill S and Messarina N (2006) Expanding microfinance for housing. *Housing Finance International* 21(2): 3–11.

Nilsson A (2008) Overview of financial systems for slum upgrading and housing. *Housing Finance International* 23(2): 19–26.

Rutherford S (2000) *The Poor and Their Money*. New Delhi, India: Oxford University Press.

Smets P (2000) ROSCAs as a source of housing finance for the urban poor: An analysis of self-help practices from Hyderabad, India. *Community Development Journal* 35(1): 16–30.

Smets P (2004) *Housing Finance and the Urban Poor*. Jaipur, New Delhi: Rawat.

Smets P (2006) Small is beautiful, but big is often the practice: Housing microfinance in discussion. *Habitat International* 30(3): 595–613.

Turner JFC (1976) *Housing by People. Towards Autonomy in Building Environments*. London: Marion.

Housing Policies in Developing Countries: Sites-and-Services and Aided Self-Help

D Mitlin, University of Manchester, Manchester, UK; The International Institute for Environment and Development, London, UK

© 2012 Elsevier Ltd. All rights reserved.

Glossary

Building standards Governments have rules and regulations that define the requirements for safe dwellings. Standards are one criterion which establish which are legal and which are not.

Collective loan finance Loans offered to a group, normally with some legal standing. In some cases, this is for individual goods such as single units constructed by housing cooperatives; however, collective loan finance is often used for infrastructure investment which is collective in nature.

Incremental development Also called progressive development, incremental development refers to the process whereby housing is constructed through many small-scale investments such as laying a concrete floor, adding a room, and/or improving the roof.

Savings-based organising Community organising methodology built around savings groups that are then networked at the city and/or national level.

Sites and services Programmes to enable households to access serviced plots with legal tenure as the first step of an incremental housing development process.

Squatter (slum) upgrading programmes Programmes to improve informal settlements that involve the regularisation of tenure and the provision of services. In some cases, there are also components related to the improvement of houses.

Toilet blocks Buildings with several toilets and washing facilities provided in low-income settlements due to high densities and/or limited investment capacity.

Introduction

As urbanisation took place without the capacity and/or will of local government to manage the situation, large-scale informal settlements grew in most cities – to the point where these often housed 30–60% of the total city population. Particularly from the early 1970s, governments came to realise that the efforts that citizens put into the building and consolidation of informal settlements were a potential solution to the problems of urban development.

In this context, sites and services programmes, along with slum and squatter upgrading programmes, emerged in response to the failures of alternative approaches by development agencies (including national government, official development aid and local government) to address deteriorating housing conditions in urban areas. Site and services programmes are much cheaper than public housing programmes because no house is built; legal tenure is provided for a residential plot together with access to basic services. They provide a partial response to housing need but one that is potentially valuable for low-income households if they can get a serviced site on which to build at a price they can afford. Unit costs may be brought down by providing only limited access to services and making an initial investment in infrastructure. The expectation is that households will build their homes and upgrade services and their dwelling over time. What distinguishes sites and services from the provision of serviced sites for higher-income families are minimal infrastructure, the possibility for delayed construction and building standards being modified to ensure affordability for the lowest-income households.

This article discusses reasons for the development of site and service programmes and explains the conceptual foundations for the approach. The discussion below reviews experiences to date with a particular emphasis on the problems that emerged and which explain the demise of these programmes. Despite this, the conceptual strength of the approach helps us understand new approaches to housing delivery; and this theme concludes the article.

The Emergence of Sites and Services Programmes

The growth in urban populations (from both migration and natural increase) has been rapid in many countries of the South in recent decades. However, city governments have struggled to identify an appropriate response to their citizens' shelter needs which takes into account both the scale of population increase and the low incomes of many urban households. As a consequence, many found accommodation in squatter settlements and other forms of informal accommodation. During the 1960s and 1970s, there were two common approaches to squatter settlements in the towns and cities of the global South (both of which continue to this day). One strategy was eviction and the eradication of informal settlements with squatters being dispossessed and moved away regardless of their claim to the land. Only rarely were those evicted provided with any help in finding new homes – and where provision was made this was usually on poor-quality sites on city peripheries far from the evictees' income-earning sources. Some such evictions were related to the management of colonial cities in Africa and the refusal of these colonial authorities to permit any uncontrolled settlement in part related to broader issues of state control (including apartheid-like controls on people's rights to live or work in urban areas). However, in other cases evictions were related simply to the reluctance to find a place for low-income residents within the city, and/or because of 'dangers' assumed to be associated with squatter communities. Such attitudes may still prevail and evictions continue to be used as a strategy to manage urban development.

For multiple reasons, local authorities came under pressure to abandon eviction strategies and find a more acceptable shelter solution. The second strategy was complete build projects in which houses or apartments were constructed for new urban residents. There are numerous examples of the lack of success of the strategy; in summary, costs were high for affordability and hence the number of units small because governments had limited resources for subsidies. Such strategies offered a significant transfer of public funds to the few who received the dwellings and they did little for the many who remained without adequate housing. Some government programmes cut the size of the subsidy on each unit but then what was built could only be afforded by higher-income households. Faced with this situation, governments gradually became more interested in sites and service programmes as they recognised the weaknesses of slum eradication and impossibility that public housing could be provided at sufficient scale.

The conceptual understanding to this approach owes much to the writers who researched and documented the ways in which low-income settlements developed without professional or governmental support. Mar, Turner, and Mangin all made contributions to influence prevailing attitudes during the 1960s and helping to legitimate more affordable and less exclusionary housing policies and associated programmes, including both serviced site programmes and upgrading programmes.

Unable to afford complete dwellings and needing to find somewhere to stay close to places of work, households squatted on available land often managing without adequate security and basic services. Settlement on agricultural or unused land on the urban periphery could take place at lower densities than inner city locations. Dwellers often anticipated the possible designation of residential areas by having grid layouts and with open spaces and pathways that might become roads. These observers recognised that households able to gain some claim over a piece of well-located land with a degree of security were able to improve their residence and, over time, negotiate for the upgrading of neighbourhoods and legal title. Independent professionals and then government officials had the idea of modelling solutions on these informal processes of land occupation. Hence, 'sites and services' programmes which sought to replicate such development processes through the provision of land, services and, in some cases, modifications of building standards (at least at the project level) to allow for a bottom-up process of shelter development were developed.

One of the few major international funding agencies interested in shelter was the World Bank which began funding sites and services programmes in the early 1970s at the very beginning of their shelter-associated lending. However, sites and services programmes existed before World Bank support in some countries where serviced sites were made available to households with existing rules and building regulations being leniently applied. Riofrio (1996: 160) suggests "... sites and services schemes were pioneered in Peru during the 1960s. Land was reserved for the poor, and when invasions of different areas took place the authorities responded by regularising these settlements." Residents received security of tenure in quasi-legal land occupation, settling in areas that were well laid out with space for public services and facilities but with permission being granted after the event. A more organised version took place in Malawi where the first planned traditional housing areas (THAs) on public land were provided with partially serviced plots offering an opportunity to urban workers who wanted to build their own houses. By 1962, a total of 2415 such plots had been demarcated and allocations to low-income residents were underway. A second phase of THAs implementation was facilitated by a World Bank loan approved in 1972. In Ghana, the shift from completed units in the early 1960s to sites and services developments was evidenced by the late 1960s.

Summary of Experience

For those governments and the few international agencies interested in addressing housing needs, sites and services programmes became popular as evidenced by their significance as a percentage of World Bank shelter lending (49% between 1972 and 1987). However, it should be added that these figures represent a relatively small number of loans with the largest total number of annual loans between 1972 and 1987 being 12.

The World Bank launched into these programmes with some enthusiasm in part because they anticipated that they could be more financially viable than the early generation of state shelter provision. "Sites and services projects blossomed in the 1970s and early 1980s; between 1972 and 1987 ... they accounted for 49 percent of all housing-related loans" (Angel, 2000: 15). Total annual shelter lending during this period was between $27 and $800 million (US$ 2001). The significance of the approach is exemplified by a recent study of land and tenure issues in six African cities which found that there had been sites and services programmes in four of them, albeit limited in some cases.

Despite the early enthusiasm for site and service programmes, as the illustrations of World Bank funding and those from the National Housing Corporation in Kenya illustrate, the significance of these programmes declined very significantly from the mid-1980s onwards. Why did they fall out of favour? Despite initial expectations, a number of problems emerged in the realisation of these programmes and some key explanations are highlighted below.

Supply of Units

One common problem has been the limited scale of programmes. Supply of serviced sites has been lacking and hence the plots have often been subject to speculation by higher-income groups who secured access. In Malawi, for example, in 1981, there were 35 000 applicants on the waiting list while the rate of serviced plot delivery was 600 plots per annum. In Botswana, by 1997 (after decades of inadequate supply), delivery had expanded to over 33 000 regularised plots in one Gaborone township alone. These were all allocated and many had been developed. However, the waiting list still stood at over 23 500 (Kalabamu, 2006: 219).

Reaching Low-Income Households

The lack of supply made the plots an attractive speculative investment. Many serviced plots have been resold at considerable profit and the rich and powerful manipulated the systems to gain from the allocation procedures. In El Salvador, the World Bank agreed to finance FUNDASAL, a locally based NGO, to provide sites and services development. However, the NGO was unable to persuade the state to scale up the programme and hence the lowest-income households did not benefit from the programme. In Nairobi, while the programme design allowed plot owners to provide rental accommodation to improve affordability, the lower-income households could not afford to repay the costs and develop the plots and they were quickly allocated illegally to higher-income households. In Botswana, the lowest-income households were unable to access serviced plots because of long waiting lists, high costs, and demands for illegal payments.

Rakodi (2006: 267) in an overview of state-supported land acquisition in six African countries concludes that serviced plots were available for some "but practice with respect to charging for the land itself and the standards adopted affects the ability of low-income households to afford the plots and never provides access for the poorest." She argues that women in particular found it difficult to establish their entitlement.

Location

The problems for low-income households were exacerbated by distant locations which ensured that the lower-income households could not afford to stay on the plots. Turner had highlighted the importance of location to ensure adequate access to both social networks and employment opportunities. One of the factors leading to the success of sites and services in Hyderabad (Pakistan) was the favourable location of the project. The World Bank modified its support, taking an explicit policy position in 1975 to favour upgrading rather than new site development which in part reflected the importance for low-income households of locations with livelihood opportunities.

Building Standards

In Malawi, standards were deliberately kept to a minimum, so that the beneficiaries could build any type of house with a chance of improving it later but this appears to be relatively unusual. Moreover, even in Malawi, this was too onerous with the lowest-income households being excluded because the regulations stipulated that the plot must be developed within 6 months from the date of acceptance. The standards adopted potentially deterred low-income households from securing access.

The Lack of Political Popularity

A related problem was that such programmes were not popular with politicians because they were not seen as producing a city of adequate status and value. Potts explained how one of the projects close to the centre of Lilongwe was demolished due to the fact that it did not fit with Banda's vision of the city.

The Impact on Urbanisation

In Peru, experiences have also been mixed. The systems may have been inefficient and slow in terms of housing development due to a lack of affordable credit and technical assistance. A further related problem has been that construction quality is sometimes poor with unsafe dwellings. In terms of the nature of neighbourhood development, the consequence has been a low-density urban sprawl often with very few services or a high-density development in more popular locations with multiple occupation of plots. (Very similar concerns are expressed in the context of Gaborone's (Botswana) urban development.) Even by 1993, only 63.6% of Lima's population enjoyed piped water in the home and only 60.2% of households were linked into main sewer.

Financial Viability

In terms of the World Bank, the declining interest was partly related to the financial crisis of the early 1980s. Sites and services and upgrading programmes were replaced by housing finance and policy interventions. The World Bank hoped that sites and services schemes would provide low-income housing without subsidies and hence that the programmes would be replicated by private sector developers. Neither of these aspirations were found to be true and a Bank study in 1987 reported large interest rate subsidies in addition to other supply-side subsidies (e.g., through the provision of land and technical assistance at a discounted cost).

Some Positive Experiences

However, it is important to recognise that the experiences were not all negative. The fact that the World Bank promoted and supported serviced sites popularised the concept and made it acceptable as a policy intervention and many city governments have implemented serviced site projects or projects with 'core housing units' without external support. Drawing on successful experiences, it appears that there is a potential for such programmes if they are carefully designed and well managed. As such, the principles of site and service programmes have been maintained and reproduced in programmes which draw upon these experiences.

Sites and Services Programmes Revisited

The continuing irrelevance of many alternative approaches to shelter acquisition and improvement helps to explain why the concept of sites and services development remains in use today. It is widely recognised that low-income households cannot afford to purchase completed dwellings. Tenure security remains a priority for households seeking to improve their housing options and access to basic services such as water and sanitation is essential. As was the case many decades ago, professionals (academics, civil society staff, and state officials) recognise that households invest considerable amounts in improving their own shelter and any strategic attempt to tackle the scale of the housing backlog will have to draw on this finance.

Reflecting these realities, a number of different strategies provide assistance to households seeking to develop housing incrementally. These strategies bear some affinity with the design principles of sites and services programmes.

Greenfield Developments with Minimal Services

Some local authorities and national governments have introduced programmes that offer Greenfield development opportunities with a varied level of service provision to maximise affordability and therefore access. The three examples below all illustrate attempts to facilitate access to serviced land: in the first case through a private developer who sells to low-income residents, in the second by offering collective loan finance to low-income residents who can purchase land and access services incrementally, and in the third with communal land and services provision from the state to organised savings schemes able to raise and manage their own development finance for incremental development.

In El Salvador, while FUNDASAL's sites and services programme financed by the World Bank was taking place, the sale of unserviced plots of land on the urban periphery continued to take place. In 1992, the legalisation of these plots began. One developer, Argoz, has made considerable efforts to provide these plots with services either directly or through the land owner if they are simply development consultants; in total, they have been involved in the provision of serviced plots for 300 000 families.

In the Philippines, the Community Mortgage Programme provides low-interest loans that allow informal settlers at risk of eviction to acquire an undivided tract of land to be purchased through a community mortgage. There are two kinds of project under the CMP: off-site and on-site projects. The on-site projects allow the illegal settlers to formalise their claim to the land they occupy already by buying it from the owner and the off-site provides finance for the relocation of residents to a Greenfield area. Loans can be used for infrastructure and housing development but this is relatively rare and most of the loan is used for the purchase of land. Communities negotiate with their local government officials and representatives (generally at the lowest level or baranguay) for incremental improvements to services. More recently, a new programme has been introduced, the Development of Poor Urban Communities Sector Project which finances local authorities to provide serviced sites to low-income families with an expectation that households will borrow directly from microfinance agencies to construct their houses (Llanto, 2007: 418).

In another example of state efforts to provide affordable tenure, in 2001 the City of Windhoek introduced seven service standards for land sales in an effort to respond to affordability levels. Lower levels of services (communal toilets and water taps) enable community groups to purchase land for later upgrading and housing construction. This policy has increased the affordability of access to tenure and enabled low-income families to have tenure security, upgrading as finance becomes available.

Civil Society Programmes to Access Serviced Land

One set of civil society initiatives is that supported by Shack/Slum Dwellers International (SDI), a transnational network with affiliates in over 30 countries in the global South. One core methodology is savings-based organising. SDI affiliates are federations of the homeless and landless poor whose membership is made up of active citizens (mainly women), saving in their local settlements. By December 2007, SDI affiliates had raised over $43 million, much of which had been lent out to the members of affiliate federations to upgrade over 100 000 plots; most of these had been acquired from governments at no or at reduced cost. In about half of these cases where state subsidies are available, housing has also been constructed. In other countries, households upgrade incrementally.

Groups negotiate for land in various ways, seeking to secure state subsidies where this is possible and/or to negotiate concessions on land development to reduce costs whether or not state subsidies are available. In Malawi, Zimbabwe, Namibia, and most recently Tanzania, savings schemes affiliated with SDI have succeeded in reducing the plot size, generally by group purchase of land with a collective title. Local groups find strategies to acquire basic services, in some cases using their own savings to invest in improvements such as the women in Namibia who installed lane sanitation and in other cases participating in government-funded schemes for toilet block construction such as in Mumbai. The flexibility of this model can be adjusted almost infinitely by local groups able to respond to what the state is able to offer. In IloIlo (the Philippines), for example, savings schemes were able to secure land from the local authority which had invested in purchasing undeveloped plots for those facing eviction. When families moved onto the plots, there were no services provided. In the following years, they negotiated improvements in water provision from the city authorities and installed their own bamboo walkway to manage the low-lying nature of the land and frequent flooding.

While SDI is unusual for the scale of its activities, there are many other initiatives that exemplify how local residents seek access to land with basic services. In Goiânia community organisations developed a specific strategy, settling on public land (common land) outside the city boundaries in organised invasions which claimed *posseiro* rights, a free right over all land which has not been subject to subdivision; over time they were able to upgrade through lobbying the municipal government for services. The process was slow and partial, but once the acquisition of land had taken place, residents negotiated for services and made investments in their housing. By 1991 (about 10 years after this activity began), 12.3% of the population of Goiânia was living in these *posseiro* areas. Such replications demonstrate the fundamental realities of urban settlement by low-income households.

Private Developers

In most nations, perhaps the largest supply of land for urban housing for low-income groups and often for large section of the middle-income population is illegal subdivisions. Illegal subdivisions might be considered semi-legal and are usually semi-serviced sites. Here, the landowner or a developer working on their behalf subdivides land into plots for housing and sells them. This is usually most evident on the urban periphery with agricultural land being subdivided. The quality and extent of provision for infrastructure and services varies a lot between different illegal subdivisions – and many such subdivisions have very little such provision. This is unlike squatter settlements in that the land is purchased (or leased) from the landowner – but like squatter settlements, these are 'illegal' because the subdivision was not approved by the local government.

In some cases, state or city government interventions have supported private efforts for services. In Bamako (Mali), for example, such unauthorised settlements housed 31% of the city's population by 1983 (compared to 5.5% in 1965) (Vaa 2000: 28). After years of neglect and insignificant intervention, in 1992 a 'comprehensive programme of legalization and upgrading was formulated' (ibid: 28) which included the provision of services in 25 of the 31 unauthorised neighbourhoods. In the peri-urban areas of São Paolo, continued land occupation is taking place as households seek affordable shelter. In this city at least, there have been attempts to provide services to these areas.

Conclusion

The concept of sites and services replicates a reality for low-income households unable to pay for housing through the market in a context in which there has been a huge under-provision of services and sites by national and local governments in the global South. State agencies have sought to support these grassroots urban development strategies with sites and services programmes. However, these programmes have not been widely associated with success and have, over time, become less popular. The problems faced by these programmes have been primarily associated with a lack of scale and insufficient considerations of the needs of the lowest-income households; in summary, too much has been offered on too limited a scale resulting in the capture of opportunities by higher-income groups. At the same time, the emphasis on rapid and/or high-standard construction deters occupation by the urban poor and/or prevents them remaining in these sites.

Nevertheless, the fundamental realities of low-income families, in particular the lack of adequate income combined with the need for public services, mean that many households seek to acquire land and negotiate for services. In this sense, self-help strategies and government programmes that want to work with local realities find themselves replicating some of the principles behind sites and services programmes even if they no longer identify with the title.

See also: Civil Sector Institutions and Informal Settlements; Housing Finance: Global South; Housing Institutions in Developing Countries; Housing Policies in Developing Countries; Self-Build: Global South; Self-Build: Latin America; Self-Help Housing Organisations; Self-Help: Policy Assistance; Self-Provided Housing in Developed Societies; Squatter Settlement Clearance; Squatting: Developing World.

References

Angel S (2000) *Housing Policy Matters: A Global Analysis*. New York: Oxford University Press.
Barbosa R, Cabannes Y, and Morães L (1997) Tenant today, posserio tomorrow. *Environment and Urbanization* 9(2): 17–46.
Buckley R and Kalarickal J (eds.) (2006) *Thirty Years of World Bank Shelter Lending: What Have We Learned?* Washington, DC: World Bank.
Centre for Housing Rights and Evictions (COHRE) (2006) *Forced Evictions: Violations of Human Rights*. Geneva: COHRE.
Dubresson A (1997) Abidjan: From the public making of a modern city to urban management of a metropolis. In: Carole R (ed.) *The Urban Challenge in Africa: Growth and Management of Its Large Cities*, pp. 252–291. Tokyo, New York and London: United Nations University Press.
Llanto G (2007) Shelter finance strategies for the poor: The Philippines. *Environment and Urbanization* 19(2): 409–424.
Manda MAZ (2007) Mchenga-urban poor housing fund: CCODE and homeless people's federation in Malawi. *Environment and Urbanization* 19(2): 337–360.
Mitlin D and Muller A (2007) Securing inclusion: Strategies for community empowerment and state redistribution. *Environment and Urbanization* 19(2): 425–441.
Porio E, Crisol CS, Magno NF, Cid D, and Paul EN (2004) The community mortgage programme: An innovative social housing programme in the Philippines and its outcomes. In: Mitlin D and Satterthwaite D (eds.) *Empowering Squatter Citizen*, pp. 54–81. London: Earthscan.
Riofrio G (1996) Lima: Mega-city and mega-problem. In: Gilbert A (ed.) *The Mega City in Latin America*. Tokyo: United Nations University Press.
Siddiqui T (2005) *Incremental Housing Development Scheme (Pakistan): An Innovative and Successful Scheme for Sheltering the Poor*. Washington, DC: World Bank Urban Research Annual Workshop.
Turner J (1976) *Housing by People: Towards Autonomy in Building Environments*. London: Marion Boyars Publishers Ltd.
Vaa M (2000) Housing policy after political transition: the case of Bamako. *Environment and Urbanization* 12(1): 27–34.

Further Reading

Alfredo S and Vance I (2008) The role of housing finance in addressing the needs of the urban poor: Lessons from Central America. *Environment and Urbanization* 20(1): 13–30.
Hardoy J and Satterthwaite D (1989) *Squatter Citizen*. London: Earthscan Publications Ltd.
Kalabamu FT (2006) The limitations of state regulation of land delivery processes in Gaborone, Botswana. *International Development Planning Review* 28(2): 209–233.
Rakodi C (1997) Residential property markets in African cities. In: Rakodi C (ed.) *The Urban Challenge in Africa: Growth and Management of Its Large Cities*, pp. 371–410. Tokyo: United Nations University Press.
Rakodi C (2006) Social agency and state authority in land delivery processes in African cities. *International Development Planning Review* 28(2): 263–285.

Housing Policy: Agents and Regulators

P Boelhouwer and J Hoekstra, Delft University of Technology, Delft, The Netherlands

© 2012 Elsevier Ltd. All rights reserved.

Glossary

Government A specific type of organisation which is expected to fulfil certain core tasks (such as providing stability) and to act as a neutral third party in regulating relations between nongovernmental actors. The government is not a homogeneous organisation. It usually consists of several territorial and functional administrative layers.

Housing system A system of interrelationships between all the actors and institutions involved in the production, consumption, and regulation of housing.

Institution A multidimensional concept that may refer to governments, nonprofit organisations, laws and regulations, and informal values and norms.

Nonprofit organisation An organisation that does not distribute any profit it makes to its owners, members, or other associated parties.

Path-dependency The belief that external developments are 'filtered' by the particular national context, as a result of which they work out differently in different countries.

Principal–agent problem The risk that individual actors exploit the organisation they are part of as a vehicle for their own ambitions, interests, and self-enrichment.

Social rental landlord Social rental landlords provide rental housing to lower- and sometimes also middle-income groups with a social purpose, as a result of which they charge rents that are below the market level.

Introduction: The Three Dimensions of Institutions

The concept 'institution' is frequently used in housing research, although the precise meaning of the term is often rather unclear. This is related to the fact that the concept 'institution' is very broad. In fact, it can have at least three different meanings.

First of all, institutions may refer to organisations that perform specific tasks within society, often with a nonprofit objective. Second, institutions may refer to laws and regulations that are formulated by the government. Third, next to formal laws and regulations, are informal values and norms that constitute an informal institutional dimension. In the last two definitions, the focus is on administrative, economic, and social rules (the rules of the game), whereas the first definition concentrates on the organisational configurations through which these rules are effectuated (the rulers of the game), or that are subject to the rules (the players of the game). Vrooman (2009) has provided an extensive overview of the different forms that institutions may take, which provides a basis to this article.

The aim of this contribution is to provide an overview of the role that institutions play within the field of housing. In addition to this, it shows how housing institutions may change over time. Examples from different, mainly European, countries are provided to illustrate both points.

Institutions as Organisations

Institutions may be seen as organisations that carry out specific tasks within society. In the most basic terms, two main types of organisations may be distinguished: government organisations (including supranational organisations) and private nonprofit organisations. It is also possible to consider commercial companies and individual agents as institutions; however, in this article, the focus is on the more conventional conceptions.

The Government as an Institution of Housing Policy and Housing Regulation

The government is a specific type of organisation which is expected to fulfil certain core tasks (such as providing security) and to act as a neutral third party which regulates relations between nongovernmental actors. The government is not a homogeneous organisation and there are several territorial and functional administrative layers. In most countries, a distinction can be made between the supranational layer of governance (European Union, United Nations), the national government, the regional government (regions or provinces), and the local government (municipalities).

As far as the formulation of housing policy is concerned, the importance of each of these government layers differs between countries. In some countries, for example France, the formulation of housing policy mainly takes place at the national level, whereas in other countries, such as Germany, housing policy is mainly formulated at the level of the regions. The importance and autonomy of local authorities with regard to housing policy decisions strongly varies between countries as well, although a general trend of decentralisation has been visible across the board in the last three decades.

Conflicts between the Different Layers of Government

Policies and regulations that are formulated at different layers of government may be in conflict with each other. In the beginning of the twenty-first century, such a conflict clearly emerged in the Netherlands, where national and local housing policies and practices in the social rental sector appeared to be at odds with the European Union regulations regarding state support and economic competition. The conflict between the Dutch national and EU government over the regulation of housing associations provides a particularly insightful case.

To a certain extent, the Dutch social rental sector is exceptional in Europe because of its large size (about 32% of the total dwelling stock) and the fact that Dutch social rental dwellings, which are built with the help of state support, have traditionally been accessible for large segments of the population (not only lower-income groups but also middle- and even higher-income groups). However, in the summer of 2005 the European Commission communicated with the Dutch government indicating that, for reasons of fair economic competition between nonprofit social rental landlords and profit-oriented private rental landlords, the state-supported Dutch social rental sector should focus more strongly on housing lower-income groups. This letter resulted in long negotiations between the European Commission and the Dutch government that only came to an end in the autumn of 2009. It was finally agreed that at least 90% of the social rental dwellings with a regulated rent (rent level below €653 in 2011) should be allocated to households with a taxable yearly income below €33 614. This target group currently covers about 40% of all households in the Netherlands.

The above agreement is expected to have serious consequences for the Dutch housing system since in 2008 and 2009 only 76% of the Dutch social rental dwellings were allocated to households that belong to the newly defined target group. It can be envisaged that the middle-income groups (especially those with an income just above the income limit) may get into trouble. After all, their access to the social rental sector will be limited, whereas an owner-occupied dwelling (57% of the Dutch housing stock) or a private rental dwelling (11% of the Dutch housing stock) is often too expensive for these households, especially so if they live in the most urbanised regions of the country such as the area around Amsterdam.

Government-Controlled Housing Organisations

Public organisations that are relevant to the field of housing are sometimes accommodated in specific organisations that are separated from the 'ordinary' territorial layers of government. Although these specific housing organisations remain government-controlled, they may also enjoy a certain degree of autonomy. On the local level, the Arms Length Management Organisations (ALMOs) in the United Kingdom are a good example of such institutions. ALMOs provide social housing at the level of local authorities. Where ALMOs are in place, the local council retains ownership of the social rental dwelling stock but the management of this stock is in the hands of a new organisation that is governed by a board of councillors, tenants, and independent persons. The French ANAH (*Agence Nationale de l'Habitat*) is an example of a government-controlled but, nonetheless, independent housing organisation that works at the national level. The ANAH is a national body that provides financial support for home refurbishment and home improvement. It has its own budget and it is partly financed through a special tax on older private rental dwellings. Also outside Europe, there are various examples of large and powerful government-controlled housing organisations that function at the national level, such as the Department of Housing and Urban Development (HUD) in the United States and the Housing and Development Board (HDB) in Singapore (which has built more than 80% of the national housing stock).

Social Rental Landlords as Nonprofit Institutions of Housing Provision

A nonprofit organisation can be defined as an organisation that does not distribute any profit it makes to its owners, members, or other associated parties. Such organisations generally come into being if the market and the government are not able to fulfil all the demand of the consumers, for instance, as a result of lack of trust in market parties or government failure. Nonprofit organisations may then arise to fill the gap left by the unfulfilled demand. The best-known nonprofit organisations within the field of housing are the social rental landlords. Social rental landlords provide rental housing to lower- and sometimes also middle-income groups with a social purpose, as a result of which they charge rents that are below the market level. Social rental landlords can have many different forms: they can be local authorities (in which case they are actually government or government-controlled institutions), private nonprofit organisations, or cooperatives of tenants, whereas mixes of these three forms are also possible.

The Principal–Agent Problem in Organisations

Organisations arise as a result of organising: the process whereby individuals or existing organisations transfer their rights and obligations to a new organisation in order to achieve a certain goal. Organisations usually have a hierarchical structure. Although organisations function as independent legal bodies in their own right, their acts are realised by individuals. These individuals (the agents) are deemed to act as representatives of the organisation (the principal) they are part of. However, despite the formal and informal rules that intend to prevent this (labour contracts, informal norms that are shared by groups within the organisation), some agents may try to exploit the organisation as a vehicle for their own ambitions, interests, and self-enrichment (Vrooman, 2009). This is generally referred to as the principal–agent problem.

Egoistic agents can seriously damage the public image of their principals. In the Netherlands, for example, the public image of housing associations has suffered badly from a few cases of fraud and the disproportionally high salaries that are paid to some housing association directors. In Germany too, lack of internal control was one of the most important reasons for the scandal surrounding the collapse of the 'Neue Heimat' – the largest German social rented housing company – in the 1980s.

Within the field of housing, individual agents that function within organisations are especially important in the process of housing allocation and/or the granting of mortgages, where the so-called 'gatekeepers' often decide who has access to housing and who does not. Gatekeepers include housing officers who work for social rental landlords or local authorities, real estate agents, and employees of mortgage providers.

Institutions as Laws and Regulations

It is generally acknowledged that an advanced society cannot function effectively and efficiently without a certain degree of government regulation. Government laws and rules provide information on what desired behaviour is and may impose sanctions when people violate the rules of the 'game' (Vrooman, 2009).

Although there are important differences between countries, the housing sector tends to be substantially regulated. A good example of how housing is regulated is the property rights endowed upon owner-occupiers and tenants. In the homeownership sector in most countries, there are formal rules dictating the content of the sales contract, the entry in the land register, agreements with the mortgage provider, the fiscal aspects, the inheritance laws, the possibilities to evict and prosecute squatters, and so on (Vrooman, 2009). In the rental sector, the property rights of tenants are reflected in the tenant security: duration of the rental contracts, protection against eviction, and so on.

Other important examples of laws and regulations that are important for housing are rent regulation, quality regulation, housing allowances, and housing allocation rules. Most housing policies and regulations have been designed with the objective to make the housing system and the housing market 'work better'. Unfortunately, this objective is not always met in practice. Sometimes, rules and regulations that are set up to combat market failure have suboptimal or even counterproductive effects (**Box 1**).

> **Box 1 Dutch housing policy: A counterproductive policy?**
>
> Dutch housing policy, although considered an exceptionally successful system in terms of achieving social housing objectives and providing high-quality housing for the vast majority of the population, shows a number of inconsistencies. The Dutch housing market can be characterised as heavily institutionalised, considering the range and depth of government interventions. Unfortunately, there has been poor coordination between different interventions, as a result of which Dutch housing policy has become rather inconsistent and ineffective. For example, the Dutch government provides strong support for the demand for housing (via mortgage interest relief for owner-occupiers and rent allowances for tenants) but, at the same time, enforces regulations and planning restrictions that hamper the supply of housing. Furthermore, the rent allowance is means-tested, whereas owner-occupiers from all income groups are eligible for fiscal support. This creates a gap between the rental sector and the homeownership sector and obstructs movement between the two.

Institutions as Values and Norms

Whereas laws and regulations are formulated by the government, values and norms are borne by groups or communities. Often, the two are complementary to each other. Given the complexity of modern societies, formal rules can never cover all possible circumstances. The rights and duties established in the formal regulation, therefore, often have to be strengthened by conventions, social norms, and internalised standards of conduct (Vrooman, 2009).

However, formal laws and regulations and informal values and norms may also be in conflict with each other. Changing values and norms within society may be an incentive for the government to change its formal rules. But the converse is also possible: informal values

> **Box 2 An example of values and norms in housing: The meaning of tenure**
>
> International comparative research has shown that the values, perceptions, and preferences associated with renting and home-owning clearly differ between countries. In other words, there are international differences in the meaning of tenure. In the English-speaking countries (the United States, the United Kingdom, and Ireland), there is a strong preference for home-owning above renting. In these societies, rent regulation and tenant security in the private rental sector are generally very limited, which makes private renting a rather insecure option for home seekers. More security may be found in the social rental sector, but this sector is only accessible to the lowest-income groups and often bears a negative stigma. Consequently, homeownership is the preferred tenure for the majority of the population.
>
> In countries with a well-developed rental sector and sufficient security of tenure in both rental segments, such as in Germany and Austria, the situation is quite different. Here, the rental sector offers a satisfactory alternative to homeownership for substantial segments of the population. Consequently, the preference for homeownership is considerably less pronounced (if such a preference exists at all).

and norms may adapt to changes in the formal institutions, possibly leading to a new equilibrium after a certain time (**Box 2**).

Institutional Change and Path Dependency

Institutions, irrespective of whether they are defined as laws and regulations, values or norms, or organisations, may change over time. The main triggers for changes in institutions are economic processes (for example, globalisation), social processes (for example, changes in the preferences of households or changes in the social stratification), demographic processes (for example, the ageing population), and scientific and technological innovations.

However, institutional change does not, generally speaking, easily come about. The transformations that have taken place in the Western welfare states are a good example of this. Although all Western welfare states have been subject to retrenchment since the late 1970s, this process has only taken place in a very gradual and incremental way, despite strong external pressures (economic crises, intensified globalisation, etc.). Next to electoral concerns of policy-makers, this is due to the fact that both recipients and providers of welfare services are organised in interest networks that are usually well placed to defend the welfare state. Their constituent organisations and individuals adapt to particular arrangements, making commitments that may render the costs of change far higher than the costs of continuity. Civil servants may further enforce this process. Officially, civil servants are loyalty bound to those with political responsibilities, but in practice they often form an 'officials elite' which is inclined to impede institutional change (Vrooman, 2009). In sum, we may therefore conclude that institutions are resilient and that, except for periods of deep social or economic crisis, they tend to change rather gradually and incrementally.

The above observations are related to the concept of 'path dependency'. This approach to understanding institutional change has arisen in contradiction to 'convergence' theories that have in the past asserted how different societies are following increasingly similar institutional and organisational patterns. Adherents of the path dependency approach object against the view that similar developments will lead to the same results everywhere. Instead, they believe that external developments are 'filtered' by the particular national institutional context, as a result of which they work out differently in different countries. The central idea of path dependency is that the existing institutional configurations in a particular country will exert a strong influence on future institutional developments. Countries may respond entirely differently to similar policy problems because the existing institutions make some institutional solutions appear more obvious than others (Kleinman, 1996).

Examples of Path Dependency within Housing

That path dependency and continuity in the institutional configurations also play an important role within housing has been convincingly illustrated in various international comparative research projects. In the early 1990s, Boelhouwer and van der Heijden (1992) compared the housing policies of seven European countries from 1970 to 1990 (The Netherlands, Belgium, West Germany, Denmark, England, France, and Sweden). They concluded that there were a number of similar factors affecting the functioning of the housing markets in these countries. They include both exogenous factors, like demographic and economic development, and policy objectives: promotion of owner-occupied housing, reduction of public expenditure on housing policy, and switch from supply to demand subsidies. However, despite these similarities, they observed that there was no strong convergence between the housing systems in the countries under review. The housing market structures, which are the product of a series of historical developments unique to each country, the institutions that have been established in the course of time, and the activities of government, which are influenced partly by tradition and ideology, are much too diverse for this to be a credible supposition. Thus, although external factors and policy objectives may be fairly similar across countries, they often lead to specific and often unique problems and institutional arrangements within each country.

This is also clearly shown in a recent comparative study by Bengtsson and Ruonavaara (2010), on the systems of housing provision in the Nordic countries (Denmark, Norway, Sweden, Finland, and Iceland). Though housing policy in all these five countries has been 'social', meaning that an important goal has been to provide decent housing to households of lesser means, the institutional arrangements chosen to achieve this goal differ fundamentally. In Denmark, housing policy has been directed towards social rental housing that is provided by public housing associations. Danish social rental housing tends to be organised in small units with a high degree of self-management for tenants. In Sweden, there is a relatively balanced distribution between the social rental sector (that is controlled by the municipalities), the cooperative sector, and the owner-occupied sector. In Norway, housing policy has been mainly based on individual and cooperative ownership, with only a very limited role for the social rental sector. This also applies to Iceland, though in this case including strong elements of individual self-build. In Finland, housing policy has not been directed at any particular form of tenure. State support, combined with means-tested allowances, has been given to both rented housing and owner-occupation.

The above differences are striking since the Nordic countries have many similarities with regard to cultural, economic, and welfare-state-related aspects. They are due to the fact that in the formative period of the Nordic housing provision systems, between 1900 and the Second World War, different solutions were chosen in order to deal with the specific housing problems in each of the countries concerned. When more comprehensive housing policy programmes were introduced after the Second World War, it was generally deemed efficient to use the existing institutions for their implementation (Bengtsson and Ruonavaara, 2010).

See also: Central Government Institutions; Cooperative Housing/Ownership; Government/Public Lending Institutions: Asia-Pacific; Housing Governance; Housing Market Institutions; Institutional Economics: New; Institutions for Housing Supply; Institutions that Represent Housing Professionals; Property Rights Approaches; Social Housing Institutions in Europe; Social Housing Landlords: Europe; Tenant Cooperatives, Shareholders' Housing Companies; Tenure as an Institution.

References

Bengtsson B and Ruonavaara H (2010) Introduction to the special issue: Path dependence in housing. *Housing, Theory and Society* 27(3): 193–203.

Boelhouwer P and van der Heijden H (1992) *Housing Systems in Europe: Part I. A Comparative Study of Housing Policy*, Housing and Urban Policy Studies 1. Delft, the Netherlands: Delft University Press.

Kleinman M (1996) *Housing, Welfare and the State: A Comparative Analysis of Britain, France and Germany*. Cheltenham, UK: Edward Elgar Publishing Limited.

Vrooman JC (2009) *Rules of Relief. Institutions of Social Security, and their Impact*. The Hague: The Netherlands Institute for Social Research (SCP).

Further Reading

Boelhouwer P and Hoekstra J (2009) Towards a better balance on the Dutch housing market? Analysis and policy propositions. *European Journal of Housing Policy* 9(4): 457–475.

Elsinga M and Hoekstra J (2005) Homeownership and housing satisfaction. *Journal of Housing and the Built Environment* 20(4): 401–424.

Elsinga M, Haffner M, and van der Heijden H (2008) Threats to the Dutch unitary rental market. *European Journal of Housing Policy* 8(1): 21–37.

Haffner M, Hoekstra J, Oxley M, and van der Heijden H (2008) *Bridging the Gap Between Social and Market Rented Housing in Six European Countries?* Housing and Urban Policy Studies 33. Amsterdam: IOS Press.

Hall P and Taylor RCR (1996) Political science and the three new institutionalisms. *Political Studies* 64: 936–957.

North DC (1990) *Institutions, Institutional Change and Economic Performance*. Cambridge, UK: Cambridge University Press.

Pierson P (1996) The new politics of the welfare state. *World Politics* 48(2): 143–179.

Williamson (2008) *The Mechanisms of Governance*. New York/Oxford, UK: Oxford University Press.

Housing Policy and Regeneration

RJ Kleinhans, Delft University of Technology, Delft, The Netherlands

© 2012 Elsevier Ltd. All rights reserved.

> **Glossary**
>
> **Empowerment** The process in which individuals gain control of and influence over their lives and become enabled to participate in various ways in society.
> **Housing career** The sequence of dwellings that a household or individual will occupy during their lifetime.
> **Neighbourhood reputation** The attributes and esteem which residents and various other actors attribute to a neighbourhood.
> **Selective migration** Occurs when highly specific groups move into and out of certain areas, that is, the socioeconomic characteristics of migrants to and from communities are different from the other residents of these areas.
> **Social cohesion** The social connections that help cement stable relationships between members of a social system (e.g., a family, organisation, or society as a whole).
> **Spillover effect** The effects of phenomena, events, or interventions in one area on (an)other area(s).
> **Regeneration** The process in which a variety of stakeholders employs a range of physical, social, and economic measures to improve the quality and future prospects of neighbourhoods or urban districts that face multiple problems.

Regeneration Policies

Urban regeneration policies have taken firm root in most Western European countries and the United States. Regeneration policies have grown in complexity, partly due to the multidimensional character of urban problems such as deteriorating housing quality, poverty, unemployment, social exclusion, segregation, low-quality public space, and so on. The content and implementation of regeneration policies differs between countries, reflecting heterogeneity in welfare systems and political context as well as variation in the physical, social, and economic structures of urban areas. Nevertheless, there are also similarities. Most regeneration policies have a strong housing policy component that can typically take two different forms. The first type is policies designed to attract and retain residents through various measures that improve the physical quality of buildings and their environment (see articles Housing and Neighbourhood Quality: Urban Regeneration; Housing and Neighbourhood Quality: Home Improvement Grants). The second type of regeneration policies is 'people focussed' and use incentives (such as housing vouchers) to motivate residents in deprived neighbourhoods to move to less deprived areas (see articles Mobility Programmes for Disadvantaged Populations: The Moving to Opportunity Programme; Policies to Address Spatial Mismatch). This second policy approach has a very different philosophy, as it aims to move residents away from deprived areas rather than tackling housing and other conditions in those areas.

Regeneration policies of the first type typically employ housing programmes to change the characteristics of the current housing stock, in ways that promote regeneration goals. The approach can extend beyond improvement of the housing stock to include the demolition, conversion, or sale of social (including public) rented housing, and the construction of new, owner-occupied, or private rented housing. These policies aim to create more variation in housing sizes, forms, quality, price, and tenure within targeted neighbourhoods. A defining feature of such measures is considerable turnover of residents since demolition, upgrading, and new construction inevitably involve displacement of existing residents, as well as the in-migration of new residents into target areas. Thus, urban regeneration programmes will generally change the composition of a neighbourhood's population, and change the behaviour of residents.

Integrating housing programmes into regeneration policies serves a broad range of policy goals. This article discusses the most common policies and identifies the regeneration benefits claimed by policy-makers in many countries. It also addresses issues of housing and neighbourhood quality, tenure diversity, residential mobility and housing careers, social interactions, social mix, reputation and stigma effects, problem dilution (i.e., a decreasing concentration of social problems in an area), spillover effects, and finally, resident empowerment.

Housing and Neighbourhood Quality

Usually, housing programmes in urban regeneration policies aim to substantially improve the general quality of the existing housing stock. 'Quality' has a broad meaning.

It includes the standard of construction, the level of maintenance, insulation, heating, comfort, size, and layout of dwellings. More recently, housing's ecological 'footprint' (i.e., carbon emissions, energy efficiency, and use of sustainable building materials) has become an increasingly important dimension of quality (see article Energy Consumption, Housing, and Urban Development Policy). Generally, regeneration is motivated by the observation that a neighbourhood's housing stock fails to comply with basic quality standards, no longer meets residential preferences, and attracts a highly segregated clientele.

There is considerable evidence of the positive impacts of housing programmes on both housing and neighbourhood quality. Improvement of the housing stock is usually also accompanied by regeneration of the surrounding physical infrastructure and public spaces, even if the original layout of the target area remains unchanged. Evaluation research consistently indicates increased resident satisfaction. The evidence on improved neighbourhood quality is somewhat less consistent, but still largely positive. For those residents who are involuntarily relocated (displaced) out of the target area, there can be costs that depend upon the standard of housing and location attributes that are affordable in their new area of residence. Residents are displaced if they cannot afford to live in the regenerated area, or no longer have access to suitable, affordable housing elsewhere. However, if forced relocation is accompanied by a housing voucher or other financial compensation, residents may move to neighbourhoods of higher quality.

Housing programmes in regeneration policies are not exclusively targeted at existing residential areas. For example, brownfield redevelopment can transform derelict industrial and commercial land sites into residential housing developments by eliminating urban blight as a possible source of neighbourhood decline (see article Brownfield Development and Housing Supply).

Tenure Diversity and Owner-Occupation

Regeneration policies can strongly alter the tenure structure of the housing stock, especially in neighbourhoods dominated by social or public rented housing. Through new construction, conversion of rental stock to owner-occupied housing and other strategies, more options for home purchasers become available. This is often in line with policy goals to attract middle- and higher-income households to provide more choice and housing career opportunities in regeneration areas and to increase social mix (see article Policies to Address Social Mix in Communities).

Increasing tenure diversity, especially the share of owner-occupied housing, can be viewed as part of a strategy to improve housing and neighbourhood quality. Much research shows that owner-occupiers are likely to have different attitudes and residential behaviour than renters, independent of socioeconomic or demographic characteristics, and are more likely to maintain and improve housing quality. There are three main reasons for this expected difference in behaviour. First of all, the sense of ownership and permanency makes them more likely than renters to put down roots, especially for households in child-rearing stages of housing careers. There is therefore a long-term financial commitment to their dwelling. Renters, on the other hand, depend on housing associations, councils, or other landlords for maintenance.

Second, the dwelling's level of maintenance is a strong determinant of its economic value. Inadequate maintenance and a deteriorating appearance will affect the value of the dwelling and the equity accumulated by the owner. This may also apply to blocks with shared ownership, in which resident associations are responsible for maintenance standards.

Third, much research shows that owner-occupiers are more prepared to organise themselves to lobby government officials about physical or social problems in their neighbourhood. This difference can be partly attributed to owner-occupiers' typically better education and higher income. They generally have more human and financial capital than renters, which enables them to deal more successfully with problems that require a proactive approach towards local authorities, estate managers, and other institutions. However, through successful lobbying for solutions to local problems, owners' efforts can be beneficial to everyone in a neighbourhood.

Residential Mobility and Housing Careers

Although the mix of problems that prompt urban regeneration may differ across urban areas, a common feature is that migration flows into and out of such neighbourhoods frequently perpetuate the problems. Middle- and higher-income households cannot access attractive housing career opportunities that match their aspirations, while low-income households cannot afford to move out of these neighbourhoods. This creates selective out- and in-migration of different income groups. Higher-income, better educated households tend to gravitate away from deprived areas, unless attractive housing alternatives become available within the same neighbourhood. Research confirms the tendency of residential mobility flows to reinforce patterns of segregation that are the result of financial constraints rather than preferences. There is an exception to this general migration pattern. Lower house prices in depressed working class neighbourhoods can attract an influx of more affluent residents that results in gentrification, a phenomenon more often associated with older neighbourhoods offering excellent access to urban amenities.

There are at least three ways that housing programmes can be helpful in addressing selective migration issues. First, tenure diversification strategies can be fruitful because some low-income households are just starting their labour and housing careers and can expect sharp rises in their disposable incomes. These households look for attractive housing career opportunities (i.e., not too expensive single-family dwellings, owner-occupation, homes with a garden, etc.) as their incomes rise, but regeneration areas often lack such opportunities. Research has demonstrated how tenure diversification strategies can retain newly emerging middle-income households through new construction of affordable owner-occupied homes, or sale of social or public rented dwellings. However, efforts to increase owner-occupation and retain middle- and higher-income households can be thwarted by discriminatory practices such as 'redlining', where financial institutions avoid lending in disadvantaged neighbourhoods (see article Policies to Address Redlining).

Second, urban regeneration may attract higher-income households from outside the area or city, especially when housing projects are favourably located near inner cities and cultural and recreational amenities. In practice, this strategy is difficult to successfully implement if regeneration areas continue to struggle with a bad reputation. However, a Dutch homesteading (*klushuizen*) project has proven to be effective. Local authorities or housing associations acquire blocks of dilapidated houses and sell them at very low prices to middle- or higher-income households, but under a contractual obligation to fundamentally renovate and upgrade the houses.

Third, the demolition of slum housing in neighbourhood regeneration areas is less disruptive if accompanied by new construction that can quickly accommodate displaced persons. An example is the construction of new, social rented apartment blocks designed for elderly people, and equipped with medical and social services. The new construction may not diversify tenure or lower rents and prices, but it will help progress the housing careers of forced movers.

The strategies mentioned above reflect the type of regeneration policies that improve the physical quality of the buildings and environment in regeneration areas. The second type of regeneration policies, mobility programmes, uses vouchers or other incentives to motivate residents to move to less deprived areas. In the United States, Moving to Opportunity programme, for example, there is evidence supporting the view that voucher users mobility allows them to benefit from strong improvements in neighbourhood quality. But voucher programmes appear to have little impact on moving families to less segregated communities, so selective migration remains a problematic issue in these cases.

Social Interactions and Social Mix

Many regeneration programmes adopt broadly defined goals of 'social cohesion', 'social mix', 'social capital', and 'social balance'. These are slippery concepts with an endless variety of definitions and meanings. The general premise is that more residential diversity in terms of income, education, social class, household type, age, and tenure can benefit neighbourhoods, especially those with concentrations of poor and deprived residents. For example, attracting middle-class residents could strengthen social networks of lower-income groups who, as a result, may obtain better information on job opportunities or other knowledge that may facilitate upward social mobility.

We use the term social interaction to capture the rationale behind policies motivated by goals of social mix, social capital, social cohesion, and social balance. Social interactions include a wide range of acts, such as saying hello in the street, borrowing from fellow residents, and to more intensive patterns such as visiting neighbours. Research has shown that these interactions may help to create a basic level of understanding and trust between neighbours.

A large body of research has also shown that housing diversification programmes do little to promote favourable social interaction. There is considerable evidence suggesting that interaction between owner-occupiers and renters in a neighbourhood or estate is infrequent, although the sale of social rented dwellings to current tenants can encourage interaction in a direct way. Scale is a very important factor. First, research findings indicate that neighbourhood contacts usually occur between neighbours who live close by. Second, the importance of building block and street level suggests that both intra-tenure and inter-tenure social interaction is subject to distance decay. As proximity between residents in different tenures increases, so does the occurrence of social networks between residents of different tenures. Tenure is not the only cause of limited cross-tenure interaction, but it may act as a clear marker of differences in socio-economic characteristics. Owners and renters may live peacefully together, but mixed neighbourhoods may engender tensions and conflicts if residents do not share values and lifestyles.

A range of nonphysical housing policies can be adopted to facilitate social interaction, as a part of a broader regeneration policy. First, housing associations may use deliberate housing allocation strategies to 'select' or tempt households to move to certain residential areas, based on the premise of a common life style or other shared characteristics that may stimulate social interaction. Another strategy is intensive social management, which may encourage residents of estates or blocks to formulate certain 'living rules' (beyond contractual obligations or bans) that every resident has to abide by. For example, residents may jointly agree that loud music is 'forbidden' after 10 o'clock in the evening. Finally, local authorities and landlords may adopt social programmes that involve residents meeting each other, such as street parties, street play events for children, street spring-cleanings, and so on. The effectiveness of such efforts is debatable, because local contexts differ and there are measurement problems, but they are potentially rewarding strategies.

Reputation and Stigma

Neighbourhood reputation is the meaning and esteem which residents and various other actors attribute to a neighbourhood or estate. Reputation is a relational concept par excellence: neighbourhoods and places acquire and develop reputations relative to each other, based on perceptions of residents (internal reputation) and 'outsiders' (external reputation). Reputations partly arise within neighbourhoods, but are generally understood to be predominantly shaped by the way neighbourhood features, events, or images are interpreted by people and institutions that live elsewhere.

Research has indicated that three general features are strong predictors of an area's reputation: physical appearance, population composition (especially the share of ethnic minorities), and the socioeconomic status of the area. These features can be strongly affected by housing programmes, so it is not surprising that improvement of an area's reputation is often a regeneration goal. However, studies have shown that lifting a neighbourhood or estate's reputation is a notoriously difficult task. There are four main reasons. First, reputations are intricately connected to the history and development of a place or area. Current reputations may be strongly affected by past events, which, especially if negatively perceived (e.g., the riots in the Parisian banlieues in 2005), continue to stick to a place until it recedes in the memories of outsiders. Second, reputation is connected to an area's surroundings. If a successfully regenerated neighbourhood is located within a wider urban area that has a bad reputation, it may be seen as 'an island of improvement in a sea of decay'. Third, reputations change slowly. The current state of affairs in regeneration areas is often far ahead of their current reputation. The main reason is that changes, even major and highly visible ones, take time to 'sink in' and then alter the perception of outsiders. Finally, small and piecemeal renewal and changes, while legitimate on their own, may not be very noticeable from the outside.

To date, there is little conclusive evidence identifying housing policies that may be successful in addressing reputation effects. Authors such as Dean and Hastings (see Further Reading) suggest several approaches. First, substantial demolition and reconstruction programmes are more likely to positively affect area features that are correlated with reputation: physical appearance, population composition, and socioeconomic status. Real change must be witnessed before it convinces outsiders; if not, efforts at image management are inevitably unconvincing. Yet, the necessary scale and scope of housing programmes targeting reputation are so substantial that they are usually not funded or only feasible over a long period of time. Second, market and communication strategies should reward outsiders for developing their understanding of the changes in regeneration areas, preferably by visiting and spending sufficient time there. Potential rewards from such knowledge are higher market values of unpopular properties, and the emergence of new markets for estate agents. Third, facilities, services, and events can be developed in regeneration areas, which attract visitors, such as supermarkets, cinema complexes, or other leisure-related facilities. The visitors may then recognise the positive changes in the area. Finally, media coverage is highly influential. Negative reports in the newspapers, on radio, television, and the Internet adversely affect an area's image, regardless of the success of improvement programmes in regeneration areas. Yet, media coverage can be used positively by offering stories or positive angles on regeneration effects to journalists, who would otherwise not get such information. Also, communication with the media should be managed very carefully, meeting journalists' need for plain language, human interest, and visual impact. In the same vein, clever advertisement campaigns, websites, billboards, and television commercials may reach an audience that is not easily impressed by newspaper stories.

Dilution and Spillover Effects

Throughout European and American policy discourses, there is a strong consensus around the idea that physical measures alone cannot solve social problems. Many residents in regeneration areas face persistent problems due to educational and language deficiencies, school absenteeism, unemployment, poverty, substance abuse, debts, illnesses, and other problems. These problems can be aggravated when disadvantaged residents are involuntarily concentrated in certain areas. While housing programmes may be inadequate in solving social deprivation or underlying processes of disadvantage and exclusion, the concentration of problems can be successfully addressed by housing programmes.

Demolition and new construction are important strategies that relocate residents that can include notorious 'trouble-makers' as well as households with multiple social problems. Both forms of problem dilution may help regeneration of a neighbourhood. Relocating 'problematic' residents and introducing owner-occupation is likely to achieve significant changes to several socioeconomic and social distress indicators by breaking up concentrations of unemployed people and deprived households, while attracting economically active households to previously depressed areas. This can significantly improve the liveability of neighbourhoods, not just in a statistical sense, but also the perception of residents remaining in those areas. Furthermore, dilution strategies have an institutional advantage. If problems associated with concentrations of disadvantaged households are addressed, dilution may relieve the work load of care and welfare organisations whose resources are frequently overstretched. For all the reasons mentioned above, problem dilution is a common motive justifying physical renewal projects, though not commonly explicitly stated or written down in these terms.

Dilution strategies can also cause undesirable side effects, that is, spillover effects. In the context of urban neighbourhood regeneration, spillover effects are the impacts of phenomena, events, or interventions in one area on (an)other area(s), typically in the same city. Demolishing rented social housing and relocating residents may inadvertently move the manifestation of social problems to other areas. Policy discourse strongly warns against such spillover effects. However, empirical research underpinning causal connections between regeneration and problem dispersion to other areas is still scarce.

Empowerment through Sale

Most regeneration policies have a clear area focus. Nevertheless, they also aim to improve the prospects for individual people. Among the more elusive effects of housing programmes in regeneration policies, is the concept of empowerment.

Psychologists define empowerment as a process in which individuals gain control of and influence over their lives and become democratically enabled to participate in society. This can raise your chances of climbing the social ladder and the way you utilise opportunities. In the context of housing, empowerment has been associated primarily with the sale of social or public housing to renters (see article Privatisation of Social Housing). A famous example is the Right to Buy scheme in the United Kingdom, executed during the 1980s. The scheme gave council tenants the right to buy their rented homes at a discount price which reflected the length of residency. The Right to Buy is a prominent and early example of tenure diversification, but it has also produced negative side effects, especially residualisation of the remaining public housing stock.

Evidence on the empowering effects of sale is mixed. But how does sale of rented housing to (sitting) tenants actually affect their empowerment? First, owner-occupation allows former tenants to accumulate equity. This benefit is now threatened in some countries following the credit crunch and global financial crisis that hit the world economy in the second half of 2008. Historically, owner-occupation has proven to have clear capital advantages in the long run. Accumulating equity offers owner-occupiers financial security as it is a store of value that can be accessed if needed.

Second, owner-occupied housing can be altered via repair and improved to the owners' taste, whereas tenants may experience restrictions over what they can alter. This increased control is thought to contribute to a more general sense of control over important life events. It provides a sense of security, as occupiers cannot be evicted, and freedom to use and modify your home in whatever way you like. The equity stake that owner-occupiers hold could also explain why they are more inclined to become involved in neighbourhood affairs.

Third, there is empowerment through perceived improvements in status. According to psychological theories, individuals assess their level of self-esteem by reflected appraisals, social comparison, and self-attribution. The principle of social comparison suggests that owning a home, particularly for low-income households, may lead them to consider themselves more successful than those who live in rental housing.

Finally, there is a process dimension of sale, apart from the issue of control in the sense of freedom and say with regard to your home. Not only the changes in the housing situation itself may be empowering, but these changes may also offer their residents opportunities to learn new skills and further self-development. Buying a home is in itself a complicated and informative experience which may open new perspectives in life.

This article has summarised the potential benefits of housing programmes within the context of urban regeneration policies. The positive impacts include improved housing and neighbourhood quality, better housing choices, more social interaction, and favourable effects on neighbourhood reputation, individual empowerment, and the incidence of several social problems. In general, the physical and residential mobility effects of housing programmes are more apparent and tangible, whereas the size and range of social effects is more context-dependent and difficult to identify.

See also: Brownfield Development and Housing Supply; Energy Consumption, Housing, and Urban Development Policy; Housing and Neighbourhood Quality: Home Improvement Grants; Housing and Neighbourhood Quality: Urban Regeneration; Mobility Programmes for Disadvantaged Populations: The Moving to Opportunity Programme; Policies to Address Redlining; Policies to Address Social Mix in Communities; Policies to Address Spatial Mismatch; Privatisation of Social Housing.

Further Reading

Allen C, Camina M, Casey R, Coward S, and Wood M (2005) *Mixed Tenure Twenty Years On – Nothing Out of the Ordinary*. Coventry/York, UK: The Chartered Institute of Housing/Joseph Rowntree Foundation.

Bolt G, van Kempen R, and van Ham M (2008) Minority ethnic groups in the Dutch housing market: Spatial segregation, relocation dynamics and housing policy. *Urban Studies* 45: 1359–1384.

Curley A (2007) Dispersing the poor: New directions in public housing policy. In: Arrighi B and Maume D (eds.) *Child Poverty in America Today, Vol. 4: Children and the State*, pp. 71–92. Westport, CT: Praeger Publishers.

Dean J and Hastings A (2000) *Challenging Images: Housing Estates, Stigma and Regeneration*. Bristol, UK: Policy Press.

Dietz R and Haurin D (2003) The social and private micro-level consequences of homeownership. *Journal of Urban Economics* 54: 401–450.

Galster G (2001) On the nature of neighbourhood. *Urban Studies* 38: 2111–2124.

Jones C and Murie A (2006) *The Right to Buy. Analysis and Evaluation of a Housing Policy*. Oxford, UK: Blackwell Publishing.

Jupp B (1999) *Living Together. Community Life on Mixed Tenure Estates*. London: Demos.

Kearns A, Hiscock R, Ellaway A, and Macintyre S (2000) Beyond four walls: The psycho-social benefits of home: evidence from west central Scotland. *Housing Studies* 15: 387–410.

Kleinhans R (2004) Social implications of housing diversification in urban renewal: A review of recent literature. *Journal of Housing and the Built Environment* 19: 367–390.

McCarthy G, van Zandt S, and Rohe W (2001) *The economic benefits and costs of homeownership: A critical assessment of the research*. America: Research Institute for Housing. Working Paper No. 01–02.

Rohe W and Basolo V (1997) Long-term effects of home ownership on the self-perceptions and social interaction of low-income persons. *Environment and Behaviour* 29: 793–819.

Somerville P (1998) Empowerment through residence. *Housing Studies* 13: 233–257.

South S and Crowder K (1998) Leaving the 'hood': Residential mobility between Black, White and integrated neighborhoods. *American Sociological Review* 63: 17–26.

Wacquant L (1993) Urban outcasts: Stigma and division in the black American ghetto and the French periphery. *International Journal of Urban and Regional Research* 17: 366–383.

Housing Policy Trends

J Doling, University of Birmingham, Birmingham, UK

© 2012 Elsevier Ltd. All rights reserved.

Introduction

The aim of this article is to present the development of housing policy, principally but not exclusively, in the economically more advanced countries of the world. These make up three broad groupings: the New World, English-speaking Western countries of North America and Australasia; the Old World, particularly Western Europe and the more advanced of the Eastern European countries; and East Asia including Japan, Korea, Taiwan, Singapore, Hong Kong, and Malaysia. Given the large numbers of countries, their wide geographical coverage and in the case of many the long historical period during which they have been industrialised, the presentation of developments will necessarily be fairly general. Indeed, for the earliest years, perhaps 150 or more years ago, when rapid industrialisation and urbanisation provided an impetus to state housing policies, the coverage will be painted with a very broad brush, glossing over the differences and exceptions to highlight general tendencies. Rather, there is detail about trends only with respect to recent decades.

Both past developments and possible future directions of housing policy are discussed within a framework that focuses on tendencies towards convergence and tendencies towards divergence. In other words, the aim is to identify not only the main policy developments and trends, but also the extent to which they can be interpreted as a narrowing of the differences between countries – are they becoming more similar – or a widening of the differences – are they becoming less similar. Such an emphasis requires that policy developments are considered against a number of theoretical perspectives that provide understandings of the origins of and influences on housing policy: why do governments have housing policies, what determines the content and aim of housing policies, and to what extent are these similar across countries – thus leading to convergence – or different – thus leading to divergence.

For the purposes of achieving these aims, the article, following this introductory section, is arranged in four sections. The first section provides a broad understanding of the meaning of convergence and divergence in policy systems with some indications of their theoretical underpinnings and of how they might be recognised empirically.

The second section presents the broad development of housing policies in the now advanced economies during the period of their initial moves towards industrialisation up to the present era, or at least up to the start of the current economic difficulties. For each of them, the timing of their economic take-off differed, as did the speed and nature of the economic, social, and political changes. But all developed state housing policies. Moreover, not only did they develop housing policies but also, at a high level of generalisation, there are at least some indications that they have tended to follow a similar trajectory characterised by an initial period of increasing state intervention followed by a second period of some withdrawal of the state with more reliance on market mechanisms. So, the (very) broad picture is: stage 1, growing reliance on the state: stage 2, growing reliance on the market. An important question, then, concerns why, as a response to the challenges of industrialisation and subsequent economic development, was there this degree of similarity, or convergence, in the field of housing?

The third, and somewhat more detailed, section focuses on housing developments over the last three or four decades. Here there have also been some across country similarities, for example, in the continuation of an active state role in housing combined with important moves towards privatisation and deregulation of housing finance markets. While these trends can be characterised in many countries by a common and increasing importance placed on homeownership, there have also been some marked differences. In other words, there is evidence of both convergence and divergence, so that part of the aim of this section is to provide an understanding of the contrary processes.

The fourth, final, and brief section provides some speculation about future developments and the likelihood of convergence or divergence in the context of two macro processes: the changes in demographic structures resulting from the ageing of populations; and the restructuring of financial markets and other changes taking place as a direct result of the global, economic hiatus occurring from 2008.

Understanding Convergence and Divergence

The terms 'convergence' and 'divergence' have long been part of the vocabulary of those engaged in the comparative study of housing policy, indeed of policies across a broad range of areas. They have come to be frequently adopted as, to use Michael Oxley's phrase, "a sort of theoretical string" that helps to tie the comparative story together, the general term that encapsulates and summarises the developments in the myriad of housing policies under review.

Meaning and Empirical Indicators

While the literal and everyday meanings of the two terms are perhaps simple and clear, the scientific meanings are arguably less so. One view, espoused by Kemeny and Lowe (1998), is that convergence refers to analysis in which it is taken, more or less for granted, that housing systems everywhere have been moulded by the same influences. Further, they recognise that underlying such analysis may be explanations of why those influences have led to similar outcomes, and thereby acknowledge that convergence refers to a process, or processes, operating over time such that housing policies in different countries are somehow moving towards a common point or model.

Empirically and theoretically this dynamic might be recognised through a narrowing of differences that might take the form of either common policy developments, such as the reduction of mortgage interest relief on housing loans or the deregulation of financial sectors, or narrowing of statistical differences, such as in the proportion of national housing stocks accounted for by social housing. The latter has been the basis of a number of studies in which the statistical variance of a number of indicators of housing systems over successive decades has been computed in order to test whether convergence had taken place.

But, convergence might be recognised in a slightly different way: each country being at a different point or stage on a common trajectory. Thus, if housing policy was a direct reflection or consequence of the stage of economic development, then countries, depending on their economic position, might be spaced widely apart but heading in the same direction, and in that sense converging. However, it is also possible, if the relationship between economic development and housing policy was nonlinear (say little investment in social housing at low and high levels of economic development, but considerable investment at medium levels of economic development), that over some periods national housing policies would statistically get further apart. In such circumstances, convergence might be happening but it might not be confirmed empirically as a reduction in statistical differences.

Divergence, in contrast, refers to differences in housing policy. This can have two distinct meanings. The one is that all countries are somehow unique and particular, and that with different social and economic circumstances, their policy responses would adapt to those different circumstances. Kemeny and Lowe (1998) argue that divergence might also be seen as classes or types of housing policy. This could be interpreted as a notion that while not all housing systems are essentially the same and proceeding in the same direction, it is possible to identify groupings of countries in which housing systems were different from those in other groupings and proceeding differently to those in other groupings, but the same as, and proceeding in the same direction as, countries in the same group.

On this basis, then, it is possible to recognise three categories of Oxley's string that ties comparative research together: particularism in which everywhere is considered unique and different; convergence in which everywhere is the same; and divergence in which there are groupings that are different from other groupings, but, within any one grouping, everywhere is the same.

Theoretical Foundations

It is possible, in turn, to attach different theoretical perspectives to each of the three categories. Kemeny and Lowe (1989) argue that particularistic approaches have tended simply to juxtapose information about different countries generally without positing explanatory frameworks that help an understanding of why there are similarities and differences. Given the tendency in such studies to present the fine detail of housing policies and outcomes – the precise dates, the precise actors, the precise percentages – their particularity is hard to resist. In their view, however, an often implicit framework in such studies is based on the notion that national governments act independently from one another, responding to different sets of circumstances effectively to determine the particular shape and direction of national housing systems.

The convergence approach, in contrast, is generally based on one or more theoretical perspectives that emphasise a deterministic response to a common process, what might be called a universal law. These high-level theories stress the significance of the logic of capitalism or the logic of industrialism, or refer to the irresistible consequences of demographic change or globalisation to provide an overarching template onto which may be mapped the development of national housing systems. It might also be said that these theories emphasise the importance of structure rather than agency.

Divergence approaches, for their part, are usually based on theories that reject the notion of the inability of nations to resist the impact of structural or universal forces, emphasising rather their capacity to impose and negotiate other outcomes. Here, politics, ideology, geography, and culture may all play a part in guiding and achieving choice. These middle-range theories inform the now large body of research that has sought to establish typologies of policy models or regimes and that received considerable encouragement with the extensive literature on more general social welfare regimes. One outcome of this research has been the frequency of attempts, on the basis of their housing systems, to locate each of the advanced economies, with some other advanced economies, in one of a set of groupings.

Broad Trends in Housing Policy: From Industrialisation to the Credit Crisis

This convergence–divergence background assists consideration of the long-run policy trends. Here, one way of approaching an understanding of the trends in housing policy is through the utilisation of the notion of the 'European Paradigm'. The value of this lies not in the fact of its Europeanness, as if European countries are somehow a model for everywhere else or even that the paradigm signifies a high degree of convergence, but simply that what we would now recognise as housing policy first developed in Europe and that this was a product of it being the birthplace of the industrial revolution and its associated urbanisation.

The Broad Trajectory of Housing Policy

The European paradigm, therefore, starts with the transition from feudal or preindustrial societies to industrial ones. In the late eighteenth and early nineteenth centuries, in a number of Western and central European countries, manufacturing enterprises were set up, mainly in urban areas that expanded with the influx of labour from rural areas. This rapid expansion of the new industrial towns and cities and the growth of a new, urban labour force was also part of the development of socio–economic–political systems based on free markets. But this also coincided with the sanitary reform movement which itself was born out of the epidemic diseases, principally cholera and typhoid, that flourished in the types of housing development that characterised the period. The free markets in land and urban development resulted, for the great mass of the new urban working classes in Europe, in housing that was built at high densities to low standards of construction and amenities frequently without adequate sanitary facilities or supplies of fresh water, and crowded onto sites that were adjacent to noisy and polluting factories.

It was against this background that European governments, particularly from the last quarter of the nineteenth century began to place constraints on the operation of the urban housing market. While the details differed, the general approach was similar: governments introduced legislation to control overcrowding at least in the sense, if not in the number of people that then lived in each dwelling, of a maximum density of development, that is, the number of dwellings per unit of area, as well as such matters as construction standards and public health provisions including sanitation facilities. In essence, these were constraints, or regulations, imposed on the supply side of the market, and intended to bring about a minimum quality or standard of the housing stock and an associated raising of the quality of housing consumed.

Moving into the early parts of the twentieth century, particularly coinciding with the time of the First World War (1914–18), there were further, and also widely common, interventions. The first involved controls over landlord–tenant relationships. Legislation in France in 1914, Britain in 1915, Denmark in 1916, and Germany and the Netherlands in 1917 took two main forms: the capping of rents so that these were lower than those that would be set by the usual market mechanism; and security of tenure. Together, these had the immediate effect of protecting tenants against high housing costs that might exceed their reasonable ability to pay out of the prevailing level of wages enjoyed by working families, alongside protection against eviction.

The second intervention also came out of a recognition that even a market subject to some regulations about minimum standards resulted in dysfunctional outcomes. European governments began to accept that if housing for the urban worker was to be of a politically and socially acceptable level, it would be necessary for even greater intervention, in the form of what has come to be known as social housing, supported by government subsidies to supply, often in the form of finance provided at an interest rate below the prevailing market rate, and made available to public bodies as well as to housing cooperatives and associations of the not-for-profit sector.

Again, as a general pattern in the European countries, support for the principle and practice of social housing expanded in the conditions prevailing in the aftermath of the First World War when generally there was a combination of housing shortage resulting from a lack of investment during and before the war years and the influx of the returning soldiers. But, such support expanded much further after the Second World War (1939–45), when the shortage of housing was even greater because added to the underinvestment and population movements that had characterised the First World War, was a third factor, the very high levels of destruction of housing stock as a direct consequence of the war effort. It was in these early, postwar years that the support for social housing was particularly large.

Once, after some decades, the housing shortages had largely been overcome; however, European government attention typically turned from questions of quantity to those of quality. This has translated into two, broad policy approaches. The first was the demolition of old dwellings, frequently built to low standards and in poor physical condition, along with the provision of new housing built to higher amenity and construction standards. In Western Europe, this occurred particularly in the 1960s and early 1970s. The second policy approach developed even more widely in the post-1970 period and took the form of the promotion of homeownership, a form of housing tenure that has been widely perceived as offering, in comparison to the position of tenants – whether of private or social landlords – distinctive financial and ontological advantages to households.

According to the European paradigm, therefore, there has been a typical, historical trajectory of state intervention in housing. This has been characterised as a progression through a number of distinct phases or stages. The first involved government efforts to ensure that the rapidly expanding number of urban workers had somewhere to live, followed by a second stage in which there were attempts to provide more than the minimum level of space, with the third stage developed when the shortages had been largely overcome and governments turned to a concern with quality, and fourthly, once quality had been widely achieved governments reverting once again to market-based housing solutions, frequently homeownership solutions.

Looking at this trajectory as a continuous progression, rather than as discrete stages, it can be described as having an inverted U shape. At first, countries have very low levels of intervention, in terms of regulation and financing, their governments leaving housing largely to the market. Gradually, over time, there are more and more interventions as governments place more restrictions on the operation of the market and then begin to intervene heavily through subsidies and even direct provision in the form of social housing. Eventually, some point is reached where the basic quantity and quality needs of the bulk of the population are met, and governments begin to draw back from intervention, again relying heavily on market solutions, particularly those supporting homeownership.

Explaining the Common Trajectory

Leaving aside the issue of how representative this paradigm is, even of European countries – that issue will be taken up later in the article – the question considered here is how can this apparent convergence be explained? Why is it that advanced economies consistently have introduced housing policies and why has housing policy consistently proceeded in the same general direction?

One view is that policies addressing housing issues, like policies addressing more general welfare concerns, are an integral part of the process of modernisation, which in turn is indicated by the transition from feudal to industrial societies. The point here is that countries have housing policies simply because it is part of the path of modernisation.

Another view, providing a more explicit explanation, is that interventions in housing, again like interventions in general welfare, are driven by the logic of industrialism. The argument here is that as countries undergo a process of industrialisation and as they then develop to more and more economically advanced levels, with higher and higher gross domestic products (GDPs), they face similar problems and opportunities. Thus, at an early stage of industrialisation, as workers are drawn into towns and cities where manufacturing plant is located, countries face new, but common, housing problems: overcrowding and unhealthy living environments. As industrialisation advances further, in order to compete with other manufacturers and other countries, it has, universally, become increasingly important that workers are productive and this in part demands that they are fit and healthy, so requiring – among other things – decent homes that keep them fit and healthy. Logic of industrialism explanations therefore envisage that at each step along the path of economic development, sets of problems and opportunities arise that are common to all countries and some of these require housing policy solutions.

One version of this – though with an emphasis on resource allocation rather than directly on policy – was developed some years ago in a study by Burns and Grebler (1977) in which they used data for the period 1963–70 covering a total of 39 countries which ranged from those at low levels of economic development – Kenya, Bolivia, and the Philippines – to those at the highest – in Western Europe as well as Japan and the United States. Fitting a regression model, they established an inverted U-shape relationship such that countries at low levels of GDP per capita typically had low total expenditure on housing, while countries at medium levels had high total expenditure on housing and those at the very highest levels, again, had only low levels of expenditure. This version thus fits broadly with the observation underlying the European paradigm and McGuire's stages. In addition, it indicates that the European paradigm may hold more widely, not only describing the European experience but also locating it in a more general process of economic development. In other words, suggesting a global paradigm.

Another version of convergence, which might more accurately be labelled a logic of capitalism explanation, is provided by Harloe (1995). Among other things, this suggests that the European paradigm is really European and not global, at least in so far as the development of mass social housing is concerned, since this has been largely specific to Western European countries. The basis of Harloe's view is that capitalism requires states to organise themselves around the pursuit of surplus value and, among other things, this means the extension of private ownership and commodification, such that generally wherever there was an opportunity to extract surplus value private markets would be established.

On this view, state welfare systems – including some housing policies – provided outside the market would be set up only as a compromise, forced on capitalism by the particular circumstances arising at historical points in time. From this, Harloe argues that social housing was initiated in many European countries prior to the First World War only as it became apparent that pure, commodified forms of housing were not capable of meeting the needs of poor people, nor of ensuring their fitness and healthiness as workers. But, it was small-scale or residual social housing with only a minimal impact on the principle of private market solutions. From this, he further argues that the shift from residual social housing to mass social housing, which occurred after each of the two world wars, was the consequence of extraordinary and temporary conditions. These were periods of system-wide crisis in which mass social housing was seen as part of the solution. In the first period, the aftermath of the First World War, the common Western-European-wide problem was to reestablish the status quo in the maintenance of the system of liberal capitalism. In the second period, from 1945 until the start of the 1970s, the challenge was the reconstruction and restructuring of national economies. In both periods, to different degrees in different countries, mass social housing was seen as part of the solution, but once the crises, the extraordinary conditions, were resolved, social housing returned to its normal, residual role.

One of the implications of this position is, therefore, that periods of mass social housing would occur only in countries which experienced system-wide crises to which it would be seen as part of the solution. So, countries like the United States, Australia, and New Zealand which did not face similar circumstances after the two world wars, or some of the countries of East Asia, for example, Korea and Taiwan, that have achieved rapid economic growth, industrialisation, and urbanisation only in the last few decades, have not developed large social housing sectors. They may – and indeed have – developed policies that regulate aspects of private housing markets and provide subsidies, so have some features of the European paradigm, but they have not adopted all the features.

Increasing the Role of Homeownership: Convergence and Divergence

Having set out the general pattern of housing policy development over the entire period from the beginnings of industrialisation to the present day, the attention paid in this section is focused on the last few decades, roughly from the mid-1970s until the start of the current credit crunch. During this period, the single most consistent development over most economically advanced countries has been the growth of homeownership. Whereas the recognition of this consistency provides a vehicle for examining the convergence processes of globalisation, the intention is also to stress differences around the common pattern, so enabling the examination of divergence processes.

Policy Trends: The General Pattern

The general pattern of housing policy developments over recent decades, then, has involved some retrenchment of state intervention with a reversion to the market and particularly homeownership (**Table 1**).

In European countries, and indeed elsewhere, a raft of policies have been involved. Some have been directed specifically at making homeownership more attractive to households, in the case of many countries explicitly for those with low incomes. These interventions, many of which have also been adopted in countries outside Europe, include tax breaks on housing-related investments, such as relief from tax on imputed rental value of owner-occupied housing and reductions on loan interest.

The policy support for homeownership has been accompanied by a general move towards the deregulation of financial markets that have resulted in increased lending to the housing sector. In some countries, for example, Australia and the US, deregulation has a history of several decades. In Western European countries, mortgage loans as a proportion of GDP have expanded considerably even over the last decade. More recently, the same general trend has been apparent in the European transition countries, where following the collapse of the Soviet Union market-based housing mortgage systems have been developed: The result in most economically advanced countries has been a large increase in the amount of residential mortgage debt as a proportion of national GDP (**Table 2**).

Other policies have been aimed at reducing the supply of, and demand for, nonmarket forms of housing often involving the privatisation of social housing stock. In fact, even if the numbers involved are not always large, most EU member states now allow the sale of social housing. The selling off of social housing has even extended to non-European countries, such as the United States, where there was only a small stock anyway. In the East European countries that had come under the control of the Soviet Union, the privatisation of former state housing has been particularly large, a result not only of the distinct change in their political systems, often with the enthusiastic embrace of private markets, but also the decision to sell them at relatively low prices. The outcome has been that social housing has largely disappeared from most of the transition countries.

Table 1 The postwar growth of homeownership: percent share of total stock by (approximate) year

Country	1960 (%)	1970 (%)	1980 (%)	1990 (%)	2002 (%)
Australia	–	–	71	72	70
Canada	–	60	62	63	65
United States	–	64	66	64	68
Austria	38	41	48	55	56
Belgium	50	55	59	67	71
Czech Republic	–	–	–	–	47
Denmark	43	49	52	51	51
France	41	45	51	54	55
Finland	57	59	61	67	58
Germany	–	–	–	38	42
Greece	–	–	70	77	83
Hungary	–	–	–	–	92
Ireland	–	71	76	81	77
Italy	45	50	59	67	80
Lithuania	–	–	–	–	84
Netherlands	29	35	42	44	53
Norway	–	53	59	59	77
Portugal	–	–	57	58	64
Slovenia	–	–	–	68	82
Spain	–	64	73	76	85
Sweden	36	35	41	42	42
United Kingdom	42	49	56	68	69
Hong Kong	–	–	–	42	56
Japan	–	–	60	61	62
Singapore	–	–	59	88	93
Taiwan	–	–	74	81	85

Sources: Catte P, Girouard N, Price R, and Andre C (2004) *Housing Markets, Wealth and the Business Cycle*, Economics Department Working Paper No. 194, OECD: Paris; Scanlon K and Whitehead C (2004) *International Trends in Housing Tenure and Mortgage Finance*. London: Council of Mortgage Lenders; National Board of Housing, Building and Planning (2004) *Housing Statistics in the EU 2004*. Karlskrona, Sweden: Boverket; UNECE (2006) *Guidelines on Social Housing: Principles and Examples*. United Nations, New York and Geneva; Lu H-c and Chen M (2006) Cultural norms and tenure choice? Investigating the high homeownership rate in Taiwan. www.fin.ntu.tw/-conference/conference 2006/powerpoint/academic7/7-1.ppt (accessed 25 July 2011).

The overall effect of these and other pro-owning policies, in Europe and elsewhere, has been continuous increase in the size of homeownership sectors. **Table 1** shows this to be the case in almost all the countries included. Notwithstanding some gaps in the data, in only a few countries, for example, Australia, Finland, and Ireland, are there exceptions to this general pattern, and even then the decreases have been small, just a few percentage points. Moreover, in some countries, the increases have been particularly large, for example, in Italy from 45% in 1960 to 80% in 2002 and in Singapore from 59% in 1980 to 93% in 2002.

Globalisation and Neoliberalism

How can this convergence towards homeownership be accounted for? One view, widely held, is that such moves towards pro-ownership policy regimes, particularly as they characterise the older EU member states, are part of a general restructuring of welfare systems brought about by the imperatives of globalisation. Specifically, the desire of governments to want to hold on to jobs, leads them to adopt business-friendly policies characterised by low taxation, low social overheads regimes as well as flexible labour markets in which workers have fewer rights vis-à-vis their employers. This 'strong' version of globalisation is thus one in which, in comparison to the past, nation-states have less autonomy over social programmes.

In this context, the pressure to reduce expenditure on social housing and to encourage homeownership becomes compelling. Insofar as social housing has mainly met the needs of lower (including the unemployed) income groups, providing them with an amount and quality of housing that exceeds the ability to pay from their own resources, there may be a perception of a heavy call on taxation to meet either production and/or consumption subsidies. Moreover, the more unemployment rises – with most economically advanced states experiencing rising unemployment in some years in recent decades – the more the income of the poorest groups in society drops and the greater the subsidies and the redistribution may

Table 2 Residential mortgage debt as percent GDP

	1992 (%)	2002 (%)	2006 (%)
Australia	24.2	50.8	-
Canada	42.7	43.1	-
New Zealand	32.6	56.2	-
United States	45.3	58.0	-
Belgium	19.9	27.9	36.3
Czech Republic	-	1.9	7.1
Denmark	63.9	74.3	100.8
Estonia	-	3.7 (1998)	32.7
Finland	37.2	31.8	43.8
France	21.0	22.8	32.2
Germany	38.7	54.0	51.3
Greece	4.0	13.9	29.3
Hungary	-	2.1 (2001)	11.4
Ireland	20.5	36.5	70.1
Italy	6.3	11.4	18.7
Latvia	-	6.7 (1999)	28.9
Lithuania	-	0.6 (1997)	12.6
Netherlands	40.0	78.8	98.4
Poland	-	1.5 (1997)	8.3
Slovenia	-	0.3 (1998)	6.6
Slovakia	-	3.9	9.6
Spain	11.9	32.3	58.6
Sweden	37.5	40.4	56.7
United Kingdom	55.5	64.3	83.2
Japan	25.3	36.8	-

Source: European Mortgage Federation (2007) *Hypostat*. Brussels: EMF.; Catte P, Girouard N, Price R, and Andre C (2004) *Housing Markets, Wealth and the Business Cycle*, Economics Department Working Paper No. 194, OECD: Paris.

appear to be. Seeing themselves compelled by the challenge of globalisation to make welfare and tax savings, one target for savings has been social housing. So, one view of national housing strategies promoting homeownership is that they reflect a wider context in which processes of globalisation are forcing policy-makers to pursue policies that involve cutting taxation and social spending.

But the view that globalisation is an irresistible force is contestable, both theoretically and empirically. For example, some forms of investment have been attracted to regimes in which there is high taxation, high social spending as well as strong labour rights. Likewise, in terms of housing outcomes, the impact of globalisation can be seen to have been quite different in different regions, for example, between Western and Eastern advanced economies, while, with respect to social housing, the reality is that some countries have maintained high production levels.

This does not mean that globalisation is not associated with convergence tendencies, nor that governments are unconstrained by international competitiveness, but rather that any convergence is indeterminate. On this view – the 'weak' model of globalisation – governments are not without choices; they do not have to rush headlong down the retrenchment path. The lesson for the politics of tenure is that the continuation and indeed strengthening of pro-owning policies, whether or not tied to antisocial housing policies, may not be inevitable.

Divergence Models

This recognition that globalisation does not necessarily constitute an inexorable and irresistible force leading to convergence in national housing policies is an appropriate point at which to consider, more fully, theories of divergence. An empirical basis for this is also provided in **Table 1**. Notwithstanding the general tendency for homeownership sectors to increase in size, wide differences in the orientation towards homeownership remain. For example, among the East Asian economies, Singapore has over 90% of its households in homeownership, whereas in Hong Kong it is 56%. Among European countries, the differences are even wider. Hungary with a 92% homeownership rate is clearly at one end of the spectrum with Germany and Sweden at the other with about 40%. And although it is not shown by **Table 1**, it is also relevant to note that social housing has been present in large numbers not only in Europe but also in some countries beyond it, most notably Hong Kong.

Examination of **Table 2** similarly shows considerable cross-country variation in the scale of mortgage lending, being particularly high in Denmark and the Netherlands and low even in some Western European countries such as France and Italy. Furthermore, there is not even a strong correlation between the size of homeownership sectors and mortgage activity, reflecting – as will be identified later in the article – different housing system models.

The significance of at least some of these differences was recognised in Jim Kemeny's seminal work in which he identified a group of English-speaking countries – Australia, Canada, New Zealand, and the United States – which he labelled home-owning societies and a second group of European mainland countries – Germany, the Netherlands, and Sweden – which he identified as cost-rental societies. As the labels implied, the first group of countries had policies and tenure outcomes that focused on homeownership, while the second had housing policies and tenure outcomes in which cost-rental housing played a significant role. In subsequent publications (e.g., Kemeny, 1995), he introduced the concept of dualist regimes to countries whose housing policies discriminated against cost renting, and unitary whose housing policies put cost renting on an equal footing with market renting.

Kemeny's thesis was that differences between these sets of countries were not simply a matter of their respective stages of industrial development, but were deeply rooted in their social structures. In his view, Australia could be characterised as having evolved a high degree of privatism, which reflected a relatively undeveloped welfare state, as well as low residential densities, which themselves derived from privatised dwelling types and housing tenure, a reliance on private transport, and a gender division of labour in which women often took 'female' roles.. By contrast, Swedish society had developed a high degree of collectivism, based on the growth of a well-developed welfare state, collective transport system that functioned well with the prevailing high-density urban form, the dominance of rental and cooperative flats, and, common gender roles based on public childcare that facilitated predominantly wage-labour roles for women. Thus, on notions such as politics, social structure, and ideology and arguing their significance in understanding divergence, Kemeny established a counterpoint to high-level theories – for example, the logic of industrialism and globalisation – of the inevitability of convergence.

With some broad similarities in approach, but directed more broadly at welfare systems, the work of Esping Andersen (1990) has nevertheless been influential in informing housing research. His identification of three worlds of welfare – Liberal (the United States, Canada, Australia, and the United Kingdom), Conservative Corporatism (Germany and France) and social democratic (Sweden and Denmark) – have been widely applied in order to analyse and interpret housing policy and outcomes.

But just as in respect of welfare in general, it has been recognised that the identification of three worlds is not sufficient to capture the diversity of housing systems across all economically advanced countries. One important addition has been the recognition of a Southern European model (Spain, Portugal, Greece, and Italy) in which the family has had a special importance in ensuring the welfare of its members and for whom, housing, in the form of homeownership, has taken on a role both as providing physical shelter and an emotional foundation of the family; homeownership is not, as in Anglo-Saxon countries, typically a financial asset but an emotional bedrock, part of the family project. A further feature of the Southern European model is that house buying is frequently financed directly from family resources rather than through a mortgage product supplied by a financial institution. So, some of these countries, for example, Italy and Greece, have quite small mortgage markets (**Table 2**).

The East Asian economies – Japan, Korea, Taiwan, Singapore, Malaysia, and Hong Kong – have been indentified as another significant grouping. In these countries, welfare has generally been subordinated to the requirement for economic growth. Consequently, there has not been the development of welfare systems based on storing social insurance principles, but rather ones based on self-reliance and family responsibilities. In this framework, the provision of decent housing has been necessary in order to maintain a productive workforce, but it has not been a means or object of redistribution. Moreover, homeownership has frequently been viewed as a financial asset on which the family could found its own welfare networks.

In addition to these groupings, the housing policy approaches in developing countries can also be seen to constitute their own grouping. The initial attempts by countries in the developing world to tackle problems of housing mainly date back to the years immediately after the end of the Second World War. Often, these attempts were heavily influenced by the European countries that were or had been their colonial masters and involved the importation of European approaches. The notion that the state should take a pivotal role in housing provision, setting standards, and providing subsidies became the norm. But, by the late 1950s and 1960s, for many developing countries the external influence switched to the United States, and to international agencies particularly the United Nations, The World Bank, and, later, the International Monetary Fund (IMF). More or less in all developing countries, mirroring the developments in the developed countries, there was a recognition that housing should not be treated as a basic right of citizenship but as a commodity to be produced and exchanged through the market. This generally meant the dismantling of public institutions formerly involved in construction and management of public housing, the selling of former public housing and a shift towards public involvement with an enabling role, promoting the functioning of land, construction, housing, and financial markets.

Whereas portrayed in these very broad terms the experience of the developing countries appears similar to those in the developed world, there are also significant differences. Notable in countries such as India, Brazil, Mexico, China, and some in Africa, for example, is the increasing concentration of poverty in the rapidly expanding urban areas. Urban slums, frequently in the form of shanty towns, are not consistently functioning as staging posts through which recent migrants slowly become absorbed into formal urban economies. While individual homeownership, albeit of low-quality physical structures, is widespread, an important focus of housing policy in many developing countries lies with assisting the poor to get access to finance and achieving the security of tenure that underlies this form of housing.

Overall, then, whereas it is possible to view the last few decades as being characterised by increasing convergence in housing policies and outcomes around a homeownership norm, there is also empirical evidence supporting the identification of a number of quite different models.

Future Trends in Housing Policy

What can be said about future housing policy trends, particularly whether they seem likely to converge or diverge? Writing in the midst of the so-called credit crunch, which appears to mark a structural break in global economic development, it seems appropriate to consider what the possible consequences for housing policy in the advanced economies might be. That is one of the aims of this final section. But before embarking on that task, recognition is given to the impact on housing policy developments of a process which transcends the precrisis and crisis periods, namely that of demographic ageing.

The Housing Consequences of Demographic Ageing

The ageing of the populations of the advanced economies is part of a worldwide trend, over the course of perhaps a century and through which there has been a shift from high rates of fertility and mortality to low rates of fertility and mortality. This demographic transition is resulting in an ageing of populations or 'age dependency', in which the share of populations accounted for by older people can be expected to grow to a level where in most advanced economies by 2050 those over the age of 65 years will constitute between 25% and 35% of the population totals, and those over 80 years between 10% and 15%.

One of the big questions facing the future for both welfare and housing policy concerns the likely impact of this changing balance. In Castles' (2004) view, "the logic of the argument is transparent." On the one hand, pensions and cash benefits to older people combined with health and social care constitute the two largest programmes in most of the larger economies, accounting for about two-thirds of total social spending. On the other hand, the proportion of older people in those same economies is growing, so that there will be increasing upwards pressure on the costs of these elements of social spending. In these circumstances, and given the twin pressures of globalisation and the fiscal implications that arise from a rise in age-dependency ratios, it seems likely that government spending on those welfare areas not directed at older people will be most vulnerable to cuts.

While Castles (2004) provides empirical evidence refuting the inevitability of such trends, it can be said, at a high level of generalisation, that the cuts in spending on social housing provision for young people and families which have characterised the housing systems of advanced economies in recent decades, nevertheless follow this logic. Moreover, the general tendency for governments to promote homeownership as a form of asset-based welfare, seeing housing equity as a source of income to meet the needs of older people, can also be seen as a response to the fiscal strains of funding state pensions. Given the continuation of demographic ageing processes, therefore, the continued support for homeownership would also seem a credible possibility.

The Housing Consequences of the Credit Crunch

At the time of writing, both the extent and future course of the current economic circumstances – often referred to as the credit crunch – are unclear, and so necessarily is its impact on housing policies in the advanced economies.

The obvious starting point for thinking about possible futures is the recognition that the credit crisis, whatever the other causes, was a consequence of developments in homeownership markets. The expansion of liquidity, itself founded on expansion of the US deficit and Asian, particularly Chinese, surpluses, was accompanied by falling interest rates, rising asset prices, and increasing levels of household indebtedness. The development in the United States in particular of sub-prime mortgages and of mortgage-backed securities which in a global financial market were sold on to banks operating in many countries, both increased and spread the risk. Once households began to default on mortgages while the extent of bad debts, hidden in the mortgage-backed securities, became untraceable, suspicion fell on banks everywhere. The combination of default and repossession along with greater reluctance to lend to house buyers led to falling house prices everywhere. Moreover, the financial and housing market crisis was followed by a more general economic crisis with rising levels of unemployment and even higher levels of mortgage default.

So, what will be the consequences for housing policy developments in the near future? On one view, it could mark the end of the trend towards ever higher levels of homeownership. With fewer people able to enter homeownership and falling house prices revealing the fragile basis of housing markets, households come to the view that homeownership is a less reliable basis for their futures. Drawing a parallel with the impact of the Asian financial crisis at the end of the 1990s, which was followed by reforms in the East Asian economies characterised by increasing reliance on Western-style social insurance-based welfare, one view is that in Western countries there could be a reassertion of their traditional approaches. Moreover, referring back to the Harloe thesis, it is also possible that this will be exactly one of those historical periods when part of the solution to the system crisis is seen to be mass social housing.

Such a view of the dampening of the promotion of homeownership is complicated, however, by the impact of the credit crunch on public finances. To varying extents, the governments of the more advanced economies have implemented rescue plans for banking sectors and other parts of their economies. These rescue plans, combined with increased demand for social spending associated with rising levels of unemployment, and lower tax receipts associated with depressed rates of economic growth, will have nationally differential consequences for the ability of governments to spend on social housing developments, or indeed other (nonrescue) subsidies for the housing sector. In such circumstances, some, but not necessarily all, governments may continue to encourage homeownership if only by failing to promote other housing opportunities.

See also: Globalisation; Home Ownership: Economic Benefits; Privatisation of Housing: Implications for Well-Being.

References

Burns L and Grebler L (1977) *The Housing of Nations: Analysis and Policy in a Comparative Framework*. London: Macmillan.
Castles FG (2004) *The Future of the Welfare State*. Oxford, UK: Oxford University Press.
Esping Andersen G (1990) *The Three Worlds of Welfare Capitalism*. Princeton, NJ: Princeton University Press.
Harloe M (1995) *The People's Home: Social Rented Housing in Europe and America*. Oxford, UK: Blackwell.
Kemeny J (1995) *From Public Housing to the Social Market: Rental Policy Strategies in Comparative Perspective*. London: Routledge.
Kemeny J and Lowe S (1998) Schools of comparative housing research: From convergence to divergence. *Housing Studies* 13: 161–176.

Further Reading

Agus R, Doling J, and Lee D (eds.) (2002) *Housing Policy Systems in South East Asia*. Basingstoke, UK: Palgrave.
Allen J, Barlow J, Leal J, Maloutas L, and Padovani L (2004) *Housing and Welfare in Southern Europe*. Oxford, UK: Blackwell.
Angel S (2000) *Housing Policy Matters: A Global Analysis*. Oxford, UK: Oxford University Press.
Doling J (1997) *Comparative Housing Policy: Government and Housing in Advanced Industrialized Countries*. Basingstoke, UK: Macmillan.
Kemeny J (1981) *The Myth of Home Ownership: Public Versus Private Choices in Housing Tenure*. London: Routledge.
Lowe S and Tsenkova S (eds.) (2003) *Housing Change in Eastern and Central Europe: Integration and Fragmentation*. Basingstoke, UK: Ashgate.
Ronald R (2008) *The Ideology of Home Ownership: Homeowner Societies and the Role of Housing*. Basingstoke, UK: Palgrave Macmillan.

Housing Preferences

HCCH Coolen and SJT Jansen, Delft University of Technology, Delft, The Netherlands

© 2012 Elsevier Ltd. All rights reserved.

Glossary

Attribute An aspect of a physical or nonphysical object, for example a dwelling, such as the type of dwelling, the number of rooms, size of the living room, a garden, and type of tenure.
Choice Actual evaluative behaviour with respect to a physical or nonphysical object.
Part-worth utility The level of satisfaction with respect to an aspect of an object – here a housing attribute, expressed in numerical terms.

Preference The relative attractiveness of an object.
Profile A combination of the attribute levels of all salient housing attributes.
Utility The level of satisfaction with an object – here the strength of preference for a dwelling, expressed in numerical terms.

Introduction

Housing is a complex process that is related to many facets of life. For many people a house forms the primary anchor in the environment, which provides such basic functions as shelter and concealment. A house also fulfils several other functions such as being an enjoyable living environment, providing privacy and territory, accommodating social contact, and being a symbol of who we are and who we would like to be. In addition to these functions, an owner-occupied dwelling can also be considered as a financial investment.

A house, whether rented or owner-occupied, is also for many people by far the most expensive item of consumption, and the decision to select a particular dwelling belongs for many households to the most crucial budget allocation decisions that they make in their life.

Furthermore, a dwelling is a special type of good, and the housing market is a very special type of market. A house is both an investment good and a consumer good. It is spatially immobile, highly durable, highly expensive, multidimensionally heterogeneous, and physically modifiable. The housing market generally lacks brands, is to a large extent a second-hand market, and many market agents typically assume simultaneously the role of buyer and seller.

Given the facts that a house is a special type of good and that housing markets are often imperfect markets, why could housing preferences be of interest? Several reasons have been mentioned in the literature. First, to improve the match between housing demand and housing supply. Although in many countries the quantitative shortage of dwellings has diminished or disappeared, a large discrepancy may still exist with regard to the qualitative match between supply and demand, which may lead to dissatisfied inhabitants. A qualitative mismatch between demand and supply may also lead to unoccupied dwellings, both in the existing stock as well as newly built housing, which may have financial and economical consequences for individual sellers, housing corporations, builders, and developers. Second, measuring housing preferences may be interesting for idealistic reasons. From the point of view of both consumer sovereignty as well as consumer emancipation, it is quite natural to take consumer preferences into account. Third, measuring preferences may improve communication, as knowledge of consumers' housing preferences can be used to improve the communication between suppliers and consumers in order to reach the potential consumer more effectively.

Although the concepts of preference and choice are widely used in housing research, these terms are frequently mistaken for each other. In contrast with this practice, in this article both concepts are conceptually distinguished from each other and the focus is on preference. Preference refers to the relative attractiveness of an object, while choice refers to actual behaviour. Preference, as an expression of attractiveness, may guide choice, but the evaluation involved in preference may take place whether or not a choice has to be made. The most important difference between housing preference and housing choice is that preference is a relatively unconstrained evaluation of attractiveness. In the case of a house, choice will always reflect the joint influences of preference, market conditions, regulations, and availability.

Housing preference has been studied from different theoretical perspectives and with a great variety of methodological approaches. It is an area of interest to researchers in fields such as economics, social geography, housing studies, and environment-behaviour studies. The emphasis in this article will be on the methodological approaches for measuring housing preferences. Apparently, what dwelling people prefer can be measured in many different ways. The choice for a particular method, though, cannot be based only on methodological aspects, but must also take the purpose of the particular measurement into account. Since the purposes of measuring housing preferences can be diverse, it will be indicated in the present article what type of information the different approaches provide, so that the reader can decide which approach is most appropriate for a particular research situation.

Dimensions of Housing Preference Approaches

In this article the following approaches to measuring housing preferences will be described:

- Descriptive method
- Means-end approach
- Decision plan nets
- Multiattribute utility method
- Conjoint approach
- Revealed preference approach.

Although these approaches are different, they have certain aspects in common. First, they all assume that houses can be described and evaluated in terms of a bundle of attributes, each of which has a limited number of levels, often two or three. Second, they all assume that people derive some satisfaction from each of the attribute levels, and in some approaches this satisfaction is expressed in terms of a part-worth utility. Third, all the approaches assume, albeit some implicitly, that people combine the satisfactions for the different attribute levels into an overall preference for a dwelling, but they may differ in the specification of the combination rule.

There are also several dimensions on which the different approaches differ from each other. With regard to the measurement of housing preferences, the main distinction is between compositional and decompositional approaches. In compositional approaches people provide an evaluation or indicate their preferred level for each housing attribute, while they may also provide an indication of the importance of the various attributes. The weighted evaluations or preferences can be aggregated into an overall evaluation of the dwelling. Decompositional approaches, on the other hand, are based on the measurement of people's evaluations of housing profiles. Each profile consists of a combination of housing attribute levels, one for each housing attribute. People indicate their preference for each profile, and statistical models may be used to derive evaluations for the separate attribute levels.

Another distinction that differentiates preference methods from each other is the one between mathematical and nonmathematical models. In mathematical preference models, an explicit rule or method for combining or decomposing the measured evaluations is used. In the case of the compositional approach, an aggregation rule may be used for combining the evaluations of the different attribute levels into an overall preference. The linear additive rule is mostly used for combining the separate preference measurements. For the decompositional approach, statistical methods, such as regression analysis and logistic regression analysis, may be used for decomposing the overall preference measurement into evaluations for separate housing attribute levels. In nonmathematical models the preference measurements are either not combined or decomposed, or this is done implicitly.

Preference models may also differ with respect to whether a trade-off between housing attributes is possible or not. In compensatory preference models a low satisfaction for a particular attribute level can, at least partially, be compensated for by higher satisfactions for one or more of the remaining attribute levels. Other preference models do not allow for compensation. This means that a low satisfaction for a particular attribute level can never be compensated, regardless of the satisfaction with the remaining attribute levels. This may be in accordance with the way in which people decide in reality; for example, it is well known that for many people a dwelling without a garden is not acceptable irrespective of the levels of the other housing attributes.

Another important distinction is the one between stated and revealed preferences. Revealed preferences are based on actual housing choices, that is, actual behaviour, in real housing markets, and the preferences are inferred from the actual choice. In contrast, stated preferences are expressions of people's evaluations of houses, when a choice still has to be made or does not have to be made at all, and may concern real or hypothetical houses. In this context, the previously mentioned distinction between preference and choice is relevant.

Finally, preference models may have two types of outcomes: utilities or another type of outcome. In utility preference models, an overall utility is attached to the house as a whole, while each of the separate attribute levels is associated with a part-worth utility. Other type of outcomes may be a set of preferred attribute levels or a ranking of preferred houses.

Preference Measurement Methods

Preliminary to every approach is the determination of the salient housing attributes and the relevant levels of these attributes. This can be done in several different ways and may be based on knowledge, experience, policy considerations, literature review, and preliminary research. For the latter, various methods are available such as the repertory grid method, less-structured interviewing, and focus groups. When describing the different housing preference models, it is assumed that the salient housing attributes and their relevant levels have already been determined.

Descriptive Method

The descriptive housing preference approach amounts to measuring people's preferred housing attribute levels for each of the salient housing attributes. For each individual the combination of preferred housing attribute levels signifies the preferred house, but often this combination is not constructed because the focus is mainly on the separate housing attributes or on simple patterns of housing preferences. Often the preferences are measured together with socio-demographic variables such as income, age, and household composition in order to be able to relate the preferences for the housing attributes to these socio-demographic variables. This type of housing preference measurement is frequently used for global segmentation purposes. A good example of this approach are the housing demand surveys often commissioned by national, regional, or local governments. Sometimes, the relative importance of each housing attribute is also measured. The measurements of both preferred housing attribute levels and weights can then be combined, according to some combination rule, to arrive at an overall preference measurement for the preferred dwelling.

Means-End Approach

In most housing preference approaches, one measures *what* people prefer, but in the means-end approach it is also determined *why* people prefer these housing attribute levels. The means-end approach relates houses and consumers. Each housing attribute is assumed to yield consequences, while the importance of consequences is based on their ability to satisfy people's personally motivating values and goals. A means-end chain relates the preference for a housing attribute to its contribution to the realisation of objectives and values. A simple means-end chain consists of the triple (housing attribute level, consequence, value). The approach, thus, uncovers both people's preferences for housing attributes as well as their motives for these preferences. After the preferred housing attribute levels have been determined, people have to indicate for each housing attribute why the preferred level is important to them or what the preferred level means to them. This *why* question is repeated as a reaction to the answer to the first *why* question. The process stops when the individual can no longer answer the *why* question, or after a predetermined number of *why* questions, depending on the goal of the research and the research design. Means-end chains have been measured by means of (semi-)structured face-to-face, telephone, or web-based interviews and with questionnaires. The aggregation of individual means-end chains and the subsequent analysis of these aggregated data may be done either by hierarchical value maps or by network analysis. The method may be used for discovering people's underlying motives, such as values, for housing preferences and has been used for marketing and advertising purposes. Although the means-end approach is relatively new in housing research, there are several applications of it.

Decision Plan Nets

A decision plan net can best be described as the underlying protocol that people use to evaluate alternative houses in terms of the housing attributes that are considered to be salient. The purpose of the method is to uncover this underlying protocol and to represent it in a tree or flow diagram. This is done by first recording the individual's preferred level for each salient housing attribute. These preferred housing attribute levels are represented on the main axis of the tree diagram. Subsequently, for each preferred housing attribute level, it is determined how hard this attribute level is. If the individual indicates that a house without this attribute level would be refused, the attribute is called a reject-inducing attribute, and this is represented in the tree diagram. The attribute is called a trade-off attribute, if the individual indicates that a different level of the attribute in question will be accepted if this is compensated for by better scores on one or more of the other housing attributes. This is subsequently recorded in the tree diagram together with the compensatory attribute levels. Finally, the individual may indicate that a different level on the attribute in question is accepted as long as the house satisfies the other housing attribute levels; such an attribute is called a relative preference attribute, which is also represented in the tree diagram. The final tree diagram clearly shows which dwellings are unacceptable. It also shows which housing alternatives are acceptable for the individual. By having the individual rank order of these alternatives, one gets a clear picture of the individual's housing preferences.

Multiattribute Utility Method

Multiattribute utility theory is designed for situations in which a decision-maker has to make an optimal choice among a set of complex alternatives while taking all the facets, criteria, or attributes of each of the alternatives into account. The multiattribute utility method amounts to valuing and weighting each of the attributes, and subsequently combining the weighted values into an overall utility per alternative. The alternative with the highest utility represents the optimal choice. Although the multiattribute utility method was intended for choice situations, it can also be used for preference measurements. Given the salient housing attributes, it involves the following procedure. First, the levels of each housing attribute have to be transformed into numerical values by each individual involved in the research. A variety of methods is available for valuing the attribute levels. A relatively easily administered method is to have individuals rate the levels of each attribute on a scale with two anchors: one extreme point of the scale 'not attractive at all' is assigned the value 0 and the other end point 'extremely attractive' gets the scale value 100. This results in individual scale values for all attribute levels. Next, individuals have to assign an importance weight to each housing attribute, for this task also several methods are available. For instance, one might ask individuals to rate each housing attribute on a numerical scale with end points 0 meaning 'not important at all' and 100 indicating 'extremely important'. The importance weights are normalised per individual in such a way that they sum to 1. For each individual an overall utility score can now be computed per housing alternative by combining the weighted valued attribute levels. The most commonly applied combination rule is the weighted linear model, in which for each attribute its value is multiplied by the attribute weight and subsequently these weighted scores are summed over all attributes. A higher overall utility score means a higher preference. In theory, for each combination of housing attribute levels, the overall utility can be computed. However, it is generally not necessary to compute the utility of every combination of housing attribute levels, as one is often only interested in a limited number of housing alternatives. The method provides the possibility to examine the importance and attractiveness of separate dwelling characteristics, to calculate utilities for single dwelling attributes, to calculate overall utilities for combinations of attribute levels, to distinguish consumer groups with different preferences, and to choose among alternatives in the case when different alternatives are available.

Conjoint Approach

The goal of conjoint analysis is to estimate utility functions for housing profiles that provide insight into the overall utility of a series of housing alternatives, into the extent to which each attribute influences overall utility, into how preferences are distributed across the levels of a housing attribute, and into the trade-off between the residential attributes. So the results indicate, among others, the preferences for a series of dwellings in terms of utilities, the weights of the housing attributes, and which of the levels of an attribute is most preferred.

Given the salient housing attributes and their relevant levels, the researcher has to determine the measurement task that individuals have to perform, must design the experiment, and has to estimate the utility function in order to arrive at the preference measurements. For the determination of the measurement task, one has to choose between a ranking task, a rating task, or a choice task. A ranking task involves that individuals have to rank order the set of housing profiles from most preferred to least preferred. In a rating task individuals have to express their strength of preference for each profile on some rating scale, for instance, on a scale which runs from 0 (extremely unattractive) to 100 (extremely attractive). So, a ranking task only measures preference order, while a rating task also measures the relative preference differences between the profiles. In a choice task the individual has to choose the most preferred dwelling profile out of a set of two or three different alternatives. This task is repeated for a specific number of predefined choice sets. Before starting the experiment the researcher must determine which profiles have to be evaluated. This is generally done according to the principles of experimental design, and typically factorial designs are used. Ideally, one would like to administer a full factorial design, since it allows the estimation of all main and all interaction effects, but with many attributes the experimental task becomes too heavy for the individuals; for instance, with seven housing attributes each having three levels, there are 2187 different housing profiles that have to be evaluated. To limit the number of profiles to manageable proportions in practice a fractional factorial design, covering only a subset of all profiles, is chosen for which one must make assumptions about which interaction effects are expected to be 0. For instance, if one assumes that all interaction effects are 0, a main effects fractional factorial design requires each individual to evaluate only 18 different housing profiles.

Finally, an appropriate estimation procedure to estimate the utility function has to be chosen. Rating tasks generate rating data, which are assumed to be of interval level measurement. These data are typically analyzed by applying ordinary least squares regression analysis, whereby the estimated regression coefficients indicate the part-worth utilities of the housing attributes. Preference measurement from a choice task is usually analyzed by means of the multinominal logit model.

Revealed Preference Approach

In the revealed preference approach the housing preferences of people are not measured directly but are inferred from other information. Two types of information are used to infer people's housing preferences. One type of information concerns the actual housing choice: the chosen housing attribute levels are considered to be the preferred ones. Sometimes, the housing attribute levels are related to each other or to an overall feature of the dwelling. For instance, in hedonic price models, the price of the dwelling is regressed on the observed housing attributes. This approach provides information about the influence of the attributes on the price. Another approach, using this type of information, is based on making assumptions about the underlying preference or utility function. A common theoretical framework in this context is random utility theory, which assumes that people's utilities for housing alternatives are based on a deterministic and a random component. Given this framework and the assumption that people's housing choices are the result of utility-maximising behaviour, the choice probabilities of the housing alternatives can be derived by means of a multinomial logit model. Alternatively, nested logit models have been used, which assume instead of a simultaneous decision process a hierarchical or sequential one, in which housing choice is considered as a number of interlinked decisions, which are modelled according to some nested structure, based on some of the housing attributes. For instance, housing choice may be considered as consisting of the interlinked choices of a location, a tenure form, and a type of dwelling, and subsequently the simultaneous choice of other salient housing attributes.

The other type of information that is used to infer housing preferences is whether or not one has moved during a certain period of time and the dwelling attributes of the house one has moved from or one is still living in if one has not moved. In so-called exit models this information is used to estimate the likelihood of a move as a function of the housing attributes, sometimes augmented with household characteristics, by means of logistic regression analysis. The estimated coefficients primarily indicate which housing attribute levels can be considered as so-called push factors.

Conclusion

The aim of the present article has been to provide a brief overview of the most popular methods for measuring housing preferences. Although these approaches are different, they have certain aspects in common, for instance they all consider a dwelling as a bundle of attributes. There are also several dimensions on which the methods differ from each other. These dimensions have been discussed in the context of the different methods for measuring housing preferences, and are summarised for each of these methods in **Table 1**. Most of the characterisations in this table follow straightforward from the description of the different housing preference methods and need no further explanation. However, it seems that this may not be the case for the characterisation of the methods in terms of the distinction between compensatory and noncompensatory approaches. This dimension is not applicable to the descriptive and means-end approach, since in these approaches people only indicate their most preferred attribute level for each of the salient housing attributes. Because no other information is available, nothing can be said about possible trade-offs. In constructing a decision plan net, it is the individual who can indicate for each attribute whether it is a reject-inducing, trade-off, or relative preference attribute. This means that it is determined on the level of each attribute whether or not it is compensatory, and consequently both types of attributes may occur in a decision plan net. For the other three approaches, whether or not trade-offs are possible depends on the combination rule that is specified either for combining the evaluations of the different attribute levels into an overall preference, or for decomposing the overall preference measurements into evaluations for separate housing attribute levels. If the linear additive rule is used, compensation is possible, but in case of a multiplicative combination rule trade-offs are farfetched since a low evaluation of one of the attribute levels will generally result in a relatively low overall utility.

A house is a complex heterogeneous good, which may have many different functions. This makes the measurement of housing preferences a delicate matter, but one that is not without importance. The way in which dwelling preferences are actually measured depends on the purpose of a particular study and on the way in which the characteristics of the various methods fit this purpose best. The present article has sketched a concise overview of the most popular methods that are currently in use and provides insight into their characteristics, so that a

Table 1 Main characteristics of housing preference methods

	Descriptive	Means-end	DPN	MAU	Conjoint	Revealed
Compositional vs decompositional	Compositional	Compositional	Compositional	Compositional	Decompositional	Decompositional
Mathematical vs nonmathematical	Both	Nonmathematical	Nonmathematical	Mathematical	Mathematical	Mathematical
Compensatory vs noncompensatory	Not applicable	Not applicable	Both	Both	Both	Both
Stated vs revealed	Stated	Stated	Stated	Stated	Stated	Revealed
Type of outcome: utility vs other	Other	Other	Other	Utility	Utility	Both

satisfactory choice can be made for a specific method. Ultimately, designing and building dwellings according to people's preferences may provide the most satisfaction to residents.

See also: Choice and Government Intervention in Housing Markets; Housing Market Search; Path Dependency; Qualitative Interviewing; Qualitative Methods in Housing Research.

Further Reading

Clark WAV and Dieleman FM (1996) *Households and Housing: Choice and Outcomes in the Housing Market*. New Brunswick: Center for Urban Research.

Coolen HCCH (2008) *The Meaning of Dwelling Features. Conceptual and Methodological Issues*. Amsterdam: IOS Press.

Jansen SJT, Coolen HCCH, Goetgeluk, RW (eds.) (2011) *The Measurement and Analysis of Housing Preference and Choice*. Heidelberg: Springer

Timmermans H, Molin E, and Van Noortwijk L (1994) Housing choice processes: Stated versus revealed modeling approaches. *Netherlands Journal of Housing and the Built Environment* 9: 215–227.

Housing Standards: Regulation

HJ Visscher and FM Meijer, Delft University of Technology, Delft, The Netherlands
JP Branco, National Laboratory for Civil Engineering, Lisbon, Portugal; Delft University of Technology, Delft, The Netherlands

© 2012 Elsevier Ltd. All rights reserved.

Glossary

Building control General term for the system of regulations, permit procedures, and monitoring compliance with regulations in design and construction phase.
Building permit procedure Procedure for checking building plan conformity with public building regulations carried out by local authorities.
Building regulations Government regulations that have to be met when new buildings and houses are being built.
Housing standards General term for public and private standards defining the physical characteristics of dwellings.

Introduction

The regulation of housing standards is an essential policy tool used by governments to assure minimal accepted living standards. The systems of requirements combined with laws about how to assure that these requirements are met are complex and extensive. Besides assuring basic living conditions, the regulations support other policies and public policy goals. Houses should be safe, healthy, usable, and comfortable for their occupants, visitors, and others. Furthermore, they are important economic assets and they contribute to environmental impact through the use of land and building materials, and because of energy consumption accompanying building construction, renovation, maintenance, as well as the occupancy of housing once it is built. Buildings are responsible for 40% of the total emissions of CO_2 and are seen as the sector where reductions can be realised most cost-effectively.

Building regulations and related laws play an important role in the building process by defining the rules of the game. By doing so, they are often considered to be an administrative burden and are therefore often the object of studies aiming for deregulation.

In addition, regulations and standards are often considered unnecessary because "An architect knows how to build a proper house, useful for everyone." But accidents and structural problems with residential buildings show that many mistakes are made. For example, research in the Netherlands has found that recently built Dutch dwellings are not achieving energy savings that had been expected, and indoor air quality is threatened by inadequate ventilation systems. It seems that high energy-saving ambitions can only be realised with the help of strict regulations and effective enforcement systems. An alternative to control and command regulations for energy use reduction might be the use of pricing mechanisms. However, without widespread and intensive information, campaigns, incentives, and subsidy schemes have shown minor results.

Purpose of and Development of Housing Standards and Building Regulations

The early origins of building regulations can be traced back to the first signs of urbanisation in most civilisations. The oldest actual building regulations can be found in Babylon's Codex Hammurabi from 1700 BC (see **Figure 1**). It contains rules that set out the responsibilities of architects and builders with respect to structural safety. Fire safety was a basic issue in the Middle Ages. Buildings should not collapse and a fire in a single building should not easily spread to other buildings. Therefore, the towns in the Middle Ages developed rules to ensure that some space was kept between individual buildings and a minimum width for streets must be provided. Aside from government building regulations, owners, designers, and builders discharge of their responsibilities was also a strong influence on the quality of buildings. In the Middle Ages, the Guilds developed rules for good craftsmanship that were of great importance.

Until the beginning of the twentieth century, public regulation of building standards was mainly in the hands of municipalities. Throughout the twentieth century there emerged an increasingly uniform and

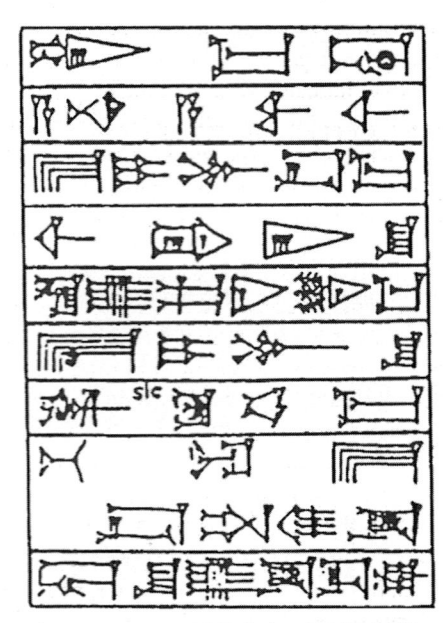

Figure 1 Codex Hammurabi, Babylon 1700 BC. "If an architect has built a house for someone which structure is not strong enough and collapses and causes the death of the owner of the house, then this architect shall be killed."

centralised regulation of building standards that are more or less independent of local circumstances. At the end of the nineteenth century, industrialisation prompted fast development of very small dwellings, built at high densities to house labourers migrating from rural locations into towns. More and more concerns were raised about the unhealthy conditions in these dwellings. Most were built back-to-back with alcoves, so very little daylight could enter and air conditions were very bad. Some progressive factory owners and manufacturers started building houses that offered better living conditions for their labourers, with the primary aim of improving productivity. Also, doctors realised that the living conditions of labourers in the towns had an increasingly important influence on their health. In the Netherlands, government responded by developing laws and regulations to provide better dwellings. This led to the introduction of the Housing Law in 1901, providing a legal base for municipalities to introduce minimum standard regulations and the right to enforce them through building permit procedures and powers to enforce improvements to dwellings that are responsible for dangerous conditions. Other countries have seen similar developments. From the early twentieth century, by the influence of national and municipal governments, the quality of housing production grew steadily, until the early 1990s. By that time, concerns about overregulation stifling developments encouraged governments to reduce the size of public administration, and this has now became a dominant factor.

While structural failure and fire safety motivated the early development of building regulations, growing concern about poor living conditions and health prompted new regulations. Concerns for safety and health were also reasons for more detailed regulations concerning the dimensions, building materials, and amenities of dwellings. Also 'usability' became a starting point to require minimal dimensions of living rooms, bedrooms, kitchens, toilets, and bathrooms. During the twentieth century, there has been a nearly continuous development in which the regulations were refined and extended to assure good basic minimum standard living conditions. Building physics in terms of damp, light, air, noise, and so on, were better controlled by requirements with respect to the quality of building exteriors and foundations. By the 1950s and 1960s, the provision of water, sewage, rainwater drains, and the provision of electricity and gas for heating and cooking were all subject to detailed regulation. However, heat insulation requirements with respect to the exterior of dwellings were only introduced in the second half of the 1970s after the oil crises first made us aware that fossil fuels were not endlessly available. Only in 1995, in the Netherlands, were modern-style energy performance regulations introduced that could take into account many options to save energy for heating. A broader anxiety about environmental sustainability also emerged during the 1980s. Until today, it has been too complicated to define public regulations to limit the environmental burden of buildings.

In general, building regulations define a minimum acceptable quality level. Of course, this does not mean that this is the desired level for all built dwellings. The actual dimensions of a building and the level of amenities provided by the building are often significantly above the level required to meet the regulations. Furthermore, required building standards were also embedded within other housing policies. For example, in the first decade after the Second World War, there was also a set of dimension requirements that were used in relation to a subsidy programme for the large building programmes. In fact, these requirements sometimes worked as maximum levels. In other European countries, the development of building regulations has been along similar lines to those in the Netherlands.

Private Standards

Besides public regulations, there are also numerous private law standards for building products, buildings, and houses. These can take the form of national widely accepted standards, but also guidelines that are the basis for certification schemes managed by industry associations, for example. National standardisation organisations are very important. They develop technical standards that can be used to calculate the performance of building materials and whole buildings. Public regulations are often based on these technical standards that are established in the private sector. The quality of building products (like concrete, bricks, and window frames) is mostly covered by private law certification schemes that are also based on the national standards. Internationally, organisations like International Organisation for Standardisation (ISO) and European Committee for Standardisation (CEN) are seeking to harmonise these standards.

The Enforcement of Building Regulations

Defining standards is on its own not enough. There should be a legal basis and procedures to enforce the regulations. The legal basis in most countries is a Building or Housing Act or Law. This law defines rules that apply when you want to build and use, change, and demolish buildings. Typically, the law makes a reference to building codes that contain the actual requirements for the specifications of buildings. The law also defines the rights, tasks, and responsibilities of some actors in the process, for example, architects. There are many differences in these rules between countries.

In nearly all countries, local municipalities administer building permit procedures. The owner, or on his/her behalf the architects, submit building plans to the municipality. In some countries only listed architects are allowed to submit building plans. Mostly, there are general or, sometimes, very detailed rules for the documents that have to be submitted, including maps, drawings, and calculations that show in what way the building meets the regulations.

Besides the national and, sometimes, local regulations for the layout and physical quality of a building, there are regulations that define specific requirements for each location. These regulations are generally called planning requirements. A local zoning plan or other local or regional development plans will define if, when and to what dimensions the housing can be built at a specific location. Can the building have a habitable function? Could it also contain a shop, an office, or an industrial function? How high can the building be and where can it be placed on the plot?

Another aspect of control by local authorities is the architecture of a building (style, shape, materials, and colours). In the United Kingdom and France, the location-dependent aspects require a specific permit, a 'planning permit', in addition to the building permit covering the physical aspects of the building. In other countries, like the Netherlands, all requirements come together in one permit. Besides the previously mentioned planning and building regulations, there may be other regulations that apply for a building development, such as permission to demolish an old building or permission to fell trees at the location. All possible public regulations were recently brought together in the Netherlands in one 'environment permit' (*omgevingsvergunning*). This reduced the administrative burden for citizens and companies that want to build.

Cuntries often define a category of minor building activities, for example, small alterations to a house that are exempt from control. One does not have to make the local authorities aware of these, but building regulations still have to be met. Another category of buildings usually follow a light procedure. Plans have to be submitted ('a building notice'), but are not effectively checked or only certain aspects are checked.

But all other buildings follow the normal procedure. Sometimes there is a preliminary consultation before the plans are actually submitted. In some countries this is even obligatory. In such cases, the plans are submitted and the municipality checks if the documentation is complete. If so, the control procedure starts. In most countries the authorities can take a maximum of 2 or 3 months to reject or accept the plans. If the plans and engineering design are accepted, the drawings and calculations that were the basis for approval will have to be checked at a later stage of development. The construction works can start. During the construction period, some form of site inspection is usually carried out, sometimes at key stages of construction, and also at random times. In some countries, there is also a formal, final inspection of the finished building and an additional permit has to be issued before the building can be used.

Although the building and planning permit are nearly always processed by municipalities, private parties play an increasing role in monitoring and policing conformity with building regulations in design as well as construction phases of a building project. There are various forms of recognition or certification that private parties must achieve if they are to legitimately carry out these responsibilities.

This whole process should ensure that all buildings meet the regulatory requirements at the beginning of their life span. For some building design features, like energy performance, for example, the regulations with respect to new buildings become stricter from time to time. As a consequence, most of the existing housing stock does not meet the current building regulation standards. However, when buildings are renovated, the standards applicable to new construction have to be met. But municipalities will relax requirements if for technical or economic reasons the current building standards are too high. Finally, there can also be a legal basis for municipalities to require improvements to old buildings in bad condition.

National or Local Regulations

As mentioned before, housing standards and building regulations were typically introduced as towns formed and urban settlements developed. While municipalities still play an important role in all countries, this role has changed. Municipalities were commonly responsible for the design of building codes and building regulations, But in many countries there has been a centralisation of regulation with respect to the physical dimensions and quality of buildings. Nowadays in half of the EU countries, technical building regulations are established by federal or national authorities, and there is no role for regional or local government in the design of building regulations. In these countries, technical building regulations are therefore uniform throughout the whole country. Due to their particular administrative divisions or legal traditions, in the other half of EU countries the responsibility for determining building regulations is divided differently. The following distributions of responsibilities can be identified: (1) central authorities set a model of technical building regulations that is adapted by regional authorities (e.g., Germany); (2) regional authorities set the technical building regulations with functional requirements and refer to the central guidelines for technical requirements (e.g., Austria).

In the last 10–15 years, the centralisation of technical building regulations has reduced the legislation and hence legal documents that architects, builders, and others must observe. This reduction is aimed mainly at simplifying the building regulations. However, in some countries there was decentralisation mainly due to the approval of new regulations for requirements or types of buildings that were not previously covered and the approval of building regulations by regional and local authorities.

Influence of Europe on National Building Regulations

In recent decades many steps have been made within the European Union (EU) to improve the conditions for an internal barrier-free construction market. However, the EU continues to regard building legislation as an internal matter for its member states, and does not claim to be directly responsible. The European Construction Products Directive 89/106/EEC (CPD) defines various standards for building products with the intent to create products of equivalent quality in all member states, while the European committees for standardisation like CEN synchronise technical regulations by enacting Eurocodes, for example. All European Directives on building and planning must be incorporated in the national laws of existing member states, and new member states will have to adopt them in the future. However, differences between the national building regulations and the technical requirements for buildings of the member states of the European Union are fundamental and numerous.

The influence of Europe on energy-related issues is growing. In 2003, the Energy Performance of Buildings Directive (EPBD) was introduced. This directive demands member states formulate energy performance regulations for new buildings, and an energy labelling system for existing buildings. Labels have to be shown each time a building is sold or leased. The design of energy performance regulation is the responsibility of individual countries. However, the EPBD gets stricter from time to time. At present, it requires member states to develop policies that guarantee only zero-energy buildings will be built from 2020.

Formulations of Technical Building Regulations

The CPD and related documents introduced the 'performance approach' as a method to formulate requirements in such a way that the goals to be reached are unambiguous, but the practical building solutions to realise these goals are not prescribed. This should stimulate innovation. Nowadays, most countries describe their regulations as 'performance based'. However, a closer look at their formulation and content reveals quite large differences between 'performance-based' requirements in different countries. The move away from prescriptive specifications towards functional requirements started over 40 years ago by introducing explanations of specifications, functional requirements, and performance standards, together with the use of deemed-to-satisfy clauses, codes of practice, the system of agreement, and information for guidance.

The CIB (International Council for Research and Innovation in Building and Construction) Taskgroup 37 'Performance-Based Building Regulatory Systems' developed a model to analyse and describe the various performance-based requirement systems. The 'Performance System Model (PSM)' was formalised in 2004. The PSM introduced a 'performance risk level', which determines the application of requirements, and a classification defined with regard to objectives like health and safety, fire safety, structure, and sustainability. It also contains a verification level, which includes design guides as well as testing or modelling techniques to establish acceptable solutions (see **Figure 2**).

This model can be used to analyse the formulation of requirements in different countries. Some countries, including the Netherlands, have consciously attempted

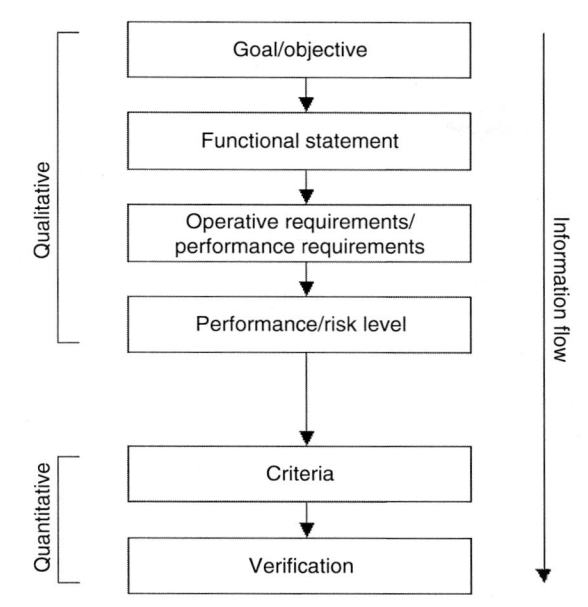

Figure 2 Performance system model CIB-TG 37.

to follow such a model. Others have devised their own performance-based systems, while some continue to use traditional systems. Analysis is difficult, even for those countries that have adopted some form of performance-based system. There are two main reasons. First, commentators vary in their understanding of these technical terms, and second, there is inconsistency within the specific systems of regulations in the countries used for different subjects.

The term 'performance requirement' is interpreted in different ways. Although it is understood by CIB to mean the qualitative formulation of requirements or goals, as opposed to prescriptive regulations with mandatory design solutions, some countries understand it to constitute a description of desired levels of performance.

Countries use a broad variation of systems and formulations of the requirements. The numerous combinations include generalised 'functional' requirements in combination with 'deemed-to-satisfy' practical design solutions (as in England and Wales); generalised 'functional' requirements with design guidance, or reference to external sources of design guidance; 'prescriptive' requirements with reference to solutions; and quantitative 'performance' requirements without reference to practical design solutions (as in the Netherlands).

Building Decree, The Netherlands

The formulation of regulations in the Dutch Building Decree, issued in 1992 and reformed in 2003, is the result of an Action Programme for deregulation that was formulated by the Dutch government in the 1980s. Briefly, the criteria that regulations are expected to meet are as follows: a regulation must be legally explicit and equitable; a regulation must be unambiguous and therefore measurable and verifiable; and a regulation should present only a minimal restriction on freedom and innovation in design. These criteria have been interpreted very strictly and led to a system of performance requirements that conform to the CIB-TG 37 model. The goal is given in the Housing Law where it is stated that in the Building Decree, regulations can be formulated relating to the building of constructions from the point of view of safety, health, useability, energy conservation, and the environment.

Each performance requirement of the Building Decree comprises a functional statement, which expresses the intention of the performance requirement; operative requirements, which elaborate the practical implications of the functional description, often including a limit value, which indicates the minimum level of performance that must be attained; a determination/verification method, usually by reference to a standard of the Dutch Standardisation Institute (NEN) or a Ministerial Regulation.

The Building Decree does not offer examples of acceptable solutions. Its formulation, using performance requirements, is intended to allow a high degree of design freedom and to stimulate innovation. The Decree allows 'equivalent solutions' if a proposal does not meet one or more operative requirements, due to the use of innovative materials or construction techniques. In such cases, the developer must demonstrate that the proposed solution meets the intention of the functional requirement and the level of performance described by the limit value or determination method. In practice, although the formulation of the Building Decree appears relatively liberal, there are numerous examples of prescription, such as limitations on stairways dimensions, to which it would be difficult to propose equivalent solutions. The formulation of the Dutch Building Decree and its relationship to other documents is described in **Figure 3**.

Building Regulations: England and Wales

In England and Wales, the structure of the Building Act, the Building Regulations, and the associated advisory Approved Documents is relatively clear, in terms of a hierarchy of elements of the regulatory system. However, there are some inconsistencies between different subjects, which are partly the result of a rolling programme of review and amendment, but also reflect the nature of the subjects.

The Building Act, 1984, is the enabling legislation for Building Regulations, 2010. It gives the Secretary of State powers to make regulations for the purpose of (1) securing the health, safety, welfare, and convenience of persons in or about buildings and of others who may be affected by

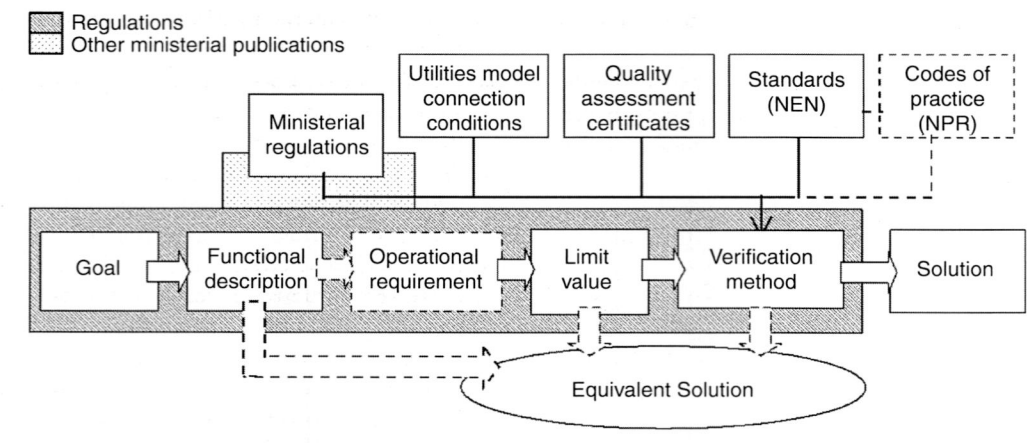

Figure 3 Formulation of the Dutch Building Decree.

buildings or matters connected with buildings; (2) furthering the conservation of fuel and power; (3) preventing waste, undue consumption, misuse, or contamination of water. Each functional requirement is brief, for instance: B1 means 'warning and escape': the building shall be designed and constructed so that there are appropriate provisions for the early warning of fire, and appropriate means of escape in case of fire from the building to a place of safety outside the building capable of being safely and effectively used at all material times. Approved Documents (ADs) are issued for each of the themes, which elaborate the requirements, discuss the underlying issues, and describe strategies that can be used to comply with the functional requirements. The ADs include guidance on operative strategies and tactics (advisory equivalent to operative requirements); various forms of verification: description of methods of measurement and verification, often by reference to British Standards; direct examples of acceptable solutions, often by means of diagrams or tables of minimum or maximum dimensions or other values; or references to external design guidance. Often, ADs offer a variety of ways of complying with requirements. Despite this relatively clear structure, the expression of requirements varies between subjects (like fire safety, energy performance, or minimal dimensions of the layout). For some subjects, the options for compliance are inherently very limited (see **Figure 4**).

The formulation of the requirements in the technical building regulations can be classified into three categories:

1. 'Functional requirements' define the main objectives, but there is no determination method, no performance level, and no reference to solutions or materials.
2. 'Performance requirements' express the level of performance in quantitative terms and define the determination method.
3. 'Prescriptive requirements' lay down a specific design or construction solutions.

Conclusions

The key trends in the regulation of housing standards can be summarised as follows: the responsibility for setting regulations has increasingly shifted from municipalities to central governments with the general aim of creating more uniformity. Differences between European countries are still considerable, but the influence of the

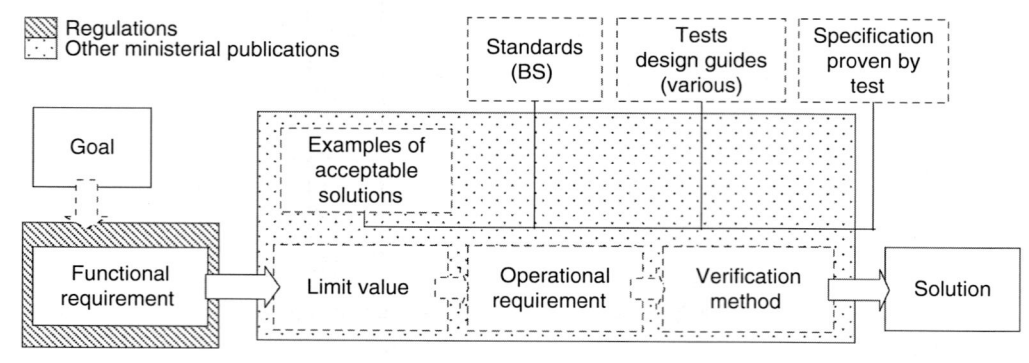

Figure 4 Formulation of the building regulations in England and Wales.

European Union is growing. The importance of energy regulations increases. The design of regulations has moved away from prescriptive to performance regulations. Another clear trend is the growing role of private parties in monitoring compliance with regulations in the design and construction of buildings.

See also: Housing Supply.

Further Reading

Bowen RP (1997) Performance-based building codes. *Final Report of CIB Task Group 11*. Rotterdam, the Netherlands: International Council for Building Research and Documentation.

Foliente GC (2000) Developments in performance-based building codes and standards. *Forest Product Journals* 50(7/8): 11–21.

Meijer FM and Visscher HJ (1998) The deregulation of building controls: A comparison of Dutch and other European systems. *Environment and Planning B: Planning and Design* 25: 617–629.

Meijer FM and Visscher HJ (2006) Deregulation and privatisation of European building-control systems. *Environment and Planning B: Planning and Design* 33(4): 491–501.

Meijer FM, Visscher HJ, and Sheridan L (2002) *Building Regulations in Europe Part 1: A Comparison of the Systems of Building Control in Eight European Countries*. Delft, the Netherlands: Delft University Press.

Meijer FM, Visscher HJ, and Costa Branco De Oliveira Pedro JA (2010) Building control systems of European Union countries: A comparison of tasks and responsibilities. *International Journal of Law in the Built Environment* 2(1): 45–60.

NKB (1978) Structure for building regulations, The Nordic Committee on Building Regulations (NKB). *Report No. 34*. Stockholm: The Nordic Committee on Building Regulations.

Sheridan L, Visscher HJ, and Meijer FM (2003) *Building Regulations in Europe Part 2: A Comparison of Technical Requirements in Eight European Countries*. Delft, the Netherlands: Delft University Press.

Tubbs B (2004) CIB World Building Congress 2004 Building for the future. *CIB TG37, Final Report*. Toronto: International Council for Building Research and Documentation.

Visscher HJ, Sheridan L, and Meijer FM (2005) The formulation of building regulations in eight European countries. *Building Research Journal* 53(4): 193–205.

Housing Statistics

M Steele, University of Guelph, Guelph, ON, Canada

© 2012 Elsevier Ltd. All rights reserved.

Glossary

Consumer Price Index (CPI) A price index for the basket of goods consumed by a typical household. The component indexes, ones for the prices of goods and services, are weighted according to the importance of the items in the expenditure of the typical household.

Flip (with reference to a housing unit) Sale shortly after a purchase, in order to realise a capital gain, sometimes after minimal renovation.

Hedonic house price index A price index derived by taking into account the effects of various characteristics of a house (e.g. number of bathrooms) on its value.

Housing starts The number of housing units on which construction has started.

Mortgage debt service Refers to a household's mortgage payment (interest and principal) plus (in the US) property tax and insurance, or (in Canada) property tax and heating cost.

Price index An indicator set equal to 1.0 or 100 in a selected base year and area which increases or decreases over time or space. Usually the value of the index is the weighted sum of component indexes.

Repeat sales house price index A price index derived, using multivariate statistical methods, from a sample which includes only houses for which there are data on at least two sales (e.g. one in January, 1990 and one in October, 2010).

Zoning Refers to bylaws and codes in North America which regulate, for a defined area of a city, the type of use permitted and constrain characteristics such as height, placement on land, and floor space of buildings.

Introduction

Housing statistics are the numbers – often averages or ratios – used to assess policies and to predict housing outcomes and other effects. Some statistics are used directly in housing analysis, and indirectly to estimate effects in housing models. Some data are measurements which are rarely used except in model estimation; these data primarily come from electronic data sets.

This article gives some general information and some that is specific to particular countries. Emphasis is placed on countries where the collection and estimation of statistics is most advanced, and among these, the English-speaking ones. This means that this article is indicative and suggestive, and not geographically comprehensive. Notably, developing countries are almost entirely omitted, as are about half the G20. Not all categories of statistics relevant to housing are covered, with demographics a notable omission. However, the information given indicates the range of possibilities and problems in housing statistics, especially for developed countries.

Commonly Used Housing Statistics

Statistics Giving the Volume of New Housing Built

The volume of new housing built is measured in terms of housing starts – that is, the start of construction – in many developed countries, including the United States, Canada, France, and Australia, and completions in others such as the United Kingdom. These statistics are a simple count, giving each dwelling – whether a one-bedroom apartment or a 16-bedroom mansion – the same weight. Obtaining even this count is problematic because housing production usually takes place on scattered sites so that its location changes from year to year, unlike the production of factory-made goods such as vehicles. Statisticians are apt to undercount if houses are built illegally or informally without obtaining proper permits or planning permission. Even in developed countries such as Canada this can be a problem. For example, a two-family house, which should count as two starts, might be disguised as one until building officials complete their inspections. In developing countries, this problem is exacerbated by the lesser reach of controls and the extent of informal building. Thus in South Africa, the only volume statistic apparently available is the number of low-cost subsidised dwellings completed or in progress, a statistic that is easy to obtain because of government subsidy records.

House Prices

House prices are important for assessing affordability and access, for information on the timing of peaks and troughs in the price cycle, and for modelling housing markets. A challenging problem is obtaining prices or estimating indexes which precisely portray the pure price change from one period to the next, without being affected by quality change or a change – in either type or location – in dwelling mix. For example, the National Association of Realtors' price of *existing houses* (see Relevant Websites) is the simple median price of all houses sold in the United States through Multiple Listing Services and is affected by a changing mix of dwellings; the Dutch Association of Real Estate Agents (NVM) also publishes median prices. In contrast, the US S&P/Case-Shiller house price indexes (see Relevant Websites), which are based on changes in prices of the same house (the repeat-sales method), are excellent indicators of pure price change, although their geographic coverage is limited to major cities.

In the United Kingdom, there are a plethora of price change indicators with broad geographic coverage. Two of these are provided by mortgage lenders using only their own data (Nationwide and Halifax) and are estimated for a standard house having a set number of bathrooms and other characteristics (the so-called hedonic method). Another is the Land Registry index (see Relevant Websites) which, on the basis of its method (repeat sales) and the coverage of its data, has a good claim to being the preferable index. A repeat sales index for the Netherlands is the Kadaster, published by the Dutch Land Registry Office. The Australian Bureau of Statistics (ABS) (see Relevant Websites), for its individual city indexes, uses a quite different approach based on sales prices in groups of suburbs. The grouping depends on the long-term price level and neighbourhood socioeconomic characteristics; the ABS has found this approach superior to its previous one which used structural characteristics and physical location in place of long-term price level.

These indexes are all based on information on transactions – and, in the case of repeat sales, only a subset of transactions – which may be a biased sample of the stock of all houses. This may lead to biased estimates of the change in the underlying value of all houses, especially at turning points in the price cycle. For example, just after the price peak, the drop in the price of houses actually sold may be less than the drop in the value of all houses, if vendors are not willing to adjust their price down and those who actually sell are the lucky ones selling to purchasers who are forced to move for job or other reasons. Indexes based on appraised values of the stock will not be affected by this problem, although they have problems of their own. A special problem in repeat sales indexes is the likelihood that cheap houses or houses bought to be flipped (i.e., for quick capital gain, often following renovation) will tend to be overrepresented among houses selling twice, biasing indexes based on them.

Which index is actually preferable will also depend on details of the data cleaning and sample selection and on the user's purpose – for example, analysis using small area data may need to use a median price index because other indexes are unavailable for such areas. Over long stretches of time, the index chosen will usually make little difference.

Price indexes are also published for 'new houses'. Some of these adjust for quality change by pricing the same model in adjacent periods. Problems may arise when builders change their models frequently because it may be difficult to distinguish between a pure price change and a change resulting from different characteristics. Builders in some markets disguise price increases by introducing a new model only slightly different from the previous one but at a substantially higher price; standard price survey methods tend to attribute the price increase to the inconsequential model change. In fact, assessment of Statistics Canada's (SC) new housing price index (see Relevant Websites) indicated that price increases it showed for some cities were distinctly lower than actual; as a consequence the method was changed to incorporate hedonic methods, as well as comparisons of project homes. The ABS' project homes index uses fundamentally the same method as that used previously by SC.

Housing analysts should be wary of using the consumer price index (CPI) component for the annual costs of homeownership to compare these costs in different countries. Conceptually different measures are used in different countries (see Relevant Websites) (Diewert et al., 2009).

Rents

Rent indexes are required for the construction of a consumer price index, which in turn is usually the basis for the reported inflation rate. For EU countries, rent indexes used for CPIs (called 'rent actually paid') are apt to be heavily affected by nonmarket rents in the social housing sector. (However, a warning is necessary because the CPI for EU countries reported by the European Central Bank is quite different in weighting and certain other respects from the CPI in the United States and Canada. In fact, in the case of the United Kingdom, the retail price index (RPI) is conceptually similar to the US CPI.) Data for 2000–04 are given in the very useful Federcasa, Italian Housing Federation (2006) (see Relevant Websites). This source also has a table showing average rents in 2004 for the two segments, market housing and social housing. Privately produced indexes for market rentals are sometimes available (e.g., see Relevant Websites), but these are of uncertain quality.

In the United States and Canada, the overwhelming majority of rental units are market units. Rents used to estimate the rent component of the CPI are collected from a random sample of units; rents are observed for the same unit in successive periods. In principle, this should result in unbiased estimates of rent change, but alternative estimates (see Relevant Websites) (Diewert et al., 2009) indicate that the US rent component understates rent changes. Among the likely reasons for this is the possible underreporting of rent change when there is tenant turnover and problems in splicing new or newly converted units into the sample. The view that there is downward bias in Canada is so widely held that analysts commonly use mean rents from Canada Mortgage and Housing Corporation's (CMHC) rental survey instead of the CPI rent component.

Input Prices

Inputs into housing include land and construction. Directly observed 'land prices' are often unavailable; for instance, they are not among the housing statistics given in Federcasa, Italian Housing Federation (2006). This is partly because land plays little role in national accounts and the latter were the frameworks for government-produced statistics in the early years of statistics agencies. Land prices are sensitive to zoning (in the United Kingdom, 'planning permission') which determines what buildings are permitted on a site. If many housing units are permitted, a given amount of land will tend to be worth much more than if only one unit is permitted. Land prices are also sensitive to location: Land for housing close to workplaces and in a desirable neighbourhood tends to be worth more than land further away.

Prices for land are available for the United Kingdom, prepared by its national office responsible for valuation (referred to as 'property assessment' in some other countries). These prices are estimates – based on land sales – by locality, of the typical value of development land with planning permission, serviced up to its borders, and with other specified characteristics (see Relevant Websites). The availability of these price data in the United Kingdom may stem from the fact that, unlike in many other countries such as the United States, (a) property assessment is performed by a federal agency and (b) land is frequently owned separately from the structure on it. Elsewhere, land prices sometimes are derived as a residual – property value net of an estimate of structure value – using, respectively, house price indexes and construction cost indexes. For example, US land price indexes derived in this way are available online (see Relevant Websites). In Canada, price indexes for land for new low-rise housing are available as a by-product of the production by Statistics Canada (see Relevant Websites) of the new housing price index.

'Housing construction costs' have three components: wages, material costs, and profit. A challenge in estimating a wage index is determining the weight each trade should be given and measuring actual wages paid rather than simply union rates. There is similar difficulty in determining a material index; in boom times actual prices may be higher than quoted prices because of the scarcity of materials and in bad times there may be discounts below list. Perhaps the most difficult component to measure (and weight, if included in an overall input index) is profits, because profits tend to go up in good times – and are higher relative to wages and material costs – and fall in bad times. If profit is given a fixed weight, or plays no role at all in an input-based construction cost index, the latter will tend to understate changes in construction costs. This is illustrated in the muted reflection of the house price boom seen in the movements in residential construction cost indexes of almost all European countries, given in Federcasa, Italian Housing Federation (2006: Table 4.5).

A better alternative is a housing construction cost output index. This is a price of a specified new house (or apartment building) excluding land (discussed earlier in the section 'House Prices' for Canada and Australia). The UK index in Federcasa, Italian Housing Federation (2006: Table 4.5), is of this type.

Homeownership and Associated Statistics

Sustainable homeownership is usually regarded as a favourable housing outcome and, in any case, the 'homeowner percentage' is an important housing indicator. Care should be taken in comparing ratios between different countries, because of the variation in rights, level of security, and equity embodied in different tenure forms. At one end of the scale is a house owned without any debt against it, but many homeowners have a mortgage and the owner's rights are dependent on keeping up mortgage payments. Some houses rest on land which the homeowner does not own. In China, the government is the landowner. In the United Kingdom, the ownership of a flat generally means owning a long lease. In the case of dwelling units owned under condominium or strata title, common in North America, the owners of units in a condominium determine as a group what changes or repairs are made to common areas, and an individual owner must pay charges levied by the condominium corporation. In the case of an equity cooperative, as it exists in Canada and the United States, the nature of title dictates that a mortgage loan for a single unit is unobtainable; also, usually owners may not rent out their units. Shared equity units in the United Kingdom are owned jointly with the government in the sense that if the price rises, the government shares in the capital gain. All of these arrangements are normally classed as homeownership, so long as there is owner-occupancy.

Swedish cooperatives are essentially similar to North American ones, but the 'owner' owns, not a share associated with a specific unit in the building, but rather the right, which the owner may sell, to inhabit the unit. In some analysis and compendiums (e.g., Federcasa, Italian Housing Federation (2006), which gives owner-occupancy rates in

European countries), such units are not counted as owner-occupied. Nonequity cooperatives in Canada are social housing; the occupier cannot sell the right to own a unit and is not classed as a homeowner.

The 'down payments' (called 'deposit' in the United Kingdom) required for the purchase of a home may constitute a barrier to homeownership. Sometimes the ratio to house value cited in official statistics is the minimum ratio required for a government-provided or insured mortgage. There is often flexibility for households willing to borrow from other sources – the rise of subprime mortgages illustrates this. Statistics on mean down payments paid are rarely available. Information on typical down payments is sometimes given in terms of the 'loan'-to-value ratio – in percentage terms, this is 100 minus the down-payment ratio (see Federcasa, Italian Housing Federation, 2006: Table 4.12). The reported ratio may be the permitted maximum rather than the mean actual.

'Mortgage interest rates' and mortgage payments have major effects on housing market cycles and on housing affordability. Standard mortgage plans vary from one country to another and, in particular, the interest term varies, bringing about comparability problems among countries. For example, in the United Kingdom a standard mortgage has a variable interest rate, while in the United States the standard term is 30 years. The US homeowner (the mortgagor) is usually able to pay off the mortgage – commonly by refinancing – without penalty, while the lender is locked in. This asymmetry means that the interest-rate risk borne by the average owner-occupier is less – and the risk borne by lenders more – in the United States than in Canada, the United Kingdom, and in most other EU countries.

Representative interest rates rather than those with a set term are given at the site of the European Mortgage Federation (EMF). A note to a table of these statistics indicates that for most countries representative rates given are variable ones, but for the United Kingdom they are an average of fixed and variable rates. The International Monetary Fund (IMF) in its International Financial Statistics database (see Relevant Websites) gives mortgage rates; those for countries in the Euro area are defined on a consistent basis – for example, interest rates for mortgages, for house purchase, new business, where the rate is fixed for between five to ten years. This source also gives a rate for the United States, but not for many countries, for example the United Kingdom, Australia, India. The IMF data are free to researchers from developing countries but not to others, although there is a five-day free trial.

Monthly payments are lower and the household takes on more risk, if the mortgage is interest-only than if interest is combined with repayment of principal. The latter is the usual case in most countries, especially for owner-occupiers; it may be termed the annuity model. Also, the longer the period over which the mortgage principal is amortised the lower is the payment; typical is 25 or 30 years but it is shorter in France and many other European countries and longer in others (Federcasa, Italian Housing Federation, 2006: Table 4.12). Lunde et al. (2008) give examples showing the effects on required payments of different noninterest mortgage terms.

Housing Need Statistics

Households may be deemed inadequately housed if they live in housing for which one or more of the following is true: physically inadequate, overcrowded, unaffordable – that is, it takes such a large part of their income that too little is left over for expenditure on food and other items. If a person is homeless, he or she is also obviously inadequately housed, but standard surveys do not cover the homeless.

An indicator of physical adequacy is the existence of basic facilities; Federcasa, Italian Housing Federation (2006: Table 2.3), gives percentages of the dwelling stock with bath or shower, with hot running water, and with central heating. These may or may not operate effectively and safely. This is recognised in the American Housing Survey (AHS) report which, for example, gives the incidence of water safe to drink and the incidence of a recent water supply stoppage (US Census Bureau, 2008: Tables 2.4, 2.6). The state of maintenance is another indicator of adequacy. This may be given in terms of 'in need of major repair' with examples, as in Canadian data. Allowing less room for interpretation is the detailed US approach in which specific problems are investigated; for example, the United States reports the incidence of dwellings with broken windows and with exposed wiring.

The oldest indicator of overcrowding – and the simplest to measure – is the incidence of housing units with more than one person per room. This is given in Federcasa, Italian Housing Federation (2006: Table 3.8), for European countries, both for low-income and quite high-income groups. For the United States, this may be calculated from US Census Bureau (2008: Table 2.3) for all households and for those living below the poverty level. Despite its simplicity, this statistic's usefulness is damaged by differences in what is classified as a room: most countries count a kitchen, but some, for example France, do not. Both these sources also give the number of square metres (in the United States, square feet) per person, but only the average (i.e., mean) is given in the first source and only the median in the US source.

Controversial but still widely used to indicate affordability problems is the criterion that a household should spend no more than 30% of its income on housing; those spending more than this are defined to have a 'heavy financial burden', and the incidence is given in Federcasa, Italian Housing Federation (2006). In the United States, paying 31–50% of income on rent is called a 'moderate' burden; the number in this class may be calculated both for all households and for those with a low income from data in US Census Bureau (2008: Tables 2-13, 2-20). For Australia, a quite similar ratio for lower-income households is available in Australian Bureau of Statistics (2007: Table 18).

Indicators of various problems are sometimes combined to produce a category of households in housing need overall, but criteria vary so much by country that statistics on this cannot be taken at face value for comparison purposes. In the United States, those in 'worst-case need' are renters (owners are assumed never to be in worst-case need) whose income is below 50% of the area median and who pay more than 50% of their income for rent and utilities or live in severely substandard housing – if the unit has severe problems in any of five areas: plumbing, heating, electrical system, upkeep, and hallways (US HUD, 2005: Appendix B). In Canada, those in 'core housing need' have a problem in their current accommodation (an affordability problem – paying more than 30% of their income for housing – physically inadequate housing or crowding), and have an income sufficiently low that the local median rent for an unproblematic dwelling would be unaffordable. For England, physical attributes alone define a 'decent' home: one in a reasonable state of repair, having no serious electrical or other hazard, having reasonably modern facilities, and a reasonable degree of thermal comfort (UK Department of Communities and Local Government, 2006).

Errors in Statistics

Some statistics, such as rent-to-income ratios, are usually calculated from sample survey data. Such data are subject to sampling error and to error resulting from nonresponse and from respondent, interviewer, and survey-designer mistakes. The first of these – the variation which occurs in an estimate because of variation from one sample to another randomly drawn from the same population – depends on the characteristics of the sampling and is almost always reported (e.g., US Census Bureau, 2008: Appendix D); it may be used to construct a confidence interval for the reported statistic. More important are the other two sources of error, but they are difficult to estimate and assess.

Many of the statistics discussed in this article are not subject to sampling error but may be biased for a host of reasons illustrated in the discussion above. In addition, comparability between countries may be prejudiced by different definitions.

Searching for Statistics

For European countries, there are many sources. CECODHAS (see Relevant Websites), an organisation of social housing providers, maintains a European Social Housing Observatory and has some housing statistics online. It also has links to housing organisations and housing ministries. One of its members was involved in publishing *Housing Statistics of the European Union, 2005/2006* (referred to here as Federcasa, Italian Housing Federation, 2006). This volume not only includes a remarkable range of data for individual EU countries, but also has a substantial appendix giving the definitions used in various countries for housing concepts, for example 'room.' It may be supplemented by more recent statistics obtained from the country of interest. For example, the current number of new homes completed in the Netherlands is available online from Statistics Netherlands (see Relevant Websites). The European Commission statistics site (see Relevant Websites) has little of direct interest to housing analysts, but the European Central Bank site (see Relevant Websites) has, among its key tables, one giving both variable and longer-term interest rates for house purchase loans by country.

For countries worldwide, the United Nations publishes a housing bulletin with a limited range of statistics, confined mostly to housing stock, construction and household distributions, and without price or rent statistics. It covers North America as well as European countries (see Relevant Websites). The Organization for Economic Co-operation and Development (OECD) brings together a remarkably wide range of demographic, economic, and other statistics for countries including Japan (stats.oecd.org), but there is little immediately related to housing.

For an individual country, one place to start searching for housing and related economic statistics is the central statistical agency. In the United States, there are three such agencies. The Bureau of Labor Statistics (BLS; see Relevant Websites) produces labour and demographic statistics based on findings from the Current Population Survey and surveys of employers, and price indexes and expenditure statistics derived from the Consumer Expenditure Survey. The Bureau of Economic Analysis (see Relevant Websites) produces gross national product (GNP) and associated statistics. The Bureau of the Census (see Relevant Websites) not only conducts the decennial Census of Housing, but many other household and business surveys, some focused on housing – such as the American Housing Survey, the Residential Finance Survey, and the Property Owners and Managers Survey. The Board of Governors of the Federal Reserve System publishes data (see Relevant Websites) on mortgage lending, interest rates, and mortgage debt servicing costs as a percentage of income. Fedstats is a comprehensive website allowing users to search for statistics from the whole array of federal agencies (see Relevant Websites). Perhaps the most useful site is the Department of Housing and Urban Development (HUD) agencies (see Relevant Websites). This has links to housing statistics produced by other agencies and has free downloadable micro data sets from the AHS and other housing surveys, ready for use by multivariate data analysis software. This site also contains detailed tables related to HUD activities.

The websites of housing bodies of US states and local governments, especially larger ones, sometimes report statistics on government programmes. For example, see Relevant Websites. The first and most important of the US panel data sets is the University of Michigan's Panel Study of Income Dynamics (see Relevant Websites).

For the United Kingdom, a basic source is the Department of Communities and Local Government (CLG) (see Relevant Websites), where statistics on a range of housing topics from house building to homelessness are available. CLG also makes microdata, from its English Housing Survey and other housing surveys, obtainable – although not downloadable – from this site. The universities' site (see Relevant Websites) has these data in downloadable form, with access restrictions; some panel survey data are also available from this site. The Office for National Statistics (ONS; see Relevant Websites) produces GNP, other national accounts series, price indexes, unemployment, and other economic and noneconomic statistics. Many are published separately for the four countries (Wales, England, Scotland, and Northern Ireland) of the United Kingdom. The ONS carries out the General Household Survey which includes sections on housing tenure and accommodation. Scotland and Ireland governments also carry out household surveys. The Bank of England publishes statistics (see Relevant Websites) on mortgage lending and interest rates, and posts links to other sources, such as the Council of Mortgage Lenders.

Canada Mortgage and Housing Corporation (CMHC) makes available tables from *Canadian Housing Statistics* through its Canadian Housing Observer link (see Relevant Websites). It also provides Housing in Canada Online which allows users to produce custom tables, mainly related to housing need; this facility is especially useful for small geographic areas. Statistics Canada has an array of free detailed housing statistics from the Census on its website but its time series database, CANSIM, microdata from the Household Expenditure Survey – which contains quite rich housing data – and other surveys are available free only through university websites. Panel data are available only on application and at special centres. The Bank of Canada (see Relevant Websites) publishes detailed mortgage interest rate series, as well as new and resale house price indexes.

For Australia, perhaps the most efficient search route would start at the Australian Housing and Urban Research Institute's site (see Relevant Websites). Most housing information links are to data produced by the Australian Bureau of Statistics (see Relevant Websites); the Reserve Bank of Australia also is a source on the AHURI site.

See also: Access and Affordability: Developed Countries; Cooperative Housing/Ownership; Econometric Modeling; Forecasting in Housing Research; Home Ownership: Economic Benefits; Home Ownership: Non-shelter Benefits; Homelessness: Measurement Questions; House Price Indexes: Methodologies; House Price Indexes; Housing Indicators; Land Owners; Maintenance and Repair; Mortgage Choice: Behavioural Finance; Mortgage Insurance; Mortgage Market Functioning; Rights to Land Tenure; Simulation Models for Housing Analysis; Small-Area Spatial Statistics; Tenure as an Institution.

References

Australian Bureau of Statistics (2007) Housing Occupancy and Costs. http://www.abs.gov.au/AUSSTATS/abs@.nsf/Lookup/4130.0.55.001Main+Features12005-06?OpenDocument or follow the link at http://www.ahuri.edu.au/housing_information/free_housing_data/ (accessed August 2009).

Crone TM, Nakamura LI, and Voith RP (2009) Hedonic estimates of the cost of housing services: Rental and owner occupied units. In: Diewert WE, Balk BM, Fixler D, Fox KJ, and Nakamura AO (eds.) *Price and Productivity Measurement, Vol. 1: Housing* ch. 4. Bloomington, IN: Trafford Press.

Diewert WE, Balk BM, Fixler D, Fox KJ, and Nakamura AO (eds.) (2009) *Price and Productivity Measurement, Vol. 1: Housing*. Bloomington, IN: Trafford Press. wwwindexmeasures.com (accessed August 2009).

European Monetary Federation (2008) Hypostat 2007: A Review of Europe's Mortgage and Housing Markets. http://www.hypo.org/Objects/6/Files/Hypostat%202007%20-%20light%20version.pdf (accessed August 2009).

Federcasa, Italian Housing Federation (2006) Housing Statistics in the European Union 2005/2006 (Ministry of Infrastructure of the Italian Republic), p. 142. www.federcasa.it (accessed August 2009).

Lunde J, Scanlon K, and Whitehead C (2008) Interest-only and longer-term mortgages: Easier access, more risk. *Hypostat 2007: A Review of Europe's Mortgage and Housing Markets*, European Mortgage Federation, November.

UK Department of Communities and Local Government (2006) A Decent Home: Definition and Guidance for Implementation. http://www.communities.gov.uk/documents/housing/pdf/138355.pdf

US Census Bureau (2008) *American Housing Survey for the United States: 2007: Current Housing Reports, Series H150/07*.

Washington DC: US Government Printing Office. http://www.census.gov/prod/2008pubs/h150-07.pdf

US Department of Housing and Urban Development (HUD) (2005) *Affordable Housing Needs: A Report to Congress on the Significant Need for Housing*, p. 103. Washington, DC: HUD. http://www.huduser.org/Publications/pdf/AffHsgNeedsRpt2003.pdf

Further Reading

Crone TM, Nakamura LI, and Voith RP (2009) Hedonic estimates of the cost of housing services: Rental and owner occupied units. In: Diewert WE, Balk BM, Fixler D, Fox KJ, and Nakamura AO (eds.) *Price and Productivity Measurement, Vol. 1: Housing*, ch. 4. Bloomington, IN: Trafford Press.

European Monetary Federation (2008)*Hypostat 2007: A Review of Europe's Mortgage and Housing Markets.* http://www.hypo.org/Objects/6/Files/Hypostat%202007%20-%20light%20version.pdf (accessed).

Relevant Websites

www.abs.gov.au – Australian Bureau of Statistics

www.ahuri.edu.au – Australian Housing and Urban Research Institute

http://bankofcanada.ca – Bank of Canada

www.bankofengland.co.uk – Bank of England

www.federalreserve.gov – Board of Governors of the Federal Reserve System

www.bea.gov – US Department of Commerce, Bureau of Economic Analysis

www.bls.gov – US Bureau of Labor, Bureau of Labor Statistics

www.cmhc-schl.gc.ca – Canada Mortgage and Housing Corporation

www.cbs.nl – Centraal Bureau voor de Statistiek

www.communities.gov.uk – Department for Communities and Local Government

www.esds.ac.uk – Economic and Social Data Service

www.ecb.int – European Central Bank

http://epp.eurostat.ec.europa.eu – European Commission Eurostat statistics

www.hypo.org – European Mortgage Federation

www.housingeurope.eu – CECODHAS Housing Europe

www.fedstats.gov – Fedstats

www.huduser.org/portal/ – US Department of Housing and Urban Development (HUD), Department of Policy Development and Research

www.imfstatistics.org/imp – International Monetary Fund (IMF) International Financial Statistics

www.indexmeasures.com – Index measures

www.voa.gov.uk – Valuation Office Agency

www1.landregistry.gov.uk/houseprices/ – Land Registry, house prices

www.lincolninst.edu/subcenters/land-values/ – Lincoln Institute of Land Policy, Land and Property Values in the US

http://lahd.lacity.org – Los Angeles Housing Department

www.realtor.org – National Association of Realtors, US

http://psidonline.isr.umich.edu – Panel study of income dynamics, US

www.findaproperty.com – Find a Property

www2.standardandpoors.com/home/en/us – Standard & Poor's Benchmarks, Research, Data and Analysis

www.statcan.gc.ca – Statistics Canada

www40.statcan.gc.ca/l01/cst01/manuf12-eng – Statistics Canada's new housing price index

www.statistics.gov.uk – UK National Statistics

www.unece.org – United Nations Economic Commission for Europe

www.census.gov – US Census Bureau

Housing Subsidies and Welfare

P King, De Montfort University, Leicester, UK

© 2012 Elsevier Ltd. All rights reserved.

Glossary

Conditionality The application of certain conditions to the receipt of welfare support.
Demand-side subsidy Subsidy provided to individuals to allow them to purchase housing in a market, which therefore encourages the demand for housing.
Merit good Goods which society believes individuals should have but which some individuals decide not to buy.
Subsidy An explicit or implicit flow of funds initiated by government activity, which reduces the relative cost of housing production or consumption below what it otherwise would have been.
Supply-side subsidy Subsidy provided to housing providers which encourages the supply of new housing or the improvement of existing stock.
Welfare The well-being, happiness, and flourishing of individuals and groups; financial and material support.

Introduction

Housing finance, as households in countries as varied as Ireland, Spain, the United Kingdom, and the United States have discovered since 2006, can seriously damage your wealth. The manner in which banks lent to households and then sold their debts to other institutions created a cat's cradle of connections which eventually triggered the collapse of global financial markets and pushed many economies into the most serious recession in over 80 years. So we can certainly argue that housing finance has not done much to further human welfare in the first decade of the twenty-first century.

But housing finance is clearly essential in enhancing welfare at both a collective and an individual level. Without the necessary finance, no household can gain or maintain a dwelling of the requisite quality. It is finance which allows households to afford good-quality housing, and in that sense it is a basic prerequisite for our individual welfare and for the more general well-being of society as a whole.

This article discusses the relationship between housing finance and welfare by looking at the nature of welfare and then what purpose housing finance has. Housing is described as a merit good and linked to the level of knowledge we are capable of requiring about our own housing need. This discussion is then linked to the appropriateness of various forms of subsidy and government intervention.

What Is Welfare?

Welfare can be defined in two distinct ways. First, we can suggest that it relates to the well-being, happiness, and flourishing of individuals or groups. But, second, we can also define welfare as the means by which this state is attained or maintained. Hence, it can relate to specific financial or material support offered to individuals and groups. So, welfare can relate to both an outcome and a means of achieving that outcome. The latter process is often referred to as welfare provision.

This suggests that we can see welfare as a quality within individuals – their need to flourish, be happy, and so on – as well as a set of institutional arrangements that seek to create, enhance, or maintain that quality. It suggests that resources are necessary for welfare to be attained and maintained and so we cannot ever fully separate the quality from the means of achieving. These means may well come from the household's own resources. They flourish through using their own income and through caring and nurturing each other. Welfare in this sense is something internal to the household.

However, welfare is not merely a matter for the individuals concerned. This is because there may be some who, for whatever reason, fail to flourish or maintain themselves adequately. This failure is not only a matter for them, but might have wider societal effects in terms of the spread of disease, a higher incidence of crime, as well as impinging on the moral sentiments of other members of society who are concerned that some of their fellow citizens are homeless or in poverty.

So welfare is as much a societal concern as it is an individual one. Hence, all states, to a greater or lesser extent, provide some form of financial or material assistance to some, or even all, of their citizens. John Hills suggests that there are five reasons for the state provision of welfare. First, the state seeks to relieve poverty and redistribute income to the long-term poor. Second, the state provides social insurance for all against long-term illness, unemployment, early retirement, family breakdown, and so on. Third, the state can redistribute income to particular groups with greater needs, be they medical, familial, or related to disability. Fourth, the state can act as a type of savings bank, smoothing out income levels over the life cycle. Households can be taxed and this money used to provide them with residential and health care. Fifth, the state can step in where the traditional family structures fail, as in the case of divorce and lone parenthood. So states are not just concerned with providing a safety net or dealing with emergencies, but can seek to offer security for all.

We should see welfare, therefore, as a combination of the use of a household's own resources and those of the state and the voluntary sector. The exact combination of the three will differ depending on the particular resources of the household as well as their place in the life cycle. This is the context in which we should view the purpose of housing finance.

What Is the Purpose of Housing Finance?

Put simply, housing finance is what allows for the production and consumption of housing. It refers to the money we use to build and maintain the nation's housing stock. But it also refers to the money we need to pay for it, in the form of rents, mortgage loans, and repayments.

There is a tendency to think that housing finance is all about government subsidies. But, the majority of households in the United Kingdom, the United States, and parts of Europe are owner-occupiers who pay for their housing from their own income. Therefore, much of housing finance is obtained from private financial institutions on the basis of a household's proven or claimed income. Indeed, the vast majority of housing finance is provided in this manner: by financial institutions offering finance at commercial rates within a competitive market.

But housing has two further qualities which are important to any discussion on welfare. First, housing is a store of wealth, and thus it is an asset that can be used by its owners. Individuals can, and do, tap into this wealth in order, say, to set up a small business, to pay school and university fees for their children, or to enjoy their retirement. Many households use their housing wealth to enhance their welfare through non-housing-related activities. But, also, these assets can be passed on to the next generation, creating what might be seen as a cascade effect of housing wealth within families. This may ensure that these households are able to provide for themselves, but it might also widen inequalities between those who inherit housing wealth and those who do not.

Second, housing is a very expensive commodity. It takes a considerable proportion of our income over a long period of time. Buying a house with a mortgage commits us to repayments over several decades, and our housing costs are often the largest item in our household budget. The long-term nature of this commitment also introduces a degree of uncertainty in that our circumstances may change; for instance, we may lose our job or become unable to work at all due to illness. Also, we are prey to changes in the financial markets, which may increase our repayments to a level we cannot afford.

One reason that housing is so expensive is because we require housing that meets particular standards. We are not concerned merely with housing of the most basic standards but that which also fulfils our expectations and aspirations. We wish to lead fulfilling lives in a civilised environment that allows us to attain our full potential. This suggests that both our notion of welfare and the level of housing necessary to achieve it are relative to our expectations. Hence, issues of housing finance often go beyond the basic level of provision.

Quality and Access

Yet, on one level housing could not be more basic. It is one of the most important items that we human beings need. There are many things that we would find difficult, if not impossible, to do without housing. We might find it hard to find and keep a job, to learn, to maintain our health, to vote, to claim benefits we are entitled to, and to initiate and maintain stable relationships.

But just because something is important, this does not mean it is always available. Like most commodities, housing comes with a price tag attached. If we want decent housing, we have to pay for it. And it follows, broadly speaking, that the better the standard of housing we want, the more it will cost us. Therefore, as standards rise, so does the cost.

One of the most important issues, then, is how we can afford the sort of housing that we want. We could say that this is simply a case of matching up our income with our aspirations and expectations, and buying or renting the best dwelling we can afford. This may be fine for those on reasonable incomes, but not for those on low incomes. Many households lack a sufficient income to provide them with a dwelling that meets their expectations. It may well be that they could find housing of some sort, but this might not be of a standard that they, or the society of which they are a part, find acceptable.

This implies that two issues are of supreme importance. The first is quality. We are not content with just any type of housing; we want good-quality housing that allows us to live a civilised and healthy life. We therefore require housing that conforms to a modern standard of amenity. This standard, of course, is a relative one, in that it depends on general expectations that exist here and now. It is no good saying that households elsewhere in the world manage with less or that our grandparents were brought up without central heating and modern appliances.

The second issue follows on from this and is about access. We might readily agree on what constitutes a good-quality dwelling for us here and now. We can describe the particular amenities and standards that the modern dwelling should have. But that does not mean that everybody has such a dwelling. Many households might not be able to afford one.

There is a clear trade-off between quality and access, in that, generally speaking, the higher the quality of housing, the fewer the number of people who are able to gain access to it. Quality comes at a cost, and this limits access. There is, then, a gap that needs to be filled between the aspirations people have for good-quality housing and their ability to access it because of a lack of income. This is where state provision comes in, by acting as a bridge over this gap.

Therefore, the true role of housing finance is to ensure that all citizens gain access to good-quality housing. For many, this will be possible using their own resources to fund a mortgage in the private sector. But for some, this will not be possible, and their welfare will be jeopardised were not some form of state provision available to assist them.

Housing as a Merit Good

However, there is an argument which suggests that the problem is not merely, or even necessarily, one of a lack of available finance. It can be argued that some goods and services are so important that their consumption ought not to be left to the decisions of individuals. Instead, society should seek to ensure that these goods are consumed at a particular level. The main reason for this is that it is for the good of the individual, and society as a whole, for this level of consumption to be achieved. Such goods are often described as merit goods and often include such items as health care, education, and housing.

The consumption of these goods benefits individuals, by making them healthier, better educated, and well housed. But there is also a benefit to society, in that healthy individuals do not pass illness and disease on to others and are able to play a full part in society; well-educated individuals can achieve their full potential and this will benefit the wider economy and a sufficient quantity of good-quality housing will enhance the environment and reduce social problems (such as antagonisms between ethnic groups caused by shortages and the need to ration access).

These benefits mean that society might decide to fund provision of these goods to a higher level than would occur if individuals were left to decide for themselves.

But there is another aspect to the merit good argument. As the benefits of high levels of provision accrue to other members of society, households may be unaware of these benefits. If we are currently healthy, we might not see the need to immunise ourselves against communicable diseases, especially if the treatment is expensive. Likewise, even though we are financially comfortable, we might choose to spend our income on things other than housing and so live in what many might consider unfit housing. Therefore, there may well be a discrepancy between what individuals wish to do and what society as a whole thinks is best, and this would apply regardless of the level of income a household currently has.

As society sees that there is considerable merit in consuming these goods at a higher level, it provides incentives. This may take the form of subsidising provision, even to the extent of making it available free at the point of use, as is the case with both health care and education in the United Kingdom.

Housing and Choice

What the merit good argument implies is that individuals may not always be the best ones to determine their own welfare. However, there is a considerable difference between the examples of merit goods we have given. While health care and education might be provided free at the point of need, this is not the case with housing. Housing may be subsidised by grants to landlords or allowances to households (or a combination of both), but there is no attempt to render the same comprehensive level of provision we find with education and health. This is arguably not mere coincidence but rather relates to the relative ability we have to make rational choices about the level of provision.

When it comes to health care, we can know that we are ill – we might be in considerable pain – but this does not help us determine the cause of our illness or the course of treatment that is necessary to relieve us. We can seldom rely on our past knowledge to assist us, and, even if we could, we would lack the expertise to treat the problem. Instead, we are forced to rely on an expert to diagnose and treat the ailment. But this is not all: The need for health care is contingent to circumstance and so our need for it is often unpredictable, in that we do not know when and if we are going to be ill. All of these issues create very difficult problems for comprehensive market provision. There may be a tendency for an underprovision in such systems, particularly among the poor who may choose, or be forced, to spend their limited resources elsewhere.

But the situation relating to housing is significantly different. Unlike our need for health care, our need for housing is permanent. We will always need to be warm, secure, and enclosed. What differs is not the need itself, but whether it is currently fulfilled by our housing. This creates a high degree of predictability, in that our needs are relatively constant and alter in ways that can be foreseen. This allows for a more regular pattern of provision as compared to the contingent situation that pertains with health care. As a result, housing is more readily understandable without the need for professional intervention. Because of these qualities of permanence and predictability we know we need it, that we always will need it and to what standard we will need it. What this suggests is that, for housing, decision making can be more readily devolved to the level of the household, and thus, generally speaking, housing is more amenable to choice than health care. This does not have to mean that we can build or maintain it ourselves, but that we have sufficient knowledge to set the parameters and determine what we need.

Like the merit good argument, this argument for choice does not depend on income. Housing is an expensive commodity and many, if not most, households will spend more in their lifetimes on housing than they would on health. Instead, what matters is the ability that individuals have to determine what they ought to spend and having the capability to do so when the need arises. Hence, the issue is an epistemic one: the greater the level of permanence, predictability, and understanding, the more decisions can be taken by individuals with the expectation that these decisions will be competent and rational and the required outcomes achieved. This is generally the case with housing, and this explains why the provision of housing is different than is the case with health care. This has important consequences for housing finance, or more particularly the manner in which governments might seek to intervene to support households.

The Effects of Housing Finance

Where governments provide financial support for housing, they tend to do it in one of two ways. First, governments may subsidise landlords to encourage them to build new dwellings of the appropriate standard or to improve their existing stock. This form of support is known as object or supply-side subsidies. Second, governments might seek to encourage the greater consumption of housing and they do this through offering demand-side subsidies. These take the form of housing allowances or vouchers paid to individual households according to a means test. Demand-side subsidies might encourage more building, but this is not necessarily the case.

These two forms of subsidies are underpinned by a number of assumptions which link to the discussions on welfare and the nature of housing. The use of supply-side subsidies links with the merit good argument by assuming that incentives have to be provided to ensure that there is a sufficient stock of high-quality and affordable dwellings. It is assumed that households are not capable of making the right decisions themselves and need the assistance of the state. This might be due to ignorance, but also it could be argued that there are structural impediments, such as inequality and discrimination, which are beyond the competence of individuals.

However, the use of demand-side subsidies takes a more benign view of individual competence. The key problem is not seen as a lack of knowledge, understanding, or even necessarily enough housing, but a sufficient income to purchase good-quality housing. The assumption is that individuals can and will make the right decisions if they are given the necessary financial support. As we have considered above, the knowledge that individuals need with regard to their housing circumstances is readily available to them and so they need only a limited form of support in order to achieve their ends. This view downplays the significance of structural factors and tends instead to focus on individual behaviour and the manner in which individuals can be encouraged or incentivised to act in particular ways.

What this suggests is that the provision of financial support is not neutral in terms of its effects on behaviour. This argument has come to the fore in debates over economic dependency and worklessness. There is the view that the provision of welfare creates dependency through the use of means testing which targets support only to the worst-off. Frank Field, a former welfare reform minister in the UK Blair government, has argued that means testing creates perverse incentives, particularly by discouraging saving, work, and honesty. This concern for the impact that welfare interventions have on individual behaviour has led to the consideration of introducing forms of conditionality into state provision, so that support is only provided if claimants meet certain conditions or commit to particular forms of behaviour. In addition, governments have sought to design welfare systems which incentivise certain types of behaviour. An example of this was the change in the UK Housing Benefit system after 2002 where private-sector households were given actual payments rather than the money being sent direct to their landlord. The logic behind this reform was that tenants would act more responsibly and be able to make choices in terms of their housing instead of taking their rent payments for granted. A further example using Housing Benefit in the United Kingdom is the proposal by the Coalition government in June 2010 to cap benefit payments to prevent households living in overly expensive dwellings at public expense.

A similar debate has occurred around the notion of time-limited tenancies for social tenants. The argument for this is that social housing in many countries is the only means tested at the point of entry. A household may be in severe housing need and so offered a tenancy. However, over the years, its situation may improve to the extent that it can provide for itself in the market. The subsidy embedded within the dwelling is therefore effectively being wasted. This can be seen as a particular problem in the United Kingdom, which allowed social tenants to purchase their dwelling at a discount. The result has been the loss of 2.5 million dwellings since 1981. The suggestion, therefore, is that tenancies only be granted for a specified period so that a further means test can be applied.

However, such a reform would itself have an impact on behaviour, as well as the nature of social provision itself. In terms of behaviour, we can speculate that individuals might alter their circumstances just as their tenancy is ending so as to pass the means test. But time-limit tenancies that ensure that only the most needy are helped will also mean a lack of diversity within social provision, with estates becoming even more polarised as places of economic dependency. So an attempt to introduce conditionality into social provision might actually have the perverse effect of encouraging even greater dependency.

Conclusions

This final point suggests that all forms of welfare provision will have an impact on behaviour, so that housing finance is never neutral in its effects. We may be able to state the purpose of housing finance fairly explicitly and link this to welfare. However, it does not follow that we shall achieve the expected outcomes or even that any particular intervention is actually beneficial. The key point here is the sheer complexity of the relation between welfare provision and individual behaviour, and the difficulty in predicting how individuals and groups will respond to incentives.

See also: Asset-Based Welfare; Health, Well-Being and Housing; Social Housing: Finance.

Further Reading

Barr N (1998) *The Economics of the Welfare State*, 3rd edn. Oxford, UK: Oxford University Press.
Department for Work and Pensions (2002) *Building Choice and Responsibility: A Radical Agenda for Housing Benefit*. London: Department for Work and Pensions.
Field F (1996) *Stakeholder Welfare*. London: Institute of Economic Affairs.
Garnett D and Perry J (2005) *Housing Finance*, 3rd edn. Coventry, UK: CIH.
Hills J (1997) *The Future of Welfare: A Guide to the Debate*, Revised edn. York, UK: Joseph Rowntree Foundation.
Kemp P (ed.) (2007a) *Housing Allowances in Comparative Perspective*. Bristol, UK: Policy Press.
King P (2009) *Understanding Housing Finance: Meeting Needs and Making Choices*, 2nd edn. Abingdon, UK: Routledge.
King P and Oxley M (2000) *Housing: Who Decides?* Basingstoke, UK: Macmillan.
Malpass P (2005) *Housing and the Welfare State*. Basingstoke, UK: Palgrave.
Schmidtz D and Goodin R (1998) *Social Welfare and Individual Responsibility*. Cambridge, UK: Cambridge University Press.

Housing Subsidies and Work Incentives

M Shroder, HUD-PD&R, Washington, DC, USA

Published by Elsevier Ltd.

Glossary

Budget constraint The whole spending power of an individual, given her resources and current prices.
Corner solution In economics, an individual's choice not to participate at all in the market for one or more goods.
Duration dependence Any tendency of a programme participant to be more (less) likely to continue participating as the length of stay in the programme grows.
Entitlement A benefit that citizens may claim as a right without the state having placed any limit on total spending for that benefit.
Guarantee The amount the state will spend in rent subsidy for a household that has no income from which it is expected to pay rent.
In-kind A benefit provided as a subsidy to a particular good, rather than in cash.
Income effect The change in an individual's readiness to consume leisure instead of market goods because the state has guaranteed payment of some part of her rent.
Reduced form An attempt to estimate the effect of one variable upon another without attempting to recover the parameters of the system of simultaneous equations that they are both part of.
Selection bias The error of estimating the effects of a housing programme without considering the unobserved characteristics causing an individual to participate in that programme.
Substitution effect The change in an individual's readiness to consume leisure instead of market goods because of changes in prices.
Tax rate or taper The amount by which the state reduces rent subsidy as a household's income rises.
Utility function In economics, the set of preferences determining an individual's choices among all alternatives.

Introduction

In most developed countries, housing assistance is a part of the larger structure of the welfare state, some parts of which reduce labour supply. In this article we discuss whether housing assistance does so as well. Arthur Okun introduced the metaphor of the leaky bucket to describe the common situation in which a dollar taken from the rich delivers less than a dollar's worth of benefit to the poor. One of Okun's four basic leaks is from changes in work effort induced by redistribution. Gary Burtless, reviewing a series of negative income tax (NIT) experiments, found that the implementation of the NIT in the United States would have caused the government to spend almost $2 in order to increase family incomes by $1, mostly due to higher transfers inducing reductions in labour supply among the assisted.

Fair assessment of programme effects is difficult. Housing assistance programmes usually target the most disadvantaged families in society. They were selected for assistance because they needed help. It is easy to confuse the effect of the selection with the effect of the programme. We first consider what economic theory predicts, then the methodological barriers to investigation, and finally the evidence relating to labour supply consequences of housing assistance programmes.

Theory

A Neoclassical Hypothesis

In general, a housing assistance programme fills the gap between the cost of decent housing and the amount the state expects a low-income household to contribute to its own shelter. In general, the amount of assistance is the higher of zero or

$$A = G - T(Y) \qquad (1)$$

where G is the amount the state will pay for a household with no income at all, Y is the household's actual income, and $T(Y)$ is the contribution function, which usually depends on Y.

The government typically sets G in response to housing market conditions and family circumstances, such as number of members in the household.

Disclaimer: Opinions expressed are the author's, and need not reflect the policy of the US Department of Housing and Urban Development.

The amount by which $T(Y)$ rises with a small increase in Y is the tax rate, or taper – the rate at which housing subsidies fall as income rises. In the United States, $T(Y)$ is a flat tax, as the tenant is expected to pay 30 cents of every dollar of income towards rent. In many countries the tax rate is graduated. For example, for UK households with less than a minimum income (more or less the basic social welfare payment), the housing programme has a tax rate of zero, but above that level benefit is withdrawn at the rate of 65 cents for each additional pound. The French housing tax is a marvel of complexity, varying between 0 and 37 cents on the marginal euro according to a five-factor formula. Most developed countries list the specific features of their programmes in OECD (2007).

Many economists and not a few noneconomists instinctively suspect that housing assistance receipt must reduce labour supply. Here we formalise that instinct; let the positive predictions that emerge from the following analysis form the 'neoclassical hypothesis'.

Suppose an assisted housing tenant is able to work. Her willingness to sell her time to an employer may change because a housing programme has both substitution and income effects.

The substitution effects are straightforward. If she gets no housing assistance, selling an hour of her time will yield her some nominal wage, net of taxes that include the benefit taper rates in other programmes. If, however, she receives assistance, her net wage will be reduced by yet another tax, representing the share of her income that she is expected to contribute towards rent. Obviously, this somewhat depresses her willingness to sell her leisure time to a potential employer.

Housing assistance also should have income effects. In principle, admission to one of the deeply targeted programmes guarantees the household the use of a standard-quality housing unit if the head of household has no income whatever. Even in the absence of a marginal tax rate on wages, the housing guarantee might make the client somewhat less interested in offering up her free time to the market.

Figure 1 gives a static view of leisure–goods trade-offs, with labour supply ('Hrs') on the X-axis and consumption ('Good') on the Y-axis. The individual has a utility function representing 'tastes and preferences' that govern her choices between consuming more market goods and having more free time, or leisure. Joining combinations of leisure and goods yielding equal amounts of utility forms indifference curves such as U and U' in **Figure 1**; when the agent's budget constraint reflects no housing assistance ('No HA'), her labour supply is A and her utility is U. When housing assistance is introduced ('HA'), the slope of the budget constraint becomes less steep because the housing programme tax reduces the net wage, and thus the slope; the guaranteed level of housing consumption raises the intercept. The agent's utility rises to U', but her labour hours fall to B.

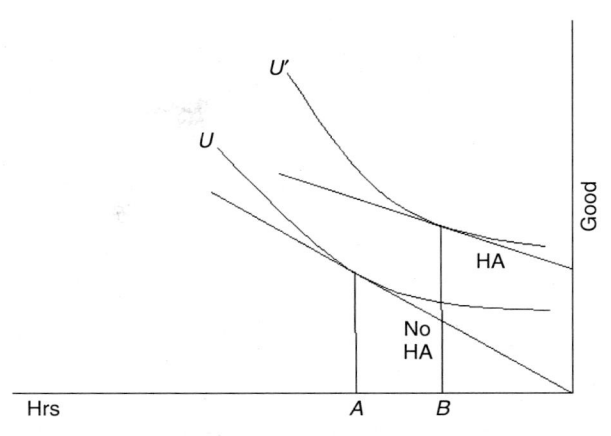

Figure 1 Static neoclassical analysis of labor supply effects of housing assistance program.
Source: Shroder M (2002) Does housing assistance perversely affect self-sufficiency? A review essay. *Journal of Housing Economics* 11: 381–417.

The neoclassical hypothesis, therefore, is that housing assistance programmes will depress a head of household's willingness to work in the short run. Although **Figure 1** presents the case of a marginal reduction in hours worked – possibly a case of little policy significance – one cannot exclude the possibility that shift in the budget constraint would lead some assistance recipients to a corner solution, that is, having no job. This case is depicted in **Figure 2**. An agent with the utility function depicted would work C hours if unassisted, but zero hours if assisted.

No reasonable housing assistance programme can readily escape the alleged negative consequences. To avoid an income effect one would have to stop helping people altogether. A programme without a tax or taper on benefits as income grows would assist everyone, whether in need or not, and tax everyone to pay for it. Some housing programmes have no taper up to a certain income Y^*, but provide no assistance at all above Y^*. These programmes have not escaped the dilemma, as the tax rate on $Y^* + 1$ might be 10 000% or more.

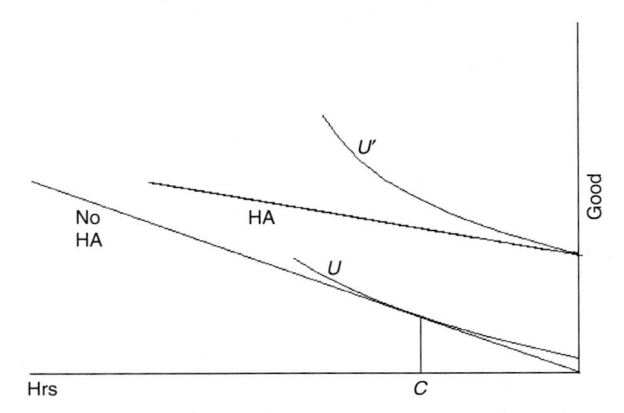

Figure 2 Static neoclassical analysis with corner solution.
Source: Shroder M (2002) Does housing assistance perversely affect self-sufficiency? A review essay. *Journal of Housing Economics* 11: 381–417.

The neoclassical hypothesis has two major theoretical weaknesses: treatment of assistance as an income supplement and neglect of selection effects.

Objection 1: In-kind character of programme. We have, up to this point, treated the assistance as an income supplement rather than as a commodity subsidy. This is a gross oversimplification; the income effect is particularly questionable because true housing assistance is not fungible. Michael Murray demonstrated in 1980 that most commodity subsidy programmes induce more work effort than equivalent cash transfer programmes, by stimulating the desire to consume more of the subsidised good with additional income. In this view, housing assistance should be modelled as a price cut to a particular good. The higher resulting real income might result in greater consumption of housing, greater consumption of other goods, and/or greater consumption of leisure. The leisure choice is indeterminate without further assumptions about preferences for consumption of other goods, which are likely to be heterogeneous.

The heterogeneity of assisted families can be considerable. Consider four cases:

1. Housing assistance might enable a parent to move away from a gang-infested area, where she need not monitor her teenager as closely. Perhaps that will lead to new employment. Or it might cause her to move to a gang area, where it is easier to use her assistance. If assistance is only available through residence in a housing project with a gang, it will be not only easier but also necessary. Perhaps that will cause her to quit her job.
2. Assistance might permit a parent to move out of the apartment where she has been living, doubled up, with her sister's family. Perhaps the reduction in background chaos will make job search easier; perhaps the increased privacy will make her feel more comfortable if she stops looking for work.
3. Suppose the head of household is caring for a sick relative, and works only enough to pay the rent. With assistance, she might stop working. But perhaps, with the rent mostly taken care of, she can get out of charity waiting rooms and into a full-time job.
4. A student recipient who is currently working part-time might be encouraged by housing subsidy payments to cut back on work hours so as to attend school full-time. Her schooling might or might not lead to full-time employment later on.

In short, so long as housing assistance is not an unconditional cash grant, the effect of housing assistance on labour supply, as a matter of either theory or practice, is ambiguous. The effect depends on which people are assisted, and how the assistance is delivered.

Objection 2: Rationing and selection effects. Housing assistance in many countries is not an entitlement, and even where it is theoretically an entitlement, as in Scandinavia, many eligible families fail to participate. In the United States, assistance is rationed to income-eligible households according to various local criteria by public housing authorities and project owners. Selection effects might mitigate any depressing effect on earnings and would certainly complicate its estimation. Blackorby and Donaldson first analysed the selection effect of a 'tagged' good in 1988. They showed that if the government cannot observe potential income, it can help ensure selection of the most needy into assistance by providing it in a form that is unappealing to those with higher potential income.

Many housing projects are unappealing to those who can afford better units. In the United States, housing vouchers are sufficiently unattractive to many landlords that a significant fraction of those who receive vouchers never use them; eligible families with the highest incomes and lowest prospective subsidies are least likely to use their vouchers. Thus, while receipt of assistance may suppress realised income, potential income may suppress receipt of assistance. The practical conditions of assistance may be such that more able workers leave or never enter the programmes.

A high marginal tax rate like the 65% charged to some tenants in the United Kingdom, for example, will on the one hand reduce labour supply from some tenants who remain in the programme but will on the other hand push other tenants out of the programme more quickly.

The use of long waiting lists or onerous admissions procedures as rationing devices would have a similar impact. People who were able to adjust to the housing market without assistance (e.g., by moving to another jurisdiction, by getting another or better job) would tend to screen themselves out of the programme. These forms of screening will eliminate the least desperate, who may include those most responsive to the potential work disincentives.

Methodological Issues

Empirical studies in this area might be subject to four different types of bias: bias from reporting error, selection bias, simultaneity bias, and general omitted variable bias.

Bias from reporting error. This is potentially fatal to certain types of study. The fact and type of housing assistance receipt are widely misreported by respondents, often in surprising directions. Researchers have to use survey data on assistance status with great caution. For example, in the 1993 American Housing Survey, the population equivalent of 2.235 million respondents informed their interviewers that they lived in public housing, which is explicitly defined in the survey instrument as units owned by a public housing authority. This is almost exactly double the true number. Thus, incorrect identification of assistance status is a threat to the validity of any study relying entirely on survey data.

Selection bias. Even if assistance status is correctly reported, selection bias may be difficult to control, for several reasons. If two households look the same, according to the data that we observe, but one has assistance and the other does not, one cannot assume that the assistance causes any observed differences in behaviour, because the difference in selection into the assistance programme may be related to other behavioural patterns.

First, selection into housing assistance is likely to be highly dependent on locality. Local housing markets dictate the degree of competition for scarce assistance resources. Programme eligibility parameters also differ from one market to another, and local administrative preferences and procedures may determine in part which families rise to the top in that competition.

Second, many of the world's housing programmes effectively exclude the full-time employed, even those with low wages. In programmes that weed out workers with strong labour force attachment, the choices of the assisted may largely reflect the selection regime. Thus, the analyst who starts out arguing, as a normative matter, for treating the current clients of a programme differently may end up arguing that the programme should serve different clients altogether.

Simultaneity bias. This is related to selection bias, but in principle may be easier to control. As noted above, housing assistance may affect labour supply, but, also, employment success affects the use of housing assistance. If one wishes to measure the former but not the latter, one strategy is not to measure them at the same time. Assuming one has the other sources of bias controlled properly, one might model the effect of housing assistance receipt in the first period on employment success in the second.

General omitted variable bias. From a very large literature in labour economics, we know that employment varies with participation in other social programmes, which have their own incentives and disincentives; with a worker's human capital; with the demands of the local labour market; with the individual's connectedness to social networks; and with sex, race, ethnicity, height, accent, personal appearance, motivation, intelligence, and many other factors. Failure to control for these factors will generally bias measurement of the specific effect of housing assistance. As we saw above, it is improbable that the effects of housing assistance on employment are uniform across different types of recipients. Omitted variable bias will naturally be lower whenever a richer set of relevant explanatory variables is available, but is inescapable in observational data.

Empirical Results: United States

In 2002 Shroder summarised nearly two dozen studies with a bearing on the effect of housing assistance on labour supply in the United States, writing that a rather large literature had failed to confirm the neoclassical hypothesis in its purest form, and that "the distribution of results from these empirical studies is consistent with a true housing assistance/short-term employment effect of zero".

That summary is obsolete. Three major reports since 2002 have made it apparent that housing assistance in the United States has a net negative impact on labour supply. However, that impact appears to vary among subgroups, may change over time, and seems rather small relative to the amounts paid out in subsidy.

In 2006 Mills and colleagues reported on a demonstration in which nearly 9000 welfare families with children in six distinct locations were randomly assigned either to receive housing vouchers or not to receive them, at least initially. In principle, use of administrative data and random assignment to treatment group eliminate all of the biases noted above. After allowing for the effects of failure by some members of the treatment group to actually use their vouchers, and for the tendency of some control group members to obtain vouchers with the passage of time, the Mills group reports a negative impact on earnings of about $960 per household actually using a voucher in the first 18 months after random assignment, but the effect is not statistically significant in the following 24 months. During the period covered, the direct cost to the government of a voucher to a welfare family for 18 months probably averaged about $9000, so the measured loss to earnings is in the neighbourhood of 10% of the subsidy outlay.

In 2008 Jacob and Ludwig reported on the experience of roughly 42 000 families in Chicago, again assigned by lottery either to receive or not receive vouchers. The Chicago sample is much more diverse in some ways than the Mills sample, containing families who never received welfare or had no children, but the danger of generalisation from Chicago to the nation is an offsetting limitation. They find a negative earnings impact of about $328 per quarter, with negative effects tending, if anything, to increase over time. As average subsidy outlays in Chicago in this period were roughly $1700 per quarter, this would be consistent with measured loss of earnings in the neighbourhood of 20% of the subsidy outlay.

Also in 2008, Carlson and coworkers exploited administrative data from the Wisconsin welfare and food stamps programmes to track the employment experience of nearly 13 000 self-reported voucher recipients, who applied at least once for either the welfare or food stamps programmes, and created a comparison group of 30 or so nonrecipients for every recipient, using the propensity score method. They find a reduction in earnings of $858 in the first year of voucher receipt, relative to the comparison group, but just $277 in the fifth year following first receipt. The former number would be consistent with measured loss of earnings in the neighbourhood of 15% of subsidy outlay. Because most families with children do not use the voucher for more than 4 years, the fifth-year estimate is consistent with no permanent impacts of the voucher on the career path of earnings once a family has relinquished it.

Together, these studies seem to establish that the US voucher programme has a negative impact on the earnings of assisted families. The 'leakage from the bucket' seems to be in the range of 10–20% of subsidy outlays. Evidence on the growth or diminution of this leakage over time is inconsistent.

The best evidence available on the relative impacts of different forms of assistance does not indicate any difference between the impact of vouchers and of public housing. In 2003 Orr and colleagues reported on the experience of about 4600 tenants of high-poverty public housing projects in five cities who applied for vouchers in a special demonstration and were randomly assigned to regular vouchers, vouchers only usable in low-poverty neighbourhoods, or to nonvoucher control status. Roughly 5 years after random assignment, there was no significant difference in earnings among the three groups.

Empirical Results Elsewhere

Empirical literature measuring the direct labour supply effects of housing assistance outside the United States is scattered and surprisingly sparse. Evidence from social experiments like those reviewed above is nonexistent outside the United States. This is not the case for other types of social interventions. The author has found significant empirical literatures only for Australia and Scandinavia. Work disincentives have been discussed elsewhere, but so far as I can tell the effects have not been measured. We omit discussion of the very complex results of Bingley and Walker (2001) in the United Kingdom.

Australia

Australia combines an entitlement housing allowance programme with a rationed public housing programme. The cash assistance (income support) programmes, such as disability pension, unemployment benefit, and so on, are the passports to eligibility for the housing allowance programme. The housing allowance is withdrawn once entitlement to the underlying pension or allowance is zero, and the taper rate is the same as that applying to the pension or allowance. This arrangement avoids adding to the multiple stacking programme, but extends the income range over which high effective marginal tax rates can persist. The entitlement programme simply adds an additional guarantee to households already receiving cash assistance; the cash assistance programmes have their own tapers and the entitlement programme does not add to them.

The extant literature is primarily concerned with labour supply impacts of the public housing programme, where the basic tax rate is 25%. Hulse and Randolph write that both entitlement and public housing programme survey respondents are well aware of work disincentives in their respective programmes, but that only public housing tenants considered them serious concerns. Whelan (2004) finds some evidence that housing assistance reduces the likelihood that assisted tenants have any employment (like the corner solution in **Figure 2**) but no evidence that it reduces the choice of hours worked (like the marginal case in **Figure 1**). In his view the programmes do not have a "sizeable or substantial impact on labour market activity" because receipt is conditional on participation in other government programmes, which have their own, more serious, work disincentive effects.

Scandinavia

Table 1 is adapted from Nordvik and Ahren (2005). It shows the percentage of households receiving housing allowances and the percentage of GDP paid out in housing allowances in the four Scandinavian nations in 2002, and we have added the United States as a reference point.

Allowances are an entitlement in Scandinavia, but differences among these four countries are large.

Table 1 Households receiving housing allowances as percent of all households and allowances as percent of GDP in four Scandinavian nations and the United States, 2002

	Denmark	Finland	Norway	Sweden	United States
Allowance recipients as per cent of all households	21	20	6	36	4
Allowances as per cent of GDP	0.64	0.12	0.61	0.69	0.21

Source: Scandinavian data from Nordvik and Ahren (2005); US data from author.

Finland, for example, gave allowances to one-fifth of its population but in doing so redistributed only one part in 800 of its national income. This implies a very low guarantee, a very low taper, and therefore a very low impact on labour supply; housing problems would need to be widespread but very shallow to justify this programme. The other three countries were redistributing about one part in 150 of national income, with very different participation rates: 6% in Norway, 21% in Denmark, and 36% in Sweden. These figures imply high guarantees in all three countries, with a high taper in Norway and lower tapers in the other two. In Sweden, for example, the tax rate is graduated but never exceeds 20%.

We have found no analyses of impact on short-term labour supply, but several on the related question of longer-term dependence on subsidy. If assistance keeps people out of the labour market, absence from the labour market keeps them poor, and poverty keeps them in assistance, then we should expect to see duration dependence in the data, that is, households would be more likely to stay in assistance if they are already assisted.

To the extent that the neoclassical hypothesis applies anywhere in Scandinavia, it must apply with greatest force in Norway, but Nordvik and Ahren reported no evidence of a dependency culture in a data set comprising all assistance recipients with children. Attrition from the programme is high and they find no sign of duration dependence.

If Norway with its high guarantee and high taper generates no signs of duration dependence, it should not be surprising that Sweden with its somewhat lower guarantee and relatively low (20%) taper does not either. Chen (2006) found no indication of duration dependence and nothing to indicate that welfare traps should be a serious concern for the Swedish housing allowance system.

Housing subsidies, like other parts of the welfare state, might discourage clients from pursuing earned income. Current literature appears to indicate that the effects of housing assistance on contemporaneous labour supply are modestly negative. Findings on long-term effects on economic self-sufficiency are not entirely consistent, but appear modestly negative at worst and negligible at best. The modest size and heterogeneity of the labour-supply response may cause a lack of robustness in findings from studies based on observational data. Controlled experiments outside the United States would therefore be highly desirable.

See also: Access and Affordability: Housing Vouchers; Housing and Labour Markets.

References

Bingley P and Walker I (2001) Housing subsidies and work incentives in Great Britain. *The Economic Journal* 111(May): C86–C103.

Blackorby C and Donaldson D (1988) Cash versus kind, self-selection, and efficient transfers. *American Economic Review* 78(4): 691–700.

Burtless G (1986) The work response to a guaranteed income: A survey of experimental evidence. In: Munnell AH (ed.) *Lessons from the Income Maintenance Experiments*, pp. 22–59. Boston, MA: Federal Reserve Bank of Boston.

Carlson D, Haveman R, Kaplan T, and Wolfe B (2008) Long-term effects of public low-income housing vouchers on work, earnings, and neighborhood quality. *Institute for Research on Poverty Discussion Paper No. 1338-08*. July.

Chen J (2006) The dynamics of housing allowance claims in Sweden: A discrete-time hazard analysis. *Uppsala University Economics Working Paper No. 2006:1*. April.

Ditch J, Lewis A, and Wilcox S (2001) Social housing, tenure and housing allowance: An international review. *In-House Report 83*. UK Department for Work and Pensions.

Finkel M and Buron L (2001) Study on section 8 voucher success rates, volume I: Quantitative study of success rates in metropolitan areas. Abt Associates. November.

Hulse K and Randolph B (2005) Workforce disincentive effects of housing allowances and public housing for low income households in Australia. *European Journal of Housing Policy* 5(2): 147–165.

Jacob B and Ludwig J (2008) The effects of housing assistance on labor supply: Evidence from a voucher lottery. *National Bureau of Economic Research Working Paper 14570*. December.

Mills G, Gubits D, Orr L, et al. (2006) *Effects of Housing Vouchers on Welfare Families*. September. Washington, DC: US Department of Housing and Urban Development.

Murray MP (1980) A reinterpretation of the traditional income-leisure model, with application to in-kind subsidy programs. *Journal of Public Economics* 14: 69–81.

Nordvik V and Ahren P (2005) The duration of housing allowance claims and labour market incentives: The Norwegian case. *European Journal of Housing Policy* 5(2): 131–146.

Okun AM (1975) *Equality and Efficiency: The Big Tradeoff*. Washington, DC: The Brookings Institution.

Organization for Economic Cooperation and Development (OECD) (2007) *Benefits and Wages: OECD Indicators*. Paris: OECD.

Orr L, Feins JD, and Jacob R, et al. (2003) *Moving to Opportunity Interim Impacts Evaluation*. September. Washington, DC: US Department of Housing and Urban Development Office of Policy Development & Research.

Shroder M (2002) Does housing assistance perversely affect self-sufficiency? A review essay. *Journal of Housing Economics* 11: 381–417.

Whelan S (2004) An analysis of the determinants of the labour market activities of housing assistance recipients. *AHURI Final Report No. 70*. October. Melbourne, VIC: Australian Housing and Urban Research Institute, University of Sydney.

Housing Subsidies in the Developing World

A Gilbert, University College London, London, UK

© 2012 Elsevier Ltd. All rights reserved.

Glossary
Subsidy Financial assistance, either through direct payments or through indirect means, such as price cuts and favourable contracts, to a person or group in order to promote a public objective (*Britannica Concise Encyclopaedia*).

Introduction

Every government faces a shelter problem, particularly in poor countries where housing conditions have often deteriorated as a result of rapid urban growth and sometimes increasing poverty. In response, most governments have devised programmes to mitigate the problem. During the twentieth century, governments in developed countries adopted policies such as building public housing in an attempt to remove slums and these policies were sometimes effective. But, in developing countries most governments found the task of improving housing conditions beyond them. Too many people lacked decent accommodation, urban growth continued apace, and public resources were always limited.

Over the years, housing policies have taken a myriad of forms but most have employed the offer of some kind of subsidy. The state, international agencies, or charities have typically provided the subsidies but in housing and infrastructure the state has sometimes forced the private sector into subsidising the poor. Rent control, for example, effectively transfers resources from landlords to tenants and this was the most common policy adopted in the first half of the twentieth century. At a time when most urban dwellers were tenants, many governments felt that rich landlords should be obliged to offer cheap accommodation for the poor. Cross-subsidisation of services was another way in which the more affluent sometimes subsidised the poor. The rich paid more for water than the poor – although many of the latter did not benefit because they did not have access to public supplies of water.

Gradually, however, most subsidies came from the state and a common practice was to build public housing for rent. Governments allocated the housing to poor families who paid a highly subsidised rent. But, many governments also offered subsidies to middle-class people, offering them income tax relief on their interest payments if they would buy their own homes. Few housing subsidy programmes have ever been targeted very accurately.

No government has ever had either the funds and/or the commitment to provide subsidies to all those without adequate shelter. Inevitably, they sought cheaper ways of addressing the housing crisis. Many governments in poor cities responded in covert ways. Some simply encouraged the poor to build their own homes by allowing them to 'invade' public land. The vast expansion in irregular housing in the 'South' could never have taken place without covert governmental support and the subsequent provision of roads and public transport. More recently, the widespread practice of upgrading self-help settlements has usually been financed with a public subsidy and the full cost of providing essential shelter elements such as transport and infrastructure has rarely been charged.

This article will limit itself to a discussion of official housing subsidies and will concentrate on those ostensibly designed for the poor. It will begin by discussing government programmes to build public housing, so-called supply-side solutions, intended first for rent and later for sale, move on to the newer and currently more fashionable concept of demand-side subsidies, before concluding with a general discussion of how to direct and target shelter subsidies. The issue of rent controls and housing vouchers is discussed in article Rental Market and Rental Policies in Less Developed Countries.

Public Housing

Over the years, many governments in developed nations and particularly those in communist countries built a great deal of public housing. Until the 1970s, this housing was usually rented out and most was highly subsidised. Since the vast majority of poor and even middle-income families in the 1930s and 1940s were tenants, this was an obvious form of response. The priority was to improve general housing conditions and to remove families from dangerous and unhygienic accommodation.

Many governments transferred this approach to their colonies and the policy of building public housing was often continued when the latter became independent. Of course, few governments had sufficient resources to build public housing on a massive scale. Only petrol-rich nations such as Saudi Arabia, socialist regimes such as China and Egypt, and countries receiving massive influxes of refugees, such as Hong Kong and Singapore, managed to build public housing in large quantities. In Latin America, financial assistance from the United States under the Alliance for Progress allowed the development of some large-scale public housing programmes, and in new cities like Brasília, a great deal of public housing was built. In apartheid South Africa, the logic of racial separation underlay large-scale public housing construction, and by 1980, much of the urban black and coloured population lived in housing rented from the state. Elsewhere, however, and particularly in Africa and much of noncommunist Asia, government rhetoric greatly exceeded any achievement on the ground.

Most poor countries' public rental housing programmes were unsuccessful (see article Rental Market and Rental Policies in Less Developed Countries). The rents charged were too low, too many tenants did not pay their rent regularly and the estates were often managed inefficiently. Maintenance was poor and, in places, such as Cape Town, the stock was taken over by gangs. Few public housing agencies were financially viable and consequently had difficulty in maintaining the stock, let alone adding to it. Many governments began to seek ways to escape the increasing problem of 'sink estates'.

The majority began to sell off the accommodation, often at a large discount to the sitting tenants. The example of the 'Right to Buy' programme of the Conservative government of Margaret Thatcher, where half of the public housing stock was privatised, was copied around the globe. In Algeria, for example, all public housing was privatised after 1980. Such an approach was even adopted by most governments in former COMECON nations 'after their political realignments during the late 1980s or early 1990s' (UNCHS, 1996: 219). Much public rental housing was sold at a large discount, a clear form of housing subsidy and one that was often ill-directed insofar as many of the beneficiaries were no longer poor.

Subsequently, most governments built social housing only for sale. Increasing the rate of owner-occupation was now an almost universal creed and if cheap housing was to be built for the masses, they should be permitted to own it. This approach also lifted the problem of collecting rents out of the hands of the state and placed the onus of maintenance on the occupants. It seemed an ideal solution until this approach also ran into problems.

First, most governments lacked the resources to build many homes, particularly because typically the housing was heavily subsidised. Public housing, therefore, was able to accommodate only a small proportion of those with serious shelter problems, and the queues for social housing grew. Government options were further limited during the 1980s debt crisis. They faced the choice of increasing already stretched government budgets or of cutting the cost of shelter programmes. Not surprisingly, most opted for the latter and many relied increasingly on prefabrication and mass construction techniques to reduce costs. Unfortunately, building quality often failed to match expectation and corruption and political favouritism in the allocation of contracts to private builders worsened the problem. Many public housing agencies were accused of building official slums. In response, some eventually opted for an even cheaper method – providing serviced sites and leaving housing construction to the poor.

Second, long queues of potential buyers put pressure on public housing allocation systems. Those with political clout, public sector workers, or those from a favoured racial or tribal group gained privileged access. As often as not, the really poor lost out. Some governments sought fairer ways of allocating the housing. In Colombia, a mixture of despair and populism led the national housing agency to employ a lottery system in the late 1980s.

By the 1980s, the whole notion of public housing was being questioned. Mayo (1999: 41) summarises the criticism levelled at most of the schemes built in the 1960s. The majority "were small in scale, largely unaffordable by the poor, poorly targeted, and largely inefficient. Moreover they followed the typical paradigm of government housing programs at the time – relying on government to design, produce, and allocate the housing 'solutions' which contributed little to addressing the needs either of the poor or of the broader economy". Both USAID and the World Bank were advocating the privatisation of housing production and praising the virtues of the market. State housing programmes did not fit into the neoliberal agenda which now dominated thinking about how to manage the economy.

The international development agencies began to recommend a new approach. Since governments had proved to be poor administrators of housing development, more scope should be given to the private sector. Governments should limit their activity to improving the planning, financial, and regulatory environment. They should not build houses or even offer subsidies. Such an approach soon became best international practice and spread even to China: "the solution is to de-politicise the housing system and restructure it into one which reflects the market principle" (Zhang, 2000: 197).

Capital Subsidies

Since housing subsidies were discouraged under the new mode of thinking, any government wishing to continue this long-established practice needed to change their practice. A new market-friendly way devised to boost demand for social housing by offering subsidies to the poor and rely on the market to increase the supply of affordable private housing. The prototype model was developed in Chile and was a direct outcome of the introduction of Chicago school economics into public administration in that country. The military regime of Augusto Pinochet wanted to reverse the 'socialist' policies of the previous government and its attempt to build public housing in massive quantities through state companies. Despite its neoliberal economic agenda, Pinochet wanted to uphold the long Chilean tradition of subsidising housing for the poor. However, the new system had to be market-led and embedded in a much more competitive economic and financial system.

The new capital subsidy scheme began operating in 1977. All social housing would be built by the private sector which would respond to market signals and compete to produce an affordable choice of housing units. The government established a rigorous mechanism for targeting the deserving poor. Points were allocated to households according to their assessed level of poverty shelter needs and on their demonstrating willingness to contribute to solving their own housing problems. The test of the latter was their ability to save over a period of time; they were encouraged to open a savings account and they were awarded points on the basis of their savings record. The allocation system was transparent and immune from political influence.

The system was not an immediate success and, ironically, its best results were achieved under the democratic governments of the 1990s when a succession of social democratic governments began to boast that Chile was the only Latin American country that was managing to cut its housing deficit.

Gradually, the influence of the Chilean housing subsidy model spread to other Latin American countries: Costa Rica, Colombia, Ecuador, and Panama. By 1995, the South African government had also independently developed a similar approach. By the 1990s, most national and international development agencies recognised that the Chilean example constituted 'best practice'. The model embraced three key elements in the new development consensus: explicit targeting of the poor, transparency, and private market provision.

Effectiveness of Capital Subsidy Programmes

Capital subsidy programmes have provided large numbers of poor families with formal homes. Between 1994 and 2007, the South African government constructed more than 2.4 million houses giving them to needy households. The Chilean government distributed 1.4 million subsidies after 1990 and claims to have cut its housing deficit. In Colombia, the government allocated almost 1.5 million subsidies between 1991 and the first half of 2006.

Despite these impressive-sounding numbers, all three countries have found it difficult to reduce the size of the queue for housing subsidies. In Chile, the number of families opening a savings account, the entry point into the system, grew from 55 000 in 1984 to 1 530 000 by 1998. Given the number of subsidies being allocated annually, this implied an average waiting time of at least 15 years.

Do the subsidies reach the poor?

Chile, Colombia, and South Africa have all succeeded in reaching poor families but there are doubts about whether they have helped the very poorest. Initially, Chile's subsidy programme favoured many middle-income families, and during the military period, almost as many beneficiaries came from the top quintile of the income distribution as from the poorest. After 1990, targeting improved but some richer families were still acquiring subsidies. The high weighting given to savings in the selection criteria has prevented those living in the greatest poverty from gaining subsidies. The Colombians have also had problems in reaching those in most need. Too few subsidies initially went to households earning less than two minimum salaries and various changes have been made to the allocation points system over the years. At times, the changes have produced unexpected results, for example, when the criteria were modified to favour women-headed households, the number of such families increased spectacularly, raising the suspicion many families were pretending to have split up. In South Africa, however, the government claims that "over 92% of subsidies granted have gone to households earning less than 1 500 rand per month" (RSA, Department of Housing, 2001). The problem is that the government does not check whether families have declared their incomes accurately.

In Chile and Colombia, the prior savings requirement has made it hard for very poor families to acquire subsidies because they are too poor to save. This is why the South African government did not embrace a savings element in its housing subsidy programme, despite considerable pressure from the World Bank and USAID.

Another problem is that most subsidy holders need to acquire housing loans to buy a home; the result of governments reducing subsidy levels to stretch their limited resources as far as possible. To facilitate this, most governments have encouraged private banks to lend to the poor and to develop microfinance facilities. Unfortunately, few banks believe that lending to the poor is profitable and tend to favour the less impoverished. In Colombia, formal sector workers near the top of the subsidy range are the only people who can access credit easily and are, therefore, the group best equipped to use their subsidies. In South Africa, a famous social contract was signed at Botshabelo in 1994, which extracted a promise from the banks to support the subsidy programme. However, ever since, they have been widely criticised for not fulfilling their promise.

Quality of the housing solutions

Social housing schemes have always been the butt of jibes about the quality of construction and the new generation of homes has not been free of that criticism. In Chile, most of the homes are very small and the basic state house in Santiago in 1990 was only 34 m^2 in size. There have also been numerous complaints about the poor design, the thinness of the walls, and the quality of construction. The homes have suffered from 'premature deterioration' and the quality issue hit the headlines in 1997 when heavy rains badly damaged as much as 10% of the social housing stock.

In Colombia, some social housing projects have offered serviced sites when the builders have claimed to have built houses with all the necessary services. In Bogotá, the thousands of new subsidies allocated have provided families with proper homes although many are very small some apartments in high-rise blocks offer only 36 sq m of living space.

Initially, in South Africa, the average floor space was only 25 m^2 and houses had no internal partitions. In 1998, the government responded to complaints by increasing the minimum size of new houses, but only to 30 m^2. The quality of construction has also been widely criticised.

Location

Most social housing schemes have been criticised for their location. Too many homes have been built in areas far from the city centre and distant from work because the builders could not find better located land at an affordable price. Occupants of distant estates have been forced into long commutes with a consequent increase in their transport costs. Everywhere, social housing has been built in the least desirable areas; in South Africa, for example, most projects have been located close to the old Black or coloured areas.

Slums of the future?

In South Africa, some suggest that the subsidy programme is creating ghettos of unemployment and poverty. The poor do not have the money to maintain their property, let alone to improve it. And, in Chile, where more criticism is heard because the subsidy policy has been operating longer, many have complained about the quality of the social housing estates. Ducci (2000: 169) argues that "the housing programs are creating neighborhoods that deteriorate rapidly, where life is unsafe, and where lack of expectations is common". Deterioration has been hastened still further by the fact that few families have been able to move out of their new neighbourhoods.

The Role of Subsidies: General Issues

According to Mayo (1999: 39), housing subsidies can be justified "on the basis of their status as merit or public goods, or because of market or 'nonmarket' failures, or because of their capacity to increase the ability to generate income and wealth. ... This is especially the case regarding 'public features' of housing such as basic infrastructure services and property rights associated with secure tenure and transferable rights. Improving basic services and the status of property rights improves the flow of current 'housing services', enhances the future flow of those services, increases property values and hence household wealth, and generates actual or potential income."

However these observations prompt several questions:

Who should receive subsidies?

While it is clear that housing subsidies should go mainly to the poor, this is not what always happens even in developed countries. In the United States, enormous sums are provided in tax relief on mortgage interest which accrue mainly to the well off. Such subsidies make housing the poor more difficult, because tax relief subsidies are partially capitalised, raising housing prices across the city. The new system of capital subsidies at least offers more help to the poor although it does not help one large group of the population, those who rent accommodation. In developed countries, most housing subsidies are directed towards tenants but capital subsidy schemes only benefit those tenants who are willing and able to become homeowners.

Do housing subsidies offer the poor what they need?

Offering subsidies for housing takes resources that could be used for other purposes. The really poor need income supplements to pay for food, education, and health; arguably housing is a lower priority. Income supplements offer families the choice of what to do with the additional income; housing subsidies help to determine poor families' priorities. In some cases too, the really poor do not seem to benefit much from their housing subsidy.

Many new owners in South Africa cannot afford to pay the charges linked to their dwellings and unable to cover the cost of water, electricity, and property tax, they sell or rent out their property, and return to informal settlements.

How large should a subsidy be?

There is a clear trade-off between the size of a housing subsidy and the number of families that can benefit from a programme. Larger subsidies can offer very poor families decent standard accommodation, but in poor countries with severe budget limitations, few families will benefit. For this reason many programmes have opted for reduced subsidies and the new one-off capital subsidies have often linked subsidies with credit programmes. Any shortfall between the size of the subsidy and the price of the housing solution can supposedly be remedied by taking out a loan.

Unfortunately, it seems that obtaining credit is a major problem confronting the poor. Few private banks in poor countries are keen to lend money to poor people: the loans are relatively small and so are expensive to administer; much self-help housing is located in dangerous places and the individuality of housing design makes it difficult to value, let alone repossess. If they lend they will do so only if interest rates are higher than normal. When other institutions have lent at low rates, they have often led to the failure of those banks. But the poor are often reluctant to borrow at any interest rate. Many do not want to borrow money because they fear that the instability of their jobs, health risks, and inflation make borrowing over anything but the short term to be extremely risky. Insofar as they are prepared to borrow, their preferred sources seem to be family, friends, or institutional pension/employment schemes.

How much should governments spend on housing?

Few governments in poor countries these days spend much on providing shelter for the poor. Direct housing subsidies are limited in size and one of the motives for adopting this approach is to control government expenditure. However, it is still unfortunate that despite the growing popularity of targeting, more assistance is often given to middle-income families than to the poor. Sometimes this is the result of failing banking and finance systems, when the government bails out the banks and mortgagees, as in Chile in the early 1980s and Colombia in the late 1990s. Sometimes it is the result of the failure to claw back the benefits that higher-income groups receive from government investment through betterment or valorisation programmes.

Summary and Conclusions

In most countries in Africa, Asia, and Latin America, the urban housing problem is worsening because the number of urban households is increasing so rapidly, because little is done to control the cost of land and building materials and, in places, because the incidence of poverty is increasing. Governments are responding to the shelter crisis in a variety of ways, notably by improving service and infrastructure provision in self-help settlements. Often the supply of electricity and water comes with a built-in subsidy, although privatisation has sometimes reversed that tendency. What is now much rarer is for governments to build social housing.

It is difficult to regret the disappearance of public housing agencies given that they were faced by so many problems and produced so few homes. The targeted capital subsidy approach is generally an improvement although it is only likely to be successful in more affluent and better administered countries like Chile. But one key error underlies this policy; the obsession with owner-occupation. Since there may be as many as 1.5 billion tenants in cities across the globe, offering subsidies to the poor only if they become homeowners appears to be a misguided approach. It offers neither an environmentally nor a socially sustainable future.

Whether governments should offer subsidies for housing at all is an open question. Of course, many such subsidies have disappeared as a result of budget cuts, structural adjustment and economic recession. But, arguably, the most beneficial way to help the poor is to provide income supplements. Poor families can then determine their own spending priorities.

See also: Economics of Social Housing; Rental Market and Rental Policies in Less Developed Countries; Social Housing: Finance.

References

Ducci ME (2000) Chile: The dark side of a successful policy. In: Tulchin JS and Garland AM (eds.) *Social Development in Latin America: The Politics of Reform*. Boulder, CO: Lynne Rienner Publishers.

Mayo SK (1999) Subsidies in housing. *Sustainable Development Department Technical Papers Series*. Washington, DC: Inter-American Development Bank.

RSA, Department of Housing (2001) The South African Housing Policy: operatonalizing the right to adequate housing. Available online at: www.un.org/ga/Istanbul+5/1-southafrica.doc (accessed 24 October 2011).

UNCHS (1996) *An Urbanising World: Global Report on Human Settlements 1996*. Oxford, UK: Oxford University Press.

Zhang XQ (2000) Privatization and the Chinese housing model. *International Planning Studies* 5: 191–204.

Further Reading

Castañeda T (1992) *Combating Poverty: Innovative Social Reforms in Chile During the 1980s*. San Francisco, CA: Institute for Contemporary Studies Press.

Dewar D and Todeschini F (2004) *Rethinking Urban Transport after Modernism: Lessons from South Africa*. London: Ashgate Publishers.

Ferguson B and Haider E (2000) Mainstreaming microfinance of housing. *Housing Finance International* 15: 3–17.

Gilbert AG (2001) *Housing in Latin America. Institute of Social Development Discussion Paper*. Washington, DC: Inter American Development Bank.

Gilbert AG (2004) Helping the poor through housing subsidies: Lessons from Chile, Colombia and South Africa. *Habitat International* 28: 13–40.

Held G (2000) Políticas de vivienda de interés social orientadas al mercado: Experiencias recientes con subsidios a la demanda en Chile, Costa Rica y Colombia. *CEPAL Serie Financiamiento del Desarrollo 96*. Santiago.

Huchzermeyer M (2003) A legacy of control: The capital subsidy for housing and informal settlement in South Africa. *International Journal of Urban and Regional Research* 27: 591–612.

Mitlin D (1997) Building with credit: Housing finance for low-income households. *Third World Planning Review* 19: 21–50.

Pérez-Iñigo González A (1999) El factor institucional en los resultados y desafíos de la política de vivienda de interés social en Chile. *CEPAL Serie Financiamiento del Desarrollo 78*.

Tomlinson MR (1999a) From rejection to resignation: Beneficiaries' views on the South African government's new housing subsidy system. *Urban Studies* 36: 1349–1359.

UN-Habitat (2005) *Financing Urban Shelter*. London and Sterling, VA: Earthscan.

World Bank (1993) *Housing: Enabling Markets to Work, A World Bank Policy Paper*. Washington, DC: The World Bank.

Housing Supply

KD Vandell, University of California Irvine, Irvine, CA, USA

© 2012 Elsevier Ltd. All rights reserved.

Glossary

Elasticity (price) of supply The percentage change in housing supply initiated by a given percentage change in the price of housing stock or services. Inelastic supply is not responsive to price changes (zero elasticity in the limit); elastic supply is highly responsive (infinitely elastic in the limit).

Equilibrium vacancy rate The vacancy rate in a real estate market that represents 'equilibrium' in that it is not too low to cause abnormal price/rent increases because of insufficient space availability (a 'tight' market) or too high to cause price/rent declines because of excess supply (a 'loose' market).

Housing stock versus housing services The distinction is drawn because housing as a physical (tangible), durable economic good which provides a specific set of intangible services over time. The stock represents the physical good (land, improvements, location, condition, quality), that produces a flow of services such as shelter and comfort. The amount of stock is often highly specialised and is directly correlated with the flow of highly specialised services.

Low-Income Housing Tax Credit (Section 42) In the United States, the primary supply-side subsidy programme for the construction or rehabilitation of affordable rental housing. It involves a tax credit for a portion of the construction costs, which is then applied to lower rents to affordable levels for qualified households. Such tax credits are awarded by states to developers on a competitive basis, but are typically sold to institutions, such as corporations or banks, that can use the credits to offset taxable income from other sources.

Marginal cost of production or operation The cost to produce the next unit of stock for new construction or redevelopment (production) or to provide one additional unit of service per unit of time (operation).

McMansion A colloquial term that has evolved to mean a new very large home on a large lot in the suburbs with embellishment in its level of finish that mimics traditional large estates (e.g., baroque balustrades and formal circular staircases). Typically intended to be derogatory.

Merchant builder A person or a company who purchases a parcel of raw land and turns it into a group of houses for sale. The major functions are land acquisition and development, construction, financing, and marketing. Unlike most manufacturers, merchant builders take their product, a house on a lot, from its virgin state directly to the consumer. There are no middle men or dealers as, for example, in the automobile business.

Rent-seeking behaviour In economics, the economic incentive of an agent to exploit economic 'rents' (i.e., excess profits) generated through market inefficiencies and noncompetitive conditions. An example would be a large landlord who controls most of the housing stock in a particular market or a builder who obtains unique concessions from local government which enhance the profitability of his project.

Spec building In real estate, construction of buildings in anticipation of future purchase. Not build to suit. Constitutes higher risk to the developer, but tends to be common in lower-priced new home subdivisions which have relatively homogeneous units and when there is a high demand velocity.

The 'American Dream' A term often used in the United States to mean achieving the goal of homeownership, which is assumed to provide attendant advantages, such as wealth accumulation, higher-quality neighbourhood environments and public amenities such as schools, and greater political stake in a community. The recent financial crisis has created a reappraisal of this definition.

Introduction

This article will deal with the 'supply side' of the housing market, that is, the production (and destruction) of housing services and stock over time. No understanding of the housing market could be complete without a study of the supply side, for it represents literally one-half of the factors influential in determining house prices/rents and vacancies and housing conditions over time (the other half being those on the demand side).

We shall first define 'housing supply' in a formal sense useful for providing a framework for any housing market analysis in the section 'What Is Housing Supply'. In the section 'Why Is Housing Supply Important?', we will identify why, when, and in what context housing supply can be particularly important. The section 'An Historical Perspective on Housing Supply' will observe housing supply in a historical context, tracing supply conditions over time and their implications for the market. The factors that can be influential in affecting the type and volume of housing supply being produced over time will be discussed in the section 'What Else Influences Housing Supply?'.

We then will turn to detailed discussions of some of these different factors and dimensions of housing supply. The section 'Inelastic versus Elastic Supply' will examine one of the most important ones: whether or not a local market is supply 'elastic' or 'inelastic', that is, whether the production of new housing stock is quickly and adequately responsive to additional demand in the market due to population growth, higher income, or changing tastes, or whether instead new housing supply is 'sticky' for one reason or another such that it takes a long time before market supply responds to new sources of demand. The next dimensions of supply analysed in the section 'Owned versus Rental and Market-Rate versus Subsidised versus Public Housing Supply' are the determinants of new housing meant for renters versus homeowners and that supply produced to be sold or rented 'at market' (i.e., at competitive market rents or sales prices), versus 'subsidised' (i.e., provided with the assistance of some financial aid from government or the for-profit or non-profit sectors), versus 'public' (i.e., produced and/or owned by a public-sector entity). Then in the section 'Who Are the 'Suppliers'? The Homebuilding and Multifamily Development Industries', we look into the institutional structure of the supply side of housing markets, specifically the homebuilders and multifamily developers, and implications for market conditions, especially demand responsiveness, price/rent levels, their adjustment, and vacancies. Finally, we draw international comparisons between the structure of the supply side of the market in the United States and that internationally in the section 'International Comparisons: Developing versus Developed Economies'. The section 'Conclusions and Prognosis for the Future' concludes and provides a prognosis for the likely evolution of housing supply.

What Is Housing Supply?

To most people, the word 'housing supply' means simply the total stock of housing units in the local market, or more frequently 'homebuilding', or the construction of new units, both single- and multifamily, as households are added to the local market. However, from an economic perspective, the 'supply side' of the market means much more. Yes, supply can mean the stock of units or flow of the production of new units. But it also matters 'what' existing or new units. What price or rent range distribution? What age? What sizes and design characteristics? What amenities? What quality levels? What locations? Supply can also mean changing the character of 'existing' units through additions, modernisation, rehabilitation, renovation, redevelopment, and other capital expenditures – or on rare occasions, the 'relocation' of the unit.

Further, supply will not always add to the stock; it can also be 'negative'. Units can be demolished or removed due to natural or man-made disasters (a flood, hurricane, earthquake, fire, arson, etc.). As with modifications and partial additions to the existing stock, we can also have partial removals from the existing stock, such as filling in a pool or not replacing obsolete or nonworking capital items (e.g., neglecting a leaking roof) or simply inadequately maintaining the facility. This latter decrease in supply is sometimes referred to as 'milking' when applied to landlords attempting to minimise maintenance expenditures. The process of additional or reduced capital expenditures or maintenance on an existing unit is referred to as upward or downward 'filtering' of the unit within the market, resulting in 'gentrification' or 'decline', respectively, when households of higher (or lower) incomes move in.

Distinguishing these different components of housing supply may seem to be unnecessary detail, but each in fact has its own unique causes and impact on the market and its own institutional structure (i.e., industrial organisation) to carry it out.

Why Is Housing Supply Important?

The supply side of the housing market and the structure of the system to influence that supply over time and space are critical to whether the local housing market is able to provide adequate and affordable shelter, within a decent living environment and to all segments of the population. These conditions include:

- the sufficient 'availability' of stock without excessive crowding or the need for 'doubling up';
- the proper mix of 'amenities' that are suitable to household needs, including both structural and site amenities: number of bedrooms and baths; room type, size, and configuration; light, heat, and ventilation; fireplace; landscaping; play areas, etc.;
- 'location' of the available stock in neighbourhoods that are safe, located appropriately relative to employment locations and accessible transportation;
- 'prices and rents' that are affordable, and do not force households into doubling up or restrict consumption of consumer necessities such as food and clothing;

- housing 'vacancies' that are not so high that deteriorating vacant and abandoned units are creating adverse neighbourhood conditions, but are not so low that rents and prices are driven outside the range of affordability; and
- a firm expectation that market conditions will remain predictable and stable without excessive speculative buying and selling activity and wildly fluctuating rents, prices, and vacancy rates; with some confidence that one will not be displaced from one's unit without just cause and compensation; with expectations that a landlord (whether public, quasi-governmental, or private) will retain the right to collect rent and restrict tenant damage to their units; and with some expectation that the surrounding neighbourhood will not change dramatically over a short period of time, especially in an undesirable way.

Housing supply, of course, is not solely responsible for the above local market conditions, but only affects them in relationship to the other half of the economic equation – the demand for housing stock and services. The gap between demand and supply represents vacancies and an upwards or downwards pressure on rents and prices. But a healthy and efficient housing supply that responds to demand pressures, which are frequently precipitated by external sources such as job growth or decline, is essential to the local housing market's smooth functioning.

The supply side of the housing market has a second and perhaps even more prominent influence through its role in the broader 'macroeconomy' (see article Housing Markets and Macroeconomic Policy). According to the US Bureau of Labor Statistics, as of the end of 2009, residential construction jobs (including both residential builders and specialist trades contractors engaged in residential building) totalled 2.36 million, 1.8% of total nonfarm employment, dropping from a high of 3.5 million jobs, or 2.5% of the total employment base in early 2006 (**Table 1**). The housing supply sector includes residential contractors and subcontractors as well as all those having anything to do with the supply of housing stock and services over time: rehabilitation specialists, sales people/brokers and leasing agents, land developers, land-use regulatory authorities, land-use attorneys, land planners, consultants, environmental remediation specialists, architects, lenders, landscapers, etc., which together would make up an even larger share of total employment. Moreover, the value of housing assets makes up a large portion of total wealth.

Between 1995 and 2008 residential construction plummeted from a high of 6.1% of gross domestic product (GDP) in 2005 to a low of 3.4% of gross domestic product (GDP) by 2008, after the housing bubble burst (see **Table 2**). Given its size and variability, it is to be expected that when the residential construction market shuts down, as it did by almost half during the 2005–08 meltdown, it can have a devastating impact on the entire economy. The demise of the housing market in the recent recession reduced the GDP growth rate during 2007–08 by an estimated 2.75% (from 3.10% to 0.44%). The spillover effects can be even greater to the extent that the decline in the residential sector is one of the prime causes of a general economic contraction. In 2006, this is exactly what happened; the dislocations in the mortgage markets, especially the subprime and nonagency issue markets, created a liquidity crisis in the broader capital markets, which in turn resulted in bankruptcies and layoffs from Wall Street to Main Street.

Just as important is the role of the residential sector in 'jump starting' an economic recovery. The residential sector today is receiving a great deal of attention from the Administration and Congress, not just because it is the expedient thing to do, but because it can be the most cost-effective way to revive asset values and create jobs, if implemented correctly.

Table 1 US employment in the housing supply sector 2001–09

Year	Total nonfarm employment (000s)	Total residential construction employment (000s)	Percent residential construction employment (%)
2001	130723.0	2649.0	2.0
2002	130183.0	2736.7	2.1
2003	130270.0	2897.5	2.2
2004	132317.0	3127.7	2.4
2005	134861.0	3401.0	2.5
2006	137000.0	3342.3	2.4
2007	138152 (p)	3068.4 (p)	2.2 (p)
2008	135074 (p)	2653.0 (p)	2.0 (p)
2009	131000.0 (e)	2360.0 (e)	1.8 (e)

p, preliminary; e, estimated.
Reproduced from US Bureau of Labor Statistics (2009).

Table 2 Residential construction's importance in the GDP US 1995–2008

Year	Real GDP ($ Billion)	Residential construction component of GDP ($ Billion)	Residential component of GDP (%)	Growth rate of real GDP (%)
1995	9093.70	456.10	5.02	2.51
1996	9433.90	492.50	5.22	3.74
1997	9854.30	501.80	5.09	4.46
1998	10 283.50	540.40	5.26	4.36
1999	10 779.80	574.20	5.33	4.83
2000	11 226.00	580.00	5.17	4.14
2001	11 347.20	583.30	5.14	1.08
2002	11 553.00	613.80	5.31	1.81
2003	11 840.70	664.30	5.61	2.49
2004	12 263.80	729.50	5.95	3.57
2005	12 638.40	775.00	6.13	3.05
2006	12 976.20	718.20	5.53	2.67
2007	13 254.10	585.00	4.41	2.14
2008	13 312.20	451.10	3.39	0.44

Reproduced from US Bureau of Economic Analysis (2009).

An Historical Perspective on Housing Supply

Traditionally, the supply process in housing has been a cyclical one, which has progressed roughly in tandem with the business cycle (**Figure 1**). In the United States, until the integration of the mortgage market with the broader capital markets and the deregulation of the savings and loan association industry in the early 1980s, deposit rate and mortgage rate ceilings were used as active tools of government policy to 'cool off' overheated markets. This was achieved through a process known as 'disintermediation', which is characterised by the restriction of capital inflows to the mortgage market, hence

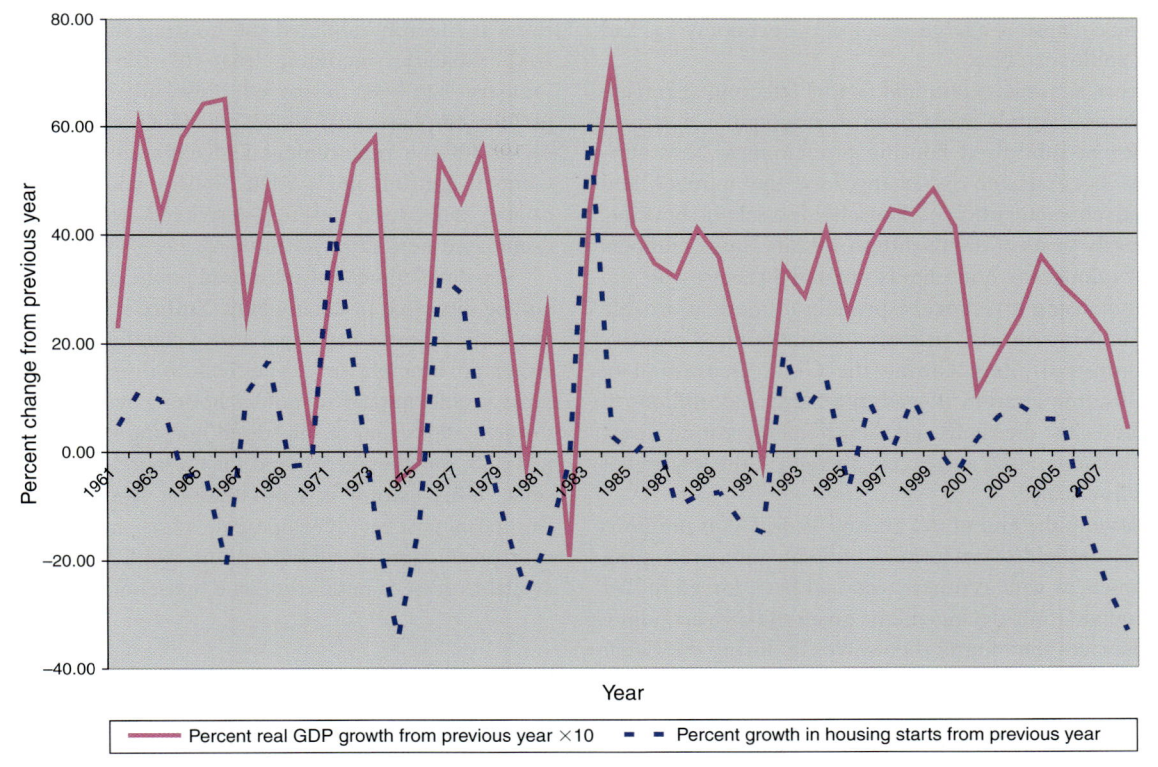

Figure 1 Housing and the economy: Percent change in new housing starts and real GDP (× 10): 1961–2008. Reproduced from US Bureau of Economic Analysis (2009) and US Census Bureau (2010).

shutting off new lending in that sector and the supply of new housing in the pipeline. Since the size of the housing construction sector was so large, economic activity in the economy slowed, the economy cooled, and inflationary pressures waned. Conversely, such credit control actions could be reversed in order to jump-start the economy after it had plunged into recession.

The residential mortgage-backed securities market developed in the early 1980s in the United States and, together with deregulation of the savings and loan industry and removal of mortgage and deposit rate ceilings, eroded the effectiveness of disintermediation in the housing market as a tool of macroeconomic policy (see article Mortgage Markets: Regulation and Intervention). Since the early 1980s, mortgage credit has generally remained available over the credit cycle, though at higher cost during tight-money periods. Typically the Federal Government has also had to rely to a greater degree on the Fed and the Fed Funds rate, to regulate the economy, which affected all sectors of the economy, not just the housing market. New housing supply, in the form of housing starts and rehabilitation expenditures, also became generally less volatile over the business cycle, with the exception of the most recent turndown, as can be seen in **Figure 1**. From a 2.2-million-unit annual rate in the second quarter of 2006, annual housing production plunged to 750 000 units per year and further to a 500 000 annual unit range by the end of 2008. Since then, it has essentially remained stagnant or grown very slowly. This dramatic collapse of a large sector of the economy has had a clear spillover effect.

Historically, two additional factors affecting aggregate new housing supply have been demographics and new government-subsidised housing programmes. New supply has been driven by changes in the number and personal characteristics of households seeking housing. In the early years of the twentieth century, huge numbers of new immigrant households created pressures on the existing housing inventory, especially of more affordable rental housing in the primary destinations, America's large industrial cities. During the Great Depression of the 1930s, immigration slowed to a crawl and millions of households lost their jobs and their homes, creating a bust in new homebuilding and excess demand at the low end of the income scale.

Following the end of the Second World War, millions of new households were formed, often by young returning servicemen, as well as others who had been forced to live in extended family arrangements given the dire economic circumstances they found themselves in during the Great Depression.

In the United States, as the new consumer economy boomed, the supply side responded, with some of the largest suburban residential developments in history. Levittown, Long Island became symbolic of this age, with 17 447 largely identical units built between 1947 and 1951. The result was 'de-densification' in the older central cities and inner neighbourhoods, as middle-income households abandoned rental basement apartments and the least desirable stock and neighbourhoods. This dramatic change in the profile of the American city was reinforced by public policies encouraging the supply-side response: The Federal Housing Administration (FHA) and Veterans Administration (VA) mortgage insurance and guarantee programmes made available low down payment (20% or less), low fixed-rate, fully amortisable long-term mortgages to middle-income households. The Interstate Highway programme, initiated in 1956, developed not only limited access highways connecting the country, but also radial and circumferential commuter access systems that reinforced the decentralisation and suburbanisation of America. The surge in new supply generated a bulge in new unit construction after the war that did not really drop off until the 1960s and 1970s, as business cycle effects and inflation created periods of severe disintermediation. One of the most recent bulges in supply occurred in the 2000s, as part of the 'bubble' discussed above, but also driven by a large influx of new immigrant families and other new households formed in response to the burgeoning economic opportunities and increases in the availability credit at lower interest rates, including the rapid expansion of subprime mortgages.

In postwar Europe, housing supply dynamics were quite different. In many countries, destruction during the war severely depleted the housing stock, and industrial capacity, including that of the homebuilding industry, had been destroyed. Politically and practically, greater emphasis had to be placed on the government sector for the replacement and expansion of the stock. Council housing and worker housing cooperatives, producing subsidised or rent-restricted worker housing, dominated new supply efforts.

The development of subsidised public housing schemes will be discussed in detail below. Suffice it to say here that the United States has never had a significant reliance on either government or explicitly subsidised housing. The most visible impact of public housing was in the 1940s through 1960s, and of subsidised housing in the late 1960s to 1970s, but they accounted for no more than 5% of the stock. This feature is very different from the Western European postwar development, which included significant production of subsidised and public housing, often available even to middle-income households.

What Else Influences Housing Supply?

We saw above that a number of factors have been important historically in influencing the level, type, and location of new supply and housing conditions in the

United States. There is no doubt that the demand for housing and factors influencing it such as migration, demographics, and general economic conditions are the major drivers of any supply response. However, from a broader economic perspective, there are a number of other factors that affect housing supply responses. Formally, the supply relationship in a local housing market is derived from the aggregate 'marginal cost' relationships for all suppliers (homebuilders and others) providing units for the market. The competitive theory of the housing market states that the market is considered in equilibrium when demand equals supply (ignoring vacancies for now), and the market price or rent per unit of housing stock or services just equals its marginal cost of production. The marginal cost is the cost of producing the next unit of stock or services. Profits are maximised when the marginal revenue from adding another unit of stock or services just equals its marginal cost of production.

What factors govern the marginal cost of production? The list is long. They include the incremental cost of any factor of production (input) going into the construction of the building or operation of a housing unit (output). It includes the costs incurred in hiring or purchasing land, labour, permits and fees, construction materials, labour, financing, taxes, lease-up or sales brokerage commissions, and 'entrepreneurial profit' – the return expected by the developer as compensation for risk. It also includes the ongoing costs of operation: property management (even if owner-managed), maintenance, capital replacement, capital appreciation/depreciation, taxes, tax benefits (such as mortgage interest and property tax deductions), insurance, utilities, and financing. An increase in any cost item (or decrease in any tax benefit) shifts the marginal cost (supply) curve upwards (see **Figure 2**), which, all things being equal, renders it more expensive to produce and operate, thus decreasing the supply of housing in the long run and increasing its price. This reduced supply could take the form of fewer units, smaller units, and/or lower-quality units. The reverse is also true for decreases in marginal costs. For example, if financing became less expensive, we would expect per-unit rents and prices to fall, and housing to become more available. Over the long run, this could become evident in the form of larger, more expensive construction, and/or a higher level of maintenance.

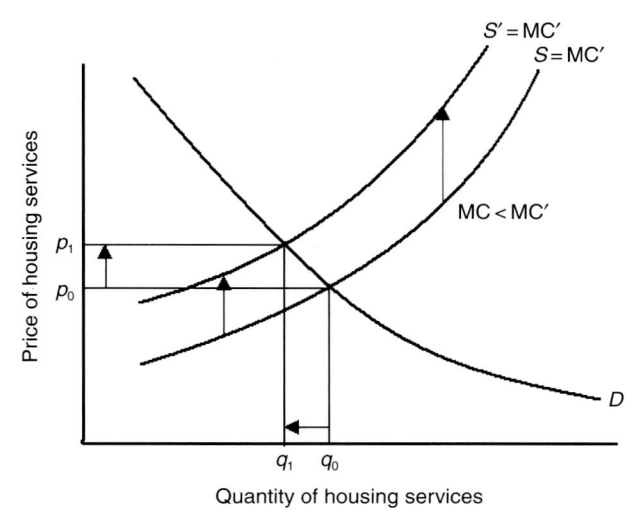

Thus far, we have considered the demand side of the market and the marginal costs influencing the supply relationship, but we have ignored vacancies. We know that vacancies always exist in the housing market and demand does not therefore equal supply, even in equilibrium; there is some extra housing left over. Is this good or bad? It turns out, it can be either. An excessively 'tight' market with few units available (considered typically in the range of 1% for owner-occupied single-family homes, and 3% for multifamily rental housing) results in lengthy and costly search by households seeking housing, multiple bids for available properties, and spikes in rent or price. These conditions create incentives for homebuilders and other suppliers to add to the stock. An excessively 'loose' market with a surplus of units available (3–5% or more for owner-occupied housing and 10% or more for multifamily housing) is a 'buyer's' or 'renter's' market. Available units languish on the market for many months (or years), and rents or prices plummet. Homebuilders and other suppliers remain on the sidelines, and existing owners may in fact begin 'milking' their units. Both are undesirable situations. A market 'in balance' is one in which the available stock of vacant units exhibits neither of the characteristics above. Sufficient units are available to meet demand as new households move into a market, previous households leave, and existing households break up and move within the market. However, this new supply is not excessive; rents and prices remain stable, growing roughly at the rate of inflation, and new unit production is such that it just meets emerging demand. Such 'equilibrium' vacancy rates are higher for markets with high rates of growth, high rates of turnover and volatility; they are lower for more stable, slower-growing markets. Vacancy, or the supply–demand imbalance in a housing market, is thus seen to be an additional important factor influencing changes in housing supply.

It is apparent from this discussion that the supply side of the market is much more complex and multifaceted than first perceived. Many factors must be considered if we are to fully understand the anticipated supply-side response to any market changes.

Figure 2 The economics of housing supply: Supply = Marginal Cost.

Inelastic versus Elastic Supply

One increasingly important supply factor is the price elasticity (or simply the elasticity) of supply (see article Supply Elasticity of Housing). It can differ considerably across local housing markets and have a significant impact on housing availability and house prices/rents and their stability over time. The (price) elasticity of supply is the percent change in housing supply for a given percent change in house prices or rents. A highly elastic market is one in which any increase in demand at the prevailing market price will be fully answered by a corresponding increase in supply, there being no increase in prices or rents (infinitely elastic supply, see **Figure 3**). A highly inelastic market is one in which any increase in demand will fail to bring forth a supply response, but instead prices or rents increase to ration the existing units (zero supply elasticity, see **Figure 3**).

Supply-elastic markets, such as Dallas or Houston, are characterised by few natural constraints on new housing development and a land-use regulatory process that is development-friendly. Supply-inelastic markets, such as Boston, New York, or San Francisco, are characterised by significant natural constraints on new housing development (such as lakes or oceans, steep slopes, or wetlands), and a land-use regulatory process that is highly restrictive (see articles Housing Supply: Urban Growth Boundaries; Housing Supply: Green Belts). House prices and rents tend to be higher in supply-inelastic markets and more volatile over the cycle, whereas the reverse is true for supply-elastic markets. Builders and other suppliers expect higher entrepreneurial profit levels in

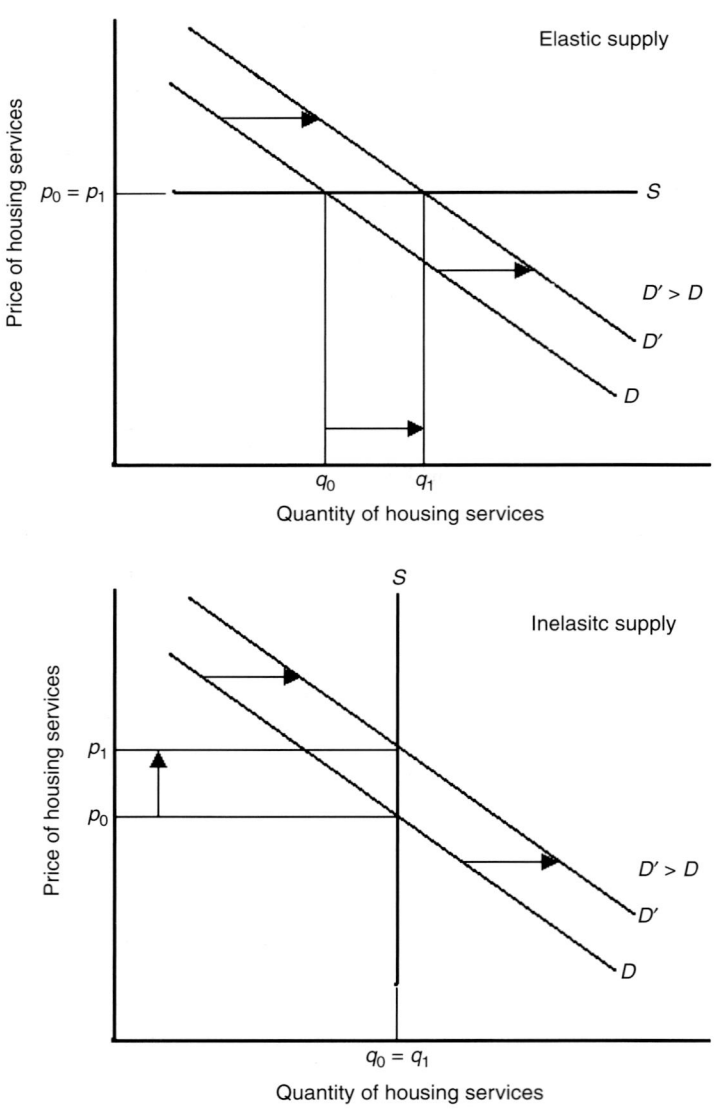

Figure 3 The economics of housing supply: Elastic vs. Inelastic supply.

supply-inelastic markets because of the greater risks they must take and greater effort they must go to in getting development approval. In an influential 2008 study, Saiz found that the dominant factor influencing supply elasticity in a local market is buildable land availability, with land-use regulation less important.

Owned versus Rental and Market-Rate versus Subsidised versus Public Housing Supply

The character of housing supply can also vary across the owner-occupied and rental tenures. The United States now has a 67.6% homeownership rate, a figure below the peak of 69.2% in the fourth quarter of 2004, before the current financial crisis. It has been in the 60s since the late 1950s. For certain units, their tenure characteristic is really a demand characteristic rather than a supply-side characteristic, since they are indistinguishable physically. However, many homes are built specifically for a certain tenure type. For example, large suburban 'McMansions' are definitely intended to attract resident buyers, and developments intended to be 'condo-sized' are often built to specifications more desired by owners, such as upgrades in appliances and better insulation. Annual Housing Starts data are commonly reported in terms of 'single family' and 'multifamily'. Condominiums are treated as 'multifamily' for reporting purposes.

Another way of categorising housing supply is according to the source of its ownership or cost structure: whether it is market-rate, subsidised, or public. In the United States, the subsidised and public housing sectors have always made up a relatively small portion of the total stock. Table 3 indicates the recent breakdown for the United States and other selected IECE countries for 'public'-sector-owned housing. The US ranks low, but ironically, some of the lowest rates of public housing ownership exist in several of the formerly Eastern Bloc communist countries that have privatised their housing stock, often selling to former tenants at prices lower than 'market prices', owing in part to the fact that the government retains ownership of the land.

Today there exist two primary subsidised housing programmes in the United States: First is the Section 42 Low Income Housing Tax Credit (LIHTC) programme, which provides tax credits up to 9% annually over a 10-year period of the cost of construction or rehabilitation of a rent-restricted multifamily rental project (see article Low-Income Housing Tax Credits). The LIHTC programme is a true supply-side subsidy programme, which provides cost reductions directly to the suppliers of housing. Second is the Section 8 voucher and certificate programmes, which provide vouchers or certificates to qualifying households. Eligible private-market rental units must have rents below affordable ceilings, the difference being met by the federal government. The Section 8 is primarily a demand-side subsidy programme in that the rent reduction is retained by an eligible tenant household, though it can be applied only to units that participate in the programme. In the past, other programmes such as the Section 236 rental and Section 235 ownership programmes subsidised financing costs to restrict rents or prices to affordable levels. However, these are no longer active, given political opposition, their adverse budgetary impact, and other problems that beset them, such as quality levels and overbuilding. The public housing programme (with the exception of elderly housing) is no longer a significant source of new supply, as it too has generated considerable public opposition over the years and has suffered from management and design/quality problems.

One thing that has always militated against a large US public or subsidised housing sector has been long-term encouragement of a large, efficient private rental sector that can meet most affordable housing needs, at least in combination with a Section 8 rent subsidy. Nonetheless, there are still considerable shortages of decent, safe housing accessible to the lowest-income segment of the population.

Who Are the 'Suppliers'? The Homebuilding and Multifamily Development Industries

In order to provide housing 'supply', there must be an industry comprising housing 'suppliers' (see article Housing Construction Industry, Competition and Regulation). The housing supply industry's industrial structure is complex and multifaceted. It is an example

Table 3 The public housing supply for selected IECE countries (percent of total housing stock)

Country	2000 (%)	2001 (%)	2002 (%)	2003 (%)	2004 (%)	2005 (%)
Denmark	1.8	1.7	1.8	1.8	1.9	
France		15.7				
Greece			0.9			
Hungary	3.8					3.1
Ireland	8.7	8.8	8.7			
Liechtenstein	1.4					
Romania	4.8	2.6	2.5	2.5	2.4	
Russian Federation	34.7	32.3	30.1			
United Kingdom					19.0	
United States			1.7		1.7	

Sources IECE, UN.

of how in a private market system, individuals can form firms that are integrated in the production process in a manner that (when the system is working correctly) responds efficiently to changes in market conditions, and provides decent, affordable, safe units and living environments to all save those at the lowest end of the income distribution. There are of course exceptions to this; there are problems concerning issues of affordability, political patronage, fraud, and shoddy workmanship, but by many measures, developed countries have dramatically improved the quality and availability of their housing stock in the course of the last century.

In the single-family sector, the 'homebuilder' plays a central role. In many countries, he often acts as both developer and contractor. As developer, he brings together the various entities that must be coordinated to supply the final product. He may take on the role of a subdivision developer himself, or more frequently work with a separate entity that specialises in such activity. For the subdivision developer, the coordination task includes obtaining the necessary permits and other entitlements, the design and assembly of roads, sewers, and other utilities, together with landscaping parks and open space in the vicinity of the development. Before being able to deliver the finished lot, the subdivision developer must typically deal with analysts who determine project feasibility, planners and landscape architects who specify the plans, attorneys to draw up the necessary documents and negotiate with planning authorities, and subcontractors who install planned infrastructure (grading, trenching, installing pipes, laying the roadway, designing and finishing public amenities, subdivision entrances, gates, walls, landscaping, etc.). He also generally requires financing that in some countries takes the form of a specialised subdivision development loan from a financial institution, and a marketing person to work with builders and other potential lot purchasers.

The homebuilder may act as either a build-to-suit builder or a speculative ('spec') builder, depending on whether or not there is a final purchaser of the home with financing that enables acquisition once it is completed, and the occupancy permit is issued (often many do both simultaneously across different projects). Spec building is obviously riskier, but constitutes a large share of the newly finished product during good times. With a spec home, the builder works with an architect on a plan that he feels will respond to market demand at the right price point, given the requirements imposed by zoning and subdivision regulations; however, in mass-market building, he often simply pulls existing plans off the shelf and uses them without an architect being involved.

Once the plans are obtained and approved, the builder lines up construction financing from a bank or savings association and engages subcontractors for the various components of the house (including clearing and grading the site, trenching for utilities, utility extensions, laying the slab and other cement work, framing, roofing, wiring, insulation and drywall, utility finish, appliances, flooring, finish electrical and carpentry, and painting). These tasks all have to be coordinated and continuously inspected to ensure the work is done properly, and timed such that down time is minimised and tasks are undertaken in sequence. Furthermore, the homebuilder must guarantee that the subcontractors are paid properly and release any mechanics liens before being paid.

Once the spec home is complete, the builder must sell it, which means he must engage brokers with specialist knowledge of the subdivision or retain his own marketing staff. Frequently the builder will assist potential purchasers to obtain financing, or arrange it himself through a lender. During this entire process, he must maintain proper accounting of all payables and receivables to monitor his profit and tax situation, being always mindful of potential bottlenecks and cost overruns.

Most builders in market economies such as the United States are small merchant builders who may build only 5–10 homes per year. Their profit margins in a mass-market are only 10% or so as a percentage of their costs (including land but often excluding their own time), so their returns are small unless they can expand their business to exploit-scale economies.

But at larger sizes, additional problems arise that increase overhead and reduce the advantages of size. Businesses require more full-time staff; they must continue to keep projects moving through the pipeline and spend substantial additional time overseeing the larger-scale output. Some builders move 'upscale' into the upper-middle to upper-income price range, since profit margins tend to be greater on the larger houses (sometimes approaching 50% or more). However, this is offset by the 'lumpiness' of sale of such homes, this market's more volatile nature, and its longer expected marketing time (approaching 1 year as opposed to 4–6 months). Nonetheless, a number of initially small-scale US builders, such as the J.F. Shea Company (sixteenth largest in the country), have grown to mid-size private firms producing several hundred to several thousand units annually.

At the other extreme of the US market are the large, publicly listed homebuilding firms, such as D.R. Horton, Pulte-Centex, Lennar, K.B. Home, and Hovnanian. They are most active in the largest cities that can support large volumes of production, where sufficient land is available, and land-use regulatory authorities are willing to work with single builders in large-scale master-planned communities. The industry is consolidating, a process accelerated by the recent global financial crisis, that has made access to capital, especially relatively cheap capital,

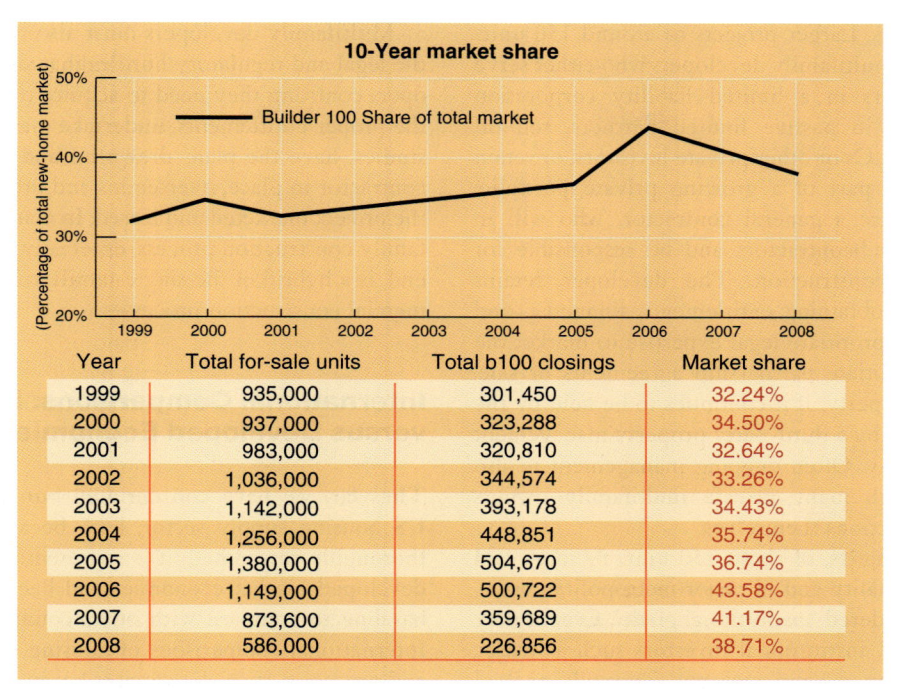

Year	Total for-sale units	Total b100 closings	Market share
1999	935,000	301,450	32.24%
2000	937,000	323,288	34.50%
2001	983,000	320,810	32.64%
2002	1,036,000	344,574	33.26%
2003	1,142,000	393,178	34.43%
2004	1,256,000	448,851	35.74%
2005	1,380,000	504,670	36.74%
2006	1,149,000	500,722	43.58%
2007	873,600	359,689	41.17%
2008	586,000	226,856	38.71%

Figure 4 The size distribution of the homebuilding industry: Builder 100 market share 1999–2008. 'Closings' represent units sold; not directly comparable to completions. Reproduced from *Builder Magazine,* "Builder 100 – 2008," May 5, 2009.

critically important. And that is the advantage of the publicly listed homebuilding firm. Both debt and equity capital is often available, and at cheaper rates, than through the private markets. Nevertheless, those large firms in financial stress can find it difficult to access capital and be forced into a merger or acquisition. Furthermore, the large public builder faces greater transparency and reporting requirements that can impede longer-term profitable investments. **Figure 4** provides a sense of the consolidation of the US homebuilding market. The top 100 homebuilding firms increased their market share from 32% in 1999 to 44% by 2006, as they took full advantage of economies of scale and their access to cheap capital. However, their market share dropped back to 39% in 2008 after the bust. It is anticipated that consolidation will continue within the industry, but that it will involve mergers and acquisitions. **Table 4** lists the 10 largest homebuilders in the United States as of 2008. Note that all of these are large publicly listed entities.

On the multifamily rental side of the market, the structure of the industry is somewhat different. At the small end of the market, rental projects from 2 to around 10 units, homebuilders often diversify their single-family construction business by constructing, owning, and

Table 4 The 10 largest homebuilding companies in the United States 2008

Rank	Company	2008 Closings	% Change	2007 Closings	2007 Ranking
1	D.R. Horton	23 915	−37	37 717	1
2	Pulte Homes	21 022	−24	27 540	4
3	Centex Corp.	18 241	−41	30 684	3
4	Lennar Corp.	15 735	−53	33 283	2
5	KB Home	12 438	−48	23 743	5
6	Hovnanian Enterprises	11 281	−25	14 928	6
7	NVR	10 741	−21	13 513	7
8	The Ryland Group	7 352	−29	10 319	9
9	Beazer Homes USA	6 642	−42	11 366	8
10	Meritage Homes Corp.	5 627	−51	7 687	12
	Total	132 994	−37	210 780	

'Closings' represent units sold; not directly comparable to completions.
Reproduced from *Builder Magazine*, "Builder 100 – 2008," May 5, 2009.

managing the units. Larger projects to around 150 units are often built by multifamily developers who either serve as general partners in a limited liability corporation (LLC) and bring in passive limited partners, sell off their projects to LLCs or other private investors, or retain full ownership as part of a growing private portfolio. They typically hire a general contractor, who will in turn recruit the subcontractors and be responsible for coordination of construction. The developer retains responsibility for obtaining entitlements, financing, and bringing in the appropriate legal expertise to market the property and negotiate partnership agreements or sale. Leasing of the property, if it continues to be held by the developer, may be by a third-party property management or leasing company. Often ongoing management is also outsourced, though many private multifamily owners conduct these functions themselves.

The largest projects, of about 150 units or more and generally of 'A' quality and in major metropolitan areas, are typically considered 'institutional grade'. Even if they are privately built, institutional investors such as trusts, foundations, insurance companies, pension funds, or Real Estate Investment Trusts (REITs) would consider purchasing them (see article Residential Real Estate Investment Trusts). They are frequently built by the institutional investor who employs the multifamily builder, often through a 'joint venture' with a developer, lender, or landowner. Other times, they are acquired from the previous owner. REITs are restricted in the amount of development they can do themselves, so they are more likely to acquire existing properties. These properties are held in institutional portfolios typically as 'core' or 'value added' properties, depending upon the extent to which incremental returns can be generated through repositioning, upgrading, or improving management of the project. In **Table 5**, we list the 10 largest builders of multifamily apartments in the United States. Note that all of these are large, private multifamily development and investment companies.

Multifamily developers must also jump over many of the legal and regulatory hurdles that single-family developers confront; they need to acquire title to a site, obtain the proper entitlements, undertake market and feasibility studies, have the plans drawn up and approved, get the contractor in place, oversee his and other's work, and get the project marketed and leased. In many ways, the multifamily construction process, especially at the institutional end, is a hybrid of the single-family residential and commercial construction processes.

International Comparisons: Developing versus Developed Economies

Thus far, we have concentrated our discussion on the US housing supply sector, both because it is the most thoroughly researched, it is representative of most other developed market economies and because it serves as a baseline to compare with other countries of the world. International comparisons of housing supply institutions and processes are rich exercises because their dimensions and behaviour are so varied, depending upon history, tradition, culture, political ideology, and the stage of development of economic institutions in each country.

At one extreme, we have the least developed countries of the world, concentrated largely in Africa, South and Southeast Asia, and the Middle East, where there is generally an 'informal' housing sector for the vast bulk of the population, supplemented by a more 'formal' sector for the upper classes (see article Housing Policies in Developing Countries). The informal sector in both rural areas and cities essentially involves nonstandardised self-construction over an extended period, as the household-builder 'owner' obtains what materials he can purchase, barter, or scavenge to obtain it. The notion of financing through a mortgage or other loan is essentially out of the question, although in certain countries such as India, microfinance tools are beginning to be employed.

Table 5 The 10 largest multifamily builders by units started 2008

Rank	Company	Public or private	Units	Units change from 2007 (%)
1	Trammell Crow Residential	private	8194	−25.07
2	Lincoln Property Co.	private	4740	−2.97
3	Hunt Building Co.	private	3476	−62.89
4	Clark Builders Group	private	3418	−41.08
5	Wood Partners	private	3369	−36.72
6	A.G. Spanos Cos.	private	3360	−17.53
7	Michaels Development Co.	private	2961	74.28
8	The Dinerstein Cos.	private	2884	22.36
9	Flournoy Construction Co.	private	2853	47.75
10	Place Properties	private	2488	−12.18

Reproduced from Builder Magazine, "Builder 100 – 2008," May 5, 2009.

In rural areas, land has often been owned or at least leased for many years by the homebuilder's family, and construction is undertaken with permission (though typically the government has little real approval power or oversight as to building standards). In urban areas, squatters' settlements are common where there is no formal title to the land. In some cases, squatters may pay some small rent to the legal owner of the land; in other cases, there is no payment involved and periodically these settlements are demolished through government 'renewal' projects. Conditions in these units are typically considered unacceptable by Western standards, with no water, sewers, indoor plumbing or baths; no electricity or gas; no heating, cooling or insulation; dirt floors; and makeshift construction. In the best cases, construction is with mud brick or cinderblock, but in the worst cases cardboard or sheets of corrugated steel are scavenged from construction sites.

The formal housing supply sector in the undeveloped world is very small, consisting of only the wealthy or business classes. Home construction is typically undertaken by commercial contractors on a build-to-suit basis, and is paid for by cash or a short-term recourse loan from the small domestic banking sector, or more frequently, foreign banks.

The developing world, including China and India and many countries in Latin America and Asia, is experiencing rapid urbanisation and high rates of migration from rural areas to the cities. These countries have taken steps to provide formal housing for its urban working class and lower-income households, although the informal sector is still prominent. In Peru, these informal neighbourhoods have taken on the name of Young Towns (*Pueblos Jovenes*), which is an appropriate descriptor in that, although land title is initially often ambiguous, over time, the communities mature and evolve. The households not only add several stories to their single-story cottages as their families grow, the communities gradually add amenities, including electricity, water, and sewers.

However, such evolution of an informal housing district is rare in most developing countries. Typically these districts are cleared, and unceremoniously razed, and replaced with mid- and high-rise flats. This abrupt change is particularly evident in India and China, where traditional *wastis* and *hutongs* are disappearing rapidly and being replaced with high-rise public housing units. In rural areas, most housing remains traditional, although public housing is gradually reaching the smaller cities and towns.

The organisation and process of development in public housing sectors of developing countries depends upon their economic history and traditions. India's programme resembles that of the traditional Council Housing system in the United Kingdom, which in turn resembles the US public housing programme, with ownership and management by a quasi-government authority or nonprofit workers' cooperative, making use of public financing but private contractors to construct the projects. Rents are maintained at levels commensurate with the income situation of individual households. However, there is a sizable middle-income private ownership housing market emerging in India. In communist systems, the production of public housing is characterised by more active direct government ownership of the construction sector and both development and ownership of the stock. The tradition that adequate housing is an entitlement in socialist economies, such as those of Cuba, China, and the former Soviet Union, has historically been responsible for this active government interventionist role, especially in the worker housing sector. It should be pointed out, however, that even in China and Russia private ownership, at least of the building structures if not the land, has become a matter of national policy (see article Policies to Promote Housing Choice in Transition Countries).

A growing middle class in developing countries is demanding improved housing conditions. These are being provided primarily through the private development of 'apartments' that are actually organised as cooperatives or condominiums. The middle-income 'market rate' private rental sector is in fact not growing in most developing countries; ownership of a flat is considered the modal aspiration. Purchase of the unit typically requires a larger down payment than is normal in the United States (sometimes as large as 50%), owing to a less-developed and less-standardised residential finance sector, but shorter-term fixed-rate or adjustable-rate loans are increasingly being offered by government-owned or private banks. 'Ownership' does not typically mean the same thing as the single-family ownership system characteristic of the United States. The household has rights to occupy the unit, use common areas, and sell rights to the unit, but the land, upon which the unit sits, and all development rights, remain in the hands of the government.

The private rental system, which is widespread in the United States, is typically not as visible in developing countries among the middle-class (see article Private Rental Landlords: Developing Countries). Such legal restrictions as rent control, limitations on eviction, and other rights skewed towards the tenant tend to limit the private rental stock. It has become a financially unattractive investment as compared to office, retail, and industrial property. The middle-class rental units that do exist tend to be public housing projects. The implications of a small private rental sector are not altogether clear. Often, the regulations limiting its development stem from past adverse experience with private landlords and exploitation of worker households, but the trade-off may be structural shortages of housing at the middle and low end of the household income scale, which tends to characterise these housing markets.

In the developed world – including the United States, Canada, Western Europe, a few countries in the Middle East, Australia and New Zealand, Japan, and increasingly, South Korea – the housing production sector has become more broadly and formally developed, though in different ways across countries. The United States has one of the most pro-ownership tax codes in the world given its mortgage interest and property tax deductions, combined with limited taxation of capital gains, and nontaxation of the implicit rent paid to oneself as an owner (see article Access and Affordability: Homeowner Taxation). It also has one of the most accommodating housing finance systems in the world, with some of the lowest down payment requirements (below 5% in some cases), lowest interest rates, and longest terms, especially for fixed-rate loans, supported further by a well-developed secondary market.

The US level of housing consumption for the middle class and above is not surprisingly among the highest in the world, in terms of unit size, low density (single-family units on their own 1/4 acre lots, though the norm in American suburbs, are rare in most other developed countries), and amenities. This is due in part to the financial and tax treatment of the ownership sector, as discussed above, but also to quite lenient development and land-use regulatory standards as well as lower population densities than many other developed countries.

Building standards in the United States also permit much greater substitution of new components for older, traditional building materials such as brick, stone, and tile. The result is that 'stick-built' multifamily projects in the United States look flimsy and of low quality to many Western Europeans used to 2-foot-thick stone and plaster walls. It takes some elaborate marketing to convince wealthy German investors to put a portion of their portfolio in the US multifamily rental sector, despite its objectively good past performance.

In spite of all of this support, however, the United States does not have the developed world's highest rate of homeownership; this honour goes to Spain, with 82%, and Ireland, with 80%, not far behind (**Table 6**). The reasons for this are several. First is that the financial and tax benefits supporting housing in the United States have in part been capitalised into higher prices, and affordability has become an issue. American households' refusal to reduce their land consumption in pursuit of the 'American Dream' of a single-family unit on its own lot, has also driven up costs, since land prices increased most dramatically in recent years. A final barrier to homeownership in the United States has been a restrictive land-use regulatory system that can act as a noose keeping younger lower-income and working class households bottled up in older inner-city rental neighbourhoods,

Table 6 Comparison of homeownership rates[a] for selected UNECE (United Nations Economic Commission for Europe) countries

Country	Year	Owner (%)
Spain	2001[b]	82.2
Ireland	2002	80.0
Norway	2001	76.7
Portugal	2001	75.4
Italy	2001	71.2
Israel	2004	70.6
United Kingdom	2004[c]	70.0
Turkey	2000	68.3
United States	2003	68.3
Poland	2002	67.4
Luxembourg	2001	66.6
Belgium	2001[d]	66.4
Canada	2001	65.8
Finland	2004	63.1
Austria	2004	56.9
France	2002	56.0
Denmark	2005[e]	51.6
Netherlands	2000	50.4
Slovakia	2001[f]	49.2
Czech Republic	2001[g]	46.9
Germany	2002	42.2
Sweden	1990	39.9
Switzerland	2000[h]	33.7

[a]There are two concepts of household, the housekeeping unit concept, and the household-dwelling concept.
[b]Includes households in nonconventional dwellings.
[c]Data at May 2004. Source: Survey of English Housing for England.
[d]Data based on the results of Census 2002.
[e]Percentage totals are not equal to 100% due to households with tenure status classification 'unknown'.
[f]Data based on the results of the Population and Housing Census 2001.
[g]Data refer to permanently inhabited dwellings only.
[h]Percentage totals are not equal to 100% due to 75 995 households with tenure status classification 'unknown'.
Sources: IECE, UN.

without an opportunity to find decent 'first-time homebuyer' units in the suburbs. Ironically, some of the highest rates of homeownership exist in the former Eastern Bloc countries, which have privatised their public housing stock at low prices (see article Policies to Promote Housing Choice in Transition Countries).

In many other developed countries, too, such as the United Kingdom and Germany, the lack of a substantial private rental housing sector and recent resistance to financing a large traditional public housing programme has led to the encouragement of 'rent-to-own' programmes (as in the UK Council Housing ownership programme in the 1980s), which have considerably increased the numbers of home-owning households (see article Privatisation of Social Housing).

Regardless of the encouragement given to homeownership versus rental in individual developed countries, however, virtually all can be characterised as having a mature development and construction industry supported by a mature housing finance system. The varying ways in which each country has structured its system of production of housing at the low, middle, and high ends of the market are reflective of the varying historical and political traditions, geographic and demographic realities, and recent economic conditions each has faced. The differences present here create a large set of 'natural experiments' to examine what seems to work and what does not.

Conclusions and Prognosis for the Future

We have seen that the institutional structure and processes surrounding the production of housing stock and services is multidimensional and complex, with a great deal of variety across different areas of the world that reflects their different stages of economic development, their historical and political traditions, the geographic and demographic realities they face, and recent economic events and conditions. These differences in structures and systems have helped shape effectiveness in housing all households in affordable, decent, and safe units and neighbourhoods. The variety in these systems and their performance permits us to learn a great deal about what works and what does not in terms of the proper design of the housing production system. We can take away certain lessons from this exercise that are universal in their applicability:

- At least in capitalist economies, the housing production system cannot ignore the realities of the market. Both the demand by households and the costs of supplying the factors of production for housing must be recognised and incorporated appropriately to maximise the efficiencies of production to obtain the 'biggest bang for the buck'. Any deviation from this objective (e.g., a separate goal of increasing local employment in construction) must be recognised and incorporated into its opportunity costs and benefits.
- The market(s) for housing and housing services must be as competitive and transparent as possible. Such conditions allow market forces to keep down costs, promote quality, and reduce inefficiencies and 'rent-seeking' behaviour. A corollary of this is that the planning and regulatory approval process must not be excessively costly or time-consuming (depending upon individual circumstances), and must monitor and police the emergence of gifts, favours, 'black money', or other illegal side payments that are not only unjust, but can also increase the cost of development substantially (estimated by some at around 50% of housing development costs in India today).
- The degree of development of the system for the production of housing is greatly dependent upon the degree of development of the economy in general. Only in a highly developed economy are the financial institutions present that can provide attractive, low-cost debt financing to purchase a working- or middle-class 'starter' home. Thus, expectations for what can be accomplished must take into account the degree of development of financial and other markets.
- Greater thought needs to be given to the appropriate role of both public and private at-market (or subsidised) rental housing in the array of housing options available. In the United States recently, the traditional pro-home-ownership bias of public policy is being questioned, given the risks and losses incurred by many households during the recent crisis. Those countries which have effectively minimised the role of the private rental housing sector in meeting housing needs should explicitly ask why and what is being given up by doing so.
- The structure of the housing production sector must be allowed to develop in such a way that it responds to the needs of the marketplace and the objectives of public policy (such as the below-market production of adequate lower-income units). Small, private merchant builders operating in a competitive market may be able to play an important role at the lower end of the market, especially in undeveloped or developing economies, where supply chains for building products are local and the infrastructure to support large firms is nonexistent. Large-scale government or private construction programmes may not only be inefficient because of their size and monopoly status, but they also have a greater likelihood of engaging in 'black money' practices.
- As an economy develops, it is important that the emerging housing production sector must be sensitive to historical and cultural traditions of the neighbourhood and housing spatial environment. Wholesale clearance of a 'slum', displacement of its residents, and relocation in a sterile high-rise project may improve a household's physical conditions but destroy its cultural and social network. Density is not necessarily achieved by isolated, high-rise structures surrounded by roads and open space; the informal neighbourhoods of Mumbai possess some of the highest urban densities on the Earth, while the high-rise apartment districts of New York City lag significantly behind. The Young Towns of Peru provide a useful case study of transition that provides some meaningful lessons.
- Technology holds the promise of continuous future improvement, both generally in the growth of economies and specifically in the efficiency and quality of housing production. Technical advances are clearly apparent in improved materials, new systems, and innovations in design construction and manufacture. Examples include insulating glass curtain walls, drywall (replacing plaster), the elevator, structural steel, zero-lot line housing, the nail gun, prefab components, CAD/CAM (computer-aided design/computer-aided

manufacture) systems, and the critical path method of scheduling construction tasks. However, it is also present in the financial markets delivering capital to the housing market: multifamily real estate investment trusts (REITs), mortgage-backed securities, new mortgage designs, and structured finance. It should be remembered, however, that not all technology offers the same potential in all housing markets in the same way and at all times. In many areas of the world, the cost of labour is still much cheaper than capital-intensive construction techniques, and the infrastructure necessary to support a highly complex mortgage finance system does not exist. Moreover, the mere presence of technology does not automatically bring reward; we have only to look at the current crisis in the capital markets to realise the truth of this.

See also: Access and Affordability: Homeowner Taxation; Housing Construction Industry, Competition and Regulation; Housing Markets and Macroeconomic Policy; Housing Policies in Developing Countries; Housing Supply: Green Belts; Housing Supply: Urban Growth Boundaries; Low-Income Housing Tax Credits; Mortgage Markets: Regulation and Intervention; Policies to Promote Housing Choice in Transition Countries; Private Rental Landlords: Developing Countries; Privatisation of Social Housing; Residential Real Estate Investment Trusts; Supply Elasticity of Housing.

References

U.S. Bureau of Economic Analysis, "National Economic Accounts: Gross Domestic Product National Income and Product Accounts Tables," 2009. Available at http://www.bea.gov/iTable/iTable.cfm?ReqID=9&step=1 (accessed 30 October 2011).

U.S. Census Bureau, *New Residential Construction*, "Table Q1. New Privately Owned Housing Units Started in the United States by Purpose and Design," 2010. Available at http://www.census.gov/const/www/newresconstindex.html (accessed 30 October 2011).

U.S. Bureau of Labor Statistics, "Occupational Employment Statistics - May 2009 National Industry-Specific Occupational Employment and Wage Estimates: NAICS 236100 – Residential Building Construction," 2009. Available at http://www.bls.gov/oes/2009/may/naics4_236100.htm (accessed 30 October 2011).

Further Reading

Apgar W and Baker K (2006) *The Evolving Homebuilding Industry & Implications for Consumers Working Paper W06-2*. Cambridge, MA: Joint Center for Housing Studies of Harvard University.

Davis MA and Heathcote JA (2005) Housing and the business cycle. *International Economic Review* 46(3): 751–784.

DiPasquale D (1999) Why don't we know more about housing supply? *Journal of Real Estate Finance & Economics* 18(1): 9–23.

Friedlander E (2009) Nationwide, housing supply still outpacing demand. *The Wall Street Journal*. January 13.

Glaeser EJ, Gyourko J, and Saiz. A (2008) *Housing Supply and Housing Bubbles*. National Bureau of Economic Research (NBER) Working Paper 14193.

Golland A (1996) Housing supply, profit, and housing production: The case of the United Kingdom, the Netherlands, and Germany. *Netherlands Journal of Housing and the Built Environment* 11(1): 5–30.

IBIS World Industry, *Single-Family Home Building in the U.S.: Report No. 23321*, September 9, 2008.

Leamer EE (2007) *Housing is the Business Cycle*. NBER Working Paper No. 13428.

Leon K (2008) *Homebuilding*. Standard & Poor's Industry Surveys, July 3, 2008.

Martín C (2006) *Technology Matters – The Costs of and Returns to Innovating Homes, or Not*. Presented at the AREUEA Mid-Year Meeting session on Home Building Technology.

Olson EA (1969) A competitive theory of the housing market. *American Economic Review* 59(4) Part 1: 612–622.

Porter ME (2003) *The U.S. Homebuilding Industry and the Competitive Position of Large Builders*. Centex Investor Conference, New York, November 18, 2003.

Quigley J and Rosenthal L (2005) The effects of land regulation on the price of housing: What do we know? What can we learn? *Cityscape* 8(1): 69–100.

Saiz A (2008) *On Local Housing Supply Elasticity*. Working Paper, Wharton School, University of Pennsylvania.

Tsuriel SC (1999) The industrial organization of housing supply: Market activity, land supply, and the size of homebuilder firms. *Real Estate Economics* 27(4): 669–694.

Housing Supply: Green Belts

K-H Kim, Sogang University, Seoul, Korea; Singapore Management University, Singapore

© 2012 Elsevier Ltd. All rights reserved.

Glossary

Elasticity of housing supply The responsiveness of housing supply to changes in housing price.

Green belt A planning tool for urban containment that keeps land near to and sometimes surrounding towns permanently open and subject to severe building controls.

Urban growth boundary A boundary, set in an attempt to control urban sprawl by mandating that the area inside the boundary be used for higher density urban development, and the area outside be used for lower-density development or preserved.

The Nature and the Evolution of Green Belts

Containing the growth of large cities and preserving agricultural land surrounding them have been an important goal for planning. Green belts, urban growth boundaries, and other regulations on the conversion of nonurban land into urban uses are examples of instruments to fulfil the policy goal of urban containment (see article Housing Supply: Urban Growth Boundaries; Brownfield Development and Housing Supply).

The green belt is designed as a planning tool for urban containment by keeping land near to and sometimes surrounding a town permanently open and subject to severe restrictions on what can be built. The first attempt to establish a green belt in England was a royal proclamation of Queen Elizabeth I in 1580 that forbade any new building on a new site within 3 miles of the city gates of London. The 1666 Great Fire forced a reappraisal and London's first green belt was subsequently developed. Modern greenbelts in England were introduced in 1935 when incorporated into an official plan by the Greater London Regional Planning Committee. New provisions for compensation in the 1947 Town and Country Planning Act allowed local authorities to include green belt proposals in their development plans. Circular 42/55 of 1955 invited local planning authorities other than London to consider establishing green belts. Currently, there are 14 district green belts in England which collectively cover 16 388 square kilometers, or about 13% of total land. London's green belt starts at about 15 miles from the centre and is 5–10 miles wide, and covers 5543 square kilometers of land.

The purposes and functions of the English green belts are spelt out in Planning Policy Guidance Note 2 (PPG2). PPG2 states five purposes that are served by including land within the green belt: To check the unrestricted sprawl of large built-up areas; to prevent neighbouring towns from merging into one another; to assist in safeguarding the countryside from encroachment; to preserve the setting and special character of historic towns; and to assist in urban regeneration, by encouraging the recycling of derelict and other urban land. It also lists six uses of land in green belts such as providing access to the open countryside for the urban population, opportunities for outdoor sport and recreation, retaining attractive landscape, and enhancing landscape near to where people live. But these are of secondary importance. In fact, as Hall (1989: 21) points out "very little of the Green Belt is actually available for the recreation of the Londoner. It may not all be very beautiful or green, but without it the town would never end". In short, the main function of green belts is that of a 'stopper'.

Quite a few other countries introduced green belts similar to the English green belts. Scotland introduced green belts in 1947. Korea established green belts around Seoul and other provincial cities between 1971 and 1977. Ottawa and the Greater Toronto Area have green belts. Boulder, Colorado has purchased land to build a green belt of farms and open space around town. Japan tried to establish green belts but did not succeed. Urban growth boundaries in Portland, Oregon and King County, Washington are similar to green belts in that their main purpose is to contain urban development. But an urban growth boundary is different from a green belt in that it is less permanent, and can be extended to provide land for urban purposes.

There are various ways green belts affect cities. Their primary goals of urban containment and the preservation of the countryside are believed to have been achieved in England. For example, the UK government's 2006 Barker Review claims that: "There is little doubt that green belt policy has played a major role in checking the unrestricted sprawl of large-built areas and safeguarding the countryside from encroachment." (p. 68). Green belts also influence the urban spatial structure and hence the pattern of land development and that of commuting. The main focus of this article is on the impact of green belts on housing supply. To this end, we will explore both theoretical and empirical literature on the relationships between growth controls, green belts in particular, and the markets for residential land and housing. We also discuss policy implications and the political economy of the regulation.

The Impact of Green Belts on Markets for Residential Land and Housing

Theoretical Predictions

A green belt or an urban growth boundary affects the markets for residential land and housing in several ways. A green belt reduces the supply of residential land by banning development inside it. This will then lead to a higher price of land and reduction of new housing supply. At the same time, housing supply becomes less elastic with respect to price. This happens because the price elasticity of new housing supply is influenced by the elasticity of developable land supply, and the latter is adversely affected by the regulation. The supply of housing becomes more elastic, the more elastic the supply of land is, given the share of land cost in total cost of housing production and the elasticity of substitution between land and nonland inputs (see article Supply Elasticity of Housing).

A green belt policy also affects the types of housing constructed. Since such a policy raises the price of residential land, the cost of producing housing that uses land extensively (detached single family houses and detached houses) increases relative to the price of housing that uses land intensively (apartments and terrace houses). As a result, the construction of the former will fall relative to that of the latter, provided other residential density controls permit increased construction of the latter.

A green belt regulation also influences the location of development, by prohibiting development at the urban fringe and instead steering development towards locations beyond the outer edge of the green belt that are further from the city centre. Such changes may also accompany changes in the composition of housing types and building densities.

There could also be dynamic impacts on the timing and density of land development, as the threat posed by regulatory initiatives such as green belts can accelerate the pace of development in the rest of the metropolitan area.

Empirical Evidence

Most studies on the impact of urban containment policies like green belts analyse effects on the prices of land and housing. The finding that such policies are associated with higher prices can be due to a decrease in housing supply, but also an increase in demand caused by the positive effect of regulations on amenities. If the green belt generates amenities such as clean air, scenic beauty, and recreational space, the benefits will be capitalised into land values. This makes it difficult to interpret the results of empirical studies.

Analysts including Monk and Whitehead (1999) argue that the typical econometric analysis of the price of land or housing is incapable of explaining the impact of regulation, because the planning system is nationwide and this therefore prevents comparisons between areas where policy applies and areas that are free of intervention. For this reason, they take a behavioural approach and analyse the trend of planning permissions granted, the price of residential land, new housing completions, house prices, as well as house types and densities for two adjoining local authority districts in the southeast of England during the period 1981–91. These two districts were within the same county structure plan but the application of planning controls differed in terms of their tightness. Their analysis confirmed that constraint in one area pushes up prices in all areas, the differences in the extent of constraints are reflected in relative land prices, and so tight constraints on land supply in the face of demand increases resulted in rising prices of land and housing, but minimal responses in housing output.

There are relatively few studies that directly analyse the impact of growth controls or green belts on the supply of urban residential land or new housing. Son and Kim (1998) analysed data on 171 cities in Korea and found that green belts contribute to urban land shortages. They first estimated the land price gradients for urban and surrounding rural areas, and then calculated the shortage or surplus of urban land as the difference between the equilibrium size of urban land area and the actual land in urban use. Finally, they investigated the factors determining the shortage or surplus of urban land by estimating a regression equation relating the calculated shortage or surplus to a set of demand side variables (e.g., population and local government revenue), infrastructure, and measures of natural and regulatory constraints on land use. Estimation results suggest that the size of green belt as a percentage of total urban area is a significant factor in determining the shortage of urban land, but natural constraints were not significant. Bramley (1993) estimated a system of five equations representing UK housing markets and used the model to analyse the impact of planning policies on the supply of residential land and housing. Bramley constructed indices of natural constraints and those measuring strictness of planning constraints. The green belt variable is included as a natural constraint considering its permanence. He found that the green belt and other natural constraints decrease housing output.

Urban containment policies are believed to have made housing supply less elastic in the United Kingdom. Pryce (1999) used the data compiled by Bramley to estimate a housing supply function. He derived estimates of the price elasticity of new housing supply as well as the elasticity of housing price with respect to land availability. He found that a 75% increase in the stock of land with outstanding permissions for housing would lead to a fall in housing price of 32.4% assuming that the price elasticity of housing demand equals −0.7.

Planning controls could also affect the type of new housing produced. Evans and Hatwich (2005) report that the share of single-storey houses in private dwelling construction fell from 12% to 5% between 1990 and 2004. Moreover, virtually no single-storey houses were built in southern England where demand for such housing is greater but the land supply constraint was more severe. Monk and Whitehead (1999) also point out that the regulatory system has limited the range of choices of housing types and densities.

Finally, Cunningham (2007) investigates the dynamic impact planning policy risk on land development. Using the data on Cooke County of the State of Washington, USA, he estimated the impact of the urban growth boundary on the timing of development. He found that the introduction of the urban growth boundary would have reduced land development by between 42% and 48% in the absence of real-option considerations, but the impact drops to between 28% and 39% once the role of real option is considered.

In sum, the literature provides some evidence for the negative impact of planning controls in general and green belts or urban growth boundaries in particular on the availability of land for housing and the supply of housing.

Implications for Housing Supply

Shortages of developable land caused by growth controls such as green belts have important implications for fulfilling housing supply targets. One measure of land shortages is the large price gap at the urban fringe between plots of agricultural land and those with planning permissions. Evans (1991: 854) reported that the price of one hectare of agricultural land near Reading was 2000 pounds while that with a development permit was 500 000 to 1 million pounds. Barker (2006b: 151) found that, as of January 2006, the multiple between the price of a plot with a development permit and that of a plot in agricultural use was as high as 260 for England and Wales excluding London. Evans (2004: 128) estimates that undeveloped land serviced with infrastructure is priced at 250 000 pounds but a comparable parcel of agricultural land has a value of less than 12 500 pounds. Such a huge gap is a symptom of strict planning controls on the conversion of agricultural land into urban use at the urban boundary in a static context. A more obvious measure of the magnitude of the constraint imposed by green belts would be the size of land demarcated as green belts compared with the size of developed or developable land. Green belts account for about 13% of all land in England, and the most optimistic estimate of the share of developed land is 13.5%. In the case of Korea, green belts used to represent 5.4% until policy reform was introduced in 1998, while the land in urban uses was 5–6%. In the case of Seoul, the amount of land designated as green belt that is not 'green' (i.e., forest) was as large as one-third of the developed land within the city boundary.

The scarcity of land for residential development must have been a major constraint on housing supply, and its magnitude has an important implication for implementing a housing supply target. Barker (2003) found that UK real house price trend growth during the period 1971–2001 was 1.3% points greater than the EU average (p. 23). She estimated that 145 000 additional houses need to be supplied per annum from 2002 to bring the long-run real house price appreciation in line with the EU average (p. 65). Barker (2004: 34) recommended that some green-belt land be re-designated where there are strong pressure points in a particular urban area, and where forcing development elsewhere would lead to perverse environmental impacts. However, the Government Housing Green Paper did not accept the recommendation and made it clear that green belts will be protected.

The British Government set a target of 240 000 new houses per year until 2016 and 3 million units by 2030. But the actual average number of new dwellings completed in England over the period 1990–2008 was about 192 000. The availability of land for new housing is a key factor in meeting the housing target. A specific question is whether brownfield land is sufficient or some greenfield land including green belt land needs to be developed. Dixon and Adams (2007) calculated the required amount of land to fulfil Barker's recommendation for housing supply increases and concluded that brown field land is not sufficient. SMF (2007) also argues that only 1 million new homes can be built on brownfield sites at the current densities and a large chunk of the 3 million homes targeted will have to be built on Greenfield sites, that is, undeveloped land, or some green belt land.

A more subtle but fundamental problem is that land use regulation in the United Kingdom is implemented with no reference to price signals. This point is highlighted by Cheshire (2008), who says, "Our planning system allocates a scarce resource-land for urban development – but without any regard for prices or any market information" (p. 51). Cheshire attributes this to the overriding objective being urban containment. The British planning system "allocates the area of developable land with the aim of deliberately restricting the spread of urban areas" (p. 52). The consequence is that restriction of land in the face of rising incomes will lead to a rise in real housing prices.

Political Economy

Green belts appear to be popular in the United Kingdom. A 60% of the respondents to a 2005 survey conducted by CPRE (Campaign to Protect Rural England), an environmental movement, agreed that green belts should be preserved. Green belts enjoy broad-based public support in Korea as well. Such public support suggests that they generate some (perceived) benefits to society as a whole, or to some segments of society, and exert influence through the political process.

One possible rationale for urban containment policies is to serve the public interest by correcting market failures. For example, the loss of open space at the urban fringe resulting from urban spatial expansion might justify a green belt or an urban growth boundary, if the benefits from open space preservation are large enough to offset the additional costs to urban residents due to a rise in housing price. However, the overall welfare of urban residents will decrease if the alleged benefits from improvement in the quality of the environment are not perceived by the residents, or accrue to a small share of the urban population.

There are some explanations of growth controls based on a political economy perspective that recognises an imbalance in the political system between existing residents, who can protect their environment, and potential new residents who have no voice. Fischel (2001) argues that homeowners try to protect the values of their homes by introducing zoning regulations that restrict the supply of developable land. Housing is typically the most important asset in household wealth portfolios, and homeowners cannot diversify their holdings of housing among several communities, or insure against some events that will lower its values. Zoning and other measures to restrict new development can be viewed as an alternative to home-value insurance in communities in which local politics is dominated by homeowners. Pennington (2000: 86–87) describes the emphasis on containment policy as "the product of a structural bias that concentrates benefits on rent-seeking interests to the detriment of a much wider population that is absent from the realm of organised politics."

Hilber and Robert-Nicoud (2009) model land use regulations as the outcome of a political game between owners of developed land and those of undeveloped land, and show that local planning authorities cater to the interests of land owners beyond those of local voters and the residential population. Their empirical analysis of 21 MSAs of the United States suggest that places with better amenities have a larger share of land developed and the more developed jurisdictions are more heavily regulated, while homeownership rate has no significant effect on the strictness of regulation. The latter result is inconsistent with Fischel's homevoter hypothesis explained above.

Finally, public perception about the functions of and the benefits from green belts or other urban containment policies may play a key role in introducing and maintaining such regulations. These perceptions may not be based on a correct calculus of direct and indirect costs and benefits, and can be described as an ideology. Kim and Kim (2000) argue that Korean green belt policy can be explained by such ideology rather than rent-seeking behaviour of land owners. If the number of people who subscribe to the belief that green belts are socially desirable is large enough, they will be able to block the efforts of those with a strong self-interest motivating removal of the regulation.

Concluding Remarks

Any land-use regulation has costs and benefits and the desirability of a particular regulation should be judged on the basis of net social benefits and the incidence of the benefits and costs among the affected people. The benefits and costs of a regulation may change over time. For example, Lee and Linneman (1998) demonstrate that the initial positive net benefit from Seoul's green belts has eroded over time as congestion increased. This finding suggests that the validity of a regulation should be reviewed as circumstances change. Barker (2006: 62) argues that green belt policy should be sensitive to the impacts in each specific case and cites some cases where green belt boundaries were reviewed in the context of growing pressure for development. In the case of Korea, the designation of green belts around medium-sized provincial cities was lifted in 1999, but adjustments to the green belt boundaries in the Seoul metropolitan area and six other major provincial cities are still ongoing. A major barrier to policy reform is public perception about the net benefits of the regulation as well as the political process of decision making based on the best estimate of the net benefits.

The empirical literature surveyed above provides some quantitative evidence that growth containment policies such as green belts decrease the availability of land for housing and the supply of housing, as well as increasing housing price and its variability. The magnitudes of the estimated impacts vary across studies, depending on the data used as well as the nature of the regulation in question. Given the importance of the magnitudes of the estimates for housing policy, measurements of the restrictiveness of policy constraints need to be improved.

See also: Brownfield Development and Housing Supply; Housing Supply: Urban Growth Boundaries; Supply Elasticity of Housing.

References

Barker K (2003) *Review of Housing Supply: Interim Report-Analysis*. London: HMSO.
Barker K (2006) *Barker Review of Land Use Planning: Final Report-Recommendations*. Norwich, UK: HMSO.
Bramley G (1993) The impact of land use planning and tax subsidies on the supply and price of housing in Britain. *Urban Studies* 30(1): 5–30.
Cheshire P (2008) Reflections on the nature and policy implications of planning restrictions on housing supply: Discussion of 'Planning policy, planning practice, and housing policy' by Kate Barker. *Oxford Review of Economic Policy* 24(1): 50–58.
Cunningham CR (2007) Growth controls, real options, and land development. *Review of Economics and Statistics* 89(2): 343–358.
Evans AW (1991) 'Rabbit hutches on postage stamps': Planning, development and political economy. *Urban Studies* 28(6): 853–870.
Evans AW and Hartwich OM (2005) *Unaffordable Housing: Fables and Myths*. London: Policy Exchange.
Fischel WA (2001) *Homevoter Hypothesis*. Cambridge, MA: Harvard University Press.
Hall P (1989) *London 2001*. Boston, MA: Unwin Hyman.
Hilber CA and Robert-Nicoud F (2009) *On the Origins of Land Use Regulations: The 'Influential Landowner' Hypothesis*. Centre for Economic Performance: Mimeo.
Kim C-H and Kim K-H (2000) The political economy of Korean government policies on real estate. *Urban Studies* 37(7): 1157–1169.
Lee C-M and Linneman P (1998) Dynamics of the greenbelt amenity effect on the land market – the case of Seoul's greenbelt. *Real Estate Economics* 26(1): 107–129.
Monk S and Whitehead CME (1999) Evaluating the economic impact of planning controls in the United Kingdom: Some implications for housing. *Land Economics* 75(1): 74–93.
Pennington M (2000) *Planning and the Political Market: Public Choice and the Politics of Government Failure*. London: Athlone.
Pryce G (1999) Construction elasticities and land availability: A two-state least-squares model of housing supply using the variable elasticity approach. *Urban Studies* 36(13): 2283–2304.
Son J-Y and Kim K-H (1998) Analysis of urban land shortages: The case of Korean cities. *Journal of Urban Economics* 43: 362–384.

Further Reading

Barker K (2004) *Review of Housing Supply: Final Report – Recommendations*. London: HMSO.
Dixon T and Adams D (2008) Housing supply and Brownfield regeneration in a post-barker world: Is there enough Brownfield land in England and Scotland? *Urban Studies* 45(1): 115–139.
Ministry of Housing and Local Government (1962) *The Green Belts*. London: HMSO.
Office of the Deputy Prime Minister (2006) *Planning Policy Guidance 2: Green belts*. London: HMSO.
Social Market Foundation (SMF) (2007) *Should the Green Belt Be Preserved?* London: SMF.

Housing Supply: Urban Growth Boundaries

M Buxton, RMIT University, Melbourne, VIC, Australia
L Groenhart, University of Sydney, Sydney, NSW, Australia

© 2012 Elsevier Ltd. All rights reserved.

Glossary

Brownfield land Land parcels within a metropolitan area available for development or redevelopment often due to a change in land use.
Greenfield land Undeveloped land on the urban fringe designated or available for urban development.
Land release The amount of land made available for urban development and the timing of its availability through landholder and developer decisions and approval processes.
Land supply The sum of land available in greenfield sites on the urban fringe and brownfield and redevelopment sites in established urban areas and regional urban centres multiplied by density.
Urban growth boundary A regulated boundary to urban development to differentiate between urban and nonurban land.

Introduction

Urban growth boundaries (UGBs) are commonly used regulatory measures aimed at limiting and redirecting outer urban growth. They are intended to increase land-use efficiency, protect the values associated with increasingly scarce peri-urban land, and provide a range of social and environmental benefits. UGBs are defined and enforced limits to urban growth intended primarily to differentiate between urban and nonurban land. They do this by distinguishing between allowable uses for the different categories of land. The two main factors influencing this differentiation are clarity in prohibiting urban-related uses on rural land and the supply of land reserved for urban purposes. The clearer the demarcation between urban and rural land and the more land available for urban purposes within the UGB or elsewhere (such as satellite towns or regional centres), the more successful a UGB is likely to be in preventing the conversion of rural land for urban purposes. A clear demarcation between uses without a sufficient supply of urban land will lead inevitably to continued pressure for a revision of institutional arrangements, such as zoning rules, to prevent rural land conversion.

UGBs are a form of urban containment policy. Other policies of this kind include urban service boundaries and greenbelts. An urban service boundary defines the area beyond which urban services, such as sewerage and piped water, will not be provided to developments. A greenbelt is a physical area of open space that surrounds or is enclosed within an urban area, where development is tightly restricted or prohibited. A greenbelt is often associated with a UGB. Greenbelts are physical barriers but, in contrast, UGBs are lines drawn around urban areas to divide them from surrounding rural land. Zoning and other regulatory tools are used to implement a UGB, with land outside the boundary zoned for rural uses and land inside the boundary zoned for urban use (see article Housing Supply: Green Belts).

UGBs and Housing Supply

The history of UGBs can be traced back to ideas about the containment of urban sprawl. They were suggested by Ebenezer Howard and the Garden City movement around 1900 and were implemented in the Greater London Plan of 1944. This plan used a greenbelt to place a boundary around London's urban development. UGBs are usually managed by a single government planning agency. If the area affected by the boundary includes multiple jurisdictions, a special authority may be created by the state or regional government to manage the boundary.

There is significant controversy over whether UGBs influence housing supply and price. The type of UGB influences housing supply. They may be hard-edged as in the European model with a clear line separating the urban from the rural or soft-edged as in the American model where there is a transitional area of mixed urban and rural uses. Different governance models apply to UGBs. Some are enforced by legislation, and others through the purchase or transfer of development rights on adjoining rural land, or by land purchase outside UGBs, or by planning or building rules. UGBs may be flexible, aimed at growth management, or inflexible, aimed at protection of nonurban land from urbanisation, or a combination of both. Growth management aims to achieve orderly land release and often to increase both development within the existing metropolitan area and public transport use. The Portland, Oregon, UGB is an example of a flexible or managed UGB; the urban boundaries associated with the greenbelts of many UK cities are examples of inflexible UGBs.

If the area within the UGB does not include enough land, the cost of residential and other development can be driven up or development can be forced to other nearby communities. If the boundary contains too much land, it will not be an effective tool for achieving community goals, including growth management. Research into the impacts of regulatory measures such as UGBs on housing supply and price, has produced variable results that are inconclusive. Many empirical studies find little or no relationship between regulation, housing supply, and price. General conclusions applicable to all cities cannot be drawn from research because of differing urban circumstances. Differences in international city types and conditions, governance, transport systems, and land supplies pose serious challenges for researchers aiming to identify and measure the strength of causal relationships. Studies on conditions applying in US cities, for example, with depressed inner urban and expanding outer urban areas, cannot be easily applied to other city types, such as networked cities or those with thriving inner-city areas characterised by high-density redevelopment. UGBs affect low-density outer urban areas with limited greenfield land differently from compact cities, which maintain adequate land supplies through metropolitan intensification. Methodological differences also help explain variable results; because many interconnected factors potentially affect land supply and price, researchers have used different techniques to disentangle their relative impacts. A general consensus on the merits of alternative methodological approaches has yet to be reached.

Housing Policies, Land and Property Taxation, and UGBs

Additional housing policy measures can help mitigate any potential negative impact from the introduction of a UGB on housing supply or price. Inclusionary zoning, a regulatory measure that requires a share of newly constructed housing to be affordable for households with low or moderate incomes, might help ensure an adequate supply of affordable housing (see article Inclusionary Zoning to Support Affordable Housing). In addition to regulatory measures, incentives can be used to reward and hence encourage developers to increase the supply of affordable housing. Density bonuses, for example, have been granted for projects on the condition that the developer includes a specified number or proportion of affordable housing units. In return, the developer is allowed to build a greater number of dwelling units than would be allowed under the planning scheme.

Government fiscal policies can also affect housing demand and property prices. Homeowner tax expenditures (see article Access and Affordability: Homeowner Taxation) and housing subsidies can be quickly capitalised into the price of buildings or land as increased demand meets an inflexible supply response or prices are manipulated by land sellers. Tax expenditures extended to landlords can also lead to increased investor competition for established housing that drives up prices. UGBs should encourage the more efficient use of metropolitan land and lead to greater housing diversity and affordability. However, they can also lead to household investment in large residential homes as repositories of private wealth. Some countries, such as the Netherlands and the United Kingdom, have curbed or removed tax allowances such as the mortgage interest deduction, while others have sought or been urged to place limits on the exemption of imputed rents and capital gains from income tax, or the exemption of residential land from land taxes, because of these contradictions. Reforms of this kind can assist achievement of urban containment goals by discouraging the overconsumption of housing that can promote urban sprawl.

Some governments have introduced user charges, betterment taxes, and impact fees on residential land and the development of residential land with a view to encouraging more compact urban development. These measures are designed to redirect residential building activity to existing metropolitan sites by requiring landowners or developers to meet, in full or part, the economic cost of new housing supply, including the need for new economic and social infrastructure, and the external costs that might arise due to loss of biodiversity, increased air pollution, and so on. They can be viewed by some as a complement or even an alternative to UGBs. There is vigorous debate around housing affordability issues as some argue that such charges, fees, and taxes are passed on into the prices and rents of housing (see article Impact Fees), while others argue that they discourage inefficient sprawl.

Housing Market Impediments to UGBs

Housing markets, and the behaviour of particular actors within them, inevitably pose challenges to the successful implementation of UGBs. Urban containment programmes, such as UGBs, are often regarded as essential elements in the intensification of cities that seek to curb outward growth and redirect development to existing metropolitan areas. However, development companies operating in outer urban areas often resist attempts to redirect their construction activities to established urban areas, and will pressure governments to revise UGBs rather than alter their own building practices. The introduction of a UGB may not be a sufficient mechanism to change established building practices on the urban fringe.

The potential for conversion of rural land to urban uses leads inescapably to rural land speculation. The lack of effective growth management may also exacerbate the effects of land speculation on short-term housing prices. Repeated relaxation of UGBs may lead paradoxically to continued land speculation outside the borders of UGBs, by signalling the direction of future urban growth to development companies, driving up rural land prices, and ultimately urban land values. Continual expansion will also tend to undermine the intent of regulatory urban containment policies that seek to redirect development to established metropolitan areas and increase outer urban land-use efficiency. Infrastructure provision, such as the building of freeways to outer urban areas, can also contradict urban consolidation policies by encouraging car-based, dispersed outer urban development, often at low densities.

The difference between housing supply and land release is an important concept in the implementation of UGBs. Governments may designate sufficient land for urban use, but development companies may limit the supply of housing by controlling the timing or amount of land made available for housing development through land banking, which raises prices. Substantial differences may also exist between the amount of land designated as future urban, land zoned urban, and residential properties placed on the market each year. In many countries, developers, in effect, determine the residential density, urban design, and location of urban uses, with public authorities exercising little oversight and ratifying developer decisions. Long time lags can occur in zoning land for urban use and issuing development approvals, and these may increase if governments transfer control of this process to development companies. Containment policies can potentially limit the number of development companies, reducing competitiveness and restricting housing choice. Other criteria, such as the extent, stage, and mix of development and broader metropolitan conditions, also influence price. A large land supply coupled with control of landownership and a slow release of developable land by a few large development companies may therefore cause housing prices to rise inside a UGB.

Governance processes also potentially affect housing supply. In many European countries, and to a lesser extent in the United Kingdom, public authorities have historically exercised a stronger role in the development approval process. This is particularly evident through land-use planning, policy and legislative traditions, active land banking policies, the provision of services and infrastructure by government agencies, and integration of land-use policy at different levels of government. All these interventions are less common in the United States and Australia. National or state plans often guide regional and local planning, with policies commonly directed at urban containment and landscape and farmland protection in urban hinterlands. Typically, outer urban densities in many northern European cities range from 35 to 120 dwellings per hectare, and the United Kingdom is seeking to increase its outer urban density from an average of 25 dwellings per hectare to the lower range of European densities. Nevertheless, in some Mediterranean cities, such as Barcelona and some southern French cities, we are now witnessing an increasing rate of development of detached outer urban housing on relatively large lots.

In contrast, local government controls the availability of urban land in areas around many US cities and this has led to extensive spatial and institutional fragmentation. Many local authorities in the United States have applied UGBs and greenbelts and introduced programmes such as the transfer of development rights or purchase of land to permanently secure UGBs, mandate higher fringe area densities, or designate future urban land in stages. However, many others effectively allow a high level of control by development companies and landowners over land releases and development type, resulting in a heterogeneous mix of unplanned uses, low-density housing, and roads. In Australia, a public authority determines the location of future urban land in the capital city, Canberra, directs development, and purchases all outer urban developable land at nonurban prices. Australian state governments control the planning of state capitals, potentially avoiding the fragmentation of US city planning, employ the use of UGBs, and designate future urban land, though in effect they divest a large amount of control to development companies.

Conclusion

Since their inception, UGBs have been criticised for increasing the cost of housing by reducing land supply for urban development. However, the research into UGB impacts shows variable results on whether they have this negative impact. As urban populations around the world grow, and the demand for urban land escalates, urban containment policies such as UGBs will be vital in protecting productive farmland and ensuring efficient use of transport and building resources. Housing policy instruments, including regulatory measures, incentives, and taxation systems, need to complement the introduction of UGBs to mitigate any adverse effects on housing affordability and supply.

See also: Access and Affordability: Homeowner Taxation; Housing Supply: Green Belts; Impact Fees; Inclusionary Zoning to Support Affordable Housing.

Further Reading

Amati M (2008) Green belts: A twentieth-century planning experiment. In: Amati M (ed.) *Urban Green Belts in the Twenty-First Century*, pp. 1–17. Aldershot, UK: Ashgate.

Bramley G (1996) Impact of land use planning on the supply and price of housing in Britain: Reply to comment by Alan W Evans. *Urban Studies* 33(9): 1733–1737.

Browder J, Bohland J, and Scarpaci J (1995) Patterns of development on the metropolitan fringe. *Journal of American Planning Association* 61(3): 310–326.

Bruegmann R (2005) *Sprawl: A Compact History*. Chicago, IL: University of Chicago Press.

Buxton M and Scheurer J (2007) Density and outer urban development in Melbourne. *Urban Policy and Research* 25(1): 91–111.

Dawkins C and Nelson A (2002) Urban containment policies and housing prices: An international comparison with implications for future research. *Land Use Policy* 19: 1–12.

European Environment Agency (EEA) (2006) Urban sprawl in Europe: The ignored challenge. *EEA Report*. Copenhagen: European Environment Agency.

Evans A (2004) *Economics and Land Use Planning*. Oxford, UK: Blackwell.

Gordon P and Richardson H (1997) Are compact cities a desirable planning goal? *Journal of the American Planning Association* 63(1): 95–106.

Ihlanfeldt K (2004) Exclusionary land use regulations within suburban communities: A review of the evidence and policy prescriptions. *Urban Studies* 41(2): 261–283.

Nelson A, Dawkins C, and Sanchez T (2007) *The Social Impacts of Urban Containment*. Aldershot, UK: Ashgate.

Patachinni E and Zenou Y (2009) Urban sprawl in Europe. *Brookings-Wharton Papers on Urban Affairs*. Washington, DC: Brookings Institution.

Pendall R (2000) Local land use regulation and the chain of exclusion. *Journal of the American Planning Association* 66(2): 125–142.

Housing Trust Funds

KE Larsen, University of Florida, Gainesville, FL, USA

© 2012 Elsevier Ltd. All rights reserved.

> **Glossary**
>
> **Affordable housing** Housing that costs a household no more than 30% of its pretax income. For owners, this includes principal, interest, taxes, and insurance. For renters, this includes rent and utility costs.
>
> **Community Development Block Grant (CDBG) program** A federal programme allocating block grants to state and local governments to improve neighbourhoods, including affordable housing initiatives.
>
> **Cost burden** When a household's housing costs exceed 30% of their pretax income, they are considered cost burdened. When that amount is 50% or more of their pretax income, the household is considered severely cost burdened.
>
> **Federal devolution** Increasing reliance of the federal or national government on local, regional, or state governments to fund and/or administer housing programmes.
>
> **HOME investment partnership program** Federal programme allocating block grants to state and local governments expressly for housing activities.
>
> **Housing linkage** The connection between employment generated by new nonresidential and market rate residential development and the demand for affordable housing it produces.
>
> **Median household income** When every household's income in a given community or area is listed in rank (ascending or descending) order, the median household income is the middle ranking income in the list.

Introduction

This government-sponsored housing resource is often tied to activity in the statewide housing market or to local land development incentives. Housing trust funds offer a flexible means for local and state governments in the United States to respond to the combined challenges of decreasing federal funding and increasing housing needs, particularly those associated with rising cost burdens among the lowest income. With the exception of the United States, most countries have not adopted housing trust funds, though the Canada Mortgage and Housing Corporation has researched their use in the United States as more communities in Canada begin to adopt them.

Federal Devolution Amidst Increasing Housing Need

Beginning in the 1970s, the United States Congress devolved responsibility, and funding, for meeting affordable housing needs to state and local governments. The perceived and real failures of the federal public housing programmes and the expanding federal budget deficit resulted in decreased attention to housing affordability on the national agenda. Major remaining federal programmes relied on state and local governments to make implementation decisions. In response, state and local governments became increasingly sophisticated in their handling of housing needs.

The availability of affordable housing persists as a critical concern in the United States, especially as unemployment rates soared following the Global Financial Crisis. Indeed, the gap between the cost of housing and the household income widened considerably in recent decades. Almost 50% of low-income households face severe housing cost burdens. This condition has become more widespread in recent years as those with moderate incomes also face cost challenges and foreclosures. At the same time, in no county across the United States can a household with one full-time minimum wage earner afford the fair market rent on a one-bedroom unit. Further, the number of rental units affordable to the lowest income groups continues to decline. In the face of these housing challenges, the breadth and sophistication of state and local housing policies and programmes has significantly increased.

Housing Trust Fund Defining Characteristics

According to a 2006 survey conducted by the Housing Trust Fund Project, the approximately 600 city, county, and state housing trust funds in the United States cumulatively generate more than $1.6 billion annually. Substantive differences exist among housing trust funds, attesting to their flexibility to meet diverse housing needs. Still, they do share some common characteristics. Generally, governments establish and fund them through an ongoing, dedicated source to ensure permanency and use them to address critical local housing issues, to leverage public and private funding, and to facilitate the role of nonprofits in the housing delivery process.

Local Housing Trust Funds

Several hundred city and county governments across the United States have local housing trust funds – many of them funded by in-lieu or housing linkage fees generated by large projects. Commercial, office, industrial, and even residential developments create jobs for lower-income workers. Local governments might adopt formulas indicating the number of affordable units required as a result of these larger projects and accept in-lieu or housing linkage fees as a means to meet these requirements. Additionally, inclusionary zoning requires developers of housing projects over a certain size to ensure that a percentage of affordable units are created alongside the market rate units in their project, either by increasing density and building these units themselves, or paying an in-lieu fee (see article Inclusionary Zoning to Support Affordable Housing). The housing trust fund created as a result of these local initiatives can then be used to build or rehabilitate affordable units or assist qualifying households to get into the housing, typically owners who require assistance with a one-time down payment or rehabilitation expense, rather than renters who would need on-going rental assistance. Programmes for the homeless and special needs populations, as well as matches for state and federally funded affordable units, are also common as is technical assistance to local nonprofits. Other sources of funding can include local taxes, such as property and hotel/motel taxes; fees, such as recording fees; and tax increment financing, where the increase in taxes associated with rising property values due to redevelopment assists affordable housing in the redevelopment area.

Over the past 30 years, hundreds of city and county governments have established housing trust funds. Concentrations of local housing trust funds exist in California, Massachusetts, New Jersey, Pennsylvania, and Washington, where state initiatives encourage cities and counties to adopt them. California's local match programme funded through a statewide bond initiative has stimulated the creation of city and county trust funds in that state. In Massachusetts, enabling legislation allows cities to increase property taxes and use these for trust funds. Local jurisdictions in New Jersey can assess developer fees based on the assessed value of new market rate development to meet their fair share of affordable housing. Pennsylvania counties can increase their document recording fees for real estate transactions to finance housing trust funds. Finally, Washington's state housing programme splits the required document recording fee between the state (40%) and the counties (60%) to be used for local affordable housing initiatives. The largest local housing trust funds exist in the largest urban areas with Chicago, Los Angeles, New York City, Philadelphia, San Francisco, and Seattle all generating over $10 million dollars in 2006 according to the Housing Trust Fund Project survey. The District of Columbia also has a housing trust fund. In a few cases, cities and counties have joined forces to create regional housing trust funds.

These programmes are typically overseen by local government housing or community development departments, although some counties turn to housing authorities or redevelopment authorities. Usually qualifying households do not have to undergo a competitive process to access funds for down payments, rehabilitation, or housing support services. On the other hand, nonprofit and for-profit developers, common recipients of assistance to support qualifying housing projects, often have to participate in a competitive process for the assistance. The form of assistance – loans or grants – may depend on the housing activity and/or income group targeted.

State Housing Trust Funds

Prior to 1980, only one state, Delaware, had created such a fund, while 17 state funds were established during the 1980s, another 19 during the 1990s, and an additional 11 so far in the 2000s. These numbers reflect 40 states that have a total of 48 state housing trust funds. Several of these programmes are unfunded at this time. Geographically, they are located throughout the nation, though certain states in the South and West do not have housing trust funds. Some of the most economically distressed areas in the South, including Alabama, Mississippi, and Arkansas, still do not have this form of statewide assistance in place.

Due to the way these funds are generated, often through increases in existing real estate transfer fees or taxes, the states with more active real estate markets tend to have larger trust funds. Most states distribute around $10 million or less annually, though a few offer as much as $25–$27 million with only three states historically providing substantially above this amount – New Jersey (at a combined total of approximately $44.7 million annually for its two trust funds), Ohio (at approximately $56 million), and Florida (previously capped at approximately $393.4 million annually, though unfunded in 2009–10). Even if this relatively high level of funding could be sustained nationally, it would be insufficient to replace the loss of tens of billions in federal support since the 1970s.

Using another measure, the Millennial Housing Commission estimated in 2002 that 250 000 units of affordable housing would have to be created every year over the next 20 years just to meet the housing gap for the extremely low-income (ELI) group. Florida, which had the largest annual distribution, assisted as many units as 14 854 (in 2002–03) at its peak, though most states are much closer to Vermont's average of 442 annually. Still, Florida's numbers reflect a broader range of income targets with some of these units intended for households earning 120% or even 140% of median income. Overall, state housing trust funds will continue to be incapable of replacing the loss in federal assistance.

Given the time these programmes have had to mature, along with the increasing capacity of the implementing state agencies and the relatively significant dissemination of state housing trust funds across the country, they have successfully addressed diverse housing needs. In order to assess performance relative to both their own policy objectives and federal programmes and policies, the author examined legislative and related documents available in early 2009, reviewing state housing trust fund structure, targets, resources, and outcomes. Key findings from this research are presented below.

Structure

The majority of states with such programmes administer them through state departments that often also administer the federal HOME Investment Partnership and Community Development Block Grant (CDBG) programs, or through some form of housing finance agency that frequently also handles housing bonds and tax credits. Increased flexibility for housing programmes; addressing the loss of federal funds through gap financing, leveraging, or matching federal assistance; and providing assistance to nonprofits are often specific goals outlined in the legislative mission or intent. Many also stipulate the goal of boosting economic activity through housing production.

Most states (over 83%) distribute the funding on a competitive basis, though a few also target certain regions or jurisdictions for assistance, with Florida distributing it as a block grant to every county and major city in the state. Just over 42% of the states specifically maintain in their trust fund documents that housing need and/or planning plays a role in funding decisions. But comprehensive housing planning responsive to other land development goals and strategies, such as transportation and land use, and integrated across levels of government from local to regional to state, is not widespread. Further, because most states disburse funds on a competitive basis, assistance might not necessarily be targeted where housing need is greatest.

Targets

Housing trust funds do allow for greater flexibility than federal programmes, which often include more restrictions and administrative requirements. In addition, some target activities or needs not typically assisted by federal funds, such as rental assistance to residents of mobile homes who are living in poverty; allow flexible enhancement of federal assistance; or offer opportunities to preserve affordable units that are nearing the end of eligible periods of assistance under federal programmes such as the Low Income Housing Tax Credit. Currently, 60.4% of state housing trust funds engage in some form of demand-side activity, with down payment assistance, some types of rental assistance, and operating or administrative support to manage these projects being the most common. While a greater variety of approaches have been implemented in recent years, innovation in and of itself does not guarantee assistance to those with the most critical housing needs. Further, the amount of assistance available appears not to have kept pace with the number of new housing strategies. Implementation can then be stymied due to lack of sufficient funding for each strategy. In fact, the policy decisions behind assistance limits (per household, per unit, and per project) – how they are set and how often they are reevaluated – are not usually clear.

Most state programmes targeting ELI households or those in poverty do not generate that much money on an annual basis, with only five having more than $10 million available annually. More state programmes target low income (serving households earning up to 80% of area median income (AMI)), and several go up to 110, 115, and even 140% of AMI.

Only five states require 'long-term' or 'perpetual' affordability as a condition of assistance with the other states that have some form of affordability requirement establishing 5- to 30-year periods. Yet, the states that use the phrase 'long-term' do not specifically define it. Further, these affordability terms do not necessarily apply to all the units assisted with housing trust funds. Affordability limits for federal programmes still exceed those established through many state housing trust funds. Those states that use these funds to match federal assistance must comply with whatever requirements are more restrictive, which tend to be federal affordability periods. Four states combine federal housing assistance with state sources in their trust funds, and 22 trust funds specifically address coordination with federal programmes.

Thus, state trust funds are commonly used for gap financing, making projects possible that might not otherwise have come to fruition or to leverage other funding sources. The 2006 Housing Trust Fund Project survey estimated that every $1 of state housing trust fund assistance typically leverages $7 of private and other public funding. The private sector is a critical partner, especially nonprofit housing providers that often assist lower-income households for-profit developers are unable to assist. In fact, almost 90% of state trust funds allow or specifically target nonprofit applicants. Recognising this fact, a number of trust funds offer some technical assistance as a means to bolster nonprofit capacity to participate in such projects.

Resources

A critical resource issue characterises housing trust funds – an ongoing, dedicated source of funding to maintain the trust fund permanently. Various studies credit a secure funding source, allowing more effective and long-range planning on both the part of agencies that administer and the developers that implement these programmes. Though this permanency is a defining characteristic of housing trust funds, at least 19 (39.6%) state programmes rely entirely or in part on annual legislative appropriations and/or general funds. Such appropriations can bolster trust funds, particularly as real estate transactions decrease. But dependence on general funds means a greater reliance on a favourable political environment to sustain the trust fund.

With the devolution of responsibility to the local and state levels, housing trust funds established a track record of flexibly meeting the nation's housing needs and demonstrated an ability to leverage significant public and private resources. Yet, for both political and financial reasons, shallow subsidies for low- and median-income households are far more common than provision of the deep subsidies needed to assist the lowest-income groups. Thus, those most in need are in effect the least served. For several years, housing advocates have promoted the establishment of a national housing trust fund to target ELI households. In 2008, that legislation was passed.

National Housing Trust Fund (Housing and Economic Recovery Act of 2008)

Support grew in the past decade for a national housing trust fund. In response to the foreclosure crisis, Congress adopted the Housing and Economic Recovery Act (Public Law No. 110-289) effective 30 July 2008, in part to protect the government-sponsored enterprises, Fannie Mae and Freddie Mac, which are responsible for up to half of the mortgage debt in the United States. In establishing the National Housing Trust Fund in this legislation, the federal government was again targeting, as it had with the public housing programme, some of the poorest households in the country, directing 75% of the programme to ELI households and the remaining 25% to very low-income (VLI) households earning up to 50% of AMI. The programme focuses on rental housing, including the production, preservation, rehabilitation, and operating costs of such housing, with only 10% of the total funds available to support homeownership activities. Over the next decade, the legislative goal is to assist 1.5 million units of housing for these income groups.

As previously outlined, many local and state programmes do not specifically target ELI or, if they do, tend to dedicate smaller amounts of assistance to this income group. In targeting this underserved group, this programme acknowledges the fact that many ELI renters have been affected by the mortgage crisis as former homeowners compete with them for limited rental units, and as tenants are evicted when their landlords lose their properties due to foreclosure. Though diverted to address foreclosure issues during the first 3 years, funds for the National Housing Trust Fund were to be generated through Fannie Mae and Freddie Mac based on a percentage of their new business. Due to the financial distress these agencies face, their ability to fund the National Housing Trust Fund has been suspended indefinitely. The National Low Income Housing Coalition, which has spearheaded advocacy for such a fund since the 1990s, is closely monitoring the situation to ensure that this critical funding source is replenished or replaced such that the Trust Fund can function as outlined in the legislation. Once funded, the Department of Housing and Urban Development (HUD) will oversee the programme, allocating assistance on a needs-based formula to designated state agencies, many of which are already managing state housing trust funds. The National Housing Trust Fund will reintroduce a greater federal role in addressing affordable housing issues, especially among the most vulnerable, and complement existing state and local housing initiatives. As housing trust funds gain credibility in the United States, Canada is also increasingly dependent on this form of housing assistance.

International Models – Canada's Housing Trust Funds

Canada is the only country other than the United States to embrace housing trust funds. Canada faces similar affordability challenges and can also generate resources based on development activity, such as development fees, in-lieu contributions, and land lease/sales. The Canada Mortgage and Housing Corporation has studied housing trust funds, particularly their application in the United States, and recommends them as a viable source of housing assistance in Canada. Prior to 2000, only five trust funds existed – Saskatoon's Social Housing Reserve, Vancouver's Affordable Housing Fund, Whistler's Employee Housing Service Charge Fund, Banff's

Reserve Fund for Affordable Housing, and Winnipeg's Housing Opportunity Partnership Loan Fund. At least 14 such regional and local trust funds exist today. A range of income groups are assisted, including the lowest income groups. Most engage nonprofits in the housing delivery process, though in some cases for-profits are also involved. Typically, Canada's housing trust funds do not generate the amount of assistance that larger urban areas do in the United States.

The Future of Housing Trust Funds

Most local and state housing trust funds do not devote significant amounts of assistance to ELI households and/or those in poverty. While demand-side strategies have increased, those that require ongoing assistance from year to year, such as housing vouchers and maintenance costs, remain minimal. Policy initiatives that address the long-term housing affordability of those with the lowest income and sustain on-going strategies require a significant depth of subsidy that many local and state programmes do not either have or use. In order to identify and meet targets, coordination with housing plans is essential. Specific funding limits may reflect more of a policy concern with maximising the number of units or households assisted as opposed to ensuring that the assistance adequately addresses critical housing needs.

Innovative housing strategies have expanded to allow state housing trust funds to address a wider range of local needs, including critical issues such as maintaining the viability and affordability of assisted housing and targeting rental assistance, and the more economically distressed such as the homeless and farm workers. In many cases, these housing programmes work in concert with federal assistance, though they tend to target a broader range of income groups.

Often, political constraints make it difficult to fully implement these programmes. Developers and local governments need to be assured that they can depend on a consistent source of assistance. With sufficient political support and funding and as part of an integrated and coordinated planning initiative, housing trust funds can accommodate truly innovative strategies to address complex housing challenges while continuing to attract private sector participation. A National Housing Trust Fund that targets the most difficult to house, the expansion of local and state programmes, and new programmes in Canada attest to the flexibility and usefulness of this funding resource.

See also: Access and Affordability: Developed Countries; Affordable Housing Strategies; Government Sponsored Enterprises in the United States; Housing Policy: Agents and Regulators; Inclusionary Zoning to Support Affordable Housing; Planning Institutions: Canada/United States.

Further Reading

Bernstine N and Saraf IB (2003) New rental production and the national housing trust fund campaign. *Journal of Affordable Housing* 12(4): 389–405.

Brooks ME (1997) Housing trust funds: A new approach to funding affordable housing. In: van Vliet W (ed.) *Affordable Housing and Urban Redevelopment in the United States*, pp. 229–245. Thousand Oaks, CA: SAGE Publications, Inc.

Brooks ME (2007) *Housing Trust Fund Progress Report 2007*. Frazier Park, CA: Housing Trust Fund Project.

Connerly CE (1993) A survey and assessment of housing trust funds in the United States. *Journal of the American Planning Association* 59(3): 306–319.

Drdla Associates Inc. (2000) *Housing Trust Funds: Their Nature, Applicability and Potential in Canada*. Toronto, ON: Canada Mortgage and Housing Corporation.

Goetz EG (1995) Potential effects of federal policy devolution on local housing expenditures. *Publius: The Journal of Federalism* 25(3): 99–116.

Katz B, Turner MA, Brown KD, Cunningham M, and Sawyer N (2003) *Rethinking Local Affordable Housing Strategies: Lessons from 70 Years of Policy and Practice*. Washington, DC: The Brookings Institution.

Larsen K (2009) Reassessing state housing trust funds – Results of a Florida survey. *Housing Studies* 24(2): 173–201.

Lubell J (2006) *Increasing the Availability of Affordable Homes: An Analysis of High Impact State and Local Solutions*. Washington, DC: Center for Housing Policy.

Orlebeke CJ (2000) The evolution of low-income housing policy, 1949 to 1999. *Housing Policy Debate* 11(2): 489–520.

Rose K and Bell J (2005) *Expanding Opportunity: New Resources to Meet California's Housing Needs*. Oakland, CA: PolicyLink.

Salsich PW (2009) National affordable housing trust fund legislation: The subprime mortgage crisis also hits renters. *Georgetown Journal on Poverty Law and Policy* 16(1): 11–51.

Schwartz AF (2006) *Housing Policy in the United States: An Introduction*. New York: Routledge.

Stegman MA (1999) *State and Local Affordable Housing Programs: A Rich Tapestry*. Washington, DC: Urban Land Institute.

Relevant Websites

www.cmhc-schl.gc.ca – Canada Housing and Mortgage Corporation.

www.communitychange.org – Center for Community Change, Housing Trust Fund Project.

www.jchs.harvard.edu – Joint Center for Housing Studies, State of the Nation's Housing.

www.nlihc.org – National Low Income Housing Coalition, Out of Reach.

Housing Wealth and Consumption

M Iacoviello, Federal Reserve Board, Washington, DC, USA

© 2012 Elsevier Ltd. All rights reserved.

Glossary

Consumption The actual and imputed expenditures of households for the purpose of acquiring goods and services.

Housing wealth The total value of the housing capital in a particular country, regardless of whether it is owned or rented, or mortgaged or not.

Wealth effect The notion that exogenous changes in wealth might affect individual behaviour.

Housing Wealth

At the aggregate level, housing wealth measures the market value of all the residential capital located in a particular country. According to this definition, aggregate housing wealth of US households at the end of 2008 was $25.4 trillion. Housing wealth is about one-half of total household net worth (which is $52.9 trillion), and is larger than the gross domestic product ($14.4 trillion). Moreover, since financial wealth is more unequally distributed than housing wealth, housing wealth accounts for almost two-thirds of the total wealth of the median household. A narrower definition of housing wealth includes only owner-occupied housing: using this definition, housing wealth in 2008 was $20.4 trillion. **Table 1** lists the balance sheet of the household sector in the United States at the end of 2008 using data from the flow of funds (FOF) accounts of the United States, using a breakdown of total household assets that differentiates housing capital from other forms of wealth. A large fraction (80%) of housing wealth is made up by the stock of owner-occupied homes. The remaining 20% (residential real estate held by non-farm, noncorporate businesses) is made up by the rental housing stock.

Figure 1 plots household consumption expenditures in the United States along with wealth divided into housing wealth and nonhousing wealth. The series have been converted in 2005 billions of dollars using the deflator for personal consumption expenditures. The stock of housing wealth is large and moves slowly over time, but it exhibits a sharp increase between 1997 and 2005, followed by a bust between 2005 and 2008: size and persistence explain why changes in housing wealth are potentially an important candidate for understanding trends and cycles in aggregate consumption expenditures.

Figure 2 plots annual changes in housing wealth and personal consumption expenditures in the United States from 1952 to 2008. The two variables tend to move together in post-Second World War US history. Their contemporaneous correlation is 0.47. This correlation is larger than the correlation between consumption and the residual components of household wealth: for instance, the contemporaneous correlation between changes in inflation-adjusted financial wealth and consumption equals 0.38.

The co-movement between housing wealth and consumption poses a challenging question for macroeconomists, policy-makers, and commentators. Do fluctuations in consumption reflect fluctuations in housing wealth, or are both variables determined by some other macroeconomic factor that moves them both, such as technological change, movements in interest rates, or other factors that contribute to business cycle fluctuations?

Housing Wealth and Consumption

A standard macroeconomics textbook contains a section presenting the economy's consumption function. In this consumption function, the standard determinants of consumption are wealth W and permanent income Y, and the consumption function reads as follows:

$$C = \alpha W + \beta Y \qquad (1)$$

where α and β measure, respectively, the marginal propensity to spend out of wealth and permanent income. This equation can be obtained as the solution to a problem where individuals maximise utility over time given a set of intertemporal trading opportunities, under very special assumptions about the set of trading opportunities and about the nature of the income process that the individual faces. An equation such as eqn [1] dates back in the history of economic thought to at least Keynes, and was given prominence in the seminal work of Milton Friedman and Franco Modigliani.

Table 1 Composition of household wealth in the United States

Household balance sheet, 2008 billion $			FOF entry
A	Assets	67 134	B100:1
B	Real estate (owner-occupied homes)	20 398	B100:3
C	Residential real estate of noncorporate business (rented homes)	4964	B103:4
D	Other tangible assets	4779	B100:2 less B100:3
E	Financial assets less residential real estate of noncorporate business	36 992	B100:8 less B103:4
F	Liabilities	14 216	B100:31
H	Household net worth	52 917	A − F
	Housing wealth	25 362	B + C
	Nonhousing wealth	27 555	D + E − F

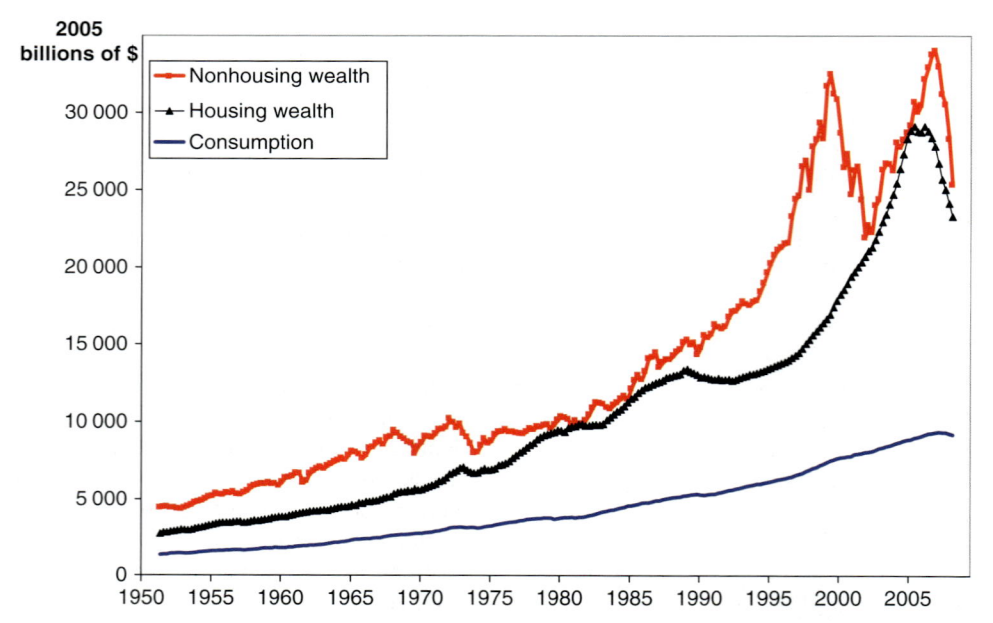

Figure 1 Housing wealth, consumption, and nonhousing wealth in the United States from 1952 to 2008. The series are expressed in 2005 billions of dollars.

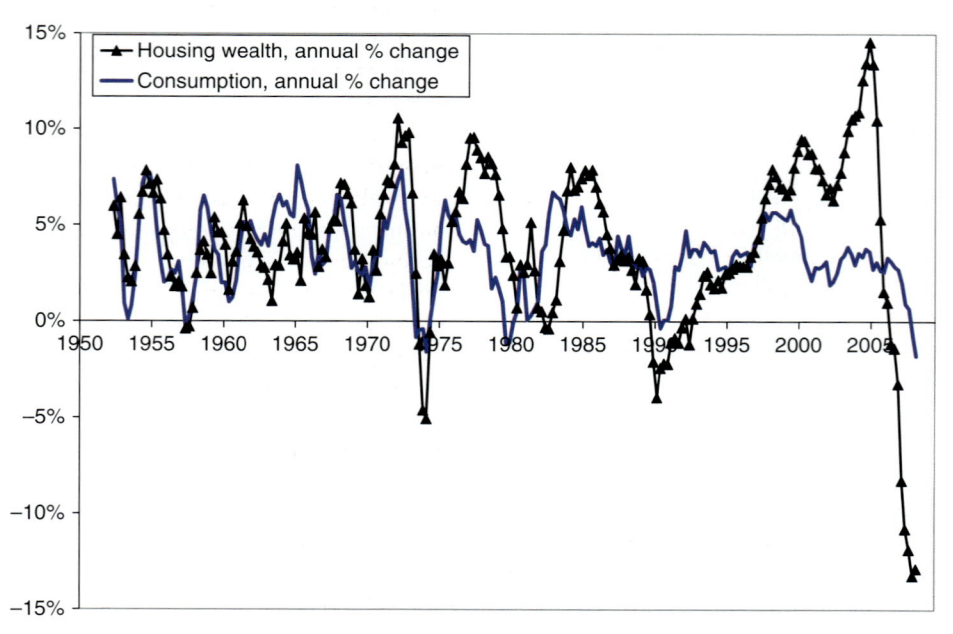

Figure 2 Annual changes in housing wealth and consumption in the United States, from 1952 to 2008.

When total wealth is broken down into housing wealth (HW) and nonhousing wealth (NW), a generalisation of the above equation that allows for different marginal propensities to consume housing and nonhousing wealth can be written as follows:

$$C = \alpha_N NW + \alpha_H HW + \beta Y \quad (2)$$

It is typical to interpret the coefficient α_H in eqn [2] as measuring the 'housing wealth effect'. At the basic level, in fact, this equation states that if housing wealth were to change by, say, $1, consumption should change by α_H dollars. This equation provides the basis to think about the connection between housing wealth and consumption. However, it is entirely silent about the reasons why housing wealth moves. One important caveat in interpreting the results from this equation is that, while it is reasonable to interpret part of changes in the two right-hand side variables as exogenous at the 'individual' level (promotions, bequests, lottery winnings, unemployment spells, gentrification, and deterioration of a neighbourhood are somewhat outside the control of the individual), the interpretation of this equation at the 'aggregate' level is more complicated, since, to a large extent, all variables of eqn [2] are endogenously determined.

Movements in nonhousing wealth, for instance, might either reflect a new view of future profits or occur because market participants apply a different set of discount factors to those expected profits, where the discount factors incorporate both risk-free interest rates and equity premiums. From a theoretical standpoint, these movements could have different effects on household spending. The same reasoning applies to housing wealth: changes in the value of the housing stock might reflect genuine shifts in tastes between housing and consumption goods, or could result from changes in availability of residential land, or from movements in sectoral technologies. It is reasonable to assume that all these changes could affect consumption, but their effects might differ.

The empirical literature (surveyed in the next section) grapples with the obvious identification problem of separating endogenous from exogenous movements in housing wealth. The theoretical literature studies instead raise the question of whether a housing wealth effect exists, what it means, and how to think about it.

The Theory

A Basic Model

To illustrate the ideas, this section considers a simple model of consumption and housing choice. A household lives forever and has preferences defined over current and future consumption c_t and housing services h_t. That is, the household problem is defined by

$$\max E_t \sum_{t=0}^{\infty} \beta^t (u(c_t) + v(h_t)) \quad (3)$$

where β is the household discount factor and E_t is the expectation operator. This preference specification is standard in models of household behaviour. Life-cycle and bequest considerations, endogenous labour supply, nonseparability between housing and consumption, and housing tenure choice are ignored here. The household faces the following budget constraint in any period t:

$$c_t + q_t h_t + s_t = Y_t + q_t h_{t-1} + R_t s_{t-1} \quad (4)$$

where q_t is the price of housing, s_t is nonhousing wealth (for instance, shares in a firm or holdings of government debt), R_t is the return on nonhousing wealth, and Y_t is labour income. In eqn [4], the right-hand side measures total resources available to the household at the end of the period t. These resources, in the absence of portfolio adjustment costs, can be used for consumption, housing wealth accumulation, and nonhousing wealth accumulation. In the absence of general equilibrium considerations, one can treat q_t, R_t, and Y_t as exogenous (and possibly random), and assume that the household chooses plans for consumption c_t, housing h_t, and financial wealth s_t. In this simple framework, random changes in q_t, R_t, and Y_t can proxy, respectively, for housing wealth shocks, nonhousing wealth shocks, and income shocks. For given initial conditions, the solution to the household problem can then be rearranged to express optimal household consumption as a function of lagged nonhousing wealth s_{t-1}, housing wealth h_{t-1}, and innovations to q_t, R_t, and Y_t. It has the interpretation of a consumption function.

What are the implications for consumption of a shock to housing wealth in this model? To gain some intuition, consider the simplest possible case where the household, because of large adjustment costs to housing, does not change house between two consecutive periods: $h_t = h_{t-1}$ for every t. It is easy to see that changes in q_t are irrelevant for consumption behaviour of this household, since $q_t h_t = q_t h_{t-1}$ in every period, so that housing wealth disappears from the household budget constraint. Intuitively, higher housing values ($q_t h_{t-1}$) result in higher housing consumption costs ($q_t h_t$) that exactly offset the housing wealth effect on nonhousing consumption; when q_t rises, wealth in units of consumption increases, but, unless the individual changes the consumption of housing services, housing wealth does not imply larger consumption. This basic logic is what leads Buiter (2008) to assert that housing wealth is not net wealth, unless individuals decrease their housing consumption in response to housing price changes.

If the household can change housing consumption between two periods (h_t needs not to equal h_{t-1}), an additional effect kicks in. When house prices rise, the so-called substitution effect will cause households to reduce their demand for housing, and will free up resources that can be spent on nonhousing consumption. In this scenario, the immediate effect of an increase in housing wealth is that of stimulating consumption. The interpretation of the rise in consumption, however, is subtle: part of the rise in consumption does reflect the result that wealth, measured in units of consumption, is larger, so that the individual will optimally reallocate part of the larger wealth among all expenditure categories. Part of the rise in consumption, instead, simply reflects the economics of asset substitution: the household can now achieve higher utility by consuming less housing and more nonhousing consumption goods than before.

Extensions

What is missing from the basic theory above?

(1) The simple theory above makes the extreme assumption that changes in the price of housing are purely exogenous. To see why modifying this assumption might change the results, consider the case where changes in the price of housing are the consequence of a shift in tastes between nonhousing and housing goods: for instance, individuals might decide that they prefer to live in larger and nicer homes rather than dining out: under this assumption, it is possible that increases in the price of housing are associated with lower consumption, since the change in house prices is the consequence of a shift in preferences away from consumption goods. Empirically, evidence in favour of a mechanism of this kind comes from the observation (at least in the United States) that movements in housing prices are positively correlated with movements in housing investment: in a simple demand–supply diagram of the housing market, this evidence would seem to support the idea that movements in housing prices (and wealth) are the consequence of shifts in housing demand, rather than housing supply.

(2) Another consideration that is missing from the basic story is the presence of borrowing constraints. The structure of financial markets in many developed economies implies that households have easy access to housing wealth through second mortgages, home equity loans, or home equity lines of credit. If liquidity-constrained households – who are believed to have a high marginal propensity to spend on average – can borrow more whenever their housing wealth rises, this channel is likely to lead to a larger correlation between movements in housing wealth and movements in aggregate consumption. Moreover, one can expect larger aggregate effects from changes in housing wealth since housing wealth is more evenly distributed across the population than non-housing wealth: if relatively poor people have higher than average propensity to consume, the aggregate consumption response to changes in housing wealth might be larger than otherwise.

(3) The basic model also sidesteps life-cycle and housing tenure considerations. The representative household of the model displays a profile of housing consumption that is constant over time. In reality, the way consumption is connected to movements in housing wealth should also depend on whether individuals expect to modify their housing consumption in the future. Cross-sectional data show that housing wealth typically increases over the life cycle, before flattening out at a relatively old age. This is true both at the extensive margin (homeownership rates increase with age) and at the intensive margin (the average size of owner-occupied houses increases with age). Taking these elements into consideration, one should expect that life-cycle considerations should imply a negative response of consumption to increases in aggregate housing prices, since – to the extent that renters plan to become homeowners at some point of their life, or homeowners plan to move to larger homes – higher housing prices require larger savings than otherwise if individuals are planning to buy a larger home.

(4) A final aspect to consider is how persistent changes in housing wealth are relative to changes in other forms of wealth. Historically, changes in housing returns have been more persistent than changes in the return to, say, stock market wealth. Household's consumption might respond more to a given size change in housing wealth if this change is not expected to reverse quickly.

Taking Stock

A message from the basic theory is that after solving the household intertemporal optimisation problem, one can derive an aggregate consumption function where consumption is expressed as a function of income and wealth, and where the marginal propensity to consume out of housing wealth is positive or negative depending on the underlying characteristics of the economy.

In a more realistic setting, however, especially when the goal is to model the economy as a whole (rather than the behaviour of a single economic agent), one should assume that wealth is endogenous, and that its fluctuations are driven by current or expected movements in technology, tastes, taxes, or some other unidentified economic fundamentals. These fundamentals, in turn, may affect at the same time both consumption and wealth itself, thus making any statement about links from wealth to consumption (or vice versa) hard to interpret.

Yet central bankers, practitioners, and policy-makers routinely think of movements in wealth as exogenous, mostly because these movements are hard to predict or explain based on movements in readily available observable variables that one can regard as purely exogenous.

Empirical Studies

The Conventional Wisdom

A simple regression on quarterly US data for the period 1952.I–2008.IV of:

$$[\Delta(\log C) = \alpha + \beta_{HW} \Delta \log(HW_{-1}) + \beta_{NW} \Delta \log(NW_{-1})]$$

where C, HW, and NW measure, respectively consumption, housing wealth, and nonhousing wealth, and Δ is the first difference operator, yields the following coefficients (standard errors below):

$$\Delta(\log C) = \underset{0.0006}{0.007} + \underset{0.035}{0.136}\Delta(\log HW_{-1}) + \underset{0.013}{0.056}\Delta(\log NW_{-1})$$

More sophisticated regressions yield similar results, at least qualitatively if not quantitatively. This simple regression has the virtue of being simple, easy to estimate, replicable, and straightforward to interpret. According to this regression, the elasticity of consumption to housing wealth is 0.14, after controlling for movements in nonhousing wealth (the elasticity of consumption to nonhousing wealth is lower, at 0.06). These estimates are more often converted into dollar-to-dollar estimates using the fact that, in the sample in question, the average ratio of housing wealth to annual consumption is about 2.3, and the average ratio of nonhousing wealth to annual consumption is about 2.75. A $1 increase in housing wealth then generates an increase in annualised consumption of about 6¢, and $1 increase in nonhousing wealth generates an increase in consumption of about 2¢.

The results of this simple regression are the basis for a series of wisdoms about wealth effects and the basis for thinking about housing wealth and consumption. In particular, the larger sensitivity of consumption to housing wealth is one of the many reasons why policy-makers might be more worried about changes in housing than nonhousing wealth.

Studies Based on Aggregate Time-Series Data

Perhaps one of the most prominent studies of the link between housing wealth and consumption is the FRB/US model, which is the econometric model of the US economy used by the Federal Reserve. One of the model blocks describes household consumption behaviour as a function of total wealth and its composition. This model predicts, among other things, a marginal propensity to consume out of net tangible assets (housing wealth and consumer durables less home mortgages) which ranges between 5 and 10¢, on the dollar (see, for instance, Brayton and Tinsley, 1996). It also predicts a marginal propensity to consume of 3¢ on the dollar for equities.

Several studies have reviewed the literature and provided additional estimates of the so-called housing wealth effect. The broad consensus from the literature based on time-series data is not very different from the FRB/US model. Poterba (2000) surveys a variety of estimates from the literature and finds values that lie in a similar range.

More recent studies corroborate the findings from the empirical literature of the 1990s. Carroll et al. (2006) propose a time-series-based method that exploits the sluggishness of consumption growth to distinguish between immediate and eventual wealth effects. Using US data, they estimate that the immediate (next-quarter) marginal propensity to consume from a $1 change in housing wealth is about 2¢, with an eventual effect around 9¢, substantially larger than the effect of shocks to financial wealth.

Case et al. (2005) found a strong correlation between aggregate house prices and aggregate consumption in a panel of developed countries. According to the central estimates, a 1% increase in housing wealth increases consumption by roughly 0.11% in the international panel. For a panel of US states, an updated version of their 2005 paper (Case et al., 2011) reports elasticities of consumption to housing wealth that range from 0.03 to 0.18, with a central estimate of 0.08.

The main problem with studies based on aggregate data is that such data do not rule out alternative explanations for the time-series correlation: either indirect wealth effects or reverse causation running from changes in household saving to changes in wealth. Iacoviello and Neri (2010) address this problem in a structural equilibrium model where both consumption and housing wealth are endogenous, and are driven by movements in technology, preferences, and monetary policy. They show that their model quantitatively replicates the positive correlation in the data between consumption growth and housing wealth growth. The bulk of this correlation simply captures common factors that move the two variables in the same direction, such as shifts in preferences, interest rates, or technology. However, a nonnegligible portion of this correlation reflects the contribution of liquidity constraints. This result echoes the conclusions of Muellbauer and Murphy (2008), who argue that housing collateral and down payment constraints are the key to understanding the role of house price variations in explaining medium-term consumption fluctuations.

Studies Based on Microdata

A growing literature has used household-level data to connect movements in consumption and movements in housing wealth. One of the main questions in this literature is to study how households respond to changes in the value of their housing wealth. A central issue concerns how to identify movements in housing wealth that are orthogonal to other factors that might also affect consumption.

Campbell and Cocco (2007) study microdata from the UK Family Expenditure Survey from 1988 to 2000. They use repeated cross-sections of household expenditure data and regional home price information to estimate a small, positive consumption response to home prices for young homeowners, and a large positive response for old homeowners. Using mean home values and consumption as reported in their paper, this translates into marginal propensities to consume out of housing wealth of 0.06 for young homeowners, and 0.11 for old homeowners.

Mian and Sufi (2009) investigate how existing homeowners respond to the rising value of their home equity, which they refer to as the home equity-based borrowing channel. They use land topography-based housing supply elasticities in order to identify exogenous variations in house price growth across different geographical areas and individual-level data on homeowner debt and defaults from 1997 to 2008. They show that existing homeowners increase their borrowing significantly in response to changes in their home equity, and use the extra borrowing mainly for real outlays, such as consumption or home improvements.

Conclusions

Housing wealth is a major component of household wealth. Housing wealth is linked to nonhousing consumption through the logic and algebra of the budget constraint: by moving to a smaller or larger house, a household can free up or use resources that would otherwise go into nonhousing consumption or other forms of saving. Empirically, housing wealth and consumption tend to move together: this could happen because some third factor moves both variables, or because there is a more direct effect going from one variable to the other. Studies based on time-series data, on panel data, and on more detailed, recent microdata point out to the possibility that a considerable portion of the effect of housing wealth on consumption reflects the influence of changes in housing wealth on borrowing against such wealth, although estimates of such effect are surrounded by considerable uncertainty.

See also: Housing and Wealth Portfolios; Housing Equity Withdrawal in the United Kingdom.

References

Brayton F and Tinsley P (1996) A guide to FRB/US: A macroeconomic model of the United States. *Finance and Economics Discussion Series 96-42.* Board of Governors of the Federal Reserve System (US). October.
Buiter WH (2008) Housing wealth isn't wealth. *CEPR Discussion Papers 6920.* CEPR Discussion Papers. July.
Campbell JY and Cocco JF (2007) How do house prices affect consumption? Evidence from micro data. *Journal of Monetary Economics* 54(3): 591–621.
Carroll CD, Otsuka M, and Slacalek J (2006) How large is the housing wealth effect? A new approach. *NBER Working Papers 12746.* National Bureau of Economic Research, Inc. December.
Case KE, Quigley JM, and Shiller RJ (2005) Comparing wealth effects: The stock market versus the housing market. *Advances in Macroeconomics* 5(1): 1235.
Case KE, Quigley JM, and Shiller RJ (2011) Wealth effects revisited 1978–2009. *NBER Working Papers 16848.* National Bureau of Economic Research, Inc. March.
Iacoviello M and Neri S (2010) Housing market spillovers: Evidence from an estimated DSGE model. *American Economic Journal: Macroeconomics* 2(2): 125–164.
Mian AR and Sufi A (2009) House prices, home equity-based borrowing, and the US household leverage crisis. *NBER Working Papers 15283.* National Bureau of Economic Research, Inc. August.
Muellbauer J and Murphy A (2008) Housing markets and the economy: The assessment. *Oxford Review of Economic Policy* 24(1): 1–33.
Poterba JM (2000) Stock market wealth and consumption. *Journal of Economic Perspectives* 14(2): 99–118.

Further Reading

Davis MA and Heathcote J (2007) The price and quantity of residential land in the United States. *Journal of Monetary Economics* 54(8): 2595–2620.
Davis MA and Palumbo MG (2001) A primer on the economics and time series econometrics of wealth effects. *Finance and Economics Discussion Series 2001–09.* Board of Governors of the Federal Reserve System (US).
Iacoviello M (2005) House prices, borrowing constraints, and monetary policy in the business cycle. *American Economic Review* 95(3): 739–764.

Housing Wealth and Inheritance in the United Kingdom

C Hamnett, Kings College London, London, UK

© 2012 Elsevier Ltd. All rights reserved.

Glossary

Equity extraction The reduction in the equity or wealth in a property as a result of remortgaging, trading down, or other strategies to unlock equity.

Estates passing at death The total assets in the estate of a deceased person.

Housing inheritance The transmission of housing assets or wealth derived from the sale of such assets from the deceased to beneficiaries.

Housing wealth The equity in a property subtracting outstanding mortgage or other debt secured on the property from its current market value. This can also be estimated at the national level using aggregate statistics.

Inequalities in housing wealth The inequalities in the value of housing wealth between regions or different social groups on the basis of occupation, income, race, gender, or age or some combination of these characteristics.

Intergenerational homeownership Where the children of homeowners are enabled to become homeowners either because of help with down payments or via housing inheritance.

Negative equity The situation where the mortgage or other debt secured on a property exceeds its market value.

Housing Wealth and the Growth of Homeownership

A major consequence of the growth of homeownership in Western countries in the post-Second World War period has been the growth and widening of housing wealth and a consequent growth in the scale and importance of housing inheritance. While housing has long been a significant component of total wealth holdings, in the nineteenth and early twentieth centuries most housing was privately rented, and housing wealth was largely concentrated in the hands of private landlords. The rapid expansion of homeownership postwar, particularly in some Western European countries, combined with the even more rapid growth of house prices over the past 40 years in some countries, has led to housing wealth becoming both more widely spread and a much larger component of overall wealth holdings. Homeownership has thus been a major driver of widening wealth ownership and a reduction in wealth inequality postwar in many countries.

In the period up until the Second World War, the majority of households owned little in the way of assets except domestic goods and chattels and had limited savings. Wealth ownership was concentrated in the hands of a relatively small minority of households, much of it in the form of land and securities. This widening of wealth ownership through homeownership has had important implications for both the structure of overall wealth ownership and for inheritance. Many more households now own a substantial property asset which they can draw on in old age or pass on to their beneficiaries. The expansion of housing wealth is, however, limited to owners and is, by definition, denied to both private rented and social housing tenants. Some argue that housing wealth is not real wealth, but this argument is flawed as owners can sell and move into rented housing, down size and release capital, borrow against or remortgage their asset, or pass it on to beneficiaries. The role of housing wealth has been documented internationally by Forrest and Murie (1995) and Smith and Searle (2010).

While large-scale ownership has long been more extensive in homesteading settler countries of North America, Australia, Canada, and New Zealand, it has been a more recent phenomenon in many European countries where private renting was the normal urban housing tenure until the 1960s. This article will focus on the trends in housing wealth and inheritance in Britain as a case study of a wider set of processes (see Zhu (2006) for an analysis of housing wealth in the United States).

The growth of homeownership in Britain (from 10% in 1914 to 25% in 1939, 50% in 1971, and 68% in 2007) combined with rapid house price inflation from 1970 onward greatly increased the value of housing in wealth holdings and widened its distribution (Hamnett and Seavers, 1996). Housing wealth is a product of the level of homeownership and the level of house prices. Sharp falls in house prices, such as those that occurred in Britain from 1989 to 2002 and from autumn 2008 to 2010, can lead to both falls in housing wealth and to substantial negative equity for those who bought near the top of the market. In this respect, housing shares many of the characteristics of other assets in that it can rise or fall in value depending on the state of the market.

The Royal Commission on the Distribution of Income and Wealth (1977) estimated that the value of dwellings as a proportion of net personal wealth in the United Kingdom increased from 18% in 1960 to 37% in 1975. Annual Inland Revenue data show that share had risen to over 50% by 1990. The share fell back in the housing market slump of the early 1990s, but has recovered since 1995 as house prices have risen. In 2005, UK residential property accounted for 52% of gross identified personal wealth (IPW). This highlights the growing importance of housing in wealth holdings. The proportionate share of other assets in wealth such as land, cash, and securities has declined correspondingly. Evidence from the United States (Zhu, 2006) also highlights the major role of housing in household wealth holdings and a comparative analysis of wealth holdings in six rich Organisation for Economic Cooperation and Development (OECD) countries confirms this (Sierminska et al., 2006). Zhu (2006) states that "Any understanding of household wealth is incomplete without considering housing's role in it" (p. 2).

The importance of housing wealth varies according to the scale of overall wealth. In 2005, housing's share of gross IPW in Britain varies from a low of 22% for those with wealth of more than £2 million to a high of 66% for those with wealth of £80 000–£300 000 and accounts for over 50% of all those with gross IPW of £40 000–£500 000 (see **Figure 1**). In the higher wealth bands, stocks and shares traditionally account for a high proportion of wealth. For many people, however, their house is their major asset and, with the reduction in fully funded company pension schemes, housing may represent an important source of insurance for old age. The figures exclude individuals with estates below a minimum size, currently £25 000 and thus most tenants. But, despite this tenure division in wealth, homeownership has been a powerful force for widening the spread of wealth ownership (Appleyard and Rowlingson 2010).

Tenants are exempt from this widening of housing wealth ownership although the introduction of the Right to Buy scheme under the Conservatives greatly increased the spread of housing wealth among ex-council tenants in Britain via a one-off sale of assets to individuals at below market price. The ownership of house property is not a guarantee of wealth accumulation in the short to medium term, however, as periods of falling prices can lead to substantial numbers of recent buyers falling into negative equity where the value of their home is less than the value of their outstanding mortgage. This happened on a large scale in Britain in the early 1990s during the housing market slump when it was estimated that some 2 million owners were in negative equity (Gentle et al., 1994) and over 500 000 were repossessed, and many of whom were left in debt. The collapse of the inflated housing market in a number of Western countries, most notably the United States, the United Kingdom, and Spain, since the financial crisis in 2007 has led to a wave of negative equity and mortgage foreclosures which has significantly reduced housing wealth, particularly among ethnic minority and low-income groups.

Given that the great majority of homeowners purchase using a mortgage, the value of their property has to be

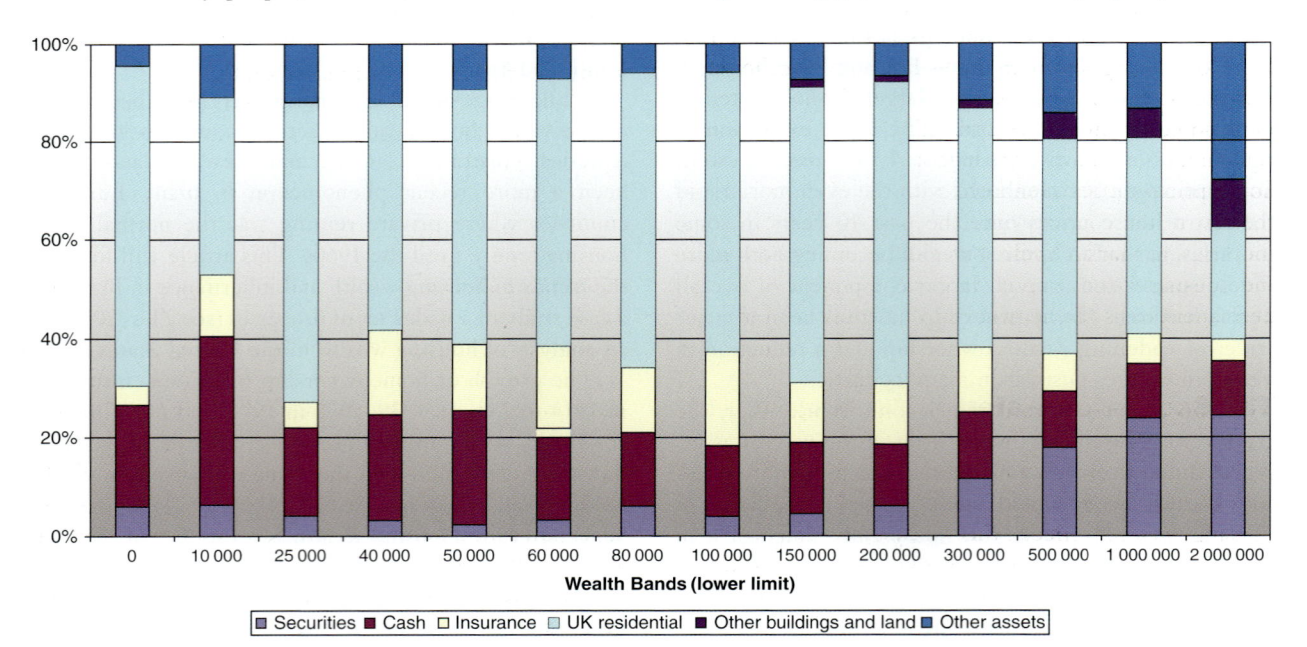

Figure 1 The distribution of assets in gross identified personal wealth, 2003.
Source: HM Revenue and Customs (2011).

measured against their outstanding mortgage debt, and this has increased very rapidly in some countries in recent years. In Britain, total household debt in 2011 totalled £1.45 trillion of which £1.2 trillion or 85% comprised lending on dwellings. Household debt as a percentage of household income in Britain rose from 100% in 1997 to 165% in 2007, largely as a result of a rapid increase in mortgage borrowing. This debt was matched by an equally large increase in the value of housing assets but the result was an inflation of overall household financial balance sheets which renders them vulnerable to sharp falls in house prices.

Geographical Differences in the Distribution of Housing Wealth

The geography of housing wealth broadly reflects the geography of house prices. Higher house prices lead to both higher levels of housing wealth in a region and often to greater affordability problems. In Britain, the gross value of the housing stock, and also housing wealth, is disproportionately concentrated in London and the South East where house prices are highest and have been for decades. Multiplying the total housing stock by average regional house prices suggests that London and the South East account for just over 40% of housing wealth in the United Kingdom. A more detailed analysis by Savills suggests that London and the South East account for 37% of housing wealth in England and Wales. However, this is not a windfall gain, as houses in London and the South East also require much larger mortgages and higher incomes to pay for them although eventually the owner is left with a larger capital asset. To some extent, the high levels of housing wealth in the South East and other high-price areas can be seen as a form of enforced saving for most domestic buyers who are not able to purchase outright and do not have ultra-high incomes. The size of the house price gap between London and the South East and the rest of the country varies depending on the stage of the housing market cycle, but there is no evidence that the housing wealth gap is widening geographically on a permanent basis (Levin and Pryce, 2010).

The Social Correlates of Housing Wealth

The incidence of homeownership increases with higher social class, income, and age, and the distribution of housing wealth reflects this. Households with higher incomes tend to buy more expensive housing which, over time, results in a higher level of housing wealth. Second, house price inflation means that the longer a household has owned, the greater the equity and embedded wealth in the property. This is generally related to age. Young households entering the home-ownership market have a high level of debt and little equity. Older households tend to have paid off most of their mortgage and have a much higher level of equity in their home. The distribution of housing wealth is also affected by cohort effects, with those purchasing in periods when house prices were lower experiencing greater levels of wealth accumulation as Hamnett (1999) has shown in Britain and Forrest (2004) has shown in a study of Hong Kong. One consequence of this is that there has been a massive intergenerational transfer of wealth towards older homeowners who have tended to have bought long ago when prices were low. The costs of this housing equity accumulation are paid for by younger buyers who have to find large deposits and pay large percentages of income in order to purchase. As Spencer Dale, the chief economist of the Bank of England, put it in a speech in 2009:

> Older households (or rather those trading down within the housing market) benefited from selling homes at much higher values. They were the winners. The big losers were younger households (or those trading up), paying more for those houses and accumulating higher debts. The money borrowed by young families ended up in bank accounts of older households.... The increase in house prices over the decade to 2007 – and the massive financial flows associated with that appreciation – represent a huge redistribution of wealth between different households within our society. (Dale, 2009)

Not surprisingly, the percentage of first-time buyers has fallen very sharply in recent years in Britain as house prices have risen. However, outright owners often tend to have lower incomes than younger mortgage buyers as many of them are retired. Therefore, high levels of housing wealth do not necessarily indicate high incomes. It may instead represent a lifetime of slow housing wealth accumulation.

Housing Wealth and Inheritance

Historically, housing wealth has been transmitted via inheritance but, recently, trading down and realisation of housing assets to fund retirement or to pay for care have become more important. Hamnett (1991) and Holmans and Frosztega (1994) have made detailed estimates of the value and incidence of housing inheritance in Britain. The data on the distribution of inheritance show a disproportionately high incidence among the higher social classes, existing homeowners, and in regions with a history of higher homeownership. This is not surprising given what we know about the history of homeownership, the lag between the growth of ownership postwar, and contemporary inheritance. Many of the homes passing on death today belonged to owners who first bought in the 1960s and 1970s, when homeownership was much more the preserve of the middle classes. This will slowly change over the next 20–30 years as widening homeownership is reflected in wider housing inheritance. The children of social housing tenants generally fail to inherit house property, however, as parents are the principal benefactors. Given that most dying owners are in their 70s or older, their children tend not to inherit until they themselves are in middle age and many may themselves be owners (Munro, 1988). A comparative analysis of housing inheritance in Britain, New Zealand, and Canada has been undertaken by Thorns (1994).

What has proved rather surprising is the low growth in the number of estates containing house property in Britain. In the 1980s, it was frequently asserted that the growth of homeownership postwar would lead to a wave of housing inheritance with Britain becoming a nation of housing inheritors. This has not happened. Annual Inland Revenue data from 1970 to 2008 show that the number of estates passing at death containing house property has risen gradually from 135–145 000 pa in the 1970s to 171 000 in 2007–08. In percentage terms, the percentage of estates containing residential property has risen from around 45–50% to 63%. This reflects the sharp growth of homeownership in the postwar period. Rather surprisingly, however, the overall number of estates passing at death has remained largely constant at around 270 000 pa. This appears to be a result of falling death rates, though it could also reflect a growth in the number of older owners selling prior to death in order to fund residential care in old age. The value of estates passing at death has increased dramatically, however, from £2 billion in 1970 to £65 billion in 2007–08. The value of housing in estates passing at death has risen from £500 million in 1970 to £32 billion in 2007–08: an average of £188 000 per estate. But, as noted earlier, much of this wealth is transmitted to existing middle-age (and often middle class) homeowners rather than to younger potential buyers.

Not all housing wealth is transmitted on death. An increasing proportion has been withdrawn via housing equity withdrawal (HEW) in recent decades. HEW can take several forms. First, some owners can sell and move into rented housing realising all the proceeds, while others can trade down to smaller and cheaper property, thus releasing some equity. Second, it is possible when a household moves to take out a larger mortgage than strictly necessary for the purchase, and to use some of the equity for consumption or investment. Third, it is also possible to remortgage a property without moving and to use some of the proceeds for general consumption. Finally, it is possible to enter into equity release schemes whereby a household can effectively take out capital against the final sale value of the property on death. The scale of HEW has risen very sharply in recent decades, notably during house price booms. Data produced by the Bank of England show that HEW rose to a peak in the late 1980s, the late 1990s, and the period up until 2007 when households withdrew some £50 billion pa or about 6% of total national posttax household income. By 2010, this had reversed into a net inflow of £25 billion a year as households sought to pay down high levels of mortgage debt (see articles Housing Equity Withdrawal in the United Kingdom and Mortgage Equity Withdrawal).

As noted earlier, there also seems to have been a growing number of older homeowners selling their property prior to death in order to fund residential care. At present, the situation in Britain is that if older people who move into a care home or who need care at home have savings or assets of over £23 000, they are liable to pay all the costs of care, and a proportion of costs if they have savings or assets of over £14 000. Given that average residential care costs are approaching £500 per week/ £25 000 pa, this can quickly exhaust savings.

Consequently, a significant proportion of older homeowners who need care may be forced to sell their home when they have exhausted their savings if they have not already sold the home and/or transferred their assets to their children. It has been estimated that this may account for over 20 000 sales pa. This is an issue of considerable political debate in Britain.

The value of accumulated housing wealth that can be transmitted on death is affected by inheritance taxation. In some countries, such as Australia, there is no inheritance tax. In Britain, the threshold for inheritance tax is currently £325 000 and, following the Conservative pledge to raise the threshold to £1 million in 2007, Labour permitted married couples a dual allowance. Thus, the great majority of estates, those under £650 000, are not liable for inheritance tax. In 2007–08, only 25 000 estates were liable for inheritance tax and the total amount raised in 2010 was only £2.4 billion, a tiny proportion of the total value of estates passing on death. It is likely, however, that a high proportion of this may have come from estates of deceased in London and the South East where wealth and house prices are much higher.

Housing Wealth, Regional Inequality, and Social Mobility

To some extent housing wealth is a reflection of achieved social mobility in that those with a sequence of good jobs and good incomes are most easily able to purchase more expensive or better-quality housing in more attractive areas. Over time, and assuming no drop into negative equity, their purchases will be transformed into housing wealth. In this sense, higher levels of housing wealth are the result of sustained prosperity and a lifetime cycle of earnings. In addition, it is more possible for those with high levels of embedded housing wealth to trade down and retire to an area of their choice which also has the effect of pushing up prices in popular retirement areas. High house prices and associated levels of housing wealth in part of the country thus have spill-over effects on other parts of the country. Conversely, those households without substantial incomes or housing wealth are unlikely to be able to achieve geographical mobility from areas of low prices to areas of high prices which can impede labour market mobility.

Housing Wealth, Credit, and Intergenerational Homeownership

Housing wealth can provide a financial resource as remortgaging can help release equity. In some cases, the cash released is used to finance housing improvement or extensions and so represents a form of investment. In other cases, cash released may be used for various forms of consumption such as car purchases. More generally, however, homeownership tends to be linked to higher credit ratings and may allow people to borrow more cheaply on credit cards and the like. This is more a function of tenure status than housing wealth per se but it may point to the existence of a two-class society where credit ratings are concerned.

What is perhaps an important development in the current era of high house prices is the role of parental housing wealth to help young people gain a foothold on the housing ladder. Parents may borrow against the security of their home or take out a larger mortgage to give money to their children to provide a down payment for their purchase and it seems to be of growing importance, particularly in high-price regions. Housing wealth is seen by some people as an alternative to company pensions and can help to fund care for the elderly. In that sense, it generates a greater sense of financial independence.

It can be argued that housing wealth should not be considered in isolation, and should instead be seen as a part of overall wealth holdings. In this respect, wider housing wealth has been a major force for wealth redistribution in Britain, especially since the growth of homeownership postwar. Housing is now a key element in more widespread popular wealth ownership. While this may have widened the wealth gap between owners and tenants, inequalities in overall wealth ownership were much greater prior to the advent of mass homeownership.

Conclusions

Housing wealth is very unequally distributed, with a minority of households in London and the South East having housing wealth of £500 000 and over at a time when most potential first-time buyers are finding it difficult to get on the housing ladder. It is important, however, not to lose sight of the fact that notwithstanding its unequal distribution, housing wealth has underpinned a significant widening of wealth ownership in Britain and has created a mass asset-owning class. Much of this wealth is now finding its way into inheritance while some is extracted by HEW when house prices are rising and some is used to fund retirement and residential care in old age. The sequence of house price booms and busts since the 1970s suggests, however, that it is misguided for buyers to see homeownership as a one-way ticket to wealth accumulation in the short term. For some buyers, ownership has led to significant capital losses.

See also: Housing Equity Withdrawal in the United Kingdom; Housing Wealth Distribution in the United Kingdom; Mortgage Equity Withdrawal.

References

Appleyard L and Rowlingson K (2010) *Home Ownership and the Distribution of Personal Wealth: A Review of the Evidence*. Joseph Rowntree Foundation. http://www.jrf.org.uk/publications/home-ownership-personal-wealth. (accessed 25 November 2011)

Dale S (2009) bankofengland.co.uk/publications/speeches/2009/speech403.pdf. (accessed 25 November 2011)

Forrest R (2004) Cohort effects, differential accumulation and Hong Kong's volatile housing market. *Urban Studies* 41(11): 2181–2196.

Forrest R and Murie A (1995) *Housing and Family Wealth: Comparative International Perspectives*. London: Routledge.

Gentle C, Dorling D, and Cornford J (1994) Negative equity in Britain: Causes and consequences. *Urban Studies* 34(2): 181–199.

Hamnett C (1991) A nation of inheritors? Housing inheritance, wealth and inequality in Britain. *Journal of Social Policy* 20(4): 509–536.

Hamnett C (1999) *Winners and Losers: The Home Ownership Market in Britain*. London: Routledge.

Hamnett C and Seavers J (1996) Home ownership, housing wealth and distribution in Britain. In: Hills J (ed.) *The New Inequality*, pp. 348–373, Oxford, UK: Oxford University Press.

HM Revenue and Customs (2011) *Personal Wealth Statistics* 2001-03 and 2005-07. http://www.hmrc.gov.uk/stats/personal_wealth/intro-personal-wealth.pdf. (accessed 25 November 2011).

Holmans A and Frosztega M (1994) *House Property and Inheritance in the UK*. Department of the Environment. London: HMSO.

Levin E and Pryce G (2010) *Delivering Changes in Housing Wealth Inequality*. Economics Paper 6, vol. 2, Department of Communities and Local Government.

Munro M (1988) Housing wealth and inheritance. *Journal of Social Policy* 17: 417–436.

Royal Commission on the Distribution of Income and Wealth (1977) *Third Report on the Standing Reference, no. 5*, Cmnd 6999. London: HMSO.

Sierminska E, Brandolini A, and Smeeding TM (2006) Cross national comparison of income and wealth status in retirement: First results from the Luxembourg Wealth Study (LWS). *8th Annual Joint Conference of the Retirement Research Consortium*. Washington, DC.

Smith SJ and Searle BA (2010) *The Economics of Housing: The Housing Wealth of Nations*. Chichester, UK: Wiley-Blackwell.

Thorns D (1994) The role of housing inheritance in selected owner occupied societies (Britain, New Zealand and Canada). *Housing Studies* 9(4): 473–492.

Zhu XD (2006) *The Role of Housing as a Component of Personal Wealth*. Joint Center for Housing Studies, Harvard university, Working Paper, 01-6.

Further Reading

Hamnett C, Harmer M, and Williams P (1991) *Safe as Houses: Housing Inheritance in Britain*. London: Paul Chapman.

Holmans A (1991) Estimates of housing equity withdrawal in the United Kingdom, 1970–1990. *Government Economic Service Working Paper*, 116, London.

Housing Wealth as Precautionary Savings

R Martin, Federal Reserve Board of Governors, Washington, DC, USA

Published by Elsevier Ltd.

Introduction

In the late 1990s, the personal savings rate (shown below) in the United States took a nose dive, falling by half or about 2% points. By the third quarter of 2005, the personal savings rate reached an all time low of 1.2%. The fall in the savings rate became a serious public policy concern: How would the boomers retire without adequate savings?

However, the personal savings rate omits the portion of the household balance sheet dedicated to residential investment. As the savings rate was falling, residential investment was booming. If we adjust the personal savings rate by adding residential investment into savings, the savings rate is roughly constant between 1995 and late 2006. While this calculation takes some liberty with the definition of personal savings, it shows that households may well take holdings of housing capital into consideration when saving for the future. (Note: Capital gains on the existing stock of housing are not included in this calculation. The calculation only includes the additional real capital stock constructed each year.) Some portions of these savings are likely precautionary: households are saving for future bad times (**Figure 1**).

Precautionary savings is defined as the increase in savings resulting from a household's exposure to risk. Precautionary savings has been extensively studied in models where households are subject to earnings shocks and savings may be used to smooth consumption across time. Although this literature was primarily interested in the determinants of wealth inequality as the outcome of uninsurable income shocks, the mechanism through which they achieved their goal was inducing households to hold precautionary buffer stocks. Accumulation of the risk-free asset has two benefits for the household: it pushes the household away from a potentially binding borrowing constraint and reduces the volatility of aggregate income. That is, the asset allows the household to self-insure in an environment that prevents full risk sharing between agents. And, because returns on the asset are risk-free, asset income reduces total income risk.

For computational purposes, the environment in these models is quite stylised. Because the state-space is potentially quite large, the models, for the most part, focus on idiosyncratic risk, abstracting from all forms of aggregate risk. However, the existence of precautionary savings extends beyond this limited framework. Precautionary savings is driven by the curvature of the utility function and the exposure of households to income risk.

The precautionary motive for households is well described by a combination of the indexes of absolute and relative prudence, $-\frac{V'''_{t+1}(A_{t+1}, \varphi_{t+1})}{V''_{t+1}(A_{t+1}, \varphi_{t+1})}$; $-\frac{V'''_{t+1}(A_{t+1}, \varphi_{t+1})A_{t+1}}{V''_{t+1}(A_{t+1}, \varphi_{t+1})}$, where V denotes the period value function, A is the household's total available assets inclusive of labour income in period $t+1$, and φ is a vector of aggregate and idiosyncratic state variables. For the class of constant relative risk aversion utility functions, the two indexes are characterised by the coefficient of relative risk aversion (when constraints are not binding). Households desire higher precautionary stocks as the indexes rise and as the variation in A and φ increases.

Housing has the potential to alter both the curvature of the value function and the variability of household income. Given this potential, does the presence of housing raise or lower the precautionary motive of agents? The answer is not immediate. The effect on the precautionary motive depends entirely on the assumptions embedded in the model and there are a myriad of ways that housing may enter the household problem. In this article, we analyse what we consider to be the three most important.

First and most straightforward, we consider housing solely as an asset. Housing services, if any, are purchased in a perfectly competitive rental market and are indistinguishable from other market consumption. Housing then is held as part of an optimal portfolio. Households use housing as a precautionary asset to a greater or lesser extent depending on its portfolio properties. In general, housing capital allows larger aggregate precautionary savings.

Second, housing is home capital and contributes importantly to the production of home goods. Consumption is the output of home production which takes as intermediate inputs both market goods and home labour. Individuals can smooth utility (although not necessarily consumption) by substituting away from the purchase of market goods and towards the production of home goods during periods of low labour income.

In the extreme, think of a retired household. Wages fall to (near) zero, implying a very small time cost and allowing households to substitute home production for market consumption. As a result, some studies have shown that the decline in utility (as opposed to market consumption) is small or negligible at retirement. All else equal, an

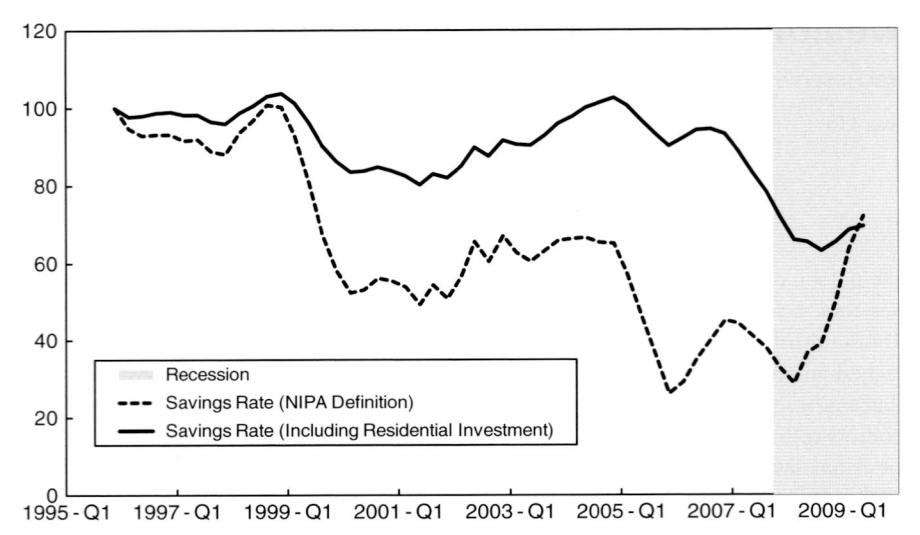

Figure 1 The savings rate including residential investment did not fall until 2007. There was a rebalancing of the housing portfolio from ordinary savings to residential buildings. Housing may be perceived by households as a true savings. Index 1995-Q1 = 100.

increase in housing capital, as an input to home production, raises the marginal product of home labour, increases the level of home output as a percent of total output, and increases the role of home production in smoothing total consumption volatility. In this environment, housing is accumulated as a precautionary asset. However, as the complementarity between the consumption of housing services and market goods increases, the ability to smooth utility fluctuations through housing capital is reduced.

Finally, housing embeds substantial transaction costs. The monetary costs of changing houses are substantial, ranging from 6 to 11% of the purchase price of a new house and the utility costs of moving (subsuming both time and inconvenience) are likely to be even higher. Housing in the presence of transaction costs can substantially increase the level of precautionary savings. When housing is only partially adjustable, households not only want to smooth the time pattern of consumption, but they also want to smooth ratio of housing and market consumption to meet the ultimate goal of smoothing fluctuations in utility. However, the precautionary motive is driven by the existence of inflexible housing capital. Households rely disproportionately on market capital as a buffer stock, reducing the relative role of housing capital.

The remainder of the article is laid out as follows. In the next section, we introduce the workhorse model, allowing us to characterise the key features of housing in one location. Over the next three sections, we refine the model to reflect the three specific ways we think about housing and precautionary savings: as an asset, as home capital, in the presence of transaction costs. Finally, we conclude.

The Workhorse Model

In this section we build a stylised real model of housing that is sufficiently general to encompass all three of our specialised cases. The model is based on the iconic endowment asset pricing model of Lucas. The economy is populated by a single, infinitely lived, representative consumer who derives positive utility from the consumption of two goods: market consumption and housing services.

There are two productive sectors. The first sector, denoted the market sector, produces output using household labour and market capital as inputs. Output from this sector may be consumed as market consumption, invested in market capital or invested as housing capital. The second sector, denoted the housing sector, produces housing services using as intermediate inputs household labour and housing capital. Investment in housing capital may be costly. Both sectors may have time-varying productivity.

We abstract from land as a factor in the production of housing services. The omission is quantitatively important as a fixed supply of land is an important friction in the ability of households to smooth consumption via home production. However, this omission is not qualitatively important.

The agent is endowed with a fixed amount of time and he/she provides labour to both the market and home sectors, receiving a fixed wage per unit of effort in each sector. The agent also accumulates market capital which he/she rents to a competitive market firm. Home capital is also accumulated.

Individual Agent Optimisation

Each agent seeks to maximise lifetime utility by choosing sequences of consumption, housing services, market and housing capital, and period-by-period labour supply decisions subject to a period-by-period budget constraint as follows:

$$\max_{c_t, b_t, B_{t,t+s}} E\left\{\sum_{t=0}^{\infty} \beta^t U(c_t, b_t)\right\}$$

s.t.

$$c_t + \text{Rent}_t b_t + \sum_{s=1}^{\infty} \rho_{t,t+s} B_{t,t+s} + K_{t+1} + p_t H_{t+1}$$
$$\leq w_t^m L_t^m + w_t^H + \sum_{s=1}^{\infty} B_{t-s,t} + (1 + r_t - \delta) K_t + p_t H_t$$
$$+ \Lambda(H_{t+1}, H_t)$$

On the left-hand side of the inequality, c is consumption of market goods, b is consumption of housing services (in this formulation rented from an aggregate rental firm), K is the holdings of market capital, and H is the holdings of home capital. Bond holdings are described below. On the income side, w is the time t wage in the sector denoted by the superscript: m for market, H for housing. The agents sell their net of depreciation market capital and sell housing capital at current price p. The function Λ embeds any transaction costs in the purchase and sale of market capital. Typically, the function is negative any time the choice of housing capital tomorrow differs from the current stock.

The bond terms are written for ease of notation. During each period, the agent chooses a portfolio of bonds. Each bond pays off one unit of consumption in a single future period and has price ρ. For example, a bond paying one unit of consumption s periods in the future is denoted, $B_{t,t+s}$. This bond trades at price, $\rho_{t,t+s}$, and represents the discount factor between t and $t+s$. Without loss of generality, the bond is not traded in the intermediate periods. These bonds are assumed to be in zero net supply.

Production

The market sector produces output via a Cobb–Douglass production function as follows:

$$Y_t = z_t K_t^{\gamma} L_t^{m(1-\gamma)}$$

The firm pays competitive rents and wages. Hence,

$$w_t^m = (1-\gamma) z_t K_t^{\gamma} L_t^{m(-\gamma)} \text{ and } r_t = \gamma z_t k_t^{\gamma-1} L_t^{m(1-\gamma)}$$

The home sector also uses a Cobb–Douglass technology to produce housing. The share of capital in production potentially differs between the two sectors, but since these differences do not play a major role, we assume the shares are the same across the two sectors.

Housing as an Asset

In this section we consider housing solely as an asset. When housing is an asset, the household accumulates housing capital as a portion of their precautionary stock. Because the production functions for market goods and housing services are separable, the total level of precautionary savings increases. We consider this a reference case relative to the next two cases considered.

Housing capital is rented to a competitive firm that pays competitive rates. The rental rate charged by the firm is also competitive. From the household's perspective, housing capital and market capital differ only in the sense that they may offer a different return. As such, the household chooses its holdings as the solution of an optimal portfolio problem.

The relevant first-order conditions are as follows:

$$H_{t+1} : 1 = \frac{\Lambda_H(H_{t+1}, H_t)}{\lambda_t p_t} + \beta E\left\{\frac{\lambda_{t+1}}{\lambda_t} \frac{p_{t+1}}{p_t}\right\}$$

$$K_t : 1 = E\left\{(1 + r_{t+1} + \delta) \frac{\lambda_{t+1}}{\lambda_t}\right\}$$

where λ_t is the t Lagrange multiplier on the budget constraint. The term $\Lambda_H(H_{t+1}, H_t)$ reflects the transaction costs inherent in housing investment. The return to housing p_{t+1}/p_t, is paid by the firm symmetrically to interest payments on capital.

All else equal, the higher the expected value of the pricing kernel, $\frac{\lambda_{t+1}}{\lambda_t}$, the higher the desired level of precautionary savings. The increased level of precautionary savings pushes down the real interest rate. Hence, the concavity of the production function in essence provides a limit to the aggregate level of precautionary savings.

The curvature of the aggregate production function is in some sense diminished because market and housing capital are accumulated proportionally. From the first-order conditions, we have the following equality:

$$E\left\{(1 + r_{t+1} + \delta) \frac{\lambda_{t+1}}{\lambda_t}\right\} = \frac{\Lambda_H(H_{t+1}, H_t)}{\lambda_t p_t} + \beta E\left\{\frac{\lambda_{t+1}}{\lambda_t} \frac{p_{t+1}}{p_t}\right\}$$

After accounting for depreciation and transaction costs, the risk-adjusted returns in the two sectors are equal. Market capital and housing capital are close to linearly related.

Consider the risk-free case when transaction costs and depreciation are zero. In this instance, the equality above reduces to $(1 + r_{t+1}) = \frac{p_{t+1}}{p_t}$, which in turn becomes

$$\gamma z_t K_t^{\gamma-1} L_t^{m(1-\gamma)} = \gamma A_t H_t^{\gamma-1} L_t^{H(1-\gamma)}$$

$$\frac{K_{t+1}}{H_{t+1}} = \left(\frac{A_{t+1}}{z_{t+1}}\right)^{\frac{1}{\gamma-1}} \frac{L_t^m}{L_t^H}$$

when we use the firm's problem to replace the return to housing capital and continue to assume equal capital shares in the two sectors. The ratio of capital then only reflects the differences in productivity in the two sectors.

As a result, if the household desires a precautionary stock, both housing and market capital are accumulated. Further, because the curvature of the joint function is less than the curvature of capital alone, the level of precautionary savings is increased relative to an economy without housing capital. The presence of housing provides an efficiency gain in the economy.

Housing as Home Capital

In this section we consider home capital as an important input into home production. Because households use the home sector to insure against fluctuations in market income, the presence of the home sector reduces the total need for precautionary savings. However, depending on the elasticity of substitution between consumption of housing services and market goods, the presence of the home sector may increase the relative use of housing capital as a precautionary buffer.

The existence of a household sector improves the household's ability to self-insure against risky outcomes. Simply put, households have two extra margins on which they can adjust: the allocation of labour between home and market and the allocation of capital. In the case where the shocks are perfectly correlated and equally important across the two sectors, these margins are meaningless.

While households will always use the home production technology to smooth utility, it turns out that the usefulness of the home sector to insure against income shocks (and the desire to disproportionately accumulate housing capital) depends on the elasticity of substitution between market goods and housing in the utility function. If the two goods are sufficiently complementary, increasing consumption of housing services does not act as a good hedge. In the following subsection we show this through the pricing equation for housing in an endowment version of the model. If prices rise when consumption falls, housing is a good hedge against future income shocks.

The Elasticity of Substitution between Market Consumption and Housing

To derive the pricing equation for housing capital, we modify the workhorse model by eliminating the rental firm and endowing households with a backyard technology for producing housing services. For simplicity, assume housing is freely transacted. All other technological parameters remain the same.

In this case, an expression for house prices can be derived by combining the first-order equations for market consumption and housing as follows:

$$p_t = \frac{U_b(c_t, b_t)}{U_c(c_t, b_t)} + \beta E\left\{\frac{U_c(c_{t+1}, b_{t+1})}{U_c(c_t, b_t)} p_{t+1}\right\}$$

The first term, $\frac{U_b(c_t, b_t)}{U_c(c_t, b_t)}$ is the utility value of holding H units of housing capital today. This is the rental value of housing. The second term is the value of selling the house in period $t+1$. This pricing equation is entirely standard.

Following standard practice we can substitute for next period's price, deriving an expression for today's house prices solely in utility terms.

$$p_t = E \sum_{s=0}^{\infty} \beta^s \frac{U_b(c_{t+s}, b_{t+s})}{U_c(c_t, b_t)}$$
$$= E \sum_{s=0}^{\infty} \beta^s \frac{U_c(c_{t+s}, b_{t+s})}{U_c(c_t, b_t)} \frac{U_b(c_{t+s}, b_{t+s})}{U_c(c_{t+s}, b_{t+s})}$$

The time t price of housing is equated to the discounted value of future rents where the term $\beta^s \frac{U_c(c_{t+s}, b_{t+s})}{U_c(c_t, b_t)}$ is the stochastic discount factor.

Do house prices increase or decrease with higher consumption expectations? If house prices increase when consumption falls, then housing is an effective hedge: households desire higher housing capital when consumption is low. Otherwise, housing is not an effective hedge and households wish to decrease housing capital stocks when consumption falls.

Higher future consumption raises both interest rates and rents. The net impact on house prices depends on which factor moves more. The dominant factor is determined by the relationship between housing and consumption in utility as given by the cross-derivative, U_{bc}.

Using the equation above, we express house prices as follows:

$$p_t = E \sum_{s=0}^{\infty} \beta^s \frac{U_b(c_{t+s}, b_{t+s})}{U_c(c_t, b_t)}$$

Then, house prices rise or fall with increases in future consumption depending on the sign of U_{bc}

$$\frac{\partial p_t}{\partial c_{t+s}} = E\beta^s \frac{U_{bc}(c_{t+s}, b_{t+s})}{U_c(c_t, b_t)} \forall s > 0$$

If U_{bc} is positive (if the marginal utility of housing is increasing with consumption), then the house prices rise with increases in consumption. If the term is negative, then they fall. This in turn is a restriction on the relative strength of intertemporal substitution of consumption and intratemporal substitution between housing and consumption.

In order for households to accumulate housing as a precautionary buffer, housing must smooth fluctuations in utility. That is, housing must be more valuable when consumption falls: house prices must fall when future consumption is expected to rise.

Transaction Costs

In this section, we consider the impact of transaction costs on precautionary savings. We find that while housing increases the total precautionary motive, housing capital makes up a smaller share of the total buffer stock. Hence, the existence of transaction costs reduces the role of housing in precautionary savings.

Habit formation into the period utility function and transaction costs work in much the same manner, although habit formation has been much more extensively studied. The presence of habits makes consumption fluctuations more painful, and those households with a small level of self-insurance will try to increase it by holding higher asset stocks. The presence of habit formation significantly increases the amount of precautionary savings and decreases the risk-free rate over an economy without habit formation. In essence, habits increase the local curvature of the utility function.

In an economy with housing capital that is traded subject to a transaction cost, precautionary savings increases. Transaction costs tend to increase the total level of precautionary savings but decrease the relative use of housing capital as the buffer stock. To see this, consider the manner in which transaction costs drive the precautionary motive. The amount of precautionary savings is driven by two factors. First, the accumulation of housing capital ties up a large portion of wealth. This wealth is no longer available for smoothing of consumption of market goods and the volatility of nondurable consumption increases. Even when the agent is free to borrow against his housing stock, this remains true. Also, because the housing stock is updated only infrequently, movements at the boundary are large. Hence, even though the adjustments are infrequent, they contribute significantly to lifetime consumption volatility and the demand for precautionary saving.

Transaction costs raise the aggregate capital stock an additional 7–17% over that found in a model without risk. However, all of this increase occurs through the accumulation of additional financial assets. The higher the transaction costs, the less the agent relies on housing as a precautionary buffer. For Cobb–Douglass preferences, the ratio of housing capital to market capital falls from 1.7 when transaction costs are zero to 1.5 when transaction costs reach about 20% of the purchase price of a new house.

Conclusions

That housing is an important and special part of the household decision problem is now well established. However, the relationship between housing and precautionary savings is less clear and depends on the manner in which housing is introduced to the model. Nonetheless, the time pattern of aggregate savings rates (with and without residential investment) given in the Introduction section points strongly toward housing as a precautionary buffer. Savings rates inclusive of residential investment did not fall substantially between 1995 and 2007, yet the share of housing capital in savings rose dramatically.

Housing certainly serves, at least in part, as an ordinary asset within the household portfolio. Households can borrow against the value of their housing stock. They can increase or decrease their holdings of housing. Therefore, it seems likely that households use their house as a part of their precautionary buffer.

Further, larger holdings of housing capital can insulate the household from temporary fluctuations in income. The household can continue to consume housing services at roughly the same rate during periods of low income. To the extent that these services can substitute for other consumption, if the two goods are sufficiently substitutable, housing capital is an excellent hedge against overall income fluctuations. Note, this consumption is independent of the leverage status of the house. Borrowing against a house reduces the household's stock of financial assets and not their stock of housing capital. Perhaps, high-leverage households are evidence of a high elasticity between consumption of housing services and market consumption: a case where the housing stock is an efficient hedge against income fluctuations.

The presence of large transaction costs in the purchase and sale reduces the efficiency of housing as a precautionary buffer stock. However, over the last 20 years, financial markets have improved substantially, reducing the cost of extracting equity from housing. These innovations allow households to bypass some of the transaction costs associated with housing. Also, housing markets themselves have likely become more efficient. Computer listing has reduced search costs and discount agents have grown in popularity. Perhaps, these improvements have shifted the balance over the last 10 years and households now prefer higher stocks of housing capital.

Acknowledgement

The views and opinions herein are solely those of the author and do not reflect the views and opinions of the Board of Governors, the Federal Reserve System, or their respective staffs.

See also: House Price Expectations.

Further Reading

Aiyagari SR (1994) Uninsured idiosyncratic risk and aggregate saving. *Quarterly Journal of Economics* 109: 659–684.

Baxter M and Jermann UJ (1999) Household production and the excess sensitivity of consumption to current income. *The American Economic Review* 89(4): 902–920.

Cagetti M (2003) Wealth accumulation over the life-cycle and precautionary savings. *Journal of Business and Economic Statistics* 21(3): 339–353.

Carroll CD and Kimball MS (2008) Precautionary savings and precautionary wealth. In: Durlaff SN and Blume LE (eds.) *The New Palgrave Dictionary of Economics,* 2nd edn. DOI:10.1057/9780230226203.1325.

Carroll CD and Samwick AA (1997) The nature of precautionary wealth. *Journal of Monetary Economics* 40: 41–71.

Davis M and Heathcote J (2003) Housing and the business cycle. *International Economic Review* 46(3): 751–784.

Davis M and Martin RF (2009) Housing, home production, and the equity and value premium puzzles. *Journal of Housing Economics* 18(2): 18–91.

Diaz A, Pijoan-Mas J, and Riso-Rull J-V (2003) Precautionary savings and wealth distribution under habit formation preferences. *Journal of Monetary Economics* 50: 1257–1291.

Hall RE (1978) Stochastic implications of the life cycle-permanent income hypothesis: Theory and evidence. *Journal of Political Economy* 86(6): 971–987.

Huggett M (1993) The risk free rate in heterogeneous-agents, incomplete insurance economies. *Journal of Economic Dynamics and Control* 17(5/6): 953–970.

Hurst E and Aguiar M (2005) Consumption vs. expenditure. *Journal of Political Economy* 113(5): 919–948.

Kimball MS (1990) Precautionary saving in the small and in the large. *Econommectrica* 58: 53–73.

Pijoan-Mas J (2003) Precautionary savings or working longer hours. *Review of Economic Dynamics* 9(2): 326–352.

Rios-Rull J-V and Sanchez-Marcos V (2006) An aggregate economy with different size houses. *Journal of the European Economic Association* 6(2–3): 705–714.

Rupert P, Rogerson R, and Wright R (1995) Estimating substitution elasticities in household production models. *Economic Theory* 6(1): 179–193.

Housing Wealth Distribution in the United Kingdom

G Pryce, University of Glasgow, Glasgow, UK

© 2012 Elsevier Ltd. All rights reserved.

Introduction

Housing wealth can be defined either as 'Gross Housing Wealth' (the current market value of a home) or as 'Net Housing Wealth' (current market value less outstanding mortgage debt). Both have become increasingly important due to financial deregulation and the growth of homeownership. Variations in house prices, over time and across space, have potent effects on the distribution of housing wealth and, indeed, of wealth per se. Demographic trends towards ageing populations will only serve to amplify further these effects. As larger proportions of national populations become income-poor (i.e., no longer participating full time in the labour market) but asset-rich (i.e. own a home), traditional measures of inequality that rely solely on income will give an increasingly incomplete picture of the true extent of financial wealth inequality.

This article is structured around three dimensions of housing wealth: (i) levels of housing wealth, (ii) socioeconomic distribution of housing wealth, and (iii) spatial distribution of housing wealth, with particular focus on the latter two. The implications of these three dimensions for a variety of social and economic outcomes, including aggregate demand, labour supply, inequality, class reproduction, labour market mobility, and the relative position of renters, are considered. A recurring theme throughout is how we measure these effects. Housing wealth is surprisingly difficult to analyse due to its transient and complex interactions with life-cycle factors and mortgage variables.

Levels of Housing Wealth

Despite the recent downturn in house prices in many countries, housing wealth remains a major financial resource for many households. Already, house prices have returned to pre-slump levels in many countries and, in others, prices are not far from their long-term trend. In any case, the cumulative increases in house prices and owner-occupation of the postwar period in the United States, Canada, Australia, the United Kingdom and more recently in China, India, and other emerging economies, are likely to overshadow the postcrisis dip. Housing wealth has, and is likely to continue to have, an important role in the functioning of the wider economy.

Prior to the 1990s, macrostudies tended to ignore or understate the role of housing markets in determining consumption – the direction of causation was implicitly assumed to run from aggregate demand to housing markets, not the other way round. Increasing recognition in the late 1980s that macromodels were failing to adequately explain aggregate consumption led to a shift in the way macromodels characterised the role of housing markets, particularly housing wealth. Subsequent national and cross-country research has confirmed that equity withdrawal (sometimes called equity extraction – the process of accessing net housing wealth by increasing the value of mortgage debt) plays a crucial role in the wider economy, and that multiple interconnected links exist between house prices and the macroeconomy (the effects of money and credit, e.g., appear to be amplified when house prices are booming).

Fluctuations in housing wealth may also have supply-side effects. For example, windfall gains in housing wealth from increases in house prices may reduce the marginal utility of income – the incremental improvement in wellbeing that individuals enjoy from each extra £1 they earn. This possible reduction in the benefit of additional income has the potential to dilute incentives to supply labour. Evidence from panel data appears to confirm this. When there are substantial increases in an individual's housing equity, reductions in hours worked tend to follow.

There may be other supply-side implications of housing capital gains, however, which offset, at least to some degree, the impact on labour supply incentives. For example, there is evidence that housing equity is an important source of funds for business start-ups. The finding in recent UK research that housing wealth tends to move in large cycles (not necessarily in sync across housing submarkets) may therefore have important implications for entrepreneurial business cycles and their impact across regions.

Socioeconomic Distribution of Housing Wealth

While the 'levels' of housing wealth have attracted the attention of macro and labour economists, it is the 'distribution' of housing wealth that has been the focus of debate in the sociology and housing policy literatures, principally because of its implications for inequality.

Growth of homeownership and the deregulation of financial markets led commentators in the 1980s to speculate on the emergence of a new socioeconomic order. Housing wealth, it seemed, could dwarf all other sources of financial wealth accumulation, and potentially become a defining force of class formation and reproduction. A debate emerged between Weberians, who emphasised the importance of housing wealth relative to other forces that stratify and segment society, and Marxists, who emphasised a person's position with respect to the means of production as the defining driver of class formation. For Weberians, homeownership was leading to new socioeconomic classifications defined with respect to a person's position in the housing market. For Marxists, the new 'housing classes' were the latest outcome of labour market differentials: inequalities across housing tenures merely reflected job market inequalities.

Empirical Evidence on the Socioeconomic Distribution of Housing Wealth

Many of the early empirical studies that attempted to test these competing theories were based on either aggregate data (and therefore unable to distinguish between different rates of house price inflation for different dwellings) or relatively small, idiosyncratic samples. As a result, firm empirical results did not really emerge until the 1990s when a number of researchers utilised panel survey data to explore how housing wealth varied across households. Even so, these data sets had two major drawbacks. First, estimating the current value of a home (essential for housing wealth analysis) is problematic in survey data. Only a fraction of houses transact in a given year (well below 10% on average in many regions in the United Kingdom) and so current house value typically has to be imputed from external data, or the researcher has to rely on the owner's own estimate (which is often highly inaccurate). Second, in order to compute net housing wealth, information is needed on outstanding mortgage debt. Again, however, this often has to be imputed, typically using amortisation equations with various implicit assumptions.

Given these caveats, survey results have to be treated with caution, but the evidence appeared to suggest that there was only a weak link between labour market income and current housing wealth, apparently refuting the Marxian view. However, this finding may partly be the result of a failure to control for life-cycle and cohort effects – elderly households, for example, were included with low or zero labour market income, but substantial housing wealth.

More recent research by the Office for National Statistics in the United Kingdom has found that, while housing wealth is unequally distributed, it is less unequal than other sources of financial wealth that are more directly linked with the labour market. This would appear to contradict the Weberian argument that homeownership was giving rise to new levels of inequality independent of, and surpassing that arising from, the labour market.

In terms of the dynamics of inequality, there remain very few studies of note, and those that exist point to a complex and sometimes inconclusive picture with regard to trends in housing wealth inequality. Research based on the British Household Panel Survey for the 1985–91 period, for example, found evidence of only a modest rise in housing wealth inequality. And studies that have explored the more recent period (2000–2004) have actually found evidence of falling housing wealth inequality.

Outside the United Kingdom, particularly the United States, research has focussed less on housing wealth inequality per se and more on inequality between particular ethnic groups and possible links with educational performance. There is evidence, for example, that children of homeowners are more likely to enter owner-occupancy sooner than are children of renters, and likely to achieve higher levels of education and income, but it is difficult to separate out the effects of homeownership and labour market status from unobserved household attributes and motivations. There is also evidence to suggest that ethnic minorities experience lower returns to homeownership than Whites, though this may be an artefact of differences in income elasticities of demand for different locations (see Spatial Distribution of Housing Wealth section), rather than evidence of racial discrimination.

While the evidence on different rates of housing wealth accumulation among homeowners is ambiguous and/or complex, the inequality between owners and renters is relatively straightforward, or at least, it was prior to the financial crisis when shifts to the right of the entire house price distribution led to an emerging gulf between the housing wealth of renters (typically zero) and the housing wealth of homeowners. Falling house prices have confused the picture somewhat as negative equity implies that some homeowners actually have less housing wealth than renters.

With respect to the impact of housing wealth on class reproduction, a critical issue is whether homeowners pass on capital gains to their children. They may instead use housing wealth to fund current consumption. Certainly, the evidence to date offers little support for the argument that homeownership has led to a major increase in housing inheritance. This may partly be the result of homeowners using up their housing wealth during their lifetimes, and partly because the cohort of households that entered homeownership during the 1980s and 1990s have yet to complete their life cycles. Continued increases in longevity will add to the delay, but housing wealth inheritance should nevertheless rise in due course. Others have had no choice but to use up their housing wealth to meet the health care costs, particularly in old age. Means-testing in state health care in countries like the United Kingdom, precludes assistance to households with substantial financial resources, including housing wealth. Others have chosen to pass on housing wealth to their children when they most need it, rather than as an inheritance.

The Bathtub Paradox

Part of the confusion and ambiguity regarding the nature of housing wealth accumulation and its class reproduction effects is the failure to distinguish between stock, flow, and life-cycle aspects. The option to draw down some or all of the equity accumulated through capital gains or amortisation complicates considerably the measurement of housing wealth. Equity withdrawal may yet exacerbate class reproduction however, particularly if that wealth is used to improve the life chances of children of homeowners. Neither should we underestimate the inequality in well-being that different rates of housing wealth accumulation and disaccumulation can produce.

To illustrate, consider the following analogy which I call 'the bathtub paradox'. Think of net housing wealth as the level of water in the bathtubs depicted in **Figure 1**. Capital gains (and amortisation) imply an inflow, raising the water level. Equity withdrawals represent an outflow, depleting the water level. Mortgage maturity is indicated by t and indicates how long a household has had a mortgage. When we compare housing wealth of four persons, represented by bathtubs A, B, C, and D, we see considerable inequality in housing wealth, with A and C having relatively low levels of net housing wealth, whereas B and D appear to have very high levels of housing wealth. The paradox is that D's housing wealth is observed to be higher than that of A, but his level of financial well-being may not be. First, it should be observed that A is early on in her housing career, whereas D is approaching retirement and is at the point of paying off his mortgage. Most importantly, over the course of its housing career, person A will enjoy much higher rates of capital gains than D. Similarly, it would be a mistake to conclude that individuals D and B are comparable in terms of how much they have benefited from homeownership. They both happen to have similar levels of housing wealth at the point of being observed, but B has enjoyed higher rates of equity withdrawal, which may have been used to enhance consumption, or pay for education, and so on.

It is oversimplistic, therefore, to assume that bequests at the point of death are the only way housing wealth can have an unequal effect on households and on class reproduction. Some homeowners may choose to pass on housing wealth to their children, increasing their access to higher education or, indeed, facilitate their access to high-return sectors of homeownership (see Spatial Distribution of Housing Wealth section). A more meaningful entity to compare across households, then, is the total level of capital gains over a person's lifetime. If we assume that people do not move (or that, when they do, that they move to areas with similar rates of capital gain), then the rate of capital gains in different areas could be used to provide a good approximation of the total gains in housing wealth over a person's lifetime as the basis for measuring total lifetime housing wealth inequality. We also have to bear in mind that households could invest in assets other than housing so it is the relative rate of return over a lifetime that should perhaps be the focus of research. And unless there are very significant systematic differences in the mortgage interest charged to one social or ethnic group as compared to another over the course of a lifetime, there is little point in computing net housing wealth – the distortions caused by (i) imputing outstanding mortgage debt from simplified amortisation equations and (ii) preclusion of interest-only mortgages, are likely to outweigh any gains in preclusion.

Spatial Distribution of Housing Wealth

While we have not precluded the possibility that different dwellings will yield different rates of housing wealth accumulation, we have yet to consider why this might actually be the case. The issue is important because, if there are no intrinsic discrepancies, spatial variation in housing wealth will simply reflect the geography of labour markets. Housing wealth will then be entirely

(i) Person A at $t=1$	(ii) Person B at $t=25$	(iii) Person C at $t=1$	(iv) Person D at $t=25$
High rate of capital gains; Net housing wealth; High rate of equity withdrawal	High rate of capital gains; Net housing wealth; High rate of equity withdrawal	Low rate of capital gains; Net housing wealth; Low rate of equity withdrawal	Low rate of capital gains; Net housing wealth; Low rate of equity withdrawal

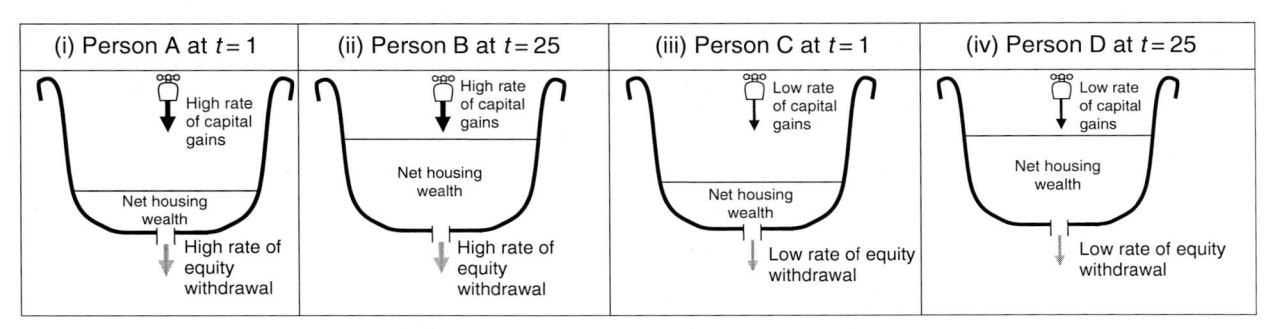

Figure 1 The bathtub paradox: How persons with low housing wealth can be better-off than those with high housing wealth.

subservient to employment inequalities and be of no particular consequence in itself. If rates of house price increase are uniform across dwellings, the solution to discrepancies between owners and renters will be to widen access to homeownership. Such a goal would not, however, fix discrepancies across low- and high-income households if there were systematic differences in rates of capital gains earned per £1 invested in housing by high-income households compared to low-income households. The crucial issue, therefore, with regard to the spatial distribution of housing wealth is whether there exist different 'rates' of house price appreciation across space.

Textbook microeconomics might provide a rationale for why we might expect different rates of house price appreciation to occur across dwellings and across income deciles. Demand theory tells us that luxury goods will have a higher-income elasticity of demand than necessity goods. That is, as income rises, the demand for luxury goods will increase relative to the demand for necessity goods. This raises the possibility that 'wealth' inequality could rise, even in the world of static 'income' inequality. It also raises the possibility that low-income homeowners may only be able to purchase dwellings that yield such low rates of return that they would be better-off renting and investing their savings in some other financial product.

Suppose, for example, the long-term trajectory of household income is upwards, but that the distribution of income remains constant. If all incomes rise at an equal rate, the price of luxury homes will nevertheless increase at a faster rate than the price of more modest accommodation because differences in income elasticities across dwellings will cause demand for luxury homes to increase relative to the demand for subsistence accommodation. If luxury homes rise in value relative to low-quality ones, the owners of luxury homes will make a higher return, per £1 invested in housing, so the distribution of housing wealth will become more unequal, even though 'income' inequality has remained unchanged.

This raises two issues. First, there is the question of what we mean by 'luxury' in the context of housing. And second, given the lumpiness of housing as an asset class, what are the implications for equality of investment opportunity across different income groups? That is, are there barriers to entry into the most lucrative sources of housing investment?

The first question is about how we conceptualise a housing unit (which also has implications for the second question). If housing is simply the linear sum of homogeneous attributes, then any home can be transformed into a luxury dwelling through home improvements. There would then be no long-term disadvantage associated with the type or location of an initial purchase in terms of the income elasticity of demand. One would receive no greater return from buying a luxury mansion, than from the purchase of a basic one-bedroom apartment which is then extended and upgraded. That is, if any low-quality dwelling can be transformed into a luxury dwelling without undue cost or time, then the inequality that might arise from unequal returns across dwelling types will be ameliorated.

Unfortunately, housing cannot be adequately described as an unbounded additive list of attributes — there are constraints on the extent to which a humble abode can be transformed into an opulent palace. Land plots are typically fixed, which imposes limits on expansion. More crucially, geography gives rise to a unique combination of access to amenities, some of which may be fixed or inert in space and time. There are 'natural amenities' (rivers, hills, coastline, etc.), 'historical amenities' (monuments, buildings, parks, and other extant aesthetically pleasing features from the past), 'economic amenities' (access to employment), 'leisure amenities' (access to shopping and recreation facilities), and 'social amenities' (neighbourhood demographic and social composition, crime rates, and social capital).

If the marginal valuation of at least some of these amenities rises sharply with income (i.e., if some amenities can be classed as luxury goods, with high-income elasticities of demand), this will cause the rich to have disproportionately higher levels of amenity demand. In other words, areas of high amenity value will attract rich households. It will also mean that, if all incomes rise at the same rate, the price of housing with access to the most prestigious amenities will rise faster than the price of dwellings with poor access to amenities, leading to differentials across home locations in the rate of housing wealth accumulation that can be earned per £1 invested.

Moreover, the fixed and inimitable nature of some amenities will place a limit on the extent to which homeowners in undesirable locations will be able to improve the income elasticity of demand for their dwelling.

Of course, one should be aware that high-income elasticities work both ways: prices of luxury homes will rise more rapidly with increases in income, but will also fall more rapidly with decreases in income. Housing wealth will become more unequal when all incomes rise, and will become less unequal when all incomes fall, ceteris paribus.

A second and related issue is that of barriers to entry into the most lucrative forms of housing investment. Given that someone on modest income can, in principle, invest in a large Blue Chip company, why would the same not be true for housing? The answer is that houses tend to be lumpy assets. Typically, people either invest in an entire dwelling or not at all. Shared ownership schemes exist but are complex and uncommon. Moreover, it is currently difficult in most countries to buy a small share in a luxury dwelling because financial vehicles have yet to emerge to make this a realistic prospect.

When we combine barriers to entry into luxury property investment, with the constraints on the extent to which a poor-quality home can be transformed into a luxury one, very real discrepancies can potentially arise in the rates of housing wealth accumulation across homeowners with different incomes, particularly during times of rising prosperity.

However, if the luxury good effect is weak, or income growth is low or negative, we would not expect inequalities in housing wealth accumulation to persist across areas, other things being equal. This is because lower-return areas will eventually experience more rapid price growth as prices become prohibitively high in high-demand areas. Cycles in housing wealth inequality would then emerge as prices in expensive areas pull away for a while, followed by periods of catch-up as demand is displaced to adjacent, less-expensive areas.

Measuring Spatial Inequality in Housing Wealth

On the extent of spatial variation in housing wealth inequality, empirical estimates vary spectacularly, even within the same country. For example, UK panel survey data estimate for the late 1980s found little change in inequality between regions. In contrast, research funded by Shelter, a UK housing charity, found evidence of huge, and apparently inexorable, increases in housing wealth inequality across space. More recent analysis by Levin and Pryce, using the same data, found pronounced cycles in spatial inequality in housing wealth but no evidence of an upward trend.

These differences in findings are attributable to the ways in which researchers address the following four key methodological challenges. First, how does one estimate current and historical home values? This is particularly problematic for survey data which are typically based on a sample of households that is not randomly distributed across space and which lacks information on the precise location of dwellings. This makes it difficult to estimate current house price, particularly if we believe home location is a key determinant of value.

Second, if one is comparing the rate of price appreciation of low-price areas with high-price areas, which time period should one use to categorise areas as low or high price? The Shelter findings, for example, are based on final period categorisation of dwellings which is likely to exaggerate the estimated inequality of housing wealth accumulation because the areas that experienced highest house price appreciation over the study period are more likely to be categorised as high house price areas, even if they were modestly priced areas at the start of the study. It is important, then, to use base-period prices to categorise areas.

Third, how many time periods should one choose to compare housing wealth? This is crucial, particularly if housing wealth inequality moves in cycles. For example, if only two periods are selected for comparison, one will obtain completely different results if the first period happens to occur at a trough in housing wealth inequality and the final period happens to occur at a peak, than if one chose two points at opposite points in the cycle. Ideally, then, changes in housing wealth inequality should be computed for every period.

Fourth, one has to decide whether to use net or gross housing wealth as the basis of inequality measurement. Computation of net housing wealth requires subtracting the estimated outstanding mortgage debt in period t from estimated house value in period t, and this introduces error, not only from amortisation approximation (particularly problematic when a significant proportion of borrowers have interest-only mortgages or when this proportion changes over time), but also from the distortions that can arise from the bathtub paradox described earlier. Namely, if the age composition of the population tends to vary systematically across space, some areas are likely to have higher levels of housing wealth entirely because of differences in mortgage maturity. As a result, genuine spatial inequalities in housing wealth accumulation will be conflated with life-cycle effects and with changes in the demographic composition of neighbourhoods.

Perhaps the most transparent way of measuring changes in the spatial inequality of housing wealth, therefore, is simply to compare cumulative rates of price appreciation between low and high house price areas (defined on the basis of base-period prices) for each and every subsequent period in the data. Research that has followed this approach found that house prices in expensive areas tend to pull away for a while, only for prices in less-expensive areas to catch up, yielding cycles in housing wealth inequality of large amplitude, with no upward trend.

There is currently no evidence that unambiguously supports the kind of spatial disparities in rates of housing wealth accumulation suggested by theoretical differences in the income elasticity of demand across dwellings. This may suggest that income elasticity of demand does not vary much across neighbourhoods. Or it may be that the effects of heterogeneous income elasticities occur over much longer time periods than those considered in existing housing wealth research, or that changes to the housing stock and the location of amenities obscure these effects, at least in the short run. It is also worth noting that, even if households across all income deciles can access similar rates of housing wealth accumulation, the long-run risk-return trade-off may be less favourable for those on lower incomes. They may, for example, face more volatile price movements, less choice in terms of the timing of entry and exit from the housing market, and higher-risk premiums on mortgage finance.

See also: Housing Equity Withdrawal in the United Kingdom; Housing Wealth and Consumption; Housing Wealth and Inheritance in the United Kingdom; Housing Wealth Over the Life Course; Monetary Policy, Wealth Effects and Housing; Mortgage Equity Withdrawal; Residential Property Derivatives.

Further Reading

Appleyard L and Rowlingson K (2010) *Home-ownership and the Distribution of Personal Wealth.* Report of the JRF Housing Market Taskforce. Joseph Rowntree Foundation. www.jrf.org.uk (accessed 1 November 2011).

Boehm TP and Schlottmann AM (2004) The dynamics of race, income, and homeownership. *Journal of Urban Economics* 55(1): 113–130.

Brueckner JK, Jacques-Francoise T, and Zenou Y (1999) Why is central Paris rich & downtown Detroit poor? An amenity-based theory. *European Economic Review* 43: 91–107.

Burbidge A (2000) Capital gains, homeownership and economic inequality. *Housing Studies* 15: 259–280.

Cameron G and Muellbauer J (1998) The housing market and regional commuting and migration choices. *Scottish Journal of Political Economy* 54: 420–446.

Goodhart C and Hofmann B (2008) House prices, money, credit and the macroeconomy. *Oxford Review of Economic Policy* 24(1): 180–205.

Henley A (1998) Changes in the distribution of housing wealth in Great Britain, 1985–91. *Economica* 65: 363–380.

Henley A (2004) Price shocks, windfall gains and hours of work: British evidence. *Oxford Bulletin of Economics and Statistics* 66(4): 439–456.

Levin E and Pryce G (2011) The dynamics of spatial inequality in UK housing wealth. *Housing Policy Debate* 21(1): 99–132.

Saunders P (1990) *A Nation of Homeowners.* London: Unwin Hyman.

Skaburskis A and Moos M (2008) The redistribution of residential property values in Montreal, Toronto, and Vancouver: Examining neoclassical and Marxist views on changing investment patterns. *Environment and Planning A* 40(4): 905–927.

Housing Wealth over the Life Course

T Davidoff, University of British Columbia, Vancouver, BC, Canada

© 2012 Elsevier Ltd. All rights reserved.

Housing Wealth over the Life Cycle: US Statistics

Data from recent surveys of US consumers highlight the importance of housing as both an asset and a liability. In the 2007 Consumer Expenditure Survey (CEX), renters allocated roughly 25% of all expenditures to shelter. Expenditures for homeowners are difficult to estimate, as tax deductions, capital gains, and opportunity costs of equity have offsetting effects ignored in the expenditure tables. The mean shelter share is deemed 19% for owners in the CEX.

The mean income of owners ($76 973) is more than double that of renters ($36 976) in CEX. In the 2000 Census (Integrated Public Use Microdata Series (IPUMS) microdata), the median homeowner household income was $49 600, as opposed to the median renter income of $26 800. This difference in incomes by ownership is consistent with a number of prominent explanations, such as the US tax code is increasingly favourable to homeownership as income and wealth rise, the normality and age profile of demand for detached homes combined with a natural tendency for detached units to be owner-occupied (see Glaeser and Shapiro, 2003), and a greater prevalence of credit constraints among those with lower income and wealth.

The greater housing expenditure for renters than owners found in the CEX is consistent with the empirical consensus that the wealth elasticity of housing demand is less than 1 (i.e., the fraction of wealth spent on housing falls with wealth; see Carliner, 1973). In the 2000 IPUMS census data, I find an elasticity of rent paid with respect to social security income of just 0.25 among retirees who rent housing aged between 65 and 76 in households with two members (unconditional on any other characteristics, such as metropolitan area housing price differences).

Survey data also provide strong support for the nearly experimental result of Hanushek and Quigley (1980) that the price elasticity of demand for housing is less than 1 (i.e., spending on housing rises as the price of housing rises). Despite similar incomes, renters in central cities in the CEX spend 22% of income on shelter, as opposed to 13% among renters in rural areas. An intriguing result of Davis and Ortalo-Magne (2007) is that despite these low income and price elasticities, the distribution of expenditure shares among renters is very close to constant across time and US metropolitan areas.

Data from the 2004 Survey of Consumer Finances (**Table 1**) show that for most homeowners of every age group, housing represents a majority of assets. For most owners under 50, the value of the home is greater than net worth. The ratio of home value to assets and net worth is declining with age and income.

Figure 1 plots the profile of mortgage status by age and homeownership by age and marital status for household heads in the 2000 US Census. Overall, 67% of household heads report owning the home in which they live, and 67% of owners report owing mortgage debt.

Figure 1 shows that throughout life, married couples are more likely to own than rent housing. A substantial portion of the increase in homeownership among household heads in their 20s and 30s comes from increasing marriage rates. Likewise, much of the decline in homeownership among household heads late in life can be explained by an increasing prevalence of widowhood. This is consistent with the finding of Venti and Wise (2000) and others that death of a spouse is among the most important triggers of exit from homeownership among the elderly. Coile and Milligan (2009) use Health and Retirement Study/Study of Assets and Health Dynamics Among the Oldest Old (HRS/AHEAD) data to show that the downward trend in homeownership in old age accelerates into the 90s, with ill health of individuals joining death of a spouse as a critical cause. They found an ownership rate among individuals of approximately 50% at age 90, but approximately 35% at age 93.

Making use of the patterns depicted in **Figure 1**, Fisher and Gervais (2009) show that homeownership rates declined sharply among younger households between 1980 and 2007, attributing this in large part to increasing age of first marriage over time. Increasing overall homeownership can be attributed largely to an ageing population and increasing homeownership among the elderly.

Among US households, the median and the modal number of residential properties owned are 1, respectively. Aizcorbe et al. (2003) found that 67% of households owned housing in 2001, but only 12.8% owned a second home or rental housing.

Housing Wealth in the Life Cycle: Theoretical Problems

The institution of homeownership presents a puzzle. Why do most households own exactly 100% of a single home,

Table 1 Home value as a fraction of assets (top panel) and net worth (bottom panel) for homeowners only, and median values are given across age and income groups

Age of head	Household income <40k	40–75k	75–125k	125–250k	250+k	Total
Median home value as fraction of assets						
Under 35	1.890	1.848	1.456	1.311	0.576	1.692
35–49	1.469	1.355	0.984	0.761	0.271	1.063
50–64	0.944	0.697	0.572	0.529	0.260	0.634
65+	0.752	0.451	0.439	0.265	0.203	0.627
Median home value as fraction of net worth						
Under 35	2.188	1.921	1.562	1.311	0.576	1.798
3549	1.488	1.367	0.990	0.761	0.271	1.070
50–64	0.944	0.697	0.572	0.529	0.260	0.637
65+	0.754	0.451	0.439	0.265	0.203	0.631
Total	0.918	0.996	0.829	0.625	0.258	0.849

Negative net worth households are excluded from the net worth panel.
Source: Data from the 2007 Survey of Consumer Finances, compiled by Todd Sinai and Moises Yi.

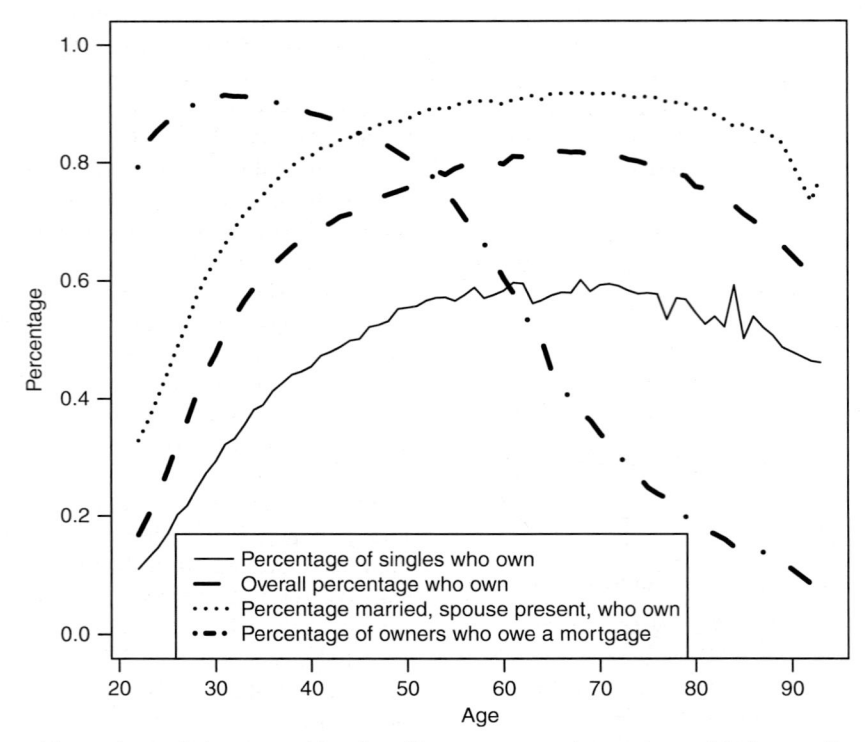

Figure 1 Homeownership rate by marital status and fraction of homeowners owing mortgage debt by age. Data for household heads from 2000 Census via IPUMS.

rather than some smaller share of a diversified bundle of homes? A variety of costs come with full ownership of a particular home, some of which are described below.

Imposition of Mobility Costs

For a given household, choosing to own rather than rent housing makes moving costlier. Finding a new occupant for a home requires maintenance and search effort independent of tenure. However, brokerage and transfer fees are significantly larger for owner units, and more marketing effort is presumably required when the next occupant is likelier to be an owner than a renter, and hence expect a longer stay in the home. Purchasing a unit suitable for owner-occupancy will thus render mobility costly, even if lifetime turnover costs are lower for owner units.

Between the effects of ex ante selection and ex post costs, it is clear empirically that owners are less mobile than renters. Schachter and Kuenzi (2002) show that in the 1996 Current Population Survey, the distribution of length of time in current residence of owners' first order dominates that of renters. The same is true in the 2000 US Census. Chetty and Szeidl (2007) find that in response to unemployment shocks, renters are more likely to move than owners, both in levels and relative to baseline mobility. In addition, homeowners decrease nonhousing consumption more in response to unemployment than do renters. To the extent that housing and other goods are poor substitutes, ownership may thus exacerbate the expected utility costs of the volatility of wealth. In the 2000 US Census, conditional on income, the number of bedrooms in respondents' units declines significantly more rapidly with age among renters than owners, consistent with a greater cost of downsizing for elderly owners.

Whether the existence of demand for changing units makes owning or renting housing relatively advantageous is an open question. The answer will depend in large part on the relative magnitudes of (1) moral hazard costs of rapid turnover and under-maintenance that arise because tenants do not pay on the margin for landlords' leasing and marketing costs upon lease termination versus (2) the expected extra financial costs of moving imposed by owner units. The cost (1) is a common rationalisation of the institution of homeownership through the mechanism of depreciation and maintenance (see Shelton, 1968). The magnitude of cost (2) will depend in part on households' ability to substitute consumption between housing and other goods and between current housing and future expenditures. To the extent that homeowners purchase homes that are particularly well suited to their idiosyncratic needs or attachment to the home grows over time in a beneficial way (e.g., through customisation), cost (2) will be smaller.

Excessive Investment in Particular Homes

Henderson and Ioannides (1983) observe that there is a welfare cost to homeownership if investment demand for a consumer's optimally chosen home is less than consumption demand for that home (in the opposite case, one can invest in housing assets beyond one's own home). There are two obvious ways in which realistic market imperfections will render investment demand relatively weak. First, homeowners may need to hold home equity greater than the amount of total savings they would otherwise choose. Second, homeowners may allocate too much portfolio weight to housing in general and the price risk of their own home in particular.

Too much saving early and late in life
Income for an individual or couple is typically hump-shaped over the life cycle. If a flat trajectory of expenditures is desirable, then transfers from middle age to earlier and later years are also desirable. As emphasised by Artle and Varaiya (1978), homeownership typically involves saving for a down payment in youth, and retaining home equity through much of retirement. Both of these characteristics of homeownership interfere with transferring resources from middle age to the early and late years of low earnings.

Both casual and formal empirical analyses demonstrate that down payment constraints are undesirable from the perspective of younger households. A first piece of evidence is the popularity of very high loan-to-value mortgages in recent years, in a period in which lenders appeared to underestimate the probability and severity of default on such loans. Many such loans featured high payments in the later years of the loan's life, suggesting a willingness to pay for the convenience of avoiding a large down payment. That housing prices increased sharply in response to expansion of mortgage credit also suggests that credit constraints are binding, as in the model of Ortalo-Magne and Rady (2006).

Using microdata covering years in which high loan-to-value ratios were unavailable or extremely costly, Englehardt (1996) shows that consumers spend less money on food in the years leading up to a first purchase of housing than they do in subsequent years. This again suggests that there is significant liquidity constraints associated with down payments.

The elderly retain a strikingly high quantity of home equity, a fact that has been documented by numerous authors such as Venti and Wise (2000). As shown in **Figure 1**, homeownership rates remain high very late into life, and mortgage debt is decreasing, not increasing, in age. As reported in Davidoff (forthcoming), in the 2004 wave of the HRS/AHEAD panel, approximately 12% of retired homeowners over 62 owe any mortgage debt, and among these, the median debt to value is just 33%. Between 1998 and 2004, despite very large increases in home values, only approximately 10% of retired homeowners increased mortgage debt. Almost all high-wealth households have substantial home equity. In the top total wealth quintile of the retired and over 62 sample, 84% held home equity greater than $100 000. To the extent that retirees wish to spend down their housing wealth before death, it thus appears that a combination of the institution of homeownership and supply problems in the markets for residential sale–leasebacks and mortgages for the elderly stand in the way.

That there is a desire to spend down financial resources before death is not at all obvious, as demonstrated by ambiguous findings on the overall savings rate of the elderly, for example, Hurd (1992), Horioka (1996), and Weil (1994). Even without a desire to bequeath wealth to heirs, a low level of consumption in retirement may be justified by a need for precautionary savings. Precautionary savings might arise for a variety of reasons, such as a stochastic need for long-term care and uncertain longevity, combined with imperfect insurance markets. Indeed, Davidoff (2009) shows that the welfare benefits of each one of home equity extraction products, annuities, and long-term care insurance depend on the presence or absence of the others.

A critical input to the retiree's financial planning problem is the question of how costly in financial and utility terms it would be to move out of one's home. If it is easy to move out of the home, then a reverse mortgage is presumably less desirable, and the need to maintain a buffer stock of other assets is lessened. Survey evidence in Bayer and Harper (2000) suggests that moves are quite costly. Engelhardt shows that random increases in social security income and support for home healthcare provision increase homeownership. Coile and Milligan (2009) show that ill health is a crucial determinant of exit from homeownership. A reasonable framework for analysing homeownership in old age would thus pose a trade-off between the liquidity and potential financial gain to selling a home versus the health-dependent utility from remaining in place. Calibration of such a model for a given household to provide normative advice on savings and optimal move date would stretch economists' tools.

Excessive portfolio weight on a particular home

The possibility that homeownership might lead to excessive portfolio weight on housing has been the subject of growing interest over the last decade (see, e.g., Flavin and Yamashita (2002) and Brueckner (1997)). Setting aside moral hazard considerations described above, it is hard to believe that massive exposure to the considerable idiosyncratic risk embodied in a particular house would be part of an optimal allocation. Establishing an optimal portfolio share for a long position in some market's housing prices in general, however, is extremely difficult. I outline some of the difficulties in determining this optimal share below.

To determine the optimal portfolio exposure to home prices, one must be able to determine whether an investor is better or worse off if home prices rise. The sign of the welfare effect of a price increase depends in part on the extent to which elderly homeowners plan to use home equity to finance retirement. If homeowners simply purchased a home when young, and then used the proceeds to finance retirement, and if rents were uncorrelated with the price of a home, then increasing price variability would reduce portfolio demand for housing, and increasing the size of the home would make the portfolio riskier.

At the other extreme, if housing demand is constant forever and prices are perfectly correlated with rents, then owning a home is a perfect hedge against expenditure risk, and increases in price variability would increase the value of homeownership relative to renting. Given the ability to substitute between housing and other consumption in an otherwise steady-state world, a familiar result is that a one-time change to housing prices must be weakly welfare increasing for a homeowner.

Not just hedging demand, but also real options associated with timing of moves, investment, default, and mortgage refinancing may make price volatility more tolerable to owners at any stage of the life cycle. In the recent boom, it seems highly likely that demand and prices were increased by owners and investors in housing who viewed high loan-to-value loans as essentially call options on volatile local prices.

The fact that many homeowners die without cashing out their home equity may be seen as evidence that capital gains risk is of limited importance. However, if housing is held as a buffer for unlikely events, price variation may impose considerable costs as the states in which the home is sold and prices are low may feature particularly high marginal utility.

Just as volatility of prices may increase or decrease the benefits of purchasing more or less housing, volatility of rents has ambiguous effects on the welfare of renters. If housing and other goods are highly substitutable within and between periods, then variability of rents may increase the welfare of renters (this is obvious in the case where housing and other goods are perfect substitutes). In this case, there may be no hedging demand for homeownership. That demand for housing is sufficiently flexible to rule out a motivation to hedge future expenditures runs counter to intuition, and seems unlikely given price elasticity estimates below 1.

Among older households, Skinner (1996) observes that it is difficult to distinguish the relative importance of bequest motives, precautionary considerations, and optimal risk-averse exercise of an option to sell in the retention of home equity in old age. Indeed, the analysis and caveats of Evans et al. (2008) suggest that just the relationship between optimal date of sale and price volatility is almost impossible to sign. Some evidence that capital gains risk matters, supportive of a precautionary motive, is provided by Banks et al. (2007) and Sinai and Souleles (2005). Both found that older households tend to sell out of high price volatility environments in old age. The authors' favoured interpretation of this evidence is that hedging considerations dominate in youth, so that volatility may boost portfolio demand for housing, but capital gains risk dominates in old age so that volatility decreases portfolio demand for housing late in the life cycle.

An easy test of the notion that homeowners are exposed to too much average price risk comes from the fact that consumers who recognise that they have excessive exposure to housing in their portfolios would seek to avoid exposing themselves to further home price risk with their other investment choices. To my knowledge, there is no study of the cross-sectional relationship between (1) the correlation of assets with real estate returns and (2) their relative prices. Such a study would face the challenge that real estate has historically had a weak correlation with financial asset prices, but crashed with the stock market in the great depression and in the recent downturn.

Active investors may or may not demand compensation for exposure to real estate price risk, but these investors are unusual. Findings from the Survey of Consumer Finances reported by Aizcorbe et al. (2003) show that many homeowners are not active investors in other markets. As of 2001, approximately 50% of households owned no equities, and many of those who did were passive investors in managed funds. Even unpriced exposure to systematic risk in housing markets does not imply that homeowners have an optimal share of their portfolio in their own particular home. Home prices are imperfectly correlated across markets, so exposure to national or international housing markets is different from exposure to individual market risk. Moreover, home price appreciation varies considerably from neighbourhood to neighbourhood within markets, and even from home to home within neighbourhoods.

Minimising Investment Constraints

A variety of products have been put forward that may help young and old homeowners reduce home equity and to help all owners reduce exposure to systematic and idiosyncratic price risk. An important open question is whether these products have proved unpopular because contracting issues pushes prices away from actuarially fair, or instead, because high savings and large housing shares in the portfolio are optimal even with fair pricing.

The obvious way to reduce savings while owning a home is to take on a mortgage. The cost of increasing loan-to-value ratios has varied considerably over time. Recent experience demonstrates that there may be no interest rate at which 100% loan-to-value is profitable to lenders. From lenders' perspective, both refinancing and default are crucial to pricing and profitability, but the optimal exercise of these options for borrowers is difficult to solve even for economists. The recent implosion of the mortgage industry and microeconomic evidence makes clear that we do not have a satisfactory model of default and prepayment, even conditional on complete histories of prices and interest rates (Deng et al. (2000) emphasise the heterogeneity of borrower behaviour across households and environments). Credit availability to younger homeowners hoping to minimise savings while retaining the hedging, contracting, or psychological benefits of homeownership is thus likely to remain cyclical.

From the discussion above, it is not clear that the elderly wish to reduce savings in the form of home equity or otherwise. The obvious products that would allow the elderly to extract equity without moving out of their homes are sale–leasebacks and reverse mortgages. The latter are somewhat more popular than the former, but even demand for reverse mortgages has been weak, with less than 1% of older homeowners owing reverse mortgage debt. Effective interest rates for reverse mortgages are quite high, with origination fees currently up to 2% of home value and historically considerably higher. Reverse mortgages are likely to feature both adverse selection (witness Mme Jean Calment who lived a record 122 years and had the French version of a reverse mortgage) and moral hazard both on the timing of sales (once a property is worth less than the loan amount, the mortgagor has no incentive to move because the loans are nonrecourse) and on maintenance (see Miceli and Sirmans, 1994) – it is not obvious that reasonable loan-to-value ratios can be attained at profitable and marketable rates.

Shiller (1993) and Caplin et al. (1997) have proposed mechanisms whereby homeowners can reduce exposure to variation in home prices. The Chicago Mercantile Exchange now allows investors to take long or short positions on changes in regional average home price indexes, calculated based on a repeated sale methodology. Several companies have devised mechanisms whereby outside investors can be given equity, rather than debt, in the home. For the latter type of contract, default risk should be lower than with debt contracts, but investment and market timing of sale may lead to problems of moral hazard. Trades on the Case–Shiller CME index avoid homeowner agency problems but do not provide insurance against individual home price risk. Given the complicated effects of home price changes on utility described above, it is not entirely surprising that there has been very limited demand for either type of product.

Summarising, it is difficult to provide households with easily understood normative advice on major life cycle housing decisions, and it is particularly difficult to characterise the optimal portfolio share for housing. The conventions of hump-shaped life cycle ownership rates, high homeownership rates, mortgage financing, and large unhedged positions in individual homes will be with us for the foreseeable future.

See also: Housing and Wealth Portfolios; Housing Wealth and Consumption; Housing Wealth and Inheritance in the United Kingdom; Housing Wealth Distribution in the United Kingdom; Monetary Policy, Wealth Effects and Housing.

References

Aizcorbe AM, Kennickell AB, and Moore KB (2003) Recent changes in U.S. family finances: Evidence from the 1998 and 2001 survey of consumer finances. *Federal Reserve Bulletin* 1–32, January.
Artle R and Varaiya P (1978) Life cycle consumption and homeownership. *Journal of Economic Theory* 18(1): 38–58.

Banks J, Blundell R, Oldfield Z, and Smith JP (2007) *Housing price volatility and downsizing in later life*. NBER Working Papers 13496. National Bureau of Economic Research, Inc.

Bayer A-H and Harper L (2000) Fixing to stay a national survey of housing and home modification issues. *Research Report*. AARP.

Brueckner J (1997) Consumption and investment motives and portfolio choices of homeowners. *Journal of Real Estate Finance and Economics* 15(2): 159–180.

Caplin A, Chan S, Freeman C, and Tracy J (1997) *Housing Partnerships: A New Approach to Markets at a Crossroads*. Cambridge, MA: MIT Press.

Carliner G (1973) Income elasticity of housing demand. *Review of Economics and Statistics* 55(4): 528–532.

Chetty R and Szeidl A (2007) Consumption commitments and risk preferences. *Quarterly Journal of Economics* 122(2): 831–877.

Coile C and Milligan K (2009) How household portfolios evolve after retirement: The effect of aging and health shocks. *The Review of Income and Wealth* 55(2): 226–248.

Davidoff T (2009) Housing, health, and annuities. *Journal of Risk and Insurance* 76(1): 31–52.

Davidoff T (2010) Home equity commitment and long-term care insurance demand. *Journal of Public Economics* 94(1): 44–49.

Davis MA and Ortalo-Magne F (2007) Household expenditures, wages, rents. *Working paper*. University of Wisconsin–Madison.

Deng Y, Quigley J, and Order RV (2000) Mortgage terminations, heterogeneity and the exercise of mortgage options. *Econometrica* 68(2): 275–307.

Englehardt G (1996) Consumption, down payments and liquidity constraints. *Journal of Money, Credit and Banking* 28: 255–271.

Evans J, Henderson V, and Hobson D (2008) Optimal timing for an indivisible asset sale. *Mathematical Finance* 18(4): 545–567.

Fisher JDM and Gervais M (2009) Why has home ownership fallen among the young? Working Paper Series WP-09-01, Federal Reserve Bank of Chicago.

Flavin M and Yamashita T (2002) Owner-occupied housing and the composition of the household portfolio. *American Economic Review* 92(1): 345–362.

Glaeser EL and Shapiro JM (2003) The benefits of the home mortgage deduction. *Tax Policy and the Economy* 17: 37–82.

Hanushek EA and Quigley JM (1980) What is the price elasticity of housing demand? *The Review of Economics and Statistics* 62: 449–454.

Henderson JV and Ioannides Y (1983) A model of housing tenure choice. *The American Economic Review* 73(1): 98–113.

Horioka CY (1996) Do the aged dissave in Japan? *Journal of the Japanese and International Economies* 10: 295–311.

Hurd MD (1992) Wealth depletion and life cycle consumption by the elderly. In: Wise D (ed.) *Topics in the Economics of Aging*, pp. 135–162. Chicago, IL: The University of Chicago Press.

Miceli T and Sirmans CF (1994) Reverse mortgage and borrower maintenance risk. *Journal of the American Real Estate and Urban Economics Association* 22(2): 257–299.

Ortalo-Magne F and Rady S (2006) Housing market dynamics: On the contribution of income shocks and credit constraints. *Review of Economic Studies* 73(2): 459–485.

Schachter JP and Kuenzi JJ (2002) Seasonality of moves and the duration and tenure of residence: 1996. *Working Paper 69*. Population Division, US Census Bureau.

Shelton JP (1968) The cost of owning vs. renting a home. *Land Economics* 44(1): 59–72.

Shiller R (1993) *Macro Markets*. Oxford, UK: Clarendon Press.

Sinai T and Souleles N (2005) Owner occupied housing as insurance against rent risk. *Quarterly Journal of Economics* 120(2): 763–789.

Skinner JS (1996) Is housing wealth a sideshow? In: Wise D (ed.) *Advances in the Economics of Aging*, pp. 241–271. Chicago, IL: NBER and University of Chicago Press.

Venti SF and Wise DA (2000) Aging and housing equity. NBER Working Paper 7882.

Weil DN (1994) The saving of the elderly in micro and macro data. *Quarterly Journal of Economics*, 99(1): 55–81.

Human Rights and Housing

P Kenna, National University of Ireland, Galway, Ireland

© 2012 Elsevier Ltd. All rights reserved.

Glossary

Commodification In relation to housing – the transformation of housing as a home to a commodity of exchange or investment, where its value is determined by the market.

General comment 4 UN clarification on State obligations stipulating that housing rights encompass legal security of tenure; availability of services, materials, facilities and infrastructure; affordability; habitability; accessibility; location and cultural adequacy.

Housing adequacy The range of housing standards required to satisfy the obligations contained within international housing rights obligations.

Housing rights The range of State obligations in international, regional, and national law which ensures a right to housing and increasing housing standards is the right of every woman, man, and child.

Progressive realisation The principle of progressive realisation recognises that all economic, social, and cultural rights will generally not be achieved in a short time, but establishes clear obligations for States to move as expeditiously and effectively as possible towards that goal, without any deliberately retrogressive measures.

Introduction

One of the primary needs of all human beings is housing. It involves shelter – essential for survival and human dignity – a place to live, a base for the development of children, and the household – home. Housing provides a psychological space for nurture, privacy, personal development, and family life, as well as a sense of personal space. The modern concept of 'home' builds on all these elements of adequate and appropriate housing, which form the core of housing rights.

The central position of housing has prompted States and political parties at the national and international levels to recognise, codify, and guarantee housing rights in law. These rights have been acclaimed by international organisations, such as the United Nations (UN), Council of Europe (CoE), Organisation of American States (OAS), and European Union (EU), as well as more than 50 Constitutions around the world. They are affirmed in numerous international declaratory and policy documents, as well as national laws, jurisprudence, and the housing policies and processes of many countries.

International housing rights derive from international human rights instruments and offer a moral compass in the development and evaluation of housing law, policy, and systems. Housing rights obligations transcend political regime types and relative primacy or hegemony of market or State provision of housing. Of course, neoliberal and social democratic governments accept the market as the primary provider of housing, with government intervention regulating excesses of the market and intervening in cases of market failure or negative market externalities. The right-to-housing default position considers that it is government's first obligation to ensure that all are decently housed, with the market managed and regulated in ways subservient to that goal. The UN Special Rapporteur on Adequate Housing has pointed out: "The belief that markets will provide housing for all has failed. The current crisis is a stark reminder of this reality. A home is not a commodity – four walls and a roof. It is a place to live in security, peace and dignity, and a right for every human being."

The Universal Declaration on Human Rights (UDHR) (1948) placed the right to housing within the right to a standard of living adequate for health and well-being. It is fundamental to the enjoyment of all economic, social, and cultural rights. Access to employment, training, and education; absence of discrimination, crime, or segregation; and enjoyment of prevailing opportunities and communal facilities are dependant on the realisation of housing rights. Indeed, people who experience homelessness, poor housing, and shelter poverty are often victims of violence and crime as well as persistent poverty. Social rights of participation and political rights are often linked to housing status, with enfranchisement often related to homeownership or housing history, address, as well as denial of such participation to homeless people.

Housing provides a gateway to other opportunities. Since housing is so central to individual, family, and community life, it determines many of the relationships and opportunities which people can enjoy. These include the availability of employment options, health care services, schools, childcare centres and other social facilities, services, materials, and infrastructure. Good housing conditions are a prerequisite to good health, which particularly affects the development of all aspects of children's lives. The location and quality of the housing environment are key features in the development of healthy and sustainable communities. *The Global Strategy for Shelter to the Year 2000* stated: "Adequate shelter means... adequate privacy, adequate space, adequate security, adequate lighting and ventilation, adequate basic infrastructure and adequate location with regard to work and basic facilities – all at a reasonable cost."

Housing also has an emotional and symbolic significance on perceptions of one's self and place in the community, and in today's world can relate to status in society. Primarily, housing offers a sanctuary from the world and a place to call home, even within a world dominated by media and financial pressures to view housing as an asset or a commodity. Indeed, one of the clearest manifestations of poverty is the lack of an adequate and affordable home. People who lack safe, secure, and healthy housing with basic infrastructure, such as piped water and adequate sanitation, suffer from 'housing poverty'.

Nature of Housing Rights

Housing rights involve more than shelter, which represents one element. Indeed, it often takes primacy in situations of housing crisis, poverty, or natural catastrophe. However, the UN, and other jurisprudence, has developed the understanding of housing rights to include legal security of tenure; availability of services, materials, and infrastructure; affordable housing; habitable housing; accessible housing; housing in a suitable location; and housing constructed and sited in a way which is culturally adequate. These also involve the absence of forced evictions, which result in individuals being rendered homeless or vulnerable to the violation of other human rights.

Housing rights obligations require that people have security of tenure, with no arbitrary evictions, fair mortgage terms and tenancy conditions. Tenure includes rental (public and private) accommodation, cooperative housing, lease, owner-occupation, emergency housing, and informal settlements, including occupation of land or property. Regardless of the type of tenure, all persons should possess a degree of security of tenure which guarantees legal protection against forced eviction, harassment, and other threats.

Adequacy and Habitability of Housing

All beneficiaries of a right to housing must enjoy habitability which facilitates a life of human dignity. The human right to adequate housing has been defined by the UN Special Rapporteur on Adequate Housing as the "right of every woman, man, youth and child to gain and sustain a safe and secure home and community in which to live in peace and dignity".

Defining housing adequacy has been contested by many States, often seeking to justify existing housing conditions as adequate. The old arguments surrounding adequacy, which differed widely between warm and cold climates, developing and modern economies, and purchased and low-cost rented housing, have been superseded by universal and holistic standards applicable to all States. Adequate and habitable housing must be of a decent physical and space standard; structurally sound; physically secure; weather and watertight; serviced with adequate electrical, water, heating, and sewage systems; free from dangerous hazards, such as asbestos and lead, vermin and pests, structural hazards and disease. An adequate house must contain certain facilities essential for health, security, comfort, and nutrition. All beneficiaries of the right to adequate housing should have sustainable access to natural and common resources; safe drinking water; energy for cooking, heating, and lighting; sanitation and washing facilities; means of food storage, refuse disposal, and site drainage; and emergency services.

Affordability

Affordable housing has been defined by the UN to require that personal or household financial costs associated with housing should be at such a level that the attainment and satisfaction of other basic needs are not threatened or compromised. In accordance with the principle of affordability, tenants should be protected by appropriate means against unreasonable rent levels or rent increases. In societies in which natural materials constitute the chief sources of building materials for housing, steps should be taken by States parties to ensure the availability of such materials. The CoE Committee for Social Rights has defined affordable housing as a situation in which the household can pay the initial costs (deposit, advanced rent); the current rent; and/or other costs (utility, maintenance, and management charges) on a long-term basis, and still be able to maintain a minimum standard of living, as defined by the society in which the household is located.

Sources of Human Rights for Housing

International Organisations

The UDHR, adopted by almost all States, recognises rights to housing in Article 25:

> Everyone has the right to a standard of living adequate for the health and well-being of himself and of his family, including food, clothing, housing and medical care and necessary social services, and the right to security in the event of unemployment, sickness, disability, widowhood, old age or other lack of livelihood in circumstances beyond his control.

Similarly, the *International Covenant on Economic, Social and Cultural Rights* (ICESCR), of 1966, now ratified by almost 150 States (though not the United States), recognises the right to housing:

> The States Parties to the present Covenant recognize the right of everyone to an adequate standard of living for himself and his family, including adequate food, clothing and housing, and to the continuous improvement of living conditions. The States Parties will take appropriate steps to ensure the realization of this right, recognizing to this effect the essential importance of international co-operation based on free consent.

Ratifying States are required to recognise, respect, protect, and fulfil these housing rights; meet 'minimum core' obligations; and ensure nondiscrimination and direct legislative measures, appropriate policies, and the maximum of available resources towards a progressive realisation of these rights. *General Comment No. 4. on the Right to Adequate Housing* sets out the minimum core guarantees which, under public international law, are legally vested in all persons.

Further relevant UN instruments include the UN *Convention on the Elimination of All Forms of Discrimination against Women* (CEDAW, 1981), the *Convention on the Rights of the Child*, 1989 and the *UN Convention Relating to the Status of Refugees* (1951).

Many other international instruments setting out rights to housing have been ratified by countries around the world. The American Declaration on the Rights and Duties of Man (1948) states:

> Art. 11. Every person has the right to the preservation of his health through sanitary and social measures relating to food, clothing, housing and medical care to the extent permitted by public and community resources.
> Art. 23. Every person has the right to own such property as meets the essential needs of decent living and helps maintain the dignity of the individual and of the home.

Article 34 of the Charter of the OAS provides for a right to housing:

> The Member States agree that equality of opportunity, the elimination of extreme poverty, equitable distribution of wealth and income and the full participation of their peoples in decisions relating to their own development are, among others, basic objectives of integral development. To achieve them, they likewise agree to devote their utmost efforts to accomplishing the following basic goals:
> ... k) Adequate housing for all sectors of the population;

The African Union (formerly the Organisation of African Unity) in its Protocol to the African Charter on Human and Peoples' Rights on the Rights of Women in Africa (2003) states:

> Article 16 – Right to Adequate Housing
> Women shall have the right to equal access to housing and to acceptable living conditions in a healthy environment. To ensure this right, State Parties shall grant to women, whatever their marital status, access to adequate housing.

The *Habitat Agenda* states: "Within the overall context of an enabling approach, Governments should take appropriate action in order to promote, protect and ensure the full and progressive realization of the right to adequate housing."

Goal 7 of the UN *Millennium Development Goals* (2000) involves halving, by 2015, the proportion of people without sustainable access to safe drinking water and basic sanitation, and by 2020, achieving a significant improvement in the lives of at least 100 million slum-dwellers.

Regional Organisations

Council of Europe

Housing rights are advanced through the CoE's *European Social Charter* and *Revised Charter* (RESC) and in an oblique way through the *European Convention for the Protection of Human Rights and Fundamental Freedoms* (ECHR) within Articles 3, 6, 8, 13, and 14 and Article 1 of Protocol No. 1.

The *European Social Charter* and the RESC contain important rights to social and medical assistance for those without adequate resources, establishing housing obligations in relation to physically and mentally disabled persons, children and young persons, migrant workers, older people, and families and people experiencing poverty or social exclusion. Article 31 of the RESC establishes a right to housing:

> With a view to ensuring the effective exercise of the right to housing, the Parties undertake to take measures designed:
>
> 1. to promote access to housing of an adequate standard;
> 2. to prevent and reduce homelessness with a view to its gradual elimination;

3. to make the price of housing accessible to those without adequate resources.

In *FEANTSA v. France*, the CoE Committee for Social Rights established that recognition of the obligations under Article 31, while not imposing an obligation of 'results', must take "a practical and effective, rather than purely theoretical form".

European Union

While the European Treaties do not refer directly to a right to housing, much EU social policy impacts on housing rights and housing policy. EU Regulations in the 1960s and 1970s ensured that migrating nonnational workers and their dependents were entitled to the same social benefits, including access to housing, as nationals of Member States on the principle of nondiscrimination. There are legally defined steps at the EU level to harmonise the conditions of asylum-seekers across Europe, including to standardise housing conditions, to recognise the rights and status of third-country nationals, and to develop a common policy on illegal immigrants.

Article 34(3) of the EU Charter of Fundamental Rights states:

> In order to combat social exclusion and poverty, the Union recognises and respects the right to social and housing assistance so as to ensure a decent existence for all those who lack sufficient resources, in accordance with the Rules laid down by Community law and national laws and practices.

Housing rights are also advanced in the Race Directive (2000), Gender Directive, and Unfair Contract Terms Directive, while the European Parliament has adopted resolutions advancing housing rights and a European Charter for Housing.

Enforcing International Housing Rights Instruments

There is a growing jurisprudence at the international and national levels on housing rights as human rights. A range of quasi-judicial and judicial bodies constantly adjudicate on the nature, extent, application, and violation of these rights, although some are promoted primarily through State policies and processes. Aspects of housing rights are regularly adjudicated upon in courts throughout the world, including in the United States. Clarifications on the contents and obligations of housing rights, including the concepts of minimum core obligations, progressive realisation of rights according to available resources, and violations of rights, are now widely understood and accepted in the context of the right to an adequate standard of living.

Human dignity, minimum core obligations of States, and a progressive realisation of these rights have become key legal concepts in advancing housing rights. Housing rights, like human rights generally, are sometimes seen as rooted in the concept of human dignity. The principle of human dignity is rooted in religious teachings across the world. However, some argue that in the contemporary interpretations of legal texts containing the term, the meaning of dignity is highly context specific, varying significantly from jurisdiction to jurisdiction and (often) over time within particular jurisdictions. Advancing housing rights on the basis of respect for human dignity alone can amount to a very meagre level of enjoyment. The rising norms and legislation for housing occupancy and standards, and the provision of social housing may surpass minimalist interpretations of housing rights.

The UN has developed the concept of minimum core obligations on States in the implementation of rights as involving at the very least, minimum essential levels of each of the rights involved. In a situation in which any significant number of individuals are deprived of basic shelter and housing the State party is failing to discharge its obligations under the Covenant. Article 2(1) of the ICESCR obligates each State party to take the necessary steps "to the maximum of its available resources".

Article 2 of the ICESCR requires States to take steps "with a view to achieving progressively the full realization of the rights recognized". The concept of progressive realisation recognises that all economic, social, and cultural rights will generally not be achieved in a short time, but establishes clear obligations for States to move as expeditiously and effectively as possible towards that goal, without any deliberately retrogressive measures.

However, while there is significant recognition of housing rights within international public law, this does not yet translate everywhere into effective domestic legislative and policy measures which implement international housing rights obligations. The impact of housing rights based on international public law depends on whether States adopt a dualist or monist approach to the applicability of such law within their internal legal system.

Much legal controversy involves the justiciability or enforceability in national courts of internationally defined housing rights. Issues arise in relation to separation of powers between the legislature and the judiciary, resource allocation powers of judges, as well as costs and access to courts. Of course, courts penalise breaches of many codified, statutory, and established socioeconomic rights. Indeed, making housing rights judicially enforceable can encourage governments to dedicate financial and policy resources to meeting housing needs. The UN views many component elements of the right to adequate housing as being at least consistent with the provision of domestic legal remedies. At an international level possible penalties and sanctions for violations of housing and other rights have been developed within the *Limburg Principles* and the *Maastricht Guidelines*.

Constitutional and Statutory Rights

Many of the world's Constitutions refer to housing or housing rights. For instance, a right to housing is set out in Article 26 of the Constitution of South Africa (1996).

1. Everyone has the right to have access to adequate housing.
2. The state must take reasonable legislative and other measures, within its available resources, to achieve the progressive realisation of this right.
3. No one may be evicted from their home, or have their home demolished, without an order of court made after considering all the relevant circumstances. No legislation may permit arbitrary evictions.

Courts have created a corpus of law establishing and consolidating these constitutional and statutory rights, with orders specifying State action to meet such obligations, including the notable case of *Government of South Africa and others v. Grootboom and others*. Many States have developed laws specifically granting housing rights, such as the *Housing (Scotland) Act 1987*, and the French Droit au logement opposable (DALO) Act of 5 March 2007. Courts across the world have developed common law housing rights in the areas of security of tenure, respect for home, nondiscrimination, decent physical standards, and fair procedures in evictions.

Some housing rights emanate from family protection laws, obligations to children, support for people with disabilities and older people, succession law, and protection for homeless people and other groups, often arising from politically inspired general public policies.

Evaluation

Dominance of Commodification and Market Approaches for Development of Human Rights to Housing?

Housing has become increasingly regarded as a consumer good and an asset across the world. Today, homeowners across the world are encouraged to view their home as an asset, a store of future and hereditable wealth and mortgage equity. Mass-produced and commodified homeownership is marketed, mortgaged, and exchanged as the *leitmotif* of settled affluent family life, and status is often attributed to housing wealth. But access to housing within local market systems requires access to housing loans, thus integrating housing availability and affordability within the global financial system, determined largely by nonhousing macroeconomic factors.

Globalisation of financial markets, with integrated housing finance, has accentuated the commodification of housing. In this climate, market or price measures determine access, location, quality, size, and value of housing rather than any measure of need or enjoyment of rights. International capital markets increasingly direct the availability of national mortgage loans and interest rates, facilitated by the encroachment of property law into housing, with an emphasis on securitisation of loans, registration of property, division between public and private interests, and so on.

Yet, housing markets are like any other asset markets, prone to booms and busts, and this has important consequences for States advancing housing rights. In any case, adequate housing has become unaffordable and inaccessible for significant numbers of households whose members are on low incomes; are in temporary or unprotected employment; and are old, disabled, or otherwise excluded. State provision has diminished across all market economies, reducing the scope of States to meet housing rights obligations. In this context, poor households have been forced to take out high interest subprime loans in many countries to secure adequate housing.

With the withdrawal of States from housing provision towards an enabling market system, it is important that housing rights are advanced within all parts of these housing systems. Angel points out that housing systems contain five essential elements involving property rights, housing finance, residential infrastructure, regulation, and subsidies/public housing.

Work on Development of a More Meaningful Concept of Housing for Human Rights

There are persistent challenges for housing rights advocates, in moving beyond the notion of housing rights from essentially the provision of social housing, to the integration of housing rights within the finance, legal, property, regulatory, infrastructural, and other elements of housing systems. Housing rights must be mainstreamed within all these key elements of housing systems to be effective, although this can present many challenges. There are dangers in seeing access to mortgage finance and homeownership as a means of implementing housing rights rather than as elements of the housing system which must result in adequate, affordable, appropriate, and sustainable housing rights. For instance, without ensuring the full ambit of housing rights, moves towards increasing access to housing finance for those previously excluded could lead to unsustainable and unaffordable homeownership, with consequent evictions and homelessness. Equally, calls for universal rights to shelter could result in dormitory style housing for all homeless people.

But there are some valuable interpretations on the intrinsic and core elements of housing rights, which transcend market and nonmarket systems. These can provide effective tools for deconstructing housing systems and creating a space for the effective and sustainable development of housing rights.

The CoE is developing precise and meaningful measures of housing rights obligations. In *FEANTSA v. France* the European Committee on Social Rights established the minimum core housing rights obligations for European States, addressing legal, budgetary, planning, social inclusion, equality, and administrative measures. The CoE Commissioner for Human Rights is also expanding the understanding of housing rights through publishing an *Issue Paper* and *Guidelines on Housing Rights*. Much work yet needs to be done to expand on the legal basis of housing rights, ensuring that clear, enforceable standards are adopted in the implementation of housing rights.

Of course, it is the rights bearers themselves who must ultimately define, advance, and ensure the implementation of housing rights. The Participation and Practice of Rights Project enabled tenants of a housing project in Northern Ireland to translate international housing rights norms to their own living conditions. Through a process of action research involving surveys, the residents established a quantifiable human rights 'baseline' of outstanding housing rights issues.

At another level, Fox raises the everyday importance of the concept of home as a social, psychological, cultural, and emotional phenomenon which has been recognised in some disciplines, but has not penetrated the legal domain. This reflects in many ways the position of housing rights, where the physical structures and capital values dominate the debate. Developing the concept of home as an encapsulation of housing rights (with some limitations) offers the possibility for developing a comparative, measurable, and people-centred definition of housing in law.

Housing rights, adopted by almost all the States of the world, are defined at the international, regional, and national levels. They offer a legal discourse based on human dignity, advancing person-centred and other values. This provides a base of legal resources which can act to temper and refocus the commercial and commodity-based interpretations of housing law, policies, and systems. Indeed, this corpus of jurisprudence can also offer a child-centred, people-centred, and feminist critique of housing systems.

See also: Feminist Perspectives on Home; Homeless People: Disasters and Displacement; Homeless People: Refugees and Asylum Seekers; Housing Standards: Regulation; Rights to Housing: Developing Societies; Rights to Housing: International Instruments; Rights to Housing Tenure; Shelter and Development; Social Justice.

Further Reading

Angel S (2000) *Housing Policy Matters – A Global Analysis*. New York: OUP.
Bratt RG, Stone ME, and Hartmann CW (2006) *A Right to Housing*. Philadelphia, PA: Temple University Press.
Commissioner for Human Rights, Council of Europe (2008) *Issue Paper Housing Rights: The Duty to Ensure Housing for All*. Strasbourg, France: Council of Europe.
Fox L (2007) *Conceptualising Home: Theories, Laws and Policies*. Oxford, UK: Hart Publishing.
Harris B (2004) *Defending the Right to a Home – The Power of Anti-Poverty Lawyers*. Aldershot, UK: Ashgate.
Kenna P (2005) *Housing Rights and Human Rights*. Brussels, Belgium: FEANTSA.
Kenna P (2008) Globalization and housing rights. *Indiana Journal of Global Legal Studies* 15(2): 397–469.
Leckie S (2000) *Legal Resources for Housing Rights*. Geneva, Switzerland: COHRE.
Limburg Principles on the Implementation of the International Covenant on Economic, Social and Cultural Rights (June 1986). UN Doc E/CN.4/1987/17.
Maastricht Guidelines on Violations of Economic, Social and Cultural Rights (January 1997) 20 HRQ 691,705.
Melish T (2002) *Protecting Economic, Social and Cultural Rights in the Inter-American Human Rights System*. New Haven, CT: Yale Law School.
Rolnik R (2009) Promotion and protection of all human rights, civil, political, economic, social and cultural rights, including the right to development. *Report of the Special Rapporteur on Adequate Housing as a Component of the Right to an Adequate Standard of Living, and on the Right to Non-discrimination in this Context*. UN General Assembly, Report to the Human Rights Council. UN Doc. A/HRC/10/7. New York: United Nations.
Westendorp I (2007) *Women and Housing: Gender makes a Difference*. Antwerp, Belgium: Intersentia.

Relevant Websites

www2.ohchr.org – Office of the United Nations High Commissioner for Human Rights.
www.ohchr.org – Fact Sheet No. 21, The Human Right to Adequate Housing.
www2.ohchr.org – Committee on Economic, Social and Cultural Rights.
www.unhabitat.org – UN Habitat. For a Better Urban Future.
www.hrea.org – Human Rights Education Associates.
www1.umn.edu – Circle of Rights. Economic, Cultural & Social Rights Activism: A Training Resource.
www.coe.int
www.cohre.org – Centre on Housing Rights and Evictions.
www.escr-net.org – International Network for Economic, Social & Cultural Rights.

Ideal Homes

T Chapman, Durham University, Durham, UK

© 2012 Elsevier Ltd. All rights reserved.

Glossary

Conspicuous consumption The process by which individuals and households project their sense of self-identity and status through the purchase of property, goods, and services to raise their sense of self-esteem in the eyes of significant others.

Cultural conservatism The tendency of individuals and households to limit their choices in terms of adventurous style or cultural experiment with patterns of consumption and lifestyle for fear of social sanction by significant others.

Manipulation of needs The process by which capitalism produces and deepens consumer desires through product design and development, marketing, and advertising.

Ontological security The popular association people make between property ownership and inclusion in mainstream society or the so-called property-owning democracy.

Show homes Properties which are fully decorated and furnished by speculative building firms to encourage consumers to imagine themselves living better lives and thereby increase the chances that they will buy a new home.

Subprime mortgages The practice by banks, building societies, and other financial institutions of making loans to people who have insufficient income or job security to repay mortgage loans.

Defining 'Ideal Homes'

In Western capitalist English-speaking nations, including Australia, Canada, New Zealand, United States of America and the United Kingdom, ideas about what constitutes an 'ideal home' have become economically and culturally embedded. This article explains the origins and consequences of this social phenomenon. It is necessary, at the outset, to recognise that popular conceptions of the ideal home in advanced industrial Western societies can be substantially different from ideas about what constitutes home in traditional societies. Anthropologist Nigel Barley (1989) illustrated this point successfully when he brought a group of Indonesians to England to look at conventional suburban homes. The visitors, who lived in traditional houses in Indonesia, asked some fundamental questions about the way Western people lived. First, why do they spend so much time tending their front gardens if they never sit in them? Second, why do they invest so much in their houses if they have to work so hard that they are rarely there? And finally, why do they invest so much in their own homes instead of building shrines for their ancestors?

Barley's work reveals that what is considered to be 'normal' in the West is, in fact, just one of many models of what constitutes the ideal home. Furthermore, Barley highlights the point that homes in the West are consumer 'products' which share common features in terms of facility, comfort, and patterns of room use. Historically, associations between home, conspicuous consumption, and status have not been as strong. In early medieval England, even the very wealthy invested much more of their resources in the building of great cathedrals than they invested in their own homes. Self-aggrandisement through the building of important houses came later, first amongst the aristocracy, later in the burgeoning middle classes as society became more affluent through the emergence of urbanism, capitalism, and industrialisation. Finally, greater affluence came to the working classes, who also subscribed to the idea of the ideal home.

Houses may have broadly the same features in cultural and functional terms, but they are differentiated by their size, expense, and the quality and quantity of artefacts they accommodate. Depending upon the economic resources of the inhabitants, there is a strong tendency for people to signal their relative affluence to significant others – particularly their families, neighbours, and friends – through the way that they furnish and decorate their homes. In affluent societies, in sum, there has been a significant shift from defining houses in terms of meeting fundamental needs such as shelter, warmth, and security to a consumer product which is more or less luxurious and is a representation of personal achievement, social aspiration, and social mobility. The home, in this sense, is less an expression of its place in the community as in traditional societies and rather an expression of individuality, privatism, and competition.

How Ideal Homes Have Changed

During the industrial revolution in England when towns grew fast to accommodate the working classes, housing conditions were notoriously inadequate. Contemporary writers such as Charles Dickens and Frederick Engels revealed that men, women, and children worked extremely long hours for low wages and lived in overcrowded and unsanitary housing with few, if any, facilities or comforts (Gauldy, 1974). As the industrial revolution progressed, the new middle classes and growing numbers of higher-paid skilled workers created unprecedented levels of consumer demand. Speculative builders put up houses of higher quality to buy or rent to meet this demand. Working people, especially in the north of England, established building societies so that people could buy their own homes and escape the sharp practices of landlords or dependence on industrial employers (Gauldy, 1974).

From about the 1860s, working-class houses, no matter how humble, were adorned with decorated tile work, portentous door cases, or bay windows to differentiate the status of the inhabitants (Girouard, 1990). People also bought furniture, carpets, and ornaments to show that they were economically secure, respectable, and fashionable. As is the case now, home had become a physical social marker of personal success, status, and style. In response to rising affluence, over the last 100 years the average size of houses has increased significantly as has the extent of their facility and scope for adornment with consumer goods.

The way that households are organised and managed has also changed over the last century. At the turn of the twentieth century, running the home was labour intensive, necessarily involving many female servants in larger middle-class homes. This changed as young women were able to find better paid work, so producing demand from middle-class women for 'labour-saving' devices. The market for household durable products or 'white goods' has since expanded greatly, and now 'basic' items such as washing machines, cookers, and refrigerators are almost universal in the homes of wealthy societies.

The home also became a principal location for leisure activity. Initially, leisure time was shared by all members of the household as they sat around the fireplace to read, play games, listen to the radio, or watch television. Electric lighting and central heating helped to open up homes so that the whole house could be used for leisure. Mass markets in televisions, hi-fi, computers, game consoles, musical instruments, and so on emerged. This shift from 'family' leisure to 'independent' leisure is reflected in the design and size of new homes.

The Ideal Home as a Consumer Product

Sociologist Thorstein Veblen (1914) introduced the concept of 'conspicuous consumption' to describe the lifestyles of the American upper classes at the turn of the twentieth century. Conspicuous consumption is the process by which people achieve self-aggrandisement by outperforming their neighbours by displaying the sophistication, fashionability, grandeur, and expense of their homes. The process Veblen identified had been prevalent in the European upper classes for several centuries as a means of gaining patronage. Conspicuous consumption soon became a popular way of placement in the social hierarchy amongst the middle and working classes as they became more affluent. In working-class homes in northern England in the early twentieth century, for example, the purchase of a piano was as important in status terms as a neogothic mansion might be to the upper classes.

In twentieth-century Britain, during the interwar years, there was a massive boom in house building for the new middle classes. In the 1920s an average of 150 000 new semidetached homes were built each year for private purchase, rising to almost 350 000 in 1936 (Oliver et al., 1981: 13). This semidetached house building boom in the new suburbs of every town and city was abhorred by the social elite because it represented, for them, the brash aspirations of their social subordinates.

These homes were designed to reflect, in miniature, the grandeur of Tudor timber-framed mansions with mock beams and high-pitched pan-tiled roofs. Gardens had impressive walls, exuberant front porches were added, and most houses had decorative stained-glass windows (see Oliver et al., 1981). The house-building boom was a physical representation of 'social mobility' for people who had come from more humble backgrounds.

New homeowners copied what they believed to be the sophisticated lifestyles of their social superordinates. This involved the purchase of many new consumer products such as matching 'three-piece suites' of heavily upholstered 'lounge furniture' to give an impression of hotel-like opulence. People bought new china tea sets with cake stands and silver trolleys to put them on to give the impression that this display had been created by a servant. In reality, few servants worked in such houses and to maintain an appropriate impression of respectability, few middle-class women retained paid employment once married (Chapman, 2004; Giles, 2004).

As women became more accustomed to the idea of maintaining home and family instead of working, they were targeted by manufacturers with a plethora of new labour-saving or status-enhancing products. Such products were displayed at the Daily Mail Ideal Home Exhibition at Olympia in London (and at similar events in Australia, Canada, and the United States). These large-scale exhibitions were visited mainly by middle-class women who were able to try out new gadgets and view the latest fashions. Then, as now, such shows aimed at the mass market and carefully positioned products to reassure consumers by not challenging 'cultural conservatism' with outlandish or adventurous products. At the same time, such shows purposefully created anxieties in the minds of viewers about being 'left behind' in fashion terms (Chapman and Hockey, 1999).

Ideal Homes as an Investment

The home can be conceptualised as an investment in two ways: as a financial investment and as an investment in social identity. The home is generally considered as a safe financial investment on the assumption that property values will continue to rise over time. This produces wealth to make retirement more comfortable or to provide inheritance for children. Owning property is also recognised by government and financial institutions as a measure of an individual's or a family's economic security, social status, and buying power.

Renting is not valued in the same way as ownership (except in the cases of the super-rich who may rent some of their homes while owning one or many others). Renting from a private landlord or a local council or housing association has, indeed, increasingly become a sign of 'failure'. People who rent are, arguably, discriminated against by finance companies, insurers, banks, and building societies because they do not have the 'security' of capital to repay a loan. But it is likely that prejudice against nonowners is deeper than this and may result in, for instance, discrimination by financial institutions and potential employers. This can result in nonproperty owners being preyed upon by unscrupulous lending companies or even loan sharks.

Owning a home signals an investment in social identity. Consequently, homeowners take steps to demonstrate that their home reflects their status by carefully choosing the area they want to live in and the type of house they will buy. Similarly, they design, furnish, and decorate their home environment in such a way as to strengthen their sense of individual identity compared with their immediate neighbours, family, and friends. Interestingly, many people who bought formerly rented council-owned homes made significant changes to the external appearance of their home to signify ownership change. Transformations could include the fitting of a new front door, adding a porch, changing the design of windows, putting up impressive gateposts, or building an extension over a garage. Such transformations are used by homeowners to demonstrate independence from the constraints imposed by local councils and to differentiate themselves from those neighbours who have remained in council houses.

The 1980 Housing Act allowed people to buy their former council houses at a discounted value. Between 1980 and 1998 about 2 million homes were sold. During the period in the United Kingdom when the 'Right to Buy' policy was at its most popular, sociologist Peter Saunders adopted the term 'ontological security' to describe this desire for independence, self-reliance, and differentiation from nonowners. His use of this terminology revealed the 'ideological' motivation of Thatcher's Conservative government to attack what was perceived to be the corporatist socialist values of the welfare state. In so doing, a burden of failure was imposed upon those who were unable to buy into the property-owning democracy.

The 'Right to Buy' policy was hugely popular and has resulted in a transformation of the housing market in the United Kingdom. But it was not without its risks for those who took on the responsibility of home ownership. By the end of the 1980s, economic crisis produced sky-high interest rates and mass unemployment. This was accompanied by a major collapse in the housing market, so producing high rates of repossession by banks and building societies. Many people suffered from 'negative equity' (where the value of their homes was lower than the cost of the loans), trapping them in homes they could no longer afford. The dream of ever-rising property values was over, temporarily at least, and for many the idea of ontological security was replaced by economic calamity and downward social mobility.

The Show Home as a Stage Set for Ideal Lives

To sell very expensive products, capital has to work very hard to encourage people to engage in the process of 'conspicuous consumption'. In contemporary Britain, in particular, companies traditionally engage in 'speculative building' whereby a house design is created and then built in large numbers on many sites across the country. In so doing, companies take a gamble that people will buy their products. To reduce their risk of failure to sell such houses, companies build 'show homes' to illustrate what it could be like to live in such a property.

Essentially, show homes are designed to create images of an ideal home life. Builders achieve this by decorating and furnishing houses in such a way as to give the impression of an affluent, stress-free, harmonious, and leisurely lifestyle. A surface analysis of show homes would reveal that the expense of the furnishing and decoration would be very substantial and that the choices designers make exaggerate impressions of the size and opulence of the house.

A deeper sociological analysis produces more interesting facets of the process of encouraging people to buy into the dream of the ideal home. For example, in contemporary British show homes, room design layouts have changed significantly from the 'universal plan' of the 1930s semidetached house. Now, the spaces in the houses which adults expect to occupy are often separated by buffer zones from children's and teenagers' spaces to afford them more privacy. This includes the almost universal introduction of *en suite* bathrooms in three- or four-bedroom houses. This idea of the promise of privacy within the family is revealing sociologically as it suggests to the buyer that the worries associated with parenting can be set aside or that their sex lives can be more exciting. Indeed, in most show homes, children's rooms are carefully designed to show that their activities are more or less isolated from the rest of the house and that in their rooms they have 'sensible' leisure activities such as horse riding or fishing. Very rarely is there evidence in a show home of children or young people in the remainder of the house.

Men's and women's activities are also separated in show homes: Often a study is decorated in an explicitly masculine way to suggest that the male will be the 'master of his own home' – rather like a fictional Victorian patriarch. This effect is often exaggerated by the building of detached garages in the fashion of a Victorian stable house. Women, in turn, are depicted as 'domestic goddesses' with fabulous kitchens and advanced culinary skills. Similarly, dining room tables are laid out with multiple place settings, flowers, and candelabra, suggesting that women host elaborate dinners with sophisticated friends.

The show home creates dreams by leaving real-life characters 'off-stage'. It is up to the viewers to imagine a lifestyle with no bills on the doorstep, medicines in the cupboards, or chaos created by children or with none of the stresses created by the sheer hard work involved in paying for such an expensive home.

The Impossible Dream of the Ideal Home

The promise of the ideal home is costly both financially and in terms of lost opportunities. Consequently, companies must engage in a process of persuading consumers to buy into this dream. The extent to which they successfully 'manipulate needs' (Lodziak, 1995) is, therefore, important to debate. As noted above, a tendency to engage in conspicuous consumption has already become embedded in the psyche of the Western mind. Consequently, capitalism does not have to work so hard to persuade people to part with their savings, or more importantly in the case of house purchases, to loan money to achieve their dreams. That said, cultural conservatism continues to be an important factor in shaping what people want and do not want. Observation at show homes or the Ideal Home Exhibition reveals that moving people out of culturally bound models of what a home should be like is very difficult. This is because people fear the consequences of disapproval or disregard from significant others.

Ultimately, this can lead to consumers 'refusing' some options presented to them by house-building companies. This process of cultural refusal is much more pronounced in times of recession. This is partly because there is less money around to spend, but it is also due to people questioning the value of overreaching themselves – especially so if they think that significant others will think them to be fools for doing so.

Most people want to be 'a little bit different' from significant others, but they can also be wary of outlandish or daring experiments in house style. Indeed, those who do not conform to expectation generally reinforce notions of cultural conservatism rather than challenge them. Television shows, such as *Grand Designs* in the United Kingdom, do not challenge convention – instead, they push the boundaries for the wealthy and titillate the aspirations of the less well off. While levels of affluence vary, sofas tend to be set out in similar ways, bedrooms are furnished in more or less the same way, and in essentials, bathrooms and kitchens are more or less identical in functional and cultural terms.

It is also important to recognise that tolerances of patterns of conspicuous consumption vary significantly between countries. In the United States, houses are very much larger than the average European home and they are characterised by their enhanced facility. If such house styles were affordable in Europe, it is a moot point as to whether people would buy them. Indeed, in much of mainland Europe, the impetus to buy detached suburban homes appears to be much lower than in the United Kingdom, as is the more limited interest in home improvement. In the United Kingdom, there has been an increased interest in city living over the last decade, especially amongst younger people who delay, forgo, or abandon the idea of conventional family life. Many older people are also eschewing the idea of the quiet garden and suburban bungalow and are instead moving into city apartment blocks where they can enjoy facility and leisure activity later in life.

The Fragility of the Ideal Home

For conventional families, living the dream of the ideal home can involve couples working much harder to pay the bills. Often families have to keep their children in nurseries to raise the income to keep their homes, which, in turn, puts more financial and emotional pressure on parents. The demands of work mean that people have to buy more expensive goods and services such as preprepared meals, ironing and laundry services, services of cleaners and gardeners. The reality can be that householders do not have time to use their fabulous kitchens, do not have energy to invite friends round for sophisticated meals, and that tiredness, worry, and stress make their relationships suffer. And the growing expectation that parents should live separate lives from their children in ideal homes – which is anathema to many cultures – may for many be a step too far down the road of conspicuous consumption. In sum, the ideal home is a 'have it all' dream which can raise expectations and increase disappointment.

The idea of home is a multilayered concept which encapsulates in idealistic terms notions of permanence, security, self-expression, personal success, and the communion of the family. But the dream of the ideal home is a relatively fragile one. Relatively few people can buy their homes outright; so most people are obliged to borrow money through long-term mortgages to achieve home ownership. For those who lose their jobs, become too ill to work, get divorced, or suffer some other economic, personal, or social calamity, the dream can quickly collapse. This often results in strong feelings of failure as people experience downward social mobility by moving to rented houses in less salubrious areas (Newman, 1999).

The housing market is characterised by cycles of booms and slumps which can result in widespread home repossession by banks and building societies. Collapse in housing markets has usually been precipitated by wider economic crises. More recently, however, collapse in the housing market has actually produced economic crisis on a global scale. This collapse in the housing market in the United States, in particular, was precipitated by the practice of selling mortgages to people who could not afford the repayments. This is known as the 'subprime' mortgage market where prospective buyers who would not normally be regarded as economically secure enough to have a mortgage were sold houses well beyond their financial means.

There has been mass repossession or abandonment of houses, especially in the United States, in the subprime market. But the question remains, has this dented people's fundamental belief that owning property is the principal way of achieving 'ontological security'? It remains likely that people will continue to seek to show significant others that they have achieved success, social mobility and become members of what Prime Minister Margaret Thatcher once famously described in the 1980s as the 'property-owning democracy'.

See also: Home as Investment; Home as Leisure Space; Meanings of Home in Popular Culture; Privacy, Sanctuary and Privatism; Suburban Homes.

References

Barley N (1989) *Native Land: The Bizarre Rituals and Curious Customs that Make the English English*. London: Longman.
Chapman T (2004) *Gender and Domestic Life: Changing Practices in Families and Households*. Basingstoke: Palgrave.
Chapman T and Hockey J (eds.) (1999) *Ideal Homes? Social Change and Domestic Life*. London: Routledge.
Gauldy E (1974) *Cruel Habitations: A History of Working-Class Housing*. London: Allen and Unwin.
Giles J (2004) *The Parlour and the Suburb: Domestic Identities, Class, Femininity and Modernity*. Oxford: Berg.
Girouard M (1990) *The English Town*. New Haven, CT: Yale University Press.
Lodziak C (1995) *Manipulating Needs: Capitalism and Culture*. London: Pluto Press.
Newman K (1999) *Falling from Grace: The Experience of Downward Mobility in the American Middle Class*. New York: Free Press.
Oliver P, Davis I, and Bentley I (1981) *Dunroamin: The Suburban Semi and Its Enemies*. London: Pimlico.
Veblen T (1914) *The Theory of the Leisure Classes*. New York: Modern Library.

Further Reading

Dovey K (1999) *Framing Places: Mediating Power in Built Form*. London: Routledge.
Forty A (1995) *Objects of Desire: Design and Society Since 1750*. London: Thames and Hudson.
Saunders P (1990) *A Nation of Homeowners*. London: Unwin Hyman.

Illicit Drug Use and Homelessness

J Neale, Oxford Brookes University, Oxford, UK

© 2012 Elsevier Ltd. All rights reserved.

Glossary

Drug consumption rooms Supervised, hygienic places where dependent drug users are allowed to bring and use illegally obtained drugs.

Harm reduction A philosophy which seeks to reduce the health, social, and economic harms associated with the use of psychoactive substances.

Hepatitis C A viral disease that leads to inflammation of the liver, including cirrhosis and liver cancer. It is mainly transmitted via direct blood-to-blood contact and is very common amongst injecting drug users.

Injecting paraphernalia A collective term which describes the equipment used in the preparation and administration of drugs for injection. In addition to needles, this might include syringes, spoons, filters, acid, swabs, and water.

Problematic drug use The use of any mind-altering drug that causes harm to either the individual user or society.

Social exclusion A complex and multidimensional process by which some individuals are excluded from the normal exchanges, practices, rights, and resources of modern society.

Substitute prescribing The controlled prescribing of opiate medication (such as methadone) to illicit opiate (usually heroin) users, as part of an overall care plan.

Introduction

It is widely accepted that homelessness and illicit drug use are two major social problems. Moreover, they commonly co-occur, with profound implications for the individuals affected. Those working within both homelessness and addiction services will routinely have contact with homeless drug users (HDUs). Yet, other more generic health, social care, and criminal justice professionals (general practitioners, hospital doctors, nurses, social workers, probation officers, the police, and prison staff, to name a few) will also encounter those who are simultaneously struggling to cope with a drug problem and lack of accommodation. Understanding the circumstances and needs of HDUs is thus directly relevant to academics, policy makers, and practitioners within, but also far beyond, the housing field.

This article will summarise some key issues and debates relating to HDUs. No attempt is made to provide a truly global perspective since this would be too ambitious an undertaking for any single article. Instead, material from Western countries, and particularly the United Kingdom, is presented. The article also focuses largely on single homeless people (rather than homeless families) and 'problematic' (rather than 'recreational') forms of drug use. These parameters are also set to keep the article manageable and because it is problematic drug use by single homeless people that has attracted most concern and research in recent years.

The Extent of the Problem

It is useful to begin by examining the extent of drug taking by homeless people. In the United Kingdom, a study of 1000 predominantly young homeless people in hostels, in day centres, and on the streets of London in the mid-1990s revealed that 88% were taking at least one drug and 35% were heroin users (Flemen, 1997). Meanwhile, a slightly later survey of homeless people in Glasgow reported that 25% were dependent on at least one drug and 18% were dependent on heroin (Kershaw et al., 2000). Subsequently, Fountain et al. (2003) conducted a survey of 389 current or recent rough sleepers in London and found that 83% had used a drug in the previous month and 36% were dependent on heroin.

A review of research conducted in Western countries between 1996 and 2007 also identified seven surveys reporting on drug dependence among homeless men and one among homeless women. This review found that the prevalence of drug dependence ranged from 4.5 to 54.2% for the men and was 24.2% for the women (Fazel et al., 2008). These data confirm that a substantial proportion of homeless people are problem drug users. However, the findings vary greatly between studies, making it impossible to provide reliable estimates of the actual numbers of HDUs. This variation likely reflects the different definitions of homelessness and drug use employed by researchers, when and where studies were undertaken, the populations sampled, and the research methods employed. Additionally, the stigma attached to both homelessness and substance misuse, combined with the illegality of much drug-related behaviour, means that the identification of HDUs may be difficult within surveys, and any findings reported will underestimate the true numbers of HDUs.

A Complex Relationship

When the separate literatures on homelessness and addiction are examined, it is evident that the factors that place individuals at an increased risk of becoming homeless are strikingly similar to those factors that place them at an increased risk of developing a problem with drugs. These shared risks include truancy, school exclusion, low educational attainment, family breakdown, childhood abuse, growing up in care, offending, imprisonment, not having a social support network, and poor mental health (Neale, 2001). It is also evident that drug misuse is a risk factor for homelessness, and homelessness is a risk factor for drug misuse. Furthermore, when homelessness and drug use co-occur, they can reinforce each other and cause or intensify other problems, such as family and relationship breakdown, ill health, and offending behaviour (Fitzpatrick et al., 2000; Hutson and Liddiard, 1994; Neale, 2001).

The relationship between homelessness and drug taking is, in other words, complex. Indeed, efforts to establish whether homelessness predates initial drug use or drug use predates initial homelessness suggest that both patterns occur. For example, Fountain et al. (2003) found that 63% of their sample of 389 homeless people in London cited drug or alcohol use as a reason for becoming homeless, and 47% reported this as a major reason. Nonetheless, drug and alcohol use, injecting, and drug dependency all increased the longer respondents had been homeless. Similarly, an American study of 303 homeless people and people at risk of homelessness found that having ever used drugs was predictive of first homelessness episodes. Meanwhile, prior homelessness experiences were also predictive of first symptoms of both alcohol and drug abuse (Johnson et al., 1997).

This complexity is further illustrated in a qualitative study of 200 drug users undertaken in Scotland in 1997–98 (Neale, 2001). Of the 136 study participants who had ever been homeless, 59 gave a main reason for their last homelessness episode, and these explanations included being asked to leave the family home because of their drug use; relationship breakdown; domestic abuse; eviction because of nonpayment of rent or drug-related antisocial behaviour (by themselves or by drug-using friends, relatives, and associates); being released from prison; local drug gang violence; and neighbourhood harassment. Whilst some participants said that becoming homeless had been a factor prompting them to start using illicit drugs, others explained how losing their home had worsened an existing drug problem. As one female participant in the study explained:

> They put me in a hostel and it was nearly all drug users. I hadn't touched drugs at all 'til I moved into that hostel and I think it was because I was stuck there and I think I was lonely.
>
> (cited in Neale, 2001)

The Harsh Reality

As is already becoming clear, HDUs frequently experience multiple and interrelated problems above and beyond their homelessness and drug taking (Craig and Hodson, 2000). These include poor health, family problems, legal problems, financial problems, harassment, and violence (Hammersley and Pearl, 1996; Neale, 2001; Reid and Klee, 1999). HDUs also tend to inject in public places, a practice associated with frequent and hasty injecting, sharing injecting equipment, poor hygiene, and using very large quantities of drugs. These behaviours in turn increase the risk of HDUs damaging their health, overdosing, and acquiring and transmitting infectious disease, including HIV and Hepatitis C (Hickman et al., 2007; Klee and Morris, 1995; Rhodes et al., 2006, 2007).

The harsh reality of being both homeless and drug dependent is also captured by data from the qualitative study of 200 drug users conducted in Scotland in 1997–98 (Neale, 2001). Being a HDU, particularly when this involved sleeping on the streets, was characterised by loneliness, depression, chronic ill health, sleep deprivation, hunger, and victimisation. Furthermore, drugs played a complex role since they aggravated the experience of being homeless, but also alleviated the physical and emotional pain that those without a home often felt. The following graphic accounts of rough sleeping were provided by two men in the study:

> I'm sleeping under this motorway bridge in this wee corner and I've got no room... I've got blankets underneath me and I'm not getting to sleep until four in the morning and I'm not eating. I'm not getting proper food, but you don't care when you're homeless.
> You need the smack [heroin]... I've been in some states, but the smack kind of kept me sane. It made me able to handle my homelessness... It was the smack that got me through it. It deadened my thoughts and just kind of froze me.
>
> (cited in Neale, 2001)

It has been argued that the concept of social exclusion is useful in understanding the difficulties often experienced by HDUs (Neale, 2008). This is because social exclusion recognises that problems (such as lack of housing, drug use, poverty, poor health, and limited access to services) frequently interact together, have composite effects, and persist over time, so excluding individuals from adequate social participation and social integration (Room, 1995). Thus, homelessness, family breakdown, poor health, limited education, unemployment, and criminal activity increase the likelihood that individuals will use drugs problematically. Meanwhile, problem drug taking can lead to further social exclusion in the form of greater housing marginalisation, more family problems, worse general health, increased likelihood of unemployment, and greater criminal involvement.

Given that HDUs tend to experience multiple problems, they also need access to a broad range of support. Alongside shelter and drug services, this can include basic essentials (such as food, clothes, and water); health care; social and emotional support; financial or legal advice; education; and training (Fitzpatrick and Kennedy, 2000; Reid and Klee, 1999). Here again, the concept of social exclusion is valuable since it emphasises that all individuals have 'rights' to the normal exchanges and practices of modern society, including housing, education, health, and access to services (Commission of the European Communities, 1993). Furthermore, it recognises that there is a duty on society to actively prevent exclusionary processes by providing support (Room, 1995).

Barriers to Accessing Support

Compounding the harsh reality of being homeless and drug dependent, HDUs do not find accessing services easy. For example, many do not know what support exists or where to go for assistance (Neale et al., 2007). Equally, they often do not stay in one place for long enough to receive help and can be excluded from services – including accommodation services – because they are a risk to others (Flemen, 1997; Liddiard and Hutson, 1991). Not having an address can create problems registering with a general practitioner and make it difficult for them to maintain contact with other professionals (Neale et al., 2007). Equally, lengthy waiting lists and strict standards of attendance and compliance at some agencies present further obstacles given the often very chaotic nature of the lives of HDUs (Pleace et al., 2000).

Research has additionally shown that many HDUs dislike hostels and nightshelters provided explicitly for homeless people. Sometimes this is because such accommodation reminds them of prison, but more commonly it relates to the high levels of alcohol consumption, illicit drug taking, and drug dealing occurring on these premises (Neale, 2001). Those who use drugs often do not like being in constant contact with other drug users since such close proximity can increase their own temptation to use and means that they are constantly encountering the negative consequences of drug taking, such as crime, violence, and overdosing. Indeed, some HDUs report feeling so vulnerable whilst in hostel accommodation that they prefer to sleep on the streets (Fitzpatrick et al., 2000; Neale, 2001):

> I've been skippering [*sleeping on the streets*] for about a year. I was in the hostels a while back, but I'm not too keen on them. It's too much like a jail and I like my own bit of space.
>
> (cited in Neale, 2001)

Beyond these specific problems, HDUs inevitably experience the many barriers to accessing services encountered by both homeless people who do not use drugs and drug users who are not homeless. These barriers include insufficient provision of services, bureaucracy, limited opening hours, lack of child care, and the hostile attitudes of service providers (Freund and Hawkins, 2004; McCollum and Trepper, 1995; Pleace et al., 2000; Wood et al., 2002). The kinds of negative attitudes that drug users have reported when seeking help from service providers include feeling judged and looked down on, being treated abruptly, not being listened to, being told that their problems are self-inflicted, and being closely observed in case they steal (Neale et al., 2007).

HDUs are, of course, not a homogeneous group, and some of the problems they experience in seeking help will depend on their personal characteristics, needs, and circumstances. For example, individuals from some black and minority ethnic groups, those with health problems, those without supporting family members, and stimulant users can all find accessing support particularly difficult (Neale et al., 2007). Drug-using parents are often reluctant to engage with services because they do not want to be separated from their children (Sterk et al., 2000) or fear losing custody of them if their ability to care is questioned (MacMaster, 2005). Equally, some HDUs might not want help because they are too ashamed, embarrassed, or guilty about their drug taking (McCollum and Trepper, 1995) or too concerned about confidentiality (Weiss et al., 1993).

Good Practice

During the 1990s, various UK researchers and organisations made important recommendations, often based on empirical research, regarding how best to provide assistance to HDUs. These recommendations included providing additional funding; offering more diverse and flexible services (especially more outreach work and early interventions); improved interagency working; increased professional training; greater use of care plans, contracts, and confidentiality policies; better publicity regarding service availability; and more service user involvement

(Flemen, 1999; London Drugs Policy Forum, 1999; O'Leary, 1997; Reid and Klee, 1999; Scottish Drugs Forum, 1993).

Building on this work, researchers in Scotland subsequently undertook a study involving qualitative interviews with professionals and HDUs to generate further information on good practice (Kennedy et al., 2001). According to the professionals interviewed, good practice meant providing easy access to a range of services (substitute prescribing, counselling, education and training, alternative leisure activities, drop-in and outreach, etc.), but also safe places within accommodation services for individuals to use drugs. In addition, the professionals advocated holistic services, partnership working, user involvement, flexible service delivery, a willingness to assist with the underlying causes of both homelessness and drug taking, and ongoing support to help those who are rehoused to maintain their new tenancies.

For their part, HDUs identified good practice as having easy access to a broad range of flexible services, immediate assistance with practical problems, social and emotional support (including help in addressing the reasons behind their homelessness and drug taking), and ongoing after care. Most of all, however, the HDUs emphasised good service delivery. In this regard, they stressed the importance of having friendly staff; creating a nonjudgmental agency environment; feeling valued, safe, and secure; and having the opportunity to be involved in service planning. Conversely, lengthy waiting lists, inflexible forms of support, feeling judged, and the dismissive attitudes of some staff were all highlighted as negative aspects.

Overall, the research by Kennedy et al. revealed that there were many similarities between the views held by professionals and HDUs on good practice. Thus, both stressed the need for a wide range of practical, social, and emotional forms of assistance. Equally, it was widely agreed that support should be accessible, delivered in a flexible manner, and provided in a safe and secure environment. Assistance should also be made available when it is needed, for as long as it is needed, and in a way that makes people feel included. In short, HDUs and the professionals working with them recognised that good practice was heavily dependent on how services were delivered and how they made service users feel.

More recently still, the Scottish Government commissioned a rapid evidence review of the international literature on effective substance misuse services for homeless people (Pleace, 2008). According to this review, services that solely seek to promote abstinence (including short-stay detoxification services) tend to have quite limited success with HDUs. This is because HDUs often cease contact with these services before treatment or rehabilitation is complete or avoid them altogether. Conversely, services that pursue a harm reduction approach appear better at engaging HDUs. For example, the US Pathways Housing First model – which uses intensive floating support delivered to ordinary accommodation, with a strong focus on service user choice and harm reduction – was identified as having demonstrated some success and cost effectiveness in resettling HDUs.

Based on his review, Pleace (2008) advocated diverse services and flexible models of service delivery that accept when harm reduction and semi-independent living are the only realistic goals, but also pursue abstinence and independent living as appropriate. Pleace also argued that services should not focus on drug taking or housing problems in isolation. Furthermore, the fact that some HDUs will need long-term support means that provision should be securely funded and not commissioned on very short contracts. His review additionally recognised that it will not always be practical to provide specialist services for HDUs, because the numbers of individuals who are both homeless and drug dependent may be very small in some locations. In such circumstances, alternative approaches might include developing specialist services that span a number of areas, modifying general homelessness and substance misuse services, and improving joint working between agencies.

Future Challenges

Over the last two decades, a growing body of literature on illicit drug use amongst homeless people has emerged. In some respects, it is reassuring that very similar findings have tended to be reported by the different studies – in particular, the complex problems of HDUs, their high support needs, barriers to accessing services, and the need for flexible service models that provide holistic care and support. This, at least, suggests that there is reliable evidence on what the key problems are and how we might begin to address them. Despite this, it is disappointing that the evidence base (and arguably also policy and practice) seems to have become stuck with no real new knowledge or theoretical developments emerging. In an attempt to move forward a little, this penultimate section now considers some of the most immediate challenges for researchers, policy makers, and practitioners.

First, and as also indicated by Pleace (2008), there is a need for more evidence on what might be done to prevent drug users from becoming homeless in the first place (and, indeed, on what might be done to prevent homeless people from becoming drug dependent). Given that drug users have reported becoming homeless as a result of their own antisocial behaviour and that of others (Neale, 2001), those who do have homes may need support in dealing with their own poor conduct as well as the disruptive activities of some of their friends, relatives, and associates. Furthermore, some drug users may be better able to maintain a tenancy if it is in an area where they are not known or where there is low drug prevalence. Clearly, these are as much issues for mainstream housing providers, particularly those allocating accommodation, as they are for addiction and homelessness specialists. Indeed, they potentially raise complex ethical and practical problems for housing managers, given that housing in areas of low drug prevalence may be limited and also highly desired by non-drug-using applicants.

In addition, it has been shown that drug users often become homeless following a relationship breakdown or when relatives can no longer cope with them living in the family home (Neale, 2001). Housing a drug user frequently places great stress on domestic relationships. Yet, the family plays an important role in preventing drug users from becoming homeless and in rehousing them after homelessness has occurred (Kemp et al., 2006). Accordingly, there is a need for more research and innovative service provision — perhaps involving professionals working in conjunction with family support groups — to explore how those who have a drug-using relative living with them might be better supported. Equally, given evidence that drug users can become homeless as a result of rent arrears, some individuals may need support (and potentially intense support) with money management. Likewise, social housing and private landlords should, whenever possible, identify strategies that address rent payment problems before crises occur.

For those working in hostels, shelters, and day centres, drug use and drug dealing are persistent concerns. This was highlighted in the United Kingdom by the Wintercomfort case, which involved two homeless workers being imprisoned after drug dealing had occurred on the premises that they managed in Cambridge during 1991. It is clear that those working in services frequented by homeless people need to find appropriate ways of supporting drug users who use their premises whilst also maintaining a safe environment for those wishing to avoid addictive behaviours. At present there is little information on how this can best be achieved. Interestingly, though, evidence that drug users often dislike hostels where drug use occurs (Fitzpatrick et al., 2000; Neale, 2001) suggests that drug-free services, drug-free areas within services, and clear policies on drug taking may be welcomed by many HDUs.

One relatively new challenge is to address the particularly high levels of Hepatitis C that research has now identified amongst HDUs (Hickman et al., 2007; Neale, 2008). Drug consumption rooms could potentially help to prevent high-risk injecting behaviours in public places. Meanwhile, all services (addiction, homelessness, generic health care, and prisons) could increase their efforts to tackle injecting (and particularly risky injecting) amongst homeless people. This might include routinely providing Hepatitis C virus (HCV)-related information and offering clean needles and sterile injecting tablets, but also other injecting paraphernalia, toothbrushes, razors, and condoms. Equally, individuals might be assisted to mark personal possessions to help prevent inadvertent sharing and virus transmission. Given that alcohol consumption accelerates progression of HCV, interventions to tackle drinking amongst homeless people are additionally required.

Finally, Pleace (2008) rightly identified the need for more randomised controlled trials and longitudinal research to assess treatment outcomes over time. It is, however, also necessary to carefully consider what types of outcome should be measured when services are evaluated. It is easy, but unhelpful, to think of success as simply being about helping HDUs to achieve abstinence or rehousing them in their own independent homes. These are important objectives, but they are not the only measures of good practice and progress. It is equally necessary to consider more intermediate and intangible outcomes, such as enabling HDUs to feel more settled, safe, confident and in control of their lives. These, after all, are also very important stages on the road to recovery.

Conclusion

In conclusion, it seems that there is a need to remain simultaneously realistic and optimistic when working with HDUs. For those whose lives are very chaotic and who are highly vulnerable because of complex ongoing physical, psychological, personal care, or other support needs, stable independent housing may seem a distant aspiration and may ultimately not be possible (Pleace, 2008). Despite this, it is important to retain hope about what HDUs can achieve in relation to their drug taking, housing, and other life goals. Accordingly, society must be prepared to invest in a wide range of high-quality specialist and generic services over the coming years. At the same time, there is a need for research that will move beyond the current evidence base to provide new insights into homelessness and substance misuse and innovative ideas for service development and evaluation.

Having a home of one's own can be associated with a sense of purpose, self-respect, and responsibility. For some, obtaining a new place to live might mean that children currently living in care will be returned to them and the family unit will be reunited. For others, feeling settled in their own accommodation can be an important first step in being able to address their addiction (Neale, 2001). Many HDUs retain a hope for improved housing circumstances in the future, and if they remain optimistic, so should we. As the personal accounts of former HDUs reveal, rehousing is not an impossible goal:

> I've had this house for nearly three years. Before that I stayed in bed and breakfasts. In between bed and breakfasts I was sleeping on the street. The last time I slept on the street would have been three years ago.
> (cited in Neale, 2001)

See also: Homelessness: Causation; Homeless People: Care Leavers; Homeless People: Care Leavers in the United Kingdom; Homeless People: Ex-Prisoners in England and Wales; Homeless People: Youth in the United Kingdom; Mental Health and Homelessness; Policies to Address Homelessness: Housing First Approaches; Social Exclusion and Housing.

References

Commission of the European Communities (1993) *Background Report: Social Exclusion – Poverty and Other Social Problems in the European Community, ISEC/B11/93*. Luxembourg: Office for the Publications of the European Communities.

Craig TKJ and Hodson S (2000) Homeless youth in London: II. Accommodation, employment and health outcomes at 1 year. *Psychological Medicine* 30(1): 187–194.

Fazel S, Khosla V, Doll H, and Geddes J (2008) The prevalence of mental disorders among the homeless in western countries: Systematic review and meta-regression analysis. *PLoS Medicine* 5(12): e225, doi:10.1371/journal.pmed.0050225.

Fitzpatrick S, Kemp PA, and Klinker S (2000) *Single Homelessness: An Overview of Research in Britain*. York: Joseph Rowntree Foundation.

Fitzpatrick S and Kennedy C (2000) *Getting by: Begging, Rough Sleeping and the Big Issue in Glasgow and Edinburgh*. Bristol: The Policy Press.

Flemen K (1997) *Smoke and Whispers: Drugs and Youth Homelessness in Central London*. London: Hungerford Drug Project.

Flemen K (1999) *Room for Drugs – Drug Use on Premises: Guidelines for Direct Access Services*. London: Release.

Fountain J, Howles S, Marsden J, Taylor C, and Strang J (2003) Drug and alcohol use and the link with homelessness: Results from a survey of homeless people in London. *Addiction Research and Theory* 11: 245–256.

Freund PD and Hawkins DW (2004) What street people reported about service access and drug treatment. *Journal of Health and Social Policy* 18: 87–93.

Hammersley R and Pearl S (1996) Drug misuse and other problems of residents in projects for the young, single homeless. *Health and Social Care in the Community* 4: 193–199.

Hickman M, Hope V, Brady T, et al. (2007) Hepatitis C virus (HCV) prevalence, and injecting risk behaviour in multiple sites in England in 2004. *Journal of Viral Hepatitis* 14: 645–652.

Hutson S and Liddiard M (1994) *Youth Homelessness*. London: Macmillan.

Johnson TP, Freels SA, Parsons JA, and Vangeest JB (1997) Substance abuse and homelessness: Social selection or social adaptation? *Addiction* 92: 437–445.

Kemp PA, Neale J, and Robertson M (2006) Homelessness among problem drug users: Prevalence, risk factors and trigger events. *Health and Social Care in the Community* 14(4): 319–328.

Kennedy C, Neale J, Barr K, and Dean J (2001) *Good Practice Towards Homeless Drug Users*. Edinburgh: Scottish Homes.

Kershaw A, Singleton N, and Meltzer H (2000) *Survey of the Health and Well-Being of Homeless People in Glasgow*. London: Office of National Statistics.

Klee H and Morris J (1995) Factors that characterise street injectors. *Addiction* 90: 837–841.

Liddiard M and Hutson S (1991) Homeless young people and runaways – agency definitions and processes. *Journal of Social Policy* 20(3): 365–388.

London Drugs Policy Forum (1999) *Housing Drug Users: Balancing Needs and Risks. Good Practice and Policy in Housing Drug Users*. London: London Drugs Policy Forum.

MacMaster SA (2005) Experiences with, and perceptions of, barriers to substance abuse and HIV services among African American women who use crack cocaine. *Journal of Ethnicity in Substance Abuse* 4: 53–75.

McCollum EE and Trepper TS (1995) Little by little, pulling me through: Women's perceptions of successful drug treatment: A qualitative inquiry. *Journal of Family Psychotherapy* 6: 63–82.

Neale J (2001) Homelessness among problem drug users: A double jeopardy explored. *International Journal of Drug Policy* 12: 353–369.

Neale J (2008) Homelessness, drug use and Hepatitis C: A complex problem explored within the context of social exclusion. *International Journal of Drug Policy* 19: 429–435.

Neale J, Godfrey C, Parrott S, Sheard L, and Tompkins L (2007) Barriers to the effective treatment of injecting drug users. Report Submitted to the Department of Health. http://www.lshtm.ac.uk/research/dmri/pdfs/neale_summary.pdf

O'Leary J (1997) *Beyond Help? Improving Service Provision for Street Homeless People with Mental Health and Alcohol or Drug Dependency Problems*. London: National Homeless Alliance.

Pleace N (2008) *Effective Services for Substance Misuse and Homelessness in Scotland: Evidence from an International Review*. Edinburgh: Scottish Government Social Research.

Pleace N, Jones A, and England J (2000) *Access to General Practice for People Sleeping Rough*. York: Centre for Housing Policy.

Reid P and Klee H (1999) Young homeless people and service provision. *Health and Social Care in the Community* 7: 17–24.

Rhodes T, Kimber J, Small W, et al. (2006) Public injecting and the need for 'safer environment interventions' in the reduction of drug-related harm. *Addiction* 101: 1384–1393.

Rhodes T, Watts L, Martin A, et al. (2007) Risk, shame and the public injector: A qualitative study of drug injecting in South Wales. *Social Science and Medicine* 65: 572–585.

Room G (ed.) (1995) *Beyond the Threshold: The Measurement and Analysis of Social Exclusion*. Bristol: The Policy Press.

Scottish Drugs Forum (1993) *Housing and Problem Drug Use – Policy Statement*. Glasgow: Scottish Drugs Forum.

Sterk CE, Elifson KW, and Theall K (2000) Women and drug treatment experiences: A generational comparison of mothers and daughters. *Journal of Drug Issues* 30: 839–862.

Weiss SH, Betts Weston C, and Quirinale J (1993) Safe sex? Misconceptions, gender differences and barriers among injection drug users: A focus group approach. *AIDS Education and Prevention* 5: 279–293.

Wood E, Tyndall MW, Spittal PM, et al. (2002) Needle exchange and difficulty with needle access during an ongoing HIV epidemic. *International Journal of Drug Policy* 13: 95–102.

Relevant Websites

http://toolkits.homeless.org.uk/cleanbreak